1997-1998
CHURCH
ALMANAC

GENERAL AUTHORITIES

1847 PIONEERS

WORLDWIDE CHURCH

MISSIONS

TEMPLES

CHRONOLOGY

NEWS IN REVIEW

FACTS, STATISTICS

Pictured on the cover are, top left, the First Presidency, October, 1996: President Gordon B. Hinckley , center; counselors President Thomas S. Monson, left; and President James E. Faust. Top right , sisters Cherrise and Cheryl Goo of Hawaii express feelings as Cherrise departs for missionary service in Japan. Below right is the Hong Kong Temple; below left is an Iowa wagon train re-enacting the Nauvoo exodus of 1846. Photos are by Tom Smart, Mike Cannon and Garry Bryant. Temple photo courtesy of LDS Church.

GENERAL AUTHORITIES, OFFICERS

1847 PIONEERS

WORLDWIDE CHURCH

MISSIONS, TEMPLES

CHRONOLOGY, NEWS IN REVIEW

FACTS, STATISTICS

FOREWORD

If I were to be sent someplace where I could only have one book to read what would I choose? Obviously my first choice would be the Scriptures.

But a strong second choice would be the Church Almanac.

This informative and helpful volume is filled with worthwhile information about the Church — past, present, and future.

Since it was first published in 1973 this biennial volume has become a standard reference work for information about the Church, its leaders, and its programs and activities.

This 1997-98 volume continues the tradition of a chronological account of important events in the Church since 1830, with more detailed information on the period from October 1994 to October 1996. Biographical information on all those who have served as General Authorities is included, plus information on general officers, stakes and missions, plus temples of the Church, and membership information.

Of particular interest in this volume is the most complete demographic information ever published on the Mormon pioneers who came to the Salt Lake Valley in 1847, 150 years ago. As the events of a sesquicentennial observance unfold this information will be of great value in understanding more about these hardy souls who established the Church in the tops of the mountains, from whence it has spread to all the world.

This almanac is a cooperative effort of the staffs of the *Church News* supplement to the *Deseret News* and the Historical Department of the Church. Sincere appreciation is expressed to all who have worked so well together to prepare the material in this volume and to ensure its accuracy.

We at the *Deseret News* hope that this volume will be instructive, enlightening and educational for you, the reader and users.

Wm. James Mortimer,
Publisher *Deseret News*

The *Deseret News Church Almanac* is prepared and edited by the staff of the Church News, a section of the Deseret News, in cooperation with the staff of the Historical Department of The Church of Jesus Christ of Latter-day Saints.

Deseret News

Deseret News President and Publisher	Wm. James Mortimer
Deseret News Managing Editor	Don C. Woodward
Church News Editor	Dell Van Orden
Church News Associate Editor	Gerry Avant
Almanac Coordinating Editor	John L. Hart
Church News Staff	R. Scott Lloyd
	Julie A. Dockstader
	Greg Hill
	Sarah Jane Weaver
	Shaun D. Stahle
	Linda Hamilton
Deseret News Pagination	Jean M. Cassidy
	Jay Hinton
Deseret News Art Department	Robert Noyce
	Craig Holyoak
	LouAnn England
	Carolyn Toronto
	Christie Jackson
	Heather Tuttle
Deseret News photo staff	Tom Smart
	Ravell Call
	Jeffrey D. Allred
	Paul Barker
	Garry Bryant
	Don Grayston
	Kristan Jacobsen
	Gary M. McKellar
	Gerald W. Silver
	Carmen Troesser
Marketing Director	Steven G. Handy

Historical Department

Executive Director	Elder Marlin K. Jensen
Assistant Executive Director	Elder John K. Carmack
Managing Director	Richard E. Turley Jr.
Almanac Chairman	Grant A. Anderson
Staff contributions	Melvin L. Bashore
	Karen S. Bolzendahl
	Linda Haslam
	William W. Slaughter

Editor's note: Information in this almanac has been gathered from a variety of sources and is believed to be the best available at the time of publication. Corrections, additional information and further country or state histories will be appreciated. Those with comments or information may write to: Church Almanac, P.O. Box 1257, Salt Lake City, UT 84110.

CONTENTS

A statistical profile of
THE CHURCH OF JESUS CHRIST
OF LATTER-DAY SAINTS
Dec. 31, 1995

CHURCH MEMBERSHIP
Total membership 9,388,000
CHURCH UNITS
Stakes 2,150
Districts 699
Missions 307
Wards, branches 22,683
Nations and territories with wards, branches 159
CHURCH GROWTH
Eight-year old children baptized in 1995 71,139
Converts baptized in 1995 304,330
MISSIONARIES
Total missionaries serving 48,631
EDUCATION
(1994-95 school year)
Cumulative total of continuing education enrollment 429,170
Students in seminary. 355,587
Students in institute. 202,920
Students in primary and secondary Church schools 8,867
Students in Church colleges and universities (fall, 1995) 37,565
TEMPLES
Temples in use. 47
Temples approved or under construction. 17
LANGUAGES
Specialty languages 2
Introductory phase languages. 48
Phase I languages 40
Phase II languages 60
Phase III languages (includes English) 25
Total languages 175
Complete translations of Book of Mormon in print 40
Translated selections of Book of Mormon in print 48
Triple combination translations 11

Oct. 1, 1996

Total membership (estimated) 9,600,000
Stakes 2,244
Missions 310
Temples in use. 49
Temples planned or under construction. 15
Missionaries 52,499

President Gordon B. Hinckley and counselors, President Thomas S. Monson and President James E. Faust, sustain themselves in solemn assembly April 1, 1995.

MAJOR EVENTS

OCTOBER 1994 — OCTOBER 1996

For more detailed listing, see News in Review section

Administrative and policy changes

• President Gordon B. Hinckley announced April 1, 1995, that the position of regional representative in the Church would be discontinued, and replaced with a new administrative position, the area authority. Area authorities will continue their current employment, reside in their own homes and serve on a Church-service basis. They will serve a flexible term, approximately six years, and will be closely tied to the area presidencies.

• A new logo design for the name of the Church, focusing on the name of the Savior, was announced by the First Presidency Dec. 20, 1995.

• In a written statement the First Presidency and Quorum of the Twelve announced Jan. 18, 1996, the withdrawal of General Authorities from boards of directors of business corporations, including Church-owned corporations.

Changes in leadership

GENERAL AUTHORITIES
First Presidency

• President Gordon B. Hinckley was ordained and set apart as the 15th president of the Church March 12, 1995, following the death of President Howard W. Hunter March 3, 1995.

• President Thomas S. Monson, second counselor to President Howard W. Hunter, was set apart March 12,

1995, as first counselor to President Gordon B. Hinckley.

• President James E. Faust was set apart March 12, 1995, as second counselor to President Gordon B. Hinckley after serving as an apostle for 16 years.

Quorum of the Twelve

• President Monson was also set apart as president of the Quorum of the Twelve March 12, 1995. President Boyd K. Packer was set apart to serve as acting president of the Twelve.

• Elder Henry B. Eyring, a General Authority for 10 years and Commissioner of the Church Educational System, was ordained an apostle April 6, 1995, filling a vacancy created when President James E. Faust was called to be second counselor in the First Presidency.

Presidency of the Seventy

• Elder Jack H Goaslind and Elder Harold G. Hillam were called to the Presidency of the Seventy. Elder Rex D. Pinegar and Elder Charles Didier were released from the presidency and called to area presidencies, effective Aug. 15, 1995.

• Elder Earl C. Tingey was called to the Presidency of the Seventy effective Aug. 15, 1996, to replace Elder Carlos E. Asay, who was given emeritus General Authority status.

First Quorum of the Seventy

• Members of the Second Quorum of the Seventy sustained to the First Quorum of the Seventy were Elders John B. Dickson, Jay E. Jensen and David E. Sorensen April 1, 1995, and Elders Dallas N. Archibald and Dieter F. Uchtdorf April 6, 1996.

• Sustained to the First Quorum of the Seventy April 1, 1995, was Elder W. Craig Zwick. Sustained April 6, 1996, was Elder Bruce C. Hafen.

• It was announced Nov. 2, 1995, that Elder Merrill J. Bateman was called from Presiding Bishopric to the First Quorum of the Seventy and appointed president of Brigham Young University. He was sustained April 6, 1996.

Emeritus General Authorities

• Elders Ted E. Brewerton and Hans B. Ringger were given emeritus status Sept. 30, 1995.

• Elder Carlos E. Asay was given emeritus status Oct. 5, 1996.

Second Quorum of the Seventy

• Elder Bruce D. Porter was sustained to the Second Quorum of the Seventy April 1, 1995.

• Released from the Second Quorum of the Seventy Sept. 30, 1995, were Elders Eduardo Ayala, LeGrand R. Curtis, Helvecio Martins, J Ballard Washburn, and Durrel A. Woolsey.

• Elders L. Edward Brown, Sheldon F. Child, Quentin L. Cook, Wm. Rolfe Kerr, Dennis E. Simmons, Jerald L. Taylor, Francisco J. Vinas and Richard B. Wirthlin were called to the Second Quorum of the Seventy April 6, 1996.

• Released from the Second Quorum of the Seventy Oct. 5, 1996, were Elders W. Mack Lawrence, Rulon G. Craven, Joseph C. Muren, Graham W. Doxey, Jorge A. Rojas, Julio E. Davila, In Sang Han, Stephen D. Nadauld and Sam K. Shimabukuro.

Presiding Bishopric

• Sustained April 6, 1996, as Presiding Bishop was Elder H. David Burton. He succeeded Presiding Bishop Merrill J. Bateman, who was called to the First Quorum of the Seventy and as BYU president.

• Sustained as counselors to Bishop Burton on April 6, 1996, were Bishops Richard C. Edgley — who had previously served as second counselor to Presiding Bishop Bateman and as second counselor to Presiding Bishop Hales — and Keith B. McMullin.

General Authority Deaths

• President Howard W. Hunter, 87, died March 3, 1995, at his Salt Lake City home.

• Elder Victor L. Brown, 81, Presiding Bishop from 1972-85 and an emeritus General Authority, died March 26, 1996, at his home in Salt Lake City.

• Elder Lloyd P. George, 75, who served in the Second Quorum of the Seventy for six years, died May 13, 1996, in Salt Lake City, Utah, at age 75.

AUXILIARIES

• Elder Harold G. Hilliam of the Presidency of the Seventy was sustained as general president of the Sunday School Sept. 30, 1995, succeeding Elder Charles Didier of the Seventy. Sustained as first and second counselors, respectively, were Elder F. Burton Howard and Elder Glenn L. Pace of

died June 15, 1996.

• Terrell H. Bell, 74, U.S. Secretary of Education under former U.S. President Ronald Reagan, died June 22, 1996, in Salt Lake City.

•Theodore Gorka, 79, prominent LDS artist, died Aug. 26, 1996, in Columbia, S.C.

• Neil W. Kooyman, 81, former mission president and manager of distribution for the Church, died Sept. 16, 1996, in Salt Lake City.

News events

• The First Presidency announced plans to build a temple in the Nashville, Tenn., area Nov. 12, 1994.

• President Howard W. Hunter installed Eric B. Shumway as the eighth president of the Brigham Young University-Hawaii campus Nov. 18, 1994.

• The 125th anniversary of the Young Women program was celebrated Nov. 28, 1994.

• A milestone was reached when President Howard W. Hunter created in Mexico City, Mexico, the Church's 2,000 stake Dec. 11, 1994.

• The Church distributed 79 tons of food for the hungry in Atlanta, Ga., through 26 religious and charitable organizations during the 1994 Christmas season.

• President Howard W. Hunter dedicated the Bountiful Utah Temple Jan. 8, 1995.

• The First Presidency announced Jan. 21, 1995, plans to build temples in Cochabamba, Bolivia and Recife, Brazil.

• The Church had reached the 9 million mark in membership, it was announced Jan. 21, 1995.

• Elder Neal A. Maxwell and Elder Russell M. Nelson of the Quorum of the Twelve traveled to Beijing, China, in February 1995, responding to an invitation extended by Vice Premier Li Lanqing when he visited the Polynesian Cultural Center in Hawaii a year earlier.

• The first stake in the Republic of Ireland was created March 12, 1995, under the direction of Elder Graham W. Doxey of the Seventy.

• Presiding Bishop Merrill J. Bateman testified March 29, 1995, before the U.S. Senate Finance Committee regarding welfare reform.

• President Gordon B. Hinckley dedicated the Tuacahn arts center and outdoor amphitheater in Ivins, Utah, April 8, 1995.

• Church members reached out to those in need after a terrorist bomb ripped through the Alfred P. Murrah Federal Building in downtown Oklahoma City April 19, 1995.

• President Gordon B. Hinckley and his counselors in the First Presidency broke ground May 1, 1995, for the BYU law library named after President Howard W. Hunter.

• It was announced May 10, 1995, in a letter from the First Presidency that the Book of Mormon is available on videotape in American Sign Language for the hearing impaired.

• Ground was broken May 13, 1995, by President Gordon B. Hinckley, accompanied by his second counselor in the First Presidency, President James E. Faust, for the Vernal Utah Temple, which will be constructed from the existing Uintah Stake Tabernacle, dedicated in 1907 by President Joseph F. Smith.

• Major exterior preservation projects at the Logan and Manti temples were announced by the First Presidency June 24, 1995.

• Elder L. Tom Perry broke ground June 29, 1995, on the John Taylor Religion Building at Ricks College.

• President Thomas S. Monson, first counselor in the First Presidency, welcomed the king and queen of Sweden to the grounds to the Stockholm Sweden Temple Aug. 23, 1995.

- The Alberta Temple was named a Canadian Historic Site by government representatives at a ceremony in Cardston Sept. 16, 1995.

- Church members in Idaho Falls, Idaho, observed the 50th anniversary of the dedication of the Idaho Falls Temple on Sept. 17, 1995.

- The First Presidency issued Sept. 23, 1995, a proclamation reaffirming gospel standards, doctrines and practices relative to the family.

- President Gordon B. Hinckley announced Sept. 30, 1995, that in place of the formerly announced temple for Hartford, Conn., two new temples would be constructed in Boston, Mass., and in White Plains, N.Y. He also announced that a third temple would likely be constructed in Venezuela.

- President Gordon B. Hinckley dedicated the new Ezra Taft Benson Science Building at BYU Oct. 20, 1995.

- The first stake in Papua New Guinea was created under the direction of Elder V. Dallas Merrell of the Seventy Oct. 22, 1995.

- President Gordon B. Hinckley met with U.S. President Bill Clinton at the White House in Washington, D.C., Nov. 13, 1995.

- The First Presidency announced Dec. 27, 1995, plans to build a new temple in Monterrey, Mexico.

- President Gordon B. Hinckley represented the Church Jan. 4 during Utah statehood centennial celebrations in Salt Lake City and other locations.

- Church members celebrated the 150th anniversary of the Saints' 1846 exodus from Nauvoo Feb. 3-4, 1996.

- Church reached a milestone Feb. 28, 1996, as the Member and Statistical Records Division estimated that for the first time, more than half of the Church membership was living outside the United States.

- President Gordon B. Hinckley announced April 6, 1996, that the Church is contemplating building a new meeting hall which will hold three to four times more people than the Salt Lake Tabernacle.

- President Gordon B. Hinckley dedicated the David O. McKay Events Center on the Utah Valley State College campus April 22, 1996.

- Elder Merrill J. Bateman of the First Quorum of the Seventy was inaugurated April 25, 1996, as the 11th president of BYU.

- President Gordon B. Hinckley dedicated the Hong Kong Temple May 17, 1996.

- President Gordon B. Hinckley became the first Church president to ever visit the mainland of China May 28, 1996.

- President Gordon B. Hinckley dedicated Cambodia for the preaching of the gospel May 29, 1996.

- President Gordon B. Hinckley broke ground June 11, 1996, for a temple in Madrid, Spain.

- The newly refurbished This Is the Place Monument and State Park was rededicated by President Gordon B. Hinckley June 19, 1996.

- At a Grand Encampment celebration in Council Bluffs, Iowa, President Gordon B. Hinckley dedicated July 12, 1996, a replica of the Kanesville Tabernacle, where Brigham Young was sustained president of the Church.

- On July 26, 1996, a new park and improved trail to the top of Ensign Peak in Salt Lake City was dedicated by President Gordon B. Hinckley.

- Elder Richard G. Scott of the Quorum of the Twelve presided at a ground-breaking for the Guayaquil Ecuador Temple Aug. 10, 1996.

- Elder Richard G. Scott presided Aug. 18, 1996, at a groundbreaking for the Santo Domingo Dominican Republic Temple, the first in the Caribbean.

- The First Presidency announced plans Aug. 31, 1996, to build the Church's 63rd temple in Billings, Mont.

GENERAL AUTHORITIES, OFFICERS

GENERAL AUTHORITIES

(Current as of Oct. 15, 1996)

THE FIRST PRESIDENCY

President Gordon B. Hinckley

President Gordon B. Hinckley was ordained and set apart as the 15th president of the Church on March 12, 1995, after serving 14 years as a counselor in the First Presidency and 20 years in the Quorum of the Twelve. Except for a short period during World War II, he has worked as an employee or General Authority of the Church on a full-time basis since completing his mission in 1935.

In his first general conference address as president, he commented: ''The time has come for us to stand a little taller, to lift our eyes and stretch our minds to a greater comprehension and understanding of the grand millennial mission of this, The Church of Jesus Christ of Latter-day Saints. It is a time to move forward without hesitation.''

President Hinckley was born June 23, 1910, in Salt Lake City, Utah, to Bryant S. and Ada Bitner Hinckley. As a young man, his ability with words won him a reputation as an outstanding speaker.

After graduating from the University of Utah in 1932 in English, he accepted a mission call to the British Isles, serving from 1933-35. He spent most of his mission in London in the office of the European Mission, under Elder Joseph F. Merrill of the Quorum of the Twelve. Upon his return, he reported to the First Presidency in an interview that led to employment as secretary of the then recently formed Radio, Publicity and Mission Literature Committee of the Church. During the next two decades he pioneered in the adapting of Church materials, particularly historical, for the media, handled and later television programming; and prepared various materials for missionaries. He has had much to do with the temples of the Church.

He married Marjorie Pay on April 29, 1937, in the Salt Lake Temple. They have five children and 26 grandchildren.

In 1937 he was called to the Deseret Sunday School Union General Board, a position he held until being called as counselor in the East Millcreek Stake in 1946. After serving 10 years in this capacity, he was called in 1956 as president of that stake, a third-generation stake president. In 1951 he was appointed general secretary of the General Missionary Committee, and assisted in introducing uniform missionary lessons.

President Hinckley was sustained an Assistant to the Twelve April 6, 1958, and as a member of the Quorum of the Twelve Sept. 30, 1961. He was ordained an apostle Oct. 5, 1961, at age 51. His service as a General Authority is characterized by a caring and personal ministry among people across the world.

President Hinckley was called as a counselor to President Spencer W. Kimball on July 23, 1981, and as second counselor Dec. 2, 1982, serving until Nov. 5, 1985. He served as first counselor to President Ezra Taft Benson from Nov. 10, 1985, to May 30, 1994. He served as first counselor to President Howard W. Hunter from June 5, 1994, to March 3, 1995.

Thomas S. Monson

President Thomas S. Monson was set apart as first counselor to President Gordon B. Hinckley on March 12, 1995. He was also set apart as president of the Twelve on that date. He was previously set apart as second counselor to President Howard W. Hunter on June 5, 1994, and as second counselor to President Ezra Taft Benson Nov. 10, 1985. He was sustained to the Quorum of the Twelve Oct. 4, 1963, and ordained an apostle Oct. 10, 1963, at age 36.

Before being called as a General Authority, he was general manager of Deseret Press. He began employment with the *Deseret News* in 1948 as an advertising executive, and was chairman of the *Deseret News* board for 19 years. Born Aug. 21, 1927, in Salt Lake City, to G. Spencer and Gladys Condie Monson, he graduated cum laude from the University of Utah in business management, and received an MBA degree from BYU. In April 1981, Brigham Young University conferred upon him the honorary degree of Doctor of Laws.

He served in the Navy during World War II. He was ordained a bishop of a Salt Lake City ward at age 22. President Monson served in the presidency of the Temple View Stake in Salt Lake City and was called as president of the Canadian Mission in 1959. He and his wife, Frances Beverly Johnson Monson, are parents of three children and have six grandchildren.

James E. Faust

President James E. Faust was set apart as second counselor to President Gordon B. Hinckley on March 12, 1995, after serving as an apostle for 16 years. He was sustained an Assistant to the Twelve Oct. 6, 1972, and to the Presidency of the First Quorum of the Seventy Oct. 1, 1976. He was sustained to the Quorum of the Twelve Sept. 30, 1978, and ordained an apostle Oct. 1, 1978, at age 58.

President Faust has served as a regional representative, stake president, and bishop, and filled a mission in Brazil from 1939-42. He served in the Air Force during World War II. Afterward, he graduated from the University of Utah with a B.A. and juris doctorate in 1948.

An attorney, he practiced law in Salt Lake City until being called as a General Authority. He is a former Utah state legislator and was appointed by President John F. Kennedy to the Lawyer's Committee for Civil Rights and Racial Unrest. He was adviser to the American Bar Journal and the president of Utah Bar Association.

In 1996, he was given the Distinguished Lawyer Emeritus Award by the Utah Bar Association. He was born July 31, 1920, in Delta, Utah, a son of George A. and Amy Finlinson Faust. He and his wife, Ruth Wright Faust, are parents of five children and have 22 grandchildren.

THE QUORUM OF THE TWELVE APOSTLES

Set apart as acting President of the Quorum of the Twelve on June 5, 1994, and again March 12, 1995. Sustained an Assistant to the Twelve Sept. 30, 1961; sustained to the Quorum of the Twelve April 6, 1970, and ordained an apostle April 9, 1970, at age 45. Former supervisor of Seminaries and Institutes of Religion; former president of the New England States Mission. Received his bachelor's and master's degrees from Utah State University, and Ph.D. in educational administration from BYU. Pilot in the Pacific Theater during World War II. Born Sept. 10, 1924, in Brigham City, Utah, a son of Ira Wright and Emma Jensen Packer. Wife, Donna Smith Packer, parents of 10 children.

Boyd K. Packer

Sustained as Assistant to the Twelve Oct. 6, 1972; sustained to the Quorum of the Twelve on April 6, 1974, and ordained an apostle April 11, 1974, at age 51. Served in the Marines in the Pacific during World War II. Graduated from Utah State University with a B.S. degree in finance; was vice president and treasurer of department store chain in Boston, Mass. Born Aug. 5, 1922, in Logan, Utah, to L. Tom and Nora Sonne Perry. Married Virginia Lee, parents of three children. She died in 1974. Married Barbara Dayton in 1976.

L. Tom Perry

Sustained an Assistant to the Twelve April 6, 1970; ordained an apostle Jan. 8, 1976, at age 69, and sustained to the Quorum of the Twelve April 3, 1976. Former regional representative, president of Scottish Mission and stake president. Attended Utah State University. Former mayor of Palo Alto, Calif., district and regional manager of large retail store chain, assistant to president of BYU; a commander in the Navy during World War II. Born Sept. 2, 1906, at Oakley, Idaho, to Hector C. and Clara Tuttle Haight. Wife, Ruby Olson Haight, parents of three children.

David B. Haight

Called as Assistant to the Twelve April 6, 1974, and to the Presidency of the First Quorum of the Seventy Oct. 1, 1976; ordained an apostle July 23, 1981, at age 55, and sustained to Quorum of the Twelve Oct. 3, 1981. Received bachelor's degree in political science and master's degree from the University of Utah; has received four honorary doctorates. Former Church commissioner of education, former YMMIA general board member and regional representative. Former executive vice president of the University of Utah. Born in Salt Lake City, Utah, on July 6, 1926, to Clarence H. and Emma Ash Maxwell. Wife, Colleen Hinckley Maxwell, parents of four children.

Neal A. Maxwell

Russell M. Nelson

Sustained to the Quorum of the Twelve April 7, 1984, and ordained an apostle April 12, 1984, at age 59. Former Sunday School general president, regional representative and stake president. Renowned surgeon and medical researcher. Received B.A. and M.D. degrees from University of Utah, and Ph.D. from University of Minnesota. Former president of the Society for Vascular Surgery and former chairman of the Council on Cardiovascular Surgery for the American Heart Association. Born in Salt Lake City, Utah, on Sept. 9, 1924, a son of Marion C. and Edna Anderson Nelson. Wife, Dantzel White Nelson, parents of 10 children.

Sustained to Quorum of the Twelve April 7, 1984, and ordained an apostle on May 3, 1984, at age 51. Graduate of BYU in accounting; received juris doctorate cum laude from University of Chicago; was law clerk to U.S. Supreme Court Chief Justice Earl Warren, practiced law in Chicago, and was professor of law at University of Chicago for 10 years, and was executive director of the American Bar Foundation for a year. Served nine years as president of BYU, and three years as Utah Supreme Court justice. Born Aug. 12, 1932, in Provo, Utah, a son of Dr. Lloyd E. and Stella Harris Oaks. Wife, June Dixon Oaks, parents of six children.

Dallin H. Oaks

Sustained to the First Quorum of the Seventy April 3, 1976, and to the presidency of the quorum Feb. 21, 1980. Sustained to the Quorum of the Twelve Oct. 6, 1985, and ordained an apostle Oct. 10, 1985, at age 57. Attended the University of Utah; previously engaged in various business enterprises, including automotive, real estate and investments. Was president of the Canada Toronto Mission; also served as counselor in a mission presidency. The grandson of Apostles Melvin J. Ballard and Hyrum Mack Smith, he was born in Salt Lake City, Utah, on Oct. 8, 1928, to Melvin Russell Sr. and Geraldine Smith Ballard. Wife, Barbara Bowen Ballard, parents of seven children.

M. Russell Ballard

Sustained as an Assistant to the Twelve April 4, 1975, to the First Quorum of the Seventy on Oct. 1, 1976, and to the presidency of the quorum Aug. 28, 1986; sustained to the Quorum of the Twelve Oct. 4, 1986, and ordained an apostle Oct. 9, 1986, at age 69. Served in the Sunday School general presidency, former stake president's counselor. Graduate of University of Utah in business management; former president of trade association in Utah. Born June 11, 1917, in Salt Lake City, Utah, to Joseph L. and Madeline Bitner Wirthlin. Wife, Elisa Young Rogers Wirthlin, parents of eight children.

Joseph B. Wirthlin

Sustained to the First Quorum of the Seventy April 2, 1977, and to the presidency of the quorum on Oct. 1, 1983; sustained to the Quorum of the Twelve on Oct. 1, 1988, and ordained an apostle Oct. 6, 1988, at age 59. Received B.S. degree in mechanical engineering from George Washington University, and completed post-graduate work in nuclear engineering at Oakridge, Tenn. Worked 12 years on the staff of Adm. Hyman Rickover, developing military and private nuclear power reactors; subsequently consultant to nuclear power industry. Born Nov. 7, 1928, in Pocatello, Idaho, to Kenneth Leroy and Mary Eliza Whittle Scott. Married, Jeanene Watkins Scott, parents of seven children, five of whom are living; She died May 15, 1995.

Richard G. Scott

Sustained an Assistant to the Twelve April 4, 1975, and to the First Quorum of the Seventy Oct. 1, 1976; sustained as Presiding Bishop April 6, 1985; sustained to the Quorum of the Twelve April 2, 1994, and ordained an apostle April 7, 1994, at age 61. Former first counselor in the Sunday School general presidency, president of the England London Mission, regional representative, and served in various leadership positions, including stake president's counselor in the United States, England, Germany and Spain. Earned bachelor's degree from the University of Utah, and master of business administration degree from Harvard; served in the U.S. Air Force as a jet fighter pilot; was an executive with four major national companies. Born Aug. 24, 1932, in New York City, N.Y., to John Rulon and Vera Marie Holbrook Hales. Wife, Mary Elene Crandall Hales, parents of two sons.

Robert D. Hales

Sustained to the First Quorum of the Seventy on April 1, 1989, while serving as president of Brigham Young University in Provo, Utah; ordained an apostle June 23, 1994, at age 53; sustained to the Quorum of the Twelve Oct. 1, 1994. Former Church Commissioner of Education and director or instructor at many institutes of religion. Received bachelor's degree in English and master's degree in religious education from Brigham Young University, and master's degree and doctorate in American studies from Yale University. Born Dec. 3, 1940, in St. George, Utah, a son of Frank D. and Alice Bentley Holland. Wife, Patricia Terry Holland, parents of three children.

Jeffrey R. Holland

Sustained to the Quorum of the Twelve April 1, 1995, and ordained an apostle April 6, 1995, at age 61. Commissioner and deputy commissioner of education for the Church Educational System. Sustained as first counselor in the Presiding Bishopric April 6, 1985, at age 51; sustained to the First Quorum of the Seventy Oct. 3, 1992. Former regional representative, member of the Sunday School General Board and bishop. Received bachelor's degree from University of Utah, and master's degree and doctorate from Harvard University. Former president of Ricks College, 1971-77. Born May 31, 1933, in Princeton, N.J., to Henry and Mildred Bennion Eyring. Wife, Kathleen Johnson Eyring, parents of six children.

Henry B. Eyring

PRESIDENCY OF THE SEVENTY

L. Aldin Porter

Sustained to the First Quorum of the Seventy April 4, 1987, at age 55, and sustained to the Second Quorum of the Seventy on April 1, 1989; sustained to the First Quorum of the Seventy April 6, 1991; called to the Presidency of the Seventy Aug. 15, 1992, and sustained Oct. 3, 1992. Former counselor in the Boise Idaho Temple presidency, president of the Louisiana Baton Rouge Mission, regional representative, stake president, and bishop. A graduate of BYU, he was an executive of a financial planning company. Born June 30, 1931, in Salt Lake City, Utah, to J. Lloyd and Revon Hayward Porter. Wife, Shirley Palmer Porter, parents of six children.

Sustained to the First Quorum of the Seventy April 1, 1989, at age 59, while serving as president of Ricks College in Rexburg, Idaho; called to the Presidency of the Seventy Aug. 15, 1993, and sustained Oct. 2, 1993. Former mission president in Mexico, president of the Missionary Training Center in Provo, Utah, counselor in the Young Men and Melchizedek Priesthood MIA; active in Scouting, serving as council commissioner and a member of the National Exploring Standing Committee. Received bachelor's degree from BYU, doctorate in education from Washington State University. Served as associate commissioner of education for the Church Educational System and has been director of several institutes of religion. Born July 21, 1929, in Banida, Idaho, to Joseph A. and Goldie Miles Christensen. Wife, Barbara Kohler Christensen, parents of six children.

Joe J. Christensen

Monte J. Brough

Sustained to the First Quorum of the Seventy Oct. 1, 1988, at age 49; sustained to the Second Quorum of the Seventy April 1, 1989; sustained to the First Quorum of the Seventy April 6, 1991; called to the Presidency of the Seventy Aug. 15, 1993, and sustained Oct. 2, 1993. Former regional representative, president of the Minnesota Minneapolis Mission, member of the Young Men General Board, and bishop. Received bachelor's degree and doctorate in business administration from University of Utah; former president and founder of financial management company. Born June 11, 1939, in Randolph, Utah, to Richard Muir and Gwendolyn Kearl Brough. Wife, Lanette Barker Brough, parents of seven children.

Sustained to the First Quorum of the Seventy April 1, 1989, at age 60; called to the Presidency of the Seventy Aug. 15, 1993, and sustained Oct. 2, 1993. Former stake president, stake Young Men president, and bishop. Graduate of Utah State University, where he received bachelor's degree in agricultural economics; received juris doctorate from the University of Utah; former trial lawyer, president of the Utah State Bar Association; served on active duty in the Army during the Korean War, and in the U.S. Army Reserve from 1950-1980. Born Aug. 23, 1928, in Tremonton, Utah, to Warren E. and Ruth Steed Hansen. Wife, Jeanine Showell Hansen, parents of six children.

W. Eugene Hansen

Young Men general president. Sustained to the First Quorum of the Seventy Sept. 30, 1978, at age 50, and served in the Presidency of the Seventy from Oct. 6, 1985 to Aug. 15, 1987; called a second time to the Presidency of the Seventy Aug. 15, 1995, and sustained Sept. 30, 1995. Former counselor in Aaronic Priesthood MIA general presidency, former president of the Arizona Tempe Mission, regional representative, stake president and bishop. Graduate of University of Utah; was vice president of a metals corporation, also served as officer in U.S. Air Force. Born April 18, 1928, in Salt Lake City, Utah, to Jack H. and Anita Jack Goaslind. Wife, Gwen Caroline Bradford Goaslind, parents of six children.

Jack H Goaslind

Sunday School general president. Sustained to the Second Quorum of the Seventy March 31, 1990, at age 54; sustained to the First Quorum of the Seventy April 6, 1991; called to the Presidency of the Seventy Aug. 15, 1995, and sustained Sept. 30, 1995. Former regional representative, president of the Portugal Lisbon Mission, stake president and counselor. An orthodontist, he has been president of the Rocky Mountain Society of Orthodontists. Born Sept. 1, 1935, at Sugar City, Idaho, to Gordon R. and Florence Evelyn Skidmore Hillam. Wife, Carol Lois Rasmussen Hillam, parents of seven children.

Harold G. Hillam

Called to the First Quorum of the Seventy Dec. 5, 1990, at age 56, and sustained April 6, 1991; called to the Presidency of the Seventy Aug. 15, 1996, and sustained Oct. 5, 1996. Former regional representative, president of the Australia Sydney Mission, counselor in the presidencies of the Eastern States, Utah North and Utah Ogden missions, and bishop. Formerly corporate attorney for Kennecott Copper Corp.; graduated from the University of Utah Law School and earned a master's degree from New York University. Born June 11, 1934, in Bountiful, Utah, to William W. and Sylvia Carr Tingey. Wife, Joanne Wells Tingey, parents of four children.

Earl C. Tingey

FIRST QUORUM OF THE SEVENTY

Sustained to the First Quorum of the Seventy April 4, 1981, at age 47; first Argentine General Authority. Former president of Argentina Rosario Mission and the Buenos Aires Argentina Temple, stake president and regional representative. Graduate of University of Buenos Aires; certified public accountant; served as secretary of the treasury in San Miguel, Argentina. Born Sept. 13, 1933, in Buenos Aires, Argentina, to Edealo and Zulema Estrada Abrea. Wife, Maria Victoria Chiapparino de Abrea, parents of three daughters.

Angel Abrea

Sustained to the Second Quorum of the Seventy April 1, 1989, at age 44; called to the First Quorum of the Seventy June 6, 1992, and sustained Oct. 3, 1992. Former president of the Guatemala Guatemala City Mission, where he was assigned to reopen the El Salvador San Salvador Mission, chairman of the Guatemala City Temple Committee, regional representative, stake president and counselor, bishop, and branch president. Received degree from the Technical Vocational Institute of Guatemala City; former technical draftsman, and later became an area director for the Church Educational System. Born Sept. 25, 1944, in Guatemala City, Guatemala, to Carlos and Rosario Funes de Amado. Wife, Mayavel Pineda Amado, parents of five children.

Carlos H. Amado

Sustained to the First Quorum of the Seventy April 3, 1993, at age 41. President of the France Bordeaux Mission from 1989-92, former stake president and stake president's counselor. Graduated cum laude with a bachelor's degree from BYU, master of business from Harvard Graduate School of Business. Born Aug. 9, 1951, in Logan, Utah, to Lyle P. and Kathryn Andersen. Wife, Kathy Sue Williams Andersen, parents of four children.

Neil L. Andersen

Called to the Second Quorum of the Seventy June 6, 1992, at age 53, and sustained Oct. 3, 1992; sustained to the First Quorum of the Seventy April 6, 1996. Former regional representative, president of the Spain Seville Mission and bishop. Was vice president of an international industrial chemical company and lived in seven other countries. Received bachelor's degree in Spanish from Weber State College, master's degree from Thunderbird Graduate School of International Management. Born July 24, 1938, in Logan, Utah, to Ezra Wilson and Marguerite Nielsen Archibald. Wife, Linda Ritchie Archibald, parents of one daughter.

Dallas N. Archibald

Sustained to the Second Quorum of the Seventy on April 1, 1989, at age 56; called to the First Quorum of the Seventy June 6, 1992, and sustained Oct. 3, 1992. Former president of the Scotland Edinburgh Mission, stake president, and bishop of three different wards. Attended the University of Utah and was owner and president of lumber company; formerly employed by two road machinery equipment companies. Born April 4, 1932, in Murray, Utah, to Ben F. and Samantha Berry Banks. Wife, Susan Kearnes Banks, parents of seven children and one foster child.

Ben B. Banks

Merrill J. Bateman

President of BYU. Called to the Second Quorum of the Seventy June 6, 1992, at age 55, and sustained Oct. 3, 1992; sustained as Presiding Bishop April 2, 1994; called to the First Quorum of the Seventy Nov. 2, 1995, and sustained April 6, 1996. Former regional representative and stake president twice. Owner of two management companies; former dean of BYU College of Business, and served as business consultant to nations in West Africa. Received bachelor's degree from University of Utah and doctorate in economics from Massachusetts Institute of Technology. Born June 19, 1936, in Lehi, Utah, to Joseph Frederic and Belva Smith Bateman. Wife, Marilyn Scholes Bateman, parents of seven children.

Sustained to the First Quorum of the Seventy Oct. 3, 1975, at age 41, while president of Chile Mission; lived in Latin America and Asia for several years while in Church leadership positions. Was in fruit growing and shipping business in Texas, and owner of a company that grew citrus and tropical fruits in Texas, Mexico and Central America for distribution in the United States and other countries; attended BYU. Born Oct. 25, 1933, in Springville, Utah, to Rawsel W. and Mary Waddoups Bradford. Wife, Mary Ann Bird Bradford, parents of six children.

William R. Bradford

F. Enzio Busche

Sustained to the First Quorum of the Seventy Oct. 1, 1977, at age 47. Former president of Frankfurt Germany Temple, Germany Munich Mission, regional representative and district president; converted to the Church in 1958. Graduate in economics and management from Bonn and Freiburg universities, and did graduate studies in technical printing; former chief executive officer of large printing and publishing company in Germany. Born April 5, 1930, at Dortmund, Germany, to Friedrich and Anna Weber Busche. Wife, Jutta Baum Busche, parents of four children.

Sustained to the First Quorum of the Seventy April 7, 1984, at age 52, while president of Idaho Boise Mission. Former regional representative, stake president. Received B.A. degree from BYU, law degree from University of California at Los Angeles; an attorney, he was legislative assistant in California Legislature; was president of a law firm in Los Angeles and past president of Westwood Bar Association. Born May 10, 1931, in Winslow, Ariz., to Cecil E. and Gladys Bushman Carmack. Wife, Shirley Fay Allen Carmack, parents of five children.

John K. Carmack

Sustained to the First Quorum of the Seventy April 3, 1993, at age 48. Former regional representative, stake president, stake president's counselor, bishop. Received bachelor's degree from BYU, juris doctorate from Duke University. Associate general counsel of NationsBank Corp. in Charlotte, N.C.; practiced law in Washington D.C. and was volunteer chairman of Middle Tennessee Literacy Coalition, and Affordable Housing of Nashville, Tenn. Born Jan. 24, 1945, in American Fork, Utah, to Paul V. and Jeanne Swenson Christofferson. Wife, Katherine Thelma Jacob Christofferson, parents of five children.

D. Todd Christofferson

Sustained as second counselor in Presiding Bishopric Oct. 1, 1976, at age 49, to the First Quorum of the Seventy April 6, 1985, and to the Presidency of the First Quorum of the Seventy Oct. 1, 1988, serving until Aug. 15, 1993. Former president of the South Africa Cape Town Mission, regional representative, stake president, counselor in a stake presidency. Graduate of BYU with B.S. in marketing, did graduate work at Stanford University; former agency manager for life insurance company in Boise, Idaho. Born April 4, 1927, at Rexburg, Idaho, to John Roland and Nora L. Redford Clarke. Wife, Barbara Jean Reed Clarke, parents of eight children.

J. Richard Clarke

Sustained to the Second Quorum of the Seventy April 1, 1989, at age 48; called to the First Quorum of the Seventy June 6, 1992, and sustained Oct. 3, 1992. Former president of the Austria Vienna Mission, regional representative, stake president and bishop of two wards. Former professor of sociology and ancient scripture at Brigham Young University. Born Aug. 27, 1940, in Preston, Idaho, to Spencer C. and Josie Peterson Condie. Wife, Dorthea Speth Condie, parents of five children.

Spencer J. Condie

Sustained to the First Council of the Seventy Oct. 3, 1975, at age 34, and to the First Quorum of the Seventy Oct. 1, 1976. Former executive secretary to the First Council of the Seventy, president of Uruguay-Paraguay Mission, and lived in Latin American countries for many years while on Church assignments. Previously was consultant, agency manager and trainer for life insurance firm, management trainer for Church employment. Received bachelor's and master's degrees in business administration from Arizona State University. Born Sept. 1, 1941, at Lehi, Utah, to Clarence H. and Myrl Johnson Cook. Wife, Janelle Schlink Cook, parents of eight children.

Gene R. Cook

Sustained to the Second Quorum of the Seventy March 31, 1990, at age 52; called to the First Quorum of the Seventy June 6, 1992, and sustained Oct. 3, 1992. Former president of the Germany Duesseldorf and Germany Munich missions, regional representative, stake president and bishop. Former president, vice president, and business manager of various universities; has worked for the Salk Institute and was involved with a company that assisted agencies and scientific institutes in the Soviet Union. Born May 10, 1937, in Salt Lake City, Utah, to Frank and Leona Conshafter Dellenbach. Wife, Mary-Jayne Broadbent Dellenbach, parents of three sons.

Robert K. Dellenbach

Called to the Second Quorum of the Seventy June 6, 1992, at age 48, and sustained Oct. 3, 1992. Sustained to the First Quorum of the Seventy on April 1, 1995. Former president of the Mexico Mexico City North Mission, stake president and stake president's counselor. Was vice president of sawmill and timber company. Received bachelor's degree from Brigham Young University in business administration. Born July 12, 1943, in Tacoma, Wash., to John H. and Helen Baird Dickson. Wife, Deloris Jones Dickson, parents of eight children.

John B. Dickson

Sustained to the First Quorum of the Seventy Oct. 3, 1975, at age 39; called to the Presidency of the Seventy Aug. 15, 1992, and sustained Oct. 3, 1992; served until Aug. 15, 1995. Sunday School general president 1994-95. Former president of France Switzerland Mission and regional representative; converted to Church in 1957; fluent in five languages, Flemish, French, German, Spanish and English. Received bachelor's degree in economics from University of Liege in Belgium; served as officer in the Belgian Air Force Reserve. Born Oct. 5, 1935, at Ixelles, Belgium, to Andre and Gabrielle Colpaert Didier. Wife, Lucie Lodomez Didier, parents of two sons.

Charles Didier

Sustained to the First Council of the Seventy April 6, 1968, at age 37, and to the First Quorum of the Seventy Oct. 1, 1976; has lived in Brazil, Australia, Philippines and New Zealand while in Church leadership positions. Former president of Australia Sydney Mission, counselor in mission presidency. Received degree in journalism and economics from BYU and M.S. in public relations from Boston University; former executive with economic development board in Boston. Born June 12, 1930, in Tooele, Utah, to Alex F. and Carol Horsfall Dunn. Wife, Sharon Longden Dunn, parents of five children.

Loren C. Dunn

First counselor in the Young Men general presidency. Sustained as second counselor in Presiding Bishopric April 6, 1972, at age 41; sustained to the First Quorum of the Seventy Oct. 1, 1976. Former Young Men general president, president of Texas San Antonio Mission, member of the YMMIA General Board and stake president; member, Boy Scouts of America National Executive Board, recipient of Silver Antelope and Silver Buffalo awards; former corporate training manager of supermarket chain based in Boise, Idaho. Born March 26, 1931, at Stockton, Utah, to Stephen E. and Emma M. Johnson Featherstone. Wife, Merlene Miner Featherstone, parents of seven children.

Vaughn J Featherstone

Sustained to the First Quorum of the Seventy April 3, 1976, at age 41. Former president of the Tonga Mission, regional representative and bishop. Has lived in South America and Hawaii while in Church leadership positions. Received bachelor's degree from BYU, master of business administration degree from Indiana University, where he also taught; formerly in real estate, development, and construction; was vice president of Idaho State Real Estate Association. Born June 17, 1934, in Idaho Falls, Idaho, to Delbert V. and Jennie Holbrook Groberg. Wife, Jean Sabin Groberg, parents of 11 children.

John H. Groberg

Sustained to the First Quorum of the Seventy April 6,1996, at age 55. Former regional representative, counselor in stake presidency, counselor in bishopric. Former president of Ricks College and provost at Brigham Young University. Received bachelor's degree in political science and humanities from Brigham Young University, juris doctorate from University of Utah. Born Oct. 30, 1940, in St. George, Utah, to Orval and Ruth Clark Hafen. Wife, Marie Kartchner Hafen, parents of seven children.

Bruce C. Hafen

Sustained to the Second Quorum of the Seventy April 1, 1989, at age 55; sustained to the First Quorum of the Seventy April 3, 1993. Former president of the Bolivia Cochabamba Mission, stake president, bishop and temple worker in the Idaho Falls Temple. Was professor of religion at Ricks College; served eight terms in the Idaho State Legislature and was minority leader for three terms. Born Dec. 19, 1933, in Blackfoot, Idaho, to Floyd Milton and Ruby Hoge Hammond. Wife, Bonnie Sellers Hammond, parents of six children.

F. Melvin
Hammond

First counselor in the Sunday School general presidency. Sustained to the First Quorum of the Seventy Sept. 30, 1978, at age 45. Former president of Uruguay Montevideo Mission and stake president; was special representative for First Presidency in Latin American affairs. Graduate of Utah State University, received law degree from the University of Utah; former assistant attorney general for Utah, chief counsel for Utah Tax Commission, legal counsel for Mexico in Intermountain Area and managing partner of Salt Lake City law firm. Born March 24, 1933, at Logan, Utah, to Fred P. and Beatrice Ward Howard.

F. Burton Howard   Wife, Caroline Heise Howard, parents of five children.

Called to the Second Quorum of the Seventy June 6, 1992, at age 50, and sustained Oct. 3, 1992. Sustained to the First Quorum of the Seventy on April 1, 1995. Former president of the Colombia Cali Mission, counselor in the Missionary Training Center presidency, stake president's counselor and bishop. Formerly director of scriptures coordination for the Church Curriculum Department. Received bachelor's, master's and doctoral degrees in Spanish and history, Church history and doctrine, and education, respectively, from BYU. Born Feb. 5, 1942, in Payson, Utah, to Ruel W. and Ethel Otte Jensen. Wife, Lona Lee Child Jensen, parents of six children.

Jay E. Jensen

Marlin K. Jensen

Sustained to the First Quorum of the Seventy April 1, 1989, at age 46. Former president of the New York Rochester Mission, regional representative, stake president and bishop. Received bachelor's degree in German from Brigham Young University and juris doctorate from the University of Utah; was attorney specializing in business and estate planning. Born May 18, 1942, in Ogden, Utah, to Keith G. and Lula Hill Jensen. Wife, Kathleen Bushnell Jensen, parents of eight children.

Sustained to the Second Quorum of the Seventy March 31, 1990, at age 49; sustained to the First Quorum of the Seventy April 3, 1993. Former regional representative and stake president; converted to the Church in 1959. Graduated from Norwich City College in England and did graduate work at the City and Guilds of London Institute of Printing; former college instructor and partner in a British insurance brokerage firm. Born July 5, 1940, at Norwich, England, to Bertie A.M. and Ada Hutson Johnson. Wife, Pamela Wilson Johnson, parents of a son.

Kenneth Johnson

Sustained to the First Quorum of the Seventy April 2, 1988, at age 56; sustained to the Second Quorum of the Seventy April 1, 1989; sustained to the First Quorum of the Seventy April 6, 1991. Former president of Florida Tampa Mission, regional representative and stake president; converted to the Church while in the U.S. Air Force in 1954. Received bachelor's, master's and doctoral degrees of education from Louisiana State University; was professor of health education and director of the Regional Training Center at East Carolina University. Born Sept. 19, 1931, in Baton Rouge, La., to Bonnie Delen and Edna Campbell Forbes Kendrick. Wife, Myrtis Lee Noble Kendrick, parents of four children.

L. Lionel Kendrick

President of Tokyo Temple. Sustained to the First Quorum of the Seventy Oct. 1, 1977, at age 36; first native-born Japanese called as General Authority. Former president of Hawaii Honolulu Mission, was stake president and counselor to mission president; converted to the Church in 1955. Graduated from Asia University of Tokyo in business psychology and management; former sales manager over Japan for a cookware company, president of a Japanese food storage company. Born July 25, 1941, to Hatsuo and Koyo Ideda Kikuchi at Hokkaido, Japan. Wife, Toshiko Koshiya Kikuchi, parents of four children.

Yoshihiko Kikuchi

Sustained to the Second Quorum of the Seventy April 6, 1991, at age 57, and to the First Quorum of the Seventy April 2, 1994. Former regional representative, president of the New York New York Mission, stake president twice and bishop. Was managing partner in a law firm. Received bachelor's degree from University of Utah, juris doctorate from the University of Southern California. Born July 11, 1933, in Santaquin, Utah, to Cree Clarence and Melba Nelson Kofford. Wife, Ila Macdonald Kofford, parents of five children.

Cree-L Kofford

Sustained to the First Quorum of the Seventy Oct. 1, 1976, at age 49, and to the quorum presidency Feb. 22, 1980, serving until Aug. 15, 1993. Served as president of the Texas South Mission, regional representative, member of the Sunday School general board, secretary of Adult Correlation Committee, member of Priesthood Missionary Committee. Graduated from Utah State University in English, was basketball coach and seminary teacher. Born May 24, 1927, at Hyrum, Utah, to Edgar Niels and Gertrude Prouse Larsen. Wife, Geneal Johnson Larsen, parents of five children.

Dean L. Larsen

Lynn A. Mickelsen

Sustained to the Second Quorum of the Seventy March 31, 1990, at age 54, and to the First Quorum of the Seventy April 3, 1993. Former president of the Colombia Cali Mission, regional representative, stake president and bishop. Attended Ricks College and graduated from BYU. Served on a hospital board and in farm associations; formerly self-employed as a farmer and potato shipper. Born July 21, 1935, at Idaho Falls, Idaho, to Lloyd P. and Reva Faye Willmore Mickelsen. Wife, Jeanine Andersen Mickelsen, parents of nine children.

Sustained to the First Quorum of the Seventy April 4, 1987, at age 56; sustained to the Second Quorum of the Seventy April 1, 1989; sustained to the First Quorum of the Seventy April 6, 1991. Former regional representative, bishop, and branch president. Received master's degrees from University of Alberta and University of Michigan, and doctorate at Cornell University, formerly professor and chairman of Food Sciences Department at University of Guelph in Canada, and was assistant deputy minister of National Health and Welfare for Canada, honored for humanitarian work. Born Dec. 22, 1930, in Edmonton, Alberta, to Alexander S. and Christina Wilson Morrison. Wife, Shirley Brooks Morrison, parents of eight children.

Alexander B. Morrison

Dennis B. Neuenschwander

Sustained to the Second Quorum of the Seventy April 6, 1991, at age 51; sustained to First Quorum of the Seventy Oct. 1, 1994. Former president of the Austria Vienna East Mission and counselor in mission presidency. Was manager of International Area of Acquisitions Division of the Church Genealogical Department. Received bachelor's degree from BYU, master's degree and doctorate in Russian literature from Syracuse University in New York. Born Oct. 6, 1939, at Salt Lake City, Utah, to George Henry and Genevieve Bramwell Neuenschwander. Wife, LeAnn Clement Neuenschwander, parents of four sons.

Second counselor in the general Sunday School presidency. Sustained as second counselor in the Presiding Bishopric April 6, 1985, at age 45; sustained to the First Quorum of the Seventy Oct. 3, 1992. Former bishop's counselor, stake clerk, elders quorum president and president of the Australia Sydney North Mission. Received bachelor's and master's degrees in accounting from BYU; was a certified public accountant, employed by a national accounting firm and was chief financial officer for a land development company; managing director of Church Welfare Services for nearly four years. Born March 21, 1940, in Provo, Utah, to Kenneth LeRoy and Elizabeth A. Wilde Pace. Wife, Jolene Clayson Pace, parents of six children.

Glenn L. Pace

Sustained to the First Quorum of the Seventy April 2, 1977, at age 48, and to the quorum presidency Aug. 15, 1987, serving until Aug. 15, 1993. Former executive secretary to the Council of the Twelve, president of the Franco-Belgian Mission. Graduate of BYU, former executive director of Utah Committee on Children and Youth, and was on board of directors of National Committee on Children and Youth. Born May 6, 1928, in Salt Lake City, Utah, to James F. and Ruth C. Martin Paramore. Wife, Helen Heslington Paramore, parents of six children.

James M. Paramore

Sustained to the First Quorum of the Seventy Oct. 1, 1994, at age 47. Former regional representative, president of the Mexico Merida Mission from 1981-84, and stake president. Received bachelor's degree from the University of Utah, and graduated from the University of Pacific Dental School; practiced dentistry in Salt Lake City for 20 years. Did volunteer work with the Lowell Bennion Community Service Center and Utah Bolivia Partners. Born June 8, 1947, in San Francisco, Calif., to Wayne Leo and Virginia Parker Peterson. Wife, Christine Ann Swensen Peterson, parents of eight children.

Andrew W. Peterson

Sustained to First Council of the Seventy Oct. 6, 1972, at age 41; sustained to First Quorum of the Seventy Oct. 1, 1976, and to the quorum presidency Sept. 30, 1989, where he served until Aug. 15, 1995. Served as counselor in the Young Men general presidency from 1979-85. Received bachelor's degree from BYU, master's degree from San Francisco State College, and doctorate in education from the University of Southern California. Former chairman of the Educational Psychology Department at BYU. Born Sept. 18, 1931, in Orem, Utah, to John F. and Grace Murl Ellis Pinegar. Wife, Bonnie Lee Crabb Pinegar, parents of six children.

Rex D. Pinegar

Sustained to the First Quorum of the Seventy Oct. 1, 1977, at age 43, and served in the quorum presidency from Oct. 4, 1986-Oct. 1, 1989; served twice as general president of the Sunday School, 1979-86 and 1989-92. Former regional representative and president of Pennsylvania Harrisburg Mission. Graduate of University of Utah, former area general agent for insurance company, president of Deseret Foundation of LDS Hospital, was appointed to serve on several governmental boards. Born Jan. 15, 1934, in Salt Lake City, Utah, to Lawrence Sylvester and Florence Boden Pinnock. Wife, Anne Hawkins Pinnock, parents of six children.

Hugh W. Pinnock

Sustained to the First Quorum of the Seventy April 1, 1978, at age 49; served in Sunday School general presidency, 1979-81, and from Oct. 3, 1992 to Aug. 15, 1994. Graduate of the University of Utah with juris doctorate; also graduated from Harvard University Graduate School of Business Administration, Advanced Management Program; was vice president, secretary and director of trucking company. Born May 10, 1928, in Salt Lake City, Utah, to Hendrick and Ella May Perkins Poelman. Married Claire Howell Stoddard, parents of four children; she died May 5, 1979. Married Anne G. Osborn June 29, 1982.

Ronald E. Poelman

Sustained to the First Quorum of the Seventy Oct. 1, 1994, at age 53. Former regional representative and stake president. He received bachelor's and master's degrees and medical degree from the University of Utah; was a physician and senior vice president of Intermountain Health Care and former vice president for health sciences and dean of the School of Medicine at the University of Utah; served as director of the Utah Chapter of the American Red Cross and Catholic Heathcare West in San Francisco. Born Aug. 1, 1941, to Cecil Osborn Sr. and Janet Brazier Mitchell Samuelson. Wife, Sharon Giauque Samuelson; parents of five children.

Cecil O. Samuelson Jr.

Called to the Second Quorum of the Seventy June 6, 1992, at age 58, and sustained Oct. 3, 1992. Sustained to the First Quorum of the Seventy April 1, 1995. Former president of the Canada Halifax Mission, stake president and counselor and bishop. Was chairman and chief executive officer of North American Health Care, a hospital chain, and board vice chairman of Nevada Community Bank in Las Vegas, Nev. Attended BYU, Utah State University and University of Utah. Born June 29, 1933, in Aurora, Utah, to Alma and Metta Amelia Helquist Sorensen. Wife, Verla Anderson Sorensen, parents of seven children.

David E. Sorensen

Sustained to the Second Quorum of the Seventy April 2, 1994, at age 53; sustained to the First Quorum of the Seventy April 6, 1996. Former stake president and stake mission president. Senior vice president for flight operations and chief pilot for Lufthansa German Airlines, and check and training captain for Boeing 747s; received wings as a jet fighter pilot in the German Air Force in 1962. Born Nov. 6, 1940, in Ostrava, Czechoslovakia, to Karl Albert and Hilde Else Opelt Uchtdorf. Wife, Harriett Reich Uchtdorf, parents of two children.

Dieter F. Uchtdorf

Sustained to the First Quorum of the Seventy Oct. 1, 1976, at age 48. Former mission president in Mexico and served as branch president, district president, regional representative in Latin America. Graduate of BYU; was former head of Central Purchasing for the Church, and former banking executive in South America for 18 years for a New York City-based bank. Born Dec. 28, 1927, in Las Vegas, Nev., to Robert Stephen and Zella Verona Earl Wells. Married Meryl Leavitt, who died in 1960. Wife, Helen Walser Wells, parents of seven children, including Sharlene Wells Hawkes, Miss America of 1985.

Robert E. Wells

Sustained to the First Quorum of the Seventy April 1, 1995, at age 47. Former president of the Chile Santiago South Mission, stake Young Men president, stake mission president's counselor, high councilor and bishop's counselor. Was executive director of the Utah Department of Transportation, former building contractor for 20 years. Received bachelor of science in business management from the University of Utah. Born June 30, 1947, in Salt Lake City, Utah, to William E. and Audrey McDonough Zwick. Wife, Janet Johnson Zwick, parents of four children.

W. Craig Zwick

THE SECOND QUORUM OF THE SEVENTY

Called to the Second Quorum of the Seventy June 6, 1992, at age 47, and sustained Oct. 3, 1992. Former regional representative, president of the Mexico Mexico City South Mission, patriarch, stake president's counselor twice and bishop. Church Educational System coordinator for Mexico. Received bachelor's degree in education from Superior School of Mexico. Born July 18, 1944, in Arteaga, Couhiula, Mexico, to Lino and Margarita Vasquez Alvarez. Wife, Argelia de Villanueva de Alvarez, parents of three children.

Lino Alvarez

Sustained to the Second Quorum of the Seventy April 6, 1996, at age 58. Former area authority in the North America Northwest Area, stake president, bishop and stake mission president. Was area director for Church Educational System; former mayor of Pocatello, Idaho. Received bachelor's degree in English and mathematics from Utah State University, master's and doctorate degrees in educational administration from University of Kansas. Born June 18, 1937, in Preston, Idaho, to Lowell and Helen Peterson Brown. Wife, Carol Ewer Brown, parents of eight children.

L. Edward Brown

Called to the Second Quorum of the Seventy June 6, 1992, at age 58, and sustained Oct. 3, 1992. Former regional representative, president of the Louisiana Baton Rouge Mission, stake president's counselor and bishop. Former associate professor of Church history at BYU. Received bachelor's degree from the University of Utah in business management and master's degree from BYU in Church history and doctrine. Born Dec. 4, 1933, in Salt Lake City, Utah, to Chellus M. and Electa J. Caldwell. Wife, Bonnie Adamson Caldwell, parents of five children.

C. Max Caldwell

Sustained to the Second Quorum of the Seventy April 6, 1996, at age 57. Former area authority in the Utah North Area, president of New York New York Mission, stake president, counselor and bishop. Was president of R.C. Willey Home Furnishings. Studied at University of Utah and Utah State University. Born May 8, 1938, in Ogden, Utah, to Mark Fay and Viola Criddle Child. Wife, Joan Haacke Child, parents of six children.

Sheldon F. Child

Called to the Second Quorum of the Seventy June 6, 1992, at age 50, and sustained Oct. 3, 1992. Former president of the California Arcadia Mission, counselor in the Utah Ogden Mission, stake president's counselor and bishop. Was associate director and instructor at Weber State University Institute of Religion. Received bachelor's degree in physical education from Washington State University, master's degree and doctorate from BYU in counseling and guidance. Born Sept. 18, 1941, Wenatchee, Wash., to Benton Joseph and Evalin Barrett Coleman. Wife, Judith Renee England Coleman, parents of six children.

Gary J. Coleman

Sustained to the Second Quorum of the Seventy April 6, 1996, at age 55. Former area authority in the North America West Area, regional representative, stake president, counselor and bishop. Was vice chairman of Sutter/California Healthcare System. Received bachelor's degree in political science from Utah State University, law degree from Stanford University Law School. Born Sept. 8, 1940, in Logan, Utah, to J. Vernon and Bernice Kimball Cook. Wife, Mary Gaddie Cook, parents of three children.

Quentin L. Cook

Sustained to the Second Quorum of the Seventy April 2, 1994, at age 45. Served as president of the Brazil Manaus Mission 1990-93, regional representative, stake president's counselor and bishop. Graduated from Colegio Pio XII, attended Paulista School of Marketing, Paulista Institute of Gems and Precious Metals. Former Church Educational System associate area director, diamond cutter, manager of jewelry store chain and finance director of diversified Almeida Prado Co. Born March 25, 1949, in Santos, Brazil, to Nelson Mendes Costa and Luzia Tassar Simoes Costa. Wife, Margareth Fernandes Morgado Mendes Costa; parents of four children.

Claudio R. M. Costa

Called to the Second Quorum of the Seventy June 6, 1992, at age 47, and sustained Oct. 3, 1992. Former regional representative, president of the Georgia Atlanta Mission, stake president and stake president's counselor. Was consultant and financial adviser to international oil and gas company. Received bachelor's and master's degrees in accounting from BYU. Born Nov. 10, 1944, in Redding, Calif., to R. Walter and Lois Manita Clayton Fowler. Wife, Marie S. Spilsbury Fowler, parents of six children.

John E. Fowler

Sustained to the Second Quorum of the Seventy April 6, 1996, at age 60. Former president of Texas Dallas Mission, stake president, high councilor, bishop's counselor and member of Sunday School general board. Was Utah State Commissioner of Higher Education. Received bachelor's degree in agriculture and master's degree in marriage and family relations from Utah State University, doctorate in educational administration from University of Utah. Born June 29, 1935, in Tremonton, Utah, to Clifton G. and Irene Pack Kerr. Wife, Janeil Raybould Kerr, parents of six children.

Wm. Rolfe Kerr

W. Don Ladd

Sustained to the Second Quorum of the Seventy April 2, 1994, at age 60. Former regional representative, stake president and counselor, bishop and branch president. Was vice president for government affairs for Marriott International, Inc., in Washington, D.C.; also served as adviser to the Church on international and governmental affairs. Born July 14, 1933, in San Mateo, Fla., to Joseph Donald and Phyllis Rose Anderson Ladd. Wife, Ruth Lynne Pearson Ladd, parents of four children.

Called to the Second Quorum of the Seventy June 6, 1992, at age 58 and sustained Oct. 3, 1992. First Filipino General Authority. Former president of the Philippines Naga Mission, regional representative, stake president, temple sealer and mission president's counselor; converted in 1964. An attorney and law professor, he received bachelor of law degree from Silliman University at Dumaguete City, Philippines. Born May 4, 1934, in Santa Cruz, Philippines, to Leon B. and Beatriz R. Alandy Lim. Wife, Myrna Garcia Morillo Lim, parents of eight children.

Augusto A. Lim

John M. Madsen

Called to the Second Quorum of the Seventy June 6, 1992, at age 53, and sustained Oct. 3, 1992. Former president of the England Southwest Mission, member of the Melchizedek Priesthood MIA general board and Young Men general board and regional representative. Was BYU religion professor. Received bachelor's in zoology from Washington State University, master's degree and doctorate in education from BYU. Born April 24, 1939, in Washington, D.C. to Louis L. and Edith Louise Gundersen Madsen. Wife, Diane Dursteler Madsen, parents of six children.

Sustained to the Second Quorum of the Seventy April 2, 1994, at age 63. Served as regional representative, member of the Young Men general board, stake president, and bishop. Received bachelor's and medical degrees from the University of Utah, master's degree and doctorate of public health from Harvard University. Was assistant secretary for health and head of U.S. Public Health Service in the U.S. Department of Health and Human Services, director of Centers for Disease Control, executive director of Utah Department of Health and Church commissioner of Health Services. Born June 19, 1930, in Salt Lake City, Utah, to A. Stanton and Neoma Thorup Mason. Wife, Marie Smith Mason, parents of seven children.

James O. Mason

Called to the Second Quorum of the Seventy June 6, 1992, at age 56, and sustained Oct. 3, 1992. Former president of the Utah Salt Lake City South Mission, regional representative, stake president's counselor and bishop. Was president and founder of leadership and consulting companies, and family and taxpayer political action organizations; candidate for U.S. Senate in Maryland. Received bachelor's and master's degrees from BYU, doctorate from University of Southern California in management and public affairs. Born Jan. 25, 1936, in Basalt, Idaho, to Victor Lybbert and Beatrice Jensen Merrell. Wife, Karen Dixon Merrell, parents of nine children.

V. Dallas Merrell

Sustained to the Second Quorum of the Seventy April 1, 1995, at age 42. He has served as stake president's counselor, stake mission president, bishop and branch president. Was an associate professor of political science at BYU and former executive director of the U.S. Board for International Broadcasting, and a research fellow at Harvard University. He has also served as a corporate analyst for the Northrop Corporation and a staff member of the U.S. Senate Armed Services Committee. Graduated from BYU and earned M.A. and Ph.D. degrees from Harvard University. Born in Albuquerque, N. M., Sept. 18, 1952, to Lyle Kay and Wilma Holmes Porter. Wife, Susan Elizabeth Holland Porter, parents of four children.

Bruce D. Porter

Sustained to the Second Quorum of the Seventy April, 6, 1996, at age 61. Former area authority in the North America Southwest Area, regional representative, president of Washington D.C. North Mission, stake president, counselor, high councilor, bishop, temple sealer. Was senior partner in his own law firm. Received bachelor's degree in music education and English from Utah State University and law degree from George Washington University Law School. Born June 27, 1934, in Beaver Dam, Utah, to Thomas Yates and Sylvia Ericksen Simmons. Wife, Carolyn Thorpe Simmons, parents of six children.

Dennis E. Simmons

Second counselor in the general Young Men presidency. Called to the Second Quorum of the Seventy June 6, 1992, at age 56, and sustained Oct. 3, 1992. Former president of the Boise Idaho Mission, regional representative, temple sealer, Young Men general board member, stake president, stake president's counselor and bishop. Was vice president and general manager of contracting company. Attended University of Utah. Born Sept. 11, 1935, in Salt Lake City, Utah, to O. Frank and Winifred Parker Stanley. Wife, Annette Shewell Stanley, parents of eight children.

F. David Stanley

Called to the Second Quorum of the Seventy June 6, 1992, at age 50, and sustained Oct. 3, 1992. Former president of the Hong Kong Mission, regional representative, stake president's counselor and branch president. Was self-employed in the import/export business and in real estate development. Graduated from the University of Sydney in Australia in chemical engineering, graduate study in management at the University of Hong Kong. Born June 30, 1941, in Hong Kong to Lung Hing and Yau Yin Chu Tai. Wife, Hui Hua Tai, parents of three children.

Kwok Yuen Tai

Sustained to the Second Quorum of the Seventy April 6, 1996, at age 59. Former area authority in the Mexico North Area, regional representative, president of Chile Santiago South Mission, stake president and bishop. Was rancher, orchardist, associate of Paquime Fruit Packing Company. Graduated from Brigham Young University in animal husbandry. Born March 22, 1937, in Colonia Dublan, Mexico, to Loren Le Roy and Lillian Hatch Taylor. Wife, Sharon Elizabeth Willis Taylor, parents of six children.

Jerald L. Taylor

Sustained to the Second Quorum of the Seventy April 6, 1996, at age 49. Former area authority in the Europe West Area, president of Argentina Salta Mission, regional representative, stake president, counselor, bishop and branch president. Was Church Educational System coordinator for Spain. Received bachelor's degree from IAVA. Born Dec. 28, 1946, in Montevideo, Uruguay, to Rafael and Sacramento Serrano de Vinas. Wife, Cristina Helenas Gaminara de Vinas, parents of three children.

Francisco J. Vinas

General counsel, office of Legal Services. Sustained to the Second Quorum of the Seventy April 2, 1994, at age 53. Served as regional representative, stake president and bishop. Received bachelor's degree from University of California at Berkeley and juris doctorate from Stanford University. Partner in the international law firm of Latham and Watkins in San Diego, Calif. Born Nov. 11, 1940, in Seattle, Wash., to Alton C. and Irene Marilyn Carlson Wickman. Wife, Patricia Farr Wickman, parents of five children.

Lance B. Wickman

Sustained to the Second Quorum of the Seventy April 6, 1996, at age 65. Former regional representative, stake president's counselor, high councilor and bishop. Was chairman, chief executive officer and founder of Wirthlin Worldwide. Received bachelor's and master's degrees from University of Utah, doctorate from University of California at Berkeley, all in economics. Born March 15, 1931, in Salt Lake City, Utah, to Joseph L. and Madeline B. Wirthlin. Wife, Jeralie Mae Chandler Wirthlin, parents of eight children.

Richard B. Wirthlin

Called to the Second Quorum of the Seventy June 6, 1992, at age 59; sustained Oct. 3, 1992. Former president of the South Africa Johannesburg Mission, stake president's counselor, bishop and branch president. Formerly director of temporal affairs for Asia and Philippines, helped found the Ezra Taft Benson Agriculture and Food Institute. Received bachelor's degree from BYU, master's degree from Montana State University and doctorate from University of California at Berkeley in agricultural economics. Born Jan. 23, 1933, in Cardston, Alberta, to Wm. Dale and Donna Wolf Wood. Wife, Lorna Cox Wood, parents of five children.

Lowell D. Wood

THE PRESIDING BISHOPRIC

Called as Presiding Bishop Dec. 27, 1995; sustained April 6, 1996. Sustained as first counselor to Presiding Bishop Robert D. Hales on Oct. 3, 1992, at age 54, and first counselor to Presiding Bishop Merrill J. Bateman on April 2, 1994. Former stake president and temple sealer. Former secretary to the Presiding Bishopric for 14 years. Received bachelor's degree in economics from the University of Utah, master's degree from University of Michigan in business administration. Born April 26, 1938, in Salt Lake City, Utah, to Harold Nelson and Blanche Mabel Swanson Burton. Wife, Barbara Matheson Burton, parents of five children.

H. David Burton

Called as first counselor in the Presiding Bishopric Dec. 27, 1995; sustained April 6, 1996. Sustained as second counselor to Presiding Bishop Robert D. Hales on Oct. 3, 1992, at age 56, and as second counselor to Presiding Bishop Merrill J. Bateman on April 2, 1994. Former stake president and bishop. Was managing director of the Church's Finance and Records Department, board member on various Church-related corporations. Received bachelor's degree in political science from BYU, master's degree in business administration from Indiana University. Born Feb. 6, 1936, in Preston, Idaho, to Phenoi Harrison and Ona Crockett Edgley. Wife, Pauline Nielson Edgley, parents of six children.

Richard C. Edgley

Called as second counselor in the Presiding Bishopric Dec. 27, 1995, at age 54; sustained April 6, 1996. Former Germany Frankfurt Mission president, stake president, bishop, counselor and high councilor. Was welfare services managing director. Received bachelor's degree in banking and finance from University of Utah. Born Aug. 18, 1941, in St. George, Utah, to Lawrence and Margaret Savage McMullin. Wife, Carolyn Jean Gibbs McMullin, parents of eight children.

Keith B. McMullin

PRESIDENTS OF THE CHURCH

1. Joseph Smith Jr. — Born Dec. 23, 1805, in Sharon, Windsor Co., Vermont, to Joseph Smith Sr. and Lucy Mack. Married Emma Hale Jan. 18, 1827, seven children. Received the  Melchizedek Priesthood (ordained apostle) in May 1829 by Peter, James and John (D&C 20:2, 27:12); sustained as First Elder of the Church April 6, 1830, at age 24; ordained high priest June 3, 1831, by Lyman Wight, sustained as president of the High Priesthood Jan. 25, 1832, at age 26 at a conference at Amherst, Lorain Co., Ohio; martyred June 27, 1844, at Carthage Jail, Carthage, Hancock Co., Illinois, at age 38.

2. Brigham Young — Born June 1, 1801, at Whitingham, Windham Co., Vermont, to John Young and Abigail Howe. Ordained  apostle Feb. 14, 1835, at age 33 by the Three Witnesses to the Book of Mormon: Oliver Cowdery, David Whitmer and Martin Harris; sustained as president of the Quorum of the Twelve Apostles April 14, 1840; sustained as president of the Church Dec. 27, 1847, at age 46; died Aug. 29, 1877, in Salt Lake City, Salt Lake Co., Utah, at age 76.

3. John Taylor — Born Nov. 1, 1808, at Milnthorpe, Westmoreland Co., England, to James Taylor and Agnes Taylor. Ordained  apostle Dec. 19, 1838, under the hands of Brigham Young and Heber C. Kimball at age 30; sustained as president of the Quorum of the Twelve Apostles Oct. 6, 1877; sustained as president of the Church Oct. 10, 1880, at age 71; died July 25, 1887, in Kaysville, Davis Co., Utah, at age 78.

4. Wilford Woodruff — Born March 1, 1807, at Avon (Farmington), Hartford Co., Connecticut, to Aphek Woodruff and Beulah Thompson. Ordained  apostle April 26, 1839, at age 32 by Brigham Young; sustained as president of the Quorum of the Twelve Apostles Oct. 10, 1880; sustained as president of the Church April 7, 1889, at age 82; died Sept. 2, 1898, in San Francisco, San Francisco Co., California, at age 91.

5. Lorenzo Snow — Born April 3, 1814, at Mantua, Portage Co., Ohio, to Oliver Snow and Rosetta Leonora Pettibone. Ordained apostle Feb. 12,  1849, at age 34 by Heber C. Kimball; sustained as counselor to President Brigham Young April 8, 1873; sustained as assistant counselor to President Brigham Young May 9, 1874; sustained as president of the Quorum of the Twelve Apostles April 7, 1889; ordained and set apart as president of the Church Sept. 13, 1898, at age 84; died Oct. 10, 1901, in Salt Lake City, Salt Lake Co., Utah, at age 87.

6. Joseph Fielding Smith — Born Nov. 13, 1838, at Far West, Caldwell Co., Missouri, to Hyrum Smith and Mary Fielding. Ordained apostle and named counselor to the First Presidency July 1, 1866, at age 27 by  Brigham Young; set apart as a member of the Quorum of the Twelve Apostles Oct. 8, 1867; released as counselor to the First Presidency at the death of President Young Aug. 29, 1877; sustained as second counselor to President John Taylor Oct. 10, 1880; released at the death of President Taylor July 25, 1887; sustained as second counselor to President Wilford Woodruff April 7, 1889; sustained as second counselor to President Lorenzo Snow Sept. 13, 1898; sustained as first counselor to Lorenzo Snow Oct. 6, 1901, not set apart to this position; released at the death of President Snow Oct. 10, 1901; ordained and set apart as president of the Church Oct. 17, 1901, at age 62; died Nov. 19, 1918, in Salt Lake City; Salt Lake Co., Utah, at age 80.

7. Heber Jeddy Grant — Born Nov. 22, 1856, in Salt Lake City, Salt Lake Co., Utah, to Jedediah Morgan Grant and Rachel Ridgeway Ivins. Ordained apostle Oct. 16, 1882, at age 25 by George Q. Cannon; became president of the Quorum of the Twelve  Apostles Nov. 23, 1916; ordained and set apart as president of the Church Nov. 23, 1918, at age 62; died May 14, 1945, in Salt Lake City, Salt Lake Co., Utah, at age 88.

8. George Albert Smith — Born April 4, 1870, in Salt Lake City, Salt Lake Co., Utah, to John Henry Smith and Sarah Farr. Married Lucy Emily Woodruff May 25, 1892 (she died Nov. 5, 1937); they had three children. Ordained apostle Oct. 8, 1903, at age 33 by Joseph F. Smith; sustained as  president of the Quorum of the Twelve Apostles July 1, 1943; ordained and set apart as president of the Church May 21, 1945, at age 75; died April 4, 1951, in Salt Lake City, Salt Lake Co., Utah, at age 81.

9. David Oman McKay — Born Sept. 8, 1873, at Huntsville, Weber Co., Utah, to David McKay and Jennette Eveline Evans. Married to Emma Ray Riggs Jan. 2, 1901 (she died Nov. 14, 1970); they had seven children. Ordained apostle April 9, 1906, at age 32 by Joseph F. Smith; sustained as second

counselor to President Heber J. Grant Oct. 6, 1934; sustained as second counselor to President George Albert Smith May 21, 1945; sustained as president of the Quorum of the Twelve Apostles Sept. 30, 1950; sustained as president of the Church April 9, 1951, at age 77; died Jan. 18, 1970, in Salt Lake City, Salt Lake Co., Utah, at age 96.

10. Joseph Fielding Smith — Born July 19, 1876, in Salt Lake City, Salt Lake Co., Utah, to Joseph Fielding Smith and Julina Lambson. Married Louie E. Shurtliff April 26, 1898 (she died March 30, 1908); they had two children. Married Ethel  G. Reynolds Nov. 2, 1908 (she died Aug. 26, 1937); they had nine children. Married Jessie Ella Evans April 12, 1938 (she died Aug. 3, 1971). Ordained apostle April 7, 1910, at age 33 by Joseph F. Smith; sustained as acting president of the Quorum of the Twelve Apostles Sept. 30, 1950; sustained as president of the Quorum of the Twelve Apostles April 9, 1951; sustained as counselor in the First Presidency Oct. 29, 1965; ordained and set apart as president of the Church Jan. 23, 1970, at age 93; died July 2, 1972, in Salt Lake City, Salt Lake Co., Utah, at age 95.

11. Harold Bingham Lee — Born March 28, 1899, at Clifton, Oneida Co., Idaho, to Samuel M. Lee and Louisa Bingham. Married Fern Lucinda Tanner Nov. 14, 1923 (she died Sept. 24, 1962); they had two children. Married Freda Joan Jensen June 17, 1963.  Ordained apostle April 10, 1941, at age 42 by Heber J. Grant; sustained as president of the Quorum of the Twelve Apostles Jan. 23, 1970; sustained as first counselor to President Joseph Fielding Smith Jan. 23, 1970; ordained and set apart as president of the Church July 7, 1972, at age 73; died

Dec. 26, 1973, in Salt Lake City, Salt Lake Co., Utah, at age 74.

12. Spencer Woolley Kimball — Born March 28, 1895, in Salt Lake City, Salt Lake Co., Utah, to Andrew and Olive Woolley Kimball. Married Camilla Eyring on Nov. 16, 1917 (she died Sept. 20, 1987); they had four children.

Ordained apostle Oct. 7, 1943, at age 48 by President Heber J. Grant; became acting president of the Quorum of the Twelve Apostles after the death of President David O. McKay in 1970; became president of the Quorum of the Twelve Apostles July 7, 1972; ordained and set apart as president of the Church Dec. 30, 1973, at age 78; died Nov. 5, 1985, in Salt Lake City, Salt Lake Co., Utah, at age 90.

13. Ezra Taft Benson — Born Aug. 4, 1899, at Whitney, Franklin County, Idaho, to George T. and Sarah Dunkley Benson. Married Flora Smith Amussen Sept. 10, 1926 (she died Aug. 14, 1992); they had six children.

Ordained an apostle Oct. 7, 1943, at age 44 by President Heber J. Grant;

served as U.S. Secretary of Agriculture, 1953-61. Became president of the Quorum of the Twelve Apostles Dec. 30, 1973; ordained and set apart as president of the Church Nov. 10, 1985, at age 86; died May 30, 1994, in Salt Lake City, Salt Lake Co., Utah, at age 94.

14. Howard William Hunter — Born Nov. 14, 1907, in Boise, Ada County, Idaho, to John William and Nellie Marie Rasmussen Hunter. Married Clara May (Claire) Jeffs June 10, 1931 (she died Oct. 9, 1983); they had three children (one died in infancy); married Inis Bernice Egan April 12, 1990.

Ordained an apostle Oct. 15, 1959, at age 51 by President David O. McKay; set apart as acting president of the Quroum of the Twelve Apostles Nov. 10, 1985, after the death of President Spencer W. Kimball; set apart as president of the Quorum of the Twelve Apostles June 2, 1988; ordained and set apart as president of the Church June 5, 1994, at age 86; died March 3, 1995, in Salt Lake City, Salt Lake Co., Utah, at age 87.

15. Gordon Bitner Hinckley — See current FIRST PRESIDENCY.

ASSISTANT PRESIDENTS OF THE CHURCH

1. Oliver Cowdery — Born Oct. 3, 1806, at Wells, Rutland Co., Vermont, to William Cowdery and Rebecca Fuller. Received Melchizedek Priesthood (ordained apostle) in May 1829, by Peter, James and John (D&C 20:2, 27:12); sustained as Second Elder of the Church April 6, 1830, at age 23; ordained high priest Aug. 28, 1831, by Sidney Rigdon; ordained assistant president of the High Priesthood Dec. 5, 1834, at age 28; sustained as assistant counselor in the First Presidency Sept. 3, 1837; excommunicated April 11, 1838; rebaptized

Nov. 12, 1848; died March 3, 1850, at Richmond, Ray Co., Missouri, at age 43.

2. Hyrum Smith — Born Feb. 9, 1800, at Tunbridge, Orange Co., Vermont, to Joseph Smith Sr. and Lucy Mack. Ordained high priest in June 1831 by Joseph Smith; sustained as assistant counselor to the First Presidency Sept. 3, 1837, at age 37; sustained as second counselor to President Joseph Smith Nov. 7, 1837; given all the priesthood formerly held by Oliver Cowdery (including apos-

tle); ordained Patriarch to the Church and assistant president Jan. 24, 1841, by Joseph Smith, at age 40; martyred June 27, 1844, at Carthage Jail, Carthage, Hancock Co., Illinois, at age 44.

FIRST COUNSELORS IN THE FIRST PRESIDENCY

1. Sidney Rigdon — Born Feb. 19, 1793, at Saint Clair Township, Allegheny Co., Pennsylvania, to William Rigdon and Nancy Bryant. Ordained high priest in June 1831 by Lyman Wight; set apart as first counselor to President Joseph Smith March 18, 1833, at age 40; excommunicated Sept. 8, 1844; died July 14, 1876, at Friendship, Allegany Co., New York, at age 83.

2. Heber Chase Kimball — Born June 14, 1801, at Sheldon, Franklin Co., Vermont, to Solomon Farnham Kimball and Anna Spaulding. Ordained apostle Feb. 14, 1835, under the hands of Oliver Cowdery, David Whitmer and Martin Harris at age 33; sustained as first counselor to President Brigham Young Dec. 27, 1847, at age 46; died June 22, 1868, at Salt Lake City, Salt Lake Co., Utah, at age 67.

3. George Albert Smith — Born June 26, 1817, at Potsdam, Saint Lawrence Co., New York, to John Smith and Clarissa Lyman. Ordained apostle April 26, 1839, by Heber C. Kimball at age 21; sustained as first counselor to President Brigham Young Oct. 7, 1868, at age 51; died Sept. 1, 1875, at Salt Lake City, Salt Lake Co., Utah, at age 58.

4. John Willard Young — Born Oct. 1, 1844, at Nauvoo, Hancock Co., Illinois, to Brigham Young and Mary Ann Angell. Ordained Feb. 4, 1864, by Brigham Young. Sustained as counselor to President Brigham Young April 8, 1873, at age 28; sustained as assistant counselor to President Young May 9, 1874; sustained as first counselor to President Young Oct. 7, 1876, at age 32; released at death of President Young Aug. 29, 1877; sustained as a counselor to the Twelve Apostles Oct. 6, 1877; released Oct. 6, 1891; died Feb. 11, 1924, at New York City, New York, at age 79.

5. George Quayle Cannon — Born Jan. 11, 1827, at Liverpool, Lancashire Co., England, to George Cannon and Ann Quayle. Ordained an apostle Aug. 26, 1860, by Brigham Young at age 33; sustained as counselor to President Young April 8, 1873, at age 46; sustained as assistant counselor to President Young May 9, 1874; released at death of President Young Aug. 29, 1877; sustained as first counselor to President John Taylor Oct. 10, 1880; released at death of President Taylor July 25, 1887; sustained as first counselor to President Wilford Woodruff April 7, 1889; sustained as first counselor to President Lorenzo Snow Sept. 13, 1898; died April 12, 1901, at Monterey, Monterey Co., California, at age 74.

6. Joseph Fielding Smith — See PRESIDENTS OF THE CHURCH, No. 6.

7. John Rex Winder — Born Dec. 11, 1821, at Biddenham, Kent Co., England, to Richard Winder and Sophia Collins. Ordained high priest March 4, 1872, by Edward Hunter; sustained as second counselor to Presiding Bishop William B. Preston

April 8, 1887, at age 65; sustained as first counselor to President Joseph F. Smith Oct. 17, 1901, at age 79; died March 27, 1910, at Salt Lake City, Salt Lake Co., Utah, at age 88.

8. Anthon Henrik Lund — Born May 15, 1844, at Aalborg, Jutland, Denmark, to Henrik Lund and Anne C. Andersen. Ordained apostle Oct. 7, 1889, by George Q. Cannon at age 45; sustained as second counselor to President Joseph F. Smith Oct. 17, 1901, at age 57; sustained as first counselor to President Smith April 7, 1910; sustained as first counselor to President Heber J. Grant Nov. 23, 1918; died March 2, 1921, at Salt Lake City, Salt Lake Co., Utah, at age 76.

9. Charles William Penrose — Born Feb. 4, 1832, at London, Surrey Co., England, to Richard Penrose and Matilda Sims. Ordained apostle July 7, 1904, by Joseph F. Smith at age 72; sustained as second counselor to President Smith Dec. 7, 1911, at age 79; sustained as second counselor to President Heber J. Grant Nov. 23, 1918; sustained as first counselor to President Grant March 10, 1921; died May 15, 1925, at Salt Lake City, Salt Lake Co., Utah, at age 93.

10. Anthony Woodward Ivins — Born Sept. 16, 1852, at Toms River, Ocean Co., New Jersey, to Israel Ivins and Anna Lowrie. Ordained apostle Oct. 6, 1907, by Joseph F. Smith at age 55; sustained as second counselor to President Heber J. Grant March 10, 1921, at age 68; sustained as first counselor to President Grant May 28, 1925; died Sept. 23, 1934, at Salt Lake City, Salt Lake Co., Utah, at age 82.

11. Joshua Reuben Clark Jr. — Born Sept. 1, 1871, at Grantsville, Tooele Co., Utah, to Joshua Reuben Clark and

Mary Louise Woolley. Sustained as second counselor to President Heber J. Grant, April 6, 1933, at age 61; sustained as first counselor to President Grant, Oct. 6, 1934; ordained apostle Oct. 11, 1934, at age 63, by President Grant; sustained as first counselor to President George Albert Smith May 21, 1945; sustained as second counselor to President David O. McKay April 9, 1951; sustained as first counselor to President McKay June 12, 1959; died Oct. 6, 1961, at Salt Lake City, Salt Lake Co., Utah, at age 90.

12. Stephen L Richards — Born June 18, 1879, at Mendon, Cache Co., Utah, to Stephen Longstroth Richards and Emma Louise Stayner. Ordained apostle Jan. 18, 1917, by Joseph F. Smith at age 37; sustained as first counselor to President David O. McKay April 9, 1951, at age 71; died May 19, 1959, at Salt Lake City, Salt Lake Co., Utah, at age 79.

13. Joshua Reuben Clark Jr. — See No. 11 above.

14. Henry Dinwoodey Moyle — Born April 22, 1889, at Salt Lake City, Salt Lake Co., Utah, to James H. Moyle and Alice E. Dinwoodey. Ordained apostle April 10, 1947, by George Albert Smith at age 57; sustained as second counselor to President David O. McKay June 12, 1959, at age 70; sustained as first counselor to President McKay Oct. 12, 1961; died Sept. 18, 1963, at Deer Park, Osceola Co., Florida, at age 74.

15. Hugh Brown Brown — Born Oct. 24, 1883, at Granger, Salt Lake Co., Utah, to Homer Manly Brown and Lydia Jane Brown. Sustained as Assistant to the Twelve Oct. 4, 1953, at age 69; ordained an apostle April 10, 1958, at age 74 by David O. McKay; sustained

as counselor in the First Presidency June 22, 1961; sustained as second counselor to President McKay Oct. 12, 1961; sustained as first counselor to President McKay Oct. 4, 1963; released at death of President McKay Jan. 18, 1970, and resumed position in the Quorum of the Twelve Apostles; died Dec. 2, 1975, at Salt Lake City, Salt Lake Co., Utah, at age 92.

16. Harold Bingham Lee — See PRESIDENTS OF THE CHURCH, No. 11.

17. Nathan Eldon Tanner — Born May 9, 1898, at Salt Lake City, Salt Lake Co., Utah, to Nathan William Tanner and Sarah Edna Brown. Sustained as Assistant to the Twelve Oct. 8, 1960, at age 62; ordained apostle Oct.  11, 1962, at age 64; sustained as second counselor to President David O. McKay Oct. 4, 1963; sustained as second counselor to President Joseph Fielding Smith Jan. 23, 1970; sustained as first counselor to President Harold

B. Lee July 7, 1972; sustained as first counselor to President Spencer W. Kimball Dec. 30, 1973; died Nov. 27, 1982, at Salt Lake City, Salt Lake Co., Utah, at age 84.

18. Marion George Romney — Born Sept. 19, 1897, in Colonia Juarez, Mexico, to George Samuel Romney and Teressa Artemesia Redd. Sustained as Church's first Assistant to the Twelve April 6, 1941, at age 43; ordained  apostle Oct. 11, 1951, at age 54; sustained as second counselor to President Harold B. Lee July 7, 1972; sustained as second counselor to President Spencer W. Kimball Dec. 30, 1973; sustained as first counselor to President Kimball Dec. 2, 1982; released at the death of President Kimball Nov. 5, 1985; became president of the Quorum of the Twelve Apostles Nov. 10, 1985; died May 20, 1988, at Salt Lake City, Salt Lake Co., Utah, at age 90.

19. Gordon Bitner Hinckley — See current FIRST PRESIDENCY.

20. Thomas Spencer Monson — See current FIRST PRESIDENCY.

SECOND COUNSELORS IN THE FIRST PRESIDENCY

1. Frederick Granger Williams — Born Oct. 28, 1787, at Suffield, Hartford, Co., Connecticut, to William Wheeler Williams and Ruth Granger. Called by revelation March 1832 to be a high priest and counselor to President  Joseph Smith (D&C 81:1); ordained high priest by Miles H. Jones; set apart as second counselor to President Smith March 18, 1833, at age 45; rejected Nov. 7, 1837; excommunicated March 17, 1839; restored to fellowship April 8, 1840; died Oct. 10, 1842, at Quincy, Adams Co., Illinois, at age 54.

2. Hyrum Smith — See ASSISTANT PRESIDENTS OF THE CHURCH, No. 2.

3. William Law — Born Sept. 8, 1809, at Tyrone Co., North Ireland. Set apart as second counselor to President Joseph Smith Jan. 24, 1841, at age 31; excommunicated April 18, 1844; died Jan. 19, 1892, at Shullsburg, Lafayette Co., Wisconsin, at age 82.

4. Willard Richards — Born June 24, 1804, at Hopkinton, Middlesex Co., Massachusetts, to Joseph Richards and Rhoda Howe. Ordained apostle April 14, 1840, by Brigham Young at age  35; sustained as second counselor to President Young Dec. 27, 1847, at age 43; died March 11, 1854, at Salt Lake City, Salt Lake Co., Utah, at age 49.

5. Jedediah Morgan Grant — Born Feb. 21, 1816, at Windsor, Broome Co., New York, to Joshua Grant and Athalia Howard. Set apart as one of the First Seven Presidents of the Seventy Dec. 2, 1845, at age 29; ordained apostle April 7, 1854, at age 38 by Brigham Young; sustained as second counselor to President Young April 7, 1854; died Dec. 1, 1856, at Salt Lake City, Salt Lake Co., Utah, at age 40.

6. Daniel Hanmer Wells — Born Oct. 27, 1814, at Trenton, Oneida Co., New Jersey, to Daniel Wells and Catherine Chapin. Set apart as second counselor to President Young Jan. 4, 1857, at age 42; released at death of President Young Aug. 29, 1877; sustained as a counselor to the Twelve Apostles Oct. 6, 1877; died March 24, 1891, at Salt Lake City, Salt Lake Co., Utah, at age 76.

7. Joseph Fielding Smith — See PRESIDENTS OF THE CHURCH, No. 6.

8. Rudger Clawson — Born March 12, 1857, at Salt Lake City, Salt Lake Co., Utah, to Hiram Bradley Clawson and Margaret Gay Judd. Ordained apostle Oct. 10, 1898, by Lorenzo Snow, at age 41; sustained as second counselor to President Snow Oct. 6, 1901, at age 44, not set apart to this position; released at death of President Snow Oct. 10, 1901, and resumed position in the Quorum of the Twelve Apostles; sustained as president of the Quorum of the Twelve Apostles March 17, 1921; died June 21, 1943, in Salt Lake City, Salt Lake Co., Utah at age 86.

9. Anthon Henrik Lund — See FIRST COUNSELORS IN THE FIRST PRESIDENCY, No. 8.

10. John Henry Smith — Born Sept. 18, 1848, at Carbunca (now part of Council Bluffs), Pottawattamie Co., Iowa, to George Albert Smith and Sarah Ann Libby. Ordained apostle Oct. 27, 1880, by Wilford Woodruff at age 32; sustained as second counselor to President Joseph F. Smith April 7, 1910, at age 61; died Oct. 13, 1911, at Salt Lake City, Salt Lake Co., Utah, at 63.

11. Charles William Penrose — See FIRST COUNSELORS IN THE FIRST PRESIDENCY, No. 9.

12. Anthony Woodward Ivins — See FIRST COUNSELORS IN THE FIRST PRESIDENCY, No. 10

13. Charles Wilson Nibley — Born Feb. 5, 1849, at Hunterfield, Midlothian Region, Scotland, to James Nibley and Jane Wilson. Ordained high priest June 9, 1901, by Joseph F. Smith; sustained as Presiding Bishop of the Church Dec. 4, 1907, at age 58; sustained as second counselor to President Heber J. Grant, May 28, 1925, at age 76; died Dec. 11, 1931, at Salt Lake City, Salt Lake Co., Utah, at age 82.

14. Joshua Reuben Clark Jr. — See FIRST COUNSELORS IN THE FIRST PRESIDENCY, No. 11.

15. David Oman McKay — See PRESIDENTS OF THE CHURCH, No. 9.

16. Joshua Reuben Clark Jr. — See FIRST COUNSELORS IN THE FIRST PRESIDENCY, No. 11.

17. Henry Dinwoodey Moyle — See FIRST COUNSELORS IN THE FIRST PRESIDENCY, No. 14.

18. Hugh Brown Brown — See FIRST COUNSELORS IN THE FIRST PRESIDENCY, No. 15.

19. Nathan Eldon Tanner — See FIRST COUNSELORS IN THE FIRST PRESIDENCY, No. 17.

20. Marion George Romney — See FIRST COUNSELORS IN THE FIRST PRESIDENCY, No. 18.

21. Gordon Bitner Hinckley — See current FIRST PRESIDENCY.

22. Thomas Spencer Monson — See current FIRST PRESIDENCY.

23. James Esdras Faust — See current FIRST PRESIDENCY.

OTHER COUNSELORS IN THE FIRST PRESIDENCY

1. Jesse Gause — Born about 1784 at East Marlborough, Chester Co., Virginia, to William and Mary Beverly Gause. Converted from the Shaker sect, he was baptized about the end of 1831. Set apart as counselor to Joseph Smith March 8, 1832; sent on a mission Aug. 1, 1832. Excommunicated Dec. 3, 1832. Died about 1836.

2. John Cook Bennett — Born Aug. 3, 1804, at Fair Haven, Bristol Co., Massachusetts, to J. and N. Bennett. Presented as assistant president with the First Presidency April 8, 1841, at age 36 (See *History of the Church* 4:341); disfellowshipped May 25, 1842; excommunicated latter part of 1842; died Aug. 5, 1867, in Polk City, Polk Co., Iowa.

3. Amasa Mason Lyman — Born March 30, 1813, at Lyman, Crafton Co., New Hampshire, to Roswell Lyman and Martha Mason. Ordained apostle Aug. 20, 1842, by Brigham Young at age 29; replaced in the Quorum of the Twelve Apostles Jan. 20, 1843, due to reinstatement of Orson Pratt; appointed counselor to the First Presidency about Feb. 4, 1843; retired from the First Presidency with death of Joseph Smith June 27, 1844; returned to the Quorum of the Twelve Apostles Aug. 12, 1844; deprived of apostleship Oct. 6, 1867; excommunicated May 12, 1870; died Feb. 4, 1877, at Fillmore, Millard Co., Utah, at age 63. Blessings restored after death.

4. Joseph Fielding Smith — See PRESIDENTS OF THE CHURCH, No. 6.

5. Lorenzo Snow — See PRESIDENTS OF THE CHURCH, No. 5.

6. Brigham Young Jr. — Born Dec. 18, 1836, at Kirtland, Geauga Co., Ohio, to Brigham Young and Mary Ann Angell. Ordained apostle Feb. 4, 1864, at age 27, by President Brigham Young; sustained to the Quorum of the Twelve Apostles Oct. 9, 1868; sustained as counselor to President Young April 8, 1873, at age 36; sustained as assistant counselor to President Young May 9, 1874; released at President Young's death Aug. 29, 1877, and resumed position in the Quorum of the Twelve Apostles; sustained as president of the Quorum of the Twelve Apostles Oct. 17, 1901; died April 11, 1903, in Salt Lake City, Salt Lake Co., Utah, at age 66.

7. Albert Carrington — Born Jan. 8, 1813, at Royalton, Windsor Co., Vermont, to Daniel Van Carrington and Isabella Bowman. Ordained apostle July 3, 1870, by Brigham Young at age 57; sustained as counselor to President Young April 8, 1873, at age 60; sustained as assistant counselor to President Young May 9, 1874; released at death of President Young Aug. 29, 1877; excommunicated Nov. 7, 1885; rebaptized Nov. 1, 1887; died Sept. 19, 1889, at Salt Lake City, Salt Lake Co., Utah, at age 76.

8. John Willard Young — See FIRST COUNSELORS IN THE FIRST PRESIDENCY, No. 4.

9. George Quayle Cannon — See FIRST COUNSELORS IN THE FIRST PRESIDENCY, No. 5.

10. Hugh Brown Brown — See FIRST COUNSELORS IN THE FIRST PRESIDENCY, No. 15.

11. Joseph Fielding Smith — See PRESIDENTS OF THE CHURCH, No. 10.

12. Henry Thorpe Beal Isaacson — Born Sept. 6, 1898, at Ephraim, Sanpete Co., Utah, to Martin Isaacson and Mary Jemima Beal. Ordained high priest Oct. 1, 1941, by Charles A. Callis; sustained as second counselor to Presiding Bishop LeGrand Richards Dec. 12, 1946, at age 48; sustained as first counselor to Presiding Bishop Joseph L. Wirthlin April 6, 1952; sustained as Assistant to the Twelve Sept. 30, 1961; sustained as counselor in the First Presidency Oct. 28, 1965, at age 67; released at death of President David O. McKay Jan. 18, 1970; resumed position as Assistant to the Twelve Jan. 23,

1970; died Nov. 9, 1970, at Salt Lake City, Salt Lake Co., Utah, at age 72.

13. Alvin Rulon Dyer — Born Jan. 1, 1903, at Salt Lake City, Salt Lake Co., Utah, to Alfred R. Dyer and Harriet Walsh. Ordained high priest Oct. 2, 1927, by Joseph Fielding Smith; sustained an Assistant to the Twelve Oct. 11, 1958, at age 55; ordained apostle Oct. 5, 1967, by David O. McKay at age 64; sustained as counselor in the First Presidency April 6, 1968; released at death of President McKay Jan. 18, 1970; resumed position as Assistant to the Twelve Apostles Jan. 23, 1970; sustained a member of First Quorum of the Seventy Oct. 1, 1976; died March 6, 1977, at Salt Lake City, Salt Lake Co., Utah, at age 74.

14. Gordon Bitner Hinckley — See current FIRST PRESIDENCY.

ASSISTANT COUNSELORS IN THE FIRST PRESIDENCY

1. Oliver Cowdery — See ASSISTANT PRESIDENTS OF THE CHURCH, No. 1.

2. Joseph Smith Sr. — Born July 12, 1771, at Topsfield, Essex Co., Massachusetts, to Asael Smith and Mary Duty. Ordained high priest June 3, 1831, by Lyman Wight; ordained Patriarch to the Church Dec. 18, 1833, at age 62; sustained as assistant counselor to the First Presidency Sept. 3, 1837, at age 66; died Sept. 14, 1840, at Nauvoo, Hancock Co., Illinois, at age 69.

3. Hyrum Smith — See ASSISTANT PRESIDENTS OF THE CHURCH, No. 2.

4. John Smith — Born July 16, 1781, at Derryfield, Hillsboro Co., New Hampshire, to Asael Smith and Mary Duty. Ordained high priest June 3, 1833, by Lyman Wight; sustained as assistant counselor to the First Presi-

dency Sept. 3, 1837, at age 56; released at the death of Joseph Smith June 27, 1844; set apart as Patriarch to the Church Jan. 1, 1849, at age 67; died May 23, 1854, at Salt Lake City, Salt Lake Co., Utah, at age 72.

5. Lorenzo Snow — See PRESIDENTS OF THE CHURCH, No. 5.

6. Brigham Young Jr. — See OTHER COUNSELORS IN THE FIRST PRESIDENCY, No. 6.

7. Albert Carrington — See OTHER COUNSELORS IN THE FIRST PRESIDENCY, No. 7.

8. John Willard Young — See FIRST COUNSELORS IN THE FIRST PRESIDENCY, No. 4.

9. George Quayle Cannon — See FIRST COUNSELORS IN THE FIRST PRESIDENCY, No. 5.

THE QUORUM OF THE TWELVE

1. Thomas Baldwin Marsh — Born Nov. 1, 1799, at Acton, Middlesex Co., Massachusetts, to James Marsh and Molly Law. Ordained apostle April 25, 1835, under the hands of Oliver Cowdery, David Whitmer and Martin Harris, at Kirtland, Ohio, at age 35; sustained as president of the Quorum of the Twelve Apostles May 2, 1835; excommunicated March 17, 1839; rebaptized in July 16, 1857; died January 1866, at Ogden, Weber Co., Utah, at 66.

2. David Wyman Patten — Born Nov. 14, 1799, at Theresa, Jefferson Co., New York, to Benenio Patten and Abigail Cole. Ordained apostle Feb. 15, 1835, under the hands of Oliver Cowdery, David Whitmer and Martin Harris, at Kirtland, Ohio, at age 35; killed Oct. 25, 1838, at the Battle of Crooked River, Missouri, at age 38.

3. Brigham Young — See PRESIDENTS OF THE CHURCH, No. 2.

4. Heber Chase Kimball — See FIRST COUNSELORS IN THE FIRST PRESIDENCY, No. 2.

5. Orson Hyde — Born Jan. 8, 1805, at Oxford, New Haven Co., Connecticut, to Nathan Hyde and Sally Thorp. Ordained apostle Feb. 15, 1835, under the hands of Oliver Cowdery, David Whitmer and Martin Harris, at  Kirtland, Ohio, at age 30; dropped from Quorum May 4, 1839; restored to Quorum June 27, 1839; sustained as president of the Quorum of the Twelve Apostles Dec. 27, 1847; Brigham Young, on April 10, 1875, took Hyde from his original position in the Quorum and placed him in the order he would have been in when he was restored to fellowship had he come into the Quorum at that time (See *"Succession in the Priesthood"* by John Taylor, p. 16.); died Nov. 28, 1878, at Spring City, Sanpete Co., Utah, at age 73.

6. William E. M'Lellin — Born Jan. 18, 1806 in Smith Co., Tenn. Ordained apostle Feb. 15, 1835, under the hands of Oliver Cowdery, David Whitmer and Martin Harris, at Kirtland, Ohio, at age 29; excommunicated May 11, 1838; died April 24, 1883, at Independence, Jackson Co., Missouri, at age 77.

7. Parley Parker Pratt — Born April 12, 1807, at Burlington, Otsego Co., New York, to Jared Pratt and Charity Dickinson. Ordained apostle Feb. 21, 1835, under the hands of Joseph Smith, Oliver Cowdery and David Whitmer, at Kirtland,  Ohio, at age 27; assassinated May 13, 1857, near Van Buren, Crawford Co., Arkansas, at age 50.

8. Luke Johnson — Born Nov. 3, 1807, at Pomfret, Windsor Co., Vermont, to John Johnson and Elsa Jacobs. Ordained apostle Feb. 15, 1835, by Oliver Cowdery, David Whitmer and Martin Harris, at Kirtland,  Ohio, at age 27; excommunicated April 13, 1838; rebaptized in 1846 at Nauvoo, Illinois; died Dec. 9, 1861, at Salt Lake City, Salt Lake Co., Utah, at age 54.

9. William B. Smith — Born March 13, 1811, at Royalton, Windsor Co., Vermont, to Joseph Smith Sr. and Lucy Mack. Ordained apostle Feb. 15, 1835, under the hands of Oliver Cowdery, David Whitmer and Martin Harris,  at Kirtland, Ohio, at age 23; dropped from the Quorum May 4, 1839; restored to Quorum May 25, 1839; dropped from the Quorum Oct. 6, 1845; excommunicated Oct. 19, 1845; died Nov. 13, 1894, at Osterdock, Clayton Co., Iowa, at age 82.

10. Orson Pratt — Born Sept. 19, 1811, at Hartford, Washington, Co.,

New York, to Jared Pratt and Charity Dickinson. Ordained apostle April 26, 1835, under the hands of Oliver Cowdery, David Whitmer and Martin Harris, at Kirtland, Ohio, at age 23;  excommunicated Aug. 20, 1842; rebaptized Jan. 20, 1843, and ordained to former office in the Quorum of the Twelve Apostles. Brigham Young took him from his original position in the Quorum in 1875 and placed him in the order he would have been in when he was restored to fellowship had he come into the Quorum at that time; died Oct. 3, 1881, at Salt Lake City, Salt Lake Co., Utah, at age 70.

11. John Farnham Boynton — Born Sept. 20, 1811, at Bradford, Essex Co., Massachusetts, to Eliphalet Boynton and Susannah Nichols. Ordained apostle Feb. 15, 1835, under the hands of Oliver Cowdery, David Whitmer  and Martin Harris, at Kirtland, Ohio, at age 23; disfellowshipped Sept. 3, 1837; excommunicated 1837; died Oct. 20, 1890, at Syracuse, Onondaga Co., New York, at age 79.

12. Lyman Eugene Johnson — Born Oct. 24, 1811, at Pomfret, Windsor Co., Vermont, to John Johnson and Elsa Jacobs. Ordained apostle Feb. 14, 1835, under the hands of Oliver Cowdery, David Whitmer and Martin Harris, at Kirtland, Ohio, at age 23; excommunicated April 13, 1838; died Dec. 20, 1856, at Prairie du Chien, Crawford Co., Wisconsin, at age 45.

13. John Edward Page — Born Feb. 25, 1799, at Trenton Township, Oneida Co., New York, to Ebenezer and Rachel Page. Ordained apostle Dec. 19, 1838, under the hands of Brigham Young and Heber C. Kimball at  Far West, Missouri, at age 39; disfellowshipped Feb. 9, 1846; excommunicated June 27, 1846; diedOct. 14, 1867, at De Kalb Co., Illinois, at age 68.

14. John Taylor — See PRESIDENTS OF THE CHURCH, No. 3.

15. Wilford Woodruff — See PRESIDENTS OF THE CHURCH, No. 4.

16. George Albert Smith — See FIRST COUNSELORS IN THE FIRST PRESIDENCY, No. 3.

17. Willard Richards — See SECOND COUNSELORS IN THE FIRST PRESIDENCY, No. 4.

18. Lyman Wight — Born May 9, 1796, at Fairfield, Herkimer Co., New York, to Levi Wight and Sarah Corbin. Ordained apostle April 8, 1841, by Joseph Smith, at Nauvoo, Illinois, at age 44. Excommunicated Dec.  3, 1848; died March 31, 1858, in Dexter, Texas, at age 63.

19. Amasa Mason Lyman — See OTHER COUNSELORS IN THE FIRST PRESIDENCY, No. 3.

20. Ezra Taft Benson — Born Feb. 22, 1811, at Mendon, Worcester Co., Massachusetts, to John Benson and Chloe Taft. Ordained apostle July 16, 1846, by Brigham Young at Council Bluffs, Iowa,  at age 35; died Sept. 3, 1869, at Ogden, Weber Co., Utah, at age 58.

21. Charles Coulsen Rich — Born Aug. 21, 1809, at Campbell Co., Kentucky, to Joseph Rich and Nancy O. Neal. Ordained apostle Feb. 12, 1849, by Brigham Young, at Salt Lake City, Utah, at age 39; died Nov. 17, 1883, at Paris, Bear Lake Co., Idaho, at age 74.

22. Lorenzo Snow — See PRESIDENTS OF THE CHURCH, No. 5.

23. Erastus Snow — Born Nov. 9, 1818, at Saint Johnsbury, Caledonia Co., Vermont, to Levi Snow and Lucina Streeter. Ordained apostle Feb. 12,

1849, by Brigham Young, at age 30; died May 27, 1888, at Salt Lake City, Salt Lake Co., Utah, at age 69.

24. Franklin Dewey Richards — Born April 2, 1821, at Richmond, Berkshire Co., Massachusetts, to Phinehas Richards and Wealthy Dewey. Or-

dained apostle Feb. 12, 1849, by Heber C. Kimball, at age 27; sustained as president of the Quorum of the Twelve Apostles Sept. 13, 1898; died Dec. 9, 1899, at Ogden, Weber Co., Utah, at age 78.

25. George Quayle Cannon — See FIRST COUNSELORS IN THE FIRST PRESIDENCY, No. 5.

26. Joseph Fielding Smith — See PRESIDENTS OF THE CHURCH, No. 6.

27. Brigham Young Jr. — See OTHER COUNSELORS IN THE FIRST PRESIDENCY, No. 6.

28. Albert Carrington — See OTHER COUNSELORS IN THE FIRST PRESIDENCY, No. 7.

29. Moses Thatcher — Born Feb. 2, 1842, at Springfield Sangamon Co., Ill., to Hezekiah Thatcher and Alley Kitchen. Ordained apostle April 9, 1879, by John Taylor, at age 37; dropped from the Quorum of the Twelve Apostles April 6, 1896; died Aug. 21, 1909, at Logan, Cache Co., Utah, at age 67.

30. Francis Marion Lyman — Born Jan. 12, 1840, at Good Hope, McDonough Co., Illinois, to Amasa Mason Lyman and Maria Louisa Tanner. Ordained apostle Oct. 27, 1880, by John Taylor, at age 40; sustained as president of the Quorum of the Twelve Apostles Oct. 6, 1903; died Nov. 18, 1916, at Salt

Lake City, Salt Lake Co., Utah, at age 76.

31. John Henry Smith — See SECOND COUNSELORS IN THE FIRST PRESIDENCY, No. 10.

32. George Teasdale — Born Dec. 8, 1831, at London, Middlesex Co., England, to William Russell Teasdale and Harriett H. Tidey. Ordained apostle Oct. 16, 1882, by John Taylor, at age 50; died June 9, 1907, at Salt Lake City, Salt Lake Co., Utah, at age 75.

33. Heber Jeddy Grant — See PRESIDENTS OF THE CHURCH, No. 7.

34. John Whittaker Taylor — Born May 15, 1858, at Provo, Utah Co., Utah, to John Taylor and Sophia Whittaker. Ordained apostle April 9, 1884, by John Taylor, at age 25; resigned Oct. 28, 1905; excommunicated March 28, 1911; died Oct. 10, 1916, at Salt Lake City, Salt Lake Co., Utah, at age 58. Blessings restored after death.

35. Marriner Wood Merrill — Born Sept. 25, 1835, at Sackville, Westmoreland Co., New Brunswick, Canada, to Nathan Alexander Merrill and Sarah Ann Reynolds. Ordained apostle Oct. 7, 1889, by Wilford Woodruff, at age 57; died Feb. 6, 1906, at Richmond, Cache Co., Utah, at age 73.

36. Anthon Henrik Lund — See FIRST COUNSELORS IN THE FIRST PRESIDENCY, No. 8.

37. Abraham Hoagland Cannon — Born March 12, 1859, at Salt Lake City, Salt Lake Co., Utah, to George Quayle Cannon and Elizabeth Hoagland. Sustained as one of the First Seven Presidents of the Seventy Oct. 8, 1882,

at age 23; ordained apostle Oct. 7, 1889, by Joseph F. Smith, at age 30; died July 19, 1896, at Salt Lake City, Salt Lake Co., Utah, at age 37.

38. Matthias Foss Cowley — Born Aug. 25, 1858, at Salt Lake City, Salt Lake Co., Utah, to Matthias Cowley and Sarah Elizabeth Foss. Ordained apostle Oct. 7, 1897, by George Q. Cannon, at age 39; resigned Oct. 28, 1905;  priesthood suspended May 11, 1911; restored to full membership April 3, 1936; died June 16, 1940, at Salt Lake City, Salt Lake Co., Utah, at age 81.

39. Abraham Owen Woodruff — Born Nov. 23, 1872, at Salt Lake City, Salt Lake Co., Utah, to Wilford Woodruff and Emma Smith. Ordained apostle Oct. 7, 1897, by Wilford Woodruff, at age 24; died June 20, 1904, at El Paso, El Paso Co., Texas, at age 31.

40. Rudger Clawson — See SECOND COUNSELORS IN THE FIRST PRESIDENCY, No. 8.

41. Reed Smoot — Born Jan. 10, 1862, at Salt Lake City, Salt Lake Co., Utah, to Abraham Owen Smoot and Anne Kestine Morrison. Ordained apostle April 8, 1900, by Lorenzo Snow, at age 38; served in the U.S. Senate, 1903-  32; died Feb. 9, 1941, at St. Petersburg, Pinellas Co., Florida, at age 79.

42. Hyrum Mack Smith — Born March 21, 1872, at Salt Lake City, Salt Lake Co., Utah, to Joseph Fielding Smith and Edna Lambson. Ordained apostle Oct. 24, 1901, by Joseph F. Smith, at age 29; died Jan. 23, 1918, at Salt  Lake City, Salt Lake Co., Utah, at age 45.

43. George Albert Smith — See PRESIDENTS OF THE CHURCH, No. 8.

44. Charles William Penrose — See FIRST COUNSELORS IN THE FIRST PRESIDENCY, No. 9.

45. George Franklin Richards — Born Feb. 23, 1861, at Farmington, Davis Co., Utah, to Franklin Dewey Richards and Nanny Longstroth. Ordained apostle April 9, 1906, by Joseph F. Smith, at age 45; sustained as acting  Patriarch to the Church Oct. 8, 1937; released from this position Oct. 3, 1942; sustained as president of the Quorum of the Twelve Apostles May 21, 1945; died Aug. 8, 1950, at Salt Lake City, Salt Lake Co., Utah, at age 89.

46. Orson Ferguson Whitney — Born July 1, 1855, at Salt Lake City, Salt Lake Co., Utah, to Horace Kimball Whitney and Helen Mar Kimball. Ordained apostle April 9, 1906, by Joseph F. Smith, at age 50; died May 16, 1931, at  Salt Lake City, Salt Lake Co., Utah, at age 75.

47. David Oman McKay — See PRESIDENTS OF THE CHURCH, No. 9.

48. Anthony Woodward Ivins — See FIRST COUNSELORS IN THE FIRST PRESIDENCY, No. 10.

49. Joseph Fielding Smith — See PRESIDENTS OF THE CHURCH, No. 10.

50. James Edward Talmage — Born Sept. 21, 1862, at Hungerford, Berkshire Co., England, to James J. Talmage and Susannah Preater. Ordained apostle Dec. 8, 1911, by Joseph F. Smith, at age 49; died July 27, 1933, at Salt Lake City, Salt Lake Co., Utah, at age 70.

51. Stephen L Richards — See FIRST COUNSELORS IN THE FIRST PRESI-

DENCY, No. 12.

52. Richard Roswell Lyman — Born Nov. 23, 1870, at Fillmore, Millard Co., Utah, to Francis Marion Lyman and Clara Caroline Callister. Ordained apostle April 7, 1918, by Joseph F. Smith, at age 47; excommunicated

Nov. 12, 1943; rebaptized Oct. 27, 1954; died Dec. 31, 1963, at Salt Lake City, Salt Lake Co., Utah, at age 93.

53. Melvin Joseph Ballard — Born Feb. 9, 1873, at Logan, Cache Co., Utah, to Henry Ballard and Margaret Reid McNeil. Ordained apostle Jan. 7, 1919, by Heber J. Grant, at age 45; died July 30, 1939, at Salt Lake City, Salt Lake Co., Utah, at age 66.

54. John Andreas Widtsoe — Born Jan. 31, 1872, at Daloe, Island of Froyen, Trondhjem, Norway, to John A. Widtsoe and Anna Karine Gaarden. Ordained apostle March 17, 1921, by Heber J. Grant, at age 49; died

Nov. 29, 1952, at Salt Lake City, Salt Lake Co., Utah, at age 80.

55. Joseph Francis Merrill — Born Aug. 24, 1868, at Richmond, Cache Co., Utah, to Marriner Wood Merrill and Mariah Loenza Kingsbury. Ordained apostle Oct. 8, 1931, by Heber J. Grant, at age 63; died Feb. 3, 1952, at Salt

Lake City, Salt Lake Co., Utah, at age 83.

56. Charles Albert Callis — Born May 4, 1865, at Dublin, Dublin Co., Ireland, to John Callis and Susanna Charlotte Quillam. Ordained apostle Oct. 12, 1933, by Heber J. Grant, at age 68.

Died Jan. 21, 1947, in Jacksonville, Duval Co., Florida, at age 81.

57. Joshua Reuben Clark Jr. — See FIRST COUNSELORS IN THE FIRST PRESIDENCY, No. 11.

58. Alonzo Arza Hinckley — Born April 23, 1870, at Cove Fort, Millard Co., Utah, to Ira Nathaniel Hinckley and Angeline Wilcox Noble. Ordained apostle Oct. 11, 1934, by Heber J. Grant, at age 64; died Dec. 22, 1936, at Salt

Lake City, Salt Lake Co., Utah, at age 66.

59. Albert Ernest Bowen — Born Oct. 31, 1875, at Henderson Creek, Oneida Co., Idaho, to David Bowen and Annie Schackelton. Ordained apostle April 8, 1937, by Heber J. Grant, at age 61; died July 15, 1953, at Salt Lake City, Salt Lake Co., Utah, at age 77.

60. Sylvester Quayle Cannon — Born June 10, 1877, at Salt Lake City, Salt Lake Co., Utah, to George Quayle Cannon and Elizabeth Hoagland. Sustained as Presiding Bishop of the Church June 4, 1925, at age 47; sustained as Associate to the Quorum of the Twelve Apostles April 6, 1938; ordained apostle April 14, 1938, by Heber J. Grant; sustained as a member of the Quorum of the Twelve Apostles Oct. 6, 1939, at age 62; died May 29, 1943, at Salt Lake City, Salt Lake Co., Utah, at age 65.

61. Harold Bingham Lee — See PRESIDENTS OF THE CHURCH, No. 11.

62. Spencer Woolley Kimball — See PRESIDENTS OF THE CHURCH, No. 12.

63. Ezra Taft Benson — See PRESIDENTS OF THE CHURCH, No. 13.

64. Mark Edward Petersen — Born Nov. 7, 1900, at Salt Lake City, Salt

Lake Co., Utah, to Christian Petersen and Christine M. Andersen. Ordained apostle April 20, 1944, by Heber J. Grant, at age 43; died Jan. 11, 1984, at Salt Lake City, Salt Lake Co., Utah, at age 83.

65. Matthew Cowley — Born Aug. 2, 1897, at Preston, Franklin Co., Idaho, to Matthias Foss Cowley and Abbie Hyde. Ordained apostle Oct. 11, 1945, by George Albert Smith, at age 48; died Dec. 13, 1953, at Los Angeles, Los Angeles Co., California, at age 56.

66. Henry Dinwoodey Moyle — See FIRST COUNSELORS IN THE FIRST PRESIDENCY, No. 14.

67. Delbert Leon Stapley — Born Dec. 11, 1896, at Mesa, Maricopa Co., Arizona, to Orley S. Stapley and Polly M. Hunsaker. Ordained apostle Oct. 5, 1950, by George Albert Smith, at age 53; died Aug. 19, 1978, at Salt Lake City, Salt Lake Co., Utah, at age 81.

68. Marion George Romney — See FIRST COUNSELORS IN THE FIRST PRESIDENCY, No. 18.

69. LeGrand Richards — Born Feb. 6, 1886, at Farmington, Davis Co., Utah, to George Franklin Richards and Alice Almira Robinson. Sustained Presiding Bishop of the Church April 6, 1938, at age 52; ordained apostle April 10, 1952, by David O. McKay, at age 66; died Jan. 11, 1983, at Salt Lake City, Salt Lake Co., Utah, at age 96.

70. Adam Samuel Bennion — Born Dec. 2, 1886, at Taylorsville, Salt Lake Co., Utah, to Joseph Bennion and

Mary A. Sharp. Ordained apostle April 9, 1953, by David O. McKay, at age 66; died Feb. 11, 1958, at Salt Lake City, Salt Lake Co., Utah, at age 71.

71. Richard Louis Evans — Born March 23, 1906, at Salt Lake City, Salt Lake Co., Utah, to John A. Evans and Florence Neslen. Sustained as member of the First Council of the Seventy Oct. 7, 1938, at age 32; ordained apostle Oct. 8, 1953, by David O. McKay, at age 47; died Nov. 1, 1971, at Salt Lake City, Salt Lake Co., Utah, at age 65.

72. George Quayle Morris — Born Feb. 20, 1874, at Salt Lake City, Salt Lake Co., Utah, to Elias Morris and Mary L. Walker. Sustained as Assistant to the Quorum of the Twelve Apostles Oct. 6, 1951, at age 77; ordained apostle April 8, 1954, by David O. McKay, at age 80; died April 23, 1962, at Salt Lake City, Salt Lake Co., Utah, at age 88.

73. Hugh Brown Brown — See FIRST COUNSELORS IN THE FIRST PRESIDENCY, No. 15.

74. Howard William Hunter — See PRESIDENTS OF THE CHURCH, No. 14.

75. Gordon Bitner Hinckley — See current FIRST PRESIDENCY.

76. Nathan Eldon Tanner — See FIRST COUNSELORS IN THE FIRST PRESIDENCY, No. 17.

77. Thomas Spencer Monson — See current FIRST PRESIDENCY.

78. Boyd Kenneth Packer — See current QUORUM OF THE TWELVE.

79. Marvin Jeremy Ashton — Born May 6, 1915, in Salt Lake City, Salt Lake Co., Utah, to Marvin O. Ashton and

Rachel Jeremy. Sustained Assistant to the Twelve Oct. 3, 1969, at age 54; ordained apostle on Dec. 2, 1971, by Harold B. Lee at age 56. Died Feb. 25, 1994, at Salt Lake City, Salt Lake Co., Utah, at age 78.

80. Bruce Redd Mc-Conkie — Born July 29, 1915, at Ann Arbor, Washtenaw Co., Michigan, to Oscar Walter McConkie and Vivian Redd. Sustained to First Council of the Seventy Oct. 6, 1946, at age 31; ordained apostle Oct. 12, 1972, by Harold B. Lee, at age 57; died April 19, 1985, at Salt Lake City, Salt Lake Co., Utah, at age 69.

81. Lowell Tom Perry — See current QUORUM OF THE TWELVE.

82. David Bruce Haight — See current QUORUM OF THE TWELVE.

83. James Esdras Faust — See current FIRST PRESIDENCY.

84. Neal Ash Maxwell — See current QUORUM OF THE TWELVE.

85. Russell Marion Nelson — See current QUORUM OF THE TWELVE.

86. Dallin Harris Oaks — See current QUORUM OF THE TWELVE.

87. Melvin Russell Ballard Jr. — See current QUORUM OF THE TWELVE.

88. Joseph Bitner Wirthlin — See current QUORUM OF THE TWELVE.

89. Richard Gordon Scott — See current QUORUM OF THE TWELVE.

90. Robert Dean Hales — See current QUORUM OF THE TWELVE.

91. Jeffrey Roy Holland — See current QUORUM OF THE TWELVE.

92. Henry Bennion Eyring — See current QUORUM OF THE TWELVE.

OTHER APOSTLES

1. Joseph Smith Jr. — See PRESIDENTS OF THE CHURCH, No. 1.

2. Oliver Cowdery — See ASSISTANT PRESIDENTS OF THE CHURCH, No. 1.

3. Hyrum Smith — See ASSISTANT PRESIDENTS OF THE CHURCH, No. 2.

4. Amasa Mason Lyman — See OTHER COUNSELORS IN THE FIRST PRESIDENCY, No. 3.

5. Jedediah Morgan Grant — See SECOND COUNSELORS IN THE FIRST PRESIDENCY, No. 5.

6. John Willard Young — See FIRST COUNSELORS IN THE FIRST PRESIDENCY, No. 4.

7. Daniel Hanmer Wells — See SECOND COUNSELORS IN THE FIRST PRESIDENCY, No. 6.

8. Joseph Angell Young — Born Oct. 14, 1834, in Kirtland, Geauga Co., Ohio, to Brigham Young and Mary Ann Angell. Ordained apostle Feb. 4, 1864, by Brigham Young, at age 29; died Aug. 5, 1875, at Manti, Sanpete Co., Utah, at age 40.

9. Brigham Young Jr. — See OTHER COUNSELORS IN THE FIRST PRESIDENCY, No. 6.

10. Joseph Fielding Smith — See PRESIDENTS OF THE CHURCH, No. 6.

11. Sylvester Quayle Cannon — See QUORUM OF THE TWELVE, No. 60.

12. Alvin Rulon Dyer — See OTHER COUNSELORS IN THE FIRST PRESIDENCY, No. 13.

PATRIARCHS TO THE CHURCH

1. Joseph Smith Sr. — See ASSISTANT COUNSELORS IN THE FIRST PRESIDENCY, No. 2.

2. Hyrum Smith — See ASSISTANT PRESIDENTS OF THE CHURCH, No. 2.

William Smith — See QUORUM OF THE TWELVE, No. 9. Ordained Patriarch to the Church May 24, 1845, by the Quorum of the Twelve and then gave patriarchal blessings, but was rejected by the Church membership at the General Conference held Oct. 6, 1845.

3. John Smith — See ASSISTANT COUNSELORS IN THE FIRST PRESIDENCY, No. 4.

4. John Smith — Born Sept. 22, 1832, at Kirtland, Geauga Co., Ohio, the eldest son of Hyrum Smith and Jerusha Barden. Ordained Patriarch to the Church Feb. 18, 1855, by Brigham Young, at age 22; died Nov. 5, 1911, at Salt Lake City, Salt Lake Co., Utah, at age 79.

5. Hyrum Gibbs Smith — Born July 8, 1879, at South Jordan, Salt Lake Co., Utah, the eldest son of Hyrum Fisher Smith and Annie Maria Gibbs. Ordained  high priest and Patriarch to the Church May 9, 1912, by Joseph F. Smith, at age 32; died Feb. 4, 1932, at Salt Lake City, Salt Lake Co., Utah, at age 52.

(From 1932 to 1937, no Patriarch to the Church was sustained.)

George Franklin Richards — (Served as acting Patriarch) See QUORUM OF THE TWELVE, No. 45.

6. Joseph Fielding Smith — Born Jan. 30, 1899, at Salt Lake City, Salt Lake Co.,  Utah, the eldest son of Hyrum Mack Smith and Ida E. Bowman. Ordained high priest and Patriarch to the Church Oct. 8, 1942, by Heber J. Grant, at age 43; released Oct. 6, 1946, due to ill health; died Aug. 29, 1964, in Salt Lake City, Salt Lake Co., Utah, at age 65.

7. Eldred Gee Smith — Born Jan. 9, 1907, at Lehi, Utah Co., Utah, the eldest son of Hyrum Gibbs Smith and  Martha Electa Gee. Ordained high priest May 23, 1938, by J. Reuben Clark Jr.; ordained Patriarch to the Church April 10, 1947, by George Albert Smith, at age 40; named emeritus General Authority Oct. 6, 1979.

(No Patriarch to the Church has been sustained since Oct. 6, 1979.)

FIRST COUNCIL OF THE SEVENTY
(Functioned from February 1835 to October 1976)

1. Hazen Aldrich — Chosen and ordained one of the First Seven Presidents Feb. 28, 1835; released April 6, 1837, having previously been ordained high priest.

2. Joseph Young — Born April 7, 1797, at Hopkinton, Middlesex Co., Massachusetts, to John Young and Abigail Howe. Ordained seventy Feb. 28, 1835, under the hands of Joseph Smith, Sidney Rigdon and Frederick G. Williams; chosen and ordained one of the First Seven Presidents Feb. 28, 1835, at age 37; died  July 16, 1881, at Salt Lake City, Salt Lake Co., Utah, at age 84.

3. Levi Ward Hancock — Born April

7, 1803, at Springfield, Hampden, Co., Massachusetts, to Thomas Hancock and Amy Ward. Ordained seventy Feb. 28, 1835, under the hands of Joseph Smith, Sidney Rigdon and Frederick G. Williams; chosen and ordained one of the First Seven Presidents Feb. 28, 1835, at age 31; released April 6, 1837, having supposedly previously been ordained high priest; restored to former place in the First Council Sept. 3, 1837, as he had not been ordained high priest; died June 10, 1882, at Washington, Washington Co., Utah, at age 79.

4. Leonard Rich — Chosen and ordained one of the First Seven Presidents Feb. 28, 1835; released April 6, 1837, having previously been ordained high priest.

5. Zebedee Coltrin — Born Sept. 7, 1804, at Ovid, Seneca Co., New York, to John Coltrin Jr. and Sarah Graham. Chosen and ordained one of the First Seven Presidents Feb. 28, 1835, at age 30; released April 6, 1837, having previously been ordained high priest; died July 20, 1887, at Spanish Fork, Utah Co., Utah, at age 82.

6. Lyman Royal Sherman — Born May 22, 1804, at Salem, Essex Co., Massachusetts, to Elkanah Sherman and Asenath Hulbert. Chosen and ordained one of the First Seven Presidents Feb. 28, 1835, at age 30; released April 6, 1837, having previously been ordained high priest; died Jan. 27, 1839, at age 34.

7. Sylvester Smith — Chosen and ordained one of the First Seven Presidents Feb. 28, 1835; released April 6, 1837, having previously been ordained high priest.

8. John Gould — Born May 11, 1808. Ordained seventy and set apart as one of the First Seven Presidents April 6, 1837, by Sidney Rigdon and Hyrum Smith, at age 28; released Sept. 3,

1837, to be ordained high priest. Died May 9, 1851, at age 42.

9. James Foster — Born April 1, 1775, at Morgan Co., New Hampshire. Ordained seventy April 6, 1837, under the hands of Sidney Rigdon and Hyrum Smith; set apart as one of the First Seven Presidents April 6, 1837, at age 62; died Dec. 21, 1841, at Morgan Co., Illinois, at age 66.

10. Daniel Sanborn Miles — Born July 23, 1772, at Sanbornton, Belknap Co., New Hampshire, to Josiah Miles and Marah Sanborn. Ordained seventy April 6, 1837, by Hazen Aldrich; set apart as one of the First Seven Presidents April 6, 1837, by Sidney Rigdon and Hyrum Smith, at age 64; died in autumn of 1845, at Hancock Co., Illinois, at age 73.

11. Josiah Butterfield — Born March 13 or 18, 1795, at Saco, York Co., Maine, to Abel Butterfield and Mary or Mercy ——-. Ordained seventy April 6, 1837, under the hands of Sidney Rigdon and Hyrum Smith; set apart as one of the First Seven Presidents April 6, 1837, at age 42; excommunicated Oct. 7, 1844; died in April 1871 at Monterey Co., California, at age 76.

12. Salmon Gee — Born Oct. 16, 1792, at Lyme, New London Co., Connecticut, to Zopher Gee and Esther Beckwith. Ordained seventy April 6, 1837, under the hands of Sidney Rigdon and Hyrum Smith; set apart as one of the First Seven Presidents April 6, 1837, at age 44; fellowship withdrawn March 6, 1838; died Sept. 13, 1845, at Ambrosia, Lee Co., Iowa, at age 52; posthumously reinstated Sept. 14, 1967.

13. John Gaylord — Born July 12, 1797, in Pennsylvania, to Chauncey Gaylord. Ordained seventy Dec. 20, 1836, by Hazen Aldrich; set apart as one of the First Seven Presidents April 6, 1837, at age 39, by Sidney Rigdon and others; excommunicated Jan. 13, 1838; rejoined the Church at Nauvoo, Illinois, Oct. 5, 1839; died July 17, 1878, at age 81.

14. Henry Harriman — Born June 9, 1804, at Rowley, Essex Co., Massachusetts, to Enoch Harriman and Sarah Brocklebank. Ordained seventy March 1835, un-  der the hands of Joseph Smith and Sidney Rigdon; set apart as one of the First Seven Presidents Feb. 6, 1838, by Joseph Young and others, at age 33; died May 17, 1891, at Huntington, Emery Co., Utah, at 86.

15. Zera Pulsipher — Born June 24, 1789, at Rockingham, Windham Co., Vermont, to John Pulsipher and Elizabeth Dutton. Ordained seventy March 6, 1838, under the hands of Joseph Young and James Foster; set apart as one of the First Seven Presidents March 6, 1838, at age 48; released April 12, 1862; died Jan. 1, 1872, at Hebron, Washington Co., Utah, at age 82.

Roger Orton was excommunicated Nov. 30, 1837; returned to the Church; sustained as one of the First Seven Presidents April 7, 1845, but was never set apart and did not function; dropped from this position Oct. 6, 1845.

16. Albert Perry Rockwood — Born June 5, 1805, at Hollis- ton, Middlesex Co., Massachusetts, to  Luther Rockwood and Ruth Perry. Ordained seventy Jan. 5, 1839, un- der the hands of Joseph Young, Henry Harriman and Zera Pulsipher; set apart as one of the First Seven Presidents Dec. 2, 1845, by Brigham Young and others, at age 40; died Nov. 26, 1879, at Sugar House, Salt Lake Co., Utah, at age 74.

17. Benjamin Lynn Clapp — Born Aug. 19, 1814, at West Huntsville, Madison Co., Alabama, to Ludwig Lewis Clapp and Margaret Ann Loy. Ordained seventy Oct. 20, 1844, under the hands of Joseph Young and Levi

W. Hancock; set apart as one of the First Seven Presidents Dec. 2, 1845, by Brigham Young and others, at age 31; excommunicated April 7, 1859; died in 1860 in California, at age 46.

18. Jedediah Morgan Grant — See SECOND COUNSELORS IN THE FIRST PRESIDENCY, No. 5.

19. Horace Sunderlin Eldredge — Born Feb. 6, 1816, at Brutus, Cayuga Co., New  York, to Alanson Eldredge and Esther Sunderlin. Ordained seventy Oct. 13, 1844, by Joseph Young; sustained as one of the First Seven Presidents Oct. 7, 1854, at age 38; died Sept. 6, 1888, at Salt Lake City, Salt Lake Co., Utah, at age 72.

20. Jacob Gates — Born March 9, 1811, at Saint Johnsbury, Caledonia Co., Vermont,  to Thomas Gates and Patty Plumley. Ordained seventy Dec. 19, 1838, under the hands of Joseph Smith and Sidney Rigdon; sustained as one of the First Seven Presidents April 6, 1860, at age 49; set apart Oct. 8, 1862, by Orson Hyde; died April 14, 1892, at Provo, Utah Co., Utah, at 81.

21. John Van Cott — Born Sept. 7, 1814, at Canaan, Columbia Co., New York, to  Losee Van Cott and Lovinia Pratt. Ordained seventy Feb. 25, 1847, by Joseph Young; sustained as one of the First Seven Presidents Oct. 8, 1862, at age 48; set apart by John Taylor; died Feb. 18, 1883, at Salt Lake City, Salt Lake Co., Utah, at 68.

22. William Whittaker Taylor — Born Sept. 11, 1853, at Salt Lake City, Salt Lake  Co., Utah, to John Taylor and Harriet Whittaker. Ordained seventy Oct. 11, 1875, by Orson Pratt; sustained as one of the First Seven Presidents

April 7, 1880, at age 26; set apart by John Taylor; died Aug. 1, 1884, at Salt Lake City, Salt Lake Co., Utah, at 30.

23. Abraham Hoagland Cannon — See QUORUM OF THE TWELVE, No. 37.

Theodore Belden Lewis — Born Nov. 18, 1843, at St. Louis, St. Louis Co., Missouri, to Thomas Anderson Lewis and Martha J. O. Belden. Ordained high priest at Nephi, Utah (date not known); sustained as one of the First Seven Presidents Oct. 8, 1882, at age 38; on Oct. 9, when he was to be set apart, he reported that he was already a high priest, so he was not set apart and did not function in this position.

24. Seymour Bicknell Young — Born Oct. 3, 1837, at Kirtland, Geauga Co., Ohio, to Joseph Young and Jane Adeline Bicknell. Or-  dained seventy Feb. 18, 1857, by Edmund Ellsworth; set apart by Franklin D. Richards as one of the First Seven Presidents Oct. 14, 1882, at age 45; sustained April 8, 1883; died Dec. 15, 1924, at Salt Lake City, Salt Lake Co., Utah, at age 87.

25. Christian Daniel Fjelsted — Born Feb. 20, 1829, at Amagar, Sundbyvester Co., Denmark, to Hendrick Ludvig Fjelsted and Ann Catrine Hen-  driksen. Ordained seventy Feb. 5, 1859, by William H. Walker; sustained as one of the First Seven Presidents April 6, 1884, at age 55; set apart by Wilford Woodruff; died Dec. 23, 1905, at Salt Lake City, Salt Lake Co., Utah, at age 76.

26. John Morgan — Born Aug. 8, 1842, at Greensburg, Decatur Co., Indiana, to Gerrard Morgan and Ann Eliza Hamilton. Ordained sev-  enty Oct. 8, 1875, by Joseph Young; sustained

as one of the First Seven Presidents Oct. 5, 1884, at age 42; set apart by Wilford Woodruff; died Aug. 14, 1894, at Preston, Franklin Co., Idaho, at 52.

27. Brigham Henry Roberts — Born March 13, 1857, at Warrington, Lancashire Co., England, to Benjamin Roberts and Ann Ever-  ington. Ordained seventy March 8, 1877, by Nathan T. Porter. Sustained as one of the First Seven Presidents Oct. 7, 1888, at age 31; set apart by Lorenzo Snow; died Sept. 27, 1933, at Salt Lake City, Salt Lake Co., Utah, at age 76.

28. George Reynolds — Born Jan. 1, 1842, at Marylebone, London Co., London, England, to George Reynolds and Julia Ann Tautz. Ordained seventy  March 18, 1866, by Israel Barlow; sustained as one of the First Seven Presidents April 5, 1890, at age 48; set apart by Lorenzo Snow; died Aug. 9, 1909, at Salt Lake City, Salt Lake Co., Utah, at age 67.

29. Jonathan Golden Kimball — Born June 9, 1853, at Salt Lake City, Salt Lake Co., Utah, to Heber Chase Kimball and Christeen Golden. Ordained sev- enty July 21, 1886, by William M. Allred; sustained as one of the First Seven Presidents April 5, 1892, at age 38; set apart by Francis M. Lyman; killed in an automobile accident Sept. 2, 1938, near Reno, Nevada, at age 85.

30. Rulon Seymour Wells — Born July 7, 1854, at Salt Lake City, Salt Lake Co., Utah, to Daniel Hanmer Wells and Louisa Free. Or-  dained seventy Oct. 22, 1875, by Brigham Young; sustained as one of the First Seven Presidents April 5, 1893, at age 38; set apart by George Q. Cannon; died May 7, 1941, at Salt Lake City, Salt Lake Co., Utah, at age 86.

31. Edward Stevenson — Born May 1, 1820, at Gibraltar, Spain, to Joseph Stevenson and Elizabeth Stevens. Ordained seventy May 1, 1844, by Joseph Young; sustained as one of the First Seven Presidents Oct. 7, 1894,  at age 74; set apart by Brigham Young; died Jan. 27, 1897, at Salt Lake City, Salt Lake Co., Utah, at age 76.

32. Joseph William McMurrin — Born Sept. 5. 1858, at Tooele, Tooele Co., Utah, to Joseph McMurrin and Margaret Leaning. Ordained seventy April 21, 1884, by Royal Barney; sustained as one of the First Seven Presidents  Oct. 5, 1897, at age 39; set apart Jan. 21, 1898, by Anthon H. Lund; died Oct. 24, 1932, at Los Angeles, Los Angeles Co., California, at age 74.

33. Charles Henry Hart — Born July 5, 1866, at Bloomington, Bear Lake Co., Idaho, to James Henry Hart and Sabina Scheib. Ordained seventy Aug. 10, 1890, by John Henry Smith; sustained as one of the First Seven Presidents April 9,  1906, at age 39; set apart by Joseph F. Smith; died Sept. 29, 1934, at Salt Lake City, Salt Lake Co., Utah, at age 68.

34. Levi Edgar Young — Born Feb. 2, 1874, at Salt Lake City, Salt Lake Co., Utah, to Seymour Bicknell Young and Ann Elizabeth Riter. Ordained seventy June 18, 1897, by Seymour B. Young; sustained as one of the First Seven Presidents Oct. 6, 1909, at age 35; set apart Jan. 23, 1910, by John Henry Smith; died Dec. 13, 1963, at Salt Lake City, Salt Lake Co., Utah, at age 89.

35. Rey Lucero Pratt — Born Oct. 11, 1878, at Salt Lake City, Salt Lake Co.,

Utah, to Helaman Pratt and Emeline Victoria Billingsley. Ordained seventy Sept. 23, 1911, by Rulon S. Wells; sustained as one of the First Seven Presidents Jan. 29, 1925, at age 46; set apart April 7, 1925, by Anthony W. Ivins;  died April 14, 1931, at Salt Lake City, Salt Lake Co., Utah at age 52.

36. Antoine Ridgeway Ivins — Born May 11, 1881, at St. George, Washington Co., Utah, to Anthony Woodward Ivins and Elizabeth A. Snow. Ordained seventy Dec. 28, 1913, by Fred E. Barker; sustained as one of the First Seven  Presidents Oct. 4, 1931, at age 50; ordained high priest June 11, 1961, by David O. McKay; died Oct. 18, 1967, at Salt Lake City, Salt Lake Co., Utah, at 86.

37. Samuel Otis Bennion — Born June 9, 1874, at Taylorsville, Salt Lake Co., Utah, to John Rowland Bennion and Emma Jane Terry. Ordained seventy March 14, 1904, by Samuel Gerrard; sustained as one of the First  Seven Presidents April 6, 1933, at age 58; set apart by Heber J. Grant; died March 8, 1945, at Salt Lake City, Salt Lake Co., Utah, at age 70.

38. John Harris Taylor — Born June 28, 1875, at Salt Lake City, Salt Lake Co., Utah, to Thomas E. Taylor and Emma L. Harris. Ordained seventy Jan. 24, 1896, by Heber J. Grant; sustained as one of the First Seven Presidents  Oct. 6, 1933, at age 58; set apart by Heber J. Grant; died May 28, 1946, at Salt Lake City, Salt Lake Co., Utah, at age 70.

39. Rufus Kay Hardy — Born May 28, 1878, at Salt Lake City, Salt Lake Co., Utah, to Rufus H. Hardy and Annie Kay. Ordained seventy July 2, 1897, by John Henry Smith; sustained to the First Council of the Seventy Oct. 6, 1934, at age 56; set apart Feb. 7, 1935, by Heber J. Grant; died March 7, 1945, at Salt Lake City, Salt Lake Co., Utah, at age 66.

40. Richard Louis Evans — See QUORUM OF THE TWELVE, No. 71.

41. Oscar Ammon Kirkham — Born Jan. 22, 1880, at Lehi, Utah Co., Utah, to James Kirkham and Martha Mercer. Ordained seventy Feb. 26, 1905, by Joseph W. McMurrin; sustained to the First Council of the Seventy

Oct. 5, 1941, at age 61; set apart by Heber J. Grant; died March 10, 1958, at Salt Lake City, Salt Lake Co., Utah, at78.

42. Seymour Dilworth Young — See FIRST QUORUM OF THE SEVENTY, No. 24.

43. Milton Reed Hunter — Born Oct. 25, 1902, at Holden, Millard Co., Utah, to John E. Hunter and Margaret Teeples. Ordained seventy Aug. 31, 1928, by Rulon S. Wells; sustained to the First Council of the Seventy April 6, 1945, at age 42; ordained high priest June 11, 1961, by David O. McKay; died June 27, 1975, at Salt Lake City, Salt Lake Co., Utah, at 72.

44. Bruce Redd McConkie — See QUORUM OF THE TWELVE, No. 80.

45. Marion Duff Hanks — See PRESIDENCY OF THE SEVENTY, No. 6.

46. Albert Theodore Tuttle — See PRESIDENCY OF THE SEVENTY, No. 4.

47. Paul Harold Dunn — See PRESIDENCY OF THE SEVENTY, No. 7.

48. Hartman Rector Jr. — See FIRST QUORUM OF THE SEVENTY, No. 25.

49. Loren Charles Dunn — See current FIRST QUORUM OF THE SEVENTY.

50. Rex Dee Pinegar — See current FIRST QUORUM OF THE SEVENTY.

51. Gene Raymond Cook — See current FIRST QUORUM OF THE SEVENTY.

On Oct. 3, 1975, the First Quorum of the Seventy was reconstituted with the sustaining of three members, Elders Charles Didier, William R. Bradford and George P. Lee. Four additional members, Elders Carlos E. Asay, M. Russell Ballard, John H. Groberg and Jacob de Jager, were sustained April 3, 1976.

On Oct. 1, 1976, the members of the First Council of the Seventy and the Assistants to the Quorum of the Twelve Apostles were released, and sustained to the First Quorum of the Seventy. A Presidency of the First Quorum of the Seventy was sustained, and the position of the members of the quorum revised.

ASSISTANTS TO THE TWELVE
(Functioned from April 1941 to October 1976)

1. Marion George Romney — See FIRST COUNSELORS IN THE FIRST PRESIDENCY, No. 18.

2. Thomas Evans McKay — Born Oct. 29, 1875, at Huntsville, Weber Co., Utah, to David McKay and Jennette Eveline Evans. Ordained high priest July 26, 1908, by

George F. Richards; sustained as Assistant to the Quorum of the Twelve Apostles April 6, 1941, and set apart May 23, 1941, by Heber J. Grant, at age 65; died Jan. 15, 1958, at Salt Lake City, Salt Lake Co., Utah, at age 82.

3. Clifford Earl Young — Born Dec. 7, 1883, at Salt Lake City, Salt Lake Co., Utah, to Seymour Bicknell Young and Ann Elizabeth Riter. Ordained high priest July 1, 1928, by Heber J. Grant; sustained as Assistant to the Quorum of the Twelve Apostles April 6, 1941, and set apart May 23, 1941, by President Grant, at age 57; died Aug. 21, 1958, at Salt Lake City, Salt Lake Co., Utah, at age 74.

4. Alma Sonne — See FIRST QUORUM OF THE SEVENTY, No. 8.

5. Nicholas Groesbeck Smith — Born June 20, 1881, at Salt Lake City, Salt Lake Co., Utah, to John Henry Smith and Josephine Groesbeck. Ordained high priest Aug. 1, 1921, by Rudger Clawson; sustained an Assistant to the Quorum of the Twelve Apostles April 6, 1941; set apart Oct. 1, 1941, by Heber J. Grant, at age 60; died Oct. 27, 1945, at Salt Lake City, Salt Lake Co., Utah, at age 64.

6. George Quayle Morris — See QUORUM OF THE TWELVE, No. 72.

7. Stayner Richards — Born Dec. 20, 1885, at Salt Lake City, Salt Lake Co., Utah, to Stephen Longstroth Richards and Emma Louise Stayner. Ordained high priest Feb. 24, 1914, by George F. Richards; sustained as Assistant to the Quorum of the Twelve Apostles Oct. 6, 1951, and set apart Oct. 11, 1951, by David O. McKay, at age 65; died May 28, 1953, at Salt Lake City, Salt Lake Co., Utah, at age 67.

8. ElRay LaVar Christiansen — Born July 13, 1897, at Mayfield, Sanpete Co., Utah, to Parley Christiansen and Dorthea C. Jensen. Ordained high priest Oct. 22, 1933, by George F. Richards; sustained as Assistant to the Quorum of the Twelve Apostles Oct. 6, 1951, and set apart Oct. 11, 1951, by

Stephen L Richards, at age 54; died Dec. 2, 1975, at Salt Lake City, Salt Lake Co., Utah, at age 78.

9. John Longden — Born Nov. 4, 1898, at Oldham, Lancashire Co., England, to Thomas Johnson Longden and Lizetta Taylor. Ordained high priest Sept. 27, 1925, by Rudger Clawson; sustained as Assistant to the Quorum of the Twelve Apostles Oct. 6, 1951, and set apart Oct. 11, 1951, by J. Reuben Clark Jr., at age 52; died Aug. 30, 1969, at Salt Lake City, Salt Lake Co., Utah, at age 70.

10. Hugh Brown Brown — See FIRST COUNSELORS IN THE FIRST PRESIDENCY, No. 15.

11. Sterling Welling Sill — See FIRST QUORUM OF THE SEVENTY, No. 9.

12. Gordon Bitner Hinckley — See current FIRST PRESIDENCY.

13. Henry Dixon Taylor — See FIRST QUORUM OF THE SEVENTY, No. 10.

14. William James Critchlow Jr. — Born Aug. 21, 1892, at Brigham City, Box Elder Co., Utah, to William James Critchlow and Anna C. Gregerson. Ordained high priest Dec. 16, 1934, by George F. Richards; sustained as Assistant to the Quorum of the Twelve Apostles Oct. 11, 1958, and set apart Oct. 16, 1958, by David O. McKay, at age 66; died Aug. 29, 1968, at Ogden, Weber Co., Utah, at age 76.

15. Alvin Rulon Dyer — See OTHER COUNSELORS IN THE FIRST PRESIDENCY, No. 13.

16. Nathan Eldon Tanner — See FIRST COUNSELORS IN THE FIRST PRESIDENCY, No. 17.

17. Franklin Dewey Richards — See PRESIDENCY OF THE SEVENTY, No. 1.

18. Theodore Moyle Burton — See FIRST QUORUM OF THE SEVENTY, No. 12.

19. Henry Thorpe Beal Isaacson — See OTHER COUNSELORS IN THE FIRST PRESIDENCY, No. 12.

20. Boyd Kenneth Packer — See current QUORUM OF THE TWELVE.

21. Bernard Park Brockbank — See FIRST QUORUM OF THE SEVENTY, No. 13.

22. James Alfred Cullimore — See FIRST QUORUM OF THE SEVENTY, No. 14.

23. Marion Duff Hanks — See PRESIDENCY OF THE SEVENTY, No. 6.

24. Marvin Jeremy Ashton — See QUORUM OF THE TWELVE, No. 79.

25. Joseph Anderson — See FIRST QUORUM OF THE SEVENTY, No. 15.

26. David Bruce Haight — See current QUORUM OF THE TWELVE.

27. William Hunter Bennett — See FIRST QUORUM OF THE SEVENTY, No. 16.

28. John Henry Vandenberg — See PRESIDING BISHOPS, No. 9.

29. Robert Leatham Simpson — See FIRST QUORUM OF THE SEVENTY, No. 18.

30. Oscar Leslie Stone — See FIRST QUORUM OF THE SEVENTY, No. 19.

31. James Esdras Faust — See current FIRST PRESIDENCY.

32. Lowell Tom Perry — See current QUORUM OF THE TWELVE.

33. John Thomas Fyans — See PRESIDENCY OF THE SEVENTY, No. 3.

34. Neal Ash Maxwell — See current QUORUM OF THE TWELVE.

35. William Grant Bangerter — See PRESIDENCY OF THE SEVENTY, No. 8.

36. Robert Dean Hales — See current QUORUM OF THE TWELVE.

37. Adney Yoshio Komatsu — See FIRST QUORUM OF THE SEVENTY, No. 22.

38. Joseph Bitner Wirthlin — See current QUORUM OF THE TWELVE.

PRESIDENCY OF THE SEVENTY

(Since April 1, 1989, serves as the Presidency of both the First Quorum of the Seventy and the Second Quorum of the Seventy)

1. Franklin Dewey Richards — Born Nov. 17, 1900, in Ogden, Weber Co., Utah, to Charles C. Richards and Louisa L. Peery. Sustained as Assistant to the Quorum of the Twelve Apostles Oct. 8, 1960, at age 59; sustained to First Quorum of the Seventy Oct. 1,  1976; served in Presidency of the First Quorum of the Seventy, Oct. 1, 1976, to Oct. 1, 1983; died Nov. 13, 1987, at Salt Lake City, Salt Lake Co., Utah, at age 86.

2. James Esdras Faust — See current FIRST PRESIDENCY.

3. John Thomas Fyans — Born May 17, 1918, at Moreland, Bingham Co., Idaho, to Joseph Fyans and Mae Farnsworth. Sustained as Assistant to the Quorum of the  Twelve Apostles April 6, 1974, at age 55; sustained to First Quorum of the Seventy Oct. 1, 1976; served in Presidency of the First Quorum of the Seventy, Oct. 1, 1976, to Oct. 6, 1985; named emeritus General Authority Oct. 1, 1989.

4. Albert Theodore Tuttle — Born March 2, 1919, in Manti, Sanpete Co., Utah, to Albert M. Tuttle and Clarice Beal. Sustained to First Council of the Seventy April 6, 1958, at age 39; sustained to First Quorum of the Seventy  Oct. 1, 1976; served in Presidency of the First Quorum of the Seventy, Oct. 1, 1976, to Feb. 22, 1980; died Nov. 28, 1986, at Salt Lake City, Salt Lake Co., Utah, at age 67.

5. Neal Ash Maxwell — See current QUORUM OF THE TWELVE.

6. Marion Duff Hanks — Born Oct.

13, 1921, in Salt Lake City, Salt Lake Co., Utah, to Stanley Alonzo Hanks and Maude Frame. Sustained to First Council of  the Seventy Oct. 4, 1953, at age 31, and as Assistant to the Quorum of the Twelve Apostles April 6, 1968; sustained to the First Quorum of the Seventy Oct. 1, 1976; served in the Presidency of the First Quorum of the Seventy from Oct. 1, 1976-April 5, 1980, and from Oct. 6, 1984-Aug. 15, 1992; named emeritus General Authority Oct. 3, 1992.

7. Paul Harold Dunn — Born April 24, 1924, at Provo, Utah Co., Utah, to Joshua Harold Dunn and Geneve Roberts. Sustained  to First Council of the Seventy April 6, 1964, at age 39; sustained to First Quorum of the Seventy Oct. 1, 1976; served in Presidency of the First Quorum of the Seventy, Oct. 1, 1976, to Feb. 22, 1980; named emeritus General Authority Oct. 1, 1989.

8. William Grant Bangerter — Born June 8, 1918, at Granger, Salt Lake Co., Utah, to William Henry Bangerter and Isabelle Bawden.  Sustained as Assistant to the Quorum of the Twelve Apostles April 4, 1975, at age 56; sustained to First Quorum of the Seventy Oct. 1, 1976; served in Presidency of the First Quorum of the Seventy from Sept. 30, 1978, to April 5, 1980, and from Feb. 17, 1985, to Oct. 1, 1989; named emeritus General Authority Oct. 1, 1989.

9. Carlos Egan Asay — Born June 12, 1926, in Sutherland, Millard Co., Utah, to A.E. Lyle Asay and Elsie Egan. Sustained to the First Quorum of the Seventy April 3, 1976, at age 49; served in Presidency of the Seventy from April

5, 1980, to Aug. 15, 1986, and from Oct. 1, 1989, to Aug. 15, 1996; named emeritus General Authority Oct. 5, 1996.

10. Melvin Russell Ballard Jr. — See current QUORUM OF THE TWELVE.

11. Dean LeRoy Larsen — See current FIRST QUORUM OF THE SEVENTY.

12. Royden Glade Derrick — Born Sept. 7, 1915 at Salt Lake City, Salt Lake Co., Utah, to Hyrum H. Derrick and Margaret Glade.  Sustained to First Quorum of the Seventy Oct. 1, 1976, at age 61; served in Presidency of the First Quorum of the Seventy, April 5, 1980, to Oct. 6, 1984; named emeritus General Authority Oct. 1, 1989.

13. George Homer Durham — Born Feb. 4, 1911, at Parowan, Iron Co., Utah, to George H. Durham and Mary Ellen Marsden.  Sustained to First Quorum of the Seventy April 2, 1977, at age 66; served in Presidency of the First Quorum of the Seventy, Oct. 1, 1981, until his death on Jan. 10, 1985, at Salt Lake City, Salt Lake Co., Utah, at age 73.

14. Richard Gordon Scott — See current QUORUM OF THE TWELVE.

15. Marion Duff Hanks — See PRESIDENCY OF THE SEVENTY, No. 6.

16. William Grant Bangerter — See PRESIDENCY OF THE SEVENTY, No. 8.

17. Jack H Goaslind Jr. — See current PRESIDENCY OF THE SEVENTY.

18. Robert LeGrand Backman — Born March 22, 1922, in Salt Lake City, Salt Lake Co., Utah, to LeGrand P. and Edith Price Backman. Sustained to the  First Quorum of the Seventy April 1, 1978, at age 56; served in the Presidency of the Seventy, Oct. 6, 1985, to

Aug. 15, 1992; named emeritus General Authority Oct. 3, 1992.

19. Joseph Bitner Wirthlin — See current QUORUM OF THE TWELVE.

20. Hugh Wallace Pinnock — See current FIRST QUORUM OF THE SEVENTY.

21. James Martin Paramore — See current FIRST QUORUM OF THE SEVENTY.

22. John Richard Clarke — See current FIRST QUORUM OF THE SEVENTY.

23. Rex Dee Pinegar — See current FIRST QUORUM OF THE SEVENTY.

24. Carlos Egan Asay — See PRESIDENCY OF THE SEVENTY, No. 9.

25. Charles Amand Andre Didier — See current FIRST QUORUM OF THE SEVENTY.

26. Lloyd Aldin Porter — See current PRESIDENCY OF THE SEVENTY.

27. Joe Junior Christensen — See current PRESIDENCY OF THE SEVENTY.

28. Monte James Brough — See current PRESIDENCY OF THE SEVENTY.

29. Warren Eugene Hansen — See current PRESIDENCY OF THE SEVENTY.

30. Jack H Goaslind Jr. — See current PRESIDENCY OF THE SEVENTY.

31. Harold Gordon Hillam — See current PRESIDENCY OF THE SEVENTY.

32. Earl Carr Tingey — See current PRESIDENCY OF THE SEVENTY.

FIRST QUORUM OF THE SEVENTY

1. Franklin Dewey Richards — See PRESIDENCY OF THE SEVENTY, No. 1.

2. James Esdras Faust — See current FIRST PRESIDENCY.

3. John Thomas Fyans — See PRESIDENCY OF THE SEVENTY, No. 3.

4. Albert Theodore Tuttle — See PRESIDENCY OF THE SEVENTY, No. 4.

5. Neal Ash Maxwell — See current QUORUM OF THE TWELVE.

6. Marion Duff Hanks — See PRESIDENCY OF THE SEVENTY, No. 6.

7. Paul Harold Dunn — See PRESIDENCY OF THE SEVENTY, No. 7.

8. Alma Sonne — Born March 5, 1884, at Logan, Cache Co., Utah, to Niels C. Sonne and Elisa Peterson. Sustained as Assistant to the Quorum of the Twelve Apostles April 6, 1941, at age 57; sustained to First Quorum of the Seventy Oct. 1, 1976; died Nov. 27, 1977, at Logan, Cache Co., Utah, at age 93.

9. Sterling Welling Sill — Born March 31, 1903, at Layton, Davis Co., Utah, to Joseph Albert Sill and Marcetta Welling. Sustained as Assistant to the Quorum of the Twelve Apostles April 6, 1954, at age 51; sustained to First Quorum of the Seventy Oct. 1, 1976; named emeritus General Authority Dec. 31, 1978. Died in Salt Lake City, Salt Lake Co., Utah, on May 25, 1994, at age 91.

10. Henry Dixon Taylor — Born Nov. 22, 1903, in Provo, Utah Co., Utah, to Arthur N. Taylor and Maria Dixon. Sustained as Assistant to the Quorum of the Twelve Apostles April 6, 1958, at age 54; sustained to First Quorum of the Seventy Oct. 1, 1976; named emeritus General Authority Sept. 30, 1978; died Feb. 24, 1987, at Salt Lake City, Salt Lake Co., Utah, at age 83.

11. Alvin Rulon Dyer — See OTHER COUNSELORS IN THE FIRST PRESIDENCY, No. 13.

12. Theodore Moyle Burton — Born March 27, 1907, at Salt Lake City, Salt Lake Co., Utah, to Theodore T. Burton and Florence Moyle. Sustained as Assistant to the Quorum of the Twelve Apostles Oct. 8, 1960, at age 53; sustained to First Quorum of the Seventy Oct. 1, 1976; named emeritus General Authority Oct. 1, 1989; died Dec. 22, 1989, at Salt Lake City, Salt Lake Co., Utah, at age 82.

13. Bernard Park Brockbank — Born May 24, 1909, at Salt Lake City, Salt Lake Co., Utah, to Taylor P. Brockbank and Sarah LeCheminant. Sustained as Assistant to the Quorum of the Twelve Apostles Oct. 6, 1962, at age 53; sustained to First Quorum of the Seventy Oct. 1, 1976; named emeritus General Authority Oct. 4, 1980.

14. James Alfred Cullimore — Born Jan. 17, 1906, at Lindon, Utah Co., Utah, to Albert Lorenzo Cullimore and Luella Keetch. Sustained an Assistant to the Quorum of the Twelve Apostles April 6, 1966, at age 60; sustained to First Quorum of the Seventy Oct. 1, 1976; named emeritus General Authority Sept. 30, 1978; died June 14, 1986, at Salt Lake City, Salt Lake Co., Utah, at age 80.

15. Joseph Anderson — Born Nov. 20, 1889, at Salt Lake City, Salt Lake Co., Utah, to George Anderson and Isabella Watson. Sustained as Assistant to the Quorum of the Twelve Apostles April 6, 1970, at age 80; sustained to First Quorum of the Seventy Oct. 1, 1976; named emeritus General Authority Dec. 31, 1978; died March 13, 1992, at Salt Lake City, Salt Lake Co., Utah, at age 102.

16. William Hunter Bennett — Born Nov. 5, 1910, at Taber, Alberta, Canada, to William Alvin Bennett and Mary

Walker. Sustained as Assistant to the Quorum of the Twelve Apostles April 6, 1970, at age 59; sustained to First Quorum of the Seventy Oct. 1, 1976; named emeritus General Authority Dec. 31, 1978; died July 23, 1980, at Bountiful, Davis Co., Utah, at age 69.

17. John Henry Vandenberg — See PRESIDING BISHOPS, No. 9.

18. Robert Leatham Simpson — Born Aug. 8, 1915, at Salt Lake City, Salt Lake Co., Utah, to Heber C Simpson and Lillian Leatham. Sustained as first counselor to Presiding Bishop John H. Vandenberg Sept. 30, 1961, at age 46; sustained as Assistant to the Quorum of the Twelve Apostles April 6, 1972; sustained to First Quorum of the Seventy Oct. 1, 1976; named emeritus General Authority Oct. 1, 1989.

19. Oscar Leslie Stone — Born May 28, 1903, at Chapin, Idaho, to Frank J. Stone and Mable Crandall. Sustained as Assistant to the Quorum of the Twelve Apostles, Oct. 6, 1972, at age 69; sustained to First Quorum of the Seventy, Oct. 1, 1976; named emeritus General Authority Oct. 4, 1980; died April 26, 1986, at Salt Lake City, Salt Lake Co., Utah, at age 82.

20. William Grant Bangerter — See PRESIDENCY OF THE SEVENTY, No. 8.

21. Robert Dean Hales — See current QUORUM OF THE TWELVE.

22. Adney Yoshio Komatsu — Born Aug. 2, 1923, at Honolulu, Honolulu Co., Hawaii, to Jizaemon Komatsu and Misao Tabata. Sustained as Assistant to the Quorum of the Twelve Apostles, April 4, 1975, at age 51;

was first General Authority of Japanese descent; sustained to the First Quorum of the Seventy Oct. 1, 1976; named emeritus General Authority Oct. 2, 1993.

23. Joseph Bitner Wirthlin — See current QUORUM OF THE TWELVE.

24. Seymour Dilworth Young — Born Sept. 7, 1897, at Salt Lake City, Salt Lake Co., Utah, to Seymour Bicknell Young Jr. and Carlie Louine Clawson. Sustained to the First Council of the Seventy April 6, 1945, at age 47; sustained to the First Quorum of the Seventy Oct. 1, 1976; named emeritus General Authority Sept. 30, 1978; died July 9, 1981, at Salt Lake City, Salt Lake Co., Utah, at age 83.

25. Hartman Rector Jr. — Born Aug. 20, 1924, at Moberly, Randolph Co., Mo., to Hartman Rector and Vivian Fay Garvin. Sustained to the First Council of the Seventy April 6, 1968, at age 43; sustained to the First Quorum of the Seventy Oct. 1, 1976; named emeritus General Authority Oct. 1, 1994.

26. Loren Charles Dunn — See current FIRST QUORUM OF THE SEVENTY.

27. Rex Dee Pinegar — See current FIRST QUORUM OF THE SEVENTY.

28. Gene Raymond Cook — See current FIRST QUORUM OF THE SEVENTY.

29. Charles Amand Andre Didier — See current FIRST QUORUM OF THE SEVENTY.

30. William Rawsel Bradford — See current FIRST QUORUM OF THE SEVENTY.

31. George Patrick Lee — Born March 23, 1943, at Towaoc, Ute Mountain Indian Reservation, Colorado, to Pete Lee and Mae K. Asdzaatchii. Sustained to First Quorum of the Seventy Oct. 3, 1975, at age 32; excommunicated Sept. 1, 1989.

32. Carlos Egan Asay — See PRESIDENCY OF THE SEVENTY, No. 9.

33. Melvin Russell Ballard Jr. — See current QUORUM OF THE TWELVE.

34. John Holbrook Groberg — See current FIRST QUORUM OF THE SEVENTY.

35. Jacob de Jager — Born Jan. 16, 1923, at The Hague, South Holland, Netherlands, to Alexander Philippis de Jager and Maria Jacoba Cornelia Scheele. Sustained to the First Quorum of the Seventy April 3, 1976, at  age 53; named emeritus General Authority Oct. 2, 1993.

36. Vaughn J Featherstone — See current FIRST QUORUM OF THE SEVENTY.

37. Dean LeRoy Larsen — See current FIRST QUORUM OF THE SEVENTY.

38. Royden Glade Derrick — See PRESIDENCY OF THE SEVENTY, No. 12.

39. Robert Earl Wells — See current FIRST QUORUM OF THE SEVENTY.

40. George Homer Durham — See PRESIDENCY OF THE SEVENTY, No. 13.

41. James Martin Paramore — See current FIRST QUORUM OF THE SEVENTY.

42. Richard Gordon Scott — See current QUORUM OF THE TWELVE.

43. Hugh Wallace Pinnock — See current FIRST QUORUM OF THE SEVENTY.

44. Friedrich Enzio Busche — See current FIRST QUORUM OF THE SEVENTY.

45. Yoshihiko Kikuchi — See current FIRST QUORUM OF THE SEVENTY.

46. Ronald Eugene Poelman — See current FIRST QUORUM OF THE SEVENTY.

47. Derek Alfred Cuthbert — Born Oct. 5, 1926, at Notting-ham, Derbyshire Co., England, to Harry Cuthbert and Hilda May Freck. Sustained to the First Quorum of the Seventy April 1, 1978, at age 51; died April 7, 1991, at Salt Lake City, Salt Lake Co., Utah, at age 64.

48. Robert LeGrand Backman — See PRESIDENCY OF THE SEVENTY, No. 18.

49. Rex Cropper Reeve Sr. — Born Nov. 23, 1914, at Hinck-ley, Millard Co., Utah, to Arthur H. Reeve and Mary A. Cropper. Sustained to First Quorum of the Seventy April 1, 1978, at age 63; named emeritus General Authority Oct. 1, 1989.

50. Fred Burton Howard — See current FIRST QUORUM OF THE SEVENTY.

51. Teddy Eugene Brewerton — Born March 30, 1925, at Raymond, Alberta, Canada, to Lee Brewerton and Jane Fisher. Sustained to the First Quorum of the Seventy, Sept. 30, 1978, at age 53; named emeritus General Authority Sept. 30, 1995.

52. Jack H Goaslind Jr. — See current PRESIDENCY OF THE SEVENTY.

53. Angel Abrea — See current FIRST QUORUM OF THE SEVENTY.

54. John Kay Carmack — See current FIRST QUORUM OF THE SEVENTY.

55. Russell Carl Taylor — Born Nov. 25, 1925, at Red Mesa, Conejos Co., Colorado, to Leo Sanford Taylor and Florence Stella Dean. Sustained to First Quorum of the Seventy April 7, 1984, at age 58; sustained to Second

Quorum of the Seventy April 1, 1989; released Oct. 1, 1989.

56. Robert B Harbertson — Born April 19, 1932, at Ogden, Weber Co. Utah, to Brigham Y. Harbertson and Gladys Venice Lewis; sustained to First Quorum of the Seventy April 7, 1984, at age 51; sustained to Second Quorum of the Seventy April 1, 1989; released Oct. 1, 1989.

57. Devere Harris — Born May 30, 1916, at Portage, Box Elder Co. Utah, to Robert Crumbell Harris and Sylvia Green. Sustained to First Quorum of the Seventy April 7, 1984, at age 67; sustained to Second Quorum of the Seventy April 1, 1989; released Oct. 1, 1989.

58. Spencer Hamlin Osborn — Born July 8, 1921, at Salt Lake City, Salt Lake Co., Utah, to William W. Osborn and Alice M. Hamlin. Sustained to First Quorum of the Seventy April 7, 1984, at age 62; sustained to Second Quorum of the Seventy April 1, 1989; released Oct. 1, 1989.

59. Phillip Tadje Sonntag — Born July 13, 1921, at Salt Lake City, Salt Lake Co., Utah, to Richard Peter Sonntag and Lena Emma Tadje. Sustained to First Quorum of the Seventy April 7, 1984, at age 62; sustained to Second Quorum of the Seventy April 1, 1989; released Oct. 1, 1989.

60. John Sonnenberg — Born April 11, 1922, at Schneidemuhle, Germany, to Otto Paul Sonnenberg and Lucille Mielke. Sustained to First Quorum of the Seventy Oct. 6, 1984, at age

62; sustained to Second Quorum of the Seventy April 1, 1989; released Oct. 1, 1989.

61. Ferril Arthur Kay — Born July 15, 1916, at Annabella, Sevier Co., Utah, to Samuel Arthur Kay and Medora Hooper. Sustained to First Quorum of the Seventy Oct. 6, 1984, at age 68; sustained to Second Quorum of the Seventy April 1, 1989; released Oct. 1, 1989.

62. Keith Wilson Wilcox — Born May 15, 1921, at Hyrum, Cache Co., Utah, to Irving C. Wilcox and Nancy Mary Wilson. Sustained to First Quorum of the Seventy Oct. 6, 1984, at age 63; sustained to Second Quorum of the Seventy April 1, 1989; released Oct. 1, 1989.

63. Victor Lee Brown — See PRESIDING BISHOPS, No. 10.

64. Harold Burke Peterson — Born Sept. 19, 1923, in Salt Lake City, Salt Lake Co., Utah, to Harold A. Peterson and Juna Tye. Sustained as first counselor in Presiding Bishopric April 6, 1972, at age 48; sustained to the First Quorum of the Seventy April 6, 1985; named emeritus General Authority Oct. 2, 1993.

65. John Richard Clarke — See current FIRST QUORUM OF THE SEVENTY.

66. Hans Benjamin Ringger — Born Nov. 2, 1925, in Zurich, Switzerland, to Carl Ringger and Maria Reif. Sustained to the First Quorum of the Seventy April 6, 1985, at age 59; was first native of Switzerland to become a General Authority; named emeritus General Authority Sept. 30, 1995.

67. Waldo Pratt Call — Born Feb. 5, 1928, at Colonia Juarez, Chihuahua, Mexico, to Charles Helaman Call and Hannah Skousen. Sustained to First Quorum of the Seventy April 6, 1985, at age 57; sustained to Second Quorum of the Seventy April 1, 1989; released Oct. 6, 1990.

68. Helio da Rocha Camargo — Born Feb. 1, 1926, at Resende, Rio de Janeiro, Brazil, to Jose Medeiros de Camargo and Else Ferreira da Rocha. Sustained to First Quorum of the Seventy April 6, 1985, at age 59; was first General Authority called from Brazil; sustained to Second Quorum of the Seventy on April 1, 1989; released on Oct. 6, 1990.

69. Hans Verlan Andersen — Born Nov. 6, 1914, in Logan, Cache Co., Utah, to Hans Andersen and Mynoa Richardson. Sustained to the First Quorum of the Seventy April 6, 1986, at age 71; sustained to the Second Quorum of the Seventy April 1, 1989; released Oct. 5, 1991; died July 16, 1992, at Orem, Utah Co., Utah, at age 76.

70. George Ivins Cannon — Born March 9, 1920, in Salt Lake City, Salt Lake Co., Utah, to George J. Cannon and Lucy Grant. Sustained to the First Quorum of the Seventy April 6, 1986, at age 66; sustained to the Second Quorum of the Seventy April 1, 1989; released Oct. 5, 1991.

71. Francis Marion Gibbons — Born April 10, 1921, in St. Johns, Apache Co., Ariz., to Andrew S. Gibbons and Adeline Christensen. Sustained to the First

Quorum of the Seventy April 6, 1986, at age 64; sustained to the Second Quorum of the Seventy April 1, 1989; released Oct. 5, 1991.

72. Gardner Hale Russell — Born Aug. 12, 1920, in Salt Lake City, Salt Lake Co., Utah, to Harry J. Russell and Agnes Gardner. Sustained to the First Quorum of the Seventy April 6, 1986, at age 65; sustained to the Second Quorum of the Seventy April 1, 1989; released Oct. 5, 1991.

73. George Richard Hill III — Born Nov. 24, 1921, in Ogden, Weber Co., Utah, to George Richard Hill Jr. and Elizabeth O. McKay. Sustained to the First Quorum of the Seventy April 4, 1987, at age 65; sustained to the Second Quorum of the Seventy April 1, 1989; released Oct. 3, 1992.

74. John Roger Lasater — Born Dec. 8, 1931, in Farmington, Davis Co., Utah, to Robert B. Lasater and Rowena Saunders. Sustained to the First Quorum of the Seventy April 4, 1987, at age 55; sustained to the Second Quorum of the Seventy April 1, 1989; released Oct. 3, 1992.

75. Douglas James Martin — Born April 20, 1927, in Hastings, New Zealand, to George Martin and Jesse Jamieson. Sustained to the First Quorum of the Seventy April 4, 1987, at age 59; first native of New Zealand to be called as a General Authority; sustained to the Second Quorum of the Seventy April 1, 1989; released Oct. 3, 1992.

76. Alexander Baillie Morrison — See current FIRST QUORUM OF THE SEVENTY.

77. Lloyd Aldin Porter — See current

PRESIDENCY OF THE SEVENTY.

78. Glen Larkin Rudd — Born May 18, 1918, in Salt Lake City, Salt Lake Co., Utah, to Charles P. Rudd and Gladys Thomas. Sustained to First Quorum of the Seventy April 4, 1987, at age 68; sustained to the Second Quorum of the Seventy April 1, 1989; released Oct. 3, 1992.

79. Douglas Hill Smith — Born May 11, 1921, in Salt Lake City, Salt Lake Co., Utah, to Virgil H. Smith and Winifred Pearl Hill. Sustained to the First Quorum of the Seventy April 4, 1987, at age 65; sustained to the Second Quorum of the Seventy April 1, 1989; released Oct. 3, 1992.

80. Lynn Andrew Sorensen — Born Sept. 25, 1919, in Salt Lake City, Salt Lake Co., Utah, to Ulric Andrew Sorensen and Ferny Boam. Sustained to the First Quorum of the Seventy April 4, 1987, at age 67; sustained to the Second Quorum of the Seventy April 1, 1989; released Oct. 3, 1992.

81. Robert Edward Sackley — Born Dec. 17, 1922, in Lismore, New South Wales, Australia, to Cecil James Sackley and Mary Duncan. Sustained to the First Quorum of the Seventy April 2, 1988, at age 65; sustained to the Second Quorum of the Seventy April 1, 1989; died Feb. 22, 1993, near Brisbane, Austrailia, at age 70.

82. Larry Lionel Kendrick — See current FIRST QUORUM OF THE SEVENTY.

83. Monte James Brough — See current PRESIDENCY OF THE SEVENTY.

84. Albert Choules Jr. — Born Feb. 15, 1926, in Driggs, Teton Co., Idaho, to Albert Choules and Rula Wilson. Sustained to the First Quorum of the Seventy Oct. 1, 1988, at age 62; sustained to the Second Quorum of the Seventy April 1, 1989; released Oct. 1, 1994.

85. Lloyd Preal George Jr. — Born Sept. 17, 1920, in Kanosh, Millard Co., Utah, to Preal George and Artemesia Palmer. Sustained to the First Quorum of the Seventy Oct. 1, 1988, at age 68; sustained to the Second Quorum of the Seventy April 1, 1989; released Oct. 1, 1994; died May 13, 1996, in Salt Lake City, Utah, at age 75.

86. Gerald Eldon Melchin — Born May 24, 1921, in Kitchener, Ontario, to Arthur and Rosetta Willis Melchin. Sustained to the First Quorum of the Seventy on Oct. 1, 1988, at age 67; sustained to the Second Quorum of the Seventy on April 1, 1989; released Oct. 1, 1994.

87. Joe Junior Christensen — See current PRESIDENCY OF THE SEVENTY.

88. Warren Eugene Hansen Jr. — See current PRESIDENCY OF THE SEVENTY.

89. Jeffrey Roy Holland — See current QUORUM OF THE TWELVE.

90. Marlin Keith Jensen — See current FIRST QUORUM OF THE SEVENTY.

91. Earl Carr Tingey — See current PRESIDENCY OF THE SEVENTY.

92. Harold Gordon Hillam — See current PRESIDENCY OF THE SEVENTY.

93. Carlos Humberto Amado — See current FIRST QUORUM OF THE SEVENTY.

94. Benjamin Berry Banks — See current FIRST QUORUM OF THE SEVENTY.

95. Spencer Joel Condie — See current FIRST QUORUM OF THE SEVENTY.

96. Robert Kent Dellenbach — See current FIRST QUORUM OF THE SEVENTY.

97. Henry Bennion Eyring — See current QUORUM OF THE TWELVE.

98. Glenn Leroy Pace — See current FIRST QUORUM OF THE SEVENTY.

99. Floyd Melvin Hammond — See current FIRST QUORUM OF THE SEVENTY.

100. Kenneth Johnson — See current FIRST QUORUM OF THE SEVENTY.

101. Lynn Alvin Mickelsen — See current FIRST QUORUM OF THE SEVENTY.

102. Neil Linden Andersen — See current FIRST QUORUM OF THE SEVENTY.

103. David Todd Christofferson — See current FIRST QUORUM OF THE SEVENTY.

104. Cree-L Kofford — See current FIRST QUORUM OF THE SEVENTY.

105. Dennis Bramwell Neuenschwander — See current FIRST QUORUM OF THE SEVENTY.

106. Andrew Wayne Peterson — See current FIRST QUORUM OF THE SEVENTY.

107. Cecil Osborn Samuelson Jr. — See current FIRST QUORUM OF THE SEVENTY.

108. John Baird Dickson — See current FIRST QUORUM OF THE SEVENTY.

109. Jay Edwin Jensen — See current FIRST QUORUM OF THE SEVENTY.

110. David Eugene Sorensen — See current FIRST QUORUM OF THE SEVENTY.

111. William Craig Zwick — See current FIRST QUORUM OF THE SEVENTY.

112. Merrill Joseph Bateman — See

current FIRST QUORUM OF THE SEVENTY.

113. Dallas Nielsen Archibald — See current FIRST QUORUM OF THE SEVENTY.

114. Dieter Friedrich Uchtdorf — See current FIRST QUORUM OF THE SEVENTY.

115. Bruce Clark Hafen — See current FIRST QUORUM OF THE SEVENTY.

SECOND QUORUM OF THE SEVENTY

The Second Quorum of the Seventy was created April 1, 1989, in response to the "continued rapid growth of the Church." (*Church News*, April 8, 1989.)

The initial members of the Second Quorum were those General Authorities serving under a five-year call (called from April 1984 to October 1988) in the First Quorum of the Seventy. General Authorities in the Second Quorum are called for five years.

1. Russell Carl Taylor — See FIRST QUORUM OF THE SEVENTY No. 55.

2. Robert B Harbertson — See FIRST QUORUM OF THE SEVENTY No. 56.

3. Devere Harris — See FIRST QUORUM OF THE SEVENTY No. 57.

4. Spencer Hamlin Osborn — See FIRST QUORUM OF THE SEVENTY No. 58.

5. Philip Tadje Sonntag — See FIRST QUORUM OF THE SEVENTY No. 59.

6. John Sonnenberg — See FIRST QUORUM OF THE SEVENTY No. 60.

7. Ferril Arthur Kay — See FIRST QUORUM OF THE SEVENTY No. 61.

8. Keith Wilson Wilcox — See FIRST QUORUM OF THE SEVENTY No. 62.

9. Waldo Pratt Call — See FIRST QUORUM OF THE SEVENTY, No. 67.

10. Helio Da Rocha Camargo — See FIRST QUORUM OF THE SEVENTY, No. 68.

11. Hans Verlan Andersen — See FIRST QUORUM OF THE SEVENTY, No. 69.

12. George Ivins Cannon — See FIRST QUORUM OF THE SEVENTY, No. 70.

13. Francis Marion Gibbons — See FIRST QUORUM OF THE SEVENTY, No. 71.

14. Gardner Hale Russell — See FIRST QUORUM OF THE SEVENTY, No. 72.

15. George Richard Hill III — See FIRST QUORUM OF THE SEVENTY, No. 73.

16. John Roger Lasater — See FIRST QUORUM OF THE SEVENTY, No. 74.

17. Douglas James Martin — See FIRST QUORUM OF THE SEVENTY, No. 75.

18. Alexander Baillie Morrison — See current FIRST QUORUM OF THE SEVENTY.

19. Lloyd Aldin Porter — See current PRESIDENCY OF THE SEVENTY.

20. Glen Larkin Rudd — See FIRST QUORUM OF THE SEVENTY, No. 78.

21. Douglas Hill Smith — See FIRST QUORUM OF THE SEVENTY, No. 79.

22. Lynn Andrew Sorensen — See FIRST QUORUM OF THE SEVENTY, No. 80.

23. Robert Edward Sackley — See FIRST QUORUM OF THE SEVENTY, No. 81.

24. Larry Lionel Kendrick — See current FIRST QUORUM OF THE SEVENTY.

25. Monte James Brough — See current PRESIDENCY OF THE SEVENTY.

26. Albert Choules Jr. — See FIRST QUORUM OF THE SEVENTY, No. 84.

27. Lloyd Preal George — See FIRST QUORUM OF THE SEVENTY, No. 85.

28. Gerald Eldon Melchin — See FIRST QUORUM OF THE SEVENTY, No. 86.

29. Carlos Humberto Amado — See current FIRST QUORUM OF THE SEVENTY.

30. Benjamin Berry Banks — See current FIRST QUORUM OF THE SEVENTY.

31. Spencer Joel Condie — See current FIRST QUORUM OF THE SEVENTY.

32. Floyd Melvin Hammond — See current FIRST QUORUM OF THE SEVENTY.

33. Malcolm Seth Jeppsen — Born Nov. 1, 1924, in Mantua, Box Elder Co., Utah, to Conrad Jeppsen and Laurine Nielsen. Sustained to the Second Quorum of the Seventy April 1, 1989, at age 64; released Oct. 1, 1994.

34. Richard Powell Lindsay — Born March 18, 1926, in Salt Lake City, Salt Lake Co., Utah, to Samuel Bennion Lindsay and Mary Alice Powell. Sustained to the Second Quorum of the Seventy April 1, 1989, at age 63; released Oct. 1, 1994.

35. Merlin Rex Lybbert — Born Jan. 31, 1926, in Cardston, Alberta, to Charles Lester Lybbert and Delvia Reed. Sustained to the Second Quorum of the Seventy April 1, 1989, at age 63; released Oct. 1, 1994.

36. Horacio Antonio Tenorio — Born March 6, 1935, in Mexico City, Distrito Federal, Mexico, to Leopoldo Horacio Tenorio and Blanca Otilia Oriza Arenas. Sustained to the Second Quorum of the Seventy April 1, 1989, at age 54; released Oct. 1, 1994.

37. Eduardo Ayala — Born May 3, 1937, in Coronel, Chile, to Magdonio Ayala and Maria Aburto. Sustained to the

Second Quorum of the Seventy March 31, 1990, at age 52; released Sept. 30, 1995.

38. LeGrand Raine Curtis — Born May 22, 1924, in Salt Lake City, Utah, to Alexander R. Curtis and Genevieve Raine. Sustained to the Second Quorum of the Seventy March 31, 1990, at age 66; released Sept. 30, 1995.

39. Clinton Louis Cutler — Born Dec. 27, 1929, in Salt Lake City, Salt Lake Co., Utah, to Benjamin Lewis Cutler and Hellie Helena Sharp. Sustained to the Second Quorum of the Seventy March 31, 1990, at age 60. Died April 9, 1994, at South Jordan, Salt Lake Co., Utah, at age 64.

40. Robert Kent Dellenbach — See current FIRST QUORUM OF THE SEVENTY.

41. Harold Gordon Hillam — See current PRESIDENCY OF THE SEVENTY.

42. Kenneth Johnson — See current FIRST QUORUM OF THE SEVENTY.

43. Helvecio Martins — Born July 27, 1930, in Rio de Janeiro, Brazil, to Honorio Martins and Benedicta Francisca. Sustained to the Second Quorum of the Seventy March 31, 1990, at age 59; released Sept. 30, 1995.

44. Lynn Alvin Mickelsen — See current FIRST QUORUM OF THE SEVENTY.

45. J Ballard Washburn — Born Jan. 18, 1929, in Blanding, San Juan Co., Utah, to Alvin Lavell Washburn and Wasel Black. Sustained to the Second Quorum of the Seventy March 31, 1990, at age 61; released Sept. 30,

1995.

46. Durrel Arden Woolsey — Born June 12, 1926, at Escalante, Garfield Co., Utah, to Willis A. Woolsey and Ruby Riddle. Sustained to the Second Quorum of the Seventy March 31, 1990, at age 63; released Sept. 30, 1995.

47. Rulon Gerald Craven — Born Nov. 11, 1924, in Murray, Utah, to Gerald and Susie Craven. Called to the Second Quorum of the Seventy Dec. 5, 1990, at age 66, and sustained April 6, 1991; released Oct. 5, 1996.

48. William McKenzie Lawrence — Born Oct. 28, 1926, in Salt Lake City, Utah, to Richard Sterling Lawrence and Thelma McKenzie. Called to the Second Quorum of the Seventy Jan. 1, 1991, at age 64, and sustained April 6, 1991; released Oct. 5, 1996.

49. Julio Enrique Davila — Born May 23, 1932, in Bucaramunga, Colombia, to Julio E. Davila Villamicar and Rita Penalosa de Davila. Sustained to the Second Quorum of the Seventy April 6, 1991, at age 58; released Oct. 5, 1996.

50. Graham Watson Doxey — Born March 30, 1927, in Salt Lake City, Utah, to Graham H. Doxey and Leone Watson. Sustained to the Second Quorum of the Seventy April 6, 1991, at age 64; released Oct. 5, 1996.

51. Cree-L Kofford — See current FIRST QUORUM OF THE SEVENTY.

52. Joseph Carl Muren — Born Feb. 5, 1936, in Richmond, Calif., to Joseph

S. Muren and Alba Maria Cairo. Sustained to the Second Quorum of the Seventy April 6, 1991, at age 55; released Oct. 5, 1961.

53. Dennis Bramwell Neuenschwander — See current FIRST QUORUM OF THE SEVENTY.

54. Jorge Alfonso Rojas — Born Sept. 27, 1940, in Delicias, Chihuahua, Mexico, to Rodolfo Rojas and Hilaria Ornelas. Sustained to the Second Quorum of the Seventy April 6, 1991, at age 50; released Oct. 5, 1996.

55. Han In Sang — Born Dec. 10, 1938, in Seoul, Korea, to Han Chang Soo and Lee Do Ho. Called to the Second Quorum of the Seventy June 1, 1991, at age 52, and sustained Oct. 5, 1991; released Oct. 5, 1996.

56. Stephen Douglas Nadauld — Born May 31, 1942, in Idaho Falls, Idaho, to Sterling Dwaine Nadauld and Lois Madsen. Called to the Second Quorum of the Seventy June 1, 1991, at age 49, and sustained Oct. 5, 1991; released Oct. 5, 1996.

57. Sam Koyei Shimabukuro — Born June 7, 1925, in Waipahu, Hawaii, to Kame and Shimabukuro Ushi Nakasone. Called to the Second Quorum of the Seventy July 13, 1991, at age 66, and sustained Oct. 5, 1991; released Oct. 5, 1996.

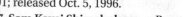

58. Lino Alvarez — See current SECOND QUORUM OF THE SEVENTY.

59. Dallas Nielsen Archibald — See

current FIRST QUORUM OF THE SEVENTY.

60. Merrill Joseph Bateman — See current FIRST QUORUM OF THE SEVENTY.

61. Chellus Max Caldwell — See current SECOND QUORUM OF THE SEVENTY.

62. Gary Jerome Coleman — See current SECOND QUORUM OF THE SEVENTY.

63. John Baird Dickson — See current FIRST QUORUM OF THE SEVENTY.

64. John Emerson Fowler — See current SECOND QUORUM OF THE SEVENTY.

65. Jay Edwin Jensen — See current FIRST QUORUM OF THE SEVENTY.

66. Augusto Alandy Lim — See current SECOND QUORUM OF THE SEVENTY.

67. John Max Madsen — See current SECOND QUORUM OF THE SEVENTY.

68. Victor Dallas Merrell — See current SECOND QUORUM OF THE SEVENTY.

69. David Eugene Sorensen — See current FIRST QUORUM OF THE SEVENTY.

70. Frank David Stanley — See current SECOND QUORUM OF THE SEVENTY.

71. Kwok Yuen Tai — See current SECOND QUORUM OF THE SEVENTY.

72. Lowell Dale Wood — See current SECOND QUORUM OF THE SEVENTY.

73. Claudio Roberto Mendes Costa

— See current SECOND QUORUM OF THE SEVENTY.

74. William Don Ladd — See current SECOND QUORUM OF THE SEVENTY.

75. James Ostermann Mason — See current SECOND QUORUM OF THE SEVENTY.

76. Dieter Friedrich Uchtdorf — See current FIRST QUORUM OF THE SEVENTY.

77. Lance Bradley Wickman — See current SECOND QUORUM OF THE SEVENTY.

78. Bruce Douglas Porter — See current SECOND QUORUM OF THE SEVENTY.

79. Lowell Edward Brown — See current SECOND QUORUM OF THE SEVENTY.

80. Sheldon Fay Child — See current SECOND QUORUM OF THE SEVENTY.

81. Quentin LaMar Cook — See current SECOND QUORUM OF THE SEVENTY.

82. Wm. Rolf Kerr — See current SECOND QUORUM OF THE SEVENTY.

83. Dennis Ericksen Simmons — See current SECOND QUORUM OF THE SEVENTY.

84. Jerald Lynn Taylor — See current SECOND QUORUM OF THE SEVENTY.

85. Francisco Jose Vinas — See current SECOND QUORUM OF THE SEVENTY.

86. Richard Bitner Wirthlin — See current SECOND QUORUM OF THE SEVENTY.

PRESIDING BISHOPS

1. Edward Partridge — Born Aug. 27, 1793, at Pittsfield, Berkshire Co., Massachusetts, to William Partridge and Jemima Bidwell. Ordained high priest June 6, 1831, by Lyman Wight; called by revelation to be the First Bishop of the Church Feb. 4, 1831, at age 37 (D&C 41:9); died May 27, 1840, at Nauvoo, Hancock Co., Illinois, at 46.

2. Newel Kimball Whitney — Born Feb. 5, 1795, at Marlborough, Windham Co., Vermont, to Samuel Whitney and Susanna Kimball. Called by revelation to be the First Bishop of Kirtland (D&C 72:8); sustained as First

Bishop of the Church Oct. 7, 1844, at age 49; sustained as Presiding Bishop of the Church April 6, 1847; died Sept. 23, 1850, at Salt Lake City, Salt Lake Co., Utah, at age 55.

George Miller — Born Nov. 25, 1794, at Orange Co., Virginia, to John Miller and Margaret Pfeiffer. Sustained as Second Bishop of the Church Oct. 7, 1844, at age 49; dropped prior to 1847; disfellowshipped Oct. 20, 1848.

3. Edward Hunter — Born June 22, 1793, at Newton, Delaware Co., Pennsylvania, to Edward Hunter and Hannah Maris. Ordained high priest Nov. 23, 1844, by Brigham Young; sustained as Presiding Bishop of the Church April 7, 1851, at age 57; died Oct. 16, 1883, at Salt Lake City, Salt Lake Co., Utah, at age 90.

4. William Bowker Preston — Born Nov. 24, 1830, at Halifax, Franklin Co., Virginia, to Christopher Preston and Martha Mitchell Clayton. Ordained high priest Nov. 14, 1859, by Orson Hyde; sustained as Presiding Bishop of the Church April 6, 1884, at age 53; released due to ill health Dec. 4, 1907; died Aug. 2, 1908, at Salt Lake City, Salt Lake Co., Utah, at age 77.

5. Charles Wilson Nibley — See SECOND COUNSELORS IN THE FIRST PRESIDENCY, No. 13.

6. Sylvester Quayle Cannon — See QUORUM OF THE TWELVE, No. 60.

7. LeGrand Richards — See QUORUM OF THE TWELVE, No. 69.

8. Joseph Leopold Wirthlin — Born Aug. 14, 1893, at Salt Lake City, Salt Lake Co., Utah, to Joseph Wirthlin and Emma Hillstead. Ordained high priest

Feb. 24, 1926, by Charles W. Nibley; sustained as second counselor to Presiding Bishop LeGrand Richards April 6, 1938, at age 44; sustained as first counselor to Bishop Richards Dec. 12, 1946; sustained as Presiding Bishop of the Church April 6, 1952, at age 58; released Sept. 30, 1961; died Jan. 25, 1963, at Salt Lake City, Salt Lake Co., Utah, at age 69.

9. John Henry Vandenberg — Born Dec. 18, 1904, at Ogden, Weber Co., Utah, to Dirk Vandenberg and Maria Alkema. Sustained as Presiding Bishop of the Church Sept. 30, 1961, at age 56; sustained as Assistant to the Quorum of the Twelve Apostles April 6, 1972; sustained to First Quorum of the Seventy Oct. 1, 1976; named emeritus General Authority Dec. 31, 1978; died June 3, 1992, at Sandy, Salt Lake Co., Utah, at age 87.

10. Victor Lee Brown — Born July 31, 1914, at Cardston, Alberta, Canada, to Gerald Stephen Brown and Maggie Calder Lee. Sustained as second counselor to Presiding Bishop John H. Vandenberg Sept. 30, 1961, at age 47; sustained as Presiding Bishop of the Church April 6, 1972; sustained to First Quorum of the Seventy April 6, 1985; named emeritus General Authority Oct. 1, 1989; died March 26, 1996, at Salt Lake City, Salt Lake Co., Utah at age 81.

11. Robert Dean Hales — See current QUORUM OF THE TWELVE.

12. Merrill Joseph Bateman — See current FIRST QUORUM OF THE SEVENTY.

13. Harold David Burton — See current PRESIDING BISHOPRIC.

FIRST COUNSELORS TO PRESIDING BISHOPS

1. Isaac Morley — Born March 11, 1786, at Montague, Hampshire Co., Massachusetts, to Thomas Morley and Editha Marsh. Ordained high priest June 3, 1831, by Lyman Wight; set apart as first counselor to Presiding Bishop Edward Partridge June 6, 1831, at age 45; released at the death of Bishop Partridge May 27, 1840; died June 24, 1865, at Fairview, Sanpete Co., Utah, at age 79.

2. Leonard Wilford Hardy — Born Dec. 31, 1805, at Bradford, Essex Co., Massachusetts, to Simon Hardy and Rhoda Hardy. Ordained high priest April 6, 1856, by John Taylor; sustained as first counselor to Presiding Bishop Edward Hunter Oct. 6, 1856, at age 50; died July 31, 1884, at Salt Lake City, Salt Lake Co., Utah, at age 78.

3. Robert Taylor Burton — Born Oct. 25, 1821, at Amhertsburg, Ontario, Canada, to Samuel Burton and Hannah Shipley. Ordained high priest Sept. 2, 1875, by Edward Hunter; sustained as second counselor to Presiding Bishop Edward Hunter Oct. 9, 1874, at age 52; sustained as first counselor to Presiding Bishop William B. Preston Oct. 5, 1884; died Nov. 11, 1907, at Salt Lake City, Salt Lake Co., Utah, at age 86.

4. Orrin Porter Miller — Born Sept. 11, 1858, at Mill Creek, Salt Lake Co., Utah, to Reuben G. Miller and Ann Craynor. Ordained high priest Aug. 8, 1886, by Angus M. Cannon; sustained as second counselor to Presiding Bishop William B. Preston Oct. 24, 1901, at age 43; sustained as first counselor to Presiding Bishop Charles

W. Nibley Dec. 4, 1907, at age 49; died July 7, 1918, at Salt Lake City, Salt Lake Co., Utah at age 59.

5. David Asael Smith — Born May 24, 1879, at Salt Lake City, Salt Lake Co., Utah, to Joseph Fielding Smith and Julina Lambson. Ordained high priest Dec. 11, 1907, by Anthon H. Lund; sustained as second counselor to Presiding Bishop Charles W. Nibley Dec. 4, 1907, at age 28; sustained as first counselor to Bishop Nibley July 18, 1918, at age 39; sustained as first counselor to Presiding Bishop Sylvester Q. Cannon June 4, 1925; released April 6, 1938; died April 6, 1952, at Salt Lake City, Salt Lake Co., Utah, at age 72.

6. Marvin Owen Ashton — Born April 8, 1883, at Salt Lake City, Salt Lake Co., Utah, to Edward T. Ashton and Effie W. Morris. Ordained high priest June 22, 1917, by Heber J. Grant; sustained as first counselor to Presiding Bishop LeGrand Richards April 6, 1938, at age 54; died Oct. 7, 1946, at Salt Lake City, Salt Lake Co., Utah, at age 63.

7. Joseph Leopold Wirthlin — See PRESIDING BISHOPS, No., 8.

8. Henry Thorpe Beal Isaacson — See OTHER COUNSELORS IN THE FIRST PRESIDENCY, No. 12.

9. Robert Leatham Simpson — See FIRST QUORUM OF THE SEVENTY, No. 18.

10. Harold Burke Peterson — See FIRST QUORUM OF THE SEVENTY, No. 64.

11. Henry Bennion Eyring — See current QUORUM OF THE TWELVE.

12. Harold David Burton — See current PRESIDING BISHOPRIC.

13. Richard Crockett Edgley — See current PRESIDING BISHOPRIC.

SECOND COUNSELORS TO PRESIDING BISHOPS

1. John Corrill — Born Sept. 17, 1794, at Worcester Co., Massachusetts. Ordained high priest June 6, 1831, by Edward Partridge; set apart as second counselor to Presiding Bishop Edward Partridge June 6, 1831, at age 36; released Aug. 1, 1837; excommunicated March 17, 1839.

2. Titus Billings — Born March 25, 1793, at Greenfield, Franklin Co., Massachusetts, to Ebenezer Billings and Esther Joyce. Ordained high priest Aug. 1, 1837, by Edward Partridge; set apart as second counselor to Presiding Bishop Edward Partridge Aug. 1, 1837, at age 44; released at the death of Bishop Partridge May 27, 1840; died Feb. 6, 1866, at Provo, Utah Co., Utah, at age 72.

3. Jesse Carter Little — Born Sept. 26, 1815, at Belmont, Waldo Co., Maine, to Thomas Little and Relief White. Ordained high priest April 17, 1845, by Parley P. Pratt; sustained as second counselor to Presiding Bishop Edward Hunter Oct. 6, 1856, at age 41; resigned summer of 1874; died Dec. 26, 1893, at Salt Lake City, Salt Lake Co., Utah, at age 78.

4. Robert Taylor Burton — See FIRST COUNSELORS IN THE PRESIDING BISHOPRIC, No. 3.

5. John Quayle Cannon — Born April 19, 1857, at San Francisco, San Francisco Co., California, to George Quayle Cannon and Elizabeth Hoagland. Ordained high priest October 1884 by John Taylor; sustained as second counselor to Presiding Bishop William B. Preston Oct. 5, 1884, at age 27; excommunicated Sept. 5, 1886; rebaptized May 6, 1888; died Jan. 14, 1931, at Salt Lake City, Salt Lake Co., Utah, at 73.

6. John Rex Winder — See FIRST COUNSELORS IN THE FIRST PRESIDENCY, No. 7.

7. Orrin Porter Miller — See FIRST COUNSELORS IN THE PRESIDING BISHOPRIC, No. 4.

8. David Asael Smith — See FIRST COUNSELORS IN THE PRESIDING BISHOPRIC, No. 5.

9. John Wells — Born Sept. 16, 1864, at Carlton, Nottinghamshire, England, to Thomas Potter Wells and Sarah Cook. Ordained high priest Feb. 12, 1911, by Richard W. Young; sustained as second counselor to Presiding Bishop Charles W. Nibley July 18, 1918, at age 53; sustained as second counselor to Presiding Bishop Sylvester Q. Cannon June 4, 1925; released April 6, 1938; died April 18, 1941, at Salt Lake City, Salt Lake Co., Utah, at age 76.

10. Joseph Leopold Wirthlin — See PRESIDING BISHOPS, No. 8.

11. Henry Thorpe Beal Isaacson — See OTHER COUNSELORS IN THE FIRST PRESIDENCY, No. 12.

12. Carl William Buehner — Born Dec. 27, 1898, at Stuttgart, Wuerttemberg, Germany, to Carl F. Buehner and Anna B. Geigle. Ordained high priest Dec. 9, 1935, by Richard R. Lyman; sustained as second counselor to Presiding Bishop Joseph L. Wirthlin April 6, 1952, at age 53; released Sept. 30, 1961; died Nov. 18, 1974, at Salt Lake City, Salt Lake Co., Utah, at age 75.

13. Victor Lee Brown — See PRESIDING BISHOPS, No. 10.

14. Vaughn J Featherstone — See current FIRST QUORUM OF THE SEVENTY.

15. **John Richard Clarke** — See current FIRST QUORUM OF THE SEVENTY.

16. **Glenn Leroy Pace** — See current FIRST QUORUM OF THE SEVENTY.

17. **Richard Crockett Edgley** — See current PRESIDING BISHOPRIC.

18. **Keith Brigham McMullin** — See current PRESIDING BISHOPRIC.

LENGTH OF SERVICE IN THE
FIRST PRESIDENCY AND COUNCIL OF THE TWELVE
(As of October 1996)

Name	Date of service, Age at time	Length of service	Total Years as General Authority†
David O. McKay	Apr 1906 (32) - Jan 1970 (96)	63 yrs 9 mos	
Heber J. Grant	Oct 1882 (25) - May 1945 (88)	62 yrs 7 mos	
Joseph Fielding Smith	Apr 1910 (33) - Jul 1972 (95)	62 yrs 3 mos	
Wilford Woodruff	Apr 1839 (32) - Sep 1898 (91)	59 yrs 5 mos	
*****Lorenzo Snow**	Feb 1849 (34) - Oct 1901 (87)	52 yrs 8 mos	
Joseph Fielding Smith	Jul 1866 (27) - Nov 1918 (80)	52 yrs 4 mos	
Franklin D. Richards	Feb 1849 (27) - Dec 1899 (78)	50 yrs 10 mos	
Ezra Taft Benson	Oct 1943 (44) - May 1994 (94)	50 yrs 7 mos	
John Taylor	Dec 1838 (30) - Jul 1887 (78)	48 yrs 7 mos	
George Albert Smith	Oct 1903 (33) - Apr 1951 (81)	47 yrs 6 mos	
Orson Pratt	Apr 1835 (23) - Aug 1842 Jan 1843 -Oct 1881 (70)	46 yrs 1 mo	
Rudger Clawson	Oct 1898 (41) - Jun 1943 (86)	44 yrs 8 mos	
George F. Richards	Apr 1906 (45) - Aug 1950 (89)	44 yrs 4 mos	
Orson Hyde	Feb 1835 (30) - May 1837 Jun 1837 - Nov 1878 (73)	43 yrs 9 mos	
Brigham Young	Feb 1835 (33) - Aug 1877 (76)	42 yrs 6 mos	
Stephen L Richards	Jan 1917 (37) - May 1959 (79)	42 yrs 4 mos	
Spencer W. Kimball	Oct 1943 (48) - Nov 1985 (90)	42 yrs 1 mo	
Reed Smoot	Apr 1900 (38) - Feb 1941 (79)	40 yrs 10 mos	
*George Q. Cannon	Aug 1860 (33) - Apr 1901 (74)	40 yrs 8 mos	
Mark E. Petersen	Apr 1944 (43) - Jan 1984 (83)	39 yrs 9 mos	
Erastus Snow	Feb 1849 (30) - May 1888 (69)	39 yrs 3 mos	
Marion G. Romney	Oct 1951 (54) - May 1988 (90)	36 yrs 7 mos	47 yrs 1 mo
George A. Smith	Apr 1839 (21) - Sep 1875 (58)	36 yrs 5 mos	
Francis M. Lyman	Oct 1880 (40) - Nov 1916 (76)	36 yrs 1 mo	
Howard W. Hunter	Oct 1959 (51) - Mar 1995 (87)	35 yrs 5 mo	
• **Gordon B. Hinckley**	Oct 1961 (51) - present	35 yrs	38 yrs 6 mos
Charles C. Rich	Feb 1849 (39) - Nov 1883 (74)	34 yrs 9 mos	
*Brigham Young Jr.	Oct 1868 (31) - Apr 1903 (66)	34 yrs 6 mos	
# Daniel H. Wells	Jan 1857 (42) - Mar 1891 (76)	34 yrs 2 mos	
Heber C. Kimball	Feb 1835 (33) - Jun 1868 (67)	33 yrs 4 mos	
• **Thomas S. Monson**	Oct 1963 (36) - present	33 yrs	
Harold B. Lee	Apr 1941 (42) - Dec 1973 (74)	32 yrs 8 mos	
John A. Widtsoe	Mar 1921 (49) - Nov 1952 (80)	31 yrs 8 mos	
Anthon H. Lund	Oct 1889 (45) - Mar 1921 (76)	31 yrs 5 mos	
John Henry Smith	Oct 1880 (32) - Oct 1911 (63)	31 yrs	
LeGrand Richards	Apr 1952 (66) - Jan 1983 (96)	30 yrs 9 mos	44 yrs 9 mos
J. Reuben Clark Jr.	Apr 1933 (61) - Oct 1961 (90)	28 yrs 6 mos	
Delbert L. Stapley	Oct 1950 (53) - Aug 1978 (81)	27 yrs 10 mos	
Anthony W. Ivins	Oct 1907 (55) - Sep 1934 (82)	26 yrs 11 mos	
• Boyd K. Packer	Apr 1970 (45) - present	26 yrs 6 mos	35 yrs
Richard R. Lyman	Apr 1918 (47) - Nov 1943 (72)	25 yrs 7 mos	
Amasa M. Lyman	Aug 1842 (29) - Oct 1867 (54)	25 yrs 2 mos	
Orson F. Whitney	Apr 1906 (50) - May 1931 (75)	25 yrs 1 mo	
George Teasdale	Oct 1882 (50) - Jun 1907 (75)	24 yrs 8 mos	
Ezra T. Benson	Jul 1846 (35) - Sep 1869 (58)	23 yrs 2 mos	
• **L. Tom Perry**	Apr 1974 (51) - present	22 yrs 6 mos	24 yrs
Parley P. Pratt	Feb 1835 (27) - May 1857 (50)	22 yrs 3 mos	
Marvin J. Ashton	Dec 1971 (56) - Feb 1994 (78)	22 yrs 2 mos	24 yrs 4 mos
James E. Talmage	Dec 1911 (49) - Jul 1933 (70)	21 yrs 7 mos	
John W. Taylor	Apr 1884 (25) - Oct 1905 (47)	21 yrs 6 mos	

Name	Service Dates	Duration	Extended
Charles W. Penrose	Jul 1904 (72) - May 1925 (93)	20 yrs 10 mos	
• David B. Haight	Jan 1976 (69) - present	20 yrs 9 mos	26 yrs 6 mos
Melvin J. Ballard	Jan 1919 (45) - Jul 1939 (66)	20 yrs 6 mos	
Joseph F. Merrill	Oct 1931 (63) - Feb 1952 (83)	20 yrs 4 mos	
N. Eldon Tanner	Oct 1962 (64) - Nov 1982 (84)	20 yrs 1 mo	22 yrs 1 mo
*# John Willard Young	Apr 1873 (28) - Oct 1891 (47)	18 yrs 6 mos	
Richard L. Evans	Oct 1953 (47) - Nov 1971 (65)	18 yrs 1 mo	33 yrs 1 mo
• James E. Faust	Oct 1978 (58) - present	18 yrs	24 yrs
Hugh B. Brown	Apr 1958 (74) - Dec 1975 (92)	17 yrs 8 mos	22 yrs 2 mos
Moses Thatcher	Apr 1879 (37) - Apr 1896 (54)	17 yrs	
Henry D. Moyle	Apr 1947 (57) - Sep 1963 (74)	16 yrs 5 mos	
Marriner W. Merrill	Oct 1889 (57) - Feb 1906 (73)	16 yrs 4 mos	
Hyrum Mack Smith	Oct 1901 (29) - Jan 1918 (45)	16 yrs 3 mos	
Albert E. Bowen	Apr 1937 (61) - Jul 1953 (77)	16 yrs 3 mos	
• Neal A. Maxwell	Jul 1981 (55) - present	15 yrs 3 mos	22 yrs 6 mos
Joseph Smith	Apr 1830 (24) - Jun 1844 (38)	14 yrs 2 mos	
Willard Richards	Apr 1840 (35) - Mar 1854 (49)	13 yrs 11 mos	
Charles A. Callis	Oct 1933 (68) - Jan 1947 (81)	13 yrs 3 mos	
Bruce R. McConkie	Oct 1972 (57) - Apr 1985 (69)	12 yrs 6 mos	38 yrs 6 mos
• Russell M. Nelson	Apr 1984 (59) - present	12 yrs 6 mos	
• Dallin H. Oaks	Apr 1984 (51) - present	12 yrs 6 mos	
Sidney Rigdon	Mar 1833 (40) - Jun 1844 (51)	11 yrs 3 mos	
• M. Russell Ballard	Oct 1985 (57) - present	11 yrs	20 yrs 6 mos
William Smith	Feb 1835 (23) - Oct 1845 (34)	10 yrs 8 mos	
• Joseph B. Wirthlin	Oct 1986 (69) - present	10 yrs	21 yrs 6 mos
John R. Winder	Oct 1901 (79) - Mar 1910 (88)	8 yrs 5 mos	22 yrs 11 mos
Matthew Cowley	Oct 1945 (48) - Dec 1953 (56)	8 yrs 2 mos	
• Richard G. Scott	Oct 1988 (59) - present	8 years	19 yrs 6 mos
George Q. Morris	Apr 1954 (80) - Apr 1962 (88)	8 yrs	10 yrs 6 mos
Matthias F. Cowley	Oct 1897 (39) - Oct 1905 (47)	8 yrs	
*Oliver Cowdery	Apr 1830 (23) - Apr 1838 (31)	8 yrs	
Lyman Wight	Apr 1841 (44) - Dec 1848 (52)	7 yrs 8 mos	
John E. Page	Dec 1838 (39) - Feb 1846 (47)	7 yrs 2 mos	
Abraham H. Cannon	Oct 1889 (30) - Jul 1896 (37)	6 yrs 9 mos	13 yrs 9 mos
*Hyrum Smith	Sep 1837 (37) - Jun 1844 (44)	6 yrs 9 mos	
* John Smith	Sep 1837 (56) - Jun 1844 (62)	6 yrs 9 mos	
Abraham O. Woodruff	Oct 1897 (24) - Jun 1904 (31)	6 yrs 8 mos	
Charles W. Nibley	May 1925 (76) - Dec 1931 (82)	6 yrs 7 mos	24 yrs
Sylvester Q. Cannon	Apr 1938 (60) - May 1943 (65)	5 yrs 1 mo	18 yrs
Adam S. Bennion	Apr 1953 (66) - Feb 1958 (71)	4 yrs 10 mos	
Frederick G. Williams	Mar 1833 (45) - Nov 1837 (50)	4 yrs 8 mos	
*Albert Carrington	Apr 1873 (60) - Aug 1877 (64)	4 yrs 4 mos	
Thorpe B. Isaacson	Oct 1965 (67) - Jan 1970 (71)	4 yrs 3 mos	23 yrs 1 mo
Thomas B. Marsh	Apr 1835 (35) - Mar 1839 (39)	3 yrs 11 mos	
David W. Patten	Feb 1835 (35) - Oct 1838 (38)	3 yrs 8 mos	
William E. M'Lellin	Feb 1835 (29) - May 1838 (32)	3 yrs 3 mos	
William Law	Jan 1841 (31) - Apr 1844 (34)	3 yrs 3 mos	
Luke Johnson	Feb 1835 (27) - Apr 1838 (30)	3 yrs 2 mos	
Lyman E. Johnson	Feb 1835 (23) - Apr 1838 (26)	3 yrs 2 mos	
* Joseph Smith Sr.	Sep 1837 (66) - Sep 1840 (69)	3 yrs	6 yrs 9 mos
Jedediah M. Grant	Apr 1854 (38) - Dec 1856 (40)	2 yrs 8 mos	11 yrs
John F. Boynton	Feb 1835 (23) - Sep 1837 (25)	2 yrs 7 mos	
• Robert D. Hales	Apr 1994 (61) - present	2 yrs 6 mos	21 yrs 6 mos
• Jeffrey R. Holland	Jun 1994 (53) - present	2 yrs 4 mos	7 yrs 6 mos
Alonzo A. Hinckley	Oct 1934 (64) - Dec 1936 (66)	2 yrs 2 mos	
Alvin R. Dyer	Apr 1968 (65) - Jan 1970 (67)	1 yr 9 mos	18 yrs 5 mos
• Henry B. Eyring	Apr 1995 (61) - present	1 yr 6 mos	11 yrs 6 mos

Bold Face denotes Church president
• Currently serving
† Includes service in the First Council of the Seventy, Assistants to the Twelve, First Quorum of the Seventy, Presiding Bishopric or as Church Patriarch
* Served as assistant counselor in the First Presidency
# Served in the First Presidency under Brigham Young; after his death sustained as counselor to Twelve Apostles

GENERAL OFFICERS OF THE CHURCH
SUNDAY SCHOOL

Though a few small Sunday School groups met regularly in Latter-day Saint communities before the Saints' westward exodus, Sunday School did not begin as a Church institution until after their arrival in the Salt Lake Valley in 1847.

Richard Ballantyne was a convert to the Church who, as a Presbyterian in his native Scotland, had organized a Sunday School. In Salt Lake City, disturbed by observing the children at play on the Sabbath day, he saw the need for a Sunday School.

In May 1849, he began plans to start a Sunday School. He built a structure on the northeast corner of 100 West and 300 South streets in Salt Lake City to serve both as his home and a place to hold the Sunday School. A monument on that corner today (now 200 West) commemorates the location of the first Sunday School.

On Sunday, Dec. 9, 1849, the first Sunday School was held, involving 50 children. The following year, a meetinghouse was built for the Salt Lake 14th Ward, in which Richard Ballantyne was second counselor in the bishopric. The expanded Sunday School was moved into the new building and divided into a number of smaller classes, with additional teachers and two assistant superintendents.

Other wards in the valley and elsewhere followed the example of Richard Ballantyne and started Sunday Schools. They were somewhat autonomous, devising their own curricula and administration, but functioned under the direction of the ward bishop.

With the coming of Johnston's Army to Utah, the Sunday School movement was suspended as many of the Saints moved south, but with the lessening of tensions in 1860, the Sunday School was resumed. By 1870, more than 200 Sunday Schools had been formed.

On Nov. 11, 1867, the Deseret Sunday School Union was organized by interested Church leaders, including President Brigham Young. Elder George Q. Cannon of the Quorum of the Twelve became the first general superintendent of the Sunday School. Its functions were to determine lesson topics and source materials and to address topics of punctuality, grading, prizes and rewards, recording and increasing attendance, music, elementary catechism, and libraries. The general Sunday School fostered uniformity in the theretofore disparate and independent Sunday Schools in the Church.

In 1866, prior to formation of the general Sunday School, a publication called the *Juvenile Instructor* was founded privately by Elder George Q. Cannon of the Twelve, who served as editor. It featured material on the scriptures, musical compositions and aids to gospel instruction. It became the official voice of the Deseret Sunday School Union, which purchased it from the Cannon family in January 1901. In 1929 the name was changed to *Instructor*. It was discontinued in 1970 when the Church magazine structure was changed.

In early 1877, the sacrament was instituted as part of Sunday School. The practice continued until 1980, when Sunday meetings were consolidated in a three-hour block, with sacrament administered only during sacrament meeting.

The Deseret Sunday School Union continued to grow through the 1900s. Stake Sunday School superintendencies were designated to supervise ward Sunday Schools. General meetings of the Sunday School were held twice a year in connection with general conference. Five new classes for older children and youth were added in the early 1900s, followed shortly by the introduction of adult classes.

A Sunday School general board was introduced in the 1870s. In the 1900s, it was expanded and members traveled extensively to provide advice and support for local Sunday School programs.

An effort in 1971 to correlate all Church functions under priesthood leadership affected the Sunday School. Dynamic changes followed, including centralized curriculum planning and writing, and an eight-year cycle of scripture instruction, later shortened to four years, for adult classes, focusing in turn on the Old Testament and Pearl of Great Price, the New Testament, the Book of Mormon, and the Doctrine and Covenants and Church History. The size of the general board was reduced, and stake boards were discontinued.

With the introduction of the consolidated meeting schedule in 1980, children's Sunday School classes were discontinued, that function being filled by the Primary. In recent years, Sunday School curriculum for adults has included a gospel doctrine class and elective courses on family history, teacher development and family relations.

A modified Church curriculum announced for implementation Jan. 1, 1995, provides that classes for youth ages 14-18 study the scriptures using the *Gospel Principles* or *Gospel Doctrine* courses of study. Under the modified plan, youth ages 12-13 on alternate years study presidents of the Church and preparing for exaltation.

Sources: *Encyclopedia of Mormonism; Jubilee History of Latter-day Saints Sunday Schools* published by the Deseret Sunday School Union; First Presidency letter to General Authorities and priesthood leaders, April 21, 1994.

SUNDAY SCHOOL OFFICERS

President

Harold G. Hillam, 30 Sep 1995 — present. See current PRESIDENCY OF THE SEVENTY.

First Counselor

F. Burton Howard, 30 Sep 1995 — present. See current FIRST QUORUM OF THE SEVENTY.

Second Counselor

Glenn L. Pace, 30 Sep 1995 — present. See current FIRST QUORUM OF THE SEVENTY.

HISTORICAL LISTING OF GENERAL SUPERINTENDENCIES AND PRESIDENCIES OF THE SUNDAY SCHOOL

(Presidents, superintendents pictured)

Superintendent, George Q. Cannon — Nov 1867-Apr 1901. See FIRST COUNSELORS IN THE FIRST PRESIDENCY, No. 5.

First Assistants, George Goddard — Jun 1872-Jan 1899, Karl G. Maeser — Jan 1899-Feb 1901.

Second Assistants, John Morgan — Jun 1883-Jul 1894, Karl G. Maeser — Jul 1894-Jan 1899, George Reynolds — Jan 1899-May 1901.

Superintendent, Lorenzo Snow (as president of the Church) — May 1901-Oct 1901. See PRESIDENTS OF THE CHURCH, No. 5.

First Assistant, George Reynolds — May 1901-Oct 1901.

Second Assistant, Jay M. Tanner — May 1901-Oct 1901.

Superintendent, Joseph F. Smith (As president of the Church) — Nov 1901-Nov 1918. See PRESIDENTS OF THE CHURCH, No. 6.

First Assistants, George Reynolds —

Nov 1901-May 1909, David O. McKay — May 1909-Nov 1918.

Second Assistants, Jay M. Tanner — Nov 1901-April 1906, David O. McKay — Jan 1907-May 1909, Stephen L Richards — May 1909-Nov 1918.

Superintendent, David O. McKay — Dec 1918-Oct 1934. See PRESIDENTS OF THE CHURCH, No. 9.

First Assistant, Stephen L Richards — Dec 1918-Oct 1934.

Second Assistant, George D. Pyper — Dec 1918-Oct 1934.

Superintendent, George D. Pyper — Oct 1934-Jan 1943.

First Assistant, Milton Bennion — Oct 1934-May 1943.

Second Assistant, George R. Hill — Oct 1934-May 1943.

Superintendent, Milton Bennion — May 1943-Sep 1949.

First Assistant, George R. Hill — May 1943-Sep 1949.

Second Assistant, Albert Hamer Reiser — May 1943-Sep 1949.

Superintendent, George R. Hill — Sep 1949-Nov 1966.

First Assistants, Albert Hamer Reiser — Sep 1949-Oct 1952, David Lawrence McKay — Oct 1952-Nov 1966.

Second Assistants, David Lawrence McKay — Sep 1949-Oct 1952, Lynn S. Richards — Oct 1952-Nov 1966.

Superintendent, David Lawrence McKay — Nov 1966-Jun 1971.

First Assistant, Lynn S. Richards — Nov 1966-Jun 1971.

Second Assistant, Royden G. Derrick — Nov. 1966-Jun 1971.

President, Russell M. Nelson — Jun 1971-Oct 1979. See current QUORUM OF THE TWELVE.

First Counselors, Joseph B. Wirthlin — Jun 1971-Apr 1975, B. Lloyd Poelman — Apr 1975-Mar 1978, Joe J. Christensen — Mar 1978-Aug 1979, William D. Oswald — Aug 1979-Oct 1979.

Second Counselors, Richard L. Warner — Jun 1971-Apr 1975, Joe J. Christensen — Apr 1975-Mar 1978, William D. Oswald — May 1978-Aug 1979, J. Hugh Baird — Aug 1979-Oct 1979.

President, Hugh W. Pinnock — Oct 1979-Aug 1986. See current FIRST QUORUM OF THE SEVENTY.

First Counselors, Ronald E. Poelman — Oct 1979-Jul 1981, Robert D. Hales — Jul 1981-Jul 1985, Adney Y. Komatsu — Jul 1985-Aug 1986.

Second Counselors, Jack H Goaslind Jr. — Oct 1979-Jul 1981, James M. Paramore — Jul 1981-Jan 1983, Loren C. Dunn — Jan 1983-Jul 1985, Ronald E. Poelman — Jul 1985-Aug 1986.

President, Robert L. Simpson — Aug 1986-30 Sep 1989. See FIRST QUORUM OF THE SEVENTY, No. 18.

First Counselors, Adney Y. Komatsu — Aug 1986-Aug. 1987, Devere Harris — Aug 1987-30 Sep 1989.

Second Counselors, A. Theodore Tuttle — Aug 1986-Nov 1986, Devere Harris — Jan 1987-Aug 1987, Phillip T. Sonntag — Aug 1987-Aug 1988, Derek A. Cuthbert — Aug 1988-30 Sep 1989.

President, Hugh W. Pinnock — 30 Sep 1989-15 Aug 1992. See current FIRST QUORUM OF THE SEVENTY.

First Counselors, Derek A. Cuthbert — 15 Aug 1988-1 Jan 1991, H. Verlan Andersen — 1 Jan 1991-5 Oct 1991, Hartman Rector Jr. — 5 Oct 1991-15 Aug 1992.

Second Counselors, Ted E. Brewerton — 30 Sep 1989-1 Oct 1990, H. Verlan Andersen — 6 Oct 1990-1 Jan 1991, Rulon G. Craven — 1 Jan 1991-5

Oct 1991, Clinton L. Cutler — 5 Oct 1991-15 Aug 1992.

President, Merlin R. Lybbert — 15 Aug 1992-15 Aug 1994. See SECOND QUORUM OF THE SEVENTY, No. 35.

First Counselor, Clinton L. Cutler — 15 Aug 1992-April 9, 1994.

Second Counselor, Ronald E. Poel-man — 15 Aug 1992-15 Aug 1994.

President, Charles Didier — 15 Aug 1994-30 Sep 1995. See current FIRST QUORUM OF THE SEVENTY.

First Counselor, J Ballard Washburn — 15 Aug 1994-30 Sep 1995.

Second Counselor, F. Burton Howard — 15 Aug 1994-30 Sep 1995.

YOUNG MEN

Today's Young Men organization has been significantly streamlined and simplified since its inception in 1875 as the Young Men's Mutual Improvement Association and has as its primary purpose furthering the work of the Aaronic Priesthood.

The YMMIA was established by President Brigham Young, who called Junius F. Wells to organize Mutual Improvement Associations in wards throughout the Church, under the direction of ward superintendencies. It was intended that the YMMIA help young men develop spiritually and intellectually and provide supervised recreational opportunities.

On June 10, 1875, Brother Wells called a meeting in the 13th Ward chapel in Salt Lake City and the first ward YMMIA was organized.

In the fall of 1875, John Henry Smith, Milton H. Hardy and B. Morris Young were called by the First Presidency to assist Brother Wells in visiting the settlements of Saints and promoting the YMMIA. By April 1876, there were 57 ward YMMIAs in existence with a membership of about 1,200 youth. That same year, a YMMIA central committee was formed with Brother Wells as president. The committee later became the General Board of the YMMIA, which has continued through the years and is now known as the Young Men General Board.

From 1876 to 1905, young men were called to serve YMMIA missions to increase membership and assist local superintendencies. Initially, all of the young men met together regardless of age. Later, the YMMIA adopted four grades or classes: Scouts (ages 12-14), Vanguards (15-16), M Men (17-23) and Adults. As the programs developed and as needs of the youth changed, further refinements were made to the class structure. Today, Young Men classes correspond with the deacons, teachers and priests quorums in the Aaronic Priesthood.

In October 1879, the monthly *Contributor* was launched with Brother Wells as editor. It served as the publication of the YMMIA until October 1899, at which time the publication of the *Improvement Era* began by the General Board.

The YMMIA met separately from the Young Women's Mutual Improvement Association (YWMIA) until around 1900 when the two joined to form the Mutual Improvement Association.

In 1913, the Church formed a formal partnership with Boy Scouts of America and was granted a national charter on May 21 of that year. Scouting exists today as a major component of the Young Men organization to help accomplish the purposes of the Aaronic Priesthood and to complement Sunday quorum instruction. Besides its partnership with BSA, the Church has established affiliations with other national Scouting organizations throughout the world whose programs, values, goals and ideals are compatible with those of the Church.

In addition to Scouting, YMMIA activities in the early and mid-1900s included sports, dance, drama and music. Athletics became a major part of the program, and stake tournament winners progressed to the All-Church tournaments in Salt Lake City, which were discontinued in the early 1970s.

Young Men, and both it and the Young Women came under the direction of the Priesthood Department.

YOUNG MEN

President, Neil D. Schaerrer — 7 Apr 1977-Oct 1979.

First Counselor, Graham W. Doxey — 7 Apr 1977-Oct 1979.

Second Counselor, Quinn G. McKay — 7 Apr 1977-Oct 1979

President, Robert L. Backman — Oct 1979-Nov 1985. See PRESIDENCY OF THE SEVENTY, No. 18.

First Counselor, Vaughn J Featherstone — Oct 1979-Nov 1985.

Second Counselor, Rex D. Pinegar — Oct 1979-Nov 1985.

President, Vaughn J Featherstone — Nov 1985-6 Oct 1990. See current FIRST QUORUM OF THE SEVENTY.

First Counselors, Rex D. Pinegar — Nov 1985-30 Sep 1989, Jeffrey R. Holland — 30 Sep 1989-6 Oct 1990.

Second Counselors, Robert L. Simpson — Nov 1985-15 Aug 1986, Hartman Rector Jr. — 15 Aug 1986-Oct 1988, Robert B Harbertson, Oct 1988-30 Sep 1989, Monte J. Brough, 30 Sep 1989-6 Oct 1990.

PRIMARY

Noting the rough and careless behavior of the boys in her Farmington, Utah, neighborhood, Aurelia Spencer Rogers asked, "What will our girls do for good husbands, if this state of things continues?" Then she continued, "Could there not be an organization for little boys, and have them trained to make better men?"

The answer was, "Yes." With the approval of President John Taylor, the encouragement of Relief Society general president Eliza R. Snow, and after receiving a calling from her bishop, Sister Rogers began planning for the first meeting of the Primary Association, and it was an overwhelming success. On Sunday, August 25, 1878, she stood at the entrance to the meetinghouse and greeted 224 boys and girls to Primary. Girls were invited because Sister Rogers thought they could help with the singing that she thought was necessary. During the first meeting, Sister Rogers instructed the children to be obedient and to be kind to one another.

Sister Rogers was not only the first Farmington Ward Primary president, but also the first Davis Stake Primary president.

Sister Snow was actively involved in the organization of the Primary Association. About the same time Sister Rogers was holding the first Primary meeting, Sister Snow was in Ogden laying the groundwork for the organization there. Upon her return to Salt Lake City, she reported to Relief Society women there about her activities with the Primary in the northern part of the state.

Over the next decade, the Primary Association was organized in almost every LDS settlement. During one trip through Southern Utah, Sister Snow and her second counselor in the Relief Society presidency, Zina Young, organized 35 Primaries.

From its beginning, Primary included songs, poetry and activities. The boys wore uniforms to the meetings. All the children met together at Primary during the first 10 years. After that, they were divided into age groups.

Sister Louie B. Felt was called as the first general president of the Primary in 1880, but the Relief Society continued to take the responsibility for organizing Primaries. Sister Felt and other general officers began taking more responsibility for Primary development after 1890.

Serving as Primary general president for 45 years, Sister Felt oversaw many developments in the organization. In 1902, publication of the *Children's Friend* magazine began. In 1913, the Primary began contributing to pediatric hospital care. That program was culminated in 1952 with the completion of the Primary Children's Hospital in Salt Lake City. Contributions from Primary children helped support the hospital.

Beginning in 1929 when the Primary took over more responsibility for the spiritual training of children, lessons were planned for three weeks of the month and an activity on the fourth week. The Cub Scout program became the responsibility of the Primary in 1952.

Primary meetings were held midweek until the Church instituted the consolidated meeting plan in 1980. Then it replaced Junior Sunday School for providing Sunday religious instruction for children ages 3 to 11. The Primary meets for one hour and forty minutes of the meeting block, dividing the time between group meetings, classroom instruction and sharing time. Although women continue to serve exclusively in Primary presidencies, men, too, are called to teach classes. Weekday activities continue on a quarterly basis.

Yearly, usually in September or October, ward and branch Primaries throughout the Church present the Children's Sacrament Meeting Presentation, during which the children share, through song and the spoken word, what they have learned during the year.

Sources: *Sisters and Little Saints,* by Carol Cornwall Madsen and Susan Oman; *Encyclopedia of Mormonism.*

PRIMARY GENERAL PRESIDENCY

| Anne G. Wirthlin First Counselor | Patricia P. Pinegar President | Susan L. Warner Second Counselor |

President — Patricia Peterson Pinegar, Oct. 1, 1994-present. Born in Cedar City, Utah, to Laurence and Wavie Williams Peterson; attended BYU in general education; served with her husband when he was president of the Missionary Training Center in Provo, Utah, and when he was president of the England London South Mission. Served as second counselor in the Young Women general presidency from April 4, 1992, until her call as Primary general president. She served on Primary general board, 1991-92. Former stake and ward Primary president and teacher, ward Relief Society president and counselor and teacher, stake Young Women counselor and adviser, and ward Young Women president and adviser; married to Ed Pinegar, parents of eight children.

First Counselor — Anne Goalen Wirthlin, Oct. 1, 1994-present. Born in Salt Lake City, Utah, to Bernard Ivan and Hettie Le Royce Thomson Goalen. Former ward Relief Society and Primary president and counselor. Graduate of the University of Utah. Member of the Young Women general board from 1993 until her call to the Primary general presidency. Served with her husband, David B. Wirthlin, while he was president of the Germany Frankfurt Mission. She and her husband are parents of six children.

Second Counselor — Susan Lillywhite Warner, Oct. 1, 1994-present. Born in Salt Lake City to Justin Bryce and Alice Mitchell Lillywhite; former stake Primary president, ward Young Women president, Relief Society president. Graduate of BYU. Member of the Primary general board from 1992 until her call to the Primary general presidency. Married C. Terry Warner, parents of 10 children.

HISTORICAL LISTING OF GENERAL PRESIDENCIES OF THE PRIMARY ASSOCIATION

(Presidents pictured)

President, Louie Bouton Felt, 19 Jun 1880-6 Oct 1925.

First Counselors, Matilda Morehouse W. Barratt — 19 Jun 1880-Oct 1888, Lillie Tuckett Freeze — Oct 1888-8 Dec 1905, May Anderson — 29 Dec 1905-6 Oct 1925.

Second Counselors, Clare Cordelia Moses Cannon — 19 Jun 1880-4 Oct 1895, Josephine Richards West — 15 Dec 1896-24 Nov 1905, Clara Woodruff Beebe — 29 Dec 1906-6 Oct 1925.

President, May Anderson — 6 Oct 1925-11 Sep 1939.

First Counselors, Sadie Grant Pack — 6 Oct 1925-11 Sep 1929, Isabelle Salmon Ross — 11 Sep 1929-31 Dec 1939.

Second Counselors, Isabelle Salmon Ross — 6 Oct 1925-11 Sep 1929, Edna Harker Thomas — 11 Sep 1929-11 Dec 1933, Edith Hunter Lambert — 11 Dec 1933-31 Dec 1939.

President, May Green Hinckley — 1 Jan 1940-2 May 1943.

First Counselor, Adele Cannon Howells — 1 Jan 1940-2 May 1943.

Second Counselors, Janet Murdock Thompson — 1 Jan 1940-May 1942, LaVern Watts Parmley — May 1942-2 May 1943.

President, Adele Cannon Howells — 29 Jul 1943-14 Apr 1951.

First Counselor, La-Vern Watts Parmley — 20 Jul 1943-14 Apr 1951.

Second Counselor, Dessie Grant Boyle — 20 Jul 1943-14 Apr 1951.

President, LaVern Watts Parmley — 16 May 1951-5 Oct 1974.

First Counselors, Arta Matthews Hale — 16 May 1951-6 Apr 1962, Leone Watson Doxey — 6 Apr 1962-23 Oct 1969, Lucile Cardon Reading — 8 Jan 1970-6 Aug 1970, Naomi Ward Randall — 4 Oct 1970-5 Oct 1974.

Second Counselors, Florence Holbrook Richards — 15 May 1951-11 Jun 1953, Leone Watson Doxey — 10 Sep 1953-6 Apr 1962, Eileen Robinson Dunyon — 6 Apr 1962-3 Jun 1963, Lucile Cardon Reading — 23 Jul 1963-8 Jan 1970, Florence Reece Lane — 8 Jan 1970-5 Oct 1974.

President, Naomi Maxfield Shumway — 5 Oct 1974-5 Apr 1980.

First Counselors, Sara Broadbent Paulsen — 5 Oct 1974-2 Apr 1977, Colleen Bushman Lemmon — 2 Apr 1977-5 Apr 1980.

Second Counselors, Colleen Bushman Lemmon — 5 Oct 1974-2 Apr

1977, Dorthea Christiansen Murdock
— 2 Apr 1977-5 Apr 1980.

President, Dwan Jacobsen Young —
5 Apr 1980-2 Apr 1988.

First Counselor, Virginia Beesley Cannon —
5 Apr 1980-2 Apr 1988.

Second Counselor,
Michaelene Packer
Grassli — 5 Apr 1980-2
Apr 1988.

President, Michaelene Packer
Grassli — 2 Apr 1988-
Oct. 1, 1994.

First Counselor, Betty
Jo Nelson Jepsen —
April 2, 1988-Oct. 1,
1994.

Second Counselor,
Ruth Broadbent
Wright — April 2, 1988-Oct. 1,
1994.

YOUNG WOMEN

President Brigham Young organized the Young Ladies Department of the Co-operative Retrenchment Association — predecessor to the Young Women program — on the evening of Nov. 28, 1869, in the parlor of the Lion House. He encouraged his older daughters, who were the charter members, to "retrench in your dress, in your tables, in your speech, wherein you have been guilty of silly, extravagant speeches and light-mindedness of thought. Retrench in everything that is bad and worthless, and improve in everything that is good and beautiful."

Thus, the Retrenchment Association was organized. Relief Society Gen. Pres. Eliza R. Snow supervised the association; Ella Young Empey was named as president.

News of the organization spread quickly. By the end of 1870, retrenchment associations had been established in several Mormon settlements. In addition, the organization had divided into senior and junior associations.

Not long after the creation of the Young Men's Mutual Improvement Association in 1875, President Young approved a name change to "Young Ladies National Mutual Improvement Association" to correspond to the young men's organization. The two organizations began holding monthly meetings together. In 1904, the word "National" was dropped since the Young Ladies' organization had become international in scope. Throughout the early years of the association's existence, the YLNMIA was directed through local ward efforts. The first stake board was organized in 1878 in the Salt Lake Stake, antedating the appointment of a general board. In 1880, Elmina S. Taylor was called as the first general president. She called as her counselors Margaret (Maggie) Y. Taylor and Martha (Mattie) Horne, with Louie Wells as secretary and Fanny Y. Thatcher as treasurer. That same year, Pres. Taylor presided over the first general conference of the YLNMIA.

Under the new general presidency's direction, the association encouraged the study of gospel principles, development of individual talents and service to those in need. General, stake and ward boards were subsequently appointed, lesson manuals were produced, and joint activities were established with the YMMIA. The *Young Woman's Journal* was inaugurated 1889 and soon began printing a series of lessons.

In 1888, the first annual June Conference for young women and young men was held. Leaders provided special training in physical activity, story-telling, and music and class instruction.

Four decades later, in 1929, a new summer camping program was announced at June Conference, and the *Young Woman's Journal* and *The Improvement Era* merged with the November issue. During the 1930s, MIA leaders gave new emphasis to music, dance and the performing arts, with an annual June Conference dance festival being held.

In the late 1940s and the 1950s, the First Presidency turned over to the YWMIA leaders a girls enrollment incentive program, previously administered by the Presiding Bishopric. It was designed to increase attendance at Church meetings.

In the early 1970s, President Harold B. Lee introduced a correlation program designed to integrate Church programs for youth. From this effort eventually came the Personal Progress program and the Young Womanhood Achievement Awards. During the 1980s, Sunday Young Women classes began meeting at the same time as priesthood meeting for Young Men.

During the tenure of general Pres. Ardeth G. Kapp, who served from 1984-1992, the Young Women motto, ''Stand for Truth and Righteousness,'' was introduced, along with the Young Women logo, represented by a torch with the profile of the face of a young woman. The torch represents the light of Christ, inviting all to ''come unto Christ.'' (D&C 20:59.)

During Pres. Kapp's administration, the Young Women theme and values were introduced. The values are faith, divine nature, individual worth, knowledge, choice and accountability, good works, and integrity.

A memorable event for the program is the Young Women Worldwide Celebration, held every three years. In 1995, the theme for the celebration was 'Experiment Upon the Word,'' taken from Alma 32:27. Young women worldwide were encouraged to study the scriptures regularly throughout the year. They then celebrated the fruits of that study Nov. 18 with local activities.

As of summer 1996, 547,000 young women ages 12 through 17 in 160 different countries were enrolled in the Young Women program as Beehives, Mia Maids or Laurels.

Sources: *Encyclopedia of Mormonism*, vols. 3-4; *A Century of Sisterhood*; *History of the YWMIA*, by Marba C. Josephson; *Deseret News 1993-1994 Church Almanac*; *Church News*, Jan. 21, April 1, 1996.

YOUNG WOMEN GENERAL PRESIDENCY

Virginia H. Pearce
First Counselor

Janette Hales Beckham
President

Bonnie D. Parkin
Second Counselor

President — Janette Callister Hales Beckham, April 4, 1992-present. Born in Springville, Utah, to Thomas L. and Hannah Gudmundson Carrick Callister; received bachelor's degree in clothing and textiles from BYU; served as second counselor to Ardeth G. Kapp in Young Women general presidency March 31, 1990 to April 4, 1992; served on the Primary general board, 1988-90; former gospel doctrine teacher and ward Relief Society president; served in the Utah State House of Representatives; married the late Robert H. Hales; parents of five children; married Raymond E. Beckham in 1995.

First Counselor — Virginia Hinckley Pearce, April 4, 1992-present. Born in Denver, Colo., to Gordon B. and Marjorie Pay Hinckley; received bachelor's degree in history from the University of Utah and master's degree in social work from the University of Utah; served on the Primary general board, 1988-92; former counselor in ward and stake Primary presidencies, gospel doctrine teacher, teacher in Primary, Relief Society and Young Women, and counselor in a ward Relief Society presidency; married James R. M. Pearce, parents of six children.

Second Counselor — Bonnie Dansie Parkin, Oct. 1, 1994-present. Born in Murray, Utah, to Jesse H. and Ruth Butikofer Dansie. Graduate of Utah State University; served on the Relief Society general board from 1990 until called to the Young Women general presidency. Former stake Young Women president's counselor, ward Relief Society and Primary president; married James L. Parkin, prents of four children.

HISTORICAL LISTING OF GENERAL PRESIDENCIES OF YOUNG WOMEN'S MUTUAL IMPROVEMENT ASSOCIATION AND YOUNG WOMEN
(Presidents pictured)

President, Elmina Shepherd Taylor — 19 Jun 1880-6 Dec 1904.

First Counselors, Margaret Young Taylor — 19 Jun 1880-1887, Maria Young Dougall — 1887-6 Dec 1904.

Second Counselor, Martha Horne Tingey — 19 Jun 1880-6 Dec 1904.

President, Martha Horne Tingey — 5 Apr 1905-28 Mar 1929.

First Counselor, Ruth May Fox — 5 Apr 1905-28 Mar 1929.

Second Counselors, Mae Taylor Nystrom — 5 Apr 1905-15 Jul 1923, Lucy Grant Cannon, 15 Jul 1923-28 Mar 1929.

President, Ruth May Fox — 28 Mar 1929-Oct 1937.

First Counselor, Lucy Grant Cannon — 28 Mar 1929-Oct 1937.

Second Counselor, Clarissa A. Beesley — 30 Mar 1929-Oct 1937.

President, Lucy Grant Cannon — Nov 1937-6 Apr 1948.

First Counselors, Helen Spencer Williams — Nov 1937-17 May 1944, Verna Wright Goddard — Jul 1944-6 Apr 1948.

Second Counselors, Verna Wright Goddard — Nov 1937-Jul 1944, Lucy T. Anderson — 6 Jul 1944-6 Apr 1948.

President, Bertha Stone Reeder — 6 Apr 1948-30 Sep 1961.

First Counselor, Emily Higgs Bennett — 13 Jun 1948-30 Sep 1961.

Second Counselor, LaRue Carr Longden — 13 Jun 1948-30 Sep 1961.

President, Florence Smith Jacobsen — 30 Sep 1961-9 Nov 1972.

First Counselor, Margaret R. Jackson — 30 Sep 1961-9 Nov 1972.

Second Counselor, Dorothy Porter Holt — 30 Sep 1961-9 Nov 1972.

AARONIC PRIESTHOOD MIA
(YOUNG WOMEN)

President, Ruth Hardy Funk — 9 Nov 1972-23 Jun 1974.

First Counselor, Hortense Hogan Child — 9 Nov 1972-23 Jun 1974.

Second Counselor, Ardeth Greene Kapp — 9 Nov 1972-23 Jun 1974.

YOUNG WOMEN

President, Ruth Hardy Funk — 23 Jun 1974-12 Jul 1978.

First Counselor, Hortense Hogan Child — 23 Jun 1974-12 Jul 1978.

Second Counselor, Ardeth Greene Kapp — 23 Jun 1974-12 Jul 1978.

President, Elaine Anderson Cannon — 12 Jul 1978-7 Apr 1984.

First Counselor, Arlene Barlow Darger — 12 Jul 1978-7 Apr 1984.

Second Counselor, Norma Broadbent Smith — 12 Jul 1978-7 Apr 1984.

President, Ardeth Greene Kapp — 7 Apr 1984-4 Apr 1992.

First Counselors, Patricia Terry Holland — 11 May 1984-6 Apr 1986, Maurine Johnson Turley — 6 Apr 1986-4 Apr 1987, Jayne Broadbent Malan — 4 Apr 1987-4 Apr 1992.

Second Counselors, Maurine Johnson Turley — 11 May 1984-6 Apr 1986, Jayne Broadbent Malan — 6 Apr 1986-4 Apr 1987, Elaine Low Jack — 4 Apr 1987-31 Mar 1990, Janette Callister Hales — 31 Mar 1990-4 Apr 1992.

RELIEF SOCIETY

In 1842, a small group of women met at the home of Sarah M. Kimball in Nauvoo, Ill., to organize a sewing society to aid Nauvoo Temple workmen. They sought the endorsement of the Prophet Joseph Smith, who praised their efforts but said the Lord had something better in mind for them. It would be an organization under the priesthood after the pattern of the priesthood. He organized the Female Relief Society on March 17, 1842. The Prophet said that the restored Church could not be perfect or complete without it. He charged members with the responsibility to save souls and taught them principles of the gospel. The women elected Emma Smith their president, and she selected two counselors.

From that original organization stemmed what is now the Relief Society, the official adult women's organization of the Church. Its motto, "Charity Never Faileth," states what has been the objective of society members from the first: to love and nurture one another and minister to the needs of Church members and others. The Female Relief Society of Nauvoo contributed to the Nauvoo Temple and supported moral reform. Members were primarily concerned with helping the poor. In July 1843, a visiting committee of four was appointed in each ward to assess needs and distribute necessities, the beginning of the visiting teaching effort that has been a part of Relief Society since then. By 1844, the society had 1,341 members.

The Female Relief Society of Nauvoo ceased to function after March 1844 amid increasing tension and persecution.

Although women carried out charitable works and a few meetings were conducted at Winter Quarters, Neb., there was no formal Relief Society during the Saints' westward trek or for several years thereafter.

In February 1854, 16 women responded to an exhortation of President Brigham Young to form a society of females to make clothing for Indian women and children. This "Indian Relief Society" met until June, when President Young encouraged such organizations in individual wards. Many remained organized to assist the poor within their wards and help provide clothing and bedding for destitute handcart companies.

In 1866, President Young reorganized the Relief Society churchwide, appointing Eliza R. Snow to assist bishops in establishing the organization in each ward.

By 1880 there was a local unit of the Relief Society in each of 300 wards, caring for the needy within its ward boundaries and using visiting teachers to collect and distribute donations. Ward Relief Societies managed their own finances, and many built their own meeting halls.

In line with the Church's move for self-sufficiency, the Relief Society sponsored in the late 1800s cooperative economic enterprises such as making and marketing homemade goods, raising silk, storing grain and financing the medical training of midwives and female doctors.

The Relief Society also promoted women's right to vote and helped organize and nurture the Young Ladies' Retrenchment Association (forerunner to the Young Women) and the Primary.

By the turn of the century, needs of women were changing, and the format of lessons was adapted and standardized to meet the needs. The *Relief Society Magazine,* introduced in 1915, contained lessons for each month on theological, cultural and homemaking topics. One week a month was spent on each topic, with time left over for charity projects and testimony bearing. The monthly format of rotating topics has remained since then, with the subject matter being varied.

Beginning in 1921, concern over high maternal and infant mortality led to the establishment of health clinics and two stake Relief Society maternity hospitals, one operated in the Snowflake (Arizona) Stake and another in the Cottonwood (Utah) Stake.

In 1944, visiting teachers ceased collecting charitable funds. Since 1921, the ward Relief Society president, under the direction of the bishop, has been responsible for assessing needs and distributing relief to the needy. Ward Relief Society presidents supervise other charitable work such as caring for the sick, called "compassionate service" to distinguish it from "welfare service."

In 1956, the Relief Society Building was dedicated after being built from contributions from LDS women and funds from the Church. Today, the building houses the general offices of the Relief Society, Young Women and Primary organizations.

In the latter 20th Century, Relief Society has become more fully coordinated under the larger Church structure. Reporting and financing systems, magazine and lesson materials and social services became the responsibility of priesthood leaders and Church departments. After September 1971, all LDS women were automatically included as members of the Relief Society.

In recent times, the Relief Society has promoted scholarly study of women's concerns by helping establish the Women's Research Center at BYU, has rallied members to contribute to the Monument to Women at Nauvoo, Ill., in 1978, and has celebrated its sesquicentennial in 1992. One aspect of this was starting a worldwide effort to improve literacy. The purpose of the Church's Gospel Literacy Effort, implemented in January 1993, was defined as two-fold: to teach basic gospel literacy skills for those who cannot read or write, and to encourage Church members to study the gospel and improve themselves and their families throughout their lives.

Sources: *Encyclopedia of Mormonism; Women of Covenant: The Story of Relief Society,* by Jill Mulvay Derr, Janath Russell Cannon, and Maureen Ursenbach Beecher, Deseret Book, 1992; *Church News,* Jan. 30, 1993.

RELIEF SOCIETY GENERAL PRESIDENCY

Chieko N. Okazaki	Elaine L. Jack	Aileen H. Clyde
First Counselor	President	Second Counselor

President — Elaine Low Jack, March 31, 1990-present. Born to Sterling O. and Lavina Anderson Low at Cardston, Alberta, Canada; attended University of Utah; former second counselor to Ardeth G. Kapp in the Young Women general presidency from April 4, 1987, to March 31, 1990; served on Relief Society general board from 1972 to 1984, former stake Relief Society president and ward and branch Young Women president; married Joseph E. Jack, parents of four sons.

First Counselor — Chieko Nishimura Okazaki, March 31, 1990-present. Born to Kanenori and Hatsuko Nishi Nishimura at Kohala, Hawaii; bachelor's degree, University of Hawaii, master's degree in curriculum, University of Colorado; served on Primary general board, 1988 to 1990; Young Women general board, 1960 to 1966, and 1971 to 1972; married Edward Y. Okazaki. He died March 20, 1992. Parents of two children.

Second Counselor — Aileen Hales Clyde, March 31, 1990-present. Born to G. Ray and M. Lesley Grooms Hales in Springville, Utah; received bachelor's degree in English from BYU, and did post-graduate work at BYU and the University of Utah; served on the Young Women general board, 1977 to 1978; involved on many community advisory boards; regent, Utah System of Higher Education; married Hal M. Clyde, parents of three sons.

HISTORICAL LISTING OF GENERAL PRESIDENCIES
OF THE RELIEF SOCIETY
(Presidents pictured)

President, Emma Hale Smith — 17 Mar 1842-16 Mar 1844.

First Counselor, Sarah Marietta Kingsley Cleveland — 17 Mar 1842-16 Mar 1844.

Second Counselor, Elizabeth Ann Smith Whitney — 17 Mar 1842-16 Mar 1844.

President, Eliza Roxey Snow — 1866-5 Dec 1887.

First Counselor, Zina Diantha Huntington Young — 19 Jun 1880-8 Apr 1888.

Second Counselor, Elizabeth Ann Smith Whitney — 19 Jun 1880-15 Feb 1882.

President, Zina Diantha Huntington Young — 8 Apr 1888-28 Aug 1901.

First Counselor, Jane Snyder Richards — 11 Oct 1888-10 Nov 1901.

Second Counselor, Bathsheba Wilson Smith — 11 Oct 1888-10 Nov 1901.

President, Bathsheba Wilson Smith — 10 Nov 1901-20 Sep 1910.

First Counselor, Annie Taylor Hyde — 10 Nov 1901-2 Mar 1909.

Second Counselor, Ida Smoot Dusenberry, 10 Nov 1901-20 Sep 1910.

President, Emmeline Woodward B. Wells — 3 Oct 1910-2 Apr 1921.

First Counselor, Clarissa Smith Williams — 3 Oct 1910-2 Apr 1921.

Second Counselor, Julina Lambson Smith — 3 Oct 1910-2 Apr 1921.

President, Clarissa Smith Williams — 2 Apr 1921-7 Oct 1928.

First Counselor, Jennie Brimhall Knight — 2 Apr 1921-7 Oct 1928.

Second Counselor, Louise Yates Robison — 2 Apr 1921-7 Oct 1928.

President, Louise Yates Robison — 7 Oct 1928-Dec 1939.

First Counselor, Amy Brown Lyman — 7 Oct 1928-Dec 1939.

Second Counselors, Julia Alleman Child — 7 Oct 1928-23 Jan 1935, Kate Montgomery Bark-

er — 3 Apr 1935-31 Dec 1939.

President, Amy Brown Lyman — 1 Jan 1940-6 Apr 1945.

First Counselor, Marcia Knowlton Howells — Apr 1940-6 Apr 1945.

Second Counselors, Donna Durrant Sorensen, Apr 1940-12 Oct 1942, Belle Smith Spafford, 12 Oct 1942-6 Apr 1945.

President, Belle Smith Spafford — 6 Apr 1945-3 Oct 1974.

First Counselor, Marianne Clark Sharp — 6 Apr 1945-3 Oct 1974.

Second Counselor, Gertrude Ryberg Garff — 6 Apr 1945-30 Sep 1947, Velma Nebeker Simonsen — 3 Oct 1947-17 Dec 1956, Helen Woodruff Anderson — Jan 1957-Aug 1958, Louise Wallace Madsen — Aug 1958-3 Oct 1974.

President, Barbara Bradshaw Smith — 3 Oct 1974-7 Apr 1984.

First Counselors, Janath Russell Cannon — 3 Oct 1974-28 Nov 1978, Marian Richards Boyer — 28 Nov 1978-7 Apr 1984.

Second Counselors, Marian Richards Boyer — 3 Oct 1974-28 Nov 1978, Shirley Wilkes Thomas — 28 Nov 1978-24 Jun 1983, Ann Stoddard Reese, 1 Oct 1983-7 Apr 1984.

President, Barbara Woodhead Winder — 7 Apr 1984-31 Mar 1990.

First Counselor, Joy Frewin Evans — 21 May 1984-31 Mar 1990.

Second Counselor, Joanne Bushman Doxey — 21 May 1984-31 Mar 1990.

1847
PIONEERS

THE PIONEERS OF 1847

Travel in frontier America in the 1830-40s was difficult at best. But movement of the Latter-day Saints from New York to Ohio, from Ohio to Missouri, and Missouri to Illinois was compounded by the hostility of their adversaries. After being expelled from Missouri in 1838, the exiles gathered at a swampy riverbank site in northern Illinois. Here they built a city that they named Nauvoo that was no sooner well underway than they were forced to leave again. Their leaving began the epic movement that settled much of Mountain West area.

The first wagons crossed the Mississippi River Feb. 4, 1846, in bitterly cold weather and set up a camp in Sugar Creek, Iowa. This group, called the Camp of Israel and led by Brigham Young, comprised about 3,000 members, many of whom were ill-prepared for the winter journey. The Camp of Israel moved laboriously across the rolling lowlands of Iowa in freezing cold and snows, and in incessant rain through deep mud.

In the spring, another 7,000 Saints comprising the main body, left Nauvoo. Traveling over dry roads, they soon caught up with the Camp of Israel. The exiles built permanent way stations at Garden Grove and Mt. Pisgah, Iowa, where they planted grain, and built fences and cabins. They exiles eventually reached the Missouri River, which they crossed and built a log city they called Winter Quarters, now part of Omaha, Neb. Winter Quarters became the staging area for the trek west that began the following spring.

In Mt. Pisgah on June 26, 1846, U.S. Army Capt. James Allen caught up with the refugees. He carried orders asking for 500 volunteers from the exiles to take part in the Mexican War. The volunteers were to form a battalion that would march across the Southwest and secure California for the United States. Brigham Young complied with the order and the Mormon Battalion was created. The money these volunteers earned was lifesaving as it was distributed to their families and the poor. The Battalion marched from Council Bluffs, Iowa, south to Fort Leavenworth, Kan., where it was outfitted. From Fort. Leavenworth, the estimated 520 men, 35 women, and 42 children of the Battalion marched to Santa Fe, N.M.

During the march, Battalion members learned of a company of some 80 Mississippi Saints wintering in Pueblo, Colo. Officers of the Battalion sent three detachments of the older or sick soldiers to Pueblo. Many of the women and children were also sent to Pueblo. The remaining soldiers marched toward California. In Tucson, Ariz., they took command of a previously Mexican post. They continued across the desert to California, arriving Jan. 29, 1847. Most were discharged in Los Angeles, Calif., July 16, 1847.

Meanwhile, those left in Nauvoo were the poor and ill who were largely unable to travel. As the thousands crossed Iowa, and as the Mormon Battalion trekked across the Southwest, time ran out for the remaining few in Nauvoo. Some 600-1,000 foes of the Church, calling themselves the "Regulators," attacked the city Sept. 10, 1846. After a four-day defense, the remaining Saints fled to the river banks while the Regulators plundered the city. The last exiles crossed the river and on the far banks set up so-called "Misery Camps."

The following spring in 1847, a vanguard company of pioneers under Brigham Young blazed the Mormon Pioneer Trail leading to the Great Salt Lake Valley. This company was followed by five companies from Winter Quarters. Most of Brigham Young's company returned to Winter Quarters that fall, while most of those in following companies remained in their new mountain home.

Within this section is information primarily about the first Mormon pioneers who arrived in the Salt Lake Valley in July 1847.

PIONEER DEMOGRAPHICS

The following charts display demographic information on the first pioneer company, and other 1847 Mormon pioneers. Because all information on all 1847 pioneers is not available, the number of subjects in this study varies accordingly.

SUMMARY OF
First pioneer company characteristics

98% male
97% 18 years of age or older
Two-thirds born in Northeastern United States
94% of those married came without their spouse
Age at death: 68.4 years
Three-fourths died in Utah

Pioneer given names

Book of Mormon names
2 Zenos
3 Moroni
4 Nephi
1 Helaman
1 Lemuel
2 Alma
1 Lamoni

Church history names
3 Joseph Smith
3 Joseph Hyrum
3 Hyrum Smith
2 Joseph Brigham
1 Joseph Lehi

Biblical names
Jezreel, Job, Hosea, Ephraim, Esther, Ezekiel, Enoch, Elijah Hezekiah, Philemon, Miriam, Moses, etc.

Most popular names
102 John
102 Mary
78 William
57 Sarah
48 Elizabeth
47 Joseph
40 James

Historical/ Literature names
7 George Washington
5 Benjamin Franklin
2 Andrew Jackson
1 Martin Luther
1 Thomas Jefferson
1 Isaac Newton
1 John Calvin
Others: Minerva (4), Pliny, Virgil

53% of pioneers had middle names

Source: Pioneer Demographic Study, Research Information Division, 1996

Place of birth

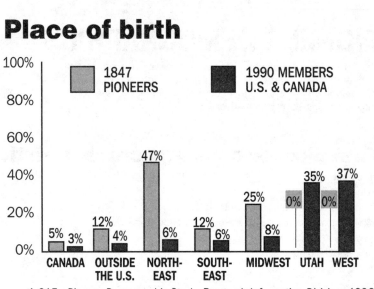

n=1,615. *Pioneer Demographic Study, Research Information Division, 1996*
n=6,244, *1990 Church Membership Study, Research Information Division*

State/place of birth

BY AGE

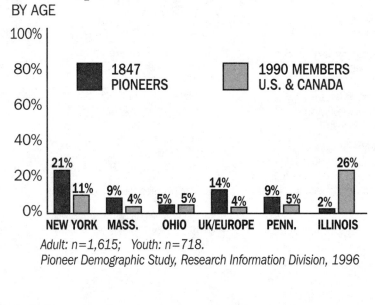

Adult: n=1,615; Youth: n=718.
Pioneer Demographic Study, Research Information Division, 1996

Gender, by company

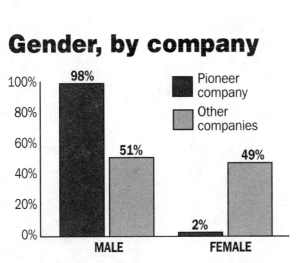

Pioneer company, n=148. Other companies, n=1,493
Pioneer Demographic Study,
Research Information Division, 1996

Gender, by age

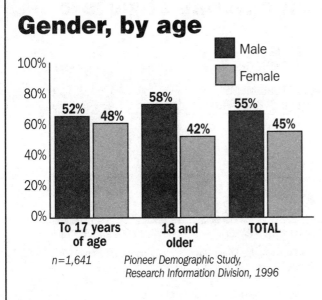

n=1,641   Pioneer Demographic Study,
Research Information Division, 1996

Marital status

1847 PIONEERS AND 1990 MEMBERS
U.S. AND CANADA, ADULTS (18+)

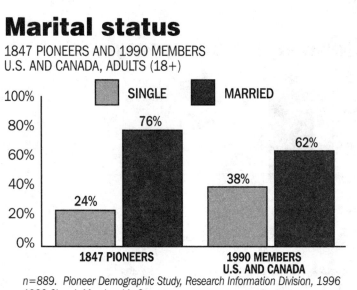

n=889. Pioneer Demographic Study, Research Information Division, 1996
1990 Church Membership Survey
1990 March Current Population Survey

Children's family structure

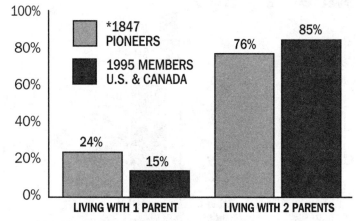

n=204. Pioneer Demographic Study, Research Information Division, 1996
n=10,600 children. Church Membership Survey

*This chart reflects the deaths that occurred
on the frontier, and during the 1846 exodus.

Mean age at time of trek and at death

PIONEER COMPANY

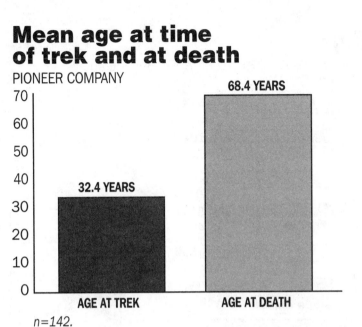

n=142.
Pioneer Demographic Study, Research Information Division, 1996

Age

1847 PIONEERS AND 1995 MEMBERS
U.S. AND CANADA

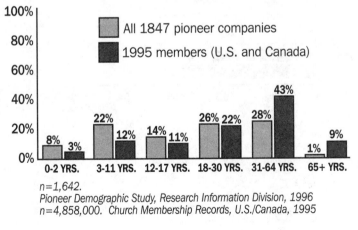

n=1,642.
Pioneer Demographic Study, Research Information Division, 1996
n=4,858,000. Church Membership Records, U.S./Canada, 1995

Age

BY GENDER, 1847 PIONEERS AND 1995 MEMBERS, U.S. AND CANADA

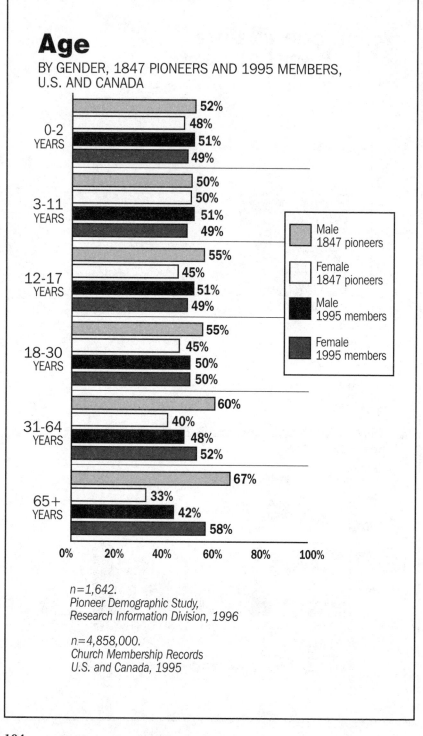

0-2 YEARS
- 52%
- 48%
- 51%
- 49%

3-11 YEARS
- 50%
- 50%
- 51%
- 49%

Legend:
- Male 1847 pioneers
- Female 1847 pioneers
- Male 1995 members
- Female 1995 members

12-17 YEARS
- 55%
- 45%
- 51%
- 49%

18-30 YEARS
- 55%
- 45%
- 50%
- 50%

31-64 YEARS
- 60%
- 40%
- 48%
- 52%

65+ YEARS
- 67%
- 33%
- 42%
- 58%

0% 20% 40% 60% 80% 100%

n=1,642.
Pioneer Demographic Study,
Research Information Division, 1996

n=4,858,000.
Church Membership Records
U.S. and Canada, 1995

Age at death

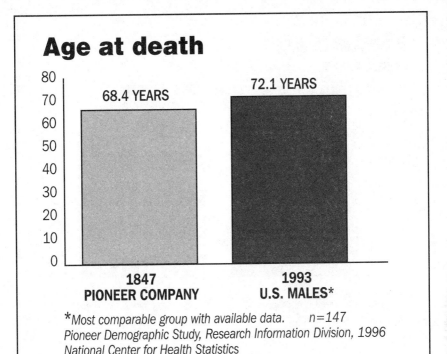

68.4 YEARS

72.1 YEARS

1847
PIONEER COMPANY

1993
U.S. MALES*

*Most comparable group with available data.   n=147
Pioneer Demographic Study, Research Information Division, 1996
National Center for Health Statistics

Place of death of
first pioneer company

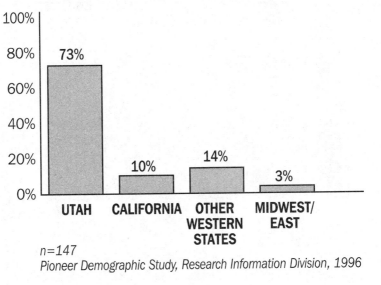

73%

10%

14%

3%

UTAH   CALIFORNIA   OTHER
WESTERN
STATES

MIDWEST/
EAST

n=147
Pioneer Demographic Study, Research Information Division, 1996

Median age

BY GENDER, ADULTS (18+)

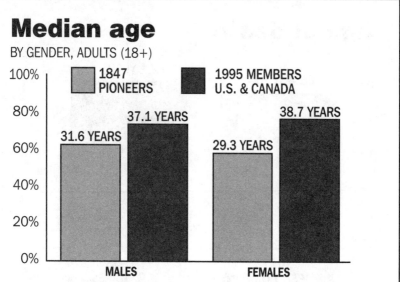

Legend:
- 1847 PIONEERS
- 1995 MEMBERS U.S. & CANADA

MALES: 31.6 YEARS (1847), 37.1 YEARS (1995)
FEMALES: 29.3 YEARS (1847), 38.7 YEARS (1995)

n=889. *Pioneer Demographic Study, Research Information Division, 1996*
n=4,858,000. *Church Membership Records*

Average age

BY COMPANY

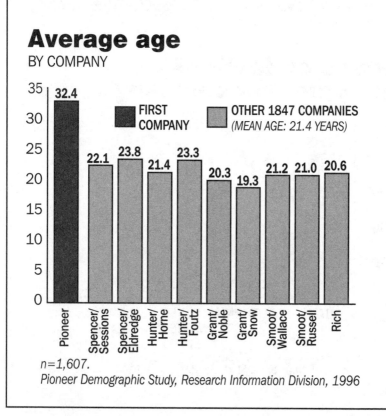

Legend:
- FIRST COMPANY
- OTHER 1847 COMPANIES *(MEAN AGE: 21.4 YEARS)*

Company	Average age
Pioneer	32.4
Spencer/Sessions	22.1
Spencer/Eldredge	23.8
Hunter/Horne	21.4
Hunter/Foutz	23.3
Grant/Noble	20.3
Grant/Snow	19.3
Smoot/Wallace	21.2
Smoot/Russell	21.0
Rich	20.6

n=1,607.
Pioneer Demographic Study, Research Information Division, 1996

Pioneer Wagon

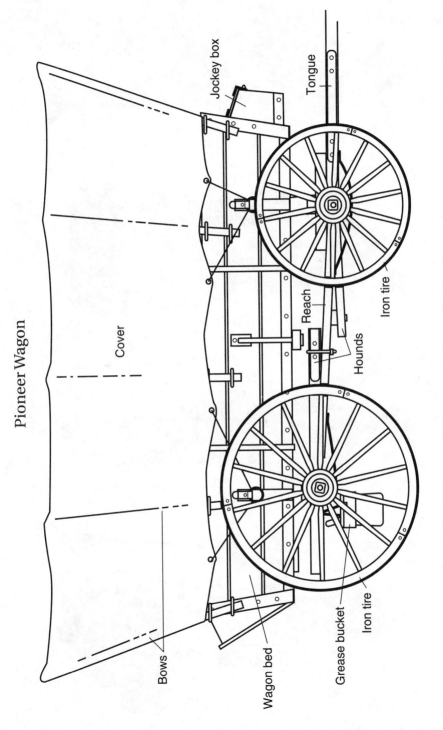

Jockey box

Tongue

Iron tire

Reach

Hounds

Cover

Bows

Wagon bed

Grease bucket

Iron tire

Typical clothing of the 1840's

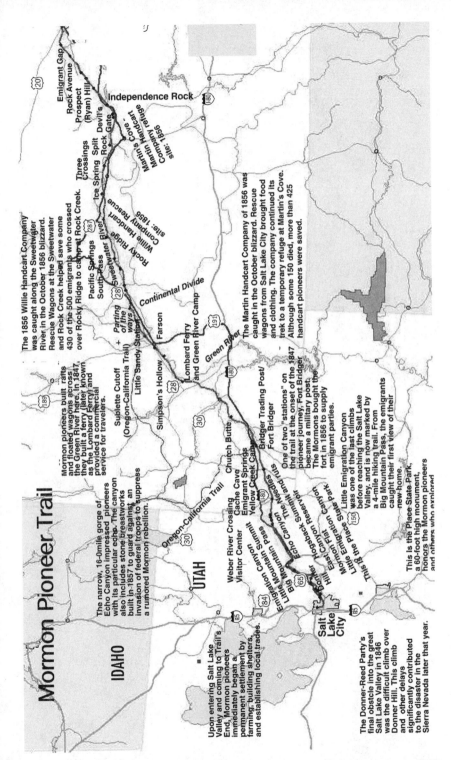

Mormon Pioneer Trail

Independence Rock

Emigrant Gap
Rock Avenue
Prospect (Ryan) Hill
Devil's Gate
Split Rock
Martin's Handcart
Martin's Cove –
Martin Handcart Company refuge site: 1856

Three Crossings
Ice Spring
Pacific Springs
South Pass
Sweetwater River
Rocky Ridge
Willie Handcart Company Rescue site: 1856

Continental Divide

Parting of the ways

Farson

Lombard Ferry and Green River Camp

Green River

Simpson's Hollow

Little Sandy Station

Sublette Cutoff (Oregon-California Trail)

Oregon-California Trail

Bridger Trading Post/ Fort Bridger

Weber River Crossing
Cache Cave
Church Butte
Visitor Center
Emigrant Springs
Yellow Creek Camp
The Needles
Little Emigration Canyon
Echo Canyon
Emigration Mountain Pass
Big Mountain Pass
Echo Summit
Donner
Hogsback Summit
Little Mountain Pass
East Canyon
East Flat
Mormon Flat State Park
Little Emigration Canyon
Little the Place

IDAHO

UTAH

Salt Lake City

This Is the Place

The 1856 Willie Handcart Company was caught along the Sweetwater River in the October 1856 blizzard. Rescue Wagons at the Sweetwater and Rock Creek helped save some 430 of the 500 emigrants who crossed over Rocky Ridge to camp at Rock Creek.

Mormon pioneers built rafts and floated wagons across the Green River here. In 1847, they built a ferry (later known as the Lombard Ferry) and provided a commercial service for travelers.

The narrow, 16.0-mile gorge of Echo Canyon impressed pioneers with its particular echo. The canyon also includes stone breastworks built in 1857 to guard against an invasion of federal troops to suppress a rumored Mormon rebellion.

The Martin Handcart Company of 1856 was caught in the October blizzard. Rescue wagons from Salt Lake City brought food and clothing. The company continued its trek to a temporary refuge at Martin's Cove. Although some 150 died, more than 425 handcart pioneers were saved.

One of two "stations" on the trail at the onset of the 1847 pioneer journey, Fort Bridger became a military post. The Mormons bought the fort in 1856 to supply emigrant parties.

Little Emigration Canyon was one of the last climbs before reaching the Salt Lake Valley, and is now marked by a 4-mile hiking trail. From Big Mountain Pass, the emigrants caught their first view of their new home.

Upon entering Salt Lake Valley and coming to Trail's End, Mormon pioneers immediately began a permanent settlement by farming, building shelters, and establishing local trades.

This is the Place State Park, a 60-foot high monument, honors the Mormon pioneers and others who explored

The Donner-Reed Party's final obstacle into the great Salt Lake Valley in 1846 was the difficult climb over Donner Hill. This climb and other delays significantly contributed to the disaster in the Sierra Nevada later that year.

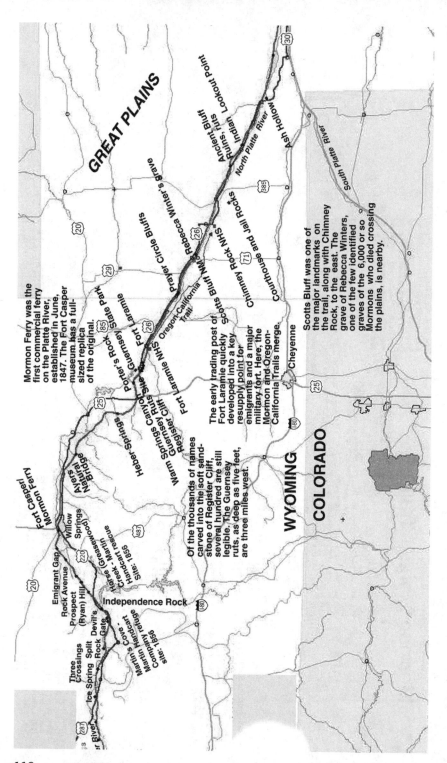

GREAT PLAINS

Mormon Ferry was the first commercial ferry on the Platte River, established in June, 1847. The Fort Casper museum has a full-sized replica of the original.

Ancient Bluff Ruins; ruts

Indian Lookout Point

North Platte River

Ash Hollow

South Platte River

Rebecca Winter's grave

Prayer Circle Bluffs

Scotts Bluff NM

Chimney Rock NHS

Courthouse and Jail Rocks

Chimney and Jail Rocks

Fort Laramie

Oregon-California Trail

Porter's Rock

Guernsey State Park

Register Cliff

Fort Laramie NHS

Warm Springs Canyon NHS

Guernsey Ruts Site

Heber Springs

The early trading post of Fort Laramie quickly developed into a key resupply point for emigrants and a major military fort. Here, the Mormon-and-Oregon-California Trails merge.

Cheyenne

Scotts Bluff was one of the major landmarks on the trail, along with Chimney Rock, to the east. The grave of Rebecca Winters, one of the few identified graves of the 6,000 or so Mormons who died crossing the plains, is nearby.

WYOMING

COLORADO

Fort Casper/ Mormon Ferry

Ayers Natural Bridge

Willow Springs

Greasewood

Horse (Greasewood) Creek - Martin rescue Handcart Site: 1856

Emigrant Gap

Rock Avenue

Prospect (Ryan) Hill

Of the thousands of names carved into the soft sandstone of Register Cliff, several hundred are still legible. The Guernsey ruts, as deep as five feet, are three miles west.

Independence Rock

Three Crossings

Split Rock

Devil's Gate

Ice Spring

Martin's Cove - Martin Handcart Company refuge site: 1856

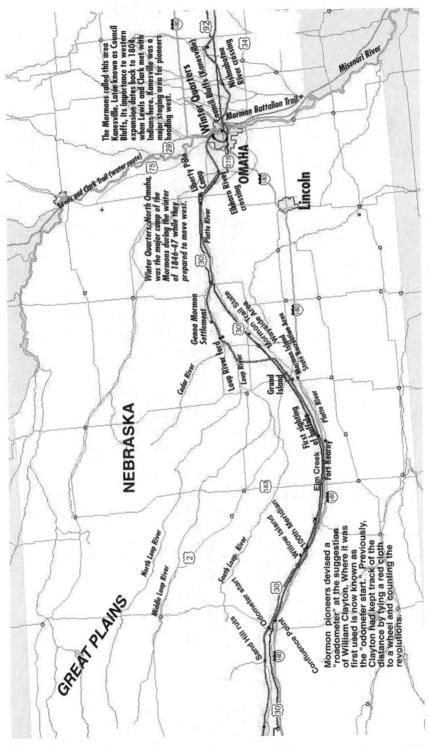

The Mormons called this area Kanesville. Later known as Council Bluffs, its importance to western expansion dates back to 1804, when Lewis and Clark met with Indians here. Kanesville was a major staging area for pioneers heading west.

Winter Quarters–North Omaha, was the major camp of the Mormons during the winter of 1846-47 while they prepared to move west.

Mormon pioneers devised a "roadometer" at the suggestion of William Clayton. Where it was first used is now known as the "odometer start". Previously, Clayton had kept track of the distance by tying a red cloth to a wheel and counting the revolutions.

Lewis and Clark Trail (water route)

Missouri River

Winter Quarters

Council Bluffs (Kanesville)

Nishnabotna River crossing

Mormon Battalion Trail

OMAHA

Liberty Pole Camp

Platte River

Elkhorn River crossing

Lincoln

Genoa Mormon Settlement

Cedar River

Loup River ford

Loup River

Mormon Trail State Wayside Area

Mormon Island State Recreation Area

Grand Island

Platte River

NEBRASKA

North Loup River

Middle Loup River

South Loup River

First sighting of buffalo

Elm Creek

Fort Kearny

100th Meridian

Willow Island

Odometer start

Commence point

Sand Hill ruts

GREAT PLAINS

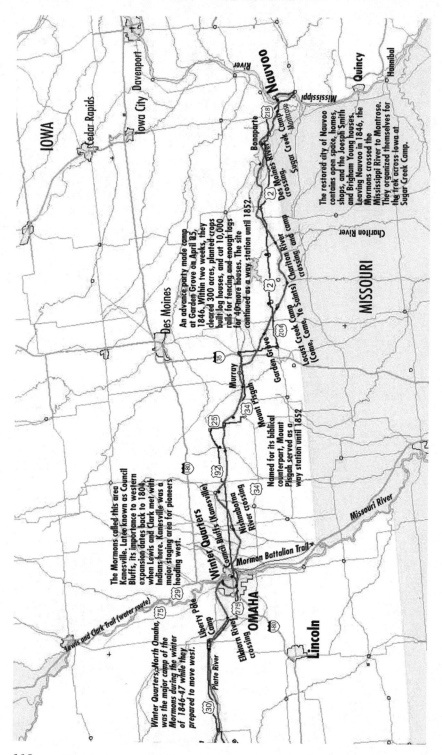

IOWA

Cedar Rapids

Davenport

Iowa City

NAUVOO

Quincy

Hannibal

Mississippi River

River

Bonaparte

218

Des Moines River

Sugar Creek Camp,
Montrose

2

The restored city of Nauvoo contains open space, homes, shops, and the Joesph Smith and Brigham Young houses. Leaving Nauvoo in 1846, the Mormons crossed the Mississippi River to Montrose. They organized themselves for the trek across Iowa at Sugar Creek Camp.

An advance party made camp at Garden Grove on April 25, 1846. Within two weeks, they cleared 300 acres, planted crops built log houses, and cut 10,000 rails for fencing and enough logs for 40 more houses. The site continued as a way station until 1852.

Chariton River

Chariton River and camp crossing

2

MISSOURI

Des Moines

35

206

Locust Creek Camp
(Come, Come, Ye Saints)

Garden Grove

Murray

34

25

Mount Pisgah

Named for its biblical counterpart, Mount Pisgah served as a way station until 1852.

80

92

Nishnabotna
River crossing

34

The Mormons called this area Kanesville. Later known as Council Bluffs, its importance to western expansion dates back to 1804, when Lewis and Clark met with Indians here. Kanesville was a major staging area for pioneers heading west.

Winter Quarters (Kanesville)

Council Bluffs (Kanesville)

29

Mormon Battalion Trail

Missouri River

Lewis and Clark Trail (water route)

75

Liberty Pole
Camp

OMAHA

275

Elkhorn River
crossing

80

Lincoln

Winter Quarters, North Omaha, was the major camp of the Mormons during the winter of 1846-47 while they prepared to move west.

Platte River

30

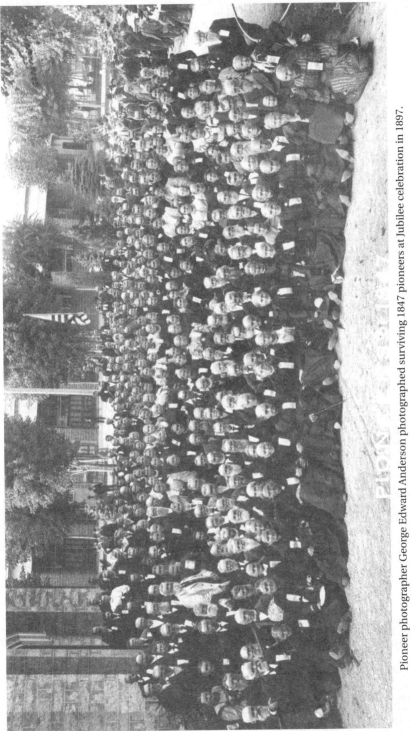

Pioneer photographer George Edward Anderson photographed surviving 1847 pioneers at Jubilee celebration in 1897.

PIONEER SUPPLIES

BILL OF PARTICULARS INCLUDED

For emigrants leaving this government next spring.

Each family consisting of five persons, to be provided with —

1 good strong wagon well covered with a light box.
2 or 3 good yoke of oxen between the ages of 4 and 10 years.
2 or more milch (milk) cows.
1 or more good beefs.
3 sheep if they can be obtained.
1000 pounds of flour or other bread or breadstuffs in good sacks.
1 good musket or rifle to each male over the age of 12 years.
1 lb. powder.
4 lbs. lead.
100 do. [ditto] sugar.
1 do. cayenne pepper.
1 do. black do.
1/2 lb. mustard.
10 do. rice for each family.
1 do. cinnamon.
1/2 do. cloves.
1 doz. nutmegs.
25 lbs. salt.
5 lbs. saleratus (bicarbonate for raising bread).
10 do. dried apples.
1 bush. beans.

A few lbs. dried beef or bacon.
5 lbs. dried peaches.
20 do. do. pumpkin.
25 do. seed grain.
20 lbs. soap for each family.
15 lbs. of iron and steel.
A few lbs. of wrought nails.
One or more sets of saw or grist mill irons to company of 100 families.
1 good seine (fishing net) and hook for each company.
2 sets of pulley blocks and ropes to each company for crossing rivers.
From 25 to 100 lbs. of farming and mechanical tools
Cooking utensils to consist of bake kettle, frying pan.
Tin cups, plates, knives, forks, spoons and pans as few as will do.
A good tent and furniture to each 2 families.
Clothing and bedding to each family, not to exceed 500 pounds.
Ten extra teams for each company of 100 families.
In addition to the above list, horse and mule teams can be used as well as oxen.
Many items of comfort and convenience will suggest themselves to a wise and provident people, and can be laid in the season; but none should start without filling the original bill. (*Nauvoo Neighbor*, Oct. 29, 1845.)

HISTORY OF THE 1847 PIONEER COMPANIES

THE FIRST COMPANY

After the exodus from Nauvoo early in 1846, Church members stayed at Winter Quarters until the spring of 1847. At that time Church leaders selected a body of men to travel by wagon to the Rocky Mountains and pioneer the way for following thousands. This group consisted of 143 men, 3 women and 2 children. They traveled in 72 wagons, 93 horses, 52 mules, 66 oxen, 19 cows, 17 dogs and some chickens. Others later joined this group, while some returned East as guides.

The first westward wagons, led by Heber C. Kimball, left Winter Quarters April 5, 1847, and traveled to a camp at the Elkhorn River, some 20 miles from Winter Quarters. Over the next few days, other wagons joined this group. Wagons led by Wilford Woodruff, Orson Pratt and Brigham Young joined the group at the Elkhorn River on April 7, after pausing for conference in Winter Quarters on the morning of April 6. On April 15, the rest of the Quorum of the Twelve arrived from Winter Quarters. On April 16, the entire company was organized with captains of hundreds, fifties and tens. The company crossed the Elkhorn River (a tributary of the Platte River), by ferrying each wagon on a raft of logs. Many westward companies were traveling to Oregon, including those from areas where the Mormons had suffered persecution, and the Mormons preferred to keep the Platte River between themselves and the Oregon-bound travelers. Thus, through Nebraska, the Mormon Pioneer Trail is on the north side of the Platte and the Oregon Trail is on the south side.

As the entire Mormon Trail was in Indian country, night guards were appointed and all in the company were instructed to have their weapons ready at all times. A piece of leather was kept over each weapon's firing mechanism to keep it dry. Wagons traveled in double file for safety. At night, the wagons formed a "circular fortification." The forward wheel of one wagon was locked into the hind wheel of the next. Animals were tethered within.

A typical day began with a bugle at 5 a.m., when each man was expected to arise and pray, prepare breakfast and lunch, care for his team, and be ready to pull out at 7 a.m. The company generally "nooned" for two hours at midday, then continued until evening. The night bugle sounded at 8:30 p.m. for prayers; fires were to be out by 9 p.m. As the company traveled, hunters most commonly bagged buffalo and antelope.

The first days of the early spring journey in April 1847 were bitterly cold with chilling prairie winds and sometimes snow. However, the weather gradually turned mild and rains replaced snows; cold nights, especially at high altitudes, accompanied the pioneers during most of the trip.

On April 19, William Clayton suggested to Orson Pratt that a set of wooden cogs, a pioneer odometer, be created and attached to the wheels of a wagon to measure the exact number of miles traveled in a day. Elder Pratt designed a set of cogs that Appleton Milo Harmon, a carpenter, built. Today, the town of North Platte, marks where pioneers began using their "roadometer."

Crossing the Loup Fork of the Platte River, the company encountered quicksand so strong they said it "rattled the wagons." Indians often approached the wagon train for food and gifts. As the wagons rumbled on, dryness replaced the rain, and clouds of dust hung over the wagon train.

Indians were said to often follow a wagon train for hundreds of miles awaiting a chance to make off with livestock. This wagon train occasionally lost animals despite the careful watching of guards.

One night the cannon carried by the party was fired twice to discourage Indians from attacking. On May 4 the near presence of a large Indian war party was so threatening that the wagons traveled five abreast. Despite such troubles on the north side of the Platte, they remained on that side of the river to make a route for those following. A group of 10-12 men worked daily to make a road for those following. Sometimes they burned old grass so companies behind would have new grass.

The first buffalo were killed for food May 1. Although the pioneers rejoiced to be in buffalo country, the huge beasts by their very numbers became a mixed blessing. While the beasts provided a ready source of fresh meat, their massive herds consumed the prairie grass and brought a constant threat of stampede. Finding grass for the stock became a constant problem.

Early in May, the pioneers' path was filled with buffalo. It appeared as if "the face of the earth was alive and moving like the waves of the sea," wrote Wilford Woodruff. The prairie was "literally black with buffalo," wrote William Clayton.

However, the men were forbidden to kill the massive bison except to provide meat for the camp. Rotting carcasses shot by other travelers created a stench in some places.

Wagons forded creeks and rivers, crossed sand dunes and jolted down bluffs. Spirits remained high, but occasionally cross words were spoken or behavior was deemed inappropriate. President Young occasionally lectured the group for such things as over-hunting and wasting meat, rowdiness, loudness, not keeping to their duties, rising late, or idleness. His lectures evidently had the desired effect because the group eventually became reformed and unified.

The pioneers reached Chimney Rock, Neb., the psychological if not actual halfway point on May 26. From then on the relentless monotony of the plains began to give way to bluffs and rock formations. On May 31 the pioneers entered what is now Wyoming, where the prairie became "naked" and some learned to enjoy eating prickly pears, a small cactus. Here they began to mount the eastern incline of the Rocky Mountain range, and the large buffalo herds disappeared behind them. The way was mostly up stream-carved canyons where they often crossed and re-crossed the same stream several times. After seven weeks on the trail, the company arrived at Fort Laramie, Wyo., where they were met by a group of 14 families, some of whom were not Mormons, who anticipated the westward trek by a year and wintered with the Mississippi Saints in Pueblo. In Pueblo, the Mississippi Saints were joined by some of the sick detachments of the Mormon Battalion. President Young sent Amasa Lyman and others to bring the group west as soon as possible. The size of the original group grew to 161 people and 15 tens.

The way became more mountainous, and wagons were rafted over streams, double-teamed to pull up steep inclines, and wheel-locked to slide down sharp hills. Camp meat changed from buffalo to blacktail deer. Geological anomalies were occasionally encountered, such as a petroleum spring, from which they greased their wagons, hot springs where they washed clothing and pure ice from a sulphur spring.

Pioneers forded the north fork of the Platte River and here joined the Oregon Trail and began to travel near Oregon pioneers. Among these companies were Missourians, some previously persecutors of the Church, with whom the Mormon pioneers had an uneasy but peaceful relationship. At Fort Laramie, Mormon pioneers learned that Lilburn Boggs, former governor of Missouri who had issued the infamous "Extermination Order," had been on the trail earlier. The Mormons fixed a wagon spring of the Missiourans, ferried them across the Platte River for a profit and even rescued one who was drowning. The Missourians occasionally assisted and fed members of the pioneer company. Thereafter relations improved a bit.

In the mountains the foresight of the pioneers was often rewarded. A boat, dubbed the "Revenue Cutter" was used as a wagon box on the plains. At streams, it was used as a ferry that carried up to 1,500-1,800 pounds. It was loaded with goods from wagon boxes so wagons crossed more easily. In addition, the boat was used to ferry Oregon immigrant companies, earning needed food and some cash. Small streams often were banked with ample grass for the livestock, although animals and humans were plagued by swarms of mosquitoes.

On June 26 the pioneers crossed the fabled South Pass, the slope that divided the East Coast drainage from the western drainage. Two days later, frontiersman Jim Bridger met the company and spent the night with them. Hoping for details, the pioneers were disappointed at the rambling accounts he offered. Another unexpected visitor met the company July 2 — Sam Brannan, captain of the ship Brooklyn, which had taken a company of Saints around the horn of South America and landed in Yerba Buena, now San Francisco. He had come from California and tried to persuade the pioneers to alter their plans and go to California instead of Salt Lake. But Brigham Young was unswayed and Brannan continued east. On July 4 soldiers from the Mormon Battalion sick detachment, traveling ahead of Amasa Lyman's Mississippi Saints, overtook the company. Three rousing cheers from the pioneer company welcomed the soldiers.

They reached Fort Bridger on July 7. During this time, "Mountain Fever" affected many in the camp. A number suffered from fever, delirium, flashes and muscle pain. When Brigham Young suffered the illness, it eventually slowed the entire company. The last leg of the journey was the most difficult. Leaving the Oregon Trail at Fort Bridger, they followed the Hastings Cutoff, a direct route to the Great Salt Lake. Traveling this route meant following the tracks of the

Donner Party wagons from the previous season, tracks barely discernible in the tall summer grass. Steep ridges and narrow openings in the mountains, compounded by large rocks and fallen trees, made the final part of the journey the most laborious.

The company halted three days when Brigham Young suffered from mountain fever in mid-July. On July 13, feeling an urgency to continue, Heber C. Kimball organized an advance guard 43 men in 23 wagons to blaze a trail to Salt Lake Valley and begin planting as soon as they arrived in the valley. A rear guard accompanied the Church president.

The advance company searched out the route down Echo Canyon in northeast Utah and spent time filling in ravines, removing tree stumps and making a road. Still the ride down the narrow canyon was hard on wagons that occasionally broke under the strain. The pioneers hacked out willows and criss-crossed mountain streams. They hauled over high ridges with disheartening views of seemingly endless ranges of mountains in all directions. They hacked their way through a tangle of willow, poplar and birch trees 20 feet high. But climbing what is now known as Big Mountain on July 21, some 12 miles above Salt Lake Valley, the landscape opened to a brief view of the valley below. To Orson Pratt, who climbed a hill to get a better look, the view was overwhelming.

"We could not refrain from a shout of joy which almost involuntarily escaped our lips," he wrote.

The pioneers' animals were near exhaustion that day as they labored upward of 10 hours without eating. Encouraged by the view, pioneers continued over Little Mountain, the last climb before the Salt Lake Valley.

They wisely cut a trail at the mouth of what is now Emigration Canyon to avoid climbing a steep mountain as the Donner Party had done a year earlier, costing it precious days.

All but the rear guard entered the valley by July 22, 1847. On July 23, the pioneers held a prayer of gratitude and began to plow, plant potatoes, corn, buckwheat and beans. They flooded the parched land with creek water.

It was Wilford Woodruff who recalled the immortal moment of Brigham Young's entry July 24. Elder Woodruff pulled his wagon to a halt to give the leader, who was still weak from mountain fever, a full view.

The ailing leader peered out over the broad valley that stretched out below. "It is enough," said Brigham Young. "This is the right place. Drive on."

THE DANIEL SPENCER COMPANY

The second company to leave on the westward trek was the 1st Hundred families. The hundred was made up of 151 wagons with about 360 men, women and children. Among the group were 63 men and boys with arms and ammunition. Of this 100 families, Peregrine Sessions was captain of the first Fifty, Ira Eldredge and Parley P. Pratt were captains of the second Fifty. The first and second fifties left the Elkhorn River June 17 and 18, 1847, respectively. Wagons were ferried across the Elkhorn River.

They learned that three men coming east had recently been attacked by Indians and one killed. Finding the remains of an Indian agent the same day led the pioneers to keep close watch on their stock. Wagons moved five abreast at first. But after a short time, the wagons resumed traveling in double file. A few Indians were seen from time to time, and a calf that lagged behind returned to the train with an arrow through its back.

The first fatality of this company occurred July 11 with the death of Ellen Holmes of the second fifty, who had been ill for six months.

Upon reaching buffalo country in Nebraska July 10, hunters killed several buffalo to provide meat for the wagon train. Buffalo created problems for the pioneers as the animals frightened the cattle into running away and mingling with buffalo. On July 22 and 23, about 100 Sioux Indians visited the wagon train and traded bread, meal and corn for buffalo robes and moccasins. The pioneers fired a cannon at their request.

Later oxen were purchased from the Indians. The company traveled without incident to Chimney Rock, Neb., which they reached July 29. On Aug. 4, they passed members of the Mormon Battalion returning toward Winter Quarters from the Salt Lake Valley, and arrived at Fort Laramie, Wyo. The day after, the train stopped to repair wagons while the women picked currants, made pies and hulled corn. Bears were seen but avoided.

On Aug. 16, Elder Ezra T. Benson, Orrin Porter Rockwell and John W. Binely had breakfast with the company as they returned east. They gave a good report of the valley. The company moved on past the Black Hills, now known as the Laramie Mountains, to the alkali area where some of the animals died, probably from drinking bad water or ingesting toxic earth while eating short grass. The company continued to find and obtain buffalo meat.

The temperatures grew colder as the company passed Independence Rock in Wyoming as it moved along Sweetwater River toward South Pass on the Continental Divide. On Aug. 27 The Spencer company heard from the Grant Company to the rear that their cattle were sick and dying. The Spencer company felt unable to give help. They labored forward, covering from 10 to 15 miles a day, crossing South Pass, and on Sept. 3 leaving the Oregon Trail and heading toward the Salt Lake Valley. Indians stole two horses but their owners followed after them and recovered both. They also met Brigham Young traveling from Salt Lake Valley with a group returning to Winter Quarters, and the Twelve held a council and rested.

Ann Agatha Walker Pratt, wife of Parley P. Pratt, wrote that while crossing quicksand near Fort Bridger, Wyo., a boy 15 months old, asleep in the wagon, awoke and found himself alone, looked out and fell between the wagon wheels. The rear wheel ran over the toddler's legs before the wagon could be stopped. But "owing to the soft sand and the great mercy of God, all the hurt was a red mark made by the iron tire across his limbs."

The weather turned cold and with rain, hailstorms and blustery winds. The company then proceeded to Green River, Wyo. When they reached Ham's Fork, the first and fifth Tens of Captain Eldredge's Fifty formed an advance party that led out, reaching the Great Salt Lake Valley Sept. 19.

On Sept. 18, Mary E. Frost gave birth to a baby girl named Catherine Frost.

After laboring down Echo and Emigration Canyons, the rest of the company arrived in the valley on Sept. 22, 1847. They immediately sent back teams of oxen to assist the company behind them.

Ann Agatha Walker Pratt, lagging behind the company, wrote of her last day's journey:

"It happened to be my turn to drive that day, Sept. 28, 1847. The reach of our wagon was broken and tied together after a fashion, and the way the front wheels wobbled about was a sight to behold. I kept expecting every minute to see the poor old concern draw apart and come to grief but it held together and when my eyes rested on the beautiful entrancing sight— the Valley — oh! how my heart swelled within me. I could have laughed and cried; such a comingling of emotions I cannot describe....

"When I drove into the Salt Lake Valley, unyoked my cattle and sat down on the wagon tongue and began to realize that in the morning I would not have to hitch up and toil through another day, such a feeling of rest — blessed rest — permeated my whole being that is was impossible to describe and cannot be realized except by those who have passed through similar scenes."

THE EDWARD HUNTER COMPANY

The 2nd Hundred wagons, the third company, were led by Captain Edward Hunter. The company started from the Elkhorn River June 17, 1847, and was comprised of 353 people in 131 wagons. Among them was Apostle John Taylor. The companies moved in fifties, under captains of Fifty Joseph Horn and Jacob Foutz. Those who could travel fastest moved out in front and had first choice of the feed for cattle.

The company rafted its wagons across the Elkhorn, hitching ropes to the raft and pulling it across with oxen. A few days later, Hunter's hundred reached the Loup Fork with its quicksand bottom. Their procedure to cross was to yoke six pair of oxen to each wagon and pull it through the river without stopping.

In the evenings, "we would gather in groups and sing the songs of Zion," wrote George Whitaker. "Sometimes we would have music and dancing and enjoyed ourselves the best we could."

"After arriving in buffalo country the company was camped close to the river one evening, when its members heard a sound like 'distant thunder.' We then knew what it was. A large herd of buffalo was crossing the river. We were frightened as they were opposite our camp. We were afraid they would run over our camp and stampede our cattle. . . .We all got down by the side of the river and shouted to try to turn them. They turned a little to one side of our camp and passed by without doing us any harm," wrote Whitaker.

About 10 days out, the train was stopped and the men repaired a bridge near an abandoned Pawnee village. Among those who helped on the project was Robert Gardner. As he worked, his son, Robert, about 5, "a thoughtful little chap" stepped down from the wagon to stand at the head of the oxen. He was kicked by an ox and fell beneath the wheel of the wagon and the oxen started up, pulling the heavy wagon over the boy's stomach. During the next months the boy grew thinner and thinner. His father, who was ill himself, held the boy in his arms much of the way. "He was hurt in the kidneys and suffered 50 deaths," wrote his father. "He lived until there was nothing left but skin and bones." The lad died Aug. 18,1847, and was buried in a shallow grave on the banks of the Platte River in Wyoming. The next year an uncle returned to retrieve his bones but wolves had scattered them.

Indians posed a constant threat but caused no serious trouble. At one time, a party of several hundred armed Indians stopped the company. Captain Horn took his wife, Mary Isabelle Horne and their baby girl, with him as he and John Taylor met the Indians before they reached the wagon train. Mary wrote in her reminiscences that one of the Indians took a fancy to her baby and offered pony after pony in trade. When the Indian went for the fourth pony, the wagon train caught up with them, to her great relief. A cannon was fired, which surprised and frightened the Indians, who were given food. Pioneers traded with them. Later the Indians danced for the pioneers.

The company reached Ft. Laramie in Wyoming and easily crossed the low Platte River to join the Oregon Trail. The company labored through what they called the Black Hills, now known as the Laramie Mountains, where they noted that meat was plentiful. They met another large party of Indians that left after being given food. Crossing an alkali desert after leaving the Platte River, a number of cattle died from poisoning. Game became very scarce.

So depleted were the oxen that when the company reached Independence Rock, Wyo., on Aug. 17, 1847, Elder Taylor wrote to Parley P. Pratt in a company ahead requesting a general council to provide extra oxen to the weaker companies to avoid a "perilous situation." He was mostly referring to the Grant company, following with the 3rd Hundred. This company had sent messengers requesting extra oxen to replace 40 oxen lost in a stampede.

Despite low supplies, on Sept. 7, while ascending the South Pass incline along the Sweetwater, the company stopped and held a feast. The feast, held in a light snowstorm, was in honor of Brigham Young and other of the original pioneers who were returning to Winter Quarters. Women of the company prepared roast beef, pies, cakes, and biscuits and afterward enjoyed the discourse of their leader.

The company labored down the west incline of the Continental Divide, but easily crossed the low Green River. When the company reached Fort Bridger, Robert Gardner's only remaining son, a baby of five months, was jostled off the wagon and fell beneath the same two wheels that had caused his brother's death, and was run over at the ankles. The baby was administered to and recovered in a few days.

Some of the pioneers sold items for "one-tenth of their value" to the trading post to buy flour and bacon.

The company proceeded "with a great many other difficulties [as] we made our way across the rivers, thru the rough canyons, and over mountains," wrote Robert Gardner.

Upon arriving in the Salt Lake Valley Oct. 1, he noted, "I unyoked my oxen and sat down on my broken wagon tongue, and I said I would not go another day's journey."

THE JEDEDIAH M. GRANT COMPANY

The fourth company, or the 3rd Hundred, was captained by Jedediah M. Grant, with Joseph B. Noble as captain of the 1st Fifty and Willard Snow as captain of the Second Fifty. The company was comprised of 331 people in 100 wagons.

Starting with great enthusiasm, this company passed the 2nd Hundred, but Elder Parley P. Pratt, captain of the 1st Hundred, reproved two captains for going out of line. The two asked for forgiveness and "all was made right."

At first, as this company left the Elkhorn June 19, 1847, wagons traveled five and six abreast for safety. The company made good progress until July 14 when in the evening at camp a boy on guard shook a buffalo robe to scare the cattle back from the wagon circle gate. The rattling skin panicked the animals which stampeded through the gate, overturning one wagon, breaking wheels and leaving broken oxhorns scattered on the ground.

Eliza R. Snow, who traveled in Captain Noble's Fifty, described the scene:

"The egress of the rushing multitude [of oxen] that thronged into the passage, piled one on top of another until the top ones were above the tops of the adjacent wagons, moving them from their stations while the inmates, at this early hour, being so unceremoniously aroused from their morning sleep, and not knowing the cause of this terrible uproar and confusion, were some of them almost paralyzed with fear. At length, those [oxen] that could, broke from the enclosure, the bellowing subsided and the quiet was restored."

At great effort, the loose oxen were recovered, but this was but a sample of worse to come. On July 17, the company suffered another stampede, one that put the entire company at risk. This time some 20 pair of oxen and another 15-22 head of cattle were lost and never recovered. The company laid over eight days searching for the lost animals. One ox made it back to Winter Quarters. Eventually the searchers gave up on the lost animals and put every cow and horse in yoke or harness in order to continue the journey. They also borrowed animals from other companies. Later, they bought additional oxen from Indians.

About a week later, on Aug. 1, the company arrived at Chimney Rock, Neb. On Aug. 4, a contingent of the Mormon Battalion going east, after being discharged in California, met the company. Among them were the husbands of several women in the company — "many female faces were lighted with unusual joy" wrote Eliza R. Snow.

She also wrote of sadness that day. "Death made its occasional inroads among us. Nursing the sick in tents and wagons was a laborious task, but the patient faithfulness with which it was performed was no doubt registered in the archives above, and an unfailing memento of brotherly and sisterly love. The burial of the dead by the wayside was a sad office. For husbands, wives, and children to consign the cherished remains of loved ones to a lone grave was enough to try the firmest heart strings. Today, a sister, Esther Ewing, who had passed away after a sickness of two weeks, was buried. The burial was attended with all the propriety that the circumstances would permit. After the customary dressing, the body was wrapped in a quilt and consigned to its narrow house. It truly seemed sad and we sorrowed deeply as we turned from the lonely grave."

Priddy Meeks, a pioneer physician, doctored the ill with local remedies such as rough elm bark, and he helped some recover. Some, he said, had diphtheria "in its worst form."

The company's progress through what they called the Black Hills (now called the Laramie Mountains) was "slow and tedious" with fewer oxen. Other companies moved farther ahead. As a result, the Grant company found less feed for its oxen and discovered the roads to be churned up and sandy.

The company ate buffalo and antelope meat to supplement their scanty supplies. However, this was not always a treat. Eliza R. Snow remarked on Aug. 23: "this morning Sister Pierce boil'd some buffalo meat which Capt. Josiah Miller killed yesterday, but it seem'd to have been the father of all buffalo and uneatable." She noted that she wrote, "A Song of the Desert" on the banks of the Platte River.

The company passed an alkali desert just beyond the Platte River, noticing the abundance of dead oxen along the trail. The 2nd Fifty was almost incapacitated from the loss of oxen as it crossed this area of poison water.

A baby of Jedediah and Caroline Grant, born the previous winter, died Sept. 2, and was buried in the alkali desert. Caroline Grant was seriously ill and never recovered. She died about three weeks later and her remains were carried to the valley for burial.

Capt. Grant was himself ill during much of the trip.

Another incident occurred while climbing the steep incline along the Sweetwater River leading to the Continental Divide on Sept. 9. The men triple teamed wagons to cross a swampy area and some boys rode by at a gallop. This startled the teams of horses and oxen into a runaway. Losses were averted during the harrowing experience. Later in the day, the company was visited by President Brigham Young's group traveling east. That evening the exhausted pioneers posted no guard. During the night, 40 horses and mules were stolen by Indians. Only five were recovered after searching up to 30 miles.

On Sept. 11, the company crossed the Continental Divide at South Pass and, over the next few days, moved along the Sandy River and to the Green River. About this location, the company broke up into tens to proceed with more flexibility, and continued down the steep canyons where the hundreds of other wagons before them had improved the road.

Eliza R. Snow on Oct. 1 described the descent through the canyons near the Great Salt Lake: "Today we traveled through brush and timber, but what was still worse, through black dust, with which we were all so densely covered that our identities might be questioned. When up the mountain we met Bro. John Taylor, who, having reached the Valley was returning to meet that portion of his company now in the rear. Riding on horseback, through the interminable dust, his face was covered with a black mask, and in his happy, jocular way, lest I should compliment him, he hastened to ask me if I had lately seen my own face! Our appearance was truly ludicrous. It mattered little to us as we went slash, mash, down the mount, over stumps, trees, ruts, etc., where no one dared ride who could walk."

On the last day of travel, the company crossed a stream 19 times. Here the valley became visible to Eliza R. Snow, "looking like a broad, rich river bottom."

The tens of the 3rd Hundred began arriving in Salt Lake City about the first week in October.

That winter, Priddy Meeks wrote that his family lived on wolf meat, flesh taken from the dead bodies of mired cattle, hawks and crows, sego lily roots and thistle roots. "I would dig until I grew weak and faint, then sit down and eat a root, and then begin again," he wrote. The next summer, as first the crops began to grow, the crickets blackened the ground in places. "My faith did not fail one partical but felt very solom[sic] on the occasion, our provisions beginning to give out," he wrote in his history.

Then he saw a flock of seven gulls, and in a few minutes, a larger flock followed. "They came faster and more of them until the heavens were darkened with them, and they would eat crickets and throw them up again and fill themselves again and right away throw them up again. A little before sundown they left for Salt Lake, for they roosted on a sandbar. A little after sunrise in the morning, they came back again and continued the course untill they had devoured the crickets, and then left, sure to die, and never returned."

ABRAHAM O. SMOOT COMPANY

The fifth company, called the 4th Hundred, under the leadership of Abraham O. Smoot, was divided into fifties under George B. Wallace and Samuel Russell. On June 19, 1847, the Wallace Fifty arrived at the Platte River camp where the first pioneer death from Indians was suffered. On that day, Jacob Weatherby, a teamster in the company, was dispatched back to Winter Quarters. He and Alfred Lambson were driving a team of oxen when three Pawnee Indians arose from the grass and halted the wagon. As Weatherby negotiated for the Indians to let them pass, one of the Indians shot him. He was taken to a tent of the Rich company of the 5th Hundred, where he died the next morning.

The 4th Hundred, with its 318 people, 500 animals and hundred wagons, roiled the prairie with dust as it moved. The heat and dust and fatigue were trying for the pioneers as they became accustomed to the rigors of the trail. Capt. Smoot helped soothe feelings as he instructed his company to be obedient and prayerful.

The company made good progress, although it had to take a 65-mile detour to cross the Loup Fork. At this quicksand-bottomed river, they drove their cattle across several times to compact the sand so it would bear the weight of the wagons. By hooking up four teams to each wagon, and being extremely careful, the company crossed the river with no accidents. Antelope were plentiful but water and firewood were scarce until July 3 when the company completed its detour. When the company reached Grand Island, Neb., a wooded area bounded by the Platte River, they paused to repair wagons. A few days later, the first buffalo were killed for meat and the food became a staple. However, members of the camp were told that "it was a disgrace to the people and displeasing to the Lord" to kill more than they could use.

On July 16, the company found a letter from Brigham Young's company left in a "chunk of wood" that raised spirits. The letter, left by the first company May 10, contained a short history of its travels.

On July 23, the camp enjoyed entertainment as 300 of the pioneers in best dress traveled throughout the camp, singing and dancing to the tune of a fife, violin and two drums. Pioneers cheered and a cannon was fired. The next day the train reached Chimney Rock, Neb., prickly pear (a small cactus) country and the near end of the prairie. That evening, Capt. Smoot exhorted the pioneers to be obedient to their officers. He told the officers to be kind to those "out of the way" unless that was not sufficient, and then to command them.

The pioneers traded with Sioux Indians and on the July 27, delivered a large batch of bread to the chief, who was "much pleased," wrote Joseph C. Kingsbury, company clerk.

As they traveled on the north side of the Platte River, this group could see on the south side of the Platte eastbound travelers returning from the Oregon Territory. They learned from these travelers as much as they could about conditions ahead. The company arrived at Fort Laramie, Wyo., on Aug. 5 and remained there for five days repairing wagons and preparing for the rest of the journey. They built kilns to cook tar from pine roots to lubricate their wagon wheels. One pioneer woman, Louisa Decker, helped to earn her passage by driving a team of horses as far as Fort Laramie. There the horses were stolen, so she drove a yoke of oxen the rest of the way, walking next to them. She milked cows at night, made mush for lunch and put milk in a churn that, through its jolting in the wagon, made butter for the next meal.

Over the next weeks, the wagons labored over the steep Laramie Mountains. When Wallace's Fifty attempted to travel on Sunday, Aug. 15, to catch up with the Russell Fifty, a "hurricane" arose that stopped the company and blew the top off one wagon. Despite the delay, the Fifty caught up with the rest of their Hundred. That evening they met Eric Glines, one of the first company who had arrived from Salt Lake Valley. He reported that a city had been laid out and fields planted. This news greatly cheered the pioneers. Elders Ezra T. Benson and John Taylor visited two days later, also cheering the company.

On Aug. 23, as the company crossed the Platte River at Mormon Ferry, Capt. John Nebeker of the fourth Ten of the Wallace Fifty had an accident. His son was bounced from the wagon and run over. The heavy wheels crushed his hip. He was given a blessing and lived.

During the trek over an alkali desert, a number of oxen died. However, other cattle were used to replace them in pulling wagons. When the company reached the Sweetwater River, Captain Wallace distributed the cattle and oxen according to need, and sent one yoke of oxen back to help Grant's company.

Laboring up the slope to the Continental Divide, the company found good roads. After it reached the first water on the west side of the Divide, called Pacific Springs because it was the first water flowing west, they met Brigham Young and a group returning to Winter Quarters. Because eight of the 12 apostles were there, a meeting was held and leaders were chosen for the Salt Lake Stake. The journey downhill from there was easier at first and in a few days they had crossed Green River, Ham's Fork, and Black's Fork, some 107 miles in a week. They reached Fort Bridger, Wyo., Sept. 15.

The pioneers labored to get to Echo Canyon where they crossed a stream several times until reaching the Weber River. On the way, a wagon "upset on a sidling place and broke the top" dumping its goods down a mountain. The pioneers battled brush and steep mountains, up Big Mountain and down Little Mountain to Emigration Canyon. Those with stronger teams continued on while some camped early and others fell behind.

At the mouth of Emigration Canyon, the pioneers shouted for joy and fired guns as the saw their new home and the infant city in the distance. They arrived in Salt Lake City on Sept. 25, 1847.

THE CHARLES C. RICH COMPANY

The Charles C. Rich Company brought up the rear guard, the smallest of the companies of 1847. His company included just three Tens, a total of 126 people in some 25 wagons. This company brought with them a cannon (later picking up the cannon left behind by the Hunter company as well), artillery and ammunition 25 kegs of black powder, the Nauvoo Temple bell, and a boat. This company included the last of the wagons from Winter Quarters.

On June 19, while camped on the Elkhorn river two days before they started, Jacob Weatherby was carried mortally wounded to the tent of Charles C. Rich. Weatherby, of the Smoot 4th Hundred, had been shot by Indians. Sarah DeArmon Pea Rich wrote of the incident:

"We fixed him a bed and did all we could to ease his pain. He suffered awful pain through the night and the next morning about nine o'clock his suffering ended in death." The young man was buried near the Elkhorn River Camp's Liberty Pole on June 20.

Later the same day, the cannon and

ammunition were ferried across the Elkhorn River. At sunrise on June 21, Capt. Rich's company fired the six-pounder cannon and the wagons started about 9 a.m., following the 1st Hundred.

As they left the campground on Fishing Slough on June 25, a near-tragedy occurred. Capt. Rich wrote: "While hitching my team one ox became unyoked, was frightened and tried to leap over the skiff [boat]. He partly fell on my son Joseph and hurt him considerably and came nigh killing him."

On June 28, Capt. Rich's company let the 2nd Hundred go in front of them. During the day, the company received word from the front company that a large hunting party of Indians was "lurking about," so the guard company fired the cannon twice but noted that night, "all things safe."

Capt. Rich's guard company reached the Loup Fork of the Platte River the next day. But because there were so many wagons ahead, the company waited until the last ones crossed the river before it crossed. On July 2, they found the "Sow" cannon carried by Capt. Hunter's 2nd Hundred abandoned on the trail with its carriage broken and tongue gone. The cannon's traveling gear was repaired the next day and the cannon brought along. A broken wagon axle further delayed the company, but by July 9 the company overtook the 1st and 2nd Hundreds. Upon arriving in buffalo country, Capt. Rich killed three large bulls for camp meat. Sarah Rich wrote: "It was very dangerous traveling through this country, but we were preserved from serious accident. It was a grand sight to see those herds of wild animals, thousands in a group, racing across the prairies. The fear was that they might attack us in their flight."

The company arrived at Chimney Rock, Neb., on Aug. 1, and reached Fort Laramie, Wyo., on Aug. 5. Here, some horses were traded for oxen and cows. The weather was hot and the women were "very sunburned" as their wagons rocked and swayed over sand, rocks and hills through clouds of dust.

Mary Rich who, with another woman, drove a wagon, wrote: "We did so well that we had our teams [ready for travel at the appointed hour] every day after that until we arrived in the Valley, as regularly as the men did. We did not grieve or mourn over it, we had some very nice times when the roads were not so bad. We would make the mountains ring with our songs, and sometimes the company would get together and we would have a dance in the evening on the grass. We did not mourn but we rejoiced that we were going to the Rocky Mountains where we would be free to practice our religion. . . ."

During the next week the guard company traveled through what they called the Black Hills, now known as the Laramie Mountains, with steep slopes and shortage of water. The "worst hill on the road" was passed safely Aug. 13 and the company had to dig in a dry stream bed for water. The following day the pioneers burned coal to repair iron wagon tires.

The company reached the Upper Ferry of the Platte River on Aug. 21. The teams were very weak and an occasional ox died as the company crossed the alkali encrusted area. On Aug. 26, four oxen died, so Capt. Rich left behind the two boats and a wagon, stripping the wagon first of its iron parts. Two days later the company was overtaken by John Taylor, in the 3rd Hundred that had fallen behind, on a quest for extra oxen. Capt. Rich gave him one yoke of oxen.

On an alkali desert, the company cut large cakes of bicarbonate of soda from Saleratus Lake, which later helped in making bread in the Salt Lake Valley. The company reached the Sweetwater River and the incline leading to South Pass, the Continental Divide, on Aug. 31. On Sept. 2, they met a small company returning from the Valley to Winter Quarters. The cool of the winter was now on them at the 7,000-foot-high mountain pass. The company noted cold winds and rain and later snow. On Sept. 6, at Pacific Springs on the west side of the Continental Divide, Capt. Rich's company and other companies halted for a meeting attended by eight of the Twelve Apostles. At this meeting, Capt. Rich was called as a counselor in the Salt Lake Stake presidency. He would be ordained to the Twelve the following winter.

On the west side of the mountains, grass and water were plentiful and the teams grew stronger. The company traveled slower for a few days following the birth of a baby. At the Big Sandy, the company lost another ox, but made steady progress to Fort Bridger, arriving Sept. 16. As the company traveled down steep, brush-choked canyons that lay beyond, wagons began to break. An axle was broken Sept. 24 going down Echo Canyon, another in East Canyon and another a day later. The repair time slowed the entire company. Crossing Big Mountain on Sept. 30, Capt. Cherry of the 1st Ten upset a wagon. The company became spread out as it traveled over the rough way.

Capt. Rich's mother, Nancy O'Neal Rich, became seriously ill. After passing Little Mountain, the company came together again and traveled down into the valley together. They reached the city Oct. 2.

On Oct. 5, Mother Rich died and was buried beside the wife of Jedediah Grant, who had died on Big Mountain a few days earlier.

BIOGRAPHIES OF THE ORIGINAL 1847 PIONEER COMPANY

Editor's note: The following are biographies of the 143 men, 3 women and 2 children comprising the first pioneer company that left the Elkhorn River April 7, 1847. They were organized into hundreds, fifties and tens. Along the way, the group's size changed several times and not all those who started completed the journey because of various changes in duties. However, Church historians have determined that the credit for blazing the trail should go equally to all who began. Drawings courtesy of the Daughters of the Utah Pioneers.

Adams, Barnabas L. — (2nd Ten) Born Aug. 28, 1812, near Perth, Upper Canada, of Vermont parentage and was converted to the Church at age 23. He came to Missouri with the "Canada Camp" under Elder John E. Page. In 1846, he married Julia Ann Bawker. Adams was selected for the original company and became a night guard over the animals. Once hired to float logs down the Mississippi River from Iowa to St. Louis, Mo., he used his experience during river fordings. After crossing the plains with Brigham Young's company in 1847, he immediately returned to Winter Quarters for his family. He brought his family to the Salt Lake Valley in 1848 and settled in the mouth of Little Cottonwood Canyon. Adams furnished lumber for the Salt Lake Tabernacle, the Salt Lake Theater, and other public buildings. In 1869, he injured himself internally while lifting the bed of a wagon and died June 2, 1869, at age 56, leaving a large family.

Allen, Rufus — (8th Ten) Born March 22, 1814, in Litchfield Co., Conn., to Gideon and Rachel Hand Allen. He joined the Church at an early age and was in Carroll Co., Mo., when a mob of 150 armed men attacked the Mormon settlement. In 1846, he was chosen to be part of the original pioneer company and was assigned to be a camp guard. Allen helped establish the new settlement in the Salt Lake Valley before returning to Winter Quarters. He later settled in Ogden, Weber Co., Utah. On Oct. 8, 1851, he accompanied Parley P. Pratt on a missionary journey to Valparaiso, Chile. Their attempt was unsuccessful and they returned May 21, 1852, to San Francisco. He was called as a senior president of the 53rd and 54th Quorums of Seventies in 1857. He died in Ogden, Utah, on Dec. 4, 1887, at age 73.

Angell, Truman Osborn — (3rd Ten) Born June 5, 1810, to James and Phebe Morton Angell at North Providence, R.I. He and his wife, Polly Johnson, joined the Church in January 1833. He helped build the Kirtland and Nauvoo temples. After crossing the plains with the original company, Angell returned the same year to get his family. When he brought them the following year, he built a small cabin and began working as a carpenter. He built the Beehive and Lion houses, and he traveled to England to learn how to build a sugar factory in Sugar House, and to study architecture. He was the architect, although not the designer, of the Salt Lake Temple. He devoted 37 years almost exclusively to the construction of the temple in Salt Lake City. He also supervised the work on the Salt Lake Tabernacle and the St. George Temple. He died Oct. 16, 1887, at age 77.

Atwood, Millen — (4th Ten) Born May 24, 1817, to Daniel and Polly Sawyer Atwood at Wellington, Tolland Co., Conn. He became interested in the Church and traveled to Nauvoo, Ill., in 1841. There, he was baptized and soon left on a mission, traveling to Illinois, Wisconsin, New York and Connecticut. A stone mason, he did considerable work on the Nauvoo Temple. After traveling to the Great Basin with Brigham Young's company, he returned to Winter Quarters that fall. He returned to Nauvoo early in 1848. He married Relief Cram. He also returned to Navuoo and recovered his temple construction tools. Atwood took part in defending against Indians, and in about 1851 was assigned to the police force in Salt Lake City. He later served a mission in Scotland and England. He returned to America with a large company of converts on the ship *Thornton* in 1856, and was a member of Capt. James T. Willie's handcart company. Atwood served on the Salt Lake Stake high council from 1873-81. He then was called

as bishop of the Thirteenth Ward, a position he held until his death in Dec. 17, 1890, in Salt Lake City at age 73.

Badger, Rodney — (14th Ten) Born Feb. 4, 1823, at Waterford, Caledonia Co., Vt., to Rodney and Lydia Chamberlain Badger. His family accepted the gospel about 1838, the year his father died. At age 15, Rodney Jr. assumed responsibility for his family and moved them, including his invalid mother, to Nauvoo, where she died. He married Nancy Garr on March 9, 1845. In 1847, he joined the first company, and his attributes as woodsman, scout and swimmer were utilized. He was among five from the original company, who, when they reached Green River in Wyoming, volunteered to return east to help guide the companies that were behind them. He joined his wife in a company at the Sweetwater River, and came with them into Salt Lake Valley on Oct. 2. He was sustained in the bishopric of the Fifteenth Ward, served in the Nauvoo Legion in defending the city and settlers against Indian attacks, and was sheriff of Great Salt Lake County. On April 29, 1853, he was assisting an emigrant company in fording the swollen Weber River when one wagon carrying a mother and six children floated off its bed. He immediately plunged into the river to help rescue them and was lost in the swirling waters. Badger was 30 at the time of his death. On April 29, 1996, the Salt Lake County Sheriff's Office posthumously recognized him as the first of their office to die in the line of duty.

Baird, Robert Erwing — (9th Ten) Born May 15, 1817, in Londonderry, Ireland, to James and Elizabeth Erwing Baird. He married Hannah McCullough in 1840. After arriving in the Salt Lake Valley, he settled in Weber Co. where he was justice of the peace and Ogden City councilman. Serving as one of the school trustees in the 5th school district of Ogden that was organized in 1860, he helped erect a log schoolhouse. He was also a member of the 33rd Quorum of Seventies and was presiding elder of the Lynne District, just north of Ogden. He died in Ogden on Aug. 24, 1875, at age 58.

Barney, Lewis — (12th Ten) Born Sept. 8, 1808, at Hollen Purchase, Niagara Co., N.Y., to Charles and Mercy Yeoman Barney. Lewis and his father moved to Ohio and then to Illinois. He took part in an Indian war after which Iowa opened up for settlements. Lewis and his

father each secured title to 2,000 acres of land in Iowa, where he heard of the persecutions of the Saints. Although he was not personally disposed toward any religion, a pair of traveling missionaries taught him and his family and others in the community. After traveling to Nauvoo to meet Joseph Smith, he was baptized in the spring of 1840, and confirmed by the Prophet. He helped in the building of the Nauvoo Temple, and later moved his family to the Nauvoo area. A neighbor took his farm and mobs burned his home. In Winter Quarters, during the winter of 1846-47, he hauled provisions from Missouri to the exiles. He crossed the plains with the original company and distinguished himself as one of their best hunters. In 1852, he brought his family west and established a lumber business in Provo. He later moved to Spanish Fork, then to Spring City, Sanpete Co., and then to Monroe. He settled for a time in Grass Valley in Sevier Co. and in Arizona. He died in Mancos, Colo., on Nov. 5, 1894, at age 86.

Barnum, Charles D. — (8th Ten) Born near Brockville, Leeds Co., Canada, May 9, 1800. He was baptized by John E. Page July 25, 1836, and ordained a teacher in September, in an area in Canada where Oliver Cowdery had proselyted. Barnum moved to Indiana two years later, and then to Far West, Mo., where he helped move some of the  persecuted Saints to Quincy, Ill. He moved to Nauvoo, but his family refused to join him. He quarried stone for the Nauvoo Temple and served in the Nauvoo Legion. Three years later his family moved to Nauvoo. When he evacuated the city, his family again refused to accompany him. He traveled alone to Winter Quarters where he remarried. After being part of the original company of 1847, he returned to Winter Quarters. In 1850, he traveled to the Salt Lake Valley in William Snow's company, and settled in the Fifteenth Ward. He served as a counselor to Bishop Andrew Cunningham from 1851-53. He died in Salt Lake City on Sept. 9, 1894, at age 94.

Benson, Ezra Taft — (Captain of 2nd Ten) Born Feb. 22, 1811, in Mendon, Worcester Co., Mass., to John and Chloe Taft Benson. He and his wife, Pamela Andrus, traveled westward to Illinois where they settled in Quincy. They encountered great debates about the

Mormons, and he heard Elders Orson Hyde and John E. Page preach on their way to dedicate Jerusalem. Benson and his wife were baptized July 19, 1840. A short time later he was ordained an elder, and then a high priest by Hyrum

Smith. The family moved to Nauvoo, Ill., in 1841. He served in the Eastern States Mission from 1842-43. He was called to the Nauvoo High Council in 1844, and after further missionary activity in the east in 1845, helped with the Nauvoo Temple and took part in the exodus of 1846. That winter, while in Mt. Pisgah, Iowa, he received notification from Brigham Young that he had been called to the Quorum of the Twelve, replacing John E. Page. He was part of the pioneer company into the valley. He decided to return east and help guide oncoming companies into the Salt Lake Valley. He then returned to Winter Quarters and ended the eventful year by beginning another mission to the East. He returned to the Salt Lake Valley in 1849 with George A. Smith. In 1856, he presided over the mission in Europe. In 1860 he was appointed to preside in Cache Valley. He left only once more, in 1864, to travel to the Sandwich Islands (Hawaii) to clear up problems after an apostate had usurped Church leadership and property. He served in many elective and political offices and died Sept. 3, 1869, in Ogden, Utah, at age 58.

Billings, George Pierce — (9th Ten) Born in Kirtland, Ohio, on July 25, 1827, to Titus and Diantha Morley Billings. His father was the second person to be baptized in Kirtland, Ohio, and later served as second counselor to the Church's first Presiding Bishop. George worked on Mississippi River boats and helped his father, a stonemason

and carpenter, build the temples in Kirtland and Nauvoo. He joined the pioneer company at age 20. He drove a wagon across the plains for his cousin, Heber C. Kimball. By the time Billings arrived in the Valley, his shoes and shirt were gone and his buckskin pants had stretched, been trimmed and shrank. Elder Kimball's wife made him a new shirt of a striped straw tick, and a pair of moccasins. Upon seeing him in his scant outfit, Heber C. Kimball felt to prophesy that soon "clothing can be bought here as cheap as in New York City." This prophecy was literally fulfilled with the arrival of California pioneers and gold seekers. Billings later went to California in search of gold. He found gold, went to Mexico and bought livestock and was bringing it to Utah when all of his stock became diseased and died. He returned poorer than he left, just as Brigham Young said would happen to those who left in search of gold. He helped settle Carson Valley, Nev. After the arrival of Johnston's army in 1858, and the abandonment of the outlying settlements, he moved to Manti, Sanpete Co, Utah. There he helped build the temple. He died in Manti on Dec. 2, 1896, at age 69.

Boggs, Francis — (8th Ten) Born May 17, 1807, in Belmont Co., Ohio, to Alexander and Hannah Martin Boggs. He was baptized by missionaries who came to his home May 17, 1841. He married Evalina Martin in 1842 and the family moved to Nauvoo where his carpentry skills were used helping to build the city. His family left Nauvoo in the exodus of 1846 and traveled to Winter Quarters. There, he was chosen to go west with the first group. His family followed, arriving in September 1847. They lived in the Salt Lake Eighth Ward, then moved to Springville in 1850, and later to Fillmore and Parowan, all in Utah. He was sent on a mission to mine lead and farm in Las Vegas, Nev. In 1861, he took his family to Washington, in Washington Co., Utah. He filled positions in various communities and served one term in the Utah legislature. He died in Washington, Utah, on Jan. 22, 1889, at age 81.

Brown, George Washington — (2nd Ten) Born Jan. 25, 1827, at Newbury, Cuyahoga Co., Ohio, to Nathaniel and Avis Hill Brown. As a child, he accompanied his father, a frontiers-man, into the West. After the death of his father in 1837, his mother returned east and settled in Chautauqua Co.,

N.Y., where she joined the Church. Brown was baptized in Sugar Creek, Iowa, and became a bodyguard of Joseph Smith. After making the journey to the Salt Lake Valley, he returned to Council Bluffs. In 1848 he went to Missouri and farmed for two years. In 1850, he returned to the Valley bringing his mother, brother, and sister with him. He married Elizabeth Amy Hancock in 1852. She died in 1862. He then married Emma Barrows. He lived in many locations in Wallsburg and Charleston, Wasatch Co., Utah, where he farmed for the rest of his life. He was ordained a high priest in 1877. He died at age 79 on Dec. 19, 1906, in Charleston.

Brown, John — (Captain of 13th Ten) Born Oct. 23, 1820, in Sumner Co., Tenn., to John and Martha Chipman Brown. Baptized by George P. Dykes in July 1841 in Perry Co. Ill., he moved to Nauvoo the following October. He served a mission in Alabama, Tennessee and Mississippi, and baptized a large number of converts. He married Elizabeth Crosby in Monroe Co., Mississippi, and became one of the leaders of the Mississippi Saints that were prominent in early Church history. He returned to Nauvoo in 1845 with others responding to a call for volunteers to help defend the city and to complete the temple. A few months later he brought his wife to Nauvoo. They stayed until January 1846. With the exodus from Nauvoo imminent, they left for Mississippi again. Because of increasing local hostility in Mississippi, they gathered a group of 60 Saints and headed west, expecting to intercept the vanguard company of Saints on the trail. Instead, they learned that the Saints had laid over a year. So Brown left his family in log cabins in Pueblo, Colo., and went to Winter Quarters where he joined the pioneer company. He was one of the advance company who first viewed the Salt Lake Valley. His family came west in 1848 and settled in the Cottonwood area. He later served as a missionary and helped explore southern Utah. He was mayor of Pleasant Grove, Utah, for 20 years and bishop of the Pleasant Grove Ward for 29 years. He died Nov. 4, 1897, at age 77 in Pleasant Grove.

Brown, Nathaniel Thomas — (10th Ten) On the way west, he associated with Porter Rockwell in hunting and in searching after lost animals. He returned to Winter Quarters in the fall of 1847. After returning to Winter Quarters, he was accidentally shot at Council Bluffs, Iowa, in February 1848, just as he was preparing to return to the Salt Lake Valley. Distressed by the accident, Brigham Young was said to have remarked, "Brown's old shoes were worth more than the whole body of the man who killed him."

Bullock, Thomas — (2nd Ten) A son of Thomas and Mary Hall Bullock, he was born Dec. 23, 1816, in Leek, Staffordshire, England. He was baptized by missionaries in the same city on Nov. 20, 1841, and emigrated on the sailing ship *Yorkshire*

and was in charge of a company of Saints. After arriving in Nauvoo, he served as clerk to Joseph Smith until the Prophet's martyrdom. He crossed the plains in 1847, then returned to Winter Quarters to get his family, whom he brought to the Salt Lake Valley the following year. He served as recorder for Salt Lake County, chief clerk of the House of Representatives and of the Church Historian's office. He was one of four men chosen to publish the first edition of the Deseret News. In 1868, he moved to Wanship, Summit Co., where he was probate court clerk and county recorder. He died in Coalville, Summit Co., Feb. 10, 1855, at age 38.

Burke, Charles Allen — (14th Ten) Born Sept. 2, 1823, at Kirtland, Ohio, to John M. and Abigail Fellows Burke. The family moved to Missouri after Abigail died in 1833. Charles joined the Church and moved to Nauvoo, Ill., where he helped construct the temple. During the exodus of the Saints from Nauvoo to Winter

Quarters, he made coffins and assisted in the burial of those who did not survive the trek. He was among the advance party that reached the valley July 22, 1847. He returned to Winter Quarters that fall and brought his relatives west the following year. An only sister died on the plains of cholera. Back in the valley, he worked for a Crosby family of the Mississippi Saints in the Cottonwood area, where he met and married Lydia Tanner on Sept. 25, 1850. He and his wife went to San Bernardino, Calif., in 1851 and remained there until being called back in 1857 to defend against Johnston's army. He then settled in Parowan, Iron Co., where he worked as a carpenter. He helped make one of the first gristmills in the area, as well as household items and coffins. He died Feb. 26, 1888, in Minersville, Beaver Co., Utah, at age 64.

Burnham, Jacob D. — (1st Ten) Born Oct. 1, 1820, in New York to Richard and Elizabeth Burnham. He was baptized Nov. 13, 1844. He received a patriarchal blessing by John Smith in Nauvoo in 1846. Although he was one of the original pioneers, he remained in the valley just a short time. He traveled to California, where records show that he paid tithing

May 21, 1850. He died later that year at Greenwood Valley while mining for gold at about age 30.

Carrington, Albert — (2nd Ten) Born Jan. 8, 1813, in Royalton, Windsor Co., Vt., to Daniel and Isabella Bowman Carrington. He grad-uated from Dartmouth College in 1833, and taught school and studied law in Penn-sylvania. He married Rhoda Maria Woods Dec. 6, 1838, He was involved in lead mining when he joined the Church in

Wiota, Wis., in July 1841. Three years later he went to Nauvoo, took part in the exodus. Shortly after his arrival in the Salt Lake Valley, he was chosen as surveyor to accompany Captain Howard Stansbury of the U.S. Topographical unit in exploring the Great Salt Lake. He also headed a committee to draft a constitution for the state of Deseret, and was editor of the Deseret News from 1854-59 and from 1863-67. He was secretary to Brigham Young for 20 years, presided over the European Mission three times. He was ordained an apostle in 1870, and was a counselor to Brigham Young. He died in Salt Lake City on Sept. 19, 1889, at age 76.

Carter, William — (7th Ten) Born Feb. 12, 1821, in Ledbury, England, to Thomas and Sarah Parker Carter. He learned glass blowing and blacksmithing as a youth. Working at a blacksmith shop, he heard the singing and preaching of Mormon missionaries, and was baptized on Dec. 27, 1840. He traveled to Nauvoo, Ill., in 1841

and assisted in the building of the Nauvoo Temple. He married Elizabeth Benbow on Dec. 5, 1843. He is credited by Wilford Woodruff with being the first to plow the land near City Creek, and the first to turn water from the stream to flood the land. He served in the bishopric of the Fourteenth Ward for a time, and in 1858 sold his horse to answer a call to serve a mission in Quebec, Canada. He used the proceeds from the horse sale to buy a handcart with which he traveled the continent eastward. He served in Quebec only briefly, being recalled because of the crisis precipitated by Johnston's army. He later settled in the St. George, Utah, area and reared a large family. He died there June 22, 1896, at age 74.

Case, James — (Captain of the 7th Ten) Born May 4, 1794, at Litchfield, Conn., to Joseph and Lydia Case. He worked at an outpost near Plum Creek, Neb., in 1845 or 1846 as a $300-a-year government farmer. When he was baptized, his Army commander refused to give him his final paycheck. When the pioneers came to this now-abandoned station while crossing the plains, Brigham Young allowed Case to take the equivalency of pay in abandoned iron, such as a stove, plows and iron bars. He was required to send a letter of explanation to his former employers, however. He later served as a missionary in the Indian Territory of Oklahoma. He arrived for service in St. Louis Nov. 10, 1855, and "all [missionaries] suffered from want of clothing and proper food, as the Indians among whom they labored were very poor." Elder Case was called to preside over the Creek Nation, and organized the Princess Branch. This branch struggled from lack of local leadership. The handful of missionaries in this mission were ill, and a few died while serving in this mission. Perhaps the effects of this illness claimed Case, as he died in Sanpete Co., Utah, in 1858, soon after returning from his mission.

Chamberlain, Solomon — (11th Ten) Born July 30, 1788, in Old Canaan, Conn., to Joel and Sarah Dean Chamberlain. He married Hopee Haskins, and learned the cooper's trade. He was baptized a few days after the Church was organized in 1830, and moved to Kirtland, Ohio, that spring, and to Jackson County, Mo., in 1831. After being driving from Missouri, his family settled in Nauvoo, "where we remained in peace for several years; but about the year 1846, we were broken up and had to flee to the Rocky Mountains." At age 59, he was the oldest of the first company of pioneers. He had mountain fever, and suffered from cholera and was near death on his original journey west. Chamberlain returned to Winter Quarters with his rations being just two quarts of parched corn and three quarts of coarse corn meal. His wife died in 1848 just as he was about to embark on the return trip to the valley. In 1850, he left for the gold fields in California, but felt impressed to return the same year. He crossed the California mountains with no weapon but a pocket knife. He died in Washington, Washington Co., Utah, on March 20, 1862, at age 74.

Chesley, Alexander Philip — (14th Ten) Born in Bowling Green, Faquier Co., Va., on Oct. 22, 1814, to John and Elizabeth Brisker Chesley. An orphan at age 3, he was reared by an uncle until 12, then by other relatives in Kentucky. He was encouraged by Henry Clay Sr. (the father of the famous legislator) to study law, which he did. He later moved to Wayne County, Ill., where he practiced law, and married Elizabeth Haws. She became a staunch convert, and after a time, he was also baptized. He joined the pioneer company and gained the reputation of being a daring Indian fighter. A member of the advance party, he entered the Salt Lake Valley on July 22, 1847. He returned to Winter Quarters for his family and brought them back to the valley in 1851. On this return trip, he guided John Taylor's wagon train carrying equipment for a sugar factory. He settled in Provo, Utah, where he taught school and was a lawyer. In 1856 he was called on a mission to Australia, from whence he never returned. He died Aug. 9, 1884, in Orange, Australia, at age 69.

Clayton, William — (9th Ten) Born July 17, 1814, at Penwortham, Lancashire, England, to Thomas and Ann Critchlow Clayton. He and his wife, Ruth Moon Clayton, heard the gospel from Elders Heber C. Kimball and Orson Hyde. She readily accepted the message, but he studied intensely before his baptism.
They left England in September 1840 and arrived in Nauvoo, Ill., in November. He was appointed secretary to Joseph Smith on Feb. 10, 1842, and later treasurer of the city of Nauvoo. While crossing the muddy fields of Iowa near what is now Corydon, he wrote the famous hymn "Come, Come, Ye Saints" which has since become well-known around the world. As scribe and historian of the pioneer journey, he recorded many of the events of the historic trek. Along the way he built a "roadometer" to count the revolutions of a wagon wheel to thus record distances. He was called on a mission to England in 1852. Upon returning to the Salt Lake Valley following his mission, he became treasurer of Zion's Cooperative Mercantile Institution; served many years as territorial recorder of marks and brands and as territorial auditor of public accounts. He died Dec. 4, 1879, at age 65 in Salt Lake City, Utah.

Cloward, Thomas Poulson — (9th Ten) Born in Chester Co., Pa., on Dec. 10, 1823, to Jacob and Anne Pluck Cloward. He was apprenticed to a shoemaker at age 15, with whom he remained for five years. He joined the Church about this time and moved to Nauvoo. He married Mary Page in 1847. After crossing the plains, he made the first pair of shoes in the Salt Lake Valley. He took an old pair of boot tops and made shoes for Ellen Kimball, Heber C. Kimball's wife. He returned to Winter Quarters with Brigham Young. He settled for two years on the east side of the Missouri River until
1852, when he brought his family west. He lived in Provo and then moved to Payson where he started a shoemaker's shop. He later helped in construction of the Salem canal. He died Jan. 16, 1909, at age 85 in Payson, Utah.

Coltrin, Zebedee — (5th Ten) Born Sept. 7, 1804, at Ovid, Seneca Co., N.Y., to John Jr. and Sarah Coltrin. He joined the Church soon after it was organized. He married Julia Ann Jennings. After she died, he married Mary Mott. After crossing with the first company, he returned for his family. However, because of lack of
sufficient funds, they did not come to the Salt Lake Valley until 1851. He settled in Spanish Fork, Utah Co., Utah, and during the Indian conflicts, moved his family into a fort there. He helped survey the city site, helped build bridges, make roads and erect schools and meetinghouses. He was described as "one of the oldest members of the Church and was identified with many of the earliest incidents in the days of Kirtland. He was closely associated with the Prophet Joseph and has often testified of having been a witness of and participant in many marvelous spiritual manifestations." He served as one of the first Seven Presidents of the Seventy until it was learned that he had earlier been ordained a high priest. He died July 21, 1887, at age 82 in Spanish Fork, Utah.

Craig, James — (6th Ten) Born in Ireland in 1821 to David and Elizabeth Craig. Known as the "Bugler of the Pioneers," he had the responsibility to awaken the camp each morning. After arriving in the Salt Lake Valley, he settled in the Millcreek area where he was appointed to a committee to eradicate poisonous reptiles and predatory animals. He was called on a mission to Great Britain where he served as president of the Preston Conference, and later labored in Ireland. He returned from his mission in 1858. In 1861, he was called to help colonize southern Utah. He settled in Santa Clara, Washington Co., Utah, where he was successful in raising cotton. He died there March 2, 1868, at about age 47.

Crosby, Oscar — (13th Ten) Born about 1815, to Vilate Crosby, an African descendant. She was a slave of William Crosby, one of the Mississippi converts. Oscar Crosby was baptized at Mormon Springs in Monroe Co., Mississippi, probably before 1845, where many other Mississippi converts were baptized. During the trip from Mississippi to Nauvoo, the company he was with encountered severe snow and ice, and two of the slaves died. He was sent ahead to assist the pioneer company. After the company's arrival in the valley, Oscar Crosby helped prepare a place for the Crosby family who were to follow. When the family arrived, they were reportedly welcomed by Crosby, a cabin, patches of potatoes, beans, buckwheat, and turnips. In 1851, he and a number of Mississippi converts helped settle San Bernardino, Calif., where they helped to establish a freight route to Los Angeles. Crosby became free in California, and his former master helped him settle. Oscar Crosby died in Los Angeles, Calif., in 1870 at age 55.

Curtis, Lyman — (13th Ten) Born Jan. 21, 1812, in New Salem, Mass., to Nahum and Millicent Waite Curtis. He was baptized March 14, 1833, and the following year married Charlotte Alvord. He and his father and brothers helped build the Kirtland Temple. In 1834, he became part of Zion's Camp, and later endured perse-  cution in Missouri and Illinois. A hunter on the Pioneer trek, he became part of the advance company that entered the valley July 22, 1847. It is said he built a large fire of sagebrush that evening that was visible to the others who were still in the canyon. He returned to Winter Quarters that fall, traveling with six pounds of flour and one horse between him and Levi Jackman, his traveling companion. He started back west in 1850 and en route, on the Nebraska plains, his wife gave birth to their ninth child. They arrived in October and lived in an adobe home the first year. The following year the family moved to Santa Clara, Utah, where he was charged to build a canal from the Little Muddy River near Moapa, Nev. After completing this task, he helped build a canal from the Santa Clara River to below St. George.

He served a five-year mission among the Indians and returned to what was called Pond Town, near Spanish Fork, Utah. Later, many people settled in the area, and they eventually changed the name of Pond Town to Salem, Curtis' home town in Massachusetts in his honor. He died in Salem, Utah Co., Utah, Aug. 5, 1898, at age 86.

Cushing, Hosea — (9th Ten) Born April 2, 1826, in Boston, Mass., to Phillip and Mary Cushing. He apprenticed to a carpenter at age 16 and stayed two years until hearing the missionaries preach. He was baptized February 1844 in Boston and soon began serving a mission. He traveled to Nauvoo, arriving April 8, 1845, where he worked on the Nauvoo Temple. He joined the exodus Feb. 15, 1846. In the spring of 1848, he and his bride, Helen Janet Murray, came to the Salt Lake Valley. He built a small cabin a block north of the temple grounds. He was called to take part in the 1853 Walker Indian War. During a skirmish, he and another man, whose name was Ging, were lost in the desert for three days without food or water. When Cushing was found, he was suffering badly, and never fully recovered. He died May 17, 1854, at age 28 in Salt Lake City.

Davenport, James — (11th Ten) Born May 1, 1802, at Danville, Caledonia Co., Vt., to Squire and Susanne Kitridge Davenport. He learned blacksmith- ing and after his marriage to Almira Phelps on Sept. 4, 1823, set up a shop and farmed as well. They joined the Church shortly after it  was organized in 1830. In 1845, they were residents of Nauvoo. He worked as a blacksmith in the first company. He was among nine men left to operate the upper ferry of the Platte River on June 18, 1847. This group was instructed to ferry the companies across, charge those who could pay. He traveled on to the Salt Lake Valley and then returned to Winter Quarters for his family. It was almost three years before they could afford to come back to the Salt Lake Valley. When he returned, he stayed a short time in Salt Lake City then moved to Grantsville, Tooele Co., Utah. He traveled across the plains twice more to help bring wagon trains of converts. He later moved to Wellsville, and finally Richmond, in Cache Co., Utah, where he died July 23, 1885, at age 83.

Decker, Isaac Perry — (3rd Ten) One of two children in the first company, he was born Aug. 7, 1840, in Winchester, Scott Co., Ill., to Isaac and Harriet Page Wheeler Decker. His mother and father divorced in March 1843, and she later married Lorenzo Dow Young, changing her name to Harriet Decker Young. His father remained a  faithful member and came to Salt Lake City in a later company, where he died in 1873. After arriving, Isaac and his mother lived in the Old Fort until Lorenzo built a cabin near the Eagle Gate in Salt Lake City. The boy saw the struggles of the members during the exodus, the trek west, the meager first years including the miracle of the gulls, and the growth of Salt Lake City. In mid-life he made his home in Provo, Utah, where his son, C.F. Decker, was mayor for a time. He died Jan. 24, 1916, among the last of the original pioneer company, at age 75.

Dewey, Benjamin Franklin — (7th Ten) Born May 5, 1829, in Westfield, Hamden Co., Mass., to Ashbell and Harriet Adams Dewey. His parents joined the Church and he was baptized when he came of age, probably in 1837. The family moved to Nauvoo in the spring of 1846. His father died at Winter Quarters. He was selected for the  original company and during the trek, became so ill with mountain fever that he and two others were left behind July 20, 1846, at East Canyon above the Salt Lake Valley. Shortly after arriving in the Salt Lake Valley, he left for the California gold fields. Two years later he came back to the Salt Lake Valley and was called to fill a mission to India. The missionaries departed Jan. 26, 1853, and arrived in Calcutta 86 days later. He traveled to Hindustan, Siam and parts of China, but was not successful. He was called in 1855 to settle in San Bernardino, Calif., where he married Alzia Smithson, also an early pioneer. They later separated and he returned to Salt Lake City, where he assisted in building the Salt Lake Tabernacle and temple. He moved to Arizona in 1885 and mined. He died Feb. 23, 1904, in Chloride, near Kingman, Ariz., at age 74.

Dixon, John — (5th Ten) Born July 26, 1818, in Cumberland, England, to Joseph and Sarah Dixon. After reaching the Salt Lake Valley, he helped in the erection of the fort and building the settlement. He was called in 1850 to accompany George Q. Morris and other missionaries to the Sandwich (Hawaiian) Islands. He returned after a short time, however. On Aug. 17, 1853, he and three others were hauling wood to Snyder's mill near Parley's Park in Salt Lake City, and a group of Indians fired on them. He and John Quayle were killed. He was 35 years old.

Driggs, Starling Graves — (2nd Ten) Born Feb. 12, 1822, in Pennsylvania to Uriel and Hannah Ford Driggs. He joined the Church in Ohio and went with his family to Nauvoo. His father died in Lee County, Iowa. The Driggses stayed near Kanesville, Iowa, in the Thomas Camp. He joined the first company and  lived in the home of Apostle Amasa Lyman for two years in Salt Lake City and here learned that his mother had died. He was called as a member of an exploring group that traveled to southern Utah with Parley P. Pratt to locate settlement sites. He later traveled to southern California and helped settle San Bernardino, where he farmed and participated in freighting. While freighting, he met Sarah Rogers, whom he married in 1855. When the San Bernardino settlers were recalled in 1857, Driggs and his family settled in Parowan, Utah. While operating a primitive threshing machine on his farm, he suffered an accident that led to his death Dec. 3, 1860, at age 38.

Dykes, William — (4th Ten) Born Nov. 18, 1815, in Philadelphia, Philadelphia, Co., Pa., to Daniel and Cynthia Dykes. He joined the Church and became a member of the 31st Quorum of Seventies in Nauvoo. He was designated a hunter in the first company. Soon after arriving in the Salt Lake Valley, Dykes returned to Winter Quarters. He applied to establish a post office on the Pottawattamie lands in Iowa in 1848. He was a member of the 31st Quorum of Seventies in Salt Lake City in 1856. However, he returned to the east in later years and died in Nebraska Nov. 24, 1879, at age 64.

Earl, Sylvester H. — (5th Ten) Born Aug. 15, 1815, to Joseph and Dorcas Wixom Earl in Ohio. He was baptized in Feburary 1837. After his baptism, he began performing missionary labors in surrounding states until 1842 when he and his family moved to Hancock Co., Ill., in a village called Morley's Settlement, near Nauvoo. On the trip west, he was a member of the gun crew that hauled a

cannon and held occasional drills. On his return trip to Winter Quarters, Earl described having 17 horses stolen, but he was able to purchase 16 from Indians. "While detained there, we became destitute of food and I, in the company of Horace Thornton, went to a small band of Indians and sold the shirt off my back for some meat. I then took my wagon cover and cut and made me another."He returned to Utah with his family, and in the fall of 1851, moved to the Nineteenth Ward. The following year, he began a two-year mission in England. In 1861, he moved to Pine Valley at the head of the Santa Clara River where he purchased a share in a sawmill. He died July 23, 1873, at age 57 in Middleton, Washington Co., Utah.

Eastman, Ozro French — (7th Ten) Born Nov. 18, 1828, in Windham Co., Vt., to James and Clarissa Goss Eastman. His parents were baptized in 1843, and he became a member of the first company but was never baptized. He was loyal to Brigham Young, Heber C. Kimball and other leaders of the Church. His father secured a

wagon and team for him and received permission for Ozro to accompany the first company. After crossing the plains in 1847, he returned with Brigham Young's company to Winter Quarters that fall. It is said he established the first harness shop in Salt Lake City. He married Mary E. Whittle on Feb. 22, 1857, and they became parents of 10 children. In 1884 he moved to Eagle Rock, later Idaho Falls, Idaho, where he continued as a harness maker. He died in Idaho Falls, Idaho, March 26, 1916, at age 87.

Egan, Howard — (Captain of the 9th Ten) Born June 15, 1815, in Tullamore, King Co., Ireland, to Howard and Ann Meade Egan. He married Tamson Parsley at age 23 in about 1838. A sailor, he immigrated to America and received his naturalization papers in 1841 and the following year was baptized at Salem, Mass., where he was working as a ropemaker. He traveled to Nauvoo, Ill., where he was appointed a major in the Nauvoo Legion and became a member of the Nauvoo police force. During the trek

west, Egan served as road scout and explorer. His journal records many of the day-to-day events of the trip. In the winter of 1849-50, he traveled to California to buy livestock and supplies. In 1860 he became a Pony Express rider and agent, and later served as a member of the Salt Lake police force and as deputy sheriff. He was a guard at the home of Brigham Young. When Brigham Young died, Egan was called on to guard his grave in Salt Lake City. In doing so, he contracted pneumonia and died March 16, 1878, at age 62.

Egbert, Joseph Teasdale — (1st Ten) Born in Vincennes, Ind., March 10, 1818, to John and Susan Hahn Egbert. The family joined the Church and eventually moved to Nauvoo. On Dec. 6, 1840, he married Caroline Allred. Selected to accompany the original pioneer company, Egbert was appointed to drive Orson Pratt's wagon

and to cook. On the trail, he once found several buffalo, and shot two. However, the other animals circled and Egbert crawled away to avoid being attacked. He returned exhausted to camp and others recovered the game. He joined the advance party that entered the valley July 22, 1847. He returned to Winter Quarters that fall and brought his family to the Great Basin. One child died while crossing the plains. He later settled in Kaysville, Davis Co., Utah, building a large home and planting some of the first fruit orchards. He was roads supervisor of the district for 35 years and constable of the town for two years. He died March 24, 1898, in Ogden, Weber Co., Utah at age 80.

Eldredge, John Sutherland — (8th Ten) Born April 30, 1831, in Canaan, Columbia Co., N.Y., to Alanson and Esther Sutherland Eldredge. He served as a teamster on the original company, crossing the plains at age 16. He is said to have been one of the first men to plow in the valley after the arrival of the pioneers. He also promoted pioneer industries.

Eldredge was called on a mission to Australia in 1852, and returned on the ill-fated ship *Julia Ann*. On board were 26 LDS immigrants and two missionaries. On Oct. 4, 1855, the ship wrecked on a coral reef and two women and three children drowned. The  others made their way on a hastily constructed raft to the Scilly Isles, 12 miles distant. They lived there nearly two months, subsisting on small shell fish and sea turtles. The group was rescued when the ship's captain traveled more than 200 miles in an open boat and returned for them in a vessel. Eldredge returned to the Salt Lake Valley in 1856. He took up farming and moved to Charleston, Wasatch Co., Utah. He died while plowing on May 7, 1873, at age 42.

Ellsworth, Edmund — (4th Ten) Born July 1, 1819, in Paris, Oneida Co., N. Y., to Jonathan and Sarah Gully Ellsworth. He was baptized Feb. 20, 1840, and three years later was ordained a seventy. He married Brigham Young's daughter Elizabeth Young. He was appointed a foot hunter, and was among 10 appointed to remain at  the upper crossing of the Platte River, near Casper, Wyo. When his family arrived at the ferry, he accompanied them to the Salt Lake Valley, where they arrived Oct. 12. He filled a mission to England in 1854-56 and on his return home, took charge of the first handcart company to cross the plains. This company left Iowa June 9, 1856, and arrived in the Salt Lake Valley Sept. 26 after considerable hardship. He was later elected alderman in Salt Lake City. In 1880, he moved his family to Arizona. He died at Show Low, Ariz., Dec. 29, 1893, at age 74.

Empey, William A. — (5th Ten) Born July 4, 1808, in Osnabrook Township, Stormont Co., in eastern Canada. He joined the Church in Canada and later gathered to Nauvoo where he was ordained a seventy in the 13th Quorum. On the trek west, while hunting May 3, 1847, he attempted to turn a drove of antelope toward hunters when he looked down a ravine and saw a hunting party of 200-300 Indians. He and others hurried back to warn the main company, and called in the other hunters. However, no problems came of the encounter. He was among those selected to remain at the upper ferry on the Platte River in Wyoming. He re-mained there helping pioneer companies and those of the Oregon Trail cross the river until Brigham Young's party returned from the Salt Lake Valley in the fall. He  went with them to Winter Quarters and brought his family to the Salt Lake Valley in 1848. He became a member of the Fifteenth Ward bishopric. From 1852 until 1854, he served a mission in England and for a time presided over the Hull Conference. When he returned to the Salt Lake Valley, he was called to settle in southern Utah. He died in St. George, Washington Co., Utah on Aug. 19, 1890, at age 82.

Ensign, Horace Datus — (7th Ten) Born May 8, 1826, at Westfield, Hampden Co., Mass., to Horace Datus and Mary Brunson Ensign. His parents joined the Church in 1843. The senior Ensign died in September 1846 in Winter Quarters. Datus, the oldest son, was baptized Dec. 6, 1846, at Winter Quarters. He was a carpenter and mechanic, and served as night guard. After arriving in the Salt Lake Valley, he started back to Winter Quarters but met his family in the Daniel Spencer company. He continued with this company to the valley, arriving Sept. 22, 1847. He was assigned to assist in repairing the Goodyear Fort in Ogden, Weber Co., Utah. In 1850, he married Eliza Jane Stewart. He participated in the so-called Echo Canyon War, delaying Johnston's army in 1856-57 from entering the Salt Lake Valley. Ensign later settled just south of the Goodyear Fort on the Weber River. Because of the river's overflow, he had to rebuild and eventually located on what became a city park. When that happened, he was given another parcel of property, where he built another home and lived there until his death, in Ogden on Sept. 1, 1866, at age 40.

Everett, Addison — (Captain of 1st Fifty; in 3rd Ten) Born Oct. 10, 1805, in Wallkill, Orange Co., N.Y., to Ephraim and Deborah Carwin Everett. He was a ship's carpenter, introduced to the gospel by Parley P. Pratt in 1837. He was called as a counselor in the branch presidency in New York April 15, 1842. He gathered with the Saints in 1844 to Nauvoo, where he was involved with events related to the martyrdom of the Prophet Joseph Smith. After arriving in the Salt Lake Valley, he returned with Brig-ham Young for Winter Quarters. On the way he met his wife,

Orpha Maria Redfield, and family near the Sweet-water River in Wyo-ming and re-turned with them to the Salt Lake Valley. He helped build Fort Supply, near Fort Bridger in Wyoming, and was called as bishop of the Eighth Ward and in 1861 was  called to the Dixie Mission. He helped build the St. George Temple and did considerable temple work after it was completed. He died in St. George, Washington Co., Utah, on Jan. 12, 1885, at age 79.

Fairbanks, Nathaniel — (10th Ten) Born at Queensbury, Washington Co., N. Y., on May 10, 1823, to Joseph and Polly White Fairbanks. He comp-leted a two-year app-renticeship as a stone-cutter before he was baptized Aug. 28, 1843. He moved to Nauvoo, in 1844. On the trek west when the comp-any stopped at a bluff near Chimney Rock,  Neb., Fairbanks was bitten by a rattlesnake. He soon began to feel extreme pain and his leg was bound in tobacco leaves and turpentine. He was given a blessing and suffered a great deal but eventually recovered. After reaching the Salt Lake Valley, he returned part way to Winter Quarters, but met his brother Jonathan en route with the Daniel Spencer company, and so he returned with them to the Salt Lake Valley. In 1853, he was driving a herd of cattle from Salt Lake to Sacramento, Calif., when he was thrown from a mule and drowned while crossing a river near Sacramento, at about age 30.

Farr, Aaron Freeman — (10th Ten) Born in Waterford, Caledona Co., Vt., on Oct. 31, 1818, to Winslow and Olive Hovey Freeman Farr. He and his younger brother Lorin were baptized in 1832 after listening to the pre-aching of Orson Pratt and Lyman John-son. He moved to Kirtland, Ohio, in 1838, and later to Nauvoo. He married  Persis Atherton Jan. 16, 1844, in the Mansion House in Nauvoo, a ceremony performed by Joseph Smith. After arriving in Salt Lake Valley, he was among a group selected to return and guide subsequent companies. Farr guided Daniel Spencer's Hundred, where his wife, with their baby in the wagon, had driven a double team of oxen from Winter Quarters. "We were in the lead of the immigration from there until we camped at some fine springs where Salt Lake City now stands," he later recalled. An attorney, he helped establish the city government after he and his family arrived in the Salt Lake Valley. In 1852-53, he served a mission to the West Indies and presided over the St. Louis Branch while returning from the West Indies. He later settled in Ogden, Utah, and practiced law and was a U.S. deputy marshal. He served a second mission to Las Vegas, Nev., then to Arizona. In 1859 he was elected probate judge of Weber Co., and also served as alderman of Ogden and as representative to the Territorial Legislature from Weber County. He died Nov. 8, 1903, at Logan, Cache Co., Utah, at age 85.

Fitzgerald, Perry — (11th Ten) Born Dec. 22, 1814, at Fayette Co., Pa., to John and Leah Phillips Fitzgerald. He was reared in Illinois where he married Mary Ann Cazot. He was bapt-ized in 1842 and moved to Nauvoo, Ill. After arriving in the valley, he returned to Winter Quarters. Fitz-gerald started across  the plains a second time with Brigham Young on May 26, 1848. He moved to Draper, Salt Lake Co., Utah, where he built a permanent home, and was among the first five families in what was then South Willow Creek. His wife, Mary Ann, died in 1851, and he later married Ann Wilson. He took part in the Walker War and assisted in building various forts. He also farmed. During his lifetime, he earned a reputation for his scrupulous honesty. He died Oct. 4, 1889, at Draper, Utah, at age 74.

Flake, Green — (14th Ten) Born in January 1828 in Anson Co., N. C., a slave of African descent on the plantation of William Jordan Flake. At age 20, he was given as a gift to James Madison Flake. He was baptized in the Mississippi River near Nauvoo by John Brown. He had traveled with the Flake family to Nauvoo, but evidently returned to his plantation before the exodus. He was sent from there with a carriage and a team of white mules to Winter Quarters and instructed to go west with the original company. He was selected to be part of the advance company that entered the valley July 22,

1847. His carriage, however, is believed to be the one that carried an ill Brigham Young into the valley. The carriage was returned to Winter Quarters that fall, but he remained and built a cabin in the Cottonwood area and planted crops for the Flake family. In 1848, he married Martha Ann Crosby, a slave of John Brown and Elizabeth Crosby Brown, newly arrived in the Cottonwood area. He remained in the area as a devout Latter-day Saint for many years. He moved to Idaho Falls, Idaho, in 1888, and lived there until his death on Oct. 20, 1903, at age 75.

Fowler, John Sherman — (1st Ten) Born July 12, 1819, in New York City, N.Y., and later baptized. He lived in Nauvoo, where he received a patriarchal blessing from Ashael Smith in February 1846 and became a member of the 2nd Quorum of Seventies. On the trek west, after leaving Fort Bridger, he caught mountain fever and was delirious for a time. He made his home in the fort in Salt Lake City, but after a few years left Salt Lake Valley and moved to San Bernardino, Calif. He died April 12, 1860, in Sacramento, Calif., at age 41.

Fox, Samuel Bradford — (4th Ten) Born Dec. 4, 1829, at Adams, Jefferson Co., N. Y., possibly to Samuel and Lucy Williams Fox. He was a teamster for Brigham Young. Three years after his arrival in the Salt Lake Valley, he went to California. There, he suffered a severe attack of smallpox and his face was disfigured. He is reported to have said that his friends should never see him in that condition, and never returned to Salt Lake City. In 1870 he moved to Oregon.

Freeman, John Monroe — (1st Ten) Born Nov. 20, 1823, in Chatham, Middlesex Co., Conn. to Israel and Deborah Freeman. He was baptized Nov. 13, 1839. In Nauvoo, Ill., he was a member of the 31st Quorum of Seventies. Three years after his arrival in the Salt Lake Valley, he went to Carson Valley, Nev., where it is said he died of cholera in 1850 at age 27.

Frink, Horace Monroe — (7th Ten) Born May 31, 1832, in Livingston Co., N.Y., to Jefferson and Emily Lathrop Frink. The family lived for a time in Nauvoo. He was chosen as a driver in the original company at age 15. After arriving in the Salt Lake Valley, he traveled in the fall of 1847 to Hangtown, Calif., where he was at Sutter's Mill when gold was discovered. He returned to Missouri on horseback and from there outfitted a wagon and brought his maternal grandmother, a sister and two half-brothers to Salt Lake Valley. They helped settle San Bernardino, California. Later, with his brother, he purchased a large tract of land in San Timoteo Valley in Calif. He married Polly Ann DeWitt on Feb. 27, 1857, and they remained in San Bernardino when the other members returned to Utah. He became one of the original orange growers in the area. He died in San Bernardino Aug. 15, 1874, at age 42.

Frost, Burr — (7th Ten) Born March 4, 1816, at Waterbury, Conn., to Alpheus and Elizabeth Frost. A blacksmith, he welded broken iron wagon parts while on the trek west. Paid for his work in flour, bacon and other provisions, he often set up his forge on the trail and welded for other wagon trains as well. He is mentioned frequently in pioneer journals for his repairs. He set up a blacksmith shop in Salt Lake City soon after arriving. He was involved in the Iron Mission of 1849-50 and made the first nails from iron ore in the area while living in Parowan, Utah. He served a mission to Australia in 1852-54. Upon returning, he brought a group of 72 Saints from Adelaide. He later became one of the presidents of the 70th Quorum of Seventy. He died in Salt Lake City Mar. 16, 1878, at age 62.

Gibbons, Andrew S. — (12th Ten) Born March 12, 1825, in Union, Licking Co., Ohio, to William Davidson and Polly Hoover Gibbons. Orphaned at an early age, he was reared by a relative of Joseph Smith. He accepted the gospel and eventually moved to Nauvoo, where he married Rispah Knight. As a member of the original pioneer company, he was chosen assistant cook. While crossing the Platte River, he jumped into the river to help steady a wagon that rolled over in midstream. He swam safely to the other side. A few days after the upper crossing of the Platte, he went out hunting and was missing for two days. He had killed a buffalo but missed the wagon train, so gave the meat to a Missouri company and stayed with them until he caught up. After reaching Salt Lake Valley, he returned east with Brigham Young. He crossed the plains westward again in 1852 and settled in Davis Co., Utah, where he farmed and planted orchards. He was called in 1854 to settle in Iron Co. In 1858, he joined an expedition to the Indians under Jacob Hamblin. In 1864, he was called to settle St. Thomas, then part of Arizona, an area now covered by Lake Mead, Nev. He was a representative of Piute Co. in the Arizona Legislature. He helped settle St. Johns, Ariz., in 1880 and planted the first orchards there. He was a high councilor in the Eastern Arizona Stake at the time of his death in St. Johns on Feb. 9, 1886, at age 60.

Gleason, John Streater — (14th Ten) Born Jan. 13, 1819, in Livonia, Livingston Co., N.Y., to Ezekiel and Polly Howard Gleason. He married Desdemona Chase while working for her father, Isaac Chase. He heard the gospel preached and was baptized June 21, 1839, and immediately served a mission in the Eastern States and  Canada, where he remained until 1841. He moved his family and Isaac Chase's family to Nauvoo, Ill., interrupting his work to serve as a missionary again in the Eastern States until 1844. At Emigration Canyon, just before entering Salt Lake Valley, he advocated clearing the brush at the mouth of the canyon and making a permanent road for following immigrants. He returned to Winter Quarters that fall and came west the following year. The family settled in Little Cottonwood and then moved to Salt Lake City where he operated a sawmill for Isaac Chase at the site of the present Liberty Park. In 1852, he moved to Tooele, Utah, and became a county commissioner. He later moved to Davis Co., Utah, and in 1857 went to Florence, Neb., with a handcart company." He was a major in the First Regiment of Militia, and later served as justice of the peace of Davis County. He served a mission in the Eastern States in 1869-70. In 1873, he traded a mine he owned, called the "Mountain Lion" in the Ophir District, for a farm in Pleasant Grove, Utah Co., Utah, where he stayed until his death Dec. 21, 1904, at age 85.

Glines, Eric — (7th Ten) Born Oct. 5, 1822, in New Hampshire to John and Maria Glines. He was reared in Churchville, Ontario, Canada, where his family stayed until 1839. He was appointed to be one of the foot hunters. He didn't follow Brigham Young's instructions when he chose to remain behind with a group at the North Platte River ferry. Later he changed his mind and followed the company, camping one night alone and then with a company of Missourians. He was among four men sent back to guide the rearward companies and pilot them across the Green River in Wyoming. After reaching Salt Lake Valley, he went to California where he pioneered in Sacramento Valley and reared a large family. He was known as a daring scout and made several trips across the continent before the railroad was built. He died in Santa Rosa, Calif., on May 4, 1881, at age 58.

Goddard, Stephen H. — (Captain of the 5th Ten) Born Aug. 23, 1810, in Clinton Co., N.Y., to Stephen G. and Sylvia Smith Goddard. Ordained a seventy June 9, 1845, he became senior member of the 27th Quorum of Seventy. On the trek west, Goddard, described as the handsomest of the pioneer company, was on the cannon crew.  He had an excellent singing voice and led the singing around the campfire. Upon arriving in the valley, he eventually became the first conductor of the choir that met in the old tabernacle. He lived at Main Street and First South until 1897 when he moved to Fruitdale, Alemeda Co., Calif., probably for his health, and died a year later. He died June 9, 1898, at San Bernardino, Calif., at age 87.

Grant, David — (8th Ten) Born July 21, 1816, in Arbroath, Scotland, to Robert and Belle Mills Grant. Apprenticed to a tailor, he became a tailor at age 19 and moved to Edinburgh. He immigrated to America in 1839, stopping first in Kentucky and then moving to Illinois. There, he was baptized. He moved to Nauvoo, about 1840 and practiced his trade as tailor. He married Mary Ann Hyde in 1843. However, his wife died in the hardships of the exodus and was buried in Winter Quarters. Selected for the original company, he helped keep clothing in repair. He was part of the advance company that entered the valley July 22, 1847. He returned east for his two children and brought them west the following year. He married Beulah Chipman Sept. 24, 1848. She died three years later. On March 8, 1852, he married Mary Hunsaker. He did considerable tailoring work for the early pioneers, including Brigham Young, and was ordinarily paid in some kind of merchandise. He was called on a mission in 1852 and traveled to England. He returned April 18, 1856, on the ship *Samuel Curling* as counselor to Dan Jones with a large company of converts. He crossed the plains as assistant to Captain

Edward Bunker in a handcart company. In 1862 he was called to help raise cotton in southern Utah. He returned to his home in Mill Creek, Salt Lake Co., Utah, where he died Dec. 22, 1868, at age 52.

Grant, George R. — (4th Ten) Born July 14, 1820, in New York. He is noted as one who captured a young eagle on the way west. He returned to Winter Quarters that fall and was one of the signers of a petition to the government requesting permission to establish a post office on Pottawattamie lands. He returned west, it is believed, with Brigham Young in 1848 and established a home in Kaysville, Davis Co., Utah, in 1852. He was among a group sent to establish the Salmon River Mission in Idaho in 1855. They preached to the Flathead, Bannock and Shoshone Indians and attempted to teach them farming and how to build houses. The mission was successful for two years but in winter of 1857-58 the mission was closed when other whites influenced the Indians to be hostile to the missionaries. He moved to Carson City, Nev., where he attempted to establish a shipping business. He died July 22, 1889, in California, at age 69.

Greene, John Young — (3rd Ten) Born Sept. 2, 1826, in New York to John P. and Rhoda Young Greene. His father was the minister to whom a Book of Mormon was given by Samuel H. Smith on the first missionary journey in 1830. This book eventually found its way to Brigham Young, an uncle of John. John joined the Church at a  young age. He was assigned to drive Brigham Young's team in the first company. Greene was called to serve a mission in Europe in 1857 and was assigned to Denmark. At the advance of Johnston's army in 1858, he was recalled to Utah, completing a successful mission. After a life of faithful service, he died at his home in Salt Lake City on May 24, 1880, at age 53.

Grover, Thomas — (2nd Ten) Born July 22, 1807, in Whitehall, N.Y., to Thomas and Polly Spaulding Grover. When he was 12 years of age, he worked as a cabin boy on an Erie Canal boat and later became captain of the boat. In 1828, he married Caroline Whiting and a few years later moved to Freedom, N.Y., where he heard the gospel preached and was baptized in 1834. He moved to Kirtland, Ohio, and helped build the temple and supported Joseph Smith financially. He helped rescue

the Prophet after a kidnapping. He served three missions from 1840-44 to Michigan, New York and southern Canada. In June 1844 he was impressed in a dream to return to Nauvoo, and arrived at Carthage, Ill., in time to escort the bodies of slain Joseph and Hyrum to Nauvoo. As a member of the first company of pioneers, he was assigned to be captain of a ferry constructed at the North Platte River crossing in Wyoming. For their labors helping an Oregon-bound company across the river, they received 20 days worth of food. He eventually entered the Salt Lake Valley in Charles C. Rich's company. His family later moved to Centerville, Davis Co., and then to Farmington, also in Davis Co. He was sent with a group of 30 men in the fall of 1848 to California to buy cattle and settle some Church debts, which he did. He also stopped in the gold fields with the group and turned over to the Church about $20,000 in gold dust. He later traveled to Iowa and brought 150 head of cattle to the Salt Lake Valley, with the help of his family. He served three terms in the Utah legislature and was probate judge of Davis Co. He served as a missionary to the Eastern States in 1874-75. He died Feb. 20, 1886, in Farmington at age 78.

Hancock, Joseph — (12th Ten) Born March 18, 1800, at Springfield, Mass., to Thomas and Amy Ward Hancock. He married Betsey Johnson and they were baptized in Mayfield, Ohio, in 1830. She died a few months after her baptism. After her death he moved to Kirtland, Ohio, where he worked as a brickmaker. He joined  Zion's Camp in 1834 and, as a successful hunter, was dubbed "Nimrod" by Joseph Smith, a nickname that stayed with him. He came down with cholera on the trip to Missouri, but was healed by the Prophet. He hauled rock for the Kirtland Temple and later moved to Missouri, where he experienced persecutions, then to Nauvoo. He was assigned to be one of the foot hunters on the trek west. Near the end of the trek, he climbed a hill, where he caught a view of the valley. After the company arrived in the valley, he helped explore for timber. He was given property near the temple site, but after returning to Winter Quarters that fall with Brigham Young, was unable to return for two years because of sickness and poverty. He was instead given land near Provo, Utah. Of a wandering nature, he traveled to California in 1852 and then to the east but returned 10 years later to stay three years in the Salt Lake Valley. He traveled to Council Bluffs, Iowa, in 1867 to visit his children. He returned to Utah in 1882. He died in Payson, Utah, on July 4, 1893, at age 93.

Hanks, Sidney Alvarus — (4th Ten) Born Aug. 17, 1820, at Madison, Lake Co., Ohio, to Benjamin and Martha Knowlton Hanks. He likely associated with the Church in Nauvoo, as did his brother Ephraim K. Hanks. He was a scout in the original company. In 1852 he was called on a mission to the Society Islands. About this time the French officials expelled the missionaries. However, Elder Hanks labored in the Tuamotu Islands, including Takaroa and Takapoto, away from contact with the main island. He remained there for 10-12 years, at least until after 1860. An 1857 letter from him indicated he was on an island of 1,100 inhabitants and 70 members. While in the islands, he was destitute of provisions or clothing, and had "almost turned native entirely." He returned to Utah where in 1862, he married Mary Ann Cook. They lived in Snyderville, near Parley's Park. In March 1870 he set out to look for a lost cow and froze to death, at age 49. His body was recovered a month later.

Hansen, Hans Christian — (13th Ten) Born Nov. 23, 1806, in Copenhagen, Denmark, to Ole Peter and Martha Margarete Osmundsen Hansen. He went to sea as a boy and occasionally visited America. The only man of Scand-inavian ancestry on the orig-inal company, he was converted to the Church while stopping over in Boston, Mass.  He was baptized in the summer of 1842. He was an accomplished violinist and often played at the campfire. On one occasion when the men danced to his music, "it was not so much for pleasure but mostly as a means of getting warm in the frigid weather." He was among the advance company to enter the Salt Lake Valley. He was a popular musician in the settlement. He later moved to Salina, Sevier Co., and filled a mission to his native land in 1862-63, earning his passage as a sailor. He never married. He died at Salina, Utah, Oct. 10, 1890, at age 83.

Harmon, Appleton Milo — (Captain of the 10th Ten) Born May 29, 1820, at Conneaut, Pa., to Jesse P. and Anna Barnes Harmon. He served a mission in 1843, and was later part of the police force of Nauvoo, He married Elmeda Stringham. A mech-anic, he was assigned to drive a team for Heber C. Kimball. He construc-ted a "road-ometer" that was designed by William  Clayton and used to measure dis-tance. The device was attached to a wagon and measured the revolutions of a wagon wheel. Harmon was among those asked to remain at the ferry at North Platte, Wyo., where he learned the craft of black-smithing. He remained at the ferry until the company returned from the Salt Lake Valley in the fall. He worked at Fort Laramie as a blacksmith until March 1848, when he returned to Winter Quarters. He returned to the Salt Lake Valley that year with his family. In 1850-53, he filled a mission to England. He later helped build sawmills in Salt Lake, Millard and Washington counties, a furniture factory at Toquerville, Washington Co., and a woolen mill at Washington in the same county. In the last two buildings, he helped set up the machinery. He spent the later years of his life in Holden, Millard Co., where he died Feb. 26, 1877, at age 56.

Harper, Charles Alfred — (12th Ten) Born Jan. 27, 1816, at Upper Providence, Montgomery Co., Pa., to Jesse and Eleanor Evans Harper. He learned the trade of wagonmaking and was a college grad-uate. He married Lovina Wollerton Dil-worth. He was kept busy with wagon repairs during the trek west. He was also  chief cook. Part of the advance company, he entered the valley July 22, 1847. He returned to Winter Quarters soon after-ward and brought his family to the Salt Lake Valley the following year. They settled in Holladay where he started the first public school in the area. He did considerable missionary work at home and abroad. He loved music and dancing. He died at his home in Holladay on April 24, 1900, at age 84.

Henrie, William — (5th Ten) Born Sept. 11, 1799, in Pennsylvania to Daniel and Sara Mendel Henrie. After his father died, he moved to Ohio and there married Myra Mayall on Nov. 16, 1823. They settled on a large tract of land and built a sawmill and gristmill. Parley P. Pratt and Samuel Smith came to their home preaching the gospel and they were soon baptized. In the first company, he became a valued scout and was a marksman and hunter. After his arrival in the Salt Lake Valley, he helped explore the regions around Salt Lake, Utah Lake, Cedar Valley, and Tooele Valley. He was chosen one of 50 to help explore the country in Utah between Salt Lake City and the Santa Clara River. He later helped found Bountiful where he constructed a pond, built a sawmill and sawed lumber. His wife and three children came to Utah with the Heber C. Kimball company in 1848. In 1865, he was called to settle Panaca, now in Nevada, but perhaps worn out at age 66, refused to go. However, his family went and experienced severe hardships for six years until returning to Panguitch, Utah. He lived the rest of his life in Bountiful and willed all his goods to the Church. He died Dec. 18, 1883, at Bountiful, Davis Co., Utah, at age 84.

Higbee, John S. — (Captain of the 11th Ten) Born March 7, 1804, in Tate Township, Clermont Co., Ohio, to Isaac and Sophie Higbee. He married Sarah Ann Voorhees Feb. 26, 1826, and in February 1832 the family joined the Church. Shortly after, the family sold its farm in New Jersey and moved to Jackson Co., Mo., where they  suffered much persecution. During difficulties in Missouri, both his parents died. In 1838, the family moved to Nauvoo. His wife died at Mt. Pisgah, Iowa, in 1846. He volunteered to go with the Mormon Battalion, but arrived a day after the men had marched away. So he traveled to Winter Quarters, where he married a widow, Judith Ball. A hunter on the first company, he remained at the upper Platte ferry, Wyo., until his family arrived. He then traveled with them to the Salt Lake Valley, arriving Sept. 26, 1847. In 1849, he helped settle Provo, Utah, and was president of the Provo Branch. That fall he was called to Great Britain on a mission and served as the president of the Newcastle Conference until Jan. 5, 1852. He presided over a company of 333 Saints on the ship *Kennebe* that sailed from Liverpool. Upon returning, he was sent to explore the Salmon River country in Idaho. He lived a time in Weber Co., and in 1865 moved to Toquerville, Washington Co., Utah, where he died Nov. 1, 1877, at age 73.

Holman, John Greenleaf — (4th Ten) Born Oct. 18, 1828, at Byron Center, Genessee Co., N.Y., to Joshua Sawyer and Rebecca Greenleaf Holman. He was baptized at age 8 and moved to Kirtland, Ohio, and afterwards to Missouri. At age 19 he accompanied the first company. Holman re-  turned east after arriving in Salt Lake Valley. He married Nancy Clark in 1849, and in 1850 returned to Salt Lake Valley. He served a mission to Great Britain in 1862-63. He lived in Pleasant Grove, Utah Co., Utah, for a time and then moved to Santaquin, also in Utah Co., before moving to Rexburg, Idaho. He served in many Church and civic positions. He died in Rexburg, Nov. 5, 1888, at age 60.

Howd, Simeon — (6th Ten) Born May 13, 1823, at Camden, Oneida Co., N.Y., to Samuel and Eunice Fuller Howd. He married Lucinda Morgan Turner on March 16, 1847, at Council Bluffs, Iowa. His bride followed him west and arrived in September. They lived in Salt Lake City for the next four years and then helped settle Parowan, Iron  Co., Utah. In 1856 he helped settle the Beaver, Utah, area. Once he met two Indians about to kill two Indian children whose parents had died. Howd traded two horses for the boys and took them to his home. He named them Charley and Jim. Charley lived with his family until marrying in his own tribe . Howd died in 1862 in Beaver, Beaver Co., Utah, at age 39.

Ivory, Mathew — (13th Ten) Born July 13, 1800, in Philadelphia, Philadelphia County, Pa., to Matthew and Ann Ivory. He was a mechanic and carpenter. He was baptized Feb. 1, 1840. He stayed in the Salt Lake Valley after arriving. He married Mary Elizabeth Bemns of Manti, Utah, in 1854. She died of palsy in 1870. In 1879 he filled a short-term mission to New Jersey. On Oct. 17, 1885, at age 85, while living in Beaver, he fitted the millstones in a newly erected grain chopper at Beaver. As he was making a final check, one of the stones came loose and killed him.

Jackman, Levi — (13th Ten) Born July 28, 1797, in Orange Co., Vt., the fifth son of Moses French and Elizabeth Carr Jackman. Three weeks before his birth, his father was killed by a falling tree. His mother sold the farm and moved to New York. She died in 1819. He married a young widow, Angeline Myers Brady, and in 1830  they moved to Portage, Ohio, where they heard and accepted the gospel and were baptized May 4, 1831. He filled a mission to the South and returned a month after the martyrdom of Joseph and Hyrum Smith. His wife died a few months later. He married Sally Plumb and joined the trek across Iowa. On the trek, he kept a daily journal. As a member of the advance company he was among the first to catch a glimpse of the valley from Little Mountain. His journal notes: "Like Moses on Pisgah's top, we could see a part of the Salt Lake Valley, our long anticipated home. We did truly rejoice at the sight." He wrote that cutting a road through the mouth of Emigration Canyon and entering the valley "seemed like bursting from the confines of prison walls into the beauties of a world of pleasure and freedom." He served as a high councilor and was later counselor to Bishop Shadrach Roundy of the Sixteenth Ward. Later, he was ordained a patriarch. He made saddle trees, chair seats, drums, and window and door frames. About 1870, he moved to Salem, Utah Co., where he died July 23, 1876, at age 78.

Jacob, Norton — (Captain of the 12th Ten) Born Aug. 11, 1804, in Sheffield, Berkshire Co., Mass., to Udney Hay and Elizabeth Hubbard Jacob. He married Emily Heaton in 1830. In 1840 he read a pamphlet that introduced him to the Church, and he was baptized that year. His family bitterly opposed his conversion,  but his father later joined the Church. He performed missionary work and after the death of Joseph and Hyrum Smith returned to Nauvoo and worked on the temple. He joined the exodus and helped make wagons. He left his wife and six small children in a cabin near Winter Quarters. A daughter was born after his departure. He kept a journal of the journey in which he noted such occurrences as choosing a camp cook, river crossings, wagons tipping over, catching mountain fever and staying with the rear company to help an ailing Brigham Young to the valley and went with them to the Salt Lake Valley. He returned to the valley with his family the following year in the Heber C. Kimball company. During the trip, his son Oliver became ill and died of black scurvy, black canker and a liver disease. He was buried along the trail. After settling in the valley, Jacob worked on the temple and various other projects, including a mill on Mill Creek and a bridge over the Weber River. He moved to Heber City, Wasatch Co., Utah, and was elected justice of the peace in 1862. He died in Glendale, Kane Co., Utah, Jan. 30, 1879, at age 74.

Johnson, Artemas — (7th Ten) Born April 18, 1809, at Remsen, Oneida Co., N.Y., to Artemas and Abia Johnson. At a conference in Nauvoo, about Oct. 6-8, 1839, he was sustained to be an elder. On June 12, 1847, he started off for hills that appeared to be a mile distant but were actually 8-10 miles away and did not return to camp. Searchers found him safe and brought back the antelope he had killed. After reaching the Salt Lake Valley, he returned to Winter Quarters that fall. He received a patriarchal blessing from Isaac Morley on Dec. 2, 1847, at Council Bluffs, Iowa. It is believed that he returned to Utah.

Johnson, Luke S. — (Captain of the 4th Ten) Born Nov. 3, 1807, at Pomfret, Windsor Co., Vt., to John and Elsa Jacobs Johnson. The family moved to Kirtland, Ohio. His father was baptized by Joseph Smith during the winter of 1830-31, and he was baptized by the Prophet May 10, 1831. He traveled to Southern Ohio where he and  Sidney Rigdon baptized 60 people and organized a branch at New Portage. He traveled through Ohio, Virginia and Kentucky baptizing more than a hundred people and organizing branches. On Nov. 1, 1833, he married Susan Harminda Poteet at Cabell Co., Va. She died later, leaving their six children. On Feb. 15, 1835, he was ordained one of the Twelve Apostles. He became involved in speculation and fell away from the Church for a time. He went to Virginia and studied medicine and returned to Kirtland as a physician. He was rebaptized in Nauvoo in

1846 in time to take part in the exodus. About this time he married America Morgan Clark. On the trek west, he was in charge of the leather boat, *Revenue Cutter,* which was carried on wagon wheels. He was a physician on the trip. He was asked to remain at the crossing at the Platte River in Wyoming with Thomas Grover. He went back to Winter Quarters in the fall of 1847 and returned west leading a company from Council Bluffs, Iowa. He and his family lived in West Jordan, Salt Lake Co., for a time then moved to Rush Valley, Tooele Co. Other families joined them in 1856 and a settlement was formed called Clover Creek. He was the first bishop. He died while on a business trip to Salt Lake City at the home of his brother-in-law, Orson Hyde, on Dec. 9, 1861, at age 54.

Johnson, Philo — (9th Ten) Born Dec. 6, 1814, at Newton, Fairfield Co., Conn., to Samuel and Abigail Johnson. He was baptized December 1841 and moved to Nauvoo on June 11, 1842, and served in the Nauvoo Legion. He wrote that "traders tried to discourage us by telling us we could not make a home in those mountain valleys for there was a frost every month of the year. In the Salt Lake Valley they had tried planting seeds several years but could not mature anything. Brigham Young said, 'We will try it and call on God to help us.'" Johnson said that after arriving, he, a mason, went to work making adobe bricks. In the fall of 1849, he married a widow with seven children, Spedy Ellsworth, and they had another seven children. He learned the hatter trade and moved to Payson, Utah Co., Utah, where he lived from 1857-1894. He made thousands of hats and at one time traded six silk hats for two city blocks. His hats were held in high repute. He died April 3, 1896, in Payson, Utah Co., Utah, at age 81.

Kelsey, Stephen — (8th Ten) Born Dec. 29, 1830, in Montville, Geauga Co., Ohio, to Stephen and Rachel Allen Kelsey. He moved from Ohio in 1842 to Nauvoo. His mother was a member of the Church but he had not been baptized. He was 16 at the time of the exodus and was selected to be in the advance company, arriving in the Salt Lake Valley July 22, 1846. One day later he

was baptized and remained faithful to the Church. He made adobe brick after arriving. He returned to Winter Quarters in the fall and found his mother and a sister had died. The following spring he came West again and brought four sisters with him. In 1849 or 1850 he traveled to California and panned $500 worth of gold in a gulch later named Kelsey's Gulch. He settled in Little Cottonwood and married Lydia Snyder, a recent immigrant from Canada. They soon moved to Brigham City, Utah, where a dozen families were involved in stock raising and farming. In the spring of 1864 he was called to settle the Bear Lake area in southeastern Idaho. They settled in Paris, Idaho, and helped build homes, schools, churches and till the land. He died May 23, 1900, in Paris, Bear Lake Co., Idaho, at age 59.

Kendall, Levi Newell — (8th Ten) Born April 19, 1822, in Lockport, Niagara Co., N.Y., to Levi and Lorena Lyman Kendall. He accepted the teachings of the Church in Michigan, and was ordained a seventy in 1844 in Nauvoo by Joseph Smith Sr. and was sent on a mission to Michigan. He was called home after the martyrdom. With the  first pioneer company, he was assigned as a guard. On June 5, 1847, he and John Eldredge were guarding the camp when they saw about 15 Pawnee Indians entering the enclosure. Kendall fired over their heads frightening them away. The stock stampeded but were turned by the alert guards and disaster was averted. He returned to Winter Quarters in the fall of 1847 and traveled west to the Salt Lake Valley the following summer. He married Eliza Clements in 1848. He moved to Springville, Utah, in 1856 and helped build canyon roads and dig irrigation canals. He was called to go east in 1861 to escort poor immigrants to the valley. Later he moved to Mapleton, Utah Co. He died March 10, 1903, in Springville, Utah Co., Utah, at age 80.

Kimball, Ellen Sanders — (9th Ten) One of three women in the original pioneer company. Born March 3, 1825, in the parish of Ten, Thelemarken, Norway, to Ysten Sondrasen. Originally named Aagaata Ystensdatter, she emigrated with her family in 1837 when she was about 13 years old. They settled in Indiana and later moved to La Salle Co., Ill., where she joined the Church in 1842. She was married to Heber C. Kimball in the Nauvoo Temple Jan. 7, 1846. At first, the original company was made up of only males, but when Harriet Young pleaded and was permitted to join the company, Ellen was also allowed to come along as well. She noted at one point that the smell of dead buffalo littering the

prairie made her sick all day. When she reached the Salt Lake Valley, her shoes were worn out so Thomas Cloward took an old pair of boot tops and made her the first shoes in Salt Lake City. She lived in Salt Lake City, where she had five children, three of whom died before reaching adulthood. She died in Salt Lake City on Nov. 22, 1871, at age 46.

Kimball, Heber C. — (9th Ten) Born June 14, 1801, in Sheldon, Franklin Co., Vt., to Solomon Farnham and Anna Spalding Kimball. He attended school through the fifth grade and at age 14 began working in his father's blacksmith shop. At age 19, Heber learned to make pottery from his brother Charles. He later bought his brother's

business and it prospered for 10 years. In 1831 he was baptized into the Baptist Church. Three weeks later he heard elders preach the restored gospel. He and Brigham Young investigated the Church together. Heber was baptized April 15, 1832, one day after Brigham Young. He moved to Kirtland, Ohio, where, on Feb. 14, 1835, he was ordained one of the original apostles. He helped build the Kirtland Temple and took part in Zion's Camp. He served a mission to the eastern states in 1835 and in England from 1837 to 1838, where he and fellow missionaries baptized some 1,500 people. Upon returning, he moved to Far West, Mo., and in 1839 to Nauvoo. In 1840-41, filled a second mission to England. He also preached in the Eastern States and was in Washington, D.C., seeking a redress of grievances when he heard of the martyrdom. He returned to Nauvoo, where he worked on the temple. He led the first six wagons from Winter Quarters to the staging area on the Elkhorn River in Nebraska. On the trek, he often preached to the men on Sundays. He was a scout for the best trail. After arriving in the valley, he returned to Winter Quarters. On the trip back, he was chased up a cliff by a mother grizzly bear. He uttered a number of prophecies, one of which was a promise that soon the Saints would be able to buy goods in the valley cheaper than in New York. This prophecy was fulfilled with the coming of wagon trains bound for California. He was called as first counselor to Brigham Young in the First Presidency in 1847. He was also lieutenant governor of the Provisional State of Deseret and a member of the legislative council. After a severe fall, he died in Salt Lake City June 22, 1868, at age 67.

King, William A. — (9th Ten) Born June 23, 1821. A member of the 25th Quorum of the Seventies in Nauvoo, he was chosen for the first company. He stayed a short time in the Salt Lake Valley, then returned to Winter Quarters. It is believed he died in Boston, Mass., in about 1862.

Kleinman, Conrad — (11th Ten) Born April 19, 1815, in Bergweiler, Lauday, Bavaria, near the French border, to Konrad and Odelia Wissing Kleinman. He immigrated to America at age 16 and settled in Rush Co., Indiana. Here he heard the gospel and was baptized Aug. 26, 1844. He traveled to Nauvoo arriving after the

martyrdom. He built a cabin and brought his wife, Elizabeth Malholm. In his journal in old Germanic script, he recorded the visit of Catholic Priest Father De Smet in Winter Quarters, who knew the West and told them of the Great Basin and the inland sea. He was among the first to reach Independence Rock in Wyoming. He recorded reaching the Continental Divide and other landmarks. After arriving in the Salt Lake Valley, he served as counselor to Bishop Pettigrew of the Tenth Ward. He moved to Lehi, Utah Co., Utah. In 1855-56, he filled a mission to New York, and was later called to settle in Dixie in southern Utah, where he resided in St. George and Toquerville, both in Washington Co. He then became one of the early settlers of Mesa, Maricopa Co., Ariz. He was counselor to two bishops in Mesa. He eventually moved back to St. George where he was ordained a patriarch in 1891. He died in St. George on Nov. 12, 1907, at age 92.

Lay, Hark — (13th Ten) Born in 1825 in Monroe Co., Miss., the son of African slaves of the William Lay household. He was baptized in Mormon Springs near his home, and was given as a marriage gift to Mormon converts William and Sytha Crosby when he was 22. He was sent on a difficult trip from Mississippi to Winter Quarters where two others died of pneumonia. Musically inclined, he danced and enjoyed the violin music of Hans Christian Hansen. He was also well-known for his singing voice. After entering the valley with the advance company on July 22, he and Oscar Crosby, another slave, built cabins and planted potatoes, beans, buckwheat and turnips. He traveled to help settle San Bernardino, Calif., where he gained his freedom. He returned to Utah and died in Union, Salt Lake Co., Utah, in about 1890 at age 65.

Lewis, Tarleton — (5th Ten) Born May 18, 1805, in Pendleton District, S.C., to Neriah and Mary Moss Lewis. In 1809, the family moved to Kentucky. He married Malinda Gimlin and they became parents of eight children. He was a skilled cabinet maker and carpenter. He heard the gospel preached by his brother, Benjamin Lewis,  and was baptized July 25, 1836. Tarlton help-ed build the Nauvoo Temple. With the first pioneer company, he helped build one of the rafts that was used to cross the quicksand-bottomed Loup Fork in Nebraska. After arriving in the Salt Lake Valley, he supervised construction of cabins in the original fort. He returned to Winter Quarters and brought his family west. He was appointed bishop of Salt Lake City, a calling he held until the city was divided into more wards. In 1850 he visited the area of Parowan, Iron Co., where he later moved and was called as bishop. He explored Beaver Valley in 1858, where were found rich deposits of lead and iron. The Lewis family opened a mine and lived in Beaver about 14 years. Then they moved to Joseph City and to Richfield in Sevier Co., Utah, and in 1877 he was set apart as bishop of the Richfield 2nd Ward, and remained in that calling until bad health led to his resignation a year later. A colorful figure, he was often referred to as "the Grand Old Man." He died at the home of his son Beason Lewis outside Teasdale, Wayne Co., Utah, on Nov. 29, 1890, at age 85.

Little, Jesse Carter — (2nd Ten) Born Sept. 26, 1815, in Belmont, Waldo Co., Maine, to Thomas and Relief Little. He joined the Church in the eastern states and was ordained a high priest in 1845. He was appointed president of the Eastern States Mission in 1846, where he helped the Saints receive a redress of grievances suffered in Missouri, by enlisting 500 LDS

men to form a battalion that would march to California. Little traveled to Nauvoo to inform leaders of this plan and then helped raise a battalion from among the members. He traveled with the enlisted men as far as Fort Leavenworth, Kan., and then returned east. Called to join the first company of pioneers, he left his wife in New Hampshire early in 1847 and traveled 3,000 miles west. He met the company April 19, 1847, about 70 miles west of Winter Quarters, then had to return to Winter Quarters for his supplies and come back to the wagon train. On the trek, he was an adjutant, and served as a scout on several occasions. After reaching Salt Lake Valley with the advance company, he immediately returned east and resumed his mission for four years. He returned to the valley with his family in 1852, and remained in Utah for the rest of his life. He held many important community and Church positions. He opened a hotel in the Warm Springs area of Salt Lake City. In 1856 he became chief engineer of a fire department. The same year he was ordained bishop and was a counselor to Presiding Bishop Edward Hunter until 1874. That year he moved to Morgan, Morgan Co., Utah, and lived in nearby Littleton for many years. He died in Salt Lake City on Dec. 26, 1893, at age 78.

Losee, Franklin G. — (7th Ten) Born in 1815 in Belmont, Waldo Co., Maine. It is believed he died in Lehi, Utah Co., Utah.

Loveland, Chauncey — (6th Ten) Born Aug. 1, 1797, in Glasgow, Conn., to Levi and Esther Hill Loveland. He married Nancy Graham at Madison, Ohio. The Loveland family moved to Carthage, Ill., in the 1840s where his wife and a son died. He had not joined the Church, but was kind toward members. In 1846 he  married Sally Horn Crockett. While living at Mt. Pisgah, Iowa, he was baptized. After arriving in the Great Basin, he returned with Brigham Young to Winter Quarters to bring his family west. The Loveland family settled on a tract in Bountiful, Davis Co., where he began farming and breeding horses. When the California gold rush began, he left the state in search of fortune. He eventually returned to Utah and resumed farming. He died in Bountiful, Utah, Aug. 16, 1876, at age 79.

Lyman, Amasa Mason — (2nd Ten) Born in Lyman Township, Grafton County, N. H., on May 30, 1813, to Boswell and Martha Mason Lyman. He was baptized April 27, 1832, and a week later left home and traveled to Hiram, Ohio, and worked on the John Johnson farm until August, after which he began missionary labors. He labored in Ohio, New York and Pennsylvania. In 1837, he was in Missouri in the company of the Prophet Joseph Smith when captured by a militia and sentenced to death. The prisoners were later released. He served additional missions to secure means to help build the Nauvoo Temple and preached in Tennessee. In 1842, he was ordained as an apostle and continued missionary work in nearby states. He returned to Nauvoo in 1844 after the martyrdom of the Prophet. When the company arrived at Chimney Rock, Neb., Elder Lyman, for diversion, rode his horse up a rock and did an impersonation of Napoleon Bonaparte crossing the Alps, and the pioneers "thought it good," wrote clerk Thomas Bullock. When the company reached Fort Laramie, Lyman was sent to Pueblo, Colo., to bring the colony of Mississippi Saints and others to Salt Lake Valley. He and the party arrived at City Creek in the Salt Lake Valley on July 29, 1847. He brought a large company west the following year. In 1851, Charles C. Rich and Elder Lyman headed a colonization effort in San Bernardino, Calif., that lasted until the threat of Johnston's army to Salt Lake City in 1857. Elder Lyman was called on a mission to Great Britain in 1860 where he preached false doctrine that eventually led to his excommunication in 1870. He died at Fillmore, Millard Co., Utah, Feb. 4, 1877, at age 63. He was posthumously restored to good standing.

Marble, Samuel Harvey — (5th Ten) Born Oct. 6, 1822, at Phelps, Ontario Co., N.Y., one of 11 children of Nathaniel and Mary (Polly) King Marble. He was baptized in Nauvoo. After crossing the plains in 1847, he returned to Winter Quarters the same year. He returned to Salt Lake City in 1849 and was shortly called as one of nine men under A. L. Lamoreaux to establish a ferry on the Green River in Wyoming to earn revenue by transporting California and Oregon immigrants. The group also established a blacksmith shop. After this assignment, he returned to Utah and

settled in Manti, Sanpete Co., where he was elected a city councilman in 1851. In 1853 he became a member of the 23rd Quorum of Seventies. He lived in Manti for several years until moving to Round Valley, Apache Co., Ariz., where he died March 16, 1914, at age 91.

Markham, Stephen — (Captain of the 1st Hundred; 12th Ten) Born Feb. 9, 1800, in Avon, Livingston Co., N.Y., to David and Dina Merry Markham. After the death of his father, his mother moved to Geauga Co., Ohio. He later followed the Church to Nauvo. During the exodus, he became captain of 200 families en route to Council Bluffs, Iowa. In the spring of 1847 he was named captain of a hundred in the first pioneer company. He took charge of the first company during a brief absence of Brigham Young and other apostles. He was also a colonel in the company. During the journey, he often joined the apostles in speaking to the men. He arrived in the Salt Lake Valley with the advance company and was soon put in charge of supplying fresh teams for plowing land along City Creek. He returned to Winter Quarters that fall and was immediately placed in charge of 140 people at Council Bluffs. He returned to Utah in 1850 in charge of a company of 50 wagons. In the fall of 1851 he and 17 other families settled in Spanish Fork, Utah Co., Utah, and formed a settlement of which he became president. A year later he was ordained the bishop of the settlement of Palmyra. He remained on his farm for the rest of his life. He served as a colonel during the Walker Indian War, and in 1856 was sent to Fort Supply in Wyoming. He died in Spanish Fork March 10, 1878, at 78 years of age.

Matthews, Joseph Lazarus — (Captain of the 14th Ten) Born Jan. 29, 1809, in Johnson Co., N.C. After his marriage to Rhoda Carroll, they moved to Neshoba Co., Miss. After hearing Elder Benjamin Clapp preach, he joined the Church and in 1845 sold his holdings in Mississippi and moved to Nauvoo. He entered the Salt Lake Valley with the advance company of the pioneers. In 1849 he took part in a company exploring southern Utah. In 1851, he joined Apostle Charles C. Rich in colonizing what became San Bernardino, Calif., where he remained until the colony was recalled in 1857. He then settled in Santaquin, Utah Co., Utah, and from there served in the Southern States Mission. He worked at farming and freighting until 1880 when he settled in Pima, Graham Co., Ariz. He died there May 14, 1886, at age 77.

Mills, George — (12th Ten) Born about 1878 in England. After arriving in the Salt

Lake Valley, he suffered from cancer. In 1854, he asked for an operation by Dr. Samuel L. Sprague in hopes of halting the incurable disease. The doctor, in consultation with three other physicians, concluded that the operation could well prove fatal. Brigham Young was consulted and gave his permission for the surgery. After arranging his will and taking care of his affairs, he was operated on Aug. 29, 1854, in Salt Lake City and died during the surgery.

Murray, Carlos — (10th Ten) Born March 12, 1829, in Ontario Co., N.Y. One of the younger members of the company and a nephew of Heber C. Kimball, he was assigned as a scout in the pioneer company. After arriving in Salt Lake Valley, he helped build the settlement, then returned to Winter Quarters that fall. He returned to the valley in 1848. He later went to California and was traveling by the Humboldt River in 1855 in what is now Nevada when he, his wife and a Mr. Redden were attacked and killed by Indians. A gold pencil and an earring were found and later identified as their property. His revolvers were found in possession of travelers who said they had bought them from Indians on the desert.

Newman, Elijah — (8th Ten) Born Sept. 17, 1793, in Hampshire Co., Va., to Solomon and Jane James Newman. He joined the Church in 1832 and followed the Saints during the next 15 years. He was named to the advance group that entered the Salt Lake Valley July 22, 1847, and afterward was one of three men to ensure that drags and plows were available for those working the land. He also helped build the first fort and provided gates for the structure. In 1850, he was among those appointed to colonize "Little Salt Lake Valley" in southern Utah. He and others traveled to Parowan, Iron Co., arriving Jan. 13, 1851. On various exploration trips, he and others found a supply of chalk, as well as locating iron, salt and coal. He was ordained a high priest in 1861 and on Feb. 13, 1869, was enrolled in the Parowan School of Prophets under Elder Erastus Snow. He served as a justice of the peace in Parowan for several years and was one of the first city councilmen. He died at Parowan on Dec. 12, 1872, at age 79.

Norton, John Wesley — (12th Ten) Born Nov. 6, 1820, near Lisbon, Wayne Co., Indiana, to David and Elizabeth Heaton Norton. Baptized March 6, 1838, and resided in Kirtland, Ohio, from 1841-43, where he was clerk of the elders quorum in the fall of 1841. He was ordained a seventy in Nauvoo, in 1845 and was endowed in the Nauvoo Temple in 1846.

While in Winter Quarters, he married Rebecca Hammer, whose father, Austin, had been killed at Haun's Mill in 1838. He served as a foot hunter with the original group of pioneers, and while traveling near Sulphur Creek, Wyo., dis-

covered an oil foun-tain. Pioneers used the oil to lubricate their wagons. After arriving in the valley, Norton returned to Winter Quarters. He worked in Missouri during the winter to earn money to bring his family to the Salt Lake Valley. They arrived in September 1848 and he worked for public works for two years. In 1854 he traveled to Australia on a mission, where he labored for three years. Upon his return, he assisted in establishing settlements in southern Utah, and for a time, resided in Panaca, Nev. He died four years later in Panguitch, Garfield Co., Utah, on Oct. 20, 1901, at age 80.

Owen, Seeley — (6th Ten) Born March 30, 1805, at Milton, Rutland Co., Vt., to Ethan and Hannah Owen. He married Lydia Ann Owen. She died during the exodus from Nauvoo in 1846 and was buried at Winter Quarters. In crossing the plains with the original company, he was assigned to the crew that hauled a cannon. The cannon was fired a few times as a warning while in Indian country, but was not used against the Indians. After arriving in Salt Lake Valley, he returned to Winter Quarters. His daughter was brought west with relatives, and he soon returned to Salt Lake Valley. For a time he lived in Provo after which he was called to help with the settlement of Wallsburg, Wasatch Co., Utah. He later moved to Arizona where he died at age 76, in 1881 near Flagstaff in an accident while working for the Atlantic Pacific Railroad.

Pack, John — (10th Ten) Born in St. John, New Brunswick, Canada, on May 20, 1809, to George and Phylotte Green Pack. He moved to Water-town, N.Y., and was baptized there March 8, 1836. A year later he and his family moved to Kirtland, Ohio, and the following year to Missouri. In 1840 he settled in Nauvoo, and was commissioned a

major in the Nauvoo Legion. He was designated a major in the original company. A member of the advance party that entered Salt Lake Valley July 22, 1847, he was chosen to ride back and report their progress to an ailing President Brigham Young. He returned to Winter Quarters that fall and returned to Salt Lake Valley in 1848 where he established a home in the Seventeenth Ward. There he opened his home for classes, the beginning of the University of Utah. Classes were held in his parlor. Orson Pratt, Cyrus W. Collins and Orson Spencer (chancellor), formed the first faculty. In 1856, he was called to assist in the settling of a colony in Carson Valley, Nev., and remained there until being recalled in 1858. He died in Salt Lake City, on April 4, 1885, at age 75.

Peirce, Eli Harvey — (4th Ten) Born July 29, 1827, in Uwchland, Chester Co., Pa., to Robert and Hannah Harvey Peirce. His parents moved to Nauvoo, in 1841 and he was baptized March 27, 1842, by Joseph Smith. He received his endowments in Nauvoo in 1846 and was ordained a seventy the same year. At age 20, he was part of the pioneer company as a teamster. After arriving, he helped build the settlement in Salt Lake Valley. On his return to Winter Quarters, he met his parents and other relatives coming west in the Edward Hunter company, so he returned with them. He was commissioned to travel to California to obtain seed grain that fall, which he did with Jefferson Hunt and others. He married Susannah Neff in 1850 and they moved to Brigham City, Box Elder Co., Utah, in 1851. After living in the Brigham City fort during Indian hostilities, they moved into their own home. He was ordained the second bishop of this settlement in 1855. He crossed the plains eastbound with a handcart in 1857 as a missionary bound for Europe. A year later he returned to his father's home and succumbed to an illness contracted while serving his mission. He died in Salt Lake City, Utah, on Aug. 12, 1858, at age 31.

Pomeroy, Francis M. — (10th Ten) Born Feb. 22, 1822, at Somers, Tollard Co., Conn., to Martin and Sybil Hunt Pomeroy. He was hired out to an uncle at a young age and when he reached 15, he joined a whaling crew. He eventually became harpoonist, and worked his way to first mate. At 21, he was in a shipwreck off Peru, of which he was the lone survivor. A Castillian family took him in and he stayed for two years, learning Spanish. He returned to Salem, Mass., where he

married Irene Ursula Haskell and was baptized in 1844. They moved to Nauvoo. With the original company June 18, 1847, he was among nine men left to operate the upper ferry of the Platte River. While at the ferry, his wife arrived in a westbound company and he continued west with them. They settled in the Twelfth Ward in Salt Lake City, but he was soon called on a mission to Lower California with Apostle Charles C. Rich that lasted a year. He returned to Salt Lake City where he acted as host and interpreter to a delegation representing Mexico President Benito Juarez, who met with Brigham Young. In 1862, moved to Weber Co., Utah, until 1864 when he helped settle Paris, Idaho. He moved to Salt River Valley in Arizona and became a founder of the city of Mesa, Maricopa Co., Ariz. He was widely respected by the Indians there and was set apart as president of the Indian Mission in 1881. Two years later, on Feb. 28, 1883, he died in Mesa at age 60.

Powell, David — (13th Ten) Born May 26, 1822, in the Edgefield District, S.C., to John and Rebecca Powell. He was ordained a seventy in Nauvoo and was at one time associated with the Mississippi Saints. On the trek west, he was in the advance party that entered the Salt Lake Valley on July 22, 1847. He returned to Winter Quarters in the fall, coming back to Salt Lake City in 1853 with his wife, Ann, and son, David Jr. He later moved to California where he died near Santa Rosa in 1883.

Pratt, Orson — (1st Ten) Born Sept. 19, 1811, in Hartford, Washington Co., N.Y., to Jared and Charity Dickinson Pratt. In 1830, his brother, Parley P., taught him the gospel and baptized him on his 19th birthday. Orson traveled to Kirtland, Ohio, to meet the Prophet, who received Section 34 calling the young man as a missionary. Within four years, he traveled nearly 8,000 miles in the Northeast, baptizing more than 150 persons and organizing several branches. He joined Zion's Camp in 1834, and a year later was called as an apostle. He extended his missionary labors to Canada and Scotland in 1841. On the trek west, he used

scientific instruments from France to determine position and altitude of the trail. He designed a mechanical mileage counter. He also determined an exact location of the South Pass on the Continental Divide. As the company neared the Great Salt Lake Valley, he was named to head the advance party. His group blazed the trail and hacked at making a road down Echo and Emigration canyons. Later he and Erastus Snow were the first to enter the valley on July 21, 1847. From 1848 to 1850, he presided over the Church in Europe during which time the membership doubled. He organized 20 ships bound for Zion, wrote 15 pamphlets, as well as lecturing to large audiences in England and Scotland. He returned to the Salt Lake Valley in 1851. In the following years he presided over the eastern branches, Europe, and divided the Book of Mormon and Doctrine and Covenants into chapters and verses, among many contributions. He died Oct. 3, 1881, in Salt Lake City, Utah, at age 70, the last of the original apostles of this dispensation.

Rappleye, Ammon Tunis — (4th Ten) Born Feb. 2, 1807, in Ovid, Seneca Co., N.Y., to John Ranson and Margaret Tillier Rappleye. He was baptized Nov. 20, 1832, and took part in building the Kirtland Temple. He married Louise Cutler. After arriving in the Salt Lake Valley, he returned with Shad-rach Roundy to Winter Quarters. Upon returning to the Salt Lake Valley the second time, he was employed as head gardener by Brigham Young. He also filled a mission in the Eastern States. He helped settle Millard Co. and died Dec. 25, 1883, in Kanosh, Utah, at age 76.

Redden, Return Jackson — (10th Ten) Born Sept. 26, 1817, in Hiram, Portage Co., Ohio, to George Grant and Adelina Higley Redden. As a boy he sold wooden clocks and worked on a Mississippi riverboat. He was baptized in the Ohio River in 1841. He was closely associated with the Prophet Joseph Smith and was one of his body guards. His wife, Laura Traske, died in childbirth. He married Martha Whiting, who died at Winter Quarters. He was a hunter and trailblazer

on the original company. Near the Bear River about at today's Utah-Wyoming border, he discovered a narrow, deep cave where trappers or others stored property. Originally named Redden's Cave, it is today called Cache Cave. After arriving in Salt Lake Valley, he assisted in planting and then returned to Winter Quarters with Brigham Young. He brought his family west the following year. He accompanied Apostle Amasa M. Lyman to California, returning by way of Carson Valley in Nevada, where he lived two years. He moved to Grantsville, Tooele Co., Utah, and then to Coalville, Summit Co., where he homesteaded 160 acres of land and owned a coal mine. He moved to Hoytsville, Summit Co., where he helped build many of the early buildings. He lived successively in Summit and Tooele counties and was justice of peace in both. He was a member of the 35th Quorum of Seventies when he died in Hoytsville on Aug. 30, 1891, at age 73.

Richards, Willard — (2nd Ten) Born June 24, 1804, in Hopkinton, Middlesex Co., Mass., to Joseph and Rhoda Howe Richards. A physician by profession, he abandoned his practice to seek the truth after reading the Book of Mormon. After reading it, he traveled to Kirtland, Ohio. He was baptized by Brigham Young, his cousin, in

Kirtland, Ohio, on Dec. 31, 1836. A year after his baptism he was sent to England with Heber C. Kimball and Orson Hyde. Shortly after his return, he was ordained an apostle and in 1841 was appointed clerk to Joseph Smith and to the Church. He was with the Prophet during the martyrdom. He used his walking stick to parry musket thrusts through the door. He escaped uninjured. His wife died in Nauvoo. Upon arriving in Salt Lake Valley with the first pioneer company, he was appointed to lead prayers, consecrating and dedicating the land to the Lord. He returned to Winter Quarters where he was chosen as second counselor to Brigham Young, in Kanesville, Iowa. He returned to Salt Lake Valley in 1848, captain of a large body of pioneers. He later served as secretary to the government of the State of Deseret, postmaster of Salt Lake City, and member of the Perpetual Emigrating Fund committee. He was the first editor of the *Deseret News*. He died of the palsy in Salt Lake City, Utah, on March 11, 1854, at age 49.

Rockwell, Orrin Porter — (10th Ten) Born June 25, 1815, in Manchester, N.Y., to Orrin and Sarah Witt Porter Rockwell, he became a good friend of Joseph Smith Jr. He was baptized early in 1830 in Fayette, Seneca Co., N.Y., and in 1831 traveled to Kirtland, Ohio, with the Prophet's mother. Charged with an assassination attempt on Gov.

Lilburn Boggs, he was imprisoned until charges were dropped by the Missourians. Rockwell provided valuable service as a hunter and scout on the trek west. He was part of the advance company that entered the Salt Lake Valley July 22, 1847. In the west, he gained considerable influence with the Indians, and often helped avoid troubles. He became a terror to the lawless elements and would ride a thousand miles in the harshest of weather in the interests of the Church. A volume of folklore has accumulated about his service as a deputy marshal of Salt Lake City. He also rode for the Pony Express and his house, 25 miles southwest of Salt Lake City, was a station for them. He died in Salt Lake City on June 9, 1878, at the age of 63.

Rockwood, Albert Perry — (Captain of the First Hundred; 3rd Ten) Born June 9, 1805, in Holliston, Middlesex Co., Mass., to Luther and Ruth Perry Rockwood. In 1837 Brigham Young and Willard Richards preached in Holliston and among their converts were Albert and his wife, Nancy Haven Rockwood. They relocated in Kirtland,

Ohio, and later in Missouri. He became one of Joseph Smith's bodyguards and a general in the Nauvoo Legion. He was set apart as one of the First Presidents of the Seventy Dec. 2, 1845. In 1847, he was chosen as a captain of a hundred in the first pioneer company. Upon arriving at the Bear River in Wyoming, he contracted mountain fever and by July 14 "was much the sickest man in camp." He recovered a few days later. After arriving in the Salt Lake Valley, he returned with Brigham Young to Winter Quarters. He brought his family west in 1849. Two years later he was in the Territorial Legislature and continued to be re-elected every term until his death. In 1862 he was elected warden of the state penitentiary. He directed prison works to open a number of roads and was also

director and organizer of the Deseret Agricultural and Manufacturing Society, watermaster of the Thirteenth Ward, road commissioner of District 11, and territory fish commissioner. He died Nov. 26, 1879, in Sugar House in Salt Lake City, Utah, at age 74.

Rolfe, Benjamin William — (11th Ten) Born Oct. 7, 1822, at Romford, Oxford Co., Maine, to Samuel and Elizabeth Hathaway Rolfe. His family accepted the gospel in Maine and moved in 1834 to Kirtland, Ohio, and later to Nauvoo, where both father and son helped in the construction of the temple. Although not a member of the Church,

he volunteered to take his father's place in the first company. He assisted in establishing the new settlement in Salt Lake and returned east with Brigham Young in the fall. When the group reached Chimney Rock, Neb., Rolfe was selected to return to the Salt Lake Valley as a mail carrier. He was baptized later and was appointed to accompany the 1855 Salmon River Mission in Idaho. When this mission ended, he pursued carpentry work in Salt Lake City. He was ordained a member of the 16th Quorum of Seventies. He died May 31, 1892, in Salt Lake City, at age 69.

Rooker, Joseph — (11th Ten) Born Jan. 22, 1818. After the trek west, he was appointed in Salt Lake Valley to be one of a committee to take teams to meet the oncoming companies, relieve them of their burdens and assist them to reach their destinations. He later resided at Black Rock, Salt Lake Co., and was a member of the 9th

Quorum of Seventy. About 1857 he left Utah and went to southern California. He died about 1895 in Oceanside, Calif.

Roundy, Shadrach — (13th Ten) Born Jan. 1, 1789, Rockingham, Windham Co., Vt., to Uriah and Lucretia Needham Roundy. He married Betsy Quimby in about 1814. After hearing the gospel preached, he traveled to Fayette, N.Y., in the winter of 1830-31 to meet Joseph Smith, after which he was bap-tized. He gave of his resources to build the Kirtland Temple. He later moved to Missouri. He was captain of the police in Nauvoo and once intercepted an attempt to kidnap

Joseph Smith. He was appointed a major in the first pioneer company. A member of the advance party, he was one of three men to plow the first furrows in the Saints' newfound home. While returning to Winter Quarters, he met his son, Lorenzo Wesley, enroute to Salt Lake Valley in the company of Orson Spencer. So father and son traded places and Shadrach spent the winter of 1847-48 in the Salt Lake Valley. There he became a member of the first high council and the Territorial Legislature. He was the first bishop of the Sixteenth Ward and served from 1849-56. He crossed the plains five times to assist poor immigrants. He was one of the founders of Zion's Cooperative Mercantile Association. He died in Salt Lake City on July 4, 1872, at age 83.

Schofield, Joseph Smith — (3rd Ten) Born Aug. 2, 1809, in Winchester Co., N.Y., to Elijah and Hannah Thompson Scofield. He became a skilled carpenter and joiner. In 1838 he married Clarissa Aurilla Terry. The couple joined the Church in New York and he became branch clerk of the 20-member branch. They soon moved to Nauvoo.

After arriving in the valley with the first company, he helped build homes and public buildings. He assisted in the building of the Salt Lake Temple, Salt Lake Theatre and Salt Lake Social Hall. He also worked on the St. George Temple. He died March 8, 1875, in Bellevue, Utah, at age 65.

Scholes, George — (5th Ten) Born Feb. 2, 1812, at Chadderton, Lancashire, England, to George and Sarah Scholes. He was baptized Nov. 3, 1839, and immigrated to Nauvoo, where he built a brick home and planted an orchard. While in Nauvoo, his wife and three children died. In the original company, he was assigned to the crew that brought the cannon. After arriving in Salt Lake Valley, he immediately prepared the land and planted vegetables and helped construct the fort. He returned to Winter Quarters and was then sent to St. Louis, Mo., to conduct business for the Church. He returned west in 1850, bringing his wife, Mary Spencer Scholes. They settled in the Cottonwood

area. He died Aug. 14, 1857, in Cottonwood, at age 45.

Sherwood, Henry G. — (5th Ten) Born April 20, 1785, in Kingsbury, N.Y. He was among those who contracted malaria when the Saints first arrived at Commerce, Ill, later to be Nauvoo. He was healed by Joseph Smith. Later he was appointed city marshal at Nauvoo. At Winter Quarters, he was appointed commissary general for the westward journey. Sherwood came down with mountain fever near the end of the trek, but recovered. After arriving in Salt Lake Valley, he made a drawing of the first city survey on a sheepskin, no paper being available. He became a member of the high council and spoke at an Independence Day celebration July 4, 1852. In 1852, he left to help colonize San Bernardino, Calif., and became surveyor for San Bernardino County. Recalled in 1856 because of Johnston's army, he became a Pony Express agent for a time. He later returned to San Bernardino, where he died Aug. 15, 1857, at age 71.

Shumway, Andrew Purley — (6th Ten) Born Feb. 20, 1833, in Millbury, Mass., to Charles and Julia Ann Hooker Shumway. His parents were baptized in 1840, and the family moved to Nauvoo, where they lived until the 1846 expulsion. His father was chosen as captain of Fifty. At Winter Quarters, his mother died. That

spring when his father prepared to leave for the trek west, Andrew burst into tears and said that because his mother had just died, it was more than he could bear to be left alone. His father received permission from Brigham Young to take the 13-year-old youth along, although they were both sick at the start of the journey. After being on the trail a while, Andrew and his father became well. He caught mountain fever near the Big Sandy Creek in Wyoming but was healed when administered to by Brigham Young. After arriving in Salt Lake Valley, he and his father returned to Winter Quarters and came back west the followig season. In 1856 he was called on a mission to England but returned prematurely because of the troubles with Johnston's army. He married Amanda S. Graham in 1859 and moved to Mendon, Cache Co., Utah. He died in Franklin, Oneida Co., Idaho, on June 12, 1909, at age 76.

Shumway, Charles — (Captain of the 6th Ten) Born Aug. 1, 1808, in Oxford, Worcester Co., Mass., to Samuel and Polly Shumway. He joined the Church in Illinois in 1841, and soon afterward moved to Nauvoo, where he took part in defending the city as a police officer. When the exodus of 1846 began, he was the first to cross the Mississippi River. His wife, Julia Ann Hooker

Shumway, died at Winter Quarters. Selected to leave with the pioneer company, Charles received permission for his son Andrew to accompany him. After completing the journey, he was one of three assigned to have plows and drags ready as land was tilled and planted along City Creek. He went back to Winter Quarters for the rest of his family and returned to Salt Lake City about a year later. In 1849, he moved to Sanpete, Sevier Co., where he started a gristmill in partnership with Brigham Young. He also built a sawmill in Sanpete and later a sawmill in Payson, Utah Co. He served a short mission in Canada and then moved to Cache Valley to help in its settlement. He settled in Wellsville and then Mendon, both in Cache Co., Utah. During his residence here, a 3-year-old daughter was carried away by Indians and never heard of again. In 1877, he moved to Kane Co., in southern Utah, and then to Shumway, near Taylor, on the Little Colorado River in Arizona. There he built his last gristmill. He returned to Johnson, Utah, where he died May 21, 1898, at 89 years of age.

Smith, George Albert — (1st Ten) Born June 26, 1817, at Potsdam, St. Lawrence Co., N.Y., to John and Clarissa Lyman Smith. He was baptized Sept. 10, 1832, and in 1833 his family moved to Kirtland, Ohio, where for the first time he met his cousin Joseph Smith. He cleared a heavily wooded 10-acre farm of his father's and soon became acquainted

with Brigham Young, then a carpenter hired to finish the Smith's home. He helped with the Kirtland Temple, hauling the first loads of rock. He took part in Zion's Camp in 1834. He became the junior member of the First Quorum of the Seventy in 1835, and for the next two years performed missionary service in the East and in Ohio. In 1838 he immigrated to Daviess Co., Mo., and from there he served another mission in Kentucky and Tennessee. He returned to Far West, Mo., and was ordained an apostle April 26, 1839. He then filled missions to England, Illinois, Indiana and Michigan. He was in Michigan when he heard of the martyrdom of Joseph and Hyrum Smith. On the journey westward, unknown to anyone else, he locked away 25 pounds of flour. As the journey wore on, "I issued my reserve flour, cup by cup, to the sick, some of whom attribute to this circumstance the preservation of their lives." In 1849, he took charge of organizing pioneer companies and brought the year's last company himself. It was a large, late-leaving and trouble-plagued company that took 155 days, a month and a half longer than the first company, and arrived Oct. 27. In 1850 he took a group of settlers 265 miles south and founded the city of Parowan, Iron Co., firing a cannon in celebration of their arrival, a celebration re-enacted annually. In 1868, he was called as first counselor to Brigham Young. He was active in territorial governments and is considered father of the southern colonies, the largest of which, St. George, Washington Co., is named in his honor. He died Sept. 1, 1875, in St. George at age 58.

Smoot, William Cockran Adkinson — (7th Ten) Born Jan. 30, 1828, in Tennessee and became the adopted son of Abraham O. and Margaret Thompson Smoot. He was baptized Feb. 8, 1836, and that same year moved with his family to Far West, Mo., and later moved to Nauvoo, where he helped with the Nauvoo Temple and was given

his temple blessings and ordained a seventy at a young age. He was assigned as a guard in the first pioneer company. He stood guard duty every three nights, missing only one night during the entire journey. He was the last man of the company to enter Salt Lake Valley, but once there assisted in laying out the city, "carrying and driving stakes." He spent the winter in the north fort, then moved to Canyon Creek and began farming. He served as a missionary to the Indians in the vicinity of Las Vegas, Nev., and made several trips across the plains to bring converts who lacked the means for transportation to Salt Lake Valley. He was set apart as counselor to his father in the Sugar House Ward, and took charge of the ward from 1866-77. He married Martha Sessions, and after she died, he married Matilda Garn. He filled a mission to the Southern States. He was the last surviving member of the company. He died Jan. 31, 1920, a day after his 92nd birthday.

Snow, Erastus — (6th Ten) Born Nov. 9, 1818, at St. Johnsbury, Caledonia Co., Vt., to Levi and Lucina Streeter Snow. He was baptized at age 14 on Feb. 3, 1833. He immediately began missionary work and in 1835 traveled to Kirtland, Ohio, where he met the Prophet Joseph Smith and lived in his home for several weeks. Soon after, he  was ordained into the 2nd Quorum of Seventy. He served additional missions, during which he faced mobs but baptized many converts. In 1838 he moved to Far West, Mo., where he helped defend the city against mob action. Later he visited Joseph Smith, who at the time was incarcerated in the Liberty Jail. Following a foiled escape attempt, Snow was imprisoned with them. He became the Prophet's attorney and, though he'd never studied law, pleaded the case. Later freed, he persuaded the judges to change the Prophet's trial venue to Boone Co. As they were being transferred, Joseph and his companions escaped from the illegal proceedings. In 1839 he moved to Illinois, then commenced about four years of missionary work in Pennsylvania and Massachusetts in which he brought in a number of converts. He returned to enjoy the winter of 1843 in Nauvoo and in the spring embarked on another missionary journey to the east. However, news of the martyrdom brought him back and he was among the exiles of Nauvoo, in 1846. In crossing the Mississippi River, the boat capsized and his family suffered additionally. A member of the first company, he carried a letter to Orson Pratt as Pratt arrived near Emigration Canyon, leading into Salt Lake Valley. The two men went ahead into the valley. "When we ascended Red Butte, near the mouth of Emigration Canyon, which gave us our first view of the blue waters of Great Salt Lake, we simultaneously swung our hats and shouted, 'Hosannah!' for the spirit told us that here the Saints would find rest," remembered Snow. They traveled a half circle in the valley of about 12 miles. He returned to Winter Quarters that fall, and then traveled to the eastern states to solicit aid for the impoverished Saints. He took his family west in 1848, and in 1849 he was ordained to the Quorum of the Twelve Apostles. He was shortly after called to open missionary work in Scandinavia, beginning in Denmark. He baptized the first 12 Danes on Aug. 12, 1850. By the time he had completed his mission in 1852, more than 600 people had been baptized by Elder Snow, his companions and other missionaries. In 1854 he organized the St. Louis, Mo., Stake, and began publication of the *St. Louis Luminary*, a Church newspaper. After 1861 he was engaged in helping and supporting the settlements of southern Utah, Arizona, New Mexico and Colorado. The town of Snowflake, Ariz., was originally named Snow Flake, in honor of Erastus Snow and William Jordan Flake. He died in Salt Lake City on May 27, 1888, at age 69.

Stevens, Roswell — (2nd Ten) Born Oct. 17, 1808, at Grand River, Upper Canada, to Roswell and Sybil Spencer Stevens. He was converted to the Church through the teachings of Joseph Smith and Sidney Rigdon and was baptized in 1834. He married Mary Ann Peterson, and they moved to Nauvoo, where he became a member of the local police force. After the exodus from Nauvoo, he enlisted in the Mormon Battalion and marched south. However, when John D. Lee and Howard Egan overtook the Battalion's march at Santa Fe, N.M., to collect and carry wages back to Winter Quarters to the soldiers' families, Stevens was sent back to accompany them. He was assigned to be a foot hunter in the first company. Upon reaching Ft. Laramie, he was one of three chosen to accompany Amasa Lyman to Pueblo, Colo., where the Mississippi Saints and sick detachments of the Mormon Battalion had wintered, and bring them to Salt Lake Valley. When he arrived in the valley, he lived first in Alpine, 30 miles south of the new city, then moved to Weber Valley, some 40 miles to the north. His daughter Martha was the first white child born in this valley. He was sent in 1879 as part of an expedition to explore southern Utah. The explorers found a location for a settlement near the San Juan River, where the town of Bluff, San Juan Co., now stands, and there he died May 4, 1880, at age 71. He was placed in a rude coffin made from his wagon box and buried in the site selected for the town cemetery.

Stewart, Benjamin Franklin — (7th Ten) Born Oct. 22, 1817, in Jackson, Monroe Co., Ohio, to Philander Barrett and Sarah Scott Stewart. He married Polly Richardson in 1837, and they moved to

Van Buren, Iowa, where they met missionaries. She was immediately converted and baptized, but he waited three years before being baptized Feb. 2, 1844. On the trek west, he was among a group left to operate a ferry for the Oregon Trail

wagon trains and oncoming Mormon wagon trains at the last crossing of the Platte River in Wyoming. He remained there until his family, traveling in the Abraham O. Smoot company, arrived and he went to the Salt Lake Valley with them. He first settled at Mill Creek near Salt Lake City and operated a sawmill for several years. He was part of an expedition to explore southern Utah led by Parley P. Pratt. From that expedition, he became interested in the area near Payson, Utah Co. He moved there and operated a sawmill in Payson Canyon for several years, then built and operated a nail factory near town. He later filled a mission to Iowa and Illinois and afterward returned to start a small settlement north of Payson. This settlement was named Benjamin in his honor. There he was struck by lightning and died on June 22, 1886, at age 68.

Stewart, James Wesley — (8th Ten) Born May 19, 1825, in Fayette Co., Ala., to George and Ruth Baker Stewart, who were baptized when Elder Benjamin Clapp came to the town and preached. They moved to Missouri where George Stewart died of fever. Chosen to accompany the first pioneers west, James Stewart was one

of the men assigned to remain at the Platte River to ferry oncoming Oregon and Mormon pioneers across the river. Upon arriving in Salt Lake Valley, he helped make the first irrigation dam on City Creek. Of the first winter, he wrote: "During the winter of 1847 it was hard picking for us, being without bread, and a thousand miles to go for flour; so we lived on cowhides at times and in the spring, sego roots." He was later sent on a mission to the Southern States where he met Jane Grover, whom he married. They built a home in Farmington, Davis Co., Utah, and later in Morgan Co., Utah. He was later ordained a high priest. He died in Cokeville, Wyo., March 22, 1913, at age 87.

Stringham, Briant — (3rd Ten) Born March 28, 1825, in Windsor, N.Y., to George and Polly Hendricksen Stringham. By 1838 the family was in Kirtland, Ohio, preparing to travel to Missouri. After arriving in Salt Lake Valley with the first company, Stringham remained and prepared for his family to come the following year with Brigham Young's company. To them he wrote: "By the time you get here, I shall be literally naked, and bareheaded, without shoes or clothing. . . . If Jed has any horses have him not fetch them, but trade them for steers and heifers, for they are the best team you can have to come through with. . . . The thought of seeing my brothers and sisters and friends, together with my aged father and dear mother, to think of you all settled in your inheritance in this goodly land fills my soul with joy I cannot express with a pen." He helped plant trees and develop the community. He was appointed probate judge in Cache County in 1856. During Indian wars, he was in charge of the commissary department. For 15 years he had charge of the tithing stock of the Church that was kept on Antelope Island in the Great Salt Lake. He lived on the island much of the time and took part in an annual round-up of the near-wild horses, described as a "thrilling event" by visitors. In 1871 as he was caring for the livestock, he was three days in a wind and rain storm, became ill, probably from pneumonia, and died a few days later, on Aug. 4, 1871, in Salt Lake City at the age of 45.

Summe, Gilbard — (14th Ten) Born Aug. 22, 1802, in Randolph Co., N.C., to John and Caroline Summe. In the first pioneer company, he joined the advance group who entered Salt Lake Valley on July 22, 1847. On April 6, 1850, he was sustained counselor in the general presidency of deacons. He was active in preserving the safety of the settlers during the Walker War. He settled San Bernardino, Calif., and later worked in the lead mines in the Mountain Spring, Nev., area. He returned with the others when recalled in 1857, and continued to assist in the southern colonies. In 1865, he was called to the Muddy Mission in Nevada's Moapa Valley. He settled in St. Joseph, a settlement that no longer exists. When this mission ended, he returned to southern Utah where he died at Harrisburg, Washington Co., on June 13, 1867, at age 64.

Taft, Seth — (Captain of the 8th Ten) Born Aug. 11, 1796, in Mendon, Worcester Co., Mass., to Seth and Lydia Staples Taft. He married Harriet Ogden in Michigan in

1826. Missionaries converted his family in 1841 and they moved to Nauvoo. In the trek west, he was among the advance company that arrived in the valley July 22, 1847. After arriving, he helped locate a site where potatoes, beans, corn and buckwheat could be grown. He began his trip back to Winter Quarters on Aug. 17, but on Sept. 4 he arrived at the Little Sandy Creek in Wyoming, and turned around when he met Daniel Spencer's company, which included his wife, who had driven an ox team across the plains. A year later he was ordained bishop of the Ninth Ward in Salt Lake City. He was called to settle the Manti area but lost his cattle during a severe winter. He returned to Salt Lake City and resumed his duties as bishop of the Ninth Ward until 1856 when he was ordained a patriarch. He died in Salt Lake City, Utah, on Nov. 23, 1863, at age 67.

Tanner, Thomas — (3rd Ten) Born March 31, 1804, in Bristol, Gloucestershire, England, to William and Judea Tanner. He immigrated to America in 1831, married in 1834 and was baptized in New Rochelle, N.Y., in 1841. He was assigned to be captain of the artillery in the first company, and placed in charge of the cannon crew. On the way across the plains, he often drilled his crew and occasionally fired the piece, especially if Indians were around. A blacksmith, his forge was useful in welding broken iron wheels and axles. After arriving in Salt Lake Valley, he built a blacksmith shop of adobe brick and worked as a blacksmith until he became foreman of the Church public works blacksmith shop. He died after a fall in Salt Lake City on Aug. 2, 1855, at age 51.

Taylor, Norman — (14th Ten) Born Sept. 15, 1828, at Grafton, Lorraine Co., Ohio, to Benjamin and Ann Mennel Talyor. He was teamster the first company and drove the second wagon that entered Salt Lake Valley. He assisted in preparing for the oncoming pioneers and then returned to Winter Quarters, where he married Laurana Forbush. He brought his family to Salt Lake Valley in 1850, and in 1851 went to southern California and settled in San Bernardino. Recalled because of the

threat of Johnston's army, he settled in Santaquin, Utah Co., Utah. He moved his family again in 1881 to settle in Moab, Grand Co., Utah. There, he set up a blacksmith's shop, operated a ranch and was owner and operator of a ferryboat across the Colorado River. He was a merchant in his later years and died Nov. 25, 1899, at Moab at age 71 years old.

Thomas, Robert T. — (8th Ten) Born Jan. 8, 1820, in Richmond Co., N.C., to Henry and Esther Covington Thomas. The family joined the Church in 1843 after listening to the preaching of Elder Benjamin L. Clapp. The family moved to Nauvoo, where Robert was ordained to the office of seventy and sent on a mission. He preached in the Southern States for a year, then returned. He was a wagonmaker in the first pioneer comany. He was in the advance party that arrived in Salt Lake

Valley July 22, 1847. After arriving in Salt Lake Valley, he worked for others, including William Stuart and Perrigrine Sessions. In 1848, he was given 60 pounds of shelled corn for his wages by Stuart and he planted in Bountiful, only to have the crickets destroy his crop. He moved back to Salt Lake City and attended school, then joined a group that went south and settled Provo, Utah Co. Just as their crops were growing a severe frost ruined most of them. His wife, Mary Ann Turner Thomas, was the first school teacher in Utah County. When Johnston's army advanced in 1857-58, he was in charge of a company called "Lost Camp" in Echo Canyon. He was also set apart as senior president of the 45th Quorum of the Seventy, a lifetime calling for him. He was elected justice of the peace in 1861, which office he held for 11 years, and was alderman of Provo from 1861-64. He served a mission to Nebraska and Iowa in 1870. Upon his return, he surveyed for a canal at the mouth of Spanish Fork to Springville, and from Provo River to Spring Creek. He organized the Upper East Union Irrigation Company. He was general watermaster of Provo from 1872-82. He died Feb. 28, 1892, at Provo at age 72.

Thornton, Horace — (8th Ten) Born May 7, 1822, at Hinsdale, Catteraugus Co., N.Y., to Ezra and Harriet Goodrich Thornton. He joined the Church in 1836 at Kirtland, Ohio, and followed the Saints to Nauvoo, and then to Winter Quarters. While crossing the plains, Thornton was a member of the cannon crew, a night guard and hunter. He was chosen for the advance company that entered Salt Lake Valley July 22, 1847. After arriving in the valley, he lived in Springville, Utah Co.; Parowan, Iron Co.; and Glenwood, Sevier Co., and then was called to do temple work in St. George and later in

Manti. He was a member of the 69th Quorum of Seventy. He died at Manti, Sanpete Co., Utah, on March 21, 1914, at age 91.

Thorpe, Marcus Ball — (1st Ten) Born June 12, 1822, at New Haven, New Haven Co., Conn. He joined the Church but remained in his hometown until the Saints were at Winter Quarters in 1846. At age 25, he joined the first company and beame part of the advance party. After arriving in the valley, he helped prepare the city for the coming wagon trains. He returned to Winter Quarters with Brigham Young's group and in 1848 came west again. He then went to California in search of gold. When he had earned enough to bring his parents and family to the valley, he placed the gold in a money belt fastened about his middle and took passage on a sailing ship, eastbound via Cape Horn. During the voyage on Jan. 9, 1849, he fell overboard and his body was not recovered.

Tippets, John Harvey — (11th Ten) Born Sept. 5, 1810, at Wittingham, Rockingham Co., N.H., to John and Abigail Pierce Tippets. In March of 1832, he heard of the Book of Mormon and walked 15 miles to read it. He was baptized in the fall of 1832. He remained with the Saints through the trials of Ohio, Missouri and Illinois. When the call came for volunteers to

serve in the Mormon Battalion, he accepted and marched with them. He accompanied a sick detachment to Pueblo, now Colo., where the Mississippi Saints had laid over for the winter. From there he carried wages, mail and dispatches back to Winter Quarters, Neb. The 52-day trip was one of great suffering and danger. He and his companion were taken prisoner by Pawnee Indians and nearly burned at the stake. Later friendly Omaha Indians guided them to Winter Quarters. In the spring he joined the first pioneer company. When the company reached Ft. Laramie, he was sent with

Apostle Amasa Lyman to go to Pueblo and bring those who had wintered there to Salt Lake. He did so and arrived in the valley on July 29. He returned to Winter Quarters that fall and brought his family west the following spring. They lived in Salt Lake City until 1856 when he was called on a mission to England. After he arrived in England, he received word that all missionaries were recalled because of Johnston's army, and he returned to find his family settled in Springville. He later moved them to Farmington, Davis Co., Utah. In 1878 he was ordained a patriarch. He suffered greatly from illness the last years of his life and died in Farmington of dropsy [edema] on Feb. 14, 1890, at age 79.

Vance, William Perkins — (6th Ten) Born Oct. 20, 1822, in Jackson Co., Tenn., to John and Sarah Perkins Vance. He was baptized into the Church in 1842 and he traveled to Nauvoo where he lived a time with the Prophet Joseph Smith. He later wrote of attending school in Ramus, five or six miles from Carthage, Ill., where he learned stenography from a Joseph Johnson. He wrote of the experience:

"Eight young fellows were put into a class, and now I am going to tell you the truth whether you believe it or not — that everyone gave it up but myself." After the Saints arrived in Salt Lake Valley, he was chosen to join Parley P. Pratt's expedition to southern Utah and became one of the first settlers in Iron County. In 1884 he moved to St. George, Washington Co., where he lived until 1892. He then moved to Lund, Nev., where he died Dec. 5, 1914, at the age of 92.

Walker, Henson — (11th Ten) Born March 13, 1820, in Manchester, Ontario Co., N.Y., to Henson and Matilda Arnell Walker. The family moved to the Michigan frontier in 1835 where he became a skilled hunter. In 1840, he was baptized and a year later he married Martha Bouk. They

moved to Salem, N.Y., where he was ordained a teacher. The following year they moved back to Michigan and visited Nauvoo, and met Joseph Smith. In 1843, his wife died and he moved to Nauvoo and lived with his father-in-law. Here he became well-acquainted with Joseph Smith and once in 1843, as a member of the Nauvoo Legion, took part in a rescue effort when the Prophet was kidnapped. After the martyrdom, he worked on the Nauvoo Temple and was married there to Elizabeth Foutz on April 10, 1846. In May, they began the exodus to Winter Quarters. He returned briefly to Nauvoo to help defend the remaining inhabitants, and then moved on to Winter Quarters. He volunteered for the Mormon Battalion, but was released. He joined the first company in the spring of 1847 as a hunter, though ill with a severe fever. He left his wife near death. After arriving in Salt Lake Valley, he started back to Winter Quarters but met his wife, now healthy, and father-in-law Bouk at the Sweetwater River in Wyoming. He returned to spend the first winter in Salt Lake Valley. That summer the crickets came and were devouring the crops. Promised by Jedediah M. Grant that "this present calamity will pass off," Walker and his family stopped fighting the crickets that came thicker than ever. That evening the miracle of the gulls occurred. "I wept for joy, as I saw how miraculously we had been saved from starvation," he said. In an 1849, he was in a skirmish with Indians. In 1850 he went to the Platte River with others and operated a ferry, earning enough that he paid $75 in tithing. He settled at Pleasant Grove, Utah Co., Utah, where he was appointed presiding elder and later bishop. When the community was incorporated, he was its first mayor. In 1863 he was called on a mission to England and presided over the Scottish Mission until returning in 1865. He later filled two missions to the Northern States, and was president of the high priests of the Alpine Stake. He died in Pleasant Grove Jan. 24, 1894, at age 73.

Wardle, George — (1st Ten) Born Feb. 3, 1820, in Cheddleton, England, to Ralph and Ann Allen Wardle. He was baptized, and immigrated to America in 1842 with his bride of two weeks, Fannie Rushton. They lived in Nauvoo, where he worked as a wheel-wright, a trade he learned in his fath-er's shop in England. On the trek west, he was  among those selected to be in the advance party. He returned to Winter Quarters for his wife, brought her to Salt Lake Valley and then settled at Sugar House. An eager student of music and dancing while in England, he soon started a dancing school in a building of logs. Among his students were Brigham Young, George Q. Cannon, and George A. Smith. He also helped organize the first choir and brass band in Salt Lake City. He was later called to Provo, Utah Co.; to Midway, Wasatch Co.; and Glenwood, Sevier Co. to teach his music arts. After John Taylor became president of the Church in 1880, Wardle was called by him to return to Midway and again teach dancing and vocal music to the members. He was later called to Vernal, Uintah Co., Utah, where he organized another school where he gave dancing and vocal lessons. He died in Vernal on Nov. 25, 1901, at age 81.

Wardsworth [or Wordsworth], William Shin — (6th Ten) Born March 5, 1810, in Salem Co., N.J., and baptized in Phil-adelphia, Pa., in the fall of 1841. He was ordained a seventy in February 1846. With the first pioneer company, he was as-signed to be a road and bridge builder. After his arrival in Utah, he continued to  make roads and build bridges and dig irrigation ditches. He also assisted in exploring the surrounding countryside. He died in Springville, Utah Co., Utah, on Jan. 18, 1888, at age 77.

Weiler, Jacob — (4th Ten) Born March 14, 1808, near Churchtown, Pa., to Joseph and Rosannah Stylers Weiler, one of 14 chil-dren. He was baptized March 16, 1841. The only mem-ber of his family to join the Church, he was sub-sequently disinheri-ted. He moved to Nauvoo, and married Anna Maria Malin. He helped in building  roads and bridges. On his return from the Salt Lake Valley, he met this family in an oncoming wagon train at Pacific Springs, near the Continental Divide in Wyoming. He brought them to the valley in Edward Hunter's company. After arriving, he built a cabin in the northeast corner of Pioneer Square in Salt Lake City. He later moved to the Third Ward after drawing for land in that area. In 1856, he was ordained a high priest and called to be bishop of the Third Ward, a position he held for nearly 40 years. He was released because of his age in 1895 and ordained to the office of patriarch. He died in Salt Lake City on March 24, 1896, at age 88.

Wheeler, John — (11th Ten) Born Feb. 3, 1802, in South Carolina, to William and

Lucy Wheeler. After arriving in Salt Lake Valley, with the first company, he returned to Winter Quarters. He came back to the valley by 1851. In 1861 he was highly commended by the Deseret Agricultural and Manufacturing Society for his fine stock exhibited at the fair in Salt Lake City. Later he went to California.

Whipple, Edson — (9th Ten) Born Feb. 5, 1805, in Dummerston, Windham Co., Vt., to Timothy and Elizabeth Safford Whipple. He married Lavinie Goss on Feb. 16, 1832. He was baptized in Philadelphia, Pa., on June 15, 1840, and was set apart as first counselor in the Philadelphia Branch. They moved to Nauvoo, in September 1842. In 1844 he was called on a mission to promote Joseph Smith's candidacy for president of the United States. During this mission, the martyrdom occurred. He returned to help complete the Nauvoo Temple and spent the winter of 1845-46 making wagons. At Council Bluffs, Iowa, he was counseled to locate at Pony Creek, 30 miles south. There, his mother died Sept. 9 and his wife died Sept. 13, and their only daughter a few weeks later. "Of the whole camp, consisting of 14 families, all but two persons were sick," he wrote in his history. "Thus my whole family died, martyrs to Christ." In the first company, he was assigned to be a night guard, taking watch half the night every third night. After arriving in Salt Lake Valley he farmed for Heber C. Kimball and raised some 400 bushels of grain. He was a member of the first high council in Salt Lake City. He started east on a business trip with 11 members of the Mormon Battalion. While there, he was called to assist Wilford Woodruff to gather out the Saints from the Eastern States. Whipple was later a captain of Fifty on a wagon train to Salt Lake Valley that arrived Oct. 13, 1850. He married again and went to Iron County with George A. Smith and helped settle Parowan. It was his city plan that was accepted and followed. He and a Brother Brimhall built the first water-powered threshing machine and threshed the first crop of grain grown in the settlement. He was elected to the Parowan City Council in 1851. Shortly after, Brigham Young visited the new colony and advised him to move to Provo, Utah Co., and he complied. He died in Colonia Juarez, Chihuahua, Mexico, on May 11, 1894, at age 89.

Whitney, Horace Kimball — (10th Ten) Born July 25, 1823, at Kirtland, Ohio, to Newel K. and Elizabeth Ann Smith Whitney. His father was later Presiding Bishop. Well-educated and an expert mathematician and musician, he joined the first company and was assigned by his father to help prepare a place for the rest of his family. He was accompanied by his brother, Orson K. Whitney. The rest of the family arrived Oct. 8, 1848. He served as a major in the Topographical Engineers of the Nauvoo Legion. When Johnston's army marched through the empty Salt Lake City in 1858, he was one of the guards who stood ready to burn the city if the army stopped. He was for many years a member of the Deseret Dramatic Association, both at the Social Hall and the Salt Lake Theatre. A gifted musician, he played in the orchestra. He learned the printer's trade while in Nauvoo and when the *Deseret News* was founded in 1850, he set the type for the first edition and became its first printer. He served in the management of the newspaper for 21 years, a period of tremendous growth for the newspaper. He died Nov. 22, 1884, in Salt Lake City, Utah, at age 61.

Whitney, Orson K. — (10th Ten) Born Jan. 30, 1830, in Kirtland, Ohio, to Newel K. and Elizabeth Ann Smith Whitney. His father was Presiding Bishop. In the first company, he assisted his brother, Horace, in Salt Lake Valley to prepare a place for the family after they arrived in the summer of 1847. After the death of his father in 1852, Orson was called on a mission to the Sandwich (Hawaiian) Islands. A cabinet maker, he earned his way to Hawaii without purse or scrip, arriving in Hawaii in August of 1854. He worked at a few jobs, such as making coffins, to support himself in his missionary work. When his mission was over, he again worked to earn passage back to the mainland. Upon his return, he assisted the Utah Infantry in Echo Canyon in November 1857. Later he fought in Indian skirmishes around Provo and Pleasant Grove in Utah Co. He was known as a daring and adventurous frontiersman. He died in Salt Lake City July 31, 1884, at age 54.

Williams, Almon M. — (8th Ten) Born Jan. 11, 1807, at New York. He arrived with the advance party on July 22, 1847, and is mentioned in the Manuscript History as directing the digging of a coal pit at the same time land was plowed for crops.

Later the same year he returned to Winter Quarters with William Clayton's company. In 1848, he was one of the signers of a petition to the U.S. Government to establish a post office on Pottawattamie lands. He died Dec. 13, 1884, at age 77.

Woodruff, Wilford — (Captain of the 1st Ten) Born March 1, 1807, in Farmington, Hartford Co., Conn., to Aphek and Beulah Thompson Woodruff. When 26, he and his brother, Azmon, heard the missionaries and he was baptized Dec. 31, 1833. Shortly after, he joined Zion's Camp, where he became acquainted with Joseph Smith. After traveling to Missouri with Zion's Camp, he remained in Missouri. He was ordained a priest and sent on a mission to Arkansas and Tennessee in the fall of 1834. He traveled some 3,200 miles to preach and was instrumental in converting many. He returned to Kirtland in the fall of 1836. He married Phoebe Carter in 1837, and left for a mission to the Fox Islands, Maine. On the way he converted many of his relatives in Connecticut. In 1838 he was called as an apostle, and traveled with a group of 50 converts to Illinois to join the Saints. In 1839 he left on a mission to England where in eight months' labor, some 1,800 people were brought into the Church. He returned to America in 1841, met his wife in Scarborough, Maine, and traveled to Nauvoo. He was on the city council of Nauvoo, and became the business manager for the newspaper *Times and Seasons*.

After the martyrdom of Joseph Smith, he went to England and presided over the British Mission during 1845. He returned, took part in the exodus, and began the trek west leading a small band, the first to pull into the prairie. He was described as the most energetic man of the entire company. Arriving at Ft. Laramie, he tied an artificial fly, and made fishing history as he did so. He later came down with mountain fever but recovered. When Brigham Young became ill a short time later, Woodruff put him and Albert Rockwood in the back of a wagon and drove the wagon that brought the Church leader into Salt Lake Valley. Later that fall he returned to Winter Quarters and soon went on a mission to the Eastern States, returning to the Salt Lake Valley in 1850. Upon his return, he was elected to the Senate of the provisional State of Deseret. In 1853 he and Ezra T. Benson took 50 families to strengthen the colonies in

Tooele County. He became Church historian in 1883 and in 1880 he became president of the Quorum of the Twelve Apostles. He became president of the Church April 7, 1889, and in 1890, issued the Manifesto discontinuing plural marriage. He also officiated at the Jubilee Celebration of the arrival of the first pioneers held July 20, 1897, at which a statue of Brigham Young was unveiled. A year later, while staying in San Francisco, Calif., seeking relief from insomnia, he died on Sept. 2, 1898, at age 88.

Woodward, George — (12th Ten) Born Sept. 9, 1817, in Monmouth Co., N. J., to George and Jemima Shinn Woodward. At age 15 he left home to be a clerk in his brother's merchandising business at Homers Town, Pa. At 18, he went to Philadelphia and learned the mason trade. There he heard missionaries and was baptized Sept.

7, 1840. In May 1841 he moved to Nauvoo, and helped with the temple and the Nauvoo House. He married Thomazin Downing in 1842 and was ordained a seventy. In the original company, he wrote near Ft. Bridger that Captain Jim Bridger "thought it a rash venture to plant so large a colony of almost destitute people in the Salt Lake or Bear River Valley." Samuel Brannan "who had come from California sought to induce the pioneers not to stop in short of that part of the country." When the company reached Green River, he recalled that President Young's anxiety for welfare of the oncoming families behind them was so intense, he sent back five men "to see how they were getting along, I being one of them." The five men advised the oncoming company to break into groups of 50, which speeded up their progress. Among those in the wagon was his wife, "to my joy." After arriving in the valley, they settled in the Salt Lake Eighth Ward where in 1850 he was called as first counselor to Bishop Elijah Sheets. In 1861, he was called to settle in St. George, Washington Co., where he worked many years as a mason and in later years was a temple worker. He died Dec. 17, 1903, in St George at age 86.

Woolsey, Thomas — (6th Ten) Born Nov. 3, 1806, in Pulaski Co., Ky., to Joseph and Abigail Schaffer Woolsey. He was baptized in 1838 in Kentucky, and soon immigrated to Illinois. In Nauvoo, he married Julia Ann Mitchell. He was among those who volunteered for the Mormon Battalion. He left his family living in a dugout in Mt. Pisgah, Iowa, and traveled with the Battalion until being sent with a sick detachment to Pueblo, Colo. From there, he carried dispatches and wages to Winter Quarters. On the way, he and John Harvey Tippets were captured by Pawnee Indians and were nearly burned. He later wrote: "We knew we were in a trap, and only through the power of God would we hope to escape, and believe me, we did send up a petition to God. Our prayers were answered." They were guided to Winter Quarters by friendly Omaha Indians. There, he joined the first pioneer company and was a member of the cannon hauling crew. He accompanied the group to Ft. Laramie where he was appointed postmaster and carried a large bundle of mail to Pueblo where the sick detachments of the Mormon Battalion had gone to winter. He was accompanied by Elder Amasa Lyman, John H. Tippets, and Roswell Stevens. Before they left, Brigham Young held a brief meeting, knelt in prayer and dedicated the four to God, and blessed them. The Pueblo group arrived in Salt Lake Valley a week after the first pioneers. He returned to Winter Quarters, where he was appointed to look after the Saints at that location, and did not return to Salt Lake Valley until 1852. After returning to the valley, he lived in several towns, including Mount Pleasant, Ephraim, Kanosh, Fort Harmony, and later in Wales, Sanpete Co., where he died Jan 5, 1897, at age 90.

Young, Brigham — (3rd Ten) Born June 1, 1801, at Whitingham, Windham Co., Vt., to John A. and Abigail Howe Young. He married Miriam Works, and in 1829 moved to Mendon, N.Y., where in the spring of 1830 he saw a copy of the Book of Mormon, distributed by Samuel H. Smith on the Church's first official missionary journey. He  was baptized April 14, 1832. His wife died Sept. 8 of the same year. He soon began missionary work and traveled to Kirtland, Ohio, to meet Joseph Smith. After that meeting, Joseph Smith said, "The time will come when Brother Brigham will preside over the Church." He went to Canada on a mission the next year. In February 1834 he married Mary Ann Angell. He took part in Zion's Camp in 1834, walking to and from Missouri, and on Feb. 14, 1835, was called to the Quorum of the Twelve Apostles. He then began preaching, organizing and supervising branches and working on the Kirtland Temple. During the next few years he stood loyal to the Prophet during the turbulent times of Kirtland and the move of the Church to Missouri. His skills in moving people were valuable as he supervised the exodus of the Saints from Missouri under extremely difficult circumstances. On Sept. 14, 1839, he left his wife, a 10-day-old baby and other children ill and departed for a mission to England. While there, a great work was opened and a stream of emigrants began to flow toward Zion. He returned in 1841, and in 1843 began another mission in the Eastern States to collect funds to help complete the Nauvoo Temple. On another short mission in 1844, he learned of the martyrdom of the Prophet. He returned to find Sidney Rigdon claiming the right to lead the Church. In a speech, Young was transfigured so he appeared like the Prophet Joseph, banishing any doubt as to who should rightfully lead the Church. He organized the exodus and established two way stations, Mt. Pisgah and Garden Grove, to support the Saints as they crossed Iowa, and then Winter Quarters, Neb. During this difficult time, he agreed to supply 500 men to the U.S. Army to receive partial redress for the grievances of Missouri, assured the government of the Saints' loyalty, and halted the U.S. government from interfering with the exodus, as had been rumored. This made necessary the waiting for a year to go to the Rocky Mountains to find a permanent home for the exiles.

In the spring of 1847, he led a company of 144 men, three women and two children the to Salt Lake Valley, an untouched frontier far from their persecutors. He organized the company into units of hundreds, fifties, and tens with captains over each.They also took considerable equipment with them, including surveying and topographical instruments used for roadmaking and laying out cities. After arriving in Indian country, he created a military organization, utilizing officers previously in the Nauvoo Legion. When the company came to buffalo, he gave strict orders that only those animals needed for meat were to be killed. As the company moved along, he acted as scout, road builder and once even constructed a raft. He used buffalo skulls and whatever else could be found as road markers. On July 12, he became ill which delayed his entry into the valley, until July 24. Fifty years later, Wilford Woodruff, who was driving the wagon carrying Brigham on that eventful day, related the immortal words of the leader upon viewing the valley: "It is enough. This is the right place. Drive on."

Recovered in health, he laid out the city in the pattern started by Joseph Smith, located a place for a temple to be built, and organized those who remained. He returned to Kanesville, Iowa, where on Dec. 5, 1847, he was sustained president of the Church. He left his home in Winter Quarters, the fifth he had abandoned for the Church, and moved to Salt Lake City in 1848. He served as the first governor of Utah. As such he successfully resisted the advance of the United States Army under Gen. Albert Sydney Johnston. Johnston came west as directed by Pres. James Buchanan, a decision known to history as "Buchanan's blunder," to quell a supposed insurrection. Finding none, the army, camped peaceably nearby the city until withdrawn. Under Brigham Young's direction, hundreds of colonies were started throughout the mountain west, missionary work extended around the world, temples built, mercantile and manufacturing efforts started, construction of telegraph and rail lines assisted, and academies and universities founded. He avoided many Indian troubles with a policy that "It is better to feed them than to fight them." He died at his home in Salt Lake City on Aug. 29, 1877, at age 76.

Young, Clarissa Decker — (3rd Ten) Born July 22, 1828, in Freedom, Catteraugus Co., N.Y., to Isaac and Harriet Page Wheeler Decker. As a child she had delicate health and, complicating that, was once struck in the head by an ax. She came on the trek west to accompany her mother, Harriet, who  said that she would die if she did not leave Winter Quarters. On the trail, she assisted the men in many ways. After arriving in Salt Lake Valley, she remained and spent the winter of 1847-48, while her husband, Brigham Young, returned to Winter Quarters. She reared her children and cared for foster children as well. She was the last surviving woman of the pioneer trek when she died Jan. 5, 1889, at age 60.

Young, Harriet Page Wheeler — (3rd Ten) Born Sept. 7, 1803, at Hillsboro, N.H., to Oliver and Hannah Ashley Wheeler. After a first marriage to Isaac Decker failed in 1843, she married Lorenzo D. Young, brother of Brigham Young. When the men were about to leave for the West, she pleaded earnestly to accompany them, saying that the climate in Winter Quarters would lead to her

death were she to remain another year. Permission was granted for her go; she was accompanied by her daughter Clarissa Decker Young and Ellen Saunders Kimball. The women proved to be ministering angels to the sick as the company traveled. She also brought two of her children, Isaac Perry Decker, son of her first husband, and Lorenzo Sobieski Young, her husband's son by a previous wife. Although she was not well during much of the journey, she did not contract the fever that afflicted so many in the camp, and was thus able to nurse the ill. She lived in Salt Lake City after her arrival. She died there on Dec. 22, 1871, at age 68.

Young, Lorenzo Dow — (3rd Ten) Born Oct. 19, 1807, at Smyrna, Chenango Co., N.Y., to John and Abigail Howe Young, a brother to Brigham Young. In 1832 he came in contact with the Church and was baptized and moved to Missouri, where he bought 160 acres of land and built a log  house but was shortly driven from his home by mobs. He then moved to Nauvoo, and took part in the exodus. His wife accompanied him on the trek west. After arriving in Salt Lake Valley, he remained until 1849, then went east to Missouri and returned the following year with 500 head of sheep, 80 head of cattle and several horses. He settled on the west side of the Jordan River and started a cattle and sheep ranch. He also raised vegetables. He was said to be the first in the valley to raise garden flowers. In 1851 he was ordained bishop of the Eighteenth Ward, serving in that office for 27 years. He later visited the settlements to encourage the well-to-do to assist and befriend the poor. He was ordained a patriarch by his brother, and he held that office until he died Nov. 21, 1895, at age 88 in Salt Lake City.

Young, Lorenzo Sobieski — (3rd Ten) Born March 9, 1841, in Winchester, Morgan Co., Ill., to Lorenzo Dow and Persis Goodall Young. He was 6 years of age when taken on the pioneer trek from Winter Quarters to Salt Lake City. He was given his second name in honor of his mother's first husband, Edwin Sobieski Little, who died in Iowa during the exodus. After arriving in the valley, Lorenzo learned horticulture from his father and became a farmer. He lived in Huntington, Emery Co., Utah, where he farmed. He died in Shelley, Bingham Co., Idaho, March 28, 1904, at age 63.

Young, Phinehas Howe — (Captain of the 3rd Ten) Born Feb. 16, 1799, in Hopkinton, Middlesex Co., Mass., to John and Abigail Howe Young, a brother of Brigham Young. He learned the printing trade and farmed. In 1818 he married Clarissa Hamilton, who later died. He then married Lucy Cowdery, half-sister of Oliver Cowdery. In 1830 he read a copy of the Book of Mormon and was baptized. In 1841 he and Franklin Richards filled a mission to Ohio. On the trek west, he

often hunted and supplied the pioneers with fresh meat. When the company reached the Green River in what is now Wyoming, Phinehas was among five men sent back to guide the oncoming companies. He later guided three additional companies across the plains to Salt Lake City. When he settled in the city, he built a two-story adobe house and planted one of the first orchards in the city. As his wife, Lucy, had refused to come west, he married an English convert, Phebe Clark. In 1853, he received his license to practice law but shortly after was called on a mission to England and Scotland. He returned in 1864 and was ordained bishop of the Second Ward. In 1871 he moved to Summit Co., where he stayed until he returned to Salt Lake City in 1875. He died in Salt Lake City Oct. 10, 1879, at age 80.

MORMON EMIGRANTS ON SHIPS FROM FOREIGN PORTS TO U.S. PORTS, 1840-1890

Some departure dates, number of passengers, and arrival dates are approximations.

Ships departed from

L - Liverpool
Lo - London
Br - Bristol, England
Au - Australia-no town
S - Sydney, Australia
N - Newcastle, Australia
M - Melbourne, Australia
W - Wellington, New Zealand
NZ - New Zealand-no town
A - Auckland, New Zealand
C - Calcutta, India
PE - Port Elizabeth, South Africa
Ca - Cape Town, South Africa
H - Hamburg, Germany
Le - LeHavre, France
Ho - Holland,Amsterdam

Ships arrived into:

NY - New York
NO - New Orleans
Q - Quebec
B - Boston
P - Philadelphia
SF - San Francisco
SP - San Pedro, Calif.

Departure		Port	Ship	Church leader	No.	Port	Arrival
1840	6 Jun	L	Britannia	John Moon	41	NY	20 July 1840
	8 Sep	L	North America	Theodore Turley	201	NY	12 Oct 1840
	15 Oct	L	Isaac Newton	Samuel Mulliner	50	NO	2 Dec 1840
1841	7 Feb	L	Sheffield	Hiram Clark	235	NO	30 Mar 1841
	Feb	Br	Caroline	Thomas Clark	181	Q	perhaps Apr 1841
	16 Feb	L	Echo	Daniel Browett	109	NO	16 Apr 1841
	17 Mar	L	Alesto	Thomas Smith and William Moss	54	NO	16 May 1841
	21 Apr	L	Rochester	Brigham Young	130	NY	20 May 1841

Year	Date		Ship	Church leader	No.	Port	Arrival
	10 May	Br	Harmony	Thomas Kington	50	Q	12 July 1841
	8 Aug	Br	Caroline	Thomas Richardson	100	Q	22 Oct 1841
	21 Sep	L	Tyrian	Joseph Fielding	207	NO	9 Nov 1841
	8 Nov	L	Chaos	Peter Melling	170	NO	14 Jan 1842
1842	12 Jan	L	Tremont	No church leader shown	143	NO	10 Mar 1842
	5 Feb	L	Hope	James Burnham	270	NO	1 Apr 1842
	20 Feb	L	John Cumming	No church leader shown	200	NO	26 Apr 1842
	12 Mar	L	Hanover	Amos Fielding	200	NO	2 May 1842
	17 Sep	L	Sidney	Levi Richards	180	NO	11 Nov 1842
	25 Sep	L	Medford	Orson Hyde	214	NO	13 Nov 1842
	29 Sep	L	Henry	John Snider	157	NO	10 Nov 1842
	29 Oct	L	Emerald	Parley P. Pratt	250	NO	Jan 1843
	Dec	L	Hope	F. Cook		NO	28 Feb 1843
1843	16 Jan	L	Swanton	Lorenzo Snow	212	NO	16 Mar 1843
	8 Mar	L	Yorkshire	Thomas Bullock and Richard Rushton	83	NO	10 May 1843
	21 Mar	L	Claiborne	No church leader shown	106	NO	13 May 1843
	5 Sep	L	Metoka	No church leader shown	280	NO	27 Oct 1843
	21 Oct	L	Champion	No church leader shown	91	NO	6 Dec 1843
1844	23 Jan	L	Fanny	William Kay	210	NO	7 Mar 1844
	6 Feb	L	Isaac Allerton	No church leader shown	60	NO	23 Mar 1844
	11 Feb	L	Swanton	No church leader shown	81	NO	5 Apr 1844
	5 Mar	L	Glasgow	Hiram Clark	150	NO	13 Apr 1844
	19 Sep	L	Norfolk	No church leader shown	143	NO	11 Nov 1844
	Oct	L	Oakland	T. Bailey		NO	20 Dec 1844
1845	17 Jan	L	Palmyra	Amos Fielding	241	NO	11 Mar 1845
	Feb	L	Walpole	No church leader shown	214	NO	16 Apr 1845
	30 Mar	L	Parthenon	Samuel Bennion		NO	12 May 1845
	20 Aug	L	Elizabeth	No church leader shown	50	NO	17 Oct 1845
	1 Sep	L	Oregon	No church leader shown	125	NO	28 Oct 1845
	20 Sep	L	Windsor Castle	No church leader shown	110	NO	22 Nov 1845
	9 Oct	L	Palmyra	No church leader shown	66	NO	26 Nov 1845
1846	16 Jan	L	Liverpool	Hiram Clark	45	NO	25 Mar 1846
	15 Feb	L	Windsor Castle	No church leader shown	54	NO	Spring 1846
	15 Aug	L	Montezuma	No church leader shown		NY	17 Sep 1846
1847	19 Jan	L	America	P.P. Pratt; John Taylor	14	NO	10 Mar 1847
	6 Jul	L	Empire	Lucius N. Scovil	24	NY	10 Aug 1847
1848	20 Feb	L	Carnatic	Franklin D. Richards	120	NO	19 Apr 1848
	9 Mar	L	Sailor Prince	Moses Martin and Uriah Hulme	80	NO	28 Apr 1848
	7 Sep	L	Erin's Queen	Simeon Carter	232	NO	28 Oct 1848
	24 Sep	L	Sailor Prince	Lorenzo D. Butler	311	NO	20 Nov 1848
	17 Nov	L	Lord Ashburton	3 emigrant families	11	NO	6 Feb 1849
	30 Dec	L	Lord Sandon	small emigrant group	11	NO	17 Feb 1849 -
1849	29 Jan	L	Zetland	Orson Spencer	358	NO	2 Apr 1849
	6 Feb	L	Ashland	John Johnson	187	NO	18 Apr 1849
	7 Feb	L	Henry Ware	Robert Martin	225	NO	8 Apr 1849
	26 Feb	L	Buena Vista	Dan Jones	249	NO	19 Apr 1849
	5 Mar	L	Hartley	William Hulme	220	NO	28 Apr 1849
	12 Mar	L	Emblem	Robert Deans	100	NO	4 May 1849
	2 Sep	L	James Pennell	Thomas H. Clark	236	NO	22 Oct 1849
	5 Sep	L	Berlin	James G. Brown	254	NO	22 Oct 1849
	10 Nov	L	Zetland	Samuel H. Hawkins	250	NO	24 Dec 1849
1850	10 Jan	L	Argo	Jeter Clinton	402	NO	8 Mar 1850
	18 Feb	L	Josiah Bradlee	Thomas Day	263	NO	18 Apr 1850
	2 Mar	L	Hartley	David Cook	109	NO	2 May 1850
	4 Sep	L	North Atlantic	David Sudworth	357	NO	1 Nov 1850
	2 Oct	L	James Pennell	Christopher Layton and Wm. L. Cutler	254	NO	22 Nov 1850
	17 Oct	L	Joseph Badger	John Morris	227	NO	22 Nov 1850
1851	8 Jan	L	Ellen	James W. Cummings	466	NO	14 Mar 1851
	23 Jan	L	George W. Bourne	William Gibson	281	NO	20 Mar 1851
	1 Feb	L	Ellen Maria	George D. Watt	378	NO	6 Apr 1851

Year	Date	Type	Ship	Leader	No.	Port	Date
	4 Mar	L	Olympus	William Howell	245	NO	27 Apr 1851
1852	10 Jan	L	Kennebec	John S. Higbee	333	NO	14 Mar 1852
	10 Feb	L	Ellen Maria	Isaac C. Haight	369	NO	5 Apr 1852
	6 Mar	L	Niagara	John Taylor, later church president	20	B	19 Mar 1852
	6 Mar	L	Rockaway	perhaps Elias Morris	30	NO	25 Apr 1852
	11 Mar	L	Italy	Ole U. C. Munster	28	NO	10 May 1852
1853	16 Jan	L	Forest Monarch	John E. Forsgren	297	NO	16 Mar 1853
	17 Jan	L	Ellen Maria	Moses Clawson	332	NO	6 Mar 1853
	23 Jan	L	Golconda	Jacob Gates	321	NO	26 Mar 1853
	5 Feb	L	Jersey	George Halliday	314	NO	21 Mar 1853
	15 Feb	L	Elvira Owen	Joseph W. Young	345	NO	31 Mar 1853
	28 Feb	L	International	Christopher Arthur	425	NO	23 Apr 1853
	28 Mar	L	Falcon	Cornelius Bagnall	324	NO	18 May 1853
	6 Apr	L	Camillus	Curtis E. Bolton	228	NO	7 June 1853
	6 Apr	S	Envelope	Charles W. Wandell	30	SF	8 July 1853
	24 Aug	L	R.ufus K. Page	Christian Binder	17	NO	28 Oct 1853
	1853	L	Miscellaneous	Miscellaneous	23	NO	1853
1854	3 Jan	L	Jesse Munn	Christian J. Larsen	335	NO	20 Feb 1854
	28 Jan	L	Benjamin Adams	Hans Peter Olsen	384	NO	22 Mar 1854
	4 Feb	L	Golconda	Dorr P. Curtis	464	NO	18 Mar 1854
	22 Feb	L	Windermere	Daniel Garn	477	NO	23 Apr 1854
	5 Mar	L	Old England	John O. Angus	45	NO	26 Apr 1854
	Mar	L	Colonel Cutts	Flewit or Flavell family	few	NO	26 Apr 1854
	12 Mar	L	John M. Wood	Robert Campbell	397	NO	2 May 1854
	22 Mar	N	Julia Ann	William Hyde	63	SP	12 June 1854
	4 Apr	L	Germanicus	Richard Cook	220	NO	12 June 1854
	8 Apr	L	Marshfield	William Taylor	366	NO	29 May 1854
	24 Apr	L	Clara Wheeler	No church leader shown	29	NO	3 July 1854
	27 Nov	L	Clara Wheeler	Henry E. Phelps	422	NO	11 Jan 1855
	1854	L	Miscellaneous	Miscellaneous	34	NO	1854
1855	6 Jan	L	Rockaway	Samuel Glasgow	24	NO	28 Feb 1855
	7 Jan	L	James Nesmith	Peter O. Hansen	441	NO	23 Feb 1855
	9 Jan	L	Neva	Thomas Jackson	13	NO	22 Feb 1855
	17 Jan	L	Charles Buck	Richard Ballantyne	403	NO	14 Mar 1855
	3 Feb	L	Isaac Jeans	George C. Riser	16	P	5 Mar 1855
	27 Feb	L	Siddons	John S. Fullmer	430	P	20 Apr 1855
	31 Mar	L	Juventa	William Glover	573	P	5 May 1855
	17 Apr	L	Chimborazo	Edward Stevenson	432	P	21 May 1855
	22 Apr	L	S. Curling	Israel Barlow	581	NY	22 May 1855
	26 Apr	L	William Stetson	Aaron Smethurst	293	NY	27 May 1855
	27 Apr	M	Tarquinia	Burr Frost	72	none	to Hawaii 5 July
	July		Williamantic		72		SF 1855
			(Tarquinia passengers from Honolulu to SF)				
	29 May	C	Frank Johnson	No church leader shown	few	SF	18 Sep 1855
	29 July	L	Cynosure	George Seager	159	NY	5 Sep 1855
	7 Sep	S	Julia Ann	John Penfold, Sr.	28	none	Wrecked 3 Oct
	3 Dec		Emma Packer	(took Julia Ann survivors to Tahiti) survivors from Tahiti	none		Tahiti 19 Dec
	5 May 1856		G. W. Kendall	took some to SF		SF	27 June 1856
	1856		Navigator	took some survivors from Tahiti to Hawaii	none		Hawaii Mar 1856
	1 Apr 1856		Francis Palmer	took some survivors from Hawaii to SF		SF	23 Apr 1856
	30 Nov	L	Emerald Isle	Philomen C. Merrill	350	NY	29 Dec 1855
	12 Dec	L	John J. Boyd	Knud Peterson	512	NY	15 Feb 1856
	1855	L	Miscellaneous	Miscellaneous	319	NY	1855
1856	18 Feb	L	Caravan	Daniel Tyler	457	NY	27 Mar 1856
	23 Mar	L	Enoch Train	James Ferguson	534	B	1 May 1856
	19 Apr	L	S. Curling	Dan Jones	707	B	23 May 1856
	4 May	L	Thornton	James G. Willie	764	NY	14 June 1856

Year	Date		Ship	Leader	Number		Arrival
	25 May	L	Horizon	Edward Martin	856	B	30 June 1856
	28 May	S	Jenny Ford	Augustus Farnham	30	SP	15 Aug 1856
	1 Jun	L	Wellfleet	John Aubrey	146	B	13 July 1856
	5 Jul	L	Lucy Thompson	James Thompson	14	NY	8 Aug 1856
	18 Nov	L	Columbia	John Williams	221	NY	1 Jan 1857
	10 Dec	C	Escort	Matthew McCune family	few	NY	30 Mar 1857
	1856	L	Miscellaneous	Miscellaneous	69	NY	1856
1857	28 Mar	L	Geo. Washington	James P. Park	817	B	20 Apr 1857
	25 Apr	L	Westmoreland	Matthias Cowley	544	P	31 May 1857
	30 May	L	Tuscarora	Richard Harper	547	P	3 July 1857
	21 Jun	L	Isaac Wright	George Gaisford family	4	NY	1 Aug 1857
	27 Jun	S	Lucas	William M. Wall	69	SP	12 Oct 1857
	18 Jul	L	Wyoming	Charles Harman	36	P	3 Sep 1857
	26 Aug	L	Dreadnought	No church leader shown	few	NY	Oct 1857
	14 Sep	S	General Cushing	Joseph A. Kelting	few	SF	1857
1858	21 Jan	L	Underwriter	Henry Herriman	25	NY	11 Mar 1858
	19 Feb	L	Empire	Jesse Hobson	64	NY	19 Mar 1858
	22 Mar	L	John Bright	Iver N. Iversen	89	NY	23 Apr 1858
	28 Mar	M	Milwaukie	No church leader shown	few	SF	21 May 1858
	Apr	PE	Gemsbok	E. Richardson	few	B	June 1858
	May	M	Marianna	Z. Snow	few	SF	July 1858
	28 Dec	M	Milwaukie	Thomas S. Johnson	30	SF	18 Mar 1859
1859	22 Jan	PE	Gemsbok	No church leader shown	5	B	18 Mar 1859
	9 Mar	PE	Alacrity	Joseph R. Humphreys	28	B	19 May 1859
	11 Apr	L	William Tapscott	Robert F. Neslen	725	NY	13 May 1859
	10 Jul	L	Antarctic	James Chaplow	30	NY	21 Aug 1859
	20 Aug	L	Emerald Isle	Henry Hug	54	NY	1 Oct 1859
1860	8 Mar	PE	Mary Pearce	N. Paul		NY	11 June 1860
	30 Mar	L	Underwriter	James S. Ross	594	NY	1 May 1860
	5 Apr	Ca	Alacrity	Charles Wood and Richard Provis		B	18 June 1860
	11 May	L	William Tapscott	Asa Calkin	731	NY	16 June 1860
	1860	L	Miscellaneous	Miscellaneous	84	NY	1860
1861	20 Feb	PE	Race Horse	H. Talbot		B	19 Apr 1861
	16 Apr	L	Manchester	Claudius V. Spencer	379	NY	14 May 1861
	23 Apr	L	Underwriter	Milo Andrus	624	NY	21 May 1861
	16 May	L	Monarch of the Sea	Jabez Woodard	955	NY	19 June 1861
1862	9 Apr	H	Humboldt	Hans Christian Hansen	323	NY	20 May 1862
	15 Apr	H	Franklin	Christian A. Madsen	413	NY	29 May 1862
	18 Apr	H	Electric	Soren Christoffersen	336	NY	5 June 1862
	21 Apr	H	Athena	Ola N. Liljenquist	484	NY	7 June 1862
	23 Apr	L	John J. Boyd	James S. Brown	702	NY	1 June 1862
	6 May	L	Manchester	John D. T. McAllister	376	NY	12 June 1862
	14 May	L	William Tapscott	William Gibson	807	NY	25 June 1862
	15 May	Le	Windermere	Serge L. Ballif	110	NY	8 July 1862
	18 May	L	Antarctic	William C. Moody	38	NY	27 June 1862
	1862	L	Miscellaneous	Miscellaneous	8	NY	1862
1863	14 Mar	PE	Rowena	Robert Grant	15	NY	22 May 1863
	31 Mar	PE	Henry Ellis	John Stock and Martin Zyderlaam	32	NY	28 May 1863
	30 Apr	L	John J. Boyd	William W. Cluff	767	NY	29 May 1863
	8 May	L	B. S. Kimball	Hans Peter Lund	657	NY	13 June 1863
	8 May	L	Consignment	Anders Christensen	38	NY	20 June 1863
	23 May	L	Antarctic	John Needham	486	NY	10 July 1863
	30 May	L	Cynosure	David M. Stuart	775	NY	19 July 1863
	4 June	Lo	Amazon	William Bramall	895	NY	18 July 1863
	1863	L	Miscellaneous	Miscellaneous	72	NY	1863
1864	5 Apr	PE	Echo	John Talbot	9	B	12 June 1864
	10 Apr	PE	Susan Pardew	William Fotheringham and Henry A. Dixon	18	B	11 June 1864
	28 Apr	L	Monarch of the Sea	John Smith, Church patriarch	974	NY	3 June 1864
	21 May	L	Gen. McClellan	Thomas E. Jeremy	802	NY	23 June 1864

Year	Date		Ship	Church Leader	No.	Port	Arrival
	3 June	Lo	Hudson	John M. Kay	863	NY	19 July 1864
	1864	L	Miscellaneous	Miscellaneous	58	NY	1864
1865	12 Apr	PE	Mexicana	Miner Grant Atwood	47	NY	18 June 1865
	29 Apr	L	Belle Wood	William H. Shearman	636	NY	31 May 1865
	8 May	H	B. S. Kimball	Anders W. Winberg	558	NY	14 June 1865
	10 May	L	David Hoadley	William Underwood	24	NY	19 June 1865
	7 June	L	Bridgewater	No church leader shown	7	NY	14 July 1865
	17 Oct	M	Albert	J. D. Spencer		SF	26 Jan 1866
	1865	L	Miscellaneous	Miscellaneous	83	NY	1865
1866	30 Apr	L	John Bright	Collins M. Gillett	747	NY	6 June 1866
	5 May	Lo	Caroline	Samuel H. Hill	389	NY	11 June 1866
	23 May	Lo	American Congress	John Nicholson	350	NY	4 July 1866
	25 May	H	Kenilworth	Samuel L. Sprague	684	NY	16 July 1866
	30 May	L	Arkwright	Justin C. Wixom	450	NY	6 July 1866
	30 May	Lo	Cornelius Grinnell	Ralph Harrison	26	NY	11 July 1866
	1 June	H	Cavour	Niels Nielsen	201	NY	31 July 1866
	2 June	H	Humboldt	George M. Brown	328	NY	18 July 1866
	6 June	L	St. Mark	Alfred Stevens	104	NY	24 July 1866
	1866	L	Miscellaneous	Miscellaneous	56	NY	1866
1867	before Mar 30	M	Unnamed ship	Australian group sailed	5	SF	Spring
	Apr or May	M	Unnamed ship	Australian group (was expected to sail)	11	SF	Spring 1867
	1 June	Lo	Hudson	No church leader shown	20	NY	19 July 1867
	21 June	L	Manhattan	Archibald N. Hill	480	NY	4 July 1867
	1867	L	Louisiana	included Ruth May Fox	3		NY 1867
	1867	L	Miscellaneous	Miscellaneous	178	NY	1867
1868	4 June	L	John Bright	James McGaw	722	NY	13 July 1868
	20 June	L	Emerald Isle	Hans Jensen Hals	876	NY	14 Aug 1868
	24 June	L	Constitution	Harvey H. Cluff	457	NY	5 Aug 1868
	30 June	L	Minnesota	John Parry	534	NY	12 July 1868
	14 July	L	Colorado	William B. Preston	600	NY	28 July 1868
	1868	L	Miscellaneous	Miscellaneous	43	NY	1868
1869	2 June	L	Minnesota	Elias Morris	338	NY	14 June 1869
	15 July	L	Minnesota	Ole C. Olsen	598	NY	28 July 1869
	28 July	L	Colorado	John E. Pace	376	NY	10 Aug 1869
	25 Aug	L	Minnesota	Marius Ensign	454	NY	5 Sep 1869
	22 Sep	L	Manhattan	Joseph Lawson	242	NY	6 Oct 1869
	6 Oct	L	Minnesota	James Needham	291	NY	17 Oct 1869
	20 Oct	L	Colorado	Charles Wilden	16	NY	1 Nov 1869
	1 Dec	L	Colorado	George Stanger	5	NY	Dec 1869
1870	28 June	L	Colorado	George Naylor	20	NY	12 July 1870
	13 July	L	Manhattan	Karl G. Maeser	269	NY	26 July 1870
	20 July	L	Minnesota	Jesse N. Smith	357	NY	1 Aug 1870
	10 Aug	L	Colorado	2 elders, small company	few	NY	Aug 1870
	7 Sep	L	Idaho	Frank H. Hyde	186	NY	21 Sep 1870
	14 Sep	L	Nevada	Richard Smyth 26 or B.N. Walter		NY26	Sep 1870
	16 Nov	L	Manhattan	Ralph Thompson	59	NY	2 Dec 1870
1871	22 Mar	L	Wisconsin	Small group from Wales	7	NY	3 Apr 1871
	26 Apr	L	Wisconsin	Small English group	8	NY	9 May 1871
	10 May	L	Wyoming	Joseph Parry	11	NY	21 May 1871
	4 June	S	Wonga Wonga	Edwin S. Kearsley		SF	8 July 1871
	21 June	L	Wyoming	George Lake	248	NY	2 July 1871
	28 June	L	Minnesota	William W. Cluff	397	NY	11 July 1871
	12 July	L	Colorado	Hamilton G. Park	146	NY	25 July 1871
	26 July	L	Nevada	Lot Smith	93	NY	7 Aug 1871
	9 Aug	L	Minnesota	William Douglass	60	NY	21 Aug 1871
	6 Sep	L	Nevada	John I. Hart	263	NY	18 Sep 1871
	18 Oct	L	Nevada	George H. Peterson	300	NY	1 Nov 1871
	30 Dec	A	Nevada (another one)	Dryden/Fawcett families	11	SF	SLC 10 Feb 1872

1872	21 Apr	W	Wellington	Henry Allington	9	SF	23 May 1872
	12 June	L	Manhattan	David Brinton	221	NY	26 June 1872
	26 June	L	Nevada	Erik Peterson	426	NY	8 July 1872
	31 July	L	Wisconsin	George P. Ward	179	NY	12 Aug 1872
	4 Sep	L	Minnesota	George W. Wilkins	602	NY	16 Sep 1872
	16 Oct	L	Minnesota	Thomas Dobson	203	NY	29 Oct 1872
	6 Nov	L	Nevada	Thomas Morley	26	none	transferred to ship Manhattan
	4 Dec	L	Manhattan	Daniel Kennedy	35	NY	21 Dec 1872
1873	4 June	L	Nevada	Charles H. Wilcken	246	NY	16 June 1873
	June	S	Unnamed ship	included John Moss	15	SF	SLC Sep 15
	2 July	L	Wisconsin	David O. Calder	976	NY	15 July 1873
	10 July	L	Nevada	Elijah A. Box	283	NY	23 July 1873
	3 Sep	L	Wyoming	John B. Fairbanks	510	NY	19 Sep 1873
	22 Oct	L	Idaho	John I. Hart	522	NY	4 Nov 1873
1874	6 May	L	Nevada	Lester J. Herrick	155	NY	21 May 1874
	11 June	L	Nevada	Joseph Birch	243	NY	23 June 1874
	24 June	L	Idaho	Peter C. Carstenson	810	NY	6 July 1874
	8 July	L	Minnesota	John Keller	81	NY	21 July 1874
	Sep	Au	Unnamed ship	John Buckle family	7	SF	SLC 8 Nov
	2 Sep	L	Wyoming	John C. Graham	553	NY	14 Sep 1874
	14 Oct	L	Wyoming	William N. Fife	155	NY	26 Oct 1874
	1874	L	Miscellaneous	Miscellaneous	11	NY	1874
1875	12 May	L	Wyoming	Hugh S. Gowans	176	NY	23 May 1875
	16 June	L	Wisconsin	Robert T. Burton	167	NY	27 June 1875
	30 June	L	Idaho	Christen G. Larsen	765	NY	13 July 1875
	29 Jul	L	City of Chester	2 elders , 1 other man	3	NY	Aug 1875
	15 Sep	L	Wyoming	Richard V. Morris	300	NY	26 Sep 1875
	14 Oct	L	Dakota	Bedson Eardley	120	NY	25 Oct 1875
1876	19 Jan	L	Montana	Isaiah M. Coombs	15	NY	31 Jan 1876
	24 May	L	Nevada	John Woodhouse	117	NY	5 June 1876
	28 June	L	Idaho	Nils C. Flygare	628	NY	10 July 1876
	16 Aug	L	Idaho	includes Enoch Stones	9	NY	Aug 1876
	23 Aug	L	Nevada	2 elders, 3 Icelandics	5	NY	5 Sep 1876
	13 Sep	L	Wyoming	William L. Binder	322	NY	23 Sep 1876
	25 Oct	L	Wyoming	Peter Barton	118	NY	4 Nov 1876
	1876	L	Miscellaneous	Miscellaneous	62	NY	1876
1877	4 Apr	L	Wisconsin	1 elder, 1 emigrant man	2	NY	Apr 1877
	Apr	Au	Unnamed ship	David Cluff	9	SF	SLC 14 May
	May	Au	Unnamed ship	Edward T. Hoagland	10	SF	SLC 6 June
	13 June	L	Wyoming	David K. Udall	186	NY	23 June 1877
	27 June	L	Wisconsin	John Rowberry	714	NY	7 July 1877
	25 July	L	Wyoming	includes Defriez family	9	NY	4 Aug 1877
	19 Sep	L	Wisconsin	Hamilton G. Park	482	NY	30 Sep 1877
	17 Oct	L	Idaho	William Paxman	150	NY	29 Oct 1877
	7 Nov	L	Montana	White family from Leeds	4	NY	22 Nov 1877
	8 Dec	L	Wyoming	1 elder and emigrants	6	NY	19 Dec 1877
	1877	L	Miscellaneous	Miscellaneous	47	NY	1877
1878	25 May	L	Nevada	Thomas Judd	354	NY	5 June 1878
	15 June	L	Montana	Theodore Braendli	221	NY	25 June 1878
	29 June	L	Nevada	John Cook	569	NY	10 July 1878
	14 Sep	L	Wyoming	Henry W. Naisbitt	609	NY	24 Sep 1878
	21 Sep	L	Nevada	John C. Christiansen	few	NY	3 Oct 1878
	19 Oct	L	Wyoming	Aurelius Miner	145	NY	29 Oct 1878
	1878	NZ	Unnamed ship	family of 4 had sailed	4	SF	Spring 1878
	1878	NZ	Unnamed ship	group of 5 will sail	5	SF	Spring 1878
	1878	NZ	Unnamed ship	James Burnett, Jr.	18	SF	1878
1879	21 Feb	S	Malay	Small Australian group	few	SF	11 May 1879
	19 Apr	L	Wyoming	Charles W. Nibley	170	NY	30 Apr 1879
	24 May	L	Wyoming	Alexander F. Macdonald	170	NY	3 June 1879
	21 June	L	Montana	Mary Foster; daughter	2	NY	2 July 1879
	28 June	L	Wyoming	William N. Williams	622	NY	8 July 1879
	30 Aug	L	Montana	2 English , 1 Welsh	3	NY	Sep 1879

Year	Date	Type	Ship	Company/Leader	No.	Port	Date
	6 Sep	L	Wyoming	Nils C. Flygare	336	NY	15 Sep 1879
	18 Oct	L	Arizona	William Bramall	224	NY	27 Oct 1879
1880	10 Apr	L	Wyoming	James L. Bunting	120	NY	22 Apr 1880
	17 Apr	L	Nevada	Joseph and Sarah May	2	NY	Apr 1880
	1 May	L	Wisconsin	Einar Johnson /Iceland	16	NY	12 May 1880
	8 May	L	Arizona	John Price from Wales	1	NY	17 May 1880
	15 May	L	Wyoming	Peter Hood	6	NY	25 May 1880
	5 June	L	Wisconsin	John G. Jones	337	NY	15 June 1880
	17 June	S	Australia	Fred J. May	30	SF	Auckland 22 June
				and Thomas A. Shreeve		SF	15 July 1880
	26 June	L	Nevada	Icelandic company	4	NY	9 July 1880
	10 July	L	Wisconsin	Niels P. Rasmussen	727	NY	20 July 1880
	4 Sep	L	Nevada	John Rider	336	NY	15 Sep 1880
	25 Sep	L	Arizona	Martin Hansen	1	NY	Oct 1880
	23 Oct	L	Wisconsin	John Nicholson	258	NY	2 Nov 1880
1881	16 Apr	L	Wyoming	David C. Dunbar	197	NY	26 Apr 1881
	23 Apr	L	Arizona	Mary Jane Thomas	1	NY	2 May 1881
	26 Apr	A	City of Sidney	George Batt	27	SF	17 May 1881
	21 May	L	Wyoming	Joseph R. Mathews	278	NY	1 June 1881
	24 May	A	Australia	Wm. Walter Day	24	SF	14 June 1881
	11 June	L	Nevada	Icelandic company	11	NY	30 June 1881
	25 June	L	Wyoming	Samuel Roskelley	775	NY	7 July 1881
	16 July	L	Nevada	John Eyvindson	24	NY	28 July 1881
	19 July	A	Zealandia	John P. Sorensen	3	SF	Aug 1881
	3 Sep	L	Wyoming	James Finlayson	644	NY	13 Sep 1881
	10 Sep	A	Australia	Small emigrant group	3	SF	Oct 1881
	22 Oct	L	Wisconsin	Lyman R. Martineau	396	NY	1 Nov 1881
	12 Nov	L	Wyoming	1 Scottish, 1 Danish	2	NY	26 Nov 1881
1882	7 Jan	L	Wisconsin	1 elder, 2 from Glasgow	3	NY	19 Jan 1882
	28 Mar	A	City of Sydney	Nioholas H. Groesbeck	18	SF	SLC 22 Apr 1882
	12 Apr	L	Nevada	John Donaldson	342	NY	24 Apr 1882
	22 Apr	L	Arizona	Scott Anderson	1	NY	May 1882
	17 May	L	Nevada	William R. Webb	392	NY	27 May 1882
	3 June	L	Abyssinia	John Fearn - emigrant	1	NY	17 June 1882
	10 June	L	Wisconsin	includes Taylor family	6	NY	21 June 1882
	21 June	L	Nevada	Robert R.. Irvine	933	NY	2 July 1882
	3 July	L	Arizona	Joseph Howell	1	NY	11 July 1882
	22 July	L	Alaska	5 English, 13 Icelandic	18	NY	31 July 1882
	19 Aug	L	Wisconsin	Fogelberg family	4	NY	Sep 1882
	2 Sep	L	Wyoming	William Cooper	662	NY	12 Sep 1882
	9 Sep	L	Arizona	David Moses	1	NY	18 Sep 1882
	7 Oct	L	Wyoming	includes 2 emigrants	16	NY	19 Oct 1882
	21 Oct	L	Abyssinia	George Stringfellow	416	NY	2 Nov 1882
	4 Nov	L	Alaska	Small emigrant group	7	NY	14 Nov 1882
	25 Nov	L	Abyssinia	A. Carrington/emigrants	6	NY	6 Dec 1882
	30 Dec	L	Abyssinia	1 elder, 2 emigrants	3	NY	15 Jan 1883
1883	6 Jan	L	Wisconsin	emigrants to Ogden	2	NY	22 Jan 1883
	20 Jan	L	Alaska	1 elder, 2 emigrants	3	NY	31 Jan 1883
	11 Apr	L	Nevada	David McKay	352	NY	23 Apr 1883
	25 Apr	A	City of New York	Wm. Burnett	48	SF	SLC 22 May
	16 May	L	Nevada	Ben E. Rich	427	NY	27 May 1883
	22 May	A	Zealandia	Arthur Bippengale	7	SF	June 1883
	2 June	L	Alaska	John Wood , Icelandic	7	NY	11 June 1883
	20 June	L	Nevada	Hans O. Magleby	697	NY	1 July 1883
	14 July	L	Wisconsin	John Sutton, Icelandic	19	NY	24 July 1883
	29 Aug	L	Nevada	Peter F. Goss	682	NY	9 Sep 1883
	6 Oct	L	Oregon	2 from Norwich	2	NY	Oct 1883
	27 Oct	L	Wisconsin	John Pickett	369	NY	7 Nov 1883
	7 Nov	A	City of New York	Walter R. Barber	3	SF	Dec 1883
	1 Dec	L	Wisconsin	1 elder, Kirby family	9	NY	Dec 1883
1884	4 Jan	L	Wisconsin	1 elder, Nickson family	5	NY	17 Jan 1884
	4 Mar	A	Zealandia	Ephraim Ralphs	13	SF	SLC 29 Mar
	9 Apr	L	Nevada	Christian D. Fjeldsted	319	NY	19 Apr 1884

Year	Date		Ship	Leader	No.	Port	Arrival
	17 May	L	Arizona	Ephraim H. Williams	287	NY	26 May 1884
	14 June	L	Arizona	Ephraim H. Nye	531	NY	23 June 1884
	24 June	L	City of Chester	N. Anderson, emigrant	1	NY	5 July 1884
	22 Jul	A	Australia	Small emigrant group	few	SF	11 Aug 1884
	2 Aug	L	Nevada	Henry W. Attley	14	NY	13 Aug 1884
	30 Aug	L	Wyoming	Benjamin Bennett	496	NY	10 Sep 1884
	23 Oct	L	City of Berlin	Carl A. Ek	93	NY	2 Nov 1884
	1 Nov	L	Arizona	J. Alma Smith	163	NY	11 Nov 1884
	Nov	A	Unnamed ship	3 elders, 11 emigrants	14	SF	Dec 1884
	6 Dec	L	Arizona	3 elders, 6 emigrants	9	NY	16 Dec 1884
1885	11 Apr	L	Wisconsin	Louis P. Lund	187	NY	22 Apr 1885
	16 May	L	Wisconsin	Nathaniel M. Hodges	274	NY	27 May 1885
	23 May	L	Wyoming	Included James Jennings		NY	3 June 1885
	20 June	L	Wisconsin	Jorgen Hansen	541	NY	1 July 1885
	27 June	L	Wyoming	John Morgan family	3	NY	8 July 1885
	21 July	A	Zealandia	Arthur Porter	17	SF	10 Aug 1885
	1 Aug	L	Wyoming	George Hunter, Icelandic	10	NY	11 Aug 1885
	20 Aug	L	Abyssinia	Svunn Erickson, Iceland	1	NY	28 Aug 1885
	29 Aug	L	Wisconsin	John W. Thornley	329	NY	8 Sep 1885
	19 Sep	L	Nevada	Thora Jensen	1	NY	Oct 1885
	24 Oct	L	Nevada	Anthon H. Lund	313	NY	4 Nov 1885
	Oct -Dec	L	Unnamed ships	2 families	7	NY	Nov 1885 to Jan 1886
1886	Jan - Feb	L	Unnamed ships	1 elder, 4 emigrants	5	NY	Jan to Mar
	17 Apr	L	Nevada	Edwin T. Woolley	179	NY	27 Apr 1886
	15 May	L	Arizona	Isaac Gadd , Icelandic	17	NY	24 May 1886
	22 May	L	Nevada	Moroni L. Pratt	279	NY	1 June 1886
	26 June	L	Nevada	Christian F. Olsen	426	NY	7 July 1886
	10 July	L	Alaska	Icelandic company	23	NY	18 July 1886
	21 Aug	L	Wyoming	David Kunz	301	NY	31 Aug 1886
	13 Oct	L	British King	Joshua Greenwood	307	P	27 Oct 1886
	30 Oct	L	Unnamed ship	Group too late		NY	SLC 17 Nov
	1 Dec	L	Unnamed ship	Small company	few	NY	Dec 1886
1887	16 Apr	L	Nevada	Daniel P. Callister	194	NY	27 Apr 1887
	21 May	L	Nevada	Edward Davis	187	NY	1 June 1887
	4 June	L	Wyoming	J. C. Neilsen	159	NY	15 June 1887
	18 June	L	Wisconsin	Quincy B. Nichols	646	NY	28 June 1887
	27 Aug	L	Wisconsin	John I . Hart	406	NY	7 Sep 1887
	8 Oct	L	Nevada	Joseph S. Wells	278	NY	18 Oct 1887
	29 Oct	L	Arizona	John V. Long	few	NY	Nov 1887
	10 Dec	L	Wisconsin	Joseph Hochstrasser	8	NY	23 Dec 1887
1888	23 Apr	A	Alameda	6 elders, emigrants	few	SF	13 May 1888
	28 Apr	L	Wisconsin	Franklin S. Bramwell	74	NY	10 May 1888
	15 May	S	New Zealandic	Alonzo L. Stewart	12	SF	June 1888
	19 May	L	Wyoming	William Wood	137	NY	29 May 1888
	26 May	L	Arizona	F. W. Schoenfeld	11	NY	4 June 1888
	2 June	L	Wisconsin	C. A. Dorius	210	NY	13 June 1888
	9 June	L	Nevada	J. S. Stucki	70	NY	20 June 1888
	23 June	L	Wyoming	Henry E. Bowring	118	NY	3 July 1888
	7 July	L	Wisconsin	Robert Lindsay, Iceland	7	NY	18 July 1888
	28 July	L	Wyoming	H. J. Christiansen	136	NY	8 Aug 1888
	11 Aug	L	Wisconsin	Levi W. Naylor	155	NY	23 Aug 1888
	1 Sep	L	Wyoming	Abraham Johnson	83	NY	11 Sep 1888
	15 Sep	L	Wisconsin	William G. Phillips	145	NY	25 Sep 1888
	6 Oct	L	Wyoming	N. P. Lindelof	123	NY	16 Oct 1888
	20 Oct	L	Wisconsin	John Quigley	125	NY	30 Oct 1888
	5 Nov	A	Mariposa	Elders and emigrants	10	SF	Dec 1888
	17 Nov	L	Arizona	L. F. Moench	7	NY	27 Nov 1888
	24 Nov	L	Wisconsin	Ole Christiansen	1	NY	Dec 1888
1889	22 Apr	A	Unnamed ship	Thomas L. Cox family	few	SF	12 May 1889
	27 Apr	Ho	Unnamed ship	M. F. Krumperman	26	NY	15 May 1889
	11 May	L	Arizona	H. C. Barrell ,Germans	few	NY	20 May 1889
	18 May	L	Wisconsin	Mayhew H. Dalley	142	NY	28 May 1889

	20 May	A	Zealandia	Alonzo L. Stewart	12	SF	SLC 12 June 1889
	8 June	L	Wyoming	Lars S. Anderson	359	NY	19 June 1889
	22 June	L	Wisconsin	John W. Volker	172	NY	3 July 1889
	17 Aug	L	Wyoming	J. C. A. Weibye	191	NY	27 Aug 1889
	31 Aug	L	Wisconsin	Wm. P. Payne	172	NY	12 Sep 1889
	21 Sep	L	Wisconsin	Rasmus Larsen	113	NY	1 Oct 1889
	5 Oct	L	Wisconsin	Edward Bennett	142	NY	17 Oct 1889
	26 Oct	L	Wyoming	A. L. Skanchy	161	NY	5 Nov 1889
	16 Nov	L	Nevada	Richard Morse	11	NY	27 Nov 1889
1890	8 Feb	Ho	Unnamed ship	Small company	few	NY	Feb 1890
	12 Apr	M	Unnamed ship	Stephen D. Chipman	20	SF	SLC 14 May
	19 Apr	L	Wisconsin	Orson H. Worthington	52	NY	1 May 1890
	3 May	L	Wyoming	Adolph Anderson	156	NY	13 May 1890
	8 May	L	Queen	Samuel Smith family	4	NY	May 1890
	24 May	L	Wisconsin	John H. Hayes	122	NY	4 June 1890
	7 June	L	Wyoming	Erastus C. Willardson	304	NY	19 June 1890
	28 June	L	Wisconsin	Abraham Maw	113	NY	10 July 1890
	2 Aug	L	Wisconsin	Leonard J. Jordan	86	NY	13 Aug 1890
	16 Aug	L	Wyoming	J. Ostlund	128	NY	26 Aug 1890
	6 Sep	L	Wisconsin	John U. Stucki	116	NY	17 Sep 1890
	20 Sep	L	Wyoming	Jens Jensen	197	NY	1 Oct 1890
	6 Oct	A	Zealandia	Angus T. Wright	13	SF	SLC 29 Oct
	11 Oct	L.	Wisconsin	Joseph J. Golighty		NY	23 Oct 1890
	25 Oct	L	Wyoming	Joseph Leaing		NY	5 Nov 1890
	1 Nov	Ho	Unnamed ship	Group from Amsterdam	5	NY	Nov 1890

Total immigrants by ship — 91,517

Pioneer Companies That Crossed the Plains, 1847-1868

Note: The information herein compiled has been obtained from journals, personal accounts and reports. Not only are there discrepancies in reports and accounts, but by its very nature, travel on the trail was unavoidably informal and disarrayed. Although the dates and other statistical information were obtained from the most reliable sources available, they should generally be considered approximations. After crossing the plains portion of the trail companies often divided into small divisions or traveled in a scattered condition, thereby arriving in Salt Lake City over the period of several days. The various companies in which Mormons traveled included freight trains, independent companies, handcart companies, and various kinds of Church companies. The Church companies were normally assigned a number at the time of their organization by which they were commonly known during that season's travel. The companies in this list are arranged by year and therein by departure date (more or less) from the outfitting location. Numbers have been assigned in this listing for convenience. Rosters noted are those that are easily accessible in the Historical Department. Other rosters may be found in journals or other records.

Asterisk (*) denotes partial roster. JH denotes Journal History; CEB denotes "Church Emigration Book," a 3-volume compilation in the Historical Department Archives.

1847

1- Capt. Brigham Young left from Winter Quarters, Neb., on 14 Apr with 148 people and 72 wagons, arrived 21-24 July. Roster, CEB 1847, D.U.P .lesson for (Pioneer Company) Apr 1959, Jenson's Biographical Encyclopedia, vol. 4, p. 693-725.

2- Capt. Daniel Spencer left from Winter Quarters, Neb., on 17 June. — Perrigrine Sessions, Capt. 1st Fifty, left from Elkhorn River, Neb., on 18 June with 185 people and 75 wagons, arrived 24-25 Sep. Roster, JH 21 Jun 1847, p. 6-11. —Ira Eldredge, Capt. 2nd Fifty [also known as Parley P. Pratt Co.], left from Elkhorn River, Neb., on 17 June with 177 or 174 people and 76 wagons, arrived 19-22 Sep. Roster, JH 21 Jun 1847, p. 11-16.

3- Capt. Edward Hunter of the 2nd Hundred left from Winter Quarters, Neb., on 17 Jun. — Joseph Horne, Capt. of 1st Fifty, left from Elkhorn River, Neb., on 17 June with 197 people and 72 wagons, arrived 29 Sep 1847. Roster, JH 21 Jun 1847, p. 17-22. Capt. 1st Fifty; —Jacob Foutz, Capt. of 2nd Fifty [also known as John Taylor Co.], left from Elkhorn River, Neb., on 19 Jun with 155 people and 59 wagons, arrived 1 Oct 1847. Roster, JH 21

Jun 1847, p. 23-27.

4- Capt. Jedediah M. Grant of the 3rd Hundred left from Winter Quarters, Neb. 17 June and arrived 29 Sep 1847. — Joseph B. Noble, Capt. of 1st Fifty, left from the Elkhorn River on 17 June with 171 people, arrived 2 Oct. Roster, JH 21 Jun 1847, p. 28-32. — Willard Snow, Capt. of 2nd Fifty, left from the Elkhorn River 19 June with 160 people, arrived 4 Oct 1847. Roster, JH 21 Jun 1847, p. 33-37.

5- Capt. Abraham O. Smoot of the 4th Hundred left from Winter Quarters, Neb., 17 June. George B. Wallace, Capt. of 1st Fifty, left the Elkhorn River, Neb., 18 June with 223 people, arrive 25,26,29 July. Roster, JH 21 Jun 1847, p. 38-44. —Samuel Russell, Capt. 2nd Fifty, left from the Elkhorn River, Neb., 17 June with 95 people, arrived 25 Sep. Roster, JH 21 Jun 1847, p. 44-47

6- Capt. Charles C. Rich left Winter Quarters, [Elkhorn River] Neb., 21 June with 126 people, arrived 2 Oct 1847. Roster, JH 21 Jun 1847, p. 48-51

1848

7- Capt. Brigham Young (Capt. 1st Division) left from Winter Quarters, Neb., 6 June with 1220 people, arrived 20-24 Sep. Roster, JH Supp. after 31 Dec 1848, p. 1-10*.

8- Capt. Heber C. Kimball (Capt. 2nd Division) left from Winter Quarters, Neb., 29 May with 662 people, arrived 24 Sep. Roster, JH Supp. after 31 Dec 1848, p. 11-16*.

9- Capt. Willard Richards (Capt. 3rd Division) left from Winter Quarters, Neb., 3 July with 526 people, arrived 10-19 Oct. Roster, JH Supp. after 31 Dec 1848, p. 17-20*.

1849

10- Howard Egan left Nebraska City, Neb., 17 May, left Pottawattamie Co. Iowa, 18 Apr with 57 people and 22 wagons, arrived 7 Aug 1849. Roster, JH Supp. after 31 Dec 1849, p. 13-14; CEB 1849.

11- Samuel Gully and Orson Spencer (1) left Kanesville, Iowa, 5-7 June with 125 people, arrived 22-24 Sep. Roster, JH Supp. after 31 Dec 1849, p. 1-2*.

12- Allen Taylor (2) left Kanesville, Iowa, 5-6 Jul with 445 people and 137 wagons, arrived 10-20 Oct. Roster, JH Supp. after 31 Dec 1849, p. 3-4*.13- Silas Richards (3) left Winter Quarters, Neb., 10 July with 72 people, arrived 25-29 Oct. Roster, JH Supp. after 31 Dec 1849, p. 5A-5I.

14- George A. Smith (4) [included Dan Jones' Welsh Company] left Winter Quarters, Neb., 14 July with 244 people and 55 wagons, arrived 26-30 Oct. Roster, JH Supp. after 31 Dec 1849, p. 6-8G.

15- Ezra T. Benson (5) left Winter Quarters, Neb., 15 July with 182 people and 63 wagons, arrived 25-29 Oct. Roster, JH Supp. after 31 Dec 1849, p. 9-12H.

1850

16- Milo Andrus (1) left Kanesville, Iowa, 3 June with 206 people and 51 wagons, arrived 29-31 Aug. Roster, JH Supp. after 31 Dec 1850 p. 1*.

17- Benjamin Hawkins left Kanesville, Iowa, 5 June with 100 people, arrived 9,12 Sep. Roster, JH Supp. after 31 Dec. 1850, p.2-3*.

18- Aaron Johnson (3) left Kanesville, Iowa, bef. 12 June with 100 people, arrived 12 Sep 1850. Roster, JH Supp. after 31 Dec 1850, p. 3-5*.

19- James Pace (4) left Kanesville, Iowa, 11 June with 100 people, arrived 20-23 Sep. Roster, JH Supp. after 31 Dec 1850 p. 5-6*.

20- Wilford Woodruff (8) left Kanesville, Iowa, 14-16 June with 209 people and 44 wagons, arrived 14 Oct 1850. Roster, JH Supp. after 31 Dec 1850, p. 17-18*.

21- David Evans left (10) Kanesville, Iowa, 15 June with 50 people, arrived 13-17 Sep. Roster, JH Supp. after 31 Dec 1850 p. 20*.

22- Warren Foote (7) left Bethlehem, Iowa, 17 June with 476 people and 105 wagons, arrived 17-18,26 Sep. Roster, JH Supp. after 31 Dec 1850, p. 15-16 CEB 1850*.

23- Justus Morse left Kanesville, Iowa, 20 June with 41 people and 13 wagons, arrived 2 Oct. No roster.

24- William Snow and Joseph Young (6) left Kanesville, Iowa, 21 June with 122 people, arrived 1-4 Oct. Roster, JH Supp. after 31 Dec 1850, p. 13-14*.

25- Warren Smith [initially a part of William Smith/Joseph Young Company, but traveled independently] left Kanesville, Iowa, 21 June with 51 people iin 14 wagons. No roster.

26- Stephen Markham (9) left Kanesville, Iowa, 20-27 June with 50 people, arrived 1-3

Oct. Roster, JH Supp. after 31 Dec 1850, p. 19*.

27- Shadrach Roundy left 22 June 26, arrived 10, 19 Sep. No roster.

28- Edward Hunter (5) [1st Perpetual Emigration Fund (P.E.F.) Company] left Kanesville, Iowa, [organized at 12-Mile Creek near Missouri River]

4 July with 261 people and 67 wagons, arrived 12-13 Oct. Roster, JH Supp. after 31 Dec 1850 p. 7-12*.

29- James Lake left Kanesville, Iowa, with 50 people, arrived 7 Oct 1850. No roster.

(In addition, independent companies captained by Andrew Perkins and Gilbert and Gerrish freight companies also brought smaller numbers of Mormon emigrants to Salt Lake City in 1850.)

1851

30- John G. Smith (1) left Kanesville, Iowa, 1 May with 150 people, arrived 15, 23 Sep. Roster, JH Supp. after 31 Dec 1851, p. 1*.

31- David Lewis [initially organized as part of John G. Smith's Company, but traveled independently] left Kanesville, Iowa, with 68 people and 15 wagons, arrived 9 Sep 1851. Roster, CR 376/1, bx. 1, fd. 4*.

32- Almon W. Babbitt left Kanesville, Iowa, 15 May with 150 people, arrived 17 Aug 1851. No roster.

33- Easton Kelsey (3) left Kanesville, Iowa, 9-10 June (1st) and 29 June (2nd) with 150 people and 100 wagons, arrived 22 Sep-7 Oct. Roster, JH Supp. after 31 Dec 1851, (1st) 29 Oct 1851 p. 4-5*.

34- Morris Phelps [initially organized as 3rd Fifty in James W. Cummings' Company, but traveled independently] left Kanesville, Iowa, 9 June with 60 people, arrived 26 Sep-1 Oct. Roster, JH Supp. after 31 Dec 1851, p. 10-12.

35- James W. Cummings (2) [also known as Orson Pratt's Company] left Kanesville, Iowa, 21 June with 100 people, arrived 30 Sep-7 Oct. Roster, JH Supp. after 31 Dec 1851, p. 2-3 CEB 1851*.

36- Harry Walton [also known as Garden Grove Company; left Garden Grove, Iowa, on 13-17 May] left Kanesville, Iowa, 23 June with 226 people and 59 wagons, arrived 24-25 Sep. Roster, JH Supp. after 31 Dec 1851, p. 7-9 CEB 1851*.

37- John Reese's Freight Train [also known as James Monroe's Train or Horner's Train] left 1 July with 40 people, arrived 29 Sep 1851. No roster.

38- John Brown (4) left Kanesville, Iowa, 7 July with 195 people and 48 wagons, arrived 28-29 Sep. Roster, JH Supp. after 31 Dec 1851, [P.E.F.] 1851 p. 6A-6G*.

39- George W. Oman left Kanesville, Iowa, arrived 1 Oct 1851. No roster.

40- Thomas S. Williams' Freight Train left Kanesville, Iowa, 3 Aug, arrived 25 Aug. Roster, JH Supp. after 31 Dec 1851, p. 10-12*.

41- Wilkins' Freight Train [included Scottish emigrants] left Kanesville, Iowa, before 12 Aug., with 10 wagons, arrived 28 Sep. Roster, JH Supp. after 31 Dec 1851, p. 10-12*.

42- Ben Holliday's Freight Train arrived 10 Aug 1851. Roster, JH Supp. after 31 Dec 1851, p. 10-12*.

43- Livingston and Kincade's Freight Company. Roster, JH Supp. after 31 Dec 1851, p. 10-12*.

1852

44- James J. Jepson (2) left Kanesville, Iowa, 29 May with 220 people and 32 wagons, arrived 10 Sep. Roster, 1852 JH Supp. after 31 Dec 1852, p. 7-11*.

45- John S. Higbee (1) [also known as James W. Bay Company] left Kanesville, Iowa, 31 May with 228 people and 66 wagons, arrived 13-20 Aug. Roster, JH Supp. after 31 Dec 1852, 1852 p. 1-6*.

46- John Parker left St. Louis, Mo., 14 Apr with 19 people and 11 wagons, arrived 28 Aug. No roster.

47- Abraham O. Smoot left Kansas City, Mo., 1 June with 250 people and 33 wagons, arrived 3 Sep. Roster, JH Supp. after 31 Dec 1852, [P.E.F.] p. 137-43*.

48- Thomas Marsden (22) [organized in St. Louis, Mo.] left Independence, Mo., 4 June with 10 wagons, arrived 2 Sep. Roster, JH Supp. after 31 Dec 1852, p. 144*.

49- John Tidwell (5) left Kanesville, Iowa, 4-9 June with 319 people and 61 wagons, arrived 10-23 Sep. Roster, JH Supp. after 31 Dec 1852, p. 25-33*.

50- David Wood (6) left Kanesville, Iowa, 6 June with 288 people and 58 wagons, arrived 20 Sep-1 Oct. Roster, JH Supp. after 31 Dec 1852, p. 34-40*.

51- Thomas C. D. Howell (3) left Kanesville, Iowa, 7 June with 293 people and 65 wagons, plus 10 families, arrived 2, 11-12, 27 Sept. Roster, JH Supp. after 31 Dec 1852, p. 12-18*.

52- Benjamin Gardner (10) left Kanesville, Iowa, 2-10 June with 241 people and 45 wagons, arrived 24,27 Sep. Roster, JH Supp. after 31 Dec 1852, 1852 p. 61B JH 24 & 27 Sep 1852*.

53- Joseph Outhouse (4) left Kanesville, Iowa, 10 June with 230 people and 50 wagons, arrived 6 Sep. Roster, JH Supp. after 31 Dec 1852, p. 19-24*.

54- Joel Edmunds [initially organized with Allen Weeks Company, but traveled independently] left Kanesville, Iowa, 10 June with 53 people and 12 wagons, arrived 8-10 Sep. No roster.

55- Henry Bryant Manning Jolly (7) left Kanesville, Iowa, 15 June with 329 people and 63 wagons, arrived 9-15 Sep. Roster, JH Supp. after 31 Dec 1852, 1852 p. 41-49*.

56- Warren Snow (8). No report/roster.

57- Isaac M. Stewart (9) left Kanesville, Iowa, 19 June with 245 people and 53 wagons, arrived 28 Aug-22 Sep. Roster, JH Supp. after 31 Dec 1852, p. 55-61*.

58- James McGaw (11) left Kanesville, Iowa, 24 June with 239 people and 54 wagons, arrived 20 Sep. Roster, JH Supp. after 31 Dec 1852, p. 67-73*.

59- Crandall Dunn [initially organized with James McGaw Company, but traveled independently] left Kanesville, Iowa, 24 June with 41 people and 12 wagons. Roster, CR 376/1, bx. 1, fd. 4*.

60- Harmon Cutler (12) left Kanesville, Iowa, & Fort Leavenworth, Kan., 27 June and 4 July with 262 people and 63 wagons, arrived Sep 4-Oct. Roster, JH Supp. after 31 Dec 1852, p. 79-84*.

61- William Morgan (13) left Kanesville, Iowa, 22-28 June with 50 people, arrived 25-30 Sep. Roster, CR 376/1, Bx. 1, fd. 4*.

62- John B. Walker (14) left Kanesville, Iowa, 26-30 June with 258 people and 50 wagons, arrived 2-7 Oct. Roster, JH Supp. after 31 Dec 1852, p. 89-95*.

63- Robert Wimmer (15) left Kanesville, Iowa, early July [organized June 23] with 230 people and 130 wagons, arrived 15 Sep. Roster, JH Supp. after 31 Dec 1852, p. 96-100*.

64- Uriah Curtis (16) left Kanesville, Iowa, 28 June with 259 people and 50 wagons, arrived 29 Sep-Oct.1. Roster, JH Supp. after 31 Dec 1852, p. 101-7*.

65- Isaac Bullock (17) left Kanesville, Iowa, with 175 people and 40 wagons, arrived 21 Sep-3 Oct. Roster, JH Supp. after 31 Dec 1852, p. 108-11*.

66- Eli B. Kelsey (19) left Kanesville, Iowa, 4 July with 100 people and 10 wagons, arrived 14-16 Oct. Roster, JH Supp. after 31 Dec 1852, p. 120-22*.

67- James C. Snow (18) left Kanesville, Iowa, 5 July with 250 people and 55 wagons, arrived 9-10 Oct. Roster, JH Supp. after 31 Dec 1852, p. 112-17*.

68- Henry W. Miller (20) left Kanesville, Iowa, 8 July with 229 people and 63 wagons, arrived 10 Sep-2 Oct. Roster, JH Supp. after 31 Dec 1852, p. 123-28*.

69- Allen Weeks (21) left Kanesville, Iowa, 18 July with 226 people, aarrived 12 Oct 1852. Roster, JH Supp. after 31 Dec 1852, p. 129-36*.

70- James Holt left Kanesville, Iowa, 27 July, arrived 27 Oct 1852. No roster.

1853

71- David Wilkin (1) left Florence, Neb. 1 June with 122 people and 28 wagons, arrived 9 Sep. Roster, JH 15 Jul 1853, p.2-5.

72- Daniel A. Miller/John W. Cooley (2) left Florence, Neb. 8 June with 282 people and 70 wagons, arrived 9-17 Sep. Roster, JH 9 Sep 1853, p. 2-24; JH 9 Aug 1853, p. 2-20.

73- Moses Clawson (4) ["St. Louis Company"] left Keokuk, Iowa, 16 May [left Kanesville, Iowa, 29 June] with 295 people and 65 wagons, arrived 15-20 Sep. Roster, JH 19 Aug 1853, p. 3-7; JH 7 Aug 1853, p. 4-5.

74- William Atkinson (3) [also known as Jesse W. Crosby Company] left Keokuk, Iowa, 18 May [left Kanesville, Iowa, 1 July] with 79 people and 12 wagons, arrived 10-11 Sep. Roster, JH 19 Aug 1853, p. 2.

75- John E. Forsgren (6) left Keokuk, Iowa, 21 May with 294 people and 34 wagons, arrived 29-30 Sep. Roster, JH 30 Sep 1853, p. 3-7*.

76- Jacob Gates (5) left Keokuk, Iowa, 3 June [left Missouri 1853 River, 15 July] with 262 people and 33 wagons, arrived 26-30 Sep. Roster, JH 9 Sep 1853, p. 25-28.

77- Henry Ettleman (7) left Keokuk, Iowa, [left Missouri River, 1 July] with 40 people and 11 wagons, arrived 1 Oct. Roster, JH 19 Aug 1853, p. 1B.

78- Vincent Shurtleff Freight Train (8) left Kanesville, Iowa, 13 July with 18 wagons, arrived 22-30 Sep. No roster.

79- Joseph W. Young (9) [included Ten Pound Company and P.E.F.] left Keokuk, Iowa, 1-7 June [left Missouri River 17 July] with 425 people and 56 wagons, arrived 10 Oct 1853. Roster, JH 22 Sep 1853, p. 1B-9.

80- Cyrus H. Wheelock (10) [included Ten Pound Company, P.E.F., and a California-bound company] left Keokuk, Iowa, 1-3 June [left Missouri River 11-14 July] with 400 people and 52 wagons, arrived 6-16 Oct. Roster, JH 19 Sep 1853, p. 2-7.

81- Claudius V. Spencer (11) [P.E.F.] left Keokuk, Iowa, 3 June [left Missouri River 4-7 July] with 250 people and 40 wagons, arrived 17-26 Sep. Roster, JH 17 Sep 1853, p. 1B-4

82- Moses Daily Freight Train left Kanesville, Iowa, 6 July with 35 people, arrived 27-29 Sep. No roster.

83- Appleton M. Harmon (12) left Keokuk, Iowa, 15-16 June [left Missouri River, 14 July] with 200 people and 22 wagons, arrived 16 Oct. Roster, CR 376/1, bx. 1, fd. 5.

84- Joshua Mecham left Kanesville, Iowa, 18 July with 10 people, arrived 16 Oct. No roster.85- John Brown (13) left Keokuk, Iowa, 1 July [left Missouri River 20-22 July] with 303 people and 35 wagons, arrived 13-17 Oct. No roster; see roster for ship Campillus in "Ms. History of British Mission," 6 Apr 1853.

1854

86- Perrigrine Sessions left Kanesville, Iowa, 23 May with 164 people and arrived Aug 1854. No roster.

87- Hans Peter Olsen (1) left Westport, Mo. [Kansas City area] 15 June with 550 people and 69 wagons, arrived 5 Oct. Roster, JH 31 Dec 1854, Supp., p. 7-9*.

88- James Brown [P.E.F.] (2) left Carroll County, Ill., 18 June [left Platte City, Mo., 7 July] with 300 people and 42 wagons, arrived 27 Sep-3. Roster, JH 31 Dec 1854, Supp., p. 9*.

89- Job Smith (4) left Westport, Mo. 16 June with 217 people and 45 wagons, arrived 23-25 Sep. Roster, JH 31 Dec 1854, Supp., p. 11*.

90- Darwin Richardson (3) [P.E.F.] left Westport, Mo. 17 June with 300 people and 40 wagons, arrived 30 Sep. Roster, JH 31 Dec 1854, Supp., p. 10*.

91- Orson Pratt, Ezra T. Benson, and Ira Eldredge "Church Train" (7) left WEstport, Mo., 21-22 June, arrived 3 Oct. Roster, JH 31 Dec 1854, Supp., p. 15*.

92- Joseph Field left 21 June with 39 wagons, 1 hc., arrived 19 Sep. No roster.

93- Daniel Garn (5) [P.E.F.] left Westport, Mo. 1-2 July with 477 people and 66 wagons, arrived 1 Oct. Roster, JH 31 Dec 1854, Supp., p. 12*.

94- William Empey (8) left Westport, Mo. 15 July with 43 people, arrived 24 Oct 1854. Roster, JH 31 Dec 1854, Supp., p. 16*.

95- Robert L. Campbell (6) left Westport, Mo., 18 July with 397 people, aarrived 28-31 Oct. Roster, JH 31 Dec 1854, Supp., p. 13-14*.

(In addition, independent companies captained by Benjamin Truman and Cyrus Snell also brought small groups of Mormon emigrants to Salt Lake City in 1854.)

1855

96- John Hindley (1) left Mormon Grove, Kan. [near Atchison, Kan.] 7 June with 206 people and 63 wagons, arrived 3 Sep 1855. Roster, JH 12 Sep 1855 JH 3 Sep 1855, p.2-12.

97- Jacob F. Secrist (2) [replaced by Noah T. Guyman after his death July 2] left Mormon Grove, 13 June with 368 people and 58 wagons, arrived 7 Sep. Roster, JH 12 Sep 1855; JH 7 Sep p.1-11.

98- Seth M. Blair (3) [due to illness, replaced by Edward Stevenson in late June] left Mormon Grove, Kan., 15 June with 89 people and 38 wagons, arrived 10-13 Sep. Roster, Ms 4806, #10, fd. 1, p. 1-2.

99- Richard Ballantyne (4) [P.E.F.] left Mormon Grove, Kan., 1-2 July with 402 people and 45 wagons, arrived 25 Sep. Roster, JH 12 Sep. 1855.

100- Moses F. Thurston (5) left Mormon Grove, Kan., 4 July with 148 people and 33 wagons, arrived 19-28 Sep. Roster, JH 12 Sep 1855.

101- Charles A. Harper (6) [P.E.F.] left Mormon Grove, Kan., 25-31 July with 305 people and 39 wagons, arrived 28-31 Oct. Roster, JH 12 Sep 1855.

102- Isaac Allred Freight Train (7) left Mormon Grove, Kan., 28-31 July with 61 people and 34-38 wagons, arrived 2,13 Nov. Roster, JH 12 Sep 1855.

103- Milo Andrus (8) Mormon Grove, Kan. 4 Aug 461 48 24 Oct 1855 JH 24 Oct 1855, p.1-13

[P.E.F.]

(In addition, the Hooper and Williams Freight Train also brought a small number of emigrants to Salt Lake City in 1855.)

1856

104- Edmund Ellsworth [1st handcart company] left Iowa City, Iowa, 9 June with 275 people and 52 wagons, arrived 26 Sep. Roster, JH 9 Jun 1856, p. 1; JH 26 Sep 1856, p. 23-30.

105- Daniel D. McArthur [2nd handcart company] left Iowa City, Iowa, 11 June with 222 and 48 handcarts, plus 4 wagons, arrived 26 Sep. Roster, JH 11 Jun 1856, p. 1; JH 26 Sep 1856, p. 31-36.

106- Edward Bunker [3rd handcart company] left Iowa City, Iowa, 23 June [left Florence, Neb., 30 July] with 300 people and 60 handcarts and 5 wagons, arrived 2 Oct. Roster, JH 2 Oct 1856, p. 6-12; JH 15 Oct 1856, p. 1.

107- James G. Willie [4th handcart company] left Iowa City, Iowa, 15 July with 500 people and 120 handcarts and 5 wagons, arrived 9 Nov 1856. Roster, JH 9 Nov 1856,p. 6-7,18-30; JH 15 Oct 1856, p. 2.

108- Edward Martin [5th handcart company] left Iowa City, Iowa, 28 July with 575 people and 145 handcarts and 7 wagons, arrivved 30 Nov 1856. Roster, JH 30 Nov 1856, p.7-8,60-76; JH 15 Oct 1856, p. 2

109- Philemon C. Merrill (1) left Florence, Neb., 5-6 June with 200 people and 50 wagons, arrived 13-18 Aug. Roster, JH 5 Jun 1856, p. 1.

110- Canute Peterson (2) left Florence, Neb., 26 June with 320 people and 60 wagons, arrived 16-21 Sep. Roster, JH 20 Sep 1856, p. 1-8; JH 15 Oct 1856, p. 2-3.

111- John Banks (3) ["St. Louis Company"] left Florence, Neb., 26-27 June [left St. Louis, 20 May] with 300 people and 60 wagons, arrived 22 Sep-2 Oct. Roster, JH 3 Oct 1856, p. 2-9; Oct 1856 JH 15 Oct 1856, p. 3.

112- Abraham O. Smoot left Mormon Grove, Kan., 10 Aug with 97 people in 43 wagons, arrived 9 Nov. Roster, CEB, 1856*

113- William B. Hodgetts (4) left Iowa City, Iowa 30 July-1 Aug [left Florence, Neb., 29 Aug] with 150 people and 33 wagons, arrived 10-15 Dec. Roster, JH 15 Oct 1856, p. 3*; JH 15 Dec 1856, p.1-6*; Ms 1066.

114- Dan Jones (5) [replaced by John A. Hunt, 11 Aug.] left Iowa City, Iowa 1 Aug [left Florence, Neb., 31 Aug] with 300 people and 56 wagons, arrived 10-15 Dec. Roster, JH 15 Dec 1856, p.7-15*; JH 15 Oct 1856, p. 2*; Ms 1066.

115- Jacob Croft left Texas [left Kansas City, Kan., May] with 58 people and 15 wagons, arrived 11 Oct. Roster, CR 376/1, fd. 7.

116- Preston Thomas left Matagorda Bay, Tex. 7 Apr with 34 people and 8 wagons, arrived 17 Sep. Roster, JH 17 Sep 1856, p. 2*.

117- Benjamin Matthews left Mississippi with 6 families, arrived 19 Jul. No roster.

1857

118- Israel Evans [6th handcart company] left Iowa City, Iowa, 22-23 May with 149 people and 28 handcarts, arrived 11-12 Sep. No roster.

119- Christian Christiansen [7th handcart company] left Iowa City, Iowa, 15 June with 330 people and 68 handcarts, and three wagons, arrived 13 Sep 1857. Roster, JH 13 Sep 1857, p. 12-26*.

120- Jesse B. Martin (1) left Iowa City, Iowa, 1-3 June [left Florence, Neb., 28-29 June] with 192 people and 31 wagons, arrived 12 Sep. No roster

121- Jacob Hoffheins/Matthew McCune (3) ["New York Company"/"St. Louis Co."] left Iowa City, Iowa, 6 June [left Florence, Neb., 1 July] with 204 people and 41 wagons, arrived 21 Sep. No roster.

122- Matthias Cowley (2) ["Scandinavian Company"] left Iowa City, Iowa, 15 June [left Florence, Neb., 6 July] with 198 people and 31 wagons, arrived 13-15 Sep. No roster.

123- William Walker's Freight Train left Florence, Neb., 14 July with 86 people and 28 wagons, arrived 4-11 Sep. No roster.

124- Homer Duncan left Texas May, arrived 14,20,25 Sep. No roster.

125- William G. Young left Iowa, City, Iowa, June [left left Florence, Neb., 1857 19 July] with 55 people and 19 wagons, arrived 25-26 Sep. No roster.

1858

126- John W. Berry left Genoa, Neb., 10-11 May with 112 people and 20 wagons, arrived 21 June. Roster, JH 21 Jun 1858, p. 30-33.

127- Horace S. Eldredge (1) left Iowa, City, Iowa, [left left Florence, Neb., 1 June] with 39 people and 13 wagons, arrived 9-11 July. Roster, CEB, 1858*.

128- Iver N. Iversen (2) left Iowa, City, Iowa, 19 May [left Florence, Neb., 5 July] with 50 people and 9 wagons, arrived 20 Sep. Roster, JH 13 Jul 1858, p. 1.

129- Russell K. Homer (3) left Iowa, City, Iowa, 19 June with 60 people and 6 wagons, arrived 6 Oct. No roster, see "Ms. History of Scandinavian Mission," 21 Feb 1858, p. 3-5.

130- Charles McCarty left Florence, Neb., 9 Aug with 24 people and 6 wagons, arrived 17 Oct. Roster, CR 376/1, bx. 1, fd. 7.

1859

131- A. S. Beckwith left Genoa, Neb., May 22, arrived 1-3 Aug. Roster, JH 1 Aug 1859.

132- George Rowley [8th handcart company] left Florence, Neb., 7-10 June with 235 people and 60 handcarts, plus 8 wagons, arrived 4-6 Sep. Roster, JH 12 Jun 1859, p. 4; Hafen's Handcarts to Zion.

133- Horton D. Haight Freight Train (2) left Florence, Neb., 6 June with 154 people and 73 wagons, arrived 1 Sep. Roster, JH 12 Jun 1859, p.4.

134- James Brown III (1) left Florence, Neb., 13-14 with 387 people and 66 wagons, arrived 29 Aug. Roster, JH 12 Jun 1859, p. 4.

135- Robert F. Neslen (3) left Florence, Neb., 23-26 June withy 380 people and 56 wagons, arrived 15 Sep. Roster, JH 12 Jun 1859, p. 4.

136- Edward Stevenson (4) left Florence, Neb., 26 June with 350 people and 54 wagons, arrived 15-16, 28 Sep. No roster.

137- Ebenezer R. Young Freight Train left Florence, Neb., 25 Aug with 12 men plus families and 10 wagons, arrived 27 Oct. No roster.

(In addition, the P.H. Buzzard and Feramorz Little freight trains and the John McNeil company also brought a small number of emigrants to Salt Lake City in 1859.)

1860

138- Warren Walling (1) left Florence, Neb., 30 May with 172 people and 30 wagons, arrived 9 Aug. Roster, JH Supp. after 31 Dec 1860, p. 7-12.

139- Daniel Robinson [9th handcart company] left Florence, Neb., 6 June with 233 people and 43 handcarts and 6 wagons, arrived 27 Aug. Roster, JH Supp. after 31 Dec 1860, p. 13-18.

140- James D. Ross (2) left Florence, Neb., 14-17 with 249 people and 36 wagons, arrived 3 Sep. Roster, JH Supp. after 31 Dec 1860, p. 19-25.

141- Jesse Murphy (3) left Florence, Neb., 19 June with 279 people and 38 wagons, arrived 30 Aug. Roster, JH Supp. after 31 Dec 1860, p. 26-33.

142- William Budge (5) left Florence, Neb., 19-20 July with 400 people and 55 wagons, arrived 5 Oct. Roster, JH Supp. after 31 Dec 1860, p. 47-57.

143- John Smith (4) left Florence, Neb., 22 June with 276 people and 41 wagons, arrived 1 Sep. Roster, JH Supp. after 31 Dec 1860, p. 38-46.

144- Franklin Brown left Florence, Neb., late June with 60 people and 14 wagons, arrived 27 Aug-4 Sep. Roster, CEB, 1860*.

145- John P. Taylor (6) ["Iowa" Company] left Iowa, City, Iowa, 24 May [left Florence, Neb., 3 July] with 116 people and 22 wagons, arrived 17-18 Sep. Roster, JH Supp. after 31 Dec 1860, p. 58-62.

146- Oscar O. Stoddard [10th handcart company] left Florence, Neb., 6 July with 126 people and 22 handcarts, and 6 wagons, arrived 24 Sep. Roster, JH Supp. after 31 Dec 1860, p. 34-37.

147- Brigham H. Young Freight Train left Florence, Neb., arrived 14 Sep. No roster.

148- Joseph W. Young Freight Train left Florence, Neb., 23 July with 100 people and 50 wagons, arrived 3 Oct. No roster.

1861

149- David H. Cannon (1) left Florence, Neb., 1 June with 225 people and 57 wagons, arrived 11-16 Aug. Roster, Ms 4210*.

150- Job Pingree left Florence, Neb., 7 June with 150 people and 33 wagons, arrived 24 Aug-5 Sep 1861. Roster, JH 24 Aug 1861.

151- Peter Ranck left Florence, Neb., 19 June with 100 people and 20 wagons, arrived 8 Sep. No roster.

152- Homer Duncan (4) left Florence, Neb., 25 June with 264 people and 47 wagons, arrived 13 Sep. Roster, JH 13 Sep 1861, p. 2-5; CEB, 1861.

153- Ira Eldredge (2) left Florence, Neb., 1 July with 514 70 13-15 Sep No roster.

154- Milo Andrus (5) left Florence, Neb., 7 July with 587 people and 72 wagons, arrived 12 Sep.. Roster, Ms 260*.

155- Thomas Woolley left Florence, Neb., July with 150 people and 30 wagons, arrived Sep. No roster.

156- Joseph Horne (3) left Florence, Neb., 1-4 July with 756 people and 63 wagons, arrived 13 Sep. No roster.

157- John R. Murdock (4) left Florence, Neb., 4 July with 300 people and 80 wagons, arrived 12-19 Sep. No roster; see "Ms. History of British Mission," 16 May 1861.

158- Joseph W. Young/Heber P. Kimball Freight Train (5) left Florence, Neb., 11 July with 300 people and 90 wagons, arrived 23 Sep 1861. No roster.

159- Ansel P. Harmon [initially a part of Joseph W. Young Company, reorganized 27 July] left Florence, Neb., 11 July with 40 wagons, arrived 23 Sep. No roster.

160- Samuel Woolley left Florence, Neb., 12-13 July with 338 people and 62 wagons, arrived 22 Sep. Roster, JH 22 Sep 1861, p.2-11.

161- Joseph Porter [initially organized as 2nd division of Samuel Woolley's company, but traveled until end of journey when they reunited] left Florence, Neb., 13 July with 28 wagons, arrived 22 Sep. Roster, JH 22 Sep 1861, p.2-11.

162- Sixtus E. Johnson left Florence, Neb., 14-15 July with 200 people and 52 wagons, arrived 27 Sep. No roster.

1862

163- Lewis Brunson left Florence, Neb., 14 June with 212 people and 48 wagons, arrived 29 Aug. Roster, *Deseret News*, 1862, vol. 12, p. 78; JH 20 Aug 1862, p. 2-7*.

164- Ola N. Liljenquist left Florence, Neb., 14 July with 250 people and 40 wagons, arrived 23 Sep. No roster.

165- James Wareham left Florence, Neb., early July with 250 people and 46 wagons, arrived 26 Sep 1862. Roster, *Deseret News*, 1862, vol. 12, p. 93; JH 16 Sep 1862, p. 1.

166- Christian A. Madsen left Florence, Neb., 14 July with 264 people and 45 wagons, arrived 23 Sep. No roster; see "Ms. History of Scandinavian Mission," Apr 1862, for Roster, of ship "Franklin".

167- Homer Duncan (1) left Florence, Neb., 22 July with 500 people and 50 wagons, arrived 21-24 Sep. Roster, JH 16 Sep 1862, p. 1; 1862 *Deseret News*, vol. 12, p. 93.

168- John R. Murdock (2) left Florence, Neb., 24 July with 597 people and 67 wagons, arrived 27 Sep. Roster, 1862 *Deseret News*, 1862, vol. 12, p. 93,109; JH 16 Sep 1862, p. 2.

169- James S. Brown left Florence, Neb., 28 July with 200 people and 46 wagons, arrived 2 Oct. Roster, *Deseret News*, 1862, vol. 12, p. 113; JH 2 Oct 1862, p. 1*.

170- Joseph Horne (3) left Florence, Neb., 29 July with 570 people and 52 wagons, arrived 26 Sep-1 Oct. Roster, *Deseret News*, 1862, vol. 12, p. 98; JH 24 Sep 1862, p. 1.

171- Isaac A. Canfield left Florence, Neb., 30 July with 120 people and 18 wagons, arrived 16-17 Oct. Roster, *Deseret News*, 1862, vol. 12, p. 93; JH 16 Sep 1862, p. 3; JH 16 Oct 1862, p. 1-16.

172- Ansel P. Harmon (4) left Florence, Neb., 1 Aug with 650 people and 36 wagons, arrived 5 Oct. Roster, JH 24 Sep 1862, p. 2; *Deseret News*, 1862, vol. 12, p. 98.

173- Henry W. Miller (5) left Florence, Neb., 5 Aug with 665 people and 49 wagons, arrived 17-18 Oct. Roster, *Deseret News*, 1862, vol. 12, p. 92.

174- Horton D. Haight (6) left Florence, Neb., 10 Aug with 650 people and 52 wagons, arrived 19 Oct. Roster, JH 24 Sep 1862, p. 2; *Deseret News*, 1862, vol. 12, p. 98.

175- William H. Dame (7) left Florence, Neb., 14 Aug with 150 people and 30 wagons, arrived 29 Oct 1862 JH 24 Sep 1862, p. 3; *Deseret News*, 1862, vol. 12, p. 98.

(In addition, a small number of emigrants traveled in the David P. Kimball, John R. Young, Benjamin Hampton, and Gilbert and Gerrish freight trains in 1862.)

1863

176- John R. Murdock (1) left Florence, Neb., 15 June with 275 people and 55 wagons, arrived 29 Aug-2 Sep. No roster.

177- Alvus H. Patterson left Florence, Neb., 29 June with 210 people and 62 wagons, arrived 4 Sep. Roster, JH 4 Sep 1863, p. 1-3.

178- John F. Sanders (2) left Florence, Neb., 6 July with 56 wagons, arrived 5 Sep. No roster.

179- John R. Young left Florence, Neb., 9 July with 200 people and 44 wagons, arrived 12 Sep. No roster.

180- William B. Preston left Florence, Neb., 10 July with 300 people and 67 wagons, arrived 10 Sep. No roster.

181- Peter Nebeker (4) left Florence, Neb., 25-26 July with 500 people and 68 wagons, arrived 23-30 Sep. No roster.

182- Daniel D. McArthur (5) left Florence, Neb., 6 Aug with 500 people and 58 wagons, arrived 3 Oct. No roster.

183- Horton D. Haight (6) left Florence, Neb., 8-9 Aug with 200 people and 42 wagons, arrived 4 Oct. No roster.

184- John W. Woolley (7) left Florence, Neb., 9 Aug with 200 people and 46 wagons, arrived 4,8 Oct. No roster.

185- Thomas E. Ricks (8) left Florence, Neb., 10 Aug with 400 people and 59 wagons, arrived 4,6 Oct. No roster.

186- Rosel Hyde (9) left Florence, Neb., 11 Aug with 300 people and 49 wagons, arrived 13 Oct. No roster.

187- Samuel D. White (10) left Florence, Neb., 14-15 Aug. with 300 people and 48 wagons, arrived 15 Oct. No roster.

1864

188- John D. Chase left Wyoming, Neb., 26 June with 85 people and 28 wagons, arrived 20 Sep. Roster, JH 20 Sep 1864, p. 2.

189- John R. Murdock (1) left Wyoming, Neb., 29 June with 78 people and 16 wagons, arrived 26 Aug. Roster, JH 26 Sug 1864.

190- William B. Preston (2) left Wyoming, Neb., 4 July with 380 people and 50 wagons, arrived 15 Sep. Roster, *Deseret News*, 17 Aug 1864, p. 369; JH 8 Jul, 14 Sep, 19 Oct 1864.

191- Joseph S. Rawlins (3) left Wyoming, Neb., 15 July with 400 people and 63 wagons, arrived 19-20 Sep. Roster, *Deseret News*, 17 Aug 1864, p. 369.

192- William S. Warren (4) left Wyoming, Neb. 21 July with 329 people and 65 wagons, arrived 4 Oct. Roster, *Deseret News*, 17 Aug 1864, p. 369.

193- John Smith left Wyoming, Neb., bef. 25 July with 150 people and 60 wagons, arrived 25 Sep-1 Oct. Roster, *Deseret News*, 12 Oct 1864, p. 13.

194- Isaac A. Canfield (5) left Wyoming, Neb., 27 July with 211 people and 50 wagons, arrived 5 Oct. Roster, *Deseret News*, 17 Aug 1864, p. 369*.

195- William Hyde (6) left Wyoming, Neb., 9 Aug with 350 people and 62 wagons, arrived 26-30 Oct. Roster, *Deseret News*, 19 Oct 1864, 1864 p. 18*.

196- Warren S. Snow left Wyoming, Neb., 13-17 Aug. with 400 people and 62 wagons, arrived 2 Nov. No roster.

(In addition, a small number of emigrants traveled with the Kimball and Lawrence, Soren Christoffersen, and Sharp and Spencer freight companies and the William E. Pritchett independent company to Salt Lake City in 1864.)

1865

197- D. J. McCann Freight Train left Nebraska City, Neb., late June, with 25 wagons, arrived 1 Nov. No roster.

198- Miner G. Atwood left Wyoming, Neb., 31 July with 557 people and 55 wagons, arrived 8-9 Nov. Roster, *Deseret News*, 1865, vol. 14, 1865 p. 403; JH 8 Nov 1865.

199- Henson Walker left Wyoming, Neb., 12 Aug with 200 people and 50 wagons, arrived 9 Nov 1865. Roster, JH 9 Nov 1865 *Deseret News*, 1865, vol. 14, p. 403.

200- William S. S. Willes left Wyoming, Neb., 12,15 Aug with 200 people and 50 wagons, arrived 11,15,29 Nov. Roster, JH 29 Nov 1865; *Deseret News*, 1865, vol. 14, p. 204,403.

1866

201- Thomas E. Ricks (1) left Wyoming, Neb., 6-10 July with 251 people and 46 wagons, arrived 29 Aug. Roster, *Deseret News*, 16 Aug 1866; JH 4 Sep 1866.

202- Samuel D. White (2) left Wyoming, Neb., 10 July with 230 people and 46 wagons, arrived 5 Sep 1866. Roster, *Deseret News*, 16 Aug 1866.

203- William Henry Chipman (3) left Wyoming, Neb., 11-12 July with 354 people and 60 wagons, arrived 15-16 Sep. Roster, JH 15 Sep 1866, p. 3-4

204- John D. Holladay (4) left Wyoming, Neb., 16-18 July with 350 people and 64 wagons, arrived 25 Sep. Roster, JH 25 Sep 1866.

205- Daniel Thompson (6) left Wyoming, Neb., 24 July with 520 people and 84 wagons, arrived 28 Sep. Roster, JH 29 Sep 1866*.

206- Joseph S. Rawlins (7) left Wyoming, Neb., 2 Aug with 400 people and 65 wagons, arrived 1-2 Oct. Roster, JH 1 Oct 1866.

207- Horton D. Haight (9) left Wyoming, Neb., 4 Aug with 4 families an 65 wagons, arrived 15 Oct. No roster.

208- Peter Nebeker (5) left Wyoming, Neb., 7 Aug with 400 people and 62 wagons, arrived 29 Sep. Roster, JH 29 Sep 1866*.

209- Andrew H. Scott (8) left Wyoming, Neb., 8-9 Aug with 300 people and 49 wagons, arrived 8 Oct. No roster.

210- Abner Lowry (10) ["Sanpete Train"] left Wyoming, Neb., 13 Aug with 300 people and 49 wagons, arrived 22 Oct. Roster, JH 22 Oct 1866.

1867

211- George Dunford left Nebraska City, Neb., late June with 23 wagons, arrived 26 Sep. Roster, No roster.

212- Leonard G. Rice left North Platte, Neb., mid-Aug with 500 people and 50 wagons, arrived 5 Oct. No roster.

213- William Streeper Freight Train left North Platte, Neb., with 11 wagons, arrived 1 Oct. No roster.

1868

214- Chester Loveland left Laramie, Wyo., 25 July with 400 people and 55 wagons, arrived 20 Aug 1868. Roster, JH 25 Jul 1868, p. 2.

215- Joseph S. Rawlins left Laramie, Wyo., 25 July with 415 people and 31 wagons, arrived 20 Aug. No roster.

216- John R. Murdock left Laramie, Wyo., 27 July with 600 people and 75 wagons, arrived 19 Aug. No roster.

217- Horton D. Haight left Laramie, Wyo., 28 July with 275 people and 30 wagons, arrived 24 Aug. No roster.

218- William S. Seeley left Laramie, Wyo., 1 Aug with 272 people and 39 wagons, arrived 29 Aug. Roster, JH 1 Aug 1868, p. 1.

219- Simpson A. Molen left Benton, Wyo., 12 Aug with 300 people and 61 wagons, arrived 2 Sep. No roster.

220- Daniel D. McArthur left Benton, Wyo., 14 Aug with 411 people and 51 wagons, arrived 2 Sep. Roster, Ms 1719*.

221- John Gillespie left Benton, Wyo., 23-24 Aug with 500 people and 54 wagons, arrived 15 Sep. Roster, Ms 1588*.

222- John G. Holman left Benton, Wyo., 1 Sep with 650 people and 62 wagons, arrived 25 Sep. Roster, JH 25 Sep 1868.

223- Edward T. Mumford left Benton, Wyo., 1 Sep with 250 people and 28 wagons, arrived 24 Sep. Roster, JH 25 Sep 1868.

224- John Doddle left from Omaha, Neb., with 20 wagons, arrived 20 Oct. No roster.

Estimated total — about 62,000 pioneers

WORLDWIDE
CHURCH

WORLDWIDE CHURCH
Areas of the World

Africa Area:
Membership, 92,000;
Stakes, 11; Wards,
56; Missions, 11;
Districts, 47;
Branches, 334;
Temples, 1;
Headquarters, Lone
Hill, South Africa.

Africa Area

NIGERIA

CENTRAL
AFRICA
REPUBLIC

UGANDA

ETHIOPIA

SOMALIA

SIERRA
LEONE

CAMEROON

LIBERIA

GHANA

IVORY
COAST

CONGO

ZAIRE

BURUNDI

KENYA

TANZANIA

MADAGASCAR

EQUATORIAL
GUINEA

ZAMBIA

ZIMBABWE

NAMIBIA

BOTSWANA

SOUTH AFRICA

MASCARENE IS.

SWAZILAND

Johannesburg

LESOTHO

Asia Area:
Membership, 59,000;
Stakes, 11; Wards,
56; Missions, 8;
Districts, 19;
Branches, 137
Temples, 2;
Headquarters, Hong
Kong.

Asia Area

MONGOLIA

CHINA

TAIWAN
Taipei

INDIA

Hong
Kong

VIETNAM

THAILAND

CAMBODIA

SINGAPORE

INDONESIA

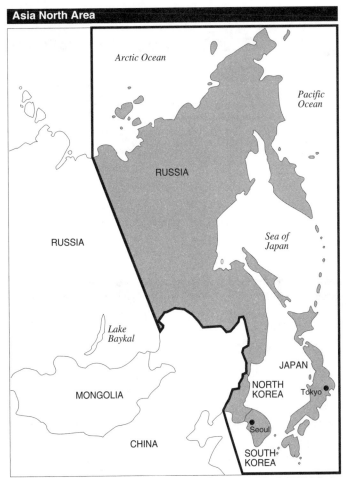

Asia North Area

Arctic Ocean

Pacific Ocean

RUSSIA

RUSSIA

Sea of Japan

Lake Baykal

JAPAN

NORTH KOREA

Tokyo

MONGOLIA

Seoul

CHINA

SOUTH KOREA

Asia North Area: Membership, 173,000; Stakes, 41; Wards, 217; Missions, 13; Districts, 27; Branches, 237; Temples, 2; Headquarters, Tokyo, Japan.

Philippines / Micronesia Area

Philippines/ Micronesia Area:
Membership, 362,000; Stakes, 46; Wards, 278; Missions, 14; Districts, 98; Branches, 761; Temples, 1; Headquarters, Manila, Philippines.

MARIANA IS.

WAKE IS.

Manila

PHILIPPINES

GUAM

MARSHALL IS.

YAP

PALAU IS.

CAROLINE IS.

Pacific Area:
Membership, 314,000; Stakes, 84; Wards, 511; Missions, 13; Districts, 32; Branches, 362; Temples, 5; Headquarters, Sydney, Australia.

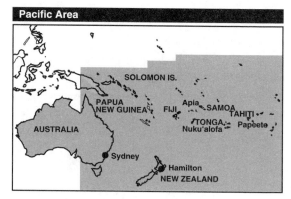

Mexico North Area: ; Membership, 354,000; Stakes, 63; Wards, 356; Missions, 10; Districts, 29; Branches, 272; Temples, 1 announced ; Headquarters, Monterrey, Mexico.

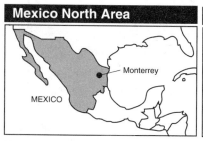

Mexico South Area: Membership, 374,000; Stakes, 75; Wards, 491; Missions, 8; Districts, 15; Branches, 263; Temples, 1; Headquarters, Mexico City, Mexico.

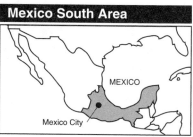

Central America Area:
Membership, 349,000; Stakes, 68; Wards, 379; Missions, 11; Districts, 70; Branches, 516; Temples, 1; Headquarters, Guatemala City, Guatemala.

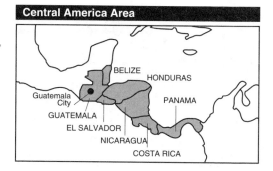

South America North Area: Membership, 682,000; Stakes, 128; Wards, 780; Missions, 19; Districts, 87; Branches, 901; Temples, 1 (4 announced; Headquarters, Quito, Ecuador.

South America North Area

Caracas
Bogota
VENEZUELA
COLOMBIA
ECUADOR
Guayaquil
PERU
Lima
Cochabamba
BOLIVIA

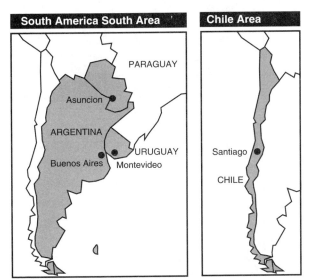

South America South Area: Membership, 718,000; Stakes, 151; Wards, 873; Missions, 19; Districts, 79; Branches, 901; Temples, 1; Headquarters, Buenos Aires, Argentina.

South America South Area

PARAGUAY
Asuncion
ARGENTINA
Buenos Aires
URUGUAY
Montevideo

Chile Area

Santiago
CHILE

Chile Area: Membership, 394,000; Stakes, 89; Wards, 516; Missions, 7; Districts, 14; Branches, 265; Temples, 1; Headquarters, Santiago, Chile

Brazil Area

Brazil Area: Membership, 548,000; Stakes, 136; Wards, 801; Missions, 23; Districts, 45; Branches, 602; Temples, 1 (1 under construction); Headquarters, Sao Paulo, Brazil.

BRAZIL

Recife

Brasilia

Sao Paulo

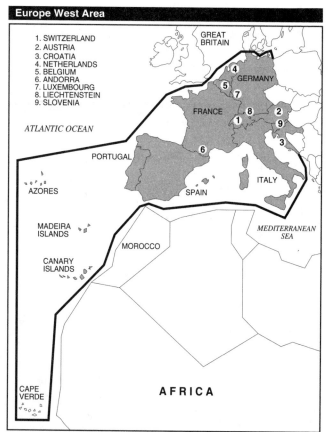

Europe West Area

1. SWITZERLAND
2. AUSTRIA
3. CROATIA
4. NETHERLANDS
5. BELGIUM
6. ANDORRA
7. LUXEMBOURG
8. LIECHTENSTEIN
9. SLOVENIA

GREAT BRITAIN

GERMANY

FRANCE

ATLANTIC OCEAN

PORTUGAL

AZORES

MADEIRA ISLANDS

CANARY ISLANDS

MOROCCO

SPAIN

ITALY

MEDITERRANEAN SEA

CAPE VERDE

AFRICA

Europe West Area: Membership, 170,000; Stakes, 41; Wards, 219; Branches, 594; Missions, 26; Districts, 58; Temples, 3, 1 under construction; Headquarters, Frankfurt, Germany

Europe North Area

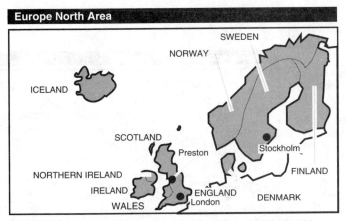

Europe North Area: Membership, 190,000; Stakes, 51; Wards, 294; Missions, 12; Districts, 11; Branches, 222; Temples, 2 (1 in construction); Headquarters, Solihull, England.

Europe East Area

1. CZECH REPUBLIC	9. MACEDONIA	18. UKRAINE
2. SLOVAKIA	10. JORDAN	19. BELARUS
3. HUNGARY	11. LEBANON	20. LATVIA
4. ROMANIA	12. CRETE	21. YUGOSLAVIA
5. BULGARIA	13. CYPRUS	22. KUWAIT
6. GREECE	14. ESTONIA	23. BAHRAIN
7. ALBANIA	15. LITHUANIA	24. U.A.E.
8. BOSNIA AND	16. POLAND	25. OMAN
HERZEGOVINA	17. MOLDOVA	26. YEMEN
		27. ARMENIA

Europe East Area: Membership, 16,000; Stakes, 1; Wards, 3; Missions, 15; Districts, 31; Branches, 232; Headquarters, Frankfurt, Germany.

North America Northwest Area:
Membership, 690,000; Stakes, 186; Wards, 1,362; Missions, 9; Districts, 3; Branches, 192; Temples, 4; Headquarters, Salt Lake City, Utah.

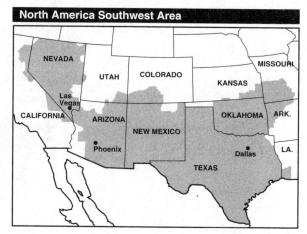

North America Southwest Area

North America Southwest Area:
Membership, 676,000; Stakes, 156; Wards, 1,115; Missions, 13; Branches, 295; Districts, 1;Temples, 3; Headquarters, Salt Lake City, Utah.

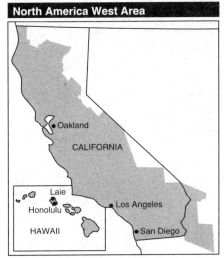

North America West Area

North America West Area:
Membership, 782,000; Stakes, 175; Wards, 1,251; Missions, 16; Districts, 2; Branches, 208; Temples, 4; Headquarters, Salt Lake City, Utah.

North America Central Area

North America Central Area:
Membership, 410,000; Stakes, 106; Wards, 732; Missions, 14; Districts, 9; Branches, 586; Temples, 4; Headquarters, Salt Lake City, Utah.

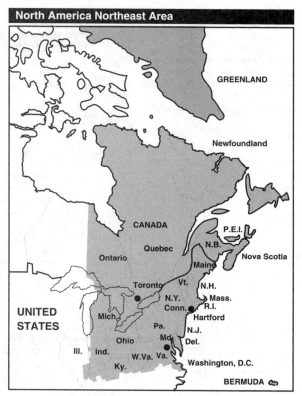

North America Northeast Area:
Membership, 422,000; Stakes, 103; Wards, 671; Missions, 27; Districts, 12; Branches, 455; Temples, 2, (2 announced); Headquarters, Salt Lake City, Utah.

North America Northeast Area

GREENLAND

Newfoundland

CANADA

Quebec

P.E.I.

N.B.

Ontario

Nova Scotia

Maine

Toronto

Vt.

N.H.

UNITED STATES

N.Y.

Mass.

Mich.

Conn.

R.I.

Pa.

Hartford

Ohio

Md.

N.J.

Del.

Ill.

Ind.

W.Va.

Va.

Ky.

Washington, D.C.

BERMUDA

North America Southeast Area:
Membership, 418,000; U.S., 333,000 Caribbean, 85,000 Stakes, 85; Wards, 559; Missions, 22; Districts, 24; Branches, 449 ; Temples, 2, (1 in construction; Headquarters, Salt Lake City, Utah.

North America Southeast Area

KY.

VA.

N.C.

TENN.

ARK.

S.C.

MISS.

ALA.

Atlanta

GA.

LA.

FLA.

Orlando

BAHAMAS

Santo Domingo

PUERTO RICO

DOM. REP.

HAITI

GRENADA

JAMAICA

TRINIDAD & TOBAGO

GUYANA

SURINAME

FR. GUIANA

BRAZIL

Utah North Area:
Membership,
1,030,000; Stakes,
280; Wards, 2,061;
Missions, 3;
Branches, 78;
Temples, 5;
Headquarters, Salt
Lake City, Utah.

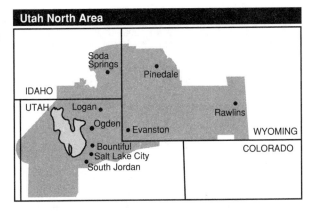

Utah South Area:
Membership,
512,000; Stakes,
151; Wards, 1,260;
Missions, 2;
Branches, 46;
Temples, 4, (1 under
construction);
Headquarters, Salt
Lake City, Utah.

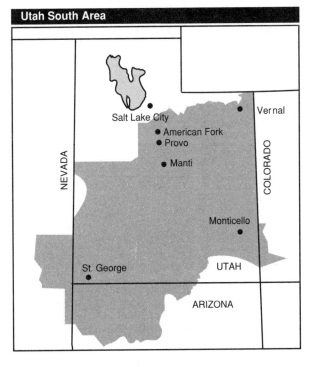

Editor's note: Information in this section has been gathered from a variety of sources and is believed to be the best available at the time of publication. Corrections, additional information and further country or state histories will be appreciated. Those with comments or information may write to: Church Almanac Histories, P.O. Box 1257, Salt Lake City, UT 84110.

UNITED STATES OF AMERICA

Year-end 1995: Est. population, 263,958,000 million; Members, 4,712,000; Stakes, 1,196; Wards, 8,719; Branches, 1,698; Districts, 20; Missions, 90; Temples, 31 (in use, under construction or announced); Percent LDS, 1.8, or one person in 56.

A few stakes and missions have headquarters in states other than that for which they are named. To simplify this listing, these stakes and missions are listed in the states for which they are named.

Numbers preceding stakes and missions are their chronological numbers assigned at the time of creation.

* Stake name changed 14 Jan 1974 or as indicated otherwise

‡ Original name

† Transferred to

Alabama

Year-end 1995: Est. population, 4,275,000; Members, 25,000; Stakes, 6; Wards, 39; Branches, 32; Missions, 1; Percent LDS, 0.6 or one person in 176

Missionaries were reported to have preached on the Montgomery County courthouse steps Oct. 7, 1839, but concerted missionary efforts waited until 1842 and 1843 with the work of Elders James Brown and John U. Eldridge. Elder Brown organized branches in Tuscaloosa (the Cybry Branch) and Perry (Bogue-Chitto Branch) counties before Aug. 24, 1842. Elder Eldridge baptized his brother, wife and mother-in-law, probably in February or March of that year.

Other early missionaries included John Brown, Peter Haws and Hayden W. Church. Early missionaries frequently passed between Alabama and Mississippi in their work.

A typical experience was that of Elder John Brown, a 17-year-old missionary in ragged clothing, who visited an inn at Tuscumbria, Colbert County, on Aug. 27, 1843. When he asked for lodging as a preacher, he was thought to be a cotton picker. His host gathered a small group to be entertained at the expense of hearing a supposed cotton picker preach. After he began, however, "they were as motionless as statues of marble." None was baptized, but the young preacher was well-treated afterward.

Elder Brown later baptized a number of people in Tuscaloosa and Perry counties, and, according to some records, baptized some of the first African-Americans to join the Church, two men named Hagar and Jack, on Oct. 24, 1843.

In early 1844, three branches, reporting a combined membership of 123, attended a conference. Three months later, in April, seven branches reported a membership of 192, although this included some members from Mississippi.

Evidently most of the members immigrated to the West to join the body of the Saints and to avoid persecution. Some Alabama members were among the group of "Mississippi" Saints that immigrated under the leadership of John Brown and William Crosby in 1846.

Missionary work resumed in the South in 1876 with the creation of the Southern States Mission. However, persecution was widespread during the 1880s. As early as 1880, attempts were made to ask the governor of Alabama to force missionaries from the state. By 1894, the persecution subsided somewhat.

In 1898, John and James Edgar joined the Church in Andalusia, Ala., and that same year immigrated to Texas, where they later founded the LDS colony of Kelsey.

Early convert Olivia Tucker McCoy recalled missionaries coming to Magnolia in 1896, and in May of 1897 a conference was held in Magnolia with 36 elders and Southern States Mission Pres. John Morgan in attendance. Evicted from family property after their conversion, the McCoy family moved from Magnolia to another community and remained faithful.

A Sunday School was organized Aug. 22, 1911, in Montgomery. In the early days, converts were baptized in the Alabama River. In 1930, membership in the state was 2,516, with branches in Bradleyton and Lamison, and Sunday Schools in Bessemer, Birmingham, Camden, Clayton, Decatur, Dothan, Elmont, McCalla, Mobile, Pine Hill, Selma and Sneed.

Elder Theron W. Borup, district president, recalled that in the mid-1930s, Sunday School groups existed in Elkmont (which had a small chapel), Gadsen, Birmingham, McCalla and Montgomery. Branches were eventually organized from these Sunday Schools. In 1937 an east-west boundary was drawn through the Alabama District and it was divided into the Alabama and North Alabama districts.

During this period, attitudes held by many people against the Church softened. In 1940, the Montgomery Branch staged a pioneer parade that attracted thousands.

Many LDS servicemen were stationed in the area as World War II proceeded, strengthening the branches. After the war, the branches began to grow. One prominent leader of the time was Stance H. Moore, president of the North Alabama District. A chapel was completed in 1955 in Montgomery, and the branch grew more rapidly after that. Alabama's first stake was created in Huntsville in 1968, the beginning of an influx of members brought by the military and the National Space and Aeronautics Administration. Membership in Alabama in 1974 was about 7,800, increasing to 14,000 in 1980 and to 20,000 in 1989, when the 150th anniversary of missionary work in Alabama was commemorated. One of the speakers at that commemoration was Chief Justice Ernest C. "Sonny" Hornsby of the Alabama Supreme Court.

Alabama members were among many to respond to storm-caused disasters in the 1990s — including Hurricane Erin and Hurricane Opal which hit the state in 1995.

Sources: *Encyclopedic History of the Church,* by Andrew Jenson; *History of the Southern States Mission, 1831-1861,* by LaMar C. Berrett, a BYU thesis of July 1960; *Sesquicentennial Star,* history published by Montgomery Alabama Stake Oct. 7, 1989, courtesy Frank W. Riggs III, with interviews of Willie Lou Greene, and others; "Alabama: The northern Saints of a southern state," April 7, 1988, *Church News*; "Members rally to help hurricane victims," *Church News*, Aug. 12, 1995; "LDS render service in wake of Opal's rage," *Church News*, Oct. 14, 1995.

Stakes — 6
(Listed alphabetically as of Oct. 1, 1996.)

No.	Name	Organized	First President
North America Southeast Area			
1362	Bessemer Alabama	12 Sep 1982	Robert Henry Shepherdson
678	Birmingham Alabama	2 Feb 1975	Fred M. Washburn
1588	Dothan Alabama 2 Mar 1986	Ned Philip Jenne	
452	*Huntsville Alabama		
	‡Alabama 3 Mar 1968	Raymond D. McCurdy	
964	Mobile Alabama 8 Oct 1978	Dean Arthur Rains	
717	Montgomery Alabama	2 Nov 1975	Gayle Dorwin Heckel

Mission — 1
(As of Oct. 1, 1996; shown with historical number. See MISSIONS.)

(166a) ALABAMA BIRMINGHAM MISSION
1560 Montgomery Highway, Suite 204
Birmingham, AL 35216
Phone: (205) 979-0686

Alaska

Year-end 1995: Est. population, 605,000; Members, 24,000; Stakes, 6; Wards, 37; Branches, 32; Missions, 1; Districts, 1; Percent LDS, 3.9, or one person in 25.

The first Latter-day Saints in Alaska, John Bigelow and Dr. Edward G. Cannon, were drawn by the gold rush of 1898. They arrived about the turn of the century. Little is known of Bigelow, but Dr. Cannon, a 79-year-old who had been converted in 1871, worked hard to establish the Church. He maintained a "tabernacle which he moved about on wheels from settlement to settlement" in the Seward Peninsula and Nome area.

On June 25, 1902, Dr. Cannon baptized a gold miner, K.N. Winnie, in the Bering Sea near Nome. Winnie reported in 1907 that they were holding gospel meetings and quite a number of people were interested. They taught Eskimos as well as miners and others. They worked together until Dr. Cannon's death in 1910, though they realized little success.

In 1913, a year after Alaska became a territory of the United States, the first two missionaries arrived in Juneau where they worked for a few weeks. The next missionaries arrived in Alaska in 1928 when Elders Heber J. Meeks, Alvin Englestead, James Judd, and Lowell T. Plowman came under the direction of Pres. William R. Sloan of the Northwestern States Mission.

The elders held 105 meetings and placed more than 1,300 copies of the Book of Mormon over the next year. They also dealt with a widespread rumor that the Church planned to colonize Alaska. Few people joined, however, and membership consisted only of a few scattered LDS homesteaders or fortune seekers.

The first branch was organized in Fairbanks on July 10, 1938, with Dr. Murray Shields as president. By 1941, membership in the territory reached 300. During the next 23 years, other branches were organized so that by 1961, membership was 3,051 with three branches in Anchorage, and additional branches in Fairbanks, Palmer, and Juneau. The Anchorage Stake was created Aug. 13, 1961, with Orson P. Millett as president.

The Alaskan-Canadian Mission was created Jan. 1, 1961. In 1964, missionaries working among the native Americans introduced the gospel to many. A massive earthquake struck Alaska on March 27, 1964, and among those killed were six members of the Valdez Branch.

As the area was rebuilt after the earthquake, the construction effort led to a building boom that brought additional members, and the stake grew along with the state. A new stake center was dedicated in Anchorage in 1966. In 1970, membership was 6,744. The Alaska Anchorage Mission was created in 1974.

Discovery of oil in the north accelerated growth. Construction of the trans-Alaska oil pipeline created a boom of membership that dropped after the construction project was completed. Special meetinghouses designed for the Arctic were built in many of the smaller branches under the leadership of mission Pres. Douglas T. Snarr in 1981. Membership in 1980 reached 14,414, and by 1990 it was 21,410. In the 1990s, members took part in community service projects that helped improve relationships for the Church.

In June 1996, for the first time in the history of the Church, a prophet visited members of the Church in Alaska. From June 17-23, President Gordon B. Hinckley spoke at a regional conference, met with missionaries of the Alaska Anchorage Mission, spoke at firesides and visited the tiny Gustavus Branch. President Hinckley was accompanied by his wife, Marjorie, and Elder LeGrand R. Curtis, then member of the Second Quorum of the Seventy, and his wife Patricia.

Sources: *Encyclopedic History of the Church,* by Andrew Jenson; *The History of the Mormons in Alaska,* by Barbara Jean Walther; *A Gathering of Saints in Alaska,* edited by Patricia B. Jasper and Beverly M. Blasongame; "The Saints in Anchorage Alaska," *Ensign,* Nov. 1987; "Alaskans: Determined Builders," Feb. 14, 1981, *Church News*; "Refuge facilities improved," *Church News,* Dec. 18, 1993; "Alaskan LDS welcome Pres. Hinckley," *Church News,* July 1, 1995.

Stakes — 6
(Listed alphabetically as of Oct. 1, 1996.)

No.	Name	Organized	First President
North America Northwest Area			
331	*Anchorage Alaska		
	‡Alaska	13 Aug 1961	Orson P. Millett
962	Anchorage Alaska North	17 Sep 1978	Wesley R. Grover
1033	Fairbanks Alaska	27 May 1979	Dennis E. Cook
2102	Juneau Alaska	8 Oct 1995	Melvin R. Perkins
1507	Soldotna Alaska	9 Dec 1984	Merrill D. Briggs
1456	Wasilla Alaska	13 Nov 1983	Elbert Thomas Pettijohn

Mission — 1
(As of Oct. 1, 1996; shown with historical number. See MISSIONS.)

(114) ALASKA ANCHORAGE MISSION
12350 Industry Way, Suite 218
Anchorage, AK 99515
Phone: (907) 345-7579

Arizona

Year-end 1995: Est. population, 4,288,000; Members, 271,000; Stakes, 64; Wards, 476; Branches, 60; Missions, 3; Temples, 1; Percent LDS, 6.3, or one person in 15.

The Mormon Battalion entered the area that is now Arizona in December 1847 and January 1848 during its famous march through the Southwest. As early as 1859, Jacob Hamblin did missionary work among the Navajos and Moquis Indians of the area. The first effort at colonization came in March 1873 when a group of Saints was sent from Utah to the Little Colorado River area under the direction of Horton D. Haight. Most returned to Utah but a few remained, including John L. Blythe. He and others established farms among the Indians at Moancopi. A second expedition under James S. Brown scouted the Little Colorado River preparing the way for a group that later colonized St. Joseph, Sunset, Obed and Brigham City. These settlers, who came in the spring of 1876, built a fort, dug canals and built dams and struggled to survive in the arid land. Most practiced the United Order. Settlers on the lower Little Colorado became discouraged after efforts failed to dam the unruly stream.

In 1876, Lot Smith and others established more colonies on the Little Colorado. A year later, Mormon colonizers settled in the Salt River Valley where Lehi and later Mesa were founded. Other colonies, such as Pima and Thatcher, were founded in Gila Valley in 1881. Eventually, some 34 Mormon colonies were started in Arizona.

The Little Colorado Stake was created in 1878, followed by the Maricopa and St. Joseph stakes in 1882 and 1883, respectively.

Members overcame severe hardships in the early years. For example, in the colony of Woodruff, members built 17 successive dams after each previous one was washed out.

Over the years, members gained prominence and were involved in the progress of the state. They earned a good reputation for their industry and integrity. Colonies continued to grow. Pres. Jesse N. Smith of Snowflake helped locate the site of the Mormon colonies in Mexico. Arizona also became a place of refuge for the settlers of Mexico during the exodus of 1912.

The Arizona Temple was completed in 1923 and dedicated Oct. 23, 1927.

By 1930, Arizona had four stakes with 18,732 members. Two stakes were created in the 1930s, and another two in the 1940s; membership in 1940 was 25,272. In 1950, membership was 33,937, and during the decade six more stakes were created. In 1960, membership had nearly doubled to 60,457; five stakes were created in the 1960s. Membership grew to 94,249 by 1970, and 21 new stakes were created in the 1970s. President Spencer W. Kimball, a long-time resident of Thatcher, Ariz., was president of the Church from 1973-1985.

To accommodate the increasing membership, the Arizona Temple was renovated and enlarged and, in 1975, became the first temple in the Church to be rededicated. A total of 205,248 members and non-members toured the renewed building during an open house held before its rededication. At that time, the temple district included 72 stakes, including 28 Spanish-speaking stakes.

The pageant "Jesus the Christ," started in 1938 and presented annually on the temple grounds, attract about 80,000 people each year. Christmas lights on the Arizona Temple grounds also attracts many from the community.

By 1980, membership reached 171,880; and by 1990, 241,000. In the last few years, about two new stakes a year have been created in Arizona.

Sources: *Encyclopedic History of the Church,* by Andrew Jenson; "Early History of Arizona," by Paul Updike, *The Pioneer,* Jan. 1981; *Heart Throbs of the West* by Kate B. Carter; "Mormons in Arizona" by Thomas Edwin Farrish, reprinted in the *Deseret News* Aug. 31, 1918.

Stakes — 64
(Listed alphabetically as of Oct. 1, 1996.)

No.	Name	Organized	First President
North America Southwest Area — 63			
1616	Apache Junction Arizona	16 Nov 1986	Charles Wray Squires
1666	Buckeye Arizona	13 Dec 1987	Charles Roy Rucker
888	Camp Verde Arizona	22 Jan 1978	John Edward Eagar
1819	Casa Grande Arizona	13 Oct 1991	Scott J. McEuen
988	Chandler Arizona	3 Dec 1978	Elone Evans Farnsworth
1513	Chandler Arizona Alma	24 Feb 1985	Martin H. Durrant
1773	Chinle Arizona	30 Sep 1990	Edwin I. Tano
963	Duncan Arizona	24 Sep 1978	Earl Adair Merrell
1627	Eagar Arizona	25 Jan 1987	Charles D. Martin
232	*Flagstaff Arizona		
	‡Flagstaff	23 Sep 1956	Burton R. Smith
703	*Gilbert Arizona Greenfield	11 Oct 1981	
	‡Gilbert Arizona	24 Aug 1975	Newell A. Barney
1295	Gilbert Arizona Stapley	11 Oct 1981	Wilburn James Brown
1661	Gilbert Arizona Val Vista	22 Nov 1987	Craig Allen Cardon
612	*Glendale Arizona		

	‡Glendale	6 May 1973	Melvin L. Huber
1236	Glendale Arizona North	15 Feb 1981	Richard Johnson Barrett
650	Globe Arizona	16 Jun 1974	Bennie Joe Cecil
536	*Holbrook Arizona		
	‡Holbrook	22 Nov 1970	Jay Barder Williams
1436	Kingman Arizona	21 Aug 1983	Louis George Sorensen
161	*Mesa Arizona		
	‡Mesa	8 Dec 1946	L.M. Mecham Jr.
1265	Mesa Arizona Central	10 May 1981	Clayton H. Hakes
224	*Mesa Arizona East		
	*Mesa East 29 May 1970		
	‡East Mesa	20 Nov 1955	Donald Ellsworth
1087	Mesa Arizona Kimball	25 Nov 1979	Allen Smith Farnsworth
1741	Mesa Arizona Kimball East	14 Jan 1990	Wayne D. Crismon
1026	Mesa Arizona Lehi	6 May 1979	Otto Stronach Shill Jr.
24	*Mesa Arizona Maricopa		
	‡Maricopa	10 Dec 1882	Alexander F. MacDonald
1628	Mesa Arizona Mountain View	25 Jan 1987	James R. Adair
558	*Mesa Arizona North 15 Mar 1978		
	*Mesa Maricopa North		
	‡Maricopa North	7 Nov 1971	Raymond L. Russell
1479	Mesa Arizona Pueblo	10 Jun 1984	E. Clark Huber
1904	Mesa Ariz Red Mountain	20 Sep 1992	James Joseph Humula
745	Mesa Arizona Salt River	15 Feb 1976	Elden S. Porter
362	*Mesa Arizona South		
	‡Mesa South	18 Nov 1962	Stanley F. Turley
555	*Mesa Arizona West		
	‡Mesa West	10 Oct 1971	Weymouth D. Pew
633	Page Arizona	10 Mar 1974	J Ballard Washburn
1061	Paradise Valley Arizona	9 Sep 1979	James David King
1631	Peoria Arizona	22 Feb 1987	Thomas G. Jones
121	*Phoenix Arizona		
	‡Phoenix	27 Feb 1938	James Robert Price
1248	Phoenix Arizona Camelback	22 Mar 1981	Ernest Widtsoe Shumway
1233	Phoenix Arizona Deer Valley	8 Feb 1981	E. Wayne Pratt
212	*Phoenix Arizona East		
	*Phoenix East 29 May 1970		
	‡East Phoenix	28 Feb 1954	Junius E. Driggs
253	*Phoenix Arizona North		
	‡Phoenix North	19 Jan 1958	Rudger G. Smith
380	*Phoenix Arizona West		
	‡Phoenix West	1 Sep 1963	Keith W. Hubbard
896	*Phoenix Arizona West Maricopa 18 May 1978		
	‡West Maricopa Arizona	5 Mar 1978	DeNelson Jones
1830	Pima Arizona	17 Nov 1991	Stephen Lavar John
2039	Pinetop-Lakeside Arizona	26 Mar 1995	Chester Trent Adams
517	*Prescott Arizona		
	‡Prescott	7 Jun 1970	Edward A. Dalton
137	*St. David Arizona		
	*Arizona South 29 May 1970		
	‡Southern Arizona	2 Mar 1941	A.B. Ballantyne
31	*St. Johns Arizona		
	‡St. Johns (Arizona, N.M.)	23 Jul 1887	David K. Udall
120	*Safford Arizona		
	‡Mount Graham		
	(Arizona, N.M.)	20 Feb 1938	Spencer W. Kimball
364	*Scottsdale Arizona		
	‡Scottsdale	9 Dec 1962	Junius E. Driggs
668	Show Low Arizona	24 Nov 1974	Elbert J. Lewis
1348	Sierra Vista Arizona	6 Jun 1982	C. Lavell Haymore
31a	*Snowflake Arizona		
	‡Snowflake	18 Dec 1887	Jesse N. Smith
1212	Taylor Arizona	30 Nov 1980	Peter Delos Shumway
391	*Tempe Arizona		
	‡Tempe	2 Feb 1964	George Isaac Dana

738	Tempe Arizona South	18 Jan 1976	Fred Dale Markham
1708	Tempe Arizona West	8 Jan 1989	Kent M. Christiansen
25	*Thatcher Arizona		
	‡Saint Joseph	25 Feb 1883	Christopher Layton
2068	Tuba City Arizona	25 June 1995	Edin I. Tano
238	*Tucson Arizona		
	‡Tucson	2 Dec 1956	Leslie Odell Brewer
878	Tucson Arizona East	6 Nov 1977	Paul Eugene Dahl
477	*Tucson Arizona North		
	‡Tucson North	2 Feb 1969	Don Hakan Peterson
1517	Tucson Arizona Rincon	3 Mar 1985	Ernest G. Blain
959	Winslow Arizona	17 Sep 1978	Thomas A. Whipple

North America West Area - 1

263	*Yuma Arizona		
	‡Yuma (Arizona, California)	27 Apr 1958	Marion Turley

Discontinued

22	Eastern Arizona	29 Jun 1879	Jesse N. Smith
	(Arizona, N.M.)		
	18 Dec 1887 †St. Johns (31), Snowflake (31a)		
21	Little Colorado	27 Jan 1878	Lot Smith
	18 Dec 1887 †Snowflake (31a)		
562	Tempe University	12 Dec 1971	Leo Rae Huish
	28 Apr 1974 †13 Salt River Valley stakes		

Missions — 3

(As of Oct. 1, 1996; shown with historical number. See MISSIONS.)

(179b) ARIZONA PHOENIX MISSION
6265 North 82nd St.
Scottsdale, AZ 85250
Phone: (602) 951-8098

(37) ARIZONA TEMPE MISSION
1871 East Del Rio Drive
Tempe, AZ 85282-2899
Phone: (602) 838-0659

(231) ARIZONA TUCSON MISSION
1840 East River Road, #102
Tucson, AZ 85718
Phone: (502) 577-7076

Arkansas

Year-end 1995: Est. population, 2,500,000; Members, 17,000; Stakes, 4; Wards, 26; Branches, 24; Missions, 1; Percent LDS, 0.7, or one person in 147.

Elders Wilford Woodruff and Henry Brown arrived as missionaries in Benton County, Ark., on Jan. 28, 1835. They held the first meeting Feb. 1, and preached to an attentive congregation. Later they were confronted by an apostate, a man who earlier endured severe persecution in Missouri but later turned bitterly against the Church. However, this man died suddenly and Elder Woodruff preached his funeral sermon. Afterward, Elder Woodruff baptized a "Brother and Sister Hubbel."

In 1838, Elder Abraham O. Smoot was called to a five-month mission to Arkansas where he preached frequently with varied results.

Elder Parley P. Pratt was murdered in the town of Van Buren, Ark., on May 13, 1857. He had just been acquitted by a court of charges pressed by the former husband of his wife Eleanor McLean Pratt. At the trial she testified that her former husband had frequently physically abused her. Disappointed with the verdict, the enraged accuser assassinated the apostle.

Little if any missionary success was realized until 1875 when Elders Henry G. Boyle and J.D.H. McAllister visited a member in Des Arc, Ark., and preached and "baptized a great many of the best citizens of the region," numbering from 80 to 90 people. In 1877, Des Arc Branch members moved a group of 27 families and 125 people to Utah by wagon train.

In 1897, Elder J.H. Peterson laboring in Arkansas reported being treated kindly while in Heber, Red River and Batesville. This changed attitude evidently paved the way for conversions in Marion and Faulkner counties about the turn of the century. Several pioneer members were baptized in March of 1900, including Benjamin Franklin Baker and his sister Emoline in Faulkner County, and Rowland William Perry and his family, as well as Mary Chapelle and Martha White in Marion County.

The Baker family established the nucleus of the Barney Branch, which was a headquarters for missionaries for many years.

Early members and missionaries faced persecution but kept the Church going. Some of these and other early converts immigrated to the West but others stayed and reared LDS families. These families were very close and held most of their social activities together.

By 1930, membership in Arkansas was 944 with branches at Barney, El Dorado and Little Rock (Faulkner County). New buildings were erected for the Little Rock and El Dorado branches in 1952, the Pine Bluff Branch in 1954, and the Barney and Rolla branches in 1956.

The first Arkansas stake was created June 1, 1969, in Little Rock, with the Ft. Smith Stake created in 1978 and the Jacksonville Stake created in 1983. The Arkansas Little Rock Mission was created in 1975.

Membership in 1980 was 9,878 and in 1990, 13,753. Arkansas members were among many to render service after storm-caused disasters — such as tornadoes which hit the state in April 1996.

Sources: *Encyclopedic History of the Church,* by Andrew Jenson; *History of the Southern States Mission,* a BYU thesis by LaMar C. Berrett, 1960; "History and Genealogy of the Early Mormon Church in Arkansas," by Emogene Tindall; "History of the Church in Marion County Arkansas," by Louise Perry Bird; *Juvenile Instructor,* 15:24; *Millennial Star,* 38:26, 59:15; Early Scenes in Church History," *Church News,* May 21, 1977; BYU Studies, 15:2; "Church members rally to help tornado victims," *Church News,* April 27, 1996.

Stakes — 4
(Listed alphabetically by area as of Oct. 1, 1996.)

No.	Name	Organized	First President
North America Southeast Area — 2			
1432	Jacksonville Arkansas	19 Jun 1983	Robert Michael McChesney
484	*Little Rock Arkansas		
	‡Arkansas	1 Jun 1969	Dean C. Andrew
North America Southwest Area — 2			
911	Ft. Smith Arkansas	30 Apr 1978	Arthur Donald Browne
1807	Rogers Arkansas	11 Aug 1991	David Allen Bednar

Mission — 1
(As of Oct. 1, 1994; shown with historical number. See MISSIONS.)

(116) ARKANSAS LITTLE ROCK MISSION
University Tower, # 210
1123 South University Ave.
Little Rock, AR 72204-1690
Phone: (501) 664-3765

California

Year-end 1995: Est. population, 31,680,000; Members, 726,000; Stakes, 160; Wards, 1,149; Branches, 203; Missions, 15; Temples, 3; Percent LDS, 2.3, or one person in 43.

Immigrants on the way to the Great Basin by way of Cape Horn were the first Latter-day Saints to set foot in California, arriving in Yerba Buena (San Francisco) July 29 or 31, 1846. They built up the community and laid important foundations for what became San Francisco. Eventually, many of the members came to Salt Lake City.

In January 1847, the Mormon Battalion arrived in San Diego and made similar if not more extensive contributions to that city, and then traveled to Los Angeles where they built a fort and raised the first American flag. Six battalion members were at Sutter's Mill Jan. 24, 1848, when gold was discovered. The attraction of gold to the Great Basin Saints was minimal, although the Church and various members did profit from its discovery.

In 1850 a Mormon colony, New Hope, was founded by Mormons who did not go to Utah. They were among California's first farmers, irrigating with a pole and bucket method. They built the first Mormon chapel in 1850. Apostle Parley P. Pratt presided over the California Mission at San Francisco from 1849-52.

The first outreach from Utah to California came in 1851 with the San Bernardino colonization effort, which was to provide a route to the coast and attract Latter-day Saints from northern California and immigrants. Apostles Charles C. Rich and Amasa M.

Lyman took charge of the effort. The San Bernardino Stake was created July 6, 1851, but was discontinued by 1857. The faithful members in this colony were eventually outnumbered by less-committed members who created considerable dissension. When the troubled colony was dissolved by the Church at the advance of Johnston's army upon Salt Lake City in 1857, some 1,400 — fewer than half the total — returned to Utah to colonize other areas.

Little missionary work took place from 1857 to 1892. Elder John L. Dalton began work in San Francisco in 1892 and organized branches. Karl G. Maeser presided over the California Mission in 1894. Missionaries began work southward and the Los Angeles Branch was created Aug. 20, 1895. The Northern California and Southern California conferences were organized in 1896, and the Sacramento Conference was added in 1898.

The land boom of the 1920s attracted many members. The Los Angeles Stake was created Jan. 21, 1923, and was divided just four years later. The Hollywood Stake was created in 1927, the same year the San Francisco Stake was formed. Membership in 1930 was 21,254.

After the 1920s, when the first three stakes were created, new stakes were added at a rapid pace. Eight were created in the 1930s, five in the 1940s and 30 in the 1950s.

During the 1930s, many members came to work in the wartime defense industry. Land for a temple was purchased in 1937 in Los Angeles and the temple was completed in 1956. A second temple in Oakland was dedicated in 1964. A third California temple was dedicated April 25, 1993, in San Diego.

Completion of the imposing Los Angeles Temple in 1956 seemed to mark the beginning of an era of Church members gaining a higher public profile. In the past few decades, Latter-day Saints throughout California have reached the highest levels of education, industry, military, medicine, entertainment, science and government.

In times of disasters, such as earthquakes, fires and floods, members have responded with organized volunteers and supplies for members and non-members alike. Members have taken leadership roles in moral issues, such as combatting pornography. They have also cooperated with other congregations in various inter-faith endeavors.

Missionary work has also prospered in the state, which has more missions than any other state. Many minority converts have been taught the gospel in their own language in California's major cities. With burgeoning population increases from Latin America, four Spanish-speaking stakes have been organized, two since 1992. Various Asian and Polynesian wards function as well, and a Tongan stake was created in San Francisco in 1992.

Membership reached 541,000 in 1980. From 1991 to 1993, because of an out-migration of members, membership dropped from 721,000 to 719,000. However, from 1993 to 1995, membership rose to 725,690. The Church is now the second largest in California.

The year 1996 marked the sesquicentennial of the arrival of the ship *Brooklyn*, carrying the first LDS settlers to California via Cape Horn. Members throughout the state commemorated the milestone with a special exhibit at the San Francisco Maritime Museum, performances of the Mormon Tabernacle Choir at the Davies Symphony Hall, a re-enactment of the arrival of the *Brooklyn* using a replica ship, dedications of plaques honoring the early settlers, and pioneer activities and parades. Attending many of these events were Elder David B. Haight of the Quorum of the Twelve, who is a former mayor of Palo Alto, Calif., and his wife, Ruby; and Elder Loren C. Dunn of the Seventy and president of the North America West Area.

In addition, to commemorate not only the arrival of early LDS settlers, but also their contributions to the development of the state, members throughout California held a statewide service blitz. Such community projects, sponsored by wards and stakes, included gathering supplies and food for the needy, cleaning parks, beaches and roadways, painting and repairing homeless shelters, and cleaning up graffiti.

Sources: *Encyclopedic History of the Church*, by Andrew Jenson; "It Started in Yerba Buena," by Richard O. Cowan, *Instructor* June 1961; "The Church in Early California," by Albert L. Zobell, *Improvement Era*, May 1964; "The Rise and Decline of Mormon San Bernardino," by Edward Leo Lyman, *BYU Studies*, Fall 1989; *Encyclopedia of Mormonism*, edited by Daniel H. Ludlow; multiple sources in *Church News*; "Spanish spoken here," by Julie A. Dockstader, *Church News*, May 15, 1993; articles on *Brooklyn* commemorative activities, *Church News*, July 6, Aug. 3, Aug. 10, Aug. 17, 1996.

(Listed alphabetically by area as of Oct. 1, 1996.)

No.	Name	Organized	First President
North America West Area — 160			
402	*Anaheim California		
	‡Anaheim	14 Mar 1965	Max V. Eliason
1514	Anaheim California East	24 Feb 1985	William E. Perron
1042	Anderson California	10 Jun 1979	Richard Miller Ericson
1263	Antioch California	3 May 1981	Clifford Spence Munns
864	Arcadia California	9 Oct 1977	Cree-L Kofford
1032	Auburn California	27 May 1979	David Oliver Montague
186	*Bakersfield California		
	‡Bakersfield	27 May 1951	E. Alan Pettit
944	Bakersfield California East	18 Jun 1978	William Horsley Davies
1622	Bakersfield California South	14 Dec 1986	Jack Ray Zimmerman
288	*Barstow California		
	‡Mojave	16 Aug 1959	Sterling A. Johnson
750	Blythe California	14 Mar 1976	Jerry Dean Mortensen
763	Camarillo California	8 Aug 1976	Victor Glenn Johnson
337	*Canoga Park California	6 Dec 1992	
	‡Canoga Park	8 Oct 1961	Collins E. Jones
	*Los Angeles California Canoga Park		
309	*Carlsbad California		
	‡Palomar	6 Nov 1960	Wallace F. Gray
1505	Carmichael California	25 Nov 1984	Marc Earl Hall
269	*Cerritos California		
	‡Norwalk	26 Oct 1958	Lewis Milton Jones
565	*Chico California		
	‡Chico	6 Feb 1972	Lloyd Johnson Cope
1072	Chino California	14 Oct 1979	Allen Clare Christensen
770	Chula Vista California	19 Sep 1976	Robert Eugene Floto
1150	Citrus Heights California	22 Jun 1980	James Barnes
378	*Concord California		
	‡Concord	23 Jun 1963	Ted Eugene Madsen
983	Corona California	19 Nov 1978	Darvil David McBride
226	*Covina California		
	‡Covina	26 Feb 1956	Elden L. Ord
502	*Cypress California		
	‡Anaheim West	15 Feb 1970	Hugh J. Sorensen
229	*Danville California 19 Jun 1989		
	*Walnut Creek California		
	‡Walnut Creek	26 Aug 1956	Emery R. Ranker
1151	Davis California	22 Jun 1980	Peter Glen Kenner
1740	Del Mar California	7 Jan 1990	Robert Geoffrey Dyer
279	*Downey California 18 Feb 1986		
	*Huntington Park California		
	‡Huntington Park	19 Apr 1959	Clifford B. Wright
179	*East Los Angeles	27 Jun 1993	
	California (Spanish)		
	*Los Angeles California East		
	*Los Angeles East 29 May 1970		
	‡East Los Angeles (California)	26 Feb 1950	Fauntleroy Hunsaker
261	*El Cajon California 30 Nov 1975		
	*San Diego California El Cajon		
	‡San Diego East	20 Apr 1958	Cecil I. Burningham
1119	El Centro California	16 Mar 1980	Robert Lamoreaux
984	El Dorado California	19 Nov 1978	Harold George Sellers
487	*Elk Grove California 30 Sep 1993		
	*Sacramento California South		
	‡Sacramento South (California)	15 Jun 1969	John Henry Huber
588	*Escondido California		
	‡Escondido	24 Sep 1972	Donald R. McArthur
1847	Escondido California South	9 Feb 1992	Louis L. Rothey
338	*Eureka California		
	‡Redwood		

	(California, Oregon)	22 Oct 1961	David DeBar Felshaw
428	Fair Oaks	12 Feb 1967	Harvey Stansell Greer
	*Fair Oaks California		
682	Fairfield California	16 Feb 1975	Byron Gale Wilson
1602	Fontana California	22 Jun 1986	Wayne Hall Bringhurst
425	*Fremont California		
	‡Fremont	11 Dec 1966	Francis B. Winkel
1584	Fremont California South	12 Jan 1986	Jerry Valient Kirk
185	*Fresno California		
	‡Fresno	20 May 1951	Alwyn C. Sessions
381	*Fresno California East		
	‡Fresno East	15 Sep 1963	Melvin P. Leavitt
1463	Fresno California North	12 Feb 1984	Stephen L. Christensen
1464	Fresno California West	12 Feb 1984	Gary R. Fogg
707	Fullerton California	21 Sep 1975	Leon Tad Ballard
330	*Garden Grove California		
	‡Garden Grove	25 Jun 1961	James Malan Hobbs
175	*Glendale California		
	‡Glendale	4 Dec 1949	Edwin Smith Dibble
786	Glendora California	14 Nov 1976	William Marshall Raymond
107	*Gridley California		
	‡Gridley	4 Nov 1934	John C. Todd
442	*Hacienda Heights California	15 Jan 1978	
	*El Monte California		
	‡El Monte	17 Sep 1967	James Cyril Brown
948	Hanford California	6 Aug 1978	Gerald Leo Thompson
228a	*Hayward California		
	‡Hayward	26 Aug 1956	Milton P. Ream
961	Hemet California	17 Sep 1978	Darrel D. Lee
1632	Hesperia California	22 Feb 1987	Larry Dale Skinner
1926	Highland California	14 Mar 1993	Dennis Alvin Barlow
420	*Huntington Beach California		
	‡Huntington Beach	5 Jun 1966	Conway W. Nielsen
802	Huntington Beach California North	16 Jan 1977	Wesley Charles Woodhouse
1477	Huntington Park California West	3 Jun 1984	Rafael Nestor Seminario
1633a	Irvine California	12 Apr 1987	Jack L. Rushton Jr.
129	*Inglewood California 21 Feb 1993		
	*Los Angeles California Inglewood		
	‡Inglewood	26 Nov 1939	Alfred E. Rohner
1784	Jurupa California	9 Dec 1990	Lester C. Lauritzen
518	*La Crescenta California		
	‡La Canada	7 Jun 1970	Robert C. Seamons
347	*La Verne California		
	‡Pomona	21 Jan 1962	Vern R. Peel
1354	Laguna Niguel California	20 Jun 1982	Donald H. Sedgwick
794	Lancaster California	28 Nov 1976	Stephen N. Hull
1798	Lancaster California East	19 May 1991	John Milloy Martz
1654	Livermore California	13 Sep 1987	Willis Arthur Sandholtz
822	*Lodi California 3 May 1981		
	‡Stockton California East	10 Apr 1977	Robert Graham Wade
1649	Lompoc California	23 Aug 1987	Billy Ray Williams
117	*Long Beach California		
	‡Long Beach	3 May 1936	John W. Jones
177	*Long Beach California East		
	*Long Beach East 29 May 1970		
	‡East Long Beach	12 Feb 1950	John C. Dalton
704	Los Altos California	24 Aug 1975	W. Kay Williams
98	*Los Angeles California		
	*Los Angeles 19 Nov 1939		
	‡Hollywood	22 May 1927	George W. McCune
188	*Los Angeles California		
	Santa Monica 14 Jan 1974		
	‡Santa Monica (California)	1 Jul 1951	E. Garrett Barlow
1249	Manteca California	22 Mar 1981	David Leon Ward

2108	Menifee California	15 Oct 1995	Timothy Rudd
156	*Menlo Park California		
	‡Palo Alto	23 Jun 1946	Claude B. Petersen
659	Merced California	15 Sep 1974	Robert D. Rowan
826	Mission Viejo California	8 May 1977	Nolan C. Draney
399	*Modesto California		
	‡Modesto	7 Jun 1964	Clifton A. Rooker
716	Modesto California North	26 Oct 1975	Charles Elwin Boice
258	*Monterey California		
	‡Monterey Bay	2 Mar 1958	James N. Wallace Jr.
1656	Moreno Valley California	27 Sep 1987	David Lowell Briggs
831	Morgan Hill California	15 May 1977	Donald Russell Lundell
1693	Murrieta California	20 Mar 1988	Ronald Miguel Peterson
297	*Napa California		
	‡Napa	17 Apr 1960	Harry S. Cargun
652	Newbury Park California	18 Aug 1974	Lavar M. Butler
453	*Newport Beach California		
	‡Newport Beach	31 Mar 1968	Ferren L. Christensen
231	*North Hollywood California	6 Dec 1992	
	*Los Angeles California North Hollywood		
	‡Burbank (California)	16 Sep 1956	James D. Pratt227a
	*Oakland California		
	‡Oakland-Berkeley	26 Aug 1956	O. Leslie Stone
1092	Ontario California	9 Dec 1979	Seth C. Baker
251a	*Orange California		
	‡Santa Ana	8 Dec 1957	Karl C. Durham
441	*Palm Springs California		
	‡Palm Springs	27 Aug 1967	Quinten Hunsaker
459	*Palmdale California		
	‡Antelope Valley	12 May 1968	Sterling A. Johnson
739	Palos Verdes California	18 Jan 1976	Merrill Bickmore
128	*Pasadena California		
	‡Pasadena	1 Oct 1939	Bertram M. Jones
1608	Penasquitos California	21 Sep 1986	Michael Lee Jensen
215	*Placentia California		
	*Fullerton 14 Mar 1965		
	‡Orange County	27 Jun 1954	John C. Dalton
675	Pleasanton California	8 Dec 1974	Dale Edwin Nielsen
2202	Porterville California	16 Jun 1996	Steven E. Tree
1056	Poway California	26 Aug 1979	Paul B. Richardson
1648	Rancho Cucamonga California 13 Aug 1987		
	‡Cucamonga California	28 Jun 1987	Steven Thomas Escher
319	*Redding California		
	‡Redding	13 Dec 1960	Albert C. Peterson
938	*Redlands California 5 May 1987		
	‡San Bernardino California East 4 Jun 1978		Donald L. Hansen
415	*Rialto California		
	‡Rialto	20 Mar 1966	Wayne A. Reeves
521	*Ridgecrest California		
	‡Mount Whitney	16 Aug 1970	AlDean Washburn
196	*Riverside California		
	‡Mount Rubidoux	26 Oct 1952	Vern Robert Peel
430	*Riverside California West		
	‡Arlington	23 Apr 1967	Clarence Leon Sirrine
1854	Rocklin California	19 Apr 1992	Jay Robert Jibson Jr.
515	*Roseville California		
	‡Roseville	17 May 1970	S. Lloyd Hamilton
108	*Sacramento California		
	‡Sacramento	4 Nov 1934	Mark W. Cram
1691	Sacramento California Antelope	6 Mar 1988	Roger William Mack
290	*Sacramento California East		
	‡American River	6 Dec 1959	Austin G. Hunt
219	*Sacramento California North		
	*Sacramento North 30 Sep 1969		
	‡North Sacramento	12 Dec 1954	Austin G. Hunt

No.	Name	Date	President
1152	*Sacramento California Rancho Cordova	17 Sep 1985	
‡	Sacramento California Cordova	22 Jun 1980	Richard W. Montgomery
111	*San Bernardino California ‡San Bernardino	3 Feb 1935	Albert Lyndon Larson
136	*San Diego California ‡San Diego	9 Feb 1941	Wallace W. Johnson
736	San Diego California East	30 Nov 1975	Philip Alma Petersen
489	*San Diego California North ‡San Diego North	22 Jun 1969	Ray Michael Brown
360	*San Diego California Sweetwater	30 Aug 1988	
	*Lemon Grove California	16 Aug 1983	
	*San Diego California South ‡San Diego South	21 Oct 1962	Cecil I. Burningham
1915a	San Fernando California (Spanish)	6 Dec 1992	Jose Gerardo Lombardo
99	*San Francisco California ‡San Francisco	10 Jul 1927	W. Aird Macdonald
1863	San Francisco California East	10 May 1992	Sione Fangu
1515	San Francisco California West	24 Feb 1985	Jeremiah I. Alip
202	*San Jose California ‡San Jose	30 Nov 1952	Vernard L. Beckstrand
693	San Jose California East	4 May 1975	Leo E. Haney
450	*San Jose California South ‡San Jose South (California)	14 Jan 1974 11 Feb 1968	DeBoyd L. Smith
329	*San Leandro California ‡San Leandro	21 May 1961	Milton R. Ream
248	*San Luis Obispo California ‡San Luis Obispo	22 Sep 1957	Arthur J. Godfrey
462	*San Rafael California ‡Marin	23 Jun 1968	Weston L. Roe
787	Santa Ana California	14 Nov 1976	Wilbur Orion Jensen
1838	Santa Ana California South (Spanish)	5 Jan 1992	Renan Ramos Disner
184	*Santa Barbara California ‡Santa Barbara	18 Mar 1951	Arthur J. Godfrey
642	*Santa Clarita California ‡Los Angeles California Santa Clarita	2 Feb 1992 19 May 1974	Norman D. Stevensen
823	Santa Cruz California	24 Apr 1977	Edwin Reese Davis
1920	Santa Margarita California	17 Jan 1993	David Michael Daly
384	*Santa Maria California ‡Santa Maria	20 Oct 1963	Clayton K. Call
181	*Santa Rosa California ‡Santa Rosa	7 Jan 1951	J. LeRoy Murdock
1582	Santee California	8 Dec 1985	Robert Earl Harper
387	*Saratoga California ‡San Jose West	10 Nov 1963	Louis W. Latimer
448	*Simi Valley California ‡Simi	10 Dec 1967	John Lyman Ballif III
171	*Stockton California ‡San Joaquin	25 Apr 1948	Wendell B. Mendenhall
1624	Thousand Oaks California	11 Jan 1987	Grant R. Brimhall
282	*Torrance California ‡Torrance	3 May 1959	Roland Earl Gagon
220	*Torrance California North ‡Redondo	29 May 1955	Leslie L. Prestwich
1591	Turlock California	23 Mar 1986	Robert Peebles Baker
877	Ukiah California	30 Oct 1977	Robert Vernon Knudsen
583	*Upland California ‡Upland	13 Aug 1972	Frank E. Finlayson
1801	Vacaville California	26 May 1991	Edwin Gordon Wells Jr.
1845	Valencia California	2 Feb 1992	Reed E. Halladay
116	*Van Nuys California		

	*San Fernando 15 Oct 1939		
	‡Pasadena	19 Apr 1936	David H. Cannon
548	*Ventura California		
	‡Ventura	30 May 1971	Joseph F. Chapman
1397	Victorville California	30 Jan 1983	Owen Dean Call
492	*Visalia California		
	‡Visalia	24 Aug 1969	Alva D. Blackburn
967	Vista California	8 Oct 1978	Jack Robert Jones
281	*Walnut California 23 July 1985		
	*La Puente California		
	‡West Covina	3 May 1959	Mark W. Smith
1587a	*Walnut Creek California 17 May 1992		
	‡Walnut Creek California East	16 Feb 1986	Williams F. Matthews
280	*Whittier California		
	‡Whittier	26 Apr 1959	John Collings
1079	Yuba City California	4 Nov 1979	Lowell R. Tingey
1969	Yucca Valley California	9 Jan 1994	Kipton Paul Madsen

North America Southwest Area — 1

1073	Quincy California	14 Oct 1979	Floyd Eugene Warren

Discontinued

159	Berkeley	13 Oct 1946	W. Glenn Harmon
	26 Aug 1956 †Oakland-Berkeley (227a)		
656	Cerritos California West	8 Sep 1974	Kenneth Laurence Davis
	19 May 1996		
806	Concord California East	23 Jan 1977	Vern W. Clark
	16 Feb 1986 †Walnut Creek California East (1587)		
1107	Lawndale California	17 Feb 1980	Silvon Foster Engilman
	21 Feb 1993		
1683	Long Beach California North	31 Jan 1988	V. Jay Spongberg
	7 Nov 1993		
817	Los Angeles California	13 Mar 1977	Clark Spendlove
	Granada Hills 6 Dec 1992		
88	*Los Angeles South 29 May 1970		
	12 Aug 1973 †Huntington Park (279)		
	*South Los Angeles 19 Nov 1939		
	‡Los Angeles	21 Jan 1923	George W. McCune
109	Oakland	2 Dec 1934	W. Aird Macdonald
	26 Aug 1956 †Oakland-Berkeley (227a)		
247	*Pacifica California		
	21 Feb 1982 †San Francisco California (99)		
	‡San Mateo	15 Sep 1957	Melvin P. Pickering
230	Reseda (California)	16 Sep 1956	Hugh C. Smith
	*Los Angeles California	14 Jan 1974	
	Chatsworth	6 Dec 1992	
4a	San Bernardino	6 Jul 1851	David Seely
	1857		
585	San Jose North (California)	20 Aug 1972	Lloyd M. Gustaveson
	*Santa Clara California 14 Jan 1974		
	10 May 1992		

Missions — 15

(As of Oct. 1, 1996; shown with historical number. See MISSIONS.)

((73a) CALIF. ANAHEIM MISSION
501 N. Brookhurst100
Anaheim, CA 92801
Phone: (714) 776-2725

(86) CALIF. ARCADIA MISSION
170 West Duarte Road
Arcadia, CA 91007
Phone: (818) 446-8519

(283) CALIF. CARLSBAD MISSION
785 Grand Ave.204
Carlsbad, CA 92008
Phone: (619)720-3430

(118) CALIF. FRESNO MISSION
2350 West Shaw Ave.123
Fresno, CA 93711
Phone: (209) 431-5510

(5) CALIF. LOS ANGELES MISSION
1591 E. Temple Way
Los Angeles, CA 90024-5801
Phone: (310) 474-2593

(235) CALIF. RIVERSIDE MISSION
3233 Arlington Ave.,107
Riverside, CA 92506-3246
Phone: (909) 788-9690

(37) CALIF. SACRAMENTO MISSION
9480 Madison Ave.2
Orangevale, CA 95662
Phone: (916) 988-7037

(113) CALIF. SAN DIEGO MISSION
3322 Sweetwater Springs Blvd.,203
Spring Valley, CA 91977-3142
Phone: (619) 660-8202

(158a) CALIF. SAN JOSE MISSION
6489 Camden Ave.,107
San Jose, CA 95120-2898
Phone: (408) 268-9411

(159) CALIF. VENTURA MISSION
260 Maple Ct.120
Ventura, CA 93003
Phone: (805) 644-1034

(85) CALIF. OAKLAND MISSION
4945 Lincoln Way
Oakland, CA 94602
Phone: (510) 531-3880

(284) CALIF. ROSEVILLE
8331 Sierra College Blvd.,208
Roseville, CA 95661
Phone: (916) 791-7558

(182) CALIF. SAN BERNARDINO
8280 Utica Ave,150
Rancho Cucamonga, CA 91730
Phone: (909) 466-1129

(299) CALIF. SAN FERNANDO
23504 Lyons Ave.,107
Santa Clarita, CA 91321
Phone: (805) 288-1614

(187a) CALIF. SANTA ROSA MISSION
3510 Unocal Place,302
Santa Rosa, CA 95403
Phone: (707) 579-9412

Colorado

Year-end 1995: Est. population, 3,790,000; Members, 101,000; Stakes, 25; Wards, 176; Branches, 34; Missions, 2; Temples, 1; Percent LDS, 2.7, or one person in 38.

In 1846, a group of 43 Saints in 19 wagons traveled to the West from Monroe County, Miss. They expected to meet Brigham Young's wagon train at the Platte River in the Iowa Territory, and accompany this train west. However, Brigham Young's pioneer train waited over a season after 500 men were enlisted in the Mormon Battalion. By the time the Mississippi company learned of this, they had reached western Nebraska. The Mississippians decided to winter at Fort Pueblo in Colorado in the upper Arkansas River Valley, where they arrived Aug. 7, 1846. During the following winter, three detachments of the Mormon Battalion, including wives and children of battalion members, and those who were ill, were sent to join the members in Pueblo.

By the end of winter in 1846, the colony had 275 people. It was soon disbanded as one party joined Brigham Young's company at Fort Laramie June 3, 1847. Others went east to bring back their families, and others joined later wagon trains going west. No remains of this settlement exist; its site is near the present-day town of Blende in metropolitan Pueblo.

In 1858, the S.M. Rooker family, traveling east from Utah, heard of a gold discovery and became the first settlers at Cherry Creek and the Platte River, which would later become Denver. As the city grew, a few members arrived, but the area was not under ecclesiastical leadership until the Colorado Mission was created Dec. 14, 1896. Presiding over the mission was Elder John W. Taylor of the Quorum of the Twelve. The first missionaries in the area were Elders John H. Broshard, Hebert A. White and William C. Clive. The Denver Branch was created Jan. 3, 1897, and a short time later, branches in Colorado Springs were organized.

In 1878, a group of 70 converts from the Southern States Mission, under the leadership of Elder James Z. Stewart, settled in Conejos County, Colo. They, and later immigrants under the direction of Church leaders from Utah, founded the communities of Manassa, Richfield and Sanford. In 1883, the San Luis Stake was created in the area.

In the summer of 1897, Bishop John I. Hart of Manassa was called to live in Pueblo and start a branch there among the handful of members. This branch was organized under the direction of Elder Taylor about mid-January, 1897.

Missionaries in this period generally found residents to be hospitable and baptized occasional converts. In 1909, missionaries campaigned against the growing number of saloons in Denver. On Nov. 23, 1911, the Tabernacle Choir gave a concert in Denver, and another later in Colorado Springs. The Young Stake was created in the Montezuma and La Plata counties in 1913.

By 1930, the Denver, Pueblo, San Luis, and Western Colorado districts, and the San Luis and Young stakes had a combined membership of 6,435 members.

A branch in Fort Collins started as LDS educators arrived to teach at Colorado State University in the 1930s.

The Denver Stake was organized in 1940. During World War II, a number of former missionaries served at military bases in the Denver area. Denver Stake Pres. Edward E. Drury and former mission Pres. Elbert R. Curtis (released at the start of the war) held a special service attended by more than 100 servicemen.

Membership continued to grow after the war, and many buildings were constructed. By 1950, membership was nearly 10,000, increasing to nearly 20,000 in 1960, nearly 40,000 in 1970, and 69,000 by 1980.

A temple to serve the LDS population in Colorado and nearby states was completed and dedicated in 1986. Membership began to emerge into public notice during the decade that the temple was dedicated. Released-time seminary was approved and seminary buildings were erected. Membership grew as jobs increased in areas of high technology and military. Agriculture continued to be a stable source of livelihood for many.

Indicative of the increasing profile of the Church, Colorado Gov. Roy Romer addressed a Church fireside in Willow Springs March 11, 1990. In August of 1993, many LDS volunteers assisted when Pope John Paul II of the Roman Catholic Church visited Denver.

Since 1989, Church members have teamed with community organizations to use the Bishops' Storehouse in Denver for efforts to aid the needy. In 1994, for example, an estimated 100,000 canned items were produced for humanitarian use.

In 1996, President Gordon B. Hinckley addressed about 4,580 youth and young adults in Colorado Springs and Denver.

Sources: *Encyclopedic History of the Church,* by Andrew Jenson; "Colorado, Mormons and the Mexican War," by John F. Yurtinus, *Essays in Colorado History,* 1983, No. 1; "A Look at the History of the Church . . . in Pueblo, Colorado," by Gail McHardy; *Comprehensive History of the Church,* by B.H. Roberts; "Pioneer Journeys," *Improvement Era,* July 1910, 802-810; "Mississippi Mormons," by Leonard Arrington, *Ensign,* June 1977; "Denver Saints Claim Spiritual Blessings," *Ensign,* Nov. 1986; *Church News,* Oct. 7, 1944; Oct. 20, 1945; Feb. 9, 1974; June 4, 1977; Aug. 24, 1986; March 24, 1990; "LDS among volunteers for papal visit," by Twila Bird, *Church News,* Aug. 21, 1993.

Stakes — 26
(Listed alphabetically by area as of Oct. 1, 1996.)

No.	Name	Organized	First President
North America Central Area — 23			
1655	Arapahoe Colorado	27 Sep 1987	Lawry Evans Doxey
287	*Arvada Colorado		
	‡Denver West	21 Jun 1959	Thomas L. Kimball
1318	Aurora Colorado	6 Dec 1981	Lawry Evans Doxey
595	*Boulder Colorado		
	‡Boulder	28 Jan 1973	C. Rodney Claridge
301	*Colorado Springs Colorado		
	‡Pikes Peak		
	(Colorado, New Mexico)	11 Sep 1960	Ralph M. Gardner
1770	Colorado Springs Colorado East	26 Aug 1990	Jack Harmon Dunn
1134	Colorado Springs Colorado North	18 May 1980	Richard Larry Williams
1214	Columbine Colorado	7 Dec 1980	David M. Brown
132	*Denver Colorado		
	‡Denver	30 Jun 1940	Douglas M. Todd Jr.
596	*Denver Colorado North		
	‡Denver North	28 Jan 1973	Gus. F. Ranzenberger

470	*Fort Collins Colorado		
	‡Fort Collins	1 Dec 1968	Raymond Price
1452	Golden Colorado	6 Nov 1983	John Marshall Simcox
223	*Grand Junction Colorado		
	‡Grand Junction	16 Oct 1955	Loyal B. Cook
1415	Grand Junction Colorado West	24 Apr 1983	Andrew H. Christensen
1528	Greeley Colorado	28 Apr 1985	Gilbert I. Sandberg
394	*Lakewood Colorado		
	‡Denver South	19 Apr 1964	R. Raymond Barnes
625	*Littleton Colorado		
	‡Littleton	2 Sep 1973	Clinton L. Cutler
1778	Longmont Colorado	11 Nov 1990	Lynn Snarr Hutchings
320	Meeker Colorado		
	‡Craig	15 Jan 1961	Loyal B. Cook
977	Montrose Colorado	5 Nov 1978	Robert M. Esplin
2236	Parker Colorado	15 Sep 1996	William Kenneth Thiess
632	Pueblo Colorado	3 Mar 1974	Louis Edward Butler
1534	Willow Creek Colorado	19 May 1985	Robert K. Bills

North America Southwest Area — 3

1425	Alamosa Colorado	29 May 1983	Gary Reese Shawcroft
557	*Durango Colorado		
	‡Mesa Verde	7 Nov 1971	Del A. Talley Sr.
26	*Manassa Colorado 31 May 1983		
	*La Jara Colorado		
	‡San Luis (Colorado, New Mexico)		10 Jun 1883

Silas S. Smith

Discontinued

21	Little Colorado	27 Jan 1878	Lot Smith
	(Colorado, Arizona)		
	18 Dec 1887 †Snowflake (31a)		

Missions — 2

(As of Oct. 1, 1996; shown with historical number. See MISSIONS.)

(286) COLORADO DENVER NORTH MISSION
11172 North Huron, Suite 21
Northglenn, CO 80234
Phone: (303) 252-7191

(17) COLORADO DENVER SOUTH MISSION
Box 2674
Littleton, CO 80161-2674
Phone: (303) 794-6457

Connecticut

Year-end 1995: Est. population, 3,275,000; Members, 11,000; Stakes, 2; Wards, 19; Branches, 12; Missions, 1; Percent LDS, 0.3, or one person in 297.

Elders Orson Hyde and Samuel H. Smith began missionary work in Connecticut in 1832 when they preached in the New England states. Evidently they did not have any converts in Connecticut. Other missionaries followed, including Elder Wilford Woodruff, a native of Farmington, Conn. He arranged to have a meeting with his family on July 1, 1838. Earlier on the day of the meeting, he wrote, "Distress overwhelmed the whole household, and all were tempted to reject the work." Later, he felt a dramatic change. "Filled with the power of God, I stood in the midst of the congregation and preached unto the people in great plainness the gospel of Jesus Christ." He afterward baptized his father, stepmother, sister and three others, and organized a small branch in Farmington.

The Eastern States Mission was created in 1839 and branches were established in Hartford and New Haven and other areas. Missionary work continued in the area until the 1850s when most members left the area, and any significant success waited until near the turn of the century. At that time missionaries throughout New England encountered prejudice and made little headway.

By 1930, branches existed in Hartford, New Haven, and Springfield. Membership was 198.

In 1932, missionaries reported "striving diligently" in Connecticut, and "large attendances" at each meeting of a conference held during the summer.

The New England Mission was created in 1937. On June 16, 1944, a meetinghouse at Bridgeport was dedicated at a branch conference. The chapel was converted from a home purchased two years earlier.

In 1952, the Hartford Branch meetinghouse was dedicated, the first meetinghouse to be erected in the New England Mission. Mission leaders began seeing growth in the 1950s and noted that membership increased following 1952, and doubled from 1955 to 1959. During this period, mission-wide youth conferences and annual Relief Society gatherings were well-attended by members.

The Hartford Stake was created in 1966 from the Connecticut Valley District, taking up most of the state and parts of western Massachusetts. The stake had a membership of nearly 3,000 with wards in Hartford, Manchester, New Haven, New London and Southington, and branches in Madison and Torrinton in Connecticut, as well as branches and wards in Massachusetts.

The Connecticut Hartford Mission was created in 1979. Membership in 1980 was 6,300. A temple announced in 1992 for Hartford was later redesignated. As no location could be found in Hartford, temples were announced Sept. 30, 1995, for White Plains, N.Y., and Boston, Mass., both areas of which had experienced recent growth.

For their youth conference July 5-7, 1995, young men and young women from the New Haven Connecticut Stake volunteered their service to the Special Olympics World Games held in and around New Haven. Their service helped make the games a success for 7,000 participants from 140 countries.

Sources: *Encyclopedic History of the Church,* by Andrew Jenson; *Church News,* July 16, 1932; Sept. 3, 1938; July 22, 1944; Oct. 4, 1952; Sept. 24, 1966; June 11, 1977; Sept. 28, 1986; *Church News,* July 15, 1995.

Stakes — 2
(Listed alphabetically as of Oct. 1, 1996.)

No.	Name	Organized	First President
	North America Northeast Area		
421	*Hartford Connecticut		
	‡Hartford (Conn., Mass.)	18 Sep 1966	Hugh S. West
1288	New Haven Connecticut	30 Aug 1981	Steven Douglas Colson

Mission — 1
(As of Oct. 1, 1996; shown with historical number. See MISSIONS.)

(169) CONNECTICUT HARTFORD MISSION
P.O. Box 378
Bloomfield, CT 06002
Phone: (860) 242-2099

Delaware

Year-end 1995: Est. population, 722,000; Members, 3,400; Stakes, 1; Wards, 7; Branches, 1; Percent LDS: 0.5, or one person in 212.

Elder Jedediah M. Grant entered Delaware and began missionary work in 1837. Little record has been made of his progress, or other missionary work. However, Wilmington was an important rendezvous for missionaries of the Eastern States Mission. Its proximity to Philadelphia and its ocean frontage made it a likely route of passage for Church leaders.

In 1843, converts throughout the region were encouraged to gather with the Saints in Nauvoo. In the years that followed, many European converts sailed up the Delaware waterway to Philadelphia where they entered the United States.

On Feb. 4, 1901, Elder John E. Baird left Brooklyn, N.Y., to visit missionaries in eastern cities including those in Wilmington. On May 26, 1914, Elders Stanley A. Lawrence and Alphonso W. Taylor reported teaching a woman who had gained a testimony of the Book of Mormon. Two years later, on Nov. 7, 1916, two missionaries reported renting a hall in Wilmington where, beginning the next Sunday, meetings were to be held during the winter.

A missionary meeting was held Feb. 2, 1925, and in 1926 another meeting was held in a local hall with attendance of about 18 people. In 1931, missionaries broadcast their message over a local radio station. Lack of success resulted in missionaries being withdrawn until 1940 when Wilmington was re-opened.

Block teaching began in 1941 among some 16 LDS families. Meetings began May 4, and the Wilmington Branch was organized Sept. 28, 1941. The branch, with nine adults and 10 children, continued with little growth for the next decade. In 1950, some 63 attended a branch party at the home of the branch president. The Salisbury Branch was organized in 1953.

A new meetinghouse was completed and the first meeting was held in the building in 1960. That same year the Philadelphia Stake was created with a ward in Wilmington. Dover and Salisbury branches were included in the stake.

Activities increased with the new meetinghouse and by 1963 the ward boundaries were reduced. In December 1974, the Wilmington Delaware Stake was created. Membership in the state in 1974 was 1,350, increasing to 1,767 in 1980, and to 3,178 in 1990. By 1988, Wilmington was home of three large wards, and Dover, Salisbury and Elkton each had large wards. Branches were organized in Smyrna (one), and Cambridge (two). Many members and leaders work for the large chemical companies that have headquarters in Delaware.

Sources: *Encyclopedic History of the Church*, by Andrew Jenson; *Journal History of the Eastern States Mission; The LDS Church in Delaware: A Book of Remembrance*, by Helen Candland Stark, published in Wilmington, Delaware, 1966; "Church grows larger in 2nd smallest state," by Kevin Stoker, *Church News*, Dec. 3, 1988.

Stake — 1
(As of Oct. 1, 1996.)

No.	Name	Organized	First President
	North America Northeast Area		
673	Wilmington Delaware	8 Dec 1974	Rulon Edward Johnson Jr.

District of Columbia

Year-end 1995: Est. population, 548,000; Members, 1,100; Districts, 1; Branches, 7; Missions, 2; Percent LDS, 0.2, or one person in 498.

The Prophet Joseph Smith, accompanied by Elias Higbee, visited the nation's capital in 1839 seeking redress of grievances suffered by the Saints in Missouri. As the coach in which they were riding approached the city, the horses began a runaway. The Prophet heroically saved his fellow passengers.

Joseph and Elias stayed in Washington for two weeks and called on President Martin Van Buren, who reportedly said, "Your cause is just, but I can do nothing for you."

The same year, Parley P. Pratt published an address setting forth the principles of the gospel and saw that a copy was presented to the President and each Cabinet member.

On Aug. 16, 1841, Samuel James was appointed to labor in Washington. Apostle John E. Page preached in Washington in 1843, baptizing one convert.

In 1843 Apostles Orson Hyde and Orson Pratt, and later joined by Apostles Heber C. Kimball, William Smith and Lyman Wight, presented the plight of the Saints to President John Tyler. Three years later Elder Jesse C. Little sought a government contract for the Church to haul freight to the West Coast. He instead won the opportunity for 500 men to join the Army and take part in a march through the Southwest. This was the genesis of the Mormon Battalion.

Elder Orson Pratt presided over the Saints in the Eastern States and served as a missionary in Washington, D.C. He was later joined by Elder Jedediah M. Grant and together they met with Pres. Millard Fillmore. They published a magazine, *The Seer*, for about 18 months.

After arriving in the Great Basin, members requested a state government, but were granted territory status instead. In pursuing statehood, members from Utah paid occasional visits to Washington, D.C. Some lived in Washington, D.C., or nearby areas while serving as Utah's delegates to Congress. After the turn of the century, Elder Reed Smoot of the Quorum of the Twelve was elected to the Senate and, after four years of well-publicized hearings, was seated. His later powerful leadership in the Senate won many friends for the Church.

During the early years of Senator Smoot's term, a handful of members who lived in Washington met in his home. In June 1919, a branch was organized. By 1927, the branch was meeting in an auditorium. Some 150 attended services upstairs while activities, such as circuses and auto shows, went on below.

Later Latter-day Saint leaders, including J. Reuben Clark Jr., Marriner S. Eccles, Edgar Brossard, J. Willard Marriott and Ezra Taft Benson, made substantial contributions to the Church in the nation's capital.

In 1930 the Church began construction on a chapel built of imported Utah marble. The building was completed in 1933 and helped establish the Church's reputation as a permanent institution. By 1940, the Washington D.C. Stake was created with Ezra Taft

Benson as president. President Benson later returned to the nation's capital as Secretary of Agriculture in the Eisenhower administration, 1953-61.

Membership in the region continued to grow as Latter-day Saints with important government jobs moved in. Additional stakes were created so that four covered the area of the original stake. In 1962, a site in suburban Kensington, Md., was purchased for a temple that was completed in 1974. The imposing temple immediately became a landmark for the Church in Washington. Within 15 years, the four stakes in the greater Washington, D.C., area became 19 stakes and membership jumped from 21,000 to 63,000. However, within the boundaries of the actual District of Columbia, membership remained slight with fewer than 100 recorded in 1980 and 434 in 1990. In the 1990s, additional efforts were made in the inner city area, and new, small branches were created. Members participated in inter-faith food drives, using the resources of the Church cannery, and other inter-faith activities. The Tabernacle Choir performed in the Kennedy Center.

Each summer, ambassadors and members of the diplomatic community are invited to a western picnic at the J. W. Marriott ranch in nearby Virginia. In addition, the diplomats also attend lighting ceremonies at the Washington Temple.

Sources: *Encyclopedic History of the Church,* by Andrew Jenson; "History of the Washington Branch," *Church News,* Nov. 4, 1933; "A Little Leavening," by Florian H. Thayn, *Brigham Young University Studies,* Spring 1981; "From Colony to Community; the Washington D.C. Saints," by Mary L. Bradford, *Ensign,* August 1974; "Membership triples in Nation's Capital," *Church News,* Dec. 2, 1989; "Pioneer members recall rich memories," *Church News,* July 20, 1991; and Oct. 26, 1991, Oct. 23, 1993; Dec. 2, 1994, Aug. 12, 1995, Feb. 2, 1994; Oct. 8, 1995, and Sept. 28, 1996.

Stake — 1

(As of Oct. 1, 1996. To simplify reference, the stake and missions in the Washington, D.C. area that carry the name of Washington, D.C., are listed in the District of Columbia rather than the state where the headquarters is located.)

No.	Name	Organized	First President
North America Northeast Area			
131	*Washington D.C.		
	‡Washington (D.C., Pa., Md.)	30 Jun 1940	Ezra Taft Benson

Missions — 2

(As of Oct. 1, 1996; shown with historical number. See MISSIONS.)

(188b) WASHINGTON D.C. NORTH MISSION
904 Wind River Lane, Suite 103
North Potomac, MD 20878
Phone: (301) 926-7977

(54) WASHINGTON D.C. SOUTH MISSION
5631 Burke Centre Parkway, Suite H
Burke, VA 22015
Phone: (703) 250-0111

Florida

Year-end 1995: Est. population, 14,270,000; Members, 98,000; Stakes, 22; Wards, 152; Branches, 28; Missions, 4; Temples 1; Percent LDS, 0.7, or one person in 146.

Elders William Brown and Daniel Cathart were called to serve in Florida in April 1843, but no record exists of them doing so. Possibly the first missionary in Florida was Phineas Young, who reported placing copies of the Book of Mormon during a two-month mission from April to June in 1845 that reached into Florida. Missionary work evidently started before Nov. 1, 1895, when the Florida Conference was organized under the direction of Pres. Elias S. Kimball of the Southern States Mission. Fifteen missionaries were assigned to labor there.

Missionaries started a number of Sunday Schools, the first of which was at Coe Mills, Liberty County, in May 1895. By September 1897, 11 Sunday Schools had been organized. The first branch was created in Jefferson County in 1897. The Sanderson Branch, probably organized Jan. 3, 1898, was the site of a missionary conference in 1898. George P. Canova, a well-to-do landowner and chairman of the Baker County Commission, was the president of the branch. On June 5, 1898, following threats of violence, Pres. Canova was martyred as he returned home from a conference. Missionaries were also temporarily driven out of Tallahassee and Orlando but returned later. They found varying degrees of success in Key West, Sanford, Starke, Peoria, Kissimmee, St. Augustine, Tampa, St. Augustine, Duck Pond, Lake City and Middleburg.

In 1900, Elder William H. Boyle reported the branches in Florida to be "in apple pie order" and that missionaries traveling without purse or scrip were hospitably received. Growth came slowly, however. In 1906, a meetinghouse was dedicated in Jacksonville, and in 1907, another was completed in Oak Grove.

In 1906, Charles A. Callis, later mission president and a member of the Quorum of the Twelve, became president of the Florida Conference. By 1920 branches in Jacksonville, Sanderson and Tampa existed. By 1925, branches or Sunday Schools had been added in Miami, Oak Grove, Oldtown, Telogia, Westville, Springfield and St. Augustine. A larger meetinghouse was completed in Jacksonville in 1926. In 1930, the Florida District had 3,164 members in four branches and eight Sunday Schools. The West Florida District was created about this time, and branches or Sunday Schools increased. By 1935, the Florida District had 22 branches, and the West Florida District had another 13 branches.

Florida's first stake was created in Jacksonville Jan. 17, 1947, by Elder Charles A. Callis, who died there four days later. The new stake had 3,000 members in the Jacksonville, Springfield, Wesconnett, Lake City, Palatka, Axson, and Waycross wards. Called as president of the new stake was Alvin C. Chace, a grandson of early leader George P. Canova.

In 1950, the Church purchased a 300,000-acre area in Central Florida, which became Deseret Ranch.

Membership increased rapidly as members from the West moved into the state, drawn by a strong commerce and the aerospace industry. Additional converts were baptized. When the Florida Mission was created in 1960, four stakes had been organized. Membership in Florida in 1977 was 30,000, increasing to 54,674 in 1980, and to 82,413 in 1990. Creation of the first Spanish-speaking stake in the Southeast in Miami on Jan, 16, 1994, reflected the increase in membership among Latin Americans and immigrants.

In February of 1990, the First Presidency announced that a temple would be built in the Orlando area. Later, a scenic location in Windermere, five miles southeast of Orlando, was selected for the temple and ground was broken June 20, 1992. The temple was dedicated Oct. 9-11, 1994, by President Howard W. Hunter. More than 20,670 members attended the 12 dedicatory sessions, which took place over three days.

Florida members were among many from Southern states to respond to storm-caused disasters in the South in the 1990s.

Sources: *Encyclopedic History of the Church*, by Andrew Jenson; *History of the Southern States Mission*, a BYU thesis by LaMar C. Berrett, July 1960; A brief summation of the growth of the Church . . . leading to the Florida Stake, by Stanley Clyde Johnson, 1986, unpublished; Church directories, 1919-1935; *Church News*, Jan. 25, 1947, Feb. 22, 1947, Dec. 1, 1956, Oct. 8, 1960, Sept, 14, 1963; March 6, 1976, July 2, 1977, and March 14, 1987; "The first Spanish-speaking stake in Southeast is created in Florida," by Kathleen Ryan, *Church News*, Feb. 19, 1994; *Church News*, May 28, 1994; "Temple is dedicated in Sunshine state, 20,670 attend sessions," by Gerry Avant, *Church News*, Oct. 15, 1994; "Members rally to help hurricane victims," *Church News*, Aug. 12, 1995.

Stakes — 23
(Listed alphabetically as of Oct. 1, 1996.)

No.	Name	Organized	First President
North America Southeast Area			
1898	Brandon Florida	23 Aug 1992	James Franklin Henry
879	Cocoa Florida	13 Nov 1977	Cleavy Eugene Waters
530	*Fort Lauderdale Florida		
	‡Fort Lauderdale	18 Oct 1970	Stanley C. Johnson
1472	Fort Myers Florida	13 May 1984	John M. Cyrocki
2151	Fort Walton Beach Florida	07 Jan 1996	Charles E. Atkinson Jr.
746	Gainesville Florida	29 Feb 1976	James R. Christianson
1842	*Homestead Florida 16 Jan 1994		
	‡South Miami Florida	19 Jan 1992	Dean Michael Madsen
465	*Jacksonville Florida East		
	‡Jacksonville	15 Sep 1968	Louis B. Vorwaller
1660	Jacksonville Florida North	15 Nov 1987	Robert Edwin Bone
163	*Jacksonville Florida West		
	‡Florida (Florida, Georgia)	19 Jan 1947	Alvin C. Chace
1590	Lake City Florida	16 Mar 1986	Ernest Robert Peacock
1380	*Lake Mary Florida 27 Oct 1987		
	‡Deland Florida	14 Nov 1982	Marvin Knowles
311	*Miami Florida		
	‡Miami	13 Nov 1960	Paul R. Cheesman
257	*Orlando Florida		
	‡Orlando	23 Feb 1958	W. Leonard Duggar
1900	Orlando Florida South	30 Aug 1992	Carl E. Reynolds Jr.

732	*Panama City Florida 4 Feb 1986		
	‡Marianna Florida	16 Nov 1975	Riley Malone Peddie
486	*Pensacola Florida		
	‡Pensacola	15 Jun 1969	S. Elroy Stapleton
1970	Pompano Beach Florida	16 Jan 1994	Richard Merlin Smith
651	St. Petersburg Florida	18 Aug 1974	Bruce Earl Belnap
1190	*Stuart Florida 16 Jan 1994		
	‡West Palm Beach Florida	12 Oct 1980	Donald Wayne Carson
594	*Tallahassee Florida		
	‡Tallahassee	21 Jan 1973	Jay Nicholas Lybbert
289	*Tampa Florida		
	‡Tampa	25 Oct 1959	Edwin H. White
1153	*Winter Haven Florida 10 Oct 1991		
	‡Lakeland Florida	27 Jun 1980	Waymon E. Meadows

Missions — 4

(As of Oct. 1, 1996; shown with historical number. See MISSIONS.)

(178b) FLA. FT. LAUDERDALE MISSION
7951 SW 6th St.,110
Ft. Lauderdale, FL 33324-3211
Phone: (954) 452-6960

(197) FLA. JACKSONVILLE MISSION
8651 Baypine Road,105
Jacksonville, FL 32256
Phone: (904) 636-0604

(96) FLA. TALLAHASSEE MISSION
1535 Killearn Center Blvd., Suite C-4
Tallahassee, FL 32308
Phone: (904) 893-4243

(139) FLA. TAMPA MISSION
13153 N. Dale Mabry,109
Tampa, FL 33618
Phone: (813) 961-7400

Georgia

Year-end 1995: Est. population, 7,273,000; Members, 51,000; Stakes, 12; Wards, 75; Branches, 36; Districts, 1; Missions, 2; Temples, 1; Percent LDS, 0.7, or one person in 142.

Elder John U. Eldredge opened missionary work in Georgia in 1843, though his service was brief. Other missionaries followed to preach and to campaign for Joseph Smith in his presidential bid. When the Prophet was martyred in 1844, the work waned, and was halted in 1846. Missionary work resumed in 1870 in the South, and in 1878 in Georgia. Southern States Mission headquarters were established in Rome, 60 miles north of Atlanta, in 1879. Pres. John Morgan wrote the pamphlet *Plan of Salvation* in Rome.

Success was realized in Rome and Axson, which was called "Little Utah," by local people. The Douglas Branch was called "Cumorah." One prominent convert, Judge Wyatt N. Williams, was baptized in Buchanan on April 25, 1879, and subsequently donated land and built a chapel in Haralson County at a place called "Mormon Springs" near his mill and cotton gin.

Missionaries were initially treated well upon their return to the South, but before long, their successes led to violent opposition. On July 21, 1879, Elder Joseph Standing was killed by a mob near Varnell's Station, Ga. His companion, Rudger Clawson, later a member of the Quorum of the Twelve, escaped serious injury. Mission leaders were unable to secure protection for missionaries, so Georgia was closed for a decade. In 1884, a small group of members from Georgia joined immigrants who went West by train from Chattanooga, Tenn. U.S. Census reports list 175 Mormons in Georgia in 1890.

Work resumed cautiously. In 1899, for example, convert Aldora Landrum Yarn was taught in a single meeting held after dark, then baptized. She did not see another missionary for three and a half years.

Disease and persecution slowed the work, the former taking a greater toll than the latter. In 1899, Ohio was added to the Southern States Mission at the request of Pres. Ben E. Rich, so he would have a place where ill missionaries could recover.

By 1908, some 6,800 converts had been baptized throughout the South during Pres. Rich's term. That year, a branch was organized and a meetinghouse constructed in Atlanta. It was replaced in 1915 with a larger building.

Pres. Charles A. Callis succeeded Pres. Rich. Pres. Callis embarked on a 25-year term that saw about 800 to 1,000 converts per year throughout the South. When then-Apostle Heber J. Grant visited Atlanta in 1911, he addressed an overflow congregation in a local Universalist church. He was favorably received.

In 1919, headquarters of the Southern States Mission was moved from Chattanooga, Tenn., to Atlanta, and a new meetinghouse was erected in that city in 1925.

Steady growth continued so that by 1930, the original Southern States Mission had some 50,000 members. The Georgia Conference, in northern Georgia, had 2,626 members in Atlanta, Augusta, Columbus, Macon and Savannah branches and in Cedar Crossing, Douglas, Empire, Glenwood, Milledgeville and Thomaston Sunday Schools. The South Georgia District had 1,686 members. The state membership was 4,311.

One of the prominent pioneer leaders in Atlanta was Homer Yarn. In 1916, he became the first local leader of a Sunday School in Atlanta. He became president of the Atlanta Branch in 1925. When the Georgia District was organized in 1937, Pres. Yarn was the first local district president. He served as mission president's counselor from 1939 to 1957.

LeGrand Richards, later a member of the Quorum of the Twelve, served as mission president from 1934-37, and wrote the outline for *A Marvelous Work and a Wonder* while in Atlanta.

In 1957, the Atlanta (later changed to Tucker) Stake was created, taking up the northern two-thirds of the state with 3,000 members with wards in Atlanta (2), Columbus, Macon and Empire, and branches in Buchanan, Athens, Givson, Milledgeville and Palmetto. Covering the rest of the state was the Georgia-Florida and South Georgia districts. Membership in Georgia in 1974 was 14,360, increasing in 1980 to 27,210 and in 1990 to 41,595.

In 1983, the Atlanta Temple was completed and dedicated, giving the South its first temple. Area headquarters in Atlanta include complete temporal and ecclesiastical distribution centers. From Atlanta, hurricane and flood relief has been shipped to many areas of disaster, including Hurricane Andrew devastation in 1992, the Albany, Ga., flooding in 1994, and Hurricane Opal destruction in 1995. In the late 1980s and early 1990s, five branches were established in the central sections of Atlanta among minorities, including Asian and Hispanic people.

In December 1994, the Church donated 158,000 pounds of food through 26 religious and charitable organizations to the hungry in Atlanta.

In 1996, hundreds of Church members from Georgia gave service during the 1996 Centennial Olympic Summer Games. During the Olympic games, Georgia hosted athletes and guests from 198 nations. Missionaries from the Georgia Atlanta Mission set up a special traveling exhibit for the Olympics called "Strong Families Can Hold Our World Together."

Sources: *Encyclopedic History of the Church,* by Andrew Jenson; "William L. Nicholls to Preside Over New Altanta Stake," *Church News,* May 11, 1957; *History of the Southern States Mission* by LaMar C. Berrett, a BYU thesis, July 1960; *A Brief History of the Southern States Mission for One Hundred Years 1830-1930,* by DeVon H. Nish, a BYU paper of 1966; Highlights of D. Homer Yarn, by David H. Yarn Jr.; "Georgia enters era of temples," by Gerry Avant, *Church News,* April 24, 1983; "Inner-city district gathers many of diverse cultures into 'gospel net,'" by Mike Cannon, *Church News,* May 29, 1993; "6,000 ease aftermath of flooding," by Gerry Avant, *Church News,* July 30, 1994; "LDS render service in wake of Opal's rage," *Church News,* Oct. 14, 1995; "Through service, members find, share Olympic Spirit," by Sarah Jane Weaver, *Church News,* July 27, 1996; "79 tons of food given to Atlanta's hungry," *Church News,* Dec. 31, 1996; "LDS display touches Olympic visitors," by Richard D. Hall, *Church News,* Aug. 3, 1996.

Stakes — 14
(Listed alphabetically as of Oct. 1, 1996.)

No.	Name	Organized	First President
North America Southeast Area			
2218	Albany Georgia	11 Aug 1996	Gregory Wayne Widman
2203	Atlanta Georgia	23 Jun 1996	John Devin Cornish
889	*Augusta Georgia 21 Aug 1988		
	‡West Columbia South Carolina	5 Feb 1978	George A. Huff Sr.
886	Columbus Georgia	15 Jan 1978	William F. Meadows Jr.
715	Douglas Georgia	26 Oct 1975	Roswald Mancil
921	*Jonesboro Georgia 29 Jan 1991		
	‡Atlanta Georgia	14 May 1978	Warren Richard Jones
241	Lilburn Georgia		
	*Tucker Georgia 1 Sep 1974		
	*Atlanta Georgia		
	‡Atlanta (Georgia)	5 May 1957	William L. Nicholls

* 23 June 1996

373	*Macon Georgia		
	‡Macon (Georgia, Alabama)	10 Mar 1963	Rayford L. Henderson
1643	Marietta Georgia East	21 Jun 1987	Paul A. Snow
1208	*Powder Springs Georgia 10 Sep 1991		
	‡Marietta Georgia	23 Nov 1980	William K. Farrar Jr.
640	*Roswell Georgia 21 Jun 1987		
	*Sandy Springs Georgia 1 Sep 1974		
	‡Tucker Georgia	12 May 1974	Richard Parry Winder
916	Savannah Georgia	7 May 1978	Robert W. Cowart
1799	Sugar Hill Georgia	26 May 1991	Donald Arthur Cazier

Missions — 2
(As of Oct. 1, 1996; shown with historical number. See MISSIONS.)

(8b) GEORGIA ATLANTA MISSION
1140 Hammond Drive , B-2110
Atlanta, GA 30328-5338
Phone: (770) 551-9626

(239) GEORGIA MACON MISSION
5082 Forsyth Road, Units A &B
Macon, GA 31210-2107
Phone: (912) 471-9205

Hawaii

Year-end 1995: Est. population, 1,192,000; Members, 55,000; Stakes, 13; Wards, 102; Branches, 8; Missions, 1; Temples, 1; Percent LDS: 4.6, or one person in 22.

Sam Brannan and his party of Mormon immigrants aboard the ship *Brooklyn* stopped in Hawaii in 1846, en route to California and the Great Basin via Cape Horn.

Although missionaries had been called in 1843 to the Sandwich Islands, as the islands were then known, they worked instead at Tubuai, one of the southern islands of French Polynesia.

In 1850, gold-mining elders serving in northern California were called to open a mission in Polynesia. They landed in Honolulu Dec. 12, 1850, under the direction of Pres. Hiram Clark. On Feb. 10, 1851, Pres. Clark baptized a 16-year-old Hawaiian young man, the first convert in Hawaii. Other missionaries were not as successful and returned discouraged to the mainland. But Elders George Q. Cannon, James Keeler, William Farrer, Henry W. Bigler and James Hawkins remained and found ample converts. Elder Cannon baptized three well-educated Hawaiians, Jonathan Napela, Uaua and Kaleohano, who later became prominent missionaries for the Church.

On Aug. 6, 1851, the Kula Branch was organized in the village of Kealakou on the island of Maui. At a conference on Aug. 18, four more branches were organized and membership was 220. A small meetinghouse was built in 1852 in Pulehu, on the island of Maui, which still stands. More missionaries arrived and by 1854, a colony and plantation were started at Lanai, a designated gathering place.

The Book of Mormon was published in Hawaiian in 1855. In 1857, missionaries were called home because of the so-called "Utah War."

In 1861 a self-appointed leader, Walter Murray Gibson, usurped Church leadership in the absence of missionaries. A recent convert called to a mission in the South Pacific, he took over the Church organization and property. Leading Hawaiian elders notified the Church of Gibson's unorthodox leadership and President Young sent Apostles Ezra T. Benson and Lorenzo Snow. They immediately excommunicated Gibson and reinstated many early members.

Defrauded of its property in Lanai, the Church purchased 6,000 acres at Laie, on the main island of Oahu, on Jan. 26, 1865, where a colony and sugar factory were started. Schools have been part of the colony since 1874.

Later, many of the Hawaiians wanted to gather to Utah to receive their temple blessings. So the Church purchased a ranch in Skull Valley, near Tooele, Utah, and the Hawaiian Saints founded the colony of Iosepa (Joseph) in 1889. By 1910 the colony was disbanded and the colonists returned to Hawaii.

The Church subsequently built a temple in the Laie settlement, dedicating the edifice Nov. 27, 1919.

In 1913, missionaries calculated that 22 percent of the Hawaiian population was LDS. Membership in Hawaii in 1920 was 11,078. By 1930, membership increased to 14,433, dropping to 9,789 in 1940 and, in 1950, following World War II, increasing to 11,855. By 1960, it increased to 18,327, and to 23,377 in 1970.

The Oahu Stake was created June 30, 1935, by Pres. Heber J. Grant. While there, the former missionary to Japan felt a need for a mission to the many Japanese in Hawaii. On

Feb. 24, 1937, the Japanese Mission (later called the Central Pacific Mission) in Hawaii was organized. Over the next dozen years, nearly 700 Japanese-Americans were converted in this effort, including Elder Adney Y. Komatsu, who was called as a General Authority in 1975. Among the missionaries and converts were many of the leaders who helped open and continue missionary work in Japan after World War II. Hawaiian members also opened the door for missionary work in South Pacific islands.

The Church College of Hawaii opened Sept. 26, 1955. Many members from the South Pacific and Asia have been educated at the school, now called BYU-Hawaii. On Nov. 12, 1963, the Polynesian Cultural Center, a cluster of villages representing various South Pacific cultures, was opened. It quickly became one of Hawaii's top attractions. In recent years the center has been host to a number of heads of state, including those of China.

During times of disasters, such as floods and hurricanes, members have been quick to assist other members and non-members. When hurricane "Iniki" struck the islands in 1992, members donated thousands of boxes of relief supplies for those on the hard-hit island of Kauai.

Also in 1992, major renovations were made to three LDS buildings at the Kalaupapa leprosy settlement on the island of Molokai. The buildings include a chapel, cultural hall and a "mission house," used for visiting General Authorities and mission presidents. A branch has existed here since the 19th century when early Church convert Kitty Napela contracted Hansen's disease and, with her husband, Jonathan, moved to the leprosy settlement in 1872. Jonathan became assistant superintendent of the colony and was later set apart as an LDS branch president. The chapel on the island today is the third such, and a small branch still exists.

In 1994, President Howard W. Hunter installed Eric B. Shumway as the eighth president of BYU-Hawaii — the first time a prophet had done so since the college was founded. On Nov. 18, hundreds lined walkways from the Aloha Center to the Cannon Activities Center for a glimpse of President Hunter during the inaugural procession. Accompanying the prophet was his wife, Inis, and Elder Neal A. Maxwell of the Quorum of the Twelve and Elder Henry B. Eyring, then of the Seventy and Church Commissioner of Education.

Among tours taken by the prophet was a visit to the Polynesian Cultural Center on Nov. 19. Greeting President Hunter was a sign with the words "Welcome home," appropriate since he served as president and chairman of the center's board of trustees from 1965-1976.

A Church president once again noted "the spirit of aloha" when President Gordon B. Hinckley spoke to some 13,500 members from nine Oahu stakes Feb. 18, 1996, during two regional conference sessions at the BYU-Hawaii Cannon Activities Center. During the prophet's Feb. 17-19 visit to the islands, he also met with two Catholic leaders who are members of a Hawaiian grassroots coalition opposed to same-gender marriage, legalized prostitution and casino gambling. Known as Hawaii's Future Today, the organization is made up of mainly Catholics and Latter-day Saints, with a broad section from the general citizenry.

Sources: *Encyclopedic History of the Church,* by Andrew Jenson; *Unto the Isles of the Sea,* by R. Lanier Britsch; *Guide to Mormon History Travel,* by William C. and Eloise Anderson; *Church News,* June 25, 1988, June 20, 1992, Sept. 19, 1992, Oct. 3, 1992, Nov. 26, 1994, Feb. 24, 1996.

Stakes — 13
(Listed alphabetically as of Oct. 1, 1996.)

No.	Name	Organized	First President
North America West Area			
807	*BYU-Hawaii 1st 22 Nov 1981		
	‡BYU-Hawaii	23 Jan 1977	Eric B. Shumway
1313	BYU-Hawaii 2nd	22 Nov 1981	Herbert Kamaka Sproat
473	*Hilo Hawaii		
	‡Hilo	15 Dec 1968	Rex Alton Cheney
222	*Honolulu Hawaii		
	‡Honolulu (Hawaii, Guam)	28 Aug 1955	J. A. Quealy Jr.
348	*Honolulu Hawaii West		
	‡Pearl Harbor (Hawaii)	4 Feb 1962	George Q. Cannon
729	Kahului Hawaii	9 Nov 1975	Evan Allan Larsen
560	*Kaneohe Hawaii		
	‡Kaneohe (Hawaii)	21 Nov 1971	Robert H. Finlayson
851	Kauai Hawaii	24 Jul 1977	Garner Dalthum Wood

669	Kona Hawaii	24 Nov 1974	Haven J. Stringham
113	*Laie Hawaii		
	‡Oahu	30 Jun 1935	Ralph E. Wooley
1395	Laie Hawaii North	16 Jan 1983	Willard Kaaihue Kekauoha
1103	Mililani Hawaii	3 Feb 1980	Kotaro Koizumi
566	*Waipahu Hawaii		
	‡Pearl Harbor West (Hawaii)	20 Feb 1972	William E. Fuhrmann

Mission — 1

(As of Oct. 1, 1996; shown with historical number. See MISSIONS.)

(9) HAWAII HONOLULU MISSION
1500 S. Beretania St., Suite 410
Honolulu, HI 96826
Phone: (808) 942-0050

Idaho

Year-end 1995: Est. population, 1,178,000; Members, 327,000; Stakes, 97; Wards, 691; Branches, 38; Missions, 2; Temples, 2; Percent LDS, 27.8, or one person in 8.

On April 7, 1855, 26 men were called by Brigham Young to locate a settlement among the Bannock and Shoshone on the Salmon River. They arrived and established Fort Lemhi on June 15, 1855. However, problems with Indians led to the settlement's abandonment in 1858.

On April 14, 1860, a party of colonizers arrived at what is now Franklin, Idaho, in northern Cache Valley. Preston Thomas became the first bishop in a ward created there in June. Franklin is both Idaho's oldest and the Church's oldest permanent settlement in Idaho. The settlers battled deep snows and extreme cold in the winter, but dug canals and began irrigating in the summer. Eventually, during the next 18 years, 16 settlements were founded in this region. They paved the way for the Oneida Stake, headquartered in Preston, near Franklin, to be created in 1884, Idaho's third.

Another colonization effort began over the mountains to the east when a party under Apostle Charles C. Rich explored Bear Lake Valley and established the settlement of Paris in the fall of 1863. About 110 people wintered there the first year. In 1864, 700 more settlers arrived and established the towns of Ovid, Liberty, Montpelier, Bloomington, St. Charles, Fish Haven and Bennington. Nine other settlements were established in the region within 13 years. The Bear Lake Stake, the first permanent stake outside Utah, was created June 20, 1869. Both Cache Valley and Bear Lake Valley were believed by the settlers to be in Utah until a survey in 1872.

In 1875, a third colonization movement came when LDS families settled in Oakley, Dayton, Elba and Almo in southcentral Idaho.

In the late 1870s, the Utah Northern Railroad line from Utah to Montana was completed. Many members were employed in the construction of the rail line. From their favorable reports of the Upper Snake River Valley, settlers soon began colonizing there, beginning in 1879. Under the leadership of Thomas E. Ricks, they established Rexburg in 1883 and 14 other colonies in Upper Snake River Valley, in Fremont and Bingham counties. Basic to their success was their expertise in irrigating. By 1910, more than 100 canals had been dug in the Upper Snake River Valley. The Bannock Stake, Idaho's second and headquartered in Rexburg, was organized in 1884.

Leaders encouraged members to continue to settle in Idaho. Many migrated to already established communities along the eastern side of Idaho, and on the western side in the Boise-Payette area. Most were farmers.

Members generally got along well with Indians and, in at least northern Cache and Bear Lake valleys, received permission from Indian leaders to settle. They preached the gospel to Native Americans, taught them agriculture and shared their supplies with them. Shoshone Chief Washakie, the most prominent chief during the early colonization effort, was baptized by Amos Wright, an early Idaho missionary.

By 1890 when Idaho was given statehood, about one-fifth of the state was LDS. Some historians suggest that without the Mormon population, Idaho's land would have been annexed by adjoining states and it would never have become a state. Despite the contributions of Mormons, however, anti-Mormon sentiment grew during the last quarter of the 19th century.

Idaho Sen William E. Borah, though non-LDS, helped neutralize this anti-Mormon sentiment after the turn of the century. Mormon women led the statewide effort for women suffrage that was attained in 1896.

Membership in the "Gem State" was 29,421 in 1900, with seven stakes in existence. Membership increased to 79,887 by 1925; 1950, 137,250; 1975, 213,106; 1980, 272,670; and 1990, 296,782.

The Idaho Falls Temple was completed in 1945 and dedicated Sept. 23-25.

Following World War II, many members migrated to the Boise area where the first Boise stake had been created in 1913. Ezra Taft Benson was its president in 1938. Other area stakes were created following the war. The second temple in Idaho was built in Boise in 1984.

In 1990, members were among the some 20,000-25,000 gathered in Franklin to celebrate Idaho's statehood centennial. Events June 26-30 included speeches by Church, civic and government leaders, pioneer cultural activities, a pageant depicting Mormon migration to the settlement and parades. Joining these activities were Elder David B. Haight of the Quorum of the Twelve, who spoke during a patriotic meeting and was the centennial parade's grand marshal; Elaine L. Jack, Relief Society general president; Ardeth Kapp, Young Women general president; Michaelene Grassli, Primary general president; and Betty Jo N. Jepsen, first counselor to Sister Grassli.

During disastrous flooding in the northwestern United States early in 1996, several members in northern Idaho were among thousands evacuated from their homes. Members here were also among thousands who reached out in relief efforts — both to LDS and non-LDS.

Born in Idaho were President Harold B. Lee, president of the Church from 1972-73, President Ezra Taft Benson, president of the Church from 1985 to 1994, and President Howard W. Hunter, president of the Church from June 1994 to March 1995.

Sources: *Encyclopedic History of the Church*, by Andrew Jenson; *Treasures of Pioneer History*, Daughters of the Utah Pioneers, 1955; "Idaho vote spells 'finish' to old feud," by Arnold Irvine, *Church News*, Nov. 13, 1982; "Idaho — A shining Gem since 1855," by Golden A. Buchmiller, *Church News*, May 8, 1983; "Centennials preserving heritage," *Church News*, May 26, 1990; "Centennial celebrations bring festivities to nation's 43rd state," *Church News*, July 7, 1990; "Mormondom in Centennial Idaho," by Leonard J. Arrington, *This People*, Fall 1990; "First LDS Bishop in Idaho: A Pioneer for Gospel's Sake," by Elinor G. Hyde, *Church News*, Dec. 15, 1990; "Paris Tabernacle," by Dean Ward, published locally; "A wake of disaster, a wave of volunteers," *Church News*, Feb. 17, 1996.

Stakes — 99

(Listed alphabetically by area as of Oct. 1, 1996.)

No.	Name	Organized	First President
North America Northwest Area — 90			
170	*American Falls Idaho		
	‡American Falls	1 Feb 1948	George R. Woolley
1481	Arimo Idaho	17 Jun 1984	Douglas Sorensen
695	Ashton Idaho	18 May 1975	Horace E. Hess
52	*Blackfoot Idaho		
	‡Blackfoot	31 Jan 1904	Elias S. Kimball
1391	Blackfoot Idaho East	12 Dec 1982	Franklin D. Transtrum
914	Blackfoot Idaho Northwest	30 Apr 1978	Reijo Laverne Marcum
214	*Blackfoot Idaho South		
	*Blackfoot South 1 Mar 1970		
	‡South Blackfoot	20 Jun 1954	Lawrence T. Lambert
504	*Blackfoot Idaho West		
	‡Blackfoot West	1 Mar 1970	Alan F. Larsen
66	*Boise Idaho		
	‡Boise	3 Nov 1913	Heber Q. Hale
1460	Boise Idaho Central	5 Feb 1984	R. Clair Miles
1041	Boise Idaho East	10 Jun 1979	Cecil Frank Olsen
409	*Boise Idaho North		
	*Boise North Jan 1966		
	‡North Boise	26 Sep 1965	L. Aldin Porter
701	Boise Idaho South	17 Aug 1975	Grant Ruel Ipsen
218	*Boise Idaho West		
	*Boise West 29 May 1970		
	‡West Boise	7 Nov 1954	David Keith Ricks
1856	Boise State University	24 Apr 1992	Robert Reed Boren
77	*Burley Idaho		
	‡Burley	27 Jul 1919	David R. Langlois

1421	Burley Idaho West	22 May 1983	Walter Ray Petersen
564	*Caldwell Idaho		
	‡Caldwell	30 Jan 1972	Talmadge C. Blacker
1446	Caldwell Idaho North	9 Oct 1983	Gerald Leland Jensen
78	*Carey Idaho 31 Oct 1977		
	*Richfield Idaho		
	‡Blaine	3 Aug 1919	William Lennox Adamson
960	*Chubbuck Idaho 8 Sep 1987		
	‡Pocatello Idaho Chubbuck	17 Sep 1978	Errol Smith Phippen
359	*Coeur d'Alene Idaho		
	‡Coeur d'Alene	14 Oct 1962	Gerald E. Browning
69	*Declo Idaho		
	*Cassia East 15 Jun 1969		
	‡Raft River	27 Apr 1915	John A. Elison
50	*Driggs Idaho		
	‡Teton (Wyoming, Idaho)	2 Sep 1901	Don Carlos Driggs
1840	Eagle Idaho	12 Jan 1992	Gary Wayne Walker
661	Emmett Idaho	22 Sep 1974	David Lee Morton
1147	Filer Idaho	15 Jun 1980	Karl E. Nelson
655	Firth Idaho	8 Sep 1974	Dale Lavar Christensen
36	*Idaho Falls Idaho		
	*Idaho Falls 16 Aug 1925		
	‡Bingham	9 Jun 1895	James E. Steele
343	*Idaho Falls Idaho Ammon		
	‡Ammon	26 Nov 1961	Harold W. Davis
825	Idaho Falls Idaho Ammon West	1 May 1977	Boyd Rencher Thomas
1448	Idaho Falls Idaho Central	16 Oct 1983	Paul Roger DeMordaunt
1665	Idaho Falls Idaho Eagle Rock	13 Dec 1987	Michael Dean Crapo
285	*Idaho Falls East 29 May 1970		
	‡East Idaho Falls	7 Jun 1959	Charles P. Birzee
	*Idaho Falls Idaho East		
1149	Idaho Falls Idaho Lincoln	22 Jun 1980	Cleon Y. Olson
112	*Idaho Falls Idaho North		
	*Idaho Falls North 29 May 1970		
	‡North Idaho Falls	12 May 1935	David Smith
157	*Idaho Falls Idaho South		
	*Idaho Falls South 29 May 1970		
	‡South Idaho Falls	30 Jun 1946	Cecil E. Hart
2183	Idaho Falls Idaho Taylor Mountain	17 Mar 1996	J Rodney Hayes
602	*Idaho Falls Idaho West		
	‡Idaho Falls West	4 Mar 1973	Terry L. Crapo
607	*Iona Idaho		
	‡Iona	15 Apr 1973	Joseph Dudley Tucker
192	*Jerome Idaho		
	‡Gooding	9 Mar 1952	Ross C. Lee
1015	Kimberly Idaho	15 Apr 1979	David LaVere Carter
2029	Kuna Idaho	26 Feb 1995	Kenneth Arthur Roetto
268	*Lewiston Idaho		
	‡Lewiston (Idaho, Wash.)	19 Oct 1958	Golden Romney
72	*McCammon Idaho 19 Feb 1983		
	*Arimo Idaho		
	‡Portneuf	15 Aug 1915	George T. Hyde
1125	Menan Idaho	30 Mar 1980	Garth Victor Hall
580	*Meridian Idaho		
	‡Meridian	11 Jun 1972	J. Richard Clarke
847	Meridian Idaho East	12 Jun 1977	Leonard E. Graham Jr.
1401	Meridian Idaho South	20 Feb 1983	Wenden Wayne Waite
79	*Moore Idaho		
	‡Lost River	18 Aug 1919	William N. Patten
641	Mountain Home Idaho	19 May 1974	Kenneth Herbert Johns
125	*Nampa Idaho		
	‡Nampa	27 Nov 1938	Peter E. Johnson
874	Nampa Idaho South	30 Oct 1977	Dean Ezra Beus
32	*Oakley Idaho		

	‡Cassia (Idaho, Utah)	19 Nov 1887	Horton D. Haight
587	*Paul Idaho		
	‡Minidoka West	24 Sep 1972	Keith C. Merrill Jr.
278	*Pocatello Idaho		
	‡Pocatello	19 Apr 1959	Roland K. Hart
40	*Pocatello Idaho Alameda 17 Jun 1984		
	*Pocatello Idaho East		
	*Pocatello East 29 May 1970		
	*East Pocatello 19 Apr 1959		
	‡Pocatello	7 Aug 1898	William C. Parkinson
1484	Pocatello Idaho Central	17 Jun 1984	Thomas William Ranstrom
971	*Pocatello Idaho East 17 Jun 1984		
	‡Pocatello Idaho South	22 Oct 1978	John Burl McNabb
377	*Pocatello Idaho Highland 17 Jun 1984		
	*Pocatello Idaho Alameda		
	‡Alameda	12 May 1963	Homer S. Satterfield
207	*Pocatello Idaho North		
	*Pocatello North 29 May 1970		
	‡North Pocatello	21 Jun 1953	Jared O. Anderson
1444	Pocatello Idaho Tyhee	25 Sep 1983	Eugene Lester Hancock
406	*Pocatello Idaho University		
	‡Idaho State University	9 May 1965	Robert E. Thompson
149	*Pocatello Idaho West		
	*Pocatello West 29 May 1970		
	‡West Pocatello	6 May 1945	Twayne Austin
28	*Rexburg Idaho		
	*Rexburg 23 Jun 1935		
	*Fremont 6 Aug 1898		
	‡Bannock	4 Feb 1884	Thomas E. Ricks
1369	Rexburg Idaho Center	24 Oct 1982	Ronald Curtis Martin
697	Rexburg Idaho East	1 Jun 1975	Keith Lester Peterson
153	*Rexburg Idaho North		
	*Rexburg North 29 May 1970		
	‡North Rexburg	28 Oct 1945	Orval O. Mortensen
405	*Ricks College 1st 7 Nov 1989		
	*Rexburg Idaho College 1st		
	*Ricks College 1st 1 Jun 1969		
	‡Ricks College	7 May 1965	J. Wendell Stucki
480	*Ricks College 2nd 7 Nov 1989		
	*Rexburg Idaho College 2nd		
	‡Ricks College 2nd	27 Apr 1969	Loren Homer Grover
690	*Ricks College 3rd 7 Nov 1989		
	‡Rexburg Idaho College 3rd	13 Apr 1975	Ray Wendell Rigby
1689	*Ricks College 4th 7 Nov 1989		
	‡Rexburg Idaho College 4th	6 Mar 1988	Jay Lufkin Risenmay
1836	Ricks College 5th	8 Dec 1991	R. Brent Kinghorn
56	*Rigby Idaho		
	‡Rigby	3 Feb 1908	Don Carlos Walker
158	*Rigby Idaho East		
	*Rigby East 29 May 1970		
	‡East Rigby	7 Jul 1946	James E. Ririe
1140	Ririe Idaho	25 May 1980	Arlo J. Moss
606	*Roberts Idaho		
	‡Jefferson	25 Mar 1973	Edwin Cutler Adamson
91	*Rupert Idaho		
	‡Minidoka	11 May 1924	Richard C. May
1476	Rupert Idaho West	3 Jun 1984	Carl B. Garner
60	*Saint Anthony Idaho		
	‡Yellowstone	10 Jan 1909	Daniel G. Miller
211	*Salmon Idaho		
	‡Salmon River	18 Oct 1953	Earl Stokes
952	Sandpoint Idaho	20 Aug 1978	Richard William Goldsberry
67	*Shelley Idaho		
	‡Shelley	16 Aug 1914	Joseph H. Dye
1180	Shelley Idaho South	14 Sep 1980	Kenneth P. Fielding

1129	Sugar City Idaho	4 May 1980	Ferron W. Sonderegger
76	*Twin Falls Idaho		
	‡Twin Falls	26 Jul 1919	Lawrence Gomer Kirkman
490	*Twin Falls Idaho West		
	‡Twin Falls West	17 Aug 1969	Joel A. Tate
1156	Ucon Idaho	29 Jun 1980	Joseph Dudley Tucker
126	*Weiser Idaho		
	‡Weiser	27 Nov 1938	Scott B. Brown
1005	Wendell Idaho	25 Feb 1979	Orlo William Stevens

Utah North Area — 9

1419	*Franklin Idaho 17 Nov 1985		
	‡Preston Idaho East	15 May 1983	Eudean Hawkins Gunnell
39	*Grace Idaho		
	‡Bannock	25 Jul 1898	Lewis S. Pond
32a	*Malad Idaho		
	‡Malad (Idaho, Utah)	12 Feb 1888	Oliver C. Hoskins
75	*Montpelier Idaho		
	‡Montpelier (Idaho, Wyoming)	23 Dec 1917	Edward C. Rich
1020	Montpelier Idaho South	22 Apr 1979	Leonard H. Matthews
8a	*Paris Idaho		
	‡Bear Lake (Idaho, Utah)	20 Jun 1869	David P. Kimball
29	*Preston Idaho North		
	‡Oneida	1 Jun 1884	William D. Hendricks
81	*Preston Idaho South		
	‡Franklin	6 Jun 1920	Samuel W. Parkinson
73	*Soda Springs Idaho		
	‡Idaho	19 Nov 1916	Nelson J. Hogan

Discontinued

70	Curlew (Idaho, Utah)	17 May 1915	Jonathan C. Cutler
	11 Feb 1940 †Malad (32), Pocatello (40)		
1273	Soda Springs Idaho North	31 May 1981	Cleston Murrie Godfrey
	27 Apr 1986 †Montpelier Idaho (75), Soda Springs Idaho (73)		

Missions — 2
(As of Oct. 1, 1996; shown with historical number. See MISSIONS.)

(111) IDAHO BOISE MISSION
2710 Sunrise Rim Road, Suite 220
Boise, ID 83705
Phone: (208) 343-9883

(264) IDAHO POCATELLO MISSION
Horizon Plaza
1070 Hiline Road, Suite 320
Pocatello, ID 83201
Phone: (208) 233-0130

Illinois

Year-end 1995: Est. population, 11,866,000; Members, 43,000; Stakes, 11; Wards, 74; Branches, 32; Missions, 2; Temples, 1; Percent LDS, 0.3, or one person in 275.

The first missionaries to Illinois were Oliver Cowdery, Parley P. Pratt, Peter Whitmer Jr., Richard Ziba Peterson and Frederick G. Williams, who visited in the fall of 1830 while on a mission to Native Americans. In 1834, Zion's Camp passed through southern Illinois, en route to Missouri. As a result of missionary work, a few branches were established in Illinois prior to 1839.

When the Saints were expelled from Missouri in 1838, they began to gather in Quincy, Springfield and other locations where they were generally received on friendly terms. One refugee, Israel Barlow, found his way to Commerce, Ill., where he laid the groundwork for the Church to purchase 660 acres of nearby property that later became Nauvoo. The city was platted and lots sold. As members poured in, the swampy land was drained and buildings erected. Converts from Canada and Europe arrived by thousands. Nauvoo grew to some 15,000 residents at its peak in 1845-46. It received a charter from the state of Illinois in 1840, and had a militia for self-defense. Members built music and cultural halls, as well as meeting halls for priesthood groups. Ten revelations of the Doctrine and Covenants were received in Illinois.

Joseph Smith planned or established in the area a network of 17 colonies, foreshadowing the colonization of the West by Brigham Young. Some of these that were founded or occupied by members included Ramus, Lima, Quincy, Mount Hope, Freedom, Geneva and Pleasant Vale.

In 1840 a site overlooking the city was selected for the Nauvoo Temple, which was completed in 1846. Proxy work for the dead began in Nauvoo, and temple endowments were first performed in 1842. The Relief Society was organized the same year.

In 1844, Joseph and Hyrum Smith were arrested and taken to jail in nearby Carthage, Ill., where they were martyred by a mob. Antagonism against the members increased, and they were expelled from Nauvoo by mobs in 1846. Members in the region left their homes, crossed the Mississippi River and traveled across Iowa to establish a temporary residence at Winter Quarters, Neb., some 300 miles away.

After the members left, the temple was destroyed by fire. The Church presence ended in Illinois for the time. After an interlude following the Saints' migration west, missionaries returned to Illinois in the 1870s. Illinois was included in the Northwestern States Mission, created in May 1878. Most converts from this mission migrated west. Mission headquarters were established in Chicago on July 20, 1889, and the name of the mission was changed to the Northern States Mission. By 1890, the mission extended into 22 states and Canada.

Following the conversions of Scandinavian settlers in Minnesota and other nearby states, Elder Christian D. Fjeldsted found success among the Scandinavians in Chicago from 1895-96.

A number of branches were created. By 1930, three conferences were organized: the Chicago, North Illinois and South Illinois. In Chicago, meetinghouses were built for the Logan Square and University branches. In 1930, state membership was 2,281. In 1933, when the World's Fair was held in Chicago, the Church's exhibit drew an estimated 10,000 people per day.

The first stake in Illinois since the Nauvoo era was organized in Chicago in 1936, followed in 1962 by the Illinois Stake (now Champaign).

In 1954, Dr. J. LeRoy Kimball purchased the Heber C. Kimball home in Nauvoo. His efforts to restore the home were well-received. Nauvoo Restoration was started by the Church in 1962 and the Kimball home was included as part of Nauvoo Restoration Inc., with Dr. Kimball serving as the first president. The Church has since re-purchased some 1,000 acres and restored 25 of the buildings and cleared and erected a monument at the pioneer cemetery. A temple was completed in the Chicago suburb of Glenview in 1985, and an addition to the temple was dedicated in 1989. Membership in 1974 was about 18,000, increasing to 29,000 in 1980 and 38,000 in 1990. Membership in recent years has increased within Chicago's multi-ethnic neighborhoods.

Members were quick to respond to assist others in the 1993 Mississippi River flooding that damaged many areas in the state and resulted in the cancellation of the Nauvoo pageant. Attention of residents throughout the state was drawn to Carthage in June, 1994, when the Church commemorated the 150th anniversary of the martyrdom of the Prophet Joseph Smith and his brother Hyrum.

Nationwide attention was focused on Nauvoo Feb. 4-5, 1996, when the sesquicentennial of the Saints' 1846 exodus was commemorated. In 1995 and 1996, tourist visitation to and news media coverage of the historic city significantly increased.

Sources: *Encyclopedic History of the Church*, by Andrew Jenson; "Spokes on the Wheel," by Donald Q. Cannon, *Ensign*, Feb. 1986; "Harvest of Faith on Chicago's South Side," by Linda Hoffman Kimball, *Ensign*, Feb. 1986; "He saved old Nauvoo from the ruin of time," *Church News*, Jan. 31, 1987; "Bittersweet memories of Ramus," by Calvin N. Smith and Joseph T. Woolley, *Church News*, Aug. 12, 1989; "A time to remember, honor, respect," by Dell Van Orden, *Church News*, July 2, 1994; "Commemorating 1846 exodus," by R. Scott Lloyd, *Church News*, Feb. 10, 1996; "Led by Spirit, not knowing beforehand," by R. Scott Lloyd, *Church News*, Sept. 7, 1996.

Stakes — 11

(Listed alphabetically by area as of Oct. 1, 1996.)

No.	Name	Organized	First President
North America Central Area			
1672	*Buffalo Grove Illinois 21 May 1991		
	‡Long Grove Illinois	24 Jan 1988	William David Johnston
370	*Champaign Illinois		
	‡Illinois	17 Feb 1963	Ross A. Kelly
646	Chicago Heights Illinois	2 Jun 1974	Robert E. Nichols
2112	Joliet Illinois	22 Oct 1995	Douglas J. Fredin
368	*Naperville Illinois		
	‡Chicago South		

	(Ill., Ind.)	3 Feb 1963	Lysle R. Cahoon
1000	Nauvoo Illinois	18 Feb 1979	Gene Lee Roy Mann
749	*O'Fallon Illinois 1 Jun 1993		
	‡Fairview Heights Illinois	14 Mar 1976	John Odeen Anderson
1163	Peoria Illinois	3 Aug 1980	Clive Edwin Ashton
1334	Rockford Illinois	11 Apr 1982	Brent L. Horsley
1094	Schaumburg Illinois	20 Jan 1980	Owen D. West Jr.
118	Wilmette Illinois		
	‡Chicago (Ill., Ind., Wis.)	29 Nov 1936	William A. Matheson

Discontinued

4	Crooked Creek [Ramus] 4 Dec 1841	4 Jul 1840	Joel Hills Johnson
8	Freedom 24 May 1841	27 Oct 1840	Henry W. Miller
9	Geneva 24 May 1841	1 Nov 1840	William Bosley
5	Lima 1845	22 Oct 1840	Isaac Morley
7	Mount Hope 24 May 1841	27 Oct 1840	Abel Lamb
2a	Nauvoo 1846	5 Oct 1839	William Marks
6	Quincy 24 May 1841	25 Oct 1840	Daniel Stanton
10	Springfield 24 May 1841	5 Nov 1840	Edwin P. Merriam

Missions — 2

(As of Oct. 1, 1996; shown with historical number. See MISSIONS.)

(9c) ILLINOIS CHICAGO MISSION
1319 Butterfield Road, Suite 522
Downers Grove, IL 60515
Phone: (630) 969-2145

(176a) ILLINOIS PEORIA MISSION
4700 North Sterling, Suite 100
Peoria, IL 61615
Phone: (309) 685-1116

Indiana

Year-end 1995: Est. population, 5,851,000; Members, 30,000; Stakes, 8; Wards, 54; Branches, 25; Missions, 1; Percent LDS, 0.5, or one person in 195.

Missionaries Samuel H. Smith and Reynolds Cahoon preached in the Indiana cities of Unionville, Madison and Vienna in the summer of 1831. Other missionaries came shortly after, including Parley P. and Orson Pratt. The first branches were organized in Sept., 1831, and the first conference was held Nov. 29, 1831. Joseph Smith spent four weeks in Greenville, Ind., in the spring of 1832.

In 1834, Zion's Camp crossed Indiana. Although trouble was predicted by their enemies, members of the group passed through Indiana peacefully. In 1838, the Kirtland Camp, a group of seventies, also crossed Indiana. It is believed that a number of Indiana converts joined the Church in the early days.

In 1882, Indiana became part of the Northwestern States Mission. Among early converts after the turn of the century were Edward and Anna Faulting of Indianapolis, in whose home meetings were held until 1910. At that time, a home was rented and membership grew from 13 people to 10 families by 1913. The first branch was organized that year and the branch met in a hired hall. John L. Thomas was branch president. In 1920 a larger hall was rented which served until a meetinghouse was erected in 1927. This meetinghouse was dedicated by President Heber J. Grant.

In 1939, a second branch was organized in Indianapolis.

The Indianapolis Stake was created May 17, 1959, from the Central Indiana District. In the stake were two Indianapolis wards, and other wards in Bloomington, Columbus, Muncie, Purdue and Richmond, with branches in Kokomo, Anderson and Connersville, and a membership of 2,287.

The Great Lakes Mission, created in 1949 from the Northern States Mission, was changed to the Indiana Indianapolis Mission in 1974. That year the state had 14,787 members, increasing to 20,738 in 1980, and to 26,169 in 1990.

Sources: *Encyclopedic History of the Church*, by Andrew Jenson; *Church News*, May 23, 1959; Indianapolis Stake Center Dedication Program, Nov. 26, 1967; "Zions Camp, Across Swamplands," *Church News*, Sept. 5, 1970, and "Zions Camp, the First Prairie," *Church News*, Sept. 12, 1970; *Discovering Mormon Trails*, by Stanley B. Kimball, Deseret Book Co., 1979.

Stakes — 9
(Listed alphabetically as of Oct. 1, 1996.)

No.	Name	Organized	First President
North America Northeast Area			
1078	Bloomington Indiana	4 Nov 1979	Hollis Ralph Johnson
712	Evansville Indiana	19 Oct 1975	Frank R. Fults Jr.
352	*Fort Wayne Indiana ‡Fort Wayne (Indiana, Ohio)	4 Mar 1962	Howard W. Thompson
283	*Indianapolis Indiana ‡Indianapolis	17 May 1959	Phillip F. Low
624a	*Indianapolis Indiana North ‡Indianapolis North	19 Aug 1973	David Val Glover
1417	Lafayette Indiana	15 May 1983	Koy Eldridge Miskin
2159	Muncie Indiana	4 Feb 1996	Michael W. Ellis
1368	New Albany Indiana	24 Oct 1982	Henry Harvey Griffith
873	South Bend Indiana	30 Oct 1977	Kenneth Bryan Fugal

Mission — 1
(As of Oct. 1, 1996; shown with historical number. See MISSIONS.)

(46) INDIANA INDIANAPOLIS MISSION
P.O. Box 495
Carmel, IN 46032
Phone: (317) 844-3964

Iowa

Year-end 1995: Est. population, 2,848,000; Members, 14,000; Stakes, 4; Wards, 27; Branches, 12; Missions, 1; Percent LDS, 0.5, or one person in 203.

Following the expulsion of the Saints from Missouri in 1838, Iowa Gov. Robert Lucas expressed sympathy for their plight and offered them refuge. Although Joseph Smith instead chose to go to the site that later became Nauvoo in Illinois, members also entered and built up Lee County, Iowa, and resided in Montrose, Augusta, Keokuk and other areas. They founded Ambrosia and started a settlement named Zarahemla. A stake was organized in Lee County in 1839.

When the Saints were expelled from Nauvoo in 1846, the exiles crossed Iowa to found Winter Quarters, just across the Missouri River in Nebraska. On their westward trek they established Garden Grove and planted grain. Farther along, they again farmed at a place they called Mount Pisgah. Noah Rogers, returning from a mission in Tahiti, died and was buried there. Eventually 2,000 Saints lived in Mount Pisgah and members of the Mormon Battalion were recruited from among its residents in 1846. Mount Pisgah was disbanded in 1852, but a cemetery is there with a monument erected by the Church in 1888. Garden Grove remains as a farming community.

Members also lived in Kanesville, Iowa, across the river from Winter Quarters, Neb., and established some 70 temporary settlements. In 1848, Winter Quarters was abandoned when Indian officials protested. Members moved back to Iowa and settled in Kanesville, the name of which was changed in 1853 to Council Bluffs.

At Kanesville, Brigham Young was formally sustained as president of the Church on Dec. 7, 1847, and the same month sent the highly influential general epistle calling upon members all over the world to gather in Great Basin of the Rocky Mountains.

After 1848, Kanesville became an important staging area for thousands of Mormon and non-Mormon overland travelers.

An estimated 8,000 members lived in Iowa at this time. The settlements were vacated as pioneers moved west. In 1856-57, many handcart pioneers crossed the plains from what is now Iowa City, Iowa, where the railway ended. Of the 2,500 handcart pioneers who crossed the plains, 200 to 300 died on the trail. A marker was placed at the site in 1980, now part of the University of Iowa campus in Iowa City.

Missionary work began in Iowa in 1869 with Elders Israel Evans and Nymphus C. Murdock. A branch was reorganized in Keokuk in 1875, and Council Bluffs in 1878. Iowa was part of the Northwestern States Mission (changed to Northern States in 1889), organized in 1878.

In 1880, Elder B.H. Roberts began his missionary work in Iowa. On one occasion, he secured a school for preaching in West Fork, Iowa, and word spread in the community that three preachers would "tie the young Mormon with questions." Elder Roberts, though, nearly missed the appointment because of being stranded behind a washed-out bridge some distance away. He waded the stream, walked 10 miles and arrived to find a standing-room only crowd and three preachers. He spoke eloquently and no one contradicted him.

In 1887, mission headquarters were moved to Council Bluffs, where it remained until 1896, when it was transferred to Chicago. By 1930, Iowa included the Eastern and Western Iowa conferences with branches in Ames, Boone, Davenport and Sioux City. The Davenport Branch had a meetinghouse. Membership then was 560.

A stake was created in 1966 in Cedar Rapids with 2,000 members in the Cedar Falls, Cedar Rapids, Davenport, Iowa City and Rock Island wards and the Fayette, Muscatine, and Washington branches. Membership in the state in 1974 was 6,111. It increased to about 9,000 in 1980 and to 11,000 in 1990.

Appreciation for the contributions of the early members increased in the state as local Latter-day Saints cooperated with many interested residents to preserve early Church sites and the Mormon Trail during the late 1980s and 1990s. In 1996, those efforts resulted in the sesquicentennial observation of the Saints' exodus from Nauvoo. Wagon trains, many community celebrations and a symposium in Des Moines commemorated the 1846 trek across Iowa. The observance was capped July 13 with the re-enactment of the Mormon Battalion mustering, and dedication by President Gordon B. Hinckley of the reconstructed Kanesville Tabernacle.

Sources: *Encyclopedic History of the Church,* by Andrew Jenson; "A meeting in Iowa," *Church News,* Nov. 24, 1973; "The LDS Legacy in Southwestern Iowa," by Gail Geo. Holmes, *Ensign,* Aug. 1988; "Handcart camp dedicated in Iowa as historic site," *Church News,* Aug. 9, 1980; "Middle Missouri Valley, 1846-1992," by Gail Geo. Holmes, *Church News,* July 18, 1992; "Iowans honor Saints' trek across 12 of their counties," by R. Scott Lloyd, *Church News,* March 30, 1996; "Tabernacle of log replicated, dedicated" and "Mormon Battalion Mustering" by Dell Van Orden, *Church News,* July 20, 1996.

Stakes — 5
(Listed alphabetically as of Oct. 1, 1996.)

No.	Name	Organized	First President
North America Central Area			
2053	Ames Iowa	21 May 1995	Robert Blaine Schafer
419	Cedar Rapids Iowa		
	‡Cedar Rapids (Iowa, Illinois)	29 May 1966	Richard F. Hagland
902	Davenport Iowa	9 Apr 1978	James Earl Campbell
525	*Des Moines Iowa		
	‡Des Moines	6 Sep 1970	Donald G. Woolley
2157	Sioux City Iowa	21 Jan 1996	David W. Roper
	Discontinued		
3a	Iowa [Zarahemla]	5 Oct 1839	John Smith
	6 Jan 1842		

Mission — 1
(As of Oct. 1, 1996; shown with historical number. See MISSIONS.)

(140) IOWA DES MOINES MISSION
8515 Douglas Ave., #19
Des Moines, IA 50322
Phone: (515) 278-9637

Kansas

Year-end 1995: Est. population, 2,572,000; Members, 22,000; Stakes, 5; Wards, 38; Branches, 22; Districts, 1; Percent LDS, 0.8, or one person in 117.

In 1831, Oliver Cowdery and Parley Pratt taught Shawnee and Delaware Indians in what is now Kansas. In 1846, the Mormon Battalion was equipped for the longest infantry march in U.S. history at Fort Leavenworth, Kan. The immigration of 1854 passed through eastern Kansas. In 1855, what is now Atchison, Kan., was chosen as a layover site for immigrants who came up the Mississippi and Missouri rivers. They needed a more healthful place to disembark to avoid the ravages of cholera. A camp called Mormon Grove was established and more than 100 acres was cultivated and crops planted for future immigrants. The camp only lasted one summer, but fulfilled its purpose.

Missionary work in Kansas began anew in 1882 when Elders Joseph F. Doxford, Marcus L. Shepherd and James Mellor labored in Dickinson, Clay, Ottawa and Salina counties. In May 1882, they organized the Meridian Branch, located on the U.S. meridian that is a border between Dickinson and Salina counties. Ten converts from the branch immigrated to Utah. Others followed, but soon a mob ordered the missionaries to leave. In 1887, Pres. William M. Palmer of the Northern States Mission began laboring with "Bickertonites," a group that earlier splintered from the Church. His success led to the transfer of Kansas to the Northern States Mission from the Southern States Mission so the missionaries could continue their work.

In 1898, Kansas was transferred to the Indian Territory Mission. Among the earliest branches was one in Kansas City. By 1930, Kansas included branches in Blau, Kansas City, Leavenworth, St. John, Topeka and Wichita, with a membership of 2,063.

The Kansas City Stake (with headquarters in Missouri) was organized Oct. 21, 1956, and it included, in Kansas, the Kansas City 1st and 2nd wards, the Topeka Ward and the Leavenworth, Hiawatha and Lawrence branches. The first stake headquartered in Kansas was in Wichita, organized June 24, 1962.

In 1974, Kansas received its first institute building, an historic estate across from Kansas State University. In that year, membership reached 8,134. In 1980, membership grew to 12,246 members; and in 1990, to 18,169 members.

On Aug. 3, 1996, at Fort Leavenworth, 500 men from 6 stakes in the Kansas City area re-enacted part of the Mormon Battalion march.

Sources: *Encyclopedic History of the Church*, by Andrew Jenson; "Martin V. Witbeck, Former Utahn, Called to Preside Over New Unit," *Church News*, Oct. 27, 1956; "Estate Home Now Building for Institute," *Church News*, Sept. 7, 1974; "Mormon Grove," by Dean L. May, *Church News*, Aug. 20, 1977; "Battalion commemorated at historic military post," by R. Scott Lloyd, *Church News*, Aug. 10, 1996.

Stakes — 5
(Listed alphabetically as of Oct. 1, 1996.)

No.	Name	Organized	First President
North America Central Area			
1994	Lenexa Kansas	16 Oct 1994	Donald D. Deshler
1610	Olathe Kansas	19 Oct 1986	Clifton D. Boyack Jr.
1696	Salina Kansas	29 May 1988	Thomas R. Coleman
747	Topeka Kansas	29 Feb 1976	Vahl W. Bodily
355	*Wichita Kansas		
	‡Wichita (Kansas, Oklahoma)	24 Jun 1962	Lee R. Meador

Kentucky

Year-end 1995: Est. population, 3,876,000; Members, 21,000; Stakes, 4; Wards, 31; Branches, 30; Missions, 1; Percent LDS, 0.5, or one person in 184.

The first missionaries known to have visited Kentucky were Samuel H. Smith and Reynolds Cahoon. Coming from Kirtland, Ohio, they passed through the northern part of the state in late June 1831 on their way to Missouri. However, it is unlikely they preached. About the same time, the Prophet Joseph Smith and several of the brethren, traveling by steamer on the Ohio River, stopped at Louisville for three days. Because of his pattern of frequent preaching, it is likely that he was the first missionary to preach in Kentucky, though no record of converts exists. The Prophet also stopped in Louisville in 1832.

After this beginning, missionary work was done in Ballards, Carlisle, McCracken, Graves, Calloway, Jefferson, Boone, Kenton, and Campbell counties, and a few branches were started. The first was in Licking River, started before May 1834 by Robert Gulbertson, a convert from Indiana. In April 1835, Elders Wilford Woodruff and Warren Parrish crossed into Kentucky. From July 1835 on, Elder Woodruff labored alone. In Kentucky and Tennessee, they found that several branches had been formed by earlier missionaries in the region. A typical diary entry indicated that they "preached on the gospel of Jesus Christ, the authenticity of the Book of Mormon and the scattering and gathering of the House of Israel."

In 1835, James Emmett and Peter Dustin baptized 22 people including Benjamin and David Lewis. Benjamin Lewis was killed at Haun's Mill in 1838.

The first conference of the Church was conducted Feb. 26, 1836, at the home of Lewis Clapp in Calloway County, Ky.

The first company of Kentucky Saints gathering to Zion left for Missouri in September 1836. This started what became a 50-year movement of the Saints from the Southern States area. Missionary work continued until the end of 1839, then began again in 1842. In July of 1843, Brigham Young and Wilford Woodruff visited Kentucky on a missionary swing through the east. Converts were still being baptized a year later when the Prophet Joseph Smith was martyred and the missionaries were called back to Illinois.

Church growth was very slow as the Saints left the Southern States through the late 1800s to gather in the West. In 1868, Jesse W. Crosby Jr. and Owen Dix worked in Kentucky "with some success."

However, post-Civil War circumstances in the South were difficult. Persecution dogged missionaries and members through the 1880s, but by mid-1890s, toleration improved for them. By 1900, some 1,170 members lived in the state. Kentucky was placed briefly in the Middle States Mission in 1903.

The history of the Lebanon Branch is typical of the growth of the Church in Kentucky. In 1907, Elder M. P. Stinson and Elder Kossnth Dyal, two traveling missionaries, visited the tiny community of Jonah, Ky., several miles east of Lebanon, and baptized Alfred Crews and his wife, Fannie. In late 1908 or early 1909, the Jonah Fork Branch of the Kentucky Conference was organized. There is no record of a branch president, but one of the first Church buildings in Kentucky was completed and dedicated at Jonah in 1910.

With the advent of the automobile and improved roads, Bradfordsville, six miles west of Jonah and seven or eight miles south of Lebanon, became the gathering place for Saints in the surrounding communities. Meetings were held in homes and outdoors into the 1920s and 1930s, as missionary activity in the region continued. One annual tradition was a July 4th fish fry, attended by up to 200 people, including many non-members of the Church. Fiddle and banjo music would accompany the meal, which was followed by "preaching" by the elders.

Membership in the state in 1930 was 2,879 in the Kentucky and East Kentucky districts, with a total of six branches with meetinghouses: Grant's Leek, Kentenia, Martin, Owingsville, Louisville and Larkin.

In 1971, the Louisville Stake was formed with wards in Fort Knox, Louisville (three), and New Albany, and branches in Lebanon, Salem, and Sulphur Well.

Membership in the state in 1980 was 13,956. In 1990, Dan Kelly was elected state senator, the the first LDS member to be elected to a state office. Membership in Kentucky in 1990 was 17,000.

Sources: *Encyclopedic History of the Church,* by Andrew Jenson; *History of the Southern States Mission,* a BYU thesis by LaMar C. Berrett, July 1960; *Church News,* Jan 30, 1971; "His first fruits," by Ronald G. Watt, *Church News,* Aug. 27, 1977; and *Church News,* "My Old Kentucky Home," by Mike Cannon, Feb. 22, 1992.

Stakes — 4
(Listed alphabetically by area as of Oct. 1, 1996.)

No.	Name	Organized	First President
North America Northeast Area — 2			
571	*Lexington Kentucky		
	‡Lexington	23 Apr 1972	Philip M. Moody
540	*Louisville Kentucky		
	‡Louisville	17 Jan 1971	Henry H. Griffith
1375	*Owingsville Kentucky 30 May 1995		
	‡Huntington West Virginia	7 Nov 1982	Grant Earl Jenson
North America Southeast Area — 1			
926	Hopkinsville Kentucky	21 May 1978	Robert Laurence Fears

Mission — 1
(As of Oct. 1, 1996; shown with historical number. See MISSIONS.)

(29) KENTUCKY LOUISVILLE MISSION
P.O. Box 4247, Baxter Ave. Station
Louisville, KY 40204
Phone: (502) 451-3010

Louisiana
Year-end 1995: Est. population, 4,355,000; Members, 24,000; Stakes, 7; Wards, 38; Branches, 28; Missions, 1; Percent LDS, 0.5, or one person in 181.

Elder Parley P. Pratt considered going to New Orleans in 1837, hoping to establish a mission there, but felt impressed to instead remain in New York. In 1841, Joseph Smith received a letter from Elam Luddington (later the first missionary to Thailand) and Eli G. Terrill of New Orleans who indicated they had a group of members and requested an elder to assist them. "Send us Peter, or an Apostle to preach unto us Jesus," they wrote, and enclosed $10 to help defray expenses. They may have been among a group from the sailing ship *Isaac Newton*, the first to carry Saints to New Orleans, which arrived from London on Dec. 21, 1840.

Elder Harrison Sagers was sent, arriving in New Orleans on March 28, 1841. Elder Sagers preached to large crowds and was troubled by mobs, but was defended on one occasion by a group of courageous women who circled him in defense. He baptized several people and ordained Terrill an elder.

In November of 1841, New Orleans became the principal port of arrival for members, 17,463 of whom emigrated from Europe via New Orleans to the gathering place of the Saints before their migration west. Most disembarked from their sailing vessel, took passage on a river steamer and traveled up the Mississippi River to Nauvoo, St. Louis or other river ports to begin their westward trek. A branch functioned in New Orleans from 1844 until 1855, when New York became the port of arrival for the Church immigrants.

Missionaries returned to Louisiana in 1896 as part of the Southern States Mission. Elder Joseph A. Cornwall arrived in Louisiana on Sept. 10, laboring on the Red River in North Louisiana with little results. In 1897, he and his companions baptized their first converts. The Red Rock Branch was organized in 1898. That year, 24 missionaries labored in Louisiana. A sawmill owner, John R. Jones, befriended the missionaries and protected them from opposition. Alexander Colman Wagley, first president of the Red Rock Branch, was baptized Sept. 4, 1898. By June 16, 1899, Elder David A. Broadbent, president of the Louisiana District from 1898 to 1899, reported that 110 people had been baptized. Pres. Wagley and missionaries were held hostage by mobs but were unharmed. When a mob threatened a missionary under the medical care of Jane Holt Clark, a midwife, she confronted the mob with a shotgun and said, "I brought a good many of you into the world and I can take you out again just as easily." The mob left.

In 1915, a wagon train of members from Pride, La., traveled to Corleyville where they settled and erected a meetinghouse in 1920. Other prominent branches were the Hardytown and Many branches. The Many Branch, which eventually absorbed the Hardytown Branch, was organized in 1933 and a meetinghouse was built in 1942.

Missionaries labored in New Orleans for 20 years before a branch was organized. Howard and Marian Bennion arrived in Louisiana in the 1920s and a branch was organized in their apartment in 1924. By 1926 the branch began meeting in a public hall. The branch faltered in the early 1930s, but members joined missionaries, and contacting through radio, newspapers and street meetings helped the branch grow. Some 100 people celebrated the branch's centennial in 1944. In 1948, the branch had grown to 300 members, due in part to an influx of LDS servicemen who came during World War II. A meetinghouse was begun in January 1951 and dedicated about two years later. That same year meetinghouses were dedicated in Hammond, Williamson and Lake Charles, and an addition on the Many Branch was dedicated.

The New Orleans Stake was created in 1955. In 1964, a new stake center was completed. Membership within the former branch area in 1973 was about 2,500.

President Spencer W. Kimball visited Baton Rouge in 1977 and addressed 12,000 people from the surrounding regions. Membership in Louisiana in 1980 was about 16,000, increasing to 22,000 in 1990.

Elder L. Lionel Kendrick of the First Quorum of the Seventy is a native of Louisiana, and was a professor of health education at the time of his calling in 1988.

Louisiana members were among many Church members to respond to storm-caused disasters in the 1990s.

Sources: *Encyclopedic History of the Church*, by Andrew Jenson; "Boats on the Mississippi are still reminder of part of LDS History," by J Malan Heslop, *Church News*, Dec. 24, 1977; "From Red Rock to Denham Springs," by Carol Ann Wagley Burnham, *Ensign*, April 1983; Branch Notes 100th Anniversary, *Church News*, Jan. 22, 1944; and *Church News*: Dec. 6, 1952; Jan. 20, 1973; Sept. 13, 1975; Sept. 3, 1977; and May 21, 1977; "Members rally to help hurricane victims," *Church News*, Aug. 12, 1995.

Stakes — 7

(Listed alphabetically as of Oct. 1, 1996.)

No.	Name	Organized	First President

North America Southeast Area

954	Alexandria Louisiana	27 Aug 1978	Jeffie Jackson Horn
476	*Baton Rouge Louisiana		
	‡Baton Rouge	26 Jan 1969	Harmon Cutler
1254	Denham Springs Louisiana	19 Apr 1981	Stephen H. Cutler
1550	Monroe Louisiana	18 Aug 1985	John Robert Falk
221	*New Orleans Louisiana		
	‡New Orleans	19 Jun 1955	Clive M. Larson
254	*Shreveport Louisiana		
	‡Shreveport (Louisiana, Texas)	26 Jan 1958	J. Milton Belisle
1575	Slidell Louisiana	17 Nov 1985	Joseph T. Kuchin

Mission — 1

(As of Oct. 1, 1996; shown with historical number. See MISSIONS.)

(31) LOUISIANA BATON ROUGE MISSION
12025 Justice Ave.
Baton Rouge, LA 70816
Phone: (504) 293-6060

Maine

Year-end 1995: Est. population, 1,242,000; Members, 7,900; Stakes, 2; Wards, 16; Branches, 9; Percent LDS, 0.6, or one person in 157.

On Sept. 19, 1832, two years after the Church was organized, Elders Orson Hyde and Samuel H. Smith crossed the Piscataqua River in a canoe to Maine. They went from door to door in search of converts, soon starting a branch in Saco, York County. One of their first converts was Timothy Smith, baptized about Oct. 31, 1832. Other missionaries followed. In 1833, additional branches were organized, including one in York County that included converts from a mass conversion of 30. The Maine Conference was created in 1835 with about 317 members.

In 1837, Elder Wilford Woodruff and Jonathan H. Hale found missionary success on the Fox Islands, where several branches were organized among some 100 converts. The converts gathered to Nauvoo a short time later.

Little missionary work was done in Maine after the martyrdom of Joseph Smith in 1844. In 1850, Brigham Young requested all the Saints in Maine to go to the West. In 1855, Elder E.B. Tripp found converts in the town of Mexico, Maine, and organized a branch that remained until 1869. Little activity occurred until after the turn of the century.

In 1904, missionaries began work in Portland. Work proceeded very slowly. The Maine Conference was reorganized in 1909, and missionaries found "practically a new field for missionary work." They visited homes near Litchfield in 1908, and met Percy E. and Annie Louise Rowe Lane. Five years later, on July 4, 1913, missionaries baptized Sister Lane and her daughter, Mildred, and the rest of the family afterward. Missionaries started a Sunday School in their home.

After 1925, when Maine was placed in the Canadian Mission, the northern part of the state was visited more often by missionaries. Bangor became a Church center for missionary work. Some 275 people, including eight converts, attended a conference in Bangor on Oct. 14, 1930.

Scattered branches continued into the 1950s before significant growth occurred. The first building was dedicated in 1957 in Portland. Another was dedicated in Bangor the same year. The Maine Stake was created in 1968 with 2,208 members. Members from the West added to the membership. In 1974, membership was 3,851; in 1980 it was 4,664, and in 1990, 7,253.

Sources: *Encyclopedic History of the Church*, by Andrew Jenson; "A Partial History of Litchfield," by Percy E. Lane, unpublished; "Wilford Woodruff's Mission to Maine," by Donald Q. Cannon, *Improvement Era*, September, 1970; "Old Mormon Palmyra and New England," by Richard Neitzel Holsapfel and T. Jeffery Cottle; *The Narrative of the Saints in Maine from 1831 to the 1990s*, an unpublished manuscript by Paul Edward Damron.

Stakes — 2

(Listed alphabetically as of Oct. 1, 1996.)

No. Name	Organized	First President
North America Northeast Area		
461 *Augusta Maine		

	‡Maine	23 Jun 1968	Olie W. Ross
1595	Bangor Maine	20 Apr 1986	Paul Herald Risk II

Maryland

Year-end 1995: Est. population, 5,063,000; Members, 30,000; Stakes, 7; Wards, 53; Branches, 13; Missions, 1; Temples, 1; Percent LDS, 0.5, or one person in 169.

Elders Jedediah M. Grant, Erastus Snow, William Bosley and John F. Wakefield began missionary work in Maryland in the summer of 1837. Elders Snow and Bosley worked in Washington County between May and October and organized a branch. Elder Snow reported preaching in Greencastle and engaging in a formal debate that lasted 10 hours in Leitersburgh, Washington County, with a Campbellite minister. He afterward baptized 11 people. He also baptized seven people in Leitersburgh. In 1838, Elder Benjamin Winchester preached in the same vicinity, traveling with Elder Snow. On this journey, Elder Snow baptized an 89-year-old man after cutting through ice 18 inches thick.

An LDS newspaper, the *Mormon Expositor,* began in 1842 in Baltimore but was discontinued. Elders Heber C. Kimball and Lyman Wight traveled to Baltimore in 1844 where they received information about the martyrdom of the Prophet Joseph Smith.

After the exodus west and the gathering of the Saints, little work was done in Maryland until the turn of the century. The Maryland Conference was reorganized June 30, 1899, with Charles A. Hardy as president. At that time, mission leadership wanted to increase the conference size, so they requested an additional four Virginia counties from the Southern States Mission. Southern States Mission Pres. Ben E. Rich humorously agreed to yield the Virginia counties on the condition that they would take six, not four.

By 1900, the conference included the Pratt and Mount Savage branches, but in 1905, the Maryland Conference was absorbed into the Eastern Pennsylvania Conference. That year a tiny group of members in Baltimore organized a Book of Mormon class that lasted several years. Sunday Schools were organized in Baltimore in 1907 and reorganized in 1917.

Missionary work picked up in 1915 as work proceeded in Havre de Grace, Baltimore, Frederick and Salisbury. In 1918, street meetings in Baltimore brought interest. Work in Annapolis began in 1920. Branch meetings in Washington and Baltimore, presided over by missionaries, and Sunday Schools and Relief Societies in other areas, were held in rented halls. One small frame meetinghouse in Capitol Heights accommodated a membership of mostly Westerners — students or those with government jobs.

The Washington Stake was created June 30, 1940, with Ezra Taft Benson as president. This stake included parts of Maryland where the first Maryland stake was later created in 1970. Maryland membership in 1980 was 17,617.

A site for the showcase Washington Temple was selected in Kensington, Md., in 1962. The temple was dedicated in 1974 and has become a prominent landmark in the region. The temple grounds have become a popular place for national leaders and diplomats to visit on special occasions, such as during the Christmas season. At the 15th anniversary of the temple in 1988, it was noted that membership around the nation's capital had increased by some 200 percent since the temple's construction, and numbered some 63,000 members in 19 stakes.

Sources: *Encyclopedic History of the Church,* by Andrew Jenson; *History of the Southern States Mission,* by LaMar C. Berrett, BYU thesis, July 1960; mission and ward histories; *Church News,* Sept. 19, 1970, Sept. 14, 1974, and Sept. 17, 1977.

Stakes — 7

(Listed alphabetically as of Oct. 1, 1996.)

No.	Name	Organized	First President
	North America Northeast Area		
1429	*Annapolis Maryland 13 Nov 1988		
	‡Columbia Maryland	12 Jun 1983	Stephen P. Shipley
674	Baltimore Maryland	8 Dec 1974	Kyle W. Petersen
1825	Columbia Maryland	10 Nov 1991	Cecil Brent Bargeron
1390	Frederick Maryland	12 Dec 1982	Earl J. Wahlquist
1566	Seneca Maryland	27 Oct 1985	David Warne Ferrel
526	*Silver Spring Maryland		
	‡Chesapeake (Maryland)	13 Sep 1970	June B. Thayn
1051	Suitland Maryland	19 Aug 1979	Thomas Bailey Kerr

(As of Oct. 1, 1996; shown with historical number. Washington, D.C., missions are listed in District of Colombia. See MISSIONS.)

(298) MARYLAND BALTIMORE MISSION
4785 Dorsey Hall Drive, Suite 105
Ellicott City, MD 21042-7728
Phone: (410) 715-0875

Massachusetts

Year-end 1995: Est. population, 6,091,000; Members, 16,000; Stakes, 3; Wards, 28; Branches, 13; Missions, 1; Temples, 1 announced; Percent LDS, 0.2, or one person in 380.

The first missionaries in Massachusetts are believed to be Elders Orson Hyde and Samuel H. Smith, who arrived in Boston June 22, 1832. They baptized four people, and, by the end of the year, had organized two branches. These branches were short-lived, however.

In 1838, Brigham Young and his brother Joseph baptized 17 people in Boston as they preached the gospel. The Eastern States Mission was created under John P. Greene in 1839 (Greene was the reverend who received a copy of the Book of Mormon during Samuel H. Smith's first missionary journey in New York in 1830). By February 1843 some 14 branches in the Boston area had been organized. Joseph Smith and others visited Boston in December 1839. They were en route to Washington, D.C., seeking redress for the injustices in Missouri.

In 1843, Elder George J. Adams preached nightly to an enthusiastic audience of some 1,200 in Charlestown. Later, eight members of the Quorum of the Twelve attended a Boston conference as part of an effort they were making to press missionary work forward in New England. Their work ended after the martyrdom of Joseph Smith in 1844. A year later the Boston Branch had some 300-400 members. In 1849, Mission Pres. William Appleby led a company of 79 members to St. Louis and on to the Great Basin. Many died of cholera.

Work slowed in 1850, and stopped in 1857 when all missionaries were called to Utah during the so-called "Utah War." Until 1893, most of New England, including Massachusetts, saw little progress in the development of the Church.

The Eastern States Mission reopened in 1893 and missionaries sought out old members. After a year, membership numbered 96. Despite emphasis on public relations, missionaries encountered substantial hostilities. Highly publicized U.S. Senate hearings on Apostle and Senator-elect Reed Smoot fanned anti-LDS sentiments. Police often refused to allow missionaries to conduct open-air meetings. President Joseph F. Smith addressed a large gathering at Deacon's Hall in Boston in 1905 on a return trip from dedicating a monument at Joseph Smith's birthplace in Vermont.

A Mutual Improvement Association was started in Boston on Jan. 5, 1908, and a branch in Lynn, Mass., was started in 1910. The Church began to grow about 1917 but the onset of World War I halted efforts.

After the war, more missionaries resumed labor in Massachusetts and the membership began to increase. On April 18, 1930, missionaries took part in a radio broadcast. At that time, membership in the Massachusetts District numbered about 356. Longtime member Naomi B. Cranney recalled that membership in the 1930s included only about 10 permanent families in the area. Returned missionaries who were students at Harvard University provided great strength, she said. The Great Depression and World War II again slowed growth. But the war also brought couples from Utah to work at the Massachusetts Institute of Technology in Cambridge. In 1947, missionaries were sent to rural areas, where they found some success.

The first meetinghouses were completed in the early 1950s. An exceptional piece of Church property was the Longfellow estate in Cambridge, Mass., that was purchased by Elder Levi Edgar Young. It later became headquarters for the New England Mission. A meetinghouse was dedicated on this site in 1956.

When mission Pres. Truman G. Madsen began serving in 1962, missionaries baptized about 1,000 per year for two years. The same year the Church purchased the shortwave radio station WRUL to beam Church-related information to Europe, Africa, and Latin America.

In 1963, some 2,200 members met in a conference in Boston, the largest LDS gathering in New England history.

The Boston Stake, the first in New England, was created in 1962. It included parts of New Hampshire and Rhode Island. During the 1960s, a number of meetinghouses were erected with beneficial effects on membership. Members enjoyed a higher profile during the next years with improved relations with government and educational figures. Additional stakes were created in Massachusetts in Hingham in 1981 and in Springfield in 1987. Membership in 1974 was 5,628, increasing to 8,174 in 1980, and 13,931 in 1990.

Shortly after he was sustained president of the Church in 1995, President Gordon B. Hinckley visited Massachusetts. He spoke to 7,500 members at the Boston Massachusetts Region Conference April 23. He also spoke to priesthood leaders and missionaries during the trip, and visited historical sites. On Sept. 30, 1995, in general conference, President Hinckley announced a temple would be built in Boston.

Sources: "Yankee Saints: The Church in New England in the Twentieth Century," by Richard O. Cowan, *Regional Studies in Latter-day Saint History*, New England; Highlights in the History of The Church of Jesus Christ of Latter-day Saints, a paper by J. D. Williams, Cambridge Branch; *Church News*, April 29, 1995.

Stakes — 3
(Listed alphabetically as of Oct. 1, 1996.)

No.	Name	Organized	First President
	North America Northeast Area		
354	*Boston Massachusetts		
	‡Boston (Mass., N.H., R.I.)	20 May 1962	Wilbur W. Cox
1287	Hingham Massachusetts	30 Aug 1981	Brent W. Lambert
1646	Springfield Massachusetts	28 Jun 1987	David O. Sutton

Mission — 1
(As of Oct. 1, 1996; shown with historical number. See MISSIONS.)

(35) MASSACHUSETTS BOSTON MISSION
385 Concord Ave., Suite 100
Belmont, MA 02178
Phone: (617) 489-3733

Michigan

Year-end 1995: Est. population, 9,578,000; Members, 33,000; Stakes, 8; Wards, 52; Branches, 41; Missions, 2; Districts, 2; Percent LDS, 0.3, or one person in 290.

Visiting her relatives in Pontiac, Lucy Mack Smith arrived in Michigan in the spring of 1831. With her was her niece, Almira Mack of Pontiac, who had been baptized in New York in 1830. They visited Lucy Mack Smith's brother, Col. Stephen Mack, considered the founder of Pontiac.

Preaching in Pontiac, she warned one unfriendly pastor that one third of his flock would soon be members, including the deacon. Upon her return to Kirtland, Ohio, the Prophet Joseph Smith sent Jared Carter and Joseph Wood to Pontiac where they arrived Jan. 7, 1833, and baptized 22 people from the pastor's congregation, including the deacon, Samuel Bent.

In 1834, Joseph Smith visited Pontiac with his father and Hyrum, the three witnesses to the Book of Mormon, Frederick G. Williams and Robert Orton. Missionary work continued in Michigan, although no records exist of how many were converted because converts often soon gathered with the body of the Church.

Parley P. and Orson Pratt visited Detroit in the fall of 1839 where they preached to crowded houses. Parley published a pamphlet, *History of the Late Persecution by the State of Missouri upon the Mormons.*

Elder Mephibosheth Serrine was a leader of the Church in southeastern Michigan, and the early 1840s saw branches in Oakland, Lapeer, Wayne, Livingston, Washtenaw and Lenawee counties. Converts from Jared Carter's efforts of 1833 continued to spread the gospel to most of western Michigan. On Jan. 12, 1844, Elder Serrine reported that in the previous six months, more than 100 converts had left to gather in Nauvoo. Visiting Church authorities created more branches in June 1844. The martyrdom of Joseph and Hyrum Smith on June 27 ended the early period of Church advancement. Many members accepted the leadership of Brigham Young and joined the westward movement. Apostate James J. Strang claimed to be the successor of the Prophet. He was denounced by leaders but attracted a group who later settled on Beaver Island in Lake Michigan before disbanding. Other splinter groups resided in Michigan as well.

In 1876, William M. Palmer served a mission in Michigan. He soon organized several branches despite serious persecution. The Northwestern States Mission was organized in 1878 with Cyrus H. Wheelock as president. Faithful converts migrated steadily to Utah. In 1889, the Northern States Mission was organized and included Michigan. After the turn of the century, the first branch in Michigan was created by German E. Ellsworth in Detroit on April 21, 1915. By 1930, membership in the East Michigan and West Michigan districts, created that year, had a combined membership of 972.

The first meetinghouse in Detroit was erected and dedicated in December 1928. In 1939, 25 missionaries who had been recalled from foreign areas because of World War II formed a chorus that performed public concerts. By 1945, some 7,183 members resided in branches in Detroit (3), Ann Arbor, Battle Creek, Grand Rapids, Jackson, Muskegon, Flint, Lansing, Pontiac, and Saginaw. Michigan's first stake was created Nov. 9, 1952, in Detroit, with later-to-be Michigan Gov. George W. Romney as president. Additional stakes were created in 1962 (Lansing), 1969, (Dearborn) and 1979 (Kalamazoo).

The Great Lakes Mission was created in 1949, and the Indiana-Michigan Mission in 1970. In 1973, the Michigan Mission (changed later to Michigan Lansing) was created. In 1980, Michigan had a membership of 22,607, and in 1990, 28,245.

On July 26, 1995, longtime national leader, Church leader, and prominent Michigan citizen George W. Romney died. He was the governor of Michigan from 1962 until he resigned in 1969 to join President Richard Nixon's cabinet. He served as president of the Detroit (Mich.) Stake and also as a regional representative. He also was a candidate for president of the United States in 1964.

Sources: *The Michigan Mormons,* written and compiled by Hilda Faulkner Browne; "The Saints Come to Michigan," by John and Audrey Cumming, *Michigan History,* March 1965; "The Mormon Era in Detroit," by John Cumming, *Detroit Historical Society Bulletin,* March 1968; *Encyclopedic History of the Church,* by Andrew Jenson; "LDS influence felt in much of Michigan history," by Frank C. Davis, *Church News,* Nov. 15, 1980, and Dec. 11, 1983; *Church News,* July 29, 1995.

Stakes — 8
(Listed alphabetically as of Oct. 1, 1996.)

No.	Name	Organized	First President
North America Northeast Area			
854	Ann Arbor Michigan	14 Aug 1977	Duane Marvin Laws
197	*Bloomfield Hills Michigan ‡Detroit (Michigan, Ohio, Canada)	9 Nov 1952	George W. Romney
940	Grand Blanc Michigan	11 Jun 1978	Trent Pickett Kitley
684	Grand Rapids Michigan	2 Mar 1975	Glenn Goodwin
1091	Kalamazoo Michigan	9 Dec 1979	Donald Lee Lykins
349	*Lansing Michigan ‡Lansing	18 Feb 1962	Sylvan H. Wittwer
469	*Midland Michigan ‡Mid-Michigan	1 Dec 1968	E. Richard Packham
474	*Westland Michigan 14 Aug 1978 *Dearborn Michigan ‡Dearborn (Michigan)	12 Jan 1969	Carl S. Hawkins

Missions — 2
(As of Oct. 1, 1996; shown with historical number. See MISSIONS.)

(164) MICHIGAN DETROIT MISSION
33505 State St., Suite 101
Farmington, MI 48335
Phone: (810) 478-8588

(104) MICHIGAN LANSING MISSION
1400 Abbott, Suite 460
East Lansing, MI 48823
Phone: (517) 351-3430

Minnesota

Year-end 1995: Est. population, 4,631,000; Members, 20,000; Stakes, 5; Wards, 35; Branches, 18; Missions, 1; Percent LDS, 0.6, or one person in 231.

In 1854, a Mormon elder, Ralph Joung, "preached at Spring Grove," according to a Minnesota county newspaper.

In 1857, missionaries baptized Minnesota settler Robert Pope and his wife, Sarah Leduc Pope, along with Edwin Theodore Pope and his wife, whose name was not recorded, in Morristown in southern Minnesota. These converts soon "gathered" to Utah.

The next missionary to Minnesota was Elder Silas Hoyt, who labored in Minnesota in

September 1868. In 1870, Ariah C. Brower and Eli Whipple worked in Minnesota and adjoining states. They were received with enthusiasm, but gained few converts. In 1875, Elder Bengt P. Wulffenstein, who spoke Swedish, German and Danish, began a systematic and successful effort to teach the many Scandinavians who had settled in Minnesota.

In 1875, Elder Wulffenstein organized Minnesota's first branch, a small group of converts in Freeborn County. By 1877, five more branches were organized, and in February 1882, mission history records indicate that Minnesota had 74 members. The town of Monticello became a center for the work as Deborah Houghton Riggs, the wife of its founder, Ashley C. Riggs, joined the Church.

Work in Minnesota was incorporated into the Northwestern States Mission in 1878, when nine missionaries served in this state. The missionaries located Mormons or those who had heard the gospel preached in their homeland. Missionaries were often the target of eggs, stones and threats as they made arduous journeys across the sparsely populated region. With few exceptions, their efforts were rewarded only with a handful of converts. During this period, several small companies of members immigrated to Utah from Minnesota, the largest being a party of 70 from Monticello.

In 1886, some 227 members belonged to the Minnesota Conference, then including Wisconsin, the Dakotas and Iowa.

Missionary work halted from 1891 until 1896. However, following the Manifesto of 1890, public opinion began to improve as people began to understand the Mormons had been maligned. In 1899, a conference was attended by Apostle Heber J. Grant. By the turn of the century most Minnesota converts had left for Zion. The handful of members who remained worked as a very small minority to build a Mormon presence.

Minnesota Conference headquarters were established in Minneapolis in 1900. A Sunday School was organized May 20, 1900, in Minneapolis. Another was organized in St. Paul on Aug. 5. The Sunday Schools were combined in 1902, and the new unit had an average attendance of 50. Mission Pres. German E. Ellsworth served from 1904-1919, and under his leadership the mission made steady progress. More Sunday Schools were started, and branches organized and divided. The first Church-owned building in Minnesota was purchased May 9, 1914, for the St. Paul Branch, and a baptismal font installed in its basement was used for baptismal services for converts from the entire state.

By 1919, membership had increased to 4,000 in 30 branches, and possibly hundreds of others migrating west. A large meetinghouse was erected and dedicated in 1924. By 1930, there were three districts in the state: the North, South and Lake districts. Over the next 20 years, many branches were established. The Minnesota Stake was organized Nov. 29, 1960, with six wards and five branches, and a membership of 2,600. By 1970, its membership had reached 4,800. The Minnesota-Manitoba Mission was created in 1970, and the Minnesota-Wisconsin Mission in 1973. When the Minnesota Stake was changed to the Minneapolis Minnesota Stake in 1974, it had 4,936 members. In 1976, the St. Paul Stake was created, and the same year the Minnesota Minneapolis Mission was created. Membership in 1980 was 11,755, and in 1990, 16,741.

Sources: *Encyclopedic History of the Church*, by Andrew Jenson; *Minnesota Mormons, a History of the Minneapolis Minnesota Stake*, by Fayone B. Willes; The Church in Minnesota, unpublished, no author listed; *Mormon Missionaries and Minnesota Scandinavians*, by Kenneth O. Bjork, *Minnesota History*, published by the Minnesota Historical Society; *Church News*, Dec. 3, 1960.

Stakes — 6
(Listed alphabetically as of Oct. 1, 1996.)

No.	Name	Organized	First President
	North America Central Area		
1562	Anoka Minnesota	20 Oct 1985	Lyle T Cottle
2192	Burnsville Minnesota	28 Apr 1996	Matthew Artell Smith
1939	Duluth Minnesota	9 May 1993	John G. Hancock
317	*Minneapolis Minnesota		
	‡Minnesota (Minn., Wis.)	29 Nov 1960	Delbert F. Wright
910	Rochester Minnesota	30 Apr 1978	Lee McNeal Johnson
744	Saint Paul Minnesota	15 Feb 1976	Thomas Albert Holt

Mission — 1
(As of Oct. 1, 1996; shown with historical number. See MISSIONS.)

Mississippi

Year-end 1995: Est. population, 2,710,000; Members, 15,000; Stakes, 4; Wards, 25; Branches, 13; Missions, 1; Percent LDS, 0.5, or one person in 180.

Missionary work in Mississippi evidently began when Elder John D. Hunter and Benjamin L. Clapp arrived in Tishomingo County in 1839. They baptized 13 people in Tishomingo County. In 1840, Elder Norvel M. Head said he visited a branch in the same county. Elders Daniel Tyler and R. D. Sheldon began work in Copiah, Miss., and baptized five people in 1841. A group of between 80 and 90 members in 40 wagons, escaping persecution, arrived in Nauvoo from Mississippi in April 1842. A small branch was organized in Monroe County in 1843, where other converts, including plantation owner James M. Flake were converted and baptized by Elder Clapp. Several branches were created and membership continued to increase.

In 1846, a company of emigrants left Monroe County expecting to join the main body of Saints in the Rocky Mountains. Instead, they became the first group of Mormons to cross the plains, wintering with fur trappers in Pueblo, Colo., that year. These members made significant contributions. They were the first to establish a religious colony in the West since the Spanish priests of 1769. They later founded the second colony in Utah at Cottonwood (once called the Mississippi Ward) and Holladay (named after a Mississippian), helped found San Bernardino, Calif., and years later, other colonies along the Little Colorado in Arizona. (Snowflake, Ariz., was originally named Snow Flake after Erastus Snow and James M. Flake.) African-American servants of these members — Green Flake, Oscar and Mark — were in the first group that entered the Salt Lake Valley. One of the children of these early pioneers from Mississippi was Alice Rowan, who taught school in Riverside, Calif., among the first African-American women to teach at a public school in the nation.

Missionary work was said to continue in Mississippi until the Civil War. It resumed in the 1870s. In 1880, enemies of the Church tried but failed to enlist the governor of Mississippi in forcing missionaries to leave the state.

A colony of African-American converts may have created a township in 1891 called Republican Square near the Mississippi Gulf Coast, but all traces of this community subsequently vanished.

Persecution increased and missionaries were often abused. Elder Alma P. Richards was murdered in 1888, though a Church investigation committee concluded the motive likely was robbery, not religious persecution.

The U.S. Census listed 123 members in Mississippi in 1890. By 1906, that number had increased to 1,018.

A meetinghouse in Quitman, Miss., was completed in 1908, and the branch had 11 members but grew in 10 years to 30 members.

By 1930, the Mississippi Conference had a membership of 2,170 in the Darburn and Red Star branches and Bay St. Louis, Meadville, Raytown, Red Hill, Sarah and Smithville Sunday Schools. New buildings were completed for the Senatobia, McNeill and Jackson branches in 1943, and for Biloxi in 1954.

The first two stakes in Mississippi were created in 1965. The first, Jackson, had a membership of 2,245 members in two Jackson wards, Meridian, Natchez, Columbus, Vicksburg and Red Star wards and the Greenville Branch. The second in Biloxi included 2,515 members in the Biloxi, Columbia, Gulfport, Hattiesburg, Liberty, and Pascagoula wards and the Bayou La Croix, Darbun, Laurel, McNiell, Sant Hill and Seminary branches.

Membership grew slowly, reaching 6,527 in 1970 and 10,403 in 1980 and 13,000 in 1990. The Kosciusko Branch, Jackson Mississippi Stake, won the "best religious entry" award in the local Christmas parade in Kosciusko, Miss., in 1993 and 1994. In May 1996, members in Monroe County, Miss., honored early pioneers from Mississippi, known as the Mississippi Saints, by dedicating a monument at Mormon Springs where many of the early converts were baptized.

Sources: *Encyclopedic History of the Church,* by Andrew Jenson; "Anniversary Noted for Old Backwoods Chapel," *Church News,* Aug. 9, 1958; *History of the Southern States Mission 1831-1861,* by LaMar C. Berrett, BYU thesis, July 1960; "Gulf States Get New Stake," *Church News,* May 8, 1965 and July 3, 1965; *A Brief History of the Southern States Mission for One Hundred Years, 1830-1930,* by DeVon H. Nish, a BYU paper, August 1966;

"Orthodoxy Versus Nonconformity: The Mormon Experience in Tennessee and Mississippi, 1875-1905," a University of Chicago paper by Mary Elizabeth Stovall, March 1976; "Mississippi Mormons," by Leonard Arrington, *Ensign*, June 1977; "Branch wins parade honor for second consecutive year," *Church News*, Dec. 24, 1994; "Mississippi Saints headed west in 1846," *Church News*, July 13, 1996.

Stakes — 4

(Listed alphabetically as of Oct. 1, 1996.)

No.	Name	Organized	First President
North America Southeast Area			
1364	Gulfport Mississippi	10 Oct 1982	John Sibbald Scott II
408	*Hattiesburg Mississippi ‡Hattiesburg	27 Jun 1965	Edwin White
404	*Jackson Mississippi ‡Jackson	2 May 1965	Neil J. Ferrell
1801	Tupelo Mississippi	9 Jun 1991	Thomas Evan Nebeker

Mission — 1

(As of Oct. 1, 1996; shown with historical number. See MISSIONS.)

(171) MISSISSIPPI JACKSON MISSION
5200 Keele St.
Jackson, MS 39206
Phone: (601) 362-1518

Missouri

Year-end 1995: Est. population, 5,262,000; Members, 43,000; Stakes, 11; Wards, 78; Branches, 32; Missions, 2; Temples, 1 under construction; Percent LDS, 0.8, or one person in 122.

Oliver Cowdery, Parley P. Pratt, Peter Whitmer Jr. and Ziba Peterson, joined by Frederick G. Williams, a convert from their stopover in Ohio, arrived in Missouri on Jan. 13, 1831, and preached to Delaware and Shawnee Indians in the adjacent Indian Territory. Indian agents soon asked them to leave. The same year, Joseph Smith received a revelation indicating that Independence, Jackson County, Mo., was to be the "New Jerusalem," and gathering site for the Saints.

This revelation led to an immediate influx of members, some of whom were ill-prepared for settling and less obedient to Church instructions. This influx laid the groundwork for what became, in essence, a battle for turf between old settlers and Mormon colonists with their strikingly different economic, political, and spiritual values. By June 1833, 1,200 members in 12 branches lived in Jackson County. On July 30, 1833, nearly 500 Missourians ordered Mormons from Jackson County. Church leaders tried to seek protection through the courts but failed. Mormons seeking to defend themselves were disarmed, and mobs drove them out.

In 1834, Joseph Smith and a group of 150-200 armed men, called Zion's Camp, arrived to protect the members. A violent storm prevented the confrontation and undoubtedly preserved the group that was subsequently disbanded at the Prophet's direction.

The Jackson County LDS refugees found safety in adjacent Clay County for two years and then, amid new adversity, moved to western, uninhabited Caldwell and Daviess counties. By 1838, Far West, the principal settlement in Caldwell County, became Church headquarters and had more than 100 homes, hotels, a printing house and a school. A temple site was dedicated here and cornerstones placed on July 4, 1838. Joseph F. Smith, president of the Church from 1901-18, was born in Far West in 1838.

It was revealed to Joseph Smith that Adam-ondi-Ahman, in Daviess County, was where Adam had lived. Twenty revelations of the Doctrine and Covenants were received in Missouri.

Apostasy fueled internal problems in 1838. Several prominent leaders were excommunicated, and unwise rhetoric against them incited Missourians again against the Church.

Violence erupted on Aug. 6, 1838, when Mormons were prevented from voting at Gallatin, Mo. Mob raids began and Mormons organized, armed themselves, and fought against the attacks as their county charter allowed. Apostle David W. Patten, who was in line to be president of the Church after Joseph Smith, was killed Oct. 25. Hearing exaggerated reports of Mormon armies, Missouri Gov. Lilburn W. Boggs, who refused to aid the Mormons or quell violence, signed the infamous order on Oct. 27 to drive out or exterminate the Mormons. Seventeen men and boys were killed at Haun's Mill on Oct. 30 by the unauthorized Livingston County Militia. On Oct. 31, Joseph Smith was arrested and the next day sentenced to death. Brig. Gen. A.W. Doniphan refused to carry out the order. On Nov. 2, the militia plundered Far West and drove out the Saints. The 12,000-15,000 LDS refugees in Missouri settled on the Mississippi River in Illinois where they established Nauvoo.

During this period, members found shelter in the more tolerant city of St. Louis, where citizens once raised funds for their aid. In 1844, a branch was started in St. Louis by LDS refugees. Shiploads of LDS immigrants used St. Louis as a port of debarkation. After the exodus from Nauvoo in 1846, more members came to St. Louis. By 1849, a district was formed with 3,000-4,000 members. The St. Louis Stake was organized in 1854. Immigrants earned money and helped build the city as they awaited overland passage. Many pioneer supplies were imported to Utah through St. Louis. The so-called "Utah War" of 1857 brought the end of the St. Louis Stake when Brigham Young called all members to Utah.

With the members gone, little missionary work occurred in Missouri until later in the century. The state became part of the Northern States Mission and in 1900 was transferred to the Southwestern States Mission, which became the Central States Mission in 1904. A branch in St. Louis was reorganized in 1898, and the Church entered an exhibit in the 1904 World's Fair at St. Louis. In 1915, as a missionary, Elder Spencer W. Kimball became president of the district and helped purchase a meetinghouse.

Mission headquarters moved to Independence in 1907 and a meetinghouse was erected in 1913.

By 1930, eight branches functioned at Independence, Joplin, Kansas City, St. Louis, Sedalia, St. Joseph, Springfield and Webb City.

The first modern stake in Missouri was the Kansas City (Missouri) Stake, created Oct. 21, 1956, and it included one Kansas City ward, the Independence Ward, Liberty Ward, St. Joseph Ward, Rock Hill Branch, and Albany and Chillicothe Sunday Schools.

The St. Louis Stake was organized June 1, 1958, and additional stakes followed in the 1970s. On June 25, 1976, Gov. Christopher S. Bond signed an executive order rescinding the extermination order issued in 1838 by Gov. Lilburn W. Boggs.

The Missouri St. Louis Mission was created in 1977. Membership in Missouri in 1974 was 13,796, in 1980, 25,243 and in 1990, 35,084. On Dec. 29, 1990, the First Presidency announced plans for a temple in St. Louis.

As the temple was constructed, community leaders enthusiastically supported the effort. The temple's location at the intersection of two major freeways raised awareness of the Church.

President Gordon B. Hinckley visited St. Louis in April 1995 to conduct his first regional conference since becoming Church president. He viewed the progress of the temple during his visit.

In Independence, local members took part in inter-faith activities and in recent years presented an annual Church pageant in June. The visit of the Tabernacle Choir in 1992, performing in the RLDS Church's Auditorium, helped solidify friendships as well.

Sources: *Encyclopedic History of the Church,* by Andrew Jenson; "Martin V. Witbeck, Former Utahn, Called to Preside over New Unit," *Church News,* Oct. 27, 1956; *Encyclopedia of Mormonism,* edited by Daniel H. Ludlow; "Missouri's Impact on the Church," by Max H Parkin, *Ensign,* April 1979; "Saints in Independence," by Janet Brigham, *Ensign,* June 1979; "The Saints in Saint Louis," by Violet Kimball, *Ensign,* March 1988; "Missouri Past Forgotten, Church Gains," by Hal Knight, *Church News,* Oct. 20, 1979; "Growth continues in river port where Church thrived in 1850s," by John L. Hart, *Church News,* Jan. 20, 1990; *Church News,* Nov. 6, 1993; *Church News,* Jan. 8, 1994; "Pres. Hinckley Greets Saints in St. Louis," *Church News,* April 22, 1995.

Stakes — 11

(Listed alphabetically by area as of Oct. 1, 1996.)

No.	Name	Organized	First President
	North America Central Area — 8		
1563	Cape Girardeau Missouri	20 Oct 1985	David E. Payne
511	*Columbia Missouri		
	‡Columbia	19 Apr 1970	Samuel D. Richards
544	*Independence Missouri		

	‡Independence	25 Mar 1971	Melvin James Bennion
234	*Kansas City Missouri		
	‡Kansas City		
	(Missouri, Kansas)	21 Oct 1956	Martin V. Witbeck
1071	Liberty Missouri	14 Oct 1979	Dell Earl Johnsen
265	St. Louis (Missouri, Illinois)	1 Jun 1958	Roy W. Oscarson
	*St. Louis Missouri		
1634	St. Louis Missouri North	15 Mar 1987	Neal C. Lewis
1118	St. Louis Missouri South	16 Mar 1980	Verner Lorenzo Stromberg Jr.

North America Southwest Area — 2

859	Joplin Missouri	28 Aug 1977	Kenneth Rae Martin
610	*Springfield Missouri		
	‡Ozark	29 Apr 1973	Carroll S. Claybrook
2052	Springfield Missouri South	21 May 1995	Robert Charles Brusman

Discontinued

2	Clay-Caldwell	3 Jul 1834	David Whitmer
3	Adam-Ondi-Ahman	28 Jun 1838	John Smith
6a	St. Louis	4 Nov 1854	Milo Andrus
	Reinstated as 265		

Missions — 2

(As of Oct. 1, 1996; shown with historical number. See MISSIONS.)

(14b) MISSOURI INDEPENDENCE MISSION
517 West Walnut
Independence, MO 64050
Phone: (816) 252-6050

(153) MISSOURI ST. LOUIS MISSION
745 Craig Road, Suite 306
Creve Coeur, MO 63141
Phone: (314) 872-8510

Montana

Year-end 1995: Est. population, 877,000; Members, 39,000; Stakes, 10; Wards, 64; Branches, 44; Missions, 1; Districts, 1; Temples, 1 announced; Percent LDS, 4.4, or one person in 22.

The Church's Fort Lemhi settlement on the Salmon River in Idaho lasted only from 1855 to 1858, but it familiarized various members with the trail to Montana that became an important trading route, known as the Montana Trail, for members following the Montana gold rush of the 1860s.

A Mormon, E.W. Van Etten, traded with Flathead Indians in the late 1850s, and a Mormon woman, Minnie Miller, wife of Henry G. Miller, was the first white woman to live in western Montana. When Col. Albert Sidney Johnston's army approached Utah in 1857, some members left Utah and moved to Montana.

After the gold discovery and subsequent gold rush, Mormon freighters hauled food and goods along the Montana Trail for substantial profit. The overland railway was completed in 1869 and afterward a Utah company was formed by Mormon leaders that constructed a narrow gauge railway from Ogden, Utah, to Butte and the Northern Pacific Railway at Garrison, Mont., in 1884.

Although some members came to Montana in the gold rush and stayed, no Church units were organized. Evidently, all of these members fell away. In 1896, the Montana Mission was organized and efforts were made to find those members who had moved to Montana earlier. However, Church leaders did not encourage members to go to Montana to live.

While exploring for a site for a settlement in the mid-1880s, Charles Ora Card traveled through Montana. He met Duncun McDonald, a Montana explorer who told him of the vast prairies east of the Rocky Mountains in Canada. His colonists often purchased supplies from Montana, a commerce that continues today. Two areas in Montana were once considered for settlements by the Saints: northern Montana, and the valleys west of the mountains in Montana and British Columbia.

Phineus Tempest was called as president of the mission. He soon organized a branch in Lima. On Oct. 27, 1897, Pres. Tempest's successor, Franklin S. Bramwell, and three missionaries met with Montana Gov. John E. Rickards and received the promise of religious freedom. Four converts were baptized near Gregson Springs on March 31, 1897. A meeting of 75 people was held in Anaconda, and a gathering of 300 met in Butte later that spring. The mission was dissolved into the Northwestern States Mission in 1898, after 71 converts had been baptized and the way paved for the establishment of the Church.

By 1930, Church organization had grown to 10 branches and a membership of 1,181 with meetinghouses in Anaconda, Butte, Allendale, Dillon, Great Falls and Sun River. Membership increased to 5,210 in 1940 and 6,416 in 1950.

Montana's first stake was created in Butte on June 28, 1953, and the first wards were created in Butte, Anaconda, Dillon, Bozeman, and Helena. Stake population was about 3,500.

Stakes were also created June 16, 1957, in Great Falls and Missoula. The Great Falls Stake had about 2,500 members and the Missoula Stake had 3,085 members. At that time, Montana had 14,223 members. That number increased to 23,890 in 1960. In 1980, membership was 30,784 and in 1990, 34,401.

In more recent years, Church members in Montana have been active in community affairs. "Project Good Turn" began in the late 1980s as an annual event led by LDS Scouts and Scouters in Montana to clean up the state's highways.

A major event occurred in August 1996 with the announcement that the Church's 64th operating temple would be built in Billings.

Sources: *Mormonism in Montana,* thesis in 1969 at Montana State University by Don Cornelius; *Encyclopedic History of the Church,* by Andrew Jenson; *Church News,* Feb. 2, 1991, p. 7 and, Aug. 31, 1996, p. 3; correspondence from Dean Snelling, Oct. 3, 1996.

Stakes — 10
(Listed alphabetically as of Oct. 1, 1996.)

No.	Name	Organized	First President
North America Central Area			
369	*Billings Montana		
	‡Billings (Montana, Wyoming)	10 Feb 1963	Howard C. Anderson
849	Billings Montana East	12 Jun 1977	Wynn J. Ferrell
1066	Bozeman Montana	16 Sep 1979	Frank Wilbert Coil
208	*Butte Montana		
	‡Butte	28 Jun 1953	Edgar T. Henderson
244	*Great Falls Montana		
	‡Great Falls	16 Jun 1957	Victor Bowen
976	Great Falls Montana East	5 Nov 1978	Howard Merle Hennebry
464	*Helena Montana		
	‡Helena	8 Sep 1968	Ronald Rex Dalley
535	*Kalispell Montana		
	‡Kalispell	20 Nov 1970	Roy K. Deming
243	*Missoula Montana		
	‡Missoula	16 Jun 1957	Grant K. Patten
1074	Stevensville Montana	21 Oct 1979	Robert H. Sangster

Mission — 1
(As of Oct. 1, 1996; shown with historical number. See MISSIONS.)

(43a) MONTANA BILLINGS MISSION
1848 Rimrock Road
Billings, MT 59102
Phone: (406) 245-6146

Nebraska

Year-end 1995: Est. population, 1,643,000; Members, 15,000; Stakes, 4; Wards, 25; Branches, 26; Missions, 1; Percent LDS, 0.9, or one person in 109.

After the Saints were driven from Nauvoo, Ill., in February 1846, they carefully skirted the entire state of Missouri and traveled 300 miles before establishing a headquarters in Indian country west of the Missouri River. They negotiated with the Indians and then built the city of Winter Quarters. Eventually, some 1,000 homes were constructed for a population of 11,800. Though most of the homes were log cabins and dugouts, the city was as carefully laid out as the many Mormon colonies later founded.

The Saints created a city government, schools, ferries, bridges, developed trades — especially those to make and outfit wagons — established a mail service, and took time for dances and concerts. Many trades were plied en route to Winter Quarters. A stockade and water-powered grist mill were added later. Crops were planted.

Before the lead company had crossed the river into Nebraska, however, the mustering of 500 men for the Mormon Battalion was completed. The departure of 500 able men in 1846 led to the advance company of pioneers waiting an extra year in Winter Quarters to prepare for the great overland journey.

It was from Winter Quarters that the first pioneer train under Brigham Young left on April 5, 1847. Nine other trains followed that year.

When Brigham Young returned from Utah in October, he received word that the Indian agent wanted the members off the Indian territory. So in the spring of 1848 the remaining members crossed back over the Missouri River and founded Kanesville in Iowa. They left Winter Quarters as a ghost settlement, which was burned in a prairie fire in the 1850s.

In 1854, the Florence Land Company, which included some Mormons, was organized to occupy the old Winter Quarters site, and from 1856 to 1864 Florence became an important Mormon pioneer staging area. An estimated 60,000 Mormon pioneers crossed the plains before the transcontinental railroad was completed in 1869. Many were outfitted in Florence, including the famous handcart companies of 1856-60. Today, Florence is part of greater Omaha. Only the pioneer cemetery and a gristmill remain from the Winter Quarters era.

While preparing to go west, Mormon travelers traded labor for food and helped establish Council Bluffs, Glenwood, Macedonia, Honey Creek and about 50 other towns. In the 1850s, Brigham Young hoped to establish settlements along the trail and started Genoa, or the "Nebraska Mission," in May 1857. Several other colonies were started. The so-called "Utah War" led to the migration west of most of these settlers, although those in Genoa remained until Indian agents forced them from the land in 1859.

Missionary work evidently started again in Nebraska in 1877 when Ferdinand F. Hintze and Anders Frandsen baptized 11 people and created a branch in Fremont, Dodge County.

The area was included in the Northwestern States Mission (later the Northern States Mission) until it became part of the Colorado Mission (later Western States Mission) in 1900. At this time the Omaha and Lincoln branches had been organized. A conference of missionaries was held April 21, 1901, for those laboring in Nebraska. In 1916, about 40 people attended a Sunday School in Lincoln. In 1921, a conference numbering from 75 to 200 was "the largest ever held by missionaries of this conference." Some 23 people were baptized under the direction of Elder Amasa Lyman. Progress was also made in Columbus, despite some opposition.

In 1930, the first meetinghouse had been erected, and districts functioned in East and West Nebraska with a total of 1,052 members. Nebraska's first stake was organized in Omaha, called Winter Quarters, on Dec. 11, 1960, with the Omaha 1st and 2nd wards, Bellevue and Lincoln wards in Nebraska. The Fremont, Grand Island, Kearney and Hastings branches were included in the stake. Membership in Nebraska in 1980 was 8,406, increasing in 1990 to 13,089, probably more than the number who ever lived at Winter Quarters at any one time.

Members in Nebraska have continued to educate their communities on the significance of historical sites. A new Church visitors center is being constructed at Historic Winter Quarters with completion expected in April 1997. In cooperation with state governments in Iowa and Nebraska and the city of Omaha, signs have been installed on interstate highways directing travelers to the Mormon Trail Center there. Plans were in place in 1996 for wagon trains to traverse the state in 1997, commemorating the sesquicentennial of the 1847 trek of the Saints to the Salt Lake Valley.

Sources: *Liahona, The Elder's Journal,* June 21, 1921; *Encyclopedic History of the Church,* by Andrew Jenson; "Winter Quarters, Nebraska," by E. Widtsoe Shumway, *Nebraska History,* June, 1954; "Proposed New Stake has Historic Setting," *Church News,* Dec. 10, 1960 and Dec. 17, 1960; "After Winter Quarters and Council Bluffs: The Mormons in Nebraska Territory, 1854-1867," by Michael W. Homer, *Nebraska History,* Winter 1984; "Mormons, Nebraska, and the Way West," by A. R. Mortensen, *Nebraska History,* Dec. 1965; *Mormons at the Missouri,* 1846-1852, by Richard E. Bennett, University of Oklahoma Press, 1987; "Reflections on Winter Quarters," by Gail Geo. Holmes, unpublished; "Seven-year epic flowed along Missouri River with tragedy, triumph," by Gail Geo. Holmes, *Church News,* July 18, 1992; "New Signs Draw Visitors to Trail Center," *Church News,* July 20, 1996.

Stakes — 4
(Listed alphabetically as of Oct. 1, 1996.)

No.	Name	Organized	First President
North America Central Area			
1803	Kearney Nebraska	16 Jun 1991	Arthur Haymore Taylor

663	*Lincoln Nebraska 2 Nov 1986		
	‡Bellevue Nebraska	27 Oct 1974	Leonard Leroy Gregory
318	*Omaha Nebraska		
	‡Winter Quarters (Nebraska, Iowa)	11 Dec 1960	William D. Hardy
1614	Papillion Nebraska	2 Nov 1986	Wayne Leon Mangelson

Mission — 1

(As of Oct. 1, 1996; shown with historical number. See MISSIONS.)

(289) NEBRASKA OMAHA MISSION
11930 Arbor Street, Suite 203
Omaha, NE 68144-2998
Phone: (402) 691-0882

Nevada

Year-end 1995: Est. population, 1,564,000; Members, 124,000; Stakes, 30; Wards, 204; Branches, 31; Missions, 1; Temples, 1; Percent LDS, 7.9, or one person in 12.

Samuel Brannan and his party became the first Latter-day Saints to set foot in Nevada as they crossed from the West Coast to Utah in the spring of 1847 to report the arrival by ship of the Brannan party in San Francisco.

Three years later, after the discovery of gold in California, 13 members joined 65 non-LDS overlanders and crossed Nevada from Utah toward California. Seven men dropped out of the party near what is now Genoa and founded a trading post. These men included Abner Blackburn, a former member of the Mormon Battalion who had found a little gold near the area on an earlier trip through. They traded profitably during the summer but sold out and returned to Utah. A year later, John Reece came with others and provisions in 13 wagons and established a trading post that became known as Mormon Station, located two miles south of the original trading post. The Reece station became a profitable trading post and site of Nevada's first colony, Genoa. Member and non-member settlers soon followed. Apostle Orson Hyde became president of the Carson Valley Stake, organized in 1856. Elder Hyde hoped to maintain the station for the assistance of immigrants coming via the West Coast, and did much to establish it. The LDS presence in the promising colony ended and the stake was dissolved when the settlers were recalled at the approach of Johnston's army to Salt Lake City.

In 1855, the same time colonists were sent to Genoa, a group of 30 men was sent to establish an Indian mission at the Meadows in southern Nevada at what is now Las Vegas. The party, under the direction of William Bringhurst, arrived June 15, 1855, and soon built a fort. They found farming difficult in the hot region, but discovered a lead mine and made friendships with the many Indians who lived nearby and on the Muddy River, a fertile area in a valley to the northwest.

Another mission was sent to mine the lead, which was partly silver, and years later became a prosperous silver mine. This metal, melted into bullets by the settlers, was the basis for a legend that Mormons used silver bullets. Both missions were recalled at the advance of Johnston's army. The abandoned fort was then named Fort Baker and served as an uninhabited but strategic outpost during the Civil War. It later became a ranch headquarters and foundation for Las Vegas, Nevada's largest city.

On May 6, 1864, colonists from St. George under the direction of Francis C. Lee arrived at what is now Panaca, a site earlier considered an alternative Church place of settlement should the Saints be driven from Salt Lake City by Johnston's army. The Lee party made a prosperous settlement, the oldest continuous Mormon colony in the state. In December 1864, Anson Call and a group established Call's landing on the Colorado River, about 12 miles above the present Hoover Dam. This settlement briefly became an important inland dock for boats that navigated the Colorado River from the Pacific Ocean with goods for Utah settlers and the U.S. Army in Arizona. The settlement continued until 1867.

The Muddy River area north of Las Vegas, known to the Church ever since the Bringhurst mission to the Meadows in 1855, was settled, beginning May 22, 1865, under the direction of Joseph Warren Foote. The long growing season and fertile land helped the settlers survive the difficulties of that frontier. Several colonies began but were eventually abandoned when the land became part of Nevada, and Nevada officials demanded back taxes. The area was re-settled in the 1880s and the Overton Branch was reorganized in 1883. Overton became headquarters of Nevada's first permanent stake, the Moapa Stake, in 1912. In 1877, Bunkerville was founded where families practiced the United Order for a time.

In 1897, the government offered the Church 15,000 acres in the White Pine area in remuneration for Church livestock that the government confiscated and lost following the 1882 Edmunds Act. Here, the present-day communities of Lund and Preston were founded.

Completion of the railroad from Salt Lake to Los Angeles in 1905 began steady growth in Nevada. The first Sunday School in Las Vegas was organized by Newell Leavitt in 1914 and became a ward in 1925. In the 1920s many Utahns moved to Nevada in search of better economic conditions. Membership in the state increased from 2,328 in 1920, to 5,319 in 1930 and to 9,139 by 1940.

Construction of the Hoover Dam in the 1940s brought an influx of people, and that same decade gaming, legalized in 1931, was widely promoted. Members did not support the move, but, as a minority, avoided confrontation. The Las Vegas Stake was created in 1954.

Substantial membership also grew in the Humboldt (Elko) and Ely areas, though these communities were not originally founded by Mormons. Eastern Nevada reflects a great deal of Utah culture. Members have increasingly greater strength today in this area where colonization efforts failed during Brigham Young's day. Members also gathered in western Nevada in Reno and nearby Sparks. Growth in "the Silver State" has been steady. The Las Vegas Nevada Temple was dedicated in 1989 as "an oasis of peace and light." On Nov. 14, 1993, a regional welfare complex was dedicated near the site of the original fort. The new facilities comprised 9,000 square feet of area for services to help care for the growing southern Nevada membership.

Nevada membership in 1950 was 14,223; in 1960, 23,890; in 1970, 44,282; in 1980, 71,462; and in 1990, 110,060.

Sources: *Encyclopedic History of the Church,* by Andrew Jenson; "The Mormons in Nevada: an Historical Portrait," by Leonard J. Arrington, *Las Vegas Sun; The Old Fort,* compiled by the Daughters of the Utah Pioneers; History of the Las Vegas First Ward, compiled by Marion B. Earl; "Panaca: Mormon Outpost Among Mining Camps, The Afterlife of St. Mary's County; or, Utah's Penumbra in Eastern Nevada," by James W. Hulse, *Utah Historical Quarterly,* Vol. 55, (1987); "Regional Welfare Center with multiple facilities dedicated in Las Vegas," by Ashley Hall, *Church News,* Nov. 20, 1993.

Stakes — 30
(Listed alphabetically as of Oct. 1, 1996.)

No.	Name	Organized	First President
	North America Southeast Area		
906	Carson City Nevada	9 Apr 1978	Edgar Gilbert Carlson
143	*Elko Nevada East 19 Mar 1995		
	*Elko Nevada		
	‡Humboldt	31 May 1942	Rodney S. Williams
2038	Elko Nevada West	19 Mar 1995	Kurt Glenn Alleman
96	*Ely Nevada		
	‡Nevada	19 Sep 1926	Carl K. Conrad
500	*Fallon Nevada		
	‡Fallon	18 Jan 1970	G. Verl Hendrix
1650	Fallon Nevada South	30 Aug 1987	Robert Floyd Weed
605	*Henderson Nevada Black Mountain 10 Mar 1992		
	*Henderson Nevada West		
	‡Lake Mead West	11 Mar 1973	Joseph Dee Reese
228	Henderson Nevada Lake Mead 2 Mar 1993		
	*Henderson Nevada		
	‡Lake Mead		
	(Nevada, Arizona, Calif.)	19 Aug 1956	James I. Gibson
216	*Las Vegas Nevada		
	‡Las Vegas	10 Oct 1954	Thomas Gay Meyers
451	*Las Vegas Nevada Central		
	‡Las Vegas Central	18 Feb 1968	Samuel M. Davis
915	Las Vegas Nevada East	30 Apr 1978	Kendall E. Jones
1519	Las Vegas Nevada Green Valley	3 Mar 1985	Roger Lee Hunt
1542	Las Vegas Nevada Lakes	23 Jun 1985	Dennis E. Simmons
1775	Las Vegas Nevada Lone Mountain	4 Nov 1990	Scott Keith Higginson
1406	*Las Vegas Meadows 4 Nov 1990		
	‡Las Vegas Nevada West	20 Mar 1983	Terry Dale Rogers

401	*Las Vegas Nevada Paradise	30 Apr 1978	
	*Las Vegas Nevada East		
	‡Las Vegas East	24 Jan 1965	Rulon A. Earl
855	Las Vegas Nevada Redrock	14 Aug 1977	E. LeGrande Bindrup
1776	Las Vegas Nevada Sandstone	4 Nov 1990	Keith R. Edwards
509	*Las Vegas Nevada South		
	‡Las Vegas South	29 Mar 1970	Erval L. Bindrup
1576	Las Vegas Nevada Sunrise	17 Nov 1985	Norman Wellington Gates
2137	Las Vegas Nevada Tule Springs	3 Dec 1995	Scott Keith Higginson
1777	Las Vegas Nevada Warm Springs	4 Nov 1990	Roger Lee Hunt
64	*Logandale Nevada		
	‡Moapa	9 Jun 1912	Willard L. Jones
1974	Mesquite Nevada	13 Feb 1994	Elwin J. Whipple
308	*North Las Vegas Nevada		
	‡Las Vegas North	6 Nov 1960	William L. Taylor
2019	Panaca Nevada	29 Jan 1995	Robert Jay Matthews
135	*Reno Nevada		
	‡Reno (Nevada, California)	9 Feb 1941	Nathan T. Hurst
635	Reno Nevada North	24 Mar 1974	Wilford Darrell Foote
339	*Sparks Nevada		
	‡Reno North		
	(Nevada, California)	22 Oct 1961	Vern Waldo
1296	Winnemucca Nevada	11 Oct 1981	Kenneth H. Lords

Discontinued

7a	Carson Valley	4 Oct 1856	Orson Hyde
	1858		

Mission — 1

(As of Oct. 1, 1996; shown with historical number. See MISSIONS.)

(127) NEVADA LAS VEGAS MISSION
3910 Pecos-McLeod, Suite B-140
Las Vegas, NV 89121-4304
Phone: (702) 435-0025

New Hampshire

Year-end 1995: Est. population, 1,155,000; Members, 6,800; Stakes, 3; Wards, 12; Branches, 5; Missions, 1; Percent LDS, 0.6, or one person in 170.

Elders Orson Pratt and Lyman E. Johnson arrived in New Hampshire in 1832. During their 26-day stay they baptized 20 people in Bath, N.H., among whom were Hazen Aldrich and Amasa M. Lyman. Later that year Elders Orson Hyde and Samuel H. Smith preached and baptized others. A branch of 15 members was created in July 1833, at Dalton, Coos County. Other branches were created in New Rowley and Lyman, Grafton County. The latter was organized in 1835 by Erastus Snow, then 17 years old. A conference held in Nashua, N.H,. on Dec. 15, 1840, was attended by 55 people.

In 1841, Zadock Parker wrote that the Grafton County Branch continued to meet and that he baptized 13 more people. Some 20-30 members continued to meet in the Gilsum Branch. Eli P. Maginn wrote that he could not "fill from one to twenty of the calls for preaching; there is the greatest excitement in the country."

The Peterborough Branch was created, and by 1843, it had 115 members. Most of the members "removed" to the West following the martyrdom of the Prophet Joseph Smith. In 1856, Solomon Mack headed the membership in New Hampshire. This state was part of the Eastern States Mission, but little work was done during the next few years. The mission was discontinued from 1869 to 1893, when New Hampshire was placed in the New England Conference. The New Hampshire Conference was created in 1909, combined with Maine, 1913-1925, with Vermont, 1925-1928, and in 1928, included in the Canadian Mission. In 1930, the New Hampshire District was headquartered at Nashua, evidently under the direction of a missionary. A branch was organized in Nashua by September 1937, the date of the creation of the New England Mission, but later dissolved. A branch in Concord was created in 1945. In 1951, Sunday Schools were held in Keene and Portsmouth.

Additional branches and Sunday Schools were subsequently organized. In 1970, the Merrimack (Nashua) Stake was created with wards in Keene, Laconia, Manchester, Portsmouth and Concord, with two wards and a branch in Massachusetts and a branch in Maine.

Wards and branches continued to be organized. A branch in Peterborough was formed in 1980. The New Hampshire Manchester Mission was created in 1987. Membership in New Hampshire in 1980 was 4,237, increasing to 6,383 in 1990.

Sources: *Encyclopedic History of the Church,* by Andrew Jenson; Church directories, 1920-1980; "4 new stakes are organized," *Church News,* April 4, 1970; "The gospel net," *Church News,* Nov. 19, 1977; "She helped nurture fledgling Church during life of service," by J Malan Heslop, *Church News,* Jan. 23, 1993.

Stakes — 3

(Listed alphabetically as of Oct. 1, 1996.)

No.	Name	Organized	First President
North America Northeast Area			
1289	Concord New Hampshire	6 Sep 1981	John Tucker Hills
1290	*Exeter New Hampshire		
	‡Portland Maine	6 Sep 1981	J. Barton Seymour
507	*Nashua New Hampshire	9 May 1980	
	*Manchester New Hampshire		
	‡Merrimack	22 Mar 1970	William A. Fresh

Mission — 1

(As of Oct. 1, 1996; shown with historical number. See MISSIONS.)

(195) NEW HAMPSHIRE MANCHESTER
6 Bedford Farms, Suite 610
Bedford, NH 03110-6532
Phone: (603) 622-0429

New Jersey

Year-end 1995: Est. population, 7,966,000; Members, 19,000; Stakes, 4; Wards, 25; Branches, 22; Missions, 2; Percent LDS, 0.2, or one person in 419.

The first missionaries to work in New Jersey were Elders Orson Pratt and Lyman E. Johnson, who arrived in the state in 1832. In 1837, Elders Parley P. Pratt, Benjamin Winchester and Jedediah M. Grant preached and converted people in New Jersey. Elder Winchester preached in Toms River, Ocean County, and baptized 11. By 1840, the branch had 90 members. Several missionaries labored in New Jersey during the next few years. At a conference in New York on Oct. 19, 1842, branches were represented from Patterson, Lodi Print Works, Wacake, Newark and Mead's Basin in New Jersey. Converts often joined the westward movement. For example, William Smith arrived in Illinois from New Jersey on April 22, 1844, with a group of 40 or 50.

Other branches were organized so that by 1848, 21 dotted the New Jersey map. After the exodus from Nauvoo, missionary work slowed. Branches in Toms Corner and Hornerstown existed in 1857. Many others had "gathered" previously.

Little work was performed until well after the trek West. In 1879, B.F. Cummings reported meeting some "old-time Saints" in Perth Amboy, N. J., whom he tried to inspire with the spirit of gathering. Ten members from there migrated to Utah in 1896.

In the 1920s, Ernest L. Wilkinson, who later became president of Brigham Young University, was among the presidents of the Newark Branch. A branch also functioned in Metuchen in the 1930s with Robert H. Daines as branch president. When the New Jersey Stake was created in 1960, it included the Montclair, North Jersey and Short Hills wards and the New Brunswick, Trenton, Monmouth and Lakehurst branches.

By 1974 membership reached 6,799. By 1980, membership was 10,512 in three stakes, and in 1990, reached 16,000. The New Jersey Morristown Mission was created in 1987. Local and state dignitaries took part in the Church's sesquicentennial in New Jersey, which was celebrated in 1988.

Sources: Eastern States Mission history; *Deseret News,* Jan. 7, 1879, and Jan. 8, 1896; *Encyclopedic History of the Church,* by Andrew Jenson; "New Stake Created By Division of New York," *Church News,* March 5, 1960; "Neighborliness: Daines Style," by Orson Scott Card, *Ensign,* April 1977; "New Jersey – Church members celebrate 100 years," *Church News,* Sept. 17,1988.

Stakes — 5

(Listed alphabetically as of Oct. 1, 1996.)

No.	Name	Organized	First President
North America Northeast Area			
1252	Caldwell New Jersey	12 Apr 1981	Weldon Courtney McGregor
1084	*Cherry Hill New Jersey	23 Sep 1986	
	‡Pitman New Jersey	18 Nov 1979	Victor Warren Hammond
429	*East Brunswick New Jersey		
	‡New Jersey Central		
	(N.J., Penn.)	26 Mar 1967	Robert H. Daines
292	*Morristown New Jersey	26 Feb 1976	
	*Caldwell New Jersey		
	‡New Jersey	28 Feb 1960	George H. Mortimer
2235	Scotch Plains New Jersey	15 Sep 1996	Andrew Kim Smith

Mission — 2

(As of Oct. 1, 1996; shown with historical number. See MISSIONS.)

(304a) NEW JERSEY CHERRY HILL MISSION
100 Century Parkway, Suite 160
Mt. Laurel, NJ 08054
Phone (609) 222-1900

(202) NEW JERSEY
 MORRISTOWN MISSION
2 Ridgedale Ave., #210
Cedar Knolls, NJ 07927-1100
Phone: (201) 326-9494

New Mexico

Year-end 1995: Est. population, 1,700,000; Members, 54,000; Stakes, 12; Wards, 82; Branches, 34; Missions, 1; Percent LDS, 3.1, or one person in 31.

In 1831, just one year after the organization of the Church, Oliver Cowdery preached to Indians in Missouri and, from that experience, reported to Joseph Smith of a civilized "Navashoes" (Navajo) tribe living 300 miles west of Santa Fe. Leaders once discussed sending a delegation to Santa Fe in 1844 to begin exploration for a possible colonization site. In 1846, the Mormon Battalion crossed what is now New Mexico during its historic march to the Pacific Coast from Fort Leavenworth, Kansas. The first part of the battalion arrived in Santa Fe Oct. 9, 1846. At Santa Fe, the battalion sent a detachment of sick to winter in Colorado.

Missionary work among the Indians perhaps began as early as the 1860s when Jacob Hamblin and James S. Brown may have traveled to New Mexico in their labors. Missionaries called to Mexico in 1875 included Ammon M. Tenney and Robert H. Smith. Elders Tenney and Smith found success while laboring among the Zuni Indians on the Little Colorado River in New Mexico, baptizing more than 100. In 1876, a colony was established among the converts. It succeeded until smallpox decimated the Indian converts. Two years later, at an adjacent site, LDS settlers founded what is now Ramah. In 1878, the settlement of Burnham (originally called Fruitland) was founded, followed in 1883 by the community of Luna. The settlers at Luna had clear title to their land, but had trouble with a cattle baron who claimed the area. The San Juan Stake, organized from settlers of the Utah "Hole-in-the-Rock" expedition of 1879-80, included members in the New Mexico settlements of Kirtland and Waterflow. During this period, settlers were troubled by outlaws. A severe drought from 1900-04 seriously affected settlers, but eliminated the outlaws.

Nearly all of the Mormon settlements in New Mexico absorbed some refugees from the Mormon colonies in Mexico during the Mexican Revolution of 1912. Other refugees founded the town of Virden, near the Mexican border.

The Young Stake was created in 1912. Other units in New Mexico were made wards and were included in Arizona and Utah stakes. By 1930, membership in the state was 1,643. The Albuquerque Stake was created in 1957. Membership increased during the 1960s and 1970s. The New Mexico Albuquerque Mission was organized in 1975.

In the 1980s, H. Vern Payne, president of the Santa Fe New Mexico Stake, served as chief justice of the New Mexico Supreme Court. A number of LDS scientists worked at the U.S. research facility at Los Alamos. In September 1996, more than 700 Church members in New Mexico joined with government officials in rededicating a monument built to honor members of the Mormon Battalion, who passed through the state 150 years earlier.

Membership in the state in 1980 was 36,881, and in 1990, 48,000. Members have learned to interact with patience and understanding in a state where three cultures meld — Indian, Hispanic and Anglo.

Sources: *Encyclopedic History of the Church,* by Andrew Jenson; "New Mexico and the Mormons," by Robert Thomas Devitt, *Southwest Heritage,* Vol. 6, Spring 1976; *Do You Remember Luna? 100 Years of Pioneer History,* published by the Luna Ward, Adobe Press, 1983; *Church News,* July 24, 1983.

Stakes — 12
(Listed alphabetically as of Oct. 1, 1996.)

No.	Name	Organized	First President
	North America Southwest Area		
250	*Albuquerque New Mexico		
	‡Albuquerque	27 Oct 1957	William J. Wilson
422	*Albuquerque New Mexico East		
	‡Albuquerque East	25 Sep 1966	George Van Lemmon
1353	Albuquerque New Mexico South	20 Jun 1982	Ivan Gary Waddoups
742	*Bloomfield New Mexico	19 Sep 1982	
	‡Farmington New Mexico East	1 Feb 1976	Marlo L. Webb
63	*Farmington New Mexico		
	‡Young (N.M., Colo.)	21 May 1912	David Halls
687	Gallup New Mexico	16 Mar 1975	Donald C. Tanner
1298	Grants New Mexico	18 Oct 1981	Elbert Leon Roundy
1363	Kirtland New Mexico	19 Sep 1982	John Scot Fishburn
654	Las Cruces New Mexico	25 Aug 1974	Harold A. Daw
816	Roswell New Mexico	13 Mar 1977	J. Allen Levie
1219	Santa Fe New Mexico	4 Jan 1981	H. Vern Payne
1409	Silver City New Mexico	17 Apr 1983	Hal Butler Keeler

Mission — 1
(As of Oct. 1, 1996; shown with historical number. See MISSIONS.)

(128) NEW MEXICO ALBUQUERQUE MISSION
6100 Seagull Lane, N.E., #109
Albuquerque, NM 87109
Phone: (505) 888-0225

New York

Year-end 1995: Est. population, 18,128,000; Members, 49,000; Stakes, 10; Wards, 55; Branches, 89; Missions, 4; Temples, 1 announced; Districts, 4; Percent LDS, 0.2, or one person in 370.

In 1820, Joseph Smith received "the glorious vision which marked the ushering in of the Dispensation of the fullness of Times" in a grove of trees near Palmyra, N.Y. Later, sacred records were received from the Hill Cumorah and were translated in Pennsylvania and Fayette, N.Y., into the Book of Mormon, published by Egbert Grandin at Palmyra in early 1830. On April 6, 1830, the Church was organized at the home of Peter Whitmer Sr. at Fayette, with some 50 people and six official members present. Samuel H. Smith began a missionary journey in late June. By year's end, membership increased to more than 100 with members from Colesville to Canandaigua. Many moved in 1831 to Kirtland, Ohio.

Twenty-five revelations in the Doctrine and Covenants were received in New York.

Among successful later missionaries were Martin and Emer Harris, who baptized 100 people in Chenango Point, N.Y., in 1832. During the next few years, missionaries organized several branches as well as the Freedom and Black River conferences. In July 1837, Parley P. Pratt was the first missionary to preach in New York City, and he organized a branch there. Branches were also organized in Long Island and Brooklyn. While there, he published his *Voice of Warning* pamphlet. In 1839, John P. Greene became the first president of the Eastern States Mission, headquartered in New York City.

A group of LDS emigrants, some 41 people, arrived from England on the ship *Britannia* July 20, 1840, the first of an estimated 50,000 to arrive between 1840 and 1890.

A newspaper, *The Prophet,* began publication in 1844 in New York. On Feb. 4, 1846, Samuel Brannan headed a company of Saints aboard the sailing ship *Brooklyn* that sailed from New York harbor to California. They also carried the press to California that was formerly used to print *The Prophet. The Mormon,* a weekly newspaper, was printed by John Taylor in 1855. Afterwards, because of the so-called "Utah War" most missionaries were withdrawn from New York. The Civil War also hindered work; little progress was realized until the 1880s. By 1890, the New York Conference was organized. New York was returned to the Eastern States Mission in 1893, when in January, Elder Job Pingree was set apart to re-open work in New York City. Headquarters at the time were established in Brooklyn. By 1900, the mission had a total membership of 975 in eight conferences within three states and Canada. When the radio came into use in the 1920s, missionaries were quick to take advantage of the new media to promote the gospel cause. By 1930, branches had been organized in Albany, Brooklyn, Erie, Hudson, Rochester and Susquehanna (including parts of Pennsylvania). By that time, the Church had purchased the Sacred Grove and the Hill Cumorah.

The first Book of Mormon pageant was produced in 1928, a forerunner to the present pageant, "America's Witness for Christ," that has attracted as many as 100,000 people during its seven-night run.

The New York Stake was created in 1934. The stake took part in Church events, including a special exhibit on the centennial of the coming of Elijah in 1936 and observance of the centennial of the sailing ship *Brooklyn* in 1946. LDS servicemen and leaders of businesses headquartered in New York helped strengthen the stake.

In 1964, the Church's pavilion at the World's Fair pioneered media technology and drew a large response to the specially made film" Man's Search for Happiness." This paved the way for future use of technology in spreading the gospel message.

Membership in New York in 1974 reached 17,000. In 1980, the sesquicentennial of the Church was held jointly in Fayette, N.Y., and Salt Lake City, Utah, as President Spencer W. Kimball spoke to the Church in conference by satellite from the rebuilt Peter Whitmer cabin at the site where the Church was organized.

Membership in New York in 1980 was 26,000, increasing to nearly 40,000 in 1990.

President Gordon B. Hinckley visited New York on Nov. 13, 1995, and again July 12, 1996. During the first trip he spoke to a group of corporate executives, representatives of the national media and heads of charitable organizations at a reception and luncheon in New York City. During the second trip, he visited Palmyra where he spoke to the cast, crew and staff of the Hill Cumorah Pageant before the opening performance. On Sept. 30, 1995, President Hinckley announced in General Conference that a temple would be built in White Plains, N.Y.

Sources: *Encyclopedic History of the Church,* by Andrew Jenson; *Church News,* May 16, 1936 and Jan. 19, 1946; "The Church in New York City," by William Woolf, *Improvement Era,* Dec. 1938; *Palmyra — a Bicentennial Celebration,* edited by Betty Troskosky, published by Historic Palmyra Inc., 1989; "LDS history unfolded in New York and Ohio," *Church News,* Jan. 7, 1989; "Legacy of the Mormon Pavilion," by Brent L. Top, *Ensign,* Oct. 1989; *Church News,* Nov. 18, 1995; *Church News,* July 20, 1996.

Stakes — 10

(Listed alphabetically as of Oct. 1, 1996.)

No.	Name	Organized	First President
North America Northeast Area			
485	*Albany New York		
	‡Hudson River	8 Jun 1969	Thomas Lorin Hicken
657	Buffalo New York	15 Sep 1974	Ronald Glen Vincent
1592	Jamestown New York	16 May 1995	
	‡Erie Pennsylvania	23 Mar 1986	Philip D. Baker
110	*New York New York		
	‡New York (N.Y., Connecticut)	9 Dec 1934	Fred G. Taylor
483	*Owego New York 9 Oct 1990		
	*Ithaca New York		
	‡Susquehanna	25 May 1969	Harold R. Capener
439	*Plainview New York		
	‡Long Island	20 Aug 1967	Gordon E. Crandall
346	*Rochester New York		
	‡Cumorah	21 Jan 1962	Bryant W. Rossiter
1543	Rochester New York Palmyra	30 Jun 1985	Kay R. Whitmore
711	Syracuse New York	19 Oct 1975	George Dale Weight
2152	Utica New York	14 Jan 1996	Dallas Williams Jones
909	*Yorktown New York 28 Aug 1978		
	‡Kitchiwan New York	30 Apr 1978	Victor B. Jex
Discontinued			
1574	New York New York East	17 Nov 1985	Mark Eliot Butler

Missions — 4

As of Oct. 1, 1996; shown with historical number. See MISSIONS.)

(290)NY NEW YORK NORTH MISSION
700 White Plains Road,34
Scarsdale, NY 10583
Phone: (914) 722-4105

(2) NY NEW YORK SOUTH MISSION
55 Northern Blvd.,206
Great Neck, NY 11021
Phone: (516) 829-1920

(77)NY ROCHESTER MISSION
P.O. Box 92580
Rochester, NY 14692
Phone: (716) 248-8570

(299) NEW YORK UTICA
P.O. Box 220
New Hartford, NY 13413-0220
Phone: (315) 733-4580

North Carolina

Year-end 1995: Est. population, 7,207,000; Members, 51,000; Stakes, 12; Wards, 77; Branches, 32; Missions, 2; Percent LDS, 0.7, or one person in 141.

Evidently the first missionary to enter North Carolina was Jedediah M. Grant. On May 18, 1838, he reported that he had preached for six months in Stokes, Surrey and Rockingham counties in North Carolina and baptized four people. In 1840, two additional missionaries joined Elder Grant, and they soon baptized another six or eight people. Missionaries also began work in other parts of the state. Writing in 1844, Elder John Eldridge said meetings he held "caused the greatest stirs imaginable. . . . I never thought that one poor mortal could make such a stir." He mentioned "some" baptisms, and also located earlier converts, whom he encouraged to gather to Zion.

Elder Grant wrote in 1845 that before he left North Carolina, he had organized a conference of 200 members in seven branches, and 150 more had joined since he left.

Following the exodus of the main body of the Church from Nauvoo, Ill., in 1846, little work was done for some time in North Carolina. In 1868, a Southern convert, Elder Henry G. Boyle, wrote that he had held 40 public meetings, baptized 30 members and organized the Surrey County Branch. This branch (soon changed to Pilot Mountain) was dissolved following migration to the West in 1870.

The Southern States Mission was created in 1875 and the Pilot Mountain Branch was reorganized in 1876. The Mount Airy Branch was organized July 28, 1879, and the Burke County Branch followed in 1885. Continuation of these branches was sporadic as converts migrated to the West. Membership in 1894 was 128, with 35 emmigrating to the West during the previous three years. Some 1,000 members from surrounding areas attended a conference held in Bradford Cross Roads on Nov. 21, 1894. After 1895, members were encouraged to remain in North Carolina.

Anti-Mormon sentiment was strong, but the majority of citizens remained above mob actions. In 1906, however, a newly completed meetinghouse on Harker's Island was burned and missionaries driven out by a mob. The meetinghouse was replaced in 1936 and the island's members remained faithful.

Occasional mobs gathered in various other locations, but after the turn of the century, public attitudes generally improved and missionaries were offered more freedom to preach.

Over the next 30 years, many local leaders presided over branches and Sunday Schools, forming a strong base of experience. In 1921, Andrew Jenson, visiting as Church historian, reported three branches and 15 Sunday Schools in North Carolina. Meetinghouses were built in Mount Airy, Hampstad, Union Ridge, Wilmington, Goldsboro and Gilreath by 1930. Membership in the state then was 2,725.

North Carolina was divided into the East and West districts in 1935. James L. Bennett Sr. was the first local member to be district president, sustained on March 26, 1939. The Central District was created July 11, 1948. A large building program was started in 1947 and 16 buildings were subsequently added.

In 1961, the North Carolina Stake was created from the East District, and the Central District was organized into the Greensboro Stake the next month.

Membership in the state in 1980 was 29,512, and in 1990, 45,960. North Carolina members were among many from Southern states to respond to storm-caused disasters in the South in the 1990s.

Sources: *Encyclopedic History of the Church,* by Andrew Jenson; *History of The Church of Jesus Christ of Latter-day Saints in North Carolina,* by Wallace R. Draughon; Members provide outpouring of help," *Church News,* Sept. 12, 1992; "Fierce storm claims lives of 3," *Church News,* March 20, 1993; "LDS render service in wake of Opal's rage," *Church News,* Oct. 14, 1995; "Members mopping up after hurricane," *Church News,* Sept. 14, 1996.

Stakes — 12

(Listed alphabetically as of Oct. 1, 1996.)

No.	Name	Organized	First President
North America Southeast Area			
1086	Asheville North Carolina	25 Nov 1979	Luther Andrew Goad
1606	Charlotte North Carolina Central	21 Sep 1986	Kenneth Larson
591	*Charlotte North Carolina South	21 Sep 1986	
	*Charlotte North Carolina ‡Charlotte	19 Nov 1972	Byron Cole Williams
1637	Durham North Carolina	3 May 1987	James L. Bennett Jr.
698	Fayetteville North Carolina	8 Jun 1975	Leland Reid Fillmore
1344	Goldsboro North Carolina	30 May 1982	James William Dixon
335	*Greensboro North Carolina ‡Greensboro	13 Sep 1961	Eugene A. Gulledge
1371	Hickory North Carolina	31 Oct 1982	Gordon M. Thornton
332	*Kinston North Carolina ‡North Carolina	27 Aug 1961	Cecil E. Reese
363	*Raleigh North Carolina ‡Raleigh	9 Dec 1962	William V. Bartholomew
574	*Wilmington North Carolina ‡Wilmington	21 May 1972	Dean Bevin Powell Jr.
881	*Winston-Salem North Carolina	25 Nov 1979	
	‡Statesville North Carolina	20 Nov 1977	Michael Stephen Bullock

Missions — 2

(As of Oct. 1, 1996; shown with historical number. See MISSIONS.)

(105) NORTH CAROLINA CHARLOTTE MISSION
6407 Idlewild Rd., Suite 3.104
Charlotte, NC 28212
Phone: (704) 563-1560

(186) NORTH CAROLINA RALEIGH MISSION
6508 Falls of Neuse, Suite 100
Raleigh, NC 27615-6845
Phone: (919) 876-2091

North Dakota

Year-end 1995: Est. population, 642,000; Members, 5,200; Stakes, 1; Wards, 3; Branches, 11; Districts, 1; Percent LDS, 0.8, or one person in 123.

Missionary work in the Dakotas began in 1883, but the first recorded work in North Dakota occurred in 1885 when four elders labored from house to house across the scattered farmland. The missionaries made friends in the "northern part, [in] Johnstown [Grand Forks County] especially. . . . The Elders are bound to leave those paths through the winter season, so as not to be exposed to the cold, which is a drawback to the Mission." In 1885, it was reported that there were three members in the Dakotas.

South and North Dakota were organized into separate conferences on July 5, 1898, and Charles A. Haacke was appointed president of the North Dakota Conference. "The Lord has seen fit to carry the Gospel to this northern state," a report in the *Deseret News* noted. Two pairs of missionaries started in Fairmont, but found little success so they planned to go north. Before leaving they held a prayer meeting in a grove of box elder trees near the train station. Afterward, one pair of elders traveled to Wahpeton and one to Fargo. In Fargo, missionaries were warned by the mayor that he would do everything he could to obstruct them. Local newspapers were more accommodating, however, and published favorable reports of the missionaries. In 1899, the missionaries transferred to South Dakota "as very little good was being done in North Dakota."

In 1900, North Dakota was taken from the Central States Mission and placed in the Colorado Mission (changed in 1907 to the Western States Mission). After the turn of the century, a convert from Montana named Sitting Eagle moved to North Dakota and explained the gospel to many people. Chief Moses White Horse corresponded with the missionaries and received a copy of the Book of Mormon. When Elders Lewis Roberts and Russell Woolf first visited Shell Village in the summer of 1914, they taught 108

Indians and baptized seven converts. Within a few years the Sully Lake Branch, under Indian leadership, included 40 members from the Fort Berthold Reservation. This unit comprised the majority of membership in the state for many years.

In 1919, a meetinghouse was completed in Sully Lake, and by 1930, a second meetinghouse had been completed in Grand Forks. Membership in 1930 was 145. In 1943, member Dorothy Hanks recalled that the Fargo Branch consisted of five to 10 people attending meetings in the basement of the YMCA building.

After 1950, the Church organizations began to increase with converts and members moving in. Buildings were erected and leaders began traveling more to nurture small branches. In the 1970s, more professionals moved in and continued strengthening the branches.

Church history was made Aug. 7, 1977; when the Fargo North Dakota Stake was created. With its creation, every state in the union had a stake within its boundaries. The new stake had a population of 2,000 with four wards and seven branches. Church membership in 1980 was 3,495 and in 1990, 4,570. In the late 1980s and 1990s, the Church became better known as members took part in many service projects in their communities.

Sources: *Church News,* Aug. 13, 1977, Dec. 24, 1977; March 11, 1989; *Encyclopedic History of the Church,* by Andrew Jenson; *Deseret News,* 57:273; Northern States Mission history.

Stakes — 2
(As of Oct. 1, 1996.)

No.	Name	Organized	First President
North America Central Area			
852	Fargo North Dakota	7 Aug 1977	John R. Price
2243	Bismarck North Dakota	22 Sep 1996	Richard A. Adsero

Ohio

Year-end 1995: Est. population, 11,740,000; Members, 43,000; Stakes, 11; Wards, 70; Branches, 35; Missions, 2; Percent LDS, 0.3, or one person in 273.

One month after Parley P. Pratt was baptized in New York on Sept. 1, 1830, he began his first missionary journey. In the company of Oliver Cowdery, Peter Whitmer Jr. and Ziba Peterson, he returned to Ohio, where he previously homesteaded, on a mission to the Native Americans. Before they reached the Native Americans, however, they taught the gospel to Sidney Rigdon, who was then a preacher, and to his congregation in Painesville, near Kirtland. Within a week, a nucleus for the Church was established in Kirtland. In a few weeks they had baptized 127 people including Rigdon and Frederick G. Williams. Later the missionaries preached to Wyandot Indians in Sandusky, Ohio, and to Delaware Indians in Missouri.

In 1831, Joseph Smith was instructed by revelation to go to Ohio. He made the trip in February, and met Newel K. Whitney at the Gilbert and Whitney store in Kirtland. He and his wife, Emma, lived with Whitney for a time. Members soon gathered to Kirtland, and in June, Joseph received the revelation naming Missouri as the gathering place. From 1831 to 1838, Kirtland was headquarters of the Church with the first stake in the Church created there in 1834. Some 46 revelations were received in the Whitney store, and an additional 16 at the nearby John Johnson farm. In all, 65 revelations of the Doctrine and Covenants were received in Ohio. Numerous visions were received here, and priesthood keys restored. The Quorum of the Twelve was restored here, as was the First Quorum of the Seventy. Newspapers were started, and missionaries sent to other areas in the United States, Canada and Great Britain. Lorenzo Snow, president of the Church from 1898 to 1901, was born in Ohio in 1814.

Construction of the Kirtland Temple began June 5, 1833, and it was dedicated March 27, 1836. In its prime, Kirtland had some 3,200 members. The Saints left Kirtland and surrounding areas for Missouri, mostly completing the exodus in 1838. Apostle Lyman Wight returned to Kirtland in 1842 and re-baptized some 200 members. The temple was acquired in the late 1800s by the Reorganized Church of Jesus Christ of Latter Day Saints and opened for tours.

Ohio was part of the Northern States Mission until 1899, when it was included in the Southern States Mission as a place were ill missionaries could go to recover. In 1926, it was returned to the Northern States Mission.

In 1930, Ohio had two conferences with branches in Akron, Cincinnati, Dayton, Middleton, Portsmouth and Toledo. The Cincinnati and Dayton branches had meetinghouses. Membership was 899.

In 1949, Ohio became part of the Great Lakes Mission. The Ohio Mission was created in 1967.

In 1954, a branch meetinghouse was dedicated in Cleveland by President David O. McKay. Work prospered in Cincinnati, Columbus and Cleveland where stakes were organized in 1958, 1961 and 1963, respectively.

Full-time missionaries returned to Kirtland in 1977, the same year the Kirtland Ward of the Cleveland Ohio Stake was created. In 1979, the Church acquired the Newel K. Whitney store, and it has since become a well-visited historic site.

In 1980, membership in the state reached 28,000, and in 1990, 38,000.

Kirtland, Ohio, hosted a large group of young single adults from several states and Canada for the "Zion's Camp Conference" May 24-27, 1996. Members of the group visited historical sites in the area and held a meeting in the Kirtland Temple. They also pulled weeds in a strawberry field for a service project as part of the conference sponsored by the Northeast Ohio Institute of Religion Council.

Sources: *Encyclopedic History of the Church,* by Andrew Jenson; "Kirtland: The Crucial Years," by Milton V. Backman Jr., *Ensign,* Jan. 1979; "Kirtland Today," by Janet Brigham, *Ensign,* Feb. 1979; "Kirtland stirs once again as Church grows in Ohio," by Hal Knight, *Church News,* Sept. 22, 1979; *Ohio History,* by Joseph H. Young, unpublished manuscript, Dec. 21, 1979; *Church News,* Nov. 29, 1958, Nov. 3, 1979, March 18, 1979 and Jan. 7, 1989.

Stakes — 11
(Listed alphabetically as of Oct. 1, 1996)

No.	Name	Organized	First President
North America Northeast Area			
696	Akron Ohio	25 May 1975	Carmen J. Libutti
270	*Cincinnati Ohio		
	‡Cincinnati (Ohio, Kentucky)	23 Nov 1958	Thomas Blair Evans
1523	Cincinnati Ohio North	17 Mar 1985	William B. Wallis
336	*Cleveland Ohio		
	‡Cleveland (Ohio, Penn.)	20 Sep 1961	E. Doyle Robison
351	*Columbus Ohio		
	‡Columbus	25 Feb 1962	James L. Mortensen
793	Columbus Ohio East	28 Nov 1976	Paul Frank Eastman
1609	Columbus Ohio North	19 Oct 1986	D. Richard McFerson
516	*Dayton Ohio		
	‡Dayton	24 May 1970	Joseph M. McPhie
1029	Dayton Ohio East	27 May 1979	Melvin Edwin Gourdin
1447	Kirtland Ohio	16 Oct 1983	Zane F. Lee
1204	Toledo Ohio	2 Nov 1980	Ronald Rufus Burke
Discontinued			
1	Kirtland	17 Feb 1834	Joseph Smith Jr.
	24 May 1841		

Missions — 2
(As of Oct. 1, 1996; shown with historical number. See MISSIONS.)

(154) OHIO CLEVELAND MISSION
24600 Center Ridge Road, #450
Westlake, OH 44145
Phone: (216) 871-0937

(77a) OHIO COLUMBUS MISSION
P.O. Box 20130
Columbus, OH 43220
Phone: (614) 451-6183

Oklahoma

Year-end 1995: Est. population, 3,295,000; Members, 31,000; Stakes, 7; Wards, 43; Branches, 30; Missions, 2; Percent LDS, 0.9, or one person in 106.

In the late 1840s, George Miller, a former bishop who delayed going to the West, traveled from Winter Quarters to visit his son in Texas. He and two other members with him, Joseph Kilting and Richard Hewitt, found construction work available in the Cherokee Nation. They arrived in Tahlequah on July 9, 1847, and began to build houses. They also began to teach others about the Church but antagonism forced Miller to leave in December. Hewitt and Kilting remained to work.

In 1855 Orson Spencer and James McGaw visited Indian Territory from St. Louis, Mo., and on April 8, 1855, five more missionaries were sent from Salt Lake City and four from St. Louis. The Indian Territory Mission was created and placed under the leadership of

Henry W. Miller on June 26, 1855. The missionaries met and re-converted followers of Lyman Wight. One of these was Jacob Croft, who had met missionaries earlier and started for Utah, but met another apostate group that told the Croft Party untruths about conditions in Utah. The discouraged Croft party had then settled in Indian Territory and built a gristmill.

As early as July, the missionaries preached to some 400 Indians, and the Cherokee Branch was started at Croft's Spavinaw Creek mill. This became mission headquarters. Croft later led a party of 56, including other former followers of Wight and some re-converted "Strangites," to Utah.

Later in the year missionaries were sent from St. Louis to southern portions of the Cherokee Nation. In 1856, the Princess Creek Branch was organized. The Lehi and Nephi branches were organized in 1858.

Illness was a problem in this mission for many years. At least four missionaries died from the effects of serving in Indian Territory, including Orson Spencer. Many suffered the effects of malaria afterward.

In 1858 and 1859 the remaining groups immigrated to Utah and by 1860 all the missionaries but John A. Richards, who had married an Indian wife, returned to Utah. The Civil War destroyed what was left of the Church. Members and leaders were scattered.

When Elders Matthew Dalton and John Hubbard returned in 1877, they found John Richards was still faithful, and they received hospitality from him. Elder Hubbard died later that year and work stopped until 1883 when the next missionaries, Elder Dalton and Elder George Teasdale, came. Tracts in the Cherokee language were printed. Plagued with ill health, these missionaries persevered and found converts in Arkansas.

Andrew Kimball, the father of President Spencer W. Kimball, presided over the mission in 1885. Although he contracted malaria, he was assisted by John Richards and later by additional full-time missionaries. In 1892, the first meetinghouse was erected in Manard, Cherokee County. Another was erected at Massey, Choctaw Nation.

Converts during this period whose descendants became stalwarts in the local branches included the families of former minister John W. Davis, Simon Peter Hubler, William Edward Roberts, and George Washington Aaron, to name a few.

In 1904, the mission became the Central States Mission. By 1921, a branch was established at Gore, Okla., with 113 members but was later dissolved. A Sunday School began in Bartlesville in 1924. Membership increased but many converts went West. By 1930, membership throughout the mission numbered 10,804.

Membership began to increase in the 1950s, and in 1960 a stake was created in Tulsa. Included in the stake were parts of Kansas, Arkansas, and Oklahoma with a membership of about 2,000. The Oklahoma City Stake was organized in the fall of the same year with James A. Cullimore as president, who later served as an Assistant to the Twelve and a member of the First Quorum of the Seventy. Other stakes followed in 1970, 1977, 1978, and three in the 1980s. Membership in 1974 was 10,105 and in 1980, 20,819 and in 1990, 26,596.

The LDS community reached out to those in need after a terrorist bomb ripped apart the nine-story Alfred P. Murrah Federal Building in downtown Oklahoma City April 19, 1995. President Gordon B. Hinckley met July 14, 1996, with 1,900 youth and leaders gathered in the auditorium of the Union High School in Tulsa.

Sources: *A History of The Church of Jesus Christ of Latter-day Saints in Eastern Oklahoma, from Oklahoma and Indian Territories to 1980* by Lynetta K. Bingham, Bonnie Lee Blamires, Clara Laster and Lenet Read, published by the Tulsa Oklahoma Stake; *Mormon Indian Missions — 1855*, a BYU thesis by Wesley R. Law, 1959; "The Cherokee Nation," by A.W. Miller, *Millennial Star*, Oct. 6, 1855, p. 637; "Faith, courage rise from the rubble," *Church News*, April 29, 1996; "Church leaders visits 5 states in 4 days," *Church News*, July 20, 1996.

Stakes — 7
(Listed alphabetically as of Oct. 1, 1996.)

No.	Name	Organized	First President
	North America Southeast Area		
777	Lawton Oklahoma	31 Oct 1976	Ralph E. Siebach
531	*Norman Oklahoma		
	‡Oklahoma South	18 Oct 1970	H. Aldridge Gillespie
305	*Oklahoma City Oklahoma		
	‡Oklahoma	23 Oct 1960	James A. Cullimore

1381	Oklahoma City Oklahoma South	14 Nov 1982	Lawrence Andrew Jackson
1277	Stillwater Oklahoma	14 Jun 1981	C. Jay Murray
298	*Tulsa Oklahoma		
	‡Tulsa (Okla., Ark., Kan.)	1 May 1960	Robert N. Sears
912	Tulsa Oklahoma East	30 Apr 1978	Raleigh L. Huntsman

Discontinued

| 1418 | Muskogee Oklahoma | 15 May 1983 | Samuel J. Hughes |
| | 11 Aug 1991 | | |

Missions — 2

(As of Oct. 1, 1996; shown with historical number. See MISSIONS.)

(248) OKLAHOMA OKLAHOMA CITY MISSION
1236 SW 89th St. Suite C
Oklahoma City, OK 73139
Phone: (405) 691-8690

(88) OKLAHOMA TULSA MISSION
5215 East 71st St., Suite 300
Tulsa, OK 74136
Phone: (918) 496-0056

Oregon

Year-end 1995: Est. population, 3,168,000; Members, 126,000; Stakes, 35; Wards, 223; Branches, 40; Missions, 2; Temples, 1; Percent LDS, 4.0, or one person in 25.

In 1838, Joseph Smith visited Washington, D.C., where, on one occasion Henry Clay, "the great compromiser," suggested the Prophet take the Mormons to Oregon Territory. The Prophet did not take the suggestion seriously. Oregon, however, was one of several locations considered for possible settlement after difficulties in Illinois in the early 1840s. At the time, Oregon was claimed by both Great Britain and the United States. Saints in both Great Britain and America offered to settle there with their government's support, but both offers were declined.

As early as Sept. 25, 1850, Elder R. Boyd Stewart, who lived in a settlement on the Sacramento River in California, was called to serve in Oregon. Additional missionaries served in 1854 and later, but were called back with their converts at the onset of the so-called "Utah War" in 1857. The exodus to Utah began March 6, 1858.

After Oregon became a state in 1858, a more favorable attitude toward members developed. During the 1860s, Mormons found work as loggers in Oregon. A few settled, but any significant Mormon presence did not occur until 1887 when LDS businessmen from Utah, David Eccles and Charles Nibley (joined in 1889 by John Stoddard), built a lumber mill on North Powder River and persuaded several hundred LDS families to migrate to Oregon. The Baker Branch was organized in 1893.

The Northwestern States Mission was organized for the second time July 26, 1897, under the direction of George C. Parkinson. Early convert Jens (James) Christensen Westergaard became the first branch president in Portland after his baptism in 1898.

Around the turn of the century, another LDS movement into Oregon occurred when ranches in eastern Oregon were purchased and divided into sugar beet farms. The Eccles partnership supported this migration effort. By June 9, 1901, enough members had migrated that the Union Stake was created. Two years later, the five original wards had increased to 12, "all in excellent working order." Completion of the Oregon Shortline Railroad led more members to migrate to the Northwest.

Both World War I and World War II defense industry efforts led to more members moving to Oregon. In 1929, a meetinghouse was completed in Portland. By 1930, membership in the state was 3,226, with wards at Baker, Imbler, LaGrande (two), Mt. Glen and Union, and branches in Bend, Eugene, Klamath Falls, Medford, Portland, Hood River and Salem.

Members continued to move in, and another stake was organized in Portland in 1938. Many members also moved into Oregon in the post-war boom and additional stakes were created.

In 1961 or earlier, the Church purchased property near Portland for eventual use for a junior college in Portland. However, the site was later chosen for the location of the Portland Oregon Temple, which was dedicated in 1989. More than 300,000 people toured the temple during its open house.

One evidence of the growing LDS population in the state was a dance festival held in July 1989 in which some 10,000 youth participated.

Members continued to support missionary work, and in 1990, the Oregon Eugene Mission was created.

In early 1996, devastating floods struck the Northwest, including parts of Oregon.

Several homes of LDS families were flooded and damaged, while some 300 other LDS families were evacuated because of potential dike failure. Members outside stricken areas joined relief efforts, including clean-up projects and working with county officials to match victims with relief crews.

Membership in 1980 was 94,093, increasing to 113,774 in 1990.

Sources: *Encyclopedic History of the Church,* by Andrew Jenson; *Mormon Migration to Oregon's Grande Ronde Valley: A Portent of Future Mormon Expansion,* by Kenneth Gerald Dull, master's thesis, Utah State University, 1981; "Enterprising beet farmers," by Bruce D. Blumell, *Church News,* Jan. 14, 1978; *Church News,* July 22, 1989, Jan. 27, 1990; *History of the Church in the Pacific Northwest,* by Leonard J. Arrington, Task Papers in LDS History, No. 18; "A wake of disaster, a wave of volunteers," *Church News,* Feb. 17, 1996.

Stakes — 35
(Listed alphabetically by area as of Oct. 1, 1996.)

No.	Name	Organized	First President
	North America Northwest Area		
386	*Beaverton Oregon		
	‡Portland West (Oregon)	10 Nov 1963	C. Carlile Carlson
2124	Beaverton Oregon West	12 Nov 1995	William Stanley Richardson
472	*Bend Oregon		
	‡Bend	15 Dec 1968	Norman K. Whitney
1373	Cedar Mill Oregon	31 Oct 1982	Edgar Lee Stone
1325a	Central Point Oregon	7 Mar 1982	Michael T. Robinson
493	*Coos Bay Oregon		
	‡Oregon West	12 Sep 1969	Edward Harold Sypher
385	*Corvallis Oregon		
	‡Corvallis	3 Nov 1963	Hugh F. Webb
191	*Eugene Oregon		
	‡Willamette	2 Dec 1951	Ralph B. Lake
1410	Eugene Oregon Santa Clara	17 Apr 1983	Terrel B. Williams
767	Eugene Oregon West	12 Sep 1976	Robert W. Hill
779	Grants Pass Oregon	31 Oct 1976	Darwin Jay Wright
643	Gresham Oregon	26 May 1974	Wilford Smith Stevenson Jr.
1365	Gresham Oregon South	10 Oct 1982	Max B. Holbrook
1200	Hermiston Oregon	26 Oct 1980	Allen D. Alder
710	Hillsboro Oregon	12 Oct 1975	H. Keith Buhler
743	*Keizer Oregon 4 Apr 1984		
	*Salem Oregon Keizer 25 Oct 1981		
	‡Salem Oregon North	8 Feb 1976	Jay Gerald Nelson
205	*Klamath Falls Oregon		
	‡Klamath (Oregon, California)	22 Mar 1953	Carroll William Smith
49	*La Grande Oregon		
	‡Union	9 Jun 1901	Franklin S. Bramwell
1469	Lake Oswego Oregon	29 Apr 1984	Thomas Dean Cottle
1102	Lebanon Oregon	3 Feb 1980	Henry Boyd Walthuis
1300	McMinnville Oregon	25 Oct 1981	Thomas Babb III
400	*Medford Oregon		
	‡Medford (Oregon, California)	23 Aug 1964	Dennis R. Hassell
999	Milwaukie Oregon	11 Feb 1979	Thomas Dean Cottle
1171	*Monmouth Oregon 21 May 1996		
	*Dallas Oregon 25 Sep 1990		
	‡Salem Oregon East	24 Aug 1980	William Paul Hyde
176	*Nyssa Oregon		
	‡Nyssa (Oregon, Idaho)	8 Jan 1950	Arvel L. Child
1504	Ontario Oregon	18 Nov 1984	Reed Neils Dame
563	*Oregon City Oregon		
	‡Oregon City	16 Jan 1972	James Hayward Bean
123	*Portland Oregon		
	‡Portland	26 Jun 1938	Monte L. Bean
190	*Portland Oregon East		
	‡Columbia River (Ore., Wash.)	2 Dec 1951	R. Spencer Papworth
1852	Ranier Oregon	8 Mar 1992	Marion Royal Johnstun
1239	*Redmond Oregon 18 Feb 1986		
	‡Prineville Oregon	1 Mar 1981	Heber D. Perrett

830	Roseburg Oregon	15 May 1977	Gary Richards Lowe
321	*Salem Oregon		
	‡Salem	22 Jan 1961	Hugh F. Webb
850	The Dalles Oregon	26 Jun 1977	Wayne B. Bush
1895	Tualatin Oregon	16 Aug 1992	Paul Walker Roberts

Missions — 2

(As of Oct. 1, 1996; shown with historical number. See MISSIONS.)

(249) OREGON EUGENE MISSION
969 Willagillespie Rd., #2
Eugene, OR 97401
Phone: (541) 342-2344

(18) OREGON PORTLAND MISSION
13635 N.W. Cornell Rd., Suite 100
Portland, OR 97229
Phone: (503) 643-1696

Pennsylvania

Year-end 1995: Est. population, 12,077,000; Members, 33,000; Stakes, 8; Wards, 59; Branches, 44; Missions, 3; Districts, 2; Percent LDS, 0.2, or one person in 366.

Joseph Smith moved to Harmony, Pa., in December 1827, and first lived in the home of Isaac Hale, his father-in-law. A few weeks later, he moved to a small cabin on an adjacent farm where he eventually translated most of the Book of Mormon. His scribes were himself, his wife Emma, Martin Harris, Oliver Cowdery and David Whitmer. At the nearby Susquehanna River, he and Oliver Cowdery were ordained to the Aaronic Priesthood May 15, 1829. The ordinance of baptism was then first performed in this dispensation as Oliver Cowdery baptized Joseph Smith. Later the Melchizedek Priesthood was restored, and 15 of the revelations in the Doctrine and Covenants were received in Harmony. The first infant son of Joseph and Emma is buried at this site. The farm was purchased by the Church Feb. 7, 1947, and a historical marker has been erected.

After the Church was formally organized in 1830, Orson Hyde, Samuel H. Smith, and a number of others began missionary work in Pennsylvania. A branch was organized in Columbia, Bradford County, by 1831. Another was created in Pittsburgh in 1832, and in 1833, in Springfield and Elk Creek. A total of 12 branches were created in the 1830s, although these branches were of short duration as members gathered to Ohio, or later Missouri and Illinois, with the body of the Saints.

Among the most prominent branches was Philadelphia, created in 1839 after initial efforts by Elders Jedediah M. Grant, Joshua Grant and Benjamin Winchester, and sustained efforts by Elders Samuel and Lewis James.

Converts from Philadelphia included Edward Hunter, a wealthy landowner who later became Presiding Bishop of the Church, and John Neff, a well-to-do businessman. Both contributed generously of their means to sustain the members during their later privations brought about by persecution. By 1840, more than 200 members belonged to the branch and 8 to 10 were baptized weekly.

From 1839 to 1846, missionary work in the Church was focused mostly in the cities of Philadelphia, Boston and New York.

Following the martyrdom of Joseph Smith in 1844, Sidney Rigdon and James J. Strang claimed leadership of the Church and established apostate groups from among Church members who had not "gathered," including those in Pennsylvania. However, many were later reclaimed. Apostate leader William Bickerton drew away members in western Pennsylvania who became known as the Bickertonites.

On March 26, 1850, Gen. Thomas L. Kane delivered a landmark address, "History of the Persecutions of the Latter-day Saints," to the Historical Society of Pennsylvania. During the 1850s, the city was a port of entry for many LDS immigrants.

Missionary work continued sporadically. The Redstone and New England (later called Wilson) branches were organized in May 1886. The Northwestern States Mission (which at the time included the Eastern states) was created in 1878, becoming the Northern States Mission in 1889. Pennsylvania was transferred to the Eastern States Mission in 1897, and the East and West Pennsylvania districts were created.

By 1930, the East District included one branch in Philadelphia. with 284 members, and a branch in Pittsburgh, which had its own meetinghouse, and another in Wilson, with a total of 510 members in the West District.

During World War II membership increased and additional branches were created. For example, missionaries arrived in Lancaster, near Harrisburg, in 1941. Their first converts were Lester D. Ross and his wife, Mary Eleanor. A branch was organized in 1943, with 10-14 members. As it grew, its members often moved to the West. After a 10-year fund drive the branch purchased property and a small meetinghouse was eventually completed. In 1970, this branch became a ward when the Gettysburg Stake was created.

The Philadelphia Stake was created Oct. 16, 1960, with 2,000 members in Pennsylvania in Philadelphia, Valley Forge and Wyncote wards, and the in Allentown, Chester and Reading branches.

The Pittsburgh Stake was created May 11, 1969, with 2,258 members in four wards in Pittsburgh, and others in Beaver Valley, Butler, Punxsutawney and Washington, and branches in Greensburg and Monongahela.

In 1970, the Pennsylvania (now Pennsylvania Harrisburg) Mission was created. The Pennsylvania Philadelphia Mission was created in July 1, 1977. Membership in Pennsylvania in 1980 was 22,211, increasing to 28,976 in 1990.

President Gordon B. Hinckley spoke to priesthood leaders, missionaries and members of the Church during a trip to Pittsburgh April 27-28, 1996. About 5,000 members attended Sunday's meeting in the Sewell Center of Pittsburgh's Robert Morris College.

Sources: *Encyclopedic History of the Church,* by Andrew Jenson; *A Study of the Origins of the Church in the States of New York and Pennsylvania, 1816-1831,* a BYU dissertation by Larry C. Porter, August 1971; *Church News,* Oct. 22, 1960, May 17, 1969, Nov. 30, 1986; *Missionary Activities and Church Organizations in Pennsylvania, 1830-1840,* a BYU thesis by V. Alan Curtis, 1976; "The Hospitable Squire," by William Hartley, *Church News,* Jan. 21, 1978; *The Church in Pennsylvania (1830-1854),* an East Stroudsburg State College thesis by Paul Zilch Rosenbaum, Dec.1982; Neff History, unpublished; Interview with Lester D. Ross by Julie Dockstader, *Church News,* Oct. 19, 1991; *Church News,* May 4, 1996.

Stakes — 8
(Listed alphabetically as of Oct. 1, 1996.)

No.	Name	Organized	First President
North America Northeast Area			
946	*Altoona Pennsylvania 31 Oct 1982		
	‡State College Pennsylvania	23 Jul 1978	Robert Armstrong Wood Sr.
1592	Erie Pennsylvania	23 Mar 1986	Philip Dale Baker
1047	Harrisburg Pennsylvania	12 Aug 1979	Charles A. Cooper
304	*Philadelphia Pennsylvania ‡Philadelphia (Penn., Del., Md., N.J.)	16 Oct 1960	Bryant F. West
481	*Pittsburgh Pennsylvania ‡Pittsburgh	11 May 1969	William P. Cook
985	*Pittsburgh Pennsylvania North 18 Feb 1992 ‡Pittsburgh Pennsylvania East	26 Nov 1978	Garth Harrison Ladle
1372	Reading Pennsylvania	31 Oct 1982	Hugh G. Daubek
1044	Scranton Pennsylvania	2 Aug 1979	Frederick Adelman Alderks
510	*York Pennsylvania 12 Aug 1979 *Gettysburg Pennsylvania ‡Gettysburg (Pennsylvania)	19 Apr 1970	Laurence L. Yager

Missions — 3
(As of Oct. 1, 1996; shown with historical number. See MISSIONS.)

(91a) PENN. HARRISBURG MISSION
3607 Rosemont Ave., #303
Camp Hill, PA 17011-6998
Phone: (717) 761-3611

(156) PENN. PHILADELPHIA MISSION
300 West State St.,107
Media, PA 19063
Phone: (610) 565-1150

(129) PENN. PITTSBURGH
MISSION
2589 Washington Road,410
Pittsburgh, PA 15241-2596
Phone: (717) 761-3611

Rhode Island

Year-end 1995: Est. population, 986,000; Members, 2,200; Stakes, 1; Wards, 5; Branches, 2; Percent LDS, 0.2, or one person in 448

Elders Orson Hyde and Samuel H. Smith arrived in Rhode Island on July 13, 1832, baptizing their first convert on July 18. They baptized another person before persecutors drove them from the state a few days afterward.

Four years later, records note the existence of a Rhode Island Branch represented by Brigham Young at a conference in Newry, Maine. The Newport Branch was organized by 1844 with 21 members.

Elder John Druce worked as an engraver and missionary in Pawtucket, R.I., in 1846, where he also preached and baptized many converts into the Church. A branch was organized June 7, 1857, in Providence, but discontinued as the members moved to the West. Druce immigrated to the West in 1861, but returned in 1876 to resume his missionary work.

In 1873, Elder Henry G. Bywater organized another branch in Providence with 25 members, and predicted many would soon emigrate. In 1876, Elder Erastus Snow wrote that he and Elder Benjamin F. Cummings met with the Saints in Pawtucket who were on their way to the Great Basin from England. A year later, Elder Cummings preached to an attentive audience in a school house in Pawtucket. In 1896, Elder Joseph A. Anderson reported illness after sleeping outside in the rain for some 12 days as he traveled in Rhode Island without purse or scrip. A conference of the Eastern States Mission was held March 22, 1899, in Providence and received favorable publicity in the *Providence Journal* and the *Telegram*. Missionaries also reported that residents treated them kindly.

The Providence Branch was organized in 1905, and by 1917 increased to about 20 people. Membership in the nation's smallest state continued to accrue gradually. In 1938, a private library was purchased for the Providence Branch, which was remodeled into a meetinghouse by the members. The facility was dedicated by Elder John A. Widtsoe of the Quorum of the Twelve on June 14, 1944. The branch was often decimated when members moved to the West to be closer to the Church. However, the branch was bolstered by converts introduced to the Church by LDS servicemen stationed at nearby military bases. The library meetinghouse was sold and another site purchased in 1960. A new building was dedicated in 1966.

The Providence Stake was created March 20, 1977, the 49th state to receive its first stake. Rhode Island wards in the stake included those in Newport and Providence, and the Davisville Branch. Also in the stake were two wards and two branches in Massachusetts and two wards in Connecticut. Membership in Rhode Island in 1974 was 799, increasing to 1,052 in 1980, and 1,701 in 1990.

July 5-7, 1995, young men and young women from the Providence Rhode Island Stake turned their youth conference into a service project. They helped make the Special Olympics World Games a success for 7,000 participants from 140 countries by helping with activities such as food services and cleanup and by cheering the athletes on in their competitions.

Sources: *Encyclopedic History of the Church,* by Andrew Jenson; Journal History of the Church, Aug. 14, 1836, Oct. 22, 1843, July 30, 1844, March 10, 1873, March 13, 1876, Feb. 5, 1977; *Deseret News,* March 31, 1877, July 12, 1877, Oct. 9, 1878, Aug 11, 1896, April 1, 1899, Dec. 3, 1932; *Church News,* March 31, 1945, March 26, 1977, and "Missionary Printer," by Ronald G. Watt, *Church News,* Jan. 28, 1978; *Church News,* July 15, 1996.

Stake — 1
(As of Oct. 1, 1996.)

No.	Name	Organized	First President
	North America Northeast Area		
818	*Providence Rhode Island	20 Mar 1977	Morgan W. Lewis Jr.

South Carolina

Year-end 1995: Est. population, 3,688,000; Members, 24,000; Stakes, 4; Wards, 37; Branches, 18; Missions, 1; Percent LDS, 0.7, or one person in 154.

While missionary work in the Southern States began as early as 1831, the first member in South Carolina is believed to be Emmanual Masters Murphy, who was baptized in Tennessee in 1836. When Elder Lysander M. Davis arrived in South Carolina about the first of November in 1839, he found the Murphys had people prepared for baptism. Seven of these were baptized.

Opposition arose and Elder Davis was briefly jailed, but progress continued with additional conversions. Murphy reportedly later visited Joseph Smith in Carthage Jail shortly before the Prophet's martyrdom. The Prophet reminded him of the prophecy that soon war would begin in South Carolina, and exhorted Murphy to warn the people of his home state.

Elder Abraham O. Smoot preached in Charleston and upstate in 1841, but failed to gain any converts. However, an "unknown missionary" traveled to Charleston earlier that year and baptized three ministers and eight others. Another missionary, Elder John Eldredge, preached in South Carolina in 1842-43.

The next missionary activity in the state began in the 1870s. The South Carolina Conference was organized in July 1882. Among the earliest branches were at King's Mountain (1882), Gaffney (1883), and among the Catawba Indian community (1885). Conference headquarters were established at the plantation of John Black, a man who remained unbaptized in order to provide refuge to the Church. Many converts, including Indians, moved onto his plantation to escape persecution. The Catawbas also shielded missionaries from persecutors. Most of the Catawbas joined the Church and remained faithful.

Stalwart missionaries braved such adversities as floggings, jailings, disease (12 missionaries died from illness from 1895-1900 in the Southern States Mission), frequent exposure to the elements, walking hundreds of miles, often missing meals, and other privations. But they continued to find converts and organize branches. From 1880 to 1888, 2,238 converts were baptized throughout the South, and 1,169 converts migrated to Utah.

Mission leaders of the 1880s and later included Henry G. Boyle, John Morgan, William Spry, J. Golden Kimball, Elias S. Kimball and Benjamin E. Rich. Later, Ephraim H. Nye, Charles A. Callis and LeGrand Richards were prominent leaders.

In the 1890s, progress and persecution continued. Mobs often gathered to punish and banish missionaries. But the members and missionaries persevered. Branches were organized in Society Hill, Columbia, Charleston and Fairfield, to name a few. About 350 members attended a conference in Society Hill in 1897. However, as converts migrated to the West, branches dwindled and some were reorganized later with new converts.

At the turn of the century, membership in the state was 1,200. That membership increased to 3,343 in 1930. The conference included six branches (four with meetinghouses) and 10 Sunday Schools. In the 1930s, mission president LeGrand Richards introduced "systematic teaching," a forerunner of today's missionary discussions. By 1937, membership in the entire mission had increased to 18,000.

South Carolina's first stake was created in Columbia in 1947. It included the entire state with wards in Columbia, Greenville, Charleston, Gaffney, Hartsville, Ridgeway and Spartanburg, and branches in Augusta (Ga.), Sumter, Society Hill, Winnsboro and Darlington. Membership totaled about 1,900 members.

Additional stakes were added in 1963, 1968, and 1972. Church membership in South Carolina in 1974 was 10,775, increasing to 17,012 in 1980, and 23,731 in 1990.

Following natural disasters from storms that occurred in the South in the 1990s, South Carolina members were among those who helped provide relief.

Sources: *Encyclopedic History of the Church,* by Andrew Jenson; *Columbia South Carolina Stake Fortieth Anniversary, Oct. 19, 1947 to 1987,* compiled under direction of stake Pres. Gary L. Fish; *History of the Southern States Mission 1831-1861,* a BYU thesis by LaMar C. Berrett, July 1960; *Brief History of the Southern States Mission for One Hundred Years, 1830-1930* by DeVon H. Nish, a BYU paper, August 1966; "Stake Birthday Notes Growth of Church in South Carolina," *Church News,* Dec. 9, 1972; *Southern States Mission and the Administration of Ben E. Rich, 1898-1908,* a thesis for BYU by Ted S. Anderson, April 1976; "Persecutor converted," by Richard L. Jensen, *Church News,* Feb. 4, 1978; "Members provide outpouring of help," *Church News,* Sept. 12, 1992; "Fierce storm claims lives of 3," *Church News,* March 20, 1993; "LDS render service in wake of Opal's rage," *Church News,* Oct. 14, 1995.

Stakes — 4
(Listed alphabetically as of Oct. 1, 1996.)

No.	Name	Organized	First President
	North America Southeast Area		
584	*Charleston South Carolina		
	‡Charleston	20 Aug 1972	Fred Ittner Harley
169	*Columbia South Carolina		
	‡South Carolina (S.C., Georgia)	19 Oct 1947	W. Wallace McBride
454	*Florence South Carolina 5 Feb 1978		
	*Columbia South Carolina East		
	‡South Carolina East	21 Apr 1968	Clyde Elmer Black Sr.

366 *Greenville South Carolina
*Greenville 19 Nov 1972
‡South Carolina West   27 Jan 1963   Ivan A. Larsen
(S.C., N.C.)

Mission — 1
(As of Oct. 1, 1996; shown with historical number. See MISSIONS.)

(130) SOUTH CAROLINA COLUMBIA MISSION
1345 Garner Lane, Suite #307
Columbia, SC 29210
Phone: (803) 798-8855

South Dakota

Year-end 1995: Est. population, 732,000; Members, 8,500; Stakes, 2; Wards, 10; Branches, 28; Missions, 1; Districts, 3; Percent LDS, 1.1, or one person in 86.

In the 1840s, Church leaders seeking a refuge in the West considered various locations for settlement. One of these locations was the Indian country of the Dakotas. An area was chosen in 1845 for settlement by a group of volunteer colonizers under maverick leader James Emmett. The group, which evidently communicated en route with Brigham Young but did not have his full approval, penetrated deep into South Dakota's Indian country and established a settlement at Fort Vermillion on the Missouri River. They arrived at the fort June 17, 1845, and immediately began building cabins and planting crops. They preached to the Sioux Indians and befriended them, but the threat of attack was constant. The colony was nearly attacked when Emmett unwisely interfered in a horse-trading deal between the Indians and traders and an argument ensued.

Emmett, who had lost some favor with Church leaders after the death of Joseph Smith, returned to Nauvoo the summer of 1845 and sought to regain favor with the Church. He was accepted in full fellowship, and on his return to Fort Vermillion, he was accompanied by two other leaders, Henry G. Sherwood and John S. Fullmer, who rebaptized the settlers. In the spring of 1846, the group received word from Brigham Young to join the Saints in the westward trek. The settlement was abandoned as most members complied with President Young's direction.

Missionary work in South Dakota began May 3, 1883, when, at a conference in Kirkhaven, Minn., Charles N. Nielsen and N.L. Lund were appointed to "open the Gospel door in the states of Dakota." Elder Nielsen arrived at Big Stone, Dakota Territory, on June 5, staying only one day. In 1885, the Dakota Conference membership was listed at "four souls," including two elders from Utah. The same year, Elder Soren Christiansen reported that he received both hospitality and threats backed up by guns as he traveled in Dakota. Missionaries reported in 1887 that Dakota was a "worn-out" territory. Missionary work continued in 1888, and in 1898, missionaries from North Dakota were transferred to the Southern Dakota Conference. The Dakotas were placed in the Colorado Mission in 1900. The mission name was changed to Western States Mission in 1907. Missionary work continued with another organization of the South Dakota Conference in 1925, and a re-opening in 1931.

The South Dakota Conference was organized for western South Dakota, and a Sunday School was organized in Sioux Falls on Aug. 17, 1930, and made a branch June 19, 1949. Another branch existed in Gettysburg. By 1950, Sunday Schools were organized at Mitchell, Aberdeen, Brookings, Ft. Thompson, and Huron. That same year ground was broken for a meetinghouse in Sioux Falls. The North Central States Mission, which included the western half of the state, was changed to the Dakota-Manitoba Mission in 1970. This mission had 230 missionaries and about 800 members. In 1974, its name was changed to the South Dakota Rapid City Mission. A number of meetinghouses were completed in the 1970s. The Rapid City South Dakota Stake was created in 1973. Membership in South Dakota in 1980 was 6,121, which grew to 7,657 in 1990.

Sources: *Encyclopedic History of the Church*, by Andrew Jenson; The Church in South Dakota, no author listed; *Church News*, July 8, 1944; "An Early Mormon Settlement in South Dakota," by Gerald E. Jones, *South Dakota State Historical Society Quarterly*, Spring of 1971; "Mormon Renegade: James Emmett at the Vermillion, 1846," by Richard E. Bennett, *South Dakota History*, Fall of 1985.

Stakes — 2
(Listed alphabetically as of Oct. 1, 1996.)

No.	Name	Organized	First President

592 *Rapid City South Dakota

‡Rapid City	10 Dec 1972	Briant LeRoy Davis
1085 Sioux Falls South Dakota	18 Nov 1979	Russell Lloyd Harward

Mission — 1

(As of Oct. 1, 1996; shown with historical number. See MISSIONS.)

(78) SOUTH DAKOTA RAPID CITY MISSION
2525 West Main, Suite 311
Rapid City, SD 57702
Phone: (605) 348-1520

Tennessee

Year-end 1995: Est. population, 5,296,000; Members, 27,000; Stakes, 8; Wards, 44; Branches, 21; Missions, 2; Temples, 1 announced; Percent LDS, 0.5, or one person in 196.

Apostle David W. Patten and Elder Warren Parrish arrived in Tennessee shortly before Oct. 11, 1834, where they preached at a large Campbellite meeting and baptized seven. Another 24 were baptized later. A small branch was organized by the end of the year. Missionary efforts took place in Henry, Benton and Humphreys counties. In 1835, Elder Parrish worked alone after Elder Patten returned to Kirtland, Ohio. Elder Parrish continued to baptize converts and was unable to fill all the requests for preaching. One of his converts was Abraham O. Smoot, who later became a prominent Church leader in Salt Lake City.

On March 27, 1835, Wilford Woodruff, then a priest, came to assist Elder Parrish. He arrived at a tavern covered with mud and identified himself as a preacher. In jest, the innkeeper urged him to preach and gathered 500 people to hear him. Elder Woodruff told the rowdy congregation individually of "their wicked deeds and the reward they would obtain." One by one, the people left until he was alone. During the next three months, he and Elder Parrish baptized 20 converts.

When Elder Parrish was called as a seventy in July 1835, he ordained Elder Woodruff an elder and placed him in charge of the work in Tennessee. At that time, membership in the district was 86 members in six branches (one in Kentucky). Elder Woodruff continued the work, reporting at year's end that he had traveled 3,248 miles, baptized 43 people, three of whom were Campbellite preachers and had three mobs rise against him. Mob activity temporarily forced missionaries from Benton County in 1836. However, work progressed well, and by 1839, 12 branches existed in Tennessee. Work continued though 1844 as missionaries promoted Joseph Smith's short-lived candidacy for president of the United States.

By 1846, missionaries had preached in 26 counties in Tennessee. Following the exodus to the West, little work was done in Tennessee. Missionaries visited the state in 1857 to call the Saints to gather in the West.

In 1870, Elder Hayden Church resumed missionary work in Tennessee. The Southern States Mission was formally organized in 1875 with headquarters in Nashville, which were moved to Chattanooga in 1882 and remained there until 1919, when Atlanta, Ga., became mission headquarters.

Elder Henry G. Boyle had established a branch at Shady Grove, Tenn., in 1875. Mob activity increased significantly in 1879. Some converts in the South left their homes and immigrated to the West in 1883. In 1884, members were fired upon in separate incidents. The worst massacre of Church members in the South occurred on Aug. 10, 1884, when mobbers shot to death Elders William S. Berry and John H. Gibbs, and local members Martin Condor and John Riley during Church services near Cane Creek, Lewis County, Tenn. Mission Pres. B.H. Roberts heroically donned a disguise, traveled to the tense area and retrieved the bodies of the slain missionaries. During this period, missionaries faced down many mobs and sometimes suffered violence. Occasionally, non-members courageously defended the missionaries. In 1888, a group of 177 Saints left Chattanooga for Colorado and Utah.

By the 1890s, public opinion became more tolerant. U.S. Census records list 136 members in Tennessee in 1890. By 1906, membership had increased to 841.

The oldest existing meetinghouse in the Southeast was dedicated in Northcutts Cove in 1909. By 1919, branches were listed in Chattanooga and Memphis.

By 1930, some 2,832 members lived in the Middle and East Tennessee districts in the Chattanooga, Memphis and Nashville branches, and Sunday Schools in Brighton, Pope, Short Creek, Silver Point and Turkey Creek.

On April 18, 1965, the Memphis Stake was created with two wards in Memphis and another in Jackson, plus wards in Mississippi and Arkansas.

The Tennessee Nashville Mission was created in 1975. Membership in Tennessee in 1980 was 15,839, increasing to 23,007 in 1990. In 1993, the Tennessee Knoxville Mission was created and on Nov. 12, 1994, a letter to priesthood leaders announced plans to build the Nashville Tennessee Temple.

In 1996, more than 150 Church members participated in the three-mile "'96 Walk for the Homeless" in downtown Nashville.

Sources: Southern States Mission directories, 1919-1935; *Encyclopedic History of the Church,* by Andrew Jenson; *History of the Southern States Mission,* a BYU thesis by LaMar C. Berrett, July 1960; *Orthodoxy Versus Nonconformity: The Mormon Experience in Tennessee and Mississippi, 1875-1905,* a University of Chicago paper by Mary Elizabeth Stovall, March 12, 1976; *Church News,* April 24, 1965, March 22, 1975, Nov. 9, 1986; "Chattanooga: LDS in Tennessee build on a firm foundation," by R. Scott Lloyd, *Church News,* May 25, 1991; "150 Church members serve the homeless," *Church News,* May 18, 1996.

Stakes — 8
(Listed alphabetically as of Oct. 1, 1996.)

No.	Name	Organized	First President
North America Southeast Area			
927	Chattanooga Tennessee	21 May 1978	Earl Eugene Callens Jr.
1089	Franklin Tennessee	2 Dec 1979	Buryl Gene McClurg
1093	Kingsport Tennessee	13 Jan 1980	William Keith Clay
581	*Knoxville Tennessee		
	‡Knoxville	25 Jun 1972	Eugene H. Perkins
1810	McMinnville Tennessee	18 Aug 1991	Gary Wayne Bradford
403	*Memphis Tennessee		
	‡Memphis	18 Apr 1965	Richard Stoddard
	(Tenn., Mo., Ark., Miss.)		
1179	Memphis Tennessee North	14 Sep 1980	Edward Victor Martin
537	*Nashville Tennessee		
	‡Nashville	6 Dec 1970	Robert N. Brady

Missions — 2
(As of Oct. 1, 1996; shown with historical number. See MISSIONS.)

(294) TENNESSEE KNOXVILLE MISSION
P.O. Box 22730
Knoxville, TN 37933-0730
Phone: (423) 671-3466

(131) TENNESSEE NASHVILLE MISSION
P.O. Box 1287
Brentwood, TN 37024
Phone: (615) 373-1836

Texas

Year-end 1995: Est. population, 18,880,000; Members, 182,000; Stakes, 39; Wards, 291; Branches, 103; Districts, 1; Missions, 6; Temples, 1; Percent LDS, 1.0, or one person in 108.

The Church's first missionary to Texas was William C. Steffey in 1843. In 1844, Joseph Smith considered Texas as an alternate location for the Saints should they be driven from Illinois. The Church negotiated with Sam Houston and considered purchasing a large tract of land in western Texas. However, the martyrdom of Joseph Smith cut short these tentative plans. Lyman Wight, an apostle who lost faith after the martyrdom, proceeded on his own to lead a colony of 100 people into central Texas, leaving Nauvoo March 25, 1845, and arriving in the spring of 1846. Although he was excommunicated in 1848, Wight and his followers pioneered in five counties in Texas and generally left a good reputation for Mormons in the area.

Among the first successful missionaries to Texas was Preston Thomas who visited the Wight colonies in 1849 and baptized some of them back into the Church. He also baptized his brother, Daniel. Preston Thomas led the first company of Texas converts to Salt Lake City in April 1853. He served six missions to Texas and led several companies to Utah.

In 1853, Thomas A. Martindale and James McGaw labored in Harris, Grimes and Montgomery counties. Two years later, Elder Benjamin L. Clapp labored in Freestone County. The Texas Conference was organized Dec. 25, 1855. Work also went forward in Washington, Milam, McLennan and Ellis counties. From 1854 to 1857, several hundred converts immigrated to Utah. Many privations accompanied some of these immigrants.

For example, Edward Wallace and Wilmirth Greer East, converts from Port Sullivan, Texas, lost four of their six young children as well as her father and brother from cholera on an 1855 trek to the West.

While records of missionary work after this period are scarce, some 276 members in Texas were on Church records after the Civil War ended. However, harsh attitudes against the members existed for many years and little growth was realized. Elder J. Golden Kimball entered the mission field in 1892, and in 1897, he reported that public opinion was by then more favorable toward the Church. The Texas Conference was reorganized June 17, 1893, and membership began a slow but steady increase. The Texas Conference was divided into several conferences in 1898, and local leaders were called.

On Dec. 31, 1898, John and James Edgar purchased property that eventually became the Mormon colony of Kelsey, where 300 members lived. In 1906, the settlements at Kelsey, Poynor, Williamson and Spurger were the largest places of LDS worship, and membership throughout the state reached 1,000. Missionaries began tracting the areas, though some were overwhelmed by the 1901 oil boom in Beaumont that brought in thousands of people.

Until 1917, members in Houston met in rented halls while branches at Williamson and Josey built their own meetinghouses. By 1930, the state had 14 branches and an additional 11 independent Sunday Schools with a total membership of 3,837. A non-member donated her home to the Houston Branch and it was remodeled and dedicated in 1933.

For about the next 20 years, membership in Texas continued to grow slowly and local members assumed more and more leadership roles. During World War II they instituted "home missions."

The El Paso Stake was created Sept. 21, 1952, and in 1953, stakes were organized in Houston and Dallas. The San Antonio Stake was created in 1958.

Growth of the Church in Texas continued and by 1977, membership totaled more than 50,000. The Dallas Texas Temple was completed in 1984 and dedicated Oct. 19-24. The temple district at the time included 46 stakes and 120,000 members in Texas and nearby states. In 1990, membership in Texas was 154,000. On Oct. 14, 1993, Richard A. Searfoss of League City, Texas, became the first Latter-day Saint to pilot a flight of a space shuttle.

In 1994, Church members rallied to assist flood-stricken southeast Texas. President Gordon B. Hinckley addressed 3,600 members of the Church at the Corpus Christi Texas multi-stake conference Jan. 7, 1996. He also addressed 14,000 members at two different regional conference in Northeast Texas March 16-17, 1996.

Sources: *Encyclopedic History of the Church,* by Andrew Jenson; Church in Texas, by Ruby Denton; *A History of the Mormon Church in Texas 1843-1906,* by Bonnie Means Durning, a master's thesis for East Texas State College; *The Houston First Ward: From Stopover to Ward in One Hundred and Ten Years,* by Robert C. Petersen, a BYU paper, 1971; "Mormon Grove Trail beset with travails," by Chris Miasnik, *Church News,* July 24, 1993; "Shuttle pilot fulfilling childhood dream," by Julie A. Dockstader, *Church News,* Sept. 18, 1993; "Texas: LDS volunteers assist victims after devastation of flood," *Church News,* Nov. 5, 1994; "Read Book of Mormon, prophet admonishes," *Church News,* Jan. 13, 1996; "Pres. Hinckley addresses 14,000," *Church News,* March 23, 1996.

Stakes — 39
(Listed alphabetically as of Oct. 1, 1996.)

No.	Name	Organized	First President
North America Southwest Area			
1262	Abilene Texas	3 May 1981	William E. Seegmiller
1272	Amarillo Texas	31 May 1981	Donald Eugene Pinnell
1594	Arlington Texas	13 Apr 1986	Richard S. Pickering
626	Austin Texas	14 Oct 1973	Amos Luther Wright
1835	Austin Texas Oak Hills	1 Dec 1991	Gary Scott Robinson
1818	Bay City Texas	13 Oct 1991	Joseph Nathanial Cannon Jr.
333	*Beaumont Texas		
	‡Beaumont (Texas, Louisiana)	3 Sep 1961	Alden C. Stout
1076	*College Station Texas 10 Oct 1989		
	‡Conroe Texas	28 Oct 1979	Nylen Lee Allphin Jr.
398	*Corpus Christi Texas		
	‡Corpus Christi	31 May 1964	Clarence Cottam
1451	Cypress Texas	6 Nov 1983	Bruce A. Nelson

210	*Dallas Texas		
	‡Dallas	18 Oct 1953	Ervin W. Atkerson
828	Dallas Texas East	15 May 1977	Arthur Eugene Gabriel
1860	Denton Texas	3 May 1992	James Boyd Martino
194	*El Paso Texas		
	‡El Paso (Texas, New Mexico)	21 Sep 1952	Edward V. Turley Sr.
1359	El Paso Texas Mount Franklin	29 Aug 1982	Gerald Merrell Pratt
443	*Fort Worth Texas		
	‡Fort Worth (Texas)	24 Sep 1967	John Kelly Jr.
843	Friendswood Texas	29 May 1977	Newell Kenneth Hill
1394	Gilmer Texas	16 Jan 1983	Von Webber Freeman
1247	Harlingen Texas	22 Mar 1981	Leonard Moore
209	*Houston Texas		
	‡Houston (Texas, Louisiana)	11 Oct 1953	Jack Byron Trunnell
456	*Houston Texas East		
	‡Houston East (Texas)	5 May 1968	Martell A. Belnap
733	Houston Texas North	16 Nov 1975	Harold Elison DeLaMare
1211	Houston Texas South	30 Nov 1980	Leo C. Smith
784	*Hurst Texas 12 Apr 1981		
	‡Fort Worth Texas North	14 Nov 1976	Richard W. Ragsdale
1834	Katy Texas	1 Dec 1991	Collins Wise Steward
986	Killeen Texas	26 Nov 1978	Stephen Brian Hutchings
1337	Kingwood Texas	18 Apr 1982	Robert Lee Ezell
1253	Lewisville Texas	12 Apr 1981	Richard W. Ragsdale
496	*Longview Texas		
	‡Texas East	9 Nov 1969	Gerald C.F. Knackstedt
446	*Lubbock Texas		
	‡Texas North	26 Nov 1967	Franklin S. Gonzalez
692	McAllen Texas	4 May 1975	Daniel Birch Larsen
1991	McKinney Texas	11 Sep 1994	Robert C. Packard
471	*Odessa Texas		
	‡Texas West	15 Dec 1968	Roland Lamar Hamblin
1360	Orange Texas	29 Aug 1982	Bernard E. Packard
616	*Plano Texas 12 Apr 1981		
	*Dallas Texas North		
	‡Dallas North	27 May 1973	Ivan Leslie Hobson Jr.
1396	Richardson Texas	30 Jan 1983	Larry Wayne Gibbons
252	*San Antonio Texas		
	‡San Antonio	19 Jan 1958	Roland C. Bremer
758	San Antonio Texas East	30 May 1976	Archie M. Brugger
1426	San Antonio Texas West	5 Jun 1983	Jan M. Sterneckert

Missions — 6

(As of Oct. 1, 1996; shown with historical number. See MISSIONS.)

(60) TEXAS DALLAS MISSION
13747 Montfort Drive, 120
Dallas, TX 75240-4454
Phone: (972) 239-5621

(189) TEXAS FORT WORTH MISSION
1331 Airport Freeway,305
Euless, TX 76040
Phone: (817) 354-7444

(142) TEXAS HOUSTON MISSION
16333 Hafer Road
Houston, TX 77090
Phone: (713) 440-6770

(254) TEXAS HOUSTON EAST MISSION
820 So. Friendswood Drive,100
Friendswood, TX 77546
Phone: (713) 992-1001

(224) TEXAS MCALLEN MISSION
3825 North 10th St.,E
McAllen, TX 78501
Phone: (210) 664-0273

(233) TEXAS SAN ANTONIO MISSION
404 E. Ramsey Rd.,105
San Antonio, TX 78216
Phone: (210) 349-3268

Utah

Year-end 1995: Est. population, 1,972,000; Members, 1,484,000; Stakes, 413; Wards, 3,199; Branches, 115; Missions, 4; Temples, 9 in use, 1 under construction; Percent LDS, 75.2, or one person in 1.3.

On Aug. 6, 1842, Joseph Smith prophesied that the Saints would be driven to the Rocky Mountains and there "become a mighty people."

The Saints were driven from Nauvoo, Ill., in 1846, and traveled as far as Winter

Quarters, Neb., that year.

On April 5, 1847, some 148 people, in a party led by Brigham Young, began their emigration from Winter Quarters. Of this group, Orson Pratt and Erastus Snow were the first to enter the Great Basin, arriving July 21, 1847, followed by the advance party, and on the 24th by the rest of the group and Brigham Young. The Saints found a habitable but unsettled place where they hoped to live in peace. They planted crops and explored, and on July 28, Brigham Young selected the site where the Salt Lake Temple now stands. Within a month, the city had been surveyed, 80 acres of land planted, 29 log houses built, nearby valleys explored, a bowry built, an adobe fort constructed, Indians befriended, and trade shops started.

Other companies of pioneers followed, starting a flood of immigration into the Great Basin that continued until the turn of the century and afterward. About 4,500 people were in the valley before the harsh winter of 1848. Many subsisted on roots of sego lilies and boiled rawhide.

On Sept. 26, 1847, Perregrine Sessions arrived in what is now Bountiful and established a colony. Nearby Farmington was founded the same year by Hector C. Haight. In 1848, Captain James Brown of the Mormon Battalion purchased the land rights of early settler Miles Goodyear and built Brown's Fort in what is now Ogden. Centerville was established in 1848, and many Salt Lake-area colonies, such as East Millcreek and Sugar House, were started the same year. Provo was founded in 1849, along with Kaysville, Granger, Tooele and the central Utah community of Manti. By 1850, Iron City in southern Utah and 28 other colonies had been started. That year, Salt Lake City had a population of more than 11,000 people and the essentials of a successful commerce.

Before the turn of the century, up to 500 settlements had been founded within the state and in the adjoining states of Idaho, Nevada, California, Arizona, New Mexico, Colorado and Wyoming. Many of the first settlers were members from the Nauvoo period — either American or British immigrants. Later colonies were made up of emigrants from Scandinavia, Europe and a variety of lands such as Australia, India, South Africa and even Hawaii. At least 236 parties or companies of pioneers crossed the plains for Utah in independent companies with wagon freighters, handcart companies and various Church companies. Many were assisted by the Church's Perpetual Emigrating Fund. An estimated 60,000 Mormons crossed the plains as pioneers. Of these, some 3,000 people crossed with handcart companies in 1856-60. Two companies, however, the late-starting Willie and Martin companies of 1856, met with tragedy in Wyoming with an unseasonably early winter, and 200 died from exposure and starvation. The majority of the people in these two handcart companies, some 875, were rescued through heroic personal effort of the Saints in Utah.

Members generally got along well with the Indians, and the most prominent local leader, Ute Chief Walker, was friendly and was baptized in 1850, though he led a brief resistance movement in 1853. Members traded with Indians and shared food with them, and the Indians helped members survive. Indian farms were established in the 1850s, but troubles between the Mormons and the government discouraged most of the Indians.

In 1857, responding to false reports of insurrection, President James Buchanan sent an army under General Albert Sidney Johnston to put down the rebellion and install a new governor in Utah. In Utah, members considered it another act of persecution (see New York, Ohio, Missouri and Illinois histories) and prepared to protect themselves. If attacked, the Saints would not fight but would burn their homes to the ground, leaving their persecutors nothing but "scorched earth," said Brigham Young. However, partly through intercession of friends of the Church, particularly Col. Thomas L. Kane, war was averted and Johnston's army passed peacefully through Salt Lake City. At the height of the war-time hysteria, a group of 120 Missouri immigrants passing through southern Utah who had provoked the Indians were killed by Indians and settlers at Mountain Meadows.

Difficulties between federal appointees and citizens continued until Utah was granted statehood in 1896. A major obstacle to statehood was the practice of plural marriage, which ended with the Manifesto issued by President Wilford Woodruff on Sept. 24, 1890.

On Feb. 14, 1853, ground was broken for the granite, six-spired temple in Salt Lake City. The edifice was constructed of stone quarried 20 miles away. The stone was hauled from the quarry by ox-drawn wagons until 1869 when the railroad was completed. Dedicated in 1892, this temple with its gilded statue of an angel and trumpet (Rev. 14:6) on the top spire has become the most recognized worldwide symbol of the Church. Before the completion of the Salt Lake Temple, three other temples in the state were built and dedicated. Three other temples were erected and dedicated in the 1970s and 1980s. The Bountiful Utah Temple was dedicated in 1995, and the Mount Timpanogos Utah Temple in American Fork became the ninth temple in the state and the second in Utah County when it was dedicated on Oct. 13, 1996, by President Gordon B. Hinckley.

The companion building to the temple, the Tabernacle on Temple Square, was built from 1863-67 and dedicated in 1875. It is among the largest timber-roofed buildings in the world, and from its impressive interior emanates the weekly broadcast of the Tabernacle Choir, the longest continuous broadcast program in the United States.

During the pioneer period and shortly after the turn of the century, many of the larger outlying communities also erected tabernacles, ornate meetinghouses built for large gatherings. Many of these stand today as outstanding examples of pioneer craftsmanship.

Completion of the overland railroad in 1869 brought many changes, including more extensive mining interests. The state's population, which reached 40,273 in 1860, jumped to 210,779 in 1890. By 1900, the population was 276,749, and Utah had 27 stakes.

Throughout this period, the Church's stakes shifted from being predominantly in Utah to being about half in Utah. In 1950 Utah gained 28 new stakes and 46 were created elsewhere. By 1992, about one stake in five was in Utah.

Converts from other nations and states continued to migrate to Utah. Many non-members also came to the state. Utah officially became a mission field with its own headquarters in 1975 when the Utah Salt Lake City Mission was organized. Previously, missionaries worked in Utah under the leadership of missions headquartered in other states. The mission proved to be successful and has been divided twice. Utah's four missions, according to mission leaders, are among the most successful in the United States.

Temple Square in Salt Lake City is visited annually by nearly 5 million people and ranks among the top tourist attractions in the nation.

Over the years, the Utah membership supplied the Church with many missionaries and leaders, and has taken a pivotal role in supporting the expansion of the Church.

On Jan. 4, 1996, Utahns celebrated 100 years of statehood with dancing in the streets, parades, speeches, fireworks and music. A special program in the Tabernacle included a re-enactment of the original celebration and remarks by the modern-day counterparts of those in the original program.

"I think it fair to say," said President Gordon B. Hinckley during the special program, "that no other community of citizens worked longer and harder for statehood or were more grateful when it was finally granted."

Other speakers included Utah Gov. Michael O. Leavitt and the Rev. Robert R. Sewell of the First United Methodist Church.

Sources: *Utah's Heritage,* by S. George Ellsworth; *Utah's History,* Richard D. Poll, general editor, BYU Press; *Pioneer Companies that Crossed the Plains,* by Melvin S. Bashore; *Encyclopedic History of the Church,* by Andrew Jenson; *Deseret News 1991-1992 Church Almanac*; multiple sources in *Church News.*

Stakes — 429

(Listed alphabetically by area as of Oct. 1, 1996.)

No.	Name	Organized	First President
Utah North Area — 266			
664	Bennion Utah	27 Oct 1974	John Labrum
1459	Bennion Utah East	29 Jan 1984	Jack L. Green
875	Bennion Utah West	30 Oct 1977	Glenn A. Weight
1482	*Bennion Heights Utah	28 Aug 1988	
	‡Bennion Utah Central	17 Jun 1984	Glen Alvin Weight
918	Benson Utah	7 May 1978	Dale Morgan Rindlisbacher
1521	Bluffdale Utah	10 Mar 1985	Michael Van Jeppson
193	*Bountiful Utah		
	‡Bountiful	23 Mar 1952	Thomas Amby Briggs
539	*Bountiful Utah Central		
	‡Bountiful Center	10 Jan 1971	Steven S. Davis
383	*Bountiful Utah East		
	‡Bountiful East	29 Sep 1963	Rendell N. Mabey

546	*Bountiful Utah Heights		
	‡Bountiful Heights	16 May 1971	Jesse Earl Godfrey
1127	Bountiful Utah Mueller Park	27 Apr 1980	Duane Bowring Welling
260	*Bountiful Utah North		
	‡Bountiful North	20 Apr 1958	Henry E. Peterson
1206	Bountiful Utah North Canyon	9 Nov 1980	Robert Heiner Garff
71	*Bountiful Utah Orchard		
	*Davis South 29 May 1970		
	‡South Davis	20 Jun 1915	James H. Robinson
262	*Bountiful Utah South		
	‡Bountiful South	20 Apr 1958	Ward C. Holbrook
1269	Bountiful Utah Stone Creek	24 May 1981	Richard Scott Lemon
501	*Bountiful Utah Val Verda		
	‡Val Verda	25 Jan 1970	Milton W. Russon
382	*Brigham City Utah		
	‡Brigham City	22 Sep 1963	Lawrence C. Taylor
148	*Brigham City Utah Box Elder		
	*Box Elder 30 Aug 1959		
	‡South Box Elder	12 Nov 1944	Abel S. Rich
147a	*Brigham City Utah North		
	*Box Elder North 29 May 1970		
	‡North Box Elder	12 Nov 1944	John P. Lillywhite
375	*Brigham City Utah South		
	*Box Elder South 29 May 1970		
	‡South Box Elder	28 Apr 1963	LeGrande Tea
1242	Brigham City Utah West	8 Mar 1981	Lowell Sherratt Jr.
575	*Centerville Utah		
	‡Centerville	21 May 1972	Joseph A. Kjar
1798	Centerville Utah Canyon View	12 May 1991	Bruce Garrett Pitt
1335	Centerville Utah North	11 Apr 1982	Richard Crockett Edgley
903	Centerville Utah South	9 Apr 1978	Robert A. Trump
277	*Clearfield Utah		
	‡Clearfield	12 Apr 1959	George Smith Haslam
966	Clearfield Utah North	8 Oct 1978	Alfred Clyde Van Wagenen
728	Clinton Utah	9 Nov 1975	Albert DeMar Mitchell
1467	Clinton Utah North	15 Apr 1984	Jay Barr Snelgrove
18	*Coalville Utah		
	‡Summit	9 Jul 1877	William W. Cluff
142	*Draper Utah		
	‡Mount Jordan	3 May 1942	Stanley A. Rasmussen
1319	*Draper Utah Eastridge 25 Aug 1991		
	‡Draper Utah North	6 Dec 1981	Richard D. Alsop
152	*Farmington Utah		
	‡Davis	14 Oct 1945	Leroy H. Duncan
1342	Farmington Utah North	16 May 1982	Richard J. White
1769	Farmington Utah Oakridge	19 Aug 1990	Jerry L. King
1750	Farmington Utah South	13 May 1990	John Leon Sorenson
1531	Fielding Utah	12 May 1985	Mark H. Jensen
1568	Fruit Heights Utah	27 Oct 1985	Newell John Law
59	*Garland Utah		
	‡Bear River	11 Oct 1908	Milton H. Welling
147	*Grantsville Utah		
	‡Grantsville	16 Jan 1944	Paul E. Wrathall
1069	Grantsville Utah West	23 Sep 1979	Don Henning Johnson
1494	Harrisville Utah	23 Sep 1984	Robert Lynn Nielsen
141	*Hooper Utah		
	‡Lakeview	22 Mar 1942	John Child
924	Huntsville Utah	14 May 1978	Marlin Keith Jensen
1559	Hyde Park Utah	22 Sep 1985	Vincent Eugene Erickson
46	*Hyrum Utah		
	‡Hyrum	30 Apr 1901	William C. Parkinson
1046	Hyrum Utah North	5 Aug 1979	J. Spencer Ward
106	*Kamas Utah		
	*Summit South 29 May 1970		
	‡South Summit	8 Jul 1934	Zach J. Oblad

1635	Kanesville Utah	19 Apr 1987	Roland B. Hadley
350	*Kaysville Utah		
	‡Kaysville	18 Feb 1962	Alan B. Blood
2101	Kaysville Utah Central	24 Sep 1995	Wesley H. Wilcox
1027	Kaysville Utah Crestwood	13 May 1979	Wallace Eldean Holliday
568	*Kaysville Utah East		
	‡Kaysville East	27 Feb 1972	Lawrence E. Welling
1010	Kaysville Utah South	11 Mar 1979	Newell John Law
255	*Kearns Utah		
	‡Kearns	2 Feb 1958	Merrill A. Nelson
1055	Kearns Utah Central	26 Aug 1979	Garth D. Mecham
990	Kearns Utah East	10 Dec 1978	Earl M. Monson
256	*Kearns Utah North		
	‡Kearns North	2 Feb 1958	Volma W. Heaton
653	Kearns Utah South	25 Aug 1974	Garth D. Mecham
1462	Kearns Utah West	12 Feb 1984	Rodney W. Bushman
1258	Kearns Utah Western Hills	26 Apr 1981	Clarence Myron White
203	*Layton Utah		
	‡Layton	25 Jan 1953	I. Haven Barlow
449	*Layton Utah East		
	‡Layton East	4 Feb 1968	Robert F. Bitner
957	Layton Utah Holmes Creek	3 Sep 1978	K. Roger Bean
2062	Layton Utah Kays Creek	11 Jun 1995	Stephen George Handy
2196	Layton Utah Layton Hills 19 May 1996		S. Clair Bankhead
1529	Layton Utah North	5 May 1985	Lorin Winslow Hurst Jr.
1657	Layton Utah Northridge	11 Oct 1987	Samuel Clair Bankhead
1629	Layton Utah South	8 Feb 1987	William C. Barney Jr.
1948	Layton Utah Valley View	27 Jun 1993	Floyd Stenquist
858	Layton Utah West	21 Aug 1977	William C. Barney Jr.
80	*Logan Utah		
	‡Logan	4 Jun 1920	Oliver H. Budge
13	*Logan Utah Cache		
	‡Cache	21 May 1877	Moses Thatcher
1422	Logan Utah Cache West	22 May 1983	Miles Peter Jensen
1241	Logan Utah Central	8 Mar 1981	Thad August Carlson
164	*Logan Utah East		
	*Cache East 29 May 1970		
	‡East Cache	2 Feb 1947	J. Howard Maughan
160	*Logan Utah Mount Logan		
	‡Mount Logan	17 Nov 1946	A. George Raymond
1347	Logan Utah South	6 Jun 1982	Ronald Skeen Peterson
259	*Logan Utah University 1st		
	‡Utah State University	13 Apr 1958	Reed Bullen
427	*Logan Utah University 2nd		
	‡Utah State University 2nd	12 Feb 1967	Reynold K. Watkins
785	Logan Utah University 3rd	14 Nov 1976	LaGrande C. Larsen
1719	Logan Utah University 4th	7 May 1989	Russell Miles Warren
2069	Logan Utah University 5th	25 Jun 1995	Bartell Cowley Jensen
90	*Magna Utah		
	‡Oquirrh	3 Jun 1923	George A. Little
1013	Magna Utah Central	8 Apr 1979	Charles Robert Canfield
410	*Magna Utah East		
	‡Oquirrh East	17 Oct 1965	William B. Martin
1510	Magna Utah South	20 Jan 1985	Hendrick Dorenbosch
246	*Midvale Utah		
	‡Midvale	30 Jun 1957	Reed H. Beckstead
457	*Midvale Utah East		
	*Midvale East 29 May 1970		
	‡East Midvale	5 May 1968	R. Kent King
1561	Midvale Utah North	13 Oct 1985	Grant Leon Pullan
96a	*Midvale Utah Union Fort		
	*Midvale Utah Fort Union		
	*Fort Union 17 Jun 1973		
	*Jordan East 29 May 1970		
	‡East Jordan	8 May 1927	Heber J. Burgon

16	*Morgan Utah		
	‡Morgan	1 Jul 1877	Willard G. Smith
1240	Morgan Utah North	8 Mar 1981	Robert Warner Poll
183	*Murray Utah		
	‡Murray	11 Feb 1951	Oral J. Wilkinson
543	*Murray Utah Little Cottonwood	8 Jan 1989	
	*Murray Utah East		
	‡Little Cottonwood	21 Feb 1971	James S. McCloy
1009	Murray Utah North	11 Mar 1979	John Mace Johnson
1849	Murray Utah Parkway	1 Mar 1992	Dan Alan Anderson
240	*Murray Utah South		
	‡Murray South	28 Apr 1957	Donald W. Challis
468	*Murray Utah West		
	‡Murray West	24 Nov 1968	Robert H.M. Killpack
528	*North Logan Utah		
	‡Cache North	11 Oct 1970	Charles L. Hyde
2244	North Logan Utah Green Canyon	22 Sep 1996	Jerry Allen Wilson
146	*North Ogden Utah		
	‡Ben Lomond	21 Nov 1943	William Arthur Budge
956	North Ogden Utah Ben Lomond	27 Aug 1978	Calvin J. Heiner
1804	North Ogden Utah Coldwater	23 Jun 1991	Eugene Jensen Low
1016	North Salt Lake Utah	15 Apr 1979	Clare Anderson Jones
57	*Ogden Utah		
	‡Ogden	19 Jul 1908	Thomas B. Evans
998	Ogden Utah Burch Creek	4 Feb 1979	James Kirk Moyes
1133	Ogden Utah Canyon View	18 May 1980	Luan Holly Ferrin
199	*Ogden Utah East		
	*Ogden East 29 May 1970		
	‡East Ogden	23 Nov 1952	Scott B. Price
198	*Ogden Utah Lorin Farr		
	‡Lorin Farr	16 Nov 1952	Elton W. Wardle
140	*Ogden Utah Mound Fort 23 Sep 1984		
	*Ogden Utah Farr West		
	‡Farr West	18 Jan 1942	Wilmer J. Maw
1157	Ogden Utah Mount Lewis	29 Jun 1980	Kenneth J. Alford
87	*Ogden Utah Mount Ogden		
	‡Mount Ogden	21 May 1922	Robert I. Burton
314	*Ogden Utah North		
	‡Ben Lomond South	20 Nov 1960	Robert M. Yorgason
798	Ogden Utah Terrace View	12 Dec 1976	Leo Neeley Harris
520a	*Ogden Utah Weber		
	‡Weber	16 Aug 1970	Nathan C. Tanner
272	*Ogden Utah Weber Heights		
	‡Weber Heights	30 Nov 1958	Keith W. Wilcox
58	*Ogden Utah Weber North		
	*Weber North 29 May 1970		
	‡North Weber	19 Jul 1908	James Wotherspoon
1191	*Ogden Utah West 23 Nov 1993		
	‡Ogden Utah Weber South	12 Oct 1980	Allan T. Clarke
1520	Park City Utah	10 Mar 1985	B. Douglas Glad
876	Plain City Utah	30 Oct 1977	Kent W. Calvert
559	*Pleasant View Utah		
	‡Ben Lomond West	21 Nov 1971	Jay Herbert Rhees
561	*Providence Utah		
	‡Providence	12 Dec 1971	Asa L. Beecher
1351	Providence Utah South	13 Jun 1982	Lanny J. Nalder
47	*Richmond Utah		
	‡Benson	1 May 1901	William H. Lewis
201	*Riverdale Utah		
	*Ogden Utah Riverdale	14 Mar 1995	
	‡Riverdale	30 Nov 1952	Rudolph L. VanKampen
303	*Riverton Utah		
	‡Riverton	18 Sep 1960	J. Harold Berrett
1067	Riverton Utah North	23 Sep 1979	Keith LeRoy Bergstrom

1843	Riverton Utah Summerhill	19 Jan 1992	L. Chad Campbell
328	*Roy Utah		
	‡Roy	26 Mar 1961	Henry Adolph Matis
1485	Roy Utah Central	24 Jun 1984	Mark Lee Angus
438	*Roy Utah North		
	‡Roy North	11 Jun 1967	Walter D. Bingham
1673	Roy Utah South	24 Jan 1988	Alonzo C Heiner
942	Roy Utah West	11 Jun 1978	Lewis R. Child
1a	Salt Lake	3 Oct 1847	John Smith
576	*Salt Lake Big Cottonwood		
	‡Big Cottonwood	28 May 1972	Robert B. Barker
115	*Salt Lake Bonneville		
	‡Bonneville	27 Oct 1935	Joseph L. Wirthlin
603	*Salt Lake Brighton		
	‡Butler South	4 Mar 1973	Alvin Don Nydegger
361	*Salt Lake Butler		
	‡Butler	18 Nov 1962	James C. Taylor
418	*Salt Lake Butler West		
	‡Butler West	8 May 1966	Sherman M. Crump
204	*Salt Lake Cannon		
	‡Cannon	1 Mar 1953	Fred H. Peck
237	*Salt Lake Canyon Rim		
	‡Canyon Rim	28 Oct 1956	Verl F. Scott
291	*Salt Lake Central		
	‡University West	7 Feb 1960	Lemonte Peterson
133	*Salt Lake Cottonwood		
	*Cottonwood 11 Feb 1951		
	‡Big Cottonwood	20 Oct 1940	Irvin T. Nelson
936	Salt Lake Cottonwood Heights	28 May 1978	R. Gordon Porter
1607	Salt Lake Eagle Gate	21 Sep 1986	W. Herbert Klopfer
150	*Salt Lake East Millcreek		
	‡East Millcreek	17 Jun 1945	L.B. Gunderson
996	Salt Lake East Millcreek North	28 Jan 1979	Joel R. Garrett
129a	*Salt Lake Emigration		
	‡Emigration	10 Mar 1940	George A. Christensen
55	*Salt Lake Ensign		
	‡Ensign	1 Apr 1904	Richard W. Young
249	*Salt Lake Foothill		
	‡Monument Park West	29 Sep 1957	Frank Carl Berg
266	*Salt Lake Granger		
	‡Granger	8 Jun 1958	Wm. Grant Bangerter
491	*Salt Lake Granger East		
	‡Granger East	24 Aug 1969	David D. Lingard
324	*Salt Lake Granger North		
	‡Granger North	26 Feb 1961	Frankland J. Kennard
764	Salt Lake Granger South	22 Aug 1976	Gordon Ward Evans
497	*Salt Lake Granger West		
	‡Granger West	4 Jan 1970	Dwayne T. Johnson
42	*Salt Lake Granite		
	‡Granite	28 Jan 1900	Frank Y. Taylor
1457	Salt Lake Granite Park	4 Dec 1983	Robert T. Fitt
92	*Salt Lake Grant		
	‡Grant	25 May 1924	Joseph J. Daynes
114	*Salt Lake Highland		
	‡Highland	8 Sep 1935	Marvin O. Ashton
154	*Salt Lake Hillside		
	‡Hillside	13 Jan 1946	Casper Hugh Parker
227	*Salt Lake Holladay		
	‡Holladay	18 Mar 1956	G. Carlos Smith Jr.
891	Salt Lake Holladay North	12 Feb 1978	John A. Larsen
460	*Salt Lake Holladay South		
	‡Holladay South	16 Jun 1968	Marvin L. Pugh
390	*Salt Lake Hunter		
	‡Hunter	5 Jan 1964	E. Verne Breeze
982	Salt Lake Hunter Central	19 Nov 1978	Evans Thomas Doxey

1533	Salt Lake Hunter Copperhill	12 May 1985	Stanley Martin Kimball
839	Salt Lake Hunter East	22 May 1977	Merrill Dimick
1539	Salt Lake Hunter South	9 Jun 1985	Morris L. Terry
582	*Salt Lake Hunter West		
	‡Hunter West	13 Aug 1972	Evans Thomas Doxey
863	Salt Lake Jordan	9 Oct 1977	Robert Bennion Arnold
162	*Salt Lake Jordan North		
	*Jordan North 29 May 1970		
	‡North Jordan	12 Jan 1947	John D. Hill
53	*Salt Lake Liberty		
	‡Liberty	26 Feb 1904	Hugh J. Cannon
68	*Salt Lake Millcreek		
	*Millcreek 11 Feb 1951		
	‡Cottonwood	29 Nov 1914	Uriah G. Miller
187	*Salt Lake Monument Park		
	‡Monument Park	24 Jun 1951	George L. Nelson
1832	Salt Lake Monument		
	Park North	24 Nov 1991	B. Lloyd Poelman
393	*Salt Lake Mount Olympus		
	‡Mount Olympus	12 Apr 1964	Orin R. Woodbury
904	Salt Lake Mount		
	Olympus North	9 Apr 1978	William Schaubel Partridge
267	*Salt Lake Olympus		
	‡Olympus	29 Jun 1958	Heber E. Peterson
145	*Salt Lake Park		
	‡Park	24 Oct 1943	J. Percy Goddard
273	*Salt Lake Parleys		
	‡Parleys	7 Dec 1958	Walter J. Eldredge Jr.
54	*Salt Lake Pioneer		
	‡Pioneer	24 Mar 1904	William McLachlan
130	*Salt Lake Riverside		
	‡Riverside	24 Mar 1940	John B. Matheson
222a	*Salt Lake Rose Park		
	‡Rose Park	9 Oct 1955	Joseph F. Steenblik
412	*Salt Lake Rose Park North		
	‡Rose Park North	28 Nov 1965	Joseph L. Lundstrom
345	*Salt Lake South Cottonwood		
	‡South Cottonwood	10 Dec 1961	James S. McCloy
144	*Salt Lake Sugar House		
	‡Sugar House	16 May 1943	Thomas M. Wheeler
178	*Salt Lake University 1st		
	*University 1st 30 Apr 1967		
	‡University	12 Feb 1950	J. Quayle Ward
433	*Salt Lake University 2nd		
	‡University 2nd	30 Apr 1967	Oscar W. McConkie Jr.
1488	Salt Lake University 3rd	19 Aug 1984	James Stuart Jardine
1857	Salt Lake University 4th	26 Apr 1992	John C. Pingree
1934	Salt Lake University 5th	18 Apr 1993	Kem C. Gardner
236	*Salt Lake Valley View		
	‡Valley View	28 Oct 1956	Lamont B. Gundersen
1928	Salt Lake Utah (Tongan)	28 Mar 1993	Pita Masaku Kinikini
1111	Salt Lake Wasatch	24 Feb 1980	Richard G. Peterson
105	*Salt Lake Wells		
	‡Wells	31 Dec 1933	Thomas E. Towler
182	*Salt Lake Wilford		
	‡Wilford	11 Feb 1951	George Z. Aposhian
274	*Salt Lake Winder		
	‡Winder	25 Jan 1959	M. Elmer Christensen
706	Salt Lake Winder West	21 Sep 1975	Wayne O. Ursenbach
276	*Sandy Utah		
	‡Sandy	12 Apr 1959	Stanley A. Rasmussen
1489	Sandy Utah Alta View	19 Aug 1984	G. Scott Dean
611	*Sandy Utah Canyon View 31 Jul 1990		
	*Sandy Utah North		
	‡Sandy North (Utah)	29 Apr 1973	Eugene D. Tenney

955	Sandy Utah Central	27 Aug 1978	Charles Alma Jones
968	Sandy Utah Cottonwood Creek	15 Oct 1978	John Robert Ruppel
627	*Sandy Utah Crescent		
	‡Crescent Utah	21 Oct 1973	Allen Eugene Hilton
1110	Sandy Utah Crescent North	24 Feb 1980	Gerald Leigh Gunnell
1639	Sandy Utah Crescent Park	17 May 1987	Brad Jensen Sheppard
981	Sandy Utah Crescent South	19 Nov 1978	Marlin Alma Fairborn
775	Sandy Utah Crescent West	24 Oct 1976	John Burton Anderson
365	*Sandy Utah East		
	‡Sandy East	13 Jan 1963	Orren J. Greenwood
972	Sandy Utah Granite	22 Oct 1978	William Stanley Bush
1367	Sandy Utah Granite South	17 Oct 1982	Charles Winston Dahquist II
1612	Sandy Utah Granite View	26 Oct 1986	Alan Snelgrove Layton
1812	Sandy Utah Hidden Valley	25 Aug 1991	Mark James Pendleton
811	Sandy Utah Hillcrest	13 Feb 1977	Arnold Christensen
1278	*Sandy Utah Midvalley 9 Oct 1988		
	‡Midvale Utah Fort	14 Jun 1981	Kenneth William Kraudy
	Union South		
579	*Sandy Utah West		
	‡Sandy West	11 Jun 1972	Reed Neff Brown
623	*Sandy Utah Willow Creek		
	‡Willow Creek	17 Jun 1973	Wayne E. Saunders
119	*Smithfield Utah		
	‡Smithfield	9 Jan 1938	Alfred W. Chambers
1384	Smithfield Utah North	21 Nov 1982	W. Noble Erickson
482	*South Jordan Utah		
	*South Jordan 30 Nov 1970		
	*Jordan South 29 May 1970		
	‡South Jordan	18 May 1969	Theron B. Hutchings
2087	South Jordan Utah		
	Country Park	13 Aug 1995	Calvin H. Newbold
1192	*South Jordan Utah Glenmoor 19 Sep 1993		
	‡South Jordan Utah West	12 Oct 1980	Calvin George Osborne
1956	South Jordan Utah Parkway	19 Sep 1993	Roger Glen Christensen
1491	*South Jordan Utah River 18 Dec 1990		
	‡South Jordan Utah East	9 Sep 1984	Charles Elmo Turner
2128	South Jordan Utah River Ridge	19 Nov 1995	William H. Webb
139	*South Ogden Utah		
	‡South Ogden	7 Dec 1941	William J. Critchlow
138	*South Salt Lake 31 May 1979		
	*Salt Lake South		
	‡South Salt Lake	2 Sep 1941	Axel J. Andresen
1705	South Weber Utah	27 Nov 1988	LeRoy Horace Poll
424	*Sunset Utah		
	‡Sunset	11 Dec 1966	John L. Nicholas
70a	*Syracuse Utah		
	*Davis North 29 May 1970		
	‡North Davis	20 Jun 1915	Henry H. Blood
1858	Syracuse Utah South	26 Apr 1992	Wesley Miller White
217	*Taylorsville Utah		
	‡Taylorsville	10 Oct 1954	Wayne Charles Player
598	*Taylorsville Utah Central		
	‡Taylorsville Central	4 Feb 1973	Richard A. Barker
629	Taylorsville Utah North	28 Oct 1973	LeVere Elihu Brady
1473	Taylorsville Utah North Central	13 May 1984	Floyd Keith Rupp
1461	Taylorsville Utah South	5 Feb 1984	Clinton D. Topham
809	*Taylorsville Utah Valley Park 4 Dec 1988		
	‡Taylorsville Utah West Central 6 Feb 1977		Floyd Keith Rupp
411	*Taylorsville Utah West		
	‡Taylorsville West	31 Oct 1965	Richard A. Barker
15	*Tooele Utah		
	‡Tooele	24 Jun 1877	Francis M. Lyman
206	*Tooele Utah North		
	*Tooele North 29 May 1970		
	‡North Tooele	29 Mar 1953	Orland T. Barrus

928	Tooele Utah South	21 May 1978	Joel James Dunn
173	*Tremonton Utah		
	*Bear River South 29 May 1970		
	‡South Bear River	1 May 1949	Clifton G.M. Kerr
1004	Tremonton Utah South	25 Feb 1979	Boyd Lee Cullimore
371	*Washington Terrace Utah		
	‡Washington Terrace	24 Feb 1963	Ernest B. Wheeler
458	Weber State University Stake 21 Aug 1990		
	*Ogden Utah College		
	‡Weber State College	12 May 1968	E. LaMar Buckner
1043	Wellsville Utah	17 Jun 1979	Donald Joseph Jeppesen Jr.
578	*West Bountiful Utah 9 Oct 1984		
	*Bountiful Utah West		
	‡Bountiful West	11 Jun 1972	Clarence D. Samuelson
97	*West Jordan Utah		
	‡West Jordan	8 May 1927	Joseph M. Holt
1511	*West Jordan Utah Bingham Creek 29 Nov 1988		
	‡West Jordan Utah Southeast	27 Jan 1985	Frederick James Haydock
735	West Jordan Utah East	30 Nov 1975	Dale P. Bateman
929	*West Jordan Utah Heritage 9 Oct 1990		
	‡West Jordan Utah West	21 May 1978	Robert B. Rowley
614	*West Jordan Utah Mountain View 21 Feb 1989		
	*West Jordan Utah South		
	‡Jordan River	20 May 1973	Max Curtis Jewkes
2155	West Jordan Utah Jordan Oaks	14 Jan 1996	Jerrald M. Jensen
1099	*West Jordan Utah		
	Mountain Shadows	6 Dec 1994	
	West Jordan Utah Central	27 Jan 1980	M. Curtis Jewkes
1311	West Jordan Utah Oquirrh	22 Nov 1981	Johannes Gerald Erkelens
1686	West Jordan Utah Prairie	7 Feb 1988	J. Kim Christensen
1443	West Jordan Utah River	18 Sep 1983	Dennis Arthur Hope
1509	West Jordan Utah Welby	20 Jan 1985	Russell Jean Abney
1512	*West Jordan Utah Westbrook 16 May 1989		
	‡West Jordan Utah North	3 Feb 1985	Henry Keonaona Chai II
1128	West Point Utah	27 Apr 1980	Vern L. Thurgood
636	*West Valley Utah 17 Jan 1989		
	‡Salt Lake Granger Central	31 Mar 1974	Norman H. Bangerter
1506	Willard Utah	25 Nov 1984	Robert Kent Lund
498	*Woods Cross Utah		
	‡Woods Cross	4 Jan 1970	D. Hatch Howard
1333	Woods Cross Utah East	21 Mar 1982	Wayne A. Beers

Discontinued

20	Box Elder	19 Aug 1877	Oliver G. Snow
	12 Nov 1944 †North Box Elder (147), South Box Elder (148)		
14	Davis	17 Jun 1877	William R. Smith
	20 Jun 1915 †North Davis (70), South Davis (71)		
41	Jordan	21 Jan 1900	Orrin P. Miller
	8 May 1927 †East Jordan (96), West Jordan (97)		
275	*Salt Lake Granite Park		
	31 May 1979 †South Salt Lake (138)		
	‡Granite Park	22 Feb 1959	Rolf Christiansen
155	*Salt Lake Temple View		
	24 June 1979 †Salt Lake Wells (105), Salt Lake Liberty (53)		
	*Temple View 14 Apr 1946		
	‡Temple	13 Jan 1946	Adiel F. Stewart
2b	Weber	26 Jan 1851	Lorin Farr
	14 Jun 1970 †Mount Ogden (87)		

Utah South Area — 163

44	*Alpine Utah		
	‡Alpine	13 Jan 1901	Stephen L. Chipman
2206	Alpine Utah North	23 Jun 1996	Terry L. Brown
1526	Altamont Utah	21 Apr 1985	Everett Dee Roberts
376	*American Fork Utah		
	‡American Fork	12 May 1963	Stanley D. Roberts

2042	American Fork Utah Central	23 Apr 1995	Paul Joseph Rasband
1022	American Fork Utah East	29 Apr 1979	Dale Orville Gunther
2154	American Fork Utah Hillcrest	14 Jan 1996	Craig B. Terry
624	*American Fork Utah North		
	‡American Fork North	17 Jun 1973	Leland Forbes Priday
1218	American Fork Utah West	14 Dec 1980	Brent Lindsay Milne
7b	*Beaver Utah		
	‡Beaver	12 Mar 1869	John R. Murdock
897	Blanding Utah	5 Mar 1978	Fred Eugene Halliday
1283	Blanding Utah West	12 Jul 1981	Preston Gardner Nielson
1690	Bloomington Utah	6 Mar 1988	Steven Howard Peterson
225	*Brigham Young University 1st		
	‡Brigham Young University	8 Jan 1956	Antone K. Romney
295	Brigham Young University 2nd	17 Apr 1960	Bryan W. Belnap
296	Brigham Young University 3rd	17 Apr 1960	William Noble Waite
395	Brigham Young University 4th	3 May 1964	William R. Siddoway
396	Brigham Young University 5th	3 May 1964	A. Harold Goodman
397	Brigham Young University 6th	3 May 1964	Wayne B. Hales
431	Brigham Young University 7th	30 Apr 1967	Dean A. Peterson
432	Brigham Young University 8th	30 Apr 1967	David H. Yarn
478	Brigham Young University 9th	27 Apr 1969	Carl D. Jones
479	Brigham Young University 10th	27 Apr 1969	Ivan J. Barrett
688	Brigham Young University 11th	13 Apr 1975	Gregory E. Austin
689	Brigham Young University 12th	13 Apr 1975	Charles Verl Clark
973	Brigham Young University 13th	29 Oct 1978	Leo Preston Vernon
974	Brigham Young University 14th	29 Oct 1978	Curtis Nicholas VanAlfen
1605	Brigham Young University 15th	31 Aug 1986	H. Donl Peterson
1688	Brigham Young University 16th	21 Feb 1988	Donald J Butler
1722	Brigham Young University 17th	21 May 1989	Stanley Armond Taylor
1889	Brigham Young University 18th	28 Jun 1992	Clark D. Webb Jr.
23	*Castle Dale Utah		
	‡Emery	Aug 1880	Christen G. Larsen
413	*Cedar City Univeristy 1st	30 Apr 1995	
	*Southern Utah University 13 Dec 1990		
	*Cedar City Utah College		
	*Southern Utah State College 12 Oct 1969		
	‡College of Southern Utah	6 Jan 1966	Robert B. White Jr.
2045	Cedar City University 2nd	30 Apr 1995	Warren Morrill Woolsey
172	*Cedar City Utah		
	‡Cedar	2 May 1948	David L. Sargent
2170	Cedar City Utah Canyon View	18 Feb 1996	Robert Browning Platt
901	Cedar City Utah North	19 Mar 1978	Robert L. Blattner
316	*Cedar City Utah West		
	‡Cedar West	27 Nov 1960	Franklin D. Day
65	*Delta Utah		
	‡Deseret	11 Aug 1912	Alonzo A. Hinckley
1068	Delta Utah West	23 Sep 1979	Glen Wilford Swalberg
62	*Duchesne Utah		
	‡Duchesne	14 Sep 1910	William H. Smart
1564	Enoch Utah	20 Oct 1985	Robert Louis Blattner
134	*Enterprise Utah		
	‡Uvada (Utah, Nevada)	15 Dec 1940	David J. Ronnow
1524	Ephraim Utah	24 Mar 1985	Joseph C. Nielsen
83	*Escalante Utah		
	‡Garfield	29 Aug 1920	Charles E. Rowan Jr.
1336	Ferron Utah	11 Apr 1982	Jerry D Mangum
6b	*Fillmore Utah		
	‡Millard	9 Mar 1869	Thomas Callister
89	*Gunnison Utah		
	‡Gunnison	6 May 1923	Allen E. Park
19	*Heber City Utah		
	‡Wasatch	15 Jul 1877	Abraham Hatch
649	Heber City Utah East	16 Jun 1974	Robert F. Clyde
1170	Helper Utah	24 Aug 1980	Robert E. Olsen
1167	Highland Utah	10 Aug 1980	Merlin B. Larson

1827	Highland Utah East	10 Nov 1991	Stephen Mark Studdert
871	Huntington Utah	23 Oct 1977	Ira Wallace Hatch
104	*Hurricane Utah		
	‡Zion Park	8 Dec 1929	Claudius Hirschi
2180	Hurricane Utah West	10 Mar 1996	Scott W. Colton
2165	Ivins Utah	11 Feb 1996	Bruce Lynn Gubler
106	*Kamas Utah		
	*Summit South 29 May 1970		
	‡South Summit	8 Jul 1934	Zach J. Oblad
11	*Kanab Utah		
	‡Kanab (Utah, Arizona)	18 Apr 1877	L. John Nuttall
1638	*Kanab Utah Kaibab 20 Aug 1991		
	‡Kanab Utah South	3 May 1987	Nils G. Bayles
1294	*La Verkin Utah 30 Nov 1984		
	‡Hurricane Utah North	11 Oct 1981	Floyd Leon Lewis
100	*Lehi Utah		
	‡Lehi	1 Jul 1928	Anchor C. Schow
637	Lehi Utah North	5 May 1974	Francis Russell Hakes
2169	Lehi Utah South	18 Feb 1996	James Earl Smith
1416	Lehi Utah West	8 May 1983	Boyd Sabey Stewart
1392	Lindon Utah	12 Dec 1982	Noel Thomas Greenwood
2091	Lindon Utah West	20 Aug 1995	James La Verle Hacking
34	*Loa Utah		
	‡Wayne	27 May 1893	Willis E. Robison
43	*Manti Utah		
	*Sanpete South 29 May 1970		
	‡South Sanpete	9 Dec 1900	Canute Peterson
714	Mapleton Utah	19 Oct 1975	Jay M. Smith Jr.
1407	Midway Utah	27 Mar 1983	Wayne Watkins Probst
553	*Moab Utah		
	‡Moab	19 Sep 1971	Leland D. Teeples
85	*Monroe Utah		
	*Sevier South 29 May 1970		
	‡South Sevier	30 Jan 1921	John E. Magleby
27	*Monticello Utah		
	‡San Juan (Utah, Colorado)	23 Sep 1883	Platte D. Lyman
102	*Moroni Utah		
	‡Moroni	16 Jun 1929	James Louis Nielsen
42a	*Mount Pleasant Utah		
	*Sanpete North 29 May 1970		
	‡North Sanpete	9 Dec 1900	Christian N. Lund
5b	*Nephi Utah		
	*Juab 1871		
	‡Nephi	20 Sep 1868	Jacob G. Bigler
1538	Nephi Utah North	9 Jun 1985	James Randy McKnight
166	Orem Utah		
	‡Orem	13 Apr 1947	Walter R. Holdaway
1668	Orem Utah Aspen	10 Jan 1988	Ross Steve Wolfley
1518	*Orem Utah Canyon View 1 Mar 1988		
	‡Orem Utah Northeast	3 Mar 1985	Jerry C. Washburn
2230	Orem Utah Cascade	08 Sep 1996	Richard Bryant Brady
271	*Orem Utah Cherry Hill 15 Apr 1988		
	*Orem Utah Sharon West		
	*Sharon West 29 May 1970		
	‡West Sharon	30 Nov 1958	Clyde M. Lunceford
751	Orem Utah East	21 Mar 1976	Mirl Blake Hymas
251	*Orem Utah Geneva Heights 5 Apr 1988		
	*Orem Utah West		
	‡Orem West	3 Nov 1957	Edward C. Bunker
1581	*Orem Utah Hillcrest 27 Nov 1988		
	‡Orem Utah Sharon South	1 Dec 1985	Wynn Howard Hemmert
867	*Orem Utah Lakeridge 1 Mar 1988		
	‡Orem Utah South Central	16 Oct 1977	Gordon Max Thomas
2204	Orem Utah Lakeridge North	23 Jun 1996	Spencer Floyd Mack
1184	Orem Utah Lakeview	28 Sep 1980	Merrill Gappmayer

533	*Orem Utah North		
	‡Orem North	1 Nov 1970	Eli Karl Clayson
1682	Orem Utah Northridge	31 Jan 1988	Larry V. Perkins
1176	Orem Utah Park	7 Sep 1980	Richard S. Johns
103	*Orem Utah Sharon		
	‡Sharon	15 Sep 1929	Arthur V. Watkins
812	*Orem Utah Sharon Park 20 Dec 1988		
	‡Orem Utah Central	13 Feb 1977	Clifton M. Pyne
1490	*Orem Utah Student 8 Jan 1991		
	Orem Utah College	26 Aug 1984	Charles E. Peterson
862	*Orem Utah Suncrest 1 Mar 1988		
	‡Utah West Central	18 Sep 1977	James Edwin Mangum
554	*Orem Utah Sunset Heights 19 Apr 1988		
	*Orem Utah South		
	‡Orem South	19 Sep 1971	Richard P. Shumway
1048	Orem Utah Timpview	12 Aug 1979	Carl Crawford
905	Orem Utah Windsor	9 Apr 1978	Dennis LeRoy Hill
12	*Panguitch Utah		
	‡Panguitch	23 Apr 1877	James Henrie
5a	*Parowan Utah		
	‡Parowan	May 1852	John C.L. Smith
45	*Payson Utah		
	‡Nebo	13 Jan 1901	Jonathan S. Page Jr.
634	Payson Utah East	24 Mar 1974	David R. Mangelson
	*Payson Utah Mountain View 9 Aug 1994		
1297	Payson Utah South	18 Oct 1981	Joe Lynn Spencer
1310	Payson Utah West	22 Nov 1981	Gerald M. Finch
529	*Pleasant Grove Utah		
	‡Pleasant Grove	11 Oct 1970	Leon R. Walker
894	Pleasant Grove Utah East	26 Feb 1978	Evan Mack Palmer
1958	Pleasant Grove Utah Grove Creek	24 Oct 1993	David Wesley Dickerson
1124	Pleasant Grove Utah Manila	23 Mar 1980	Grant Kay Fugal
101	*Pleasant Grove Utah Timpanogos		
	‡Timpanogos	1 Jul 1928	Wilford W. Warnick
61	*Price Utah		
	‡Carbon	8 May 1910	Gustave A. Iverson
151	*Price Utah North		
	*Carbon North 29 May 1970		
	‡North Carbon	24 Jun 1945	Cecil Broadbent
127	*Provo Utah		
	‡Provo	19 Feb 1939	Charles E. Rowan Jr.
1437	Provo Utah Bonneville	28 Aug 1983	Norman Dean Anderson
3b	*Provo Utah Central		
	*Utah 1855		
	‡Provo	19 Mar 1851	Isaac Higbee
165	*Provo Utah East		
	*Provo East 29 May 1970		
	‡East Provo	13 Apr 1947	Charles E. Rowan
541	*Provo Utah Edgemont		
	‡Edgemont	17 Jan 1971	Richard A. Call
1692	Provo Utah Edgemont North	20 Mar 1988	Clayton S. Huber
899	Provo Utah Edgemont South	19 Mar 1978	Keith Hale Hoopes
1209	Provo Utah Grandview	23 Nov 1980	Laren R. Robison
547	*Provo Utah North		
	‡Provo North	30 May 1971	Wayne Alvin Mineer
2187	Provo Utah North Park	21 Apr 1996	Brent A. Gines
821	Provo Utah Oak Hills	10 Apr 1977	John R. Christiansen
200	*Provo Utah Sharon East		
	*Sharon East 29 May 1970		
	‡East Sharon	23 Nov 1952	Henry D. Taylor
1090	Provo Utah South	2 Dec 1979	Moorlan Wayne Snow
1424	Provo Utah Sunset	29 May 1983	Glen Howard Snyder
167	*Provo Utah West		
	*Utah West 29 May 1970		

	‡West Utah	4 May 1947	J. Earl Lewis
10a	*Richfield Utah		
	‡Sevier	24 May 1874	Joseph A. Young
848	Richfield Utah East	12 Jun 1977	Warren T. Harward
82	*Roosevelt Utah		
	‡Roosevelt	26 Jun 1920	William H. Smart
1458	Roosevelt Utah East	11 Dec 1983	Earl V. Allred
685	Roosevelt Utah West	2 Mar 1975	Alvin Leonard Bellon
9a	*St. George Utah		
	‡Saint George (Utah, Arizona)	7 Nov 1869	Joseph W. Young
1623	*St. George Utah		
	Bloomington Hills	20 Nov 1994	
	Bloomington Hills Utah	4 Jan 1987	James Grey Larkin
759	St. George Utah College	30 May 1976	Peter A. Nyberg
1814	St. George Utah Dixie Downs	25 Aug 1991	Thomas Randy Judd
322	*St. George Utah East		
	‡St. George East	5 Feb 1961	Rudger C. Atkin
1813	St. George Utah Green Valley	25 Aug 1991	La Rell David Muir
1999	St. George Utah Morningside	20 Nov 1994	James Grey Larkin
1625	*St. George Utah Pine View 12 Dec 1989		
	‡Washington Utah West	18 Jan 1987	H. Carlyle Stirling
895	St. George Utah West	5 Mar 1978	Dale Gubler
686	*Salem Utah 8 Dec 1976		
	‡Spanish Fork Utah Salem	9 Mar 1975	Kent Blaine Hansen
2205	Salem Utah West	23 Jun 1996	Stanley W. Green
84	*Salina Utah		
	*Sevier North 29 May 1970		
	‡North Sevier	30 Jan 1921	Moroni Lazenby
1361	Santa Clara Utah	29 Aug 1982	Dale Gubler
74	*Santaquin Utah		
	*Santaquin-Tintic 2 Apr 1939		
	‡Tintic	22 Apr 1917	Erastus Franklin Birch
1525	*Snow College Utah 1st 28 Apr 1996		
	‡Snow College Utah	24 Mar 1985	Allen P. Jacobson
2193	Snow College Utah 2nd	28 Apr 1996	Richard Wheeler
233	*Spanish Fork Utah		
	‡Spanish Fork	30 Sep 1956	Joseph Y. Toronto
2179	Spanish Fork Utah East	10 Mar 1996	Allen Dredge Ward
94	*Spanish Fork Utah Palmyra		
	‡Palmyra	23 Nov 1924	Henry A. Gardner
1115	Spanish Fork Utah South	9 Mar 1980	Wilbur Angus Stephenson
900	Spanish Fork Utah West	19 Mar 1978	Clair O. Anderson
235	*Springville Utah		
	‡Springville	21 Oct 1956	Leo A. Crandall
1483	Springville Utah Hobble Creek	17 Jun 1984	Donald Blaine Hadley
93	*Springville Utah Kolob		
	‡Kolob	23 Nov 1924	George R. Maycock
705	*Springville Utah Spring Creek 21 Jun 1988		
	‡Springville Utah North	31 Aug 1975	F. Calvin Packard
239	*Vernal Utah Ashley		
	‡Ashley	2 Dec 1956	William Budge Wallis
1434	Vernal Utah Glines	19 Jun 1983	Gayle F. McKeachnie
913	Vernal Utah Maeser	30 Apr 1978	Venil P. Johnson
30	*Vernal Utah Uintah 10 Jun 1986		
	*Vernal Utah		
	‡Uintah	11 Jul 1886	Samuel R. Bennion
991	Washington Utah	7 Jan 1979	Lorel Wynn Turek
1193	Wellington Utah	12 Oct 1980	Charles V. Bradshaw
		Discontinued	
122	Moon Lake	24 Apr 1938	Edwin L. Murphy
	10 Nov 1957 †Duchesne (62)		

9 Dec 1900 †North Sanpete (42), South Sanpete (43)

Missions — 4
(As of Oct. 1, 1996; shown with historical number. See MISSIONS.)

(132) UTAH OGDEN MISSION
2133 Washington Blvd.
Ogden, UT 84401
Phone: (801) 392-9325

(222) UTAH PROVO MISSION
2500 N. University Ave., #100
Provo, UT 84604
Phone: (801) 377-1490

(187) UTAH SLC MISSION
7938 South 3500 East, Suite H
Salt Lake City, UT 84121
Phone: (801) 942-7983

UTAH SLC TEMPLE SQUARE MISSION
P.O. Box 112110
Salt Lake City, UT 84147-2110
Phone: (801) 240-3011

MISSIONARY TRAINING CENTER
2005 North 900 East
Provo, UT 84604
Phone: (801) 378-2602

Vermont

Year-end 1995: Est. population, 587,000; Members, 3,400; Stakes, 1; Wards, 6; Branches, 5; Percent LDS, 0.6, or one person in 172.

The Prophet Joseph Smith was born in Sharon, Vt., on Dec. 23, 1805. Other prominent leaders born in this state include Oliver Cowdery, Brigham Young, Heber C. Kimball and Erastus Snow. In all, about a dozen of the early Church leaders were born in Vermont.

Jared Carter arrived in Benson, Rutland County, Vt., about Oct. 25, 1831, and after preaching, baptized 27 converts. Most of these members, and those baptized later, remained faithful, migrating to the West in 1833.

Elders Orson Pratt and Lyman E. Johnson supposedly preached in Vermont in early 1832. Other missionaries followed. By 1835, branches were organized in St. Johnsbury, Danville, Charleston, Andover, and Benson. Additional branches were organized in Irasburg in 1836, Addison in 1840, and Woodstock in 1843. Elders Erastus Snow and William Hyde were laboring in Woodstock in 1844 when they heard of the martyrdom.

Members of these branches dispersed in large numbers to join the westward movement, and missionary work did not resume until many years later. Membership in the mostly rural state, which is the third least populated in the United States, has remained sparse. On Dec. 23, 1905, at the centennial of Joseph Smith's birth, a 100-ton granite shaft 50 feet 10 inches tall was dedicated. Community members supported the construction and the dedication was well-attended. Some 30,000 people visit the marker and its attendant historic site facility each year. The monument was a frequent site for missionary conferences in the early years.

The Eastern States Mission, reopened in 1893, maintained responsibility for Vermont until the state was transferred to the Canadian Mission in 1927. The Vermont Conference was organized in 1909, though no branches were organized. In 1916, 30 people attended a conference at Barre. The Morrisville Branch existed by 1924. In 1930, a small branch functioned at Burlington, organized in 1927 or after. Responsibility for the state was placed with the New England Mission when it was created in 1937. Its first conference was held at the Joseph Smith monument in July 1938 with 60 missionaries in attendance. Beginning in 1987, lights were placed around the Joseph Smith Monument during the Christmas season, attracting thousands of visitors. About 70,000 visitors, including those at Christmas, come to the site annually.

The Montpelier Vermont Stake, where the bulk of the state's LDS membership resides today, was created April 11, 1976, with a membership of 2,116 members. (Two of its wards were in New Hampshire.) In 1980, statewide membership was 2,196. It increased to 2,758 in 1990.

Church membership today is almost entirely converts and a large percentage of them are natives of Vermont.

Sources: "Proceedings at the Dedication of the Joseph Smith Memorial Monument," distributed at the dedication Dec. 23, 1905; *Encyclopedic History of the Church,* by Andrew Jenson; "The Benson Exodus of 1833: Mormon Converts and the Westward Movement," by Erik Barnouw, Summer, 1986, *Vermont Journal History;* "Gospel Brothers," by James L. Kimball, *Church News,* March 11, 1978; "Yankee Saints: The

Church in New England during the Twentieth Century," by Richard O. Cowan, 1988, "Members reflect spirit of pioneers in state rich in Church history," by Sheridan R. Sheffield, *Church News,* Dec. 21, 1991; *Regional Studies in Latter-day Saint History,* BYU; *Church News,* Dec. 18, 1993.

Stake — 1

(Listed alphabetically as of Oct. 1, 1996.)

No.	Name	Organized	First President
North America Northeast Area			
753	Montpelier Vermont	11 Apr 1976	C. Lynn Fife

Virginia

Year-end 1995: Est. population, 6,652,000; Members, 61,000; Stakes, 16; Wards, 93; Branches, 31; Missions, 1; Percent LDS, 0.9, or one person in 109.

Elder Jedediah M. Grant preached in Patrick County, Va., from 1837 to 1838, establishing a small branch there. In 1838, Elder George A. Smith preached in Montgomery County and realized some success. Francis Gladden Bishop labored in various locations in Virginia from 1838-39 and baptized many converts. Other missionaries also worked in Wythe and Nelson counties.

Elder Grant returned to Virginia in 1840 and preached successfully in Smyth, Washington and Tazewell counties. He was in high demand as a preacher and had three invitations for every one he could fill. He frequently read Joseph Smith's prophecy of the Civil War. His listeners gave him a horse, clothing and funds to assist him in preaching in more locations.

In 1841, Elder Grant's companion, his brother Joshua, reported a membership of 80 in the state, including a branch of 25 in Rich Valley, Smyth County. After the Grant brothers left in 1842, Elder R.H. Kinnamon traveled to nine counties and baptized more than 100 persons. Prominent Southern States missionary and mission president, Henry G. Boyle, was among those converted from Tazewell County. He preached in his home state in 1844-45 and baptized a number of converts.

Work progressed well until the martyrdom of the Prophet Joseph Smith, when some elders returned to Nauvoo. Membership at the time was probably in excess of 350. Most of these faithful early members migrated west.

Missionary work resumed with some success in 1870. In 1879, when Elders Mathias F. Cowley and Frank A. Benson preached in Tazewell, Bland and Smyth counties, they baptized a few children and grandchildren of those who first heard the gospel preached by Elder Grant. Some of these people recalled the prophecy of the Civil War that was fulfilled 20 years after it was given.

In 1886, the Virginia Conference was divided and the West Virginia Conference created. The state was briefly placed in the Middle States Mission from 1902 until 1903 when it was returned to the Southern States Mission.

By 1919, branches existed in Danville, Petersburg, Portsmouth and Richmond. In 1929, the state was transferred to the East Central States Mission. In 1930, the Virginia Conference had a membership of 2,267 in the Danville, Norfolk, Richmond and Roanoke branches and Sunday Schools in Mt. Lake, Petersburg, Portsmouth, Scholfield, Vinton and Oilville. The Virginia East District was created in 1944. The Virginia Stake was created June 30, 1957, with about 1,600 members in the Dutch Gap, Petersburg, Newport News, Norfolk, Richmond, and Portsmouth wards, and the Franklin Branch in Virginia. Missionary work and an influx of members involved in military and industrial fields accounted for the recent growth of the district. Growth also came as members assumed roles in governmental agencies headquartered in Washington, D.C.

Commemorating the 500th anniversary of Columbus' voyage to the America's, the Tabernacle Choir performed in the Mosque Theater in Richmond, July 20, 1992.

Sources: *Encyclopedic History of the Church,* by Andrew Jenson; Southern States Mission, manuscript history; *Church News,* July 6, 1957; *History of the Southern States Mission,* a BYU thesis by LaMar C. Barrett, July 1960; "Church blossoms where history's roots run deep," by Mike Cannon, *Church News,* April 21, 1990; "Choir launches tour in historic Virginia," by Gerry Avant, July 25, 1992.

Stakes — 16

(Listed alphabetically as of Oct. 1, 1996.)

No.	Name	Organized	First President
North America Northeast Area			
512	*Annandale Virginia		

	‡Mount Vernon	26 Apr 1970	Allen Claire Rozsa
740	*Centrerville Virginia	29 Jan 1995	
	Fairfax Virginia	1 Feb 1976	Ed Mordue Hayward
1671	Chesapeake Virginia	17 Jan 1988	Joseph Craig Merrell
1198	Fredericksburg Virginia	26 Oct 1980	Douglas Lynn Marker
1325	McLean Virginia	14 Feb 1982	Earl John Roueche
1583	Mount Vernon Virginia	5 Jan 1986	Keith Alan Gulledge
922	*New River Virginia 24 Oct 1989		
	‡Bluefield Virginia	14 May 1978	Norman Perry Tyler Jr.
846	Newport News Virginia	12 Jun 1977	Kirk Thomas Waldron
372	*Oakton Virginia		
	‡Potomac (Virginia, D.C., Md.)	3 Mar 1963	Miller F. Shurtleff
245	*Richmond Virginia		
	‡Virginia (Va., N. C.)	30 Jun 1957	Cashell Donahoe Sr.
1450	Richmond Virginia Chesterfield	30 Oct 1983	John Leonard Ruckart Jr.
499	*Roanoke Virginia		
	‡Roanoke	11 Jan 1970	Russell B. Maddock
392	*Virginia Beach Virginia	21 Jun 1994	
	*Norfolk Virginia		
	‡Norfolk (Virginia, North Carolina)	12 Apr 1964	Walter H. Hick
2018	Warrenton Virginia	29 Jan 1995	Richard L. Brown
934	*Waynesboro Virginia 16 Dec 1982		
	‡Charlottesville Virginia	28 May 1978	Wilford John Teerlink
837	Winchester Virginia	22 May 1977	Harold S. Harrison

Mission — 1

(As of Oct. 1, 1996; shown with historical number. See MISSIONS. Washington D.C. missions, though headquarters are located in Virginia and Maryland are listed under District of Columbia.)

(42) VIRGINIA RICHMOND MISSION
9327 Midlothian Tpk, Suite 1-B
Richmond, VA 23235
Phone: (804) 330-9620

Washington

Year-end 1995: Est. population, 5,478,000; Members, 211,000; Stakes, 50; Wards, 398; Branches, 47; Missions, 3; Temples, 1; Percent LDS, 3.8, or one person in 26.

In 1854, four missionaries serving in California, Elders John Hughes, Clark Faben, Alfred Bybee and Silas Harris, were sent to labor in the Washington and Oregon territories. One of these, Elder Hughes, converted enough people to start a branch on the Lewis River.

One early convert who remained in Washington despite persecution was Louisa A. Johns Bozarth. She was faithful throughout her life. When she died in 1911, animosity against the Church was still so pronounced that her grave was dedicated secretly at night.

Many Mormons worked on the construction of the Northern Pacific Oregon Short Line railroads in the 1880s and a few later moved into the Northwest.

In 1886, a mission was organized under the direction of George C. Parkinson, president of the Oneida Stake in southeastern Idaho. He wanted to search for the members of his stake who had moved into Washington, Oregon and Montana. The first full-time missionaries were active in Spokane by 1896. A second Northwestern States Mission was created in that city July 26, 1897. (The first Northwestern States Mission, created in 1878, had its headquarters in Chicago, Ill.)

A meeting held in a Church facility in Colfax, Wash., on Jan. 3, 1898, had an attendance of 65 people. Missionaries began working in Walla Walla on Jan. 17, 1898.

A year later, an Eastern Washington Conference was held with one elder and 20 members in attendance. On Sept. 9, 1906, a Sunday School was organized in Spokane, and a branch was organized on March 12, 1916. The branch obtained a meetinghouse in 1920. In Seattle, a Sunday School was started in 1915, and a branch organized Sept. 12, 1920. A building for this branch was purchased in 1927. Many people joined the Church, and many members moved in. Many came to work in defense industries.

In 1930, membership was 1,855 in eight branches, with chapels in Everett, Spokane,

Seattle and Olympia. World War II brought an influx of members to Washington to take part in the war effort. The Seattle Stake was created July 31, 1938. Membership in the state reached 5,000 in 1940.

The completion of the Grand Coulee Dam on the Columbia River in the early 1940s opened the way for additional farming in the Columbia River Basin, and many members flocked to the state. Membership increased to 11,000 by 1960. Growth continued, and by 1970, membership reached 67,203. Membership reached 138,000 in 1980. The Seattle Temple was dedicated that year. By 1990, membership reached 189,000. In 1992, Washington became the fifth state in the United States with at least 50 stakes.

In February 1996, floods devastated parts of Washington and other northwestern states. Among thousands displaced during the week of Feb. 5 were hundreds of LDS families. Two LDS meetinghouses, one in Washington, were flooded. Facing "massive amounts of mud and debris," members joined with neighbors in rescue and relief efforts. Several members of the Olympia Washington Stake risked their lives in pulling from 50 to 70 victims by boat to safety. Other members in unaffected areas joined clean-up efforts and volunteered with such organizations as the Red Cross.

Sources: *Encyclopedic History of the Church*, by Andrew Jenson; *Latter-day Saints in the Great Northwest*, by J. Arthur Horne, published by Graphic Arts Press, Seattle, Wash.; *History of the Church in the Pacific Northwest*, by Leonard J. Arrington, task papers in LDS History, No. 18; "A wake of disaster, a wave of volunteers," *Church News*, Feb. 17, 1996.

Stakes — 50
(Listed alphabetically as of Oct. 1, 1996.)

No.	Name	Organized	First President
North America Northwest Area			
1388	Auburn Washington	28 Nov 1982	Alan Warner Bolles
388	*Bellevue Washington ‡Seattle East	1 Dec 1963	Raymond W. Eldredge
1266	Bellingham Washington	10 May 1981	Eugene Clifford Hatch
1312	Bothell Washington	22 Nov 1981	Arnold R. Parrott
299	*Bremerton Washington ‡Puget Sound	19 Jun 1960	Herbert S. Anderson
958	Centralia Washington	10 Sep 1978	Frank Edward Berrett
1299	Colville Washington	18 Oct 1981	Garnett Russell Port
1438	Elma Washington	28 Aug 1983	Lou Elwin Green
1148	Ephrata Washington	15 Jun 1980	Robert A. Hammond
532	*Everett Washington ‡Cascade South	25 Oct 1970	Wesley K. Duce
883	Federal Way Washington	20 Nov 1977	Jack Lynn Smith
776	Kennewick Washington	24 Oct 1976	Elton Elias Hunt
1374	Kennewick Washington East	31 Oct 1982	Donald LeRoy Brunson
1495	Kent Washington	14 Oct 1984	Owen Edvin Jensen
1855	Kirkland Washington	19 Apr 1992	Peter Gideon Condie
1565	Lakewood Washington	20 Oct 1985	James Rolland Ely
599	*Longview Washington ‡Columbia River West	4 Feb 1973	Walter Lee Robinson
925	Lynnwood Washington	14 May 1978	Robert C. Barnard
1251	Marysville Washington	29 Mar 1981	Verle George Call
213	*Moses Lake Washington ‡Grand Coulee	18 Apr 1954	Elmo J. Bergeson
379	*Mount Vernon Washington ‡Cascade	30 Jun 1963	Robert E. Jones
440	*Olympia Washington ‡Olympia	27 Aug 1967	Herbert S. Anderson
1049	Othello Washington	12 Aug 1979	Jay L. Christensen
437	*Pasco Washington ‡Pasco (Washington, Oregon)	21 May 1967	David K. Barber
1848	Port Angeles Washington	23 Feb 1992	Richard Ernest Shaw
638	Pullman Washington	5 May 1974	John Leo Schwendiman
542	*Puyallup Washington ‡Mount Rainier	17 Jan 1971	Owen H. Dickson
1389	Puyallup Washington South	28 Nov 1982	Dennis Tripp Sampson
844	Redmond Washington	29 May 1977	Arnold R. Parrott
514	*Renton Washington ‡Renton	3 May 1970	Harris A. Mortensen

1244	Renton Washington North	15 Mar 1981	Denzel Nolan Wiser
180	*Richland Washington		
	‡Richland		
	(Washington, Oregon)	25 Jun 1950	James V. Thompson
124	*Seattle Washington		
	‡Seattle	31 Jul 1938	Alex Brown
242	*Seattle Washington North		
	*Seattle North 29 May 1970		
	‡North Seattle	19 May 1957	Wilford H. Payne
1496	Seattle Washington Shoreline	14 Oct 1984	Brent Isaac Nash
1023	*Selah Washington 31 Aug 1982		
	‡Yakima Washington North	29 Apr 1979	Robert Atwood Hague
1057	Silverdale Washington	26 Aug 1979	David Junior Jones
1890	Snohomish Washington	28 Jun 1992	Craig L. Morrison
168	*Spokane Washington		
	‡Spokane	29 Jun 1947	Albert I. Morgan
556	*Spokane Washington East		
	‡Spokane East	17 Oct 1971	James B. Cox
992	Spokane Washington North	7 Jan 1979	Dwaine E. Nelson
1841	Spokane Washington West	12 Jan 1992	Elroy C. McDermott
195	*Tacoma Washington		
	‡Tacoma	28 Sep 1952	Elvin E. Evans
1052	Tacoma Washington South	19 Aug 1979	James Rolland Ely
389	*Vancouver Washington		
	*Columbia River North 29 May 1970		
	‡North Columbia	1 Dec 1963	Wallace V. Teuscher
1570	Vancouver Washington North	3 Nov 1985	Bruce A. Schreiner
979	Vancouver Washington West	5 Nov 1978	Earl Clifford Jorgensen
1011	Walla Walla Washington	11 Mar 1979	David L. Hafen
426	*Wenatchee Washington 7 Dec 1978		
	*Quincy Washington		
	‡Grand Coulee North	29 Jan 1967	Leslie H. Boyce
284	*Yakima Washington		
	‡Yakima	24 May 1959	F. Edgar Johnson

Missions — 3

(As of Oct. 1, 1996; shown with historical number. See MISSIONS.)

(78a) WASHINGTON SEATTLE MISSION
13353 Bel-Red Road, Suite 103
Bellevue, WA 98005-2329
Phone: (206) 641-5050

(166) WASHINGTON SPOKANE MISSION
P.O. Box 14808
Spokane, WA 99214-0808
Phone: (509) 924-8932

(255) WASHINGTON TACOMA MISSION
4007-D Bridgeport Way W.
Tacoma, WA 98466-4330
Phone: (206) 566-5480

West Virginia

Year-end 1995: Est. population, 1,830,000; Members, 11,000; Stakes, 2; Wards, 17; Branches, 18; Missions, 1; Percent LDS, 0.6, or one person in 166.

Missionaries entered what is now West Virginia in 1832 when Luke S. Johnson and William W. M'Lellin preached in Cabell County, which lies just over the Ohio River from Ohio on the western tip of the state. The Prophet Joseph Smith visited Wheeling on April 4, 1832, and purchased paper for the Church's press that was then in Jackson County, Mo. The paper was used to publish the *Book of Commandments*, which was later mostly scattered by a mob. That same year, Elder Amasa M. Lyman and an Elder Johnson baptized 40 converts. In 1836, Elders Lorenzo D. Barnes and Samuel James baptized enough converts to start a branch in Shinnston, Harrison County. In 1837, some 1,200 (mostly non-members) attended a meeting there. Elder George A. Smith taught a grammar school at or near Shinnston, which had 75 members.

One convert was Bathsheba Wilson Bigler Smith, sister of Jacob G. Bigler and later the wife of Apostle George A. Smith, who was baptized Aug. 21, 1837, along with a number of other family members including parents, brothers and sisters. "The spirit of gathering with the Saints in Missouri came upon me, . . ." she wrote in her autobiography. "About this time my father sold his farm in West Virginia and we started for Far West." She later served as Relief Society general president.

Others felt the same spirit and emigrated to the West with the Saints, and the branches were discontinued.

Missionary work did not resume until 1881 when Elder John E. Carlisle and Elder Joseph L. Townsend toured in McDowell County and baptized three adults.

Laboring in Logan County in June 1884, Elders Andrew W. Spence and an Elder Vickers were served with a warrant for suspicion of being part of a band of robbers. The pair opened their satchels and not only convinced the officers that they were innocent, but also distributed tracts that opened the way for the missionaries to teach at the courthouse. From this opening, a branch of 26 people was organized. The West Virginia Conference was organized Sept. 18, 1886. A year later, missionaries from the Northern States Mission searched out and taught "Bickertonites" (see Pennsylvania history) but failed to make any headway among them. In 1889, a local newspaper wrote of the "serious" success of the missionaries among other residents in the Wheeling area.

West Virginia was placed in the Eastern States Mission in 1897. It became part of the Middle States Mission in 1902, but was soon after reunited with the Eastern States Mission.

In 1906, Elder George D. Ward and a companion completed a small chapel for the Franklin Branch. One of the early converts in this branch was William Perry Hartman, and three branches later developed from his family's influence.

The West Virginia Conference was divided and the West Virginia North and South conferences were created. In 1930, the North conference had 888 members and the South conference 1,397 members, for a statewide total of 2,285.

The membership built up gradually and the first stake was created in 1970 in Charleston, comprised of the West Virginia South District with a membership of 3,966. Units in West Virginia included the Asheland, Charleston, Charleston 2nd, Huntington and Parkersburg wards and the Beckley, Logan, Portsmouth, Ripley, Point Pleasant and Webster Spring branches. Additional stakes were created in 1979 and 1982. Membership in West Virginia in 1974 was 9,149, growing to 9,734 in 1980, and 10,000 in 1990.

Sources: *Encyclopedic History of the Church,* by Andrew Jenson; *Autobiography,* Bathsheba Wilson Bigler Smith; Southern States, Eastern States and Northern States Missions histories; *Church News,* Sept. 5, 1970; West Virginia and Mormonism's Rarest Book, by Lisle G. Brown, *West Virginia History,* January/April 1978, Vol. 39; "'Bell-snickeled' builders," by Richard L. Jensen, *Church News,* April 1, 1978; "West Virginia," by Mike Cannon, *Church News,* Oct. 2, 1989.

Stakes — 2
(Listed alphabetically as of Oct. 1, 1996.)

No.	Name	Organized	First President
North America Northeast Area			
522	*Charleston West Virginia		
	‡West Virginia (W. Va., Ky.)	23 Aug 1970	David L. Atkinson
1025	Fairmont West Virginia	6 May 1979	David Glen Williams

Mission — 1
(As of Oct. 1, 1996; shown with historical number. See MISSIONS.)

(188) WEST VIRGINIA CHARLESTON MISSION
405 Capitol St., #406
Charleston, WV 25301-1727
Phone: (304) 342-8332

Wisconsin

Year-end 1995: Est. population, 5,143,000; Members, 16,000; Stakes, 3; Wards, 24; Branches, 19; Missions, 1; Districts, 1; Percent LDS, 0.3, or one person in 321.

Settlement of the Saints in Wisconsin was suggested as early as 1836 at a citizens meeting in Liberty County, Mo. The suggestion was not acted upon, however.

Missionary work in Wisconsin began in 1841. In that year, Elder Elisha H. Groves opened a small branch in Vienna, Dane County. William O. Clark also baptized 17 people at Mineral Point, Lafayette County. Amasa Lyman also labored in Wisconsin that year.

After Nauvoo, Ill., was settled, a group of 14 members was sent in 1841 to obtain lumber from the pine forests along Black River in Wisconsin Territory, some 600 miles to the north. Workers in this "pinery expedition" floated logs to Nauvoo for the temple and other buildings. By 1843, the camp at Black River had more than 150 people and was a settlement. But members learned then that they were on Indian territory. Bishop George Miller met with Menominee Indian Chief Oshkosh and reached an agreement to pay for the wood. He also preached to the Indians.

After the 1847 exodus from Nauvoo, little work was done in Wisconsin until the Northwestern States Mission was organized in 1878. Cyrus H. Wheelock, laboring in Fond du Lac, Wis., in 1877, was called to organize the mission. Some converts likely were gained over the next decade who migrated to Utah, but work proceeded slowly in the early 1890s with few or no missionaries serving. The Milwaukee District was organized in 1896, and the Milwaukee Branch on April 16, 1899. Christopher Leonard Rueckert, a former missionary in Wisconsin, was assigned by the Church to return to the city with his family and head the new branch.

On March 23, 1907, a chapel was dedicated for the branch. The branch was later divided. By 1930, membership in the state was 932 in the Eleva, La Crosse, Milwaukee and Racine branches. When the Chicago (Illinois) Stake was organized in 1936, the Milwaukee Ward was created and included in the stake. This ward was divided in 1958. The Milwaukee Stake was created in 1963, and a stake center dedicated in 1967. Membership in 1974 was more than 6,000. In 1980, Wisconsin had 9,855 members, and in 1990, 13,159 members.

Efforts in recent years to enhance the visibility of the Church in Wisconsin have included a three-year exhibit beginning in 1995 at the Sun Prairie Historical Library and Museum. Assembled by the Sun Prairie Ward, Madison Wisconsin Stake, it highlights Church history and doctrine.

Sources: *Encyclopedic History of the Church,* by Andrew Jenson; "Brief History of the Milwaukee Stake," published at the dedication of the Milwaukee Stake Center, Aug. 27, 1967; "The Pinery Expedition," by Jill Mulvay Derr, *Church News,* April 8, 1978; "Minnesota Mormons," by Fayone B. Willes, published by the Minnesota Stake, 1990; "Exhibit Acquaints Visitors with Church," *Church News,* July 15, 1995.

Stakes — 3
(Listed alphabetically as of Oct. 1, 1996.)

No.	Name	Organized	First President
	North America Central Area		
1597	Appleton Wisconsin	11 May 1986	Nevin Richard Limburg
702	*Madison Wisconsin 11 Apr 1982		
	‡Beloit Wisconsin	24 Aug 1975	Arval Lewis Erikson
367	*Milwaukee Wisconsin		
	‡Milwaukee	3 Feb 1963	DeWitt C. Smith

Mission — 1
(As of Oct. 1, 1996; shown with historical number. See MISSIONS, p. 286.)

(167) WISCONSIN MILWAUKEE MISSION
5651 Broad St.
Greendale, WI 53129-1889
Phone: (414) 421-7506

Wyoming

Year-end 1995: Est. population, 482,000; Members, 54,000; Stakes, 16; Wards, 120; Branches, 15; Percent LDS, 11.2, or one person in 9.

In 1846, a group of Mississippi converts came West hoping to join the Saints en route to the Great Basin. However, they stopped a few miles below Fort Laramie in July 1846. There, they learned that the Saints had waited a year at Winter Quarters, Neb., so the Mississippians decided to winter in Colorado. Some of these Mississippi members joined Brigham Young's pioneer wagon train, which entered Wyoming May 31, 1847, near Fort Laramie. The Mississippi group included members of the Mormon Battalion sick detachments as well. On June 28, the combined company under Brigham Young met mountainman Jim Bridger, who gave them a generally optimistic appraisal of the Great Basin area.

Most later emigrant companies crossed Wyoming without incident, but the Willie and Martin Handcart companies of 1857 were trapped in snows before reaching South Pass, Wyo., and about 200 of the 1,075 in the companies died. The rest were saved by rescue parties from Utah.

Fort Supply was erected near Fort Bridger and a colony started in 1853. It provided supplies for wagon companies coming from the East. This flourishing colony was abandoned and burned at the advance of Johnston's army in 1856. Fort Bridger, which the Church had purchased in 1855, was partially burned at the same time. The army subsequently camped at Fort Bridger before a peaceful settlement was reached in Utah the following summer.

In 1877, seeking areas to colonize, Moses Thatcher and William Preston came to western Wyoming, then known as Salt River Valley. Thatcher re-named the area Star Valley. Apostle Brigham Young Jr. visited the area the following year and dedicated it as a gathering place. The first settlers from Bear Lake Valley, Idaho, stayed the winter of 1879-80 near what is now Auburn. In the 1880s, the colonies of Grover, Afton, Freedom, Smoot, Thayne, Bedford, and Fairview were established. Others followed. Star Valley today remains primarily LDS and has two stakes.

The Big Horn Basin was settled in 1900 after a request for settlers by Wyoming Gov. DeForrest Richards to President Lorenzo Snow. The first settlement of Burlington was founded by LDS settlers from Uintah County, Utah, and organized under Apostle Abraham O. Woodruff. Also founded near the turn of the century were the settlements of Byron, Cowley, Lovell, and others after the turn of the century. The settlers dug a 37-mile canal to provide irrigation water only to find that irrigation lifted underground alkali to the surface. Settlers persevered, however, and the problem abated. The Big Horn Basin presently has three stakes.

In 1930, about 12,000 members lived in Wyoming. Most lived in the western part of the state, but members began moving into other areas as well. By 1980, membership in Wyoming reached 47,314, increasing to 51,692 in 1990.

During the observance of Wyoming's state centennial in 1990, the LDS heritage of the state, including the Mormon Trail, were included in commemorations.

In 1992, the Riverton Wyoming Stake erected three monuments in memory of the Willie and Martin handcart pioneer companies. The monuments were dedicated Aug. 15, 1992, by President Gordon B. Hinckley of the First Presidency. Later purchased by the Church was the site surrounding a monument at the mouth of Sweetwater Canyon where 21 people perished in one night, and was dedicated in 1994 by President Hinckley.

In 1996, Wyoming Church members continued to honor their legacy. More than 700 descendants and friends of LDS settlers at what became known as "Mormon Row" near Jackson Hole gathered there July 11-14 to commemorate their ancestors' lives. When the planned Montana Billings Temple is completed, it will serve members in northern Wyoming.

Sources: *Encyclopedic History of the Church,* by Andrew Jenson; "Star Valley and Its Communities," by Lee Roland Call, Afton, Wyo., *Star Valley Independent,* 1970; *Lovell, Our Pioneer Heritage,* by Rosa Vida Bischoff Black; "Fort Supply: Brigham Young's Green River Experiment," by Frederick R. Gowans and Eugene E. Campbell, BYU, 1976; *Wyoming Place Names,* by Mae Urbanek, Mountain Press Publishing Co., 1988; *Church News,* May 26, 1990, Dec. 15, 1990, Dec. 22, 1990; "Mormon Settlers helped make Wyoming a state," *Church News,* May 26, 1990; " 'Second rescue' of handcart pioneers," by Dell Van Orden, *Church News,* Aug. 22, 1992; "Project stands as reminder of legacy," by Julie A. Dockstader, *Church News,* July, 30, 1994.

Stakes — 16
(Listed alphabetically by area as of Oct. 1, 1996.)

No.	Name	Organized	First President
North America Central Area — 8			
357	*Casper Wyoming ‡Casper	14 Oct 1962	W. Reed Green
286	*Cheyenne Wyoming ‡Cheyenne (Wyo., Colo.)	21 Jun 1959	Archie R. Boyack
593	*Cody Wyoming ‡Cody	7 Jan 1973	Parley J. Livingston
1158	Gillette Wyoming	29 Jun 1980	Marion A. Dalene
1420	Laramie Wyoming	15 May 1983	Philip Munro Hoyt
48	*Lovell Wyoming ‡Big Horn	26 May 1901	Byron Sessions
358	*Riverton Wyoming ‡Wind River	14 Oct 1962	J. Rex Kocherhans
1194	Worland Wyoming	12 Oct 1980	David Harris Asay
Utah North Area — 8			
33	*Afton Wyoming		

	‡Star Valley	14 Aug 1892	George Osmond
38	*Evanston Wyoming		
	‡Woodruff (Wyoming, Utah)	5 Jun 1898	John M. Baxter
1493	Evanston Wyoming South	23 Sep 1984	Harold Sidney Stock
660	Green River Wyoming	22 Sep 1974	Ronald Clyde Walker
708	Kemmerer Wyoming	12 Oct 1975	Merrill R. Anderson
790	Lyman Wyoming	21 Nov 1976	Ronald C. Walker
95	*Rock Springs Wyoming		
	‡Lyman (Wyoming, Utah)	18 Jul 1926	H. Melvin Rollins
975	Thayne Wyoming	29 Oct 1978	Marlow C. Bateman

WORLDWIDE CHURCH

U.S. territories or possessions are listed by their own name in this section. Other territories are listed under the name of the administering country.

Numbers preceding stakes and missions are their chronological numbers assigned at the time of creation.

* Name changed 14 Jan 1974 unless indicated otherwise

‡Original name

†Transferred to

ALBANIA

Year-end 1995: Est. population, 3,413,000; Members, fewer than 100; Branches, 5; Europe East Area; Missions, 1.

Albania is a small mountainous country in southeastern Europe's Balkan Peninsula where the Albanian- and Greek-speaking people are 70 percent Sunni Muslim, with 20 percent Greek Orthodox and 10 percent Roman Catholic.

Elder Hans B. Ringger of the Seventy and president of the Europe Area, accompanied by Pres. Kenneth D. Reber, president of the Austria Vienna Mission, visited Albania in 1991. In June 1992, four full-time missionaries arrived in Albania: Elders Matthew Wirthlin, Mark Slabaugh, Paul McAlister and Jonathan Jarvis. In addition, Elder George Niedens and Sister Nancy Niedens were transferred from Austria to assist in agriculture.

On May 17-20, 1992, Elder Dallin H. Oaks of the Quorum of the Twelve participated in a major international consultation on religious liberty and ethnic rights. Held in Budapest, Hungary, the consultation brought together 72 participants to discuss problems and share ideas pertaining to church-state issues in east central European nations that were once part of the communist bloc, particularly Albania, Bulgaria, Czechoslovakia, Hungary, Latvia, Poland, Romania, Croatia, Slovenia and Russia. The consultation helped emphasize religious freedom in many countries.

Elder Oaks visited Albania in April 1993, and spoke to a gathering of 78 people, including 55 Albanian members.

In 1994, Albania was among eastern European nations receiving shipments of food and other humanitarian relief supplies from the Church.

Albania was once part of the Zurich Switzerland Mission. The Albania Tirana Mission was created in July 1996.

Sources: *Church News,* June 22, 1992; *Church News,* June 12, 1993; *Church News,* March 16, 1996; *The Universal Almanac* 1996, Andrew's and MS Meel, a Universal Press Syndicate Company.

Mission — 1

(308) ALBANIA TIRANA MISSION
P.O. Box 2984
Tirana, Albania
Phone: (011-35-5) 423-2234

AMERICAN SAMOA

Year-end 1995: Est. population, 53,000; Members, 12,000; Stakes, 3; Wards, 24; Branches, 3; Percent LDS, 22.6, or one in 4; Pacific Area Samoa Apia Mission.

Located in the South Pacific Ocean, American Samoa is a U.S. territory. The people are Protestant, 50 percent; LDS, 25 percent; and Roman Catholic, 20 percent.

In 1863, two missionaries from Hawaii arrived in Samoa. The two, Kimo Pelia and Samuela Manoa, however, had been sent by an unauthorized leader, Walter Murray Gibson, excommunicated by the Church. The pair labored faithfully for nearly 20 years without the knowledge or support of the Church. They baptized a few people on Tutuila, which is now American Samoa. Later, after Elder Joseph H. Dean and his wife, Florence, arrived in Samoa in 1888, missionaries were again sent to Tutuila. The first branch was started in Pago Pago on May 27, 1893, and before the turn of the century, 11 branches had been organized on the island.

On April 27, 1900, the U.S. flag was raised over Tutuila and conflict between the German and U.S. governments that had hindered missionary work was largely resolved.

On Nov. 26, 1906, a Relief Society was founded at Mapusaga with Malia as president, and 14 members were enrolled. Malia later served a full-time mission in Tonga. A Primary was organized May 24, 1908. An LDS village with a school and a supporting plantation was founded at Mapusaga May 10, 1903.

In 1938, the Boy Scout organization was started at Mapusaga.

Missionaries were recalled in 1940 prior to World War II because of troubled conditions, and local members assumed more leadership. After the war, the work quickened considerably. The Pago Pago Stake was created in 1969.

In 1989, Eni F. [Hunkin Jr.] Faleomavaega, former lieutenant governor of American Samoa, was elected as a non-voting member of 101st U.S. Congress, the first Samoan LDS member to do so.

During hurricanes in February 1990 and December 1991, members suffered considerable losses but local units responded well in dealing with the devastation. Membership in 1990 was 7,500, increasing to about 12,000 in 1994.

Sources: *Encyclopedic History of the Church,* by Andrew Jenson; *Unto the Isles of the Sea,* by R. Lanier Britsch; *Samoa Apia Mission History, 1888-1983,* published by R. Carl Harris, president of the Samoa Apia Mission; *Church News,* Feb. 25, 1989; *Church News,* Feb. 17, 1990; *Church News,* Dec. 21, 1991; "Church responds swiftly to Samoa disaster," *Church News,* Dec. 28, 1991.

Stakes — 3
(Listed alphabetically as of Oct. 1, 1996.)

No.	Name	Organized	First President
Pacific Area			
488	*Pago Pago Samoa		
	‡Pago Pago	15 Jun 1969	Patrick Peters
1972	Pago Pago Samoa Central	6 Feb 1994	Beaver T. Ho Ching
1169	Pago Pago Samoa West	24 Aug 1980	William T. Geleai

ANGOLA

Year-end 1995: Est. population, 10,170,000; Members, fewer than 100; Branches, 1; Africa Area.

A country on the southwest coast of Africa, the People's Republic of Angola has a population of about 11 million. The nation's official language is Portuguese, although the majority of black Angolans speak a language that belongs to the Bantu language group. About 90 percent of the people are Christians, mostly Roman Catholic, with the remainder practicing mainly indigenous beliefs. Some three-fourths of the people of Angola live in rural areas, mainly as farmers and herders.

The Church was officially recognized in Angola in 1993, with the first branch being created in 1996. Some 86 members and investigators attended the services in the capital city of Luanda, with Elder J. Richard Clarke of the Seventy, then president of the Africa Area, presiding. Called as the first branch president was Tshaka Mbenza Vuamina, a professor at the University of Angola.

Latter-day Saints had been living in the area since 1985. However, many had been baptized while living for a short time in France or Portugal. After their return to Angola, they formed the nucleus of the Church. Records indicate that some 400 members baptized in Europe during the previous 15 years had returned to cities in Angola. Elder Clarke praised the members for their faith while living in an area burdened by civil war. They had been meeting in the homes of priesthood holders and had been functioning as a group, not a branch.

Sources: *World Book Encyclopedia,* published by World Book, Inc., 1993, vol. 1, pp. 464-65; *Church News,* Sept. 7, 1996.

ANTIGUA AND BARBUDA

Year-end 1995: Est. population, 101,000; Members, fewer than 100; Branches, 1; North

America Southeast Area; West Indies Mission.

These eastern Caribbean islands are a constitutional monarchy with a British type of parliament. The population speaks English and is mostly members of the Church of England.

Missionary work began in St. John's, Antigua, on May 19, 1984, when President Kenneth Zabriskie of the West Indies Mission visited the governor of Antigua and received permission to station missionaries on the island.

The first missionaries, Elder Ralph and Sister Aileen Tate arrived on July 28, 1984, under the direction of Pres. Zabriskie. They were followed in late August by Elders Gill W. Halford, Jay R. Schroeder, Carl Read and Russell T. Hansen. The first baptism was Evelyn Shaw, on Sept. 15, 1984. On Dec. 2, Ezzard Weston received the Aaronic Priesthood, the first to receive it on Antigua.

Elder Rex B. Blake, serving with his wife, Ruth, was the first president of the St. John's Branch, which was organized Jan. 6, 1985, in a rented conference room of a bank. The Church slowly grew to about 70 members in 1995. That year, hurricanes Luis and Marilyn caused widespread damage and many members lost homes and jobs because of the storm.

Sources: Journal of Pres. Kenneth L. Zabriskie and his wife, LeOra; interview with Rex and Ruth Blake; *Church News*, Dec. 11, 1993, Sept. 30, 1995; unpublished St. John's Branch history.

ARGENTINA

Year-end 1995: Est. population, 34,318,000; Members, 235,000; Stakes, 46; Wards, 271; Branches, 426; Missions, 10; Districts, 47; Temples, 1; Percent LDS, .60, or one person in 146.

Located in southern South America, the Republic of Argentina has a Spanish-speaking population that is about 92 percent Roman Catholic.

Church members Wilhelm Friedrichs and Emil Hoppe and their families emigrated from Germany to Argentina about 1923. Brother Friedrichs was particularly missionary-minded and began announcing gospel messages in local newspapers. He also sent letters to the First Presidency requesting missionaries.

In response, Elder Melvin J. Ballard of the Quorum of the Twelve and Elders Rulon S. Wells (German-speaking) and Rey L. Pratt (Spanish-speaking) were sent to Argentina, arriving in Buenos Aires Dec. 6, 1925. On Dec. 13, they baptized six persons who had been taught by Brother Friedrichs: Anna and Jacob Kullick and their adoptive daughter, Herta; Ernst and Maria Biebersdorf and their daughter, Maria. On Dec. 25, Elder Ballard dedicated South America for the preaching of the gospel. He later prophesied that "the work will go forth slowly just as the oak grows from an acorn. . . . [But] the South American Mission will become a power in the Church."

Reinhold Stoof, the first mission president, arrived in 1926 to preside over the South American Mission. The mission was divided into the Brazilian and Argentine missions in 1936. A decade later, after a slowing of activity during World War II, membership in Argentina was 800. Branches had been established ranging up to 500 miles south of Buenos Aires and 700 miles to the north and west.

The Argentine Mission was divided in 1962, and additional missions have been created since then, including two in 1990. The Buenos Aires Stake was organized in Nov. 20, 1966, with Angel Abrea, now a member of the First Quorum of the Seventy, as stake president. By 1978, membership had reached about 40,000 members. The Buenos Aires Argentina Temple was announced in 1980, and dedicated Jan. 17, 1986.

Buenos Aires was designated presidency headquarters of the South America South Area in 1984. Three new missions in 1990 — Mendoza, Resistencia, and Trelew, and the Buenos Aires West in 1992, reflect the continuing growth in Argentina. Membership in 1990 was 171,000, growing to 235,000 in 1995.

Sources: *Encyclopedic History of the Church,* by Andrew Jenson; *From Acorn to Oak Tree,* by Frederick S. Williams and Frederick G. Williams; *LDS Beginnings in South America, A Look at Argentina,* BYU paper by Denise H. Williams; *50 Años de la Iglesia in Argentina — Cronologia,* by Nestor Curbelo, seminary system, 1986.

Stakes — 54

(Listed alphabetically as of Oct. 1, 1996.)

No.	Name	Organized	First President
	South America South Area		
1097	Bahia Blanca Argentina	23 Jan 1980	Daniel Humberto Fucci

2117	Bahia Blanca Argentina Villa Mitre	5 Nov 1995	Jorge Horacio Cizek
2172	Bariloche Argentina	25 Feb 1996	Miguel Angel Reginato
1797	*Buenos Aires Argentina Aldo Bonzi 2 Jun 1996 ‡Buenos Aires Argentina Ezeiza	12 May 1991	Carlos Ernesto Aguero
2239	Buenos Aires Argentina Avellandeda	22 Sep 1996	Oscar Altera
920	Buenos Aires Argentina Banfield	14 May 1978	Heber Omar Diaz
1992	Buenos Aires Argentina Belgrano	18 Sep 1994	Nestor Esteban Curbelo
1143	Buenos Aires Argentina Castelar	8 Jun 1980	Jorge H. Michalek
423	*Buenos Aires Argentina East ‡Buenos Aires	20 Nov 1966	Angel Abrea
2200	Buenos Aires Argentina Gonzalez Catan	02 Jun 1996	Pedro Emilio Ayala
1178	Buenos Aires Argentina Litoral	12 Sep 1980	Jorge Fernandez
950	Buenos Aires Argentina Merlo	13 Aug 1978	Enrique Alfredo Ibarra
1824	Buenos Aires Argentina Monte Grande	10 Nov 1991	Hugo Vicente Riccinti
1405	Buenos Aires Argentina Moreno	20 Mar 1983	Carlos Domingo Marapodi
995	Buenos Aires Argentina North	28 Jan 1979	Tomas Federico Lindheimer
1946	Buenos Aires Argentina Sarmiento	27 Jun 1993	Carlos Antonio Moure
639	Buenos Aires Argentina West	12 May 1974	May Hugo Angel Catron
1975	Comodoro Rivadavia Argentina	20 Feb 1994	Jorge EstebanDetlefsen
569	*Cordoba Argentina ‡Cordoba	28 Feb 1972	Arturo Palmieri
1021	Cordoba Argentina North	29 Apr 1979	Juan Aldo L.
2228	Cordoba Argentina West	08 Sep 1996	Ruben B. Luis Spitale
1959a	Cordoba Argentina Sierras	7 Nov 1993	Roberto Jose Echegaray
1951	Florencio Varela Argentina	22 Aug 1993	Jorge Luis del Castillo
2059	General Roca Argentina	4 Jun 1995	Ruben Sabatino Tidei
1036	Godoy Cruz Argentina	6 Jun 1979	Salvador Molt'o
1978	Guaymallen Argentina	17 Apr 1994	Angel Licursi
1642	Jujuy Argentina	7 Jun 1987	Pedro Horacio Velazquez
1207	La Plata Argentina	23 Nov 1980	Hector Alejandro Olaiz
2058	Maipu de Cuyo Argentina	4 Jun 1995	Luis Wachman
997	Mar del Plata Argentina	31 Jan 1979	Hector Luis Catron
2049	Mar del Plata Argentina North	21 May 1995	Eduardo Bautista Ferrari
570	*Mendoza Argentina ‡Mendoza	1 Mar 1972	Mario A. Rastelli
1918	Neuquen Argentina	20 Dec 1992	Ruben Sabatino Tidei
2210	Neuquen Argentina West	07 Jul 1996	Sergio Marcelo Redaelli
1902	Posadas Argentina	20 Sep 1992	Manuel Aristides Franco
694	Quilmes Argentina	15 May 1975	Hugo Nestor Salvioli
1237	Resistencia Argentina	17 Feb 1981	Leopoldo Oscar Fuentes
2160	Rio Cuarto Argentina	11 Feb 1996	Esteban Eliseo Colaberardino
636a	Rosario Argentina	5 May 1974	Hugo Ruben Gazzoni
1177	Rosario Argentina North	10 Sep 1980	Daniel Arnoldo Moreno
2055	Rosario Argentina West	28 May 1995	Esteban Gabriel Resek
1260	Salta Argentina	29 Apr 1981	Victor Hugo Machado
2104	Salta Argentina West	15 Oct 1995	angel Eleodoro Caceres
2166	San Juan Argentina Chimbas	18 Feb 1996	Ruben Dario Romeu
1871	San Juan Argentina Nuevo Cuyo	24 May 1992	Jorge Eduardo Chacon
1001	San Nicolas Argentina	22 Feb 1979	Deolindo Antonio Resek
2023	San Rafael Argentina	19 Feb 1995	Armando Hector Scorziello
1161	Santa Fe Argentina	20 Jul 1980	Raimundo Eduardo Rippstein
2085	Santa Fe Argentina North	13 Aug 1995	Pedro Manuel Zapata

1945	Santiago Del Estero Argentina	20 Jun 1993	Jose Badami
1727	Trelew Argentina	11 Jun 1989	Oscar Daniel Filipponi
1095	Tucuman Argentina	21 Jan 1980	Ronaldo Juan Walker
2004	Tucuman Argentina West	18 Dec 1994	Ricardo Ismael Rodriguez
2208	Zapala Argentina	30 Jun 1996	Humberto Nakad Saade

Discontinued

1250 Parana Argentina   29 Mar 1981   Carlos Arturo Sosa
     15 Apr 1990
1096 San Juan Argentina   22 Jan 1980   Ricardo N. Ontiveros
     30 Jul 1989 †Argentina Cordoba Mission

Missions — 10

(As of Oct. 1, 1996; shown with historical number. See MISSIONS.)

(180) ARG. BAHIA BLANCA MISSION
Casilla de Correo 70
(8000) Bahia Blanca, Buenos Aires
Argentina
Phone: (011-54-91) 517-633

(112) ARG. BUENOS AIRES SO. MISSION
Italia 26, 4 Piso
1832 Lomas de Zamora
Buenos Aires, Argentina
Phone: (011-54-1) 292-4380

(73) ARG. CORDOBA MISSION
Casilla de Correo 17 - Suc. 9
(5009) Cordoba
Argentina
Phone: (011-54-543) 20699

(230) ARG. NEUQUEN MISSION
Casilla de Correo Suite 321
8300 Neuquen, Neuquen
Argentina
Phone: (011-54-99) 432413

(100) ARG. ROSARIO MISSION
Casilla de Correo 341
2000 Rosario, Santa Fe
Argentina
Phone: (011-54-41) 514-503

(32) ARG. BUENOS AIRES NO. MISSION
Ituzaingo 355, C.C. 46
1642 San Isidro
Buenos Aires, Argentina
Phone: (011-54-1) 743-2450

(269) ARG. BUENOS AIRES W. MISSION
Bonpland No. 2349/55
1425 Capital Federal
Buenos Aires, Argentina
Phone: (011-54-1) 777-7539

(228) ARG. MENDOZA MISSION
Casilla de Correo 631
5500 Mendoza
Argentina
Phone: (011-54-61) 22-20-04

(229) ARG. RESISTENCIA MISSION
Casilla de Correo 1
3500 Resistencia - CHACO
Argentina
Phone: (011-54-722) 31722

(206) ARG. SALTA MISSION
Casillo de Correo 429
(4400) Salta
Argentina
Phone: (011-54-87) 31-06-68

ARMENIA

Year-end 1995, Est. population, 3,557,000; Members, 200; Branches, 6; Districts 1; Europe East Area; Ukraine Kiev Mission.

Missionaries worked among Armenian people in Turkey and Syria as early as the 1880s. However, units established among the Armenians were discontinued following unsettled conditions in 1909. Some converts immigrated to the United States.

In modern times, the Church provided assistance in Armenia following the devastating earthquake of 1988 that killed 55,000 people and left half a million people homeless.

The Church and LDS industrialist Jon Huntsman worked together to help provide housing. Huntsman's company built a factory to build cement panels for homes. In response, Armenia donated property where the Church built a multipurpose building for the factory workers.

In 1992, Utah farmers donated tons of milk for Armenian children.

In 1993, the area presidency invited BYU's International Folk Dance Ensemble to perform.

In 1995, missionary couples helped distribute to 200,000 people food donated by the Huntsman family.

Sources: *Church News*, April 28, 1981, July 4, 1981, July 6, 1991, Sept. 28, 1991, April 2, 1992.

AUSTRALIA

Year-end 1995: Est. population, 18,322,000; Members, 87,000; Stakes, 25; Wards, 146; Branches, 101; Missions, 6; Districts, 14; Temples, 1; Percent LDS, 0.4, or one LDS in 210.

Southeast of the Indian Ocean and in the southwest South Pacific, the island-continent of Australia is a democratic federal state in the British commonwealth. Australia's population speaks English, and is Anglican, 26 percent; other Protestant, 25 percent; and Roman Catholic, 25 percent.

In 1840, William Barratt was called at age 17 from England to serve as a missionary in Australia. He found circumstances difficult, but evidence suggested that he baptized converts, including Robert Beauchamp, who later became an influential mission president in Australia. Historians believe Barratt was unable to contact the Saints in England or the United States after the martyrdom of Joseph Smith, and so married and remained in Australia until his death in 1891. The next missionary was Andrew Anderson, a Scottish immigrant to Australia who had been baptized by Orson Pratt in Scotland and given license to preach before sailing to Australia. He and his family arrived in 1841. He found converts and by the end of 1844, organized a branch in the private township of Montefiores, some 220 miles northwest of Sydney. Elder James Wall also served and baptized converts about this time, but information about his work is largely unknown.

Missionaries from Utah, Elders John Murdock and Charles Wandell, arrived Oct. 30, 1851, in Sydney, which became mission headquarters. They published tracts, began preaching and found a few converts among a people very distracted by a gold rush. A year later, 47 members were in the mission when Elder Murdock left because of ill health. On April 6, 1853, Elder Wandell left with a company of Saints. A few days later, another 10 missionaries arrived under the direction of Elder Augustus Farnham to continue the work. More branches were established but emigrations of converts continued, and at least two voyages involved serious mishaps. The most serious ship accident among all the LDS emigrants occurred Oct. 3, 1855, when the bark *Julia Ann*, carrying 350 tons of coal in addition to 28 Saints, broke up on shoals near the Scilly Islands. Five people were drowned, but the rest managed to survive. In 1856, among the emigrants was Joseph Ridges, who carried with him the first of the Tabernacle organs.

Work continued in the 1860s and 1870s with a great emphasis on emigrating to Utah. During one period, mission headquarters were moved to New Zealand and little work was done in Australia. On Jan. 1, 1898, the Australasian Mission was divided, forming a mission in Australia and a mission in New Zealand, and work resumed. At the time, membership was about 200.

The first LDS meetinghouse built in Australia was completed in Brisbane in 1904. Emigrating members continually depleted numbers and upset the Australian government, who in 1918 forbade "emigration propaganda."

The Church grew slowly, and the lack of buildings was a serious hindrance. In 1920, membership was about 1,000, and in 1940, 2,000. World War II particularly slowed the work. However, activity resumed in 1950-55, as President David O. McKay visited in 1955 and authorized building of many more meetinghouses. The mission was divided in 1955, with a second mission in Melbourne. The new meetinghouses proved the base for further growth. Membership reached 7,071 in 1960, 25,063 in 1970, and 40,000 in 1980.

Australia's first stake was organized in Sydney March 27, 1960, with Dell C. Hunt as president. Additional missions were created in 1958 (Adelaide), 1973 (Brisbane) and 1975 (Perth). The Sydney Australia Temple was dedicated Sept. 20, 1984. Membership in 1990 was 76,000.

Members in Brisbane helped computerize government genealogy records in 1992, and Australia's sixth mission was created that year in Sydney. Elder Robert E. Sackley, who served in the Second Quorum of the Seventy from 1989 until his death in 1993, was a native of Australia. In the 1993 brush fires that burned 1.5 million acres, members responded with food for firefighters and stranded motorists. In 1994, a group of 40 aborigine members gathered to do temple work and enjoy their culture. In 1996, the Australian National Maritime Museum in Sydney announced that it would prepare an exhibit to feature a shipwreck of the *Julia Ann*, with its load of Mormon emigrants in 1855.

Sources: *History of the Church*, Vol. 4, p. 154; *Encyclopedic History of the Church*, by Andrew Jenson; *Unto the Islands of the Sea*, by R. Lanier Britsch; *Church News*, Feb. 12, 1955, Dec. 27, 1958, Oct. 28, 1967, July 29, 1978; "The Church in Australia," by Garry P. Mitchell, *Ensign* February 1976, pp.13-19; "Australia Today: And Now the Harvest," by Michael Otterson, *Ensign*, October 1986; "Pioneering in the Gospel," by Marjorie A.

Newton, *Ensign*, October 1986; *Church News*, Aug. 15, 1992; *Church News*, Nov. 29, 1992,; *Church News*, Feb. 27, 1993; *Church News*, Jan. 15, 1994; "Aborigines gather for temple work," *Church News*, Feb. 5, 1994; *Church News*, March 26, 1994, May 4, 1996.

Stakes — 25

(Listed alphabetically as of Oct. 1, 1996.)

No.	Name	Organized	First President
	Pacific Area		
2129	Adelaide Australia Firle	26 Nov 1995	Philip F. Howes
414	*Adelaide Australia Marion 6 Jan 1982		
	*Adelaide Australia Payneham 23 Apr 1978		
	*Adelaide Australia		
	‡Adelaide	23 Feb 1966	Dudley Russell Tredrea
907	Adelaide Australia Modbury	23 Apr 1978	Douglas E. Hann
306	*Brisbane Australia		
	‡Brisbane	23 Oct 1960	William E. Waters
1684	Brisbane Australia North	7 Feb 1988	Douglas Walter Hill
2022	Canberra Australia	19 Feb 1995	Perter John Moir
2141	Devonport Australia	10 Dec 1995	John Robert Hargreaves
892	*Eight Mile Plains Australia 10Dec 1995		
	‡Brisbane Australia South	19 Feb 1978	John D. Jeffrey
2140	Gold Coast Australia	10 Dec 1995	Robert Gordon
860	Hobart Australia	14 Sep 1977	John Douglas Jury
1279	*Ipswich Australia 6 May 1986		
	‡Brisbane Australia West	21 Jun 1981	John D. Jeffrey
551	*Melbourne Australia Braeside 5 Apr 1994		
	*Melbourne Australia Dandenong 18 Mar 1986		
	*Melbourne Australia Moorabbin		
	‡Melbourne South	22 Aug 1971	Bruce James Opie
1175	*Melbourne Australia Deer Park 18 Mar 1986		
	‡Melbourne Australia		
	Fairfield West	7 Sep 1980	Edward Anderson
307	*Melbourne Australia Heidelberg 2 Jul 1995		
	*Melbourne Australia Fairfield		
	‡Melbourne	30 Oct 1960	Boyd C. Bott
2070	Melbourne Australia Pakenham 2 Jul 1995		J. Murray Lobley
1617	*Melbourne Australia Maroondah 2 Jul 1995		
	*Melbourne Australia Waverly	7 Dec 1986	Ian Frank Davenport
1106	*Newcastle Australia 15 Jul 1986		
	‡Sydney Australia Newcastle	15 Feb 1980	Peter R. Barr
447	*Perth Australia Dianella 6 Jul 1980		
	*Perth Australia		
	‡Perth	28 Nov 1967	Donald W. Cummings
1159	Perth Australia Southern River	6 Jul 1980	Roy B. Webb
2033	Perth Australia Warwick	12 Mar 1995	Peter Fletcher Meurs
1988	Sydney Australia Campbelltown 28 Aug 1994		Ma'a Ma'a Jr.
293	*Sydney Australia Greenwich		
	‡Sydney	27 Mar 1960	Dell C. Hunt
1105	Sydney Australia Hebersham	15 Feb 1980	Peter J. Moir
435	*Sydney Australia Mortdale 2 Jun 1992		
	*Mortdale Australia 31 Mar 1992		
	*Sydney Australia Mortdale 15 Feb 1980		
	*Sydney Australia South		
	‡Sydney South	14 May 1967	John Daniel Parker
495	*Sydney Australia Parramatta 2 Jun 1992		
	*Parramatta Australia 31 Mar 1992		
	*Sydney Australia Parramatta 15 Feb 1980		
	*Parramatta Australia 14 Jan 1974		
	‡Parramatta (Australia)	2 Nov 1969	Stanley Owen Gray

Missions — 6

(As of Oct. 1, 1996; shown with historical number. See MISSIONS.)

82) AUSTRALIA ADELAIDE MISSION
P.O. Box 97
Marden, South Australia 5070
Australia
Phone: 011-61-8 332-2588

(106) AUSTRALIA BRISBANE MISSION
P.O. Box 348
Hamilton, Brisbane
Queensland 4007, Australia
Phone: 011-61-7 3268-7077

(43c) AUSTRALIA MELBOURNE MISSION
1216 Old Burke Road
North Balwyn 3104, Victoria
Australia
Phone: 011-61-3 9819-7000

(117) AUSTRALIA PERTH MISSION
P.O. Box 185
Tuart Hill, Western Australia 6060
Australia
Phone: 011-61-9 275-7177

(278) AUSTRALIA SYDNEY NORTH MISSION
P.O. Box 60
Epping, N.S.W. 2121
Australia
Phone: 011-61-2 869-0022

10) AUSTRALIA SYDNEY SOUTH MISSION
P.O. Box 403
Mortdale, NSW 2223
Australia
Phone: 011-61-2 580-9700

AUSTRIA

Year-end 1995: Est. population, 7,986,000; Members, 4,000; Stakes, 1; Wards, 6; Branches, 5; Missions, 1; Percent LDS, 0.05, or one person in 1,996.

Austria, which is 98 percent German-speaking, is in south-central Europe. Some 85 percent of the people in the parliamentary democracy are Roman Catholic.

Elder Orson Pratt of the Quorum of the Twelve and Elder William W. Ritter arrived in Austria on Jan. 18, 1865, but were soon banished. The first Austrian convert was Joseph A. Oheim, baptized Jan. 22, 1870, in Munich, Germany. The first convert baptized in Austria was Paul Haslinger on Nov. 25, 1883. In 1883, Elders Thomas Biesinger and Paul E. B. Hammer arrived and baptized a few converts. These elders were also expelled. By 1901 a branch was established in the Haag am Hausruck. A second branch was established in Vienna in 1909. Government restrictions then stopped work for a time.

The Church began to grow at the end of World War I when religious freedom was allowed. Missionaries were withdrawn during World War II and local members carried on. Missionary work began again in 1946 when Elder Ezra Taft Benson, then of the Quorum of the Twelve and president of the European Mission, established the Austrian District of the Swiss Austrian Mission. The Austrian government officially recognized the Church in 1955. In 1965, the centennial of the Church in Austria was celebrated, and by 1972, there were 2,675 members in Austria. By 1979, there were 2,756 members. President Benson presided on April 20, 1980, at the creation of the Vienna Austria Stake, with Johann A. Wondra, former Vienna District president, as its first president.

In the late 1980s and 1990s, the Austria mission supervised developing areas in Eastern Europe. During the subsequent difficult economic times for various countries, including the conflict in the former country of Yugoslavia, members donated food and clothing for relief. In October 1992, members began receiving general conference live via satellite. Membership in 1990 was 3,700.

Sources: *Encyclopedic History of the Church,* by Andrew Jenson; "Austria gains 1st new stake," *Church News,* May 3, 1980; "Humanitarian relief in Europe," *Church News,* Feb. 29, 1992; *Church News,* Oct. 3, 1992.

Stake — 1
(As of Oct. 1, 1996)

No. Name	Organized	First President
Europe Area		
1126 Vienna Austria	20 Apr 1980	Johann Anton Wondra

Mission — 1
(As of Oct. 1, 1996; shown with historical number. See MISSIONS.)

(53) AUSTRIA VIENNA MISSION
Fuerfanggasse 4
A-1190 Vienna, Austria
Phone: (011-43-1) 37-31-69

(309) AUSTRIA VIENNA SOUTH
Rugirstrasse 1213
Vienna, Austria 1220

BAHAMAS

Year-end 1995: Est. population, 256,000; Members, 400; Branches, 2; Percent LDS, 0.1, or one person in 640; North America Southeast Area; West Indies Mission.

A Caribbean commonwealth, the Bahamas is made up of nearly 800 islands and has a population that speaks English. They are Baptist, 29 percent; Anglican, 23 percent; and Roman Catholic, 22 percent.

Two LDS families, Larry and Marge McCombs and Albert and Karen Ballard, moved to Nassau in the summer of 1979. Missionaries arrived in December of that year but were refused visas and were asked to leave, which they did the following May. Full-time missionaries were allowed to return in March 1985. Alexandre Paul, consul general from Haiti to the Bahamas, and his wife were baptized Jan. 6, 1980. Some 48 investigators and members attended the first branch conference Sept. 12, 1981. A missionary couple, Dr. Thomas E. and Donna Bauman, arrived Dec. 11, 1982. A number of members from the Bahamas have served full-time missions.

A new meetinghouse was dedicated May 8, 1988, and within a few weeks the Soldiers Road and Nassau branches began to outgrow the building. The Soldiers Road Branch is made up of French Creole-speaking Haitians. In 1992, a collection of LDS books was donated to the College of the Bahamas library.

Sources: Personal journal, Margery McCombs; *Church News*, April 22, 1984, Nov. 9, 1986, March 19, 1988, June 18, 1988; *Church News*, Dec. 5, 1992.

BANGLADESH

Year-end 1995: Est. population, 129,000,000; Members, fewer than 100; Branches, 1; Asia Area.

Located on the northern coast of the Bay of Bengal, the People's Republic of Bangladesh is a parliamentary republic and member of the commonwealth of nations. Its people are Islam, 83 percent and Hindi, 16 percent.

Among the first members here were Kenneth and Beatrice Nielsen, an LDS couple working for the Canadian government in 1985. A year or two later, the Nielsens' former cook, Bono Barua, and his family were baptized, the first converts in the country. Also baptized was Roseline Gomes, a young woman who later became the first of her nationality to serve a full-time mission. She left her homeland at age 19 to live in Canada with Church members who had lived in Bangladesh.

In 1995, there was one branch, in Dacka, consisting mainly of expatriates.

Sources: "Welcome mat is out in several countries," by Sheridan R. Sheffield, *Church News*, Oct. 23, 1993; *Church News*, May 15, 1993.

BARBADOS

Year-end 1995: Est. population, 257,000; Members, 500; Branches, 4; Percent LDS, 0.19, or one LDS in 514; North America Southeast Area; West Indies Mission.

A Caribbean independent sovereign state of Great Britain, English-speaking Barbados is made up of one island and a population where some 70 percent are Anglican.

Among the first LDS in Barbados were John and Norman Namie, who served as presidents of the Black Rock and Christ Church branches. The island was in the Puerto Rico San Juan Mission and transferred to the West Indies Mission when that mission was created in 1983. In 1994, headquarters of the West Indies Mission were transferred from Barbados to Tobago.

The Christ Church Branch was created Oct. 20, 1979, and the Black Rock Branch was organized Aug. 24, 1983.

BELARUS

Year-end 1995: Est. population, 10,437,000; Members, 200, Branches, 4; Europe East Area; Ukraine Kiev Mission.

Formerly Byelorussia (also spelled Belorussia) or White Russia, Belarus is a hilly lowland with forests, rivers and lakes. It is bordered by Latvia, Lithuania, Ukraine, Russia and Poland. Its people speak Belarusian and are mostly Russian Orthodox.

Belarus is part of the Ukraine Kiev Mission, which was created July 1, 1991. The country was visited by Church leaders in May 1993. Two branches in Minsk, the Minsk Pushkinsky and the Minsk Tsentralny, were created in January 1994.

Three children from Belarus, affected by radioactivity from the 1986 Chernobyl Nuclear Power Station explosion, were guests of the Solihull (England) Ward for a day in April 1995. The Belarusian Military and Utah National Guard have a sister-state relationship.

Sources: *Church News*, June 12, 1993.

BELGIUM

Year-end 1995: Est. population, 10,082,000; Members, 6,000; Stakes, 2; Wards, 9;

Branches, 13; Missions, 1; Percent LDS, 0.05, or one person in 1,680.

Located in northwest Europe on the North Sea, Belgium is a parliamentary democracy under a constitutional monarch. Its population speaks Flemish, 55 percent, French, 33 percent and minority languages. About 75 percent of the population is Roman Catholic.

Mischa Markow, a Hungarian converted in Turkey, is believed to be the first member to have come to Belgium. Markow, baptized in Turkey in 1887, visited Antwerp in 1888. He preached to a family named Esselman, and baptized the mother, Henreite, and her oldest son, Frederick, on Oct. 17, 1888. Four other members of the family were baptized later.

Three missionaries from the Swiss and German Mission were then sent, and within two months they had baptized 80 people and organized branches in Liege, Brussels and Antwerp. In 1891, Belgium became part of the Netherlands Mission.

Opposition was manifest in 1896 when a mob estimated at nearly 500 people threatened to kill Elder John Ripplinger in Liege. The mob stormed the home where he was staying, but was dispersed by police. However, he remained in the city and eventually baptized some 10 people.

Several branches were transferred to the French Mission in 1924, with the Flemish-speaking branches remaining in the Netherlands Mission.

Work stopped during World War I, and by 1930, just a few scattered members remained in the country. Members in six branches remained active during World War II, during the German occupation of Belgium. However, when the Flemish section of Belgium was re-opened in January 1948 by the Netherlands Mission, there were no known members in Antwerp. Work progressed slowly, and in 1963 the Franco-Belgian Mission was organized. Ten years later, there were some 3,500 members in three districts in Belgium. The Belgium Antwerp Mission (232) was organized in 1975, discontinued in 1982, and reorganized in 1990 and discontinued again in 1994.

A second stake, Antwerp Belgium Stake, was organized in October 1994 with Johan A. Buysse as president. Elder Charles Didier of the Seventy is a native of Ixelles, Belgium. Members in Brussels received a boost with the visit of President Gordon B. Hinckley in June 1996, the first president in some 40 years to travel to the city.

Sources: *Encyclopedic History of the Church*, by Andrew Jenson; *Ensign*, Aug. 1973; *Church News* Oct. 22, 1977; "Anti-LDS Boomerang," by William Hartley, *Church News*, Aug. 12, 1978; "Missionary to the Balkans: Mischa Markow," by William Hale Kehr, *Ensign*, June 1980; *Church News*, Jan. 10, 1981; June 22, 1996.

Stakes — 2

(As of Oct. 1, 1996.)

No.	Name	Organized	First President
Europe West Area			
1993	Antwerp Belgium	16 Oct 1994	Johan A. Buysse
813	Brussels Belgium	20 Feb 1977	Joseph Scheen

Mission — 1

(As of Oct. 1, 1996; shown with historical number. See MISSIONS.)

(76) BELGIUM BRUSSELS MISSION
87, Blvd. Brand Whitlock
1200 Bruxelles, Belgium
Phone: (011-32-2) 736-99-33

BELIZE

Year-end 1995: Est. population, 216,000; Members, 1,800; Districts, 3; Branches, 10; Percent LDS, 0.8, or one person in 120; Central America Area; Guatemala Guatemala City North Mission.

Located on the eastern coast of Central America, Belize formerly was known as British Honduras; a parliamentary government with a population that speaks English, Spanish and Creole. They are Roman Catholic, 60 percent; Protestant, 40 percent. Belize received independence from Great Britain in 1981.

Missionary work opened in Belize on May 5, 1980, when President Samuel Flores of the Honduras Tegucigalpa Mission and Elder Robert Henke arrived to prepare for 10 additional missionaries coming the following day. On the day of their arrival, Elder

Merlin Mikkelson was set apart as president of a newly organized branch, and the first Sunday meeting was held May 11, 1980. Elders Larry Pinnock and Scott Harries baptized Ernesto Alay on June 1, 1980. Elder Hugh W. Pinnock of the Seventy visited the country Aug. 30, 1980.

The Belize District was organized April 17, 1983, with Harold Smith as president. Meetinghouses were completed in Orange Walk in August of 1987, and in San Ignacio in September 1987. By 1987, some 1,000 members in seven branches comprised the Belize District. On July 1, 1990, the Honduras Tegucigalpa Mission was divided, and Belize was placed in the new Honduras San Pedro Sula Mission.

Elder Russell M. Nelson of the Quorum of the Twelve visited and dedicated a meetinghouse in December 1992, at which some 289 members attended.

Sources: Honduras Tegucigalpa Mission history; *Church News,* Feb. 16, 1990; *Church News,* Dec. 19, 1992; Corrrespondence from Ralph D. and Dawnetta A. Erickson, Nov. 30, 1994.

BERMUDA

Year-end 1995: Est. population, 61,600; Members, fewer than 100; Branches, 1; North America Northeast Area; New York New York South Mission.

Bermuda consists of 360 small coral islands, 20 of which are inhabited, located 580 miles east of North Carolina. Most of the residents of the United Kingdom dependency are Protestant.

Church members serving in the Air Force and Navy and their families created the first LDS presence in Bermuda. On July 16, 1953, a group of servicemen's wives organized a Relief Society, which was brought under the Eastern States Mission on Oct. 11, 1956. Sacrament meetings and Sunday School were held beginning Oct. 8, 1961, among the military personnel.

Arthur L. McMullin and his wife, Melba, arrived April 19, 1966, and received permission to proselyte on May 3, 1966. On May 31, Elders Kenneth R. French and Curt S. Call arrived and began tracting and proselyting. The Bermuda Branch, which had about 50 in attendance, was organized June 25, 1966, by mission Pres. W. Jay Eldredge. This branch was made part of the New York New York Mission in 1974.

Native Bermudans began to join the branch in the 1980s. Vernon Every, converted in 1982, became the first Bermudan priesthood holder, and the first called to the branch presidency in 1985. In 1993, Bermuda was placed in the New York New York South Mission.

Sources: *Church News,* Dec. 14, 1957; Bermuda Branch manuscript history; "Bermuda Branch sprouts in gentle island climate," by Heidi Waldrop, *Church News,* Aug. 25, 1985; *Church News* March 13, 1993.

BOLIVIA

Year-end 1995: Est. population, 7,974,000; Members, 89,000; Stakes, 16; Wards, 95; Districts, 10; Branches, 99; Missions, 2; Temples, 1 under construction; Percent LDS, 1.1, or one person in 90.

Bolivia, located in central South America, is a republic with a population that speaks Spanish, Quechua, and Aymara. Some 95 percent are Roman Catholic.

Three LDS families who lived in Bolivia in 1963 — Duane Wilcox and Dube Thomas in La Paz, and Norval Jesperson in Cochabamba — helped the Church gain legal status. On Nov. 24, 1964, missionaries arrived from the Andes Mission. They baptized Victor Walter Vallejos at Cochabamba just before Christmas in 1964. In two years, branches opened in Oruro and Santa Cruz. In 1968, the Church had about 350 members, among whom was the first Bolivian to serve a mission, Desiderio Arce Cano, who left a singing career in Argentina to serve in his native land. He was called April 25, 1967. The first missionary called from Bolivia was Carlos Pedraja, baptized May 30, 1965, and called to the Andes South Mission in 1968.

By 1977, membership in Bolivia numbered 9,700. Church education, including seminary, helped prepare many young people for leadership positions. The Andes South Mission was organized in 1966, later named the Bolivia La Paz Mission. In 1977, the Bolivia Santa Cruz Mission was organized, and has since been re-named the Bolivia Cochabamba Mission. Some 4,373 members attended an area conference in La Paz on March 3, 1977. President Kimball also met with the head of state, President Hugo Bonzer Suarez.

The Santa Cruz Bolivia Stake, the first stake in Bolivia, was organized Jan. 14, 1979, with Noriharu Ishigaki Haraguichi as president.

In recent years, a number of Church-sponsored humanitarian projects have improved the health of members and non-members in various rural areas. Membership in 1990 was 64,000. A temple was announced for Cochabamba Jan. 21, 1995, and ground was scheduled to be broken for the temple by President Gordon B. Hinckley on Nov. 10, 1996.

Sources: *Improvement Era*, Jan. 1965; 'Bolivia," *Ensign*, Feb. 1977; "Love, respect and emotion end area conference series," by Dell Van Orden, *Church News*, March 12, 1977; *Church News*, Jan. 27, 1979, Feb. 24, 1990, May 26, 1990, June 8, 1991.

Stakes — 19

(Listed alphabetically as of Oct. 1, 1996.)

No.	Name	Organized	First President
South America North Area			
1465	Cochabamba Bolivia Cobija	19 Feb 1984	Guillermo Rivero Paz Soldan
2143	Cochabamba Bolivia Jaihuayco	10 Dec 1995	Ivan Jorge Gutierrez
1062	*Cochabamba Bolivia Universidad	19 Feb 1984	
	‡Cochabamba Bolivia	11 Sep 1979	Carlos L. Pedraja
1940	Cochabamba Bolivia Los Alamos	16 May 1993	Jose Ruben Rivero Zeballos
1831	El Alto Bolivia	24 Nov 1991	Edmundo Chavez Vasquez
1227	*El Alto Bolivia Satelite	6 Mar 1992	
	‡La Paz Bolivia El Alto	18 Jan 1981	Victor Hugo Saravia R.
2207	La Paz Bolivia Alto San Pedro	30 Jun 1996	Juan Carlos Mogrovejo Rocabado
1112	*La Paz Bolivia Constitucion	18 Jan 1981	
	‡La Paz Bolivia West	24 Feb 1980	Victor Hugo Saravia R.
1007	*La Paz Bolivia Miraflores	18 Jan 1981	
	‡La Paz Bolivia	11 Mar 1979	Jorge Leano
1670	La Paz Bolivia Sopocachi	17 Jan 1988	Eduardo Gabarret I.
2120	Montero Bolivia	12 Nov 1995	Hugo Walter Sandoval Pinto
1213	Oruro Bolivia	1 Dec 1980	J. Adrian Velasco C.
2063	Potosi Bolivia	18 Jun 1995	Edgar Medardo Lopez Loayza
993	*Santa Cruz Bolivia Canoto	15 Feb 1981	
	‡Santa Cruz Bolivia	14 Jan 1979	Noriharu Ishigaki Haraguichi
1782	Santa Cruz Bolivia Equipetrol	2 Dec 1990	Antonio Rolando Oyola
1235	Santa Cruz Bolivia Paraiso	15 Feb 1981	Erwin Birnbaumer
1981	Santa Cruz Bolivia Piray	19 June 1994	Rolando A. Oyola Suarez
2191	Sucre Bolivia	28 Apr 1996	Esteban Portillo Rios
2184	Tarija Bolivia	24 Mar 1996	Juan Garcia Vargas

Missions — 2

(As of Oct. 1, 1996; shown with historical number. See MISSIONS.)

(150) BOLIVIA COCHABAMBA MISSION
Casilla de Correo 1375
Cochabamba
Phone: (011-591-4) 117-207

(75a) BOLIVIA LA PAZ MISSION
20 de Octubre 2550
Casilla 4789Bolivia
La Paz, Bolivia
Phone (011-591-2) 43-17-22

BOTSWANA

Year-end 1995: Est. population, 1,405,000; Members, 300; Branches, 3; Districts,1; Africa Area; South Africa Johannesburg Mission.

Located north of South Africa, Botswana is a parliamentary democracy with a population that speaks English and Setswana. The majority follow indigenous beliefs, and 15 percent are Christian.

Missionary work in Botswana began in 1990 with the arrival in Gabarone of Pres. R.J. Snow of the South Africa Johannesburg Mission, followed by occasional visits by Elder Karl and Sister Marjorie Jenkins. The first missionaries assigned to Botswana were Elder Bruce Midgley and his wife, Patricia, who established a group in Gabarone on June 24, with Elder Midgley as the presiding elder.

Members living in Botswana at the time included two returned missionaries who had become Peace Corps workers, Patricia Lutz of Levittown, Pa., in Molepolole, and Javotte Pickering of Enterprise, Utah, stationed in Kang. The Maurice Mzwinila and Anthony Mogare families, who had joined the Church while studying in the United States, were later located through a newspaper article.

In September 1990, a baptismal service was held. Among the converts was Kwasi Agyare Dwomoh, an architect from Ghana working for the Botswana government. When the Church registration was filed in August 1991 and the first branch was organized, Brother Dwomoh was called as its first president. By March 1992, the fast-growing branch was ready to be divided into two branches, and Brother Dwomoh was called as the first district president in Botswana. He also was the first member in Botswana to receive his endowments at the Johannesburg South Africa Temple.

By August 1992, membership had grown to 160, with a number of baptisms planned for the city of Lobatse. A third unit was added to the district in 1992.

On Feb. 18, 1996, members from Botswana were among the 5,000 people who gathered for the Johannesburg South Africa Regional Conference at Soweto.

Sources: Correspondence from Pres. R.J. and Sister Marilyn M. Snow; "Missionary work begins in Botswana," by Elder Darwin and Sister Maureen Cook, *Church News*, Sept. 15, 1990; "Four nations in central, southern Africa," by Mary Mostert and Gerry Avant, *Church News*, Sept. 26, 1992; *Church News*, March 2, 1996.

BRAZIL

Year-end 1995: Est. population, 160,810,000; Members, 548,000; Stakes, 136; Wards, 801; Branches, 597; Missions, 23; Districts, 45; Temples, 1 and 1 planned; Percent LDS, 0.3, or one LDS in 293.

Brazil, a federal republic, covers almost half the continent of South America, and has a population that speaks Portuguese and is 89 percent Roman Catholic.

The first Church members in Brazil were German immigrants, Augusta Kuhlmann Lippelt and her four children. Her husband, Roberto, was baptized several years later. They arrived in Brazil in 1923. The first missionaries were Elders William Fred Heinz and Emil A.J. Schindler, accompanied by Pres. Rheinold Stoof of the South American Mission in Buenos Aires, Argentina. Pres. Stoof first visited Brazil in 1927, and returned with the elders to begin proselyting among German-speaking people in September 1928. Bertha Sell and her children, Theodore, Alice, Seigfried and Adell, were the first converts, baptized April 14, 1929. The first Church-owned meetinghouse in South America was dedicated Oct. 25, 1931, in Joinville.

A mission was created and headquartered in Brazil on May 25, 1935. At first, missionaries taught only in German. However, the Book of Mormon was translated into Portuguese in 1937, and missionaries began teaching in Portuguese a year later. By 1940, there were still fewer than 200 members in the country. Missionary work progressed very slowly during World War II. More than a decade later, in 1957, the Church had reached about 1,000 members.

In the next decade, however, the work began to accelerate. By 1959, membership was 3,700. The Sao Paulo Stake, the first in Brazil, was organized in 1966 with Walter Spat as president. Ten years later, Brazil had 10 stakes, and a temple had been announced for Sao Paulo. President Spencer W. Kimball attended a cornerstone ceremony for the temple March 9, 1977, at which 3,000 people attended. President Marion G. Romney of the First Presidency performed the ceremonial mortaring of the cornerstone.

The Sao Paulo Temple was dedicated Oct. 30, 1978, by President Spencer W. Kimball. The Brazil Area was created in August 1987.

On Feb. 2, 1986, Brazil became the third country outside the United States to have 50 stakes. With the creation of the Sao Leopoldo Stake Dec. 5, 1993, Brazil reached 100 stakes, the second country out of the United States to do so. Elder Helio A. Camargo was the first Brazilian to serve as a General Authority. Brazilian Elders Helvecio Martins, released in 1995, and Claudio R.M. Costa of the Seventy have served as General Authorities. Membership in 1990 was 368,000.

In October 1993, construction began on Brazil's missionary training center, the Church's second largest. With 23 missions in 1996, Brazil has the largest number of missions outside the United States. A temple for Recife was announced Jan. 21, 1995, and President Gordon B. Hinckley broke ground for the temple Nov. 15, 1996. He also visited members in Porto Alegre, Campinas, Sao Paulo, and Manaus during his visit.

Sources: *From Acorn to Oak Tree,* by Frederick S. Williams and Frederick G. Williams;

Deseret News, Nov. 14, 1935; "Brazil, A new frontier for the Restored Gospel," by Rulon S. Howells, *Improvement Era,* May 1936 and Sept. 1938; "Brazilian Missions," *Improvement Era,* May 1963; "Sao Paulo Temple cornerstone laid by President Romney," by Dell Van Orden, *Church News,* March 19, 1977; "Gospel story in Brazil begun by German Family," by Jason Souza Garcia, *Church News,* May 31, 1980; *Church News,* Sept. 18, 1993; *Church News,* Feb. 19, 1994.

Stakes — 140
(Listed alphabetically as of Oct. 1, 1996.)

No.	Name	Organized	First President
Brazil Area			
1292	Alegrete Brazil	20 Sep 1981	Waldomiro Siegfried Radtke
2066	Americana Brazil	25 Jun 1995	Donizetti de Paul Tavares
1851	*Aracajo Brazil Bela Vita	8 Mar 1995	
	Aracaju Brazil	8 Mar 1992	Manuel Durval Andrade Neto
2077	Aracaju Brazil America	23 Jul 1995	Valdeilson de Oliveira
2078	Aracaju Brazil Cidade Nova	23 Jul 1995	Raulino Gairao LIma Jr.
1886	Aracatuba Brazil	14 June 1992	Paulo Henrique Itinose
2100	Arapiraca Brazil	17 Sep 1995	Antonio de A. de Banos
970	Araraquara Brazil	22 Oct 1978	Marcio Rodrigues Galhardo
1959	Bage Brazil	31 Oct 1993	Cecer Ronaldo Loureiro Dutra
1893	Bauru Brazil	2 Aug 1992	Lazaro Beteto
1837	Belem Brazil	29 Dec 1991	Luiz Carlos Silva De Franca
2067	Belem Brazil Cabanagem	25 Jun 1995	Jaime Carneiro Costa
1234	*Belo Horizonte Brazil 6 Mar 1990		
	*Belo Horizonte Brazil De Siao 10 Jan 1989		
	‡Belo Horizonte Brazil	15 Feb 1981	Ernani Teixeira
1963a	Belo Horizonte Brazil West	12 Dec 1993	Rodrigo de Lima e Myrrha
2074	Birigui Brazil	09 Jul 1995	Sebastiao Henrique Neto
1189	Brasilia Brazil	12 Oct 1980	Daniel Alberta da Gloria
1393	*Brasilia Brazil Alvorada 22 Mar 1983		
	‡Alvorada Brazil	9 Jan 1983	Manoel Francisco Clavery G.
2147	Brasilia Brazil Taguatinga	17 Dec 1995	Jose Claudio de Almeida
1984	Camaragibe Brazil	24 Jul 1994	Altair Roque da Silva
1442	Campina Grande Brazil	18 Sep 1983	Jose Francisco Barbosa
621	*Campinas Brazil		
	‡Campinas	9 Jun 1973	Nelson de Genaro
1586	Campinas Brazil Castelo	2 Feb 1986	S. Lourenco de Oliveira
1897	Campinas Brazil Flamboyant	23 Aug 1992	Luiz Antonio Cairo
1805	Campo Grande Brazil	30 Jun 1991	Ricardo Kasimerczak
1962	Canoas Brazil	5 Dec 1993	Raul Anibal Proenca Krieger
1963	Caxias Do Sul Brazil	5 Dec 1993	Alvacir Luiz Siedschlag
1942	Contagem Brazil	6 June 1993	Evandro Chevitarese Parada
2032	Cuiaba Brazil	5 Mar 1995	Ildemar Ferreira Vilas Boas
552	*Curitiba Brazil		
	‡Curitiba	12 Sep 1971	Jason Garcia Souza
1302	Curitiba Brazil Bacacheri	1 Nov 1981	Casemiro Antunes Gomes
1243	*Curitiba Brazil Boqueirao 14 Mar 1989		
	‡Curitiba Brazil East	15 Mar 1981	Francisco Reguim
1468	Curitiba Brazil Iguacu	29 Apr 1984	Waldemar de Lima
1974a	Curitiba Brazil Novo Mundo	29 Feb 1994	Valdemiro Skraba
893	*Curitiba Brazil Portao 14 Mar 1989		
	‡Curitiba Brazil South	26 Feb 1978	Albina Bruno Schmeil
2073	Curitiba Brazil Taruma	9 Jul 1995	Ildefonso de Castro Dues Neto
2231	Feira de Santana Brazil	15 Sep 1996	Vaguiner Cruciol Tobias
1569	Florianopolis Brazil	3 Nov 1985	Cesar A. Seiguer Milder
1284	Fortaleza Brazil	19 Jul 1981	Orville Wayne Day Jr.
1828	Fortaleza Brazil Bom Sucesso	17 Nov 1991	Manoel A. De Carvalho Filho
1935	Fortaleza Brazil Ceara	2 May 1993	Jose Vieira de Matos Filho
1454	Fortaleza Brazil Montese	13 Nov 1983	Fernando J. Duarte D.
1578	Fortaleza Brazil West	24 Nov 1985	Antenor Silva Junior
1952	Franca Brazil	5 Sep 1993	Donizete Pugliesi Braz
2048	Garanhuns Brazil	21 May 1995	Jose Ciaudio Furtado Campos
1641	Goiania Brazil	24 May 1987	Antonio Casado Rodriguez
2142	Gravatai Brazil	10 Dec 1995	Fabiano Ribeiro Barreto

2221	Guaruja Brazil	18 Aug 1996	Carlos Roberto Couto E. Silva
1891	*Jaboatao Brazil Dos Guararapes	15 May 1994	
	‡Recife Brazil Jaboatao	26 Jul 1992	Jose Antonia da Silva
1979	Jaboatao Brazil Litoral	15 May 1994	Domingos Savio Linhares
1185	Joao Pessoa Brazil	2 Oct 1980	Jose Francisco Barbosa
1896	Joao Pessoa Brazil Rangel	23 Aug 1992	
1338	Joinville Brazil	21 Apr 1982	Heins Dorival Halter
1833	Jundiai Brazil	1 Dec 1991	Domingos Fatobene Jr.
1821	Livramento Brazil	27 Oct 1991	Clademir Elton Trage
1080	Londrina Brazil	11 Nov 1979	Carlos Roberto Moeller
1322	Maceio Brazil	21 Jan 1982	Abelardo Rodrigues Camara
1923	Maceio Brazil Litoral	7 Feb 1993	Gilberto C. da Silva Moraes
2030	Maceio Brazil Pajucara	5 Mar 1995	Jose Domingues Silva
1700	Manaus Brazil	16 Oct 1988	Eduardo A. Soares C.
2116	Manaus Brazil Cidade Nova	5 Nov 1995	Walter Braga De Souza
1941	Manaus Brazil Rio Negro	30 May 1993	Divino Presenca
2145	Maracanau Brazil	17 Dec 1995	Raimundo Vieira de Oliveira
1449	Marilia Brazil	23 Oct 1983	Wilson de Souza Novelli
2095	Maringa Brazil	27 Aug 1995	Dirceu Freire
2065	Mogi Mirim Brazil	25 Jun 1995	Milton Cenko
1964	Monte Cristo Brazil	19 Dec 1993	Adelson de Paula Parrella
1894	Natal Brazil	16 Aug 1992	Ricardo Gueiros
987	Novo Hamburgo Brazil	3 Dec 1978	Paulo R. Grahl
1282	Olinda Brazil	12 Jul 1981	Reinhold Kraft
2020	*Olinda Paulista Brazil	22 Aug 1995	
	Paulista Brazil	5 Feb 1995	Reginaldo de Morais Junior1932
	Osasco Brazil	18 Apr 1993	Marcos Anthony Aidu Kaitis
1604	Passo Fundo Brazil	10 Aug 1986	Helio Rodrigues Severo
1658	Pelotas Brazil	18 Oct 1987	Marco Antonio Rais
2080	Pelotas Brazil North	23 Jul 1995	Victor Afranio Asconavieta da Silva
1377	Petropolis Brazil	14 Nov 1982	Antonio Jose Mendoza
2012	Piracicaba Brazil	22 Jan 1995	Marcos Tadeu Michailuca Nolli
1182	*Ponta Grossa Brazil Parana	7 Apr 1992	
	‡Ponta Grossa Parana Brazil	22 Sep 1980	Silvina Mendes de Jesus
601	*Porto Alegre Brazil		
	‡Porto Alegre	13 Feb 1973	Miguell Sorrentino
1858	Porto Alegre Brazil		
	Moinhos De Vento	3 May 1992	Claudio Weihert
1256	Porto Alegre Brazil North	21 Apr 1981	Silvio Geschwasdtner
1793	Porto Alegre Brazil Partenon	5 May 1991	Ulisses Pereira Filho
1201	Recife Brazil	31 Oct 1980	Iraja Bandeira Soares
1332	*Recife Brazil Boa Viagem	26 Jul 1992	
	*Boa Viagem Brazil	21 Mar 1982	Iraga Bandeira Soares
2135	Recife Brazil Imbiribeira	3 Dec 1995	Marcone Magalhaes Santos
1811	*Recife Brazil Jardim Sao Paulo	10 May 1994	
	‡Recife Brazil Southwest	25 Aug 1991	Herbert Otto Homolka
1916a	Ribeiro Pires Brazil	13 Dec 1992	Guilherme Tell Peixoto
1645	Ribeirao Preto Brazil	28 Jun 1987	Moises Barreiro Damasceno
1888	Ribeirao Preto Brazil Centro	21 Jun 1992	Augusto Martinez Perez
1953	Ribeirao Preto Brazil Ipiranga	5 Sep 1993	Jose Alberto Borges da Silva
1954	Ribeirao Preto Brazil Quintino	5 Sep 1993	Euclides Jose Maggio
2136	Rio Branco Brazil	3 Dec 1995	Tarciso Barboza Friere
1135	Rio Claro Brazil	21 May 1980	Marcio Rodriques Galhardo
589	*Rio de Janeiro Brazil		
	‡Rio de Janeiro	22 Oct 1972	Veledmar Cury
1028	Rio de Janeiro Brazil Andarai	20 May 1979	Nelson Gennari
1378	Rio de Janeiro		
	Brazil Madureira	14 Nov 1982	Atilio Pinto Maio
769	Rio de Janeiro Brazil Niteroi	19 Sep 1976	Joao Eduardo Kemeny
2079	Rio Grande Brazil	23 Jul 1995	Carlos William Ramires de Oliveira
2031	Rosario Do Sul Brazil	5 Mar 1995	Jean Jaques
1862	Salvador Brazil	10 May 1992	Carlos Shunji Obata
1934a	Salvador Brazil North	2 May 1993	Sandro Silva Quatel
1922	Santa Maria Brazil	31 Jan 1993	Aires Luciano
2227	Santa Rita Brazil	01 Sep 1996	Jose Joel Alves Fernandes

1136	Santo Andre Brazil	23 May 1980	Ademar Leal
620	*Santos Brazil		
	‡Santos	8 Jun 1973	Jose Gonzalez Lopes
523	*Sao Bernardo Brazil	23 May 1980	
	*Sao Paulo Brazil South		
	‡Sao Paulo South	6 Sep 1970	Saul Messias de Oliveira
1909a	Sao Carlos Brazil	15 Nov 1992	Justino Carlos Atchiza Peres
2081	Sao Joao da Boa Vista Brazil	30 Jul 1995	Izaias Pivato Nogueira
1965	Sao Jose Brazil	19 Dec 1993	Jose Jorge Cordeiro Campos
1917	Sao Jose Do Rio Preto Brazil	13 Dec 1992	Guilherme Tell Peixoto
1516	Sao Jose Dos Campos Brazil	3 Mar 1985	Eric Brito Correa
1961	Sao Leopoldo Brazil	5 Dec 1993	Valmir Severo Dutra
2071	Sao Luis Brazil	2 Jul 1995	Jose Benicio Pereira
417	*Sao Paulo Brazil		
	‡Sao Paulo	1 May 1966	Walter Spat
1846	Sao Paulo Brazil		
	Campo Limpo	9 Feb 1992	Dejanir Hadleck de Castro
2076	Sao Paulo Brazil Cotia	16 Jul 1995	Ulisses Soares
1868	Sao Paulo Brazil Guarulhos	24 May 1992	Gilmar Silva Diasta
1536	Sao Paulo Brazil Interlagos	26 May 1985	Walter Guedes de Queiroz
1137	Sao Paulo Brazil Ipiranga	25 May 1980	Demar Staniscia
1869	Sao Paulo Brazil Itaquera	24 May 1992	Vanderlei Zanchetta
2198	Sao Paulo Brazil Jacana	02 Jun 1996	Jorge Luiz de Oliveira
1870	Sao Paulo Brazil		
	Mogi Das Cruzes	24 May 1992	Gilberto Vicente da Silva
815	Sao Paulo Brazil North	20 Feb 1977	Jorge Flavio de Moraes
467	*Sao Paulo Brazil Penha	24 May 1992	
	*Sao Paulo Brazil East		
	‡Sao Paulo East	24 Nov 1968	Helio da Rocha Camargo
1138	Sao Paulo Brazil Perdizes	25 May 1980	Oswaldo Silva Camargo
1913	Sao Paulo Brazil Piratininga	6 Dec 1992	Luiz Carlos Coronetti
1082	Sao Paulo Brazil Santo Amaro	12 Nov 1979	Wilson Sanchez Netto
1823	Sao Paulo Brazil		
	Sao Miguel Paulista	10 Nov 1991	Gilberto Vicente Da Silva
1441	Sao Paulo Brazil Taboao	18 Sep 1983	Octavio Baptists de Carvalho
1921	Sao Paulo Brazil Vila Sabrina	24 Jan 1993	Jose Olimpio Fabrizio
622	*Sao Paulo Brazil West		
	‡Sao Paulo West	10 Jun 1973	Jose Benjamin Puerta
1291	Sao Vincente Brazil	20 Sep 1981	Vicente Verta Jr.
989	Sorocaba Brazil	10 Dec 1978	Nelson de Genaro
1892	Sorocaba Brazil Barcelona	26 Jul 1992	Mauro Junot De Maria
2146	Sorocaba Brazil Trujillo	17 Dec 1995	Valdimir Fernandes Tasso
1960a	Teresina Brazil	28 Nov 1993	Alexandre J. Gomes da Cruz
1966	Tubarao Brazil	19 Dec 1993	Gelson Januario
2017	Uberlandia Brazil	29 Jan 1995	Raimundo Walter Tavares A.
1912	Uruguaiana Brazil	29 Nov 1992	Saul E. Seiguer Milder
2094	Vila Velha Brazil	27 Aug 1995	Washington Luiz Lima
1630	Vitoria Brazil	15 Feb 1987	Pedro J. da Cruz Penha

Discontinued

1030	Curitiba Brazil North	27 May 1979	Alfredo Heliton de Lemos

30 Apr 1989 †Curitiba Brazil Iguacu (No. 1468)

Missions — 23

(As of Oct. 1, 1996; shown with historical number. See MISSIONS.)

(296) BRAZIL BELEM MISSION
Avenida Nazare532 Sala 412
Royal Trade Center
66035-170 Belem, PA
Brazil
Phone: 011-55-91 223-7316

(213) BRAZIL BELO HORIZONTE MISSION
Rua Sao Paulo, 1781, 10 Andar
Edif. 17 de Maio, Sala 1001
Barrio Lourdes
30170-132 Belo Horizonte - MG, Brazil
Phone: 011-55-31 335-7553

(295a) BRAZIL BELO HORIZONTE EAST MISSION
Rua Paraiba, 1174, Sala 401
Funcioncarios
30130-141 Belo Horizonte - MG
Brazil
Phone: 011-55-31 261-6775

(190) BRAZIL CAMPINAS MISSION
Caixa Postal 1814
13001-970 Campinas - SP
Brazil
Phone: 011-55-192 33-53-66

(281) BRAZIL FLORIANAPOLIS MISSION
Caixa Postal: 361
88010-970 - Florianapolis - SC
Brazil
Phone: 011-55-482 22-8350

(233) BRAZIL MANAUS MISSION
Caixa Postal No 3461
Alvorada I
69042-010 Manaus, AM
Brazil
Phone: 011-55-92 238-5433

(256) BRAZIL PORTO
 ALEGRE NORTH MISSION
ACF Princesa Isabel
Caixa Postal 20256
90620-970 Porto Alegre - RS
Brazil
Phone: 011-55-51 223-5744

(167a) BRAZIL RECIFE MISSION
Rua Sao Francisco, 110 Sala 102
Derby
52010-020 - Recife - PE
Brazil
Phone: 011-55-81 221-3280

(279) BRAZIL RIBEIRAO PRETO MISSION
Caixa Postal 388
14001-970 Ribeirao Preto - SP
Brazil
Phone: 011-55-16 610-3141

(280) BRAZIL RIO
 DE JANEIRO NORTH MISSION
Rua da Gloria, 344 Sala 904
20241-180 - Rio de Janeiro - RJ, Brazil
Phone: 011-55-21 221-3316

(298) BRAZIL SALVADOR SOUTH MISSION
Caiza Postal 7384
Pituba
41811-970 - Salvador - BA
Brazil
Phone: 011-55-71 334-0140

(185a) BRAZIL BRASILIA MISSION
SAS Quadra 5, Bloco "N"
Ed. OAB, Salas 201-204
70438-900 Brasilia - DF
Brazil
Phone: 011-55-61 322-5881

(181) BRAZIL CURITIBA MISSION
Caixa Postal 9501
Portao
80613-991 Curitiba - Parana Brazil
Phone: 011-55-41 345-1010

(200) BRAZIL FORTALEZA MISSION
Rua Barao de Aracati, No. 1145
Aldeota, 60115-081 Fortaleza - CE
Brazil
Phone: 011-55-85 221-1335

(302) BRAZIL MARILIA MISSION
Rua Maranhao, 75 Salas 61 E 62
Centro
17500-000 - Marilia - SP
Brazil
Phone: 011-55-144 33-6130

(48) BRAZIL PORTO
 ALEGRE SOUTH MISSION
ACF Princesa Isabel
Caixa Postal 20251
90620-970 - Porto Alegre - RS
90631-730 Brazil
Phone: 011-55-51 223-0288

(282) BRAZIL RECIFE
 SOUTH MISSION
Rua General Joaquim Inacio, 412
Sala 1202
50070-270 Recife - PE, Brazil
Phone: 011-55-81 221-0982

(80) BRAZIL RIO
DE JANEIRO MISSION
Av. das Americas, 1155, salas 502/503
(Barra Space Center) - Barra da Tijuca
22631-000 Rio de Janeiro - RJ, Brazil
Phone: 011-55-21 439-9243

(234) BRAZIL SALVADOR MISSION
Caixa Postal 3046
Pituba
41811-970 - Salvador, BA
Brazil
Phone: 011-55-71 358-7345

(102) BRAZIL SAO PAULO
 EAST MISSION
Caixa Postal 13339
Mooca
03198-970 - Sao Paulo - SP Brazil
Phone: 011-55-11 264-5185

2) BRAZIL SAO PAULO
INTERLAGOS MISSION
Rua Comendador Elias Zarzur, 311
Santo Amaro
04736-000 Sao Paulo - SP Brazil
Phone: 011-55-11 522-3677

(101) BRAZIL SAO
PAULO NORTH MISSION
Caixa Postal 26095
05599-970 - Sao Paulo - SP
Brazil
Phone: 011-55-11 211-5920

(102) BRAZIL SAO PAULO
SOUTH MISSION
Caixa Postal 46031
04046-970 - Sao Paulo - SP
*Brazil
Phone: 011-55-11 5589-5278

BULGARIA

Year-end 1995: Est. population, 8,775,000; Members, 700; Branches, 9; Missions, 1; Districts, 2; Europe East Area.

Located on the eastern Balkan peninsula on the Black Sea, Bulgaria has a population that speaks Bulgarian, Turkish and Greek, and they have an Orthodox background in religion.

Mischa Markow, prominent early missionary to the Balkans, visited Bulgaria in about 1900 when he registered with the police and received permission to preach. Soon he was challenged by a Protestant minister, which had the effect of bringing in many more curious people. He preached to many, but was soon banished by the police.

The first missionaries to Bulgaria in recent times were two couples and two sisters, who arrived Sept. 10, 1990. The first missionary couples were Elder Delbert and Sister Marilyn Fowler who taught English in the town of Pravets, and Elder Morris and Sister Annetta Mower who served in Sofia. Sisters Judy Gubler and Rose Marie Daigle were the first sister missionaries. They taught English in the city of Smolyan. The first elders arrived Nov. 13, 1990, from the Austria Vienna East Mission. The elders also took part in charitable endeavors.

Elder Russell M. Nelson of the Quorum of the Twelve and Elder Hans B. Ringger of the Seventy visited government officials Feb. 13, 1990. Following their visit, the Bulgaria Sofia Mission was created July 1, 1991, at which time there were about 50 members, mostly in Sofia. President of the mission was Kiril P. Kiriakov, 68, of Manassas, Va., a native of Bulgaria.

Missionaries were also brought from Yugoslavia because they spoke Serbo-Croatian, a language similar to Bulgarian, which helped them overcome the language barrier. The Lamanite Generation from BYU toured the country in 1991.

In 1993, pediatricians, ophthalmologists, audiologists and others, working through the Europe Area presidency and Church humanitarian services, went to Bulgaria to help train doctors and nurses in efforts to improve health care of children. Other LDS volunteers served in hospitals and educational institutions. Also, through Church humanitarian services, educators went to Bulgaria to help strengthen special education programs, and two Bulgarian school administrators were brought to Utah and Idaho for a tour of training facilities. In May 1993, Elder M. Russell Ballard of the Quorum of the Twelve and Elder Dennis B. Neuenschwander of the Seventy visited Church humanitarian projects in Sofia.

Sources: "Missionary to the Balkans, Mischa Markow," by William Hale Kehr, *Ensign*, June 1980; *Church News*, May 18, 1991; June 5, 1993.

Mission — 1
(As of Oct. 1, 1996; shown with historical number. See MISSIONS.)

(259) BULGARIA SOFIA MISSION
Blvd. Tsar Boris III No. 94
1612 Sofia, Bulgaria
Phone: (011 359-2) 954-1105

BURUNDI

Year-end 1995: Est. population, 6,320,807; Members, fewer than 100; Branches, 1; Africa Area; Zaire Kinshasa Mission.

About the size of Maryland, Burundi is a republic bordered by Tanzania, Zaire and

Rwanda. Its people speak Kirundi and French, the official language, and are 62 percent Roman Catholic, 5 percent Protestant and 32 percent indigenous beliefs.

The Church established a branch in the capital city of this East Central African country following its adoption of a new constitution in 1992. After its first six months of organization, the Bujumbura Branch in Burundi continued to flourish with 36 members and four full-time missionaries.

The first branch president, Pres. Egide Nzojibwami, was set apart by Elder J Ballard Washburn of the Africa Area presidency and a member of the Seventy on Nov. 27, 1992. The first branch meeting was held two days later with 39 in attendance. Pres. Homer M. LeBaron of the Zaire Kinshasa Mission and his wife, Aleene, met with the Nzojibwami family and arranged for the organization. Pres. Nzojibwami and his wife, Beatrice, were baptized in Liege, Belgium, in 1984 while pursuing studies in that country. He was dean of the school of Geological Engineering at the University of Burundi.

Soon after the branch was organized, missionaries from the Ivory Coast Abidjan Mission (formerly Cameroon Yaounde Mission) arrived and began teaching the pool of investigators. These missionaries were Elders Francois Boue, Felix Gnamba, Aime Cesar Kipre and Bassin Kouhon.

Source: *Church News*, Aug. 21, 1993.

CAMBODIA

Year-end 1995: Est. population, 10,561,000; Members, 200; Branches, 3; Districts, 1; Asia Area.

Many Cambodian refugees in the United States joined the Church in the 1970s following the Vietnam War. Cambodian branches were also established in a number of metropolitan centers in other countries.

On March 4, 1994, the government of Cambodia granted legal recognition to the Church. Missionary couples serving there do not proselyte but perform Christian service work. The announcement of the legal recognition was made by President Gordon B. Hinckley, first counselor in the First Presidency, on March 6, 1994.

On May 28-29, 1996, President Gordon B. Hinckley visited Cambodia, traveling with his wife, Marjorie, and Elder Joseph B. Wirthlin of the Quorum of the Twelve and his wife, Elisa, and Elder John H. Groberg of the Seventy and his wife, Jean. On the evening of May 28, President Hinckley spoke at a fireside attended by 439 people at the Cambodiana Hotel in Phnom Penh, where there are three branches. Before departing Cambodia the morning of May 29, President Hinckley and his party went to a hillside overlooking the Mekong River.

Source: *Church News*, March 12, 1994; *Church News*, June 8, 1996.

CAMEROON

Year-end 1995: Est. population, 13,540,000; Members, 200; Branches, 1; Africa Area; Ivory Coast Abidjan Mission.

Located on the western coast of Africa on the Gulf of Guinea, Cameroon is a republic where the people speak tribal languages, including Bamileke and Fulani. The people follow Animist, Christian and Moslem beliefs.

A few members lived in Cameroon representing various health organizations in the 1980s and earlier. Cameroon Pres. Paul Biya approved the Church's request for legal recognition on Sept. 9, 1993. At the time, two missionary couples, Elder Gerard and Sister Georgette Gagne of Montreal, Quebec, and Elder Ken and Sister Bea Nielsen from Calgary, Alberta, were serving in the French-speaking country. Up to the time the government granted recognition, about 30 people had been baptized, and another 60 investigators were attending Sunday meetings.

The Cameroon Yaounde Mission was created on July 1, 1992, with Robert L. Mercer as its first president. The mission headquarters were moved to Abidjan, Ivory Coast, on May 18, 1993, which is also French-speaking.

Representatives from Cameroon have participated in widely publicized LDS events. On Oct. 8, 1994, Cameroon was among 40 nations represented at the fourth annual "Western Family Picnic" at the Marriott Farm in Hume, Va. In addition, the Cameroon ambassador attended the lighting ceremony for the Festival of Lights at the Washington Temple Visitors Center in 1995. The African nation was among some 50 nations represented at the ceremony.

In 1996, a Church group was created in Duoala.

Sources: *Church News*, Feb. 2, 1992; *Church News*, Jan. 22, 1994; *Church News* Oct. 15, 1994; *Church News*, Dec. 9, 1995; correspondence from Elder James O. Mason of the Seventy and president of the Africa Area, Sept. 26, 1996.

CANADA

Year-end 1995: Est. population, 28,435,000; Members, 143,000; Stakes, 39; Wards, 261; Branches, 161; Missions, 7; Districts, 8; Temples, 2; Percent LDS, 0.5, or one person in 198.

At the northern end of North America, Canada is a confederation with a parliamentary democracy and a population speaking English and French, and is Roman Catholic, 46 percent; and Protestant, 41 percent.

ALBERTA

Year-end 1995: Est. population, 2,716,000; Members, 60,000; Stakes, 18; Wards, 132; Branches, 41; Missions, 1; Districts, 1; Temples, 1; Percent LDS, 2.20, or one person in 45.

Mormon railway crews from northern Utah helped lay track for the Canadian Pacific Railway as early as 1883 and were familiar with southern Alberta. They evidently readily supported later colonization efforts. In 1886, Charles O. Card, president of the Cache Valley Stake in Logan, Utah, explored southern Alberta, seeking a location to colonize in Canada. In March 1887, he left with a small advance party, arrived at Lee's Creek on June 3, and started a settlement that later became Cardston. The Cardston Ward was organized in 1888. Others welcomed the opportunity for land away from the burgeoning population of the Great Basin. Soon settled were Mountain View and Aetna (1890); Beazer (1891); Leavitt (1893); Kimball (1897); Caldwell, Taylorville, Magrath and Stirling, (1898); and after the turn of the century, Woolford, Welling, Orton, Raymond, Barnwell, Welling, Taber, Frankburg, Glenwood and Hill Spring.

Completion of some 115 miles of irrigation canal by 1900, contracted to the Church by C.A. McGrath, and considerable investment from Utahn Jesse Knight in starting a sugar beet industry facilitated development of the prairie.

The Alberta Stake was created in 1895, the Taylor Stake in 1903 and the Lethbridge Stake in 1921. By 1914, more than 10,000 members lived in the vicinity. In 1913, ground was broken in Cardston for the Alberta Temple, which was dedicated in 1923. In 1920, membership was 8,896, increasing to 10,067 in 1930.

The Edmonton Branch began in 1933. Headquarters of the Western Canadian Mission was established in Edmonton in September 1941. In 1951, the first meetinghouse in Edmonton was dedicated. Membership in 1940 was 11,343, and in 1950, 14,583.

Members began dispersing to population centers, including Calgary, Alberta, the province of British Columbia, and to eastern Canada, where they continue to provide stability and leadership. The Calgary Stake was created in 1953. Over the next decades membership increased in 1960 to 19,985 and in 1970, 27,989. In 1981, membership in Alberta was 41,444, increasing to 56,000 in 1990. Nathan Eldon Tanner, who served as first counselor in the First Presidency, was a resident of Alberta at the time of his calling as a General Authority. General Authorities from Alberta have included Elders Ted E. Brewerton, Presiding Bishop Victor L. Brown, Alexander B. Morrison and Lowell D. Wood. In addition, former Young Women's Gen. Pres. Ardeth Kapp and Relief Society Gen. Pres. Elaine Jack were born in Alberta.

Sources: *Encyclopedic History of the Church*, by Andrew Jenson; *A History of the Mormon Church in Canada*, compiled and published by the Lethbridge Stake in 1968; "Canada," by Richard E. Bennett, *Ensign*, Sept. 1988; "The Alberta Settlements, 1887-1925," chapters by Brigham Y. Card and Leonard Arrington, *The Mormon Presence in Canada*, published by the University of Alberta Press, 1990.

Stakes — 17

(Listed alphabetically as of Oct. 1, 1996.)

No.	Name	Organized	First President
North America Central Area			
211a	*Calgary Alberta		

	‡Calgary	15 Nov 1953	N. Eldon Tanner
1924	Calgary Alberta East	14 Feb 1993	Geoffrey Bryan Grunewald
416	*Calgary Alberta North		
	‡Calgary North	17 Apr 1966	Gerald E. Melchin
1101	Calgary Alberta South	3 Feb 1980	Clarence Lee Robertson
1031	Calgary Alberta West	27 May 1979	Lynn Albert Rosenvall
35	*Cardston Alberta		
	‡Alberta	9 Jun 1895	Charles O. Card
1455	Cardston Alberta West	13 Nov 1983	Brent L. Nielson
655	*Edmonton Alberta Bonnie Doon 6 Nov 1983		
	‡Edmonton Alberta East	3 Nov 1974	Bryant L. Stringham
1453	Edmonton Alberta Millwoods	6 Nov 1983	Kenneth Orland Higginbotham
312	*Edmonton Alberta Riverbend 6 Nov 1983		
	*Edmonton Alberta		
	‡Edmonton	15 Nov 1960	Leroy Rollins
1560	Fort Macleod Alberta	29 Sep 1985	Heber James Beazer
189	*Lethbridge Alberta		
	*Lethbridge 15 Nov 1953		
	*East Lethbridge	28 Oct 1951	Grant G. Woolley
667	Lethbridge Alberta East	24 Nov 1974	Bryce C. Stringham
1199	Magrath Alberta	26 Oct 1980	James Dickson Bridge
1998	Medicine Hat Alberta	20 Nov 1994	Robert Albin Gehmlich
51	*Raymond Alberta		
	‡Taylor	30 Aug 1903	Heber S. Allen
1350	Red Deer Alberta	13 Jun 1982	Dennis William Guenther
302	*Taber Alberta		
	‡Taber	11 Sep 1960	Ray B. Evenson

Discontinued

86	Lethbridge	10 Nov 1921	Hugh B. Brown

15 Nov 1953 †Calgary (No. 211a), Lethbridge (No. 189)

Mission — 1

(As of Oct. 1, 1996; shown with historical number. See MISSIONS.)

(36a) CANADA CALGARY MISSION
6940 Fisher Road S.E., #122
Calgary, Alberta T2H 0W3
Canada
Phone: (403) 252-1141

BRITISH COLUMBIA

Year-end 1995: Est. population, 3,668,000; Members, 26,000; Stakes, 7; Wards, 41; Branches, 35; Missions, 1; Districts, 2; Percent LDS, 0.7, or one person in 141.

Vancouver Island was one of several locations Brigham Young considered as a western settlement site for the Saints. In a letter to the members published Nov. 1, 1845, he mentioned the island as "one of many good locations for settlement on the Pacific." The letter sparked a petition by the members in England to Queen Victoria to support them in settling the island. However, the petition was ignored, and no LDS immigrants settled on the island until 1875. That year William Francis and Maria Judson Copley and their three children settled at Shawigan. For the next 15 years they were the only members here. The first convert on the island was Anthony Maitland Stenhouse, a member of the legislative assembly of British Columbia who chose to resign from the assembly and be baptized in 1887. He became a vigorous defender of the faith, living in Cardston, Alberta, and eventually returning to his homeland of Great Britain.

On March 15, 1902, most of British Columbia was placed in the Northwestern States Mission. On May 13, 1903, seven missionaries, led by mission Pres. Nephi Pratt, arrived. The Victoria Conference was organized the next day. Their first converts were unbaptized members of the Copley family. By 1918 membership on the island was 21. A Sunday School was organized on Vancouver Island but later dissolved when several families moved away. It was resumed in 1937.

World War II brought members to the island, and a branch was started in Victoria. A second group began meeting in Nanaimo in 1946. Missionaries arrived following the war, and additional branches were started. Membership over the years has increased. In 1920,

British Columbia had 200 members, growing to 584 in 1930 and 455 in 1940.

Work in Vancouver City on the mainland began in 1904 when Pres. Pratt visited and located an LDS family, that of Edward Neill. A conference with 12 in attendance was held in 1909 and a branch was organized in Feb. 12, 1911. By 1925 the branch had a chapel. The branch was made a ward and included in the new Seattle Stake in 1938. The Vancouver District of the new Western Canadian Mission was created in 1948. From then on, the area grew significantly as members moved in and more converts joined the Church. Membership in the province grew to 1,582 in 1950, 4,104 in 1960, and 10,123 in 1970.

On Nov. 21, 1960, the Vancouver Stake was created with wards in Vancouver (two), North Shore, New Westminister, Fleetwood, Richmond, White Rock, Langley and Chilliwack. A new stake center was started in 1966.

Membership in Vancouver has grown increasingly international. Membership in British Columbia in 1981 was 15,494, and reached 24,000 in 1990.

Sources: *A History of the Mormon Church in Canada,* compiled and published by the Lethbridge Stake in 1968; "The Church of Jesus Christ of Latter-day Saints and Vancouver Island: The Establishment and Growth of the Mormon Community," by Robert J. McCue, *BC Studies,* Summer 1979; "No One Is an Island," by Giles H. Florence Jr., *Ensign,* August 1990.

Stakes — 7

(Listed alphabetically as of Oct. 1, 1996.)

No.	Name	Organized	First President
	North America Northwest Area		
1980	Abbottsford British Columbia	12 Jun 1994	Andrew Howard Rattray
994	Cranbrook British Columbia	14 Jan 1979	Brian James Erickson
1905	Prince George British Columbia	26 Sep 1992	A. Brice Gurney
315	*Vancouver British Columbia		
	‡Vancouver	21 Nov 1960	Ernest E. Jensen
1014	*Surrey British Columbia	12 Jun 1994	
	Vancouver B.C. South	8 Apr 1979	Richard Bulpitt
709	Vernon British Columbia	12 Oct 1975	James Ronald Burnham
679	Victoria British Columbia	9 Feb 1975	Howard Lowell Biddulph

Mission — 1

(As of Oct. 1, 1996; shown with historical number. See MISSIONS.)

(58) CANADA VANCOUVER MISSION
P.O. Box 149
Point Roberts, WA 98281
Phone: (604) 271-3585

MANITOBA

Year-end 1995: Est. population, 1,131,000; Members, 3,900; Stakes, 1; Wards, 5; Branches, 6; Missions, 1; Percent LDS, 0.34, or one person in 290.

A request from John Sherman, a member who lived in Souris, Manitoba, to Pres. Charles O. Card of the Canadian Mission led to missionaries coming to Manitoba. Elder Niels Hansen supervised six other missionaries who were called in 1896 and who arrived in Manitoba in 1897 and made progress in spreading the gospel. Soon another dozen elders arrived to help. Several converts immigrated to Alberta. In 1899, Manitoba was placed in the Northern States Mission. A conference organized in 1901 was later discontinued but re-opened in 1906. That year, missionaries vigorously sold copies of the Book of Mormon, with eight missionaries selling 308 copies. A year later their efforts bore fruit, and five in the province were baptized. Many of the converts later moved to LDS centers in other areas.

In 1910, the Winnipeg Sunday School was organized with 37 members. The branch was organized in 1922.

Membership in the district in 1930 was 197, including the Winnipeg and Bergland, Ontario, branches. The Brandon Branch was created in 1955, and a second branch in Winnipeg was created in 1961. Other branches were organized in Portage La Prairie (for U.S. Air Force personnel in 1951), Kenora (1955), Thompson (a nickel mining center, in 1963), Dauphin (a Sunday School in 1957). Membership in the province in 1966 was 1,368.

The Canada Winnipeg Mission was created in 1976 with about 4,200 members in four districts, including those in Saskatchewan and western Ontario. The Winnipeg Manitoba Stake was created Nov. 12, 1978. A new stake center was dedicated in 1988, and stake membership reached 2,500. Membership in Manitoba in 1981 was 2,136. Membership in 1990 was 3,700.

Sources: *Encyclopedic History of the Church,* by Andrew Jenson; Northern States Mission, manuscript history, 1899-1908; *A History of the Church of Jesus Christ of Latter-day Saints in Canada, 1830-1963,* a BYU dissertation by Melvin S. Tagg, May 1963; *A History of the Mormon Church in Canada,* compiled by the Lethbridge Stake, 1968; "North Star Harvest," by Carol Cornwall Madsen, *Church News,* May 13, 1978; "Thompson Saints Sink Roots in Manitoba Soil," by Bruce Northcott, *Ensign,* August 1986; "In Winnipeg: An Exciting Time to be a Member," by Raman Job, *Ensign,* May 1989.

Stake — 1
(As of Oct. 1, 1996.)

No. Name	Organized	First President
North America Central Area		
980 Winnipeg Manitoba	12 Nov 1978	Lorne Leslie Clapson

Mission — 1
(As of Oct. 1, 1996; shown with historical number. See MISSIONS.)

(136) CANADA WINNIPEG MISSION
1661 Portage Avenue, #306
Winnipeg, Manitoba R3J 3T7
Phone: (204) 775-0466

NEW BRUNSWICK

Year-end 1995: Est. population, 760,700; Members, 2,200; Stakes, 1; Wards, 5; Branches, 3; Percent LDS, 0.3, or one person in 345; Canada Halifax Mission.

Missionary work in the Maritime provinces began in 1833 when Lyman E. Johnson and James Heriot began proselyting in Nova Scotia and New Brunswick. Elder Johnson preached in Saint John, New Brunswick, in the spring of 1836 and later in Sackville, where he baptized 18 people and organized the first branch in the Maritimes.

Among those baptized in Sackville was Marriner W. Merrill, who later preached extensively in Canada and eventually become a member of the Quorum of the Twelve.

In 1920, a branch was organized in Saint John, New Brunswick. The branch was discontinued, and then reorganized and has been continuous since 1948. A meetinghouse was completed in 1954. The Fredericton Branch was organized in 1940, later discontinued and started again in 1957, and completed a meetinghouse in 1963. The Moncton Branch, created in 1966, included the Sackville area where the first branch of the Church in the Maritimes was created. Membership in this branch reached 160 in 1974. The St. John New Brunswick Stake was created in 1988. Growth of the Church in the Maritimes has fluctuated over time, but the work of missionaries and members has pushed efforts along in the 1990s. Membership in 1990 was 2,100.

Sources: *Encyclopedic History of the Church,* by Andrew Jenson; *A History of the Mormon Church in Canada,* published in 1968 by the Lethbridge Alberta Stake under the direction of Dr. Melvin S. Tagg; "Portrait of a New Mission," by Jack E. Jarrard, *Church News,* Sept. 22, 1973; "The Saints in Canada's Maritime Provinces," by Eleanor Knowles, *Ensign,* June 1974; and "LDS in Canada — Growth through faithfulness," *Church News,* Oct. 23, 1983; "Maritime provinces," by Sheridan R. Sheffield, *Church News,* Oct. 24, 1992.

Stake — 1
(As of Oct. 1, 1996.)

No. Name	Organized	First President
North America Northeast Area		
1698 Saint John New Brunswick	26 Jun 1988	Blaine E. Hatt

NEWFOUNDLAND

Year-end 1995: Est. population, 582,700; Members, 500; Branches, 4; Percent LDS, 0.08, or one person in 1,164; North America Northeast Area; Canada Halifax Mission.

The St. John's Branch in Newfoundland was created Feb. 7, 1957, and in 10 years grew to 92 members. Other branches in the province include Cornerbook and Gander.

About half of the converts in this area are immigrants, often from eastern European countries. Retention of converts in the area is extremely high. Unemployment and economic difficulties are challenges that hamper growth.

Sources: *Encyclopedic History of the Church,* by Andrew Jenson; *A History of the Mormon Church in Canada,* published in 1968 by the Lethbridge Alberta Stake under the direction of Dr. Melvin S. Tagg; "Portrait of a New Mission," by Jack E. Jarrard, *Church News,* Sept. 22, 1973; "The Saints in Canada's Maritime Provinces," by Eleanor Knowles, *Ensign,* June 1974; and "LDS in Canada — Growth through faithfulness," *Church News,* Oct. 23, 1983; "Maritime provinces," by Sheridan R. Sheffield, *Church News,* Oct. 24, 1992.

NOVA SCOTIA

Year-end 1995: Est. population, 937,000; Members, 4,000; Stakes, 1; Wards, 6; Branches, 10; Missions, 1; Percent LDS, 0.4, or one person in 234.

Lyman E. Johnson and James Heriot began proselyting in the Maritime Provinces in 1833 when they arrived in Nova Scotia and New Brunswick. Two missionaries were sent to Nova Scotia by Joseph Smith in 1843. A conference there was attended by 18 members under district Pres. Robert Dixon. The Halifax Branch was created Nov. 14, 1843, and smaller branches began in Preston, Popes Harbour, and Onslow.

In 1845, John Sherry, a member from Nova Scotia, preached on Prince Edward Island. Branches were organized at Beddeque and Charlottetown. Persecution followed the members and most left for the West by 1855. One group of 50, most of the Halifax Branch, traveled with their branch president, John A. Jost, aboard the ship *Barque Halifax,* which left May 12, 1855, and took them the first leg of their journey around Cape Horn to San Francisco. This exodus ended organized branches in the Maritimes until work resumed under the Canadian Mission in 1920. Membership in the area after this time was often depleted when converts moved to be closer to the established Church.

After missionary work resumed, missionaries presided over groups in Halifax, Windsor, and New Glasgow in Nova Scotia. The Halifax Branch in Nova Scotia was organized in July 1947 by mission Pres. S. Dilworth Young. In 1974, the Halifax and Dartmouth branches numbered about 750. A meetinghouse was started in 1958 and completed in 1959.

In 1959, converts were baptized in Bridgewater, Nova Scotia. The branch, created in 1961, grew to 135 in 1967. A meetinghouse was completed in 1966. A branch in Sydney was created in 1958. Membership in Nova Scotia is among the most rapidly growing in Canada. With 250 members in 1972, it increased more than 800 percent in 10 years, reaching 2,331. The Dartmouth Nova Scotia Stake was created in 1985. The Dartmouth/Halifax area in Nova Scotia continues to serve as the center of Church activity in the Maritimes. Membership in Nova Scotia in 1990 was 3,800.

Sources: *Encyclopedic History of the Church,* by Andrew Jenson; *A History of the Mormon Church in Canada,* published in 1968 by the Lethbridge Alberta Stake under the direction of Dr. Melvin S. Tagg; "Portrait of a New Mission," by Jack E. Jarrard, *Church News,* Sept. 22, 1973; "The Saints in Canada's Maritime Provinces," by Eleanor Knowles, *Ensign,* June 1974; and "LDS in Canada — Growth through faithfulness," *Church News,* Oct. 23, 1983; "Maritime provinces," by Sheridan R. Sheffield, *Church News,* Oct. 24, 1992.

Stake — 1
(As of Oct. 1, 1996.)

No.	Name	Organized	First President
	North America Northeast Area		
1530	Dartmouth Nova Scotia	12 May 1985	Terry Lee Livingstone

Mission — 1
(As of Oct. 1, 1996; shown with historical number. See MISSIONS.)

(107) CANADA HALIFAX MISSION
202 Brownlow Ave., Unit F, Bldg F
Dartmouth, Nova Scotia B3B 1T5
Canada
Phone: (902) 468-2718

ONTARIO

Year-end 1995: Est. population, 10,928,000; Members, 34,000; Stakes, 8; Wards, 56; Branches, 35; Missions, 2; Districts, 2; Temples, 1; Percent LDS, 0.3, or one person in 321.

Seeking ways to finance the publication of the Book of Mormon, the first Mormons to enter Canada were Hiram Page and Oliver Cowdery, who crossed the border from New York in the winter of 1829-30, before the Church was organized. In 1830, Phinehas Young traveled to Earnestown. Though unbaptized, he preached about the Book of Mormon.

Joseph Smith Sr. and Don Carlos Smith entered Canada briefly in September 1830, visiting a few villages north of the St. Lawrence River. Early in June 1832, Phinehas Young returned to Canada, this time as an ordained elder in the company of five others. Before the last of these missionaries had left Canada, four branches had been organized. Other missionaries soon followed, including Joseph Smith, who visited in October 1833 and again in July 1837. Two of the most successful missionaries were John E. Page and Parley P. Pratt. Elder Page baptized almost a thousand converts. Elder Pratt brought in such future Church leaders as John Taylor, who later became president of the Church; and Isaac Russell, John Snider, John Goodson and Joseph Fielding. These four opened the highly successful work in Great Britain. Missionaries organized a district in Toronto that was placed under the direction of John Taylor.

Between 1830 and 1850, an estimated 2,500 Canadians, mostly from Ontario, joined the Church. Most of these who remained faithful gathered with the Saints in the Great Basin in the West. By 1861, the Ontario census lists only 74 members.

Little work progressed in eastern Canada until the Canadian Mission was organized in 1919, with conferences in Toronto and Ottawa. That same year, branches were organized in Toronto and Hamilton. Another was organized in Kitchener in 1923. The Ottawa Branch was created in July 1926. The St. Catherine's Branch was organized in 1933. The Oshawa Branch began in 1947 after functioning off and on as a Sunday School since 1944. Membership in all of eastern Canada reached 1,974 in 1950.

The first meetinghouse in eastern Canada was dedicated in Toronto in 1939, and the first eastern stake was organized in 1960 in Toronto, while President Thomas S. Monson, now first counselor in the First Presidency, was mission president. The Toronto Temple was announced April 7, 1984, and dedicated Aug. 25-27, 1990. On July 1, 1993, Toronto's second mission was created. Missionaries may potentially work with people from upwards of 100 nations who come in hopes of immigrating. From Toronto, efforts to increase the profile of the Church through media led to a television series in 1994 during prime time across Canada. Membership in 1981 was 16,138, and in 1990, 28,000.

On May 5, 1996, President Thomas S. Monson, first counselor in the First Presidency, and Elder M. Russell Ballard of the Quorum of the Twelve created the Sudbury Ontario Stake out of the last mission district remaining in Ontario. President Monson and Elder Ballard had previously been based in Toronto while presiding over Canadian missions.

Sources: *Encyclopedic History of the Church,* by Andrew Jenson; *A History of the Mormon Church in Canada,* compiled and published by the Lethbridge Stake, 1968; "Canada: From Struggling Seed, The Church Has Risen to Branching Maple," by Richard E. Bennett, *Ensign,* Sept. 1988; "Toronto, A Growing Light in the East," by Richard Robertson, *Ensign,* Sept. 1988; "Plucking not Planting," by Richard E. Bennett, *The Mormon Presence in Canada,* published by the University of Alberta Press, 1990; " 'Our treasure,' a new temple is dedicated," and "Past legacy builds today's faith," both by Dell Van Orden, *Church News,* Sept. 1, 1990; *Church News,* March 13, 1993; "Church begins series on TV across Canada," by William B. Smart, *Church News,* Feb. 5, 1994; *Church News,* May 18, 1996.

Stakes — 9
(Listed alphabetically as of Oct. 1, 1996.)

No.	Name	Organized	First President
North America Northeast Area			
1222	Brampton Ontario	11 Jan 1981	Cecil Malcolm Warner
524	*Hamilton Ontario ‡Niagara	6 Sep 1970	Eldon C. Olsen
1600	Kitchener Ontario	22 Jun 1986	Graeme K. Hingston
752	London Ontario	11 Apr 1976	Harold Crookell
1907	Mississauga Ontario	18 Oct 1992	Lawrence R. Fuller
761	*Oshawa Ontario 22 Jun 1986 ‡Toronto Ontario East	13 Jun 1976	John Bruce Smith
796	Ottawa Ontario	12 Dec 1976	Boyden E. Lee
2194	Sudbury Ontario	05 May 1996	G. Boyd McGinn
300	*Toronto Ontario ‡Toronto	14 Aug 1960	William M. Davies

Missions — 2

(285) CANADA TORONTO EAST MISSION
2025 Sheppard Avenue East, Suite 2300
Willowdale, Ontario M2J 1V7
Canada
Phone: (416) 490-6869

(23a) CANADA TORONTO WEST MISSION
338 Queen Street East, Suite 214
Brampton, Ontario L6V 1C5
Canada
Phone: (905) 452-7484

PRINCE EDWARD ISLAND

Year-end 1995: Est. population, 134,000; Members, 300; Branches, 3; Percent LDS, 0.22, or one person in 446; North America Northeast Area; Canada Halifax Mission.

The first missionary to preach in the province was John Sherry, coming to Prince Edward Island in 1845. Branches were organized in Bedeque and Charlottetown, but were disbanded in 1850 when all members immigrated to Utah.

The first modern presence of the Church in Prince Edward Island came in 1964 when Ralph and Gerda Waugh, converts from New York, returned to the land of Brother's Waugh's birth. They contacted another member and began holding Sunday School.

Elder Boyd K. Packer, then an Assistant to the Twelve, was president of the New England Mission at the time, which included Prince Edward Island. Elder Packer visited the Waugh home with missionaries in July 1966. About two weeks later full-time missionaries were transferred to the island and missionaries have been here since then.

Brother Waugh was called as the first branch president of the Summerside Branch on Dec. 21, 1969. In 1974 the branch was divided and the Charlottetown Branch was formed.

The Church continued to grow on the island, and in 1982 the Prince Edward Island District was formed. Excavation also began in Summerside on construction of the island's first meetinghouse. The building was completed on June 18, 1983. A second meetinghouse in Charlottetown was started in 1983 and completed on July 14, 1984. The Montague Branch was formed in November 1985 and a meetinghouse was completed in June 1988. The three branches became part of the St. John New Brunswick Stake on June 26, 1988.

One of the most popular tourist locations in the Maritimes, this area is home to the smallest number of members of any province in Canada. Membership on Prince Edward Island in 1990 was 300.

Sources: *A History of the Mormon Church in Canada,* published in 1968 by the Lethbridge Alberta Stake under the direction of Dr. Melvin S. Tagg; "The Saints in Canada's Maritime Provinces," by Eleanor Knowles, *Ensign,* June 1974; "Prince Edward Island: Members find peace in 'little land' where 'you find your soul,' " by Sheridan R. Sheffield, *Church News,* July 10, 1993.

QUEBEC

Year-end 1995: Est. population, 7,281,000; Members, 7,600; Stakes, 2; Wards, 11; Branches, 11; Missions, 1; Districts, 1; Percent LDS, 0.1, or one person in 958.

Early missionaries in the 1830s frequently traveled through but found little success in Lower Canada, as the province of Quebec was then called. They found proselyting difficult among its largely French-speaking people. In 1836, however, Hazen Aldrich and Winslow Farr labored in Stanstead County and baptized a number of people. Twenty-three of these emigrated July 20, 1837. Converts also came from the community of Eardley, north of Ottawa. After the 1840s, missionary work experienced an interlude until the next century.

The Canadian Mission was organized in 1919. By 1930, an English-speaking branch began meeting in Montreal. A meetinghouse for this branch was purchased from another faith in 1942 and served the branch until the late 1970s.

The Ottawa-Montreal District was created in 1953 as part of the Canadian Mission. The same year a mission district was created in Quebec. In 1961, then-Mission Pres. Thomas S. Monson sent six French-speaking missionaries into the area around Quebec. The missionaries found converts and established a base that attracted LDS French-speaking immigrants. From this effort, missionaries entered Quebec City where a branch was started in 1969. The Quebec (later changed to the Canada Montreal) Mission was created in 1972, and by 1974, a French-speaking district was created. By 1987, membership among the French-speaking people was 2,753, some 65 percent of the total membership in the province. These converts tended to stay in Quebec where their roots were instead of moving to the West as did many of their English-speaking counterparts.

The Tung Fong Branch was created in 1975 for the many Chinese people in the Montreal area.

The Montreal Quebec Stake, considered the first French-speaking stake in North America, was created in 1978. A high councilor was Kitchner Young, one of the first French-speaking missionaries. A stake center for this stake was completed, following an open house, in 1993.

In addition, French-speaking members from Quebec have made contributions as missionaries in French-speaking countries in West Africa and other developing nations of the world.

The Quebec District consists of the Quebec (1969), Alma (1984), Chicoutimi (1976) and Rimouksi (1979) branches. In 1975, membership in this district was 977 members.

In 1980, the English-speaking Montreal Mt. Royale Quebec Stake was created. Membership in Quebec reached 3,246 in 1981. In 1990, membership was 6,800.

Sources: *Encyclopedic History of the Church*, by Andrew Jenson; *The Mormon Church in Canada*, compiled and published by the Lethbridge Stake, 1968; "History of the Church in Quebec and Ontario," *Culture for Missionaries*, Missionary Training Center, 1977; "Converts in Quebec," *Church News*, by Maureen Ursenbach Beecher, June 24, 1978; *Church News*, July 8, 1978; "Canada, From Struggling Seed, the Church has Risen to Branching Maple," by Richard E. Bennett, *Ensign*, Sept. 1988; "Canadian Mormon Identity and the French Fact," by Dean R. Louder, in *The Mormon Presence in Canada*, published by the University of Alberta Press, 1990; *Church News*, June 5, 1993.

Stakes — 2
(Listed alphabetically as of Oct. 1, 1996.)

No.	Name	Organized	First President
North America Northeast Area			
943	Montreal Quebec	18 Jun 1978	Gerard C. Pelchat
1160	Montreal Quebec Mount Royal	6 Jul 1980	Ian Gillespie Wilson

Mission — 1
(As of Oct. 1, 1996; shown with historical number. See MISSIONS.)
(99a) CANADA MONTREAL MISSION
1320 Blv. Graham, Suite 310
Ville Mont-Royal, Quebec H3P 3C8
Canada
Phone: (514) 731-0612

SASKATCHEWAN

Year-end 1995: Est. population, 1,016,000; Members, 4,500; Stakes, 1; Wards, 5; Branches, 12; Districts, 1; Percent LDS, 0.4, or one person in 226; Canada Winnipeg Mission.

In the early 1920s, G. Gordon Whyte of Moose Jaw encountered a copy of the Book of Mormon, accepted it as true and requested baptism. He was baptized Aug. 17, 1923, in Moose Jaw and later lived in Regina. His membership was kept in the Raymond 1st Ward, under Bishop John G. Allred. That same year, Bishop Allred, who later was to serve as president of the North Central States Mission from 1925-29, and Brother Whyte held a street meeting in Regina where they placed 16 copies of the Book of Mormon.

The first missionaries in Saskatchewan were Elders Leo E. Nielsen and John A. Ward in Saskatoon and Reuben T. Reynolds and Raymond L. Allen in Regina, who arrived in 1925. The North Saskatchewan and South Saskatchewan conferences were organized Aug. 6 of that year.

Missionaries found progress slow, but a Sunday School was organized May 8, 1927, in Saskatchewan which became a branch on May 27, 1934, under Pres. Whyte. The north and south conferences were combined by 1930 and had a membership of 145. A meetinghouse was dedicated for the Regina Branch in 1939.

In 1934, LDS farmers in southern Alberta and their non-LDS neighbors, donated two boxcars of vegetables and food to 200 families in Saskatchewan suffering from the effects of a severe drought. Among them were 20 families in the Regina Branch.

Saskatchewan became part of the Western Canadian Mission Dec. 6, 1942, and a mission home was purchased in Saskatchewan on Dec. 9. At that time, the district had 173 members including 79 in the Regina Branch.

During this time, Brother Whyte continued to do missionary work among various Indians on nearby reserves. An Indian seminary program began in 1965 with 45 Lamanite children on the Piapot, Carry-the-Kettle and Cowesses reserves east of Regina.

In 1949, the Saskatoon Branch functioned for a short time with no actual membership as members had moved away and investigators held positions. Later missionary work and baptisms led to the normalization of the branch.

By 1961, branches in Regina (May 27, 1934), Moose Jaw (a Sunday School functioned from 1929 until a branch was organized in 1945), Saskatoon (1944), Swift Current (1952), Prince Albert (1959) and Silver Park (re-named Melfort; organized in 1947) were included in the Saskatchewan District, with a total of about 600 members. On Sept. 3, the district was divided into the North and South districts. The Yorktown and Carry-the-Kettle branches were organized in 1966.

The Saskatoon Saskatchewan Stake was created Nov. 5, 1978, combining two districts, with 2,101 members. At that time, Saskatoon and Regina had two wards each. Membership in Saskatchewan in 1980 was 2,857, increasing to 4,200 in 1990.

Sources: *Encyclopedic History of the Church,* by Andrew Jenson; *Liahona,* Oct. 20, 1925, p. 182; North Central States Mission Manuscript History, 1925-40; *History of the Western Canadian Mission,* by Wilbur Gordon Hackney, a BYU thesis, May 17, 1950; *A History of the Mormon Church in Canada,* compiled and published by the Lethbridge Stake, 1968; "The Christian Way," by Carol Cornwall Madsen, *Church News* July 1, 1978; *Church News,* Feb. 10, 1945, Feb. 2, 1949, July 5, 1950, Nov. 18, 1978, Oct. 23, 1983.

Stakes — 1
(As of Oct. 1, 1996.)

No.	Name	Organized	First President
	North America Central Area		
978	Saskatoon Saskatchewan	5 Nov 1978	Noel W. Burt

NORTHWEST TERRITORIES

Year-end 1995: Est. population, 64,000; Members, 100; Branches, 1; Percent LDS, 0.1, or one person in 640; North America Central Area; Canada Calgary Mission.

The Yellowknife Branch in the Northwest Territories covers half a million square miles and is called the largest branch in area in the Church. Half the members live in Yellowknife and half are scattered in the communities of Hay River, Fort Smith, Coppermine, Inuvik, Rankin Inlet and Iqaluit. Members occasionally travel hundreds of miles to meet for socials and meetings.

Sources: *A History of the Mormon Church in Canada,* published in 1968 by the Lethbridge Alberta Stake under the direction of Dr. Melvin S. Tagg; "Northern Hospitality," by Ronald G. Watt, *Church News,* July 8, 1978; "Largest Branch in the World," *Ensign,* September 1988.

YUKON TERRITORY

Year-end 1995: Est. population, 30,000; Members, 200; Branches, 1; Percent LDS, 0.6, or one person in 150; North America Northwest Area; Alaska Anchorage Mission.

A branch was created in Whitehorse, Yukon Territories, on Oct. 15, 1963, and meetings were held in rented quarters with a mostly 100 percent attendance of the 35 members. The branch now has a meetinghouse.

A highlight in branch history came in 1968 when Apostle LeGrand Richards visited and witnessed the baptism of four people. His was the first known visit of a General Authority to the branch.

Sources: *A History of the Mormon Church in Canada,* published in 1968 by the Lethbridge Alberta Stake.

CAPE VERDE

Year-end 1995: Est. population, 440,000; Members, 3,000; Districts, 3; Branches, 17; Percent LDS, 0.7 or one LDS in 146; Europe West Area; Portugal Lisbon South Mission.

The Republic of Cape Verde is made up of 10 main islands, 400 miles west of Senegal off the African coast. The people, who are mostly Roman Catholics influenced by indigenous beliefs, speak Portuguese and Criuolo.

Spain Canary Islands Mission Pres. Marion K. Hamblin opened the Cape Verde area by visiting the islands in November 1988 and sending Elders Christopher Lee and Ken Margetts there a short time later to create the Praia/Lajes Branch on Cape Verde. The ambassador of Cape Verde attended the lighting ceremony of the Washington Temple in 1993. In September 1994, Elder Dallin H. Oaks visited the islands and made courtesy visits to the president of the republic, Antonio Mascarenhas, and Paia mayor Jacinto Santos.

By September 1994, some 50 members from Cape Verde had been called to serve full-time missions.

Sources: Spain Canary Islands Mission correspondence; *Church News,* Dec. 7, 1991; *Church News,* Dec. 11, 1993; *Church News,* Sept. 24, 1994.

CENTRAL AFRICA REPUBLIC

Year-end 1995: Est. population, 3,240,000; Members, 100; Branches, 1; Africa Area; Ivory Coast Abidjan Mission.

Located in Central Africa along the northern border of Zaire, the Central Africa Republic is a republic with a population that speaks French and local dialects. The population is Protestant, 25 percent; Catholic, 25 percent; tribal beliefs, 24 percent; and other beliefs.

The first known member living in Central Africa Republic was Carol Forrest of the U.S. Peace Corps, a returned missionary and one of the medical personnel, who arrived in June 1991. She shared the gospel with many of her associates and in September 1991 was set apart as a district missionary. Elder J Ballard Washburn of the Seventy and a counselor in the Africa Area presidency visited Sister Forrest and a group of investigators in September 1992.

Traveling with Elder Washburn was Pres. Robert L. Mercer of the Cameroon Yaounde Mission. On Sept. 19, 1992, 20 converts were baptized and two branches organized. Celestin N'Gakondou was called as president of the Bangui 1st Branch, and Gaspard Lapet was called to preside over the Bangui 2nd Branch.

A French couple, Elder and Sister Frutina, arrived in January of 1993.

An ambassador from the Central Africa Republic attended the lighting ceremony for the 1995 Festival of Lights at the Washington Temple Visitors Center. The African republic was among some 50 nations represented at the widely publicized event.

Sources: "Medical officer ministers to souls," by Mary Mostert, *Church News,* Dec. 5, 1992; Correspondence from the Ivory Coast Abidjan Mission, March 1994; *Church News,* Dec. 9, 1995.

CHILE

Year-end 1995: Est. population, 14,170,000; Members, 394,000; Stakes, 89; Wards, 516; Branches, 265; Missions, 7; Districts, 14; Temples, 1; Percent LDS, 2.8, or one person in 35.

On the west coast of South America, the Republic of Chile has a Spanish-speaking population that is 89 percent Roman Catholic.

Parley P. Pratt, his wife, Phebe, and Elder Rufus C. Allen traveled to Chile, arriving Nov. 8, 1851, but remained only five months. Their inability to speak the language and their meager funds, along with continuing civil turbulance in the country proved insurmountable obstacles. The next LDS presence began with LDS families living in Santiago in the early 1950s. President David O. McKay visited the William Fotheringham family, residents of Santiago, on Feb. 8, 1954. On May 26, 1956, Chile became part of the Argentine Mission. At that time, Elders Joseph Bentley and Verle Allred crossed the Andes from Argentina and arrived in Chile June 23, 1956, beginning missionary work in Chile. They stayed with the Fotheringhams and on July 5, the first branch was organized. A few months later they baptized Ricardo and Perla Garcia and others on Nov. 2, 1956. Six more branches were created by 1959.

When Elder Spencer W. Kimball, then of the Quorum of the Twelve, visited in 1959, the country had about 450 members. In October of that year, 45 more people were baptized, a 10 percent increase in one month. The Chile Mission was organized Oct. 8, 1961, with 1,100 members. When the first stake was organized 11 years later with Carlos A. Cifuentes as president, membership had grown to more than 20,000 members.

On Feb. 27, 1977, President Spencer W. Kimball visited Santiago and addressed nearly 7,000 members. At the same gathering, Elder Bruce R. McConkie of the Quorum of the Twelve predicted that in the future, the Church would become the most powerful influence in the nation. President Kimball returned to Santiago on May 30, 1981, to break ground for a temple, attended by 6,000 people who waited in the rain for several hours.

The temple was completed in 1983, and dedicated on Sept. 15. At that time, the country had 140,400 members in 27 stakes. On Oct. 29, 1988, Chile became the fourth country in the world to reach 50 stakes. Chile has strong local leadership, a high percentage of local missionaries and a number of local mission and temple presidents.

Chile's first General Authority was Elder Eduardo Ayala of the Seventy. Membership in 1990 was 298,000. At the commemoration of the 10th anniversary of the temple in 1994, it was noted that Chile, with the fastest growing membership in South America, had doubled membership and the number of stakes during the decade. Continued growth, including the creation of 26 stakes from 1994-96, led to the creation of the Chile Area in 1996.

Sources: *Encyclopedic History of the Church*, by Andrew Jenson; "Chile," by Steven J. Iverson, *New Era*, February 1977; "Love, respect and emotion end area conference series," by Dell Van Orden, *Church News*, March 12, 1977; *Los Mormones in Chile*, by Rodolfo Acevedo Acevedo, published in Santiago, Chile, 1989; *Church News*, Sept. 25, 1993, *Church News*, June 15, 1996, and *Church News*, Aug. 13, 1996, by Nestor Curbelo.

Stakes — 93
(Listed alphabetically as of Oct. 1, 1996.)

No.	Name	Organized	First President
Chile Area			
1499	Achupallas Chile	28 Oct 1984	Luis Alino Pereira P.
1075	Andalien Chile	28 Oct 1979	Pedro E. Arias
2005	Angol Chile	18 Dec 1994	Juan Carlos Morales Vasquez
1165	Antofagasta Chile	10 Aug 1980	Octavio Araya Y.
1955	Antofagasta Chile Portada	5 Sep 1993	Miguel A. Gonzalez Romero
1100	Arica Chile	29 Jan 1980	Jose Ulloa C.
2035	Arica Chile Azapa	12 Mar 1995	Arnando Ernesto Perez M.
1598	Arica Chile El Morro	18 May 1986	Sergio Alberto Funes
2026	Buin Chile	26 Feb 1995	Jorge H. Herrera Carmona
1522	Calama Chile	17 Mar 1985	Ivan Gonzalez Castillo
1501	Caliche Chile	4 Nov 1984	Ricardo Manuel Palma F.
2006	Chiguayante Chile	18 Dec 1994	Carlos Andrews Puig Iguatt
1398	Chillan Chile	13 Feb 1983	Sergio Rios S.
808	Concepcion Chile	30 Jan 1977	Claudio Signorelli G.
1929	Copiapo Chile	11 Apr 1993	Sergio Orlando Mora Oviedo
1960b	Coquimbo Chile	5 Dec 1993	Marco Oyarzun Vera
2167	Coyhaique Chile	18 Feb 1996	Feberico Sanchez G.
1264	Curico Chile	10 May 1981	Jose Luis Ferreira P.
1931	El Belloto Chile	11 Apr 1993	Hugo L. Garrido Gonzalez
1621	Iquique Chile	14 Dec 1986	Nelson C. Mondaca I.
1702	La Serena Chile	23 Oct 1988	Ricardo Thomas Rubina
2196a	La Union Chile	26 May 1996	Lautaro Roberto Sanchez Cerda
1694	Linares Chile	24 Apr 1988	Alberto Ariosto Alveal V.
1949	Los Andes Chile	4 Jul 1993	Vicente E. Zuniga Figueroa
1599	Los Angeles Chile	1 Jun 1986	Mario Carlos Escobar
1950	Melipilla Chile	18 Jul 1993	Natanael Toro Navarrete
1267	Osorno Chile	17 May 1981	Raul Hernan Paredes P.
1976	Ovalle Chile	20 Feb 1994	Wilson B. Nunez Castillo
1320	*Penaflor Chile 18 Jul 1993		
	*Santiago Chile Penaflor 10 Apr 1990		
	‡Penaflor Chile	10 Dec 1981	Sergio Venegas Pacheo
1268	Penco Chile	24 May 1981	Abel Poblete Flores
1339	Puerto Montt Chile	25 Apr 1982	Juan Carlos Lopez L.
1478	Punta Arenas Chile	10 Jun 1984	Luis Elqueda C.
1275	Quillota Chile	7 Jun 1981	Maximo Ananias Iribarren I.
791	Quilpue Chile	28 Nov 1976	Eduardo Lamartine A.
1285	Rancagua Chile	26 Aug 1981	Hector Verdugo Radrigan
1930	Rancagua Chile Tupahue	11 Apr 1993	Juan Carlos Fredes Duran
1731	San Antonio Chile	2 Jul 1989	Sergio Enrique Gonzalez S.
1703	San Fernando Chile	30 Oct 1988	Jose Luis Ferreira P.
1286	San Pedro Chile	30 Aug 1981	Juan Cuevas I.
2089	Santiago Chile Alicahue	20 Aug 1995	Patricio R. Ortega Hernandez
1960	Santiago Chile Cerro Navia	7 Nov 1993	Juan David Huaiguinir Castro
1038	Santiago Chile Cinco de Abril	10 Jun 1979	Poblibio Gonzalez Gutierrez
1077	Santiago Chile Conchali	4 Nov 1979	Juan Castro Duque

2036	Santiago Chile Cordillera	19 Mar 1995	Jorge Andres Pedero
1216	Santiago Chile El Bosque	14 Dec 1980	Eduardo Ayala Aburto
1933	Santiago Chile Gran Avenida	18 Apr 1993	Andres Maja Basaez
1024	Santiago Chile Independencia	6 May 1979	Wilfredo Lopez G.
1902	Santiago Chile Javiera Carrera	20 Sep 1992	Patricio LaTorre Orellana
1995	Santiago Chile Jose Miguel Carrera	6 Nov 1994	Patricio G. Latorre O.
2075	Santiago Chile La Bandera	9 Jul 1995	Felix Reinaldo Cofre Quezada
672	*Santiago Chile La Cisterna	18 Apr 1976	
	‡Santiago Chile South	8 Dec 1974	Eduardo Ayala
1039	Santiago Chile La Florida	10 Jun 1979	Carlos G. Zuniga Campusano
1899	Santiago Chile La Granja	30 Aug 1992	Arturo del Carmen Jorquera M.
1947	Santiago Chile La Reina	27 June 1993	Santiago Vicente Vera Barrera
2090	Santiago Chile Las Araucarias	20 Aug 1995	Luis Enrique Moya Basaez
1402	Santiago Chile Las Condes	12 Mar 1983	E. Gustavo Flores Carrasco
2086	Santiago Chile Lo Blanco	13 Aug 1995	Eric Alejandro Nunez Yevenes
2024	Santiago Chile Lo Espejo	19 Feb 1995	David Ormeno Parra
2178	Santiago Chile Lo Prado	10 Mar 1996	Raul Alfredo Dote
2082	Santiago Chile Los Cerrillos	30 Jul 1995	Renato Alejandro Ruz Leon
2121	Santiago Chile Los Manantiales	12 Nov 1995	Luis Arturo Inostroza Gomez
1915	Santiago Chile Maipu	6 Dec 1992	Julio Cesar Valdivia Marin
792	Santiago Chile Nunoa	28 Nov 1976	Gustavo Alberto Barrios C.
2126	Santiago Chile Ochagavia	19 Nov 1995	Gerardo Gabezas Leyton
1919	Santiago Chile O'Higgins	20 Dec 1992	Victor A. Cifuentes Droguett
1403	Santiago Chile Pudahuel	13 Mar 1983	Enrique Espinoza
1548	Santiago Chile Puente Alto	18 Aug 1985	Jorge A. Pedrero Martinez
1205	*Santiago Chile Quilicura	13 Dec 1988	
	‡Santiago Chile Huechuraba	9 Nov 1980	Juan Humberto Body B.
590	*Santiago Chile Quinta Normal	10 Jan 1980	
	*Santiago Chile Providencia	18 Apr 1976	
	*Santiago Chile ‡Santiago (Chile)	19 Nov 1972	Carlos A. Cifuentes
1492	Santiago Chile Renca	16 Sep 1984	Eduardo Cabezas O.
754	Santiago Chile Republica	18 Apr 1976	Julio Jaramillo
1003	Santiago Chile San Bernardo	25 Feb 1979	Hugo Balmaceda
1549	Santiago Chile San Miguel	18 Aug 1985	Hector G. Carvajal Arenas
1927	Santiago Chile Vicuna Mackenna	21 Mar 1993	Jorge Andres Pedrero Martinez
1379	*Santiago Chile Zapadores	13 Dec 1988	
	‡Santiago Chile Las Canteras	14 Nov 1982	Juan Castro Duque
1083	*Talca Chile Lircay	11 Jun 1995	
	Talca Chile	17 Nov 1979	Emilio Diaz
2060	Talca Chile El Mirador	11 Jun 1995	Gaston Alberto Rocha Fernandez
866	Talcahuano Chile	16 Oct 1977	Claudio Daniel Signorelli G.
2047	Talcahuano Chile Colon	7 May 1995	Daniel Marcelo Canoles M.
1146	*Talcahuano Chile Hualpen	7 May 1995	
	*Hualpen Chile	26 Jul 1988	
	‡Talcahuano Chile Hualpen	15 Jun 1980	Fernando Aguilar
1245	Temuco Chile Nielol	26 Nov. 1995	
	Temuco Chile	18 Mar 1981	Eleazar F. Magnere D.
2133	Temuco Chile Cautin	26 Nov 1995	Hector L.F. Sandoval
1667	Valdivia Chile	10 Jan 1988	Armando Ambrosio Linco P.
882	Valparaiso Chile	20 Nov 1977	Abel Correa Lopez
2014	Valparaiso Chile Oriente	22 Jan 1995	Sergio Ignacio Padovani T.
2013	Valparaiso Chile Playa Ancha	22 Jan 1995	Bernardo Felix Gallegos B.
1230	Valparaiso Chile South	1 Feb 1981	Juan Rios R.
1037	Villa Alemana Chile	8 Jun 1979	Eduardo Adrian LaMartine
2212	Villa Alemana Chile West	14 Jul 1996	M. Gonzalo Sepulveda Moya
671	Vina del Mar Chile	5 Dec 1974	Jose Leyton
2016	Vina del Mar Chile		

	Agua Santa	22 Jan 1995	Dinar Michael Reyes Barbe
2015	Vina del Mar Chile Forestal	22 Jan 1995	Edgardo Ramon Salina H.
1967	*VIna Del Mar Chile Miraflores		
	Miraflores Chile	19 Dec 1993	Jorge Bernardo Toro

Missions — 7

(As of Oct. 1, 1996; shown with historical number. See MISSIONS.)

(214) CHILE ANTOFAGASTA MISSION
Casilla 704
Antofagasta
Chile
Phone: (011-56-55) 22-28-41

(119) CHILE CONCEPCION MISSION
Casilla 2210
Concepcion
Chile
Phone: (011-56-41) 227-613

(151) CHILE OSORNO MISSION
Casilla 7-0
Osorno
Chile
Phone: (011-56-64) 23-76-26

(148) CHILE SANTIAGO NORTH MISSION
Casilla 172
Santiago 29, Providencia
Chile
Phone: (011-56-2) 223-6466

(67) CHILE SANTIAGO SOUTH MISSION
Casilla 137, Providencia
Santiago 29
Chile
Phone: (011-56-2) 223-5366

(303) CHILE SANTIAGO WEST
Casilla 73, Santiago 29
Chile
Phone: (011-56-2) 225-3098

(168) CHILE VINA DEL MAR MISSION
Casilla 24-D
Vina del Mar, Chile
Phone: (011-56-32) 976-080

CHINA

Year-end 1995: Est. population, 1,263,000,000; Members, 200; Branches, 3; Asia Area; Hong Kong Mission.

Encompassing most of east Asia, the People's Republic of China has a population that speaks Mandarin Chinese, Yue, Wu Minbei, Minnan and Xiang. Population inlcudes atheists, and traditional Confucians, Buddhists and Taoists.

In 1853, Hosea Stout, James Lewis and Chapman Duncan were called to teach the gospel to the Chinese. They arrived in Hong Kong April 27, 1853, and stayed only four months, finding access to the country impossible. They may have baptized one convert.

On a world tour, Elder David O. McKay, then of the Quorum of the Twelve, visited China in January 1921.

In more recent times, annual visits by BYU performing groups beginning in 1979 have led to warmer relations. The Chinese ambassador, Chai Zemin, visited Church headquarters Jan. 9-11, 1981. His visit was followed by a visit to the Polynesian Cultural Center by Premier Zhao Ziyang Jan. 7, 1984. President Li Xiannian visited the cultural center July 31, 1985.

Further exchanges were made as Elder Russell M. Nelson of the Quorum of the Twelve was named an honorary professor in 1985 by a Chinese medical college in appreciation for his earlier work in China.

As cultural exchanges continued, a few expatriate LDS families began living in China. For these families and Chinese people who joined the Church while living abroad, branches were established in Beijing and Shanghai.

Elder Nelson and Elder Dallin H. Oaks of the Quorum of the Twelve continued discussions with Chinese leaders in the late 1980s.

A group of high-ranking Chinese educators visited Elder Oaks in his office in the Church Administration Building Nov. 10, 1989, and received a set of LDS books that will be placed in their institutions' libraries. On Feb. 21, 1990, on behalf of the First Presidency, Elder Nelson presented to the Chinese ambassador to the United States a check for $25,000 to help in reconstruction efforts after a major earthquake caused extensive damage in China.

While in Beijing Jan. 19-23, 1990, Elder Dallin H. Oaks was invited by the Chinese

Academy of Social Sciences to deliver an hour-and-a-half lecture about the Church.

David Hsiao Hsin Chen, a professor at BYU-Hawaii who was born and raised in China, was set apart as the first traveling elder in China at the Beijing Branch Jan. 21, 1990, by Beijing Branch Pres. Timothy Stratford. Elder Chen's responsibility was to go to China several times a year to train LDS Chinese leaders and to oversee the Church's membership in China.

Most of the LDS members in China are foreign teachers, foreign businessmen or diplomats and their families, and Chinese members who have returned to their homeland after having studied or worked in North America, Europe or other parts of the world. There is no proselyting in the People's Republic of China.

President Gordon B. Hinckley visited Shenzhen May 27-28, 1996, becoming the first Church president to go to China. With him were President Thomas S. Monson, first counselor in the First Presidency; Elders Neal A. Maxwell and Joseph B. Wirthlin of the Quorum of the Twelve; and Elder Kwok Yuen Tai of the Seventy. Sisters Marjorie Hinckley, Frances Monson, Colleen Maxwell, Elisa Wirthlin and Hui Hua Tai accompanied their husbands to China. The invitation to visit China was arranged through the Church-owned Polynesian Cultural Center in Hawaii, which helped officials in China establish a similar cultural center in Shenzhen.

Sources: *Encyclopedic History of the Church,* by Andrew Jenson; *Church News,* Jan. 17, 1981, Jan. 15, 1984, Nov. 18, 1989, Feb. 3, 1990; "President Hinckley visits China," *Church News,* June 1, 1996.

COLOMBIA

Year-end 1995: Est. population, 36,500,000; Members, 113,000; Stakes, 13; Wards, 85; Branches, 191; Missions, 4; Districts, 21; Temples, 1 under construction; Percent LDS, 0.3, or one person in 323.

Located in the northwest corner of South America, Colombia is a republic with a Spanish-speaking population that is predominantly Roman Catholic.

In early 1966, some 45 members, mostly North Americans, were meeting in branches in Bogota and Cali. Elders Randall Harmsen and Jerry Broome of the Andes Mission were assigned to Bogota in May of that year. Among the first converts was Antonio Vela. Aura Ivars was the first convert in Cali. The Colombia-Venezuela Mission was created in 1968, and by 1971, 27 branches had been established in 10 cities, and the Venezuela Mission was divided from Colombia, where the mission headquarters were in Bogota. In 1975, the Colombia Cali Mission was created. President Spencer W. Kimball visited Colombia and addressed a gathering of 4,600 at an area conference on March 5, 1977.

Seminaries and institutes were begun in 1972, and by 1976, 900 students were taking part in the educational programs, and membership reached 6,178. By 1986, membership mushroomed to 45,800.

A temple was announced for Colombia on April 7, 1984, and a site for the temple was announced in 1988. Ground was broken for the Bogota Colombia Temple on June 26, 1993, by Elder William R. Bradford of the Seventy, but construction had been delayed pending government approvals.

In September 1988, internal political difficulties led to a withdrawing of North American missionaries. Despite these problems, missionary work continued to progress. The Colombia Barranquilla Mission was formed in 1988, in a city where the first stake was created in 1985. Since then, three other stakes have been created in Barranquilla. Membership in Colombia in 1990 was 83,000. The first General Authority from Colombia was Julio Davila, who was called to the Second Quorum of the Seventy in 1991. He was president of the first stake in Colombia.

Following countrywide fasts of Latter-day Saints, government approvals were received and the long-awaited construction of the Bogota Colombia Temple was started in late spring of 1995.

Sources: "Church in Colombia moving ahead," by Jack E. Jarrard, *Church News* Feb. 1, 1969; "The Saints in Colombia," by Colleen J. Heninger, *Ensign,* October, 1976; "Colombia," *Ensign,* February 1977; "Love, respect and emotion end area conference series," by Dell Van Orden, *Church News,* March 12, 1977; *Church News,* Oct. 23, 1976, March 19, 1988; *Church News,* June 3, 1995.

Stakes — 15
(Listed alphabetically as of Oct. 1, 1996.)

No.	Name	Organized	First President

South America North Area

1878	Barranquilla Colombia Cevillar	31 May 1992	Carlos M. Lopez Mangones
1537	*Barranquilla Colombia El Carmen	30 May 1992	
	‡Barranquilla Colombia	30 May 1985	Libardo Rodriguez
1879	Barranquilla Colombia Hipodromo	31 May 1992	Donaldo Antonio Osorio Perez
1880	Barranquilla Colombia Paraiso	31 May 1992	Jose Peralbo Aparicio
805	Bogota Colombia	23 Jan 1977	Julio E. Davila P.
1113	Bogota Colombia Ciudad Jardin	2 Mar 1980	Miguel Oswaldo Porras
1659	Bogota Colombia El Dorado	18 Oct 1987	Humberto Lopez S.
1008	Bogota Colombia Kennedy	11 Mar 1979	Miguel A. Vargas
1308	Bucaramanga Colombia	22 Nov 1981	Horacio Julio Insignarez
937	Cali Colombia	4 Jun 1978	Luis Alfonso Rios
1054	Cali Colombia Americas	24 Aug 1979	Libber A. Montoya O.
1697	Medellin Colombia	5 Jun 1988	Arnold Porras Martinez
2213	Medellin Colombia Belen	14 Jul 1996	Harold Cristian Cruz Arango
2161	Pasto Colombia	11 Feb 1996	Jose Luis Santacruz Fernandez
1968	Pereira Colombia	19 Dec 1993	Jose Luis Gonzalez

Missions — 4

(As of Oct. 1, 1996; shown with historical number. See MISSIONS.)

(270) COLO. BOGOTA SOUTH MISSION
Calle 72 No. 10-07 Oficina 1001
A.A. 77604
Santafe de Bogota 2
D.C. Colombia
Phone: (011-57-1) 210-4663

(79a) COLO. BOGOTA
NORTH MISSION
Apartado Aereo 90746
Bogota 8, D.E.
Colombia
Phone: (011-57-1) 210-1396

(215) COLO. BARRANQUILLA MISSION
Calle 82 No. 55-20, Apt. 2
A.A. 50710
Barranquilla - Atlantico
Colombia
Phone: (011-57-53) 56-22-16

(120) COLO. CALI MISSION
Apartado Aereo 4892
Cali, Valle
Colombia
Phone: (011-57-23) 667-1816

CONGO

Year-end 1995: Est. population, 2,530,000; Members, 1,000; Branches, 6; Districts, 1; Africa Area; Ghana Accra Mission.

Congo is a West African republic, where the people speak French and Kongo. A slight majority of the population is Christian but many follow tribal beliefs.

Congo granted the Church formal recognition Dec. 23, 1991. Missionaries were subsequently assigned to Congo from the Zaire Kinshasa Mission. Branches have been established in the capital city of Brazzaville.

For a period in 1992, missionaries to the Congo were withdrawn because of political turmoil.

Source: *Church News,* Dec. 28, 1991; *Church News,* Dec. 18, 1993.

COOK ISLANDS (RAROTONGA)

Year-end 1995: Est. population, 17,000; Members, 900; Districts, 1; Branches, 6; Percent LDS, 5.3, or one person in 19; Pacific Area; New Zealand Auckland Mission.

Located in the South Pacific, about 400 miles southwest of French Polynesia, the Cook Islands are self-governing, and 75 percent of the population are Protestants. The islands maintain close ties with New Zealand.

The first missionaries arrived in 1899, but failed to gain converts. Elder Osborne J.P. Widtsoe and a companion, Elder Mervin Davis, arrived in Rarotonga May 23, 1899, becoming the first LDS missionaries in the Cook Islands. During World War II, Matthew Cowley, then president of the New Zealand Mission, assigned Fritz Kruger, a New Zealand baker who owned a business at Avarua, Rarotonga, to help establish the Church on the Cook Islands. He and his family subsequently moved to Rarotonga, and their first convert was Samuel Glassie and his family.

In 1947, a couple, Elder and Sister Trevor Hamon, and later Elders Donlon DeLaMar and John L. Sorenson were sent to Avarua. By 1949, 160 Cook Islanders had joined the Church.

During the next decades, the Cook Islands were transferred to several missions in an attempt to maintain better communication with the remote location. The islands were part of the Samoan Mission (1954), New Zealand North Mission (1966), Fiji Mission (1971), and the Tahiti Papeete Mission (1975). The Islands are now part of the New Zealand Auckland Mission.

President David O. McKay visited in 1955. A Rarotonga Mission was created Nov. 20, 1960, but later became part of the New Zealand Mission. In the early 1960s, the Book of Mormon was translated into Cook Island Maori. In 1979, there were 718 members in 10 branches in the Cook Islands.

President Spencer W. Kimball visited Rarotonga in February 1981 during a trip to the South Pacific, and held a short service with members there in an airport hangar.

In 1990, the government issued a series of stamps featuring the first missionaries to the Cook Islands of various denominations. The LDS stamp featured a painting of Elder Widtsoe in the foreground and a drawing of an LDS meetinghouse in the background. On Sept. 4-7, 1996, Church members celebrated the 50th anniversary of the Church in the Cook Islands. During the 4-day celebration, members participated in dances, exhibits, sporting events, district conference, and a special fireside.

Sources: *Unto the Islands of the Sea,* by R. Lanier Britsch; "New day dawns for temples in Pacific," by Dell Van Orden, *Church News,* Feb. 28, 1981; "Island stamp honors LDS elder," *Church News,* June 23, 1990; interview with Fritz Kruger; *Church News,* Feb. 28, 1991; Aug. 29, 1992; interview with Mere Fiore.

COSTA RICA

Year-end 1995: Est. population, 3,450,000; Members, 25,000; Stakes, 4; Wards, 23; Branches, 45; Missions, 1; Districts, 6; Percent LDS, 0.7, or one LDS in 138.

A Central American democratic republic, Costa Rica has a population that speaks Spanish, and is 95 percent Roman Catholic.

Pres. Arwell L. Pierce of the Mexican Mission was authorized by the First Presidency to add Costa Rica to the Mexican Mission on July 8, 1946. He visited the country on Sept. 12, 1946, staying at the home of a member, H. Clark Fails.

Elders Robert B. Miller and David D. Lingard arrived in Costa Rica about Sept. 10, 1946. They presented the president of the republic with a copy of the Book of Mormon. The missionaries left to avoid being in the nation during a revolution in 1948, but Elder Lingard and Elder Jack M. Farnsworth returned in 1949 and enjoyed a Pioneer Day celebration of the members on July 24. The first conference was held in Costa Rica June 7, 1950, and about 70 attended. A branch was organized Aug. 25, 1950. Property for a meetinghouse was purchased in 1951.

General Authorities visited several times in the 1950s as the Church grew slowly. The Central American Mission was organized from the Mexican Mission Nov. 16, 1952. When the Guatemala-El Salvador Mission was created in 1965, it included Costa Rica. The first district conference was held in August 1968, with 296 people in attendance. The Costa Rica Mission was organized June 20, 1974.

The San Jose Costa Rica Stake was created Jan. 20, 1977, with Manuel Najera Guzman as president, and a month later an area conference was held in San Jose. At that time, there were 3,800 members in the country. By 1986, Costa Rica had 7,100 members. Eight years later, by 1995, this number had reached 25,000.

Sources: San Jose Branch manuscript history; Address by Pres. Manuel Najera at San Jose, Costa Rica, area conference Feb. 23, 1977.

Stakes — 4
(Listed alphabetically as of Oct. 1, 1996.)

No.	Name	Organized	First President
Central America Area			
1783	*Alajuela Costa Rica	20 Jun 1995	
	San Jose Costa Rica Alajuela	9 Dec 1990	Milton Perez Ruiz
1826	San Jose Costa Rica La Paz	10 Nov 1991	Max Enrique Urena Fallas
917	San Jose Costa Rica La Sabana	7 May 1978	Jorge Arturo Solano Castillo

803   *San Jose Costa Rica Los Yoses 10 Nov 1991
    ‡San Jose Costa Rica   20 Jan 1977   Manuel Najera G.

Mission — 1

(As of Oct. 1, 1996; shown with historical number. See MISSIONS.)

(43b) COSTA RICA SAN JOSE MISSION
Apartado Postal 2339-1000
San Jose, Costa Rica
Phone: (011-506) 234-1940

CROATIA

Year-end 1995: Est. Population, 4,666,000; Members, fewer than 100; Branches, 3; Districts, 1; Europe East Area ; Austria Vienna Mission.

Located on the Balkan Peninsula in southeast Europe, Croatia is a republic made up of what was a northern internal division of Yugoslavia.

Mischa Markow, a Hungarian who had immigrated to Salt Lake City, Utah, arrived as a missionary in Yugoslavia in May 1899. He was banished to Hungary a month later because government authorities objected to his preaching.

Some 70 years passed before members returned. By the early 1970s, a few Latter-day Saints were living in Yugoslavia, some of whom had joined the Church while working or studying abroad. Their first testimony meeting was held in Zadar Sept. 11, 1972.

In early 1975, Neil D. Schaerrer, president of the Austria Vienna Mission, established the Church as a legal entity in Yugoslavia and organized a branch in Zadar. He met with members in Zadar and Zagreb during the following months.

Among those who joined the Church while studying abroad was Kresimir Cosic, a BYU basketball star who returned to play on and coach the Yugoslavia Olympic team. He served as president of the Yugoslavia District. Following the dissolution of Yugoslavia, he persuaded the United States to send a representative to Croatia, and he was appointed deputy ambassador to the United States from Croatia in 1992.

Humanitarian relief has been provided Croatia by the Church and Church members in the United States and Europe. Thousands of tons of food, clothing, bedding and medical supplies were shipped between 1993-96.

Sources: Yugoslavia manuscript history; "Missionary to the Balkans, Mischa Markow," by William Hale Kehr, *Ensign*, June 1980; Zagreb Branch history, published by the branch at dedication of meetinghouse, Oct. 30, 1985; "Tears of joy," by Richard L. Jensen, *Church News*, Dec. 8, 1979; "Yugoslavia's bright future," *Church News*, March 2, 1986; Sept. 26, 1992; Feb. 26, 1993; April 24, 1994; Dec. 3, 1994; and Feb. 25, 1995.

CYPRUS

Year-end 1995: Est. population, 737,000; Members, fewer than 100; Branches, 2; Europe East Area; Greece Athens Mission.

Located in the Mediterranean Sea off the Turkish coast, the republic has groups speaking Greek and Turkish and following the Greek Orthodox and Muslim religions.

The Cyprus LDS group was organized in 1962 among member families living in Cyprus on government service. The group, also called the Nicosia Branch, was dissolved in 1969, reorganized in 1971, temporarily dissolved in 1980 and later reorganized. The members are part of an English-speaking community residing in Cyprus, and they occasionally meet with other religious denominations for interdenominational meetings.

On Sept. 14, 1993, Elder Joseph B. Wirthlin of the Quorum of the Twelve and Elder Hans B. Ringger of the Seventy and their wives, Elisa Wirthlin and Helen Ringger, met with a small group of members at Larnaca.

CZECH REPUBLIC

Year-end 1995: Est. population, 10,500,000; Members, 1,200; Branches, 18; Missions, 1; Districts, 4; Europe East Area.

In east-central Europe, the Czech Republic's people speak Czech and Slovak, both of which are official languages. Some 65 percent of the population is Roman Catholic.

Elder Thomas Biesinger, the first missionary to enter what was then Czechoslovakia, arrived in 1884. However, he was imprisoned and banished following a trial. After his release and before his departure, he baptized and confirmed Anthon Just, one of his previous investigators and a witness at his trial, on June 21, 1884.

After Elder Biesinger left, the work awaited his return in 1928, at the age of 84. On his second attempt, he obtained legal permission for the Church. The Czechoslovakia Mission was organized July 24, 1929, by Elder John A. Widtsoe, president of the European Mission. Arthur Gaeth, one of the elders in the German-Austrian Mission, was chosen to preside over the new mission. At that time, there were seven members in the nation. Among them were Franziska Brodil, a widow whose two daughters, Frances and Jane, were baptized in Czechoslovakia in 1921.

Lectures on the Church were delivered over radio, and at a cultural fair in 1931 missionaries handed out more than 150,000 tracts. The Book of Mormon was translated in 1933, and additional materials were later translated and published. A shortage of missionaries during the Great Depression slowed the work. With the approach of World War II, missionaries were recalled from the country. The mission was left under the direction of a young convert, Josef Roubicek. During the war, Pres. Roubicek kept the Saints together, added 28 members, and published a mission circular letter. Missionary work resumed in 1946 and continued until April 6, 1950, when the mission was closed. Roubicek immigrated to America in 1949.

The Czechoslovakia District was organized Feb. 3, 1982. Local missionaries began having success after about 1985. After the democratization of the nation in 1989-90, the first full-time missionaries arrived in 1990. About that time, the Church applied for recognition. According to President Thomas S. Monson, second counselor in the First Presidency, "The government leaders had said to us, 'Don't send an American, a German or a Swiss. Send us a Czech.'" Acknowledging Church leadership during the prohibition of religion was tantamount to imprisonment, Pres. Jiri Snederfler, Czechoslovakia district president, answered the call and faced this risk as he applied to the government for recognition.

Pres. Snederfler met in Prague on Feb. 6, 1990, with Deputy Prime Minister Josef Hromadka, and recognition that was first granted to the Church in 1928 was officially renewed on Feb. 21, 1990. The Czechoslovakia Prague Mission was reorganized July 1, 1990, from a division of the Austria Vienna East Mission, with Richard W. Winder as president. He had served a mission in Czechoslovakia 40 years earlier. By 1990, there were more than 200 members. The Tabernacle Choir performed in Prague in 1991. In 1993, Czech broadcasters visited Salt Lake City and broadcast a nationwide feature on the Church.

Sources: *Encyclopedic History of the Church,* by Andrew Jenson; *Church News,* Feb. 22, 1936, Feb. 29, 1936, March 7, 1936, March 14, 1936; Feb. 14, 1951, March 3, 1990; "A Missionary's Two Months in Jail," by William G. Hartley, *New Era,* Nov. 1982; "Prayed for a mission," by Davis Bitton, *Church News,* Oct. 28, 1978; Swiss Mission history, May 8, 1968; "Czech broadcasters see Church close-up," by R. Scott Lloyd, *Church News,* May 22, 1993; Correspondence from Kahlile Mehr, Dec. 29, 1992.

Mission — 1
(As of Oct. 1, 1996; shown with historical number. See MISSIONS.)

(236) CZECH PRAGUE MISSION
Milady Horakove 8595
170 00 Praha 7
Czech Republic
Phone: (011-42-2) 329 314

DENMARK

Year-end 1995: Est. population, 5,200,000; Members, 4,700; Stakes, 2; Wards, 13; Branches, 11; Missions, 1; Percent LDS, 0.09, or one person in 1,106.

Located in northern Europe on the Baltic Sea, Denmark is a constitutional monarchy with a population that speaks Danish, 90 percent of whom are Evangelical Lutherans.

Elder Erastus Snow was called in October 1849 to open the work in Scandinavia. He and Elders John E. Forsgren and George P. Dykes traveled to Denmark, arriving in Copenhagen June 14, 1850. Another member, Peter O. Hansen, had arrived about a month earlier.

The first baptism took place Aug. 12, 1850, and within two months, the elders had established the headquarters of the mission in Copenhagen and baptized 15 people. The first branch was organized Sept. 15, 1850, in Copenhagen. Elder Dykes opened a second branch in Aalborg Nov. 25, 1850.

Work continued to progress as the elders pushed into every corner of Denmark, but heavy persecution was waged against members. In Aalborg in 1851, a mob vandalized the hall where the Saints were meeting. Soon conferences (districts) were established in eight areas to accommodate the multiplying branches. The first converts to emigrate left Jan. 31, 1852. Of about 26,000 people who were converted during this early period, 13,984 converts immigrated to the United States by 1930.

The Danish Mission was organized April 1, 1920. Convert baptisms varied from 50 to 200 a year between 1966 and 1974. In 1971, the Church membership in Denmark consisted of about 4,193 people in three districts. Although members were limited in number, they took part in home seminary, served missions and attended the Swiss Temple after it was dedicated in 1955.

The Copenhagen Denmark Stake, the first in the country, was organized June 16, 1974, with Johan H. Benthin as president. In 1983, membership totaled 4,097, and in 1990, 4,200.

Church presidents have visited the country several times in later years. The most recent visit was by President Gordon B. Hinckley on June 14, 1996. There, he challenged the Saints to double their membership in five years.

Sources: *Encyclopedic History of the Church*, by Andrew Jenson; *History of the Danish Mission, 1850*; "Prophet visits 5 European countries, asks Saints to keep commandments," by John L. Hart, *Church News*, June 22, 1996.

GREENLAND

Year-end 1995: Population, 57,000; Members, fewer than 100; North America Northeast Area.

This very large island, slightly larger than Mexico, in the North Atlantic between Canada and Iceland is a province of Denmark under home rule. Greenland has a parliamentary government with a population that speaks Danish and Greenlandic, and most are members of the Evangelical Lutheran Church.

A branch of LDS servicemen was organized in 1953 and functioned for at least five years. The branch was discontinued in 1989, but a military group continues to meet at Thule Air Base.

Sources: *Church News*, April 19, 1958; Jan. 9, 1960.

Stakes — 2
(Listed alphabetically as of Oct. 1, 1996.)

No.	Name	Organized	First President
Europe Area			
945	Aarhus Denmark	2 Jul 1978	Knud Bent Andersen
648	Copenhagen Denmark	16 Jun 1974	Johan Helge Benthin

Mission — 1
(As of Oct. 1, 1996; shown with historical number. See MISSIONS.)

(23b) DENMARK COPENHAGEN MISSION
Boqupsalle 128, 1.tv
200 Frederiksberg Denmark
Phone: (011-45) 38-11-39-39

DOMINICAN REPUBLIC

Year-end 1995: Est. population, 8,030,000; Members, 54,000; Stakes, 8; Wards, 42; Branches, 99; Missions; 3; Districts, 11; Temples, 1 under construction; Percent LDS, 0.6, or one LDS in 148.

An island in the West Indies, Dominican Republic is about the size of Vermont and New Hampshire combined, but has nearly five times their combined populations. The Dominican Republic is a representative democracy. Its population speaks Spanish, and is mostly Roman Catholic.

The Eddie and Mercedes Amparo family arrived in the Dominican Republic on June 9, 1978, the day the revelation was announced that allowed all worthy men to hold the priesthood. They and another newly arrived family, John and Nancy Rappleye, began doing missionary work. An associate of the Amparos, Rodolfo Bodden, was the first convert, baptized in August 1978. Among the first missionaries were John A. and Ada Davis of Provo, Utah. The Dominican Republic Santo Domingo Mission was organized Jan. 1, 1981. At that time, membership was at 2,500. A highlight came March 8-9, 1981, when President Spencer W. Kimball visited.

Membership increases have been rapid. In 1979, 354 people were baptized. By 1986, membership reached 11,000. The Santo Domingo Dominican Republic Stake was organized March, 23, 1986. A second mission was organized in Santiago on July 1, 1987, when the country's membership was about 13,000. A second stake was organized Oct. 16, 1988, and a third on Nov. 5, 1989. Membership in 1990 was 31,000. In 1992, the Dominican members received satellite transmissions of general conference.

The first temple in the Caribbean was announced for Santo Domingo, Dominican Republic by President Gordon B. Hinckley of the First Presidency on Dec. 4, 1993. More than 4,000 Church members gathered Aug. 18, 1996, to witness the temple groundbreaking by Elder Richard G. Scott of the Quorum of the Twelve.

Sources: *Church News*, Dec. 6, 1980; March 21, 1981; "Dominican Growth: From Zero to Thousands since 1978," *Ensign*, January 1987; "2 families bring gospel to a nation," by William B. Smart, *Church News*, July 11, 1981; *Church News*, Aug. 25, 1985; July 15, 1989; Jan 26, 1986; "Rendering Service to Others," an address by Pres. Spencer W. Kimball, *Ensign*, May 1981; Conversion account of Eric Olivero delivered May 26, 1991, and conference report by Elder Stan Bradshaw; "Dominican Republic, a Second Decade for Dominican Saints," by Elizabeth and Jed VanDenBerghe, *Ensign*, October 1990; *Church News*, Dec. 4, 1993; "Ground broken for Caribbean's first temple," *Church News*, Aug. 24, 1996.

Stakes — 9
(Listed alphabetically as of Oct. 1, 1996.)

No.	Name	Organized	First President
North America Southeast Area			
1800	San Francisco de Macoris Dominican Republic	26 May 1991	Eric Edison Olivero P.
1701	*Santo Domingo Dominican Republic Geronimo 18 Oct 1992 ‡San Geronimo Dominican Republic	16 Oct 1988	Victor Alejandro Navarro M.
1786	*Santiago Dominican Republic South 8 Jan 1995 Santiago Dominican Republic	17 Feb 1991	Ramon Matias Lantigua
2009	Santiago Dominican Republic North	8 Jan 1995	Roberto Antonio Rodriguez
1593	Santo Domingo Dominican Republic	23 Mar 1986	Jose Delio Ceveno
1906	Santo Domingo Dominican Republic Independencia	18 Oct 1992	Felix Sequi-Martinez
1735a	*Santo Domingo Dominican Republic Oriental 2 Feb 1992 *Oriental Dominican Republic 29 Oct 1991 *Santo Domingo Dominican Republic Oriental 24 Sep 1991 ‡Santo Domingo Dominican Republic East	5 Nov 1989	Pedro Arturo Abreu C.
1844	Santo Domingo Dominican Republic Ozama	2 Feb 1992	Jose Andres Taveras Arias
2182	Santo Domingo Dominican Republic Villa Mella	17 Mar 1996	Domingo Antonio Aybar A.

Missions — 3
(As of Oct. 1, 1996; shown with historical number. See MISSIONS.)

(196) DOMINICAN REPUBLIC
SANTIAGO MISSION
Apartado 1240
Santiago,
Dominican Republic
Phone: (809) 241-1145

(188a) DOMINICAN REPUBLIC
SANTO DOMINGO WEST MISSION
Edificio Manuel Arsenio Urena,
Quinto Piso
Avenida 27 de Febrero #514
Santo Domingo
Dominican Republic
Phone: (809) 537-3758

(259) D.R. SANTO DOMINGO
EAST MISSION
50 E. North Temple
Salt Lake City, UT 84150
(Pouch)
Phone: (809) 687-9085

ECUADOR

Year-end 1995: Est. population, 11,000,000; Members, 128,000; Stakes, 21; Wards, 128; Branches, 138; Missions, 3; Districts, 11; Temples, 1 under construction; Percent LDS, 1.10, or one LDS in 85.

Located on the equator on the Pacific Coast side of South America, the Republic of Ecuador is divided into three zones by two ranges of Andes mountains. Its Spanish- and Quechua-speaking population is 95 percent Roman Catholic.

A letter from Elder Spencer W. Kimball, then of the Quorum of the Twelve, received by Pres. J. Averil Jesperson of the Andes Mission in Lima, Peru, on Sept. 22, 1965, suggested opening missionary work in Ecuador. Elders Craig Carpenter, Bryant R. Gold, Lindon Robinson and Paul O. Allen were sent to Quito two weeks later, and on Oct. 9, Elder Kimball visited Quito. Work progressed rapidly, and when the Ecuador Mission, with headquarters in Quito, was created Aug. 1, 1970, membership was 1,000.

Some of the first proselyting was done among the Otavalo Indians near Quito, among whom the first all-Lamanite stake in South America was organized in 1981.

Others in Ecuador eagerly accepted the gospel. By the end of 1975, membership had tripled to 3,226. Ecuador's first stake was organized in Guayaquil June 11, 1978, under the direction of Pres. Lorenzo A. Garaycoa, and a second mission was organized in Guayaquil, on July 1, 1978. Membership at the beginning of 1979 was 19,000.

A temple was announced for Guayaquil by President Gordon B. Hinckley on March 31, 1982. Ground was broken by Richard G. Scott of the Quorum of the Twelve, Aug. 10, 1996 for the temple. Members continued to prepare family names for temple work.

The headquarters for the South America North Area was moved from Lima, Peru, to Quito, Ecuador, in 1989. Membership in 1986 reached 43,000, and in 1995, 128,000.

Sources: *The Improvement Era*, May 1966; "Ecuador", *Ensign*, February 1977; "Language no barrier," *Church News*, Nov. 11, 1978; "Tip your Panama hat, this is Ecuador," by Gerry Avant, *Church News*, Feb. 14, 1981; *Church News*, July 8, 1978; "In the Andes, Lehi's children grow strong in the gospel," by Elayne Wells, *Church News*, Feb. 17, 1990; *Church News*, June 25, 1994.

Stakes — 24
(Listed alphabetically as of Oct. 1, 1996.)

No.	Name	Organized	First President
South America North Area			
2144	Ambato Ecuador	10 Dec 1995	Jorge Humberto Verde
1882	Duran Ecuador North	31 May 1992	Mark Roy Kent
1883	Duran Ecuador South	31 May 1992	Jimmy Winston Olvera
2110	Esmeraldas Ecuador	22 Oct 1995	Jorge Miguel Arroyo Jacombe
2162	Guayaguil Ecuador Alborada	11 Feb 1996	Henry Alejandro Mora
1808	Guayaquil Ecuador Centenario	18 Aug 1991	Luis Guillermo Granja G.
2163	Guayaquil Ecuador El Cisne	11 Feb 1996	Melvin Merchan
1716a	*Guayaquil Ecuador Garcia Moreno 11 Feb 1996		
	Guayaquil Ecuador Central	30 Apr 1989	Gonzalo Eduardo Alvarado R.
1809	Guayaquil Ecuador East	18 Aug 1991	Jimmy Winston Olvera C.
939	*Guayaquil Ecuador El Salado 11 Feb 1996		
	‡Guayaquil Ecuador West 22 Mar 1987		
	‡Guayaquil Ecuador	11 Jun 1978	Lorenzo A. Garaycoa
1916	Guayaquil Ecuador Huancavilca	6 Dec 1992	Jose Eladio Paredes Garcia
1117	*Guayaquil Ecuador Prosperina 11 Feb 1996		
	‡Guayaquil Ecuador North 22 Mar 1987		
	‡Guayaquil Ecuador Febres Cordero	16 Mar 1980	Douglas Alarcon Arboleda
1006	*Guayaquil Ecuador South 22 Mar 1987		
	Guayaquil Ecuador Centenario	4 Mar 1979	Vincente de la Cuadra S.
1853	Machala Ecuador	22 Mar 1992	Manuel Andres Galan Pereira
2173	Manta Ecuador	25 Feb 1996	Wilson Marino Chinga Holguin
1796	Milagro Ecuador	5 May 1991	Alberto W. Guillen Fuentes
1316	Otavalo Ecuador	6 Dec 1981	Luis Alfonso Morales C.
1224	Portoviejo Ecuador	13 Jan 1981	Jorge Vicente Salazar H.
1259	Quevedo Ecuador	27 Apr 1981	Pedro Jose Cantos J.
2050	Quito Ecuador Chillgallo	21 May 1995	Eduardo Calderon Poveda

1053	*Quito Ecuador Colon 15 Jan 1981		
	‡Quito Ecuador	22 Aug 1979	Ernesto Franco
1839	Quito Ecuador Inaquito	12 Jan 1992	Horacio Araya Olivares
1225	Quito Ecuador Santa Ana	15 Jan 1981	Cesar Hugh Cacuango C.
2096	Santo Domingo Ecuador	3 Sep 1995	Wilson Alcides Echanique Cueve

Discontinued

1116	Guayaquil Ecuador Duran	16 Mar 1980	Lorenzo Augusto Garaycoa
	22 Mar 1987 †Guayaquil Ecuador West (939), Guayaquil		
	Ecuador South (1006), Guayaquil Ecuador North (1117)		
1221	Guayaquil Ecuador Kennedy	11 Jan 1981	Fausto Montalvan Morla
	22 Mar 1987 †Guayaquil Ecuador West (939), Guayaquil		
	Ecuador South (1006), Guayaquil Ecuador North (1117)		

Missions — 3

(As of Oct. 1, 1996; shown with historical number. See MISSIONS.)

(261) ECUADOR GUAYAQUIL NORTH MISSION
Casilla de Correo 16160
Guayaquil
Ecuador
Phone: (011-593-4) 399-446

(160) ECUADOR GUAYAQUIL SOUTH MISSION
Casilla 8757, 8750
Guayaquil
Ecuador
Phone: (011-593-4) 289-570

(93) ECUADOR QUITO MISSION
Casilla 17-03-078
Quito
Ecuador
Phone: (011-593-2)508-526

EGYPT

Year-end 1995: Est. population, 63,000,000; Members, fewer than 100; Branches, 1; District 1; Europe East Area.

Located in the northeast corner of Africa, the republic has a population that speaks Arabic and English, and is 94 percent Sunni Muslim.

The Cairo Branch functioned from 1971-74 as part of the Switzerland Mission. In 1974, two students arrived in Cairo for intensive study of Arabic. Dilworth B. Parkinson and John Sharp, met with Carol Azeltine, a teacher at an international school in suburban Digla, and began holding LDS meetings in the garden area of the American University in downtown Cairo.

From 1974 to 1987, the branch was in the International Mission until the mission was dissolved and the branch was placed in the Austria Vienna East Mission. Membership of the branch is made up of about 100 expatriates, most of whom are in the country on U.S. or other government service projects, or for BYU's ongoing archaeology studies. The members met in each other's homes until 1982, when a villa was rented in Maadi. On Feb. 1, 1985, the branch began meeting in a larger, two-story villa in the same community. They hold outings in historic places and ways, such as camel rides and boating on the Nile.

Beginning in 1980, a continual string of couples has come to Egypt specifically to serve as special Church representatives, who make friends for the Church but do not proselyte.

Among those who helped make significant contributions in Egypt in recent years are members who have worked on mechanization for small farms, modern drip irrigation methods, various farm production projects, dental service projects, medical technology training, and a significant on-going BYU archaeology excavation performed under the direction of Dr. C. Wilfred Griggs.

Sources: *Church News*, Nov. 26, 1988; "Benson Institute improves lives," *Church News*, Nov. 18, 1989; "Branch in land of pyramids is 'home away from home' " By Edwin O. Haroldsen, *Church News*, June 12, 1993.

EL SALVADOR

Year-end 1995: Est. population, 5,920,000; Members, 64,000; Stakes, 13; Wards, 71; Branches, 49; Missions, 2; Districts, 2; Percent LDS, 1.0, or one person in 92.

El Salvador, in Central America, is a republic with a Spanish- and some Nahuatl-speaking population of mostly Roman Catholics.

On Aug. 20, 1948, Pres. Arwell L. Pierce of the Mexican Mission visited El Salvador and explored the possibility of proselyting. On May 26, 1949, he assigned Elders Glenn Whipple Skousen and Omer Farnsworth to go to El Salvador and open the work. A conference was held at San Salvador on Feb. 16, 1951, attended by Elder Albert E. Bowen of the Quorum of the Twelve, at which 63 people were present. A short time later, on March 2, 1951, Ana Villasenor became the first person baptized in the country. Elder Vance Whipple performed the baptism at Apulo Beach at Lake Ilopango. Eleven others were baptized at the same time.

The country was transferred from the Mexican Mission on Nov. 16, 1952, when the new Central America Mission was created. The San Salvador District was organized in January 1965, and was soon followed by the Guatemala-El Salvador Mission. Membership then numbered 4,200. On June 3, 1973, the district was organized into the San Salvador Stake, which had a membership of 5,600. President of the stake was former district president Mario Edmundo Scheel. The El Salvador San Salvador Mission was organized July 1, 1976, at which time the nation had 4,745 members. Ten years later in 1986, membership had climbed to 15,100, and the number of stakes increased to six. The nation reached self-sufficiency in local missionaries in 1989. In 1990, the El Salvador San Salvador East Mission was created and membership was 38,000, nearly doubling in five years to 64,000.

Sources: El Salvador San Salvador Mission history, year ending Dec. 31, 1976; *El Salvador District Manuscript History*; *Church News*, Feb. 3, 1990.

Stakes — 15
(Listed alphabetically as of Oct. 1, 1996.)

No.	Name	Organized	First President
Central America Area			
1817	Ahuachapan El Salvador	22 Sep 1991	Juan Antonio Merlos V.
2219	Atiquizaya El Salvador	11 Aug 1996	Jose Salvador Molina Linares
2114	Chalchuapa El Salvador	20 Oct 1995	Jose Salvador Molina
2122	Juayua El Salvador	12 Nov 1995	Oswaldo Rodriguez Villata .
1223	San Miguel El Salvador	11 Jan 1981	Carlos Antonio Hernandez
618	*San Salvador El Salvador		
	‡San Salvador (El Salvador)	3 Jun 1973	Mario Edmundo Scheel
1035	San Salvador El Salvador Cuzcatlan	3 Jun 1979	Franklin Henriquez Melgar
741	*San Salvador El Salvador Ilopango	3 Jun 1979	
	‡San Salvador El Salvador East	1 Feb 1976	Alfonso Octavio Diaz
2111	San Salvador El Salvador La Libertad	22 Oct 1995	H. Edgardo Alvarado Renderos
2241	San Salvador El Salvador Layco	22 Sep 1996	E. Leonardo Rivera Herrera
1745a	San Salvador El Salvador Los Heroes	8 Apr 1990	Cristobal A. Hernandez
1744	San Salvador El Salvador Soyopango	8 Apr 1990	Rene Francisco Esquivel G.
1217	Santa Ana El Salvador Modelo	14 Dec 1980	Jorge Alberta Benitez M.
1088	*Santa Ana El Salvador Molino	14 Dec 1980	
	‡Santa Ana El Salvador	2 Dec 1979	Elmer Barrientos
1816	Sonsonate El Salvador	22 Sep 1991	Rolando Arturo Rosales H.

Missions — 2
(As of Oct. 1, 1996; shown with historical number. See MISSIONS)

(137a) EL SALVADOR SAN SALVADOR EAST MISSION
Apartado Postal #3362
San Salvador
El Salvador C.A.
Phone: (011-503-2) 26-12-15

(181a) EL SALVADOR SAN SALVADOR WEST MISSION
Apartado Postal 367
San Salvador
El Salvador C.A.
Phone: (011-503) 243-3208

ENGLAND
(See United Kingdom)

EQUATORIAL GUINEA
Year-end 1995: Est. population, 424,000; Members, fewer than 100; Africa Area; Ivory Coast Abidjan Mission.

Located near the equator on the west coast of Africa, Equatorial Guinea is a unitary republic with a population that is mostly Roman Catholic.

Equatorial Guinea was included in the Ivory Coast Abidjan Mission when it was created Feb. 1, 1992.

ESTONIA

Year-end 1995: Est. population, 1,625,000; Members, 200; Branches, 4; Europe East Area; Lithuania Vilnius Mission.

The first contacts in recent times in Estonia were established by Finnish members who worked in Tallinn, Estonia. Among these were Valtteri Rotsa and Enn Lembit, who were baptized in Helsinki, Finland.

LDS Finnish businessman Pekka Uusituba, who was visiting in Estonia, taught the gospel to a group of 10 investigators at Lembit's home in November 1989. The first Estonians baptized in Estonia were Alari Allik, Eva Reisalu, Jaana Lass and Kristi Lass, on Dec. 17, 1989. Later, Jaanus Silla from Tallinn, was baptized Jan. 6, 1990. He was the first missionary from Estonia, and was called to the Utah Salt Lake City Mission. At that time, the branch had an attendance of some 50 people.

In May 1991, the Estonian and Russian branches (both in Tallinn) had 130 members. Humanitarian relief was supplied to members in Estonia from Europe and the United States during 1990-92. During the summer of 1993, BYU's Young Ambassadors toured Estonia and other Eastern European countries, helping raise the Church's profile.

In July 1993, Estonia was placed in the newly created Latvia Riga Mission, relocated in Lithuania Vilnius in 1996.

During a summer tour in 1995, members of BYU's women's volleyball team attended Church in Tallinn.

Sources: Interview and records of Elder Jaanus Silla; correspondence from Mission Pres. Gary L. Browning; correspondence from Kahlile Mehr, Dec. 29, 1992; "Y. troupe tours Russia, Baltic states," *Church News*, July 17, 1993; "Growth of Church in 'that vast empire' " by Gary L. Browning, *Church News*, Nov. 6, 1993; *Church News*, March 6, 1993; "European trip unites BYU volleyball team," *Church News*, Sept. 23, 1995.

ETHIOPIA

Year-end 1995: Est. population, 56,700,000; Members, 200; Branches, 1; Africa Area; Kenya Nairobi Mission.

In east central Africa, Ethiopia has a population that speaks Amharic, English, Orominga, and Tigrigna and who are primarily Ethiopian Orthodox, Islam and animist (a belief of conscious life within objects).

The first members in Ethiopia were expatriates attached to embassies who held Church meetings in homes in Addis Ababa. In March 1985, Elders M. Russell Ballard and Glenn L. Pace visited Addis Ababa with LDS relief supplies. They held a sacrament meeting in the home of Harry Hadlock, an expatriate airline consultant, on March 17, 1985. The Church donated some $2.8 million for famine relief and irrigation development in Ethiopia and neighboring countries, such as Sudan.

After the Kenya Nairobi Mission was created in 1991, Robert DeWitt, serving with the American embassy, and his wife arrived and stayed for two years. The first official meeting was held in the DeWitt home in August 1992 with Brother Dewitt presiding. The Church was legally registered Sept. 16, 1993, in Addis Ababa. The first missionaries were Elder Eugene and Sister Ruth Hilton, who arrived Feb. 28, 1993. The first convert was Dereje Ketsahu, baptized April 16, 1993. The Addis Ababa Branch was created Jan. 5, 1994.

The first Ethiopian branch president was Girma Denisa, who was baptized while attending Ricks College in 1973.

The seminary program was instituted in Ethiopia in 1995. In addition, later in the year, a representative from Ethiopia attended the lighting ceremony for the 1995 Festival of Lights at the Washington Temple Visitors Center. Ethiopia was among some 50 nations represented at the widely publicized event.

Source: Correspondence from Larry K. Brown, president of the Kenya Nairobi Mission, April 12, 1994; *Church News*, Dec. 9, 1995; *Church News*, March 9, 1996.

FIJI

Year-end 1995: Est. population, 780,000; Members, 11,000; Stakes, 2; Wards, 14;

Branches, 20; Missions, 1; Districts, 2; Percent LDS, 1.4, or one LDS in 70.

Located in western South Pacific, the republic of Fiji has a population speaking English, Hindustani and Fijian. The archipelago has 322 islands, of which 106 are inhabited.

In the 1950s, LDS Tongan and Samoan families, including Cecil B. Smith and Mele Vea Ashley and their families, held Church meetings in Suva, Fiji. When the first missionaries, Elders Boyd L. Harris and Sheldon L. Abbott, arrived, they began working with this group and organized the Suva Branch Sept. 5, 1954.

Work proceeded slowly. Missionaries were limited by the multiple languages spoken in Fiji and by restrictions of only two missionary visas at a time. In January 1955, President David O. McKay had a airplane layover in Suva, and he met the missionaries and attended services at the Smith home. Twenty-eight people attended that day. He urged missionaries to proceed and to purchase property for a meetinghouse. The meetinghouse that was later built was a nearly normal-sized stake center, anticipating future growth. Fiji was placed in the Tonga Mission on Jan. 15, 1958, and 93 people attended the conference that day. Later in 1958, 300 attended dedicatory services for the new meetinghouse. About that time, the quota of missionaries was increased by six. Gideon Dolo was the first Fijian to serve a mission, leaving in February 1959.

Growth continued in the 1960s. In 1966, 150 attended district conferences in Suva. Three years later, the attendance at conference reached 500, and the district was divided. The Fiji Mission was created July 23, 1971. In 1972, Mission Pres. Eb L. Davis expanded the mission into several new areas. By 1972, the meetinghouse was filled with Fijians, Indians, Rotumans, Tongans, Samoans, New Zealanders, Australians, Europeans, and Americans.

Educational efforts were also strengthened. In 1969, a Church school was held in the meetinghouse, and in 1973, it had more than 100 students. In 1975, the LDS Fiji Technical College was opened. By 1984, 372 students were enrolled at the college.

The Suva Fiji Stake was organized June 12, 1983, with Inosi Naga as president. At year-end 1983, membership in Fiji was 2,722. By 1995, membership was 11,000.

Sources: *Unto the Isles of the Sea,* by R. Lanier Britsch; *Church News,* Sept. 14, 1991; "Fiji: Church gaining prominence in isle cultures," *Church News,* Nov. 2, 1991.

Stakes — 3
(As of Oct. 1, 1996.)

No.	Name	Organized	First President
	Pacific Area		
2216	Lautoka Fiji	11 Aug 1996	Jone Sovasova
2040	Nasinu Fiji	16 Apr 1995	Vilikesa Ravia
1428	Suva Fiji	12 Jun 1983	Inosi Naga

Mission — 1
(As of Oct. 1, 1996; shown with historical number. See MISSIONS.)

(99) FIJI SUVA MISSION
GPO Box 215
Suva, Fiji Islands
Phone: (011-679) 314-277

FINLAND
Year-end 1995: Est. population, 5,085,000; Members, 4,400; Stakes, 2; Wards, 11; Branches, 18; Missions, 1; Districts, 3; Percent LDS, 0.08, or one LDS in 1,155.

Located in northern Europe, the Republic of Finland has a population that speaks Finnish and Swedish, and 90 percent are Lutherans.

The first Latter-day Saints in Finland were Finnish emigrants who had been baptized in Sweden in the early 1870s. The first missionaries were Swedish brothers Carl A. and John E. Sundstrom. They preached in Vaasa and found converts in 1876. During the first decade in Finland, the missionaries worked among Swedish-speaking Finns, and by 1886 had baptized 25 people. Because Finnish law forbade "getting up and preaching," missionaries learned to preach while sitting.

In 1903, Elder Francis M. Lyman of the Quorum of the Twelve visited Finland.

Efforts were made to establish branches in several areas, but the branches were not permanent. When Anders and Lovis Stromberg were converted in Larsmo, a permanent branch eventually grew up around them. Membership in the country was 35 in 1930. As late as 1941, all Church members in Finland had their records in Larsmo.

In 1946, seven missionaries from Sweden were sent to Finland, the first being Mark E. Anderson. In 1947, Henry A. Matis, an American with Finnish roots, was called as president of the Finnish Mission. Membership in Finland was 129 when he arrived. During the seven years that he served, the Church gained legal status (July 1, 1948), began microfilming Finnish church records (December 1948-November 1955) and translated and published the Book of Mormon in Finnish (December 1954). Missionaries taught English, played basketball and did everything they could to raise the Church's profile.

After 1954, local Finnish members served missions. A building program was started and more people were converted. By 1957, membership was 904. The first temple trip to Switzerland was made in June 1960.

The Helsinki Stake was organized Oct. 16, 1977, with Kari Haikkola as president. At that time there were 3,642 members. Ten years later, it had increased to 4,100.

Finnish members were the first to introduce the gospel to Estonia and parts of Russia (see Estonia history). The Helsinki East Mission was created in 1990 to serve members in Leningrad and other areas in the Soviet Union. It was discontinued with the creation of the Russia missions in 1991, although Finnish leaders were among those called to serve in Russia. Membership in 1990 was 4,200.

Sources: *Ensign*, May 1973; "A man worth the wait," by John L. Hart, *Church News*, Nov. 14, 1987; *Church News*, Nov. 16, 1991; "Finland," *Church News*, Feb. 15, 1992.

Stakes — 2
(Listed alphabetically as of Oct. 1, 1996.)

No.	Name	Organized	First President
Europe North Area			
865	Helsinki Finland	16 Oct 1977	Kari Juhani Aslak Haikkola
1408	Tampere Finland	17 Apr 1983	Kari Juhani Aslak Haikkola

Mission — 1
(As of Oct. 1, 1996; shown with historical number. See MISSIONS.)

(41) FINLAND HELSINKI MISSION
Neitsytpolku 3 A 4
00140 Helsinki, Finland
Phone: (011-358-9) 177-311

FRANCE

Year-end 1995: Est. population, 58,110,000; Members, 28,000; Stakes, 7; Wards, 35; Branches, 87; Missions, 3; Districts, 7; Percent LDS, 0.04, or one LDS in 2,075.

In western Europe, France has a population that speaks French, and includes minorities who speak Breton, Alsatian, German, Flemish, Italian, Basque and Catalan. The population of France is mostly Roman Catholic.

A Welsh member named William Howells arrived in Le Havre, France, in July 1849, and on July 30, 1849, baptized Augustus Saint d'Anna. After a short detour to the Island of Jersey, Howells returned to France and baptized a man named Pebble and a young woman, Anna Browse. The Boulogne-sur-Mer Branch with six members was organized April 5, 1850. On June 18, Apostle John Taylor and Elder Curtis E. Boulton arrived. The party traveled to Paris, and on Dec. 8, 1850, a branch of eight members was organized in that city. The Book of Mormon was translated and published in French in January 1852. By July 24, 1853, nine branches had been organized, with 337 members including 289 from the Channel Islands.

Government restrictions by French Emperor Louis Napoleon prohibited gathering of any more than 20 people, making it difficult for missionaries to hold meetings. Louis Bertrand, a member of the original branch in Paris, published a periodical and tried to extend missionary work. In 1859, Pres. Bertrand was called to preside over the mission but in 1864, the work in France was closed. The work re-opened in 1912 when the French Mission was reorganized. Sixty-two converts joined that year, but World War I halted the work until 1923 when the French Mission was re-established. In 1924, the first year of mission activity, some 200 converts joined. By 1930, there were two meetinghouses in the French Mission (both were in the Belgian sector of the French Mission) and missionaries were working in 33 cities in the two countries.

Missionaries worked hard to build the Church's image and some helped by singing in groups while others played on successful basketball teams. During World War II, a local leader, Leon Fargier, conducted the affairs of the Church. After World War II, missionary work resumed. The Tabernacle Choir visited in 1955. In 1959, membership reached 1,909 members. The first meetinghouse in France was constructed in Nantes in 1962. In 1974, 29 French members were serving full-time missions. The Paris France Stake, the first stake in France, was created Nov. 16, 1975, with Gerard Giraud-Carrier as president. At that time, membership in the nation was about 10,000. A decade later, it had grown to 16,500 in three stakes. By 1996, 28,454 members were organized into seven stakes.

The France Bordeaux Mission was created in 1989, and the France Marseille Mission was created July 1, 1991. On Aug. 15, 1992, the Europe Mediterranean Area was created and headquarters were established in Thoiry, France, later tranferred to Frankfurt, Germany, when the area boundaries were changed.

The Tabernacle Choir performed in Strasbourg, June 11, 1991.

Sources: "Moments in History," *Church News*, July 31, 1971; "Church in Europe," *Ensign*, August, 1973; "Church's Second Generation Growth is Strong in France," by J Malan Heslop, *Church News*, Dec. 1, 1973; *Church News* Feb., 25, 1989; "His Faith Wouldn't Go Underground," by Alain Marie, *Ensign*, Sept. 1991; *Church News*, Sept. 7, 1991.

Stakes — 7

(Listed alphabetically as of Oct. 1, 1996.)

No.	Name	Organized	First President
Europe West Area			
1867	Bordeaux France	24 May 1992	Jacquie Simonet
1669	Lille France	17 Jan 1988	Dominique Degrave
1772	Lyon France	9 Sep 1990	Pierre-Marie Brenders
1413	Nancy France	24 Apr 1983	John Keith Bishop
1130	Nice France	14 May 1980	Joseph Michel Paya
731	Paris France	16 Nov 1975	Gerard Giraud-Carrier
1850	Paris France East	8 Mar 1992	Dominique Calmels

Missions — 3

(As of Oct. 1, 1996; shown with historical number. See MISSIONS.)

(221a) FRANCE BORDEAUX MISSION
67 Rue Furtado
33800 Bordeaux
France
Phone: (011-33-56) 91-78-11

(262) FRANCE MARSEILLE MISSION
48, Ave Robert Schumann
F-13090 Aix-en-Provence,
France
Phone: (011-33-42) 26-88-63

(6) FRANCE PARIS MISSION
23, rue du Onze Novembre
78110 Le Vesinet
France
Phone: (011-33-01)3480-0483

FRENCH GUIANA

Year-end 1995: Est. population, 145,000; Members, 200; Branches, 2; North America Southeast Area; West Indies Mission.

French Guiana is an overseas department of France located in northern South America. Charles Fortin, a native of French Guiana, was baptized in France and returned to his homeland. Rosiette Fauvette, also baptized in France, returned to French Guiana July 8, 1981, and sacrament meetings with the two were held at Brother Fortin's home in Cayenne. Brother Fortin introduced the Church to many people before his death in April 1986. By then several other members were attending services including Gerard Charpentier, who later became branch president. Meetings were then held in the home of the Masinski family until January 1987 when the metings were moved to Sister Fauvette's home in Kourou, which had a special room added for the meetings.

Elder Charles Didier of the Seventy visited on March 4, 1988, and organized a group. On Nov. 5, 1988, Serge and Christie Bonnoit of France became the first converts in French Guiana. On June 26, 1989, the Kourou Branch was divided and the Cayenne Branch created. On July 1, 1989, Michaela Papo, the first native Guyanaise convert, was baptized.

The first missionary couple was Elder Wilbur and Sister Jacqueline Wortham, followed in November 1989 by Elder A. Edward and Sister Louise P. Schmidt. The newly organized branch in Cayenne had about 23 members in 1989.

Source: "History of the Church in French Guiana," supplied by Pres. Elden L. Wood, 1994; Interview with Elder A. Edward and Louise P. Schmidt.

FRENCH POLYNESIA
(Tahiti)

Year-end 1995: Est. population, 220,000; Members, 14,000; Stakes, 5; Wards, 28; Branches, 34; Missions, 1; Districts, 2; Temples, 1; Percent LDS, 6.4, or one LDS in 16.

Located in the South Pacific midway between South America and Australia, the French Polynesia archipelago is a French overseas territory. Tahiti's population speaks French and Tahitian. Most of the French Polynesians are Protestants.

Elders Benjamin F. Grouard, Addison Pratt, Noah Rogers and Knowlton F. Hanks were sent by Joseph Smith to the Pacific Islands. They boarded the whaling ship *Timoleon* Oct. 10, 1843, and sailed around the Cape of Good Hope. During the voyage, Elder Hanks died of tuberculosis and was buried at sea. When the ship reached Tubuai, an island about 500 miles south of Tahiti, on April 30, 1844, Elder Pratt disembarked and remained to preach. He is considered the first missionary to a foreign language area in modern Church history. He baptized many people and established a branch.

Elders Grouard and Rogers went on to Tahiti, where initially they found proselyting difficult. Elder Rogers returned to the United States, while Elder Grouard visited the Tuamotu Islands and was successful, though at great personal sacrifice and effort. He was later joined by Elder Pratt, and their converts numbered in the hundreds. Elder Pratt returned to United States in 1848, and came back with his family in 1850. This promising start for the Church was halted when French government restrictions led to the mission being closed in May 1852.

Work was re-opened in 1892, with Elders Joseph W. Damron and William A. Seegmiller, who found most of the early members had fallen away. They started branches again among those who had remained stalwart, and built meetinghouses that helped speed the work.

Completion of the New Zealand Temple in 1958 was a blessing for the Tahitian Saints, who proved to be faithful attenders.

On May 23, 1963, in the worst-recorded sea disaster for Latter-day Saints in the South Pacific, 15 members of the Maupiti Branch, about 160 miles northwest of Tahiti, lost their lives when the boat in which they were returning from a meetinghouse dedication cracked up on the Maupiti reef. Elder Gordon B. Hinckley, then of the Quorum of the Twelve, visited the bereaved branch members to offer solace and comfort.

In 1964, the Church constructed an elementary school in Tahiti, and in 1972 the Tahiti Stake was organized. The Papeete Tahiti Temple was dedicated Oct. 27, 1983. Tahiti's second stake was created in 1982, and its third stake in 1990.

In 1991, a group of members from the Maupiti Branch, many of them aged, made their first trip to the new Papeete Temple.

In 1991, Saints in Takaroa in the Tuamotu islands observed the 100th anniversary of a meetinghouse built by early members, the oldest meetinghouse in the South Pacific. The imposing building took 20 years to complete and has withstood tropical storms. On Jan 6, 1991, the Takaroa Branch was divided, with a total membership of more than 300. Some of the members are descendants of those converted in the 19th century.

In 1994, members celebrated the 150th anniversary of the missionaries arriving in their islands. Closer relations with other religions resulted as Elder Russell M. Nelson of the Quorum of the Twelve was formally introduced to the territory's president and full cabinet. President Gaston Flosse and other top government leaders attended several events.

Sources: *Encyclopedic History of the Church*, by Andrew Jenson; *Histoire de l'Eglise Mormone en Polynesie Francaise de 1844 a 1982*, by Yves R. Perrin; "A bright new future dawns for Polynesian atoll and 100-year-old meetinghouse," by Kathleen C. Perrin, *Church News*, Feb. 2, 1991; "Temple Blessings broaden view of paradise," by Kathleen C. Perrin, *Church News*, Aug. 24, 1991; "150th year of Church in Tahiti," by Kathleen C. Perrin, *Church News*, May 7, 1994; "LDS note 150 years in French Polynesia," by John L. Hart, *Church News* May 14, 1994; "Sesquicentennial: 'Spiritual feast,'" by John L. Hart, *Church News*, May 21, 1996.

Stakes — 5
(Listed alphabetically as of Oct. 1, 1996.)

No.	Name	Organized	First President
Pacific Area			
1747	Paea Tahiti	15 Apr 1990	Jean Alexis Tefan
573	*Papeete Tahiti		
	‡Tahiti	14 May 1972	Raituia Tehina Tapu
1355	Pirae Tahiti	20 Jun 1982	Lysis G. Terooatea
2054	Punaauia Tahiti	28 May 1995	Tetuanui Marama Tarati
1962a	Uturoa Tahiti Raiatea	5 Dec 1993	Michel Just Doucet

Mission — 1

(As of Oct. 1, 1996; shown with historical number. See MISSIONS.)

(3) TAHITI PAPEETE MISSION
B.P. 93
Papeete, Tahiti
French Polynesia
Phone: (011-689) 50-55-21

MARTINIQUE AND GUADELOUPE

Year-end 1995: Est. population, 798,000; Members, fewer than 100; Branches, 2; North America Southeast Area; West Indies Mission.

The Caribbean Islands of Martinique and Guadeloupe are departments (states) of France. Guadeloupe has a population of 400,000. Martinique is the northernmost of the windward islands and has a population of 400,000. Martinique and Guadeloupe each have one branch with fewer than 100 members.

Andre Condoris, a young man baptized in France while serving in the military, returned to his homeland Aug. 9, 1980. He encouraged Mission Pres. Kenneth Zabriskie to send missionaries. French-speaking Elders Mark Richards, Stan Jones and David Simons were transferred from missions in Paris, France, and Brussels, Belgium, to open the work in Martinique and Guadeloupe. Joell Joseph-Agathe, a young woman baptized in France, returned to Martinique and also welcomed missionaries to the country. They arrived May 4, 1984, and held the first meeting May 6. The branch first met in Case Pilote, then Ducos and then in Chateau Boef. The branch now meets in Lamentin.

By 1985, five converts had been baptized. By 1994, the branch in Martinique had 80 members. Among the first converts in Guadeloupe were the Claire Dinane family, who soon moved to the the small island of St. Martin.

St. Martin

The island of St. Martin in the Caribbean, with 20 square miles, was part of the France Toulouse Mission when the St. Martin Branch was organized Jan. 9, 1979. The mission was discontinued a short time later, and work resumed under the West Indies Mission in 1983. Elders Thad Ariens and Victor Quarty began working in St. Martin, the administration of which is divided between two governments, French and Dutch. The Claire Dinane family, which was baptized on Guadeloupe, moved to St. Martin and helped re-open the St. Martin Branch on Jan. 31, 1984. In September 1995 Hurricane Luis and Hurricane Marilyn struck the island of St. Martin, destroying at least 80 percent of the homes on the island. Members, many who lost their homes and jobs because of damage done by the hurricanes, rallied to help each other.

Sources: Journal of Pres. Kenneth and Sister LeOra Zabriskie; "A religion, the Mormons," by Albert Albicy, *France-Antilles*, Jan. 27, 1994, courtesy Pres. J. Richard Toolson; *Manuscript history of France Toulouse Mission*, "Extensive hurricane damage, but LDS safe," Church News, Sept. 30, 1995.

NEW CALEDONIA

Year-end 1995: Est. population, 200,000; Members, 1,000; Branches, 5; Districts, 1; Percent LDS, 0.5, or one in 200; Pacific Area; Fiji Suva Mission.

An overseas territory of France, New Caledonia is a group of islands in the South Pacific.

Church activity in New Caledonia began in the 1950s as a few Tahitian members migrated to work in a nickel smelter. They were organized into the Noumea Branch on Oct. 21, 1961. However, visas for missionaries were not obtained until 1967. On July 15, 1968, the first two missionaries arrived, Harold and Jeannine Richards, and their daughter, Jacquelina.

In June 1975, administration over the island group was transferred to the Fiji Suva

Mission, and more progress was realized. The Noumea Branch was divided, and the small meetinghouse was enlarged. In July 1978, the Tontouta Branch was organized. In 1990, there were 382 members in New Caledonia.

Source: *Unto the Islands of the Sea*, by R. Lanier Britsch.

REUNION

Year-end 1995: Est. population, 666,000; Members, 600; Districts, 1; Branches, 4; Percent LDS, 0.09, or one LDS in 1,110; Africa Area; South Africa Durban Mission.

A volcanic Island in the Indian Ocean, Reunion is a department of France.

Missionary work began in Reunion in 1979 under the direction of the International Mission. In 1986, the islands were transferred to the South Africa Johannesburg Mission. Among the first members in Reunion were Alain and Danielle Chion-Hock, converted in France. On Nov. 4, 1979, Chion-Hock baptized his sister, Rose Tahi Soui Tchong, the first convert on Reunion.

Elder Joseph T. Edmunds and his wife, Ruth, were the first modern missionaries on the islands in 1979. They were joined by Elder Theo and Sister Nita Verhaarens. The first branch was established on Dec, 30, 1979. The Mascarene Islands Mission was created July 1, 1988, at which time there were 400 members on the islands with three branches in Reunion and two on the nearby island of Mauritius, which is included in the same district. Headquarters of the mission was transferred to Durban, South Africa, in January 1992.

Sources: *Church News*, Sept. 21, 1986; Feb. 7, 1987; Oct. 24, 1987; March 19, 1988; Nov. 5, 1987; Dec. 17, 1988; "Tropical Isles receive best news as mission opens," by Allen W. Palmer, *Church News*, Nov. 5, 1988; "At Home on the Island of Mauritius," by Lori Palmer, *Ensign*, March, 1991, Feb. 1986, March 1989.

GABON

Year-end 1995: Est. population, 1,157,000; Members, fewer than 100; Africa Area; Ivory Coast Abidjan Mission.

Gabon is a republic on the Atlantic coast of west central Africa where the people speak French and Bantu dialect, and follow tribal beliefs, although some are Christians. Some 100,000 expatriate Europeans, as well as Africans, live in Gabon, including about 18,000 of French ancestry.

Jerome Obounou-Mbogo, a diplomat of the the Embassy of Gabon, traveled to Utah and had a favorable visit with Elder Neal A. Maxwell of the Quorum of the Twelve and Elder Richard P. Lindsay of the Seventy in their offices as part of his visit Aug. 4-6, 1990. The Church received permission to enter the country in 1992.

Jean Mickouma, a member of the Church from Gabon, accompanied Obounou to Salt Lake City. Mickouma joined the Church several years previous while working in Washington, D.C.

Gabon was included in the Cameroon Yaounde Mission that was created on Feb. 1, 1992, and later transferred to the Ivory Coast Abidjan Mission.

Sources: *Church News*, Aug. 25, 1990; correspondence with Elder James O. Mason of the Seventy and president of Africa area, Sept. 26, 1996.

GERMANY

Year-end 1995: Est. population, 81,338,000; Members, 36,000; Stakes, 14; Wards, 88; Branches, 88; Missions, 6; Districts, 1; Temples, 2; Percent LDS, 0.04, or one LDS in 2,259.

A central European nation divided following World War II and reunited in October 1990, Germany is composed of Catholics, 45 percent, and Protestants, 44 percent.

The first Latter-day Saint into Germany was James Howard, a British convert working in Germany in 1840. He tried to preach but was unsuccessful. Elder Orson Hyde spent 10 months in Germany in 1841-42, but was unsuccessful in preaching, although he did study German and introduce the language to the Prophet Joseph Smith. He saw the translation of a tract into German completed.

Another missionary, Johan Greenig, is often credited with having established the first German branch, in Darmstadt, Germany, in 1843.

In 1849, apostles and other missionaries were sent to Scandinavia, Italy and France. Each of these mission efforts also reached into Germany. George P. Dykes, assigned to the Scandinavian Mission, went to Schleswig-Holstein, which was at that time under Danish rule, and may have baptized the first two German converts on Sept. 15, 1851. Elder John Taylor, assigned to France, went to Hamburg in October 1851, where he joined

Elder Dykes and supervised translation of the Book of Mormon into German.

Daniel Carn was called by Brigham Young to be the first mission president in Germany. Pres. Carn arrived in Hamburg April 3, 1852. By Aug. 1, he had baptized 12 and organized the Hamburg Branch. Pres. Carn was exiled but continued to supervise the German Saints, and strengthened Danish branches as well. Five additional missionaries from the United States arrived, but within four months went to England, discouraged by constantly being called before the police.

The first converts to emigrate left Germany Aug. 13, 1852. In 1854, apostates and police halted missionary work as the missionaries were imprisoned and exiled. Most of the local faithful converts emigrated and the branch was dissolved.

A prominent convert of this period from Dresden was Karl G. Maeser, who was attracted to the Church by an anti-Mormon tract. He was taught by Elder William Budge, a native of Scotland who later became president of the Logan Temple. On Oct. 21, 1855, the Dresden Branch was established with Maeser as president. The branch lasted until 1857, when opposition led to the emigration of most members of the branch, including its president.

Southern Germany's first branch was organized in Karlsruhe in 1860, under the direction of the Swiss-German Mission. During the next seven years, missionaries were halted by rigid law and frequently prevented from effective proselyting. The faltering mission was boosted in 1867 by the return of Karl G. Maeser as a missionary. More than 600 people joined the Church in the next three years. However, for the next decades, work proceeded slowly amid opposition. As the Church seemed poised for progress, World War I began. Nearly 200 missionaries left some 60 branches in Switzerland and Germany. Despite the war, most branches remained intact. By 1925, the German Mission was divided, leaving 6,125 members in the German-Austrian Mission, and 5,305 members in the Swiss-German Mission.

On Sept. 16, 1939, the First Presidency ordered missionaries to be evacuated from Germany. During World War II, more than 600 German Saints were killed, 2,500 were missing, and 80 percent were homeless.

Relief efforts by the Church, supervised by Elder Ezra Taft Benson, then of the Quorum of the Twelve, and neighboring members including the Dutch, helped sustain German members during the difficult post-war period. Missionaries returned in 1947. In the next 20 years, five stakes were organized, three missions created, and European headquarters were established for the Church in Frankfurt.

Membership in Germany in 1975 was 13,829. In 1985, it had increased to 29,900. A temple in Frankfurt was announced in 1981, and was dedicated Aug. 28, 1987. Following the publicity of the dedication and an increased missionary effort, missionary work increased in the late 1980s. The Germany Dusseldorf Mission, started in 1961 but dissolved in 1982, was re-organized in July 1990.

The German Democratic Republic, which existed following World War II until reunification in 1990, was the home of many faithful members cut off from the rest of the Church. These members continued in faithfulness despite many difficult problems, strengthening each other through fellowship. "The war cost us everything," said one. "But there was something they couldn't take — our testimonies."

Among the leaders to visit in the 1960s was Elder Thomas S. Monson, then of the Quorum of the Twelve, who promised the Saints they would eventually have every blessing of members elsewhere. A patriarch was ordained, and plans for a meetinghouse were made and completed. Later, following prayers and fasting of the members, government relations improved and German Democratic Republic leaders gave permission for a temple to be built in Freiberg. After the temple was completed, 89,789 people toured the public open house. It was dedicated June 29, 1985. Government approval was later given for missionary work to begin. On March 30, 1989, foreign missionaries arrived in the country, and on May 28, 1989, missionaries from the German Democratic Republic entered the Missionary Training Center to begin foreign missions.

The Berlin Wall separating East and West Berlin for 28 years fell Nov. 9, 1989, and the two Germanys were reunified on Oct. 3, 1990. When American military personnel were withdrawn in 1993, overall membership was reduced. In October of that year, the first offical broadcast of general conference to Germany was completed.

Elder F. Enzio Busche of the First Quorum of the Seventy was called as a General Authority on Oct. 1, 1977, and Elder Dieter Uchtdorf was sustained to the Second Quorum of the Seventy on April 2, 1994.

On Aug. 27, 1995, President Thomas S. Monson, first counselor in the First Presidency, dedicated the Goerlitz Branch meetinghouse in what had been East Germany.

President Gordon B. Hinckley conducted a Berlin Regional Conference in June 1996 as part of a five-country tour. Member participation was high with an estimated 50 percent of the members in the former German Democratic Republic attending.

Sources: *Encyclopedic History of the Church*, by Andrew Jenson; *Mormonism in Germany*, by Gilbert W. Scharffs, Deseret Book, 1970; "Memories of West German Evacuation," by J. Richard Barnes, unpublished; interview with Emil Fetzer; correspondence from Tim T. Brosnahan Jr., June 15, 1985; multiple newspaper sources, 1989-91; *Church News*, Oct. 2, 1993; April 9, 1994; Sept. 2, 1995; June 22, 1996.

Stakes — 14
(Listed alphabetically as of Oct. 1, 1996.)

No.	Name	Organized	First President
Europe Area			
334	*Berlin Germany		
	‡Berlin	10 Sep 1961	Rudi Seehagen
768	Dortmund Germany	19 Sep 1976	Klaus Fritz K. Hasse
1358	*Dresden Germany 21 Oct 1990		
	‡Freiberg German		
	Democratic Republic	29 Aug 1982	Frank Herbert Apel
577	*Duesseldorf Germany		
	‡Duesseldorf	4 Jun 1972	Frerich Jakob Emil Goerts
766	Frankfurt Germany	12 Sep 1976	Magnus R. Meiser
342	*Hamburg Germany		
	‡Hamburg	12 Nov 1961	Michael Panitsch
845	*Hanover Germany 25 Jan 1993		
	‡Hannover Germany	12 Jun 1977	Michael Schulze
466	*Kaiserslautern Germany Military		
	‡Servicemen Stake Europe		
	(W. Germany)	30 Oct 1968	Herbert B. Spencer
1475	*Leipzig Germany 21 Oct 1990		
	‡Leipzig German		
	Democratic Republic	3 Jun 1984	Hermann M. Schutze
1324	Mannheim Germany	7 Feb 1982	Baldur H.H. Stoltenberg
870	Munich Germany	23 Oct 1977	August Schubert
1305	*Neumuenstern Germany 9 Apr 1985		
	‡Hamburg Germany North	8 Nov 1981	Karl-Heinz Danklefsen
1651	Nueremnberg Germany	6 Sep 1987	Jon Paul Baker
	Servicemen		
340	*Stuttgart Germany		
	‡Stuttgart	26 Oct 1961	Hermann Moessner

Discontinued

No.	Name	Organized	First President
824	Frankfurt Germany Servicemen 1 May 1977		Kenneth Alvin Nessen
	20 Feb 1994		
765	Stuttgart Germany Servicemen 12 Sep 1976		Gary K. Spencer
	15 Nov 1992		

Missions — 6
(As of Oct. 1, 1996; shown with historical number. See MISSIONS.)

(263) GERMANY BERLIN MISSION
P.S.F. 480-418
12254 Berlin 48
Germany
Phone: (011-49-30) 711-3645

(240) GERMANY DUSSELDORF MISSION
Morsenbroicherweg 184 A
40470 Duesseldorf
Germany
Phone: (011-49-211) 611-042

(35a) GERMANY FRANKFURT MISSION
Kurfuerstenstrasse 60
60486 Frankfurt am Main
Germany
Phone: (011-49-69) 97-06-43-10

(36) GERMANY HAMBURG MISSION
Rugenbarg 7A
22549 Hamburg
Germany
Phone: (011-49-40) 804-027

(225) GERMANY LEIPZIG MISSION
Springerstrasse 16
04105 Leipzig
Germany
Phone: (011-49-341) 5646 723

(49) GERMANY MUNICH MISSION
Boschetsrieder Str. 10a
81379 Munich
Germany
Phone: (011-40-89) 724-2044

GUAM

(See also Micronesia)

Year-end 1995: Est. population, 150,000; Members, 1,400; Branches, 5; Missions, 1; Districts, 1; Percent LDS, .73, or one LDS in 136; Philippines/Micronesia Area.

The largest of the Mariana islands in the South Pacific, the self-governing U.S. territory of Guam has a population that is mostly Roman Catholic.

The first LDS members on Guam probably came as members of the armed forces during World War II. Guam branches of from 50 to 300 servicemen began functioning in 1944, acting under the Far East Mission. In 1945, four groups were organized on the island. On one occasion, they dedicated the graves of fallen LDS servicemen.

In 1951, fund-raising events by the members raised enough money to purchase land and two quonset huts, which they used for a chapel and classrooms. The facilities were dedicated in 1953 and Guam became a dependent branch of the Oahu Hawaii Stake.

In 1952, Ethel T. Kurihara, a native of Guam, became the first local Relief Society president.

Elders Danny Gallego and Paul Ray arrived on Aug. 25, 1955, and served for a year and a half.

As more LDS military personnel arrived, land for another meetinghouse was purchased. A new meetinghouse in Barrigada was dedicated March 10, 1970, and the Guam Branch became a ward. Open houses were frequently held, but few joined the Church. In May 1976, the Guam Ward was divided. The first Chamorro couple to join, Don Calvo and his wife, Maria, were baptized in May 1977. The Agat Branch was created in 1978. And in 1979, Herbert J. Leddy, the first missionary of Chamorro lineage, was called to the Tennessee Nashville Mission.

The Micronesia Guam Mission was created April 1, 1980. In June, the Guam District was created with four branches.

In 1989, selections of the Book of Mormon were translated into Chamorro, and the same year, Herbert J. Leddy became the first Chamorro member to be called as district president. Membership in 1995 was 1,400.

Sources: "A Brief History of the Micronesia-Guam Mission, 1980-1990," published by the Micronesia Guam Mission, 1990; *Unto the Islands of the Sea*, by R. Lanier Britsch.

Mission — 1

(As of Oct. 1, 1996; shown with historical number. See MISSIONS.)

(178) MICRONESIA GUAM MISSION
P.O. Box 21749 GMF
Barrigada, GU 96921
Phone: 011-671 734-3526

GUATEMALA

Year-end 1995: Est. population, 11,500,000; Members, 148,000; Stakes, 30; Wards, 171; Branches, 118; Missions, 4; Districts, 30; Temples, 1; Percent LDS, 1.3, or one LDS in 77.

The northernmost isthmus country in Central America, the Republic of Guatemala has people who speak Spanish and various Indian dialects, and are mostly Roman Catholics.

John F. O'Donnal from the Mormon colonies in Mexico moved to Central America in 1942 as an agricultural adviser of the U.S. government. He paved the way for the arrival of the first missionaries in 1947. Pres. A. L. Pierce of the Mexican Mission assigned Elders Seth G. Mattice, Earl E. Hansen, Robert B. Miller and David D. Lingard, who arrived in Guatemala on Sept. 4, 1947. They held a sacrament meeting, and with the assistance of Brother O'Donnal, visited several government leaders. A year later, on Aug. 12, Brother O'Donnal was set apart as district president. Some 66 people attended the first meeting in a rented building on Aug. 22, 1948. On Nov. 13, 1948, Pres. O'Donnal baptized his wife, Carmen, the first convert in Guatemala.

On Nov. 16, 1952, Elder Spencer W. Kimball, then of the Quorum of the Twelve, visited and organized the Central American Mission. By 1956, three branches with a membership of about 250 had been established. The Guatemala-El Salvador Mission was created Aug. 1, 1965.

When the Church received official recognition in November 1966, there were 10,000 members. On May 21, 1967, the Guatemala City Stake was organized with Udine

Falabella as president. The stake was divided in 1972, and the mission was divided in 1976, creating separate missions in Guatemala and El Salvador. By 1977, the mission had been divided again with the creation of the Guatemala Quetzaltenango Mission, with John F. O'Donnal as president. Four stakes had been established and membership was more than 17,000. A temple was announced for Guatemala City in 1981, and completed and dedicated Dec. 14-16, 1984. Called as president of the temple was John F. O'Donnal. At that time, membership was 40,000 in eight stakes and 13 districts. A third mission, the Guatemala City North, was created Jan. 1, 1988. The fourth, Guatemala Central, was created July 1, 1993. Membership in 1990 was 125,000, increasing to 148,000 in 1995.

On April 1, 1989, Elder Carlos H. Amado, former temple committee chairman, was called to the Second Quorum of the Seventy, becoming the first Guatemalan General Authority.

On Jan. 22, 1994, Elder Boyd K. Packer of the Quorum of the Twelve dedicated a new 36,400-square-foot missionary training center.

Sources: Guatemala Branch manuscript history; *Encyclopedic History of the Church* by Andrew Jenson; Guatemala City conference report, Feb. 21-22, 1977; *Church News,* Jan. 13, 1979, Nov. 10, 1966, Sept. 10, 1966, Aug. 20, 1966, June 30, 1985, Nov. 27, 1993, Feb. 12, 1994.

Stakes — 33
(Listed alphabetically as of Oct. 1, 1996.)

No.	Name	Organized	First President
Central America Area			
1611	*Chimaltenango Guatemala 22 Mar 1988 Guat. Chimaltenango		
	‡Guatemala City	26 Oct 1986	Mario Salazar Moran
1738	Coatepeque Guatemala	10 Dec 1989	Ricardo Rolando Morales
2115	Coban Guatemala	29 Oct 1995	Jorge Rafael Cabrera Galindo
1681	*Escuintla Guatemala 3 Apr 1990 Guatemala Escuintla		
	‡Guatemala City	31 Jan 1988	Enrique Leveron L.
436	*Guatemala City Guatemala		
	‡Guatemala City	21 May 1967	Udine Falabella
1618	Guatemala City Guatemala Atlantico	7 Dec 1986	Luis Alvarez Ovando
2105	Guatemala City Guatemala Bosques de San Nicolas	15 Oct 1995	Cesar Antonio de Leon
1619	Guatemala City Guatemala Central	7 Dec 1986	Armando G. Diaz L.
1768	Guatemala City Guatemala El Molino	19 Aug 1990	Jose Julio Aguilar
1620	Guatemala City Guatemala Florida	7 Dec 1986	Miguel A. Gomez L.
1704	Guatemala City Guatemala La Laguna	27 Nov 1988	Carlos Estrado Mouna M.
778	Guatemala City Guatemala Las Victorias	31 Oct 1976	Carlos Enrique Soto D.
1040	Guatemala City Guatemala Mariscal	10 Jun 1979	Samuel Ramirez Abrego
1745	Guatemala City Guatemala Milagro	15 Apr 1990	Victor Manuel Canenguez P.
2106	Guatemala City Guatemala Monserrat	15 Oct 1995	Sam Mino Galvez Orellana
1733	Guatemala City Guatemala Nimajuyu	9 Jul 1989	Rene Humberto Oliva L.
2010	Guatemla City Guatemala Palmita	15 Jan 1995	Carlos Francisco Arredondo C.
699	*Guatemala City Guatemala Utatlan 31 Oct 1976		
	‡Guatemala City Guatemala West	8 Jun 1975	Mario Antonio Lopez
2043	Guatemala City Guatemala Villa Hermosa	30 Apr 1995	Bruno Emilio Vasquez R.
1706	*Huehue Tenango Guatemala Zachuteu	19 Jun 1994	
	Huehuetenango Guatemala	4 Dec 1988	Edgar Leonardo Fuentes P.
1982	Huehuetenango	19 Jun 1994	Victor M. Rodas Corado

	Guatemala Calvario		
1937	Jalapa Guatemala	9 May 1993	Luis Daniel Aragon Aquino
1938	Malacatan Guatemala	9 May 1993	Edilzar Joel Barrios Rodriguez
1737	Mazatenango Guatemala	10 Dec 1989	Mario Antonio de Leon S.
2195	Momostenango Guatemala	12 May 1996	Francisco de J. Rosales Santiago
713	Quetzaltenango Guatemala	19 Oct 1975	Jorge Herminio Perez C.
1996	Quetzaltenango	6 Nov 1994	Melvin Enrique Recinos D.
	Guatemala El Bosque		
1497	Quetzaltenango	24 Oct 1984	Amilcar Raul Robles A.
	Guatemala West		
1168	Retalhuleu Guatemala	17 Aug 1980	Manuel Efrain Barrios F.
1955a	San Felipe Guatemala	19 Sep 1993	Mario A. Monterroso Gonzalez
1498	San Marcos Guatemala	24 Oct 1984	Abraham Raymundo Juarez C.
1785	Villa Nueva Guatemla	27 Jan 1991	Luis Gomez Garcia
2153	Zacapa Guatemala	14 Jan 1996	Arnulfo Franco Martinez

Missions — 4

(As of Oct. 1, 1996; shown with historical number. See MISSIONS.)

(287) GUA. GUATEMALA CITY
CENTRAL MISSION
8-60 Avenida Reforma
Edf. Galeria Reforma 5to,
nivel 505, Zona 9
Guatemala City, Guatemala C.A. 01909
Phone: (011-502-2) 31-86-17

(205a) GUATEMALA GUATEMALA CITY
NORTH MISSION
Apartado Postal 332-A
Guatemala City, Guatemala
Phone: (011-502-3) 34-5543

(76a) GUATEMALA GUATEMALA CITY
SOUTH MISSION
Apartado Postal 340-A
Guatemala City, Guatemala
Phone: (011-502-2) 331-8611

(152) GUATEMALA QUETZALTENANGO
MISSION
Apartado Postal 206
Quetzaltenango, Guatemala 09001
Phone: (011-502) 761-6736

GUYANA

Year-end 1995: Est. population, 724,000; Members, 500; Branches, 2; North America Southeast Area; West Indies Mission.

On the northern coast of South America, Guyana is a republic in the United Kingdom commonwealth of nations. Its population speaks English and Amerindian dialects, and is Christian, 57 percent, and Hindu, 37 percent.

Elder Benjamin Hudson and his wife, Ruth, entered Guyana Aug. 19, 1988, and held a sacrament meeting in September 1988. Among those who attended was the Majid Abdulla family, which had been baptized previously in Canada. The first convert was Indra Sukhdeo, baptized Oct. 23, 1988, by Brother Abdulla.

The Church gained recognition in February 1989, and a small branch in Georgetown was organized in March with about 23 in attendance.

In February 1990, Elder M. Russell Ballard of the Quorum of the Twelve visited the branch, and, along with missionary couples Carvel G. and Lois N. Jackson and Joseph W. and Florence B. Allen, attended services with 45 members and investigators.

Kenrick Latchmansingh was called as the first local branch president in 1990.

On Sept. 15, 1992, President Desmond Hoyte, Guyana's head of state, was a special guest at a luncheon hosted by Elder Stephen D. Nadauld of the Seventy and a member of the North America Southeast Area presidency, and Pres. J. Richard Toolson of the Trinidad Tobago Mission.

Sources: History, personal histories, other information submitted by Joseph and Florence Allen, Benjamin and Ruth Hudson, and Carvel and Lois Jackson; "Taking root in 'Land of Waters,'" *Church News*, May 18, 1991; *Church News*, Nov. 7, 1992.

HAITI

Year-end 1995: Est. population, 6,560,000; Members, 5,100; Branches, 19; Missions, 1; Districts, 2; Percent LDS, 0.07, or one person in 1,286; North America Southeast Area.

On the west side of Hispaniola Island in the West Indies, Haiti has a people who speak French and Creole. Eighty percent are Roman Catholic and 10 percent are Protestant;

voodoo is influential.

The first LDS member in Haiti was Alexandre Mourra, who traveled to Florida from his home to be taught and baptized by the missionaries on June 30, 1977. Earlier, he had read a pamphlet and the Book of Mormon in Haiti.

On July 2, 1978, 22 Haitians were baptized in Hatte-Maree, near Port-au-Prince. In September of that year, J. Frederick Templeman of the Canadian embassy arrived. He and Alexandre Mourra worked to start the first branch, which was created in October 1980 in Port-au-Prince.

Missionary work opened in Haiti in May 1980 under the direction of Pres. Glen E. Stringham of the West Indies Mission. In 1982, 12 missionaries were serving in Haiti.

A branch was created in Petion-ville on March 31, 1981, with Alexandre Mourra as president, and divided in 1982. At that time, the Haiti District was created and four missionaries were sent to open the city of Cap Hatien. Called as president was Ludner Armand. Missionaries had more referrals than they could teach. In August 1981, Fritzner Joseph, called to Puerto Rico, was the first Haitian to serve a full-time mission. In 1992, he was called as the first Haitain mission president, serving in the Haiti mission.

Selections of the Book of Mormon were translated into Haitian Creole in 1983, and that year, Haitian convert Luckner Huggins translated several hymns into Creole. Year-end membership was 485. The Haitian mission was created Aug. 4, 1984. By 1986, membership reached 1,500, and by 1988 it was 2,200. At a Port-au-Prince District conference in May 1989, 1,200 of the total 3,000 members attended district conference, and 49 men were ordained elders. Due to troubled internal conditions, foreign missionaries were removed from Haiti on Oct. 25, 1991. Haitian members rejoiced when ground was broken Aug. 18, 1996, for a temple in Dominican Republic, a more accessible location.

Sources: *Church News,* June 10, 1989, April 22, 1984, July 10, 1983, May 22, 1983, Nov. 29, 1980; Kenneth and LeOra Zabriskie journals; "Haitian Saints See Hope in Gospel," by Elizabeth and Jed VandenBerge, *Ensign,* March 1991; correspondence from Margene Stringham, Oct. 9, 1991; correspondence from Dr. Michael T. Johnson, Feb. 16, 1993; *Church News,* June 27, 1992 and March 26, 1994; "Ground broken for Caribbean's first temple," *Church News,* Aug. 24, 1996.

Mission — 1
(As of Oct. 1, 1996; shown with historical number. See MISSIONS.)

(180a) HAITI PORT-AU-PRINCE MISSION
Boite Postale 15319
Petion-ville,
Port-au-Prince, Haiti, F.W.I.
Phone: (011-509) 46-4476

HONDURAS
Year-end 1995: Est. population, 5,500,000; Members, 65,000; Stakes, 16; Wards, 89; Branches, 60; Missions, 2; Districts, 11; Percent LDS, 1.2 or one LDS in 84.

In Central America between Nicaragua and Guatemala, Honduras has a population that speaks Spanish and Indian dialects, and most are Roman Catholic.

Elders Spencer W. Kimball and Marion G. Romney, then of the Quorum of the Twelve, were instrumental in promoting missionary work in Central America. Early in the 1950s, they visited and left a tract and a copy of the Book of Mormon with a hotel waiter, who was later baptized. Missionary work in Honduras began Dec. 10, 1952, a month after the Central America Mission was opened in Guatemala City, Guatemala. Elders James T. Thorup and George W. Allen, the first two missionaries in Honduras, baptized Jose Ortega, Alicia Castanado, Corina de Bustamante, Mario A. de Chotria and Carmen B. Corina on March 21, 1953. They organized a branch in Tegucigalpa March 22, 1953. Missionaries opened San Pedro Sula on Oct. 4, 1954, and a branch was organized there in 1955. The San Pedro Sula District was organized June 4, 1961.

The first stake in Honduras was created April 10, 1977. The Honduras Mission was created Jan. 1, 1980, with 6,300 members in the country.

By the end of 1987, membership had increased to 23,000. The mission was divided July 1, 1990, and the country's ninth stake was created in September 1990. Membership in 1995 was 65,000, ten times what it was just 15 years earlier.

Sources: *Church News,* Sept. 28, 1974, April 23, 1977, Oct. 27, 1979, July 20, 1986, Nov. 30, 1986, Oct. 3, 1987, April 16, 1988, Feb. 3, 1990; *Ensign,* Aug. 1977, June 1990; Honduras

Tegucigalpa manuscript history.

Stakes — 19
(Listed alphabetically as of Oct. 1, 1996.)

No.	Name	Organized	First President
Central America Area			
2051	Choluteca Honduras	21 May 1995	Edwin Raul Ferman Zelaya
2150	Comayagua Honduras	17 Dec 1995	Carlos Armando Zepeda Hernandez
1383	Comayaguela Honduras	21 Nov 1982	Jorge Alberto Sierra B.
2097	Comayaguela Honduras Country	3 Sep 1995	Carlos Martin Velasquez Aceituno
1990	Comayaguela Honduras Torocagua	4 Sep 1994	Luis Gustavo Duarte Fonseca
2027	Danli Honduras	26 Feb 1995	Rodolfo Diaz Ortiz
1757	El Merendon Honduras	17 Jun 1990	Jose Francisco Funes R.
2061	Fesitranh Honduras	11 June 1995	Victor Guillermo Sierra Barahona
1647	La Ceiba Honduras	28 Jun 1987	Luis Alfredo Salazar V.
1601	La Lima Honduras	22 Jun 1986	Rodolfo Arguello A.
820	San Pedro Sula Honduras	10 Apr 1977	Samuel Ben-Zion Ventura
2224	San Pedro Sula Honduras El Progresso	25 Aug 1996	Sami G. Medrano Ramiriz
2168	Satelite Honduras	18 Feb 1996	Marvin Ivan Gudiel Castillo
947	Tegucigalpa Honduras	30 Jul 1978	Jose Miguel Dominguez C.
1709	Tegucigalpa Honduras Guaymuras	29 Jan 1989	Armando Antonio Sierra
2099	Tegucigalpa Honduras La Esperanza	10 Sep 1995	Jose Benigno Triminio Rodriguez
2197	Tegucigalpa Honduras Uyaca	26 May 1996	Moises Abraham Molina Guillen
1771	*Tequcigapa Honduras Toncontin‡ Toncontin Honduras	4 Sep 1994 2 Sep 1990	Ricardo Valladares B.
1732	Valle de Sula Honduras	2 Jul 1989	Solomon Jaar Welchez

Missions — 2
(As of Oct. 1, 1996; shown with historical number. See MISSIONS.)

(242) HONDURAS SAN PEDRO SULA MISSION
Apartado Postal 1970
San Pedro Sula, Honduras
Phone: (011-504) 53-48-90

(177) HONDURAS TEGUCIGALPA MISSION
Apartado Postal 556 (o 3539)
Tegucigalpa, Honduras, C.A.
Phone: (011-504) 36-66-23

HONG KONG
Year-end 1995: Est. population, 5,800,000; Members, 19,000; Stakes, 5; Wards, 24; Branches, 11; Missions, 1; Temples, 1; Percent LDS, 0.3, or one LDS in 305.

At the mouth of the Canton River on the southern coast of mainland China, Hong Kong is a British Crown Colony acquired in 1841, which reverts to China in 1997. Its people speak Cantonese and English, and are mostly Buddhists and Taoists, although small groups of Christians, Hindus and Jews also live in Hong Kong.

In 1852, Hosea Stout, James Lewis and Chapman Duncan were called to teach the gospel to the Chinese. They arrived in Hong Kong April 27, 1853. They stayed only four months, finding access to the country impossible. They may have baptized one convert.

On a world tour, Elder David O. McKay visited China in 1921. However, because of internal problems in China, a mission was not opened in Hong Kong until 1949. Hilton A. Robertson was president of the new China Mission.

The first two missionaries, H. Grant Heaton and William K. Paalani, arrived Feb. 25, 1950, and later their ranks increased to eight. Three converts were baptized Dec. 31, 1950. Soon, an average of 30 people attended weekly meetings. Work in Hong Kong was interrupted by the Korean War and did not reopen until 1955, when Grant Heaton returned as mission president of the new Southern Far East Mission. Leaders emphasized language training and translation. By November of that year, two branches were opened. On April 26, 1956, 11 converts were baptized.

Four years later, there were 91 full-time foreign and 12 full-time local missionaries serving, with eight branches and a membership of about 1,700.

Membership grew to 3,000 over the next five years, but continuing emigration took a heavy toll on both membership and leadership. A district was established in 1965. That same year, the Book of Mormon was printed in Chinese, and work began to increase. The first meetinghouse was completed in 1966. Area conferences were held in 1975 and 1980. The Hong Kong Stake was organized April 25, 1976, and the stake had a membership of 3,410. Membership remained at that number for about five years, but by 1986 had jumped to 12,200 members in four stakes.

On May 26, 1996, President Gordon B. Hinckley dedicated the Hong Kong Temple. There were seven dedicatory sessions attended by 5,000 members of the Church. The temple in Kowloon Tong on the Kowloon Peninsula serves more than 20,000 members in Hong Kong, Macao and Singapore. The temple occupies the top three floors of the building and the baptismal font is in the basement. A meetinghouse, mission office, apartments for the temple president and the mission president and a small outlet of Beehive clothing are located on the other floors.

Sources: *The Church Encounters Asia,* by Spencer J. Palmer, Deseret Book, 1970; Hong Kong, Pearl of the Orient, by Jay A. Parry, *Ensign,* August 1975; *Church News,* May 15, 1976; *Culture for Missionaries, Taiwan, Hong Kong,* Missionary Training Center, 1980; "Saints throng to area meetings in the Far East," by Dell Van Orden, *Church News,* Nov. 1, 1980; "Pearls of the Orient," by Kellene Ricks, *Ensign,* Sept. 1991; *Church News,* Feb. 5, 1994; *Church News,* May 25, 1996; "Hong Kong Temple dedicated," by Gerry Avant, *Church News,* June 1, 1996.

Stakes — 5
(Listed alphabetically as of Oct. 1, 1996.)

No.	Name	Organized	First President
Asia Area			
756	*Hong Kong Island	29 May 1980	
	‡Hong Kong	25 Apr 1976	Shiu-Tat Sheldon Poon
1141	Homg Kong Kowloon East	20 Mar 1994	
	*Hong Kong Kowloon	11 Nov 1984	
	‡Kowloon Hong Kong	29 May 1980	Patrick Chung-hei Wong
1502	*Hong Kong Tolo Harbour	20 Mar 1994	
	Hong Kong Kowloon North	11 Nov 1984	Fu Man Yau
1977	Hong Kong Kowloon West	20 Mar 1994	Poon Yin Sang Peter
1503	Hong Kong New Territories	11 Nov 1984	Johnson Ma

Mission — 1
(As of Oct. 1, 1996; shown with historical number. See MISSIONS.)

(44a) HONG KONG MISSION
#2 Cornwall Street
Kowloon Tong, Kowloon
Hong Kong
Phone: (011-852) 2857-1098

HUNGARY

Year-end 1995: Est. population, 10,318,000; Members: 2,100; Branches, 20; Missions, 1; Districts, 2; Europe East Area.

In east central Europe, Hungary's population speaks Hungarian (Magyar), and is Roman Catholic, 67 percent, and Protestant, 25 percent.

The first missionary effort into Hungary was made by Elders Thomas Biesinger and Paul E.B. Hammer in Vienna, in what was then in the dual sovereignty of Austria-Hungary. Elder Biesinger labored in Prague, but was eventually banished from the country.

Mischa Markow, a native of Hungary who was converted near Constantinople in 1887, preached the gospel in Belgium, Hungary, Romania, Bulgaria, Germany, Turkey, Russia and Serbia, which later became part of Yugoslavia. He visited Hungary the year of his baptism to preach to his parents, but they were not converted. He immigrated to America, and returned as a missionary in about May 1899 and preached in Serbia until banished to Hungary three months later. In about July 1899, he was banished from Hungary after being imprisoned in solitary confinement. He went to Temesvar, Hungary, Sept. 3, 1900. He and his companion, Elder Hyrum Lau, were soon ordered to surrender their passports. In the few days afterward, while they could legally remain in the country, they worked feverishly, and the day before they were banished they baptized 12 people and ordained leaders to watch over a branch of 31 people.

Missionaries worked among German-speaking Hungarians in 1908, and the Church received legal recognition in 1911. However, missionary work among Hungarian-speaking people was not successful, and the area was closed by March 10, 1913.

The Book of Mormon was translated into Hungarian in 1933, but selections were not published until 1979.

In modern times, the Church received legal recognition from Hungary on June 24, 1988. A fireside on that day was attended by Elder Russell M. Nelson of the Quorum of the Twelve, as well as a congregation of 85 people. Two converts were baptized the next day. The first meetinghouse in Hungary was dedicated Oct. 17, 1989, by President Thomas S. Monson, second counselor in the First Presidency.

Yuri and Ludmilla Terebenin and their daughter Anna of Leningrad, then in the Soviet Union, heard about the Church during a trip to Budapest, Hungary, where they were baptized on July 1, 1989. They were among the first converts in Russia. One of Lithuania's first converts, Irute Meskiene of Vilnius, also heard the gospel preached in Szeged, Hungary, where she was later baptized.

The Hungary Budapest Mission was created from the Austria Vienna East Mission on June 1, 1990. At the time there were some 75 members in one district. The Tabernacle Choir performed in Budapest's elegant Opera House in June 1991 to an enthusiastic audience, which gave it eight curtain calls.

In 1992, the Hungary-based Democracy After Communism Foundation helped sponsor a major international consultation on religious liberty and ethnic rights for eastern European nations May 17-20, and it was attended by Elder Dallin H. Oaks of the Quorum of the Twelve.

In June 1996, Elder Jeffrey R. Holland of the Quorum of the Twelve and Elder Dennis B. Neuenschwander of the Seventy met with nearly 1,000 members in an all-mission conference in Budapest. The two General Authorities were interviewed by Hungarian national television. They met with LDS service personnel in Taszar.

Sources: *Millennial Star*, March 13, 1913; "Hungary — Then and Now," by Kahlile Mehr, *Ensign*, June 1990; German and Swiss mission manuscript histories; *Church News*, June 22, 1991, May 30, 1992, June 27, 1992, and Aug. 24, 1996.

Mission — 1
(As of Oct. 1, 1996; shown with historical number. See MISSIONS.)

(243) HUNGARY BUDAPEST MISSION
H-1029 II Ker.
Kinizsi Pal Utca 37
Budapest, Hungary
Phone: (011-36-1) 176-5174

ICELAND

Year-end 1995: Est. population, 266,000; Members, 200; Branches, 3; Districts, 1; Percent LDS, 0.07, or one LDS in 1,330; Europe North Area; Denmark Copenhagen Mission.

Located between Scandinavia and Greenland, the constitutional Republic of Iceland has a people who speak Icelandic and who are 95 percent Evangelical Lutheran.

Converted in Denmark while learning trades, Thorarinn Thorason and Gudmund Gudmundson of Iceland were baptized in 1851. They returned to Iceland that year and began preaching on Westmann Island. A number believed, and Benedikt Hanson and his wife were among the first baptized by Thorason. Unfortunately, Thorason drowned a short time later and Gudmundson, who had been ordained a teacher, was not authorized to baptize. He continued his work, but not until 1853 did other missionaries receive permission to enter and assist him. Missionaries and members endured severe persecution. Johan P. Lorentzen arrived and ordained Gudmundson an elder, baptized several more converts and organized a branch June 19, 1853. Soon after, nearly all the members immigrated to America.

In 1873, Elders Magnus Bjarnason and Loptur Johnson of the Scandinavian Mission returned to Westmann Island and baptized a few more converts and reorganized a branch. In 1874, 11 converts immigrated to America. Missionary work continued in 1875 with the return of Samuel Bjarnason and Thordar Dedikson. In 1879, a pamphlet was translated, printed in Denmark, and distributed in Iceland. Small emigrating companies left Iceland throughout the early 1880s. Many of the Icelandic members settled in Spanish Fork, Utah. An Icelandic Mission was organized for a short time, from about

1894 until after 1900. Proselyting in Iceland was discontinued in 1914.

Missionary work, under the direction of the Denmark Copenhagen Mission, resumed in Iceland in 1975, building on the efforts of LDS servicemen who had been stationed in Iceland. A branch was organized on a military base at Keflavik with 130 servicemen and their families. Byron and Melva Geslison, with their twin sons, returned missionaries David and Daniel, were called from Utah to re-open the work. In two years, some 40 Icelanders were baptized and a branch was organized at Reykjavik Aug. 8, 1976, with about 10 members. A year later, it had grown to 40 members. A meetinghouse was dedicated in 1981 by Elder David B. Haight of the Quorum of the Twelve.

The Book of Mormon was translated into Icelandic in 1980, and the other standard works followed. By 1986, membership had reached 180.

Sources: *Encyclopedic History of the Church*, by Andrew Jenson; Denmark Mission manuscript history, "Fire and Ice," by Flint J. Stephens, *New Era*, Dec. 1981; correspondence from D.B. Timmins; "Gospel touches remote Iceland," by Tod Harris, *Church News*, Aug. 6, 1994.

INDIA

Year-end 1995: Est. population, 937,000,000; Members, 1,800; Missions, 1; Districts, 5; Branches, 20; Asia Area.

Occupying the Indian subcontinent in south Asia, India is a federal republic with a population that speaks 16 languages including the official Hindi and associate official English, and is Hindu, 83 percent; Muslim, 11 percent; Christian, 3 percent; and Sikh, 2 percent.

Church members Benjamin Richey and George Barber, British sailors converted in 1849, visited Calcutta, India, in 1850 and shared their testimonies. They were followed in 1851 by Elder Joseph Richards, who also preached in Calcutta. He baptized James Patrick Meik, Mary Ann Meik, Matthew McCune and Maurice White, and set them apart as missionaries. Soon after, White was appointed to preside over the branch, and he baptized Anna, a native. The little branch was depleted by emigration, but additional missionaries arrived and baptized a few more people, and a small meetinghouse was built.

In 1853, additional missionaries took the gospel message to Madras, Bombay, Rangoon, Karatchi, Poona and other areas, and several small branches were established.

However, when these missionaries returned to Utah in 1858, some of the converts also emigrated. Although other missionaries and conversions followed, the India Mission was not considered a successful one. At least one branch existed through 1903. Missionaries were not successful in learning the Hindustani, Tamil, Telugu or other native languages.

In 1954, S. Paul Thiruthuvadoss, an accountant for a cement company in Coimbatore in southern India, found an LDS tract, and through it found the Church. He was not baptized until Feb. 7, 1965, when missionaries from the Southern Far East Mission visited. His baptism was performed by mission Pres. Jay A. Quealy Jr., grandson of early India convert Matthew McCune.

Thiruthuvadoss held schools for underprivileged children, and shared the message of the gospel with many people. In 1967, Pres. G. Carlos Smith of the Singapore Mission visited and baptized 24 of the people prepared by Thiruthuvadoss. As of 1980, the Coimbatore branch had 225 members and regular services are conducted in Tamil.

In Delhi, northern India, Baldwin Das was baptized by Charles Redford in 1968, and was joined by the Roshan Juriel family. In 1972, Maureen Das was the first to serve a mission from India. In 1981, government regulations allowed a missionary couple, Horace and Edna Hayes, to establish a branch. A visit by the BYU Young Ambassadors in 1983, and the arrival of LDS families involved in diplomatic service strengthened the branch. Later, the branch was divided for Indian and American members. By 1987, a congregation of 50 met in the Indian branch with all the auxiliaries functioning.

In 1977, Edwin and Elsie Dharmaraju of Hyderabad, India, living in Samoa, were converted to the Church. They received permission to return to India and teach the gospel to their family. They arrived in December 1978, and on Dec. 27, eighteen members of their family were baptized. A branch was organized with Victor David as president. In 1981, the Dharmarajus delivered a 700-page manuscript to the Church, the Book of Mormon translated into Telegu by her father, the Rev. P. Sreenivasam. This translation of the Book of Mormon was printed in 1982, as was another full translation in Hindi, and translated selections of the Book of Mormon in Tamil.

In the 1980s, the Church microfilmed genealogical records in India. In December 1992, Elaine L. Jack, Relief Society general president, visited branches in Bangalore and reported that members met in homes three times a month and in a rented building on the fourth Sunday.

The India Bangalore Mission was created Jan. 1, 1993. Gucharan Singh Gill, a native of India, was called as mission president. At that time, India had 1,150 members in 13 branches.

Sources: *Encyclopedic History of the Church* by Andrew Jenson; Church History in North India, report by Baldwin Das and Douglas Rose, Aug. 1987; Testimony of S. Paul Thiruthuvadoss; *The Church in Asia,* by J. Spencer Palmer, Deseret Book, 1970; "India fills genealogy link," by William B. Smart, *Church News,* Jan. 9, 1988; *Church News,* Dec. 19, 1992; "Asia Area: Welcome mat is out in several countries," by Sheridan R. Sheffield, *Church News,* June 19, 1993.

Mission — 1

(As of Oct. 1, 1996; shown with historical number. See MISSIONS.)

(277) INDIA BANGALORE MISSION
1117, 13th Cross
Indiranagar, Stage II
Bangalore 560 038
India
Phone: (011-91-80) 525-3823

INDONESIA

Year-end 1995: Est. population, 204,000,000; Members, 5,000; Missions, 1; Districts, 3; Branches, 20, Asia Area.

An archipelago of more than 13,500 islands, including Java, one of the world's most densely populated areas, Indonesia is a republic whose population speaks Bahasa, Indonesian (the official language), Javanese and up to 100 other Austronesian languages.

Six missionaries entered Indonesia on Jan. 5, 1970, and began work on Jan. 20. The Jakarta Branch was organized Feb. 15, 1970, and first converts were baptized March 29, 1970. Door-to-door tracting was halted by the government in April 1970, but it resumed in May after the Church was granted clearance. The Church was officially recognized Aug. 11, 1970.

The first missionaries to the city of Solo in Central Java arrived on June 27, 1972. After only a few weeks, they had more than 100 people in attendance at their English classes and were also teaching English on radio, but proselyting was limited due to government regulations.

During the next few years, branches were organized throughout Java, where the work was performed. The Indonesia Jakarta Mission was organized July 1, 1975. By 1977, when the Book of Mormon was published in Indonesian, membership reached 1,200 and local missionaries carried on the work.

However, difficulties with missionary visas and government limitations continued to restrict missionaries. Indonesia's difficult internal religious conflicts and activities by others against missionary work made progress difficult.

On Aug. 1, 1978, the government issued restrictions on proselyting.

The mission was discontinued Jan. 1, 1981. In 1982, some 30 local missionaries maintained efforts and were finding success. An Indonesian, Effian Kadarusman, was called as mission president and the mission was reopened July 1, 1985. A new mission home was dedicated July 24, 1988, but all foreign missionaries were restricted from the country on Nov. 26, 1988, and the Indonesia Mission was consolidated with the Singapore Mission on July 1, 1989.

In 1993, Dr. Dean and Sister Elan Belnap entered Indonesia to work with the medical school in Jakarta, and help with the local branches. Their service helped raise the Church's profile. The Indonesia Jakarta Mission was re-opened July 1, 1995; districts are in Jakarta, Surabaya and Kurakarta.

Highly illustrated cloth batiks created by Indonesian members regularly contributed to art displays at the Museum of Church History and Art in the 1990s.

The Hong Kong Temple, dedicated on May 26, 1996, serves Indonesian members.

Sources: *Spreading the Gospel in Indonesia: Organizational Obstacles and Opportunities,* a university paper by Garth N. Jones, Winter 1982; *Church News,* Aug. 3,

1991; "Asia Area: Welcome mat is out in several countries," by Sheridan R. Sheffield, *Church News,* June 19, 1993; *Church News,* June 19, 1993; *Deseret News,* May 27, 1996.

IRELAND

(See also Northern Ireland, under United Kingdom)

Year-end 1995: Est. population, 3,600,000; Members, 2,300; Stakes, 1; Wards, 4; Branches, 11; Missions, 1; Districts, 1; Percent LDS, 0.06, or one LDS in 1,565; Europe North Area.

The island of Ireland lies in the Atlantic Ocean, west of Great Britain. It is a parliamentary republic where English is the dominant language, but Irish (Gaelic) is also spoken. The population is Roman Catholic, 95 percent, and Anglican, 3 percent. Northern Ireland, part of the United Kingdom, has a population of 1.6 million, of whom about half are Protestant.

The first missionary to Ireland was Reuben Hedlock, who arrived in Belfast in May 1840, but stayed only three days before sailing to Paisley. He was followed on July 28 by Apostle John Taylor, who was accompanied by James McGuffie and William Black, a native Irishman. A non-member Irishman, Thomas Tait (or Tate), also accompanied them. More than 600 people heard Elder Taylor preach that evening in Newry. On July 31, as the party walked between towns and arrived at a lake called Loughbrickland, Tait was baptized, becoming Ireland's first convert.

Two months later, Elder Theodore Curtis arrived in Ireland and established a branch of 35 in Hillsborough. A second branch, organized in Crawfordsburn, had 22 members by July 21, 1841.

In 1842, many of the 71 members in Ireland emigrated. Membership declined over the next years, despite renewed efforts in 1843. The 1845-47 famine prompted the emigration of most of the remaining 51 members.

Early missionaries remarked that proselyting was slowed by opposition, particularly that of landholders who threatened sharecroppers with expulsion if they welcomed LDS missionaries. However, historians believe that a good number of the British converts during the 1840s and '50s were expatriated Irish.

In the early 1850s, missionaries established a few branches, but in 1853 most missionaries left for America. Another group arrived in 1854, found new converts and saw membership increase from some 20 to 210 in 1855, and to nearly 300 in 1856. However, the 1857 "Utah War" led to the recall of the missionaries and the branches were unsupervised for four years. Missionary work was discontinued in 1867.

In 1884, a few native Irish members were called as missionaries in their homeland. They found some success despite opposition and established a branch in Belfast that by the end of 1884 had 50 members. Political unrest prompted most of the converts to emigrate. By 1900, about 90 had left Ireland for Utah.

However, a branch grew up in Dublin after 1900, made up of Germans. By 1920, there were about 225 members in the Belfast Conference (District) and 60 in and around Dublin.

The Emerald Isle was divided in 1949, amid continued unrest, into an independent Ireland and Northern Ireland, which remained under the British government.

As part of the 150th anniversary of the Church in the British Isles in 1987, markers were dedicated at the site of the first baptism and at the birthplace in Dublin of Elder Charles A. Callis of the Council of the Twelve, once president of the Irish Conference while a missionary about 1894. Membership in 1990 was 1,800.

Indicative of the strength of the Church, Pres. Van F. Dunn noted in 1994 that seven missionaries from Ireland were serving at the same time in the England London South Mission.

President Gordon B. Hinckley visited Ireland Sept. 1-2, 1995, the first Church president to do so since President David O. McKay in August 1953. He spoke to members from the newly created Dublin Ireland Stake, Cork Ireland District and Belfast Northern Ireland Stake.

Sources: *Encyclopedic History of the Church,* by Andrew Jenson; "Emerald Isle Hosts Beauty, Friendliness," by Gerry Avant, *Church News,* Feb. 25, 1978; "The Saints in Ireland," by Orson Scott Card, *Ensign,* Feb. 1978; *Church News,* July 6, 1974, Dec. 1, 1985; "Markers tell where history was made," by Dell Van Orden and Gerry Avant, *Church News,* Aug. 1, 1987, and *Church News,* Aug. 8, 1987; *Church News,* Aug. 27, 1994; "Visit to Ireland caps 'whirlwind trip' " by Mike Cannon, *Church News,* Sept. 9, 1995.

(Listed alphabetically as of Oct. 1, 1996.)

No. Name	Organized	First President
Europe North Area		
2034 Dublin Ireland	12 Mar 1995	Liam Gallagher

Mission — 1

(As of Oct. 1, 1996 shown with historical number. See MISSIONS.)

(70) IRELAND DUBLIN MISSION
The Willows, Finglas Road
Glasnevin, Dublin 11, Ireland
Phone: (011-353-1) 830-6899

ITALY

Year-end 1996: Est. population, 58,262,000; Members, 17,000; Stakes, 2; Wards, 9; Branches, 109; Missions, 4; Districts, 16; Percent LDS, 0.03, or one person in 3,427.

In southern Europe jutting into the Mediterranean Sea, the boot-shaped Republic of Italy has a population that speaks Italian, and is nearly all Roman Catholic.

The first missionaries in Italy were Elders Lorenzo Snow of the Quorum of the Twelve, Joseph Toronto and Thomas B.H. Stenhouse. They arrived in Genoa, Italy, on June 25, 1850. They traveled to the Piedmont Valley to work among a group of Protestants of French origin called the Waldenses. They were joined there by Elder Jabez Woodard.

On Oct. 27, 1850, Elder Snow baptized Jean Antoine Box at La Tour. Other baptisms followed and three branches of the Church were organized in Angrogne, St. Germain and St. Bartholomew, all in Piedmont. Tracts were published in the French language for the Waldenses. The Book of Mormon was published in 1852. By 1855, 50 members had immigrated to America and membership was 64.

Proselyting outside the Piedmont Valley was very difficult, due to a great deal of anti-Mormon activity. Missionaries labored with little success in Italy, departing for Switzerland in 1857. Elder Daniel B. Hill Richards tried to re-open the work in 1900, but was refused legal permission.

In 1965, the Church was given legal status and missionary work resumed. The first modern convert of Italy was Leopoldo Larcher, who later served as the first Italian mission president and as regional representative. On Aug. 2, 1966, the Italian Mission was re-established.

By that time, there were two Italian branches and seven combined servicemen and Italian branches, and a membership of 66. By 1978, membership had increased to 7,271, and the nation had four missions. Italy's first stake was created June 7, 1981, in Milan, under the direction of Pres. Mario Vaira.

Local missionaries and leaders contributed to increased growth in the 1980s. By mid-1985, membership increased to 12,000. Membership in 1990 was 14,000.

A milestone was reached May 12, 1993, when Italy formally granted legal status to the Church for the first time. The application to have the Italian government officially recognize the Church was filed four to five years earlier, underwent several reviews and an investigation, and was signed by Italy's president, Oscar Luigi Scalfaro, on Feb. 22, 1993. Italian law does not require legal status for proselyting.

On Dec. 19, 1993, a group of 50 missionaries was invited to sing on Vatican Radio from St. Peter's Basilica at the Vatican.

During May 1996, the District of Turin celebrated the 30-year anniversary of the Church being organized in the northwestern area of Italy with an emphasis on missionary work. Activities included opening and closing ceremonies and a presentation by the BYU Lamanite Generation.

Sources: *Millennial Star,* Dec. 15, 1850; *Encyclopedic History of the Church,* by Andrew Jenson; *The Scriptural Allegory,* by Dr. Daniel B. Richards, Magazine Publishing Company, Salt Lake City, Utah, April 1931; *History of the French Mission of the Church, 1850-1960,* by Gary Ray Chard, master's thesis at Utah State University, 1965; *Church News,* June 12, 1993; *Church News,* Jan. 15, 1994.

(Listed alphabetically as of Oct. 1, 1996)

No.	Name	Organized	First President
	Europe West Area		
1274	Milan Italy	7 Jun 1981	Mario Vaira
1556	Venice Italy	15 Sep 1985	Claudio E. Luttmann

Missions — 4

(As of Oct. 1, 1996 shown with historical number. See MISSIONS.)

(158) ITALY CATANIA MISSION
Via Corsaro 84 (Parco Inglese)
95030 S. Agata Li Battiati (Ct.), Italy
Phone: (011-39-95) 411009

(98) ITALY MILAN MISSION
Via Gramsci No. 13
20090 Opera (MI), Italy
Phone: (011-39-2) 5760-0860

(244) ITALY PADOVA MISSION
Via Caldonazzo, #10
35030 Selvazzano Dentro (PD), Italy
Phone: (011-39-49) 805-5629

(74) ITALY ROME MISSION
C.P. 11/282
I-00414 Rome. Italy
Phone: (011-39-6)827-2708

IVORY COAST

Year-end 1995: Est. population, 16,300,000; Members, 2,800; Missions, 1; Districts, 2; Branches, 14; Africa Area.

Located on the Gulf of Guinea on the west coast of Africa next to Ghana, Ivory Coast has a population that speaks tribal languages and French and belongs to tribal religions and Islam.

Isolated LDS families lived in Ivory Coast in the 1970s and earlier, including Baernard and Cherry Silver and Terry and Bobby Broadhead.

Lucien Yapi Affoue and his wife, Agathe, joined the Church in 1980 in Lyon, France, where he was a student. They were sealed in the Swiss Temple and served in the Bordeaux Branch. They returned to Abidjan in March 1984, and eventually helped establish four branches. They were joined by Philippe Assard and his wife, Anelise Noetzel Assard, and their two children in 1986. There were 16 members in the country in 1987.

In 1988, the Church donated $60,000 to Rotary International for polio vaccinations of children in Ivory Coast.

The Affoue family moved to Bouake, where another branch was established on Oct. 4, 1988. The Abidjan Branch was created on June 1, 1989.

The first missionaries to Ivory Coast were Elder Barnard Stewart Silver and his wife, Cherry, who arrived in April 1988. Elder Robert M. and Sister Lola Walker arrived in April 1989, and introduced the gospel to some 100 members. A U.S. expatriate, Douglas Arnold, was called as the first district president in October 1989.

The first district conference was held March 10-11, 1990, in Abidjan with about 200 people from the branches of Abidjan and Boauke. At the time, local records indicated a membership of 350. Two missionary couples from the Ghana Accra Mission continued baptizing about 30-35 a month. The Plateau Dokui Branch, Ivory Coast's fourth, was organized at the conference. At the time, 35 men held the Melchizedek Priesthood.

The Church received legal recognition on April 19, 1991.

Eighteen local elders were called to serve in the mission in December 1991. On June 30, 1992, Ivory Coast was transferred from the Ghana Accra Mission to the Cameroon Yaounde Mission. Mission Pres. Robert L. Mercer moved the Cameroon Yaounde Mission headquarters to Ivory Coast and this became the Ivory Coast Abidjan Mission on May 1993.

The mission concentrated its resources in the Abidjan area to establish a center of the Church here for French-speaking Africa.

In 1993, Mayor Alan Dawson of Midrand, South Africa, a Church member, initiated a sister city partnership with Yamoussoukro, Ivory Coast. In 1995, Sister Jennie Kallunki, wife of mission Pres. J. Thomas Kallunki, directed a sister missionaries' training conference, the first-ever such conference in Ivory Coast, which included workshops on community service, strengthening branches and teaching about the Book of Mormon.

Early in 1996, the symbolic "first stone," a ceremonial start of construction, was held for the first meetinghouse in Ivory Coast. More than 60 members and friends gathered for the ceremony for the Yopugon meetinghouse, which was to hold two branches and the offices of the Abidjan District presidency.

Sources: "When a Woman Is Alone," by Cherry Silver, *Ensign*, June 1978; *Church News*, Oct. 17, 1987, June 25, 1988, June 10, 1989, April 28, 1990; correspondence from Chirley Roundy Arnold, April 19-23, 1991; *Church News*, Dec. 4, 1993; correspondence from the Ivory Coast Abidjan Mission, March 1994; *Church News*, Dec. 30, 1995; Feb. 24, 1996.

Mission — 1
(As of Oct. 1, 1996; shown with historical number. See MISSIONS.)

(271) IVORY COAST ABIDJAN MISSION
06 B.P. 1077
Abidjan 06
Cate d'Ivoire
West Africa, Ivory Coast
Phone: (011-225) 412933

JAMAICA

Year-end 1995: Est. population, 2,575,000; Members, 3,300; Districts, 2; Branches, 15; Missions, 1; Percent LDS, 0.1, or one LDS in 780; North America Southeast Area.

Located in the West Indies, south of Cuba, Jamaica is an independent state where English and Jamaican Creole are spoken, and 70 percent of the people are Protestants.

The first LDS elder on Jamaica was Harrison Sager, who preached here briefly in 1841. Twelve years later, Elders James Brown, Aaron F. Farr, Alfred B. Lambson, Darwin Richardson and Elijah Thomas returned to preach, but found a great deal of antagonism and stayed only six weeks.

In modern times, two LDS families, the John L. Whitfields and Jay P. Bills families, began holding meetings in Mandeville, and the Mandeville Branch was created March 22, 1970. One of the first converts was Victor Nugent and his family, baptized Jan. 20, 1974. As new converts, the Nugents remained faithful when the branch's priesthood leaders moved away. They introduced the gospel to soccer star Errol Tucker and his family, who helped them maintain the branch. Full-time missionaries began work again in Jamaica in November 1978, under the direction of Pres. Richard L. Millett of the Florida Ft. Lauderdale Mission. By 1983, membership had increased to 300, and by 1985, to 520.

The first Jamaican branch president was Joseph Hamilton. Vaughn and Mary Soffe microfilmed the statistical records of Jamaica in 1982. Seminary began in Jamaica in the mid-1980s and by 1989, 141 students were taking seminary. Membership in 1990 was 1,900.

Sources: *Millennial Star*, April 2, 1853; *Encyclopedic History of the Church*, by Andrew Jenson; "A Trusted Friend," by Ronald W. Walker, *Church News*, March 17, 1979; Kenneth and LeOra Zabriskie journals; "Jamaicans nurture new gospel tradition," by Wanda Kenton Smith, *Church News*, Jan. 29, 1984; *Church News*, Aug. 28, 1976; Nov. 29, 1980; April 22, 1984, Nov. 24, 1985, May 27, 1989.

CAYMAN ISLANDS

In September 1985, missionaries from the West Indies Mission opened work in the Grand Cayman Islands, located in the Caribbean Sea some 400 miles south of Florida. One branch with fewer than 100 members is organized here. It was created on Nov. 25, 1981.

Mission — 1
(As of Oct. 1, 1996; shown with historical number. See MISSIONS.)

JAMAICA KINGSTON MISSION
Box 2316
Kingston 8, Jamaica, West Indies
Phone: (809) 924-0116

JAPAN

Year-end 1995: Est. population, 125,507,000; Members, 106,000; Stakes, 25; Wards, 130; Branches, 163; Missions, 9; Districts, 21; Temples, 1; Percent LDS, 0.08, or one LDS in 1,184.

Off the eastern coast of Asia, Japan is a parliamentary democracy with people who are primarily Buddhists and Shintoists.

The history of the Church in Japan dates back to the turn of the century when Elder Heber J. Grant of the Quorum of the Twelve, and missionaries Horace S. Ensign, Louis A. Kelsch and Alma O. Taylor arrived in the country Aug. 12, 1901.

Under Elder Grant's direction, the first Church mission was established in Asia with headquarters in Tokyo. The first baptism came March 8, 1902, when Elder Grant baptized Hijime Nakazawa, a former Shinto priest, in Tokyo Bay. A second baptism came on March 10, 1902, when Saburo Kikuchi was baptized.

Elder Taylor began translating the Book of Mormon into Japanese in 1904, and continued that work for 51/2 years, while he served as president of the Japanese Mission. The book was printed in October 1909.

Missionary work came to a halt in 1924 when President Heber J. Grant, then president of the Church, closed the mission to await a more "favorable time," which came following World War II. Fujiya Nara was one of the converts who saw the missionaries off, later being appointed a presiding elder over the small group that remained. He visited them and published a newsletter, "Shuro" (Palm). In 1926 the MIA was organized. The Japan Mission was re-opened in 1937 with headquarters in Honolulu, Hawaii. Hilton Robertson was named president. Then in 1947, Edward L. Clissold was called to preside over the Japan Mission and in 1948 was given permission to return to Japan to do missionary work. He found a group of about 50 meeting with Brother Nara each Sunday. The first five missionaries arrived in June that year.

During the time the mission was closed, LDS servicemen had prepared the way for proselyting by baptizing Tatsui Sato on July 7, 1946. His wife, Chiyo, and son, Yasuo, were also baptized. One serviceman, Boyd K. Packer, later of the Quorum of the Twelve, baptized Sister Sato. This was the first baptism of local members in Japan in more than 20 years and was the beginning of a new era for the Church in the Far East.

Sato re-translated the Book of Mormon, the Doctrine and Covenants, the Pearl of Great Price, and other important works. Work went forward, and the Japanese Mission was divided in July 1955 to form the Northern Far East and the Southern Far East missions.

The first Mormon meetinghouse in Asia, housing the Tokyo North Branch, was dedicated by Elder Gordon B. Hinckley, then of the Quorum of the Twelve, on April 26, 1964.

Hawaii native Adney Y. Komatsu was called as mission president in 1965, the first mission president of Japanese ancestry. Ten years later, in April 1975, he was called to be the first General Authority of Japanese ancestry. The first General Authority from Japan was Elder Yoshihiko Kikichi, who was called to the First Quorum of the Seventy in 1977.

The first stake of the Church in Asia, the Tokyo Stake, was organized on March 15, 1970, with Kenji Tanaka as president.

The Japan Nagoya Mission was formed from the Japan Mission and the Japan Central Mission in 1973.

Plans for the Tokyo Temple were announced in August 1975, and the completed building was dedicated on Oct. 27, 1980. The Japan Okinawa Mission was created in 1985. In 1991, the Asia North Area was created and the area offices were established in Tokyo.

The Church provided extensive assistance after a major earthquake devastated the Kobe/Osaka area in the predawn hours of Jan. 17, 1995. The Kobe Ward meetinghouse and adjoining Japan Kobe Mission Home were used as shelters for members and others. One member of the Church died in the earthquake and 35 LDS families were left homeless.

President Gordon B. Hinckley presided over six meetings in Japan May 17-21, 1996, during an extended visit to Asia. It was the first visit of a Church president to Japan in 16 years. He spoke to members and missionaries in Tokyo, Osaka, Fukuoka and Naha, Okinawa. He also met with the U.S. ambassador to Japan, Walter Mondale, and with the media.

Sources: *Encyclopedic History of the Churc,* by Andrew Jenson; *A History of the Church in Japan from 1948 to 1980,* by Terry G. Nelson, a BYU thesis August 1986; "Kyoto, the cultural center of Japan," by Sheridan Sheffield, *Church News,* June 22, 1991; "Growth reflected in Asia areas," by Sheridan Sheffield, *Church News,* Nov. 16, 1991; "The Blossoming of the Church in Japan," by R. Lanier Britsch, *Ensign,* Oct. 1992; "Fujiya Nara, Twice a Pioneer," by Yukikon Konn, *Ensign,* April 1993; *Church News,* Jan. 28, 1995; "President Hinckley visits Japan for a fast-paced three days," *Church News,* May 25, 1996.

Stakes — 25
(Listed alphabetically as of Oct. 1, 1996.)

No.	Name	Organized	First President

Asia North Area

No.	Name	Organized	First President
1901	Abiko Japan	13 Sep 1992	Shigejiro Akamatsu
1018	Fukuoka Japan	20 Apr 1979	Yoshizawa Toshiro
1271	Hiroshima Japan	31 May 1981	Satoshi Nishihara
1120	Kobe Japan	19 Mar 1980	Keiichi Mizuno
1874	*Kyoto Japan 25 Apr 1993		
	‡Kyoto Japan North	31 May 1992	Kaatsuichiro Fukuyama
1197	Machida Japan	26 Oct 1980	Koichi Aoyagi
919	Nagoya Japan	10 May 1978	Masaru Tsuchida
1203	Nagoya Japan West	2 Nov 1980	Take Shi Nakamura
1195	Naha Okinawa Japan	23 Oct 1980	Kensei Nagamine
1404	Okayama Japan	20 Mar 1983	Akira Watanabe
586	*Osaka Japan		
	‡Osaka (Japan)	12 Sep 1972	Noboru Kamio
1873	Osaka Japan East	31 May 1992	Ryochi Tanaka
872	Osaka Japan North	30 Oct 1977	Noboru Kamio
1328	Osaka Japan Sakai	17 Mar 1982	Hiroshi Takayoshi
949	Sapporo Japan	13 Aug 1978	Geiji Katanuma
1154	Sapporo Japan West	29 Jun 1980	Bin Kikuchi
1202	Sendai Japan	2 Nov 1980	Shigenori Funayama
1255	Shizuoka Japan	21 Apr 1981	Tadachika Seno
1164	Takasaki Japan	10 Aug 1980	Masataka Kitamura
505	*Tokyo Japan		
	‡Tokyo	15 Mar 1970	Kenji Tanaka
1121	Tokyo Japan East	23 Mar 1980	Ryotaro Kanzaki
869	Tokyo Japan North	23 Oct 1977	Ryo Okamoto
1270	Tokyo Japan South	30 May 1981	Kazutoshi Ono
1329	Tokyo Japan West	21 Mar 1982	Koichi Aoyagi
662	Yokohama Japan	27 Oct 1974	Hitoshi Kashikura

Discontinued

No.	Name	Organized	First President
1875	Kyoto Japan South 25 Apr 1993	31 May 1992	Kenichiro Kimura
1257	Takamatsu Japan 2 June 1991	23 Apr 1981	Takejiro Kanzaki

Missions — 8

(As of Oct. 1, 1996; shown with historical number. See MISSIONS.)

(91) JAPAN FUKUOKA MISSION
46 Josui-machi, Hirao, Chuo-ku
Fukuoka, 810
Japan
Phone: (011-81-92) 522-0386

(108) JAPAN NAGOYA MISSION
1-304 Itakadai
Meito-ku Nagoya-shi T 465
Japan
Phone: (011-81-52) 773-0755

(90) JAPAN SAPPORO MISSION
Kita 2 jo Nishi 24 Chome 1-25
Chuo-ku, Sapporo-Shi, Hokkaido 064
Japan
Phone: (011-81-11) 643-6411

(82a) JAPAN TOKYO NORTH MISSION
4-25-12 Nishi Ochiai
Shinjuku-ku
Tokyo 161, Japan
Phone: (011-81-33) 952-6802

(83) JAPAN KOBE MISSION
6-28 4-Chome, Shinohara Honmachi
Nada Ku, Kobe, T 657
Japan
Phone: (011-81-78) 881-2712

(144) JAPAN OKAYAMA MISSION
87-4 Koku Ichiba
Okayama Shi, Okayama Ken
Japan 703
Phone: (011-81-862) 75-4833

(109a) JAPAN SENDAI MISSION
Yagiyama Minami 3 Chome 1-5
Taihaku-Ku Sendai-Shi
Japan 982
Phone: (011-81-222) 45-8851

(162) JAPAN TOKYO SOUTH MISSION
1-7-7 Kichijoji-Higashi Machi
Musashino-Shi
Tokyo T 180, Japan
Phone: (011-81-422) 21 2619

KENYA

Year-end 1995: Est. population, 30,000,000; Members, 2,200; Missions, 1; Districts, 2; Branches, 14; Africa Area.

American USAID employees and their families serving in Kenya in the 1970s held Church services in their own homes. The first African converts in Kenya were baptized Oct. 21, 1979, Elizaphan Osaka and his wife, Ebisiba, and their two oldest children, Margaret and Jairo. Brother Osaka, a former minister, was ordained a priest the same day.

The first missionaries were Elder Farrell and Sister Blanch McGhie of Palo Alto, Calif., who arrived Sept. 6, 1980.

The Kenya District, with two branches in Nairobi and Kiboko, was created May 10, 1981. The first Kenyan called as a full-time missionary was Benson Kasue, who served in the Los Angeles, Calif., area from 1983-85.

In 1988, the Church donated funds that were collected on special fasts to bring water to 15 Kenyan villages, located 100 miles from Nairobi. The water systems were installed by 1989. The first branch was organized in Nairobi March 15, 1989.

The Church received official recognition in Kenya Feb. 25, 1991, following a visit to Kenya by Judge Clifford Wallace of San Diego, Calif., a member who made the request to proper authorities. The Kenya Nairobi Mission, which includes Kenya, Uganda, and Tanzania, was created in July 1991. In February 1992, more than 200 members and investigators from five branches attended a district conference in Nairobi, in the Parklands Branch meetinghouse. The meeting was conducted by district Pres. Joseph Sitati. Pres. Sitati, a convert since 1985, and his wife, Gladys, and their children were the first Kenyans to go through the temple. More than 30 missionaries served during the first year of the mission.

In 1992, the Church provided food staples to Somalian and Kenyan refugees affected by severe drought conditions. On Oct. 21, 1992, a six-acre plot of Church land was planted under the direction of LDS agronomist Joel K. Ransom, and the self-help project expanded later to members' own property and saw vital crops harvested.

By 1994, four districts had been created and large congregations attended many of the meetings. The first meetinghouse was completed in July 1994 for the Langata Branch in Nairobi.

Church humanitarian projects have blessed the lives of Kenyans, including a community water project in 1994 that provided personal water taps to hundreds of families.

Sources: *Church News*, March 18, 1989, March 23, 1991, April 25, 1992, Sept. 26, 1992, Nov. 21, 1992, Feb. 11, 1995; Journals and correspondence of Kirk P. Lovenbury, June 10, 1993; correspondence from Pres. Larry K. Brown, Kenya Nairobi Mission, April 12, 1994.

Mission — 1

(As of Oct. 1, 1996; shown with historical number. See MISSIONS.)

(265) KENYA NAIROBI MISSION
P.O. Box 39634
Nairobi, Kenya
Phone: (011-254-2) 740-444

KIRIBATI

Year-end 1995: Est. population, 80,000; Members, 5,100; Districts, 1; Branches, 17; Percent LDS, 6.4, or one LDS in 16; Pacific Area; Fiji Suva Mission.

Made up of 36 Micronesian islands in the mid-Pacific where the equator and international dateline meet, Kiribati is a republic that became independent in 1979. The islands' population speaks Gilbertese and English. About half of the population is Protestant and half Roman Catholic.

The Church was introduced to Kiribati when Waitea Abiuta, a school teacher and headmaster of a school, asked to have graduates from his school attend Liahona High School in Tonga. Fijian mission Pres. Eb L. Davis visited Kiribati in September 1972, and approved 12 students to come to the Church school. Students were converted at the high school and they began serving as missionaries in Kiribati on Oct. 19, 1975.

Among those who joined the Church were Waitea Abiuta and several of the staff and students of the school. However, when opposition to the Church arose, enrollment at the school declined. In August 1976, Grant and Pat Howlett, LDS educators at Liahona High, were called to teach at the Kiribati school. Through their efforts, enrollment increased and government relations improved. Later, the Church purchased the school and renamed it Moroni Community School, and other teachers arrived from Tonga as enrollment continued to increase. In 1984, the student body reached 240, and has remained at that number.

In 1982, a new meetinghouse was completed, and Buren Ratieta, Gilbertese branch president, held services in February of that year. Among the 250 who attended the dedicatory services was the president of the Kiribati Republic, Ieremia T. Tabai. He said government leaders at first feared the Church would divide the people, but when he saw the great social contribution the Church made, he became happy to cooperate with the Church.

Since that time, missionary work has expanded to more distant islands in Kiribati. Selections of the Book of Mormon were translated into Gilbertese in 1988.

In the fall of 1993, a group of first-time basketball players from Moroni High School, the age of U.S. high school sophomores and juniors, won the championship of Kiribati in their division. They also defeated the 20-30-year-olds division champions. Membership in 1990 was 2,300.

In 1994, Teatao Teanaki, president of the Republic, was the main speaker at the graduation ceremony at Moroni High School.

On Aug. 9, 1996, Elder L. Tom Perry of the Quorum of the Twelve dedicated Moroni High School. On Aug. 11, 1996, Elder Perry created the Tarawa Kiribati Stake, the first stake in the country.

Sources: *Unto the Isles of the Sea,* by R. Lanier Britsch; interviews with various missionaries; *Church News,* Oct. 23, 1993; *Church News,* Feb. 5, 1994; "Elder Perry creates first Kiribati stake, dedicates islands," Church News, Sept. 21, 1996.

Stakes — 1
(Listed alphabetically as of Oct. 1, 1996.)

No.	Name	Organized	First President
	Pacific Area		
2215	Tarawa Kiribati	8 Aug 1996	Atunibeia Mote

KOREA

Year-end 1995: Est. population, 45,600,000; Members, 67,000; Stakes, 16; Wards, 87; Branches, 74; Missions, 4; Districts, 6; Temples, 1; Percent LDS, 0.15, or one LDS in 680.

In northern east Asia, the Republic of Korea, or South Korea, has a population that speaks Korean and principally follows Buddhism, Confucianism and Christianity.

LDS servicemen performed the first missionary work during the Korean War in 1951. Among the first Korean members was Ho Jik Kim, converted while earning a doctorate in the United States. Kim became an influential leader in the Korean government and paved the way for missionaries to enter Korea. His children, Tai Whan and Young Sook, were among the first four baptized on Aug. 3, 1952. He died of a stroke in 1959.

The first missionaries, Elders Richard L. Detton and Don G. Powell, arrived in Korea in 1954. At that time, membership in Korea was 64. The missionaries learned to speak Korean and taught many young students.

The Korean Mission was created on July 8, 1962, with Gail C. Carr, one of the early missionaries to Korea, as president. The new mission had seven branches, in Seoul, Pusan and Taegu. By 1964, membership had reached 1,800. The Book of Mormon was printed in Korean in 1967. By 1968, significant increases in membership began to develop. From 1974 to 1977, a girls choir in an orphanage operated by LDS member Whang Keun-Ok was promoted on national media, increasing the percent of those who recognized the name of the Church from 10 to 70 percent. The first stake was created in Seoul on March 8, 1973, with Ho Nam Rhee as president. He later served as mission president. Membership increased to 9,000 in 1975, and by 1983, it had reached 28,795. Membership in Korea in 1990 was 59,000, increasing to 62,000 the next year.

A temple was announced for Seoul, Korea, on April 1, 1981, and was dedicated Dec. 14, 1985. Following the temple's dedication, many of the Korean members did the temple work for their ancestors.

When the 1988 Olympic games were held in Korea, the BYU Folk Dancers performed at opening ceremonies, viewed by an estimated audience of 1 billion worldwide.

Elder In Sang Han, called to the Second Quorum of the Seventy on June 1, 1991, was the first Korean General Authority.

In 1992, a record of the testimonies of the early Korean converts was published by Spencer J. and Shirley Palmer.

In May 1996, President Gordon B. Hinckley conducted meetings for members and missionaries in Seoul and Pusan during an extended visit to Asia. He also attended a press conference and luncheon with members of the media in Korea.

Sources: *History of the Church in Korea,* by John D. Nash; *The Church Encounters Asia,* by Spencer J. Palmer, Deseret Book, 1970; *Ensign,* Nov. 1985; *Church News,* Oct. 1, 1988; *Church News,* Feb. 5, 1992; "Whang Keun-Ok: Caring for Korea's Children," by Shirleen Meek Saunders, *Ensign,* Oct. 1993; *Church News,* June 8, 1996.

Stakes — 16

(Listed alphabetically as of Oct. 1, 1996.)

No.	Name	Organized	First President
Asia North Area			
1865	Anyang Korea	24 May 1992	Young Hwan Lee
1385	*Chong Ju Korea 23 Sep 1986		
	‡Seoul Korea Chong Ju	28 Nov 1982	Chung Yul Hwang
1306	Inchon Korea	12 Nov 1981	Chea Huo
1596a	Jeon Ju Korea	27 Apr 1986	Ju In Pak
1196	Kwang Ju Korea	25 Oct 1980	Bjong Kyu Pak
1382	*Ma San Korea	13 Apr 1995	
	Pusan Korea West	20 Nov 1982	Gil Whe Do
1059	Pusan Korea	6 Sep 1979	Chaewhan Chang
604	*Seoul Korea		
	‡Seoul	8 Mar 1973	Ho Nam Rhee
1412	Seoul Korea Dong Dae Mun	24 Apr 1983	Son Awunf Ju
1017	Seoul Korea East	18 Apr 1979	Won Yong Ko
1386	Seoul Korea Kang Seo	28 Nov 1982	Do Hwan Lee
1060	Seoul Korea North	9 Sep 1979	Moo Kwang Hong
834	Seoul Korea West	22 May 1977	Chang Sun Kim
1387	Seoul Korea Yung Dong	28 Nov 1982	Jae Am Park
1866	Suwon Korea	24 May 1992	Yong Hwan Lee
1435	*Tae Gu Korea 29 Jun 1993		
	*Dae Gu Korea 3 Dec 1990		
	‡Daegu Korea	24 Jun 1983	Chan Tae Kwon

Missions — 4

(As of Oct. 1, 1996; shown with historical number. See MISSIONS.)

(124) KOREA PUSAN MISSION
Tongnae P.O. Box 73
Pusan 607-600, Korea
Phone: (011-82-51) 552-7011

(71) KOREA SEOUL MISSION
Gwang Hwa Moon
Seoul 110-602, Korea
Phone: (011-82-2) 734-3653

(170) KOREA SEOUL WEST MISSION
Songpa P.O. Box 31
Seoul, 138-600, Korea
Phone: (011-82-2) 409-4164

(191) KOREA TAEJON MISSION
Taejon P.O. Box 38
Taejon, 300-600, Korea
Phone (011-82-42) 628-1482

LATVIA

Year-end 1995: Est. population, 2,763,000; Members, 200; Branches, 5; Europe East Area; Lithuania Vilnius Mission.

Latvia is a republic on the eastern shore of the Baltic Sea.

Mischa Markow, a Hungarian who had previously pioneered missionary work in Serbia, Hungary, Romania and Bulgaria, was the first to preach in Latvia. Elder Markow registered with the district court and then preached to Germans in Riga, Latvia, on Oct. 9, 1903, and three families requested baptism. However, when he was summoned to court, he chose to comply with instructions from Pres. Francis M. Lyman of the European Mission: leave the country if he were summoned to court.

In modern times, Elder Dallin H. Oaks of the Quorum of the Twelve addressed Latvian and other leaders at a major international consultation on religious liberty and ethnic rights held in Budapest, Hungary, May 17-20, 1992.

Recent missionary work in Lativa began June 17, 1992, with the arrival of four missionaries serving under Pres. Charles H. Creel, Elders Dale Franklin, Dennon Ison, Matthew H. Lyman and Michael G. Van Patten. They were followed on June 30 by the arrival of a missionary couple, Elder Boris A. and Sister Liselotte Schiel. The first convert in Latvia, Gunars Kavals, was baptized July 25, 1992.

In March 1993, Latvia was visited by Elder James E. Faust of the Quorum of the Twelve, and at that time, some 40 Latvian members comprised the membership of the Church in this land. LDS humanitarian assistance has been given to Latvia.

The Latvia Riga Mission was created July 1, 1993, and included Latvia, Lithuania and Estonia. On April 16, 1996, the mission was transferred and the name changed to the Lithuania Vilnius Mission.

Source: "Missionary to the Balkans: Mischa Markow" by William Hale Kehr, *Ensign*, June 1980; *Church News*, Nov. 16, 1991, June 27, 1992; March 6, 1993, and June 12, 1993.

LESOTHO

Year-end 1995: Est. population, 2,000,000; Members, 300; Branches, 1; Africa Area; South Africa Johannesburg Mission.

Completely surrounded by South Africa, Lesotho is a mountainous kingdom where the people speak English and Sotho, and are primarily Roman Catholic, 38 percent and Protestant, 42 percent.

Scattered LDS families from the United States lived in Lesotho during the 1980s. In July 1988 at a meeting attended by 15 people, the Maseru Branch was organized by Pres. R. J. Snow of the South Africa Johannesburg Mission at the home of expatriates Garry and Mary Massey. Brother Massey was called as president. John and Elaine Scott later moved to Lesotho from Swaziland. The Church was registered July 6, 1989, and the first missionaries, Elders Marc Modersitzki of Bancroft, Idaho, and Bradley Saunderson of Durban, South Africa, entered in September. They baptized Paul Khobutle and Lawrence van Tonder Dec. 17 of that year. As the branch grew, facilities were rented in a local school. A home was purchased to be remodeled into a meetinghouse and the first meeting in it was held Jan. 2, 1994.

A seminary program functioned in the country as early as 1991. On July 31, 1993, six converts traveled to the Johannesburg South Africa Temple. The first full-time missionary from Lesotho was Patrick Molapo, 23, who began serving in the Durban mission Dec. 21, 1993.

A second branch was created July 4, 1993, at Mazenod, which functioned for a short time before being disbanded because facilities for meeting were not available.

On Feb. 18, 1996, members from Lesotho were among some 5,000 who attended the Johannesburg Regional Conference — the largest LDS gathering assembled to this point in South Africa.

Sources: Correspondence from R.J. Snow; *Church News*, Dec. 12, 1989, March 10, 1990, Dec. 15, 1990, Jan. 26, 1991, April 25, 1992, March 2, 1996; Lesotho historical information, by Peter Daubney, May 1994.

LIBERIA

Year-end 1995: Population, 3,073,000; Members, 1,600; Districts, 2; Branches, 7; Africa Area; Ivory Coast Abidjan Mission.

On the southwest coast of West Africa, the republic has a marshy coastline that gives way to low mountains and plateaus; the interior is forested. It is 20 percent Muslim, 20 percent Christian and 60 percent tribal beliefs.

Among the early Church members in Liberia were Joan Raily, baptized in New Jersey in 1986, and expatriates Steven P. and Barbara Wolf, who were in Liberia on a military assignment. Meetings were held in their home in 1986. A year earlier, Thomas Peihopa of New Zealand began teaching a Sunday School class for Joe Jawloh, a school principal in New Kru Town. Peihopa brought some 80 investigators to a social in the Wolf's home. Bihise "Biz" Kajunju and his family, converts from Zaire, also joined the group.

Missionary couples opened missionary work in Liberia in 1987. Among the early couples were J. Duffy and Jacelyn Palmer, who arrived July 3, 1987, and Philander and Juanita Smartt. The first convert was John Tarsnoh, baptized Aug. 22, 1987. The missionaries baptized 47 people Aug. 27, 1987, in a lagoon. The New Kru Town and Congo Town branches were organized that day. On Feb. 21, 1988, Joseph Forkpah became the first Liberian branch president. The Liberia Monrovia Mission was created March 1, 1988, when missionary couples were working with some 133 members in Congo Town and New Kru Town.

Under the direction of Pres. Miles Cunningham, a handful of newly converted young men served full-time missions in 1990. At the beginning of 1990, the mission had one district and 8 branches.

The mission was closed in April 1991 because of civil war that started Dec. 24, 1989. Missionaries from Liberia were transferred to Freetown, Sierra Leone, on May 8, 1990. David A. Tarr, then first counselor in the Monrovia District, was left in charge. During that time, about 400 members remained, another 400 fled to neighboring countries and another 400 were unaccounted for. When the war began to abate, some of the members returned. While conditions remained unsettled, no missionaries were assigned to Liberia.

In 1992, a second outbreak of serious hostilities occurred. Members started regrouping in 1991, however, and by the spring of 1993, seven of the eight branches had been reorganized.

With a renewal of hostilities, members in Liberia experienced additional hardships and suffering.

Sources: Interview with Miles Cunningham, correspondence from James C. Palmer, Bill K. Jarkloh, June, 1994, and information from David A. Tarr; *Church News*, July 9, 1994, March 9, 1996, April 27, 1996.

LITHUANIA

Year-end 1995: Est. Population, 3,876,000; Members, 100; Missions, 1; Branches, 3; Europe East Area.

Lithuania is a republic on the eastern shore of the Baltic Sea. Several expatriates have joined the Church and live in various countries.

One of the first converts in modern Lithuania was Irute Meskiene of Vilnius. She heard the gospel preached in Szeged, Hungary, and was baptized in 1988 in Hungary. Robert and Ruth Rees, retired literature and music teachers, respectively, were called to Lithuania as missionaries in October 1992.

BYU's Young Ambassadors performed in Lithuania and stayed three nights with host families from the Neamanus Folk Ensemble in Kaunas.

In late 1993 and 1994, Lithuanian media presented Church-produced programs and also focused on missionaries and their work. In November 1994, Elder Marek Vasilkov of Vilnius became the first native Lithuanian to be called on a mission. He served in the Utah Salt Lake City Mission.

By November 1995, the Church in Lithuania had grown enough to create three branches, two in Vilnius and one in Kaunas. In 1996, the Latvia Riga Mission was relocated and renamed the Lithuania Vilnius Mission.

Source: *Church News*, June 12, 1993, and July 17, 1994; correspondence from Elder Robert A. Rees and Gabriele Sirtle, May 2, 1994.

Mission — 1
(As of Oct. 1, 1996; shown with historical number. See MISSIONS.)

(288) LITHUANIA VILNIUS MISSION
A/D 1289
2056 Vilnius, Lithuania
Phone: (011-370-2) 625-523

LUXEMBOURG

Year-end 1995: Est. population, 371,000; Members, 100; Branches, 1; Europe West Area; Belgium Brussels Mission.

Located in western Europe, the Grand Duchy of Luxembourg's population speaks French, German, and Luxembourger. The people are 97 percent Roman Catholic.

On Nov. 19, 1963, Elders Hyrum M. Smith and Gerald E. Malmrose of the Franco-Belgian Mission went into the city of Luxembourg to help new missionaries there get started in their labors. They were there four days and left several missionaries to continue the work.

A branch was formed in the mid-1960s, and in 1965 Sunday meetings were conducted in the Hotel Kons. Attendance varied from one to three members and six missionaries. The branch remained small and struggled until it was discontinued in 1971.

The city and country of Luxembourg became part of the newly created Belgium Brussels Mission June 20, 1974, and continues as part of that mission today.

In late 1989 more than 1,000 people from 23 countries attended a nine-day exhibition titled "The Origin of Man" at the Luxembourg municipal hall. The event was hosted by area Church members and full-time missionaries. Of the 1,000 guests, nearly 200 signed the visitors book, leading to the placement of 190 copies of the Book of Mormon. In about June 1994, Luxembourg became part of the newly created Metz France District, which was divided from the Nancy France Stake.

Sources: *Church News*, Jan. 6, 1990; Belgian Mission manuscript history; *Church News*, July 9, 1994.

MADAGASCAR

Year-end 1995: Est. population, 15,250,000; Members, 400; Branches, 2; Africa Area; South Africa Durban Mission.

Located in the Indian Ocean off Mozambique, Madagascar is the world's fourth largest island. Its population speaks Malagasy and French, and 52 percent follow traditional beliefs, while 41 percent are Christian and 7 percent are Islam.

The first member in Madagascar was Razanapanala Rameandricso, who was baptized in Bordeaux, France, in about 1986. He returned to Madasgascar in 1989 and began teaching the gospel to a small group of people in his home. He contacted Pres. Girard Giraud-Carrier of the Mascarene Islands Mission, who visited. The first five converts were baptized upon his visit, near the end of 1990.

The first missionaries to Madagascar were Elder Fred L. and Sister Eileen Forsgren, who arrived March 3, 1991. The Antananarivo Branch was organized in February 1991 in a restaurant in Antananarivo. When the second couple, Elder Marvyn and Sister LaVeeta Hogenson, arrived in May 1991, the branch had 33 members. During their stay, the Church continued to grow. They completed their mission in September of 1992 and there were more than 130 attending meetings.

The first young full-time missionaries, Elders Jason Tarbet and Jeffry Gifford, arrived Sept. 25, 1992. The Hogensons returned for a second mission, and served from December 1993 to August 1994. During that period, seminary was started and the auxiliaries functioned.

The Church received legal status in Madagascar on July 13, 1993. At the end of August 1994, membership was at 375.

Source: Journal of Eileen Forsgren, interview with LaVeeta Hogensen and journal of Elder Jason Tarbet.

MALAYSIA

Year-end 1995: Est. population, 20,500,000; Members, 700; Districts, 1; Branches, 7; Asia Area; Singapore Mission.

On the southeast tip of Asia and the northern half of the island of Borneo, Malaysia is a federal parliamentary democracy with a constitutional monarch. Its people speak Malay, Chinese, English and Indian languages, and practice primarily Muslim, Hindu, Buddhist, Confucian, Taoist and local religions.

When the Singapore Mission opened in 1974, with Malaysia a part of the mission, missionaries were rotated in and out of the country on 30-day tourist visas to comply with the law of the land. The first missionaries came to Kuala Lumpur on June 27, 1972.

Elder and Sister Werner Kiepe of Salt Lake City, Utah, special representatives of the International Mission, were sent to Malaysia shortly after the government granted the Church a recognition status in 1977. They helped acquire the first property owned by the Church in Malaysia in a suburb of Kuala Lumpur, the capital of Malaysia. Church membership was small, with many members being Americans and Australians temporarily working in the country, as well as some Chinese members living in the country.

In 1981, a milestone was reached when two native Malaysian elders were called to serve as missionaries in 1981 in the Singapore Mission. A district was organized in Malaysia.

In 1986, the seminary and institute program was established with groups of young people attending in Pinang, Ipoh and Kuala Lumpur.

On Oct. 20, 1990, King Syed Putra Jamallai, the rajah of Perlis state in Malaysia, was honored during a visit at the Polynesian Cultural Center in Laie, Hawaii.

Elder Halvor P. Hansen, serving in the Singapore Mission with his wife, Colleen, presented a copy of the *Encyclopedia of Mormonism* to the National Library of Malaysia in 1993.

Elder Monte J. Brough of the Seventy, then Asia Area president, reported in 1993 that while proselyting is not allowed, members and leaders were very devoted to the Church.

In 1994, local Church leaders were invited to dine with the Tenth King and Queen of Malaysia, Tuanku Ja'afar and Tuanku Najihah in the royal couple's coronation events. The meeting in the dining hall of the Royal Palace in Kuala Lumpur was arranged by Vincent and Sandra Gordacan of Las Vegas, Nevada, close personal friends of the king and queen.

Sources: *The Church Encounters Asia,* by Spencer J. Palmer, Deseret Book, 1970; *Church News,* May 23, 1981; Aug. 14, 1982; Dec. 9, 1984; March 10, 1985; "Specific Prayers led him to specific answers," by Gerry Avant, *Church News,* Jan. 20, 1985; *Church News,* May 11, 1986, Nov. 3, 1990; *Church News,* Aug. 21, 1993; "Welcome mat is out in several countries," by Sheridan R. Sheffield, *Church News,* June 19, 1993; "Members dine with royalty," *Church News,* Dec. 17, 1994.

MALTA

Year-end 1995: Est. population, 400,000; Members, fewer than 100; Branches, 2; Europe West Area; Italy Catania Mission.

Located in the Mediterranean Sea, Malta is a republic with a population that speaks Maltese and English, and is mostly Roman Catholic. For the third time in recent history, the gospel is being taught in Malta.

When Apostle Lorenzo Snow was in charge of missionary work in Italy in the early 1850s, he saw the island as a possible pojnt of beginning for carrying the gospel to other countries in the region.

After a visit to Malta in 1852, he left Elders Jabez Woodard and Thomas Obray in charge of missionary efforts here. Between 1852 and 1856, some proselyting progress was made, and a branch of about 25 people came into existence. But there was intense opposition to the work, and when the Crimean War scattered most of the British military personnel who had joined the Church, missionary efforts on the island ceased.

More than a century later, in 1979, a second effort on Malta was undertaken when the Italy Catania Mission sent Elders Victor Bonnici (of Maltese descent) and Paul Anderson to the island. They had good contacts among the island's nearly 350,000 inhabitants, but because of visa problems were unable to stay long enough to establish a branch.

Then in early 1988, Elder Rodger and Sister Helen Gunn were sent as a missionary couple to Malta. Assisted by two elders from the mission, they baptized several Maltese people, established a branch and sponsored cultural evenings and a family history seminar.

The branch, under early convert Pres. Emanuel d'Emanuele, met in an old villa near Naxxar. Another milestone in 1993 came when the Malta Branch held its first branch conference, presided over by Pres. G. Robert Dewitt of the Italy Catania Mission.

Sources: *Encyclopedic History of the Church,* by Andrew Jenson; *Church News,* Jan. 12, 1974; "Soldier converts," by Ronald W. Walker, *Church News,* April 21, 1979; "A Valiant Little Band: LDS Soldiers in the Crimean War," by Wilford Hill LeCheminant, *Ensign,* Jan. 1981; *A History of the Discontinued Mediterranean Missions of the Church,* by Ralph L. Cottrell Jr., a BYU master's thesis, 1983; *Church News,* Dec. 3, 1993.

MARSHALL ISLANDS

Year-end 1995: Est. population, 60,000; Members, 2,900; Districts, 2; Branches, 10; Percent LDS, 4.8, or one LDS in 20; Philippines/Micronesia Area; Micronesia Guam Mission.

Made up of two atoll chains in the South Pacific, the Marshall Islands are a republic.

MAJURO

Elders William Wardel and Steven Cooper arrived in Majuro Feb. 3, 1977, and they baptized Misao Lokeijak, who had been introduced to the Church in Hawaii. By the end of 1977, there were 27 converts on the island. The Laura Branch was created May 11, 1978, with Misao Lokeijak as president. By the end of 1979, there were 177 members. Meetinghouses for the Laura and Rita branches were started in September 1984 and dedicated Jan. 13 and 14, 1986, respectively. By 1987, Majuro had a district with five branches. By 1990, Majuro had 1,100 members.

In May 1992, BYU and the Republic of Marshall Islands agreed to have BYU give special training for government administrators and teachers.

KAWJALEIN/EBEYE

The Kwajalein Island Branch in the Marshall Islands was organized in 1978, made up entirely of U.S. citizens serving in the military or as civil service personnel. Missionaries opened the island of Ebeye on May 16, 1989, and Elders Kepiloni Foliaki and Michael Steele baptized Mary Kekuhuna on Jun 11, 1989.

ARNO AND MILI

Arno and Mili, located at the eastern end of Micronesia, some 2,200 miles west of Hawaii, are part of the 28-island Marshall group. In 1994, the Church had four branches in the Marshall Islands and three Church-owned meetinghouses.

Source: *Brief History of the Micronesia-Guam Mission,* published by the Micronesia Guam Mission, 1990, Lewis V. Nord, president;

MAURITIUS

Year-end 1995: Est. population, 1,130,000; Members, 200; Branches, 1; Africa Area; South Africa Durban Mission.

East of Madagascar in the Indian Ocean, Mauritius is a subtropical island with a parliamentary democracy, composed of an English, French, Creole, Hindi, Urdu, Hakka and Bojpoori speaking population that is 51 percent Hindu, 30 percent Christian and 16 percent Muslim.

Elder George Kershaw, an LDS settler in South Africa, served two months in Mauritius in 1856. His only known converts were an army private and seven or eight members of the crew of the ship he arrived on.

In modern times, missionary work began in the Mascarenes in 1979 under the direction of the International Mission. In 1986, the islands were transferred to the South Africa Johannesburg Mission.

Elder Joseph T. Edmunds and his wife, Ruth, and Elder Theo and Sister Nita Verhaarens visited the island briefly. The first branch was established on Feb. 25, 1982, by Elder Preston and Sister Isabelle Gledhill, the first full-time missionaries on the island. The Mascarene Islands Mission was created July 1, 1988, at which time there were 400 members on the islands in three branches in Reunion and two in Mauritius. Headquarters of the mission was transferred to Durban, South Africa, in January 1992.

Sources: *Church News,* Sept. 21, 1986, Feb. 7, 1987, Oct. 24, 1987, Nov. 5, 1987, March 19, 1988, Dec. 17, 1988; "Tropical Isles receive best news as mission opens," by Allen W. Palmer, *Church News,* Nov. 5, 1988; "At Home on the Island of Mauritius," by Lori Palmer, *Ensign,* March, 1991.

MEXICO

Year-end 1995: Est. population, 94,924,000; Members, 728,000; Stakes, 138; Wards, 847; Branches, 535; Missions, 18; Districts, 44; Temples, 1 and 1 announced; Percent LDS, 0.8, or one LDS in 130.

In southern North America, Mexico is a federal republic with a Spanish-speaking population that is 97 percent Roman Catholic.

In 1875, a party of six was called by Brigham Young to take materials, translated into Spanish by convert Meliton Trejo, from Salt Lake City to Mexico. On the way, they preached to Indians and gave a favorable colonization report that led to the founding of Mesa, Ariz.

Rebuffed at first in Mexico in 1876, the missionaries divided into two groups. The first, Daniel W. Jones and Ammon N. Tenney, traveled to Chihuahua, where they were well-received. There, they scouted settlement sites and mailed pamphlets containing translated sections of the Book of Mormon to 500 influential leaders throughout Mexico. They found many listeners among the mountain villages and Indians, but did not baptize. The second group of missionaries attempted to preach to the fierce Yaqui Indians and were nearly killed.

In 1876, Helaman Pratt and Meliton Trejo traveled to Hermosillo, Sonora, where they baptized the first five members in Mexico,and returned home.

Dr. Plotino C. Rhodakanaty of Mexico City received a tract from the original Jones expedition and began corresponding with Meliton Trejo. Rhodakanaty claimed a group of 20 believers and asked for missionaries to baptize them. Apostle Moses Thatcher and Elders Trejo and James Z. Stewart were sent to Mexico City, where on Nov. 20, 1879, they baptized Rhodakanaty and Silviano Arteaga, organized a branch and placed Rhodakanaty over it. By 1880, more literature had been translated. Political difficulties in Utah and changing moods in Mexico resulted in less success in Mexico City. Missionaries left Mexico City, and found converts in the small rural town of Ozumba. Additional missionaries arrived, and despite setbacks, the work moved forward in Ozumba and the surrounding villages near Mount Popocateptl.

In 1885, a group of nearly 400 colonists from Utah arrived at the northern Mexico Casas Grandes River and acquired property. Mexico's first stake was created in Colonia Juarez in 1895. In 1887, members from central Mexico arrived at the colonies but found circumstances difficult and returned to their homes. By 1912, more than 4,000 members had settled in Chihuahua and Sonora.

In 1901 Ammon M. Tenney became president of the Mexican Mission. Visiting village branches in central Mexico, he found early converts were still faithful. Branches were re-organized and by 1911, membership in the region reached 1,000.

The Mexican Revolution halted much of the Church's progress, as colonists in the north left Mexico in the 1912 exodus to avoid the conflict, and members in central Mexico were left without leaders and were abused by conflicting armies. Two local leaders, Rafael Monroy and Vicente Morales, were executed because of their faithfulness to the Church.

When Rey L. Pratt returned to central Mexico in November 1917, he found the members had remained faithful despite extreme hardship. Work again progressed, but in 1926 all foreign clerics were expelled from Mexico. Local Mexican leaders again maintained stability and expanded the work, calling six local missionaries in 1930. In 1936, however, a group called the Third Convention broke away from the Church for a period, but was reunited under the leadership of mission Pres. Arwell Pierce. In 1946 Church President George Albert Smith visited the members. Membership then was more than 5,300.

During the next two decades membership increased as local leaders were called to more leadership positions, and the missionary zeal of the Mexican members was manifest.

On June 10, 1956, the mission was divided. On Dec. 3, 1961, the Mexico Stake was created, with Harold Brown as president. He was shortly succeeded by pioneer member Agricol Lozano. Membership then was about 25,000.

Church schools were established in 1959; the capstone of these was the large preparatory school, Benemerito, which was established in 1963. This flagship of the Church in Mexico helped the Church advance in leadership and reputation.

In the late 1960s, membership began to expand rapidly. By 1972, it reached 100,000. On April 3, 1976, a temple was announced for Mexico City and the completed temple was dedicated Dec. 2-4, 1983. At that time, membership in Mexico was conservatively placed about 240,000. Mexico was the first country outside the United States to reach 100 stakes. When the 100th stake was created at Tecalco in 1989, membership in Mexico was estimated to be more than half a million. In 1992, Mexico made Church history when it became the first nation outside the United States to be divided into two areas, Mexico North and Mexico South.

Elder Waldo Call of the Seventy, called in 1985 from the original Mexican colonies, was the first Mexican General Authority. He was followed in 1989 by Elder Horacio Tenorio, the first of Mexican ancestry to be called. Elder Jorge A. Rojas Ornales was called in 1991, and Elder Lino Alvarez was called in 1992.

An historic moment came June 29, 1993, when the Mexican government formally registered the Church, allowing it to own property. The recognition was granted at a rarely held ceremony presided over by Patrocinio Gonzalez Garrido, Secretary of Government. Instrumental in gaining the recognition was Agricol Lozano H., the Church's legal counsel, who bore his testimony at the ceremony. The effort was under the direction of Elders F. Burton Howard and Angel Abrea of the Seventy, presidents of the Mexico North and Mexico South areas. They were supervised by Elder Russell M. Nelson of the Council of the Twelve, who worked under the direction of the First Presidency on the project.

President Howard W. Hunter visited Mexico to create the Mexico City Contreras Stake, the Church's 2,000th, on Dec. 11, 1994. President Gordon B. Hinckley visited Veracruz Jan. 27-8, 1996, for a regional conference and addressed 9,000 members.

Sources: *Historia Del Mormonismo en Mexico,* by Agricol Lozano; Tecalco history, unpublished history by "Ixta" and "Popo" wards; extensive selections from journals, publications and histories courtesy Gerry R. Flake; multiple other published and unpublished papers and books and *Church News* articles; "Mexico formally registers Church," *Church News* July 17, 1993; *Church News*, Dec. 17, 1994, Feb. 3, 1996.

Stakes — 145
(Listed alphabetically by area as of Oct. 1, 1996.)

No.	Name	Organized	First President
Mexico North Area — 66			
1640	Aguascalientes Mexico	17 May 1987	Jose Luis Rios A.
941	Celaya Mexico	11 Jun 1978	Armando Gaona
782	Chihuahua Mexico	13 Nov 1976	Gustavo Ulises Cortez S.
1633	*Chihuahua Mexico Chuviscar	14 Nov 1989	
	‡Chihuahua Mexico East	1 Mar 1987	Humberto Enrique Serna G.
1736a	Chihuahua Mexico Tecnologico	26 Nov 1989	Arturo Galindo Rubalcava
1109	Ciudad Juarez Mexico East	24 Feb 1980	Armando Arzate Saldana
1699	Ciudad Juarez Mexico North	9 Oct 1988	Luis Carlos Gomez M.
783	*Ciudad Juarez Mexico South	9 Oct 1988	
	‡Ciudad Juarez Mexico	14 Nov 1976	Sergio Armando de la Mora M.
1301	*Ciudad Mante Mexico	25 Jan 1982	
	‡Mante Mexico	1 Nov 1981	Humberto Noriega F.
772	Ciudad Obregon Mexico	10 Oct 1976	Jorge Mendez I.
1712	Ciudad Obregon Mexico Nainari	19 Feb 1989	Jesus Angulo Montoya
1500	Ciudad Obregon Mexico Yaqui	28 Oct 1984	Jorge Mendez Ibarra
797	Ciudad Victoria Mexico	12 Dec 1976	Jesus Martinez T.
1742	Colonia Dublan Mexico	25 Feb 1990	Carl L. Call
37	*Colonia Juarez Mexico		
	‡Juarez	9 Dec 1895	Anthony W. Ivins
838	Culiacan Mexico	22 May 1977	Federico Fragoza Diaz
1710	Culiacan Mexico Humaya	12 Feb 1989	Jose Exaltacion Astorga E.
1644	Culiacan Mexico Tamazula	21 Jun 1987	Rosario Lobo
1707	Delicias Mexico	18 Dec 1988	Sergio Trejo L.
1228	Durango Mexico	21 Jan 1981	Ernesto Padilla Lozano
2057	Durango Mexico Del Valle	28 May 1995	Miguel Angel Martinez Macias
1761	*Ensenada Mexico	8 Aug 1990	
	‡Tijuana Mexico Ensenada	24 Jun 1990	Jose Pedroza A.
935	Gomez Palacio Mexico	28 May 1978	Ruben Martinez A.
1749	Gomez Palacio Mexico	6 May 1990	Magdaleno Sanchez S.
	La Laguna		
1183	Guadalajara Mexico	27 Sep 1980	Felipe Covarrubias S.
	Independencia		
1753	Guadalajara Mexico Reforma	3 Jun 1990	Jose Saavedra T.
683	*Guadalajara Mexico Union	28 Sep 1980	
	‡Guadalajara Mexico	23 Feb 1975	Emilio Garcia L.
2044	Guadalajara Mexico Victoria	30 Apr 1995	Luis Ruben Castrejon Bonilla
1779	Guaymas Mexico	18 Nov 1990	Ruben A. Palestino
771	Hermosillo Mexico	8 Oct 1976	Hector Ceballos L.
1636	Hermosillo Mexico Pitic	26 Apr 1987	Carlos Pineda O.
1232	*Irapuato Mexico	24 Mar 1992	
	‡Leon Mexico	8 Feb 1981	Armando Gaona J.
1734b	*La Paz Mexico	30 Jan 1990	
	‡Finisterra Mexico	10 Sep 1989	Antonio Aguilar V.
2220	Leon Mexico	11 Aug 1996	Alberto Galo de Jesus Romo Gonzalez
1139	Los Mochis Mexico	25 May 1980	Victor Manuel Soto
1714	Los Mochis Mexico El Fuerte	5 Mar 1989	Ezequiel Fernando Ramirez Q.
795	Madero Mexico	11 Dec 1976	Gabriel Raymundo Saldivar F.
1131	Matamoros Mexico	18 May 1980	Luciano Ramirez
1718	Mazatlan Mexico	7 May 1989	Jose Alberto Holcombe I.
819	Mexicali Mexico	20 Mar 1977	Eduardo Del Rio P.
1626	Mexicali Mexico Los Pinos	18 Jan 1987	Jose de Jesus Ruelas U.
644	Monclova Mexico	26 May 1974	Francisco Aragon Garza
774	Monterrey Mexico Anahuac	17 Oct 1976	Lehi Gracia L.
572	*Monterrey Mexico Libertad	17 Oct 1976	
	*Monterrey Mexico East		
	‡Monterrey East	7 May 1972	Jose Humberto Gonzalez
1765	Monterrey Mexico Los Angeles	22 Jul 1990	Carlos Charles Plata
508	*Monterrey Mexico Mitras	8 Jun 1980	
	*Monterrey Mexico		
	‡Monterrey	22 Mar 1970	Guillermo G. Garza
1114	Monterrey Mexico Moderna	9 Mar 1980	Mauro Garcia Herrera
1144	Monterrey Mexico Morelos	8 Jun 1980	Carlos R. Merino D.
908	Monterrey Mexico Paraiso	23 Apr 1978	Alfredo Gallegos L.

773	Monterrey Mexico Roma	16 Oct 1976	Jose Humberto Gonzalez G.
1615	Monterrey Mexico Valle Verde	2 Nov 1986	Jose F. Torres M.
857	Piedras Negras Mexico	21 Aug 1977	Fidencio Guzman Lugo
2037	Queretaro Mexico	19 Mar 1995	Glendon Lyons Castillo
1132	Reynosa Mexico	18 May 1980	Noe Flores Silva
1767	Saltillo Mexico Miravalle	12 Aug 1990	Edmundo Rodriguez Pena
1155	Saltillo Mexico Republica	29 Jun 1980	Roberto Teodoro Guzman R.
1231	San Luis Potosi Mexico	1 Feb 1981	Guillermo G. Soubervielle R.
2214	*San Luis Potosi Benito Juarez Mexico	4 Aug 1996	Victor Joaquin Herrejon Faburrieta
567	*Tampico Mexico		
	‡Tampico	27 Feb 1972	Guillermo Garmendia
2123	Tampico Mexico Bosque	12 Nov 1995	Luis Eduardo de Leon de Leon
757	Tijuana Mexico	23 May 1976	Carlos Mendez S.
1587	*Tijuana Mexico La Mesa	15 Apr 1986	
	‡La Mesa Mexico	9 Feb 1986	Angel Luevano Cordova
781	Torreon Mexico	12 Nov 1976	David Limon Miranda
1532	Torreon Mexico Jardin	12 May 1985	Rafael Leon Miranda
1736	Torreon Mexico Reforma	15 Oct 1989	Miguel Angel Rivera C.
628	*Valle Hermosa Mexico		
	‡Valle Hermosa	28 Oct 1973	Benjamin Morales

Mexico South Area — 79

1735	Acapulco Mexico	24 Sep 1989	Francisco Javier Torres G.
1971	Atlixco Mexico	16 Jan 1994	Hector Garcia Ceballos
1474	Campeche Mexico	27 May 1984	Gabriel Francisco Ramos G.
2056	Cancun Mexico	28 May 1995	Victor Sebastian Roca Gomez
722	Chalco Mexico	9 Nov 1975	Ruben Valenzuela G.
1822	Chetumal Mexico	27 Oct 1991	Raul Gaspar Rodriguez F.
1043a	Coatzacoalcos Mexico	1 Jul 1979	Raymundo Madris Carbajal
1766	Coatzacoalcos Mexico Puerto	29 Jul 1990	Raul Munoz Z.
721	Cuautla Mexico	9 Nov 1975	Juan Angel Alvaradejo
1983	*Cuautla Mexico Palmas	23 Jan 1996	
	‡Cuautla Mexico Aguahedionda	19 Jun 1994	Luis F. Rodriguez Trejo
1427	Cuernavaca Mexico	5 Jun 1983	Sergio Rojas Espinoza
2107	Iguala Mexico	15 Oct 1995	Alberto Saucedo Roa
1589	Jalapa Mexico	2 Mar 1986	Jorge Sanchez
1764	Juchitan Mexico	22 Jul 1990	Gerardo Castellanos A.
804	Merida Mexico	22 Jan 1977	Abel R. Ordaz R.
1728	Merida Mexico Centro	11 Jun 1989	Joaquin Eduardo Carrillo V.
1754	Merida Mexico Itzimna	10 Jun 1990	Mauro Jose Luis Gil P.
923	Merida Mexico Lakin	14 May 1978	Benigno Pena Pech
1603	Mexico City Mexico Anahuac	29 Jun 1986	Luis Manuel Angel B.
617	*Mexico City Mexico Aragon		
	‡Mexico City Aragon	27 May 1973	Agricol Lozano H.
658	Mexico City Mexico Arbolillo	15 Sep 1974	Guillermo Torres
1317	Mexico City Mexico Azteca	6 Dec 1981	Juan Alberta Ramos B.
719	Mexico City Mexico Camarones	8 Nov 1975	Jorge Rojas O.
1357	Mexico City Mexico Chapultepec	27 Jun 1982	Jose Ismael Ruiz G.
716a	Mexico City Mexico Churubusco	8 Nov 1975	Juan Casanova C.
2000	Mexico City Mexico Contreras	11 Dec 1994	Victor Manuel Salinas G.
1752	Mexico City Mexico Cuautepec	20 May 1990	Salvador Aguirre Osorio
1763	Mexico City Mexico Cuautitlan	8 Jul 1990	Victor M. Cardenas L.
1759	Mexico City Mexico Culturas	17 Jun 1990	Octavio Saul Morales A.
1663	Mexico City Mexico Ecatepec	6 Dec 1987	Juan Manuel Rodriguez C.
718	Mexico City Mexico Ermita	8 Nov 1975	Aurelio Valdespino O.
723	Mexico City Mexico Industrial	9 Nov 1975	Juan Roberto Alva
1070	*Mexico CIty Mexico Meyehualco	11 Dec 1994	
	Mexico City Mexico Iztapalapa	14 Oct 1979	Aurelio Valdespino
1760	Mexico City Mexico La Perla	24 Jun 1990	Pedro Espinosa C.
965	Mexico City Mexico Linda Vista	8 Oct 1978	Fernando R. Dorantes T.
726	Mexico City Mexico Moctezuma	9 Nov 1975	Filiberto Ledezma M.
727	Mexico City Mexico	9 Nov 1975	Jaime Garay M.

	Netzahualcoyotl		
1433	Mexico City Mexico Oriental	19 Jun 1983	Felipe Gerardo Ramirez N.
717a	Mexico City Mexico Tacubaya	8 Nov 1975	Roman Gomez I.
720	*Mexico City Mexico Tlalnepantla 10 Oct 1978		
	‡Mexico City Mexico Satelite	9 Nov 1975	Horacio Tenorio O.
1356	Mexico City Mexico Tlalpan	27 Jun 1982	Jose Alberto Rasales G.
1579	Mexico City Mexico	28 Nov 1985	Arturo Lopez G.
	Valle Dorado		
1980	Mexico City Mexico Vergel	15 May 1994	Ernesto Rosas Vazquez
724	Mexico City Mexico	9 Nov 1975	Juan Manuel Cedeno R.
	Villa de las Flores		
715a	Mexico City	8 Nov 1975	Bonaerges Rubalcava E.
	Mexico Zarahemla		
829	Minatitlan Mexico	15 May 1977	Ignacio Cruz S.
1280	Oaxaca Mexico	21 Jun 1981	M. Ociel Bengoa Vargas
2209	Oaxaca Mexico Mitla	30 Jun 1996	Jose Luis Alonso Trejo
1685	Oaxaca Mexico Monte Alban	7 Feb 1988	Valentin Cruz B.
801	Orizaba Mexico	16 Jan 1977	Humberto Sanchez R.
1466	*Pachuca Mexico 13 Nov 1990		
	‡Mexico City	18 Mar 1984	Alejandro Chavez Rodriguez
	Mexico Pachuca		
2158	Pachuca Mexico Centro	28 Jan 1996	Ismael Mendoza Regino
1716	Papantla Mexico	23 Apr 1989	Antonio Casino C.
730	Poza Rica Mexico	13 Nov 1975	Jose Luis Pichardo M.
799	Poza Rica Mexico Palmas	15 Jan 1977	Angel Valle G.
2225	Puebla Mexico Amalucan	25 Aug 1996	Jose Manuel de la Rosa Rojas
1293	Puebla Mexico Fuertes	11 Oct 1981	Francisco Pineda Salazar
680	Puebla Mexico La Paz	16 Feb 1975	Santiago Mejia M.
1758	Puebla Mexico Nealtican	17 Jun 1990	Marcelino Osorio P.
898	Puebla Mexico Popocateptl	12 Mar 1978	Zeferino Tlatelpa
681	Puebla Mexico Valsequillo	16 Feb 1975	Ramiro Goana M.
2021	Salina Cruz Mexico	5 Feb 1995	Jose Ceferino Castillo Cupil
951	Tapachula Mexico	20 Aug 1978	Jorge David Arrevilla M.
1762	Tapachula Mexico Izapa	8 Jul 1990	Guillermo Sanchez R.
1730	Tecalco Mexico	25 Jun 1989	Felipe Hernandez L.
2164	Tlaxcala Mexico	11 Feb 1996	Mosiah Saul Delgado Gonzalez
1829	Toluca Mexico	17 Nov 1991	Gilberto Lopez D'Antin
725	Tula Mexico	9 Nov 1975	Silvino Mera U.
1943	Tuxtepec Mexico	6 June 1993	Marcelo Valis Medina
1174	Tuxtla Gutierrez Mexico	31 Aug 1980	Enrique Sanchez Casillas
2028	Tuxtla Gutierrez		
	Mexico Grijalva	26 Feb 1995	Moises Ulloa Solis
1653	Valle del Mezquital Mexico	13 Sep 1987	Joel Gandara Salazar
700	Veracruz Mexico	15 Jun 1975	Leon Lopez Alavez
1751	Veracruz Mexico Mocambo	20 May 1990	Fernando Lagunez V.
800	Veracruz Mexico Reforma	16 Jan 1977	Leon Lopez A.
2119	Veracruz Mexico Villa Rica	5 Nov 1995	Marco Antonio Caarrillo Bogard
1166	Villahermosa Mexico	10 Aug 1980	Jose Luis Madrigal N.
1746	*Villahermosa Mexico Gaviotas 5 Oct 1993		
	‡Villahermosa Mexico	15 Apr 1990	Joaquin Gonzalez L.
	Las Gaviotas		
2242	Zamora Mexico	22 Sep 1996	Juan Lopez Tejeda

Discontinued

344 ‡Mexico City Mexico
8 Nov 1975 †Mexico City Mexico Churubusco (716a), Mexico City Mexico
Tacubaya (717a), Mexico City Mexico Ermita (718), Mexico City
Mexico Chapultepec (No. 1357)
*Mexico City   7 May 196
‡Mexico

534 *Mexico City Mexico East   15 Nov 1970   Agricol Lozano
8 Nov 1975 †Chalco Mexico (No. 722), Mexico City Mexico Villa de las
Flores (No. 724), Mexico City Mexico Moctezuma (726), Mexico City
Mexico Netzahualcoyotl (727)
‡Mexico City Mexico East   3 Dec 1961   Harold Brown

434 *Mexico City Mexico North

‡Mexico City North   7 May 1967   Agricol Lozano
8 Nov 1975 †Tampico Mexico (No. 567), Mexico City Mexico Camarones
(No. 719), Mexico City Mexico Satelite (No. 720)

Missions — 18
(As of Oct. 1, 1996; shown with historical number. See MISSIONS.)

(208) MEXICO CHIHUAHUA MISSION
Sucursal "3" de Correos
Apartado Postal 3-41
Chihuahua, Chihuahua
C.P. 31250 Mexico
Phone: (011-52-14) 13-77-76

(201) MEXICO CULIACAN MISSION
A.P. 645 Rio Mocorito 251 Ote.
Colonia Guadalupe
Culiacan, Sinaloa
C.P. 80000 Mexico
Phone: (011-52-67) 15-12-48

(125) MEXICO GUADALAJARA MISSION
Apartado Postal 22-3
C.P. 44290
Guadalajara, Jalisco Mexico
Phone: (011-52-3) 651-49-15

(56) MEXICO HERMOSILLO MISSION
Apartado Postal 557
Hermosillo, Sonora, C.P. 83000
Mexico
Phone: (011-52-62) 14-15-02

(222a) MEXICO LEON MISSION
Apartado Postal 1-1125
Leon, Guanajuato
37000 Mexico
Phone: (011-52-47) 70-12-21

(126) MEXICO MERIDA MISSION
Apartado Postal #26 y 27 Sucursal C
97000, Merida, Yucatan
Mexico
Phone: (011-52-99) 23-58-60

(193) MEXICO MEXICO CITY
 EAST MISSION
Fuente de Piramides No. 1
Piso 10, Lomas de Tecamachalco
Edo. de Mexico C.P. 53950
Mexico
Phone: (011-52-5) 245-9287

(163) MEXICO MEXICO CITY
 NORTH MISSION
Fuente de Piramides #1, Piso #1
Lomas de Tecamachalco,
Edo. de Mexico
C.P. 53950 Mexico
Phone: (011-52-5) 245-9288

(20) MEXICO MEXICO CITY
 SOUTH MISSION
Monte Caucaso 1110
Lomas de Chapultepec
Mexico D.F., C.P. 11000 Mexico
Phone: (011-52-5) 540-3797

(45) MEXICO MONTERREY
 NORTH MISSION
Calle Cerralvo #134
Colonia Libertad
Cd. Guadalupe, Nuevo Leon Mexico
Phone: (011-52-8) 379-6858

(276) MEXICO MONTERREY SOUTH
MISSION
Calle Chiapas #2202
Colonia Roma Sur
Monterrey, Nuevo Leon, 64700
Mexico
Phone: (011-52-8) 358-1044

(246) MEXICO OAXACA MISSION
Huerta de los Ciruelos esquina con
Huerta de los Olivos #100
Fracc. Trinidad de las Huertas
Oaxaca, Oaxaca,Mexico
C.P. 68120
Phone: (011-52-951) 4 20 17

(217) MEXICO PUEBLA MISSION
Calle 25 Sur #907
Col. La Paz
Puebla, Puebla 72160
Mexico
Phone: (011-52-22) 49-88-07

(218) MEXICO TAMPICO MISSION
Apartado Postal 241
Cd. Madero, Tamaulipas
A.P. 89460
Mexico
Phone: (011-52-12) 16-65-50

(247) MEXICO TIJUANA MISSION
Apartado Postal 3379
Tijuana, B.C.N. 22000
Mexico C.P. 27000
Phone: (011-52-66) 85-72-78

(209) MEXICO TUXTLA GUTIERREZ
MISSION
Apartado 278
Tuxtla Guitierrez, Chiapas
Mexico C.P. 29000
Phone: (011-52-961) 2-14-41

(81) MEXICO TORREON MISSION
Apartado Postal 792
Torreon, Coahuila
Mexico
Phone: (011-52-17) 12-33-92

(75) MEXICO VERACRUZ MISSION
Apartado Postal 103
Veracruz, Veracruz
C.P. 91700
Mexico
Phone: (011-52-29) 31-35-66

MICRONESIA

Year-end 1996: Est. population, 123,000; Members, 3,000; Districts, 5; Branches, 23; Percent LDS, 2.4, or one LDS in 41; Philippines/Micronesia Area; Micronesia Guam Mission.

Extending along the 1,800-mile Caroline Islands archipelago, the Federated States of Micronesia has a culturally diverse population that speaks eight island dialects.

CHUUK

In Chuuk (Truk), two missionaries, Elders Dan Baldwin and Torlik Timaarrived, July 7, 1977. They baptized T. M. Conrad Mailo and his wife, Nisor Cerly David, on Oct. 22, 1977. The first Trukese missionary was Happiness Ichin, the second convert on the island. By 1980, membership reached 170, and on May 31, 1981, the Truk-Pohnpei District was created. A meetinghouse was dedicated April 24, 1983. By 1990, the district had been divided, and two meetinghouses dedicated.

A visit to Micronesia by Michaelene P. Grassli, Primary general president, and Virginia H. Pearce, board member, in June 1991, included stops in Chuuk, Pohnpei, Kosrae, and Kwajalein.

KOSRAE

Work in Kosrae began in March 1985, but missionaries found little success. They worked hard to break down public opinion against the Church. The first Kosrean, Isidro Abraham, was baptized April 26, 1986. By October 1989 when a branch conference was held at Lela, 72 people attended. Kosrae became a district on March 14, 1990. The first seminary graduation took place on Aug. 1, 1990. Ground was broken for the Malem meetinghouse on Dec. 21, 1989, and the completed facility was dedicated Dec. 3, 1992. The Lelu meetinghouse was dedicated in January 1993.

POHNPEI

Pohnpei Island was opened to missionary work on Oct. 23, 1976, when Elders George L. Mortensen and Aldric Porter arrived. The first baptism on the island, however, did not occur until Feb. 7, 1981. Missionary work progressed steadily and the Pohnpei District was created Nov. 22, 1985. In 1990, membership was 464. In late 1993, 18 young women in the Pohnpei District held their first camp on the island of Madolenihmn.

YAP

The Church came to Yap in 1977, with Charles Keliikipi, under contract to organize a police department on the island, assigned to organize the Church here. The first missionaries, Elders David S. Ige and Douglas Andrews, came that year as well. The first convert was baptized in March 1978, and afterwards several families came into the Church. The first missionary couple was Elder and Sister Stewart, who arrived Aug. 2, 1979. A meetinghouse was completed Jan. 13, 1981. By 1990, membership on the island was 150. The first seminary graduation on Yap was held Aug. 16, 1990.

Sources: *Church News*, Jan 9, 1952; *Unto the Isles of the Sea*, by R. Lanier Britsch; *Church News*, March 4, 1989; *Brief History of the Micronesia-Guam Mission*, published by the Micronesia Guam Mission, 1990, Lewis V. Nord, president; "Visit to area reveals growing gospel roots," by Sheridan R. Sheffield, *Church News*, June 22, 1991; *Church News*, Nov. 13, 1993.

MONGOLIA

Year-end 1995: Est. population, 2,500,000; Members, 400; Missions, 1; Branches, 3; Asia Area.

In east central Asia between Russia and China, Mongolia is a socialist country with a population that speaks Mongolian and traditionally follows Lama Buddhist beliefs.

Elder Monte J. Brough of the Asia Area presidency met with top government officials and the directors of five universities in May and August 1992. Afterward, six missionary couples were sent to assist the country's higher education program and to teach others about the Church. The first couples arrived Sept. 16, 1992, and lived in Ulaanbaatar, which is home to half the population of Mongolia. Elder Kenneth H. Beesley, former president of LDS Business College, and his wife, Donna, headed the couples. The first sacrament meeting was held Sept. 20, 1992, in Elder and Sister Beesley's apartment. The Ulaanbaatar Branch was organized in 1993. The first converts were Lamjav Purevsuren and Tsendkhuu Bat-Ulzii, baptized Feb. 6, 1993.

The first six missionary couples to arrive included the Beesleys, Royce P. and Mary Jane Flandro, Richard G. and Anna M. Harper, Stanley B. and Marjorie Smith, C. DuWayne and Alice C. Schmidt, and Gary and Barbara L. Carlson. The first full-time elders were Bart Jay Birch, Duane Lee Blanchard, Brett Andrew Hansen, Jared K. Meier, Curtis Dee Mortensen and Bradley Jay Pierson.

On April 15, 1993, Elder Neal A. Maxwell of the Quorum of the Twelve and Elder Kwok Yuen Tai of the Seventy visited Mongolia. Fifty government officials attended a reception that evening hosted by the Church.

A foundation representing the Church was legally registered Jan. 17, 1994, and efforts continue to have the Church fully recognized.

By March 1, 1996, attendance at the branch averaged between 85 and 110. Among the early converts were a professor at Mongolian University of Art, editor of an English-language newspaper, a veterinarian, a physician and a computer operator. The Mongolia Ulaanbaatar Mission was created July 1, 1995, with Richard E. Cook serving as president.

Source: *Church News,* Sept. 19, 1992; correspondence from Elder Kenneth H. Beesley to Asia Area presidency, Feb. 24, 1994.

Mission — 1
(As of Oct. 1, 1996; shown with historical number. See MISSIONS.)

(307) MONGOLIA ULAANBAATAR MISSION
Box #258
Ulaanbaatar 210644
Mongolia
Phone: (011-976-1) 313-789

MOZAMBIQUE
Year-end 1995: Est. population, 18,385,000; Members, fewer than 100, Africa Area.

A country on the southeast coast of Africa, Mozambique covers 309,496 square miles and has a population of about 17 million. Almost all Mozambicans are Africans and speak one of the Bantu languages, although fewer than 1 percent of the population are minorities. The country's official language is Portuguese.

About 55 percent of the people practice tribal African religions. About 30 percent are Christians, mostly Roman Catholics. Many are Muslims.

The Church was legally recognized in Mozambique in 1996. But prior to that, people in Mozambique benefited from Church humanitarian aid. A deadly drought, the worst in 100 years, caused great suffering in Mozambique and in neighboring countries. In 1992, the Church shipped 1 million pounds of food and relief items for victims of the drought in this area.

Sources: World Book Encyclopedia, vol. 13, pp. 904-905; 1996 correspondence from Elder James O. Mason, Africa Area president and member of the Seventy; "Deadly drought," *Church News,* Sept. 26, 1992.

NAMIBIA
Year-end 1995: Est. population, 1,677,000; Members, 200; Branches, 1; Africa Area; South Africa Cape Town Mission.

The Republic of Namibia in Southern Africa became an independent nation March 20, 1990, and has a population that speaks Afrikaans, English, and indigenous languages. Namibians are Lutheran, 50 percent, and other Christian, 30 percent.

Namibia, which prior to independence was known as South West Africa, did not have a formal LDS Church organization until 1973, when Otto Krauss was called as the presiding elder. The first Church meeting had been held in the Krauss home in April

1972. The first missionaries in Namibia were Elders Daniel Gustafson and Douglas Stone, who arrived in 1978. The first baptism was Vernon Collett, and the first branch was organized in Windhoek in 1983, with Dieter Greiner as the first branch president. The first missionary called from Namibia was Andre Van der Merwe, who began serving in the South Africa Johannesburg Mission in 1992. The first district was formed in 1991, with Elder A. Eugene Hilton as the first district president. However, the district was dissolved in 1992.

A few weeks before Namibia gained its independence, four elders and one couple began proselyting in Windhoek. At the time there were fewer than 20 members in the entire country. Namibian Pres.-elect Sam Nujoma had stated at the time of independence that missionaries were welcome in his country.

Converts were steadily added to the Windhoek and Rehoboth branches, and about 100 people attended each branch as of October 1991.

Leaders reported that the branches frequently have more people attending than are on the record books. A Scouting program was organized in Windhoek that provides wholesome activities for the young men. Relief Society sisters took part in an educational program for less-fortunate women during a service project in 1992-93.

In 1995, the seminary program was begun. On Feb. 18, 1996, members from Namibia joined some 5,000 other Latter-day Saints for the Johannesburg Regional Conference — the largest such gathering in South Africa.

Sources: Brief history of Namibia prepared in 1994 by Elder Darol D. Allred, executive secretary of the Windhoek Branch and full-time missionary with his wife, Beth; "Gospel springs forth in harsh desert land of new Africa nation," by Mark Newman and Greg Hagen, *Church News*, Oct. 5, 1991; "Four nations in central, southern Africa," by Mary Mostert and Gerry Avant, *Church News* Sept. 26, 1992, March 2, 1996, March 9, 1996

NETHERLANDS

Year-end 1995: Est. population, 15,453,000; Members, 7,500; Stakes, 3; Wards, 15; Branches, 22; Missions, 1; Percent LDS, 0.04, or one LDS in 2,060.

In northwest Europe on the North Sea, The Netherlands, also known as Holland, is a constitutional monarchy with a Dutch-speaking population that is 36 percent Roman Catholic and 19 percent Dutch Reformed.

The Church's presence in The Netherlands goes back to1841, when Elder Orson Hyde, while on a missionary journey to Jerusalem, spent more than a week in Rotterdam and Amsterdam explaining the gospel to Jewish rabbis.

The first missionaries assigned to labor in The Netherlands arrived Aug. 5, 1861. By May 10, 1862, they had baptized 14 people in Amsterdam, and organized the first branch here.

For the first three years, the area was part of the Swiss-German Mission. The Netherlands Mission was established Nov. 1, 1864. The mission also serves the Flemish-speaking northern half of Belgium.

For many years, the Church was not allowed to own property in The Netherlands, and it remains difficult to obtain permits to purchase land for meetinghouses. Official recognition of the Church was received in August 1955, after nearly 20 years of petitioning. This was considered a major breakthrough, since legal recognition gives the Church the right to hold property, exemption from taxation on Church properties and a certain degree of stature.

In the first 100 years of the Church in The Netherlands, some 4,500 missionaries served there, and more than 14,000 people were baptized. A large percentage of those converts emigrated to the United States.

In recent years, however, with temples more accessible, few members have emigrated, and today there are many second-, third- and even fourth-generation members in the wards and branches. The first non-English-speaking stake in the Church was organized in The Hague in 1961, with Johan Paul Jongkees as president. Elder Jacob de Jager, an emeritus member of the Seventy, was the first General Authority born in Holland.

More than 2,000 people attended the first regional conference held in the Netherlands in June 1984.

In 1990, Church members organized a food drive among members and non-members that resulted in the shipment to Romania of 12 large truckloads of food. LDS member Jeane Henny Kirschbaum received a royal golden medal of honor from the burgomaster of Heemstede in 1993 for her community service.

During the summer of 1995, members organized displays, offered workshops and presented theme-centered entertainment for 650 visitors interested in learning to deal with youth problems, different lifestyles and pressures affecting children. The purpose was to educate parents and increase their influence with their children while acquainting them with the Church.

Sources: *Encyclopedic History of the Church,* by Andrew Jenson; *Church News,* March 11 and 25, 1961; *History of the Netherlands Mission 1861-1966,* by Keith C. Warner, a BYU thesis, August 1967; "Netherlands," *Ensign,* August, 1973; *Church News,* June 24, 1984, March 17, 1990; *Church News,* Nov. 20, 1993; *Church News,* July 29, 1995.

Stakes — 3
(Listed alphabetically as of Oct. 1, 1996.)

No.	Name	Organized	First President
Europe West Area			
1720	Apeldoorn Netherlands	14 May 1989	Max Henning Van Der Put
326	*The Hague Netherlands	12 Aug 1976	
	*The Hague Holland		
	‡Holland	12 Mar 1961	Johan Paul Jongkees
933	*Rotterdam Netherlands	16 Oct 1994	
	Utrecht Netherlands	28 May 1978	Eugene M. Engelbert

Mission — 1
(As of Oct. 1, 1996; shown with historical number. See MISSIONS.)

(8a) NETHERLANDS AMSTERDAM MISSION
Noordse Bosje 16
1211 BG Hilversum, Netherlands
Phone: (011-31-35) 624-8346

NETHERLANDS ANTILLES
Year-end 1995: Est. population, 207,000; Members, fewer than 100; Branches, 3; North America Southeast Area; West Indies Mission.

Made up of two groups of islands in the Caribbean, the Netherlands Antilles are considered part of The Netherlands. Work was opened and closed on Curacao in 1978-79 by the Venezuela Caracas Mission. However, a branch was created on Curacao Oct. 31, 1979. The branch was divided in April 1987, but rejoined in January 1988. A meetinghouse was dedicated in August 1988.

Sources: Venezuela Caracas Mission manuscript history; "Book of Mormon now in 80 Languages," *Ensign,* March 1988; *Church News,* April 2, 1988.

ARUBA
Year-end 1995: Est. population, 64,000; Members, fewer than 100; Branches, 1; North America Southeast Area; West Indies Mission.

An autonomous member of The Netherlands, Aruba lies 18 miles off the coast of Venezuela. A branch was organized on Aruba Aug. 13, 1986, and missionaries were sent in January 1987. Selections of the Book of Mormon were translated into Papiamento in 1987, and coupled with activity by missionaries, brought a successful reactivation effort.

Sources: Venezuela Caracas Mission manuscript history; "Book of Mormon now in 80 Languages," *Ensign,* March 1988; *Church News,* April 2, 1988.

ST. MAARTEN
Year-end 1995: Est. population, 4,500; Members, fewer than 100; Branches, 1; North America Southeast Area; West Indies Mission.

The Island of St. Maarten in the Caribbean, with 20 square miles and an estimated population of 4,500, was part of the France Toulouse Mission when the St. Maarten Branch was organized Jan. 9, 1979. The mission was discontinued and work resumed with the West Indies Mission. Elders Thad Ariens and Victor Quarty began working in St. Maarten, the administration of which is divided between the Dutch and French governments. The Claire Dinane family, which was baptized on Guadeloupe, moved to St. Maarten and helped re-open the St. Maarten Branch on Jan. 31, 1984.

Source: Manuscript History of the France Toulouse Mission.

NEW ZEALAND
Year-end 1995: Est. population, 3,405,000; Members, 82,000; Stakes, 20; Wards, 121; Branches, 79; Missions, 2; Districts, 5; Temples, 1; Percent LDS, 2.4, or one LDS in 41.

Located in the South Pacific in the Tasman Sea, New Zealand has a parliamentary government. Its English-speaking population is Anglican, 29 percent; Presbyterian, 18 percent; and Roman Catholic, 15 percent.

Augustus Farnham, president of the Australian Mission, accompanied by William Cooke, arrived in New Zealand Oct. 27, 1854, and preached with little success in Auckland and Nelson for two months. Elder Cooke then remained alone and in March 1855, baptized 10 people, and organized a branch at Karori in April. A few other missionaries followed, and a handful of converts emigrated to Utah. Persecution arose, and in 1871 the New Zealand parliament briefly considered the "Mormon invasion."

At first missionary work centered among Europeans. At the end of 1880, seven branches had been established with 133 members. However, at this time President Joseph F. Smith of the First Presidency instructed missionaries to concentrate on the indigenous Maori people.

Mission Pres. William F. Bromley subsequently assigned Elders Alma Greenwood and Ira N. Hinckley Jr. to teach Maoris in the southern tip of the North Island.

Prior to the arrival of the missionaries to the Maoris, at least five Maori leaders, some of whom were Tohungas (spiritual leaders) while others were tribal wise men, had told of a "true religion" that would come. Because many beliefs of the Maoris and missionaries were similar, a number of Maoris were converted. The first conversions came in the Waikato region, but others soon followed. The first Maori baptized was Ngataki, on Oct. 18, 1881.

By the end of 1884, membership included 265 Europeans and 811 Maoris. Membership among the Maoris increased to nearly 4,000 in 79 branches by the turn of the century, an almost all-Maori membership.

The Book of Mormon was translated into Maori in April 1889. The New Zealand Mission was created Jan. 1, 1898. In 1907, the First Presidency authorized a secondary school to add to the primary educational program that was previously established. The Maori Agricultural College was completed in 1913. It operated until 1931, when it was damaged beyond repair by an earthquake. Elder Matthew Cowley of the Quorum of the Twelve made many contributions to the Church as he served as missionary, mission president and supervising General Authority of New Zealand.

By the mid-1930s, the Church had grown to 8,600. After World War II ended, the Church expanded beyond its primarily Maori membership, as many of European ancestry joined.

In 1948, Elder Cowley announced plans for a new school, and in February 1955, the First Presidency announced plans for a temple near Hamilton. Both facilities were largely constructed by labor missionaries. Dedicated in 1958 were the newly built temple on April 20, and the Church College of New Zealand on April 26. The first stake in New Zealand was created in Auckland May 18 of the same year. Membership at the time was 17,000 but grew to 26,000 in the next eight years. In 1968-70, the seminary program was established. Some 12,000 members attended an area conference in 1976 at which President Spencer W. Kimball spoke.

In 1987, Elder Douglas J. Martin, a former stake president from Hamilton, was called to the Second Quorum of the Seventy. Membership in 1990 was 76,000.

Sources: *Zion in New Zealand* by Brian W. Hunt; *Encyclopedic History of the Church*, by Andrew Jenson; Origin of the Maori People in New Zealand, by Stewart Meha; *Church News*, Jan. 18, 1964, p. 6; *Church News*, May 9, 1936, p. 1; The Church in New Zealand, by Mervyn Dykes, *Ensign*, February 1976.

Stakes — 22
(Listed alphabetically as of Oct. 1, 1996.)

No.	Name	Organized	First President
Pacific Area			
630	Auckland New Zealand Harbour	4 Nov 1973	Kenneth M. Palmer
1304	Auckland New Zealand Henderson	8 Nov 1981	Alan Robert Patterson
861	Auckland New Zealand Manukau	18 Sep 1977	Oscar Westerlund
455	*Auckland New Zealand Manurewa ‡Auckland South	5 May 1968	Geoffrey R. Garlick
264	*Auckland New Zealand Mount Roskill ‡Auckland	18 May 1958	George R. Biesinger

1973	Auckland New Zealand Panmure	13 Feb 1994	Stephen Aubrey Keung
2222	Auckland New Zealand Papakura	25 Aug 1996	Moses Christopher Armstrong
2223	Auckland N.Z. Papatoetoe	25 Aug 1996	Ephraim Cooper
1664	Auckland N.Z. Tamaki	13 Dec 1987	Clark W. Palmerston Larkins
953	Christchurch New Zealand	27 Aug 1978	Bardia Pine Taiapa
1104	Gisborne New Zealand	14 Feb 1980	William Pakimana Taurima
310	*Hamilton New Zealand ‡Hamilton	13 Nov 1960	Wendell H. Wiser
2001	Hamilton New Zealand Glenview	18 Dec 1994	Richard Saxon Ball
313	*Hastings New Zealand ‡Hawkes Bay	20 Nov 1960	Joseph Alvin Higbee
2103	Hastings N.Z. Flaxmere	15 Oct 1995	Lawrence Victor Maxwell
475	*Kaikohe New Zealand ‡New Zealand North (New Zealand)	19 Jan 1969	Stanley J. Hay
1012	Palmerston North N.Z.	18 Mar 1979	James Dunlop
884	Rotorua New Zealand	27 Nov 1977	Paul Robert Thomas
445	*Temple View New Zealand ‡Hamilton South	19 Nov 1967	Harry S. Peckham
853	Upper Hutt New Zealand	14 Aug 1977	Trevor A. Beatson
407	*Wellington New Zealand ‡Wellington	12 May 1965	Keith A. Harrison
2002	Whangarei New Zealand	18 Dec 1994	Hira Paea Nepia Christy

Missions — 2

(As of Oct. 1, 1996; shown with historical number. See MISSIONS.)

(20) NEW ZEALAND AUCKLAND MISSION
P.O. Box 33-840
Takapuna, Auckland 9
New Zealand
Phone: (011-64-9) 489-5102

(143) NEW ZEALAND WELLINGTON MISSION
P.O. Box 50448
Porirua
New Zealand
Phone: (011-64-4) 237-8248

NICARAGUA

Year-end 1995: Est. population, 4,225,000; Members, 18,000; Missions, 1; Districts, 13; Branches, 96; Percent LDS, 0.4, or one LDS in 234; Central America Area.

Located in Central America, the Republic of Nicaragua has a Spanish-speaking population that is 95 percent Roman Catholic.

Elder Spencer W. Kimball, then of the Quorum of the Twelve, promoted work in Central America that led to the opening of the Central America Mission in 1952. Two missionaries from that mission, Elders Manuel Arias and Archie R. Mortensen, entered Nicaragua in 1953. They encountered difficulties at first, but on April 11, 1954, baptized Jose D. Guzman. Other conversions followed. The Nicaraguan District was organized in 1959. The Managua Stake was organized March 22, 1981, with Jose R. Armando Garcia A. as president, but it was discontinued on Oct. 15, 1989.

Missionary work was interrupted in September 1978, as internal conflicts and a civil war led to missionaries being withdrawn. Work continued under local missionaries, and full-time work resumed in the late 1980s. During the periods when few outside leaders entered the country, the local members continued faithfully. In the summer of 1987, members of the Managua Stake received government permission and traveled by bus to the Guatemala City Temple for their temple work.

When the Nicaragua Managua Mission was organized Oct. 15, 1989, following normalization of the government, membership was 3,453. By December 1990, membership had increased to 8,000 members, and by 1995, to 18,000. The members had 100 percent home teaching in the last three months of 1990, and 800 men were ordained to the Melchizedek Priesthood, reported Elder Ted E. Brewerton of the Seventy, area president.

Sources: "LDS Scene," *Ensign*, November, 1978; "Church Continues to Progress in Nicaragua," *Ensign*, Feb. 1979; "A Prayer Answered," by William Hale Kehr, *Church News* May 19, 1979;"Nicaraguans eager to learn, improve lives through gospel," by Gerry Avant, *Church News*, Nov. 22, 1980; "Church Denies Charges in Nicaragua," *Ensign*, Oct. 1982; "Work is booming as members eagerly share their testimonies with friends," *Church News*, Feb. 16, 1991.

		Stakes — 0	
No.	Name	**Organized**	**First President**
		Discontinued	
1246	Managua Nicaragua	22 Mar 1981	Jose R. Armando Garcia A.
	15 Oct 1989 †Nicaragua Managua Mission		

Mission — 1

(As of Oct. 1, 1996; shown with historical number. See MISSIONS.)

(227) NICARAGUA MANAGUA MISSION
Apartado Postal 3527
Managua, Nicaragua C.A.
Phone: (011-505-2) 66-19-50

NIGERIA

Year-end 1995: Est. population, 101,245,000; Members, 28,000; Stakes, 3; Wards, 19; Branches, 109; Missions, 3; Districts, 16; Percent LDS, 0.02, or one LDS in 3,615.

On the west coast of Africa bordering the Gulf of Guinea, the Federal Republic of Nigeria has a military government with a population that speaks English, Hausa, Yoruba and Ibo. Three-fourths of the population is Muslim, with a large number of Christians in the southern half.

The restored gospel took root spontaneously in Nigeria two decades before it was formally preached in that country. From the late 1950s on, some Nigerians learned about the Church through magazine articles and acquired Church literature.

Groups of people began meeting unofficially in the Church's name, and through the years some of them wrote to Church headquarters requesting missionaries. Glen G. Fisher, returning from serving as president of the South Africa Mission, visited Nigeria in 1960 and reported that the groups were sincere, and recommended sending missionaries. However, attempts to send missionaries were thwarted because visas were unavailable.

The historic revelation on the priesthood, announced June 9, 1978, was the catalyst for the start of missionary work in Nigeria. In November of that year, two couples — Elder and Sister Rendell N. Mabey and Elder and Sister Edwin Q. Cannon Jr. — were sent to Nigeria and Ghana as special representatives of the Church's International Mission. They arrived Nov. 8, and soon searched out and taught the gospel to people who had been meeting in the Church's name and praying for the coming of Church representatives. The first baptized was Anthony Ozodimma Obinna, one of those who had waited many years for the coming of the missionaries. By early 1980, more than 1,700 converts were baptized in the two countries.

Brother Obinna died Aug. 25, 1995. His funeral in Aboh Mbaise, Nigeria, drew a huge congregation, and a homemade mortar provided a gun salute.

The Africa West Mission was organized July 1, 1980. The name was changed to Nigeria Lagos Mission July 1, 1985.

Less than 10 years after the Church's establishment in Nigeria, membership approached 10,000 in 1987. Twin milestones occurred in 1988, with the creation of the Aba Nigeria Stake May 15, under the direction of Elder Neal A. Maxwell of the Quorum of the Twelve, and the division July 1 of the Nigeria Lagos Mission to create the Nigeria Aba Mission. The Jos and Ilorin missions, with Nigerian mission presidents Ato Kwamina Dadson and John Agbonkonkon Ehanire, respectively, were organized July 1, 1992. In the local branches, self-help was emphasized. By 1994, Nigeria had three stakes and 12 districts. Church programs continue to bless the lives of Nigerian Saints, such as young women in the Port Harcourt (Nigeria) 2nd Ward, who held their first Young Women in Excellence program. In addition, Relief Society sisters in Port Harcourt are participating in the Church's Gospel Literacy Effort to increase spiritual and temporal self-reliance. Saints in this African country are faithful despite challenges. Benin City Nigeria Stake members do home teaching though few families have cars or telephones. Sacrament meeting attendance is high despite political turmoil and frequent transportation disruptions.

Sources: Swiss Mission manuscript history; "Nigeria and Ghana", by Janet Brigham, *Ensign*, Feb. 1980; *Brother to Brother*, by Rendell N. Mabey and Gordon T. Allred, Bookcraft, 1984; "Nigeria marks twin milestones," *Church News*, May 21, 1988; *All Are Alike unto God*, edited by E. Dale LeBaron, Bookcraft, 1990; *Church News*, Oct. 8, 1994, Dec. 2, 1995, June 1, 1996, Sept. 7, 1996.

(Listed alphabetically as of Oct. 1, 1996.)

No.	Name	Organized	First President
Africa Area			
1695	Aba Nigeria	15 May 1988	David William Eka
1957	Benin City Nigeria	24 Oct 1993	Alexander Afamefuna Odume
2237	Etinan Nigeria	22 Sep 1996	Emmanuel Sunday Ekaete
1781	Port Harcourt Nigeria	25 Nov 1990	Ephriam Sobere Etete
2211	Qua River Nigeria	14 Jul 1996	Udo David Umoh
2238	Umuahia Nigeria	22 Sep 1996	Godwin E. Woko

Missions —3

(As of Oct. 1, 1996; shown with historical number. See MISSIONS.)

(275) NIGERIA ENUGU MISSION
83 Ogui Road
P.O. Box 4133
Enugu, Enugu State
Nigeria
Phone: (011-234-42) 251-820

(179) NIGERIA LAGOS MISSION
50 E. North Temple
Salt Lake City, UT 84150
Phone : (011-234-1) 497-4712

(221) NIGERIA PORT HARCOURT MISSION
P.O. Box 7116, Trans-Amadi
Port Harcourt, Rivers State,
Nigeria
Phone: (011-234-84) 238-633

NIUE

Year-end 1995: Est. population, 1,750; Members, 300; Districts, 1; Branches, 2; Percent LDS, 17, or one LDS in 6; Pacific Area; New Zealand Auckland Mission.

Niue, located in the South Pacific about 300 miles south of the Samoan Islands, is a self-governing island under New Zealand protection. Most residents speak Niuean, and belong to the London Missionary Society religion. The island has a -6 percent growth rate.

The first LDS members in Niue were Fritz Bunge-Kruger and his family, who arrived in 1952 to do missionary work. He traveled about the island and showed movies, and then, with the contacts he made, started a home Sunday School. It soon grew to an attendance of 80. They moved to a local dance hall for meetings and on May 29, 1952, a Mutual Improvement Association was organized. The following August, 26 converts were baptized by Elder Thayne Christensen. Other baptismal services followed, and a total of 65 were baptized the first year. Because of persecution during open air meetings, activities were held quietly at first, but at times entire villages attended. The first Niuean missionary was Sionemologa Tagavaitau.

On Feb. 12, 1955, work commenced on the Alofi Chapel with a handful of members raising money and doing much of the building by hand. They were assisted by labor missionaries. The building was completed in 1958. Additional Church buildings were erected later.

About a third or more of the Niuean members have moved to New Zealand. Devastating hurricanes hit the island in 1959, 1960 and 1990. Many homes were leveled. Members in Niue, particularly the youth, have often distinguished themselves in island competitions.

Sources: *History of the Church in Niue* by Sister Relva R. Price, May 1973; *Unto the Islands of the Sea,* by R. Lanier Britsch; correspondence from Adelia Shumway from Niue Island, Aug. 24, 1990; interview with Fritz Kruger, 1991; *Church News*, Aug. 29, 1992.

NORTHERN IRELAND

(See United Kingdom)

NORTHERN MARIANA ISLANDS

Year-end 1995: Est. population, 43,000; Members, 500; Branches, 4; Percent LDS, 0.1, or one LDS in 86; Philippines/Micronesia Area; Micronesia Guam Mission.

The Northern Mariana Islands are a commonwealth administered by the United

States. Its population is primarily of Chamorro people.

SAIPAN

Among the first church members to Saipan were American servicemen in 1944, including L. Tom Perry, later a member of the Quorum of the Twelve. Missionary work in Saipan began in the early 1970s, but was stopped because of local hostility. In February 1975, Elders Jeff Frame and Callis Carlton began full-time missionary work. One of the first group meetings on the island was held July 24, 1975.

LDS member Alfred "Mustang" Gonzalez became construction manager of the new airport, arriving July 16, 1975, and brought his family the following October. They brought a small vacant quonset hut that had been abandoned in the jungle and used it for a meetinghouse. After this building was too small, meetings were held in the elders' kitchen and living room. Sunday School classes were held outside under the coconut trees. A small building was completed in 1983. Brad T. Nago and his wife, Jean, were converts in Saipan, baptized Jan. 24, 1976, and became president of Saipan's Chalan Laulau Branch after the Gonzalez family returned to Hawaii. At the time the Micronesia Guam Mission was created in 1980, the Saipan Branch had 85 members.

President Gordon B. Hinckley, Elder Joseph B. Wirthlin and their wives visited briefly with 10 missionaries and about 60 of Saipan's 300 members during a refueling stop en route home from Asia June 1, 1996.

ROTA — TINIAN

Elders Stephen Jones and Kamealoha Kaniho were assigned to open Rota, an island in the Northern Marianas, for proselyting on Sept. 5, 1986. Work was opened on Tinian Aug. 14, 1992, by Elder James Adamson and an Elder McCune.

Source: *Brief History of the Micronesia-Guam Mission,* published by the Micronesia Guam Mission, 1990, Lewis V. Nord, president; unpublished "History of the Chalan Laulau Branch of the Guam Micronesia Mission."

NORWAY

Year-end 1995: Est. population, 4,330,000; Members, 4,100; Stakes, 1; Wards, 7; Branches, 17; Missions, 1; Districts, 3; Percent LDS, 0.09, or one LDS in 1,056.

In western Scandinavia on the Norwegian Sea, the kingdom of Norway is a hereditary constitutional monarchy. Its people speak Norwegian and Lappish and 94 percent are Evangelical Lutheran.

Missionary work in Norway grew out of the effort in Denmark. Hans F. Petersen, one of the first converts in Denmark, was sent as a missionary to Norway in September 1851. Other elders followed, and the first baptisms took place at Osterrisor on Nov. 26, 1851. A branch was organized there July 16, 1852, and another in Frederikstad July 25, 1852.

Church units in Norway were part of the Scandinavian Mission until 1905, when the Danish-Norwegian Mission was organized. Norway was separated from Denmark into a mission of its own in 1920.

In the early days, many missionaries in Norway were arrested and imprisoned because of their preaching. By 1930, 8,555 baptisms had been performed in Norway, with about 3,500 converts immigrating to Zion. Members remained under local leadership during World War II, and some missionary work was done. Many Church members immigrated to the United States after the war.

Until 1950, members and missionaries in Norway used the Danish translation of the Book of Mormon. That year, a Norwegian translation was published, and Norwegian translations of the Doctrine and Covenants and the Pearl of Great Price followed in 1954 and 1955, respectively.

The Oslo Norway Stake was created on May 22, 1977, with Osvald Bjareng as its first president. Elder John A. Widtsoe of the Quorum of the Twelve was born in Norway.

In the 1980s, member-missionary work proceeded. Pres. Stein Pedersen called 30 stake missionaries to assist missionaries of the Norway Oslo Mission. Membership in 1990 was 3,700. At the same time, stake public affairs director Rigmor Heistoe helped improve relationships between university professors and the Church. In 1988, Elder Russell M. Nelson of the Quorum of the Twelve presented Kjell Eliassen, Norwegian ambassador to the United States, with a book containing his family history.

In the 1990s, work also progressed in the Tromso District, made up of four small branches: Tromso, Alta/Hammerfest, Bodo and Harstad/Narvik, headquartered in the largest city in the part of Norway above the Arctic Circle.

Sources: *Encyclopedic History of the Church,* by Andrew Jenson; "Norway Saints Note Anniversary," *Church News,* July 1950; "Beyond the Arctic Circle," by Elder Dennis Mead, *Church News,* Jan. 17, 1959; *The Mormon Migration from Norway,* a University of Utah thesis by Helge Slejaas, August 1972; "Norway," *Ensign,* July 1974; "First Stakes for Norway. . ." *Church News,* June 11, 1977; "Norway — Land of the Blue Fjords," *Relief Society Course of Study,* 1979-80; *Church News,* Jan. 16, 1988; " 'Field is white' in Norway's Arctic region," by R. Scott Lloyd, *Church News,* March 16, 1991; "Inner peace can come during time of war," by John Floisand, *Church News,* Feb. 26, 1994.

Stake — 1
(As of Oct. 1, 1996.)

No.	Name	Organized	First President
Europe North Area			
835	Oslo Norway	22 May 1977	Osvald Bjareng

Mission — 1
(As of Oct. 1, 1996; shown with historical number. See MISSIONS.)

(24) NORWAY OSLO MISSION
Baerumsveien 373
Postboks 145
1346 Gjettum, Norway
Phone: (011-47-67) 56-84-80

PANAMA

Year-end 1995: Est. population, 2,700,000; Members, 26,000; Stakes, 5; Wards, 25; Branches, 38; Missions, 1; Districts, 5; Percent LDS, 0.9, or one LDS in 103.

Located in southern Central America, the Republic of Panama has a population that speaks Spanish and some English. The country is 93 percent Roman Catholic.

The first members in Panama were LDS servicemen associated with the Panama Canal. In 1941, the first branch in Panama was organized for the military personnel. The branch reached a membership of 100 in its first year. Because the Panamanian government did not recognize the Church until 1965, missionary work was limited. In 1961, Elder Marion G. Romney, then of the Quorum of the Twelve, presented a copy of the Book of Mormon to the president of the republic, Roberto F. Chiari. In 1965, the Church was officially recognized and proselyting began in Panama.

Word of the Church spread to the San Blas Islands, located just off the coast and considered part of Panama, when various San Blas Indians heard of the Church while visiting the Canal Zone. In 1965, mission Pres. Ted E. Brewerton visited San Blas and started full-time missionary work. Because the people there had traditions that corresponded closely with Book of Mormon events, many joined the Church. The first meetinghouse, completed in April 1970, was built on the island of Ustopo. The Panama Stake was created Nov. 11, 1979, with Nelson L. Altamirano as president.

The Panama Panama City Mission was created July 1, 1989. At the time, some 10,400 members lived in Panama. Most North American missionaries were withdrawn from the country in 1988, but local leaders and missionaries continued the work.

Cuna Indians from the San Blas Islands have regularly contributed outstanding molas, or fabric paintings, to the Church's international art competitions.

Sources: "Elder Romney sets busy schedule in Canal Zone," *Church News,* Dec. 2, 1961; "San Blas Indians," by Ronald K. Esplin, *Church News,* June 2, 1979; "Panama gains first stake from Costa Rica mission," *Church News,* April 25, 1970, Dec. 22, 1979; "New Missions," *Church News,* Feb. 25, 1989 and *Church News* Aug. 8, 1993.

Stakes — 4
(Listed alphabetically as of Oct. 1, 1996.)

No.	Name	Organized	First President
Central America Area			
2118	Colon Panama	5 Nov 1995	Eugenio Antonio Rodriguez Jacclos
1634a	David Panama	19 Apr 1987	Manuel Salvador Arauz
1734	*La Chorrera Panama	5 Nov 1995	
	*Bella Vista Panama 25 Jan 1993		
	‡Bellavista Panama	23 Jul 1989	Gustavo Brandaris Vergara
1081	Panama City Panama	11 Nov 1979	Nelson Altamirano Lopez
1596	San Miguelito Panama	20 Apr 1986	Domingo Estribi

(226) PANAMA PANAMA CITY MISSION
Apdo 55-0036
Paitilla, Panama
Phone: (011-507) 260-2411

PAPUA NEW GUINEA

Year-end 1995: Est. population, 4,314,000; Members, 4,700; Stakes, 1; Wards, 6; Missions, 1; Districts, 1; Branches, 11; Percent LDS, 0.1, or one LDS in 917; Pacific Area.

On the eastern half of the island of New Guinea in the Coral Sea and spreading across hundreds of smaller islands, Papua New Guinea is a parliamentary democracy. Its population speaks up to 700 village languages. They are 63 percent Protestant and 31 percent Roman Catholic.

Members visited Papua New Guinea long before the first missionaries arrived in 1980. The Port Moresby Branch was organized Oct. 10, 1979, with Athol Pike as branch president. Attending were mostly expatriates of Australia. Elder L. Douglas and Sister Eva Johnson of the Australia Brisbane Mission arrived Aug. 15, 1980. On Oct. 19, 1980, Maria Biai, Komara Nana, Sarah Nana and Rhoda Baka were baptized. Some 63 investigators attended services the following Sunday. Elder Douglas and Sister Nita Campbell succeeded the Johnsons, and during their service, property was obtained for a mission home and meetinghouse. Membership at that time had grown to 280. By October 1982, membership had reached 475 in three branches. Many of those converted had heard of the Church by word of mouth and contacted the missionaries to learn more.

By 1983, five branches had been organized under the direction of mission Pres. Dennis D. Flake. A meetinghouse was completed in 1984. Also that year, two Papuans, Elders George Mauhi and Robert Goisisi, were called as full-time missionaries.

Despite opposition, membership continued to increase. By March 1987, there were 1,450 members in nine branches. As the Church grew, more and more contacts were made in remote villages where many were interested in learning about the gospel. For example, residents of the Daru Village asked for missionaries, who arrived in July, 1990. Just three months later, the Daru Branch had 160 members. During this short time, two full-time missionaries, Elders Brian Mott of Washington and Benjamin Lish of Ohio, were involved in the conversion of approximately 100 of the new branch members.

District Pres. Valba Rome, one of the early converts, led some 138 Papuans to the Sydney Australia Temple in late 1991.

The Papua New Guinea Port Moresby Mission was created Feb. 13, 1992, and includes the Solomon Islands. The Relief Society continues to make contributions to the branches. Some sisters have learned to read the scriptures through the Relief Society's gospel literacy effort. And in a Relief Society service project in the 1990s, sisters in the Popondetta Branch, completed a service project of donating bandages for the hospital in their city. On Oct. 21, 1995, Elder V. Dallas Merrell of the Seventy created the Papua New Guinea Port Moresby Stake, the first stake on the island. The stake had 2,200 members in six wards and one branch.

Sources: Manuscript History of Church in Papua New Guinea; *Unto the Islands of the Sea,* by R. Lanier Britsch; "Light and Truth pouring into nation 10 years following Church's arrival," by Carol West, *Church News,* Sept. 16, 1989; *Church News,* Feb. 2, 1992; "Literacy opened 'whole new world' for her," *Church News,* Feb. 6, 1993; *Church News,* May 15, 1993; "Faith leads to first Papua New Guinea stake," by Sarah Jane Weaver, *Church News,* Nov. 11, 1995.

Stake — 1
(Listed alphabetically as of Oct. 1, 1996.)

No.	Name	Organized	First President
Pacific Area			
2109	Port Moresby Papua New Guinea	22 Oct 1995	Valba Rome

Mission — 1

(275) PAPUA NEW GUINEA PORT MORESBY MISSION
P.O. Box 6947
Boroko, N.C.D.
Papua New Guinea
Phone: (011-675) 325-2191

PARAGUAY

Year-end 1995: Est. population, 5,400,000; Members, 24,000; Stakes, 4; Wards, 23; Branches, 79; Missions, 1; Districts, 10; Percent LDS, 0.4, or one LDS in 225.

The Republic of Paraguay in central South America has a population that speaks Spanish and Guarani. They are 87 percent Roman Catholic.

Among the first Latter-day Saints to visit Paraguay was Frederick S. Williams, president of the Argentine Mission, who came in 1939. Samuel J. Skousen, a former missionary in Argentina working for the U.S. government in Rio de Janeiro and later in Asuncion, Paraguay, introduced the gospel to Carlos Alberto Rodriguez and his wife, Mafalda. Rodriguez was baptized in Asuncion Aug. 21, 1948, and his wife, awaiting the birth of their baby, followed Jan. 15, 1949. A branch with Brother Skousen as president was organized in Asuncion on July 26, 1948. The first missionaries arrived Jan. 9, 1950. Their efforts proceeded slowly, but by 1951 two branches had been organized. Their first baptism was Clara Ans de Krisch.

The Paraguay Mission was organized July 1, 1977, with a membership of 2,063, and the first stake was organized Feb. 25, 1979, with Carlos Ramon Espinola as president. Membership then was about 2,900.

An interesting development occurred in 1980 when a colony of 200 Nivacle Indians, who returned to their ancestral homeland in the Gran Chaco, joined the Church. The colony, under its own leadership for 10 years, continued to progress into the 1990s.

The Church in the population centers continued to progress, indicated by the creation of the Asuncion Paraguay North Stake in late 1992. Membership in 1990 was 12,000, and increased to 24,000 in 1995. The recent increases have come from expanding missionary work into the interior, with missionaries speaking Spanish, Portuguese and Guarani.

Sources: *From Acorn to Oak Tree,* by Frederick S. Williams and Frederick G. Williams; "The Church in Uruguay and Paraguay," *Ensign,* Feb. 1975; "Unexpected Welcome," by William Slaughter, *Church News,* June 9, 1979; *Church News,* Nov. 27, 1983; "Chulupi colony, Mistolar, thrives deep in interior," by Nestor Curbelo, *Church News,* June 2, 1990; *Church News,* Jan. 2, 1993, "'Heart' of South America opening to the gospel," by Nestor Curbelo, *Church News,* May 27, 1995.

Stakes — 5
(Listed alphabetically as of Oct. 1, 1996.)

No.	Name	Organized	First President
South America South Area			
1002	Asuncion Paraguay	25 Feb 1979	Carlos Ramon Espinola
1911	Asuncion Paraguay North	22 Nov 1992	Gregorio Figueredo Servian
2199	Ciudad Del Este Paraguay	02 Jun 1996	Juan Ramon Ocampos Gonzalez
1142	Fernando de la Mora Paraguay	1 Jun 1980	Guillermo M. Riveros A.
1997	San Lorenzo Paraguay	20 Nov 1994	Jorge Daniel Colina

Mission — 1
(As of Oct. 1, 1996; shown with historical number. See MISSIONS.)

(155) PARAGUAY ASUNCION MISSION
Casilla de Correo 818
Asuncion, Paraguay
Phone: (011-595-21) 601-392

PERU

Year-end 1995: Est. population, 24,100,000; Members, 279,000; Stakes, 63; Wards, 393; Branches, 368; Missions, 7; Districts, 34; Temples, 1; Percent LDS, 1.1, or one LDS in 86.

Located on the Pacific Coast side of South America, Peru is a constitutional republic with a population that speaks Spanish, Quechua and Aymara. Some 90 percent are Roman Catholic.

Prior to 1956, LDS families living in Peru held group meetings, but no organized missionary work was done. A Peruvian copper mine owned by a member in Salt Lake City, Utah, Alfred W. McCune, also brought a few members to Peru. On Jan. 1, 1956, Frederick S. Williams, a former mission president in Argentina and Uruguay, and his family moved to Peru and contacted Church headquarters for permission to organize a branch and begin missionary work. A branch was organized July 8, 1956, by Elder Henry D. Moyle, then of the Quorum of the Twelve. Elders Darwin Thomas, Edward T. Hall,

Donald L. Hokanson and Shirrel M. Plowman arrived Aug. 7, 1956, and began proselyting. A building for branch meetings was purchased Nov. 30. At the first branch conference held Feb. 24, 1957, 44 attended, 22 of whom were investigators. Missionaries were sent to Arequipa later in the year. The Andes Mission, headquartered in Lima, was established Nov. 1, 1959. At the time, there were five branches and 300 members.

The mission was divided Oct. 1, 1961. After the division, the Chile and Andes missions (comprising Bolivia and Peru) each had 12 branches and more than 2,000 members. The number of members in Peru increased to 6,391 in 1965. When the first stake was organized in Lima on Feb. 22, 1970, membership in Peru was 10,771. Called as president was Roberto Vidal, an early convert. That same year, the mission was divided and renamed the Peru Mission.

Growth continued as local leaders assumed priesthood leadership, and by 1977 there were 17,000 members. At an area conference presided over by President Spencer W. Kimball held in Lima Feb. 26-27, 1977, 7,900 attended. Four years later in 1981, President Kimball announced a temple for Lima, which was completed and dedicated Jan. 10-12, 1986.

On Jan. 30-31, 1988, just 32 years after missionary work started in Peru, seven stakes in Lima were created in one weekend by Elder M. Russell Ballard of the Quorum of the Twelve, and Lima became the city with the second largest number of stakes of any metropolitan area outside the United States.

In July, 1993, Peru's sixth mission was created, the Peru Chiclayo, which includes the highland Andes, where many of Lamanite descent live, and land bordering Ecuador. Seven additional stakes were created from October 1992 to October 1994, and 18 from October 1994 to October 1996. A seventh mission in Peru was created July 1, 1994.

Sources: Andes Mission manuscript history; Peru, *Ensign*, February 1977; *From Acorn to Oak Tree*, by Frederick S. Williams and Frederick G. Williams; *Church News*, Jan. 19, 1986; "Resourceful people of Lima making Church 'blossom,'" by Lee Warnick, *Church News*, Feb. 6, 1988; *Church News*, Jan. 28, 1996.

Stakes — 73
(Listed alphabetically as of Oct. 1, 1996.)

No.	Name	Organized	First President
South America North Area			
1815	Arequipa Peru Central	15 Sep 1991	Cesar Leoncio Gamarra G.
1540	Arequipa Peru Manuel Prado	20 Jun 1985	Efrain Jorge Rodriguez M.
1985	Arequipa Peru Selva Alegre	24 Jul 1994	Elias A. Rebaza Rado
1108	*Arequipa Peru Umacollo	20 Jun 1985	
	‡Arequipa Peru	21 Feb 1980	Victor H. Gamero
2189	Ayacucho Peru	21 Apr 1996	Job Edwin Quintanilla Pretel
2156	Cerro de Pasco Peru	21 Jan 1996	Bernardo Cristocal Santiago
1145	Chiclayo Peru	8 Jun 1980	Jorge Humberto del Carpio M.
1567	Chiclayo Peru Central	27 Oct 1985	Franklin D. Orroyo S.
1820	*Chiclayo Peru Eldorado	29 Oct 1995	
2113	Chiclayo Peru Latina	29 Oct 1995	Oswaldo Tello Mier y Teran
	Chiclayo Peru North	20 Oct 1991	Javier Delgado Torres
1122	Chimbote Peru	23 Mar 1980	Carlos Santos Lopez O.
1790	Chimbote Peru South	17 Mar 1991	Julio Arturo Leiva P.
1860	Chincha Peru	8 May 1992	Alfonso Eduardo Ormeno Villa
1527	Cuzco Peru	28 Apr 1985	Jose U. Coacalla
1910	Cuzco Peru Inti Raymi	15 Nov 1992	Miguel A. Vallenas Frisancho
1725	Huacho Peru	4 Jun 1989	Carlos Manuel Zapata P.
1471	Huancayo Peru	6 May 1984	Moises Sanchez T.
1756	Huanuco Peru	17 Jun 1990	Raul Rodriguez S.
2148	Huanuco Peru Amarilis	17 Dec 1995	Jesus Antonio Epinoza Solorzano
1739	Ica Peru	17 Dec 1989	Alexander Alfonso Nunez T.
2041	Ilo Peru	23 April 1995	Miguel Fernando Neyra M.
1162	Iquitos Peru	3 Aug 1980	Carlos Rojas Romero
2131	Iquitos Peru Mi. Peru	26 Nov 1995	Roger Braga Llerena
2132	Iquitos Peru Nueve de Octubre	26 Nov 1995	Johnny Padilla Bustos
1864	Iquitos Peru Punchana	23 May 1992	Alfonso Frederico Rojas R.
1541	Iquitos Peru Sachachorro	23 Jun 1985	Jorge Diaz Suarez
2007	Juliaca Peru	18 Dec 1994	Jesus Mario Barreda Ponze
1924a	Lima Peru Bayovar	7 Mar 1993	Augusto R. Ordinola Salva
1063	Lima Peru Callao	16 Sep 1979	Manuel Paredes

1743	*Lima Peru Canto Grande 7 Mar 1993		
	‡Canto Grande Peru	18 Mar 1990	Augusto Ordinalo S.
2181	Lima Peru Carabayllo	17 Mar 1996	Johnny Enrique Tunque Carrasco
789	Lima Peru Central	21 Nov 1976	Oscar H. Aguayo U.
1679	Lima Peru Chorrillos	31 Jan 1988	Israel Antonio Gonzalez B.
1794	Lima Peru Chosica	5 May 1991	Ricardo Enrique Lazo T.
1675	Lima Peru Comas	31 Jan 1988	Grover Pinto R.
1680	Lima Peru El Olivar	31 Jan 1988	Antero Miguel Sanchez M.
788	Lima Peru Lamanita	21 Nov 1976	Rafael de la Cruz
1677	Lima Peru Las Flores	31 Jan 1988	Miguel Fernando Rojas A.
1674	Lima Peru Las Palmeras	31 Jan 1988	Albina Isidro Chagua C.
503	*Lima Peru Limatambo 21 Nov 1976		
	*Lima Peru		
	‡Lima	22 Feb 1970	Roberto Vidal
670	*Lima Peru Magdalena 21 Nov 1976		
	‡Lima Peru West	1 Dec 1974	Manuel Paredes L.
1678	Lima Peru Maranga	31 Jan 1988	Benedicto S. Pacheco M.
1486	Lima Peru Palao	1 Jul 1984	Rene Loli
2201	Lima Peru Rimac	16 Jun 1996	Gustavo Guillermo Andrade Brouseet
1439	Lima Peru San Felipe	11 Sep 1983	Mauro Luis Artica Q.
2185	Lima Peru San Gabriel	24 Mar 1996	Juan Carlos Mercado Briceno
1064	Lima Peru San Juan	16 Sep 1979	Jorge Salazar
1440	Lima Peru San Luis	11 Sep 1983	Philippe J. Kradolfer
1065	Lima Peru San Martin	16 Sep 1979	Rene Loli
2149	Lima Peru Santa Anita	17 Dec 1995	Jose Humberto Naupori Velez
2186	Lima Peru Surco	24 Mar 1996	Alejandro Julian Llanos Morales
1795	Lima Peru Tahuantinsuyo	5 May 1991	Albino Isidro Chagua C.
1553	Lima Peru Villa Maria	25 Aug 1985	Juan Maguina Colquis
1881	Lima Peru Villa Salvador	31 May 1992	Victor Nicolas Anicama
1676	Lima Peru Vitarte	31 Jan 1988	Luis E. Stiglich S.
1734a	Mantaro Peru	30 Jul 1989	Manuel Moises Sanchez T.
2008	Moquegua Peru	18 Dec 1994	Claudio Luis Zeballos Flores
1925	Pisco Peru	13 Mar 1993	Marcelo P. Munante Salguero
1755	Piura Peru Castilla	17 Jun 1990	Oscar Alfredo Galvez C.
1400	†Piura Peru Central 10 Mar 1996		
	‡Piura Peru	16 Feb 1983	Pedro Puertas Rojas
2177	Piura Peru Miraflores	10 Mar 1996	Jose Alberta Castillo Saldarriaga
1961a	Pucallpa Peru	5 Dec 1993	Ferrando Vela Lopez
2130	Puno Peru Bellavista	26 Nov 1995	Pedro Tito Huanca
1872	*Puno Peru Titicaca	26 Nov 1995	
	Puno Peru	28 May 1992	Adan Bravo Mathens
1399	Tacna Peru	13 Feb 1983	Abraham La Torre Parades
2233	Tacna Peru Alameda	15 Sep 1996	Roger Valdivia
1914	Tacna Peru Arias Araguez	6 Dec 1992	Derliz Guzman Tejadi
2234	Tacna Peru Los Angeles	15 Sep 1996	Rolando Melchor
1987	*Trujillo Peru Central	14 Aug 1994	Pedro Gerardo Rodriguez H.
887	Trujillo Peru	22 Jan 1978	Teofilo Puertas Vega
	*Trujillo Peru North 19 Aug 1984		
	‡Trujillo Peru	22 Jan 1978	Teofilo Puertas Vega
1802	Trujillo Peru East	16 Jun 1991	Raymundo Aponte Garcia
1487	Trujillo Peru Palermo	12 Aug 1984	Jose Neyra
2229	Ventanilla Peru	08 Sep 1996	Luis Arnaldo Alvarado Zegarra

Missions — 7

(As of Oct. 1, 1996; shown with historical number. See MISSIONS.)

(165) PERU AREQUIPA MISSION
Casilla 1884
Arequipa,Peru
Phone: (011-51-54) 22-98-84

(291) PERU CHICLAYO MISSION
Casilla de Corrreo #630
Chiclayo, Peru
Phone: (011-51-14) 234-948

(302) PERU LIMA CENTRAL
MISSION
Av. Arequipa 660, Piso 11
Lima, Peru
Phone: (011-51-14) 33-08-06

(210) PERU LIMA EAST MISSION
Apartado 14-0196
Lima 14, Peru
Phone: (011-51-1) 433-1566

(149) PERU LIMA NORTH
MISSION
Casilla de Correo 11-0123
Lima 11, Peru
Phone: (011-51-14) 33-15-96

(50) PERU LIMA SOUTH
MISSION
Casilla de Correo 14-0293
Lima 14, Peru
Phone: (011-51-14) 4335-982

(184a) PERU TRUJILLO MISSION
Casilla 10
Urbanizacion California
Trujillo, Peru
Phone: (011-51-44) 28-41-74

PHILIPPINES

Year-end 1996: Est. population, 74,000,000; Members, 354,000; Stakes, 46; Wards, 278; Branches, 717; Missions, 13; Districts, 89; Temples, 1; Percent LDS, 0.4, or one LDS in 209.

An archipelago off the southeast coast of Asia, the Republic of the Philippines has a population that speaks Tagalog and English. They are Roman Catholic, 83 percent; Protestant, 9 percent; and Muslim, 5 percent.

The Church was introduced in the Philippines during the Spanish-American War in 1898. Two artillery batteries from Utah were sent to the Philippines, and Willard Call and George Seaman were set apart as missionaries, making them the first Mormon elders to preach the gospel among the people of the Philippine islands.

There was no missionary activity in the Philippines until the end of World War II, when Maxine Grimm, wife of a U.S. Army colonel, serving in the American Red Cross in the Philippines, introduced the gospel to Aniceta Pabilona Fajardo, the first Filipino to join the Church in the islands. Sister Fajardo was baptized in 1945. Dean Franklin Clair, a U.S. Army medic, was another LDS pioneer in the Philippines when he married Filipina Leona H. Seno.

The Church experienced a growth spurt in the area in 1953 during the Korean War when the Luzon Servicemen's District was organized.

On April 28, 1961, Elder Gordon B. Hinckley, then of the Quorum of the Twelve, met with a small group of local servicemen, American residents, Filipino members and their families at the American War Memorial Cemetery to offer a prayer for the islands and open the islands for missionary work. The first missionaries, Elders Ray Goodson, Harry Murray, Kent Lowe and Nestor Ledesma, arrived in Manila on June 5, 1961.

The first two to be baptized by the missionaries were Jose Gutierez Sr. and Lino Brocka. By the end of 1961, there had been eight baptisms.

In 1967, the Philippine Mission was organized with Paul S. Rose as president. Two years later the Church had spread to eight major islands of the country and the mission had the highest number of baptisms in the Church.

The Philippines Mission was divided into two missions in 1974, creating the Philippines Manila Mission, under the leadership of Pres. Raymond L. Goodson, and the Philippines Cebu City Mission, under the direction of Pres. Carl D. Jones. In the next 12 years, seven more missions were created.

The Manila Missionary Training Center was established in 1983 to train missionaries, and in September 1984 the Manila Philippines Temple was dedicated. At that time, membership was 76,000.

In 1987, the Philippines/Micronesia Area was created with headquarters in Manila. Nine new missions were created in the Philippines between 1986-92.

During 1990-91, members experienced volcanic eruptions, earthquakes, flooding and conflicts between insurgent and government forces. Church relief efforts were sent to help in the recovery of the natural disasters. Membership continued to grow, reaching 237,000 in 1990.

The first Filipino General Authority, Elder Augusto A. Lim, was called to the Second Quorum of the Seventy June 6, 1992. The Church became more prominent as Christmas lights on the temple grounds attracted more people, and its youth become involved in more service projects.

President Gordon B. Hinckley returned to this land where he had served for 36 years on May 16, 1996. The trip was part of an eight-nation tour that included the dedication of the Hong Kong Temple. His visit to the Philippines served to renew long-time acquaintances. Many traveled long distances to hear the prophet.

Sources: "The Philippines," *The Improvement Era*, March 1964; *History of the Church in the Philippines*, compiled by the Luzon District, 1965; "Philippines: the Land of Joyous Service," *Ensign*, August 1975; "Missionaries in Khaki," by Carol Cornwall Madsen, *Church News*, June 23, 1979; "Gospel flourishes in soil of Filipino faith," by Francis M. Orquiola, *Ensign*, Sept. 1984; "Dateline Philippines," *Tambuli*, April 1991; *Church News*, Dec. 25, 1993.

Stakes — 49
(Listed alphabetically as of Oct. 1, 1996.)

No.	Name	Organized	First President
Philippines/Micronesia Area			
1226	Angeles Philippines	18 Jan 1981	Orlando D. Aquilar
1281	Bacolod Philippines	5 Jul 1981	Remus G. Villarete
1323	Bacolod Philippines North	7 Feb 1982	Rufino Alvarez Villanueva Jr.
1573	Baguio Philippines	17 Nov 1985	Carlos F. Chavez
1806	Balanga Philippines	7 Jul 1991	Torbio Nuguid Santos
1788	Binalbagan Philippines	3 Mar 1991	Jose Vicente Pioquinto
1711	Butuan Philippines	19 Feb 1989	Henry Ferrer Acebedo
1340	Cabanatuan Philippines	9 May 1982	Arsenio A. Pacaduan
1884	Cabuyao Philippines	7 June 1992	Tomas S. Merdegia Jr.
1572	Cadiz Philippines	10 Nov 1985	Carmelino M. Cawit
1535	Cagayan De Oro Philippines	26 May 1985	Loreto Balanta Libid
1748	Cagayan de Oro Philippines East	6 May 1990	Danilo D. De La Vega
1807	Camiling Philippines	14 Jul 1991	Celso Arenzana Nicolas
1545	Cavite Philippines 24 Oct 1989		
	‡Makiling Philippines	18 Aug 1985	Jose Trinidad Aguilar
1220	Cebu City Philippines	11 Jan 1981	Jacob Torres Lopez
1229	Dagupan Philippines	25 Jan 1981	Bernardo G. Reamon
1307	Davao Philippines	15 Nov 1981	George S. Lavarino
1544	Davao Philippines Buhangin	18 Aug 1985	Patrick Hartford M. Clair
1876	Digos Philippines	31 May 1992	Paul Farinas Bunoan
2084	General Santos Philippines	6 Aug 1995	Fabian L. Simamban
1908	Iligan Philippines	18 Oct 1992	William C. Garife
1508	Iloilo Philippines	20 Jan 1985	Hannibal Delgado D.
1238	*Kalookan Philippines 17 Feb 1996		
	‡Caloocan Philippines	22 Feb 1981	Godofredo Hilario Esguerra
1877	Kidapawan Philippines	31 May 1992	Rodolfo Bergado Estrella
1547	La Carlota Philippines	18 Aug 1985	Antonio V. Custodio
1715	Laoag Philippines	23 Apr 1989	Jose Miguel Tumaneng
1555	Las Pinas Philippines	15 Sep 1985	Delfin T. Justiniano
1551	Legazpi Philippines	19 Aug 1985	Jose P. Leveriza
1557	Lingayen Philippines	22 Sep 1985	Oberlito R. Cantillo
841	Makati Philippines	29 May 1977	Ruben Moscaira Lancanienta
1726	Malolos Philippines	11 Jun 1989	Rogelio C. Coronel
1735b	Mandaue Philippines	19 Nov 1989	Cesar Abina Perez Jr.
613	*Manila Philippines		
	‡Manila	20 May 1973	Augusto Alandy Lim
1210	Marikina Philippines	30 Nov 1980	Augusto Alandy Lim
1546	Naga Philippines	18 Aug 1985	Avelino S. Babia Sr.
1713	Olongapo Philippines	5 Mar 1989	Richard Noboru Kivabu
1309	Paranaque Philippines	22 Nov 1981	Ruben M. Lacanienta
1554	Pasig Philippines	15 Sep 1985	Macario Molina Yasona Jr.
842	Quezon City Philippines	29 May 1977	Augusto Alandy Lim
2176	Rosales Philippines 10 Mar 1996		Emmanuel Vallejos Damasco
1789	San Fabian Philippines	17 Mar 1991	Loreto D. Querimit
1315	San Fernando Philippines La Union	6 Dec 1981	Angel B. Salanga Jr.
1552	San Pablo Philippines	20 Aug 1985	Cleofas S. Canoy
1875	Santa Cruz Philippines	31 May 1992	Rolando Pramis Nueva
1330	*Talisay Philippines 10 Aug 1989		
	‡Cebu City Philippines South	21 Mar 1982	Bienvenido Pangilinan Flores
1321	Tarlac Philippines	13 Dec 1981	Mario de Jesus
1721	Tuguegarao Philippines	21 May 1989	Quirino Sumabat Donato

| 1558 | Urdaneta Philippines | 22 Sep 1985 | Felino Caparas Ocampo |
| 1571 | Zamboanga Philippines | 10 Nov 1985 | Catalino A. Dugupan Sr. |

Discontinued

| 1577 | Munoz Philippines 31 May 1992 | 24 Nov 1985 | Juanito Wytangooy Tanedo |
| 1780 | Ozamiz Philippines 7 Nov 1993 | 25 Nov 1990 | Wilfredo Tumampos Romero |

Missions — 13
(As of Oct. 1, 1996; shown with historical number. See MISSIONS.)

(110) PHILIPPINES BACOLOD MISSION
P.O. Box 660, Bacolod City
6100 Negros Occidental
Philippines
Phone: (011-63-34) 433-3001

(268) PHILIPPINES CABANATUAN MISSION
P.O. Box 176,
Kapitan Pepe Subdiv.
3100 Nueva Ecija, Philippines
Phone: (011-63-44) 463-0017

(194) PHILIPPINES CEBU MISSION
P.O. Box 338
Cebu City 6000
Philippines
Phone: (011-63-32) 311-153

(256) PHILIPPINES ILAGAN MISSION
LDS Church
National Highway
Guinatan, Ilagan
3300 Isabela, Philippines
Phone: (011-63-76) 624-2185

(223) PHILIPPINES NAGA MISSION
P.O. Box 885
Naga City
4400 Camarines Sur, Philippines
Phone: (011-63-5421) 736209

(219) PHILIPPINES SAN FERNANDO MISSION
P.O. Box 1198, Ortigas Center
Emerald Avenue, Pasig
Metro Manila 1600, Philippines
Phone: (011-63-912) 302-8547

(251) PHILIPPINES TACLOBAN MISSION
Diversion Road
Banezville, Maras Baras
Tacloban City, P.O. Box 69,
6500 Leyte, Philippines
Phone: (011-63-53) 323-4063

(172) PHILIPPINES BAGUIO MISSION
P.O. Box 380
Baguio City
Philippines
Phone: (011-63-74) 442-5951

(211) PHILIPPINES CAGAYAN DE ORO
P.O. Box 0400
Cagayan de Oro City
9000 Philippines
Phone: (011-63-88) 22 6531

(157) PHILIPPINES DAVAO MISSION
P.O. Box 82624
8000 Davao City,
Philippines
Phone: (011-63-82) 7-22-36

(76b) PHILIPPINES MANILA MISSION
P.O. Box 1997
Makati Central Post Office
Makati, Metro Manila
0714 Philippines
Phone: (011-63-2) 899-9128

(192) PHILIPPINES QUEZON CITY MISSION
Ortigas Center P.O. Box 13873
Emerald Avene, Pasig
Metro Manila 1600, Philippines
Phone: (011-63-2) 631-5763

(250) PHILIPPINES SAN PABLO MISSION
Mabini Street Extension
P.O. Box 38
San Pablo City, 4000 Laguna, Philippines
Phone: (011-63-93) 562-0778

POLAND

Year-end 1995: Est. population, 38,792,000; Members, 700; Missions, 1; Districts, 1; Branches, 12; Europe East Area.

On the Baltic Sea in east central Europe, Poland has a population that speaks Polish, and is mostly Roman Catholic.

In 1928, the Selbongen Branch meetinghouse was erected in Germany. After World War II, the town of Selbongen was part of the area ceded to Poland, and its name was changed to Zelbak.

President Ezra Taft Benson, then a member of the Quorum of the Twelve, was the first priesthood leader to visit Zelbak after the war. Upon his arrival, more than 100 members and friends gathered in a quickly convened meeting to bear their testimonies, sing and pray and receive his counsel.

While the branch struggled to stay alive during the subsequent years, the spirit of the Saints did not falter. In 1947, government officials ordered the Zelbak meetings discontinued on the grounds that only the Polish language could be spoken in public meetings of any kind. Three years later, the branch was re-opened. The branch continued until 1978, when priesthood leaders made the decision to discontinue the branch. The meetinghouse there still stands, but is no longer used for LDS functions.

President Spencer W. Kimball visited Poland Aug. 24, 1977, after official recognition of the Church by the Polish government, which came on May 30, 1977.

A number of couple missionaries served in Poland following 1977. The first elders arrived in January 1988. Sister Urzula Adamska, the first Polish missionary, was called in 1989.

On June 15, 1989, ground was broken for a meetinghouse in Warsaw. The ceremony was attended by more than 200 people, including government and religious leaders of different faiths. Elder Russell M. Nelson of the Quorum of the Twelve presided over and addressed the groundbreaking ceremony. The day after the groundbreaking, Elder Nelson and other Church leaders met with Poland's minister of religious affairs, who shared copies of a new law guaranteeing freedom of conscience and belief. The meetinghouse was dedicated June 22, 1991, in a service attended by more than 400 people, including government leaders. At the time work on the Warsaw meetinghouse was begun, Poland was part of the Austria Vienna East Mission. The Poland Warsaw Mission was created July 1, 1990.

Church Welfare Service workers served on a non-denominational consulting company helping Poland modernize its agriculture. The Church donated medical supplies, clothing and bedding to Poland in 1991. The Tabernacle Choir performed in Warsaw June 22, 1991. In 1995, members of BYU's women's volleyball team participated in a fireside in Warsaw.

Sources: Swiss Mission manuscript history; *Church News,* July 13, Aug. 17, and Aug. 24, 1946; "New Branch Organized in Red Poland," *Church News,* Oct. 1, 1966; "The Branch that Wouldn't Die," by Gilbert W. Scharffs, *Ensign,* 1971; *Church News,* Sept. 17, 1977; "Zelwagi survives," by Richard L. Jensen, *Church News,* June 30, 1979; "Church in Poland: Small but Strong," *Ensign,* August 1979; "Reunion revives spirit of Selbongen," *Church News,* Oct. 14, 1989; "The Book of Mormon in Polish," by Kerril Sue Rollins, *Ensign,* June 1982; *Church News,* July 1, 1989; July 6, 1991; Sept. 23, 1995.

Mission — 1
(As of Oct. 1, 1996; shown with historical number. See MISSIONS.)

(252) POLAND WARSAW MISSION
ul. Wolska 142
P1-01-258 Warsaw, Poland
Phone: (011-48-22) 36-19-39

PORTUGAL

Year-end 1995: Est. population, 10,563,000; Members, 34,000; Stakes, 5; Wards, 23; Branches, 81; Missions, 3; Districts, 12; Percent LDS, 0.3, or one LDS in 310.

At the southwest corner of Europe, the Republic of Portugal is a parliamentary democracy. Its population is 97 percent Roman Catholic.

The first members of the LDS Church in Portugal were members in the U.S. Armed Forces stationed in the country in the early 1970s. The first known regularly held Church meetings were conducted by military personnel John C. Peterson and Steven Lindsey, who in the spring of 1974 visited the Spain Madrid Mission to see if missionary work could begin in Portugal. Official recognition of the Church was not gained. However, a revolution in May 1974 led to a new government, which gave recognition to religious entities. Shortly thereafter, President Spencer W. Kimball and David M. Kennedy, special representative of the First Presidency, visited Portugal, and received assurances that the Church could enter the country.

In August 1974, Church member Ray E. Caldwell was assigned by the Canadian government to be first secretary of the Canadian embassy in Lisbon. He stopped en route in Salt Lake City, Utah, and was set apart as the group leader over any members he might find.

Church meetings were soon held in the Caldwell home. In November 1974, Pres. Wm. Grant Bangerter, later of the Presidency of the Seventy, arrived in Lisbon to preside over the newly created Portugal Lisbon Mission. Four missionaries were transferred from a mission in Brazil to begin the work, and they found many people who were interested in the gospel. By July 1975, there were 100 Portuguese members.

From those beginnings, the Church reached its first thousand members by July 1978. The Lisbon Portugal Stake was created July 10, 1981, with Jose Manuel da Costa Santos as president. The Portugal Porto Mission was formed from the Portugal Lisbon Mission in July 1987. The Portugal Lisbon Mission was divided in 1989 to create the Lisbon North and Lisbon South missions.

Sources: Culture for Missionaries: Portugal, 1984; "Discovering Gospel Riches in Portugal," by Don L. Searle, *Ensign*, Oct. 1987; *Church News*, Feb. 16, 1989; "Brotherly Love," *Ensign*, August 1989.

Stakes — 5

(Listed alphabetically as of Oct. 1, 1996.)

No.	Name	Organized	First President
Europe West Area			
1276	Lisbon Portugal	10 Jun 1981	Jose Manuel da Costa Santos
1729	Lisbon Portugal Oeiras	25 Jun 1989	Vitor Manuel Pereira M.
1723	Matosinhos Portugal	28 May 1989	Alexandre Rocha Benidio
1613	Porto Portugal	2 Nov 1986	Alcino Pereira Da Silva
1652	Setubal Portugal	6 Sep 1987	Octavio Da Silva Melo

Missions — 3

(As of Oct. 1, 1996; shown with historical number. See MISSIONS.)

(253) PORTUGAL LISBON NORTH MISSION
Apartado 40054
500 Lisboa, Portugal
Phone: (011-351-1) 760-3369

(115) PORTUGAL LISBON SOUTH MISSION
Largo Com. Augusto Madureira, 7B
1495 Alges, Portugal
Phone: (011-351-1) 410-2064

(203) PORTUGAL PORTO MISSION
Rua de Amalia Luazes, 23 - Sala 1
4200 Porto
Portugal
Phone: (011-351-2) 521-575

AZORES AND MADEIRA ISLANDS

Year-end 1995: Est. population, 250,000; Members, 1,900; Districts 3; Branches, 8; Europe West Area; Portugal Lisbon North Mission.

The Azores Islands, located 800 miles off the coast of Portugal in the North Atlantic, includes nine main islands that are populated.

Both archipelagos are Portuguese territories where Portuguese is spoken. The first branch was organized in Funchal on Sept. 4, 1983. In 1991 a group of Boy Scouts from Madeira took part in the Church's first Boy Scout encampment in Portugal. One district with four branches has been established in the Madeira Islands, and two districts in the Azores in the Europe Area.

Sources; French Mission correspondence; Portugal Lisbon North Mission; *Church News*, March 19,1988; *Church News*; Oct. 5, 1991.

MACAO

Year-end 1995: Est. population, 400,000; Members, 700; Branches, 1; Asia Area; Hong Kong Mission.

An enclave at the mouth of the Canton River in China, Macao is administered by Portugal.

In 1964, Pres. Jay Quealey of the Southern Far East Mission sent Elders Darryl Thomander and Gilbert Montano to labor in Macao. They arrived July 2, 1964, and held the first LDS services July 12 in their rented quarters. Ten investigators were present. Their first convert was Gary Lau, baptized Aug. 21, 1964.

After an interlude, missionaries under Pres. Jerry D. Wheat of the Hong Kong Mission resumed work on Macao Sept. 6, 1976, after they learned of a constitutional amendment that allowed religious freedom to meet, teach and proselyte.

The Macao Branch of the Hong Kong Island Stake was organized Jan. 1, 1977, and had about 300 members in 1990, and increased to 676 members in 1995.

Sources: *Church News*, Dec. 4, 1976; Journal, correspondence from Darryl Thomander, Sept. 26, 1992.

PUERTO RICO

Year-end 1995: Est. population, 3,801,000; Members, 20,000; Districts, 8; Branches, 52; Missions, 1; Percent LDS, 0.5, or one LDS in 190.

The easternmost island of the Greater Antilles in the east Caribbean Sea, Puerto Rico is a U.S. commonwealth with a population that speaks Spanish. Most of the people are Roman Catholic.

Gardner H. Russell (who was called to the Seventy in 1986) began holding Church meetings with his family and LDS servicemen at Guajataca in 1947, and later in San Juan. For the first few years, those who attended the meetings were LDS servicemen. Later, other members moved to Puerto Rico. In 1953, Reginald R. Dorff, military group leader, presided at the baptism of Dorothy Tate.

Florida Mission Pres. Ned Winder visited Puerto Rico in October 1963 on a routine visit and felt inspired to send missionaries. In January 1964, Elders Verl Tolbert and Dwight K. Hunter arrived in Puerto Rico under his direction. They visited several branches in the Puerto Rico District, which had been organized earlier for military personnel. They baptized a serviceman, Dennis Wayne Hart, on Feb. 8, 1964. The first Puerto Rican baptized was Ilka Josephina Frau, baptized at the Naval Beach on March 2, 1964.

The next mission president was Pres. Glen L. Rudd (who was called to the Seventy in 1987), who sent Spanish-speaking missionaries to the island. The first Spanish-speaking branch was organized in 1970. On March 8 of that year, the first meetinghouse in the Caribbean District of the Florida Mission was dedicated in San Juan. On Oct. 17, home seminary was started. The Spanish branch became an independent branch a year later. Members' spirits were lifted March 8, 1981, by a visit from President Spencer W. Kimball.

The Puerto Rico San Juan Mission was created in 1979 with a membership of 1,892. The first stake was created in San Juan on Dec. 14, 1980, by President Ezra Taft Benson, then of the Quorum of the Twelve, at a meeting attended by 81 percent of the membership. Called to lead the stake was Pres. Herminio de Jesus.

New stakes were added in 1982, 1984 and 1985. President Benson visited again on April 12, 1987, and noted that membership had increased to more than 12,000. Four stakes were discontinued in December 1993 following the reduction of military personnel stationed in Puerto Rico. In 1996, two stakes were reinstated because of the increase in local members.

The Church's administrative office in Puerto Rico sent relief supplies to help hurricane victims in the Caribbean. Hurricane Luis and Hurricane Marilyn both hit the area in September 1995.

Sources: "Puerto Rico organizes two branches," by Elder Delbert Goates, *Church News*, June 25, 1955; Florida Mission manuscript history; "The Saints in Puerto Rico," by Orson Scott Card, *Ensign*, March 1978; "Caribbean beginnings," by Gordon Irving, *Church News*, April 22, 1978; "First Puerto Rican stake organized," *Church News*, Dec. 27, 1980; "History is made: prophet visits Caribbean islands," by Gerry Avant, *Church News*, March 21, 1981; "President Benson visits Puerto Rico," by Gerry Avant, *Church News*, April 18, 1987; "Outline of Historical Events . . . in Caribbean Nations," *VASAA Newsletter*, by Virgil N. Kovalenko; "Extensive hurricane damage, but LDS safe," *Church News*, Sept. 30, 1995.

		Stakes — 2	
No.	Name	Organized	First President
North America Southeast Area			
2217	Mayaguez Puerto Rico Reinstated from No. 1580	11 Aug 1996	Tomas Olmo
2240	Ponce Puerto Rico Reinstated from No. 1349	22 Sep 1996	Rafael Ortiz

1480	Carolina Puerto Rico 5 Dec 1993	17 Jun 1984	Jesus Nieves
1580	Mayaguez Puerto Rico 5 Dec 1993	1 Dec 1985	Heriberto Hernandez Vera
1349	Ponce Puerto Rico 5 Dec 1993	13 Jun 1982	Noah Jefferson Burns
1215	San Juan Puerto Rico 5 Dec 1993	14 Dec 1980	Herminio De Jesus

Mission — 1
(As of Oct. 1, 1996; shown with historical number. See MISSIONS.)

(157) PUERTO RICO SAN JUAN MISSION
Urb. Villa Andalucia
A-14 Ronda Street #201
Rio Piedras, PR 00926
Phone: (787) 755-2670

ROMANIA

Year-end 1995: Est. population, 23,200,000; Members, 600; Missions, 1; Districts, 2; Branches, 9; Europe East Area.

In July 1899, Mischa Markow, a prominent missionary to the Balkans, arrived in Constanta, Romania, with a Bulgarian companion, Argir Dimitrov, whom he baptized on Aug. 30, 1899. The pair traveled to Bucharest where they baptized another person. They made no further progress until Elder Markow had a dream about meeting a mother and daughter who would hear the gospel. The dream was realized in every detail and the mother and daughter were eventually baptized. Five others were later baptized as well and a branch organized.

Elder Markow was arrested a short time later. During his trial, Elder Markow defended the gospel and a dispute about the apostasy broke out in the courtroom. Elder Markow was confined to a jail for few days and banished.

In modern times, Elder Russell M. Nelson of the Quorum of the Twelve and Elder Hans B. Ringger of the Seventy met with the ministers of justice, health and religion, and other dignitaries, including the mayor of Bucharest and members of the district council on Feb. 8-9, 1990. Following this meeting, the Church began assisting with the Romanian orphanages and supplying medical supplies to the country.

Romania became part of the Austria Vienna East Mission in 1990, where it remained until the mission was discontinued in 1992. Missionaries serving in Romania provided humanitarian services under the Hungary Budapest Mission until the Romania Bucharest Mission was created July 1, 1993.

Assistance to Romania continued from European stakes through the early 1990s. By the end of 1995, Romania had nine branches in two districts.

Sources: "Began with one," by William Slaughter, *Church News*, July 21, 1979; "Mischa Markow, Missionary to the Balkans," by William Hale Kehr, *Ensign*, June 1980; *Church News*, Aug. 18, 1990; Aug. 17, 1991, Dec. 7, 1991, Jan. 11, 1992, correspondence from Kahlile Mehr, Dec. 29, 1992.

Mission — 1
(As of Oct. 1, 1996; shown with historical number. See MISSIONS.)

(292) ROMANIA BUCHAREST MISSION
B-Dul Unirii Nr. 10
BL. 7B Sc. 1 Et. 2 Apt. 5
Sector 4 Bucharest,
Romania
Phone: (011-40-1) 410-3437

RUSSIA

Year-end 1995: Est. population, 149,909,000; Members, 3,700; Missions, 6; Districts, 8; Branches, 59; Europe East Area.

Russians speak Slavic languages, including Russian, and local dialects. Non-religious or atheists make up 51 percent of the population, with Russian Orthodox 31 percent, and Muslim, 11 percent.

As early as 1843, Russia was considered a prospective mission field. Orson Hyde and George J. Adams were called to go to Russia by the Prophet Joseph Smith, but their mission was aborted by the Prophet's martyrdom a year later.

In 1895, Elder August Joel Hoglund, a native of Sweden, was sent to St. Petersburg where he arrived June 9. He met with the Johan M. Lindelof family and baptized Johan and his wife, Alma, on June 11 in the river Neva. The Lindelof family was visited periodically and in 1903, Elder Francis M. Lyman of the Council of the Twelve and then president of the European Mission, accompanied by Joseph J. Cannon, visited the family in St. Petersburg. The Lindelof family was later dispersed during the revolution of 1918.

On April 27, 1919, Andrew Hasberg, a member of the U.S. Expeditionary Forces in World War I, was baptized in a lake about four miles south of Vladivostok, Russia's easternmost port city, by Thomas E. Hunsaker.

In 1959 Elder Ezra Taft Benson of the Quorum of the Twelve, then U.S. Secretary of Agriculture, visited the Central Baptist Church in Moscow and preached to an attentive congregation.

Missionary work resumed tentatively in 1989. Among the first to be baptized were Yuri, Liudmilla and Anna Terebenin, who heard about the Church and were baptized during a trip to Budapest, Hungary. Olga Smolyanova, then 18, was baptized in Italy. Others were baptized by Finnish member-missionaries. One of these was Leena Laitinen, who taught a group of investigators in her home in Leningrad. During this period, visits were made to Leningrad and Moscow by Elder Hans B. Ringger of the Seventy and mission presidents Steven R. Mecham of the Finland Helsinki Mission and Dennis B. Neuenschwander (called in April 1991 to the Seventy) of the Austria Vienna East Mission. In September of 1989, Pres. Neuenschwander authorized U.S. Embassy worker Dohn Thornton to begin holding group meetings in his apartment. Two missionaries, Elders David S. Reagan and Kevin A. Dexter, arrived in Leningrad on Jan. 26, 1990. They taught Sister Laitinen's investigators and baptized Anton Skripko Feb. 3, 1990, the first member baptized in Russia in modern times. He later became the first to serve a full-time mission from Russia, arriving at the Missionary Training Center, in Provo, Utah, on July 26, 1991, and serving in the Utah Ogden Mission.

The first missionaries stationed in Leningrad were Elder Reagan and Elder Burt Dover. The Vyborg Branch was created in February 1990.

Elders Russell M. Nelson and Dallin H. Oaks of the Quorum of the Twelve visited a number of times and continued efforts to strengthen the Church in Russia and its neighboring countries.

By mid-summer 1990, the Leningrad Branch, which had been created Dec. 3, 1989, numbered 100 members, and the Vyborg Branch 25 members. In September, the St. Petersburg Branch was recognized by the government and in October, a religious freedom law was passed.

The Russia Moscow and Russia St. Petersburg missions were created Feb. 3, 1992, with the membership of Russia numbering about 750. The first Russian branch president was Andrei Petrov, sustained in March 1991. A year later, the Moscow Branch was divided into six branches, and in 1993, these became 15 branches. At that time, there were as many members in the Moscow area as in the whole of Russia a year earlier. A third mission, Russia Samara, was created July 1993, and two additional ones, Russia Novosibirsk and Russia Rostov were created July 1, 1996. The sixth mission, Russia Yekaterinburg, was created July 1995.

In June 1991, the Tabernacle Choir received publicity "beyond its wildest expectations" as it performed in the Bolshoi Theater in Moscow, and in Leningrad (now St. Petersburg) and recorded songs later broadcast to a potential audience of 339 million. The Church was officially recognized by Russia on May 28, 1991, and announcement of this was made at a dinner following the Choir's Moscow performance on June 24.

During 1991 and afterward, humanitarian relief to members in Russia was supplied by members in Europe and the United States. Tons of food and clothing were distributed to members and non-members, including shipments to Kommi and Ossetia regions in the fall of 1994; 160,000 pounds of food and 40,000 pounds of winter clothing sent to Partizansk in December 1994.

Sources: *Times and Seasons*, 4:218; *Millennial Star*, Aug. 27, 1903; *Improvement Era*, November, 1903; "Mischa Markow, Missionary to the Balkans," by William Hale Kehr, *Ensign*, June 1980; *Journal of Mormon History*, Vol. 13, 1986-87; *Ezra Taft Benson, A Biography*; "Choir leaves trail of joyful tears," by Gerry Avant, *Church News*, July 7, 1991; *Church News*, Oct. 12, 1991; "Converts pioneer frontier in Russia," by Steve Fidel, *Church News*, Sept. 19, 1992; "Many families in Russia are blessed by relief effort," *Church News*, Jan. 28, 1995; and "Victims of hardship 'full of gratitude,' " *Church News*, April 27, 1996; "1989-90, The Curtain Opens," by Kahlile Mehr, *Ensign*, Dec. 1993 and correspondence from Kahlile Mehr, Dec. 29, 1992; "Growth of the Church in 'that vast empire,' " an address by Gary L. Browning, *Church News*, Nov. 6, 1993.

Missions — 6
(As of Oct. 1, 1996; shown with historical number. See MISSIONS.)

(272) RUSSIA MOSCOW MISSION
Rossiia, 101000 Moskova
Glavpochtampt a/ia 257
Russia
Phone: (011-7-502) 224-5544

(301) RUSSIA NOVOSIBIRSK MISSION
Mochishchenskava Shosse 18, 2 etazh
Pochtamt a/ai 208
630123 Novosibirsk, Russia
Phone: (011-7-3832) 28-50-25

(302) RUSSIA ROSTOV MISSION
344007 g. Rostov-na-Donu
Pochtamt no. 96, Russia
Phone: (011-7-8632) 67-946-83

(273) RUSSIA ST. PETERSBURG
Nab. Reki Moiki 11-11
St. Petersburg, Russia 191065
Phone: (011-7-812) 325-6148

(293) RUSSIA SAMARA MISSION
Studenchesky Periulok d 2a, kv 7
443001 Samara
Russia
Phone: (011-7-8461) 42-41-47

(305) RUSSIA YEKATERINBURG MISSION
620151 Yekaterinburg
ul. Rabochikh 9, Office 1
Russia
Phone: (011-7-3432) 46-56-27

ST. KITTS AND NEVIS (ST. CHRISTOPHER-NEVIS)

Year-end 1995: Est. population, 40,000; Members, fewer than 100; Branches, 1; North America Southeast Area; West Indies Mission.

Located in the Eastern Caribbean in the Leeward Islands, St. Kitts and Nevis has a population that speaks English, and is mostly Protestant.

Pres. Kenneth Zabriskie of the West Indies Mission and his wife, LeOra, were introduced to the government officer of St. Kitts through a mutual acquaintance, Kutaba Alghanin, who sailed about the Caribbean in his yacht and employed two returned missionaries as tutors to his children.

In July 1984, Elders Douglas Myers and Robert J. Molina arrived on St. Kitts and were soon followed by Reuel and Alice Lambourn on Oct. 20, 1984. They adapted a home into a meetinghouse and the St. Kitts-Nevis Branch was organized on Sept. 10, 1985, with Elder Lambourn as the first president. On Feb. 2, 1985, Dianna Ermintude Johnson was baptized, the first convert on the island. A weekly open house was held on Thursdays where the newly baptized members and investigators could study together.

A local member, Carol Pamela Heather Thomas, became the first missionary from the islands when she was called June 14, 1991, to the New Jersey Morristown Mission. Three other missionaries served from St. Kitts and Nevis in the next two years. In 1994, the branch had about 70 members taking part in all the programs, including seminary. Two choirs regularly took part in the meetings. In February 1995, a small group of Church members went to the government and asked permission to clean up a park in the center of town. This act help change many people's attitudes about the Church. Terry Lewellyn Hanley became the first native branch president to serve on St. Kitts in early 1996.

Sources: Kenneth and LeOra Zabriskie journals; correspondence from West Indies Mission, 1994; "Caribbean members plan to celebrate achievements of pioneers — those on island and of 1847 trek," *Church News*, June 22, 1996.

ST. VINCENT AND THE GRENADINES

Year-end 1995: Est. population, 117,000; Members, 300; Branches, 1; Percent LDS, 0.25, or one LDS in 390; North America Southeast Area; West Indies Mission.

In the eastern Caribbean and part of the Windward Island chain, the Grenadines are a parliamentary democracy. Most of the population speaks English. Major religions are Methodist, Anglican and Roman Catholic.

The Grenadines were under the Puerto Rico San Juan Mission until 1983, when the islands were placed in the West Indies Mission. The Kingstown Branch was organized Oct. 22, 1980. Under the direction of Pres. Edmund Israel the branch developed. Missionaries cleared the land for a meetinghouse and a site dedication was held June 16,

1985, and a building was subsequently constructed. A former prime minister of St. Vincent, Ebeneezer Joshua, joined the Church and served in the branch presidency. Sharon Nichols was the first local member called on a full-time mission in 1983.

When Brother Joshua died in 1991, from 30,000 to 40,000 people, including top government officials, viewed or attended his televised funeral in the Kingstown meetinghouse and learned of the plan of salvation.

Sources: Kenneth and LeOra Zabriskie journals; correspondence from Pres. A. Dean Jeffs, West Indies Mission; *Church News*, March 30, 1991.

SCOTLAND

(See United Kingdom)

SERBIA

Year-end 1995: Est. population, 8,400,000; Members, 100; Districts, 1; Branches, 2; Europe East Area; Austria Vienna Mission.

Located on the Balkan Peninsula in southeast Europe, Serbia is a republic made up of what was the easternmost internal division of Yugoslavia.

Mischa Markow, a Hungarian who had immigrated to Salt Lake City, Utah, arrived as a missionary in Belgrade, Yugoslavia, in June 1899. He was taken to court where he preached. Even his arresting officer pled his case. But one judge was so irate that he reportedly said the missionary should be "thrown in to the Danube to drown." Elder Markow was banished to Hungary. He wrote that he shed tears of joy that he was privileged to testify before a magistrate and a high court.

In modern times, missionary work has proceeded slowly. A few members live in Belgrade, where a branch was organized in 1988.

The Church provided members and non-members in Serbia with humanitarian supplies in 1992, which included food, clothing, blankets and medical supplies.

Sources: "Tears of joy," by Richard L. Jensen, *Church News*, Dec. 8, 1979; Yugoslavia, manuscript history; "Missionary to the Balkans, Mischa Markow," by William Hale Kehr, *Ensign*, June 1980; Zagreb Branch history, published by the branch at dedication of meetinghouse, Oct. 30, 1985; *Church News*, Sept. 26, 1992.

SIERRA LEONE

Year-end 1995: Est. population, 4,800,000; Members, 2,400; Districts, 3; Branches, 14; Africa Area; Ghana Accra Mission.

On the west coast of West Africa, the Republic of Sierra Leone has a population that speaks English and tribal languages, and is Muslim, 30 percent; Animist, 30 percent; and Christian, 10 percent.

Michael Samura was baptized in Holland in 1981, and later returned to Freetown, Sierra Leone, where he stayed until 1984. He later returned to Sierra Leone. Elizabeth Bangura and Monica Orleans were baptized in Ghana and formed a study group in Freetown in January 1988. Christian George was baptized outside the country and returned to preside over the first approved meeting, held Jan. 18, 1988, at Goderich, a suburb of Freetown. In May 1988, Elder and Sister Clair Fisher, and Elder and Sister Erwin Waite arrived and took part in a service on June 11, 1988, where the first 14 converts were baptized.

The Liberia Monrovia Mission, which included Sierra Leone, was created on March 1, 1988. The Goderich Branch was organized Aug. 7, 1988, with Brother Samura as a counselor in the branch presidency. On Oct. 6, 1989, Abu H. Conteh was called as the first full-time missionary and assigned to serve in Sierra Leone.

The Freetown District was created December 1990 by Elder Robert E. Sackley of the Africa Area presidency and a Seventy. Michael Samura was called as its president. Seminary was introduced into the country by 1991, and two more districts, Bo and Wellington, were created Aug. 25 of that year.

The Liberia mission offices were moved to Freetown, Sierra Leone, in May 1990 because of the unrest in Liberia. Later, as civil war developed, the Liberia Monrovia Mission was discontinued April 22, 1991, and the area transferred to the Ghana Accra Mission. In May and August 1992, two missionary couples were temporarily removed from Sierra Leone because of unrest.

By year-end 1993, 89 Sierra Leonians were serving full-time missions, including 41 from the six branches of the Freetown District.

In 1994, quilts from young women of the Frederick Maryland Stake were shipped to Sierra Leone through the Church's Washington, D.C., welfare complex. With each quilt was a letter, signed by the young women, that explained that individual pieces of the quilt represent acts of love and service.

In 1994, an artist from Sierra Leone, Abu Hassan Conteh, entered a textile in the Third International Art Competition sponsored by the Museum of Church History and Art in Salt Lake City. His work was again exhibited in the museum in 1995 among other award-winning entries from the competition.

Sources: Pres. Miles Cunningham of the Liberia Monrovia Mission; *Church News*, Jan. 26, 1991; correspondence from Pres. Christopher N. Chukwurah, Ghana Accra Mission, March 14, 1994; *Church News*, Jan. 8, 1994, April 2, 1994, Feb. 4, 1995.

SINGAPORE

Year-end 1995: Est. population, 2,900,000; Members, 1,900; Stakes, 1; Wards, 5; Branches, 2; Missions, 1; Percent LDS, .06; or one LDS in 1,526.

On the tip of the Malay Peninsula in southeast Asia, Singapore is a parliamentary democracy. Its population speaks Chinese, Malay, Tamil and English (all are official languages). The people are Buddhist, Christian, Islam, Taoist and Hindu.

Members in the British military and Chinese members who moved from Hong Kong began holding meetings in Singapore in 1963. On March 19, 1968, four missionaries from the Southern Far East Mission arrived in Singapore. A branch was organized Oct. 13, 1968, with John McSweeney as president and Sheila Hsia, a member from Hong Kong, as Relief Society president. The Southeast Asia Mission was created Nov. 1, 1969.

About a year later the branch membership numbered approximately 100.

In 1970, the government restricted tracting and visas, and work progressed through the local members. By 1976, membership was 309. The Singapore Mission was re-opened Jan. 1, 1980. In 1985, membership increased to 960. Three meetinghouses were completed in 1990.

In August 1992, a returned missionary from Taiwan, Jon Huntsman Jr., was sworn in as U.S. ambassador to Singapore. He served until June 15, 1993, the youngest-ever U.S. ambassador to Singapore and the first to speak Mandarin.

By mid-1993, membership had increased to 1,750 members in seven branches.

On Feb. 25, 1995, Elder Neal A. Maxwell of the Quorum of the Twelve created the Singapore Stake from the Singapore District. Woo Hoi Seng Leonard, 39, was called as stake president.

Sources: LDS Scene, *Improvement Era*, June 1969; "Help from members," *Church News*, Aug. 18, 1979; *Church News*, March 10, 1985; address by Elder Marion D. Hanks, Salt Lake Institute devotional April 5, 1981; *Church News*, Nov. 17, 1973, Nov. 16, 1991, Sept. 5, 1992; *Church News*, June 5, 1993; "Asia area: Welcome mat is out in several countries," by Sheridan R. Sheffield, *Church News*, June 19, 1993; "New Stakes," *Church News*, April 27, 1995.

Stake — 1
(Listed alphabetically as of Oct. 1, 1996.)

No.	Name	Organized	First President
Asia Area			
2025	Singapore Singapore	26 Feb 1995	Woo Hoi Seng Leonard

Mission — 1
(As of Oct. 1, 1996; shown with historical number. See MISSIONS.)

(89) SINGAPORE MISSION
711 Lorong 37 Geylang
#04-04
Oriental Venture Building
Singapore 389626
Phone: (011-65) 842-0931

SLOVAKIA

Year-end 1995: Est. Population, 5,432,000; Members, fewer than 100; Branches, 2; Europe East Area; Czech Republic Prague Mission.

The east side of the former state of Czechoslovakia, Slovakia is a federal republic with a population that speaks Slovak, Czech and Hungarian, and which is mostly Roman

Catholic, Protestant and Orthodox Jewish.

The first member in Slovakia was Valerie Ruzena Frantiska Zizkova, born to members in the Czech Republic and baptized July 1939, just before the missionaries departed prior to World War II. She regained contact with missionaries for a brief period after the war, and then, from the pressure of the Communist government, lost contact with the Church. She later married and moved to Central Slovakia and remained faithful, renewing contact with the Church in 1992. Other members who had been baptized as expatriates included Alzbeta Domotorova, who had been baptized in Germany in 1977; and Pavel Pirovits, who had requested political asylum in Germany prior to the fall of the Communist regime. Other influential converts were Peter and Hanka Vaclav. Brother Vaclav had been baptized in March 1991 stemming from contact with members in Moravia. His wife joined several months later following an accident after which she began to have a deeper interest in God. The first Church meeting held in modern times in Slovakia was at the home of Brother and Sister Vaclav. The meeting was held in the latter part of October 1991 with visiting missionaries from the Czech Republic presiding. The family interest led to the establishment of the first branch in Slovakia, the Trencin Branch. This branch was created under the direction of Pres. Richard W. Winder of the Czechslovakia Prague Mission on Jan. 24, 1993. A group of members began meeting in Bratislava, and a second branch was created there later in the year.

Elders David Backman and Christopher Williams arrived to work in Trencin on March 29, 1992, and they baptized Martin and Zuzana Blaskova on July 25, 1992, in Trencin.

In 1993, producer Radim Smetana and reporter Premysl Cech of Czechoslovak Television visited Salt Lake City to make a documentary featuring the Church for broadcast in the Czech Republic and Slovakia. Mr. Smetana came in contact with the Church in June 1991 when the Tabernacle Choir performed in Prague; his contact then led to subsequent programs featuring the Church.

On April 30, 1994, a translation team with Elder Marcello de Oliveira as coordinator began translating basic Church materials into Slovak.

Sources: Unpublished history of the Church in Slovakia, courtesy Pres. Phil J. Bryson; "Czech broadcasters see Church close up," *Church News*, May 22, 1993.

SLOVENIA

Year-end 1995: Est. Population, 2,051,000; Members, fewer than 100; Districts, 1; Branches, 3; Europe West Area; Austria Vienna Mission.

Located on the Balkan Peninsula in southeast Europe, Slovenia is a republic made up of what was the northernmost internal division of Yugoslavia.

Mischa Markow, a Hungarian who had immigrated to Salt Lake City, Utah, arrived as a missionary in Yugoslavia in May 1899. He was banished to Hungary a month later because government authorities objected to his preaching.

Some 70 years passed before members returned. By the early 1970s, a few Latter-day Saints were living in Yugoslavia, some of whom had joined the Church while working or studying abroad.

In early 1975, Neil D. Schaerrer, president of the Austria Vienna Mission, established the Church as a legal entity in Yugoslavia. He met with members in Ljubljana, a major city in central Slovenia, during the following months. In 1993, Elder Matjaz Juhart became the first full-time missionary called from the Republic of Slovenia. He was called to the Utah Salt Lake City Mission and entered the Missionary Training Center Sept. 15, 1993.

Boza Gardner, 22, and Albin Lotric, 24, president of the Ljubljana Branch, were to be the first couple to marry in the temple from Slovenia. They even found a wedding dress for her among clothing donated from members in other countries. The two were married in the Frankfurt Germany Temple July 8, 1992.

The presence of BYU's men's basketball team, on a European tour in 1994, led to many referrals for the 20 missionaries and 60 members residing in Slovenia. Team members, seven of whom are returned missionaries, attended sacrament meeting in a hotel in Ljubjana.

Sources: Yugoslavia, manuscript history; "Missionary to the Balkans, Mischa Markow," by William Hale Kehr, *Ensign*, June 1980; Zagreb Branch history, published by the branch at dedication of meetinghouse, Oct. 30, 1985; *Church News*, Sept. 26, 1992; "Cinderella story: A dress for bride-to-be," *Church News*, Feb. 6, 1993; *Church News*, Jan 22, 1994; *Church News*, Sept. 10, 1994.

SOMALIA

Year-end 1995: Est. population, 7,360,000; Members, fewer than 100. Africa Area.

The easternmost country in Africa, the Somalia Democratic Republic covers more than 246,000 square miles and has a population of about 8 million. Almost all Somalians speak the Somali language and are Sunni Muslims.

Somalia gained its independence in 1960. Prior to that, Great Britain ruled the northern section and Italy ruled the south.

There are fewer than 100 members in the country and, as yet, no official Church group. In 1992, the Church shipped 1 million pounds of food and relief supplies to Somalia and neighboring countries to help alleviate suffering from drought. A large portion of Church aid went to Somalians, victims of not only the drought, but also of civil war.

Sources: World Book Encyclopedia, vol. 18, p. 588; Church membership records; "Deadly drought," *Church News,* Sept. 26, 1992.

SOUTH AFRICA

Year-end 1995: Est. population, 45,140,000; Members, 24,000; Stakes, 6; Wards, 25; Branches, 61; Missions, 3; Districts, 3; Temples, 1; Percent LDS, 0.05, or one LDS in 1,880.

At the southern end of the continent of Africa, the Republic of South Africa is a tricameral parliament. Its people speak Afrikaans, English and Bantu, and are mainly Christian, with Hindu and Muslim minorities.

Elders Jesse Haven, Leonard L. Smith and William H. Walker began missionary labors in Cape Town, South Africa, on April 19, 1853. On May 23, 1853, the trio officially organized the Church in the Cape of Good Hope. Elder Haven was appointed the first mission president of the South African Mission. Despite immediate, heavy persecution, they baptized Henry Stringer, the first convert, on June 15, 1853.

On Aug. 16, 1853, the first branch of the Church in South Africa was organized at Mowbray, four miles from Cape Town. A second branch was organized Sept. 7, 1853, at Newlands, six miles from Cape Town. A third branch was organized Feb. 23, 1854, at Beaufort, Cape Colony. These branches later formed the the Cape Conference. At a conference held in Port Elizabeth on Aug. 13, 1855, the "Church in the Cape of Good Hope" (South African Mission) was reported to consist of three conferences, six branches and 126 members.

Due to proselyting restrictions and lack of knowledge of the Afrikaans language, the South African Mission was closed from 1865 to 1903. Elder Warren H. Lyon reopened and presided over the mission. The first LDS meetinghouse in South Africa was built in 1916-17 as an addition to the first mission home at Mowbray. In 1950, missionary work was extended to Rhodesia (now Zimbabwe), where several branches of the Church were established.

The first stake in South Africa, the Transvaal Stake, was organized on March 22, 1970, with Louis P. Hefer as president. The Afrikaans translation of the Book of Mormon was first introduced to the South African Saints on May 14, 1972.

The first-ever area conference in South Africa was held in Johannesburg Oct. 23-24, 1978, attended by 3,450 of the subcontinent's 7,200 members living in South Africa, Rhodesia (now Zimbabwe) and South West Africa (now Namibia). Five General Authorities attended the conference, the first time ever that more than one General Authority was in South Africa at the same time.

The Johannesburg South Africa Temple was completed and dedicated in 1982 and has been visited by members throughout the southern part of the continent.

The South African Mission was divided on July 1, 1984, creating the South Africa Johannesburg and South Africa Cape Town missions.

Work in townships and other areas in South Africa progressed significantly in the 1980s. At a regional conference held Feb. 8-9, 1992, in Johannesburg, attendance reached 4,200, including a choir of 140 youths from three area stakes. Membership in the Soweto township continued to grow as members and missionaries worked closely together. Following the abolition of apartheid (apartness), members of all origins worked together to overcome cultural barriers.

Among Church or Church-affiliated programs active in South Africa is the Scouting organization. Iin 1996, some 5,000 gathered for the Johannesburg Regional Conference — the largest such LDS gathering in South Africa.

Sources: *Encyclopedic History of the Church*, by Andrew Jenson; "South Africa,", *Relief Society Magazine*, June 1969; "Mission Opening — 117 Years Ago," by Jack E. Jarrard, *Church News*, June 20, 1970; "The Saints in South Africa," by Lawrence E. Cummins, *Ensign*, March 1973; "South Africans greet prophet at conference," by Dell Van Orden, *Church News*, Nov. 4, 1978;"Early MormonImprints in South Africa", by David J. Whittaker, *Brigham Young University Studies*, spring 1980; Saints in South Africa, by Marjorie E. Woods, September 1986; *Church News*, Feb. 29, 1992, Sept. 26, 1992; "South Africa: Land of Good Hope," by R. Val Johnson, *Ensign*, February 1993; *Church News*, Nov. 11, 1995, March 2, 1996.

Stakes — 6

(Listed alphabetically as of Oct. 1, 1996.)

No.	Name	Organized	First President
Africa Area			
1662	Benoni South Africa	29 Nov 1987	Jan G. Hugo
1470	Cape Town South Africa	6 May 1984	Otto Wilhelm Miessner
1314	Durban South Africa	29 Nov 1981	Percy E.A. Winstanley
506	*Johannesburg South Africa		
	‡Transvaal (South Africa)	22 Mar 1970	Louis P. Hefer
969	*Pretoria South Africa	29 Nov 1987	
	‡Sandton South Africa	22 Oct 1978	Johannes P. Brummer
2046	Roodepoort South Africa	7 May 1995	Christoffel Golden Jr.

Missions — 3

(As of Oct. 1, 1996; shown with historical number. See MISSIONS.)

(177a) S. AFR.CAPE TOWN MISSION
P.O. Box 217
Howard Place
7450 Cape Town
Republic of South Africa
Phone: (011-27-21) 531-6903

(216) S. AFR. DURBAN MISSION
8 Windsor Ave.
Westville, 3630
Republic of South Africa
Phone: (011-27-31) 267-0250

(14) S. AFR. JOHANNESBURG MISSION
Private Bag X7
Weltevreden Park 1715
Republic of South Africa
Phone: (011-27-11) 475-3130

TRANSKEI

Year-end 1995: Est. population, 3,500,000; Members, fewer than 100; Branches, 1; Africa Area; South Africa Cape Town Mission.

Transkei, one of 10 homelands established for the Xhosa people by South Africa, is on the southwest coast of South Africa. In March 1988, a member, Dr. Emmanuel Danso and his wife, Akosua Seiwa, moved to Port Saint Johns, where they met with missionaries and Akosua Seiwa was baptized. The Umtata Branch was organized with Dr. Danso as branch president on April 8, 1989. The branch is part of the East London South Africa District and part of the South Africa Cape Town Mission.

Sources: South Africa Johannesburg Mission manuscript history; "Gospel takes root in Africa's Wild Coast," by Jay H. Buckley, *Church News*, June 16, 1990.

SPAIN

Year-end 1996: Est. population, 39,404,000; Members, 27,000; Stakes, 4; Wards, 19; Branches, 126; Missions, 5; Districts, 17; Temples, 1 under construction; Percent LDS, 0.06, or one LDS in 1,459.

Located in southwest Europe, Spain is a constitutional monarchy. Its people speak Spanish, Catalan, Galician and Basque, and 90 percent are Roman Catholic.

Regular Church services began in Spain among LDS servicemen after World War II when the United States established relations with that country. Two American branches were functioning in 1966, and a district presidency operated under the French Mission. One of the first converts in Spain, Jose Maria Oliveira, was baptized in France in March 1966.

The Spanish Religious Liberty Law passed in 1967 paved the way for the organization of the Madrid Branch on the first Sunday in February 1968. Some 40 attended, including Spanish wives of American servicemen, other Spanish-speaking members, and investigators.

Official recognition for the Church in Spain was formalized on Oct. 22, 1968. A mission was organized July 11, 1970. During this period, many Spanish-speaking members were transferred by their businesses to Spain and helped strengthen the new branches. By 1974, 17 branches, with a total membership of 619, were operating in Spain.

Elder Gordon B. Hinckley, then of the Quorum of the Twelve, accompanied by Elder Neal A. Maxwell of the Presidency of the First Quorum of the Seventy, visited King Juan Carlos de Bourbon in August 1978.

Spain's first stake was created in Madrid on March 14, 1982, with Jose Oliveira as president. Additional stakes followed. When the Seville Spain Stake was created in 1988, one area within the stake reported 98 percent activity among Melchizedek Priesthood holders, and noted that 54 members of the stake were serving full-time missions.

President Hinckley visited King Juan Carlos I and Queen Sofia March 9, 1992, and presented the couple with a personalized, leather-bound copy of the Book of Mormon. About that time, Spain was among the countries to receive satellite broadcasts of general conference. At the April 1993 general conference, as first counselor in the First Presidency, President Hinckley announced that the Church was acquiring property for a temple in Spain, the Church's fifth in continental Europe.

President Hinckley returned on June 11, 1996, as the first president of the Church to visit Spain where he broke ground for the Madrid Spain Temple. The ceremony was held in 113-degree heat on a graded site in Moratalez.

Sources: *Encyclopedic History of the Church,* by Andrew Jenson; "The Church Grows in Spain," by J Malan Heslop, *Church News,* Oct. 30, 1971; "Spain," *Ensign,* August 1973; "This is Spain," by Betty Ventura, *Ensign,* April 1975; "The Restored Church in Spain," unpublished history by David B. Timmons; "Relief Society Offers New Outlook for Spanish Women," by Gerry Avant, *Church News,* May 17, 1975; "Mormons meet king of Spain," *Church News,* Oct. 14, 1978; "Lead their own," by Jill Mulvay Derr, *Church News,* Sept. 1, 1979; *Church News,* March 20, 1982; March 28, 1992; *Church News,* June 22, 1996.

Stakes — 4
(Listed alphabetically as of Oct. 1, 1996.)

No.	Name	Organized	First President
Europe West Area			
1370	Barcelona Spain	31 Oct 1982	Jose Lara Straube
2022a	Cadiz Spain	19 Feb 1995	Cristobal Rodriguez Vasquez
1327	Madrid Spain	14 Mar 1982	Jose Mario Oliveira Aldamiz
1687	Seville Spain	14 Feb 1988	Jesus Manuel Benitez S.

Missions — 5
(As of Oct. 1, 1996; shown with historical number. See MISSIONS.)

(137) SPAIN BARCELONA MISSION
Calle Calatrava 10-12, bajos
08017 Barcelona, Spain
Phone: (011-34-3) 211-6558

(220) SPAIN LAS PALMAS MISSION
Avenida Rafael Cabrera 4-6oA
35002 Las Palmas de Gran Canaria
Spain
Phone: (011-34-28) 36-87-62

(141) SPAIN MALAGA MISSION
Edf. Ofisol
Avda. Jesus Santos Rein 4, Planta 3 D-E
29640 Fuengirola (MALAGA)
Spain
Phone: (011-34-5) 246-9392

(199) SPAIN BILBAO MISSION
c/Bidearte 6, 4o dcha
48930 Las Arenas (Vizcaya)
Spain
Phone (011-34-4) 464-8687

(92) SPAIN MADRID MISSION
Calle San Telmo, 26
28016 Madrid (Madrid)
Spain
Phone: (011-34-1) 359-2634

CANARY ISLANDS

Year-end 1995: Est. population, 1,343,000; Members, 3,500; Districts, 3; Branches, 18; percent LDS, 0.26, or one LDS in 384; Africa Area; Spain Las Palmas Mission.

The Canary Islands, in the South Atlantic off the coast of Africa, are rugged, volcanic mountainous islands with rich soil and long beaches where sand from the western Sahara Desert has drifted.

The first converts on the Canary Islands were Francisco Dominguez Pena; his wife, Francisca; and their son, Javier, who were baptized June 13, 1979. They were introduced to the Church by Jesus Gomez y Vega, a resident of the islands who had moved to Spain and been baptized in 1973. Meetings were subsequently held in their home. The first missionaries were Elders David L. Gill and Scott C. Jensen.

The first branch was organized in Las Palmas on Jan. 29, 1980. The first district, Las Palmas Gran Canarias, was organized Oct. 2, 1984, with eight branches. The second district, Santa Cruz de Tenerife Canaria, was organized Aug. 8, 1989, with six branches. The Spain Las Palmas Mission, with headquarters in the Canary Islands, was created July 1, 1988, under the leadership of Pres. Marion K. Hamblin.

Sources: The Begininnings of the Church in the Canary Islands, by Maria Torio de Gomez Vega, unpublished; Spain Las Palmas Mission history; *Church News*, Nov. 10, 1990.

SURINAME

Year-end 1995: Est. population, 430,000; Members, 300; Branches, 1; North America Southeast Area; West Indies Mission.

Located on the Atlantic Coast at the top of South America, the Republic of Suriname has a population that speaks Dutch, Creole and English. They are Hindu, 27 percent; Muslim, 23 percent; and Christian, 25 percent.

Elder John Limburg and his wife, Beverly, arrived in Paramaribo in October 1988 and started the Paramaribo Branch. By the start of 1989, some 16 people were attending services. The first convert was baptized March 26, 1989, in services attended by about 25 people.

By 1990, attendance at the branch averaged about 100 people. Meetings were also held in the rural communities of Lelydorp and Uitkijk.

Sources: Interview with John M. and Beverly Limburg; manuscript history of Suriname; *Church News*, April 29, 1989, March 10, 1990; "Work flourishing among a people without guile," by Elayne Wells, *Church News*, Dec. 1, 1990.

SWAZILAND

Year-end 1995: Est. population, 975,000; Members, 700; Branches, 3; Percent LDS, 0.09, or one LDS in 1,393; Africa Area; South Africa Johannesburg Mission.

The second smallest country in Africa, Swaziland is a mountainous kingdom located in southern Africa near the Indian Ocean. The people speak Siswati and English, and 57 percent of the people are Christian while 43 percent have indigenous beliefs.

A group of LDS non-Africans living in Swaziland in 1984 included the Herman Van Thiel Berghuijs, George Gardner and John Scott families. The Mbabane Branch was organized Nov. 5, 1985, with Brother Gardner as president. The Church was recognized by the government in February 1987, and Elder Kenneth Edwards and his wife, Betty, the first missionaries, arrived that year and converts came into the Church.

The first called on a mission from Swaziland was Elder Paulo Cipriano Zandamela, baptized July 31, 1988, a Mozambican. Sister Fikile Dlamini was the first Swazi to serve a full-time mission. By 1990, converts were serving full-time missions and of the 115 members, only Branch Pres. Larry Brown and his family were non-Africans.

On Feb. 24, 1991, three more branches were organized under local priesthood leadership. By then, several members from Swaziland had been through the temple, and seven local missionaries had been called. Swaziland's first meetinghouse was dedicated July 18, 1993, in a ceremony attended by government representatives, and presided over by Elder Richard P. Lindsay of the Seventy and president of the Africa Area. At the time, in Swaziland, there were 650 members in five branches. Other branches have been established in Ezulwini, Manzini and Nhlangano.

Members and residents here have benefited from both giving and receiving service. In 1993, young adults from the Johannesburg South Africa Stake spent three days giving service to orphans at the Swaziland Government Hospital, cleaning the local meetinghouse and training prospective elders. Full-time missionaries in the Mbabane Swaziland District served at the SOS Children's Village for Orphans. In 1996, members from Swaziland joined some 5,000 others at the Johannesburg Regional Conference — the largest such gathering of LDS in South Africa.

Sources: Manuscript history of South Africa Johannesburg Mission; correspondence from mission Pres. R.J. and Marilyn M. Snow; *Church News*, Jan. 27, 1990, March 10, 1990; Sept. 25, 1993; Nov. 13, 1993; March 2, 1996.

SWEDEN

Year-end 1995: Est. population, 8,700,000; Members, 8,400; Stakes, 3; Wards, 14; Branches, 38; Missions, 1; Districts, 3; Temples, 1; Percent LDS, 0.1, or one LDS in 1,035.

In northern Europe on the east side of the Scandinavian Peninsula, the kingdom of Sweden is a constitutional monarchy; its population speaks Swedish and Finnish, and is 95 percent Lutheran.

The first missionary to Sweden was John E. Forsgren, a Swedish seaman who joined the Church in Boston, Mass., and then moved to Nauvoo, Ill., to be with the Saints.

After migrating to the Salt Lake Valley with the pioneers, he answered a mission call to Sweden. He went first to his hometown of Gavle, where his brother, Peter, was healed by the power of the priesthood. He then baptized Peter on July 26, 1850, as the first convert to the Church in Sweden.

After baptizing a few more converts, Elder Forsgren was arrested and banished from the country for preaching. Thereafter, missionaries occasionally visited Sweden from Denmark. In 1853, successful missionary operations were commenced in southern Sweden by Anders W. Winberg and others.

On April 24, 1853, the first branch of the Church was organized in Skonaback by Elder Winberg, and another branch was soon started in Malmo. From there, the Church extended northward, with many converts immigrating to the United States.

In 1905, Sweden was taken from the Scandinavian Mission and the Swedish Mission was organized.

Notable events of the Church in Sweden in recent times include the first Nordic area conference Aug. 16-18, 1974, in Stockholm and organization of stakes in Stockholm on April 20, 1975, and in Goteborg Nov. 20, 1977. On March 17, 1984, ground was broken for a temple near Stockholm, which was dedicated July 2-4, 1985.

On March 24, 1988, President Thomas S. Monson, second counselor in the First Presidency, took part in Sweden's observance of the 350th anniversary of the first Swedish settlement in the United States. President Monson and his wife, Frances, exchanged greetings with King Carl XVI Gustaf and Queen Silvia. Also taking part was Gregory J. Newell, the U.S. ambassador to Sweden, a member of the Church.

As Eastern Europe opened to the preaching of the gospel, the temple in Sweden offered an opportunity for the Swedish members to host many visitors. The first group of Russian Saints to come to the temple arrived Aug. 30, 1993.

On Aug. 23, 1995, King Carl XVI Gustaf and Queen Silvia were hosted on a visit to the Stockholm Temple grounds by President Thomas S. Monson, first counselor in the First Presidency.

Sources: *Encyclopedic History of the Church*, by Andrew Jenson; *History of the Church in Sweden 1850-1905*, by A. Dean Wengreen, a BYU dissertation, August 1968; *History of the Swedish Mission of the Church, 1905-1973*, by Carl-Erik Johansson, a BYU thesis August 1973; *Church News*, Nov. 21, 1987; *Church News*, Nov. 20, 1993; "Royal couple visits at Swedish temple with Pres. Monson" by Gerry Avant, *Church News*, Sept. 2, 1995.

Stakes — 4

(Listed alphabetically as of Oct. 1, 1996.)

No.	Name	Organized	First President
Europe North Area			
880	*Goeteborg Sweden 7 Jan 1991		
	‡Goteborg Sweden	20 Nov 1977	Arne Lennart Hedberg
691	Stockholm Sweden	20 Apr 1975	Evert W. Perciwall
2088	Stockholm Sweden South	20 Aug 1995	Ulf Arne Gilhammer
2226	Malmoe Sweden	01 Sep 1996	C. Urban Girhammar

Mission — 1

(As of Oct. 1, 1996; shown with historical number. See MISSIONS.)

SWITZERLAND

Year-end 1995: Est. population, 7,085,000; Members, 6,900; Stakes, 3; Wards, 15; Branches, 24; Missions, 2; Temples, 1; Percent LDS, 0.10, or one LDS in 1,026.

In central Europe, Switzerland is a federal republic with a population that speaks German, 65 percent; French, 18 percent; Italian, 12 percent; and Romansch, 1 percent. The Swiss people are 49 percent Roman Catholic and 48 percent Protestant.

Missionary work began in Switzerland on Nov. 24, 1850, as an outgrowth of the work in Italy. Elder Lorenzo Snow of the Quorum of the Twelve, laboring in Italy, set apart Thomas B.H. Stenhouse as the first president of the Swiss Mission. The *Millennial Star* reported that 20 converts were baptized in 1851 in Switzerland. Many Church members emigrated from Switzerland to America until the 1950s.

In August 1914 and again in September 1938, missionaries were evacuated from Switzerland due to World War I, and World War II, respectively, and during both wars, local priesthood holders were placed in leadership of the missions, branches, and districts in Switzerland.

After World War I, programs of the Church steadily developed in Switzerland as many Church publications and manuals were translated.

President David O. McKay visited in 1952 and a building site for the Swiss Temple was selected in Zollikofen, near Bern. The completed temple was dedicated in several sessions beginning Sept. 11, 1955, and served Church members in Western Europe and the Nordic countries, as well as Switzerland.

The first stake in Switzerland was organized Oct. 28, 1961, in Zurich. The first General Authority from Switzerland was Elder Hans B. Ringger, who was called to the Seventy in 1985.

After refurbishment of the Swiss Temple, European Saints from many countries attended the rededication by President Gordon B. Hinckley on Oct. 23-25, 1992. At the dedication, he commented that while those of every nationality had different passports, their temple recommends were similar.

President Howard W. Hunter visited Switzerland Aug. 8-16, 1994, the first country he visited as Church president. He spoke to members and missionaries and attended to matters at the recently rededicated temple.

Sources: *Encyclopedic History of the Church*, by Andrew Jenson; *Church News*, Nov. 11, 1961; *History of the Church in Switzerland*, by Dale Z. Kirby, a BYU thesis, May 1971; "Switzerland," *Ensign*, April 1973; "Switzerland: land of peace, precision and great progress," by Gerry Avant, *Church News*, Dec. 22, 1979; "Thousands tour London and Swiss temples," and "LDS officials rededicate Swiss Temple," by Gerry Avant, *Church News*, Oct. 24, 1992; *Church News*, Aug. 20, 1994.

Stakes — 3

(Listed alphabetically as of Oct. 1, 1996.)

No.	Name	Organized	First President
Europe West Area			
1261	Bern Switzerland	3 May 1981	Peter Lauener
1352	Geneva Switzerland	20 Jun 1982	Denis Bonny
341	*Zurich Switzerland ‡Swiss (Switzerland, Germany)	28 Oct 1961	Wilhelm Friedrich Lauener

Missions — 2

(As of Oct. 1, 1996; shown with historical number. See MISSIONS.)

(59) SWITZERLAND GENEVA MISSION
8, chemin William Barbey
CH-1292 Chambesy (GE)
Switzerland
Phone: (011-41-22) 758-1535

(8) SWITZERLAND ZURICH MISSION
Pilatusstrasse 11
CH-8032 Zurich
Switzerland
Phone: (011-41-1) 252-5114

TAHITI
(See French Polynesia under FRANCE)

TAIWAN

Year-end 1995: Est. population, 21,601,000; Members, 22,000; Stakes, 4; Wards, 22; Branches, 35; Districts, 4; Temples, 1; Percent LDS, 0.1, or one LDS in 981.

Off the southeast coast of China, the Republic of China has a population that speaks Mandarin Chinese and Taiwan and Hakka dialects. They mostly adhere to Buddhism, Taoism and Confucianism.

An American servicemen's group was functioning in Taipei when the first four missionaries departed from Hong Kong to open the work in Taiwan (then called Formosa). Elders Weldon J. Kitchen, Keith Madsen, Duane W. Dean and Melvin C. Fish arrived in June 1956. Progress was slow at first, and anti-American riots hindered the work in 1957. However, by the end of 1957 almost 50 people had been baptized. After another year, nearly 200 had been converted and 31 missionaries were working in six cities. By the end of 1959, eight branches had been organized. Two large meetinghouses were completed in the 1960s in Taipei and Kaohsiung. Translation of the Book of Mormon into Chinese in 1965 also helped the work. Local leadership presided over most of the branches. In 1975, 30 branches in three districts, with a membership of 7,000, had been reached. Church educational programs were established, and many young people grew up taking seminary and institute classes. Some 2,500 members attended an area conference held in Taipei Aug. 13-14, 1975, and in 1980.

The Taipei Taiwan Stake was created April 22, 1976. A temple was announced for Taipei in April 1982 and was dedicated Nov. 17-18, 1984. At the time, membership numbered about 13,000. Membership in 1990 was 18,000.

Missionaries performing service projects in the 1990s have earned favorable publicity for the Church.

In 1993, some 20,300 members were in 57 units, three stakes and three districts in two missions. In December 1994, Jien-Nien Chen, a pharmacist and former branch president, became the first elected LDS governor in Taiwan.

President Gordon B. Hinckley addressed more than 3,000 members at a meeting May 23, 1996, in the Taipei International Convention Center. June 4, 1996, marked the 40-year anniversary of the Church in Taiwan.

Sources: "Mormon Missionaries Now Labor in Formosa," *Church News*, June 23, 1956; China and the Restored Church, by William Heaton, *Ensign*, August 1972; "My Sheep Know My Voice," *Church News*, April 28, 1973; "Taiwan: Steep Peaks and Towering Faith," by Janice Clark, *Ensign*, August 1975; "Relative Freedom of Taiwan Allows Growth of Church," by Gerry Avant, *Church News*, Dec. 6, 1975; "Saints throng to area meetings in the Far East," by Dell Van Orden, *Church News*, Nov. 1, 1980; "First Temple in Chinese Realm," by Gerry Avant, *Church News*, Nov. 25, 1984; *Church News*, July 9, 1994; "He bears testimony of blessings," *Church News*, June 8, 1996; "40-year anniversary in Taiwan," *Church News*, June 22, 1996.

Stakes — 4
(Listed alphabetically as of Oct. 1, 1996.)

No.	Name	Organized	First President
Asia Area			
1303	Kaohsiung Taiwan	6 Nov 1981	Ho Tung Hai
2003	Taichung Taiwan	18 Dec 1994	Chou, Wen Tsung
1326	Taipei Taiwan East	14 Mar 1982	Yuan-Hu Yen
755	*Taipei Taiwan West 14 Mar 1982		
	‡Taipei Taiwan	22 Apr 1976	I-Ch'ing Chang

Missions — 2
(As of Oct. 1, 1996; shown with historical number. See MISSIONS.)

(146) TAIWAN TAICHUNG MISSION
498-11 Wu Chuan Road
Taichung 40415
Taiwan ROC
Phone: (011-886-4) 226-7181

(94) TAIWAN TAIPEI MISSION
Floor 4, No. 24, Lane 183
Chin Hua Street
Taipei 106-06, Taiwan ROC
Phone: (011-886-2) 393-3285

TANZANIA

Year-end 1995: Est. population, 29,000,000; Members, 100; Branches, 1; Africa Area; Kenya Nairobi Mission.

On the east coast of Africa, Tanzania is a republic with its people speaking Swahili and English. The people are Muslim, 35 percent, Christian, 30 percent, and the balance follow tribal beliefs.

One of the first families to hold Church meetings was D.E. Tapie Rohm Jr. from Los Angeles, Calif., a Fulbright scholar assigned to Dar es Salaam from 1988-1989. In August 1991, Bruce Wilson and his family from Smith Falls, Ontario, Canada, arrived in Dar es Salaam. He was employed by International Development Co. The Wilson family began holding meetings in September 1991.

The Kenya Nairobi Mission, which includes Kenya, Uganda and Tanzania, was created in July 1991. Application for legal recognition was made March 15, 1992, and was approved Oct. 8, 1992. This recognition was assisted by a visit by Chief Judge J. Clifford Wallace of the U.S. Court of Appeals in San Diego, Calif., to Tanzania. An official who had been hosted by LDS members in Portland, Ore., facilitated Judge Wallace's request. Robert Muhile, a Tanzanian, was baptized in Cairo, Egypt, before the arrival of the missionaries. On Dec. 15, 1992, the Dar es Salaam Branch was created, and Brother Muhile called as its president on March 13, 1994.

A missionary couple, Elder Lervae and Sister Joyce Cahoon, arrived in February, 1992. The first converts were Projest S. Captain, Dickson and Japhet Kiiza, Dishon Z. Makunge and Mariam Mohamed-Chui, all baptized March 15, 1992.

Sources: *Church News*, March 23, 1991; correspondence from Pres. Larry K. Brown, Kenya Nairobi Mission, April 12, 1994.

THAILAND

Year-end 1995: Est. population, 60,770,000; Members, 6,300; Stakes, 1; Wards, 5; Branches, 21; Districts, 4; Missions, 1.

On the Indochinese and Malay Peninsula, Thailand is a constitutional monarchy. The Thai-speaking population is 95 percent Buddhist and 4 percent Muslim.

Elder Elam Luddington arrived in Bangkok, Thailand, April 6, 1854, as the first missionary to preach the gospel in the Asian country. Four elders had been assigned to preach the gospel in Thailand, then known as Siam, but only Elder Luddington reached the country. After laboring under difficult circumstances, he was able to baptize a ship's captain, James Trail, and his wife. When Elder Luddington left Thailand four months later, missionary work came to a halt for more than a century.

Six missionaries were transferred to Thailand from the Taiwan and Hong Kong zones of the Southern Far East Mission on Feb. 2, 1968. Thanks to the help of Anan Eldredge, a Thai who had been adopted by an American family and subsequently baptized, the elders were able to learn the language and teach the people the gospel. Brother Eldredge was the first Thai to hold the priesthood, the first to be a full-time missionary, and the first to be called as a mission president on July 1, 1988. Another early convert, Srilaksana Gottsche, was largely responsible for translating the Book of Mormon into Thai.

Thailand continued to grow as an important part of the Southern Far East Mission, which was divided Nov. 1, 1969. The new Southeast Asian Mission included Thailand with G. Carlos Smith as president. Under his direction, construction began on the country's first meetinghouse, located in Bangkok. Church leaders spent several years overcoming challenges and finally, on July 19, 1973, Thailand became its own mission with Paul D. Morris as president of the Thailand Bangkok Mission. The first sister missionaries arrived in the country in 1974, the same year that Elder David B. Haight of the Quorum of the Twelve dedicated the first meetinghouse in Thailand.

In 1987, three new meetinghouses were dedicated for the Bangnaa, Thonburi and Chiang Mai branches of the Church. The Church in Thailand noted a milestone in June 1990, when 201 Thai members went to the Manila Temple to receive their endowments or to be sealed to their families.

In 1993, long-term visas were extended to the Church by the government of Thailand.

Missionaries in the mission translated for the Utah Army National Guard in providing volunteer medical and dental services to residents near Ubon, Thailand, in 1993.

In July 1994, The Church's Thailand Bangkok office purchased and sent rice by a three-truck caravan over the Mekong River to Vientiane, Laos, as humanitarian service. The Church also contributed cash to aid in distribution of the rice, and agreed to send a shipment of clothing.

On June 18, 1995, Elder Neal A. Maxwell of the Quorum of the Twelve created the Bangkok Thailand Stake from the Bangkok Thailand District, with Thipparad Kitsaward, 52, called as president. Wards are Asoke, Bangkapi, Bangkhan, Bangnaa and Thonburi;

branches are Bangkok (English), Chonburi and Lopburi.

Thailand is now in the Hong Kong Temple district.

Sources: *Encyclopedic History of the Church,* by Andrew Jenson; Culture for Missionaries: *The Church Encounters Asia,* by Spencer J. Palmer, Deseret Book, 1970; "Thailand," prepared by Language Training Mission, 1978; *Church News,* Jan. 16, 1988, Feb. 13, 1988, July 16, 1988; Sept. 3, 1988; *Church News,* May 23, 1993; "Asia Area: Welcome mat is out in several countries," by Sheridan R. Sheffield, *Church News,* June 19, 1993.

Stake — 1
(Listed alphabetically as of Oct. 1, 1996.)

No.	Name	Organized	First President
Asia Area			
2064	Bangkok Thailand	18 Jun 1995	Thipparad Kitsaward

Mission — 1
(As of Oct. 1, 1996; shown with historical number. See MISSIONS.)

(109) THAILAND BANGKOK MISSION
50/829-832 Muang Thong Thani
Chaengwatana Road
T. Ban Mai, A Pakkret
Nonthaburi, Thailand 11120
Phone: (011-66-2) 503-3422

TONGA

Year-end 1995: Est. population, 106,000; Members, 40,000; Stakes, 13; Wards, 86; Districts, 1; Branches, 52; Missions, 1; Temples, 1; Percent LDS, 38, or one LDS in 3.

In the western South Pacific, the kingdom of Tonga is a constitutional monarchy whose population speaks Tongan and English. Tongans are Free Wesleyan, LDS, Roman Catholic, Church of Tonga, and Free Church of Tonga.

The first missionaries to Tonga were Brigham Smoot and Alva J. Butler, sent by the Samoan Mission Pres. William O. Lee. The missionaries arrived July 15, 1891, and soon visited King Jiaoji (George) Tubou and received permission to preach. They purchased property and erected a mission home and school, and also purchased a boat to travel between islands. The first convert was Alipate, baptized July 15, 1892. The mission made some progress, but was closed in 1897.

In 1907, the Tonga Mission was re-opened by Elders William O. Facer and Heber J. McKay. They opened a school in Nieafu on the island of Vava'u and by 1908, there were 28 day students and 13 night students. Elder Facer later was stationed in Ha'alaufuli where he found success, organizing a branch with 32 converts. Missionary work opened on the main island of Tongatapu on March 17, 1911, and by December 1912, a meetinghouse and school had been completed and a conference organized. A mission for Tonga was organized July 8, 1916, and more missionaries began serving.

Relationships with the government became strained as more people joined the Church. In 1921, Elder David O. McKay, then of the Quorum of the Twelve, visited, but was quarantined on a nearby island for 11 days before he was allowed to enter the country. Later, visas were denied to missionaries for two years. Local missionaries were called to do the work and served in positions of leadership.

Publication of the Book of Mormon in 1946 also helped strengthen the Church. All foreign missionaries were called home during World War II, but many LDS servicemen were stationed near Tonga and attended local meetings. After the war, foreign missionaries were once again restricted, with the exception of the mission president and his family. Membership in Tonga in 1946 was 2,422. From among them, mission presidents called local missionaries in what became one of the most successful local missionary programs in the Church.

Much of the progress on the islands has been through Church schools. The establishing of schools in 1892 and 1908 proved significant, and led to other schools starting. The Makeke School was opened Feb. 20, 1926, and it was the principal method of advancing the Church for many years. A new educational complex, the Liahona High School, was opened in 1952. Its building in 1949 was the beginning of the Church's labor missionary program and probably the catalyst for expansion of the Church.

In 1968, a jubilee celebration was held under the direction of mission Pres. John H. Groberg, now of the Seventy. Tonga's first stake was created Sept. 5, 1968. After that, the

Church in Tonga became nearly all led by local members, including its mission, many of the schools and the stakes.

Membership reached 10,000 in 1967, and increased to 14,355 in 1970, 18,484 in 1980, and 27,400 in 1985.

A highlight came Aug. 9-11, 1983, when the Tonga Nuku'alofa Temple was dedicated. In 1991, LDS and other Tongans joined in celebrating the centennial of the Church in Tonga. Among the most significant parts of the lengthy celebration was a dance festival in which 3,000 youths performed for King Taufa'ahau Topou IV.

Sources: *Unto the Islands of the Sea,* by R. Lanier Britsch; *Mighty Missionary of the Pacific,* by David W. Cummings, Bookcraft, 1961; *Tongan Saints, Legacy of Faith,* translated and edited by Eric B. Shumway, Institute for Polynesian Studies, Laie, Hawaii; *From Tonga to Zion,* prepared by Ella Mae Judd from journals of Fa'aki K. A. Richter; "Celebrating 100 years in Tonga," *Church News,* Aug. 31, 1991.

Stakes — 16
(Listed alphabetically as of Oct. 1, 1996.)

No.	Name	Organized	First President
Pacific Area			
2174	Eua Tonga	26 Feb 1996	Tuifio Finau
1430	Ha'apai Tonga	14 Jun 1983	Fanongonongo Vaitai
737	Neiafu Vava'u Tonga	4 Dec 1975	Mosese Hetau Langi
1172	Neiafu Vava'u Tonga North	27 Aug 1980	Mosese Hetau Langi
2092	Neiafu Vava'u Tonga West	27 Aug 1995	Tukia'i Vava'u Havea
463	*Nuku'alofa Tonga ‡Nuku'alofa	5 Sep 1968	Orson Hyde White
1986	Nuku'alofa Tonga Central	31 Jul 1994	Filimone Fie'eiki
550	*Nuku'alofa Tonga East ‡Nuku'alofa East	21 Jul 1971	Viliami Pele Folau
2175	Nuku'alofa Tonga Ha'akame	10 Mar 1996	Sosaia Lehonitai Mateaki
2083	Nuku'Alofa Tonga Halaliku	3 Aug 1995	Staleki Tonga Faemani
1173	Nuku'alofa Tonga Liahona	31 Aug 1980	Vaikalafi Lutui
2188	Nuku'alofa Tonga Mu'a	21 Apr 1996	J. William Harris
1445	Nuku'alofa Tonga North	9 Oct 1983	Sione Moala Fineanganofa
519	*Nuku'alofa Tonga South ‡Nuku'alofa South	26 Jul 1970	Tevita Folau Mahuinga
1431	Nuku'alofa Tonga Vaini	15 Jun 1983	Samuela Iloa
520	*Nuku'alofa Tonga West ‡Nuku'alofa West	26 Jul 1970	Orson H. White

Mission — 1
(As of Oct. 1, 1996; shown with historical number. See MISSIONS.)

(22c) TONGA NUKU'ALOFA MISSION
P.O. Box 58
Nuku'alofa, Tonga
Phone: (011-676) 21577

TRINIDAD AND TOBAGO

Year-end 1995: Est. population, 1,276,000; Members, 1,000; Districts, 1; Branches, 4; Missions, 1; Percent LDS, 0.05, or one LDS in 1,857; North America Southeast Area; West Indies Mission.

Off the east coast of Venezuela in the Caribbean Sea, both Trinidad & Tobago is a parliamentary democracy where the people speak English as the official language. The major religions are Roman Catholic, 32 percent; Protestant, 29 percent; and Hindu, 25 percent.

Among the first converts to the Church were Blasil D. and Felicia Borde, baptized in 1977 by Elder Daniel Rector. A branch in Port of Spain was organized June 5, 1980, under the Venezuela Caracas Mission. The area was transferred to the West Indies Mission in September 1983. The first missionaries from the West Indies Mission were Elders Chris Doty, Doug Mathews, Randy Clark and David Roos, who helped organized a citywide cross-country race that raised the Church's profile. In 1991, Elder Newell Anderson and his wife, Cora Gene, taught agriculture and developed ways to grow row crops of vegetables. Sister Anderson taught sewing classes.

On Sept. 2-5, 1991, LDS basketball players Danny Ainge, Greg Kite, Jeff Chatman and

Scott Runia held a series of basketball clinics on both islands of Trinidad and Tobago. They also appeared on television talk shows to discuss family values. The Trinidad Tobago Mission was created July 1, 1991, but discontinued in 1994. That year, however, the West Indies Mission was headquartered in Trinidad.

Sources: Kenneth and LeOra Zabriskie journals; *Church News*, March 6, 1983, July 10, 1983, March 10, 1990, Sept. 21, 1991; March 26, 1994.

UGANDA

Year-end 1995: Est. population, 19,592,000; Districts, 2; Branches, 7; Members, 13,000; Africa Area; Kenya Nairobi Mission.

Uganda, in east central Africa, has a military government and a population that speaks Luganda, Acholi, Lango and other languages. English is the official language and in understood by about 70 percent of the population. Its people are Christian, 63 percent; Muslim, 6 percent and tribal beliefs.

Expatriate Latter-day Saints lived in Uganda and held meetings as early as the 1960s. The first Ugandan to join the Church was Charles Osinde, who was baptized in Scotland, and returned to his homeland. Guy Denton and his wife, Peggy, arrived in Uganda in March 1990 as part of a USAID program. The Dentons held meetings in their home and Osinde and others joined them. The first Ugandan baptized was Mugisa James Collins, baptized Aug. 25, 1990, by Brother Denton.

A branch was soon created in Kampala and the people met in the Osinde's home. In December 1990, the first missionaries, Elder Lark and and Sister Arlea Washburn of Mesa, Ariz., arrived in Uganda. By March 1991, an average of 30 to 35 people attended branch meetings.

The Kenya Nairobi Mission, which includes Kenya, Uganda and Tanzania, was created in July 1991.

Church humanitarian efforts have benefited Ugandans through such projects as delivering clothing to the Kitgum District in Northern Uganda for victims of fighting between political factions.

Sources: History provided by LuDean Worthen; *Church News*, March 30, 1991; Feb. 11, 1995.

UKRAINE

Year-end 1995: Est. population, 51,900,000; Members, 3,100; Missions, 2; Districts, 6; Branches, 37; Europe East Area.

Bordering the Black Sea, Ukraine is a member of the Commonwealth of Independent States.

Missionary work began in October 1991 in Ukraine under the direction of Pres. Gary L. Browning of the Finland Helsinki East Mission. The Ukraine Kiev Mission was created Feb. 3, 1992, under the direction of Pres. Howard L. Biddulph, formerly president of the Austria Vienna East Mission. The mission, with 35 missionaries in 1992, served the entire Ukraine population.

On Sept. 12, 1991, Elders Boyd K. Packer and Dallin H. Oaks of the Quorum of the Twelve visited Ukraine and met with about 40 people, including members, missionaries and investigators. The Kiev Branch was created in June 1991.

Humanitarian assistance to people in Kiev was offered by members in Germany and the United States, who shipped thousands of pounds of food and clothing in 1991, 1992 and 1993. In July 1993, Ukraine received its second mission in Donetsk as work moved forward rapidly. Membership increased to 3,100 in 1995 from 1,700 in 1993.

Sources: *Church News*, Feb. 15, 1992, Feb. 29, 1992.

Missions — 2

(As of Oct. 1, 1996; shown with historical number. See MISSIONS.)

(295) UKRAINE DONETSK MISSION
P.O. Box 3494
340050 Donetsk
Ukraine
Phone: (011-380-622) 63-91-99

(274) UKRAINE KIEV MISSION
P.O. Box 144
252001 Kiev
Ukraine
Phone: (011-380-44) 228-0276

UNITED KINGDOM

Year-end 1995: Est. population, 58,295,000; Members, 168,000; Stakes, 43; Wards, 249; Branches, 135; Missions, 8; Temples, 1, 1 near completion; Percent LDS, 0.28, or one person in 346.

The United Kingdom consists of England, Scotland, Wales and Northern Ireland, and is located off the northwest coast of Europe. The population speaks English, Welsh, and Gaelic. Most belong to the Church of England or are Roman Catholics.

Sources: *Truth Will Prevail*, editors V. Ben Bloxham, James R. Moss and Larry C. Porter; A History of the Church in Cambridgeshire, unpublished history by Leonard Reed; *Church News*, July 6, 1974, Dec. 1, 1985; "Markers tell where history was made," by Dell Van Orden and Gerry Avant, *Church News*, Aug. 1, 1987, Aug. 8, 1987; *Church News*, Nov. 24, 1990; "Temples rededicated, lives renewed," by Gerry Avant, *Church News*, Oct. 31, 1992; "Ground broken for Preston temple," by Bryan J. Grant, *Church News*, June 18, 1994; "Prophet returns to beloved England" *by Mike Cannon, Church News*, Sept. 2, 1995.

ENGLAND

Year-end 1995: Est. population, 46,293,000; Members, 127,000; Stakes, 34; Wards, 201; Branches, 82; Missions, 6; Temples, 1, 1 near completion; Percent LDS, 0.3, or one LDS in 364.

On July 1, 1837, seven Canadian and American missionaries set sail for England on the packet ship *Garrick*. The seven, Elders Heber C. Kimball and Orson Hyde of the Quorum of the Twelve; and Willard Richards, Joseph Fielding, John Goodson, Isaac Russell and John Snider, arrived July 19, 1837. They preached at Preston on Sunday, July 23, and on July 30, a baptismal service was held at nearby River Ribble that was viewed by some 8,000 curious onlookers. Nine converts were baptized by Elder Kimball, the first of whom was George D. Watt. A week later, the number of converts reached 50. The first conference was held on Christmas. Missionaries began working in Alston and Bedford, where branches were established, but the greatest work was done in the Preston area. Opposition began to mount through ministers and the press, but within nine months, more than a thousand had been baptized.

From 1840-41, seven members of the Quorum of the Twelve labored in England, finding significant success. Some 800 converts emigrated during the apostles' stay. The flow of British converts was life-sustaining for the struggling Church in America.

By 1850, 42,316 people had been baptized, and 6,832 had emigrated; from 1851-60, 37,215 converts were baptized, and 12,972 had emigrated; from 1861-70, 14,977 had joined and 10,094 emigrated.

The Church faced considerable opposition during the next several decades and the work was slowed. Missionary work increased after the turn of the century. With the onset of World War I, local sisters took over missionary work. The Relief Society was particularly active during the war. After the war, missionary work increased and anti-Mormon activity waned. Membership increased and in the mid-1930s, a large building program began and local leadership and missionaries became stronger. Members were urged to stay in England rather than emigrate.

World War II again interrupted missionary work, and British Saints took charge of their affairs. Despite difficulties finding leaders, they persisted in "home missionary work." When American leadership resumed in 1944, the number of branches had increased from 68 to 75, although they were later consolidated into 29. After the war, the missionary force was bolstered and conversions increased. Many members immigrated to America.

The announcement of a temple for London Aug. 1, 1953, along with visits of authorities and the Tabernacle Choir during the next few years, lifted members' spirits. Many aspects of the Church were strengthened during this period. More than 12,000 members attended the dedication of the London Temple Sept. 7-9, 1958. On March 27, 1960, the Manchester Stake, under the leadership of Pres. Robert G. Larson, was created and the British Mission was divided. Growth continued, more missions were created, and a large building program started. By 1971, membership was nearly 70,000, increasing in 1980 to 91,000.

The celebration of the Church's 150th anniversary in Great Britain in 1987 underscored the maturity of the Church in this land. President Ezra Taft Benson and President Gordon B. Hinckley of the First Presidency joined former Prime Minister Edward Heath at a celebration which viewed a videotaped message from U.S. President Ronald Reagan. Eight public markers were dedicated honoring important Church sites in the British Isles. Membership in 1990 was 151,000.

In November 1990, Terry Rooney of the Bradford 2nd Ward, Huddersfield England Stake, became the first LDS member elected to Parliament.

In October 1991 area president Elder Jeffrey R. Holland of the Seventy presented to the Federation of Family History Societies microfiche containing the 1881 census of the

British Isles, which had been placed on microfiche by members.

Natives of England who have been called as General Authorities through the years include John Taylor, president of the Church 1880-87; George Q. Cannon, John R. Winder, George Teasdale, James E. Talmage, John Longden, B. H. Roberts, George Reynolds, Joseph W. McMurrin, Derek A. Cuthbert. Elder Kenneth Johnson is currently serving in the Seventy.

The London Temple was rededicated Oct. 18, 1992. And another temple for England, to be built in the Preston area, was announced Oct. 19, 1992, by President Hinckley. Ground was broken for the Preston England Temple on June 12, 1994, by President Hinckley, with 10,500 in attendance.

On a trip Aug. 24-Sept. 2, 1995, to England and the Republic of Ireland, President Gordon B. Hinckley created the Canterbury England Stake, rededicated the Hyde Park Chapel, and met with members, missionaries and news media in Liverpool and elsewhere.

Stakes — 35
(Listed alphabetically as of Oct. 1, 1996.)

No.	Name	Organized	First President
Europe North Area			
1345	Ashton England	6 Jun 1982	Brian Ashworth
760	*Billingham England 10 Jun 1986		
	‡Hartlepool England	13 Jun 1976	Craig Lithgow Marshall
494	*Birmingham England		
	‡Birmingham	14 Sep 1969	Derek A. Cuthbert
609	*Bristol England		
	‡Bristol	29 Apr 1973	Donald V. Norris
2093	Canterbury England	27 Aug 1995	Christopher Brian Munday
1331	Cheltenham England	21 Mar 1982	Warrick N. Kear
1346	Chester England	6 Jun 1982	Peter Furniss Lee
1936	Coventry England	9 May 1993	Thomas William Phillips
856	Crawley England	19 Aug 1977	J.A. Casbon
327	*Huddersfield England		
	‡Leeds	19 Mar 1961	Dennis Livesey
608	*Hull England		
	‡Hull	26 Apr 1973	Ian David Swanney
1423	Ipswich England	29 May 1983	Brian Arthur Frank Watling
780	Leeds England	12 Nov 1976	Douglas Rawson
325	*Leicester England		
	‡Leicester	5 Mar 1961	Derek A. Cuthbert
814	Lichfield England	20 Feb 1977	Robert James Mawle
748	Liverpool England	14 Mar 1976	Michael R. Otterson
	‡London	26 Feb 1961	Donald W. Hemingway
928a	London England Hyde Park	28 May 1978	Vance R. Leavitt
	‡London North	20 Sep 1970	Thomas Hill
929a	London England Wandsworth	28 May 1978	John Dodd
930	Maidstone England	28 May 1978	William J. Joliffe III
294	*Manchester England		
	‡Manchester	27 Mar 1960	Robert G. Larson
677	Newcastle-Under-Lyme England	17 Jan 1975	
	James Kenneth Cork		
810	Northampton England	13 Feb 1977	Michael J. Wade
549	*Norwich England 28 May 1978		
	*Ipswich England		
	‡East Anglia	20 Jun 1971	Dennis R. Reeves
597	*Nottingham England		
	‡Nottingham	4 Feb 1973	Ernest Hewitt
885	Plymouth England	27 Nov 1977	Leonard Eden
1343	Poole England	23 May 1982	Peter J. Crockford
600	*Portsmouth England 6 Feb 1990		
	*Southampton England		
	‡Southampton	11 Feb 1973	Reginald V. Littlecott
762	Preston England	17 Jun 1976	Eric Cryer
615	*Reading England		
	‡Thames Valley	24 May 1973	Peter B.C. Brighty
666	Romford England	24 Nov 1974	Arthur James Turvey

932	Saint Albans England	28 May 1978	Roland Edward Elvidge
1376	Sheffield England	14 Nov 1982	Kenneth Jones
931	Staines England	28 May 1978	Peter Benjamin C. Brighty
374	*Sunderland England		
	‡Sunderland	17 Mar 1963	Fred W. Oates
2190	Watford England	28 Apr 1996	Michael John Plant

Discontinued

323	*London England
	28 May 1978 †London England Hyde Park (928a), London England Wandsworth (929a), Staines England (931)
527	*London England North
	28 May 1978 †Saint Albans England (932), Romford England (666), Staines England (931), London England Hyde Park (928a)

Missions — 6

(As of Oct. 1, 1996; shown with historical number. See MISSIONS.)

(183) ENG.BIRMINGHAM MISSION
187 Penns Lane
Sutton Coldfield
West Midlands B76 1JU England
Phone: (011-44-21) 384-2032

(68) ENGLAND BRISTOL MISSION
Southfield House
#2 Southfield Road
Westbury-on-Trym
Bristol BS9 3BH, England
Phone: (011-44-1179) 621-939

(52) ENGLAND LEEDS MISSION
Techno Centre, Station Road
Horsforth, Leeds LS18 5BJ
West Yorkshire, England
Phone: (011-441132) 584-221

(1) ENGLAND LONDON MISSION
64-68 Princes Gate
Exhibition Road
London SW7 2PA England
Phone: (011-44-71) 938-1330

(79) ENGLAND LONDON SOUTH MISSION
484 London Road
Mitcham, Surrey CR4 4ED
England
Phone: (011-44-181) 640-6018

(138) ENG. MANCHESTER MISSION
Trafalger House
110 Manchester Road
Altrincham, Cheshire WA14 1NU, England
Phone: (011-44-61) 980-8015

NORTHERN IRELAND

Year-end 1995: Est. population, 1,600,000; Members, 5,700; Stakes, 1; Wards, 8; Branches, 7; Percent LDS, 0.35, or one LDS in 280; Ireland Dublin Mission.

Located in the northeast corner of Ireland, Northern Ireland is part of the United Kingdom. About 66 percent of the people are Protestant and 33 percent are Roman Catholic.

Northern Ireland remained in the United Kingdom when Ireland became an independent republic in 1949. Most of the Church membership is centered in and around Belfast.

When the London Temple was dedicated in 1958, it marked a "new era" for the Saints in Northern Ireland, who then numbered 540 in 10 branches. The Irish Mission was organized July 7, 1962. Twelve years later, June 9, 1974, the Belfast Ireland Stake was organized with Andrew Renfrew, former president of the Ulster District, as president.

On Sept. 7, 1986, some 1,350 attended a regional conference in Belfast, the largest-ever gathering of Saints in this area.

Stake — 1

(As of Oct. 1, 1996)

No.	Name	Organized	First President
Europe North Area			
1647	*Belfast Northern Ireland	13 Jan 1987	
	‡Belfast Ireland	9 Jun 1974	Andrew Renfrew

SCOTLAND

Year-end 1995: Est. population, 5,000,000; Members, 26,000; Stakes, 5; Wards, 24; Branches, 26; Missions, 1; Percent LDS, 0.5, or one LDS in 192.

Native Scots converted in Canada, Alexander Wright and Samuel Mulliner, were the first missionaries to Scotland, arriving in Glasgow Dec. 20, 1839. Alexander and Jessie Hay were baptized by Elder Mulliner in the River Clyde on Jan. 9, 1840. By May 3, membership had increased to 80. Elder Orson Pratt arrived and organized a branch at Paisley on May 8, and labored in Edinburgh, where he found a number of converts. During this period, he wrote an influential pamphlet, *An Interesting Account of Several Remarkable Visions.* By March 1841, more than 200 had joined the Church in Edinburgh. Another branch had been organized in Glasgow. By 1850, membership had risen to 3,257 in more than 50 branches. By 1855, four conferences had been organized. However, membership began a decline in the 1850s that lasted for many years.

One missionary about the turn of the century was Elder David O. McKay, who experienced little success; membership in the country was 338. Discouraged, he saw engraved in stone the words: "What e'er thou art, act well thy part." The inspiration from this had a great impact on his life, and the future of the Church as well.

Low conversions and frequent emigration reduced Church membership in Scotland. The Scottish-Irish Mission was created in 1961, and re-named Scottish Mission the following year. Scotland's first stake was created in Glasgow Aug. 26, 1962, with Archibald R. Richardson as president.

Members in Scotland celebrated the 150th anniversary of the Glasgow Branch as members of five Scotland stakes formed a chorus and took part in Glasgow's prestigious European Year of Culture 1990, receiving a standing ovation for their Oct. 21, 1990, performance.

Membership in Scotland was 12,000 in 1980, and 22,000 in 1990, 10,000 more than ever joined the Church during the 19th century.

In the 1990s, missionary work continued to progress as membership reached 25,000 by the end of 1993.

Stakes — 5
(Listed alphabetically as of Oct. 1, 1996.)

No.	Name	Organized	First President
Europe North Area			
1186	Aberdeen Scotland	12 Oct 1980	William Albert Wilson
734	Dundee Scotland	23 Nov 1975	John Keogh
1187	Edinburgh Scotland	12 Oct 1980	Alexander Mutter Clark
356	*Glasgow Scotland		
	‡Glasgow	26 Aug 1962	Archibald R. Richardson
1188	Paisley Scotland	12 Oct 1980	Alexander Cumming

Mission — 1
(As of Oct. 1, 1996; shown with historical number. See MISSIONS.)

(61) SCOTLAND EDINBURGH MISSION
51 Spylaw Road
Edinburgh, Scotland
EH10 5BP
Phone: (011-44-131) 337-1283

WALES
Year-end 1995: Est. population, 2,947,000; Members, 7,400; Stakes, 2; Wards, 12 Branches, 9; Percent LDS, 0.24, or one LDS in 398; England Bristol Mission.

It is supposed that the first Welshman was converted at the lectures of Wilford Woodruff in Herfordshire in 1840, but records cannot confirm this. Possibly the first member to preach in Wales was James Morgan. The first known missionary was Elder Henry Royle and his companion, Frederick Cook. They met with immediate success in Flintshire in North Wales. Just three weeks after their arrival, a branch of 32 members was organized on Oct. 30, 1840. In four months, there were two congregations totaling 150 members, but the missionaries experienced active opposition from ministers. Evidently, most of these early converts promptly emigrated.

In South Wales, work proceeded more slowly at first. Elder James Palmer labored there with little success late in 1840. Two years later, 44 Welshmen had been baptized. In 1843, Elder William Henshaw began proselyting in the Merthyr Tydfil area, and a branch of 50 was eventually organized. In 1844, the first Welsh-language materials were printed and work began to progress. A converted Welshman and associate of the Prophet Joseph Smith, Dan Jones, arrived in 1845. After a disappointing year in North Wales, he found success in the south and by 1849, left for America as captain of 300 Saints. He was later called to a second mission in Wales, which he completed in 1856, again leaving with a company, this one of 560 members.

The work slowed considerably afterwards, but began to build up in the 1900s. By 1950, there were 1,500 members in two districts. The first stake was created Jan. 12, 1975, in Merthyr Tydfil. Membership in 1990 was 6,500.

Stakes — 2
(Listed alphabetically as of Oct. 1, 1996.)

No.	Name	Organized	First President
	Europe North Area		
1341	Cardiff Wales	9 May 1982	Barry Derek Roy Whittaker
676	Merthyr Tydfil Wales	12 Jan 1975	Ralph Pulman

URUGUAY

Year-end 1995: Est. population, 3,335,000; Members, 64,000; Stakes, 12; Wards, 63; Branches, 81; Missions, 1; Districts, 8; Percent LDS, 1.9, or one person in 52.

On the eastern coast of South America, the Republic of Uruguay has a people who speak Spanish. Some 66 percent of the population is Roman Catholic.

The first Church contact in Uruguay came in 1940 when Elder Rolf L. Larson of the Argentina Mission starred on the championship Argentine basketball team in games held in Montevideo. His example and the publicity about him led to Uruguayan contacts.

The Montevideo Branch was organized June 25, 1944, by Frederick S. Williams, former president of the Argentine Mission, for his family and a few North Americans living here while on government service. Pres. Williams was called as mission president and opened the Uruguay Mission on Aug. 31, 1947. By the year's end, 24 missionaries were serving in Uruguay, though few spoke Spanish fluently. By the end of 1948 there were 14 branches, all well-attended by investigators.

The first converts in Uruguay were Avelino Juan Rodriguez and his wife, Maria Esther, baptized by Pres. Williams on Nov. 4, 1948. Baptismal services were held regularly after that, and eight new branches were created in 1949. By 1957, the mission was baptizing 500 converts a year. The Montevideo Stake was organized Nov. 12, 1967, with Vicente C. Rubio as its first president. At that time, there were 14,800 members in the country. In 1979, membership reached 26,000 members in Uruguay.

In 1990, Elder Luis Alberto Ferrizo, a regional representative, was elected as national deputy in the Uruguayan government, equivalent to a governor in the United States. Membership in Uruguay in 1990 was 52,000, growing to 64,000 in 1995. Local leaders in Uruguay have continued to emphasize missionary work among their youth.

On April 6, 1996, Francisco J. Vinas of an LDS pioneer family in Uruguay, was sustained as a member of the Second Quorum of the Seventy.

Sources: *From Acorn to Oak Tree,* by Frederick S. Williams and Frederick G. Williams; *50 Anos de la Iglesia in Argentina — Cronologia,* by Nestor Curbelo, seminary system, 1986; *Church News,* Nov. 9, 1986, March 17, 1990, Aug. 24, 1995, April 6, 1996.

Stakes — 13
(Listed alphabetically as of Oct. 1, 1996.)

No.	Name	Organized	First President
	South America South Area		
1123	Artigas Uruguay	23 Mar 1980	Luis Gonzalez
1098	Durazno Uruguay	25 Jan 1980	Luis Alberto Ferrizo
2072	Las Piedras Uruguay	2 Jul 1995	Gustavo Eduardo Sarasua
2232	Maldonado Uruguay	15 Sep 1996	Louise Laurito
1033a	Melo Uruguay	2 June 1979	Santiago Gonzalez
1944	Mercedes Uruguay	20 Jun 1993	Milton Jose Airala Perez
1058	Montevideo Uruguay Cerro	2 Sep 1979	Nester Rivera M.
631	Montevideo Uruguay East	17 Feb 1974	Ariel A. Fedrigotti
1034	Montevideo Uruguay Maronas	3 Jun 1979	Jorge Washington Ventura
890	Montevideo Uruguay North	12 Feb 1978	Ariel Omar Fedrigotti
444	*Montevideo Uruguay West	17 Feb 1974	
	*Montevideo Uruguay ‡Montevideo	12 Nov 1967	Vincente C. Rubio
832	Rivera Uruguay	20 May 1977	Ormesindo Correa

1019	Salto Uruguay	22 Apr 1979	Atilio Silveiro
		Discontinued	
836	Minas Uruguay	22 May 1977	Alberto E. Hernandez
	12 Nov 1989		
833	Paysandu Uruguay	21 May 1977	Atilio Silveira
	22 Oct 1989 †Uruguay Montevideo Mission		
840	Santa Lucia Uruguay	23 May 1977	Hector Julio Vigo
	20 Aug 1989 †Uruguay Montevideo Mission		

Mission — 1

(As of Oct. 1, 1996; shown with historical number. See MISSIONS.)

(40) URUGUAY MONTEVIDEO MISSION
San Carlos de Bolivar 6178
Carrasco, Montevideo
Uruguay 11.500
Phone: (011-598-2) 60-44-11

VENEZUELA

Year-end 1995: Est. population: 21,526,000; Members, 73,000; Stakes, 15; Wards, 77; Branches, 100; Missions, 4; Districts, 10; Temples, 1 planned; Percent LDS, 0.3, or one LDS in 294.

On the Caribbean coast of South America, Venezuela is a federal republic where the people speak Spanish and Indian languages, and are 96 percent Roman Catholic.

A group of members, most expatriates working in Venezuela, held Church meetings in the home of Carl C. Wilcox in 1966 and earlier. On Nov. 2, 1966, a branch of 45 members was organized by Elder Marion G. Romney, then of the Quorum of the Twelve. Pres. Wilcox, a top financial officer of Del Monte Corp., was called to preside. A week before the dedication, Pres. Ted E. Brewerton (now of the Seventy) of the Costa Rica Mission sent four missionaries to open Venezuela for missionary work. The first missionaries were Elders Floyd Baum, Neil Gruwell, David Bell and Fred Podlesny. Maracaibo was opened July 7, 1967, by Elders Baum and Bell and Elders Steve Jensen and Stephen Edmunds.

Work progressed very slowly as missionaries at first sought out converts who had leadership ability, and tried to introduce the Church through the media and the family home evening program. On Feb. 12, 1967, Elders Fred Podlesny and David Bell baptized Hernan Sepulveda, the first convert. Though initial converts were few, work progressed to the point where the Colombia-Venezuela Mission was created in 1968. Soon the Caracas 1st, 2nd and 3rd branches in the Caracas District were organized with 150 members. Other small branches began in Merida, San Cristobal and Maracaibo in the Venoc District. The first district conference was held Oct. 15, 1968, with 28 missionaries then serving in Caracas and Maracaibo.

When the Venezuela Mission was created July 1, 1971, membership had reached 1,259, and the Church entered a new phase. Under the leadership of mission Pres. Clark D. Webb, the mission began to average 40 converts a month. Emphasis was placed on bringing in entire families, which greatly strengthened local branches.

In 1977, some 4,000 members were in 23 branches in five districts. Successive mission presidents emphasized building programs and leadership preparation. President Spencer W. Kimball visited Venezuela in January 1975.

On July 1, 1977, Alejandro Portal Campos, an early leader in Venezuela, became president of the Venezuela Caracas Mission.

The Church Educational System started in Venezuela in 1972, under the direction of Brother Portal, and has involved many youths continually since then. The Maracaibo Venezuela Mission was created in 1979, with membership at nearly 5,000. By 1986, membership was 23,516 in five stakes, two missions and eight districts. Within four years, that membership doubled.

The likelihood for a temple to be built in Venezuela was announced in general conference on Sept. 30, 1995, by President Gordon B. Hinckley, and later confirmed for Caracas by the First Presidency. Some 1,000 members in Caracas had the opportunity to hear that conference announcement live at the Caurimare meetinghouse in Caracas, where conference was carried as a donation by a television cable company, SuperCable.

Sources: "Venezuela,", *Ensign* 1977; "Perseverance pays," *Church News*, Nov. 10, 1979; *La Historia de la Iglesia en Venezuela 1966 a 1986*, published by the Church Educational System in Venezuela; *Church News*, Oct. 7, 1995 and Nov. 4, 1995.

(Listed alphabetically as of Oct. 1, 1996.)

No.	Name	Organized	First President
South America North Area			
1724	Barcelona Venezuela	4 Jun 1989	Angel Luis Fajardo C.
1989	Barquisimeto Venezuela	28 Aug 1994	Julio Ramon Davila Duran
827	Caracas Venezuela	15 May 1977	Adolfo F. Mayer G.
1887	Caracas Venezuela Palo Verde	14 June 1992	Edgardo Angulo de la Paua
1717	Caracas Venezuela Urdaneta	7 May 1989	Hector Manuel Arraez R.
1787	Ciudad Ojeda Venezuela	24 Feb 1991	Juan Silfrido Carrizo C.
1585	Guayana Venezuela	15 Jan 1986	Luis A. Aguilar Guevara
1181	Maracaibo Venezuela	15 Sep 1980	Francisco Giminez S.
1862	Maracaibo Venezuela Central	17 May 1992	Ruben Dario Blanco Valles
1414	Maracaibo Venezuela South	24 Apr 1983	Omar Alvarez
1774	Maracay Venezuela	4 Nov 1990	Jairo R. Herrera
1885	Puerto La Cruz Venezuela	7 June 1992	Luis Jose Gonzalez
2127	San Cristobal Venezuela	19 Nov 1995	Javier Ibanez Leon
1050	Valencia Venezuela Los Sauces	19 Nov 1995	
	Valencia Venezuela	19 Aug 1979	Teodoro Hoffman
2125	Valencia Venezuela Candelaria	19 Nov 1995	Gamaliel de Jesus Osorno Flores

Missions — 4

(As of Oct. 1, 1996; shown with historical number. See MISSIONS.)

(303) VENEZUELA BARCELONA MISSION
Apdo. Postal 295
Barcelona 6002, Estado Anzoatequi,
Venezuela
Phone: (011-58-81) 76-77-74

(95) VENEZUELA CARACAS MISSION
Apartado 69204
15Caracas 1060-A
Venezuela
Phone: (011-58-2) 985-3431

(174) VENEZUELA MARACAIBO MISSION
Apartado 10020 Bella Vista
Maracaibo, Estada Zulia CP 4002A
Venezuela
Phone: (011-58-61) 922-751

(267) VENEZUELA VALENCIA MISSION
Apartado Postal 1249
Valencia, Estado Carabobo,
Venezuela
Phone: (011-58-41) 236-937

VIETNAM

Year-end 1995: Est. population, 74,765,000; Members, fewer than 100; Branches, 1; Asia Area.

LDS servicemen arrived in Vietnam in the early 1960s in sufficient numbers to establish groups. An LDS serviceman's group was organized as part of the Southern Far East Mission on June 30, 1962, by mission Pres. Robert D. Taylor with Cecil Cavender as president.

On Nov. 3, 1962, U.S. Air Force Capt. John T. Mullennex was baptized in Saigon by Maurice H. Lee of the Saigon Group presidency. Converts Nguyen Thi Thuy and Duong Thuy Van, baptized in early 1963 by Capt. Loring B. Bean, were the first Vietnamese to join the Church.

The size of the LDS group began to grow as the Vietnam War became more intense and more servicemen arrived. Other groups were added, and several General Authorities visited. A small meetinghouse was erected at Bien Hoa Air Base. By 1971, three districts had been organized under the Hong Kong Mission.

When the cease-fire was reached Jan. 27, 1973, the Saigon Branch numbered about 100 under branch Pres. Nguyen Van The. Elders were sent to Vietnam immediately afterward. Elders Colin B. Van Orman, James L. Christensen, David T. Posey and Richard C. Holloman were transferred to Saigon from Hong Kong, arriving April 6, 1973.

These elders and those who came later found success, but on April 30, 1975, South Vietnam was defeated in war. Many of the members in Vietnam were able to leave and were relocated in America by the Church. Some 83 members were assigned to sponsors in the United States and Canada by Church refugee workers, along with 672 of their relatives and friends. Following the relocation, many refugees joined the Church and a number of full-time missionaries came from their ranks.

LDS veterans from that period helped locate many former branch members and reunify families.

At the end of 1991, the Church donated medical equipment that enabled Vietnamese surgeons to use microsurgery. Presenting the gift was Elder Merlin R. Lybbert of the Seventy, the first General Authority to enter Vietnam since 1975.

A year later, two LDS couples entered Hanoi on Jan. 6, 1993, to teach English. The couples, Elder James L. and Sister Helen Ream Bateman and Elder Stanley G. and Sister Mavis Lynnette Steadman, were warmly welcomed in ceremonies at Tran Hung Dao Hospital and at the Children's Palace. The couples taught English to many people and also set up the first-ever presentation of Handel's Messiah in Vietnam, an unusual event partly funded by professional Vietnamese musicians who donated 70 cents at each rehearsal.

President Gordon B. Hinckley and his wife, Marjorie, Elder Joseph B. Wirthlin of the Quorum of the Twelve and his wife, Elisa, Elder John H. Groberg of the Seventy and his wife, Jean, visited Ho Chi Minh City (formerly Saigon) and Hanoi on May 29, 1996.

Sources: *Church News*, March 30, 1963; history by Virgil N. Kovalenko; "Church donates medical gift to Vietnam," *Church News*, Jan. 11, 1992; "Asia Area: Welcome mat is out in several countries," by Sheridan R. Sheffield, *Church News*, June 19, 1993; "Vietnam: Musicians perform 'Messiah' " *Church News*, Dec. 4, 1993; "Pres. Hinckley dedicates Cambodia — Gives addendum to prayer during his visit to Vietnam," *Church News*, June 8, 1996.

VIRGIN ISLANDS

Year-end 1995: Est. population, 97,000; Members, 300; Branches, 2; Percent LDS, 0.3, or one LDS in 323; North America Southeast Area; Puerto Rico San Juan Mission.

The Virgin Islands are made up of three large and 50 small islands located 70 miles east of Puerto Rico. The residents speak English and have a republican form of government that operates under the United States.

The first missionaries to St. Croix were Elders Thomas Williams, Eric Leach, Gregory Collier and Kurtis Gibbons, who arrived Jan. 28, 1981. They held meetings in the home of a member, Jack Cluett, with about 15 attending. A branch was organized Feb. 8, 1981, with Stephen L. Whitmer as the first president. Missionaries baptized several converts the first year. A meetinghouse was later built on the island. Branches have also been established on St. John and St. Thomas.

On St. Thomas, various expatriate families lived on the island. In 1969, one of these was the Earl Keele family. He arrived May 1969, and his wife, Celia, and two children followed in August. The family held a home Sunday School as part of the San Juan Branch in Puerto Rico. In 1970 another family, James and Carolyn Boykin, joined the group. Debra Rybacki, met with the family and received permission to be baptized in Brewer's Bay in January 1976. Other families arrived and the St. Thomas Branch was created Dec. 13, 1977. The first missionaries came in June 1978, Elders John Sorensen and D.E. Blomquist. They baptized the supervisor of Sister Rybacki, Aubrey Nelthropp, and his wife, Carol, on July 16, 1978. The first branch meetinghouse was used July 16, 1978.

A devastating hurricane, Hugo, struck St. Croix in September 1989, destroying the homes of many members. A shipment of food from the mainland and use of the branch meetinghouse helped alleviate emergency conditions. Damage to the islands was reported repaired within a year.

Sources: Kenneth and LeOra Zabriskie journals; *Church News*, Sept. 9, 1989; *Ensign*, November 1989; unpublished historical sketch of the Church in St. Thomas, by Celia Keele.

WALES
(See United Kingdom)

WESTERN SAMOA

Year-end 1995: Est. population, 211,000; Members, 54,000; Stakes, 15; Wards, 86; Branches, 27; Missions, 1; Districts, 1; Temples, 1; Percent LDS, 26, or one in 4.

Located in the South Pacific, Western Samoa is a parliamentary democracy. The people are Protestant, 45 percent; LDS, 29 percent; and Roman Catholic, 20 percent.

In 1863, two missionaries from Hawaii arrived in Samoa. The two, Kimo Pelia and

Samuela Manoa, however, had been sent by an unauthorized leader, Walter Murray Gibson, excommunicated by the Church. The pair labored faithfully for nearly 20 years without the support of the Church.

Elder Joseph H. Dean and his wife, Florence, arrived June 21, 1888. The mission was organized June 17, 1888. The Deans found that Pelia had died but Manoa was still very supportive. He was re-baptized and re-ordained. The same day, Elder Dean baptized a woman named Malaea, who is considered his first convert. Within four months 40 others had joined, and Elder Dean received additional help as more missionaries arrived. Missionaries visited all the islands and baptized converts. A local member, Polonga, was called as the first local missionary.

By 1896, members began to join in greater number. Missionaries also helped educate youths in small chapel schools. As local members filled leadership positions, they were assigned to distant branches, a pattern unique to Samoa. Local members also served missions and contributed toward the growth of the Church.

Proselyting continued, but was made difficult by internal political conflicts. In 1899, the Samoan islands were divided up between Germany and the United States. Western Samoa became a German colony. Soon, the Germans banned English-language schools, an act that temporarily slowed missionary work. The German control ended in 1914.

By June 1903, the Book of Mormon had been translated. At the end of 1920, membership numbered 3,500, about 5 percent of the total population of the islands.

A visit by Elder David O. McKay, then of the Quorum of the Twelve, in May 1921, had great impact upon the membership. Conversions increased afterward and some entire villages joined the Church.

By 1950, membership had grown to more than 7,000, and by 1961, to more than 16,000. By 1974, the country had six stakes and became the first country of the world to be entirely covered by stakes.

On Oct. 15, 1977, a temple was announced to be built in Apia, Western Samoa, and was dedicated Aug. 5, 1983. At that time, membership reached an estimated 40,000, about 20 percent of the population of the islands. In 1980, membership was 27,000, increasing to 41,000 in 1990.

Members suffered considerable property losses and one member died during tropical storm in 1991. However, local units responded well to dealing with the disaster. A number of former missionaries to Samoa helped in preserving a 30,000-acre rain forest in Falealupo, and in restoring and preserving the historic home of Robert Louis Stevenson. In June 1995, Tufuga Samuelu Atoa of the Pesega 5th Ward, Pesega Samoa Stake, was awarded the Western Samoa Order of Merit by Head of State Malietoa Tanumafili II for his service to the Samoan Olympic team. Six new stakes were created in Western Samoa from 1994-96.

Sources: *Encyclopedic History of the Church,* by Andrew Jenson; *Unto the Isles of the Sea,* by R. Lanier Britsch; *Samoa Apia Mission History, 1888-1983,* published by R. Carl Harris, president of the Samoa Apia Mission; "Samoan rain forest reprieved from ruin," *Church News,* Aug. 19, 1989; *Deseret News,* Oct. 14, 1990; "Stevenson's historic home and grave to get a face lift," *Deseret News,* July 24, 1994; "Member is honored by government leader," *Church News,* July 22, 1995.

Stakes — 16
(Listed alphabetically as of Oct. 1, 1996.)

No.	Name	Organized	First President
Pacific Area			
353	*Apia Samoa ‡Apia	18 Mar 1962	Percy John Rivers
1045	Apia Samoa East	5 Aug 1979	Daniel Afamasaga Betham
2134	Apia Samoa Navu	3 Dec 1995	Tigi Manumaluena
513	*Apia Samoa West ‡Apia West	26 Apr 1970	Percy J. Rivers
2138	Fagamalo Samoa	4 Dec 1995	Rama Endemann
2011	Pesega Samoa	22 Jan 1995	Meliula Meafou Fata
538	*Savai'i Samoa ‡Savai'i	8 Jan 1971	Amuia W. Hunt
2098	Savai'i Samoa Sagone	10 Sep 1995	Paulo Sofeni Matofai
1366	Savai'i Samoa South	17 Oct 1982	Malina Ropeti Ti'a
619	*Savai'i Samoa West ‡Savai'i West	3 Jun 1973	Fa'afoi Tuitama

868	Upolu Samoa East	23 Oct 1977	Kovana Pauga
2171	Upolu Samoa Faleasiu	25 Feb 1996	Pouono Lameko
1909	Upolu Samoa North	25 Oct 1992	Sofeni Pilimai
2139	Upolu Samoa Saleilua	5 Dec 1995	Polesi Avauli Salani
645	Upolu Samoa South	1 Jun 1974	William Richard Schwalger
545	*Upolu Samoa West		
	‡Upolu West	25 Apr 1971	Tua'ifaiva O. Aiono

Mission — 1

(As of Oct. 1, 1996; shown with historical number. See MISSIONS.)

(13c) SAMOA APIA MISSION
P.O. Box 1865
Apia, Western Samoa
Phone: (011-685) 20-311

ZAIRE

Year-end 1995: Est. population, 45,000,000; Members, 5,300; Districts, 6; Branches, 22; Missions, 1; Percent LDS, 0.01 percent, or one LDS in 8,490; Africa Area.

Formerly Belgian Congo in central Africa, Zaire became an independent republic in 1960 and was named Zaire in 1971. The people speak French and Bantu dialects, and are Christian, 70 percent, and Muslim, 10 percent.

Elder R. Bay and Sister Jean Hutchings arrived in Kinshasa in February 1986, when the Church received legal status through the efforts of David M. Kennedy, special representative of the First Presidency. Pres. Hutchings was soon called as president of the Zaire Kinshasa Mission, created July 1, 1987. Meetings were first held in the home of Michael C. Bowcutt, an employee of the U.S. Embassy, and later at the home of Nkita Bungi Mbuyi, a returned missionary from England, converted in Belgium. The Church purchased a villa and had it remodeled into a meetinghouse in September 1986. At the first meeting in the 200-seat facility, 208 attended. The first baptisms in Zaire were Banza Jr. and Philippe Muchioko, sons of Banza Muchioko, who were converted in Switzerland seven years earlier.

Many young men and young families were converted in the first year. In July 1987, membership reached 300. Some 20 of the new converts were to be called as local missionaries to extend the work.

The first full-time missionaries from Zaire were Banza Muchioko Jr., Diamany Ngalamulume, Mutombo Nkadi Thomas and Maly-malu Kanda, who began serving in their homeland before April 1991.

Church Educational System missionaries Phyll and Betty Hansen introduced seminary to Zaire in late 1991. Elder Hansen trained Kabwika Natambwe, a member of the Zaire mission presidency, who carried the work forward throughout the country.

Sources: *Church News*, April 25, 1987; "Zaire's people, thirsty for the gospel," *Church News*, July 18, 1987; "A new day dawns on African nations," by Dell Van Orden and Gerry Avant, *Church News*, Oct. 17, 1987; *Church News*, April 25, 1992, Sept. 9, 1992.

Mission — 1

(As of Oct. 1, 1996; shown with historical number. See MISSIONS.)

(198) ZAIRE KINSHASA MISSION
Africa Area Office
P.O. Box 1218
Lonehill 2062
Republic of South Africa
Phone: (011-243-88) 40-557

ZAMBIA

Year-end 1995: Est. population, 10,000,000; Members, 400; Africa Area; Zimbabwe Harare Mission.

A republic in southcentral Africa, Zambia has a population that speaks English and local dialects. Most of the population follows Christian beliefs, with smaller numbers who have indigenous and Muslim beliefs.

In the 1960s, a meetinghouse was built in Kwekwe, Zimbabwe, for a branch composed almost totally of expatriates working in what was then northern Rhodesia in the copperbelt, and farmers from South Africa. Those original members left, presumably across the border into Zambia. However, when none were located, Pres. Vern Marble of the Zimbabwe Harare Mission went to Zambia in 1991 to search for members.

He searched for, but could not find, a man who had been baptized in England, Johnson Makombe, and his wife, Noria. However, a taxi driver in Lusaka offered to find them and deliver a message. When Pres. Marble returned a short time later, Noria Makombe went to the hotel where he was staying. When she met him in the lobby, her first words were, "Where can I pay my tithing?"

The first missionary couple, Elder Dean and Sister Ruth Harrison, were assigned to open the work in Zambia in April 1992, and the Church was formally registered July 10, 1992. When a branch of the Church was organized in Lusaka on July 14, 1992, by Pres. Marble, the congregation of about 50 was almost the same size as when the meetinghouse was built in Kwekwe in the early 1960s.

By 1993, the Church had stored in computers alphabet characters in Bemba, one of Zambia's 70 indigenous languages, in preparation for publishing scriptures in that language.

The seminary program was established in Zambia in 1995.

Sources: "Four nations in central, southern Africa," by Mary Mostert and Gerry Avant, *Church News*, Sept. 26, 1992; "Alphabets of the world at fingertip," by John L. Hart, *Church News*, May 5, 1993; "Seminary thrives in Africa," by Sarah Jane Weaver, *Church News*, March 9, 1996.

ZIMBABWE

Year-end 1995: Est. population, 10,000,000; Members, 6,200; Districts, 3; Branches, 23; Missions, 1; Percent LDS, 0.06, or one LDS in 1,602; Africa Area.

In southern Africa, Zimbabwe is a one-party socialist state where the people speak English (official language), Shona and Sindebele. Traditional tribal beliefs dominate, with a Christian minority.

Missionary work began in what was then Rhodesia in the early 1930s but soon slowed, continued by only short visits by missionaries from South Africa. In 1950, under the direction of mission Pres. Evan P. Wright, eight missionaries began working in Salisbury and Bulawayo. Hugh Hodgkiss was the first convert, baptized Feb. 1, 1951.

On April 17, 1951, the missionaries distributed 3,000 handbills, and a fairly large crowd attended an introductory meeting. The first services were held in a pre-school building and prospective members sat on tiny chairs. Later, they met in the cloak room of a primary school.

During that period, Sir John Kennedy, governor of Southern Rhodesia, invited the missionaries to teach square dancing. They attended four large dances and made many contacts, but few conversions, as they taught dancing.

In 1980, the government changed and the nation of Zimbabwe was formed. A new mission was established in Zimbabwe. At the time, membership was 1,014. Missionary work increased as local missionaries began serving full-time missions.

On July 26, 1990, mission president George T. Brooks died in a car-truck accident near Kwekwe, Zimbabwe. His wife, Sister Lillis Remington Brooks, was seriously injured.

Since 1988, the Church has had an ongoing humanitarian project in Zimbabwe that included funds, a mill for grinding grain, a dam near Masvingo, gardening materials, and two large shipments of new textbooks for Zimbabwe's school children.

In 1996, LDS teenagers enjoyed participating in the seminary program. One teacher, Wilson Athgten, walked eight miles every morning to teach seminary, and, when students were involved in evening activites, he walked each home.

Sources: A History of the South African Mission, by Evan P. Wright; "Preached by Dancing," *Church News*, July 14, 1979; *Church News*, March 14, 1987, March 23, 1991; "Seminary thrives in Africa," by Sarah Jane Weaver, *Church News*, March 9, 1996.

Mission — 1
(As of Oct. 1, 1996; shown with historical number. See MISSIONS.)

(204) ZIMBABWE HARARE MISSION
65 Enterprise Road
Highlands, Harare, Zimbabwe
Phone: (011-263-4) 737-297

Editor's note: Information in this section has been gathered from a variety of sources and is believed to be the best available at the time of publication. Corrections, additional information and further country or state histories will be appreciated. Those with comments or information may write to: Church Almanac Histories, P.O. Box 1257, Salt Lake City, UT 84110.

MISSIONS, TEMPLES

FULL-TIME MISSIONS

Missions are listed here in chronological order and according to the name under which they were originally organized. On June 20, 1974, most mission names were changed under the Church's current naming system; these and other name changes are indicated on the lines beneath the "Name" column.

* Denotes a name change; capital letters indicate the mission's new name.

The number immediately preceding the name of the mission indicates the total number of missions in existence at the time of its organization. A letter after the number indicates that the number was reached previously; the letter is added to clarify cross-references. This number is also placed with the mission in the "Worldwide Church" section.

By using this list it is possible to trace the "family tree" of each mission. Included in each mission entry is the number, in parenthesis, of the "parent" mission from which it was created, and, in the "See also" entry, the numbers of "offspring" missions that were created from divisions of this mission. Also included are the numbers of missions that this mission may have been transferred to when it was discontinued, and the number the mission was assigned when it was re-opened.

	NAME	ORGANIZED	FIRST PRESIDENT
1	BRITISH *10 Jun 1970 ENGLAND EAST *20 Jun 1974 ENGLAND LONDON See also 4, 52, 62, 68, 79, 161	20 Jul 1837	Heber C. Kimball
2	EASTERN STATES Discontinued Apr 1850 Reopened 1854 (15) Discontinued 1858 Reopened 1865 (9a) Discontinued 1869 Reopened from Northern States Jan 1893 (15b) *20 Jun 1974 NEW YORK NEW YORK *1 JUL 1993 NEW YORK NEW YORK SOUTH See also 23a, 29, 35, 54, 77, 202	6 May 1839	John P. Greene
3	SOCIETY ISLANDS Discontinued 15 May 1852 Reopened 29 Apr 1892 (13d) *1907 TAHITIAN *25 Nov 1959 FRENCH-POLYNESIAN *10 Jun 1970 FRENCH-POLYNESIA *20 Jun 1974 TAHITI PAPEETE	30 Apr 1844	Noah Rogers
4	WELSH Organized from British (1) Discontinued 26 Mar 1854, transferred to British (1)	15 Dec 1845	Dan Jones
5	CALIFORNIA Discontinued 1858 Reopened 23 Aug 1892 (14c) *20 Jun 1974 CALIFORNIA LOS ANGELES See also 37, 73a, 86, 159	31 Jul 1846	Samuel Brannan
5a	SCANDINAVIAN Discontinued 1 Apr 1920, transferred to Danish (23b), Norwegian (24) See also 22a	11 May 1850	Erastus Snow
6	FRENCH Discontinued 1864 Reopened 15 Oct 1912 (22b) Discontinued 18 Sep 1914 Reopened 20 Aug 1923 (26) from Swiss-German (8) *10 Jun 1970 FRANCE *20 Jun 1974 FRANCE PARIS See also 59, 76, 92, 121, 221a	18 Jun 1850	John Taylor
7	ITALIAN Discontinued 1 Jan 1854, transferred to Swiss and Italian (8) Reopened 2 Aug 1966 (74a) from Swiss (8)	1 Nov 1850	Lorenzo Snow

```
      *10 Jun 1970 ITALY
      *1 Jul 1971 ITALY SOUTH
      *20 Jun 1974 ITALY ROME
      See also 98, 123, 158, 244

8     SWISS                            24 Nov 1850      Thomas B.H. Stenhouse
      *1 Jan 1854 SWISS AND ITALIAN
      *1 Jan 1861 SWISS, ITALIAN AND GERMAN
      *1 Jan 1868 SWISS AND GERMAN
      *1 Jan 1898 SWISS
      *22 May 1904 SWISS-GERMAN
      *1 Jan 1938 SWISS AUSTRIAN
      *21 Nov 1938 SWISS
      *25 May 1946 SWISS AUSTRIAN
      *18 Sep 1960 SWISS
      *10 Jun 1970 SWITZERLAND
      *20 Jun 1974 SWITZERLAND ZURICH
      See also 6, 7, 13, 8a, 19, 26, 30, 53

9     SANDWICH ISLANDS                 12 Dec 1850      Hiram Clark
      Discontinued 1 May 1858
      Reopened 27 Mar 1864 (7a)
      *1900 HAWAIIAN
      *1 Apr 1950 HAWAII
      *20 Jun 1974 HAWAII HONOLULU
      See also  34, 178

10    AUSTRALIAN                       30 Oct 1851      John Murdock
      *1854 AUSTRALASIAN
      *1 Jan 1898 AUSTRALIAN
      *10 Jun 1970 AUSTRALIA EAST
      *20 Jun 1974 AUSTRALIA SYDNEY
      *1 Jan 1993 AUSTRALIA SYDNEY SOUTH
      See also 20, 43c, 106

11    EAST INDIAN                          1851         Lorenzo Snow
      Discontinued 2 May 1856
      Reopened 1 Aug 1884 (12a)
      Discontinued 10 Jun 1885

12    MALTA                            26 Feb 1852      Lorenzo Snow
      Discontinued 1856

13    GERMAN                           3 Apr 1852       Daniel P. Garn
      Discontinued 1 Jan 1861, transferred to Swiss, Italian and German (8)
      Reopened 1 Jan 1898 (19) from Swiss and German (8)
      Discontinued 22 May 1904, transferred to Swiss-German (8)
      Reopened 23 Aug 1925 as German-Austrian (27) from Swiss-German (8)
      Discontinued 1 Jan 1938, transferred to West German (35a), East German
        (36), Swiss Austrian (8)
      See also 30

13a   GIBRALTAR                        7 Mar 1853       Edward Stevenson
      Discontinued 5 Jul 1854

14    SOUTH AFRICAN                    19 Apr 1853       Jesse Haven
      Discontinued 12 Apr 1865
      Reopened 25 Jul 1903 (23)
      *10 Jun 1970 SOUTH AFRICA
      *20 Jun 1974 SOUTH AFRICA JOHANNESBURG
      See also 177a, 204, 216

15    EASTERN STATES (See 2)               1854         John Taylor
14a   SIAM                             6 Apr 1854       Elam Luddington
      Discontinued 12 Aug 1854

15a   EUROPEAN (Administrative)        28 Jun 1854      Franklin D. Richards
      Discontinued 14 Feb 1950
      Reopened 17 Jan 1960 (51)
      Discontinued 14 Sep 1965
      See also 64

14b   INDIAN TERRITORY                 26 Jun 1855      Henry W. Miller
      Discontinued 23 May 1860
```

Reopened Mar 1877 (9b)
Discontinued 12 Sep 1877
Reopened 20 Apr 1883 (11a)
*29 Mar 1898 SOUTHWESTERN STATES
*4 Apr 1904 CENTRAL STATES
*10 Jun 1970 KANSAS-MISSOURI
*20 Jun 1974 MISSOURI INDEPENDENCE
See also 31, 88, 140, 153

7a	SANDWICH ISLANDS (See 9)	27 Mar 1864	Joseph F. Smith
8a	NETHERLANDS	1 Nov 1864	Joseph Weiler

Organized from Swiss, Italian and German (8)
*31 Jan 1891 NETHERLANDS-BELGIUM
*15 May 1914 NETHERLANDS
*20 Jun 1974 NETHERLANDS AMSTERDAM
See also 135, 232

9a	EASTERN STATES (See 2)	1865	John Taylor
8b	SOUTHERN STATES	Nov 1876	Henry G. Boyle

*Jun 1971 GEORGIA-SOUTH CAROLINA
*20 Jun 1974 GEORGIA ATLANTA
See also 22, 29, 55, 130, 166a, 239

9b	INDIAN TERRITORY (See 14b)	Mar 1877	Matthew W. Dalton
9c	NORTHWESTERN STATES	6 May 1878	Cyrus H. Wheelock

*20 Jul 1889 NORTHERN STATES
*1 Jul 1973 ILLINOIS
*20 Jun 1974 ILLINOIS CHICAGO
*1 Jul 1980 ILLINOIS CHICAGO NORTH
*1 Jul 1983 ILLINOIS CHICAGO
See also 23a, 26a, 43a, 46, 97, 167, 184

10a	MEXICAN	16 Nov 1879	Moses Thatcher

Discontinued Jun 1889
Reopened 8 Jun 1901 (20a)
*10 Jun 1970 MEXICO
*20 Jun 1974 MEXICO MEXICO CITY
*1 Jul 1978 MEXICO MEXICO CITY SOUTH
See also 33, 43b, 45a, 75, 125, 163, 193

11a	INDIAN TERITORY (See 14b)	20 Apr 1883	George Teasdale
12a	EAST INDIAN (See 11)	1 Aug 1884	William Willis
13b	TURKISH	30 Dec 1884	Jacob Spori

Discontinued 1 Oct 1909
Reopened 6 Nov 1921 (25)
*23 Jan 1924 ARMENIAN
*12 Aug 1933 PALESTINE-SYRIAN
Discontinued 1939
Reopened 8 Nov 1947 (43)
*25 Jan 1950 NEAR EAST
Discontinued Jan 1951

13c	SAMOAN	17 Jun 1888	Joseph H. Dean

*10 Jun 1970 SAMOA
*20 Jun 1974 SAMOA APIA
See also 22c, 57, 99

13d	SOCIETY ISLANDS (See 3)	29 Apr 1892	Joseph W. Damron
14c	CALIFORNIA (See 5)	23 Aug 1892	John L. Dalton
15b	EASTERN STATES (See 2)	Jan 1893	Job Pingree
16	MONTANA	10 Sep 1896	Phineas Tempest

Discontinued 12 Jun 1898, transferred to Northwestern States (18)
See also 43a

17	COLORADO	15 Dec 1896	John W. Taylor

*1 Apr 1907 WESTERN STATES
*10 Jun 1970 COLORADO-NEW MEXICO
*10 Oct 1972 COLORADO
*20 Jun 1974 COLORADO DENVER
*01 Jul 1993 COLORADO DENVER SOUTH

See also 26a, 33, 43a, 132, 286

18 NORTHWESTERN STATES   26 Jul 1897   George C. Parkinson
    *10 Jun 1970 OREGON
    *20 Jun 1974 OREGON PORTLAND
    See also 26a, 36a, 43a, 78a, 249

19 GERMAN (See 13)   1 Jan 1898   Peter Loutensock

20 NEW ZEALAND   1 Jan 1898   Ezra F. Richards
    Organized from Australasian (10)
    *10 Jun 1970 NEW ZEALAND NORTH
    *20 Jun 1974 NEW ZEALAND AUCKLAND
    See also 47, 99

20a MEXICAN (See 10a)   8 Jun 1901   Ammon N. Tenney

21 JAPAN   12 Aug 1901   Heber J. Grant
    Discontinued 31 Jul 1924
    Reopened 6 Mar 1948 as Japanese (44)
    Discontinued 28 Jul 1955, transferred to Northern Far East (43d), Southern
      Far East (44a)

22 MIDDLE STATES   28 Jun 1902   Ben E. Rich
    Organized from Southern States (8b)
    Discontinued 7 Aug 1903, transferred to Southern States (8b)

23 SOUTH AFRICAN (See 14)   25 Jul 1903   Warren H. Lyon

22a SWEDISH   15 Jun 1905   Peter Matson
    Organized from Scandinavian (5a)
    *10 Jun 1970 SWEDEN
    *20 Jun 1974 SWEDEN STOCKHOLM
    See also 41, 145

22b FRENCH (See 6)   15 Oct 1912   Edgar B. Brossard

22c TONGAN   8 Jul 1916   Willard L. Smith
    Organized from Samoan (13c)
    *10 Jun 1970 TONGA
    *20 Jun 1974 TONGA NUKU'ALOFA
    See also 99

23a CANADIAN   1 Jul 1919   Nephi Jensen
    Organized from Eastern States (15b), Northern States (9c)
    *10 Jun 1970 ONTARIO-QUEBEC
    *1 Jul 1972 ONTARIO
    *20 Jun 1974 CANADA TORONTO
    *01 Jul 1993 CANADA TORONTO WEST
    See also 26a, 35, 99a, 285

23b DANISH   1 Apr 1920   Carl E. Peterson
    Organized from Scandinavian (5a)
    *10 Jun 1970 DENMARK
    *20 Jun 1974 DENMARK COPENHAGEN

24 NORWEGIAN   1 Apr 1920   Andrew S. Schow
    Organized from Scandinavian (5a)
    *10 Jun 1970 NORWAY
    *20 Jun 1974 NORWAY OSLO

25 TURKISH (See 13b)   6 Nov 1921   Joseph Wilford Booth

26 FRENCH (See 6)   20 Aug 1923   Russell H. Blood

26a NORTH CENTRAL STATES   12 Jul 1925   John G. Allred
    Organized from Northern States (9c), Western States (17),
    Northwestern States (18), Canadian (23a)
    *10 Jun 1970 MANITOBA-MINNESOTA
    *1 Jul 1973 MINNESOTA-WISCONSIN
    *20 Jun 1974 MINNESOTA MINNEAPOLIS
    See also 36a, 43a, 167

27 GERMAN-AUSTRIAN (See 13)   23 Aug 1925   Fred Tadje

28 SOUTH AMERICAN   6 Dec 1925   Melvin J. Ballard
    Discontinued 25 May 1935, transferred to Brazilian (31a), Argentine (32)

29 EAST CENTRAL STATES   9 Dec 1928   Miles L. Jones
    Organized from Southern States (8b), Eastern States, (15b)

*10 Jun 1970 KENTUCKY-TENNESSEE
*20 Jun 1974 KENTUCKY LOUISVILLE
See also 42, 131

30   CZECHOSLOVAK   24 Jul 1929   Arthur Gaeth
Organized from German-Austrian (27), Swiss (8)
Discontinued 6 Apr 1950
Reopened 1 Jul 1990, see 236
Organized from Austria Vienna East (205)
*2 Mar 1993 CZECH PRAGUE
*26 Aug 1993 CZECH REPUBLIC PRAGUE
*15 May 1995 CZECH PRAGUE

31   TEXAS   11 Jan 1931   Charles Elliott Rowan Jr.
Organized from Central States (11a)

*May 1945 TEXAS-LOUISIANA
*19 Jun 1955 GULF STATES
*20 Jun 1974 LOUISIANA SHREVEPORT
*1 Jul 1975 LOUISIANA BATON ROUGE
See also 60, 116, 171

31a BRAZILIAN   25 May 1935   Rulon S. Howells
Organized from South American (28)
*10 Jun 1970 BRAZIL CENTRAL
Discontinued 17 Oct 1972, transferred to Brazil North Central (101),
Brazil South Central (102)
See also 48, 80

32   ARGENTINE   14 Aug 1935   W. Ernest Young
Organized from South American (28)
*10 Jun 1970 ARGENTINA SOUTH
*20 Jun 1974 ARGENTINA BUENOS AIRES NORTH
See also 40, 50, 73, 100, 112, 269

33   SPANISH-AMERICAN   28 Jun 1936   Orlando C. Williams
Organized from Mexican (20a)
Discontinued Dec 1967, transferred to Texas (60), Texas South (77b),
Western States (17)
See also 46a, 77b

34   JAPANESE   24 Feb 1937   Hilton A. Robertson
Organized from Hawaiian (7a)
*14 May 1944 CENTRAL PACIFIC
Discontinued 1 Apr 1950, transferred to Hawaii (9)
(Administrative headquarters different from 21)

35   NEW ENGLAND   24 Sep 1937   Carl Eyring
Organized from Eastern States (15b), Canadian (23a)
*20 Jun 1974 MASSACHUSETTS BOSTON
See also 107, 169, 195, 299

35a WEST GERMAN   1 Jan 1938   Philemon M. Kelly
Organized from German-Austrian (27)
*10 Jun 1970 GERMANY WEST
*20 Jun 1974 GERMANY FRANKFURT
See also 49, 63, 240

36   EAST GERMAN   1 Jan 1938   Alfred C. Rees
Organized from German-Austrian (27)
*12 Sep 1957 NORTH GERMAN
*10 Jun 1970 GERMANY NORTH
*20 Jun 1974 GERMANY HAMBURG
See also 65

36a WESTERN CANADIAN   15 Sep 1941   Walter Miller
Organized from North Central States (26a), Northwestern States (18)
*10 Jun 1970 ALBERTA-SASKATCHEWAN
*20 Jun 1974 CANADA CALGARY
See also 58, 136

37   NORTHERN CALIFORNIA   2 Jan 1942   German E. Ellsworth
Organized from California (14c)
*15 Jul 1966 CALIFORNIA NORTH

```
        *20 Jun 1974 CALIFORNIA SACRAMENTO
        See also 85, 127, 187a
38      NAVAJO-ZUNI                           7 Mar 1943    Ralph W. Evans
        *1 Jan 1949 SOUTHWEST INDIAN
        *10 Oct 1972 NEW MEXICO-ARIZONA
        *20 Jun 1974 ARIZONA HOLBROOK
        Discontinued 1 Jul 1984, transferred to Arizona Phoenix (179b)
        See also 78, 128, 132

39      PACIFIC (Administrative)              7 Dec 1946    Matthew Cowley
        Discontinued 27 Nov 1948

40      URUGUAY                               31 Aug 1947   Frederick S. Williams
        Organized from Argentine Mission (32)
        *10 Jun 1970 URUGUAY-PARAGUAY
        *20 Jun 1974 URUGUAY MONTEVIDEO
        See also 50, 155

41      FINNISH                               1 Sep 1947    Henry A. Matis
        Organized from Swedish (22a)
        *10 Jun 1970 FINLAND
        *20 Jun 1974 FINLAND HELSINKI
        See also 238

42      CENTRAL ATLANTIC STATES               26 Oct 1947   Robert J. Price
        Organized from East Central States (29)
        *10 Jun 1970 NORTH CAROLINA-VIRGINIA
        *1 Jul 1973 VIRGINIA
        *20 Jun 1974 VIRGINIA ROANOKE
        *25 Feb 1992 VIRGINIA RICHMOND
        See also 105, 188

43      PALESTINE-SYRIAN (See 13b)            8 Nov 1947    Badwagan Piranian
44      JAPANESE (See 21)                     6 Mar 1948    Edward L. Clissold
45      CHINESE                               10 Jul 1949   Hilton A. Robertson
        Discontinued 9 Feb 1953

46      GREAT LAKES                           31 Oct 1949   Carl C. Burton
        Organized from Northern States (9c)
        *10 Jun 1970 INDIANA-MICHIGAN
        *1 Jul 1973 INDIANA
        *20 Jun 1974 INDIANA INDIANAPOLIS
        See also 77a, 104

43a     WEST CENTRAL STATES                   11 Nov 1950   Sylvester Broadbent
        Organized from North Central States (26a), Northwestern States (18),
          Western States (17)
        *10 Jun 1970 MONTANA-WYOMING
        *20 Jun 1974 MONTANA BILLINGS
        See also 111

43b     CENTRAL AMERICAN                      16 Nov 1952   Gordon M. Romney
        Organized from Mexican (20a)
        *10 Jun 1970 CENTRAL AMERICA
        *20 Jun 1974 COSTA RICA SAN JOSE
        See also 76a, 79a, 177, 226

43c     SOUTH AUSTRALIAN                      3 Jul 1955    Thomas S. Bingham
        Organized from Australian (10)
        *Nov 1958 SOUTHERN AUSTRALIAN
        *1 Aug 1968 AUSTRALIA SOUTH
        *20 Jun 1974 AUSTRALIA MELBOURNE
        See also 82

43d     NORTHERN FAR EAST                     28 Jul 1955   Hilton A. Robertson
        Organized from Japanese (44)
        Discontinued 31 Aug 1968, transferred to Japan (82a), Japan-Okinawa (83)
        See also 71

44a     SOUTHERN FAR EAST                     17 Aug 1955   Herald Grant Heaton
        Organized from Japanese (44)
        *1 Nov 1969 HONG KONG TAIWAN
        *11 Jan 1971 HONG KONG
        See also 76b, 89, 94
```

45a NORTHERN MEXICAN   10 Jun 1956   Joseph T. Bentley
     Organized from Mexican (20a)
     *10 Jun 1970 MEXICO NORTH
     *20 Jun 1974 MEXICO MONTERREY
     *2 Sep 1992 MEXICO MONTERREY WEST
     *3 Nov 1992 MEXICO MONTERREY NORTH
     See also 56, 81, 193, 218

46a WEST SPANISH-AMERICAN   8 Mar 1958   Leland M. Perry
     Organized from Spanish-American (33)
     *10 Jun 1970 WEST SPANISH AMERICA
     Discontinued 1 Jul 1970, transferred to California (5)
     California South (73a), Arizona (87)

47   NEW ZEALAND SOUTH   1 Sep 1958   Alexander P. Anderson
     Organized from New Zealand (20)
     *20 Jun 1974 NEW ZEALAND WELLINGTON
     Discontinued 1 Jul 1981, transferred to New Zealand Christchurch (143),
       New Zealand Auckland (20)

48   BRAZILIAN SOUTH   20 Sep 1959   Asael T. Sorensen
     Organized from Brazilian (31a)
     *10 Jun 1970 BRAZIL SOUTH
     *20 Jun 1974 BRAZIL PORTO ALEGRE
     *25 Jan 1991 BRAZIL PORTO ALEGRE SOUTH
     See also 80, 181, 256a, 258

49   SOUTH GERMAN   4 Oct 1959   John A. Buehner
     Organized from West German (35a)
     *10 Jun 1970 GERMANY SOUTH
     *20 Jun 1974 GERMANY MUNICH
     See also 69, 240

50   ANDES   1 Nov 1959   J. Vernon Sharp
     Organized from Uruguay (40), Argentine (32)
     *10 Jun 1970 PERU-ECUADOR
     *1 Aug 1970 PERU
     *Feb 1971 PERU ANDES
     *Apr 1971 ANDES PERU
     *20 Jun 1974 PERU LIMA
     *1 Jan 1977 PERU LIMA SOUTH
     See also 67, 75a, 79a, 93, 149, 165, 300

51   EUROPEAN (Administrative) (See 15a) 17 Jan 1960   Alvin R. Dyer

52   NORTH BRITISH   27 Mar 1960   Bernard P. Brockbank
     Organized from British (1)
     *10 Jun 1970 ENGLAND NORTH
     *20 Jun 1974 ENGLAND LEEDS
     See also 61, 72, 138

53   AUSTRIAN   18 Sep 1960   W. Whitney Smith
     Organized from Swiss Austrian (8)
     *10 Jun 1970 AUSTRIA
     *20 Jun 1974 AUSTRIA VIENNA
     See also 205

54   EASTERN ATLANTIC STATES   16 Oct 1960   George B. Hill
     Organized from Eastern States (15b)
     *10 Jun 1970 DELAWARE-MARYLAND
     *20 Jun 1974 WASHINGTON D.C.
     *1 Jul 1986 WASHINGTON D.C. SOUTH
     See also 91a, 188b, 298

55   FLORIDA   1 Nov 1960   Karl R. Lyman
     Organized from Southern States (8b)
     *10 Jun 1971 FLORIDA SOUTH
     *20 Jun 1974 FLORIDA FT. LAUDERDALE
     Discontinued 20 Jun 1983, transferred to Florida Tampa (139), West Indies (178a)
     Reopened 1 Jul 1984 (178b)
     See also 96, 175

56   WEST MEXICAN   1 Nov 1960   Harold E. Turley
     Organized from Northern Mexican (45a)

*10 Jun 1970 MEXICO WEST
*20 Jun 1974 MEXICO HERMOSILLO
See also 125, 247

57   RAROTONGA   20 Nov 1960   Joseph R. Reeder
      Organized from Samoan (13c)
      Discontinued 15 Apr 1966, transferred to New Zealand (20)

58   ALASKAN-CANADIAN   21 Nov 1960   Milton L. Weilenman
      Organized from Western Canadian (36a)
      *10 Jun 1970 ALASKA-BRITISH COLUMBIA
      *20 Jun 1974 CANADA VANCOUVER
      See also 114

59   FRENCH EAST   19 Jan 1961   Henry D. Moyle Jr.
      Organized from French (26)
      *10 Jun 1970 FRANCE-SWITZERLAND
      *20 Jun 1974 SWITZERLAND GENEVA
      See also 221a, 262

60   TEXAS   16 Feb 1961   Ralph J. Hill
      Organized from Gulf States (31)
      *10 Jun 1970 TEXAS NORTH
      *20 Jun 1974 TEXAS DALLAS
      See also 77b, 189

61   SCOTTISH-IRISH   28 Feb 1961   Bernard P. Brockbank
      Organized from North British (52)
      *8 Jul 1962 SCOTTISH
      *10 Jun 1970 SCOTLAND
      *20 Jun 1974 SCOTLAND EDINBURGH
      See also 70, 74, 147

62   CENTRAL BRITISH   6 Mar 1961   James A. Cullimore
      Organized from British (1)
      *10 Jun 1970 ENGLAND CENTRAL
      *20 Jun 1974 ENGLAND BIRMINGHAM
      Discontinued 1 Jul 1983, transferred to England Coventry (183)

63   CENTRAL GERMAN   15 Mar 1961   Stephen C. Richards
      Organized from West German (35a)
      *10 Jun 1970 GERMANY CENTRAL
      *20 Jun 1974 GERMANY DUSSELDORF
      Discontinued 1 Apr 1982, transferred to Germany Frankfurt (35a), Germany
       Munich (49)
      Reopened 1 Jul 1990, Germany, Duesseldorf; from Germany Frankfurt (35a), Germany
       Munich (49) See 240

64   WEST EUROPEAN (Administrative)   30 Apr 1961   N. Eldon Tanner
      Organized from European (51)
      Discontinued 14 Sep 1965

65   BERLIN   14 Jul 1961   Percy K. Fetzer
      Organized from North German (36)
      Discontinued 31 May 1966, transferred to North German (36)

66   SOUTH AMERICA (Administrative)   25 Aug 1961   A. Theodore Tuttle
      Discontinued 17 Jul 1965

67   CHILEAN   8 Oct 1961   A. Delbert Palmer
      Organized from Andes (50)
      *10 Jun 1970 CHILE
      *20 Jun 1974 CHILE SANTIAGO
      *1 Jan 1977 CHILE SANTIAGO SOUTH
      See also 119, 148, 214, 303a

68   SOUTHWEST BRITISH   1 Feb 1962   A. Ray Curtis
      Organized from British (1)
      *10 Jun 1970 ENGLAND SOUTHWEST
      *20 Jun 1974 ENGLAND BRISTOL
      See also 79

69   BAVARIAN   4 Mar 1962   Owen Spencer Jacobs
      Organized from South German (49)
      Discontinued 10 Jun 1965, transferred to South German (49)

70	IRISH	8 Jul 1962	Stephen R. Covey

70   IRISH   8 Jul 1962   Stephen R. Covey
Organized from Scottish-Irish (61)
*10 Jun 1970 IRELAND
*20 Jun 1974 IRELAND BELFAST
*11 Sep 1976 IRELAND DUBLIN

71   KOREAN   8 Jul 1962   Gail Edward Carr
Organized from Northern Far East (43d)
*10 Jun 1970 KOREA
*20 Jun 1974 KOREA SEOUL
See also 124, 170

72   NORTHEAST BRITISH   1 Sep 1962   Grant S. Thorn
Organized from North British (52)
Discontinued May 1965, transferred to North British (52)

73   NORTH ARGENTINE   16 Sep 1962   Ronald V. Stone
Organized from Argentine (32)
*10 Jun 1970 ARGENTINA NORTH
*20 Jun 1974 ARGENTINA CORDOBA
See also 100, 206, 228

74   NORTH SCOTTISH   24 Nov 1962   William N. Waite
Organized from Scottish (61)
Discontinued 31 May 1965, transferred to Scottish (61)

75   SOUTHEAST MEXICAN   27 Mar 1963   Carl J. Beecroft
Organized from Mexican (20a)
*10 Jun 1970 MEXICO SOUTHEAST
*20 Jun 1974 MEXICO VERACRUZ
See also 126, 193

76   FRANCO-BELGIAN   1 Oct 1963   Joseph T. Edmunds
Organized from French (26)
*10 Jun 1970 FRANCE-BELGIUM
*20 Jun 1974 BELGIUM BRUSSELS
See also 135

77   CUMORAH   26 Jan 1964   N. Lester Petersen
Organized from Eastern States (15b)
*20 Jun 1974 NEW YORK ROCHESTER

78   NORTHERN INDIAN   8 Apr 1964   Grant Roper Farmer
Organized from Southwest Indian (38)
*1 Jul 1973 DAKOTA-MANITOBA
*20 Jun 1974 SOUTH DAKOTA RAPID CITY
See also 136

79   BRITISH SOUTH   27 Dec 1964   Don K. Archer
Organized from British (1), Southwest British (68)
*10 Jun 1970 ENGLAND SOUTH
*20 Jun 1974 ENGLAND LONDON SOUTH

76a   GUATEMALA-EL SALVADOR   1 Aug 1965   Terrance L. Hansen
Organized from Central American (43b)
*20 Jun 1974 GUATEMALA GUATEMALA CITY
*29 Mar 1988 GUATEMALA GUATEMALA CITY SOUTH
See also 137a, 152, 205a, 227

73a   CALIFORNIA SOUTH   10 Jul 1966   D. Crawford Houston
Organized from California (14c)
*20 Jun 1974 CALIFORNIA ANAHEIM
See also 86, 87, 113, 182

74a   ITALIAN (See 7)   2 Aug 1966   John Duns Jr.

75a   ANDES SOUTH   14 Nov 1966   Franklin Kay Gibson
Organized from Andes (50)
*1969 BOLIVIA
*20 Jun 1974 BOLIVIA LA PAZ
*10 Jun 1970 PHILIPPINES
*20 Jun 1974 PHILIPPINES MANILA
See also 110, 172, 194, 250, 268

77a   OHIO   31 Jul 1967   E. Garrett Barlow

Organized from Great Lakes (46)
*31 Aug 1972 OHIO-WEST VIRGINIA
*20 Jun 1974 OHIO COLUMBUS
See also 154, 188, 179a

Organized from Texas (60), Spanish-American (33)
*20 Jun 1974 TEXAS SAN ANTONIO
See also 142, 224

78a	PACIFIC NORTHWEST	1 Jan 1968	Joe E. Whitesides

Organized from Northwestern States (18)
*10 Jun 1970 WASHINGTON
*20 Jun 1974 WASHINGTON SEATTLE
See also 166, 255

79a	COLOMBIA-VENEZUELA	1 Jul 1968	Stephen L. Brower

Organized from Central American (43b), Andes (50)
*1 Jul 1971 COLOMBIA
*20 Jun 1974 COLOMBIA BOGOTA
*1 Jul 1992 COLOMBIA BOGOTA NORTH
See also 95, 120, 215, 270

80	BRAZILIAN NORTH	7 Jul 1968	Hal Roscoe Johnson

Organized from Brazilian (31a), Brazilian South (48)
*10 Jun 1970 BRAZIL NORTH
*20 Jun 1974 BRAZIL RIO DE JANEIRO
See also 167a, 185a

81	MEXICO NORTH CENTRAL	5 Aug 1968	Arturo R. Martinez

Organized from Northern Mexico (45a)
*20 Jun 1974 MEXICO TORREON
See also 125, 208

82	AUSTRALIAN WEST	7 Aug 1968	Milton J. Hess

Organized from Southern Australian (43c)
*10 Jun 1970 AUSTRALIA WEST
*20 Jun 1974 AUSTRALIA ADELAIDE
See also 117

82a	JAPAN	1 Sep 1968	Walter R. Bills

Organized from Northern Far East (43d)
*20 Jun 1974 JAPAN TOKYO
*1 Jul 1978 JAPAN TOKYO NORTH
See also 90, 108, 109a, 162

83	JAPAN-OKINAWA	1 Sep 1968	Edward Y. Okazaki

Organized from Northern Far East (43d)
*16 Mar 1970 JAPAN CENTRAL
*20 Jun 1974 JAPAN KOBE
See also 91, 108, 144, 185, 245

84	GERMANY DRESDEN	14 Jun 1969	J. Henry Burkhart

Discontinued Dec 1978
*12 Mar 1984

GERMANY DEMOCRATIC REPUBLIC DRESDEN
Discontinued 3 Jun 1984
Reopened 1 Jul 1989, see 225
*6 Sep 1990 GERMANY DRESDEN
*13 Jan 1994 GERMANY LEIPZIG
See also 263

85	CALIFORNIA CENTRAL	1 Jul 1969	Wilbur Wallace Cox

Organized from California North (37)
*20 Jun 1974 CALIFORNIA OAKLAND
See also 118, 158a, 187a

86	CALIFORNIA EAST	7 Jul 1969	William L. Nicholls

Organized from California South (73a), California (14c)
*20 Jun 1974 CALIFORNIA ARCADIA
See also 182, 297

87	ARIZONA	1 Aug 1969	Clark M. Wood

Organized from California South (73a)
*20 Jun 1974 ARIZONA TEMPE

See also 127, 132, 179b, 231

88 SOUTH CENTRAL STATES   4 Aug 1969   Albert B. Crandall
    Organized from Central States (11a)
    *10 Jun 1970 OKLAHOMA
    *20 Jun 1974 OKLAHOMA TULSA
    See also 116, 248

89 SOUTHEAST ASIA   1 Nov 1969   G. Carlos Smith
    Organized from Southern Far East (44a)
    *20 Jun 1974 SINGAPORE
    Discontinued 1 Jul 1978, transferred to Indonesia Jakarta (122)
    Reopened 1 Jan 1980 (176)
    See also 109

90 JAPAN EAST   15 Mar 1970   Russell N. Horiuchi
    Organized from Japan (82a)
    *20 Jun 1974 JAPAN SAPPORO

91 JAPAN WEST   18 Mar 1970   Kan Watanabe
    Organized from Japan-Okinawa (83)
    *20 Jun 1974 JAPAN FUKUOKA
    See also 144

91a PENNSYLVANIA   1 Jul 1970   George M. Baker
    Organized from Delaware-Maryland (54)
    *20 Jun 1974 PENNSYLVANIA HARRISBURG
    See also 129, 156

92 SPAIN   11 Jul 1970   R. Raymond Barnes
    Organized from French (26)
    *20 Jun 1974 SPAIN MADRID
    See also 137, 141, 199

93 ECUADOR   1 Aug 1970   Louis W. Latimer
    Organized from Peru-Ecuador (50)
    *20 Jun 1974 ECUADOR QUITO
    See also 160

94 TAIWAN   11 Jan 1971   Malan R. Jackson
    Organized from Hong Kong-Taiwan (44a)
    *20 Jun 1974 TAIWAN TAIPEI
    See also 146

95 VENEZUELA   1 Jul 1971   Clark D. Webb
    Organized from Colombia-Venezuela (79a)
    *20 Jun 1974 VENEZUELA CARACAS
    *1 Jul 1991 VENEZUELA CARACAS EAST
    *25 Mar 1994 VENEZUELA CARACAS
    See also 174, 267, 303

96 ALABAMA-FLORIDA   1 Jul 1971   Hartman Rector Jr.
    Organized from Florida (55)
    *20 Jun 1974 FLORIDA TALLAHASSEE
    See also 166a, 197

97 NAUVOO   1 Jul 1971   J. LeRoy Kimball
    Organized from Northern States (9c)
    Discontinued 1 Jul 1974, transferred to Illinois Chicago (9c)

98 ITALY NORTH   6 Jul 1971   Dan Charles Jorgensen
    Organized from Italy (74a)
    *20 Jun 1974 ITALY MILAN
    See also 244

99 FIJI   23 Jul 1971   Sherman A. Lindholm
    Organized from Samoa (13c), New Zealand North (20), Tonga (22c)
    *20 Jun 1974 FIJI SUVA
    See also 178

99a QUEBEC   14 Jul 1972   John K. M. Olsen
    Organized from Ontario-Quebec (23a)
    *20 Jun 1974 CANADA MONTREAL

100 ARGENTINA EAST   30 Jul 1972   Joseph T. Bentley
    Organized from Argentina North (73), Argentina South (32)
    *20 Jun 1974 ARGENTINA ROSARIO

See also 229

101 BRAZIL NORTH CENTRAL   17 Oct 1972   Leroy A. Drechsel
   Organized from Brazil Central (31a)
   *20 Jun 1974 BRAZIL SAO PAULO NORTH
   See also 190, 257

102 BRAZIL SOUTH CENTRAL   17 Oct 1972   Owen Nelson Baker
   Organized from Brazil Central (31a)
   *20 Jun 1974 BRAZIL SAO PAULO SOUTH
   See also 181, 257

103 INTERNATIONAL   9 Nov 1972   Bernard P. Brockbank
   Organized for "unattached" members worldwide
   Discontinued 15 Aug 1987
   See also 179, 205

104 MICHIGAN   3 Jul 1973   C. Russell Hansen
   Organized from Indiana-Michigan (46)
   *20 Jun 1974 MICHIGAN LANSING
   See also 164

105 NORTH CAROLINA   18 Jul 1973   Charles M. Alexander
   Organized from North Carolina-Virginia (42)
   *20 Jun 1974 NORTH CAROLINA GREENSBORO
   *1 Jul 1980 NORTH CAROLINA CHARLOTTE
   See also 186

106 AUSTRALIA NORTHEAST   26 Jul 1973   J. Martell Bird
   Organized from Australia East (10)
   *20 Jun 1974 AUSTRALIA BRISBANE
   See also 275

107 CANADA-MARITIMES   27 Jul 1973   Thurn J. Baker
   Organized from New England (35)
   *20 Jun 1974 CANADA HALIFAX

108 JAPAN-NAGOYA   1 Aug 1973   Satoru Sato
   Organized from Japan (82a), Japan Central (83)
   *20 Jun 1974 JAPAN NAGOYA

109 THAILAND   1 Aug 1973   Paul D. Morris
   Organized from Southeast Asia (89)
   *20 Jun 1974 THAILAND BANGKOK

109a JAPAN SENDAI   1 Jul 1974   Walter Teruya
   Organized from Japan Tokyo (82a)

110 PHILIPPINES CEBU CITY   1 Jul 1974   Carl D. Jones
   Organized from Philippines Manila (76b)
   *3 Aug 1984 PHILIPPINES CEBU
   *1 Jul 1988 PHILIPPINES BACOLOD
   See also 157, 194, 223

111 IDAHO POCATELLO   1 Jul 1974   Ernest Eberhard Jr.
   Organized from Montana Billings (43a)
   *29 May 1979 IDAHO BOISE
   See also 132, 264

112 ARGENTINA BUENOS AIRES SOUTH   22 Jul 1974   Juan Carlos Avila
   Organized from Argentina South (32)
   See also 180, 269

113 CALIFORNIA SAN DIEGO   1 Aug 1974   Frank M. Bradshaw
   Organized from California Anaheim (73a)

114 ALASKA ANCHORAGE   15 Oct 1974   Weston F. Killpack
   Organized from Canada Vancouver (58)

115 PORTUGAL LISBON   19 Nov 1974   Wm. Grant Bangerter
   * 1 Jul 1990 PORTUGAL LISBON SOUTH
   See also 203, 253

116 ARKANSAS LITTLE ROCK   1 Jul 1975   Richard M. Richards
   Organized from Louisiana Shreveport (31), Oklahoma Tulsa (88)

117 AUSTRALIA PERTH   1 Jul 1975   Bruce James Opie
   Organized from Australia Adelaide (82)

118 CALIFORNIA FRESNO   1 Jul 1975   Robert B Harbertson
   Organized from California Oakland (85)

119   CHILE CONCEPCION   1 Jul 1975   Lester D. Haymore
Organized from Chile Santiago (67)
See also 151

120   COLOMBIA CALI   1 Jul 1975   Jay E. Jensen
Organized from Colombia Bogota (79a)

121   FRANCE TOULOUSE   1 Jul 1975   George W. Broschinsky
Organized from France Paris (26)
Discontinued 1 Jul 1982, transferred to France Paris (26), Switzerland Geneva (59)

122   INDONESIA JAKARTA   1 Jul 1975   Hendrik Gout
Organized from Singapore (89)
Discontinued 1 Jan 1981, transferred to Singapore (89)
Reopened 1 Jul 1985 (182b)
Discontinued 1 Jul 1989
Reopened 1 Jul 1995 See 306

123   ITALY PADOVA   1 Jul 1975   John Anthony Grinceri
Organized from Italy Rome (7)
Discontinued 1 Jul 1982, transferred to Italy Milan (98)
Reopened 1 Jul 1990; organized from Italy Milan (98), Italy Rome (7)see 244

124   KOREA PUSAN   1 Jul 1975   Han In Sang
Organized from Korea Seoul (71)
See also 191

125   MEXICO GUADALAJARA   1 Jul 1975   Isauro Gutierrez
Organized from Mexico Mexico City (20a), Mexico Torreon (81),
Mexico Hermosillo (56)
See also 201

126   MEXICO VILLAHERMOSA   1 Jul 1975   Abraham Lozano
Organized from Mexico Veracruz (75)
*1 Jul 1978 MEXICO MERIDA
See also 193, 209

127   NEVADA LAS VEGAS   1 Jul 1975   Ronald M. Patterson
Organized from Arizona Tempe (87), California Sacramento (37)

128   NEW MEXICO ALBUQUERQUE   1 Jul 1975   Stanley D. Roberts
Organized from Arizona Holbrook (38)
See also 231

129   PENNSYLVANIA PITTSBURGH   1 Jul 1975   Kenneth W. Godfrey
Organized from Pennsylvania Harrisburg (91a)
See also 188

130   SOUTH CAROLINA COLUMBIA   1 Jul 1975   Ronald L. Knighton
Organized from Georgia Atlanta (8b)
See also 239

131   TENNESSEE NASHVILLE   1 Jul 1975   Emerson Taylor Cannon
Organized from Kentucky Louisville (29)

132   UTAH SALT LAKE CITY   1 Jul 1975   Ernest Eberhard Jr.
Organized from Idaho Pocatello (111), Colorado Denver (17),
Arizona Tempe (87), Arizona Holbrook (38)
*1 Jul 1980 UTAH SALT LAKE CITY NORTH
*1 Jan 1989 UTAH OGDEN
See also 187, 222

133   YUGOSLAVIA ZAGREB   1 Jul 1975   Gustav Salik
Discontinued 1 Jul 1976

134   IRAN TEHRAN   4 Jul 1975   D. Burton Fransworth
Discontinued 1 Jan 1979

135   BELGIUM ANTWERP   16 Jul 1975   Larry Hyde Brim
Organized from Belgium Brussels (76), Netherlands Amsterdam (8a)
Discontinued 1 Jul 1982, transferred to Netherlands Amsterdam (8a)
Reopened 1 Jul 1990, Organized from Netherlands Amsterdam (8a)
Discontinued 1 Jul 1995, Transferred to Netherlands Amsterdam (8a)
See 232

136   CANADA WINNIPEG   15 Feb 1976   Howard L. Lund
Organized from Canada Calgary (36a), South Dakota Rapid City (78)

137   SPAIN BARCELONA   8 May 1976   Smith B. Griffin

Organized from Spain Madrid (92)
See also 199

137a EL SALVADOR SAN SALVADOR   1 Jul 1976   Eddy L. Barillas
Organized from Guatemala Guatemala City (76a)
Discontinued 1 Apr 1981, transferred to Guatemala Guatemala City (76a)
Reopened 1 Oct 1984 (181a)
*1 Jul 1990 EL SALVADOR SAN SALVADOR WEST

138 ENGLAND MANCHESTER   1 Jul 1976   O. Louis Alder
Organized from England Leeds (52)

139 FLORIDA TAMPA   1 Jul 1976   A. Sterling Workman
Organized from Florida Ft. Lauderdale (55)
See also 178a, 197

140 IOWA DES MOINES   1 Jul 1976   Erwin E. Wirkus
Organized from Missouri Independence (11a), Illinois Chicago (9c)

141 SPAIN SEVILLE   3 Jul 1976   Hugo A. Catron
Organized from Spain Madrid (92)
12 Jan 1993 SPAIN MALAGA
See also 220

142 TEXAS HOUSTON   3 Jul 1976   George L. Merrill
Organized from Texas San Antonio (77b)
See also 254

143 NEW ZEALAND CHRISTCHURCH   5 Jul 1976   Ivan G. Radman
Organized from New Zealand Wellington (47)
*15 Jan 1991 NEW ZEALAND WELLINGTON

144 JAPAN OKAYAMA   9 Jul 1976   William H. Nako
Organized from Japan Fukuoka (91), Japan Kobe (83)

145 SWEDEN GOTEBORG   26 Jul 1976   Paul Kent Oscarson
Organized from Sweden Stockholm (22a)
Discontinued 1 Jul 1982, transferred to Sweden Stockholm (22a)

146 TAIWAN KAOHSIUNG   3 Aug 1976   P. Boyd Hales
Organized from Taiwan Taipei (94)
*28 Sep 1983 TAIWAN TAICHUNG
See also 173

147 SCOTLAND GLASGOW   1 Nov 1976   Roy W. Oscarson
Organized from Scotland Edinburgh (61)
Discontinued 1 Jul 1981, transferred to Scotland Edinburgh (61)

148 CHILE SANTIAGO NORTH   1 Jan 1977   Berkley A. Spencer
Organized from Chile Santiago (67)
See also 168, 214, 303a

149 PERU LIMA NORTH   1 Jan 1977   Jose A. Sousa
Organized from Peru Lima (50)
See also 165, 184a, 210, 300

150 BOLIVIA SANTA CRUZ   1 Jul 1977   DeVere R. McAllister
Organized from Bolivia La Paz (75a)
*1 Feb 1982 BOLIVIA COCHABAMBA

151 CHILE OSORNO   1 Jul 1977   Lester D. Haymore
Organized from Chile Concepcion (119)

152 GUATEMALA QUETZALTENANGO   1 Jul 1977   John F. O'Donnal
Organized from Guatemala Guatemala City (76a)

153 MISSOURI ST. LOUIS   1 Jul 1977   Norman W. Olsen
Organized from Missouri Independence (11a)
See also 176a

154 OHIO CLEVELAND   1 Jul 1977   Donald S. Brewer
Organized from Ohio Columbus (77a)
See also 179a

155 PARAGUAY ASUNCION   1 Jul 1977   Mearl K. Bair
Organized from Uruguay Montevideo (40)

156 PENNSYLVANIA PHILADELPHIA   1 Jul 1977   Lewis K. Payne
Organized from Pennsylvania Harrisburg (91a)
See also 304a

157 PHILIPPINES DAVAO   1 Jul 1977   Layton B. Jones
    Organized from Philippines Cebu City (110)
    See also 211

158 ITALY CATANIA   10 Jul 1977   Leopoldo Larcher
    Organized from Italy Rome (7)

158a CALIFORNIA SAN JOSE   1 Jul 1978   Lysle R. Cahoon
    Organized from California Oakland (85)

159 CALIFORNIA VENTURA   1 Jul 1978   Hyrum S. Smith
    Organized from California Los Angeles (14c)
    See also 182, 297

160 ECUADOR GUAYAQUIL   1 Jul 1978   William J. Mitchell
    Organized from Ecuador Quito (93)
    *25 Apr 1991 ECUADOR GUAYAQUIL SOUTH
    *16 Jun 1995 ECUADOR GUAYAQUIL
    *25 Apr 1996 ECUADOR GUAYAQUIL SOUTH
    See also 261, 310

161 ENGLAND LONDON EAST   1 Jul 1978   Carl D. Jones
    Organized from England London (1)
    Discontinued 1 Jul 1983, transferred to England London (1), England
    London South (79)

162 JAPAN TOKYO SOUTH   1 Jul 1978   Delbert H. Groberg
    Organized from Japan Tokyo (82a)

163 MEXICO MEXICO CITY NORTH   1 Jul 1978   John B. Dickson
    Organized from Mexico Mexico City (20a)
    See also 193, 218, 222a

164 MICHIGAN DEARBORN   1 Jul 1978   William R. Horton
    Organized from Michigan Lansing (104)
    * 1 Dec 1989 MICHIGAN DETROIT

165 PERU AREQUIPA   1 Jul 1978   Norval C. Jesperson
    Organized from Peru Lima North (149), Peru Lima South (50)

166 WASHINGTON SPOKANE   1 Jul 1978   Norwood C. McKoy
    Organized from Washington Seattle (78a)

167 WISCONSIN MILWAUKEE   1 Jul 1978   L. Flake Rogers
    Organized from Minnesota Minneapolis (26a), Illinois Chicago (9c)

166a ALABAMA BIRMINGHAM   1 Jan 1979   William J. Attwooll
    Organized from Georgia Atlanta (8b), Florida Tallahassee (96)

167a BRAZIL RECIFE   1 Jul 1979   Harry Eduardo Klein
    Organized from Brazil Rio de Janeiro (80)
    See also 200, 234

168 CHILE VINA DEL MAR   1 Jul 1979   Gerald J. Day
    Organized from Chile Santiago North (148)
    See also 214

169 CONNECTICUT HARTFORD   1 Jul 1979   Gerald L. Ericksen
    Organized from Massachusetts Boston (35)
    See also 195, 299

170 KOREA SEOUL WEST   1 Jul 1979   D. Brent Clement
    Organized from Korea Seoul (71)

171 MISSISSIPPI JACKSON   1 Jul 1979   Frank W. Hirschi
    Organized from Louisiana Baton Rouge (31)

172 PHILIPPINES QUEZON CITY   1 Jul 1979   Robert E. Sackley
    Organized from Philippines Manila (76b)
    *1 Jan 1981 PHILIPPINES BAGUIO
    *11 Feb 1991 PHILIPPINES LA UNION
    *22 Aug 1991 PHILIPPINES BAGUIO
    See also 192, 219

173 TAIWAN T'AICHUNG   1 Jul 1979   Frederick W. Crook
    Organized from Taiwan Kaohsiung (146)
    Discontinued Jul 1982, transferred to Taiwan Kaohsiung (146), Taiwan Taipei (94)

174 VENEZUELA MARACAIBO   1 Jul 1979   Alejandro Portal
    Organized from Venezuela Caracas (95)

175 PUERTO RICO SAN JUAN   7 Jul 1979   Richard L. Millett
     Organized from Florida Ft. Lauderdale (55)
     See also 178a, 188a

176 SINGAPORE (See 89)   1 Jan 1980   J. Talmage Jones
     Organized from Indonesia Jakarta (122)

177 HONDURAS TEGUCIGALPA   1 Feb 1980   Samuel Flores
     Organized from Costa Rica San Jose (43b)
     See also 242

178 MICRONESIA GUAM   1 Apr 1980   Ferron C. Losee
     Organized from Hawaii Honolulu (7a), Fiji Suva (99)

179 AFRICA WEST   1 Jul 1980   Bryan Espenschied
     Organized from International (103)
     *1 Jul 1985 NIGERIA LAGOS
     See also 183a, 221, 276

180 ARGENTINA BAHIA BLANCA   1 Jul 1980   Allen B. Oliver
     Organized from Argentina Buenos Aires South (112)
     See also 230

181 BRAZIL CURITIBA   1 Jul 1980   Dixon D. Cowley
     Organized from Brazil Sao Paulo South (102), Brazil Porto Alegre (48)
     See also 302a

182 CALIFORNIA SAN BERNARDINO   1 Jul 1980   Howard C. Sharp
     Organized from California Anaheim (73a), California Arcadia (86),
      California Ventura (159)
     See also 235, 297

183 ENGLAND COVENTRY   1 Jul 1980   Quinn G. McKay
     Organized from England Birmingham (62)
     *22 Aug 1991 ENGLAND BIRMINGHAM
     See also 62

184 ILLINOIS CHICAGO SOUTH   1 Jul 1980   Charles E. Petersen
     Organized from Illinois Chicago (9c)
     Discontinued 1 Jul 1983, transferred to Illinois Chicago (9c)

185 JAPAN OSAKA   1 Jul 1980   Shigeki Ushio
     Organized from Japan Kobe (83)
     Discontinued 1 Jul 1995, transferred to Japan Kobe

186 NORTH CAROLINA RALEIGH   1 Jul 1980   Joel N. Gillespie
     Organized from North Carolina Greensboro (105)

187 UTAH SALT LAKE CITY SOUTH   1 Jul 1980   Jonathan W. Snow
     Organized from Utah Salt Lake City (132)
     *1 Jan 1989 UTAH SALT LAKE CITY
     See also 222, 304

188 WEST VIRGINIA CHARLESTON   1 Jul 1980   O. Rex Warner
     Organized from Ohio Columbus (77a), Virginia Roanoke (42),
      Pennsylvania Pittsburgh (129)

188a DOMINICAN REPUBLIC SANTO DOMINGO 1 Jan 1981   John A. Davis
     Organized from Puerto Rico San Juan (175)
     *1 Jul 1991 DOMINICAN REPUBLIC SANTO DOMINGO WEST
     See also 178a, 196, 260

178a WEST INDIES   20 Jun 1983   Kenneth L. Zabriskie
     Organized from Florida Tampa (139), Dominican Republic Santo
      Domingo (188a), Puerto Rico San Juan (175)
     See also 180a, 186a, 266

176a ILLINOIS PEORIA   1 Jul 1983   Brent Reed Rigtrup
     Organized from Missouri St. Louis (153)

177a SOUTH AFRICA CAPE TOWN   1 Jul 1984   G. Philip Margetts
     Organized from South Africa Johannesburg (23)

178b FLORIDA FT. LAUDERDALE (See 55) 1 Jul 1984   Claud Darwin Mangum

179a OHIO AKRON   1 Jul 1984   Stanley M. Smoot
     Organized from Ohio Columbus (77a)
     Discontinued 1 Jul 1989, transferred to Ohio Cleveland (154)

179b ARIZONA PHOENIX   1 Jul 1984   Francis M. Bay
    Organized from Arizona Holbrook (38), Arizona Tempe (87)
    See also 231

180a HAITI PORT-AU-PRINCE   1 Aug 1984   James S. Arrigona
    Organized from West Indies (178a)

181a EL SALVADOR SAN SALVADOR   1 Oct 1984   Manuel Antonio Diaz
    See also 137a, 237

182b INDONESIA JAKARTA (See 122)   1 Jul 1985   Effian Kadarusman
    Organized from Singapore (89)

183a GHANA ACCRA   1 Jul 1985   Miles H. Cunningham
    Organized from Africa West (179)

184a PERU TRUJILLO   1 Jul 1985   Roberto Vidal
    Organized from Peru Lima North (149)

185a BRAZIL BRASILIA   1 Jul 1985   Demar Staniscia
    Organized from Brazil Rio de Janeiro (80), Brazil Recife (167)
    See also 200, 213, 233

186a JAMAICA KINGSTON   1 Jul 1985   Richard L. Brough
    Organized from West Indies (178a)

187a CALIFORNIA SANTA ROSA   1 Jul 1985   Robert C. Witt
    Organized from California Sacramento (37), California Oakland (85)

188b WASHINGTON D.C. NORTH   1 Jul 1986   Dennis E. Simmons
    Organized from Washington D.C. (54)
    See also 298

189 TEXAS LUBBOCK   1 Jul 1986   Lyle L. Wasden
    Organized from Texas Dallas (60)
    *20 Jan 1988 TEXAS FT. WORTH

190 BRAZIL CAMPINAS   1 Jul 1986   Sheldon R. Murphy
    Organized from Brazil Sao Paulo North (101)
    See also 213, 302a

191 KOREA TAE JON   1 Jul 1986   Moo-Kwang Hong
    Organized from Korea Pusan (124)

192 PHILIPPINES QUEZON CITY   1 Jul 1986   Joel E. Leetham
    Organized from Philippines Baguio (172)
    See also 219, 256, 268

193 MEXICO MEXICO CITY EAST   1 Jan 1987   Enrique Moreno
    Organized from Mexico Mexico City North (163), Mexico Mexico City South (20a),
     Mexico Monterrey (45a), Mexico Merida (126), Mexico Veracruz (75)
    See also 217

194 PHILIPPINES CEBU EAST   1 Jul 1987   C. Elliott Richards
    Organized from Philippines Cebu (110), Philippines Manila (76b)
    *1 Jul 1988 PHILIPPINES CEBU
    See also 251

195 NEW HAMPSHIRE MANCHESTER   1 Jul 1987   Lynn E. Thomsen
    Organized from Massachusetts Boston (35), Connecticut Hartford (169)

196 DOMINICAN REPUBLIC SANTIAGO   1 Jul 1987   Michael D. Stirling
    Organized from Dominican Republic Santo Domingo (188a)

197 FLORIDA JACKSONVILLE   1 Jul 1987   Douglas W. DeHaan
    Organized from Florida Tampa (139), Florida Tallahassee (96)

198 ZAIRE KINSHASA   1 Jul 1987   R. Bay Hutchings
    Organized from International Mission (103)

199 SPAIN BILBAO   1 Jul 1987   Garth J. Wakefield
    Organized from Spain Madrid (92), Spain Barcelona (137)

200 BRAZIL FORTALEZA   1 Jul 1987   Helvecio Martins
    Organized from Brazil Recife (167a), and Brazil Brazilia (185a)
    See also 233

201 MEXICO MAZATLAN   1 Jul 1987   Samuel Lara M.
    Organized from Mexico Guadalajara (125)
    *21 Feb 1995 MEXICO CULIACAN

202 NEW JERSEY MORRISTOWN   1 Jul 1987   Dan J. Workman

Organized from New York New York (15b)
See also 304a

203 PORTUGAL PORTO 1 Jul 1987 Dan Copeland
Organized from Portugal Lisbon (115)
See also 220

204 ZIMBABWE HARARE 1 Jul 1987 Joseph Hamstead
Organized from South Africa Johannesburg (23)

205 AUSTRIA VIENNA EAST 1 Jul 1987 D.. Neuenschwander
Organized from Austria Vienna (53), International (103)
*3 Feb 1992 UKRAINE KIEV
See also 236, 241, 243, 252, 259, 274

205a GUATEMALA GUATEMALA CITY NORTH 1 Jan 1988 Gordon W. Romney
Organized from Guatemala Guatemala City South (76a)

206 ARGENTINA SALTA 8 Jan 1988 Francisco Jose Vinas
Organized from Argentina Cordoba (73)

207 BOLIVIA LA PAZ (See 75a) 8 Jan 1988 Steven R. Wright

208 MEXICO CHIHUAHUA 8 Jan 1988 Victor M. Cerda
Organized from Mexico Torreon (81)

209 MEXICO TUXTLA-GUTIERREZ 8 Jan 1988 Alberto D. Gamboa
Organized from Mexico Merida (126)
See also 246

210 PERU LIMA EAST 8 Jan 1988 Douglas K. Earl
Organized from Peru Lima North (149)
See also 300

211 PHILIPPINES CAGAYAN DE ORO 8 Jan 1988 Rufino A. Villanueva Jr.
Organized from Philippines Davao (157)

212 LIBERIA MONROVIA 1 Mar 1988 J. Duffy Palmer
Discontinued 12 Feb 1991, transferred to Ghana Accra (183a)

213 BRAZIL BELO HORIZONTE 1 Jul 1988 Nivio Varella Alcover
Organized from Brazil Brasilia (185a), Brazil Campinas (190)
*25 Apr 1994 BRAZIL BELO HORIZONTE EAST
*2 Aug 1994 BRAZIL BELO HORIZONTE
See also 295a

214 CHILE ANTOFAGASTA 1 Jul 1988 Carlos Ramon Espinola
Organized from Chile Santiago North (148), Chile Santiago South (67),
Chile Vina del Mar (168)

215 COLOMBIA BARRANQUILLA 1 Jul 1988 Frank Berrett
Organized from Colombia Bogota (79a)

216 MASCARENE ISLANDS 1 Jul 1988 Gerard Giraud-Carrier
Organized from S. Africa Johannesburg (23)
*22 Apr 1991 SOUTH AFRICA DURBAN

217 MEXICO PUEBLA 1 Jul 1988 George G. Sloan
Organized from Mexico Mexico City East (193)

218 MEXICO TAMPICO 1 Jul 1988 Hector Ceballos
Organized from Mexico Mexico City North (163), Mexico Monterrey (45a)
*2 Sep 1992 MEXICO MONTERREY EAST
*3 Nov 1992 MEXICO TAMPICO

219 PHILIPPINES QUEZON CITY WEST 1 Jul 1988 Robert J. Kennerley
Organized from Philippines Baguio (172), Philippines Quezon City (192)
*1 Jul 1991 PHILIPPINES SAN FERNANDO
*7 Jun 1994 PHILIPPINES OLONGAPO

220 SPAIN LAS PALMAS 1 Jul 1988 M. K. Hamblin
Organized from Spain Seville (141), Portugal Porto (203)

221 NIGERIA ABA 1 Jul 1988 Arthur W. Elrey Jr.
Organized from Nigeria Lagos (179)
*1 May 1995 NIGERIA PORT HARCOURT
See also 277

222 UTAH PROVO 1 Jan 1989 George E. Magnusson
Organized from Utah Salt Lake City South (187)

221a FRANCE BORDEAUX   1 Jul 1989   Neil L. Andersen
    Organized from France Paris (6), Switzerland Geneva (59)
    See also 262

222a MEXICO QUERETARO   1 Jul 1989   Scott T. Lyman
    Organized from Mexico Mexico City North (163)
    *24 Mar 1992 MEXICO LEON

223 PHILIPPINES NAGA   1 Jul 1989   Augusto A. Lim
    Organized from Philippines Cebu (110)

224 TEXAS CORPUS CHRISTI   1 Jul 1989   S. Gibbons Frost
    Organized from Texas San Antonio (77b)
    *24 Feb 1994 TEXAS MCALLEN

225 GERMAN DEM. REPUBLIC DRESDEN   1 Jul 1989   Wolfgang Paul
    Reopened, see 84

226 PANAMA PANAMA CITY   1 Jul 1989   Pedro E. Abularach
    Organized from Costa Rica San Jose (43b)

227 NICARAGUA MANAGUA   15 Oct 1989   Luis A. Alvarez O.
    Organized from Guatemala Guatemala City South (76a)

228 ARGENTINA MENDOZA   1 Jul 1990   Charles W. Eastwood
    Organized from Argentina Cordoba (73)

229 ARGENTINA RESISTENCIA   1 Jul 1990   Wilfredo R. Lopez G.
    Organized from Argentina Rosario (100)

230 ARGENTINA TRELEW   1 Jul 1990   Antonio Cappi
    Organized from Argentina Bahia Blanca (180)
    *25 May 1993 ARGENTINA NEUQUEN

231 ARIZONA TUCSON   1 Jul 1990   James E. Mangum
    Organized from Arizona Tempe (87), Arizona Phoenix (179b), New
     Mexico Albuquerque (128)

232 BELGIUM ANTWERP   1 Jul 1990   R. Bruce Barrett
    See 135

233 BRAZIL MANAUS   1 Jul 1990   Claudio R. Mendes C.
    Organized from Brazil Brasilia (185a), Brazil Fortaleza (200)
    See also 294a

234 BRAZIL SALVADOR   1 Jul 1990   Jairo Massagardi
    Organized from Brazil Recife (167a)
    See also 296

235 CALIFORNIA RIVERSIDE   1 Jul 1990   Jerry M. Hess
    Organized from California San Bernardino (182)

236 CZECHOSLOVAKIA PRAGUE   1 Jul 1990   Richard W. Winder
    organized from Austria Vienna East (205)
    See 30

237 EL SALVADOR SAN SALVADOR EAST   1 Jul 1990   Ramon E. Turcios D.
    Organized from El Salvador San Salvador (181a)

238 FINLAND HELSINKI EAST   1 Jul 1990   Gary L. Browning
    Organized from Finland Helsinki (41)
    *2 Jan 1992 RUSSIA MOSCOW
    See also 272, 273, 293

239 GEORGIA MACON   1 Jul 1990   John H. Cox
    Organized from South Carolina Columbia (130), Georgia Atlanta (8)

240 GERMANY DUESSELDORF   1 Jul 1990   Edgar Wolferts
    Reopened, see 63; organized from Germany Frankfurt (35a), Germany Munich (49)

241 GREECE ATHENS   1 Jul 1990   R. Douglas Phillips
    Organized from Austria Vienna East (205)
    See also 308

242 HONDURAS SAN PEDRO SULA   1 Jul 1990   Lehi Gracia
    Organized from Honduras Tegucigalpa (177)

243 HUNGARY BUDAPEST   1 Jul 1990   James L. Wilde
    Organized from Austria Vienna East (205)

244 ITALY PADOVA   1 Jul 1990   Vicenzo Conforte

Reopened, see 123

245 JAPAN OKINAWA   1 Jul 1990   Evan Allan Larsen
Discontinued 1 Jul 1996
Organized from Japan Kobe (83)

246 MEXICO OAXACA   1 Jul 1990   Miguel Hidalgo N.
Organized from Mexico Tuxtla-Gutierrez (209)

247 MEXICO TIJUANA   1 Jul 1990   Arturo de Hoyos
Organized from Mexico Hermosillo (56)

248 OKLAHOMA OKLAHOMA CITY   1 Jul 1990   Duane Beazer
Organized from Oklahoma Tulsa (88)

249 OREGON EUGENE   1 Jul 1990   Lloyd M. Rasmussen
Organized from Oregon Portland (18)

250 PHILIPPINES SAN PABLO   1 Jul 1990   Dean O. Peck
Organized from Philippines Manila (76b)

251 PHILIPPINES TACLOBAN   1 Jul 1990   Leonardo S. Mina
Organized from Philippines Cebu (194)

252 POLAND WARSAW   1 Jul 1990   Walter Whipple
Organized from Austria Vienna East (205)

253 PORTUGAL LISBON NORTH   1 Jul 1990   Vitor Martins
Organized from Portugal Lisbon (115)

254 TEXAS HOUSTON EAST   1 Jul 1990   Allen S. Farnsworth
Organized from Texas Houston (142)

255 WASHINGTON TACOMA   1 Jul 1990   Sidney R. Henderson
Organized from Washington Seattle (78)

256 PHILIPPINES ILAGAN   1 Sep 1990   Reynaldo Ibanez Vergara
Organized from Philippines Quezon City (192)

256a BRAZIL PORTO ALEGRE NORTH 1 Jul 1991   Joseph Larry Memmott
Organized from Brazil Porto Alegre (48)

257 BRAZIL SAO PAULO EAST   1 Jul 1991   Willis C. Fails
Organized from Brazil Sao Paulo North (101) , Brazil Sao Paulo South (102)

258 BRAZIL SAO PAULO INTERLAGOS 1 Jul 1991   Frederick G. Williams
Organized from Brazil Sao Paulo South (102)

259 BULGARIA SOFIA   1 Jul 1991   Kiril P. Kiriakov
Organized from Austria Vienna East (205)

260 DOM. REPUBLIC SANTO DOMINGO EAST 1 Jul 1991   Mark Allen Jarman
Organized from Dominican Republic Santo Domingo (188a)

261 ECUADOR GUAYAQUIL NORTH   1 Jul 1991   Daniel L. Johnson
Organized from Ecuador Guayaquil (160), Ecuador Quito (93)
Discontinued 16 Jun 1995
reopened 1 Jul 1996 (310)

262 FRANCE MARSEILLE   1 Jul 1991   Richard W. Thatcher
Organized from Switzerland Geneva (59), France Bordeaux (221a)

263 GERMANY BERLIN   1 Jul 1991   Manfred H. Schutze
Organized from Germany Dresden (84)

264 IDAHO POCATELLO   1 Jul 1991   Wayne W. Probst
Organized from Idaho Boise (111)

265 KENYA NAIROBI   1 Jul 1991   Larry King Brown

266 TRINIDAD TOBAGO   1 Jul 1991   J. Richard Toolson
Organized from West Indies (178a)
Discontinued 1 Jul 1994, transferred to West Indies (178a)

267 VENEZUELA CARACAS WEST   1 Jul 1991   Charles M. Hunter
Organized from Venezuela Caracas (95) Venezuela Maracaibo (174)
*25 Mar 1994 VENEZUELA VALENCIA
See also 303

268 PHILIPPINES CABANATUAN   1 Jan 1992   Martin D. Openshaw
Organized from Philippines Quezon City (192),Philippines Manila (76b)
Philippines San Fernando (219)

269 ARGENTINA BUENOS AIRES WEST   27 Jan 1992   Lloyd H. Richmond
Organized from Buenos Aires North (32) Buenos Aires South (112)

270 COLOMBIA BOGOTA SOUTH   27 Jan 1992   Jerry P. Cahill
Organized from Colombia Bogota (79a)

271 CAMAROON YAOUNDE   1 Jul 1992   Robert L. Mercer
*1 June 1993 IVORY COAST ABIDJAN

272 RUSSIA ST. PETERSBURG   3 Feb 1992   Thomas S. Rogers
Organized from Russia Moscow (238, 272)

273 PAPUA NEW GUINEA PORT MORESBY   13 Feb 1992   Joseph Jones Grigg
Organized from Australia Brisbane Mission (106)

274 NIGERIA ILORIN   1 Jul 1992   John A. Ehanire
*Organized from Nigeria Lagos (179)
2 Aug 1993 NIGERIA IBADAN
Discontinued 1 Jul 1995

275 NIGERIA JOS   1 Jul 1992   Ato Kwamina Dadson
Organized from Nigeria Aba (221)
*14 Dec 1993 NIGERIA ENUGU

276 MEXICO MONTERREY SOUTH   3 Nov 1992   Garry R. Flake
Organized from Mexico Monterrey East (218)

277 INDIA BANGALORE   1 Jan 1993   Gurcharan Singh Gill
Organized from Singapore (89)

278 AUSTRALIA SYDNEY NORTH   1 Jan 1993   Glenn L. Pace
Organized from Australia Sydney (10)

279 BRAZIL RIBEIRO PRETO   1 Feb 1993   Cesar A. Seiquer Milder
Organized from Brazil Campinas

280 BRAZIL RIO DE JANEIRO NORTH   1 Feb 1993   Moises B. Damasceno
Organized from Brazil Rio de Janeiro (80)

281 BRAZIL FLORIANOPOLIS   1 Jul 1993   Jose Benjamin Puerta
Organized from Brazil Curitiba (181)

282 BRAZIL RECIFE SOUTH   1 Jul 1993   Jorge Moreira
Organized from Brazil Recife (167a)

283 CALIFORNIA CARLSBAD   1 Jul 1993   Merlyn K. Jolley
Organized from California San Diego (113)

284 CALIFORNIA ROSEVILLE   1 Jul 1993   John Hoybjerg
Organized from California Sacramento (37)

285 CANADA TORONTO EAST   1 Jul 1993   Harold Roger Boyer
Organized from Canada Toronto (23a)

286 COLORADO DENVER NORTH   1 Jul 1993   Lynn M. Paulson
Organized from Colorado Denver (17)

287 GUATEMALA CITY GUATEMALA CENTRAL   1 Jul 1993   Denis Roy Morrill
Organized from Guatemala City North (205a), Guatemala City South (294),
Guatemala Quetzaltenango (152)

288 LATVIA RIGA MISSION   1 Jul 1993   Robert W. Blair
Organized from Russia St. Petersburg (272)
*16 Apr 1996 LITHUANIA VILNIUS

289 NEBRASKA OMAHA   1 Jul 1993   Reed B. Maw
Organized from Missouri Independence (14b)

290 NEW YORK NEW YORK NORTH   1 Jul 1993   Parley L. Howell
Organized from New York New York (2)

291 PERU CHICLAYO   1 Jul 1993   Rene Loli
Organized from Peru Trujillo (184a) and Peru Lima North (149)

292 ROMANIA BUCHAREST   1 Jul 1993   John Rolph Morrey
Organized from Hungary Budapest (243)

293 RUSSIA SAMARA   1 Jul 1993   Arlo R. Nelson
Organized from Russia Moscow (238)
See also 305

294 TENNESSEE KNOXVILLE   1 Jul 1993   Richard Karl Sager
Organized from Tennessee Nashville (131)

295 UKRAINE DONETSK   1 Jul 1993   Leo Merrill
Organized from Ukraine Kiev (205)

294a	BRAZIL BELEM Organized from Brazil Manaus (233)	1 Jul 1994	Pedro J. D. Penha
295a	BRAZIL BELO HORIZONTE SOUTH Organized from Brazil Belo Horizonte (213)	1 Jul 1994	Thomas P. Smith
296	BRAZIL SALVADOR SOUTH Organized from Brazil Salvador (234)	1 Jul 1994	Marcos A.C. Prieto
297	CALIFORNIA SAN FERNANDO Organized from California Arcadia (86), California San Bernardino (182), California Ventura (159)	1 Jul 1994	Steven E. Snow
298	MARYLAND BALTIMORE Organized from Washington D.C. North (188b), Washington D.C. South (54)	1 Jul 1994	Bruce M. Ballard
299	NEW YORK UTICA Organized from Connecticut Hartford (169), Massachusetts Boston (35)	1 Jul 1994	Robert Noel Hatch
300	PERU LIMA CENTRAL Organized from Peru Lima North (149), Peru Lima East (210), Peru Lima South (50)	1 Jul 1994	Carlos A. Cuba Q.
301	RUSSIA NOVOSIBIRSK See also 305	1 Jul 1994	Jerald C. Sherwood
302	RUSSIA ROSTOV NA DONU 24 Apr 1995 RUSSIA ROSTOV	1 Jul 1994	Vladimir Siwachok
303	VENEZUELA BARCELONA Organized from Venezuela Caracas East (95), Venezuela Caracas West (267)	1 Jul 1994	Ned B. Roueche
304	UTAH SALT LAKE CITY TEMPLE SQUARE Organized from Utah Salt Lake City (187)	5 Apr 1995	Robert C. Witt
302a	BRAZIL MARILIA Organized from Brazil Campinas (190)	1 Jul 1995	Gutenberg G. Amorim
303a	CHILE SANTIAGO WEST Organized from Chile Santiago North (148), Chile Santiago South (67)	1 Jul 1995	Ronald N. Walker
304a	NEW JERSEY CHERRY HILL Organized from New Jersey Morristown (202), Pennsylvania Philadelphia (156)	1 Jul 1995	John Glen Sanford
305	RUSSIA YEKATERINGBURG Organized from Russia Samara (293), and Russia Novosibirsk (301)	1 Jul 1995	Vyacheslav I. Efimov
306	INDONESIA JAKARTA (See 122)	1 Jul 1995	Vern M. Tueller
307	MONGOLIA ULAANBATAAR	1 Jul 1995	Richard Cook
308	ALBANIA TIRANA Organized from Greece Athens (241)	1 Jul 1996	Laurel L. Holman
309	AUSTRIA VIENNA SOUTH Organized from Austria Vienna (53)	1 Jul 1996	Johann A. Wondra
310	ECUADOR GUAYAQUIL NORTH (see 261)	1 Jul 1996	B. Renato Maldonado

FIRST STAKE IN EACH STATE OF THE UNITED STATES

STATE	NAME OF STAKE	DATE ORGANIZED	CURRENT NAME
ALABAMA	Alabama (452)	3 Mar 1968	Huntsville Alabama
ALASKA	Alaska (331)	13 Aug 1961	Anchorage Alaska
ARIZONA	Little Colorado (21)	27 Jan 1878	‡18 Dec 1887
	*Maricopa (24)	10 Dec 1882	Mesa Arizona Maricopa
ARKANSAS	Arkansas (484)	1 Jun 1969	Little Rock Arkansas
CALIFORNIA	San Bernardino (4a)	6 Jul 1851	‡By 1857
	*Hollywood (98)	22 May 1927	Los Angeles California
COLORADO	San Luis (26)	10 Jun 1883	Manassa Colorado
CONNECTICUT	Hartford (421)	18 Sep 1966	Hartford Connecticut
DELAWARE	Wilmington Delaware (673)	8 Dec 1975	Same
DIST. OF COLUMBIA	Washington (131)	30 Jun 1940	Washington D.C.
FLORIDA	Florida (163)	19 Jan 1947	Jacksonville Florida West
GEORGIA	Atlanta (241)	5 May 1957	Tucker Georgia
HAWAII	Oahu (113)	30 Jun 1935	Laie Hawaii
IDAHO	Bear Lake (8a)	20 Jun 1869	Paris Idaho
ILLINOIS	Nauvoo (2a)	5 Oct 1839	‡By 1846
	*Chicago (118)	29 Nov 1936	Wilmette Illinois
INDIANA	Indianapolis (283)	17 May 1959	Indianapolis Indiana
IOWA	Iowa (3a)	5 Oct 1839	‡6 Jan 1842
	*Cedar Rapids (419)	29 May 1966	Cedar Rapids Iowa
KANSAS	Wichita (355)	24 Jun 1962	Wichita Kansas
KENTUCKY	Louisville (540)	17 Jan 1971	Louisville Kentucky
LOUISIANA	New Orleans (221)	19 Jun 1955	New Orleans Louisiana
MAINE	Maine (461)	23 Jun 1968	Augusta Maine
MARYLAND	Chesapeake (526)	13 Sep 1970	Silver Spring Maryland
MASSACHUSETTS	Boston (354)	20 May 1962	Boston Massachusetts
MICHIGAN	Detroit (197)	9 Nov 1952	Bloomfield Hills Michigan
MINNESOTA	Minnesota (317)	29 Nov 1960	Minneapolis Minnesota
MISSISSIPPI	Jackson (404)	2 May 1965	Jackson Mississippi
MISSOURI	Clay-Caldwell (2)	3 Jul 1834	‡By 1839
	*Kansas City (234)	21 Oct 1956	Kansas City Missouri
MONTANA	Butte (208)	28 Jun 1953	Butte Montana
NEBRASKA	Winter Quarters (318)	11 Dec 1960	Omaha Nebraska
NEVADA	Carson Valley (7a)	4 Oct 1856	‡By 1858
	*Moapa (64)	9 Jun 1912	Logandale Nevada
NEW HAMPSHIRE	Merrimack (507)	22 Mar 1970	Nashua New Hampshire
NEW JERSEY	New Jersey (292)	28 Feb 1960	Morristown New Jersey
NEW MEXICO	Young (63)	21 May 1912	Farmington New Mexico
NEW YORK	New York (110)	9 Dec 1934	New York New York
NORTH CAROLINA	North Carolina (332)	27 Aug 1961	Kinston North Carolina
NORTH DAKOTA	Fargo North Dakota (852)	7 Aug 1977	Same
OHIO	Kirtland (1)	17 Feb 1834	‡24 May 1841
	*Cincinnati (270)	23 Nov 1958	Cincinnati Ohio
OKLAHOMA	Tulsa (298)	1 May 1960	Tulsa Oklahoma
OREGON	Union (49)	9 Jun 1901	La Grande Oregon
PENNSYLVANIA	Philadelphia (304)	16 Oct 1960	Philadelphia Pennsylvania
RHODE ISLAND	Providence R.I. (818)	20 Mar 1977	Same
SOUTH CAROLINA	South Carolina (169)	19 Oct 1947	Columbia South Carolina
SOUTH DAKOTA	Rapid City (592)	10 Dec 1972	Rapid City South Dakota
TENNESSEE	Memphis (403)	18 Apr 1965	Memphis Tennessee
TEXAS	El Paso (194)	21 Sep 1952	El Paso Texas
UTAH	Salt Lake (1a)	3 Oct 1847	Same
VERMONT	Montpelier Vermont (753)	11 Apr 1976	Same
VIRGINIA	Virginia (245)	30 Jun 1957	Richmond Virginia
WASHINGTON	Seattle (124)	31 Jul 1938	Seattle Washington
WEST VIRGINIA	West Virginia (522)	23 Aug 1970	Charleston West Virginia
WISCONSIN	Milwaukee (367)	3 Feb 1963	Milwaukee Wisconsin
WYOMING	Star Valley (33)	14 Aug 1892	Afton Wyoming

( ) **Chronological number of stake; ‡ Discontinued; * First permanent stake**

FIRST STAKE ORGANIZED IN COUNTRIES OF THE WORLD

COUNTRY	NAME OF STAKE	DATE ORGANIZED	CURRENT NAME
AMERICAN SAMOA	Pago Pago (488)	15 Jun 1969	Pago Pago Samoa
ARGENTINA	Buenos Aires (423)	20 Nov 1966	Buenos Aires Argentina East
AUSTRALIA	Sydney (293)	27 Mar 1960	Sydney Australia Greenwich
AUSTRIA	Vienna Austria (1126)	20 Apr 1980	Same
BELGIUM	Brussels Belgium (813)	20 Feb 1977	Same
BOLIVIA	Santa Cruz Bolivia (993)	14 Jan 1979	Santa Cruz Bolivia Canoto
BRAZIL	Sao Paulo (417)	1 May 1966	Sao Paulo Brazil
CANADA	Alberta (35)	9 Jun 1895	Cardston Alberta
CHILE	Santiago (590)	19 Nov 1972	Santi. Chile Quinta Normal
COLOMBIA	Bogota Colombia (805)	23 Jan 1977	Same
COSTA RICA	San Jose Costa Rica (803)	20 Jan 1977	Same
DENMARK	Copenhagen Denmark (648)	16 Jun 1974	Same
DOMINICAN REPUBLIC	Santo Domingo Dominican Republic (1593)	23 Mar 1986	Same
ECUADOR	Guayaquil Ecuador (939)	11 Jun 1978	Guayaquil Ecuador West
EL SALVADOR	San Salvador (618)	3 Jun 1973	San Salvador El Salvador
ENGLAND	Manchester (294)	27 Mar 1960	Manchester England
FIJI	Suva Fiji (1428)	12 Jun 1983	Same
FINLAND	Helsinki Finland (865)	16 Oct 1977	Same
FRANCE	Paris France (731)	16 Nov 1975	Same
GERMANY	Berlin (334)	10 Sep 1961	Berlin Germany
GHANA	Accra Ghana (1791)	21 Apr 1991	same
GUATEMALA	Guatemala City (436)	21 May 1967	Guatemala City Guatemala
HONDURAS	San Pedro Sula Honduras (820)	10 Apr 1977	Same
HONG KONG	Hong Kong (756)	25 Apr 1976	Hong Kong Island
IRELAND	Dublin Ireland (2034)	12 Mar 1995	Same
ITALY	Milan Italy (1274)	7 Jun 1981	Same
JAPAN	Tokyo (505)	15 Mar 1970	Tokyo Japan
KOREA	Seoul (604)	8 Mar 1973	Seoul Korea
KIRIBATI	Tarawa Kiribati (2215)	08 Aug 1996	Same
MEXICO	Juarez (37)	9 Dec 1895	Colonia Juarez Mexico
NETHERLANDS	Holland (326)	12 Mar 1961	The Hague Netherlands
NEW ZEALAND	Auckland (264)	18 May 1958	Auckland N.Z. Mt. Roskill
NICARAGUA	Managua Nicaragua (1246)	22 Mar 1981	‡15 Oct 1989
NIGERIA	Aba Nigeria (1695)	15 May 1988	Same
NORTHERN IRELAND	Belfast Ireland (647)	9 Jun 1974	Belfast Northern Ireland
NORWAY	Oslo Norway (835)	22 May 1977	Same
PANAMA	Panama City Panama (1081)	11 Nov 1979	Same
PAPUA NEW GUINEA	Port Moresby Papua New Guinea (2109)	22 Oct 1995	same
PARAGUAY	Asuncion Paraguay (1002)	25 Feb 1979	Same
PERU	Lima (503)	22 Feb 1970	Lima Peru Limatambo
PHILIPPINES	Manila (613)	20 May 1973	Manila Philippines
PORTUGAL	Lisbon Portugal (1276)	10 Jun 1981	Same
PUERTO RICO	San Juan Puerto Rico (1215)	14 Dec 1980	Same
SCOTLAND	Glasgow (356)	26 Aug 1962	Glasgow Scotland
SINGAPORE	Singapore Singapore (2025)	26 Feb 1995	Same
SOUTH AFRICA	Transvaal (506)	22 Mar 1970	Johannesburg South Africa
SPAIN	Madrid Spain (1327)	14 Mar 1982	Same
SWEDEN	Stockholm Sweden (691)	20 Apr 1975	Same
SWITZERLAND	Swiss (341)	28 Oct 1961	Zurich Switzerland
TAHITI	Tahiti (573)	14 May 1972	Papeete Tahiti
TAIWAN	Taipei Taiwan (755)	22 Apr 1976	Taipei Taiwan West
THAILAND	Bangkok Thailand (2064)	18 Jun 1995	Same
TONGA	Nuku'alofa (463)	5 Sep 1968	Nuku'alofa Tonga
UNITED STATES	Kirtland (1)	17 Feb 1834	‡24 May 1841
	*Salt Lake (1a)	3 Oct 1847	Same
URUGUAY	Montevideo (444)	12 Nov 1967	Montevideo Uruguay West
VENEZUELA	Caracas Venezuela (827)	15 May 1977	Same
WALES	Merthyr Tydfil Wales (676)	12 Jan 1975	Same
WESTERN SAMOA	Apia (353)	18 Mar 1962	Apia Samoa

( ) Chronological number of stake; ‡ Disorganized; * First permanent stake

TEMPLES OF THE WORLD

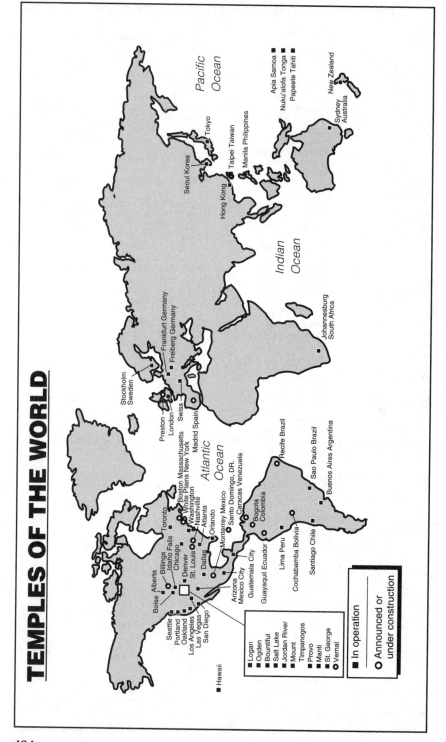

TEMPLES OF THE CHURCH
Listed by order of completion

TEMPLE	LOCATION	DEDICATED	BY WHOM
Kirtland*	Kirtland, Ohio	27 Mar 1836	Joseph Smith
Nauvoo**	Nauvoo, Ill.	30 Apr 1846	Joseph Young (private)
		1 May 1846	Orson Hyde (public)
1 St. George	St. George, Utah	6 Apr 1877	Daniel H. Wells
Rededicated after remodeling		11 Nov 1975	Spencer W. Kimball
2 Logan	Logan, Utah	17 May 1884	John Taylor
Rededicated after remodeling		13 Mar 1979	Spencer W. Kimball
3 Manti	Manti, Utah	17 May 1888	Wilford Woodruff (private)
		21 May 1888	(His prayer read by Lorenzo Snow; public)
Rededicated after remodeling		14 Jun 1985	Gordon B. Hinckley
4 Salt Lake	Salt Lake City, Utah	6 Apr 1893	Wilford Woodruff
5 Hawaii	Laie, Oahu, Hawaii	27 Nov 1919	Heber J. Grant
Rededicated after remodeling		13 Jun 1978	Spencer W. Kimball
6 Alberta	Cardston, Alberta, Canada	26 Aug 1923	Heber J. Grant
Portions rededicated after remodeling		2 Jul 1962	Hugh B. Brown
Rededication after remodeling		22 Jun 1991	Gordon B. Hinckley
7 Arizona	Mesa, Ariz.	23 Oct 1927	Heber J. Grant
Rededicated after remodeling		15 Apr 1975	Spencer W. Kimball
8 Idaho Falls	Idaho Falls, Idaho	23 Sep 1945	George Albert Smith
9 Swiss	Zollikofen, near Bern, Switzerland	11 Sep 1955	David O. McKay
Rededicated after remodeling		23 Oct 1992	Gordon B. Hinckley
10 Los Angeles	Los Angeles, Calif.	11 Mar 1956	David O. McKay
11 New Zealand	Hamilton, New Zealand	20 Apr 1958	David O. McKay
12 London	Newchapel, Surrey, England	7 Sep 1958	David O. McKay
Rededicated after remodeling		18 Oct 1992	Gordon B. Hinckley
13 Oakland	Oakland, Calif.	17 Nov 1964	David O. McKay
14 Ogden	Ogden, Utah	18 Jan 1972	Joseph Fielding Smith
15 Provo	Provo, Utah	9 Feb 1972	Joseph Fielding Smith (His prayer read by Harold B. Lee)
16 Washington	Kensington, Md.	19 Nov 1974	Spencer W. Kimball
17 Sao Paulo	Sao Paulo, Brazil	30 Oct 1978	Spencer W. Kimball
18 Tokyo	Tokyo, Japan	27 Oct 1980	Spencer W. Kimball
19 Seattle	Bellevue, Wash.	17 Nov 1980	Spencer W. Kimball
20 Jordan River	South Jordan, Utah	16 Nov 1981	Marion G. Romney
21 Atlanta Georgia	Sandy Springs, Ga.	1 Jun 1983	Gordon B. Hinckley
22 Apia Samoa	Apia, Western Samoa	5 Aug 1983	Gordon B. Hinckley
23 Nuku'alofa Tonga	Nuku'alofa, Tonga	9 Aug 1983	Gordon B. Hinckley
24 Santiago Chile	Santiago, Chile	15 Sep 1983	Gordon B. Hinckley
25 Papeete Tahiti	Pirae, Tahiti	27 Oct 1983	Gordon B. Hinckley
26 Mexico City	Mexico City, Mexico	2 Dec 1983	Gordon B. Hinckley
27 Boise Idaho	Boise, Idaho	25 May 1984	Gordon B. Hinckley
28 Sydney Australia	Carlingford, Australia	20 Sep 1984	Gordon B. Hinckley
29 Manila Philippines	Quezon City, Philippines	25 Sep 1984	Gordon B. Hinckley
30 Dallas Texas	Dallas, Texas	19 Oct 1984	Gordon B. Hinckley
31 Taipei Taiwan	Taipei, Taiwan	17 Nov 1984	Gordon B. Hinckley
32 Guatemala City	Guatemala City, Guatemala	14 Dec 1984	Gordon B. Hinckley
33 Freiberg Germany	Freiberg, Germany	29 Jun 1985	Gordon B. Hinckley
34 Stockholm Sweden	Vasterhaninge, Sweden	2 Jul 1985	Gordon B. Hinckley
35 Chicago Illinois	Glenview, Ill.	9 Aug 1985	Gordon B. Hinckley
36 Johannesburg South Africa	Johannesburg, South Africa	24 Aug 1985	Gordon B. Hinckley
37 Seoul Korea	Seoul, Korea	14 Dec 1985	Gordon B. Hinckley
38 Lima Peru	Lima, Peru	10 Jan 1986	Gordon B. Hinckley
39 Buenos Aires Argentina	Buenos Aires, Argentina	17 Jan 1986	Thomas S. Monson

40 Denver Colorado	Littleton, Colo.	24 Oct 1986	Ezra Taft Benson
41 Frankfurt Germany	Friedrichsdorf, Germany	28 Aug 1987	Ezra Taft Benson
42 Portland Oregon	Lake Oswego, Ore.	19 Aug, 1989	Gordon B. Hinckley
43 Las Vegas Nevada	Las Vegas, Nev.	16 Dec 1989	Gordon B. Hinckley
44 Toronto Ontario	Brampton, Ontario, Canada	25 Aug 1990	Gordon B. Hinckley
45 San Diego California	San Diego, Calif.	25 Apr 1993	Gordon B. Hinckley
46 Orlando Florida	Windermere, Fla.	9 Oct. 1994	Howard W. Hunter
47 Bountiful Utah	Bountiful, Utah	8 Jan. 1995	Howard W. Hunter
48 Hong Kong	Hong Kong	26 May 1996	Gordon B. Hinckley
49 Mount Timpanogos	American Fork, Utah	13 Oct. 1996	Gordon B. Hinckley
50 St. Louis Missouri	Town and Country, Missouri		

Temples announced or under construction:

Billings Montana
Bogota Colombia
Boston Massachusetts
Caracas Venezuela
Cochabamba Bolivia

Guayaquil Ecuador
Madrid Spain
Monterrey Mexico
Nashville Tennessee
Preston England

Recife Brazil
Santo Domingo Dominican Rep.
Vernal Utah
White Plains New York

* No longer in use by the Church **No longer stands

TEMPLES OF THE CHURCH
(Listed alphabetically)

ALBERTA TEMPLE

Location: Cardston, about 185 miles south of Calgary in southern Alberta; 348 3rd St. West, Cardston, Alberta. Telephone: (403) 653-3552.

Site: In 1887, eight-acre site laid out and given to the Church by Charles Ora Card, leader of the first group of Mormons to Canada. It was then called the Tabernacle Block.

Exterior finish: White granite quarried near Kootenai Lakes in Nelson, British Columbia. Each stone was hand-hewn at the quarry or temple site.

Temple design: Octagonal shape, similar to Maltese cross, with no spire.

Architects: Hyrum C. Pope and Harold W. Burton.

Number of rooms: Approximately 40 in original structure; four ordinance, five sealing.

Total floor area: Originally 29,471 square feet, now 65,000 square feet.

Dimensions of building: 100 feet by 100 feet; height, 85 feet.

District: Alberta, Saskatchewan, Manitoba, southeastern British Columbia, northern Montana; 24 stakes.

Groundbreaking, site dedication: July 27, 1913, President Joseph F. Smith dedicated

site in the presence of about 1,500 people. Ground broken Nov. 9, 1913, by Daniel Kent Greene of Glenwoodville, Alberta.

Dedication: Aug. 26-29, 1923, by President Heber J. Grant; 11 sessions. Rededicated after remodeling July 2, 1962, by President Hugh B. Brown of the First Presidency; closed for remodeling May 1988-June 1991; toured by 101,000 people during an open house June 6-15, 1991. Rededicated by President Gordon B. Hinckley June 22-24, 1991; 12 sessions.

Rededicatory prayer excerpt: "*Bless the Latter-day Saints of Canada that they may be good citizens of the nation, men and women of integrity worthy of the respect of the people of this nation, and contributing of their talents and strength to its well-being.*"

APIA SAMOA TEMPLE

Location: Near the school and mission home in Pesega; P.O. Box 1621, Apia, Western Samoa, Telephone: (011-685) 21018.

Site: 1.7 acres.

Exterior finish: "R-wall" exterior finish and insulation system on concrete block; split cedar shake shingles on roof.

Temple design: Modern.

Architect: Emil B. Fetzer, Church architect.

Construction advisers: Dale Cook and Richard Rowley.

Contractor: Utah Construction and Development.

Number of rooms: Three sealing rooms, two ordinance rooms; 31 total rooms.

Total floor area: 13,020 square feet.

Dimensions of building: 142.88 feet by 115.32 feet; statue of Angel Moroni on top spire, 75 feet high.

District: Western Samoa and American Samoa; 19 stakes.

Groundbreaking, site dedication: Feb. 19, 1981, by President Spencer W. Kimball, assisted by the head of state, Malieotoa Tanumafil II. Nearly 4,000 people attended.

Dedication: Aug. 5-6, 1983, by President Gordon B. Hinckley; 7 sessions.

Dedicatory prayer excerpt: *"We pray for thy blessings upon those who govern these islands and the people who dwell here that principles of peace and equity may prevail and that the citizens of these islands may have cause to rejoice in the liberty that is theirs."*

ARIZONA TEMPLE

Location: In Mesa, 16 miles east of Phoenix, in central Arizona's Valley of the Sun. Mesa's Main Street passes the site on the north; 101 S. LeSueur, Mesa, AZ. 85204. Telephone: (602) 833-1211.

Site: 20-acre site selected Feb. 1, 1920, by President Heber J. Grant, Apostles David O. McKay and George F. Richards. Purchased in 1921.

Exterior finish: Concrete reinforced with 130 tons of steel. Exterior is faced with a terra cotta glaze that is egg-shell in color and tile-like in finish.

Temple design: Modification of the classic style, suggestive of pre-Columbian temples and even the Temple of Herod.

Architects: Don C. Young and Ramm Hansen.

Construction supervisor: Arthur Price.

Construction chairman: Executive building committee: J.W. LeSueur, chairman; O.S. Stapley, John Cummard, Andrew Kimball.

Number of rooms: four ordinance, nine sealing; 193 total rooms.

Total floor area: 72,712 square feet.

Dimensions of building: 128 feet by 184 feet, and 50 feet in height above the foundation.

District: Most of Arizona and New Mexico; El Paso Texas region; 74 stakes.

Site dedication, groundbreaking: Site dedicated Nov. 28, 1921; ground broken April 25, 1922, by President Heber J. Grant.

Dedication: Oct. 23, 1927, by President Heber J. Grant; services broadcast by radio. Rededicated after extensive remodeling April 15-16, 1975, by President Spencer W. Kimball; 8 sessions.

Dedicatory prayer excerpt: *"Accept the dedication of this house, and these grounds, which we have dedicated unto thee by virtue of the Priesthood of the Living God which we hold."*

ATLANTA GEORGIA TEMPLE

Location: In Sandy Springs, on the northeastern outskirts of Atlanta; 6450 Barfield Rd.; Atlanta, GA 30328. Telephone: (770) 393-3698.

Site: 5.9 acres.

Exterior finish: Pre-cast stone walls, built-up roof.

Temple design: Modern.

Architect: Emil B. Fetzer, Church architect.

Construction adviser: Michael Enfield and Ronald Prince.

Contractor: Cube Construction Company.

Number of rooms: Five sealing rooms, four ordinance rooms; 54 total rooms.

Total floor area: 27,360 square feet.

Dimensions: 187 feet 8 inches by 166 feet 3 inches; statue of Angel Moroni on top spire.

District: Most of southeastern U.S. except Florida, and extreme south of Georgia; 54 stakes (10 of these stakes will be included in the St. Louis Missouri Temple District when that temple is completed).

Groundbreaking, site dedication: March 7, 1981, by President Spencer W. Kimball, attended by 10,000 people.

Dedication: June 1-4, 1983, by President Gordon B. Hinckley; 11 sessions.

Dedicatory prayer excerpt: *"May the very presence of this temple in the midst of thy people become a reminder of the sacred and eternal covenants made with thee. May they*

strive more diligently to banish from their lives those elements which are inconsistent with the covenants they have made with thee.

"May all who enter these holy precincts feel of thy spirit and be bathed in this marvelous, sanctifying influence. May they come ... in a spirit of love and dedication."

BILLINGS MONTANA TEMPLE

Announced: Aug. 31, 1996

District: Montana, No. Dakota, So. Dakota, Wyoming: 18 stakes.

Status: Awaiting groundbreaking.

BOGOTA COLOMBIA TEMPLE

Announced: April 7, 1984, by President Gordon B. Hinckley. Site announced May 28, 1988, by the First Presidency.

Site: 3.75 acres.

Location: In the Niza section of Bogota, about 10 miles from downtown.

Exterior finish: Colombian limestone.

Temple design: Modern.

Architects: Cuellar, Serrano Gomez, SA.

Number of rooms: four ordinance, three sealing, 138 total rooms.

Total floor area: 45,000 square feet

Dimensions of building: 154 feet by 76 feet.

District: Colombia; 13 stakes.

~~**Groundbreaking, site dedication:** June~~ 26, 1993, by Elder William R. Bradford of the First Quorum of Seventy and president of the South America North Area.

Status: Under construction.

BOISE IDAHO TEMPLE

Location: Just off Interstate 84 on South Cole Road in the west end of Boise; 1211 S. Cole Road, Boise, ID 83709-1781. Telephone: (208) 322-4422.

Site: 4.8 acres.

Exterior finish: Faced with light colored marble and has a slate roof. It is surrounded by three detached towers on each end; 8-foot statue of the Angel Moroni tops highest spire.

Temple design: Modern adaptation of six-spire design.

Architects: Church architectural staff, with assistance from Ron Thurber & Associates of Boise.

Construction adviser: Jerry Sears.

Contractor: Comtrol Inc. of Midvale, Utah.

Number of rooms: Four ordinance rooms, three sealing rooms, 42 total rooms.

Total floor area: 32,269 square feet, following 1987 addition.

Dimensions of building: 236 feet by 78 feet; statue of Angel Moroni on top spire.

District: Southwestern Idaho, eastern Oregon; 34 stakes.

Groundbreaking, site dedication: Dec. 18, 1982, by Elder Mark E. Petersen of the Council of the Twelve.

Dedication: May 25-30, 1984, by President Gordon B. Hinckley; 24 sessions. Addition dedicated by Elder James E. Faust of the Council of the Twelve, May 29, 1987.

Dedicatory prayer excerpt: *"May thy faithful Saints of this and future generations look to this beautiful structure as a house to which they will be made welcome . . . for the making of eternal covenants with thee, for inspiration and sanctification, as they serve unselfishly."*

BOSTON MASSACHUSETTS TEMPLE

Announced: Sept. 30, 1995 by the First Presidency.

Site: 8.86 acres

District: Maine, New Hampshire, Vermont, Rhode Island, New Brunswick, Massachusetts; 13 stakes.

Status: Awaiting groundbreaking.

BOUNTIFUL UTAH TEMPLE

Location: In the Bountiful foothills on east bench, 640 S. Bountiful Blvd, Bountiful, Utah. (1650 East). Telephone: (801) 296-2100

Site: 9 acres.

Exterior finish: Bethel white granite.

Temple design: Modern, with single spire.

Architect: Church architectural staff.

Contractor: Okland Construction Co.

Construction adviser: Michael

Enfield.

Number of rooms: Four endowment rooms, eight sealing rooms.

Total floor area: 104,000 square feet.

Dimensions of building: 195 feet by 157 feet; statue of Angel Moroni on top spire; 176 feet high.

District: Central and south Davis County, Utah; 29 stakes.

Groundbreaking, site dedication: May 2, 1992, by President Ezra Taft Benson.

Dedication: Jan. 8-14, 1994, by President Howard W. Hunter; 28 sessions.

Dedicatory prayer excerpt: *"May this house provide a spirit of peace to all who observe its majesty, and especially to those who enter for their own sacred ordinances and to perform the work for their loved ones beyond the veil. Let them feel of thy divine love and mercy. May they be privileged to say, as did the Psalmist of old, 'We took sweet counsel together, and walked unto the house of God in company.'"*

BUENOS AIRES ARGENTINA TEMPLE

Location: On southwest outskirts of Buenos Aires; Autopista Richieri y Puente 13, 1778 Ciudad Evita, Buenos Aires, Argentina. Telephone: (011-54-1) 487-1520.

Site: 3 acres.

Exterior finish: Light gray native granite.

Temple design: Modern adaptation of earlier six-spire design.

Dimensions: 178 by 71 feet. Angel Moroni statue is atop tallest spire, 112 feet.

Architects: Church architectural staff; local architect Ramon Paez.

Construction adviser: Gary Holland.

Contractor: Benito Roggio and Sons.

Number of rooms: Four ordinance rooms, three sealing rooms.

Total floor area: 11,980 square feet.

District: Argentina, Uruguay; 67 stakes.

Groundbreaking, site dedication: April 20, 1983, by Elder Bruce R. McConkie of the Council of the Twelve.

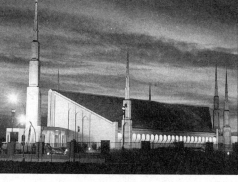

Dedication: Jan. 17-19, 1986, by President Thomas S. Monson; 11 sessions.

Dedicatory prayer excerpt: *"We remember that it was in this very city of Buenos Aires, on Christmas Day in the year 1925, just 60 years ago, that Elder Melvin J. Ballard, an apostle of the Lord, dedicated all of South America for the preaching of the gospel. What a fulfillment to an inspired prayer is evident today."*

CARACAS VENEZUELA TEMPLE

Announced: Sept. 30, 1995 by President Gordon B. Hinckley.

District: Venezuela, 9 stakes.

Status: Awaiting groundbreaking.

CHICAGO ILLINOIS TEMPLE

Location: 20 miles north of Chicago; 4151 West Lake Ave., Glenview, IL 60025. Telephone: (847) 299-6500.

Site: 13 acres.

Exterior finish: Gray buff marble, gray slate roof.

Temple design: Modern adaptation of earlier six-spire design.

Architects: Church architectural staff; local architect, Wight & Co.

Construction adviser: Virgil Roberts.

Contractor: Pora Construction Co., Des Plaines, Ill., with Utah Construction and Development Co.

Number of rooms: Five ordinance rooms, three sealing rooms.

Total floor area: Originally 17,850 square feet; 37,060 square feet following addition.

Dimensions of building: 236 feet by 78 feet; seven-foot-tall Angel Moroni statue is atop tallest spire, 112 feet high.

District: Michigan, Minnesota, Wisconsin; parts of Illinois, Iowa, Indiana, North Dakota, South Dakota; and Ohio; 57 stakes (15 of these stakes will be in the St. Louis Missouri Temple District when that temple is completed).

Groundbreaking, site dedication: Aug. 13, 1983, by President Gordon B. Hinckley.

Dedication: Aug. 9-13, 1985, by President Gordon B. Hinckley; 19 sessions.

Dedicatory prayer excerpt: *"We are mindful that thy Prophet Joseph and his brother Hyrum were martyred in Carthage, Ill., at a time of terrible conflict and persecution. May there now be peace and goodwill in the land. Bless the officers of this state and nation that they shall stand firmly for those principles of freedom and equity which were written into the Constitution of the United States under thine inspiration."*

COCHABOMBA BOLIVIA TEMPLE

Announced: Jan. 21, 1995.
District: Bolivia; 7 stakes.
Groundbreaking: Nov. 10, 1996, by President Gordon B. Hinckley.
Status: Under construction.

DALLAS TEXAS TEMPLE

Location: 12 miles north of the downtown area, at 6363 Willow Lane, Dallas, TX 75230. Telephone: (972) 991-1273.

Site: 6 acres.

Exterior finish: Light-colored marble tile walls, dark gray slate roof.

Temple design: Modern adaptation of earlier six-spire design.

Architects: Church architectural staff, with assistance from West & Humphries of Dallas.

Construction adviser: Virgil Roberts.

Contractor: Comtrol Inc. of Midvale, Utah.

Number of rooms: Five ordinance rooms, three sealing rooms; total rooms 43.

Total floor area: Originally 17,850 square feet; 42,383 square feet following addition.

Dimensions of building: 236 by 78 feet; tower, 95 feet; statue of Angel Moroni on top spire.

District: Texas (except El Paso region) and parts of Oklahoma, Arkansas, and Louisiana; 59 stakes (3 of these will be in

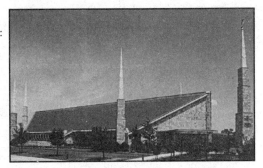

the St. Louis Missouri Temple District when that temple is completed).

Groundbreaking, site dedication: Jan. 22, 1983, by President Gordon B. Hinckley.

Dedication: Oct. 19-24, 1984, by President Gordon B. Hinckley; 23 sessions.

Dedicatory prayer excerpt: *"May this beautiful temple, standing in this community, become a declaration to all who shall look upon it of the faith of thy Saints in the revealed things of eternity, and may they be led to respect that which is sacred unto us, thy people."*

DENVER COLORADO TEMPLE

Location: In Littleton, a suburban community in Arapahoe County, about 20 miles south of Denver, at County Line Road and South University Boulevard; 2001 E. Phillips Circle, Littleton, CO 80122. Telephone: (303) 730-0220.

Site: 7.5 acres.

Exterior finish: Modern design; precast stone walls and built-up roof.

Dimensions: 187 by 160 feet; single 90-foot spire capped with statue of Angel Moroni.

Temple design: Modern.

Architects: Church architectural staff.

Supervising architect: Local architect, Bobby R. Thomas.

Construction adviser: Michael Enfield.

Contractor: Langley Constructors.

Number of rooms: Four ordinance rooms, six sealing rooms; total of 54 rooms.

Total floor area: 29,117 square feet.

District: Most of Colorado, eastern Wyoming, western North and South Dakota; part of Kansas, Nebraska, Oklahoma and New Mexico; 34 stakes (1 of these

stakes will be included in the Vernal Utah Temple District when that temple is completed).

Groundbreaking, site dedication: May 19, 1984, by President Gordon B. Hinckley.

Dedication: Oct. 24-28, 1986, by President Ezra Taft Benson; 18 sessions.

Dedicatory prayer excerpt: *"Touch the hearts of thy people that they may look to this temple as a refuge from the evil and turmoil of the world. May they ever live worthy of the blessings here to be found. May they be prompted to seek the records of their forebears and to serve here in their behalf, under that plan which thou hast revealed for the salvation and exaltation of thy children of all generations."*

FRANKFURT GERMANY TEMPLE

Location: In the center of Friedrichsdorf, a small town nine miles north of Frankfurt; Talstrasse #10, D-61381 Friedrichsdorf/TS, Germany. Telephone: (011-49-61) 72-5900-0.

Site: 5.2 acres.

Exterior finish: White granite, copper roof.

Architects: Church architectural staff; local architect, Borchers-Metzner-Kramer; project architect, Hanno Luschin.

Construction adviser: Henry Haurand.

Contractor: Hochtief AG.

Number of rooms: Four ordinance rooms, five sealing rooms; total rooms, 63.

Total floor area: 24,757 square feet.

Dimensions of building: 93 feet by 232 feet; statue of Angel Moroni on top spire, 82 feet high.

District: Belgium, the Netherlands, Luxembourg, northern France, much of Germany, and a small part of Austria; 21 stakes.

Groundbreaking, site dedication: July 1,

1985, by President Gordon B. Hinckley.

Dedication: Aug. 28-30, 1987, by President Ezra Taft Benson; 11 sessions.

Dedicatory prayer excerpt: *"The presence of this house, on the soil of this nation, is an answer to the prayers of thy people."*

FREIBERG GERMANY TEMPLE

Location: In Freiberg, about 120 miles south of Berlin; Hainchener strasse 64, 009599 Freiberg, Germany. Phone: (011-49-3) 731-23546.

Site: 1 acre.

Exterior finish: Exterior white German stucco over 24-inch thick brick walls, blue gray slate stone slab roof.

Temple design: Modern design with German influence; two high arches, reminicent of Gothic style, are parallel with front of building and bisected by two similar arches to form a single spire.

Architect: Emil B. Fetzer.

Government construction adviser: Dr. Dieter Hantzche, architect director of Bauakademie of Dresden.

Number of rooms: One ordinance room, two sealing rooms; 32 total rooms.

Total floor area: 7,840 square feet.

Dimensions of building: Square, 98 feet by 98 feet.

District: Eastern Germany and most of eastern Europe; 3 stakes.

Groundbreaking, site dedication: April 23, 1983, by Elder Thomas S. Monson.

Dedication: June 20-30, 1985, by President Gordon B. Hinckley; 7 sessions.

Dedicatory prayer excerpt: *"On this day of dedication our hearts turn to thee. We thank thee for this holy temple in this land and nation. We thank thee for all who have made possible its building — the officers of the government who have who have given encouragement and made available land and materials, the architects and the builders, and all who have made possible this glorious day of dedication."*

GUATEMALA CITY TEMPLE

Location: At the base of hills in southeastern Guatemala City; 24 Avenida 2-20, Zona 15, Vista Hermosa 1, Guatemala City, Guatemala. Telephone: (011-502) 369-3426.

Site: About 1.4 acres.

Exterior finish: Natural white Guatemala marble.

Temple design: Modern adaptation of earlier six-spire design.

Architects: Church archectural staff, assisted by Jose Asturias, Guatemala City.

Construction adviser: David Judd.

Contractor: Isa Constructors Aires Y Cia Ltd.

Number of rooms: Four ordinance rooms, three sealing rooms; 32 total rooms.

Total floor area: 11,610 square feet.

Dimensions of building: 178 feet by 72 feet, six spires; statue of Angel Moroni tops

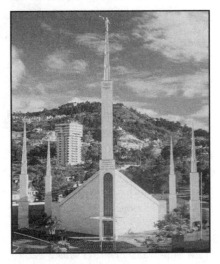

126-foot spire.

District: Guatemala, Nicaragua, Costa Rica, El Salvador, Honduras, Belize, southern Mexico; 75 stakes.

Groundbreaking, site dedication: Sept. 12, 1982, by Elder Richard G. Scott of the First Quorum of the Seventy.

Dedication: Dec. 14-16, 1984, by President Gordon B. Hinckley; 10 sessions.

Dedicatory prayer excerpt: *Bless our land, O Father, this nation of Guatemala where stands thy holy house. May those who govern do so in righteousness. . . . Bless them as they act to preserve the liberties. . . and enhance the prosperity of the people. May there be peace in the land."*

GUAYAQUIL ECUADOR TEMPLE

Announced: March 31, 1982, by President Gordon B. Hinckley.

Location: El Principado - De Las Lomas.

Site: 6.2 acres

Exterior finish: Granite.

Temple design: Modern.

Architects: Rafael Velez Calisto, Architects & Consultants.

Number of rooms: four ordinance rooms; three sealing; 138 total rooms.

Total floor area: 45,000 square feet.

Dimensions of building: 154 feet by 76 feet.

District: Ecuador; 17 stakes.

Groundbreaking, site dedication: Aug. 10, 1996, by Elder Richard G. Scott.

Status: Under construction.

HARTFORD CONNECTICUT TEMPLE

On Sept. 30, 1995, President Gordon B. Hinckley announced that two temples would replace the one announced previously for Hartford, Conn. New temples will be built in White Plains, N.Y., and Boston, Mass. During the years of searching for a suitable temple site in the Hartford area, the Church grew appreciably in the areas to the north and south of Hartford.

HAWAII TEMPLE

Location: In Laie, on the northeast side of the island of Oahu, formerly a 6,000-acre plantation purchased by the Church in 1865, 32 miles from Honolulu; P.O. Box 988, 55-600 Naniloa Loop, Laie, HI 96762. Telephone: (808) 293-2427.

Site: 11.4 acres, a portion of original property purchased by Church.

Exterior finish: Built of concrete made of the crushed lava rock of the area, reinforced with steel. After hardening, it was dressed on the exterior by pneumatic stone cutting tools that produced a white cream finish.

Temple design: The first of three temples built with no tower; shaped like a Grecian cross and suggestive of the ancient temples found in South America.

Architects: Hyrum C. Pope and Harold W. Burton.

General superintendent: Samuel E. Woolley. Much of the work on this temple was done by the Polynesian Saints.

Number of rooms: Three ordinance rooms, six sealing rooms; total rooms after remodeling, 163.

Total floor area: 10,500 square feet originally; approximately 40,971 square feet after remodeling.

Dimensions of building: 140 feet by 282 feet, rising to a height of 50 feet above the upper terrace. Very similar "cubical contents" as ancient temple of Solomon.

District: Hawaii and some central Pacific islands, 13 stakes.

Groundbreaking, site dedication: June 1, 1915, site dedicated by President Joseph F. Smith.

Dedication: Thanksgiving Day, Nov. 27, 1919, by President Heber J. Grant.

Rededicated June 13-15, 1978, by President Spencer W. Kimball after extensive remodeling; nine sessions.

Dedicatory prayer excerpt: *"May all who come upon the grounds which surround this temple, in the years to come, whether members of the Church or not, feel the sweet and peaceful influence of this blessed hallowed spot."*

HONG KONG TEMPLE

Location: Cornwall Street, Kowloon Tong on the Kowloon Peninsula. 2 & 4a Cornwall St., Kowloon Tong, Kowloon, Hong Kong. Telephone: (011-852) 2339-8100.

Announced: Oct. 3, 1992, by President Gordon B. Hinckley.

Site: .3 acres.

Exterior finish: Polished granite.

Temple design: Hong Kong colonial.

Architects: Liang Peddle Thorpe Architects.

Number of rooms: 2 ordinance rooms, two sealing rooms.

Total floor area: 22,600 square feet.

Dimensions of building: 70 feet by 92 feet; statue of Angel Moroni is 135 feet above main floor.

District: Hong Kong and Macau; 6 stakes.

Groundbreaking, site dedication: Jan. 22, 1994 by Elder John K. Carmack of the Seventy and Asia Area president.

Dedication: May 26-27, 1996; by President Gordon B. Hinckley; 7 sessions.

Dedicatory prayer excerpt: *"Thy Church in this area now comes to full maturity with the dedication of this sacred temple. We pray that this harvest of souls may continue, that in the future as in the present, Thy people may be free and secure in their worship and that none shall hinder the service of missionaries called to this area. We pray that Thy work may grow and prosper in the great Chinese realm, and may those who govern be ever receptive to those called and sent as messengers of revealed truth."*

IDAHO FALLS TEMPLE

Location: In northwestern Idaho Falls on the banks of the Snake River; 1000 Memorial Drive, Idaho Falls, ID 83402. Telephone: (208) 522-7669.

Site: 7 acres.

Exterior finish: Built of reinforced concrete. A mixture of white quartz aggregate and white cement called cast stone covers the 16-inch thick exterior walls in slabs two inches thick.

Temple design: Modern-contemporary.

Architects: Church board of temple architects: Edward O. Anderson, Georgius Y. Cannon, Ramm Hansen, John Fetzer, Hyrum C. Pope, Lorenzo S. Young.

Construction adviser: Arthur Price.

Contractor: Birdwell Finlayson of Pocatello, Idaho.

Number of rooms: 1 ordinance room, 9 sealing rooms; total of 38 rooms in original plans; 84 following various additions.

Total floor area: 86,972 square feet.

Dimensions of building: 175 feet by 190 feet; tower 148 feet high. Two annexes added 7,700 square feet. A 12-foot statue of Angel Moroni was added to the tower Sept. 5, 1983.

District: Most of eastern Idaho, parts of Montana and Wyoming; 65 stakes.

Groundbreaking, site dedication: Dec. 19, 1939, ground broken by David Smith, North Idaho Falls Stake president. Site dedicated Oct. 19, 1940, by President David O. McKay of the First Presidency.

Dedication: Sept. 23-25, 1945, by President George Albert Smith.

Dedicatory prayer excerpt: *"We pray that thou wilt accept this temple as a freewill offering from thy children, that it will be sacred unto thee."*

JOHANNESBURG SOUTH AFRICA TEMPLE

Location: 2 miles north of city center; 7 Jubilee Rd., Parktown, Johannesburg, 2193, South Africa. Telephone: (011-27-11) 642-4952.

Site: One acre.

Exterior finish: Masonry exterior.

Temple design: Modern adaptation of earlier six-spire design.

Architects: Church architectural staff; local architect, Halford & Halford.

Construction adviser: Stanley G. Smith.

Contractor: Tiber Bonvac.

Number of rooms: Four ordinance rooms, three sealing rooms.

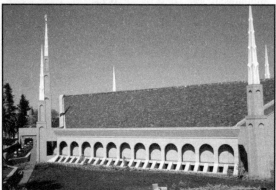

Total floor area: 13,025 square feet.

Dimensions of building: 178 feet by 71 feet; Angel Moroni statue is atop tallest spire at 112 feet.

District: Africa south of the Sahara; 14 stakes.

Groundbreaking, site dedication: Nov. 27, 1982, by Elder Marvin J. Ashton of the Council of the Twelve.

Dedication: Aug. 24-25, 1985, by President Gordon B. Hinckley; 4 sessions.

Dedicatory prayer excerpt: *"Almighty God, wilt thou overrule for the blessing and safety of thy faithful Saints. We pray for peace in this troubled land. Bless this nation which has befriended thy servants. May those who rule in the offices of government be inspired to find a basis for reconciliation among those who now are in conflict one with another. May the presence of thy house on the soil of this land bring blessings to the entire nation."*

JORDAN RIVER TEMPLE

Location: About 15 miles south of Salt Lake City in South Jordan, with access from Redwood Road and 13th West; 10200 South 1300 West, South Jordan, UT 84095. Telephone: (801) 254-3003.

Site: 15 acres, announced Feb. 3, 1978, by the First Presidency.

Exterior finish: Cast stone containing white marble chips. Tower appears same as the rest of the building, but in order to reduce weight it contains fiberglass in a product called cemlite.

Temple design: Modern.

Architect: Emil B. Fetzer, Church architect.

Resident project inspector: Jerry Sears.

Construction superintendent: Lawrence

O. Dansie for Layton Construction Co.

Number of rooms: Six ordinance rooms, 17 sealing rooms.

Total floor area: 153,641 square feet.

Dimensions of building: Basement and main floor, 211 by 218 feet; two upper levels, 140 by 166 feet. Height to square is 58 feet, to top of tower, 199 1/2 feet. Tower topped with a 20-foot figure of the Angel Moroni.

District: Southern Salt Lake County in Utah; 94 stakes.

Groundbreaking, site dedication: June 9, 1979, by President Spencer W. Kimball.

Dedication: Nov. 16-20, 1981, by President Marion G. Romney; 15 sessions.

Dedicatory prayer excerpt: *"May all who enter have clean hands and pure hearts, and may they participate with faith in the ordinances to be given herein."*

KIRTLAND TEMPLE*

*No longer in use by the Church.

Location: Kirtland, Ohio, 25 miles east of Cleveland, on a hill west of the Chagrin River.

Site: Selected March 1833; deed recorded Aug. 4, 1834.

Exterior finish: Sandstone covered with stuccoed plaster.

Temple design: Adaptation of Federal Georgian and New England Colonial.

Architect: Joseph Smith.

Building committee: Hyrum Smith, Reynolds Cahoon and Jared Carter.

Master builder: Artemis Millett.

Number of rooms: Originally 15.

Total floor area: Approximately 15,000 square feet.

Dimensions of building: 79 feet by 59 feet; walls 50 feet high; tower height above ground, 110 feet.

Start of work: Hauling of sandstone to site began June 5, 1833.

Cornerstones: July 23, 1833.

Dedication: March 27, 1836, by President Joseph Smith.

Dedicatory prayer excerpt: *"And we ask thee, Holy Father, that thy servants may go forth from this house, armed with thy power and that thy name may be upon them. . . ."*

LAS VEGAS NEVADA TEMPLE

Location: On the east side of Las Vegas at edge of a residential area on the slope of Frenchman Mountain, 827 Temple View Drive, Las Vegas, NV 89110. Telephone: (702) 453-1263.

Site: 10.3 acres; announced April 7, 1984.

Exterior finish: White precast stone walls and copper roof and detailing.

Temple design: Six spires

Architects: Tate & Snyder.

Construction adviser: Gary Holland

Contractor: Hogan & Tingey.

Number of rooms: four ordinance rooms, 6 sealing rooms.

Total floor area: 80,900 square feet.

Dimensions of building: 260 feet by 127

feet; statue of Angel Moroni on top spire, 119 feet.

District: Southern Nevada, parts of Arizona and California; 22 stakes.

Groundbreaking, site dedication: Nov. 30, 1985, by President Gordon B. Hinckley.

Dedication: Dec. 16-18, 1989, by President Gordon B. Hinckley; 11 sessions.

Dedicatory prayer excerpt: *"Within its walls are to be tasted the refreshing waters of living and eternal truth. For all who enter the portals of thy house may this be an oasis of peace and life and light, in contrast with the clamor and evil and darkness of the world."*

LIMA PERU TEMPLE

Location: Southwest part of Lima, in the Molina district; Avenida Javier Prado Este y Av. Los Ingenieros, La Molina, Lima, Peru. Telephone: (011-51-13) 48-0418.

Site: 4.5 acres.

Exterior finish: Local granite, Oriental design.

Temple design: Modern adaptation of earlier six-spire design.

Dimensions of building: 178 by 71 feet. Angel Moroni statue is atop tallest spire at 112 feet.

Architects: Church architectural staff; local architect Jose Asturias.

Construction adviser: Sergio Gomez.

Number of rooms: Four ordinance rooms, three sealing rooms.

Total floor area: 10,052 square feet.

District: Peru and most of Bolivia, Colombia, Ecuador and Venezuela; 141 stakes until Ecuador, Colombia and Venezuela temples are completed.

Groundbreaking, site dedication: Sept. 11, 1982, by Elder Boyd K. Packer.

Dedication: Jan. 10-12, 1986, by President Gordon B. Hinckley; 11 sessions.

Dedicatory prayer excerpt: *"We are particularly mindful this day of the sons and daughters of Lehi. They have known so much of suffering and sorrow in their many generations. They have walked in darkness and in servitude. Now thou hast touched them by the light of the everlasting gospel. The shackles of darkness are falling from their eyes as they embrace the truths of thy great work."*

LOGAN TEMPLE

Location: On eastern bench overlooking Cache Valley; 175 N. 300 East, Logan, UT 84321. Telephone: (801) 752-3611.

Site: 9 acres, selected by Brigham Young, May 15, 1877.

Exterior finish: Dark-colored, siliceous limestone, extremely hard and compact in texture, was used for the major portion of the temple. Buff-colored limestone, more easily carved, was used wherever intricate shaping was necessary.

Temple design: Castellated style.

Architect: Truman O. Angell.

Construction heads: Superintendent of construction, Charles O. Card; master mason, John Parry; plastering foreman, William Davis. Labor needs met by 25,000 people who worked on Logan Temple.

Number of rooms: four ordinance rooms, 11 sealing rooms; five stories, total rooms, 60.

Total floor area: Originally 59,130 square feet; 115,507 square feet after remodeling.

Dimensions of building: 171 feet by 95 feet; 86 feet high. The east tower is 170 feet high; west tower, 165 feet high; four octagonal towers, each 100 feet high.

District: Northern Utah, southeastern Idaho; 41 stakes.

Groundbreaking, site dedication: May 17, 1877; site dedicated by Elder Orson Pratt, ground broken by President John W. Young of the First Presidency.

Dedication: May 17-19, 1884, by President John Taylor; 3 sessions.

On March 13-15, 1979, after extensive remodeling, the temple was rededicated by President Spencer W. Kimball; 9 sessions.

Dedicatory prayer excerpt: *"We ask that in this house a more full knowledge of thee and thy laws may be developed.... And, as all wisdom dwells with thee, and, as all light, truth and intelligence... we humbly seek unto thee for thy learning under thy guidance, direction and inspiration."*

LONDON TEMPLE

Location: 25 miles south of London, formerly an Elizabethan farm; Newchapel, Nr. Lingfield, Surrey, England, RH7 6HW. Telephone: (011-441-342) 832759.

Site: In June 1952, President David O. McKay and Elder Stayner Richards, president of the British Mission, selected site at Newchapel. Purchased several months later in 1953; 32 acres.

Exterior finish: Reinforced concrete and structural steel skeleton, walls of brick masonry faced with cut Portland limestone, white in color. Spire sheathed in lead-coated copper.

Temple design: Modern-contemporary.

Architect: Edward O. Anderson, Church architect.

Supervising architects: T.T. Bennett and Son, London.

Contractor: Kirk and Kirk, Ltd., London.

Number of rooms: four ordinance rooms, seven sealing rooms, total rooms, 64.

Total floor area: Originally 34,000 square feet; now 42,652 square feet.

Dimensions of building: 84 feet wide, 159 feet long, 56 feet to the square. The tower rises 156 feet 91/2 inches from ground level, spire 33 feet above that.

District: England, Scotland, Wales, Northern Ireland, Ireland and the Canary Islands; 44 stakes (20 of these will be in the Preston England Temple District when

that temple is completed).

Groundbreaking, site dedication: Aug. 10, 1953; site dedicated by David O. McKay, who broke ground on Aug. 27, 1955.

Dedication: Sept. 7-9, 1958, by President David O. McKay; 6 sessions. Rededicated Oct. 18-20, 1992, by President Gordon B. Hinckley; 10 sessions.

Dedicatory prayer excerpt: *"With humility and deep gratitude we acknowledge thy nearness, thy divine guidance and inspiration. Help us, we pray thee, to become even more susceptible in our spiritual response to thee.*

"Temples are built to thy holy name as a means of uniting thy people, living and dead, in bonds of faith, of peace and of love throughout eternity."

LOS ANGELES TEMPLE

Location: Atop a hill near Westwood Village, two miles west of Beverly Hills, 10777 Santa Monica Blvd., Los Angeles, CA 90025. Telephone: (310) 474-5569.

Site: On 13 of the original 24.23 acres purchased from the Harold Lloyd Motion Picture Company on March 23, 1937, by President Heber J. Grant.

Exterior finish: The exterior is covered with 146,000 square feet of Mo-Sai stone facing, a mixture of crushed quartz and white Portland cement quarried in Utah and Nevada. Wainscot around exterior is Rockville granite from Minnesota.

Temple design: Modern.

Architect: Edward O. Anderson, Church

architect. (Millard F. Malin, sculptor of 15-foot statue of Angel Moroni on spire.)

Superintendent: Vern Loder.

Contractor: Soren N. Jacobsen.

Number of rooms: four ordinance rooms, 10 sealing rooms; total rooms, 90.

Total floor area: 190,614 square feet, or approximately 4.5 acres.

Dimensions of building: 364 feet by 241 feet; overall height is 257 feet 11/2 inches.

District: Part of Southern California; 76 stakes.

Groundbreaking, site dedication: Sept. 22, 1951, by President David O. McKay.

Dedication: March 11-14, 1956, by President David O. McKay; 8 sessions.

Dedicatory prayer excerpt: *"May all who come within these sacred walls feel a peaceful, hallowed influence. Cause, O Lord, that*

even people who pass the grounds, or view the temple from afar, may lift their eyes from the groveling things of sordid life and look up to thee and thy providence."

MADRID SPAIN TEMPLE

Location: Barrio of Moratalez, corner of Hacienda DePaudres and Valdeberrando.

Announced: Country announced at general conference on April 4, 1993, by President Gordon B. Hinckley; city announced at groundbreaking of Mt. Timpanogos Utah Temple on Oct. 9, 1994.

Site: 12,846 square meters.

Exterior finish: Camaro Marble from Italy.

Temple design: Modern Classic.

Architects: Arquitechior Langdon, SA.

Number of rooms: four ordinance; four sealing; 100 total.

Total floor area: 5405.9 square meters.

Dimensions of building: 36.9 meters by 46 meters.

District: Spain, Portugal; 8 stakes.

Groundbreaking, site dedication: June 11, 1996, by President Gordon B. Hinckley.

Status: Under construction.

MANILA PHILIPPINES TEMPLE

Location: In Quezon City; 13 Temple Drive, Greenmeadows Subdivision, Quezon City, Metro Manila, Philippines 1110. Telephone: (011-63-2) 635-0954.

Site: About 3.5 acres.

Exterior finish: Ceramic tile.

Temple design: Modern adaptation of earlier six-spire design.

Architect: Church architectural staff, with assistance from Felipe M. Mendoza & Partners, Manila.

Construction adviser: Wayne Tuttle.

Contractor: A. C. K. Construction of Manila.

Number of rooms: four ordinance rooms, three sealing rooms; 34 total rooms.

Total floor area: 19,388 square feet.

Dimensions of building: 200 feet by 75 feet, six spires; tallest is 115 feet high, including statue of Angel Moroni.

District: Philippines, Micronesia, Indonesia, Singapore, Thailand, India, and part of Burma; 49 stakes.

Groundbreaking, site dedication: Aug. 25, 1982, by President Gordon B. Hinckley. Despite the threat of a typhoon, 2,000 members attended groundbreaking.

Dedication: Sept. 25-27, 1984, by President Gordon B. Hinckley; 9 sessions.

Dedicatory prayer excerpt: *"Lift the blight of poverty from which so many suffer. Particularly bless thy faithful Saints who live honestly with thee in the payment of their* tithes and offerings. Bless them that neither they nor their generations after them will go hungry, nor naked, nor without shelter from the storms that beat about them.

"We thank thee for this beautiful edifice and for all who have worked to make it possible. May it stand as a pillar of truth and as an invitation to all who look upon it to learn of the purposes for which it has been created."

MANTI TEMPLE

Location: Hill above U.S. Highway 89 in Sanpete Valley in Manti, Utah, 120 miles south of Salt Lake City; Temple Hill, Manti, UT 84642. Telephone: (801) 835-2291.

Site: 27 acres. "Manti Stone Quarry" had been prophesied as site for a temple since area's settlement in 1849. President Brigham Young on June 25, 1875, announced the temple would be built there. It then became known as "Temple Hill."

Exterior finish: Fine-textured, cream-colored oolite limestone obtained from quarries in hill upon which it is built.

Temple design: The castellated style reflecting influence of Gothic Revival, French Renaissance Revival, French Second Empire and colonial architecture.

Architect: William H. Folsom.

Construction heads: William H. Folsom from Oct. 15, 1877, to Aug. 7, 1888, when Daniel H. Wells took his place as supervisor; master mason, Edward L. Parry.

Number of rooms: Four floors including basement, one ordinance room and eight sealing rooms; 43 total rooms.

Total floor area: 86,809 square feet.

Dimensions of building: 171 feet by 95 feet; 86 feet high. The east tower is 179 feet high, west tower 169 feet high, building at ground level 60 feet above highway below.

District: Central and southeastern Utah and southwestern Colorado; 29 stakes.

Groundbreaking, site dedication: April 25, 1877, by President Brigham Young.

Dedication: May 17, 1888, private dedication held; dedicated by President Wilford Woodruff. Three public dedicatory services held May 21-23, 1888; Elder Lorenzo Snow, then of the Council of the Twelve, read prayer.

Rededicated June 14-16, 1985, by President Gordon B. Hinckley; 9 sessions.

Dedicatory prayer excerpt: *"May this holy temple be to them as one of the gates of heaven, opening into the straight and narrow path that leads to endless lives and eternal dominion."*

MEXICO CITY TEMPLE

Location: Near Aragon public park and zoological gardens, bounded by Calle Ignacio Allende and Calle Emiliano Capata; Avenida 510 #90, Col. San Juan de Aragon, Mexico D.F. 07950. Telephone: (011-52-5) 551-4347.

Site: 7 acres.

Exterior finish: White cast stone, ornate with adaptations of ancient Mayan designs, especially on upper portion of the structure.

Temple design: Modern adaptation of ancient Mayan architecture.

Architect: Emil B. Fetzer, Church architect.

Resident project inspector: Ricardo Espiriti.

Construction superintendent: Jose Ortiz for Urbec Construction Co.

Number of rooms: Four ordinance rooms, 11 sealing rooms.

Total floor area: 117,133 square feet.

Dimensions of building: Basement and

first floors, 178 by 214.5 feet; two upper levels, 119.5 by 157 feet. Height to square, 70 feet; to top of tower, 152 feet. Statue of Angel Moroni stands on top tower.

District: Most of Mexico; 138 stakes.

Groundbreaking, site dedication: Nov. 25, 1979, by Elder Boyd K. Packer of the Council of the Twelve, 10,000 people attended.

Dedication: Dec. 2-4, 1983, by President Gordon B. Hinckley; 9 sessions.

Dedicatory prayer excerpt: *"Bless thy Saints in this great land and those from other lands who will use this temple. Most have in their veins the blood of Father Lehi. Thou hast kept thine ancient promises."*

MONTERREY MEXICO TEMPLE

Announced: In December 1995 by the First Presidency.

District: Northern Mexico; 49 stakes.
Status: Awaiting groundbreaking.

MOUNT TIMPANOGOS UTAH

Location: 742 North 900 East, American Fork, Utah 84003. Telephone: (801)763-4540.

Announced: Oct. 3, 1992, by President Gordon B. Hinckley and President Thomas S. Monson.

Site: 16.7 acres, part of a larger parcel of land that was once a welfare farm.

Exterior finish: Sierra white granite clad temple with art glass windows and bronze doors.

Temple design: Traditional, with a single spire.

Architects: Church physical facilities staff.

Contractor: Okland Construction Company.

Number of rooms: four ordinance, eight sealing; total 239 rooms.

Total floor area: 104,000 square feet.

Dimensions of building: 195 feet by 157 feet; 190 foot spire, including statue of Angel Moroni.

District: Northern Utah County and Wasatch County; 43 stakes.

Groundbreaking, site dedication: Oct. 9, 1993, by President Gordon B. Hinckley.

Dedication: Oct. 13-19 1996, by President Gordon B. Hinckley; 27 sessions.

Dedicatory prayer excerpt: *"May it be a beacon of peace and a refuge to the troubled. May it be an holy sanctuary to those whose burdens are heavy and who seek Thy consoling comfort."*

NASHVILLE TENNESSEE TEMPLE

Announced: Nov. 9, 1994, by the First Presidency.

District: Tennessee, Alabama, West Virginia, Ohio, Indiana, Mississippi, Kentucky; 19 stakes.

Status: Awaiting groundbreaking.

NAUVOO TEMPLE**

**No longer stands; burned by arson fire in 1848 after Nauvoo exodus; walls later destroyed by a tornado.

Location: In Nauvoo, Ill., on a high bluff on the east side of the Mississippi River. Temple block bounded by Woodruff, Mulholland, Knight and Wells streets.

Site: Selected in October 1840 by Joseph Smith on property known as the Wells addition, slightly less than 4 acres.

Exterior finish: Light gray limestone quarried to the north and south of the city.

Temple design: Incorporated several types of architecture, no single style dominating.

Architect: William Weeks.

Temple building committee: Alpheus Cutler, Elias Higbee and Reynolds Cahoon. After the death of Elias Higbee in 1843, Hyrum Smith replaced him until his own death.

Number of rooms: Approximately 60.

Total floor area: Approximately 50,000 square feet.

Dimensions of building: Approximately 128 feet by 88 feet; 65 feet high, with the tower and spire reaching to 165 feet.

Cornerstones: April 6, 1841, President Joseph Smith presiding.

Dedication: Portions of the temple were dedicated and used as soon as completed. To avoid possible violence, a private dedication was held April 30, 1846, with Orson Hyde and Joseph Young officiating. The temple was dedicated publicly May 1-3, 1846, with the dedicatory prayer offered by Orson Hyde.

Dedicatory prayer excerpt: *"We thank thee that thou hast given us strength to accomplish the charges delivered by thee. Thou hast seen our labors and exertions to accomplish this purpose. By the authority of the Holy Priesthood now we offer this building as a sanctuary to thy worthy name. We ask thee to take the guardianship into thy hands and grant thy spirit shall dwell here and may all feel a sacred influence on their hearts that His Hand has helped this work."*

NEW ZEALAND TEMPLE

Location: At site of Church College of New Zealand in Temple View, outside of Hamilton, New Zealand. Hamilton is 75 miles south of Auckland; Private Bag 3003, Hamilton, New Zealand. Telephone: (011-64-7) 846-2750.

Site: Temple site and college grounds, 86 acres.

Exterior finish: Reinforced concrete block, manufactured at site, structural steel; painted white.

Temple design: Modern-contemporary.

Architect: Edward O. Anderson, Church architect.

Construction chairman: Wendell B. Mendenhall.

Construction supervisor: E. Albert Rosenvall and George R. Biesinger.

Number of rooms: one ordinance room, three sealing rooms, 75 total rooms.

Total floor area: 34,000 square feet.

Dimensions of building: 159 feet by 84 feet; total height of tower, 215 feet above highway, 157 feet above ground line.

District: New Zealand and nearby South Pacific islands; 22 stakes.

Groundbreaking, site dedication: Dec. 21, 1955. First sod turned by Ariel Ballif, Wendell B. Mendenhall, and George R. Biesinger.

Dedication: April 20, 1958, by President David O. McKay.

Dedicatory prayer excerpt: *"We invoke thy blessing particularly upon the men and women who have so willingly and generously contributed their means, time and effort to the completion of this imposing and impressive structure. Especially we mention all those who have accepted calls as labor missionaries and literally consecrated their all upon the altar of service."*

NUKU'ALOFA TONGA TEMPLE

Location: At site of Church's Liahona College, several miles outside of Nuku'alofa; Loto Rd., Tongatapu, Nuku'alofa, Tonga. Telephone: (011-676) 29-255.

Site: 5 acres.

Exterior finish: "R-wall" exterior finish and insulation system on concrete block; split cedar shake shingles on roof.

Temple design: Modern.

Architect: Emil B. Fetzer, Church architect.

Construction adviser: Richard Westover and Richard Rowley.

Contractor: Utah Construction & Development.

Number of rooms: Three sealing rooms, two ordinance rooms; 31 total rooms.

Total floor area: 13,020 square feet.

Dimensions of building: 142.88 feet by 115.32 feet; statue of Angel Moroni on top spire, 75 feet high.

District: Tongan islands, Fiji; 20 stakes.

Groundbreaking, site dedication: Feb. 18, 1981, by President Spencer W. Kimball with Tonga's King Taufa'ahau Tupou IV. Nearly

7,000 people attended.

Dedication: Aug. 9-11, 1983, by President Gordon B. Hinckley; 7 sessions.

Dedicatory prayer excerpt: *"We ask that thou wilt accept this temple as the gift of thy people presented unto thee with love for the accomplishments of thy holy purposes with reference to thy children. It is thy house. It is the house of thy Son. May it always be held in reverence by thy people."*

OAKLAND TEMPLE

Location: On hill overlooking Oakland, Berkeley, San Francisco and the Bay, near intersection of Lincoln Avenue and Warren Freeway; 4700 Lincoln Ave., Oakland, CA 94602. Telephone: (510) 531-3200.

Site: Inspected and approved by President David O. McKay in 1942; 14.5 acres purchased Jan. 28, 1943; additional land acquired later to make 18.3 acres.

Exterior finish: Reinforced concrete faced with Sierra white granite from Raymond, Calif.

Temple design: Modern, with an Oriental motif.

Architect: Harold W. Burton. Resident architect supervisor, Arthur Price.

Construction chairman: W. B. Mendenhall.

Construction supervisor: Robert C. Loder. Contractors: Leon M. Wheatley

Co., Palo Alto, Calif., and Jacobsen Construction Co., Salt Lake City.

Number of rooms: four ordinance rooms, 7 sealing rooms; 265 total rooms.

Total floor area: 82,417 square feet.

Dimensions of building: Temple proper, 210 feet by 190 feet with a central tower rising 170 feet; other towers 96 feet.

District: Northern California and western Nevada; 67 stakes.

Groundbreaking, site dedication: May 26, 1962, by President David O. McKay.

Dedication: Nov. 17-19, 1964, by President David O. McKay, 6 sessions.

Dedicatory prayer excerpt: *"This temple is a monument testifying to the faith and loyalty of the members of thy Church in the payment of their tithes and offerings. We thank thee for every effort that has been put forth by the members, from every sacrifice that has been made by the young boys and girls who have given of their dimes and dollars, to the millionaire who gave of his thousands."*

OGDEN TEMPLE

Location: In downtown Ogden, between Grant Avenue and Washington Boulevard; 350 22nd Street, Ogden, UT 84401. Telephone: (801) 621-6880.

Site: Approved by President David O. McKay and announced Aug. 14, 1967; 18.3 acres.

Exterior finish: White cast stone with a fluted appearance, gold anodized aluminum grillwork, gold directional glass windows.

Temple design: Modern and functional.

Architect: Emil B. Fetzer, Church architect.

Construction chairman: Mark B. Garff and Fred A. Baker, vice chairman.

Contractor: Okland Construction Company.

Number of rooms: 6 ordinance rooms, 11 sealing rooms, 4 floors; 283 total rooms.

Total floor area: 115,000 square feet.

Dimensions of building: 200 feet by 184 feet; tower 180 feet above ground level; single tower of 180 feet.

District: Part of northeastern Utah, southwestern Wyoming; 67 stakes (2 of these will be included in the Vernal Utah Temple District when that temple is completed).

Groundbreaking, site dedication: Sept. 8, 1969, President N. Eldon Tanner conducted; prayers given by President Alvin R. Dyer and President Joseph Fielding Smith; ground broken by President Hugh B. Brown.

Dedication: Jan. 18-20, 1972, by President Joseph Fielding Smith; 6 sessions.

Dedicatory prayer excerpt: *"It has been our privilege, as guided by the whisperings of thy Spirit, to build unto thee this temple, which we now present unto thee as another of thy holy houses."*

ORLANDO FLORIDA TEMPLE

Location: On a knoll overlooking Butler chain of lakes at Apopka-Vineland Road on the edge of Orlando suburb of Windermere, five miles southwest of Orlando near Florida Turnpike and Interstate 4; 9000 Windy Ridge Road, Windermere, FL 34786. Telephone: (407) 876-0022.

Site: 13 acres.

Exterior finish: White precast concrete with marble chips.

Temple design: Classic modern with one spire.

Architects: Scott Partnership Architects.

Church project manager: Ralph Cluff.

Contractor: Brice Building Company.

Number of rooms: Four ordinance rooms, five sealing rooms.

Total floor area: 70,000 square feet.

Dimensions of building: 180 feet by 182 feet; tower with statue of Angel Moroni is 165 feet high.

District: Florida, part of southern Georgia; 34 stakes (10 of these will be included in the Santo Domingo Dominican Repub-lic Temple District when temple is completed).

Groundbreaking, site dedication: June 20, 1992, by Elder James E. Faust of the Council of the Twelve.

Dedication: Oct. 9-11, 1994, by President Howard W. Hunter; 12 sessions.

Dedicatory prayer excerpt: *"To all who look upon it, including those who reside in this area, may it ever present a picture of peace and beauty, a structure partaking of thy divine nature."*

PAPEETE TAHITI TEMPLE

Location: In Pirae, adjacent to Papeete, on Rua de Pierri Loti, Titioro; B.P. 5682, (Allee Pierre Loti, Titioro) Pirae, Tahiti, French Polynesia. Telephone: (011-689) 43-9118.

Site: 5 acres.

Exterior finish: Stucco, using imported white sand.

Temple design: Shows some European elements of French influence as well as Polynesian culture.

Architect: Emil B. Fetzer, Church architect; adapted by Temples and Special Projects Architecture.

Construction adviser: George Bonnet.

Contractor: Comtrol Inc., a Midvale, Utah, construction firm.

Number of rooms: 2 ordinance rooms, two sealing rooms; 29 total rooms.

Total floor area: 10,658 square feet.

Dimensions of building: 125 feet by 105 feet, with an eight-foot statue of Angel Moroni on a 66-foot spire.

District: French Polynesia; 5 stakes.

Groundbreaking, site dedication: Feb. 13, 1981, by President Spencer W. Kimball, who also offered a prayer of dedication

that the temple would be "a light to all in these islands."

Dedication: Oct. 27-29, 1983, by President Gordon B. Hinckley; 6 sessions.

Dedicatory prayer excerpt: *"We ask that thou wilt preserve [the temple]. . . as thy house. May it be protected by thy power from any who would defile it. May it stand against the winds and the rains."*

PORTLAND OREGON TEMPLE

Location: In a wooded suburb about 10 miles southwest of downtown Portland, in the northwest corner of Oswego, adjacent to Interstate 5; 13600 SW Kruse Oaks Blvd., Lake Oswego, OR 97035. Telephone: (503) 639-7066.

Site: The land was purchased by the Church in mid-1960s for a junior college, but 7.3 acres was later chosen as a temple site.

Exterior finish: White marble walls and slate roof.

Temple design: 6 spires.

Architects: Leland A. Gray, architect; Lee/Ruff/Waddle, site and local architects.

Construction adviser: Michael Enfield

Contractor: Zwick Construction Co.

Number of rooms: four ordinance, fourteen sealing rooms.

Total floor area: 65,000 square feet.

Dimensions of building: 270 feet by 183 feet, four towers 124 feet tall; statue of Angel Moroni on east spire, 169 feet tall.

District: Includes most of Oregon and parts of Washington and California; 37 stakes.

Groundbreaking, site dedication: Sept. 20, 1986, by President Gordon B. Hinckley.

Dedication: Aug. 19-21, 1989, by President Gordon B. Hinckley; 11 sessions.

Dedicatory prayer excerpt: *"May a spirit of solemnity rest upon all who enter herein. Open to their vision a glimpse of thy great and everlasting designs."*

PRESTON ENGLAND TEMPLE

Location: A6/M61 Link road, Hartwood Green, Chorley; Lancashire.

Announced: Oct. 19,1992, by President Gordon B. Hinckley.

Site: 15 acres or 6 hectares.

Exterior finish: Olympia white granite from Sardinia.

Temple design: Modern.

Architects: Church physical facilities staff.

Number of rooms: four ordinance rooms; four sealing rooms; 147 total.

Total floor area: 210,033 square feet (6482.53 square meters).

Dimensions of building: 102.3 feet by 174.9 feet (31 meters by 53 meters); 155 foot high spire (47 meters), including statue of Angel Moroni.

District: Parts of England, Scotland; 22 stakes.

Groundbreaking, site dedication: June 12, 1994, by President Gordon B. Hinckley.

Status: Under construction.

PROVO TEMPLE

Location: At the entrance of Rock Canyon on the east bench of Provo; 2200 Temple Hill Drive, Provo, UT 84604. Telephone (801) 375-5775.

Site: 17 acres. Announced by President David O. McKay on Aug. 14, 1967.

Exterior finish: White cast stone, gold anodized aluminum grills, bronze glass panels, and single spire finished in gold and anodized aluminum; similar to Ogden Temple.

Temple design: Modern and functional.

Architect: Emil B. Fetzer, Church architect.

Construction chairman: Mark B. Garff,

with Fred A. Baker, vice chairman.

Construction supervisor: Hogan and Tingey, general contractors.

Number of rooms: Six ordinance, 12 sealing rooms, 283 total rooms.

Total floor area: 115,000 square feet.

Dimensions of building: 200 by 184 feet; 175 feet high with a 118-foot spire on top of the building.

District: Central and eastern Utah; 59 stakes (47 of these will be included in the Mt. Timpanogos and Vernal Utah temple districts when those temples are completed).

Groundbreaking, site dedication: Sept. 15, 1969, ground broken by President Hugh B. Brown.

Dedication: Feb. 9, 1972; dedicatory prayer written by President Joseph Fielding Smith and read by President Harold B. Lee; 2 sessions.

Dedicatory prayer excerpt: *"We dedicate this temple to thee, the Lord. We dedicate it as a house of baptism, a house of endowment, a house of marriage, a house of righteousness for the living and the dead."*

RECIFE BRAZIL TEMPLE

Announced: Jan. 21, 1995, by the First Presidency.

Site: 5.36 acres

District: Northern Brazil; 21 stakes.

Groundbreaking: Nov. 15, 1996, by President Gordon B. Hinckley.

Status: Under construction.

ST. GEORGE TEMPLE

Location: near the center of St. George; 250 E. 400 South, St. George, UT 84770. Telephone: (801) 673-3533.

Site: 6 acres, selected by Brigham Young in 1871.

Exterior finish: Native red sandstone quarried north of the city was used for the temple which was then plastered white.

Temple design: Castellated Gothic style.

Architect: Truman O. Angell.

Construction superintendent: Miles P. Romney; Edward L. Parry, head stone mason.

Number of rooms: three ordinance rooms; eight sealing rooms, 64 rooms in original structure; 135 rooms after remodeling.

Total floor area: 56,062 square feet in original building; 110,000 square feet after remodeling completed in 1975.

Dimensions of building: 142 feet by 96 feet. To the top of the buttresses, the height is 80 feet, and to the top of the vane, 175 feet.

District: Southwestern Utah, small part of Nevada, Arizona; 34 stakes.

Groundbreaking, site dedication: Nov. 9, 1871, by President Brigham Young; site dedication prayer by George A. Smith.

Dedication: Jan. 1, 1877, completed portions were dedicated. Final dedication, April 6-8, 1877, President Brigham Young presiding, and Daniel H. Wells offered

prayer.

On Nov. 11-12, 1975, after extensive remodeling, the temple was rededicated by President Spencer W. Kimball; 5 sessions.

Dedicatory prayer excerpt: *"We implore thy blessings upon the various congregations of thy people who may assemble in this house from time to time."*

ST. LOUIS MISSOURI TEMPLE

Location: 12555 North Forty Drive, Town and Country, Missouri.

Site: 14 acres.

Exterior finish: Cast stone and Bethal white granite with thermal finish.

Temple design: Modern.

Architects: Chiodini Associates.

Number of rooms: four ordinance four sealing; eight total rooms.

Total floor area: 58,749 square feet.

Dimensions of building: 88 feet by 189 feet

District: Missouri, Nebraska, Kansas, Illinois, Indiana, Arkansas; 20 stakes.

Groundbreaking, site dedication: Oct. 13, 1993.

Dedication: pending completion.

SALT LAKE TEMPLE

Location: On Temple Square in the center of Salt Lake City; 50 W. North Temple St., Salt Lake City, UT 84150. Telephone: (801) 240-2640.

Site: 10 acres. Selected July 28, 1847, by Brigham Young.

Exterior finish: Granite from Little Cottonwood Canyon, 20 miles to the southeast of Salt Lake City. The chapel and office annex are reinforced concrete faced with Utah granite.

Temple design: Suggestive of Gothic and other classical styles, but unique and distinctive.

Architect: Truman O. Angell, Church architect, worked out plans under direction of Brigham Young. During Angell's illness, William Folsom temporarily filled his post. After Angell's death in 1887, Don Carlos Young completed work on the temple.

Construction supervisor: Daniel H. Wells supervised construction; "Public Works," was organized Jan. 26, 1850, to provide labor and materials.

Number of rooms: One ordinance room, 1four sealing rooms; 177 total rooms.

Total floor area: 253,015 square feet in the temple, including the annex.

Dimensions of building: 118 feet 6.75 inches by 181 feet 7.25 inches. At east end of the building, the height of the center pinnacle is 210 feet. The center of the three

towers on the west end is 204 feet high.

District: Tooele County and part of Salt Lake and Summit counties in Utah; 58 stakes.

Groundbreaking, site dedication: Feb. 14, 1853, President Brigham Young broke ground and Heber C. Kimball dedicated the site.

Dedication: April 6-24, 1893, by President Wilford Woodruff; 31 sessions.

On April 5, 1893, more than 600 non-LDS residents of Salt Lake City toured the temple, which had taken more than 40 years to complete.

Dedicatory prayer excerpt: *"When thy people. . . are oppressed and in trouble . . . we beseech thee, to look down from thy holy habitation in mercy and tender compassion."*

SAN DIEGO CALIFORNIA TEMPLE

Location: In the northern part of city of San Diego near the suburb of La Jolla on a ridge above the San Diego Freeway; 7474 Charmant Dr., San Diego, CA 92122. Telephone: (619) 622-0991.

Site: 7.2 acres.

Exterior finish: Marble chips in plaster.

Temple design: Modern, with two major towers.

Architects: Deems, Lewis & McKinnley-William Lewis, and Hyndman & Hyndman.

Project representative: Stanley G. Smith.

Contractor: Okland Construction Co.

Number of rooms: Four ordinance and eight sealing rooms.

Total floor area: 82,447 square feet.

Dimensions of building: 165 feet by 194 feet; roof 62 feet high; statue of Angel Moroni on top spire, 200 feet high.

Groundbreaking, site dedication: Ground broken Feb. 27, 1988, by President Ezra Taft Benson; site dedicated the same day by President Thomas S. Monson of the First Presidency.

District: Parts of Southern California and northwestern Mexico; 27 stakes.

Dedicated: April 25-30, 1993, by President Gordon B. Hinckley in 23 sessions.

Dedicatory prayer excerpt: *"We thank*

thee that hundreds of thousands of men and women of various faiths and philosophies have had the opportunity of walking through this sacred house prior to this time of dedication. May an attitude of respect and reverence grow within them. May very many of them be stirred to seek and learn the truths of thy restored work that they too might become eligible to enjoy the blessings offered herein. May any voices of criticism be stilled and any words of disrespect be silenced."

SANTIAGO CHILE TEMPLE

Location: At site of former Church school headquarters in Santiago suburb of Providencia on Pedro de Valdivia 1423; Pocuro #1940 Providencia, Santiago, Chile. Telephone: (011-56-2) 223-9976.

Site: 2.61 acres.

Exterior finish: Stucco on concrete block.

Temple design: Modern.

Architect: Emil B. Fetzer, Church architect.

Construction adviser: Gary Holland.

Contractor: H. Briones Y Cia & The Church of Jesus Christ of Latter-day Saints.

Number of rooms: Two ordinance rooms, three sealing

rooms; 31 total rooms.

Total floor area: 13,020 square feet.

Dimensions of building: 142.88 feet by 115.32 feet; statue of Angel Moroni on top spire, 76.5 feet high.

District: Chile; 93 stakes.

Groundbreaking, site dedication: May 30, 1981, by President Spencer W. Kimball, in a cold rain, attended by 6,000 members.

Dedication: Sept. 15-17, 1983, by President Gordon B. Hinckley; 10 sessions.

Dedicatory prayer excerpt: *"Bless thy work upon this great continent of South America which is part of the land of Zion. Bless thy work in this nation of Chile. May all that has been done in the past be but a prologue to a far greater work in the future. May thy people be recognized for the virtue of their lives."*

SANTO DOMINGO DOMINICAN REPUBLIC TEMPLE

Location: Avenidz Bolivar and Avenida Genesis.

Announced: Dec. 4, 1993, by the First Presidency.

Site: 6.58 acres.

Exterior finish: Granite.

Temple design: Modern.

Architects: The Scott Partnership.

Number of rooms: four ordinance rooms; four sealing room; 149 total.

Total floor area: 64,406 square feet.

Dimensions of building: 203 feet by 88 feet.

District: Caribbean; 7 stakes.

Groundbreaking, site dedication: August 18, 1996, by Elder Richard G. Scott.

Status: Under construction.

SAO PAULO TEMPLE

Location: In the Butanta section of Sao Paulo; Av. Prof. Francisco Morato 2390, CEP 05512-300, Sao Paulo, Brazil. Telephone: (011-55-11) 813-9622.

Exterior finish: Reinforced concrete faced with cast stone composed of quartz and marble aggregates set in special white-base cement.

Temple design: Modern design with Spanish influence.

Architect: Emil B. Fetzer, Church architect.

Construction chairman: Christiani Nielsen, general contractor.

Construction supervisor: Ross Jensen and James Magleby.

Number of rooms: Two ordinance rooms, four sealing rooms, 76 total rooms.

Total floor area: 51,279 square feet.

Dimensions of building: 116 feet by 256 feet, with tower reaching 101 feet, 4 inches.

District: Brazil, Paraguay, part of Bolivia; 149 stakes.

Groundbreaking, site dedication: March 20, 1976, by Elder James E. Faust, then an Assistant to the Twelve; attended by 2,000 Church members.

Dedication: Oct. 30-Nov. 2, 1978, by President Spencer W. Kimball; 10 sessions.

Dedicatory prayer excerpt: *"Our Father, may peace abide in all the homes of thy*

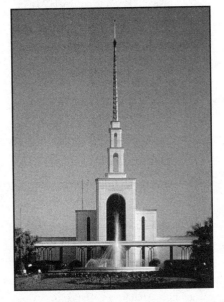

saints. May holy angels guard them. May prosperity shine upon them and sickness and disease be rebuked from their midst. May their land be made fruitful. May the waters be pure and the climate tempered to the comfort and well-being of thy people.

"Bless the poor of thy people, that the cry of want and suffering may not ascend unto thy saints."

SEATTLE TEMPLE

Location: Across from Bellevue Community College, near the Eastgate Interchange on Interstate 90; 2808 148th Ave. SE, Bellevue, WA 98007. Telephone: (206) 643-5144.

Site: 23.5 acres, selected June 1975.

Exterior finish: Reinforced concrete faced with white marble aggregate and cast stone.

Temple design: Modern.

Architect: Emil B. Fetzer, Church architect.

Project representative: Michael Enfield.

Construction superintendent: Kent Carter for Jacobsen Construction Co. of Salt Lake City.

Number of rooms: four ordinance rooms, 12 sealing rooms.

Total floor area: 110,000 square feet.

Dimensions of building: Ground level is 142 feet by 194 feet; upper levels are 117 feet by 163 feet. Height to square is 70 feet; to top of the Angel Moroni, 179 feet.

District: Most of Washington, British Columbia, Alaska, northern Idaho; 59 stakes.

Groundbreaking, site dedication: May 27, 1978, by President Marion G. Romney of the First Presidency.

Dedication: Nov. 17-21, 1980, by President Spencer W. Kimball; 13 sessions.

Dedicatory prayer excerpt: *"Bless, we pray thee, the presidency of this temple and the matron and all the officiators herein. Help them to create a sublime and holy atmosphere so that all ordinances may be performed with love and a sweet, spiritual tone that will cause the members to greatly desire to be here, and to return again and again."*

SEOUL KOREA TEMPLE

Location: 500-23 Chang Chun-dong, Seodaemun-Ku, Seoul, Korea 120-180. Telephone: (011-82-2) 332-9526.

Site: 1 acre.

Exterior finish: Granite exterior.

Temple design: Modern adaptation of earlier six-spire design.

Dimensions of building: 178 feet by 71 feet; Angel Moroni statue is atop tallest spire at 112 feet.

Architects: Church architectural staff; local architect, Komerican Architects.

Construction adviser: Calvin Wardell.

Contractor: Woo Chang.

Number of rooms: Four ordinance rooms, three sealing rooms.

Total floor area: 12,780 square feet.

District: South Korea; 16 stakes.

Groundbreaking, site dedication: May 9, 1983, by Elder Marvin J. Ashton of the Council of the Twelve.

Dedication: Dec. 14-15, 1985, by President Gordon B. Hinckley; 6 sessions.

Dedicatory prayer excerpt: *"This is the*

first such house of the Lord ever constructed on the mainland of Asia, this vast continent where through the generations of the past have lived unnumbered hosts whose lives have not been touched by the saving principles of the gospel."

STOCKHOLM SWEDEN TEMPLE

Location: Vasterhaninge, about 13 miles southeast of Stockholm; Box 153, (Tempelvagen 5) S-13732 Vasterhaninge, Sweden. Telephone: (011-46) 8500-65500.

Exterior finish: Masonry exterior, copper roof.

Temple design: Modern adaptation of earlier six-spire design.

Architects: Church architectural staff; local architect, John Sjostrom.

Construction adviser: Henry Haurand.

Contractor: Johnson Construction Co.

Number of rooms: Four ordinance rooms; three sealing rooms.

Total floor area: 14,508 square feet.

Dimensions of building: 178 feet by 71 feet; Angel Moroni statue is atop tallest spire at 112 feet.

District: Sweden, Finland, Denmark, Norway; 9 stakes.

Groundbreaking, site dedication: March 17, 1984, by Elder Thomas S. Monson of the Council of the Twelve.

Dedication: July 2-4, 1985, by President Gordon B. Hinckley; 11 sessions.

Dedicatory prayer excerpt: *"Bless this nation where is found thy temple, and its sister nations. . . .*

"Save these nations from war and oppression, and may their people look to thee and open their doors and hearts to thy messengers of eternal truth."

SWISS TEMPLE

Location: In a northern suburb of Bern in a setting with the Alps on the south, and the Jura Mountains on the west and north; Tempelstrasse 4, Ch - 3052 Zollikofen, Switzerland. Telephone: (011-41-31) 911-0912.

Site: 7 acres, selected July 1952, by President David O. McKay and President Samuel E. Bringhurst of the Swiss-Austrian Mission.

Exterior finish: Built of reinforced concrete with a creamish gray terra cotta facing trimmed in white. Tower is white base and spire is gold-colored.

Temple design: Modern-contemporary, but similar to lines of early Church temples.

Architect: Edward O. Anderson, Church architect. Re-drawn into German specifications by Wilhelm Zimmer of Bercher and Zimmer Architects.

Contractor: Hans Jordi of Bern.

Number of rooms: four ordinance rooms, seven sealing rooms; total rooms, 82.

Total floor area: Originally 34,750 square feet; now 39,063 square feet.

Dimensions of building: 152 feet by 84 feet; top of tower rises 140 feet.

District: Switzerland, Austria, Spain, Portugal, Italy, southern France; 18 stakes.

Groundbreaking, site dedication: Aug. 5, 1953, by President David O. McKay.

Dedication: Sept. 11-15, 1955, by President David O. McKay; 10 sessions, Taber- nacle Choir participated. Rededicated Oct. 23-25, 1992, by President Gordon B. Hinckley; 10 sessions.

Dedicatory prayer excerpt: *"Increase our desire, O Father, to put forth even greater effort towards the consummation of thy purpose to bring to pass the immortality and eternal life of all thy children."*

SYDNEY AUSTRALIA TEMPLE

Location: In suburban Carlingford, 15 miles northwest of downtown Sydney; Pennant Hill Road & Moseley Street, Carlingford, NSW Australia 2118. Telephone: (011-61-2) 984-5471.

Area of site: 3 acres.

Exterior finish: Precast panels, white quartz finish, terra cotta roof tiles.

Temple design: Modern.

Architect: Emil B. Fetzer, Church architect, and R. Lindsay Little.

Construction adviser: D. Crosbie and Richard Rowley.

Contractor: J.P. Cordukes Pty. Ltd.

Number of rooms: Three sealing rooms, two ordinance rooms; 31 total rooms.

Total floor area: 13,020 square feet.

Dimensions of building: 145.11 feet by 115.14 feet; statue of Angel Moroni added to top spire.

District: Australia and Papua New Guinea; 26 stakes.

Groundbreaking, site dedication: Aug. 13, 1982, by Elder Bruce R. McConkie of the Council of the Twelve.

Dedication: Sept. 20-23, 1984, by President Gordon B. Hinckley; 14 sessions.

Dedicatory prayer excerpt: *"May this temple with its grounds be a place of beauty to all who look upon it. May they be touched by thy spirit."*

TAIPEI TAIWAN TEMPLE

Location: In the Taipei business district; 256 Ai Kuo East Road, Taipei, Taiwan, R.O.C. Telephone: (011-886-2) 351-0218.

Site: 0.5 acres.

Exterior finish: White ceramic tile.

Temple design: Modern adaptation of earlier six-spire design.

Architect: Church architectural staff with assistance from Philip Fei & Associates of Taipei.

Construction adviser: Harold Smith.

Contractor: I. Cheng Construction & Development Corp.

Number of rooms: four ordinance rooms, three sealing rooms; 32 total rooms.

Total floor area: 16,214 square feet.

Dimensions of building: 178 feet by 72 feet, six spires; statue of Angel Moroni rises to height of 126 feet.

District: Taiwan, 9 stakes.

Groundbreaking, site dedication: Aug. 27, 1982, by President Gordon B. Hinckley.

Dedication: Nov. 17-18, 1984, by President Gordon B. Hinckley; 5 sessions.

Dedicatory prayer excerpt: *"We thank thee for the firm foundation on which thy Church is now established in this part of the earth. We thank thee for this day when those who will use this temple may turn their hearts to their fathers, participating in this thy holy house in those ordinances which will make it possible for their deceased forebears to move forward on the way that leads to eternal life."*

TOKYO TEMPLE

Location: Opposite the Arisugawa Park; 5-8-10 Minami Azabu, Minato-Ku, Tokyo, Japan 106. Telephone: (011-813-3) 442-8171.

Site: 18,000 square feet (about 0.5 acre).

Exterior finish: Structural steel and reinforced concrete faced with 289 panels of precast stone, having the appearance of light gray granite.

Architect: Emil B. Fetzer, Church architect. Architect's local representative, Masao Shiina.

Resident engineer: Sadao Nagata.

Construction superintendent: Yuji Morimura for the Kajima Corporation.

Number of rooms: Two ordinance rooms, five sealing rooms.

Total floor area: 58,000 square feet.

Dimensions of building: Ground floor is 103 feet by 134 feet; upper levels are 103 by 105 feet. Height to square is 701.5 feet, to top of tower, 178.5 feet.

Design: Modern, one spire.

District: Japan; 25 stakes.

Groundbreaking, site dedication: Neither was held.

Dedication: Oct. 27-29, 1980, by President Spencer W. Kimball.

Dedicatory prayer excerpt: *"Kind Father,*

bless all those who come to this temple, that they may do so with humble hearts, in cleanliness, and honor, and integrity. We are grateful for these Saints, for their devotion and their faith, for their worthiness and their determination to be pure and holy."

TORONTO ONTARIO TEMPLE

Location: On the outskirts of Brampton, about 20 miles west of Toronto; 10060 Bramalea Rd, Brampton, Ontario, Canada L6R 1A1. Telephone: (905) 799-1122.

Site: Announced April 15, 1984; 13.4 acres.

Exterior finish: White cast stone.

Temple design: Modern.

Architects: Allward-Gouinlock Inc.

Supervising architects: Alfred T. West Jr. and Dagmar Wertheim.

Construction adviser: Jer-

ry Sears

Contractor: Milne & Nicholls Ltd.

Number of rooms: four ordinance rooms, six sealing rooms.

Total floor area: 56,000 square feet.

Dimensions of building: 154 feet by 208 feet; spire, 105 feet high with 11-foot statue of Angel Moroni.

District: Northeastern Canada and parts of Ohio, Michigan, New York, Pennsylvania, Maine and Vermont; 27 stakes.

Groundbreaking, site dedication: Oct. 10, 1987, by President Thomas S. Monson.

Dedication: Aug. 25-27, 1990, by President Gordon B. Hinckley; 11 sessions.

Dedicatory prayer excerpt: *"This nation has become a gathering place for people from scores of other lands. In their veins flows the blood of Israel. Many have hearkened to the testimony of thy servants and been favored with a knowledge of the principles and ordinances of thine everlasting gospel."*

VERNAL UTAH TEMPLE

Location: The temple is the remodeled 87-year-old Tabernacle on 200 South and 500 West, Vernal, Utah, some 180 miles east of Salt Lake City.

Announced: Feb. 13, 1994, in a letter to local Church leaders from the First Presidency.

Site: 1.6 acres.

Exterior finish: Face brick.

Temple design: Adaptation of Uintah Stake Tabernacle.

Architects: FFKR Architects of Salt Lake City, Utah.

Number of rooms: Two ordinance, three sealing.

Total floor area: 33,400 square feet.

District: East central Utah and parts of

Wyoming and Colorado; 12 stakes.

Groundbreaking, site dedication: June 11, 1996, by President Gordon B. Hinckley.

Dedication: Pending completion

WASHINGTON TEMPLE

Location: Wooded site in Kensington, Md., near Exit 20 of the Capital Beltway (Interstate 495), a half-hour drive from downtown Washington, D.C.; 9900 Stoneybrook Dr., Kensington, MD 20895. Telephone: (301) 588-0650.

Site: Selected in 1962; 52 acres.

Exterior finish: Reinforced concrete sheathed in 173,000 square feet of Alabama white marble.

Temple design: The total design portrays the Church as "a light to the world," with three towers to the east representing the Melchizedek Priesthood leadership, and those to the west, the Aaronic Priesthood leadership, said principal architect Keith W. Wilcox.

Architects: Fred L. Markham, Henry P. Fetzer, Harold K. Beecher, Keith W. Wilcox, under general direction of Church architect Emil B. Fetzer.

Contractor: Jacobsen, Okland, and

Sidney Foulger construction companies.

Number of rooms: Six ordinance rooms, fourteen sealing rooms, seven floors, 294 total rooms.

Total floor area: 160,000 square feet.

Dimensions of building: 248 feet long, 136 feet wide, not including annex or bridge to temple proper. Statue of Angel Moroni on highest spire 288 feet above ground.

District: Most of eastern United States, including some of New England; 64 stakes.

Groundbreaking, site dedication: Dec. 7, 1968, by President Hugh B. Brown.

Dedication: Nov. 19-22, 1974, by President Spencer W. Kimball; 10 sessions.

Dedicatory prayer excerpt: *"We are so grateful, our Father, that thy Son has thrown wide open the doors of the prisons for the multitudes who are waiting in the spirit world."*

WHITE PLAINS NEW YORK TEMPLE

Announced: Sept. 30, 1995, by President Gordon B. Hinckley.

District: Connecticut, Pennsylvania, New York; 14 stakes.

Status: Awaiting groundbreaking.

PROGRESS DURING ADMINISTRATIONS OF THE PRESIDENTS

	At beginning		At end	
	Stakes	Members*	Stakes	Members*
JOSEPH SMITH	0	280	2	26,146
BRIGHAM YOUNG	2	34,694	20	115,065
JOHN TAYLOR	23	133,628	31	173,029
WILFORD WOODRUFF	32	180,294	40	267,251
LORENZO SNOW	40	267,251	50	292,931
JOSEPH F. SMITH	50	292,931	75	495,962
HEBER J. GRANT	75	495,962	149	954,004
GEORGE ALBERT SMITH	149	954,004	184	1,111,314
DAVID O. MCKAY	184	1,111,314	500	2,807,456
JOSEPH FIELDING SMITH	500	2,807,456	581	3,218,908
HAROLD B. LEE	581	3,218,908	630	3,306,658
SPENCER W. KIMBALL	630	3,306,658	1,570	5,920,000
EZRA TAFT BENSON	1,570	5,920,000	1,980	8,688,511
HOWARD W. HUNTER	1,980	8,689,619	2,029	9,025,914
GORDON B. HINCKLEY	2,029	9,025,914		

* Nearest year-end total

CHRONOLOGY,
NEWS IN
REVIEW

HISTORICAL CHRONOLOGY OF THE CHURCH

This chronology gives a selected listing of important dates in Church history. Among the items excluded are many that can be found elsewhere in this Almanac, including information on General Authorities and the establishment of stakes and missions. Italicized entries are secular events that were taking place during the time.

1805

April 27 — *The U.S. Marines captured the port city of Derna in the Tripolitan War; the phrase "to the shores of Tripoli" in the official Marine hymn comes from this campaign.*

Dec. 23 — Joseph Smith Jr. was born in Sharon, Windsor Co., Vt., the fourth child of Joseph and Lucy Mack Smith.

1816

After living in several villages in central Vermont and New Hampshire, the Joseph Smith Sr. family moved to Palmyra, N.Y., and a couple of years later to a farm in nearby Manchester, N.Y.

1820

Spring — In Joseph Smith's First Vision, Jesus Christ answered his question about which church to join. Joseph had prayed for guidance in response to a religious revival in the area.

March 3 — *The Missouri Compromise, allowing slavery in Missouri but not anywhere else west of the Mississippi, was passed by Congress.*

1823

Sept. 21-22 — In five visits with Joseph Smith, the resurrected Moroni revealed the existence of ancient gold plates and instructed him on his role in restoring the gospel and translating the Book of Mormon.

Dec. 2 — *The Monroe Doctrine, stating opposition to European intervention in the Americas, was announced by President James Monroe in his annual message to Congress.*

1827

Jan. 18 — Joseph Smith married Emma Hale in South Bainbridge, N.Y. The couple met while Joseph was working in Harmony, Pa., for Josiah Stowell and boarding with Emma's father, Isaac Hale.

Aug. 6 — *The United States and Great Britain signed a treaty, continuing joint occupation of the Oregon country, which extended from the California border to Alaska.*

Sept. 22 — Joseph Smith received the plates of the Book of Mormon from the Angel Moroni at the Hill Cumorah. He also received the Urim and Thummim, which was used to assist in translation.

1828

February — Martin Harris took a transcript and partial translation of the Book of Mormon to Professor Charles Anthon of Columbia College and to Dr. Samuel L. Mitchell of New York. In June, Harris borrowed and lost 116 manuscript pages.

July 4 — *The age of railroading began in the United States when the first passenger railroad in the country, the Baltimore & Ohio, started operation.*

1829

May 15 — Joseph Smith and Oliver Cowdery received the Aaronic Priesthood from John the Baptist along the banks of the Susquehanna River, near Harmony, Pa. (See D&C 13.) The two baptized one another, as instructed.

May/June — Peter, James and John conferred the Melchizedek Priesthood upon Joseph Smith and Oliver Cowdery near the Susquehanna River between Harmony, Pa., and Colesville, N.Y.

June — The Book of Mormon translation was completed, and the three witnesses — Oliver Cowdery, David Whitmer and Martin Harris — viewed the plates in a vision (see D&C 17). Soon afterward, the plates were shown to eight other witnesses —Christian Whitmer, Jacob Whitmer, Peter Whitmer Jr., John Whitmer, Hiram Page, Joseph Smith Sr., Hyrum Smith and Samuel H. Smith.

1830

The first covered wagons, led by Jedediah Smith and William Sublette of the Rocky Mountain Fur Company, made the trek from the Missouri River to the Rocky Mountains.

March 26 — The Book of Mormon was published in Palmyra, N.Y., by Joseph Smith. E.B. Grandin printed 5,000 copies for $3,000.

April — The revelation on Church government (see D&C 20) outlined procedures for organizing the Church, duties of members and officers, need for record-keeping and procedures for baptism and sacrament administration.

April 6 — Joseph Smith organized the "Church of Christ" at the Peter Whitmer Sr. home in Fayette, N.Y., with six incorporators as required by law — Joseph Smith, Oliver Cowdery, Hyrum Smith, Peter

Whitmer Jr., David Whitmer and Samuel H. Smith.

April 11 — Oliver Cowdery preached the first public discourse of the new Church at a meeting in the Peter Whitmer home.

June — The "Words of Moses," later incorporated in the Pearl of Great Price, were revealed to Joseph Smith. The prophecy of Enoch was revealed to the Prophet in December.

June — Joseph Smith was arrested on charges of disorderly conduct but was acquitted in a trial at South Bainbridge, N.Y. This was the first of what would be many trumped-up charges against the Prophet.

June 9 — The first conference of the Church, which now numbered 27 members, convened in Fayette, N.Y.

June 30 — Samuel H. Smith left on a mission to neighboring villages, including Mendon, N.Y., where the Young and Kimball families resided.

Oct. 17 — Following a revelation received by the Prophet Joseph Smith (See D&C 32), Parley P. Pratt, Oliver Cowdery, Peter Whitmer Jr. and Ziba Peterson began a mission to the Lamanites, leaving copies of the Book of Mormon with the Cattaraugus Indians in New York, the Wyandots in Ohio and the Shawnees and Delawares on the Missouri frontier. They stopped en route to teach and baptize Sidney Rigdon and a congregation of his followers in the Kirtland, Ohio, area.

Dec. 30 — The Saints were commanded in a revelation (See D&C 37) to gather in Ohio, the first commandment concerning a gathering in this dispensation.

1831

Feb. 4 — Edward Partridge was named "bishop unto the Church." (See D&C 41.) This was the first revelation given through the Prophet Joseph Smith at Kirtland, Ohio.

June 3-6 — At a conference in Kirtland, the first high priests were ordained, and elders were called to go to Jackson County, Mo. (See D&C 52.)

Aug. 2 — During a ceremony in Kaw Township, 12 miles west of Independence in Jackson County, Mo., Sidney Rigdon dedicated the Land of Zion for the gathering of the Saints. Joseph Smith dedicated a temple site the following day on Aug. 3.

Dec. 12 — *The Republican Party held the first nominating convention of a major party in the United States.*

1832

Jan. 25 — Joseph Smith was sustained president of the high priesthood at a conference at Amherst, Ohio. Sidney Rigdon and Jesse Gause were named counselors in March 1832. Gause's service in this capacity is unconfirmed by historical records. Frederick G. Williams was called by revelation (see D&C 81) to replace him.

Feb. 16 — While working on the inspired revision of the Bible, Joseph Smith and Sidney Rigdon received a vision of the three degrees of glory. (See D&C 76.)

May 21 — *The Democratic Party formally adopted its present name at a convention in Baltimore, Md.*

June — Elders began teaching in Canada, the first missionary effort outside the United States.

June 1 — The *Evening and Morning Star*, the first LDS publication, was issued at Independence, Mo., with William W. Phelps as editor.

Dec. 25 — Revelation and prophecy on war (see D&C 87), commencing with the Civil War some 28 years later, was given to the Prophet Joseph Smith.

Dec. 27 — The revelation known as the "Olive Leaf" (D&C 88) was presented to the Church. Included were instructions leading to the organization of the School of the Prophets.

Dec. 28 — *John Calhoun became the first U.S. vice president to resign. Afterward, he won an election to fill a vacant Senate seat representing South Carolina.*

1833

Feb. 27 — The revelation known as the "Word of Wisdom" (D&C 89) was received at Kirtland, Ohio.

March 18 — The First Presidency of the Church was organized when Sidney Rigdon and Frederick G. Williams were appointed and set apart by Joseph Smith to be his counselors.

May 6 — The Saints were commanded by revelation to build a House of the Lord at Kirtland. (See D&C 94.) Further instructions concerning the building of the temple were given by revelation on June 1. (See D&C 95.)

July 2 — The Prophet Joseph Smith finished the translation of the Bible.

July 20 — A mob destroyed the *Evening and Morning Star* printing office in Independence, Mo., interrupting the printing of the Book of Commandments. The *Evening and Morning Star* began publication again on Dec. 18 in Kirtland.

Oct. 5 — The Prophet Joseph Smith left Kirtland, Ohio, for Canada, the only country outside the United States where the Prophet preached.

November — The Saints left Jackson

County, Mo., in response to mob threats and attacks.

Dec. 3 — *Oberlin College in Ohio opened, becoming the first co-educational college in the U.S.*

Dec. 18 — The Prophet Joseph Smith gave the first patriarchal blessings in this dispensation to his parents, three of his brothers and Oliver Cowdery. Joseph Smith Sr. was ordained the first Patriarch to the Church.

1834

Feb. 17 — The first high council of the Church was organized by revelation (see D&C 102) for the stake in Kirtland, Ohio, which was created on the same day. The Kirtland Stake was the first stake organized in the Church. A similar organization was created in Clay-Caldwell counties, Missouri, on July 3, 1834.

May 3 — At a conference of elders in Kirtland, the Church was first named "The Church of Jesus Christ of Latter-day Saints."

May 8 — Zion's Camp commenced its march from New Portage, Ohio, to Clay County, Mo., to assist the exiled Missouri Saints. The camp dispersed June 30.

June 30 — *The Indian Territory was created by an act of Congress.*

October — The *LDS Messenger and Advocate* began publication at Kirtland and continued until the Mormon evacuation of Ohio in 1838.

1835

The Church published a collection of hymns and sacred songs selected by Emma Smith. She had been appointed to the work in July 1830 (see D&C 25), but destruction of the Independence, Mo., printing press in 1833 had delayed publication.

Feb. 14 — The three witnesses to the Book of Mormon selected 12 apostles at a meeting of the members of Zion's Camp in Kirtland, Ohio, and the Quorum of the Twelve was organized.

Feb. 28 — The First Quorum of the Seventy was organized in Kirtland, and its first seven presidents named.

March 28 — A revelation in which various priesthood offices and powers were defined (See D&C 107) was received during a meeting of the First Presidency and Twelve in Kirtland.

May 4 — The Twelve left Kirtland for the eastern states on their first mission as apostles.

July 3 — Michael H. Chandler arrived in Kirtland to exhibit four Egyptian mummies and some scrolls of papyrus. Joseph

Smith's work with the scrolls resulted in the Book of Abraham, later included in the Pearl of Great Price.

Aug. 17 — A general assembly of the Church in Kirtland accepted the revelations selected for publication as the Doctrine and Covenants. This volume contained the revelations gathered for the Book of Commandments in 1833 and others received since that time, along with articles on marriage and government and a series of Lectures on Faith written for the School of the Prophets.

1836

March 27 — The Kirtland Temple, the first temple built in this dispensation, was dedicated after being under construction for nearly three years. The dedicatory prayer was given to the Prophet Joseph Smith by revelation. (See D&C 109.)

April — Apostle Parley P. Pratt was set apart for a mission to upper (eastern) Canada, the first area outside the United States opened for the preaching of the gospel.

April 3 — The Savior and also Moses, Elias and Elijah appeared in the Kirtland Temple and committed the keys of their respective dispensations to Joseph Smith and Oliver Cowdery. (See D&C 110.)

June 29 — A mass meeting of citizens at Liberty, Mo., passed a resolution to expel the Saints from Clay County. By December many had relocated on Shoal Creek (later known as Far West) in the newly established Caldwell County, located northeast of Clay County.

1837

Parley P. Pratt issued his pamphlet *Voice of Warning*, the first tract published for missionary use in the Church.

June 13 — Apostles Heber C. Kimball and Orson Hyde and Elders Willard Richards and Joseph Fielding left Kirtland, Ohio, on their missions to England, opening up the missionary work outside North America. They and two brethren from Canada, John Goodson and Isaac Russell, left New York on July 1 aboard the ship *Garrick*.

June 20 — *Victoria became Queen of Great Britain.*

July 30 — Nine persons were baptized in the River Ribble at Preston, England, the first converts to the Church in Great Britain. By December, there were 1,000 LDS members in England.

1838

April 23 — *The first transatlantic steamship service began, although scheduled service was not established until*

1840.

May 19 — Joseph Smith and others visited a place on Grand River, about 25 miles north of Far West, Mo., called Spring Hill by the Saints, which by revelation was named Adam-ondi-Ahman because "it is the place where Adam shall come to visit his people, or the Ancient of Days shall sit, as spoken of by Daniel the prophet." (See D&C 116, Dan. 7:9-14.)

July 6 — The exodus from Kirtland, Ohio, began under the direction of the First Council of the Seventy as planned three months earlier. The Kirtland Camp arrived at Far West, Mo., Oct. 2 and at Adam-ondi-Ahman two days later.

July 8 — Revelation on law of tithing (see D&C 119) was given at Far West, Mo.

Aug. 6 — A scuffle at the polls at Gallatin, Daviess County, Mo., intensified the mounting tension between Latter-day Saints and other area settlers.

Oct. 27 — Acting upon reports of civil war and rebellion among the Mormons, Gov. Lilburn W. Boggs issued an order to exterminate or expel the Saints from Missouri.

Oct. 30 — Seventeen Latter-day Saints were killed in the Haun's Mill Massacre at a small settlement on Shoal Creek, 12 miles east of Far West. The attack, by the Livingston County militia, was a reaction to the extermination order of Gov. Boggs.

Oct. 31 — Joseph Smith and others were made prisoners of the militia. The next day, a court-martial ordered the Prophet and the others shot, but Brig. Gen. A.W. Doniphan refused to carry out the order.

Nov. 9 — Joseph Smith and the other prisoners arrived in Richmond, Mo., where they were put in chains and suffered much abuse by the guards. An arraignment and a two-week trial followed, resulting in their being sent Nov. 28 to the Liberty Jail in Liberty, Mo., where they were imprisoned about Dec. 1.

1839

Jan. 26 — Brigham Young and the Twelve organized a committee to conduct the removal of the Saints from Missouri.

March 20 — While in Liberty Jail, Joseph Smith wrote an epistle to the Saints, which contained fervent pleadings with the Lord regarding the suffering of the Saints and words of prophecy. (See D&C 121.) A few days later, he continued the epistle, parts of which became Sections 122 and 123 of the Doctrine and Covenants.

April 16 — Joseph Smith and four other prisoners were allowed to escape while being transferred from Daviess to Boone counties under a change of venue in their case.

April 20 — The last of the Saints left Far West, Mo. A whole community, numbering about 15,000, had been expelled from their homes on account of their religion.

April 25 — Commerce, Ill., was selected as a gathering place for the Church. On May 1, two farms were purchased by Joseph Smith and others, the first land purchased in what later became Nauvoo.

June 11 — Joseph Smith began the task of compiling his *History of the Church*. He had the help of scribes and, later, Church historians. Segments of his history were published in Church periodicals in Nauvoo and later in Salt Lake City, and appeared in book form beginning in 1902.

Oct. 29 — Joseph Smith left Illinois for Washington, D.C., to seek redress from the president of the United States for wrongs suffered by the Saints in Missouri.

November — The first issue of the *Times and Seasons* was published in Nauvoo.

Nov. 29 — In a meeting with U.S. President Martin Van Buren in Washington, D.C., Joseph Smith was told by the president that he [Van Buren] could do nothing to relieve the oppressions in Missouri. Petitions were also presented to Congress, and a second interview was held with Van Buren, all to no avail.

1840

January — *Wilkes expedition discovered the Antarctic continent.*

April 15 — The Twelve in England named Parley P. Pratt editor of a proposed monthly periodical to be named the *Latter-day Saints Millennial Star*. The first issue was published in Manchester, England, on May 27; the publication would continue until 1970.

June 6 — Forty-one members of the Church sailed for the United States from Liverpool, England, on the ship *Britannia*, being the first Saints to gather from a foreign land. By 1890, some 85,000 LDS emigrants crossed the Atlantic in about 280 voyages.

Dec. 16 — Gov. Thomas Carlin of Illinois signed a bill creating a charter for Nauvoo, defining the city boundaries and establishing its government. Provisions included a university and a militia, the Nauvoo Legion.

1841

Jan. 19 — A revelation (See D&C 124)

given at Nauvoo outlined instructions for building a temple in Nauvoo. Baptism for the dead was introduced as a temple ordinance.

Jan. 24 — Hyrum Smith was ordained Patriarch to the Church, replacing his father, who had died Sept. 14, 1840, and also assistant president, replacing Oliver Cowdery, who had been excommunicated.

April 4 — *John Tyler was the first vice president to become U.S. president due to death of a predecessor.*

Oct. 24 — At a site on the Mount of Olives in Jerusalem, Orson Hyde dedicated Palestine for the gathering of the Jews.

1842

Elder Lorenzo Snow presented a British edition of the Book of Mormon to Queen Victoria of England, the first head of government in the world to receive a copy of the Book of Mormon. The book, printed in Liverpool in 1841, is now in the Royal Library at Windsor.

March 1 — The Articles of Faith were published for the first time in the *Times and Seasons,* a publication of the Church in Nauvoo, Ill. Joseph Smith, in response to a request from John Wentworth, editor of the *Chicago Democrat,* wrote a summary of the Church's history, ending with 13 declarations of LDS belief.

March 17 — Joseph Smith organized the Female Relief Society of Nauvoo, with Emma Smith, Sarah M. Cleveland and Elizabeth Ann Whitney as its presidency, to look after the poor and sick.

May 4 — Joseph Smith introduced the temple endowment to seven men at a meeting in the room over his store in Nauvoo. A few others received endowments before completion of a temple.

Aug. 6 — Joseph Smith prophesied that the Saints would be driven to the Rocky Mountains, but that he would not go with them.

Nov. 8 — The *Times and Seasons* published a brief history of the Church and the Articles of Faith, written at the request of John Wentworth, editor of the Chicago Democrat.

1843

Jan. 10 — *The first impeachment resolution was introduced in Congress; Virginian John Botts charged President John Tyler with corruption, misconduct in office and high crimes. It was rejected 127-83.*

May 3 — The *Nauvoo Neighbor* began publication and was voice for the Church for 2 1/2 years.

June 21 — Illinois agents, armed with a warrant from Gov. Thomas Ford, arrested Joseph Smith at Dixon, Lee County, Ill. He was released July 1, 1843, under a writ of habeas corpus.

July 12 — A revelation received in Nauvoo, Ill., on the "Eternity of the Marriage Covenant and Plural Marriage" (see D&C 132) was recorded, giving fuller meaning to the "new and everlasting covenant," which had been mentioned as early as 1831.

1844

Jan. 29 — A political convention in Nauvoo nominated Joseph Smith as a candidate for the president of United States.

Feb. 20 — Joseph Smith instructed the Twelve to organize an exploratory expedition to locate a site for the Saints in California or Oregon. A group of volunteers was organized for the trip in meetings over the next several days.

March 26 — Joseph Smith prepared a message for Congress asking for a law protecting United States citizens immigrating to the unorganized territories, known as California and Oregon, and offered volunteers to serve in such a protective force.

May 11 — Joseph Smith organized the Council of Fifty, a secret political body that directed the westward migration of the Saints and served as a "shadow government" in Utah during the 19th century.

May 24 — *Samuel Morse transmitted the first public message by telegraph from Washington, D.C., to Baltimore, opening the way for development of the first means of rapid communications.*

June 7 — The first and only edition of the *Nauvoo Expositor* appeared. The city council declared the paper a nuisance three days later, and the city marshal forced entry into the print shop and destroyed the type and papers.

June 11 — Joseph Smith and the city council were charged with riot in the destruction of the *Expositor* press. A Nauvoo court absolved them of the charge, but the complainant asked for the issue to be examined by the Carthage court.

June 22 — Joseph and Hyrum Smith crossed the Mississippi River to flee to the Great Basin. Gov. Ford had promised the Prophet safety, and so at the pleadings of others, the pair returned to Nauvoo and turned themselves over to government agents.

June 27 — Joseph and Hyrum Smith were killed by a mob that rushed the Carthage jail in Carthage, Ill. John Taylor was injured in the attack; Willard Richards escaped injury.

Aug. 4 — Sidney Rigdon advocated appointment of a guardian for the Church at a meeting in Nauvoo.

Aug. 8 — At a meeting designated for the appointment of a guardian, Rigdon again stated his views, after which Brigham Young announced an afternoon meeting. During the latter session, Young claimed the right of leadership for the Twelve and was sustained by vote of the Church.

1845

January — The Illinois Legislature repealed the city charter of Nauvoo.

April 14 — A wall was started around the Nauvoo Temple Block.

May — The nine accused murderers of Joseph and Hyrum Smith were acquitted upon instructions of the court.

May 18 — The attic story was begun on the Nauvoo Temple.

Fall — A limestone baptismal font replaced a temporary wooden font in the basement of the Nauvoo Temple.

Sept. 9 — Church leaders stated their intent to move to the Rocky Mountains to establish a refuge for the Saints.

Sept. 22 — Citizens at a mass meeting in Quincy, Ill., endorsed a proposal requesting that the Saints leave Illinois as quickly as possible. The Twelve's reply reiterated the Latter-day Saints' intention to move to a remote area and asked for cooperation and an end of molestation in order to prepare for the move early the following summer.

Sept. 23 — *The first U.S. baseball club, the New York Knickerbocker Club, was organized.*

Dec. 10, 1845-Feb. 7, 1846 — Some 5,000 endowments were performed in the

---

150 YEARS AGO:1847-1848

1847

Jan. 14 – Brigham Young presented instructions at Winter Quarters for the westward trek, including patterns for organizing the wagon companies (see D&C 136).

Jan. 27 – The Mormon Battalion arrived at San Luis Rey, Calif., within view of the Pacific Ocean.

April 7 – The first pioneer company, numbering 143 men, 3 women and 2 children, left Winter Quarters under the leadership of Brigham Young.

June 1 – The Mormon Pioneers arrived at Ft. Laramie, Wyo.

July 16 – The Mormon Battalion was discharged at Los Angeles, Calif.

July 22-24 – Brigham Young's pioneer company arrived in the Great Salt Lake Valley to select a settlement site for the Saints. Eleven companies arrived in the valley in 1847.

July 28 – Brigham Young selected a site for the Salt Lake Temple and instructed surveyors to lay out a city on a grid pattern square with the compass.

Dec. 5 – The First Presidency was reorganized by the Quorum of the Twelve in Kanesville, Iowa, with Brigham Young sustained as president, and Heber C. Kimball and Willard Richards as counselors. The action was ratified in a conference in Kanesville three weeks later.

1848

Jan. 24 – Gold was discovered at Sutter's Mill in California. The millrace, or canal to the millwheel, was dug by members of the Mormon Battalion. Four of them witnessed the discovery.

Feb. 2 – *The Treaty of Guadalupe Hidalgo ended the war between Mexico and the United States that had begun in 1846. By terms of the treaty, Mexico gave up what are now the states of California, Nevada, Utah, most of Arizona, and parts of New Mexico, Colorado and Wyoming, and relinquished all rights to Texas north of the Rio Grande.*

May – Millions of crickets descended into Salt Lake Valley and devoured the crops of the Pioneers. The "miracle of the sea gulls" saved what was left of the crops by devouring the crickets.

June – Brigham Young started for Salt Lake Valley again from Winter Quarters, Neb., with a company of 1,229 people.

Aug. 10 – A thanksgiving feast was held in Great Salt Lake Valley to celebrate harvest.

Aug. 13 – A conference in Manchester, England, was attended by more than 17,000 members of the British Mission.

November – The High Council at Kanesville, Iowa, voted to accept Oliver Cowdery back into the Church by his own request.

Nauvoo Temple.

1846

Jan. 30 — A wind vane in the shape of an angel was put on the tower of the Nauvoo Temple.

Feb. 4 — The Mormon migration from Nauvoo began. The same day, the ship *Brooklyn* left New York for California under the direction of Samuel Brannan.

April 24 — A temporary settlement of the westward-moving Saints was established at Garden Grove, Iowa. Other permanent camps were established at Mount Pisgah, Iowa, on May 18; at Council Bluffs, Iowa, on June 14; and at Winter Quarters, Neb., in September.

May 1 — The Nauvoo Temple was dedicated by Apostle Orson Hyde in public services.

Mid-June — Brigham Young and advance vanguard reached the Missouri River at Council Bluffs, Iowa Territory.

July 7 — *Annexation of California was proclaimed by the United States after the surrender of Mexico in the Mexican War.*

July 13 — The first of the volunteer companies of the Mormon Battalion was enlisted in response to a request delivered to Brigham Young two weeks earlier by Capt. James Allen of the United States Army. The battalion left for Fort Leavenworth on July 20, and arrived in San Diego, Calif., on Jan. 29, 1847.

August — *The Donner party blazed a trail from Henefer, Utah, to Salt Lake Valley that was used the following summer by Brigham Young's party of the original Mormon pioneers. The delay to build the road cost the Donner party 42 lives when they became snowbound in the Sierra Nevada, California.*

Sept. 17 — The remaining Saints in Nauvoo were driven from the city in violation of a "treaty of surrender" worked out with a citizens' committee from Quincy, Ill. The siege became known as the Battle of Nauvoo.

Dec. 28 — Iowa became the 29th U.S. state.

1849

March 3 — *Congress authorized coinage of the gold dollar and $20 gold piece (double eagle).*

March 5 — A provisional State of Deseret was established and appeals made for self-government.

October — A Perpetual Emigrating Fund was established during general conference to assist the poor. The system, which was incorporated one year later, continued until it was disincorporated by the Edmunds-Tucker Act in 1887.

Dec. 9 — The Sunday School was started by Richard Ballantyne in Salt Lake City. George Q. Cannon became the first general superintendent in November 1867.

1850

Missionary work took on a wider scope as missions were opened overseas in Scandinavia, France, Italy, Switzerland and Hawaii; most were discontinued after a few years.

June 15 — The first edition of the *Deseret News* was published in Salt Lake City.

September — Brigham Young was appointed governor of the Territory of Utah.

Sept. 18 — *The U.S. Congress passed the Fugitive Slave Act, permitting slave owners to reclaim slaves who had escaped into other states.*

1851

The Book of Mormon was published in Danish, the first language other than English in which the book was printed.

March 24 — A company of 500 settlers called to settle in California departed from Payson, Utah. The group settled in San Bernardino, Calif., which became the first Mormon colony outside the Great Basin since the arrival of the pioneers in 1847.

Aug. 12 — *Isaac Singer was granted a patent for his sewing machine. Singer set up business in Boston with $40 capital.*

September — Three federally appointed officials, Judge Lemuel C. Brandenbury, Judge Perry C. Brochus and Secretary Broughton D. Harris, left Utah in protest against plural marriage, as well as what they considered unjustified influence of the Church in political affairs in the territory.

1852

March 20 — *Harriet Beecher Stowe's influential novel about slavery, Uncle Tom's Cabin, was published.*

Aug. 28-29 — At a special conference in Salt Lake City, the doctrine of plural marriage was first publicly announced, although several of the leading brethren of the Church had been practicing the principle privately since it had been taught to them by Joseph Smith in Nauvoo.

1853

April 6 — The cornerstones were laid for the Salt Lake Temple.

June 29 — *The U.S. Senate ratified the $10 million Gadsden Purchase from Mexico, which completed the modern geographical configuration of the United*

States.

July 18 — The so-called Walker War began near Payson, Utah. This was one of several incidents of tension between Mormons and Indians in Utah Territory. The war ended in May 1854.

1854

Jan. 19 — The official announcement adopting the Deseret Alphabet was made in the *Deseret News.*

May 26 — *The Kansas-Nebraska bill passed, giving territories or states freedom of choice on the question of slavery.*

1855

Feb. 17 — *Congress authorized construction of a telegraph line from the Mississippi River to the Pacific.*

May 5 — The Endowment House in Salt Lake City was dedicated.

July 23 — The foundation of the Salt Lake Temple was finished.

Oct. 29 — In a general epistle, the First Presidency proposed that Perpetual Emigrating Fund immigrants cross the plains by handcart.

1856

During this year a general "reformation" took place throughout the Church, in which Church members were admonished forcefully from the pulpit to reform their lives and rededicate themselves to the service of the Lord. As a symbol of renewed dedication, many members renewed their covenants by rebaptism. The reformation movement continued into 1857.

Feb. 10 — *An important change in U.S. citizenship laws provided that all children born abroad to U.S. citizens were assured of citizenship.*

June 9 — The first handcart company left Iowa City, Iowa. Later that year two handcart companies, captained by James G. Willie and Edward Martin, suffered tragedy due to an early winter. More than 200 in the two companies died along the trail.

1857

March 6 — *The U.S. Supreme Court handed down its landmark ruling that a slave, Dred Scott, could not sue in federal court for his freedom.*

March 30 — Territorial Judge W.W. Drummond, who had earlier left the Territory of Utah, wrote a letter to the attorney general of the United States, charging Mormon leaders with various crimes.

May 13 — Elder Parley P. Pratt of the Quorum of the Twelve was assassinated while on a mission in Arkansas.

May 28 — Under instructions from President James Buchanan, the United States War Department issued orders for an army to assemble at Fort Leavenworth, Kan., to march to Utah. It was assumed that the people of Utah were in rebellion against the United States. This was the beginning of the so-called "Utah War."

July 24 — While participating in the 10th anniversary celebration in Big Cottonwood Canyon of the arrival of the Pioneers, Brigham Young received word that the army, under the command of Gen. Albert S. Johnston, was approaching Utah.

Sept. 7 — The Mountain Meadows Massacre took place, in which Arkansas immigrants on their way to California were killed by a group of misguided Mormons in Southern Utah. Twenty years later, John D. Lee was executed for his part in the crime.

Sept. 15 — Brigham Young declared Utah to be under martial law and forbade the approaching troops to enter the Salt Lake Valley. An armed militia was ordered to go to various points to harass the soldiers and prevent their entry. Brigham Young also called the elders home from foreign missions and advised the Saints in many outlying settlements to return to places nearer the headquarters of the Church.

1858

June 26 — After having been stopped for the winter by the delaying tactics of the Mormons, Gen. Johnston's army finally entered the Salt Lake Valley, but peacefully. The army's permanent encampment, until 1861, was at Camp Floyd in Cedar Valley in Utah County. Meanwhile, most of the Saints north of Utah County had moved south, and they only returned to their homes when peace seemed assured.

Aug. 5 — *The first transatlantic cable was completed.*

1859

July 13 — Horace Greeley, founder and editor of the *New York Tribune*, had a two-hour interview with Brigham Young, covering a variety of subjects from infant baptism to plurality of wives. The substance of his interview was published a year later in Greeley's *Overland Journey from New York to San Francisco.*

Aug. 27 — *The first oil well in the United States was drilled near Titusville, Pa.*

1860

April 3 — *The Pony Express mail service began.*

Sept. 24 — The last of 10 groups of Saints to cross the plains by handcarts entered Salt Lake City.

November — *Abraham Lincoln defeated Stephen A. Douglas in the presidential election.*

1861

April 12 — *The Civil War began as Confederate forces fired on Ft. Sumter in South Carolina.*

April 23 — The first of several Church wagon trains left the Salt Lake Valley with provisions for incoming Saints, whom they would meet at the Missouri River. This was the beginning of a new program to help immigrating Saints that lasted until the railroad came in 1869.

Oct. 1 — The first baptisms in the Netherlands took place near the village of Broek-Akkerwoude in the northern province of Friesland. A monument marking the site was erected in 1936.

1862

March 6 — The Salt Lake Theater, which became an important cultural center for Mormon people in the area, was dedicated. It was opened to the public two days later.

May 20 — *The Homestead Act, granting free family farms to settlers, was passed.*

July 8 — A federal law was passed defining plural marriage as bigamy and declaring it a crime. Mormons considered the law unconstitutional and refused to honor it.

1863

March 10 — President Brigham Young was arrested on a charge of bigamy and placed under a $2,000 bond by Judge Kinney. He was never brought to trial, however.

April 14 — *A continuous roll printing press was patented, the first press to print both sides of a sheet.*

1864

April 5 — A small group of Saints bound for Utah sailed from Port Elizabeth, South Africa. Five days later another group set sail for Utah from South Africa.

1865

A war with the Indians in central Utah, known as the Black Hawk War, began. It lasted until 1867.

Feb. 1 — *Abraham Lincoln signed the document abolishing the institution of slavery in the United States. After ratification by 27 states, the necessary three-fourths, the measure became the 13th Amendment to the Constitution on Dec.*

18, 1865.

April 10 — In a special conference, the Church agreed to build a telegraph line connecting the settlements in Utah. The line was completed in 1867.

April 14 — *U.S. President Abraham Lincoln was assassinated by John Wilkes Booth in Ford's Theatre in Washington, D.C., while watching a performance of "Our American Cousin."*

1866

Jan. 1 — The first edition of the *Juvenile Instructor*, the official organ of the Sunday School, was published. Its name was changed to the *Instructor* in 1930, and it continued publication until 1970.

July 27 — *The first permanent transatlantic cable between the United States and Great Britain was completed.*

1867

July 1 — *The Dominion of Canada was created.*

Oct. 6 — The first conference to be conducted in the newly completed Tabernacle on Temple Square in Salt Lake City began. The building was dedicated eight years later on Oct. 4, 1875.

Dec. 8 — Brigham Young requested that bishops reorganize Relief Societies within their wards. The societies had been disbanded during the Utah War.

1868

Jan. 29 — The name Great Salt Lake City was changed to simply Salt Lake City.

May 26 — *President Andrew Johnson was acquitted of impeachment charges by one vote. Johnson had been accused of "high crimes and misdemeanors."*

1869

March 1 — ZCMI opened for business. The Church-owned institution was the forerunner of several cooperative business ventures in Utah territory.

May 10 — The transcontinental railroad was completed with the joining of the rails at Promontory Summit, Utah. The railroad had great impact on immigration policy and on the general economy of the Church in Utah.

Nov. 17 — *The Suez Canal, linking the Mediterranean Sea and the Red Sea, was opened.*

Nov. 28 — The Young Ladies' Retrenchment Association, later renamed the Young Women's Mutual Improvement Association, was organized by Brigham Young in the Lion House in Salt Lake City. The first president, called June 19, 1880, was Elmina Shepherd Taylor. This was the forerunner of today's Young Women organization.

1870

Jan. 13 — A large mass meeting was held by the women of Salt Lake City in protest against certain anti-Mormon legislation pending in Congress. This and other such meetings demonstrated that, contrary to anti-Mormon claims, Mormon women were not antagonistic to the ecclesiastical power structure in Utah.

February — The "Liberal Party" was formed, which generally came to represent the anti-Mormon political interests, as opposed to the "People's Party," which generally represented Church interests until the end of the century.

Feb. 12 — An act of the Territorial Legislature giving the elective franchise to the women of Utah was signed into law. Utah became one of the first American states or territories to grant woman's suffrage.

July 24 — *The first railroad car from the Pacific Coast reached New York City, opening the way for transcontinental train service.*

1871

February — Judge James B. McKean, who had arrived in Utah in August 1870, made several rulings regarding naturalization that began a bitter and antagonistic relationship between himself and Church members.

Oct. 2 — President Brigham Young was arrested on a charge of unlawful cohabitation. Various legal proceedings in the court of Judge James B. McKean lasted until April 25, 1872, during which time President Young was sometimes kept in custody in his own home. The case was dropped, however, due to a U.S. Supreme Court decision that overturned various judicial proceedings in Utah for the previous 18 months.

Oct. 8 — *Fire broke out in Patrick O'Leary's barn, which later became known as the Chicago fire, and before the blaze was put out 27 hours later, 300 persons died, 18,000 buildings were destroyed and 90,000 were left homeless.*

1872

June – The first issue of the *Woman's Exponent*, a paper owned and edited by Mormon women, was published. This periodical continued until 1914.

Nov. 5 — *Susan B. Anthony was fined $100 for voting in the presidential election, because women did not then have the right to vote.*

1873

April 6 — Due to failing health, President Brigham Young called five additional counselors in the First Presidency.

1874

May 8 — *Massachusetts enacted the first effective 10-hour day law for women.*

May 9 — At general conference, which began on this date, the principal subject discussed was the "United Order." This resulted in the establishment of several cooperative economic ventures, the most notable of which were communities such as Orderville, Utah, where the residents owned no private property but held all property in common.

June 23 — The so-called Poland Bill became a federal law. It had the effect of limiting the jurisdiction of probate courts in Utah. These courts had been authorized to conduct all civil and criminal cases and were generally favorable toward members of the Church, but now Mormons accused of crimes had to be tried in federal courts.

1875

March 18 — Judge James B. McKean, with whom the Mormons had been unhappy, was removed from office by U.S. President Ulysses S. Grant.

May 19 — *The first Kentucky Derby was run at Louisville, Ky.*

June 10 — The first Young Men's Mutual Improvement Association was organized in the Thirteenth Ward in Salt Lake City. On Dec. 8, 1876, a central committee was formed to coordinate all such associations. Junius F. Wells was the first superintendent. This was the forerunner of today's Young Men organization.

Oct. 16 — Brigham Young Academy, later to become Brigham Young University, was founded in Provo, Utah.

1876

March 7 — *The patent was issued for Alexander Graham Bell's telephone.*

March 23 — Advance companies of Saints from Utah who were called to settle in Arizona arrived at the Little Colorado. This was the beginning of Mormon colonization in Arizona.

1877

April 6 — The St. George Temple was dedicated by President Daniel H. Wells in connection with the 47th Annual Conference of the Church that was held in St. George. This was the first temple to be completed in Utah. The lower portion of the temple had been dedicated earlier, on Jan. 1, 1877, and ordinances for the dead had commenced.

April 24 — *Northern post-Civil War rule in the South ended as federal troops were removed from New Orleans.*

Aug. 29 — President Brigham Young died at his home in Salt Lake City at age 76.

Sept. 4 — The Quorum of the Twelve, with John Taylor as president, publicly assumed its position as the head of the Church.

1878

May 19 — The Church had previously provided for the purchase of land in Conejos County, Colo., for settlements of Saints from the Southern States. On this date the first settlers arrived, thus opening Mormon settlements in Colorado.

Aug. 25 — The Primary, founded by Aurelia Rogers, held its first meeting at Farmington, Utah. The movement spread rapidly and on June 19, 1880, a Church-wide organization was established, with Louie B. Felt as the first president.

Dec. 1 — *The first telephone was installed in the White House.*

1879

Jan. 6 — The Supreme Court of the United States, in the important Reynolds case, upheld the previous conviction of George Reynolds under the 1862 anti-bigamy law. With the ruling, the court paved the way for more intense and effective prosecution of the Mormons in the 1880s.

Oct. 4 — The first edition of the *Contributor*, which became the official publication of the Young Men's Mutual Improvement Association, was issued. It was published until 1896.

Oct. 21 — *Thomas Edison tested an electric incandescent light bulb in Menlo Park, N.J., that burned for 13 1/2 hours, marking the beginning of a new era of electric lighting.*

1880

April 6 — At general conference, a special jubilee year celebration was inaugurated. Charitable actions, reminiscent of Old Testament jubilee celebrations, included rescinding half the debt owed to the Perpetual Emigrating Fund Company, distribution of cows and sheep among the needy and advice to the Saints to forgive the worthy poor of their debts.

Oct. 10 — The First Presidency was reorganized and John Taylor was sustained as third president of the Church, with George Q. Cannon and Joseph F. Smith as counselors.

Dec. 20 — *One mile of Broadway Street in New York City was electrically illuminated by arc lighting.*

1881

May 21 — *The American Red Cross was organized, with Clara Barton as president.*

1882

Jan. 8 — The Assembly Hall on Temple Square in Salt Lake City was dedicated.

March 22 — The Edmunds Anti-Polygamy bill became law when U.S. President Chester A. Arthur added his approval to that of the Senate and House of Representatives. The law defined polygamous living as "unlawful cohabitation" and made punishable the contracting of plural marriage as well as disenfranchisement of those who continued to live it. Serious prosecution under this law began in 1884.

July 17 — The Deseret Hospital, the second hospital in Utah and the first Church hospital, was opened by the Relief Society in Salt Lake City.

Aug. 18 — The Utah Commission, authorized in the Edmunds law, arrived in the territory. The five members of the commission, appointed by the U.S. president, had responsibility of supervising election procedures in Utah. Since the result of its activities was to enforce the disfranchisement of much of the Mormon population, Church members considered its work unfair.

Sept. 30 — *The first hydroelectric power station in the United States was opened at Appleton, Wis.*

1883

January — *The Pendleton Act established the U.S. Civil Service System.*

June 21 — The Council House, the first public building erected in Salt Lake City, was destroyed by fire. The structure was completed in December 1850 and was designed as a "general council house" for the Church, but was also used by the provisional State of Deseret as a statehouse. It also housed the University of Deseret for a number of years.

Aug. 26 — The first permanent branch of the Church among the Maoris in New Zealand was organized at Papawai, Wairarapa Valley, on the North Island. The first baptism of a Maori in New Zealand was on Oct. 18.

Dec. 26 — Thomas L. Kane, long a friend of the Church and a champion for Mormon people, died in Philadelphia, Pa.

1884

May 1 — *Work began in Chicago on a 10-story building called a "skyscraper."*

May 17 — The Logan Temple, the second temple constructed after the Saints came west, was dedicated by President John Taylor.

June 9 — The building known as the "Cock Pit," in Preston, England, in which the first Mormon missionaries to England held meetings in 1837, tumbled down.

1885

Extensive prosecution under the Edmunds law continued in both Utah and Idaho. Many who practiced polygamy were imprisoned, while others fled into exile, some to Mexico in 1885 and to Canada in 1887. Most of the Church leaders went into hiding, which was referred to as the "underground." Similar conditions continued for the next few years. These years are sometimes called the years of the "Crusade."

Feb. 1 — President John Taylor delivered his last public sermon in the Tabernacle in Salt Lake City. It was also his last appearance in public before he went to the "underground."

Feb. 3 — An Idaho law was approved by the governor that prohibited all Mormons from voting through the device of a "test oath." The Idaho "test oath" was upheld five years later by the U.S. Supreme Court on Feb. 3, 1890.

Feb. 21 — *The 555-foot high Washington Monument was dedicated 37 years after the cornerstone was laid.*

March 22 — The U.S. Supreme Court annulled the "test oath" formulated by the Utah Commission, thus restoring the right to vote to a number of Saints in the territory.

May 13 — A delegation, appointed by a mass meeting held in the Tabernacle in Salt Lake City on May 2, met with U.S. President Grover Cleveland in the White House in Washington, D.C. They presented to the president a "Statement of Grievances and Protest" concerning injustices brought about because of the Edmunds law.

1886

Jan. 31 — The first Church meeting was held in the first meetinghouse built in Mexico on the Piedras Verdes River in a settlement named Colonia Juarez.

March 6 — A mass meeting of 2,000 LDS women assembled in the Salt Lake Theater to protest the abuse heaped upon them by the federal courts and to protest the loss of their vote.

Oct. 28 — *The Statue of Liberty, a gift from the French people symbolizing the friendship between the United States and France, was dedicated in New York Harbor.*

1887

Feb. 17-18 — The Edmunds-Tucker Act passed Congress, and it became law without the signature of U.S. President Grover Cleveland. Among other stringent provisions, the law disincorporated the Church, dissolved the Perpetual Emigrating Fund Company and escheated its property to the government, abolished female suffrage and provided for the confiscation of practically all the property of the Church.

June 3 — Charles O. Card, leading a contingent of eight families, pitched camp on Lee's Creek in southern Alberta, marking the beginning of the Mormon colonies in Canada. Under instructions from President John Taylor, a gathering place for Latter-day Saints in Canada was selected, and on June 17 a site was chosen for what later became Cardston.

July 25 — President John Taylor died while in "exile" at Kaysville, Utah, at age 78. The Quorum of Twelve Apostles assumed leadership of the Church until 1889.

July 30 — Under provisions of the Edmunds-Tucker Act, suits were filed against the Church and the Perpetual Emigrating Fund Company and Church property was confiscated. A receiver for the property was appointed in November 1887, but the government allowed the Church to rent and occupy certain offices and the temple block.

Aug. 31 — *Thomas A. Edison was awarded a patent for a device he called a "kinetoscope," used to produce pictures representing objects in motion.*

1888

March 11 — *More than 400 people died as a snowstorm crippled the eastern United States during the legendary "Blizzard of '88," the most noted snowstorm in U.S. history.*

May 17 — The Manti Temple was dedicated in a private service by President Wilford Woodruff; a public service was held May 21.

June 8 — The Church General Board of Education sent a letter instructing each stake to establish an academy for secondary education. From 1888 to 1909, 35 academies were established in Utah, Idaho, Wyoming, Arizona, Mexico and Canada. The academy in Rexburg, Idaho, later became Ricks College.

June 21 — The first authorized missionary to Samoa, Elder Joseph Dean, accompanied by his wife, arrived on the island of Anunu'u in Samoa.

1889

April 6 — The first Relief Society general conference was held in the Assembly Hall in Salt Lake City. Twenty stakes were represented.

April 7 — Wilford Woodruff was sustained as fourth president of the Church, with George Q. Cannon and Joseph F. Smith as counselors.

May 6 — *The Eiffel Tower in Paris was officially opened.*

October — The *Young Woman's Journal*, official organ of the Young Ladies' Mutual Improvement Association, began publication. It was merged with the *Improvement Era* in 1929.

November — The Endowment House in Salt Lake City was torn down.

1890

Sept. 24 — President Wilford Woodruff issued the "Manifesto," now included in the Doctrine and Covenants as "Official Declaration — 1," that declared that no new plural marriages had been entered into with Church approval in the past year, denied that plural marriage had been taught during that time, declared the intent of the president of the Church to submit to the constitutional law of the land and advised members of the Church to refrain from contracting any marriage forbidden by law.

Oct. 6 — The "Manifesto" was unanimously accepted by vote in the general conference of the Church. This marked the beginning of reconciliation between the Church and the United States, which effectively paved the way to statehood for Utah a little more than five years later.

Oct. 25 — The First Presidency sent a letter to stake presidents and bishops directing that a week-day religious education program be established in every ward where there was not a Church school. It was recommended that classes be taught, under the direction of the Church's General Board of Education, after school hours or on Saturdays .

Dec. 31 — *Ellis Island in New York Harbor was opened as an immigration depot.*

1891

March — At the first triennial meeting of the National Council of Women of the United States, the Relief Society attended and became a charter member of that council.

1892

Jan. 4 — The new Brigham Young Academy building at Provo, Utah, was dedicated.

April 19 — *Three million acres of Cheyenne and Arapaho lands in Oklahoma were opened for settlement by presidential proclamation.*

Oct. 12 — Articles of incorporation for the Relief Society were filed, after which it became known as the National Women's Relief Society. The name was again changed in 1945 to Relief Society of The Church of Jesus Christ of Latter-day Saints.

1893

Jan. 4 — The president of the United States, Benjamin Harrison, issued a proclamation of amnesty to all polygamists who had entered into that relationship before Nov. 1, 1890. The Utah Commission soon ruled that voting restrictions in the territory should be removed.

April 6 — The Salt Lake Temple was dedicated by President Wilford Woodruff. The dedicatory services were repeated almost daily until April 24 with a total of 31 services held.

May 23 — The first ordinance work, baptisms for the dead, was performed in the Salt Lake Temple. On May 24, the first endowment work and sealings were performed.

June 27 — *The stock market crashed, resulting in four years of economic depression.*

Sept. 8 — The Salt Lake Tabernacle Choir, while competing in the choral contest at the Chicago World's Fair won second prize, ($1,000). While on this tour, the choir also held concerts at Denver, Colo.; Independence, Kansas City and St. Louis, Mo.; and Omaha, Neb. The First Presidency, consisting of Wilford Woodruff, George Q. Cannon and Joseph F. Smith, accompanied the choir.

Oct. 25 — President Grover Cleveland signed a resolution, passed by Congress, for the return of the personal property of the Church. Three years later, on March 28, 1896, a memorial passed by Congress and approved by the president provided for the restoration of the Church's real estate.

1894

January — *The railroad age continued with railroad building by far the nation's single largest economic enterprise.*

April — President Wilford Woodruff announced in General Conference that he had received a revelation that ended the law of adoption. The law of adoption was the custom of being sealed to prominent Church leaders instead of direct ancestors. He re-emphasized the need for genealogical research and sealings along natural family lines. With the termination of this type of sealings, genealogical work to trace direct ancestry increased among the members of the Church.

July 14 — President Grover Cleveland signed an act that provided for statehood for Utah. This culminated 47 years of effort on the part of Mormons in Utah to achieve this status.

Aug. 27 — President Grover Cleveland issued a proclamation granting pardons and restoring civil rights to those who had been disfranchised under anti-polygamy laws.

Nov. 13 — The genealogical society of the Church, known as the Genealogical Society of Utah, was organized.

1895

March 4 — The Utah Constitutional Convention met in Salt Lake City. John

Henry Smith, a member of the Council of the Twelve, was elected president of that convention.

Nov. 5 — By a vote of 31,305 to 7,687, the people of Utah ratified the constitution and approved statehood. The documents were later hand-delivered to President Grover Cleveland.

Nov. 28 — *The first automobile race in the U.S. took place from the heart of Chicago to its suburbs, 54 miles at 7 1/2 miles an hour.*

1896

Jan. 4 — President Grover Cleveland signed the proclamation that admitted Utah to the Union as the 45th state. Until statehood, the affairs of the Church in the Utah Territory had been closely associated with the affairs of the civil government. With statehood and the rights of self-government secured to the people, the Church could become separate from po-

---

100 YEARS AGO:1897–1898

1897

June 4 — Historian Andrew Jenson returned to Salt Lake City after circling the world in the interest of Church history.

July 5 — *Soft coal miners, as ordered by the United Mine Workers, went on strike, eventually winning an 8-hour day and abolition of the company store.*

July 20-25 — The Jubilee anniversary of the arrival of the Pioneers into the Salt Lake Valley was held in Salt Lake City for six days. The celebration began with the dedication by President Wilford Woodruff of the Brigham Young Monument at the intersection of Main and South Temple streets on July 20, and ended with a celebration for the Pioneers in the Tabernacle on July 24 and memorial services honoring all deceased Pioneers on July 25.

November — The *Improvement Era* began publication as the official organ of the Young Men's Mutual Improvement Association. Other Church organizations later joined in sponsoring the monthly magazine, which continued as the official voice of the Church until 1970. It was replaced by the *Ensign* magazine.

1898

January 24 — Four aged members of the Mormon Battalion took part in the 50th anniversary of the discovery of gold in California, which they wit-

nessed.

Feb. 15 — *Battleship* Maine *was sunk by a mine in the harbor of Havana, Cuba.*

May 9 — George P. Canova, a branch president in Florida, was murdered.

April 24 — *Spain declared war on the United States, and the Spanish-American War began. The war formally ended Feb. 10, 1899.*

April 28 — A First Presidency statement encouraged Latter-day Saint youths to support the American War effort in the Spanish-American war. This placed the Church firmly on the side of the war declarations of constituted governments and ended a policy of selective pacifism.

Sept. 2 — President Wilford Woodruff died at age 91 in San Francisco, Calif., where he had gone to seek relief from his asthma problems.

Sept. 13 — Lorenzo Snow became fifth president of the Church. He chose George Q. Cannon and Joseph F. Smith as counselors. Both had served as counselors to President Brigham Young, President John Taylor and President Wilford Woodruff.

Oct. 15 — President Lorenzo Snow announced that the Church would issue bonds to lighten the burden of its indebtedness.

litical struggles.

Aug. 17— *Gold was discovered in Alaska on the Klondike River, sparking the second great gold rush in U.S. history.*

Nov. 5 — The First Presidency issued a formal letter of instruction directing that the first Sunday in each month be observed as fast day, rather than the first Thursday, which had been observed as fast day since the early days of the Church in the Utah territory.

1899

May 8 — President Lorenzo Snow announced a renewed emphasis concerning the payment of tithing, which members had been neglecting for some time, at a conference in St. George, Utah. "The time has now come for every Latter-day Saint . . . to do the will of the Lord and pay his tithing in full," President Snow told the conference.

July 2 — A solemn assembly was held in the Salt Lake Temple, attended by the Church's 26 General Authorities and presidencies of the 40 stakes and bishops of the 478 wards of the Church. The solemn assembly accepted the resolution that tithing is the "word and will of the Lord unto us."

Oct. 14 — *The U.S. declared an "Open Door Policy" toward China, opening it as an international market.*

1900

Jan. 8 — President Lorenzo Snow issued an official statement reaffirming the Church ban on polygamy.

Jan. 25 — The U.S. House of Representatives voted to deny Utahn B.H. Roberts of the First Council of the Seventy his seat in Congress following an investigation of the right of polygamists to hold office under the Constitution.

Aug. 14 — *Anti-saloon agitator Carry Nation began attacking bars with a hatchet.*

1901

Aug. 12 — Elder Heber J. Grant of the Quorum of the Twelve dedicated Japan and opened a mission there as a first step in renewed emphasis on preaching the gospel in all the world.

Sept. 6 — *U.S. President William McKinley was shot by Leon Czolgosz; McKinley died eight days later.*

Oct. 10 — President Lorenzo Snow died at his home in the Beehive House in Salt Lake City at age 87.

Oct. 17 — Joseph F. Smith was ordained the sixth president of the Church, with John R. Winder and Anthon H. Lund as counselors.

1902

The Church published in book form the first volume of Joseph Smith's *History of the Church,* edited by B.H. Roberts. Publication continued over the next decade, with a seventh volume added in 1932.

January — The *Children's Friend* began publication as an organ for Primary Association teachers. The magazine later widened its audience to include children, then eliminated the teachers' departments. It was published until 1970 when it was replaced by the *Friend* magazine.

March 6 — *The Bureau of the Census was created by an act of Congress.*

Aug. 4 — The First Council of the Seventy opened a Bureau of Information and Church Literature in a small octagonal booth on Temple Square. It was replaced by a larger building in March 1904 and by the present visitors centers in 1966 and 1978.

1903

Nov. 5 — The Church announced purchase of the Carthage Jail as a historic site.

Dec. 17 — *Orville and Wilbur Wright became the first men to fly when they managed to get their powered airplane off the ground near Kitty Hawk, N.C., for 12 seconds. They made four flights that day, the longest lasting for 59 seconds.*

1904

April 5 — President Joseph F. Smith issued an official statement upholding provisions of the 1890 Manifesto and invoking excommunication against persons violating the "law of the land" by contracting new plural marriages.

July 23 — *The first Olympic games to be held in the U.S. opened as part of the St. Louis, Mo., Exposition.*

1905

Jan. 1 — The Dr. William H. Groves Latter-day Saints Hospital opened in Salt Lake City and was dedicated three days later, the first in the Church hospital system. In 1975, the Church divested itself of its hospitals and turned them over to a private organization.

Sept. 5 — *The Treaty of Portsmouth ended the Russian-Japanese War.*

Oct. 28 — Elders John W. Taylor and Matthias F. Cowley, finding themselves out of harmony with Church policy on plural marriage, submitted resignations from the Council of the Twelve that were announced to the Church April 6, 1906.

Dec. 23 — President Joseph F. Smith

dedicated the Joseph Smith Memorial Cottage and Monument at Sharon, Windsor Co., Vt., the site of the Prophet's birth 100 years earlier.

1906

The Sunday School introduced a Church-wide parents' class as part of an increased emphasis on the importance of the home and of the parents' role in teaching their children the gospel.

April 18 — *San Francisco was hit by a major earthquake, measuring 8.25 on the Richter scale, which leveled 490 city blocks.*

Summer — President Joseph F. Smith traveled to Europe, the first such visit of a Church president to the area. President Smith also visited Hawaii, Canada and Mexico during his presidency.

1907

Jan. 10 — President Joseph F. Smith announced payment of the last two $500,000 bond issues sold by President Lorenzo Snow in December 1899 to fund the Church debt. The first had been paid in 1903.

February — The United States Senate agreed to seat Utah Sen. Reed Smoot, a member of the Quorum of the Twelve. The vote culminated a three-year investigation, during which Church officials testified concerning polygamy and Church involvement in politics.

April 5 — A vote of the general conference approved the First Presidency's 16-page summary statement of the Church position in the Smoot hearings.

Aug. 1 — *An aeronautical division, consisting of one officer and two enlisted men, was established by the U.S. Army, the forerunner of the U.S. Air Force.*

1908

April 8 — The First Presidency created a General Priesthood Committee on Outlines, which served until 1922. In fulfillment of its assignment, the committee created definite age groupings for Aaronic Priesthood offices, provided systematic programs for year-round priesthood meetings, and in other ways reformed, reactivated and systematized priesthood work.

Oct. 1 — *Henry Ford introduced his famous Model-T Ford automobile.*

1909

April 6 — *The North Pole was discovered by an expedition led by Robert E. Peary.*

November — The First Presidency issued an official statement on the origin of man.

1910

The Bishop's Building, an office building for the Presiding Bishopric and auxiliary organizations at 50 N. Main St., opened. It was used for more than 50 years.

January — The first issue of the *Utah Genealogical and Historical Magazine* was published. This quarterly publication served as the voice of the Genealogical Society of Utah. It was discontinued in October 1940.

Feb. 8 — *The Boy Scouts of America was founded. It was chartered by the U.S. Congress in 1916.*

1911

The Church adopted the Boy Scout program and has since become one of the leading sponsors of this movement for young men.

April 15 — *Collier's* magazine published a letter from Theodore Roosevelt refuting many charges made against Utah Sen. Reed Smoot and the Church. This action helped defuse an anti-Mormon propaganda surge of 1910-11.

Dec. 14 — *Norwegian explorer Roald Amundsen became the first man to reach the South Pole.*

1912

Aug. 14 — *The United States sent Marines to Nicaragua, which was in default on loans from the U.S. and Europe.*

Fall — A seminary at Granite High School in Salt Lake City opened, marking the beginning of a released-time weekday education program for young Latter-day Saints. As the seminary program grew, the Church phased out its involvement in academies, which were Church-sponsored high schools or junior colleges. By 1924, only the Juarez Academy in Mexico remained.

Nov. 8 — The First Presidency created a Correlation Committee, headed by Elder David O. McKay, and asked it to coordinate scheduling and prevent unnecessary duplication in programs of Church auxiliaries. A Social Advisory Committee of the General Boards was merged with it in 1920. The combined committee issued a major report April 14, 1921, offering proposals for correlating priesthood and auxiliary activities; many of its recommendations were thereafter adopted.

1913

The Church established the Maori Agricultural College in New Zealand. It was destroyed by an earthquake in 1931 and was never rebuilt.

Feb. 25 — *The 16th Amendment, creating the income tax, became a part of the U.S. Constitution, the first constitutional amendment adopted in the 20th century.*

May 21 — The Boy Scout program was officially adopted by the Young Men's Mutual Improvement Association and became the activity program for boys of the Church.

1914

January — The *Relief Society Magazine* appeared as a monthly publication containing lesson material for use in the women's auxiliary of the Church. The magazine carried stories, poetry, articles, homemaking helps, news and lesson material until it ceased publication in December 1970, when the *Ensign* magazine became the magazine for adults in the Church.

The Relief Society also introduced its first uniform courses of study, organized around four general themes. The pattern was altered in 1921 to include theology, work and business meetings, literature and social service.

Aug. 15 — *The Panama Canal, connecting the Atlantic Ocean to the Pacific, was officially opened. Twelve days before, on Aug. 3, an ocean steamer, the SS Acon, passed through the canal.*

1915

May 7 — *A German submarine sank the British liner* Lusitania, *enroute from New York to Liverpool, off the coast of Ireland, killing 1,198 persons.*

September — James E. Talmage's influential book *Jesus the Christ* was published.

1916

Feb. 21 — *The longest and bloodiest battle of World War I, the Battle of Verdun, began in France, resulting in the death of one million soldiers.*

June 30 — The First Presidency and Council of the Twelve issued a doctrinal exposition clarifying the use of the title "Father" as it is applied to Jesus Christ.

1917

Oct. 2 — The Church Administration Building at 47 E. South Temple was completed.

Nov. 7 — *Nikolai Lenin and the Bolsheviks overthrew the Kerensky regime in Russia.*

1918

May — Wheat that Relief Society sisters had been gathering and storing since 1876 was sold to the U.S. government at a government price, with approval of the First Presidency and the Presiding Bishopric, to alleviate shortages during World War I.

Oct. 3 — While contemplating the meaning of Christ's atonement, President Joseph F. Smith received a manifestation on the salvation of the dead and the visit of the Savior to the spirit world after His crucifixion. A report of the experience was published in December and was added to the Doctrine and Covenants June 6, 1979, as Section 138.

Nov. 11 — *World War I ended, as the Allies signed an armistice with Germany.*

Nov. 19 — President Joseph F. Smith died six days after his 80th birthday. Because of an epidemic of influenza, no public funeral was held for the Church president.

Nov. 23 — Heber J. Grant was sustained and set apart as the seventh president of the Church during a meeting of the Twelve in the Salt Lake Temple. He selected Anthon H. Lund and Charles W. Penrose as counselors.

1919

January — The 18th Amendment to the United States Constitution established prohibition. Church leaders supported the movement toward nationwide prohibition and opposed the amendment's repeal in 1933.

April — The April general conference of the Church was postponed due to the nationwide influenza epidemic. The conference was held June 1-3.

May 27 — *The first transatlantic flight (with two stopovers) was completed by a U.S. Navy seaplane.*

Nov. 27 — President Heber J. Grant dedicated the temple at Laie, Hawaii, the first Latter-day Saint temple outside the continental United States. Construction had begun soon after the site was dedicated in June 1915.

1920

Jan. 10 — *The League of Nations, the first permanent international body encompassing many of the nations of the world, was established as the World War I Treaty of Versailles went into effect.*

1920-1921

Elder David O. McKay of the Council of the Twelve and President Hugh J. Cannon of the Liberty Stake in Salt Lake City traveled 55,896 miles in a world survey of Church missions for the First Presidency. The pair visited the Saints in the Pacific Islands, New Zealand, Australia and Asia, and then made stops in India, Egypt and

Palestine, before visiting the missions of Europe.

1921

The M-Men and Gleaner departments in the MIA were introduced Churchwide to serve the special needs of young people from ages 17 to 23.

Oct. 5 — *The World Series was broadcast on radio for the first time.*

1922

May — The Primary Children's Hospital opened in Salt Lake City.

Nov. 26 — *King Tutankhamen's tomb was opened in Egypt.*

1923

The Church purchased a part of the Hill Cumorah. Additional acquisitions in 1928 gave the Church possession of the entire hill and adjacent lands.

Aug. 26 — President Heber J. Grant dedicated the Alberta Temple, in Cardston, Alberta, Canada, which had been under construction for nearly a decade.

Sept. 29 — *Britain began to rule Palestine under a mandate from the League of Nations.*

1924

March 21 — A First Presidency statement answered criticism of unauthorized plural marriages by once again confirming the Church's policy against the practice. Polygamist cliques within the Church were excommunicated when discovered.

June 2 — *The U.S. Congress granted citizenship to all American Indians.*

Oct. 3 — Radio broadcast of general conference began on KSL, the Church-owned station. Coverage was expanded into Idaho in 1941.

1925

July 24 — *In the famous "Scopes Monkey Trial," John T. Scopes, a Tennessee school teacher, was found guilty of teaching evolution in a public school.*

Dec. 6 — Elder Melvin J. Ballard of the Quorum of the Twelve established a mission in South America with headquarters in Buenos Aires, Argentina, opening the Church's official work in South America.

1926

Weekday religious education was expanded to include college students with the building of the first institute of religion adjacent to the University of Idaho at Moscow.

May 9 — *Richard Byrd and Floyd Bennett became the first men to make an airplane flight over the North Pole.*

1927

May 21 — *Charles Lindbergh, aboard his "Spirit of St. Louis" monoplane, completed the first transatlantic solo flight from New York City to Paris, a distance of 3,610 miles, in 33 1/2 hours.*

Oct. 23 — President Heber J. Grant dedicated the Arizona Temple at Mesa, completing a project begun six years before.

1928

The YMMIA introduced a Vanguard program for 15- and 16-year-old boys. After the National Boy Scout organization created the Explorer program in 1933, patterned in part after the Vanguards, the Church adopted Explorer Scouting.

January — Priesthood quorums began meeting during the Sunday School hour for gospel instruction under a correlated experiment lasting 10 years. This priesthood Sunday School experiment included classes for all age groups, with Tuesday evening reserved as an activity night for both priesthood and young women.

May 11 — *The first regularly scheduled television programs were begun by Station WGY in Schenectady, N.Y.*

1929

July 15 — The Tabernacle Choir started a weekly network radio broadcast on NBC. Richard L. Evans joined the program with his sermonettes in June 1930. "Music and the Spoken Word" eventually switched to KSL Radio on the CBS network and has since become one of the longest continuing programs in broadcasting history.

Oct. 29 — *The New York Stock Market collapsed in frantic trading, a dramatic beginning of the Great Depression.*

1930

April 6 — The centennial of the Church's organization was observed at general conference in the Tabernacle in Salt Lake City. B.H. Roberts prepared his *Comprehensive History of The Church of Jesus Christ of Latter-day Saints* as a centennial memorial.

July 21 — *The U.S. Veterans Administration was established.*

1931

March 21 — A 10-reel film of the history of the Church was completed.

April 6 — The first edition of the *Church News* was printed by the Church's *Deseret News.*

May 1 — *The Empire State Building was opened in New York City.*

June — The Church Music Committee outlined a proposal to have better choirs in every ward and stake in the Church.

1932

Jan. 10 — The first missionary training classes began, which were to be organized in every ward throughout the Church.

February — The Lion House, home of Brigham Young and a noted landmark of Salt Lake City, was turned over to the Young Ladies Mutual Improvement Association by the Church for a social center for women and young ladies. The Beehive House was previously placed under the direction of the YLMIA as a girls' home.

April 2 — A campaign against the use of tobacco was launched by the Church.

May 12 — *Infant* Charles *Lindbergh Jr., kidnapped March 1, was found dead.*

May 15 — Utah Gov. George H. Dern proclaimed a special fast day in the depths of the Great Depression to gather funds for the poor.

June 12 — A marker at the site of the "Great Salt Lake Base and Meridian" was dedicated on the southeast corner of Temple Square. Apostle Orson Pratt on Aug. 3, 1847, established the base line from which all government measurements and surveys began for the West.

July 16 — The first of the Mormon Trail markers were unveiled in Henefer, Utah, and Casper, Wyo.

1933

Jan. 30 — *Adolf Hitler was named chancellor of Germany, capping a phenomenal 10-year rise to power.*

Feb. 21 — The Church began a six-day commemoration of the 100th anniversary of the Word of Wisdom revelation with special observances in every ward throughout the Church.

June 1 — The Church opened a 500-foot exhibit in the Hall of Religions at the Century of Progress World's Fair in Chicago, Ill. The exhibit was prepared by famed LDS sculptor Avard Fairbanks.

July 26 — The first effort to mark the historic sites in Nauvoo, Ill., was made by the Relief Society when it placed a monument at the site of its organization in 1842 in Joseph Smith's store.

Nov. 5 — The First Presidency and four members of the Quorum of the Twelve participated in the dedication of the Washington, D.C., chapel, which was adorned by a statue of the Angel Moroni atop its 165-foot spire.

1934

The general board of the Sunday School officially recognized the Junior Sunday School, which had been part of some ward programs for many years.

Jan. 17 — New headquarters of the Genealogical Society of Utah, located in the Joseph F. Smith Memorial Building on North Main Street in Salt Lake City, was formally opened. The building previously was part of the campus of the LDS College.

Feb. 3 — Stake seventies were instructed in a letter from the First Council of the Seventy that they have a duty, under the direction of the stake president, to do missionary work in the stakes.

Aug. 2 — *Adolf Hitler took control of Germany after the death of President Paul von Hindenburg.*

1935

Jan. 11 — *American aviatrix Amelia Earhart became the first woman to fly over the Pacific, from Hawaii to California.*

Feb. 24 — The YMMIA general superintendency was released to allow the General Authorities serving in those posts more time for other duties. In April, Albert E. Bowen, George Q. Morris and Franklin West were sustained as the new superintendency.

March 3 — First of a series of six "Church of the Air" broadcasts was carried nationwide by the Columbia Broadcasting Co.

July 21 — President Heber J. Grant dedicated the Hill Cumorah Monument near Palmyra, N.Y.

1936

A separate Aaronic Priesthood program for adults, recommended by the General Priesthood Committee on Outlines 20 years earlier, was introduced.

Jan. 29 — *Ty Cobb, Walter Johnson, Christy Mathewson, Babe Ruth and Honus Wagner became the first five men to be elected to the Baseball Hall of Fame.*

April — The Church introduced a formal welfare program to assist needy Church members and those unemployed in emergency situations. Called the Church Security Program at first, it was renamed the Church Welfare Program in 1938 and has continued to expand its services with the addition of local production programs.

Also in April, supervision of stake missions was given to the First Council of the Seventy, and stake missions were soon organized in all stakes. The work had previously been under stake presidency direction.

1937

January — The First Presidency officially adopted the practice widely utilized over several preceding decades of ordaining young men in the Aaronic Priesthood at specific ages. The recommended ages for advancement from deacon to teacher to priest to elder has changed from time to time since 1937.

Feb. 20 — A portion of the Nauvoo Temple lot in Nauvoo, Ill., returned to Church ownership when Wilford C. Wood, representing the Church, purchased the property.

April 27 — *The first Social Security payment in the U.S. was made.*

July — The Hill Cumorah pageant, "America's Witness for Christ," began on an outdoor stage on the side of the Hill Cumorah in New York. A Bureau of Information opened at the base of the hill.

Sept. 12 — President Heber J. Grant returned to Salt Lake City after a three-month tour of Europe, where he visited with Church members and missionaries in 11 countries. He dedicated nine meetinghouses and gave some 55 addresses, including the principal address at the British Mission Centennial Conference at Rochdale, England, on Aug. 1.

1938

Aug. 14 — The first Deseret Industries store opened in Salt Lake City to provide work opportunities for the elderly and handicapped. Part of the Welfare Program, a growing network of stores still offers used furniture, clothing, and other items.

Oct. 30 — *Orson Welles' fantasy radio program "War of the Worlds" was so realistic that it caused nationwide panic.*

1939

Feb. 18 — A miniature Salt Lake Tabernacle, with a seating capacity of about 50 persons, was built by the Church for its exhibit at the San Francisco World's Fair. The exhibit attracted 1,400 persons on opening day.

June 19 — Wilford Wood purchased the Liberty Jail in Missouri on behalf of the Church.

Aug. 24 — The First Presidency directed all missionaries in Germany to move to neutral countries. Later the missionaries were instructed to leave Europe and return to the United States. The last group arrived in New York Nov. 6, 1939.

Sept. 1 — *World War II began when Nazi Germany invaded Poland. Britain and France declared war on Germany two days later.*

Oct. 6 — The First Presidency message

on world peace was delivered in general conference by President Heber J. Grant.

1940

Jan. 28 — The Mormon Battalion Monument was dedicated in San Diego, Calif.

Sept. 16 — *U.S. President Franklin D. Roosevelt signed the Selective Service Act, setting up the first peacetime military draft in the nation's history.*

1941

The Presiding Bishopric inaugurated a new membership record system. Under the new system, a master record for each member was established in the Presiding Bishopric's Office, eliminating the need for personal membership certificates.

April 6 — In general conference, the First Presidency announced the new position of Assistant to the Twelve, and the first five Assistants were called and sustained.

May — The First Presidency appointed Hugh B. Brown as the Church Army coordinator. His work with the LDS servicemen and military officials led to the development of the Church servicemen's program.

Dec. 7 — *The Japanese bombed Pearl Harbor, killing 2,403 Americans and wounding 1,178. The next day, President Franklin D. Roosevelt asked Congress for a declaration of war against Japan. Four days later, Germany and Italy declared war on the United States, and on the same day the U.S. declared war on the European dictatorships.*

1942

The Girls' Activity Program of the Church was introduced.

Jan. 4 — The Church observed a special fast Sunday in conjunction with a national day of prayer called by President Franklin D. Roosevelt.

Jan. 17 — The First Presidency asked all general boards and auxiliary organizations to discontinue institutes, conventions and auxiliary stake meetings to help members meet wartime restrictions on travel and to help reduce personal expenses under increased war taxes.

Feb. 28 — It was announced that due to World War II, the Relief Society general conference scheduled for April, which had been planned to commemorate the centennial anniversary of the founding of the Relief Society, along with centennial celebrations in the stakes, would not be held. Rather, celebrations were to be held on the ward and branch level.

March 23 — The First Presidency announced that for the duration of World War II it would call only older men who have been ordained high priests and seventies on full-time missions.

March 23 — *The forced movement of Japanese-Americans from their homes on the U.S. West Coast to inland camps during World War II began.*

April 4-6 — Because of limitations on travel, the annual April general conference was closed to the general Church membership and confined to General Authorities and presidencies of the 141 stakes. The First Presidency on April 5, 1942, closed the Tabernacle for the duration of the war. Conference sessions were held in the Assembly Hall on Temple Square and in the assembly room of the Salt Lake Temple.

April 18 — May Green Hinckley, general president of the Primary Association, announced that the presiding officers of the Primary on all levels would henceforth be known as "presidents" rather than "superintendents."

July — Church Welfare leaders urged members to plant gardens, to bottle as many fruits and vegetables as they could utilize and to store coal.

Aug. 17 — *The USS Brigham Young was christened. It was of the Liberty ship class.*

1943

March 7 — The Navajo-Zuni Mission was formed, the first mission designated only for Indians.

May — The Church announced that a pocket-size Church directory had been printed for distribution in the armed forces, along with a pocket-size Book of Mormon and a compilation titled *Principles of the Gospel.*

May 22 — *USS Joseph Smith,* a Liberty class ship, was launched in Richmond, Calif. Ceremonies included a tribute to Joseph Smith and a description of the Church's part in the war effort.

July 24 — The MIA completed a war service project to purchase aircraft rescue boats by purchasing war bonds. The project began May 11 and ended with 87 stakes raising a total of $3.1 million, enough to purchase 52 boats, which cost $60,000 each.

Sept. 9 — *United States troops invaded Italy.*

1944

March — The Church announced the purchase of Spring Hill in Missouri, known in Church history as Adam-ondi-Ahman. Final deeds for the purchase were dated June 27, 1944, the 100th anniversary of the martyrdom of the Prophet Joseph Smith. The deed to the land was passed on to the Church by Eugene Johnson, whose family had been in possession of the property for a century.

May 15 — A 12-page monthly *Church News* for the 70,000 LDS servicemen was inaugurated by the First Presidency in order to keep more closely in touch with the servicemen. This edition contained inspirational material, vital messages, answers to questions and a summary of important news in the Church.

June 6 — *Allied forces, numbering 130,000 men, invaded Europe at Normandy, France, on "D-Day" breaking the Nazi stranglehold on the Continent and leading to the eventual surrender of Germany.*

June 25 — Memorial services were held in each ward to commemorate the 100th anniversary of the martyrdom of the Prophet Joseph Smith and Hyrum Smith. Special services were also held in Carthage Jail on June 27.

July — The Church organized the Committee on Publications comprised of General Authorities to supervise the preparation and publication of all Church literature. This committee controlled all auxiliary lessons and all publications published by and for the Church.

November — The name of the Genealogical Society of Utah was changed to the Genealogical Society of The Church of Jesus Christ of Latter-day Saints.

Nov. 28 — Young Women's Mutual Improvement Association celebrated its 75th anniversary. A plaque was dedicated by President Heber J. Grant and placed in the Lion House where the initial organization had taken place.

1945

May 14 — President Heber J. Grant died in Salt Lake City at age 88.

May 21 — At a special meeting of the Quorum of the Twelve in the Salt Lake Temple, the First Presidency was reorganized with George Albert Smith sustained and set apart as the eighth president of the Church. Presidents J. Reuben Clark Jr. and David O. McKay, counselors to President Grant, were called also as counselors to President Smith.

July 16 — The First Presidency authorized monthly priesthood and auxiliary leadership meetings if they could be held without violating government restrictions concerning use of gas and rubber.

September — The First Presidency began calling mission presidents for areas

50 YEARS AGO: 1947-1948

1947

April 11 — *Jackie Robinson broke Major League Baseball's previous all-white color barrier when he began playing for the Brooklyn Dodgers.*

May — The vast project of revising early scripture translations and translating the scriptures into additional languages was begun by the Church Offices.

July 22 — A caravan of wagon-canopied automobiles of the same number of people as the original pioneer company, completed following the Mormon Pioneer Trail.

July 24 — Church members celebrated the 100th anniversary of the Pioneers' arrival in Salt Lake Valley. The "This Is the Place" monument was dedicated by President George Albert Smith.

Aug. 7 — *The Kon-Tiki raft sailed by ethnologist Thor Heyerdahl arrived at the Marquesa Islands from Peru, to support his theory of the origination of the South Pacific Islanders.*

Oct. 12 — The Tabernacle Choir returned from a trip to San Bernardino, Calif.

November — Some 75 tons of potatoes raised and donated by Dutch members were delivered to needy families in Germany. A year later, the German Saints would harvest their own crop of potatoes.

December — Fast day was set aside for the relief of those in need in Europe. About $210,000 was collected and then distributed to Europeans of all faiths by an agency not connected with the Church.

Also in December, more than one million people visited Temple Square in one year for the first time.

Dec. 1 — An ambitious project to microfilm European records was started by the Genealogical Society.

Dec. 20 — President George Albert Smith announced that in the century following the end of World War II, the Church had the responsibility to carry the gospel to the people at home and abroad, a missionary posture leading to the internationalization of the Church.

1948

Jan. 23 — Members of the Church in California took part in the centennial of the discovery of gold at the site where members of the Mormon Battalion worked under foreman John Marshall at Sutter's Mill.

April — Mission presidents from around the world reported increasing numbers of baptisms. An expanded building program was started.

May 14 — *Britain ended its rule in Palestine, and the independent state of Israel was proclaimed.*

June — It was announced that Ricks College in Rexburg, Idaho, would become a four-year college in the 1949-50 school year.

Oct. 17 — The Tabernacle Choir performed its 1,000th national broadcast over radio.

December — Significant increases were made among the Indian membership in the Southwest states.

---

vacated during the war. This process continued through 1946. The sending of missionaries soon followed the appointment of mission presidents. By the end of 1946, 3,000 missionaries were in the field.

Also, the Tabernacle was opened to the general public for the first time since March 1942.

Sept. 2 — *Formal ceremonies of surrender, ending World War II — history's deadliest and most far-reaching conflict — were held aboard the battleship* Missouri *in Tokyo Bay. Japan had surrendered on Aug. 14 (V-J Day); Germany on May 8 (V-E Day).*

Sept. 23 — The Idaho Falls Temple was dedicated by President George Albert Smith.

Oct. 5-7 — The first general, unrestricted conference of the Church in four years was held in the Tabernacle in Salt Lake City. (During World War II, general conferences were limited to general, stake and ward priesthood leaders.)

Nov. 3 — President George Albert Smith met with U.S. President Harry S. Truman in the White House and presented the Church's plans to use its welfare facilities to help relieve the suffering of Latter-day Saints in Europe.

1946

January — The Church began sending supplies to the Saints in Europe. This continued for the next several years.

Jan. 7 — *The United Nations General*

Assembly held its first session in London.

Feb. 4 — Elder Ezra Taft Benson of the Quorum of the Twelve, newly called as president of the European Mission, left New York for Europe to administer to the physical and spiritual needs of members there. He traveled throughout Europe for most of the year, visiting Saints who had been isolated by the war, distributing Church welfare supplies and setting the branches of the Church in order.

May — President George Albert Smith became the first president of the Church to visit Mexico. While in the country, he met with Manuel Avila Camacho, president of Mexico, and presented to him a copy of the Book of Mormon.

May 2 — The First Presidency instructed local Church leaders that in meetings where the the sacrament is passed, it should be passed to the presiding officer first.

December — The Relief Society announced the creation of an enlarged social service and child welfare department.

1949

April 5 — At a special welfare meeting held in conjunction with general conference, the Welfare Program was declared a permanent program of the Church.

May 12 — *The Berlin Blockade ended as the Soviet Union announced reopening of East German land routes.*

October — For the first time, general conference was broadcast publicly over KSL television, although since April 1948 it had been carried by closed-circuit television to other buildings on Temple Square.

Also in October, the centennial conference of the Deseret Sunday School Union was held.

1950

July 1 — The responsibility of the LDS girls' program was transferred from the Presiding Bishopric to the Young Women's Mutual Improvement Association, where it remained until 1974.

September — Early morning seminaries were inaugurated in Southern California. This was the beginning of a movement that spread seminary throughout the Church on an early morning, nonreleased-time basis.

Nov. 8 — *American jets were attacked by North Korean jets in the opening days of the Korean War.*

1951

A new edition of the Servicemen's Directory was published. In addition, it was announced that the United States armed forces had authorized the use of special "LDS" identification tags (called "dog tags") for Church members in the service.

March 29 — *Julius Rosenberg and his wife, Ethel, were convicted of wartime espionage. They were executed June 19.*

April 4 — President George Albert Smith died in Salt Lake City at age 81.

April 9 — David O. McKay was sustained as ninth president of the Church, with Stephen L Richards and J. Reuben Clark Jr. as counselors.

July 20 — Because the Korean War reduced the number of young elders being called as missionaries, the First Presidency issued a call for seventies to help fill the need. Many married men subsequently served full-time missions.

1952

A Systematic Program for Teaching the Gospel was published for use by the missionaries of the Church. This inaugurated the use of a standard plan of missionary work throughout the Church, although the specific format of the various lessons was modified from time to time after this.

March 2 — The new Primary Children's Hospital in Salt Lake City was dedicated. Half the cost of the building had been raised by children of the Church through the continuing Primary penny drive.

April 5 — The Church began carrying the priesthood session of general conference by direct wire to buildings beyond Temple Square.

June — President David O. McKay made a six-week tour of European missions and branches in Holland, Denmark, Sweden, Norway, Finland, Germany, Switzerland, Wales, Scotland and France. During this trip he announced the selection of Bern, Switzerland, as site of the first European temple.

Oct. 6 — A letter from the Presiding Bishopric introduced a new Senior Aaronic Priesthood program, with men over 21 years of age organized into separate Aaronic Priesthood quorums. Subsequently, special weekday classes were encouraged in each stake to prepare these brethren for the Melchizedek Priesthood and temple ordinances.

Nov. 1 — *The United States announced "satisfactory" experiments in developing the world's first hydrogen bomb.*

Nov. 25 — Elder Ezra Taft Benson of the Quorum of the Twelve was chosen Secretary of Agriculture by Dwight D. Eisenhower, newly elected president of the United States. Elder Benson served in that capacity for eight years.

Dec. 31 — A letter from the First Presidency announced that the Primary Association had been assigned the duty of establishing the Cub Scout program of the Boy Scouts of America for boys of the Church.

1953

March 25 — The First Presidency announced that returning missionaries would no longer report directly to General Authorities but, rather, to their stake presidency and high council.

May 29 — *Sir Edmund Hillary of New Zealand became the first person to reach the top of Mount Everest.*

July 9 — Organization of the United Church School System, with Ernest L. Wilkinson as administrator, was publicly announced.

October — The semiannual conference of the Church was broadcast by television for the first time outside the Intermountain area.

1954

Utahns debated the question of ownership of Dixie, Snow and Weber State Colleges, which had once been owned by the Church. Though the Church expressed a willingness to resume control, and the state was hard-pressed financially to operate them, voters rejected the transfer in a referendum.

Jan. 2 — President David O. McKay left Salt Lake City on a trip to London, England; South Africa; and South and Central America. He returned in mid-February, and at that point had officially visited every existing mission of the Church. He was the first president of the Church to visit the South African Mission.

April 7 — The Church Board of Education announced that Ricks College, which had been a four-year college since 1949-50, would revert back to being a junior college, effective fall semester 1956. The final graduation of a four-year class was Aug. 10, 1956.

May 17 — *The U.S. Supreme Court ruled that racial segregation in public schools was unconstitutional.*

July — The Church announced the inauguration of the Indian Placement Program, whereby Indian students of elementary and secondary age would be placed in foster homes during the school year in order for them to take advantage of better educational opportunities.

July 21 — The First Presidency announced the establishment of the Church College of Hawaii. The college commenced operation Sept. 26, 1955.

Aug. 31 — The First Presidency approved a plan to ordain young men to the office of teacher at age 14 and priest at age 16. The previous ages were 15 and 17.

1955

A special program of missionary work among the Jewish people was organized. It continued until 1959.

January-February — President David O. McKay took a trip covering more than 45,000 miles to the missions of the South Pacific, selected a site for the New Zealand Temple and discussed plans for the building of a Church college in New Zealand.

April 5 — *British Prime Minister Winston Churchill resigned.*

July — The Church Building Committee was organized to supervise the now-vast building program of the Church throughout the world.

August-September — The Tabernacle Choir made a major concert tour of Europe.

Sept. 11 — The Swiss Temple, near Bern, was dedicated by President David O. McKay.

Dec. 27 — A letter from the Presiding Bishopric announced that students at BYU would be organized into campus wards and stakes commencing Jan. 8, 1956. This move set the pattern for student wards to be organized at Church colleges and institutes of religion wherever their numbers warranted it.

1956

March 11 — President David O. McKay dedicated the Los Angeles Temple.

Oct. 3 — The new Relief Society Building in Salt Lake City was dedicated.

December — A new program for training priesthood leaders was inaugurated. It included quarterly stake priesthood meetings, quarterly leadership meetings and various special leadership sessions in connection with stake conferences.

1957

Ward education committees were organized throughout the Church to encourage and enroll young people in a seminary, organize their transportation and encourage them to attend a Church college or a college with an institute of religion. These committees functioned until 1964, when their duties were transferred to home teachers.

April — The First Presidency announced plans to move Ricks College from Rexburg to Idaho Falls, Idaho. This created much local concern and started a long debate that ended in a reversal of the decision and the announcement on April 26, 1962, of a major expansion program for the Rexburg campus.

July — The Pacific Board of Education was organized to supervise all Church schools in the Pacific area.

October — For the first time in the history of the Church, the semiannual general conference was canceled due to a flu epidemic.

Oct. 4 — *The Space Age began when the Soviet Union put the first man-made satellite into orbit around the earth.*

1958

A new program for convert integration was adopted during the year, having been previously tried on a pilot basis in several stakes.

April 20 — The New Zealand Temple was dedicated by President David O. McKay.

Aug. 3 — *The world's first atomic-powered submarine, the* USS Nautilus, *made the first voyage underneath the North Pole.*

Sept. 7 — The London Temple was dedicated by President David O. McKay.

Dec. 17 — The Church College of Hawaii in Laie, Hawaii, was dedicated by President David O. McKay. The college became a branch of Brigham Young University in 1974 and renamed Brigham Young University-Hawaii Campus.

1959

June 19 — The First Presidency issued a statement, entitled "The Sabbath," admonishing Latter-day Saints to keep the Sabbath day holy, and particularly to avoid shopping on Sundays.

Aug. 21 — *Hawaii was admitted as the 50th state; Alaska had been added to the United States Jan. 3.*

Nov. 29 — The Tabernacle Choir received a Grammy award for its recording of the "Battle Hymn of the Republic" at the first television awards show of the National Academy of Recording Arts and Sciences in Los Angeles, Calif.

1960

Jan. 3 — The First Presidency inaugurated a three-month series of weekly Sunday evening fireside programs for youth. President David O. McKay addressed an estimated 200,000 youth at the opening fireside, carried by direct wire to 290 stake centers in the United States, western Canada and Hawaii.

Also in January, the Church began setting up the administrative framework for a large building program in Europe. By early 1961, administrative building "areas" outside North America had been established for all parts of the world where the Church existed, and the labor missionary program, which originated in the South Pacific in the early 1950s, was utilized in each area.

March — The First Presidency requested the General Priesthood Committee, with Elder Harold B. Lee of the Council of the Twelve as chairman, to make a study of Church programs and curriculum with the object of providing for better "correlation."

May 1 — *A U.S. U-2 reconnaissance airplane was shot down over the Soviet Union, typifying worsening relations between the two superpowers.*

1961

March 12 — The first non-English-speaking stake of the Church was organized at The Hague in The Netherlands.

June-July — A number of significant developments took place that revamped the missionary program of the Church. The first seminar for all mission presidents was held June 26-July 27 in Salt Lake City, at which new programs were outlined. Also, a new teaching plan of six lessons to be used in every mission of the Church was officially presented, as was the "every member a missionary" program. The missions of the world were divided into nine areas, and a General Authority was called to administer each area.

Aug. 13 — *The Soviet Union began building the Berlin Wall, dividing East and West Germany.*

November — A Language Training Institute was established at Brigham Young University for missionaries called to foreign countries. In 1963, it became the Language Training Mission.

1962

Feb. 20 — *John Glenn became the first American to orbit the earth, a feat he accomplished in one hour and 37 minutes aboard the Friendship 7 space capsule.*

March — The age at which young men became eligible for missions was lowered from 20 to 19.

April — At the 132nd Annual Conference, the first seminar of General Authorities and presidents of stakes outside North America was held.

October — The Church purchased a shortwave radio station, WRUL, with a transmitter in Boston and studios in New York City. It was subsequently used to transmit Church broadcasts to Europe and South America.

Dec. 3 — The first Spanish-speaking stake was organized, headquartered in Mexico City.

1963

July — The labor missionary program was expanded to include the United States and Canada.

Oct. 12 — The Polynesian Cultural Center, located near the temple in Laie, Hawaii, was dedicated.

Nov. 22 — *John F. Kennedy became the fourth U.S. president to be assassinated; he was fatally wounded while riding in a motorcade in Dallas, Texas.*

December — Church storage vaults for records in Little Cottonwood Canyon were completed. They were dedicated on June 22, 1966.

1964

January — A new program of home teaching was officially inaugurated throughout the Church after having been presented in stake conferences during the last half of 1963.

Jan. 28 — Temple Square and the Lion House were recognized as National Historic Landmarks by the federal government.

March — Two LDS schools were opened in Chile, one in Santiago and the other in Vina del Mar. During the early 1970s, the Church opened an elementary school in Paraguay, one in Bolivia and one in Peru.

April — The Mormon Pavilion opened at the New York World's Fair. The Church also built elaborate pavilions for subsequent expositions in San Antonio, Texas (1968); Japan (1970); and Spokane, Wash.(1974).

July 31 — *The U.S.* Ranger 7 *spacecraft transmitted to earth the first close-up pictures of the moon.*

October — The Pacific Board of Education was discontinued. Schools under its direction became part of the Unified Church School System.

Nov. 17 — The Oakland Temple was dedicated by President David O. McKay.

1965

January — The home evening program was inaugurated. A weekly home evening had been encouraged before by Church leaders, but now the Church published a formal home evening manual, which was to be placed in every LDS home. In October 1970, Monday was designated for home evening throughout the Church; no other Church activity was to

be scheduled during that time.

Jan. 18 — The Tabernacle Choir sang at the inauguration of U.S. President Lyndon B. Johnson in Washington, D.C.

February — The Italian government gave permission for LDS missionaries to proselyte in the country. No missionary work had been done there since 1862.

March — The three-generation genealogical family group-sheet program was initiated.

June 3 — *Astronaut Ed White made the first American "walk" in space during the* Gemini 4 *orbital flight.*

September — Because of the war in Vietnam, a missionary quota of two per ward was established within the United States to comply with Selective Service requests.

October — With the appointment of President Joseph Fielding Smith and Elder Thorpe B. Isaacson as counselors, President David O. McKay announced that the First Presidency would be increased to five, instead of three.

1966

May 1 — The first stake in South America was organized at Sao Paulo, Brazil.

June 29 — *North Vietnam's capital, Hanoi, and principal seaport, Haiphong, were bombed for the first time by the U.S. in the Vietnam War.*

August — A new visitors center on Temple Square was opened to tourists in August. While this would be the most elaborate center, it represented a trend of building new visitors centers at historic sites and temples and at various other locations during the 1960s and 1970s.

1967

April — For the first time, seven Mexican television and radio stations carried a session of general conference.

June 10 — *The Six-Day War in the Middle East ended with Israel holding conquered Arab territory four times its own size.*

Sept. 1 — The beginning of the Church year was changed to Sept. 1 instead of Jan. 1 in the Southern Hemisphere, to coincide with the public school year.

Sept. 29 — The new administrative position of regional representative of the Twelve was announced, and 69 regional representatives were called and given their initial training.

November — Part of the Egyptian papyri owned by Joseph Smith while he was translating the Pearl of Great Price was given to the Church by the New York Metropolitan Museum of Art.

1968

Jan. 22 — *The* USS Pueblo *and its 83 crew members were seized in the Sea of Japan by North Korea.*

August — A large LDS educational complex was dedicated in Mexico City. The school, Benemerito de las Americas, contained 11 grades for more than 1,200 students.

Oct. 17 — Relief Society Gen. Pres. Belle S. Spafford was named president of the National Council of Women for a two-year term.

1969

January — Two-month language training missions began. Language training for missionaries prior to their departure to their mission field first began during the early 1960s for Spanish, Portuguese, and German language missions.

Jan. 20 — The Tabernacle Choir sang at U.S. President Richard M. Nixon's inauguration in Washington, D.C.

June — The first missionaries were sent to Spain.

July 20 — *U.S. astronaut Neil Armstrong became the first man to walk on the moon when he descended from the lunar module* Eagle; *he was followed 18 minutes later by Edwin Aldrin, pilot of the lunar module.*

Aug. 3-8 — A world conference on records was held in Salt Lake City, sponsored by the Church's Genealogical Society.

Nov. 1 — The Southeast Asia Mission formally opened with headquarters in Singapore. In January 1970, the first missionaries were sent to Indonesia, which was part of the mission.

1970

January — A computerized system for recording and reporting Church contributions went into operation.

Jan. 18 — President David O. McKay died in Salt Lake City at age 96.

Jan. 23 — Joseph Fielding Smith became the 10th president of the Church and chose Harold B. Lee and N. Eldon Tanner as his counselors.

March 15 — The first stake in Asia was organized in Tokyo, Japan.

March 22 — The first stake in Africa was organized in Transvaal, South Africa.

April 22 — *Earth Day, organized to call attention to environmental concerns, was first celebrated.*

May — The Beehive House was placed on the register of National Historic Sites.

September — A new Aaronic Priesthood Personal Achievement Program was started, which gave young men the opportunity to set their own goals in consultation with their bishop. A similar program for young women commenced in January 1971.

1971

January — Distribution of the new Church magazines began: the *Ensign* for adults, the *New Era* for youth, and the *Friend* for children.

Also in January, a bishops' training program conducted by stake presidents commenced, and a new correlated teacher development program began operation.

July — The medical missionary program (later called the health missionary program) began.

Aug. 27-29 — The first Area Conference of the Church was held in Manchester, England. Before the program of holding large area conferences ended, 44 were held throughout the world.

September — All LDS women were automatically enrolled as members of the Relief Society; dues were eliminated.

Sept. 30 — *The United States and the Soviet Union signed pacts designed to avoid accidental nuclear war.*

1972

Church sports tournaments and dance festivals were directed to be held on a regional basis instead of an all-Church basis.

Jan. 14 — The Church Historical Department was formed in a reorganization of the Church Historian's Office. Church library, archives and history divisions were created within the new department.

Jan. 18 — The Ogden Temple was dedicated by President Joseph Fielding Smith.

Feb. 9 — The Provo Temple was dedicated by President Joseph Fielding Smith.

Feb. 27 — J. Spencer Kinard became the commentator for the Tabernacle Choir's "Music and the Spoken Word," succeeding Elder Richard L. Evans of the Council of the Twelve, who had been the program's spokesman for nearly 40 years.

July 2 — President Joseph Fielding Smith died in Salt Lake City at age 95.

July 7 — Harold B. Lee became the 11th president of the Church, with N. Eldon Tanner and Marion G. Romney as his counselors.

Sept. 5 — *Eleven Israeli athletes and five of their assailants were killed in an attack on the Olympic Village at Munich, West Germany, by Arab terrorists.*

November — The MIA was realigned into the Aaronic Priesthood and Melchizedek Priesthood MIA and placed directly under priesthood leadership.

Nov. 4 — Church departments began moving into the newly completed 28-story Church Office Building at 50 E. North Temple in Salt Lake City.

1973

A new set of missionary lessons was completed for use in all missions. It was the first change in missionary lessons since 1961.

February — The first Church agricultural missionaries to leave the United States were sent to the Guatemala-El Salvador Mission.

Feb. 4 — The Marriott Activities Center at BYU was dedicated. Seating 22,000, it was the largest such arena on any university campus in the United States.

March 8 — The first stake on mainland Asia was organized in Seoul, Korea.

April 7 — The creation of the Welfare Services Department was announced in general conference. The new organization brought the three welfare units — health services, social services, and welfare — into full correlation.

Sept. 20 — *The British-French supersonic airliner, Concorde, made its first landing in the United States at the Dallas-Fort Worth International Airport.*

Dec. 26 — President Harold B. Lee died in Salt Lake City at age 74.

Dec. 30 — Spencer W. Kimball was set apart as the 12th president of the Church, with N. Eldon Tanner and Marion G. Romney as counselors.

1974

Jan. 14 — Names of stakes Church-wide were changed to reflect a consistent style identifying them with the geographical area served. Mission names were changed June 20, 1974.

March 23 — In an exchange of pioneer homes, the Church traded the Brigham Young Forest Farm home in Salt Lake City to the state of Utah for use in the state's Pioneer State Park. The Church acquired the Brigham Young winter home in St. George and the Jacob Hamblin home in Santa Clara, Utah, for use as visitor and information centers.

May 9 — *Impeachment hearings began against U.S. President Richard M. Nixon.*

June 23 — MIA was dropped from the name of Church youth programs, and further modifications were implemented in the administrative structure of the Aaronic Priesthood and the Young Women organizations.

Sept. 1 — Church College of Hawaii became a branch of Brigham Young University and was given the name Brigham Young University-Hawaii Campus.

Oct. 3 — Seventies quorums were authorized in all stakes, and all quorums in the Church were renamed after the stake. Stake mission presidencies were also reorganized, with all seven presidents of seventies serving in the calling, instead of three of the presidents.

Nov. 19-22 — President Spencer W. Kimball dedicated the Washington Temple at Kensington, Md. Visitors during pre-dedication tours September through November totaled 758,327, topping the previous record of 662,401 at the Los Angeles Temple in 1956.

1975

March 21 — The Church completed legal steps to divest itself of 15 hospitals operated by its Health Service Corporation in three western states. A nonprofit, non-Church organization, Intermountain Health Care Inc., assumed ownership.

April 20 — *South Vietnam unconditionally surrendered to North Vietnam, and the Vietnam War was officially at an end.*

May 3 — The First Presidency announced the creation of an area supervisory program and the assignment of six Assistants to the Twelve to oversee Church activities while residing outside of the United States and Canada. The number of these foreign areas was increased to eight later in the year.

May 17 — A supervisory program for missions in the United States and Canada was announced, along with the assignment of members of the Quorum of the Twelve as advisers and other General Authorities as supervisors of the 12 areas.

June 27 — The end of auxiliary conferences was announced during the opening session of the 1975 June Conference. These conferences would be replaced with annual regional meetings for priesthood and auxiliary leaders.

July 24 — The 28-story Church Office Building was dedicated by President Spencer W. Kimball.

Oct. 3 — President Spencer W. Kimball announced in general conference the organization of the First Quorum of the Seventy, and three members of the quorum were sustained.

Oct. 6-11 — Brigham Young University observed its 100th anniversary during homecoming week.

Nov. 18 — The Church Genealogical Department was organized with five divisions, two of which were formerly known as the Genealogical Society.

1976

April 3 — Members attending general conference accepted Joseph Smith's Vision of the Celestial Kingdom and Joseph F. Smith's Vision of the Redemption of the Dead for addition to the *Pearl of Great Price*. The scriptures on June 6, 1979, became part of the Doctrine and Covenants.

June 5 — The First Presidency published an official statement reaffirming the Church policy against abortion. The statement supplemented a filmstrip placed in distribution in March.

June 25 — Missouri Gov. Christopher S. Bond signed an executive order rescinding the extermination order issued in 1838 by Gov. Lilburn W. Boggs.

July 4 — President Spencer W. Kimball spoke at a Church-sponsored U.S. Bicentennial devotional attended by more than 23,000 people at the Capitol Centre in Landover, Md. Numerous additional activities involved Church members in the United States during the year-long Bicentennial observance.

Sept. 3 — Viking 2, *an American spaceship, made a successful landing on Mars.*

Oct. 1 — Members of the First Council of the Seventy and the Assistants to the Twelve were released in general conference and called to the new First Quorum of the Seventy. Franklin D. Richards was named the first presiding president.

1977

Jan. 1 — The First Presidency announced a new format for general conferences, with general sessions on the first Sunday of each April and October and on the preceding Saturday and regional representative seminars on the preceding Friday.

Jan. 14 — The first Presiding Bishopric area supervisor, called to direct temporal affairs of the Church in Mexico, began work in Mexico City. Presiding Bishopric area supervisors for eight other areas outside the United States and Canada were announced June 4.

Feb. 5 — The First Presidency announced that the Quorum of the Twelve would oversee ecclesiastical matters, and the Presiding Bishopric would have responsibility for temporal programs.

Feb. 21-March 11 — President Spencer W. Kimball met with heads of state in Mexico, Guatemala, Chile and Bolivia during a tour of Latin America to attend area conferences, and then visited at the White House with U.S. President Jimmy Carter March 11.

March 27 — *The worst airline disaster in history killed 581 people, as two jumbo jets collided on a runway in the Canary Islands.*

May 14 — A bishops central storehouse, the second in the Church and first outside of Salt Lake City, opened at Colton, Calif. Also, the Young Men program was restructured. Young Men presidency and general board were given responsibility for Aaronic Priesthood curriculum, leadership training and quorum work.

May 22 — Formation of a new Church Activities Committee, with responsibility for coordinating cultural arts and physical activities, was announced. Similar groups were organized on the stake and local level.

July 1 — In response to continued growth in membership worldwide, the geographic subdivisions of the Church, previously known as areas, were renamed zones, and the 11 zones were subdivided into areas. Members of the First Quorum of the Seventy were assigned as zone advisers and area supervisors.

July 30 — The Church Educational System was placed in the ecclesiastical line organization of the Church through an Education Executive Committee of the Council of the Twelve.

Oct. 1 — The Church published *A Topical Guide to the Scriptures of The Church of Jesus Christ of Latter-day* Saints, the first product of a continuing scriptural-aids project established by the First Presidency.

1978

March 31 — President Spencer W. Kimball announced that semiannual rather than quarterly stake conferences would be held starting in 1979.

April — The Church published an eight-page removable insert about Church programs in the *Reader's Digest*, the first of a series aimed at nearly 50 million *Digest* readers.

April 1 — President Spencer W. Kimball emphasized the four-generation program, which later became the basis for the Church's computerized Ancestral File.

June 9 — In a letter dated June 8 and made public the following day, the First Presidency announced the revelation that worthy men of all races would be eligible to receive the priesthood. On Sept. 30, members accepted the revelation by sustaining vote at general conference. The

First Presidency's announcement is now "Official Declaration - 2" in the Doctrine and Covenants.

July 1 — The Relief Society Monument to Women was dedicated in Nauvoo, Ill., by President Spencer W. Kimball.

July 22 — The United States Senate passed a bill, earlier approved by the House of Representatives, designating the Mormon Trail from Nauvoo, Ill., to Salt Lake City as a national historic trail.

Sept. 9 — A new missionary training program was announced: Missionaries to English-speaking missions would receive four weeks training while those learning other languages would continue to receive eight weeks training at the new Missionary Training Center in Provo, Utah, which replaced the Language Training Mission and the Mission Home in Salt Lake City.

Sept. 16 — Women and girls 12 years of age and over gathered for a first-ever special closed-circuit audio conference, similar to general conference priesthood broadcasts.

Sept. 30 — A new special emeritus status for General Authorities was announced in general conference, and seven members of the First Quorum of the Seventy were so designated.

Oct. 22 — *Pope John Paul II formally assumed the papal throne.*

Oct. 30 — The Sao Paulo Temple in Brazil was dedicated by President Spencer W. Kimball.

1979

Jan. 1 — *The United States and China established diplomatic relations after decades of animosity.*

Feb. 3 — The Church Genealogical Department announced a new "family entry system" to allow submissions of names of deceased ancestors for temple work whose birthplaces and birthdates are unknown.

Feb. 18 — The Church's 1,000th stake was created at Nauvoo, Ill., by President Ezra Taft Benson.

June 6 — Joseph Smith's Vision of the Celestial Kingdom and Joseph F. Smith's Vision of the Redemption of the Dead were transferred from the Pearl of Great Price to the Doctrine and Covenants, becoming Sections 137 and 138, respectively.

Sept. 12-14 — The Tabernacle Choir, which celebrated the golden anniversary of its nationally broadcast radio program in July, toured Japan and Korea.

Sept. 29 — A new 2,400-page edition

of the King James version of the Bible, with many special features, including a topical guide, a Bible dictionary and a revolutionary footnote system, was published by the Church.

Oct. 24 — President Spencer W. Kimball, on a tour of the Middle East, dedicated the Orson Hyde Memorial Gardens on the Mount of Olives in Jerusalem.

1980

Feb. 22 — The Presidency of the First Quorum of the Seventy was reorganized to strengthen the lines of administration at Church headquarters. The executive directors of the Missionary, Curriculum, Priesthood and Genealogy departments replaced former members of the presidency.

March 2 — U.S. and Canadian members began a new consolidated meeting schedule that put priesthood, sacrament and auxiliary meetings into one three-hour time block on Sundays.

April 6 — To celebrate the Church's 150th anniversary, President Spencer W. Kimball conducted part of general conference from the newly restored Peter Whitmer farmhouse at Fayette, N.Y., the site where the Church was organized. The proceedings in Fayette were linked with the congregation in the Tabernacle in Salt Lake City via satellite, the first time a satellite was used in the Church for transmitting broadcasts of general conference.

May 18 — *Mt. St. Helens in Washington, one of the few active volcanoes in the United States, erupted in a violent explosion that left 10 dead and scores of others homeless.*

Oct. 27 — The Tokyo Temple was dedicated by President Spencer W. Kimball.

Nov. 17 — The Seattle Temple was dedicated by President Spencer W. Kimball.

1981

Jan. 20 — The Tabernacle Choir participated in the inaugural festivities for President Ronald Reagan.

April 1 — Plans to build nine smaller temples in the United States, Central America, Asia, Africa and Europe were announced by President Spencer W. Kimball: Chicago, Ill.; Dallas, Texas; Guatemala City, Guatemala; Lima, Peru; Frankfurt, Germany; Stockholm, Sweden; Seoul, Korea; Manila, Philippines; and Johannesburg, South Africa.

May 5 — The First Presidency publicly voiced its opposition to the proposed basing of the MX missile system in the Utah-Nevada desert.

July 23 — Elder Gordon B. Hinckley was called as a counselor in the First Presidency, the first time since the administration of President David O. McKay that a president had more than two counselors.

Sept. 12 — A smaller, less-expensive ward meetinghouse, called the Sage Plan, was announced by the First Presidency.

Sept. 26 — The first copies of a new version of the Triple Combination (Book of Mormon, Doctrine and Covenants and Pearl of Great Price), with extensive scripture helps, were made available to the public.

Oct. 3 — A network of 500 satellite dishes for stake centers outside of Utah was announced. The receivers linked Church headquarters in Salt Lake City with members in the United States and Canada.

Nov. 16 — The Jordan River Temple was dedicated by President Marion G. Romney of the First Presidency.

1982

March 9 — The Spencer W. Kimball Tower, the tallest building on the BYU campus, was dedicated during ceremonies that featured President Kimball's first public appearance in six months because of illness.

March 18 — Three Church executive councils were created: the Missionary Executive Council, the Priesthood Executive Council and the Temple and Genealogy Executive Council.

April 1 — It was announced that Church membership had reached the 5-million member mark.

April 2 — At general conference, major changes in financing Church meetinghouses were announced, shifting construction costs to general Church funds and utility costs to local units. Also, the term of service for single elders serving full-time missions was reduced from two years to 18 months.

June 30 — *The Equal Rights Amendment was defeated after a 10-year struggle for ratification.*

Sept. 5 — The Mormon Tabernacle Choir celebrated 50 years of continuous weekly broadcasts over the CBS radio network.

Sept. 10 — U.S. President Ronald Reagan visited Utah to tour a Church cannery and see the Church Welfare Program in action.

Oct. 3 — Elder Boyd K. Packer of the Quorum of the Twelve and a member of the Scriptures Publication Committee announced that a subtitle was being added

to the Book of Mormon: "Another Testament of Jesus Christ."

Oct. 30 — A visitors center and historic site opened its doors in the three-story Grandin printing building in Palmyra, N.Y., where the first copies of the Book of Mormon were printed in 1830.

1983

Feb. 27 — The 150th anniversary of the Word of Wisdom was observed throughout the Church and at the Newel K. Whitney store in Kirtland, Ohio, where the original revelation was received in 1833.

June 1 — The Atlanta Georgia Temple was dedicated by President Gordon B. Hinckley of the First Presidency.

Aug. 5, 9 — For the first time in Church history, two temples were dedicated within a week's time: the Apia Samoa Temple on Aug. 5 and the Nuku'alofa Tonga Temple on Aug. 9; both by President Gordon B. Hinckley.

Sept. 15 — The Santiago Chile Temple was dedicated by President Gordon B. Hinckley.

Oct. 16 — The first of a series of multi-stake (later known as regional) conferences was held in London, England.

Oct. 25 — *U.S. Marines and Rangers invaded the Caribbean island of Grenada, deposing the island's Marxist government.*

Oct. 27 — The Papeete Tahiti Temple was dedicated by President Gordon B. Hinckley.

Dec. 2 — The Mexico City Temple was dedicated by President Gordon B. Hinckley.

1984

Jan. 7 — Premier Zhao Ziyang of the People's Republic of China visited the BYU-Hawaii campus and the adjacent Polynesian Cultural Center during the first visit of a Chinese premier to the United States since the People's Republic of China was formed in 1949.

March 25 — A new program — the Four-Phase Genealogical Facilities Program — was announced to allow wards and branches to establish genealogical facilities in their meetinghouses.

April 7 — The first members of the First Quorum of the Seventy called for temporary three- to five-year terms, were sustained. These Brethren were later sustained to the Second Quorum of the Seventy, created in 1989, and their term of service standardized at five years.

May 10 — *A federal judge in Salt Lake City ruled that the U.S. government was negligent in its above-ground testing of* *nuclear weapons at the Nevada test site in the 1950s and early 1960s.*

May 25 — President Gordon B. Hinckley dedicated the Boise Idaho Temple.

June 24 — Members of the First Quorum of the Seventy were appointed to serve as area presidencies in 13 major geographical areas of the Church — seven in the United States and Canada and six in other parts of the world.

Sept. 20 — The Sydney Australia Temple was dedicated by President Gordon B. Hinckley.

Sept. 25 — The Manila Philippines Temple was dedicated by President Gordon B. Hinckley.

Oct. 19 — The Dallas Texas Temple was dedicated by President Gordon B. Hinckley.

Oct. 28 — The Church's 1,500th stake was created 150 years after the first stake was organized in Kirtland, Ohio. The landmark stake was the Ciudad Obregon Mexico Yaqui Stake.

Nov. 17 — The Taipei Taiwan Temple was dedicated by President Gordon B. Hinckley.

Nov. 26 — The First Presidency announced that, beginning Jan. 1, the term of full-time missionary service for single elders would again be 24 months. It had been shortened from two years to 18 months in April 1982.

Dec. 14 — The Guatemala City Temple was dedicated by President Gordon B. Hinckley.

1985

Jan. 2 — BYU's football team was voted No. 1 in the nation for the 1984 season by every major poll, and was named National Champions. The Cougars had just completed a perfect 13-0 season.

Jan. 27 — Latter-day Saints in the United States and Canada participated in a special fast to benefit victims of famine in Africa and other parts of the world. The fast raised more than $6 million.

April 12 — U.S. Senator Jake Garn became the first Church member to fly in space. He was aboard the space shuttle *Challenger.* Another Church member, Don Lind, was a crew member on a space shuttle mission that blasted off April 29.

June 29 — The Freiberg Temple, located in the German Democratic Republic, then communist-controlled, was dedicated by President Gordon B. Hinckley.

July 2 — The Stockholm Sweden Temple was dedicated by President Gordon B. Hinckley.

July 31 — Li Xiannian, president of the

People's Republic of China, and his wife, Madame Lin Jiamei, toured the Church's Polynesian Cultural Center in Hawaii as part of his tour of the United States and Canada.

Aug. 2 — A new LDS hymnbook, the first revision in 37 years, came off the presses.

Aug. 9 — The Chicago Illinois Temple was dedicated by President Gordon B. Hinckley.

Aug. 24 — The Johannesburg South Africa Temple was dedicated by President Gordon B. Hinckley. With the dedication of this building, there was now a temple on every continent except Antarctica.

Oct. 23 — The Church Genealogical Library was dedicated by President Gordon B. Hinckley.

Nov. 5 — President Spencer W. Kimball died in Salt Lake City at age 90.

Nov. 10 — President Ezra Taft Benson was set apart as the 13th president of the Church, with President Gordon B. Hinckley and President Thomas S. Monson as counselors.

Dec. 14 — The Seoul Korea Temple was dedicated by President Gordon B. Hinckley.

1986

Jan. 10, 17 — The Lima Peru Temple was dedicated by President Gordon B. Hinckley, and the Buenos Aires Argentina Temple was dedicated by President Thomas S. Monson.

Jan. 28 — *The space shuttle* Challenger *exploded shortly after liftoff, killing all seven people aboard, including Christa McAuliffe, the first teacher in space.*

April 30 — Church membership was estimated to have reached the 6-million member milestone.

June 22 — The 1,600th stake of the Church was created by President Thomas S. Monson in Kitchener, Ontario.

July 6 — New missionary discussions, which focus on "teaching from the heart," were approved for use in all English-speaking missions.

Oct. 4 — Seventies quorums in stakes throughout the Church were discontinued. Brethren serving as seventies returned to elders quorums or were ordained high priests.

Oct. 5 — The First Presidency issued a statement opposing the legalization of gambling and government sponsorship of lotteries.

Oct. 11 — In the first Churchwide Young Women activity, an estimated 300,000 gathered at sites around the world to release helium-filled balloons containing personal messages from the young women.

Oct. 24 — The Denver Colorado Temple was dedicated by President Ezra Taft Benson.

1987

Jan. 23 — Documents dealer Mark Hofmann was imprisoned after a plea bargain arrangement in which he admitted responsibility for the bombing deaths of two people in Salt Lake City in October 1985. He also confessed that he had forged the so-called Martin Harris "Salamander Letter" and other documents relating to the Church.

Jan. 27 — *Soviet Union leader Mikhail Gorbachev proposed a series of economic and social reforms that signaled the start of an era of "glasnost," or openness, in the Communist country.*

Feb. 15 — The Tabernacle Choir marked its 3,000th radio broadcast in a series that had become the longest-running network program in the free world.

March 12 — It was announced that the Church-owned Hotel Utah, a landmark in downtown Salt Lake City for 76 years, would close as a hotel Aug. 31 and be renovated as a meetinghouse and office building.

April 25 — The First Presidency announced a realignment of the Church's worldwide administrative areas, including creation of four new areas.

June 20 — The First Presidency sent a letter to priesthood leaders defining the organizational structure of ward Young Women presidencies and calling for consistent midweek activities for young women.

July 15 — The Genealogical Library celebrated the conversion of the last card from its card catalog to computer.

July 24-26 — LDS throughout Britain commemorated the 150th anniversary of the first missionary work in Great Britain. Thirteen General Authorities, including President Ezra Taft Benson and President Gordon B. Hinckley, attended various events, which included dedication of historical sites, firesides and conferences.

Aug. 15 — The Church's Genealogical Department was renamed the Family History Department.

Aug. 25 — A national Emmy award, the first-ever awarded to a public service spot, was given to the Church by the National Academy of Television Arts and Sciences.

Aug. 28 — The Frankfurt Germany Temple was dedicated by President Ezra Taft Benson.

Sept. 4 — A letter from the First Presidency announced the discontinuance of the International Mission. Responsibility for its areas reverted to the respective area presidencies of the Church.

1988

March 24 — President Thomas S. Monson, second counselor in the First Presidency, and his wife, Frances, were guests of the king and queen of Sweden at a dinner commemorating the 350th year of the first Swedish settlement in the United States.

April 2 — Ricks College officially inaugurated its centennial celebration.

May 15 — Elder Neal A. Maxwell organized the Aba Nigeria Stake, the first Church stake in West Africa.

May 28 — The First Presidency issued a statement on the subject of AIDS, stressing chastity before marriage, fidelity in marriage and abstinence from homosexual behavior.

June 1 — The Church was granted legal recognition in Hungary, the first of several such steps in Eastern European nations during the next two years.

July 4 — The Tabernacle Choir completed a 21-day, 19-concert tour of Hawaii, Australia and New Zealand.

July 16 — Monuments commemorating where the Mormon Battalion was mustered and where LDS pioneers established Nebraska's first community were dedicated near Council Bluffs, Iowa, and Florence, Neb.

Mid-August — The Church reached the milestone of having completed 100 million endowments for the dead.

Sept. 17 — The Church joined an interfaith television network (VISN) sponsored by 18 religious organizations. Also, the BYU Folk Dancers were the only North American dance company that performed at Opening Ceremonies of the 1988 Olympic Games in Seoul, Korea, viewed by an estimated 1 billion people worldwide.

Oct. 16 — Elder David B. Haight created the 1,700th stake of the Church. The new stake was in Manaus, Brazil, a city of 1.5 million in the heart of the Amazon jungle.

Oct. 24-28 — President Thomas S. Monson, second counselor in the First Presidency, led a delegation of Church leaders that met with the German Democratic Republic's top government officials. It was announced Nov. 12 that the Church had been granted rights to send missionaries to the DDR and for LDS members from the DDR to serve as missionaries in other countries.

1989

Jan. 19 — The Mormon Tabernacle Choir, called "The Nation's Choir," performed at events during the inauguration of President George Bush.

Jan. 28 — Elders Russell M. Nelson and Dallin H. Oaks of the Quorum of the Twelve completed an eight-day visit to China and were assured by high-level Chinese leaders that people are free to practice religious beliefs in that country.

Feb. 15 — One hundred fifty years after Quincy, Ill., residents gave aid to Church members forced to flee from Missouri, the city's mayor presented Elder Loren C. Dunn of the First Quorum of the Seventy with a key to the city and proclaimed this date "Latter-day Saints Day."

March 24 — *The* Exxon Valdez *struck a reef in Alaska's Prince William Sound and spilled 240,000 barrels of oil, the largest oil spill in U.S. history.*

April 1-2 — The Second Quorum of the Seventy was created and all General Authorities serving under a five-year call were sustained as members, along with another eight newly called General Authorities.

May 16 — The BYU Jerusalem Center for Near Eastern Studies was dedicated by President Howard W. Hunter.

June 14 — LDS missionaries and those of the Jehovah's Witnesses were expelled from Ghana, a western Africa nation where 6,000 Church members live. The Church had no advance notice of the ban. The LDS missionaries were able to return to Ghana in 1990.

June 15 — Ground was broken for the first LDS meetinghouse in Poland.

June 25 — The 100th stake in Mexico was created in Tecalco. Mexico became the first country outside the United States with 100 or more stakes.

June 27 — The renovated Carthage Jail complex in Illinois, where the Prophet Joseph Smith was martyred, was dedicated by President Gordon B. Hinckley, highlighting activities commemorating the 150th anniversary of the Mormon settlement of Nauvoo, Ill.

Aug. 19 — The Portland Oregon Temple was dedicated by President Gordon B. Hinckley.

Sept. 9 — Because of threats expressed against Americans in Colombia during increasing drug-related violence, Church leaders decided to give early releases or transfers to North American missionaries serving in that country.

Sept. 30 — The first General Authorities called under a plan to serve for five years were released in general conference.

Oct. 17 — The first LDS meetinghouse in the Republic of Hungary, located in the capital city of Budapest, was dedicated by President Thomas S. Monson, second counselor in the First Presidency.

Nov. 9 — *The Berlin Wall came down, paving the way for eventual unification of East and West Germany.*

Nov. 25 — A major change in policy for financing local Church units in the United States and Canada was announced by the First Presidency. Ward members would no longer have stake and ward budget assessments.

Dec. 16 — The Las Vegas Nevada Temple was dedicated by President Gordon B. Hinckley.

1990

Jan. 19-23 — Elder Dallin H. Oaks of the Quorum of the Twelve met with Chinese leaders and delivered a 90-minute address about the Church to the Chinese Academy of Social Sciences.

Jan. 21 — David Hsiao Hsin Chen, a professor at BYU-Hawaii who was born and raised in China, was sustained as the Church's "traveling elder" to oversee Church affairs in China.

April 2 — A new Church software package called FamilySearch, designed to simplify the task of family history research, was released by the Church.

April 27-29 — Soviet Union's ambassador to the United States, Yuri V. Dubinin, made a historic visit to Utah Church sites and spoke at a conference of the Salt Lake Monument Park Stake.

May 21 — The U.S. Supreme Court handed down a unanimous decision that money given directly to missionaries is not a deductible donation under federal tax law. The Church encouraged members to follow established procedures of contributing through their wards.

July — New missions in the Eastern European countries of Czechoslovakia, Hungary and Poland highlighted the record 29 missions created in 1990.

Aug. 7 — *International forces of "Operation Desert Shield" left for Saudi Arabia following the invasion of Kuwait by Iraq.*

Aug 25 — The Toronto Ontario Temple was dedicated by President Gordon B. Hinckley.

Sept. 13 — Registration of the

Leningrad Branch of the Church was approved by the Council on Religious Affairs of the Council of Ministers in the Soviet Union.

Sept. 15 — President Gordon B. Hinckley spoke at a memorial service at Cedar City, Utah, that brought together descendants of the pioneers involved with and the victims of the Mountain Meadows Massacre. He also dedicated a monument that had recently been erected at the site.

Sept. 19 — President Ezra Taft Benson underwent surgery to remove two subdural hematomas. After a recurrence of problems, President Benson was operated on again Sept. 23.

November — The First Presidency announced in November a new policy for United States and Canada, effective Jan. 1, 1991, that would equalize contributions required to maintain a full-time missionary.

Nov. 30 — The government of Ghana gave permission for the Church to resume activities in that West African country.

1991

Jan. 15. — Latter-day Saints were among the servicemen and women who were mobilized as part of the war in the Persian Gulf, "Operation Desert Storm." More than 100 LDS groups, spread out across the Arabian Peninsula, saw to the spiritual needs of LDS servicemen and women.

Late February — Delivery of 1,800 packages of food and vitamins, designated for Church members and non-members in the Soviet Union republics of Russia and Estonia, was completed.

April 19 — Recognition of the Church in the Ivory Coast, the center of French West Africa, was announced at a special meeting of Church members in Abidjan. The announcement was made by Elder Richard P. Lindsay, a member of the Seventy and president of the Africa Area.

April 27 — Fifty years after the Church began keeping individual membership records, it computerized membership records worldwide.

May 1 — The 500,000th full-time missionary in this dispensation was called.

May 26 — The 1,800th stake in the Church, the San Francisco de Macoris Dominican Republic Stake, was created.

June 8 — The Tabernacle Choir embarked on a 21-day tour of eight European countries, including five countries in which the choir had not performed before: Hungary, Austria, Czechoslovakia, Poland and the Soviet Union.

June 22-24 — The Alberta Temple, after three years of renovation, was rededicated by President Gordon B. Hinckley, first counselor in the First Presidency, in 12 sessions.

June 24 — The Russian Republic, the largest in the Soviet Union, granted formal recognition to the Church following the Tabernacle Choir's concert in Moscow's Bolshoi Theater.

Aug. 13-27 — The 100th anniversary of the founding of the Church in Tonga was observed with events in Tonga. King Taufa'ahau Tupou IV attended the major events on the main island of Tongatapu.

Sept. 1 — Membership in the Church reached 8 million, about two years after membership hit the 7 million mark in December 1989.

Nov. 5 — Twenty-two members of the Church were killed in the Philippines when a typhoon unleashed flash floods, sending a wall of mud and water through the central Philippine city of Ormoc.

December — The *Encyclopedia of Mormonism,* promoted by its New York publisher as "a landmark reference work," was published. A 13-member board of editors at BYU compiled the encyclopedia under commission from Macmillan Publishing Co.

Dec. 25 — *The Soviet Union broke up; U.S., and other western countries recognized Commonwealth of Independent States.*

1992

March 14 — The sesquicentennial of the founding of the Relief Society on March 17, 1842, was celebrated in an international satellite telecast.

May 2-3 — In the aftermath of rioting and looting in Los Angeles, Calif., sparked by the April 29 acquittal of four policemen charged in the physical abuse of a motorist, hundreds of Church members joined thousands of volunteers in clean-up and relief efforts.

May 13 — Elder Dallin H. Oaks of the Quorum of the Twelve appeared before the U.S. House Subcommittee on Civil and Constitutional Rights advocating legislation that would restore freedom of religion that was diminished in a 1990 Supreme Court decision. He testified Sept. 18 before the Senate advocating the same legislation.

May 31 — Attending specially called meetings in four Utah cities, six members of the Quorum of the Twelve and three members of the Seventy counseled stake presidents and regional representatives on moral issues.

June 9 — The new Social Hall Memorial and walkway — featuring the unearthed foundation of the historic Social Hall of Brigham Young's era — was dedicated by President Gordon B. Hinckley, first counselor in the First Presidency, in downtown Salt Lake City.

Aug. 15 — Commemorating the "second rescue" of the ill-fated Willie and Martin handcart pioneers, President Gordon B. Hinckley, first counselor in the First Presidency, dedicated three monuments near South Pass, Wyo. The Riverton Wyoming Stake researched family histories and performed temple ordinances for those pioneers whose work was not previously done.

Aug. 23-26 — Hurricane Andrew, the most powerful hurricane in more than 60 years, caused $30 billion in damage, including homes of Church members and some Church buildings, particularly in the Homestead Florida Stake near Miami.

Aug. 30 — The Church's 1,900th stake, the Orlando Florida South Stake, was organized by Elder Neal A. Maxwell of the Council of the Twelve.

Sept. 26 — The First Presidency authorized the use of humanitarian relief funds to be sent to Somalia and other African nations in the grip of the drought of the century. In an initial response, one million pounds of food was shipped.

Oct. 18-20, 23-25 — The London and Swiss Temples were rededicated following extensive remodeling and refurbishing.

Dec. 6 — The Church reached a milestone of 20,000 wards and branches with the creation of the Harvest Park Ward in the Salt Lake Granger South Stake.

Dec. 15 — A gospel literacy effort sponsored by the Relief Society to help increase literacy throughout the Church was announced in a letter from the First Presidency to priesthood and Relief Society leaders.

Dec. 26 — The Tabernacle Choir left on a tour of the Holy Land. Concerts were later held in Jerusalem, Tel Aviv and Haifa.

1993

Jan. 6 — Four Church-service missionaries entered Hanoi, Vietnam, to give humanitarian service, teaching English to doctors and staff at a children's hospital and to teachers, staff and children at a school for young children.

April 6 — The centennial of the Salt Lake Temple was observed at a Tabernacle Choir special program, and a special mural was placed in the temple.

April 25-30 — The San Diego California Temple was dedicated by President Gordon B. Hinckley.

June 27 — After being refurbished and remodeled, the former Hotel Utah was rededicated and renamed the Joseph Smith Memorial Building, housing office and meeting facilities for the Church and a theater showing the new film "Legacy"

June 29 — The government of Mexico formally registered the LDS Church, granting it all the rights of a religious organization, including the right to own property.

Nov. 8 — TempleReady, a long-awaited software making it possible to rapidly clear names from family history research for temple work, was announced in a letter to priesthood leaders from the First Presidency.

Nov. 16 — Church leaders hailed the Religious Freedom Restoration Act passed by Congress. This act was signed into law by the U.S. president on this date as "the most historic piece of legislation dealing with religious freedom in our lifetime."

December — Members in Spanish-speaking countries received the Triple Combination of the scriptures with the scripture aids in their language. The Book of Mormon with scripture aids was published in 1992.

1994

January — A yearlong commemoration of the 100th anniversary of the Church's Genealogical Society of Utah — now the Family History Department — began with an effort to invite the non-member international genealogical community to join the effort in preserving, automating and sharing genealogical information for the benefit of all mankind.

Feb. 13 — The First Presidency announced that the 87-year-old Uintah Stake Tabernacle in Vernal, Utah, would be renovated and dedicated as Utah's 10th temple. It was the first existing building to be renovated into a temple.

May 30 — President Ezra Taft Benson, 94, president of the Church for 8 1/2 years, died in Salt Lake City.

June 5 — President Howard W. Hunter was set apart and ordained as the 14th president of the Church.

June 26 — President Howard W. Hunter, President Gordon B. Hinckley and Elder M. Russell Ballard spoke at three separate commemorative events in Nauvoo and Carthage, Ill., on the 150th anniversary of the martyrdom of the Prophet Joseph Smith.

Aug. 6 — It was announced by the Missionary Department that fully one-third of the population of the United States has been visited by Church representatives, and 36 percent have friends or relatives that are LDS.

Sept. 24 — President Howard W.

Hunter asked the women of the Church to stand with and for the Brethren in stemming the "tide of evil that surrounds us, and in moving forward the work of our Savior" at the annual General Relief Society Meeting.

NEWS IN REVIEW
October 1994 – September 1996

October 1994

In a solemn assembly at general conference in the Tabernacle, Oct. 1, President Howard W. Hunter was sustained as the 14th president of the Church. Also sustained were his first counselor, President Gordon B. Hinckley, and his second counselor, President Thomas S. Monson.

Elder Jeffrey R. Holland, ordained an apostle on June 23, was sustained a member of the Council of the Twelve.

Called from the Second Quorum of the Seventy to the First Quorum was Elder Dennis B. Neuenschwander. Two others called to the First Quorum of the Seventy were Elders Andrew W. Peterson and Cecil O. Samuelson Jr.

Elder Hartman Rector Jr. of the First Quorum of the Seventy, a General Authority since 1968, was given emeritus status. Members of the Second Quorum of the Seventy who were released at the conclusion of their five-year term of service were: Elders Albert Choules Jr., Lloyd P. George, Malcolm S. Jeppsen, Richard P. Lindsay, Merlin R. Lybbert, Gerald E. Melchin and Horacio A. Tenorio.

Sustained as the new Sunday School general president was Elder Charles Didier of the Presidency of the Seventy. His first and second counselors, respectively, were Elders J Ballard Washburn and F. Burton Howard of the Seventy. They succeed Elder Merlin R. Lybbert, former Sunday School general president, and his second counselor, Ronald E. Poelman. Elder Clinton L. Cutler, former first counselor, died April 9, 1994.

Sustained as new Primary general president was Patricia Peterson Pinegar, formerly second counselor in the Young Women general presidency. Her first and second counselors, re-

Oct. 9, 1994: President Howard W. Hunter, center, and his counselors President Gordon B. Hinckley and President Thomas S. Monson take part in dedication of Orlando Florida Temple.

spectively, were Anne Goalen Wirthlin and Susan Carol Lillywhite Warner.

Bonnie Dansie Parkin was sustained as second counselor in the Young Women general presidency, succeeding Sister Pinegar. Michaelene P. Grassli and her counselors, Sisters Betty Jo N. Jepsen and Ruth B. Wright, were released.

Also in the news in October, 1994:

Oct. 9-11 : The Orlando Florida Temple was dedicated in 12 sessions, with President Howard W. Hunter pronouncing the prayer of dedication, the first Church president to do so for a temple dedication since 1989.

Oct. 15-16 : President Howard W. Hunter returned for a weekend conference and reception to the Pasadena California Stake, over which he presided from 1950 to 1959.

Oct. 16 : About 200 LDS families were among thousands in southeast Texas forced to evacuate their homes as flood waters and subsequent fires destroyed or damaged homes, farmland and businesses. Church members engaged in relief efforts for flood victims.

November 1994

In a letter to stake presidents in Nashville, Tenn., and vicinity, the First Presidency announced plans to build a temple in that area.

Also in the news in November 1994:

Nov. 3: An open house for the newly constructed Bountiful Utah Temple began with tours for news media representatives, VIPs and others.

Nov. 10: A reception in the Relief Society Building in Salt Lake City commemorated the 125th anniversary of the Young Women, which was organized Nov. 28, 1869.

Nov. 13: A century of efforts to identify and redeem the dead was celebrated with a program in the Salt Lake Tabernacle commemorating the 100th anniversary of the Genealogical Society of Utah. Members of the First Presidency and Elder Russell M. Nelson of the Council of the Twelve spoke at the program. President Howard W. Hunter was given birthday honors as his 87th birthday was the following day. He is a former president of the society.

Nov. 17: President Thomas S. Monson, second counselor in the First Presidency, was honored by Catholic Community Services of Utah for humanitarian care and concern.

Nov. 18: Eric B. Shumway was officially installed as the eighth president of the Brigham Young University-Hawaii campus by President Howard W. Hunter.

Nov. 30: More than 40 ambassadors were welcomed by Elder Neal A. Maxwell of the Council of the Twelve to the 17th annual Festival of Lights at the Washington Temple Visitors Center.

December 1994

In December, relief supplies consisting of 80 tons of food, 20 tons of winter clothing and 2,000 winter blankets were donated to some 3,000 families of flood victims in Partiznask, Russia. Also, 79 tons of food were donated by the Church to feed the homeless in Atlanta, Ga.

Also in the news in December, 1994:

Dec. 3: It was announced in the *Church News* Dec. 3 that more than 20,000 food packages for families in Bosnia, Croatia and Albania were being prepared by hundreds of Church members for shipment during the next few months.

Dec. 4: At the annual First Presidency Christmas Devotional telecast by satellite from the Tabernacle on Temple Square in Salt Lake City, members of the First Presidency shared their feelings concerning the Savior and the Christmas season.

Dec. 11: The 2,000th Stake in the Church was created in Mexico City, Mexico, with President Howard W. Hunter presiding.

Dec. 17: A total of 870,361 people toured the Bountiful Utah Temple during its open house, Nov. 5-Dec. 17.

January 1995

On Jan. 8-14 the Bountiful Utah Temple was dedicated by President Howard W. Hunter in the first of 28 sessions. He had dedicated the Orlando Florida Temple the previous October. During the week President Hunter attended six sessions and addressed four sessions.

In other news in January, 1995:

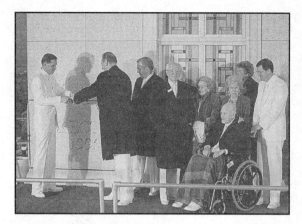

Jan. 8, 1995: On frosty morning, First Presidency participates in cornerstone laying at Bountiful Utah Temple.

Jan. 13-14: Elder Dallin H. Oaks of the Quorum of the Twelve and six LDS scholars were featured at a BYU seminar on the Joseph Smith Translation of the Bible. The seminar underscored the validity of the Prophet's translation for use by Church members in study and teaching.

Jan. 17: Church leaders and members rallied quickly to aid victims of an earthquake in Kobe, Japan, which killed more than 5,000 people. One Church member was killed, and 35 member families were left homeless after the quake.

Jan. 21: The Church reached the 9 million mark in membership, it was announced. Plans to build two new temples in South America : in Cochabamba, Bolivia, and Recife, Brazil : were announced by the First Presidency.

Jan. 24: President Thomas S. Monson, second counselor in the First Presidency, joined other religious leaders and Utah officials in welcoming the Most Rev. George H. Nieder-

auer as the bishop of the Catholic Church's Diocese of Salt Lake City.

February 1995

A missionary satellite telecast on **Feb. 26** was accompanied by simultaneous open houses in many parts of the Church. It featured Elder Jeffrey R. Holland of the Quorum of the Twelve, who narrated a video presentation about the ministry of the Savior and invited all to "come unto Christ."

Feb. 5: President Thomas S. Monson, second counselor in the First Presidency, spoke to more than 23,000 young adults in BYU's Marriott Center and to thousands of others watching a satellite telecast. His message focused on President Howard W. Hunter.

Feb. 15-22: For the first time in 37 years the Tabernacle Choir made a recording of Handel's "Messiah," the complete oratorio. It was conducted by eminent British choral conductor, David Willcocks. The album on compact disc and audio cassette, was re-

Jan. 24, 1995: President Thomas S. Monson, accompanied by his wife, Frances, welcomes incoming Bishop George H. Niederauer of the Salt Lake Catholic Diocese. Also at the ceremony are Elder James E. Faust and his wife, Ruth.

March 8, 1995: Funeral services are held for President Howard W. Hunter, who died March 3, 1995.

leased in mid-May.

Feb. 21: President Gordon B. Hinckley, first counselor in the First Presidency, was honored by the Utah Region of the National Conference of Christians and Jews. At a dinner attended by more than 1,000 people of various religious faiths, he was honored for promoting high moral values

and culture.

March 1995

President Howard W. Hunter died **March 3** at his Salt Lake City home. His was the shortest tenure of any Church president—less than nine months—but he was praised for having an enormous impact on Church members during that time.

President Gordon B. Hinckley was ordained and set apart **March 12** as the 15th president of the Church. Called as first counselor in the First Presidency was President Thomas S. Monson and as second counselor President James E. Faust. President Monson was also set apart as president of the Quorum of the Twelve. President Boyd K. Packer was named acting president of that quorum, a position he held during President Howard W. Hunter's tenure.

Also in the news in March 1994:

March 4: After extensive remodeling, the South Visitors Center on Temple Square in Salt Lake City reopened with a new look and a new function as a tour center.

March 12: The first stake in the Republic of Ireland was created under the direction of Elder Graham W. Doxey of the Seventy.

March 25: At the General Young Women Meeting originating from the Tabernacle on Temple Square in Salt Lake City, President Gordon B. Hinck-

March 13, 1995: The Church's 15th president, President Gordon B. Hinckley addresses the press. On his right is President Thomas S. Monson, first counselor; on his left is President James E. Faust, his second counselor. President Boyd K. Packer, acting president of the Quorum of the Twelve Apostles, is seated far right.

May 13, 1995: About 13,000 people gather for the groundbreaking of the Vernal Utah Temple, the first to be constructed from an existing building.

ley endorsed the yearlong emphasis of the Young Women organization "to experiment upon the word" of God.

March 29: In testimony at a U.S. Senate Finance Committee hearing regarding welfare reform, Presiding Bishop Merrill J. Batemen highlighted Church welfare programs and shared the history, principles and lessons learned while establishing these programs.

April 1995

For the second time in six months, Church members met in solemn assembly to sustain a new First Presidency of the Church in connection with the 165th Annual General Conference **April 1-2**.

Also at the conference:

• Elder Henry B. Eyring was sustained as a member of the Quorum of the Twelve.

• Elders John B. Dickson, Jay E. Jensen, David E. Sorensen and W. Craig Zwick were sustained to the First Quorum of the Seventy. (Elders Dickson, Jensen and Sorensen were serving at the time as members of the Second Quorum.) Also, Elder Bruce D. Porter was sustained to the Second Quorum of the Seventy.

• Creation of a new administrative position in the Church, area authority, and the discontinuance of the position of regional representative, effective Aug. 15, was announced by President Gordon B. Hinckley.

Also in the news in April 1995:

April 8: President Gordon B. Hinckley dedicated Tuacahn, an outdoor amphitheater and arts center 10 miles north of St. George in southern Utah. The Tabernacle Choir performed at the dedication, attended by more than 2,000 people.

April 15-16: President Gordon B. Hinckley participated in his first regional conference since becoming Church president. He spoke to more than 7,000 members of the St. Louis Missouri Region.

April 22-23: President Gordon B. Hinckley attended the Boston Massachusetts Regional Conference and spoke to 7,500 Church members.

May 1995

President Gordon B. Hinckley broke ground **May 13** at the Uintah Stake Tabernacle in Vernal, Utah, to signal remodeling that will turn the pioneer building into the new Vernal Utah Temple. President James E. Faust, second counselor in the First Presidency, also participated in the groundbreaking.

Also in the news in May 1995:

May 1: Ground was broken on the BYU campus for a law library to be named in honor of the late President Howard W. Hunter. President Gordon B. Hinckley presided at the ceremony, in which all three members of the First Presidency participated.

May 13: Church members throughout Utah helped clean up the state as they took part in "Take Pride in Utah Day" designated by Utah Gov. Mike Leavitt.

May 20-21: President Gordon B. Hinckley addressed some 13,000 members at a regional conference in the Santa Rosa/Vacaville, Calif., area.

June 1995

The International Olympic Committee announced **June 16** that Salt Lake City had been selected as the site for the Winter Olympics in 2002. The announcement was cheered at a celebration featuring the Tabernacle Choir. Later in the day, the First Presidency stated that the Church would cooperate with state and city officials in their effort to be hospitable hosts for the games.

Also in the news in June 1995:

June 16: Rex E. Lee, president of BYU for six years, announced that he had been granted a release from his post due to health considerations.

June 17-23: In the first visit of a Church president to Alaska, President Gordon B. Hinckley spoke to 7,700 people at a regional conference in Anchorage.

June 22: A new musical production commemorating the 1996 Utah Centennial premiered at the Church's Promised Valley Playhouse. It was titled "Unspoken Song : a Celebration of 100 Years of Utah Spirit."

June 24: Major exterior preservation projects at the Logan and Manti temples were announced by the First Presidency. They will include replacement or restoration of deteriorating stone, mortar joints and window woodwork.

June 29: Elder L. Tom Perry of the Quorum of the Twelve broke ground for the new John Taylor Religion Building at Ricks College in Rexburg, Idaho.

July 1995

The First Presidency announced changes in the Presidency of the Seventy on **July 1**, effective Aug. 15. Elder Jack H Goaslind and Elder Harold G. Hillam were called to the presidency, while Elder Rex D. Pinegar and Elder Charles Didier were released.

Also in the news in July 1995:

July 16: President Gordon B. Hinckley addressed 1,176 Church members in a combined sacrament meeting of three wards in Jackson, Wyo.

July 17: A milestone in progress in the construction of the Mount Timpanogos Temple was reached with

June 16, 1995: Mormon Tabernacle Choir sings as announcement is made that Salt Lake City is chosen as the site for the 2002 Winter Olympics.

August, 1995: Former members of opposing forces in World War II are now unified by their Church membership. From left are Erich Vergin, German air force; Norman Sharples, British infantry; Masao Watabe, Japanese air force; and Lowell Christensen, U.S. Navy.

the placement of a statue of the Angel Moroni atop the temple's 190-foot spire.

July 22-26: Pioneer Day observances in Utah included dedication of the restored Miles Goodyear cabin in Ogden, parades, a sunrise service, marathon race, and a hike up Ensign Peak in Salt Lake City.

August 1995

President Thomas S. Monson, first counselor in the First Presidency, and his wife, Frances, helped welcome the king and queen of Sweden to the grounds of the Stockholm Sweden Temple on **Aug. 23.** The king and queen visited the temple site in a revival of a tradition dating back to the 13th century in which the king traveled through the country to be met by its citizens. President and Sister Monson also visited sites of significance to the Church in Germany, where President Monson dedicated a meetinghouse in Goerlitz, Germany, on Aug. 27, fulfilling a 27-year-old promise that the Saints would receive all the blessings any other member of the Church would receive.

Also in the news in August 1995:

Aug. 4-5, 8-9: In performances at the John F. Kennedy Center for the Performing Arts in Washington, D.C., the Tabernacle Choir premiered "An American Requiem" by James De-Mars. The choir also performed in New York City in the famed Cathedral of St. John the Divine, the sixth largest cathedral in the world.

Aug. 20: President Gordon B. Hinckley spoke to 17,328 Church members at a regional conference in Tacoma, Wash.

Aug. 24-Sept. 2: In a whirlwind 10-

Aug. 23, 1995: President Thomas S. Monson, first counselor in the First Presidency, accompanied by his wife, Frances, shakes hands with Sweden's Queen Silvia, standing next to King Carl XVI Gustaf on the Stockholm Sweden Temple grounds.

Sept. 23, 1995: The sanctity of the family was emphasized in a proclamation on the family issued by the First Presidency.

day tour of England and Ireland, President Gordon B. Hinckley, accompanied by his wife, Marjorie, created a stake in Canterbury, England; rededicated the Hyde Park Chapel in London; visited significant Church history sites; and spoke at many member firesides and meetings with missionaries.

September 1995

The First Presidency issued a proclamation **Sept. 23** to the Church and to the world reaffirming gospel standards, doctrines and practices relative to the family. The proclamation was presented by President Gordon B. Hinckley at the General Relief Society meeting.

Also in the news in September 1995:

Sept. 16: The Alberta Temple was named a Canadian Historic Site by government representatives at a ceremony in Cardston.

Sept. 17: Church members in Idaho Falls, Idaho, observed the 50th anniversary of the dedication of the Idaho Falls Temple at a special service, which was addressed by Elder W. Eugene Hansen of the Seventy and executive director of the Temple Department.

Sept. 28: President Gordon B. Hinckley received the Distinguished Service to Humanity Award from the Association of Mormon Counselors and Psychotherapists.

October 1995

At the 165th semiannual general conference held **Sept. 30-Oct. 1**:

• Two new temples were announced by President Gordon B. Hinckley, one in Boston, Mass., and the other in White Plains, N.Y. The possibility of one in Venezuela was also announced. President Hinckley said the two new temples will be built instead of one previously announced for Hartford, Conn. President Hinckley also said the Church was working on sites in six more areas.

• A new Sunday School general presidency was sustained, consisting of Elder Harold G. Hillam as president and Elders F. Burton Howard and Glenn L. Pace as counselors. They succeeded Elders Charles A. Didier, J Ballard Washburn and F. Burton Howard in the respective positions in the presidency.

• Elders Ted E. Brewerton and Hans B. Ringger of the First Quorum of the Seventy were granted emeritus status.

• Released from the Second Quorum of the Seventy were Elders Eduardo Ayala, LeGrand R. Curtis, Helvecio Martins, J Ballard Washburn and Durrell A. Woolsey.

Also in the news in October 1995:

Oct. 2: Two new adjoining parks in Salt Lake City — one constructed by the city and the other by the Church, were dedicated by President Gordon

B. Hinckley on property once belonging to President Brigham Young. The Brigham Young Historic Park, built by the Church, memorializes the work of the Latter-day Saint settlers of the Salt Lake Valley. City Creek Park complements the Church park.

Oct. 17: President Gordon B. Hinckley honored outgoing BYU Pres. Rex E. Lee in his address at the BYU devotional assembly.

Oct. 18: President James E. Faust rededicated the Church-owned cannery in Murray, Utah.

Oct. 20: The new Ezra Taft Benson Science Building at BYU was dedicated by President Gordon B. Hinckley in a service attended by all three members of the First Presidency.

Oct. 22: The first stake in Papua New Guinea was created under the direction of Elder V. Dallas Merrell of the Seventy.

Oct. 29: President Gordon B. Hinckley spoke to nearly 10,000 people at a regional conference of the five Ricks College stakes in Rexburg, Idaho.

November 1995

Presiding Bishop Merrill J. Bateman was named the 11th president of BYU on **Nov. 2**, effective Jan. 1, 1996. President Gordon B. Hinckley, who made the announcement at a media conference in the Joseph Smith Memorial Building, said that Bishop Bateman had also been called to the First Quorum of the Seventy.

Also in the news in November 1995:

Nov. 13: President Gordon B. Hinckley met with U.S. President Bill Clinton at the White House in Washington, D.C., at the request of the chief executive. The two conversed on the importance of strong families. While in the eastern United States, President Hinckley also met with corporate executives, representatives of the national media and heads of charitable organizations at a reception and luncheon in New York City.

Nov. 18: The Young Women Worldwide Celebration culminated a yearlong emphasis on the admonition and promises in Alma 32 to "experiment upon the word." Various activities were held in wards and stakes.

Nov. 25: Ambassadors from about 50 nations and 12 members of U.S. congress attended a ceremony to turn on 300,000 Christmas lights at the Washington D.C. Temple, where Ambassador Siddhartha Shankar Ray of India displayed a remarkable knowledge of Church history and doctrine before turning on the lights.

Nov. 29: President Thomas S. Monson and President James E. Faust of the First Presidency hosted Catholic leaders in Utah on a special tour of the Church's Deseret Industries Sort Center and Welfare Square.

December 1995

The First Presidency announced a new Presiding Bishopric **Dec. 27**, consisting of Presiding Bishop H. David Burton and his counselors, Bishop Richard C. Edgley and Bishop Keith B.

Dec. 18, 1995: President Gordon B. Hinckley hosts Mike Wallace of CBS "60 Minutes" during an inteview that was later used in a telecast in April 1996.

Feb. 3, 1996: Horses and covered wagons wait on banks of frozen Mississippi River during re-enactment of 1846 Nauvoo exodus.

McMullin.

Also in the news in 1995:

Dec. 18: President Gordon B. Hinckley was interviewed by CBS Television Network's Mike Wallace for the popular weekly program "60 Minutes." The segment would be shown in April 1996.

Dec. 20: A new logo design for the name of the Church, focusing on the name of the Savior, was announced by the First Presidency.

Dec. 27: The First Presidency announced plans for a temple in Monterrey, Mexico.

January 1996

Church members joined other Utah residents in celebrating the state centennial, beginning **Jan. 4** with a program in the Salt Lake Tabernacle, parades, a musical gala, fireworks and other events and continuing throughout the year. President Gordon B. Hinckley represented the Church at the Tabernacle program.

Also in the news in January 1996:

Jan. 13-14: Continuing a busy schedule of travel and meetings, President Gordon B. Hinckley visited the southern Utah communities of Parowan and St. George for a variety of Church and civic events.

Jan. 18: In a written statement, the First Presidency and Quorum of the Twelve announced the pending withdrawal by General Authorities from boards of directors of business corporations, including Church-owned corporations, effective at the next regular annual meetings of the respective corporations.

Jan. 21: President Gordon B. Hinckley invited young adults attending a Salt Lake Valley-wide institute fireside in the Salt Lake Tabernacle to walk with him on "the path of faith" and to "stand for that which is right and true and good."

Jan. 27-28: On a whirlwind trip to Veracruz and Mexico City, Mexico, President Gordon B. Hinckley spoke to some 9,000 Saints, instructed some 1,200 priesthood leaders and missionaries and met with top government officials and media representatives.

February 1996

In bitterly cold weather, some 1,000 people huddled in a large tent at the edge of the Mississippi River in Nauvoo, Ill., for a program **Feb. 3** to commemorate the beginning of the Saints' forced exodus from the city 150 years before. The following day, Sunday, **Feb. 4,** a fireside was held in Nauvoo to mark the anniversary date.

Also in the news in February 1996:

Feb. 2: The Tabernacle Choir was featured on "CBS This Morning," a national news program, in a special telecast from Salt Lake City.

Feb. 4: In the Pacific island nation of Kiribati, 80 men were ordained to the Melchizedek Priesthood, indicating phenomenal growth of the Church there in recent years.

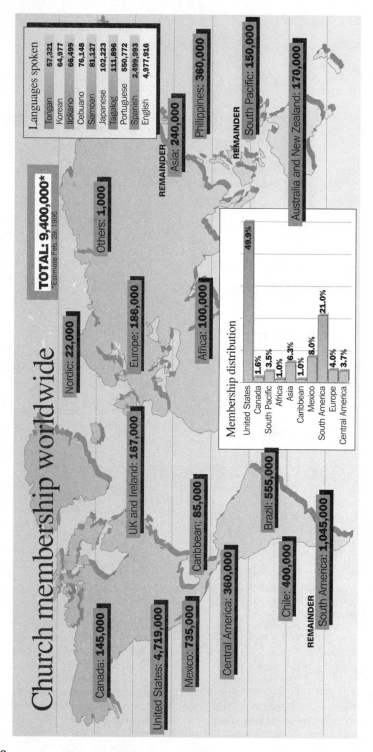

Church membership worldwide

TOTAL: 9,400,000*
*Estimate Feb. 29, 1996

Languages spoken

Tongan	57,321
Korean	64,977
Ilokano	66,499
Cebuano	76,148
Samoan	81,127
Japanese	102,223
Tagalog	111,896
Portuguese	550,772
Spanish	2,499,993
English	4,977,916

Canada: 145,000

United States: 4,719,000

Mexico: 735,000

Central America: 360,000

Caribbean: 85,000

Brazil: 555,000

Chile: 400,000

REMAINDER South America: 1,045,000

UK and Ireland: 167,000

Europe: 186,000

Nordic: 22,000

Others: 1,000

Africa: 100,000

REMAINDER Asia: 240,000

Philippines: 360,000

REMAINDER South Pacific: 150,000

Australia and New Zealand: 170,000

Membership distribution

United States	49.9%
Canada	1.6%
South Pacific	3.5%
Africa	1.0%
Asia	6.3%
Caribbean	1.0%
Mexico	8.0%
South America	21.0%
Europe	4.0%
Central America	3.7%

Feb. 10: Addressing couples in five BYU married stakes, President Gordon B. Hinckley shared four cornerstones on which to build homes: mutual respect, the soft answer, financial honesty with the Lord and prayer.

Feb. 17-19: President Gordon B. Hinckley visited Laie, Hawaii, for regional conferences and priesthood leadership and missionary meetings. He met with Catholic leaders with whom Church members have worked on legislative issues of a moral nature.

Feb. 18: At the largest LDS gathering ever assembled in South Africa, Elder M. Russell Ballard of the Quorum of the Twelve encouraged nearly 5,000 listeners to declare the gospel to all the world.

Feb. 25: A dozen well-known Church members in entertainment, sports, industry, business, opera and government shared their testimonies at the annual missionary satellite fireside transmitted as part of locally organized open houses.

Feb. 28: The Church reached a milestone in its history as the Member and Statistical Records Division estimated that for the first time, more than half of the Church membership was living outside the United States.

Feb. 24-25: President Gordon B. Hinckley met with 9,000 Church members from six stakes in the western part of North Carolina at regional meetings, including priesthood leadership and missionary meetings.

Feb. 28: During a visit with U.S. Vice President Al Gore in Washington, D.C., Elder Neal A. Maxwell and Elder M. Russell Ballard presented him with a copy of his family history.

March 1996

President Gordon B. Hinckley counseled Young Women of the Church to be true to their faith, heritage, parents and God at the annual General Young Women Meeting **March 30.**

Also in the news in March 1996:

March 1-8: During a visit to Utah, former British Prime Minister Margaret Thatcher attended a Tabernacle Choir broadcast, visited Temple Square and the Museum of Church History and Art, spoke at BYU on the moral basis of a free society and was hosted by the First Presidency at a luncheon.

March 11: Former BYU Pres. Rex E. Lee, released Dec. 31, 1995, died at age 61, having battled various health problems, including cancer.

March 16-17: President Gordon B. Hinckley visited two regional conferences at Denton and Plano Texas and spoke to almost 300 missionaries at a combined conference of the Texas Fort Worth and Dallas missions.

March 23-24: President Gordon B. Hinckley spoke to more than 4,200 youth and young adults in three firesides in San Diego, Calif., encouraging them to strengthen their belief in God and themselves.

March 26: Elder Victor L. Brown, General Authority emeritus and former Presiding Bishop, died at age 81.

April 1996

At the 166th Annual General Conference **April 6-7,** nine new General Authorities were called. Elder Bruce C. Hafen was called to serve in the First Quorum of the Seventy and the others to serve in the Second Quorum of the Seventy were Elders L. Edward Brown, Sheldon F. Child, Quentin L. Cook, Wm. Rolfe Kerr, Dennis E. Simmons, Jerald L. Taylor, Francisco J. Vinas and Richard B. Wirthlin. Also, Elders Dallas N. Archibald and Dieter F. Uchtdorf, who had been serving in the Second Quorum of the Seventy, were sustained to the First Quorum. Elder Merrill J. Bateman was sustained to the First Quorum of the Seventy, a move announced the previous November when he was named president of BYU. He was thus released as Presiding Bishop with his counselors Bishop H. David Burton and Bishop Richard C. Edgley. Sustained as the Presiding Bishopric were Bishop Burton as Presiding Bishop, Bishop Edgley as first counselor and Bishop Keith B. McMullin as second counselor.

Also in the news in April 1996:

April 6: President Gordon B. Hinckley announced in the opening session of general conference that a new meeting hall was being designed that would hold three to four times more people than the Salt Lake Tabernacle.

April 14: President Gordon B. Hinckley delivered three addresses as he met with 4,850 young adults and youth in Colorado.

April 22: A new building on the campus of Utah Valley State College, named the David O. McKay Events Center in honor of the ninth president of the Church, was dedicated by President Gordon B. Hinckley.

April 25: Elder Merrill J. Bateman of the First Quorum of the Seventy was inaugurated as the 11th president of BYU in a ceremony conducted by President Gordon B. Hinckley.

April 26: Speaking via satellite telecast to some 18,000 missionaries in the 101 missions of the United States, Canada and the Caribbean, President Gordon B. Hinckley told them they

May 26, 1996: Members leave Hong Kong Temple following its dedication.

will affect generations to come with their service. The balance of the Church's 50,000 missionaries were to view the telecast on video cassette.

April 27-28: President Gordon B. Hinckley attended the Pittsburgh Pennsylvania Regional Conference, speaking to members of three stakes and a mission district as well as 170 missionaries in the Pennsylvania Pittsburgh Mission.

May 1996

President Gordon B. Hinckley became the first Church president ever to visit the mainland of China. He and associates among the General Authorities visited Shenzhen on **May 27-28,** a sister facility to the Church's Polynesian Cultural Center in Hawaii.

Also in the news in May 1996:

May 1: David M. Kennedy, a special representative of the First Presidency for nearly 20 years and a former U.S. Secretary of the Treasury, died at age 90.

May 3-4: At a symposium in Des Moines, Iowa, scholars and enthusiasts from Iowa, Utah and elsewhere assembled for two days of lectures and presentations on the part Latter-day Saints played in the history of Iowa during the 1846 portion of the westward trek from Nauvoo, Ill., to the Salt Lake Valley.

May 13: Elder Lloyd P. George, who served in the Quorums of the Seventy for six years, died at age 75.

May 17-21: En route to Hong Kong for a temple dedication, President Gordon B. Hinckley visited Tokyo, Japan, speaking to Church members, visiting U.S. ambassador Walter Mondale and meeting with news media representatives.

May 26-27: The Hong Kong Temple was dedicated in seven sessions presided over by President Gordon B. Hinckley.

May 28-29: President Gordon B. Hinckley visited Cambodia and Vietnam. In Cambodia, he offered a prayer to dedicate the land for the

May 28, 1996: President Gordon B. Hinckley receives warm welcome during visit to Chinese Folk Villages in Shezhen, China.

preaching of the gospel; in Vietnam, he gave an "addendum" to the prayer he offered there in 1966, at the height of the Vietnam War.

June 1996

President Gordon B. Hinckley revisited the most sacred sites of the Holy Land during a stay in Israel **June 16-22.**

Also in the news in June 1996:

June 4-28: A wagon train commemorating the centennial of Utah traversed the state from Logan to Cedar City. Elder M. Russell Ballard spoke to wagon train participants on the eve of their departure, and President Gordon B. Hinckley addressed the group at his restored ancestral home of Cove Fort, Utah.

June 11: President Gordon B. Hinckley broke ground for a temple in Madrid, Spain. The occasion was the first visit by a Church president to Spain.

June 11-16: President Gordon B. Hinckley visited five European nations, stopping in Madrid, Spain; Brussels, Belgium; The Hague, Netherlands; Copenhagen, Denmark; and Berlin, Germany. He encouraged the Saints he addressed to find happiness through keeping the commandments and having loving families.

June 16: President Thomas S. Monson addressed a Utah Centennial Fireside in Moroni, Utah.

June 17-July 12: Two wagon trains and a handcart group conceived and organized largely by non-Latter-day Saints left Nauvoo, Ill., and traced the Pioneers' 1846 route across 12 Iowa counties. Communities along the way put on celebrations marking the sesquicentennial of the Nauvoo exodus.

June 19-23: The largest group of new mission presidents ever assembled — 138 — and their wives received four days of instruction at the annual Seminar for New Mission Presidents at the Missionary Training Center in Provo, Utah. All three members of the First Presidency and other General Authorities spoke to them.

June 29: President Gordon B. Hinckley rededicated the newly refurbished This Is the Place Monument and state park at a ceremony that featured the Tabernacle Choir. Old Deseret Village, a living-history facility at the park, was enlarged and improved with extensive participation from Church members, as a state centennial project.

June 29: President Gordon B. Hinckley was honored in Sun Valley, Idaho, by the American Academy of Achievement with the Golden Plate Award for exceptional accomplishment in the area of public service. Eight others of national prominence also received the award.

July 1996

On a five-state tour, President Gordon B. Hinckley spoke to Church members in Nauvoo, Ill.; attended the Hill Cumorah pageant in Palmyra, N.Y.; attended the Grand Encampment celebration in Council Bluffs,

July 13, 1996: A re-enactment of the 1846 mustering of the Mormon Battalion is held in Council Bluffs, Iowa.

Iowa; and spoke to missionary and youth groups in Tulsa, Okla., and Kansas City, Mo.

At the Grand Encampment celebration in Council Bluffs, Iowa, **July 13**, President Gordon B. Hinckley dedicated a new replica of the Kanesville Tabernacle, where Brigham Young was sustained as president of the Church. The mustering-in of the Mormon Battalion was also re-enacted at the celebration, to commemorate the 150th anniversary of the Mormon Trail, Iowa statehood, and the founding of Council Bluffs as Kanesville by the Saints on their way from Nauvoo to the Rocky Mountains.

Also in the news in July 1996:

July 26: A new park and improved trail to the top of Ensign Peak in Salt Lake City was dedicated by President Gordon B. Hinckley. It is the site where Brigham Young and eight others raised a figurative and scriptural "ensign to the nations" two days after they arrived in the Salt Lake Valley.

July 29-31: In a celebration featuring the Tabernacle Choir, Church members and others in San Francisco, Calif., commemorated the arrival of the ship *Brooklyn,* carrying Latter-day Saints there on July 31, 1846. A ship similar to the *Brooklyn* was used in a re-enactment at San Francisco Bay.

August 1996

At the U.S. Army post in Fort Leav-enworth, Kan., where the Mormon Battalion was outfitted and trained 150 years ago, 500 costumed re-enactors commemorated their march **Aug. 3**, a ceremony sponsored by the post and six stakes of the Church.

Also in the news in August 1996:

Aug. 2: King Taufa'ahau Tupou IV of Tonga met with the First Presidency in Salt Lake City during a visit to accept an award from the Seacology Foundation based in Springville, Utah.

Aug. 4: At a community service in Provo commemorating the Utah centennial, President Gordon B. Hinckley decried the "secularizing of America" in which any mention of God is removed from national institutions.

Aug. 10: Elder Richard G. Scott of

July 30, 1996: A replica of the ship *Brooklyn* sails into the San Francisco harbor in commemoration of the 150th anniversary of the arrival of the first group of Saints in 1846.

the Quorum of the Twelve presided at a groundbreaking for the Guayaquil Ecuador Temple.

Aug. 11: Elder L. Tom Perry of the Quorum of the Twelve created the Tarawa Kiribati Stake, the first in that nation.

Aug. 18: Elder Richard G. Scott of the Quorum of the Twelve presided at a groundbreaking for the Santo Domingo Dominican Republic Temple, the first in the Caribbean.

Aug. 31: The First Presidency announced plans for the Church's 63rd temple to be built in Billings, Mont.

September 1996

Sept. 1: President Gordon B. Hinckley delivered the keynote address in the Salt Lake Tabernacle at a religious service of the American Legion national convention in Salt Lake City. He expressed the concern that America is forsaking God and the fear "that He may forsake us."

Sept. 17: In a devotional address at BYU, President Gordon B. Hinckley praised the students for having been designated second on a list of "stone-cold sober" schools around the nation. He also urged them to pursue greatness and stand for the right.

Sept. 20: President Gordon B. Hinckley broke ground for a massive underground addition to the Harold B. Lee Library at BYU.

Sept. 21: President Thomas S. Monson, first counselor in the First Presidency, spoke to 12,000 at a two-day Jamboral at Park City, Utah, sponsored by the Great Salt Lake Council, Boy Scouts of America.

Sept. 27: At a Scout Jamboral in Fillmore, Utah, similar to the one the previous week in Park City, President Gordon B. Hinckley spoke to 28,000 Scouts from the Utah National Parks Council.

Sept. 27: A statue of President David O. McKay was unveiled near the new David O. McKay Events Center on the Utah Valley State College campus. It was sculpted by Ortho Fairbanks, who made a portrait bust of President McKay nearly 30 years previously.

Sept. 28: As "noble daughters of God," the sisters of the Church have stood true in the faith through the history of the Church, President James E. Faust, second counselor in the First Presidency said at the General Relief Society Meeting in the Salt Lake Tabernacle.

October 1996

Oct. 6: At the 166th Semiannual General Conference, emeritus status was granted to Elder Carlos E. Asay of the Presidency of the Seventy and the call of Elder Earl C. Tingey to fill the vacancy was sustained. Also, nine members of the Second Quorum of the Seventy were given honorable releases: Elders Rulon G. Craven, Julio E. Davila, Graham W. Doxey, In Sang Han, W. Mack Lawrence, Joseph C. Muren, Stephen D. Nadauld, Jorge A. Rojas and Sam K. Shimabukuro. Elder Nadauld was released as first counselor in the general Young Men presidency. He was succeeded by Elder Vaughn J Featherstone of the Seventy, former second counselor. Called as second counselor was Elder F. David Stanley.

Church growth

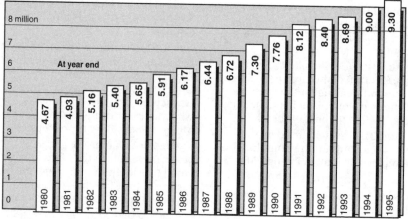

8 million

At year end

1980	1981	1982	1983	1984	1985	1986	1987	1988	1989	1990	1991	1992	1993	1994	1995
4.67	4.93	5.16	5.40	5.65	5.91	6.17	6.44	6.72	7.30	7.76	8.12	8.40	8.69	9.00	9.30

Nations, Territories

At year end *(Where the church has wards or branches)*

| 1981 | 1982 | 1983 | 1984 | 1985 | 1986 | 1987 | 1988 | 1989 | 1991 | 1992 | 1993 | 1994 | 1995 |
| 86* | 105 | 107 | 114 | 115 | 122 | 122 | 125 | 128 | 130 | 146 | 149 | 156 | 159 |

Stakes

At year end

| 1980 | 1981 | 1982 | 1983 | 1984 | 1985 | 1986 | 1987 | 1988 | 1989 | 1990 | 1991 | 1992 | 1993 | 1994 | 1995 |
| 1,218 | 1,321 | 1,392 | 1,458 | 1,507 | 1,582 | 1,622 | 1,666 | 1,707 | 1,738 | 1,784 | 1,837 | 1,919 | 1,968 | 2,008 | 2,150 |

FACTS,
STATISTICS

MEMBERSHIP STATISTICS

Membership and units by Church area

(As of Dec. 31, 1991; area boundaries do not necessarily follow country, state or province boundaries. Membership totals may not agree with individual entries due to rounding; Totals are from original, not rounded, numbers)

Area	Membership	Stakes	Wards	Branches in stakes	Missions	Districts	Missions branches	Total wards, branches
Total Church	"9,342,000	2,150	14,337	4,061	306	698	4,287	22,685
Africa Area	92,000	11	56	65	11	47	269	390
Asia Area	59,000	11	56	30	8	19	107	193
Asia North Area	173,000	41	217	101	13	27	136	454
Brazil Area	548,000	136	801	278	23	45	315	1,394
Central America Area	349,000	68	379	164	11	70	352	895
Chile Area	394,000	89	516	178	7	14	87	781
Europe East Area	16,000	1	3	14	15	31	218	235
Europe North Area	190,000	51	294	167	12	11	55	516
Europe West Area	170,000	41	219	252	26	58	342	813
Mexico North Area	354,000	63	356	83	10	29	189	628
Mexico South Area	374,000	75	491	149	8	15	114	754
North America Central Area	410,000	106	732	270	14	9	78	1,080
North America Northeast Area	422,000	103	671	365	27	12	90	1,126
North America Northwest Area	690,000	186	1,362	175	9	3	17	1,554
North America Southeast Area	419,000	85	559	272	22	24	177	1,008
Caribbean	86,000	8	42	37	7	23	173	252
U.S.A. Only	333,000	77	517	235	15	1	4	756
North America Southwest Area	676,000	156	1,115	292	13	1	3	1,410
North America West Area	782,000	175	1,251	197	16	2	11	1,459
Pacific Area	314,000	84	511	184	13	32	178	873
Philippines/ Micronesia Area	362,000	46	278	150	14	98	611	1,039
South America North Area	682,000	128	780	340	19	87	561	1,681
South America South Area	718,000	151	873	385	19	79	467	1,725
Utah North Area	1,030,000	280	2,061	78	3	0	0	2,139
Utah South Area	512,000	151	1,260	46	1	0	0	1,306
USA	4,712,000	1,196	8,719	1,552	91	20	155	10,417
Outside US	4,630,000	954	5,617	2,505	216	679	4,144	12,266
Total Church	9,342,000	2,150	14,336	4,057	307	699	4,290	22,683

Membership and units by lands

Land	Member-ship	Stakes	Wards	Bran-ches in stakes	Miss-ions	Dis-trics	Miss-ions bran-ches	Total wards, bran-ches
AFRICA								
Botswana	300	0	0	3	0	0	0	3
Cameroon	200	0	0	0	0	0	1	1
Cape Verde	3,000	0	0	0	0	3	17	17
Central African Republic	100	0	0	0	0	0	1	1
Congo	1,000	0	0	0	0	1	6	6
Egypt	*	0	0	0	0	0	1	1
Ethiopa	200	0	0	0	0	0	1	1
Ghana	14,000	2	12	8	1	5	28	48
Ivory Coast	2,800	0	0	0	1	2	14	14
Kenya	2,200	0	0	0	1	2	14	14
Lesotho	300	0	0	1	0	0	0	1
Liberia	1,600	0	0	0	0	2	7	7
Madagascar	400	0	0	0	0	0	2	2
Mauritius	200	0	0	0	0	0	1	1
Namibia	200	0	0	0	0	1	1	1
Nigeria	28,000	3	19	7	3	16	102	128
Reunion	600	0	0	0	0	1	4	4
Sierra Leone	2,400	0	0	0	0	3	14	14
Somalia	*	0	0	0	0	0	0	0
South Africa	24,000	6	25	43	3	3	18	86
Swaziland	700	0	0	3	0	0	0	3
Tanzania	100	0	0	0	0	0	1	1
Tunisia	*	0	0	0	0	0	1	1
Uganda	1,300	0	0	0	0	2	7	7
Zaire	5,300	0	0	0	1	6	22	22
Zambia	400	0	0	0	0	0	2	2
Zimbabwe	6,200	0	0	0	1	3	23	23
Africa Total	**95,000**	**11**	**56**	**65**	**11**	**50**	**289**	**410**
ASIA								
Armenia	200	0	0	0	0	1	6	6
Bangladesh	*	0	0	0	0	0	1	1
Cambodia	200	0	0	0	0	1	3	3
China	200	0	0	0	0	0	3	3
Cyprus	*	0	0	0	0	0	2	2
Diego Garcia	*	0	0	0	0	0	1	1
Hong Kong	19,000	5	24	11	1	0	0	35
India	1,800	0	0	0	1	5	20	20
Indonesia	5,000	0	0	0	1	3	20	20
Japan	106,000	25	130	62	9	21	101	293
Macao	700	0	0	1	0	0	0	1
Malaysia	700	0	0	0	0	1	7	7
Mongolia	400	0	0	0	1	0	3	3
Myanmar	*	0	0	0	0	0	1	1
Papua New Guinea	4,700	1	6	1	1	1	10	17
Philippines	354,000	46	278	150	13	89	567	995
Singapore	1,900	1	5	2	1	0	0	7
South Korea	67,000	16	87	39	4	6	35	161
Sri Lanka	200	0	0	0	0	0	1	1
Taiwan	22,000	4	22	13	2	4	22	57
Thailand	6,300	1	5	3	1	4	18	26
Vietnam	*	0	0	0	0	0	1	1
Asia Total	**593,000**	**100**	**560**	**296**	**35**	**138**	**834**	**1,690**
CANADA								
Alberta	60,000	18	132	33	1	1	8	173
British Columbia	26,000	7	41	19	1	2	16	76
Manitoba	3,900	1	5	6	1	0	0	11
New Brunswick	2,200	1	5	3	0	0	0	8

Land	Membership	Stakes	Wards	Branches in stakes	Missions	Districts	Missions branches	Total wards, branches
Newfoundland	500	0	0	0	0	0	3	3
Northwest Territories	100	0	0	0	0	0	1	1
Nova Scotia	4,000	1	6	5	1	1	5	16
Ontario	34,000	8	56	26	2	2	9	91
Prince Edward Island	300	0	0	0	0	0	3	3
Quebec	7,600	2	11	5	1	1	6	22
Saskatchewan	4,500	1	5	8	0	1	4	17
Yukon	200	0	0	1	0	0	0	1
Canada Total	**143,000**	**39**	**261**	**106**	**7**	**8**	**55**	**422**

CARIBBEAN

Land	Membership	Stakes	Wards	Branches in stakes	Missions	Districts	Missions branches	Total wards, branches
Antigua	*	0	0	0	0	0	1	1
Aruba	200	0	0	0	0	0	2	2
Bahamas	400	0	0	0	0	0	2	2
Barbados	500	0	0	0	0	0	4	4
Bermuda	*	0	0	0	0	0	1	1
Bonaire	*	0	0	0	0	0	1	1
Cayman Island	*	0	0	0	0	0	1	1
Cuba	*	0	0	0	0	0	1	1
Curacao	300	0	0	0	0	0	2	2
Dominican Republic	54,000	8	42	37	3	11	62	141
Grenada	*	0	0	0	0	0	1	1
Guadeloupe	*	0	0	0	0	0	1	1
Haiti	5,100	0	0	0	1	2	18	18
Jamaica	3,300	0	0	0	1	2	15	15
Martinique	*	0	0	0	0	0	1	1
Netherlands Antilles	*	0	0	0	0	0	0	0
Puerto Rico	20,000	0	0	0	1	8	52	52
Saint Kitts-Nevis	*	0	0	0	0	0	1	1
Saint Maarten	*	0	0	0	0	0	1	1
Saint Vincent	300	0	0	0	0	0	1	1
Trinidad and Tobago	1,000	0	0	0	1	0	4	4
Virgin Islands, US	300	0	0	0	0	0	2	2
Caribbean Total	**85,000**	**8**	**42**	**37**	**7**	**23**	**174**	**253**

CENTRAL AMERICA

Land	Membership	Stakes	Wards	Branches in stakes	Missions	Districts	Missions branches	Total wards, branches
Belize	1,800	0	0	0	0	3	10	10
Costa Rica	25,000	4	23	18	1	6	27	68
El Salvador	64,000	13	71	35	2	2	14	120
Guatemala	148,000	30	171	79	4	30	139	389
Honduras	65,000	16	89	19	2	11	41	149
Nicaragua	18,000	0	0	0	1	13	96	96
Panama	26,000	5	25	13	1	5	25	63
Central America Total	**349,000**	**68**	**379**	**164**	**11**	**70**	**352**	**895**

EUROPE

Land	Membership	Stakes	Wards	Branches in stakes	Missions	Districts	Missions branches	Total wards, branches
Albania	400	0	0	0	0	0	5	5
Andorra	*	0	0	0	0	0	1	1
Austria	4,000	1	6	5	1	1	12	23
Belgium	6,000	2	9	13	1	1	6	28
Bulgaria	700	0	0	0	1	2	9	9
Byelorussia (Belarus)	200	0	0	0	0	0	4	4
Corsica	*	0	0	0	0	0	1	1
Croatia	*	0	0	0	0	1	3	3
Czech Republic	1,200	0	0	0	1	4	18	18
Estonia	200	0	0	0	0	0	4	4
France	28,000	7	35	46	3	7	41	122
Germany	36,000	14	88	83	6	1	5	176

Land	Membership	Stakes	Wards	Branches in stakes	Missions	Districts	Missions branches	Total wards, branches
Greece	400	0	0	0	1	1	6	6
Hungary	2,100	0	0	0	1	2	20	20
Italy	17,000	2	9	16	4	16	93	118
Latvia	200	0	0	0	1	0	5	5
Lithuania	100	0	0	0	0	0	3	3
Luxembourg	100	0	0	0	0	0	1	1
Malta	*	0	0	0	0	0	2	2
Netherlands	7,500	3	15	22	1	0	0	37
Poland	700	0	0	0	1	1	12	12
Portugal	34,000	5	23	22	3	12	59	104
Romania	600	0	0	0	1	2	9	9
Russia	3,700	0	0	0	6	8	59	59
Serbia	*	0	0	0	0	1	2	2
Slovakia	*	0	0	0	0	0	2	2
Slovenia	*	0	0	0	0	1	3	3
Spain	27,000	4	19	22	5	17	103	144
Switzerland	6,900	3	15	23	2	0	1	39
Ukraine	3,100	0	0	0	2	6	37	37
Europe Total	**181,000**	**41**	**219**	**252**	**41**	**84**	**526**	**997**
MEXICO								
Mexico Total	**728,000**	**138**	**847**	**232**	**18**	**44**	**303**	**1,382**
SCANDINAVIA								
Scandinavia Total	**22,000**	**8**	**45**	**43**	**4**	**10**	**44**	**132**
Denmark	4,700	2	13	11	1	0	0	24
Finland	4,400	2	11	7	1	3	11	29
Greenland	*	0	0	0	0	0	0	0
Iceland	200	0	0	0	0	1	3	3
Norway	4,100	1	7	3	1	3	14	24
Sweden	8,400	3	14	22	1	3	16	52
SOUTH AMERICA								
Argentina	235,000	46	271	148	10	47	278	697
Bolivia	89,000	16	95	34	2	10	65	194
Brazil	548,000	136	801	278	23	45	315	1,394
Chile	394,000	89	516	178	7	14	87	781
Colombia	113,000	13	87	42	4	22	149	278
Ecuador	128,000	21	128	64	2	11	74	266
Falkland Islands	*	0	0	0	0	0	0	0
French Guiana	200	0	0	0	0	0	2	2
Guyana	500	0	0	0	0	0	2	2
Paraguay	24,000	4	23	21	1	10	59	103
Peru	279,000	63	393	169	7	34	199	761
Suriname	300	0	0	0	0	0	1	1
Uruguay	64,000	12	63	38	1	8	43	144
Venezuela	73,000	15	77	31	4	10	69	177
South America Total	**1,948,000**	**415**	**2,454**	**1,003**	**61**	**211**	**1,343**	**48,000**
SOUTH PACIFIC								
American Samoa	12,000	3	24	3	0	0	0	27
Australia	87,000	25	146	46	6	14	55	247
Cook Islands	900	0	0	0	0	1	7	7
Fiji	11,000	2	14	4	1	2	16	34
French Polynesia	14,000	5	28	15	1	3	19	62
Guam	1,400	0	0	0	1	1	5	5
Johnston Atoll	*	0	0	0	0	0	1	1
Kiribati	5,100	0	0	0	0	1	17	17
Marshall Islands	2,900	0	0	0	0	2	10	10
Micronesia	3,000	0	0	0	0	5	23	23
Nauru	*	0	0	0	0	0	1	[1]Land

Membership	Stakes	Wards	Branches in stakes	Districts	Missions	Total missions, branches	Total wards, branches
New Caldonia	1,100	0	0	0	0	1	5	5

Membership	Stakes	Wards	Branches in stakes	Districts	Missions	Total missions, branches	Total wards, branches
New Caldonia	1,100	0	0	0	0	1	5
New Zealand	82,000	20	121	50	2	6	29	200
Niue	300	0	0	0	0	1	2	2
North Mariana Islands	500	0	0	0	0	0	4	4
Palau	400	0	0	0	0	1	2	2
Tonga	40,000	13	86	43	1	1	9	138
Tuvalu Islands	*	0	0	0	0	1	0	1
Vanuatu	500	0	0	0	0	0	2	2
Western Samoa	54,000	15	86	22	1	1	5	113
South Pacific Total	**317,000**	**83**	**505**	**183**	**13**	**40**	**213**	**901**
U.K./IRELAND								
England	127,000	34	201	82	6	0	0	283
Ireland	2,300	1	4	4	1	1	7	15
Northern Ireland	5,700	1	8	7	0	0	0	15
Scotland	26,000	5	24	22	1	0	4	50
Wales	7,400	2	12	9	0	0	0	21
U.K./Ireland Total	**168,000**	**43**	**249**	**124**	**8**	**1**	**11**	**384**
UNITED STATES								
Alabama	25,000	6	38	32	1	0	0	70
Alaska	24,000	6	37	25	1	1	7	69
Arizona	271,000	64	476	60	3	0	0	536
Arkansas	17,000	4	26	24	1	0	0	50
California	726,000	162	1,149	193	15	2	10	1,352
Colorado	101,000	25	176	33	2	0	1	210
Connecticut	11,000	3	19	12	1	0	0	31
Delaware	3,400	1	7	1	0	0	0	8
District of Columbia	1,100	0	0	0	0	1	7	7
Florida	98,000	21	152	28	4	0	0	180
Georgia	51,000	12	75	32	2	1	4	111
Hawaii	55,000	13	102	8	1	0	0	110
Idaho	327,000	99	721	45	2	0	0	766
Illinois	43,000	11	74	32	2	0	0	106
Indiana	30,000	8	54	25	1	0	0	79
Iowa	14,000	4	27	12	1	0	0	39
Kansas	22,000	5	38	15	0	1	7	60
Kentucky	21,000	5	31	30	1	0	0	61
Louisiana	24,000	7	38	28	1	0	0	66
Maine	7,900	2	16	9	0	0	0	25
Maryland	30,000	9	53	13	2	0	0	66
Massachusetts	16,000	3	28	13	1	0	0	41
Michigan	33,000	8	52	31	2	2	10	93
Minnesota	20,000	5	35	18	1	0	0	53
Mississippi	15,000	4	26	16	1	0	0	42
Missouri	43,000	11	78	32	2	0	0	110
Montana	39,000	10	64	34	1	1	10	108
Nebraska	15,000	4	25	18	1	0	1	44
Nevada	124,000	30	204	31	1	0	0	235
New Hampshire	6,800	3	12	5	1	0	0	17
New Jersey	19,000	4	25	22	2	1	4	51
New Mexico	54,000	12	82	34	1	0	0	116
New York	49,000	10	55	56	4	4	33	144
North Carolina	51,000	12	77	32	2	0	0	109
North Dakota	5,200	1	3	3	0	1	8	14
Ohio	43,000	10	70	35	2	0	0	105
Oklahoma	31,000	7	43	29	2	0	1	73
Oregon	126,000	35	223	40	2	0	0	263
Pennsylvania	33,000	8	59	25	3	2	19	103
Rhode Island	2,200	0	5	2	0	0	0	7
South Carolina	24,000	4	37	18	1	0	0	55
South Dakota	8,500	2	9	10	1	1	14	33
Tennesee	27,000	8	44	21	2	0	0	65
Texas	182,000	39	291	118	6	1	3	412
Utah	1,484,000	413	3,199	115	3	0	0	3,314

Vermont	3,400	1	6	5	0	0	0	11
Virginia	61,000	15	99	33	2	0	0	132
Washington	211,000	49	398	47	3	0	0	445
West Virginia	11,000	2	17	18	1	0	0	35
Wisconsin	16,000	3	24	19	1	1	7	50
Wyoming	54,000	16	120	15	0	0	0	135
United States Total	**4,712,000**	**1,196**	**8,719**	**1,552**	**90**	**20**	**146**	**10,417**

CHURCH STATISTICS

As of Dec. 31	Members, stakes	Members, missions	Total members	Stakes	Wards, branches	Missions	Mission branches
1830							
Apr. 6	0	0	6	0	0	0	0
Dec. 31	280	0	280	0	4	0	0
1831	680	0	680	0	6	0	0
1832	1,318	1,313	2,661	0	27	0	6
1833	1,805	1,335	3,140	0	23	0	17
1834	3,050	1,322	4,372	2	22	0	18
1835	7,500	1,335	8,835	2	22	0	26
1836	12,000	1,293	13,293	2	25	0	29
1837	14,400	1,882	16,282	2	25	1	42
1838	15,300	2,581	17,881	2	26	1	65
1839	13,700	2,760	16,460	3	16	2	70
1840	11,962	4,903	16,865	10	18	2	69
1841	12,475	7,381	19,856	2	19	2	84
1842	13,549	10,015	23,564	2	26	2	199
1843	15,601	10,379	25,980	2	31	2	238
1844	16,374	9,772	26,146	2	33	3	239
1845	17,020	13,312	30,332	1	34	4	277
1846	18,960	15,033	33,993	0	30	5	311
1847	17,263	17,431	34,694	1	48	5	357
1848	16,749	23,728	40,477	1	55	5	426
1849	17,654	30,506	48,160	1	75	5	515
1850	18,756	33,083	51,839	1	61	9	637
1851	16,069	36,096	52,165	4	60	11	717
1852	15,627	37,013	52,640	5	65	13	795
1853	25,537	38,617	64,154	5	75	14	885
1854	30,817	37,612	68,429	6	79	13	859
1855	28,654	35,320	63,974	6	99	14	858
1856	31,762	32,119	63,881	7	124	12	841
1857	32,529	22,707	55,236	6	77	12	742
1858	33,880	21,875	55,755	4	81	9	661
1859	36,481	20,557	57,038	4	98	9	635
1860	39,338	21,744	61,082	4	110	8	611
1861	42,417	23,794	66,211	4	126	7	588
1862	45,565	23,215	68,780	4	135	7	563
1863	49,283	22,487	71,770	4	143	7	524
1864	53,006	21,342	74,348	4	161	8	471
1865	56,562	20,209	76,771	4	164	8	436
1866	59,803	18,081	77,884	4	167	8	420
1867	63,071	18,053	81,124	4	175	8	407
1868	66,589	18,033	84,622	5	178	8	385
1869	70,157	18,275	88,432	9	187	7	383
1870	73,747	16,383	90,130	9	195	7	363
1871	78,458	17,138	95,596	9	200	7	342
1872	81,821	16,331	98,152	9	206	7	347
1873	85,194	16,344	101,538	9	213	7	348
1874	88,567	15,349	103,916	10	216	7	309
1875	91,992	15,175	107,167	10	222	7	302
1876	95,773	15,338	111,111	10	230	8	307
1877	99,780	15,285	115,065	20	252	8	285
1878	109,894	15,152	125,046	21	254	9	272
1879	112,705	15,681	128,386	22	263	10	289
1880	117,773	15,855	133,628	23	272	10	287
1881	123,918	16,815	140,733	23	283	10	293

As of Dec. 31	Members, stakes	Members, missions	Total members	S takes	Wards, branches	Missions	Mission branches
1882	128,779	16,825	145,604	24	292	10	291
1883	135,128	16,465	151,593	27	317	11	292
1884	142,417	15,825	158,242	29	340	13	296
1885	147,557	16,573	164,130	29	348	12	311
1886	150,602	16,051	166,653	30	342	12	315
1887	155,654	17,375	173,029	31	360	12	326
1888	162,424	17,830	180,294	32	373	13	336
1889	164,834	18,310	183,144	32	388	12	339
1890	170,653	17,610	188,263	32	395	12	330
1891	177,489	17,956	195,445	32	409	12	332
1892	182,623	18,338	200,961	33	439	14	350
1893	194,352	20,182	214,534	34	451	15	356
1894	201,047	21,322	222,369	34	457	15	356
1895	208,179	22,937	231,116	37	479	15	356
1896	215,514	25,913	241,427	37	489	17	348
1897	222,802	32,934	255,736	37	493	18	374
1898	229,428	37,823	267,251	40	516	20	401
1899	229,734	41,947	271,681	40	506	20	412
1900	236,628	47,137	283,765	43	529	20	438
1901	243,368	49,563	292,931	50	577	21	442
1902	249,927	49,178	299,105	50	595	22	481
1903	257,661	47,240	304,901	51	612	23	477
1904	275,681	48,608	324,289	55	619	21	475
1905	281,162	50,886	332,048	55	627	22	514
1906	289,377	55,637	345,014	55	636	22	541
1907	298,847	59,066	357,913	55	634	22	558
1908	307,308	64,164	371,472	59	666	22	595
1909	308,094	69,185	377,279	60	684	21	590
1910	327,017	71,461	398,478	62	699	21	611
1911	334,643	72,648	407,291	62	706	21	632
1912	341,278	76,277	417,555	65	716	22	647
1913	350,321	81,286	431,607	66	749	22	650
1914	371,729	82,989	454,718	68	772	21	601
1915	381,336	84,902	466,238	72	783	21	608
1916	390,449	86,872	477,321	73	808	22	559
1917	397,933	90,105	488,038	75	875	22	578
1918	404,030	91,932	495,962	75	893	22	559
1919	413,563	94,398	507,961	79	888	23	554
1920	426,167	99,820	525,987	83	904	24	623
1921	441,472	107,331	548,803	86	933	25	665
1922	451,762	114,596	566,358	87	946	25	661
1923	463,578	112,318	575,896	90	962	26	697
1924	479,498	118,363	597.861	94	969	25	716
1925	490,688	122,884	613,572	94	985	28	720
1926	494,536	129,373	623,909	96	992	28	739
1927	510,910	133,835	644,745	99	1,005	28	758
1928	516,986	138,700	655,686	101	1,004	29	813
1929	520,339	143,313	663,652	104	1,004	30	823
1930	532,877	137,140	670,017	104	1,000	30	868
1931	544,453	143,982	688,435	104	1,004	31	861
1932	554,462	149,487	703,949	104	1,012	31	867
1933	564,042	153,577	717,619	105	1,014	31	875
1934	579,118	151,620	730,738	110	1,035	31	892
1935	595,071	151,313	746,384	115	1,064	32	900
1936	607,202	153,488	760,690	118	1,081	33	933
1937	616,088	151,664	767,752	118	1,101	35	951
1938	632,994	151,770	784,764	126	1,137	36	947
1939	645,618	157,910	803,528	129	1,154	35	1,002

As of Dec. 31	Members, stakes	Members, missions	Total members	Stakes	Wards, branches	Missions	Mission branches
1940	703,017	159,647	862,664	134	1,191	35	728
1941	736,544	155,536	892,080	139	1,224	36	757
1942	754,826	162,889	917,715	143	1,242	37	776
1943	774,161	162,889	937,050	146	1,261	38	807
1944	792,362	161,642	954,004	148	1,273	38	773
1945	811,045	168,409	979,454	153	1,295	38	909
1946	823,819	172,686	996,505	161	1,340	39	959
1947	843,021	173,149	1,016,170	169	1,425	43	1,149
1948	854,099	187,871	1,041,970	172	1,451	44	1,323
1949	876,661	202,010	1,078,671	175	1,501	46	1,327
1950	898,478	212,836	1,111,314	180	1,541	43	1,370
1951	933,792	213,365	1,147,157	191	1,666	42	1,414
1952	974,118	214,935	1,189,053	202	1,767	43	1,551
1953	1,034,381	211,981	1,246,362	211	1,884	42	1,399
1954	1,079,583	222,657	1,302,240	219	1,993	42	1,476
1955	1,126,265	213,009	1,357,274	224	2,082	44	1,471
1956	1,177,856	238,875	1,416,731	239	2,210	45	1,854
1957	1,233,397	254,917	1,488,314	251	2,362	45	1,740
1958	1,292,098	263,701	1,555,799	273	2,513	47	1,757
1959	1,336,675	279,413	1,616,088	290	2,614	50	1,895
1960	1,408,722	284,408	1,693,180	319	2,882	58	1,811
1961	1,514,551	309,110	1,823,661	345	3,143	67	1,872
1962	1,626,965	335,821	1,965,786	364	3,423	74	1,802
1963	1,736,567	380,884	2,117,451	389	3,615	77	1,782
1964	1,801,571	433,345	2,234,916	400	3,749	79	2,016
1965	1,977,418	418,514	2,395,932	412	3,897	76	2,137
1966	2,032,359	448,540	2,480,899	425	4,022	75	2,053
1967	2,144,766	469,574	2,614,340	448	4,166	77	1,987
1968	2,207,976	476,097	2,684,073	473	4,385	83	2,112
1969	2,344,635	462,821	2,807,456	496	4,592	88	2,016
1970	2,485,525	445,285	2,930,810	537	4,922	92	1,943
1971	2,645,419	445,534	3,090,953	562	5,135	98	1,942
1972	2,794,731	424,177	3,218,908	592	5,394	101	1,891
1973	2,904,244	402,414	3,306,658	630	5,707	108	1,817
1974	2,999,536	410,451	3,409,987	675	5,951	113	1,822
1975	3,188,062	384,140	3,572,202	737	6,390	134	1,761
1976	3,352,535	390,214	3,742,749	798	6,903	149	1,422
1977	3,618,331	350,889	3,969,220	885	7,486	157	1,694
1978	3,829,385	337,469	4,166,854	990	8,064	165	1,790
1979	4,059,044	345,077	4,404,121	1,092	9,365	175	1,121
1980	4,328,521	311,301	4,639,822	1,218	10,324	188	2,267
1981	4,621,688	298,761	4,920,449	1,321	11,063	188	2,030
1982	4,832,158	330,461	5,162,619	1,392	11,492	180	1,979
1983	5,013,541	338,183	5,351,724	1,458	11,952	178	1,991
1984	5,278,192	362,862	5,641,054	1,507	12,422	182	2,046
1985	5,555,407	364,074	5,919,483	1,582	12,939	188	2,068
1986	5,785,324	381,650	6,166,974	1,622	13,318	193	2,064
1987	5,974,239	420,075	6,394,314	1,666	13,727	205	2,307
1988	6,271,311	449,889	6,721,210	1,707	14,069	222	2,470
1989	6,794,428	514,016	7,308,444	1,739	14,533	228	2,751
1990	7,141,477	619,702	7,761,179	1,784	15,003	256	3,079
1991	7,423,426	666,417	8,089,843	1,837	15,513	267	3,325
1992	7,673,980	730,107	8,404,087	1,919	16,292	276	3,819
1993	7,911,694	777,925	8,689,619	1,968	17,048	295	4,049
1994	8,160,113	865,801	9,025,914	2,008	17,528	303	4,343
1995	8,469,191	871,259	9,340,450	2,150	18,398	307	4,287

MISSIONARY STATISTICS

Year	Set apart in year	Year	Set apart in year	Year	Set apart in year	Year	Set apart in year
1830	16	1840	80	1850	50	1860	96
1831	58	1841	100	1851	44	1861	19
1832	72	1842	45	1852	158	1862	27
1833	41	1843	374	1853	33	1863	50
1834	111	1844	586	1854	119	1864	52
1835	84	1845	84	1855	65	1865	71
1836	80	1846	32	1856	130	1866	32
1837	52	1847	40	1857	88	1867	133
1838	16	1848	55	1858	0	1868	32
1839	67	1849	58	1859	18	1869	250
1870	96	1880	219	1890	283	1900	796
1871	167	1881	199	1891	331	1901	522
1872	132	1882	237	1892	317	1902	848
1873	35	1883	248	1893	162	1903	658
1874	98	1884	205	1894	526	1904	699
1875	197	1885	235	1895	746	1905	716
1876	211	1886	209	1896	922	1906	1,015
1877	154	1887	282	1897	943	1907	930
1878	152	1888	242	1898	1,059	1908	919
1879	179	1889	249	1899	324	1909	1,014
1910	933	1920	889	1930	896	1940	1,194
1911	822	1921	880	1931	678	1941	1,257
1912	769	1922	886	1932	399	1942	629
1913	858	1923	812	1933	525	1943	261
1914	684	1924	867	1934	843	1944	427
1915	621	1925	1,313	1935	960	1945	400
1916	722	1926	1,236	1936	899	1946	2,297
1917	543	1927	1,017	1937	1,079	1947	2,132
1918	245	1928	1,193	1938	1,146	1948	2,161
1919	1,211	1929	1,058	1939	1,088	1949	2,363

Year	Set apart in year	Year	Set apart in year	Total in Field	Year	Set apart in year	Total in Field
1950	3,015	1960	4,706	9,097	1970	7,590	14,387
1951	1,801	1961	5,793	11,592	1971	8,344	15,205
1952	872	1962	5,630	11,818	1972	7,874	16,367
1953	1,750	1963	5,781	11,653	1973	9,471	17,258
1954	2,022	1964	5,886	11,599	1974	9,811	18,109
1955	2,414	1965	7,139	12,585	1975	14,446	22,492
1956	2,572	1966	7,021	12,621	1976	13,928	25,027
1957	2,518	1967	6,475	13,147	1977	14,561	25,264
1958	2,778	1968	7,178	13,018	1978	15,860	27,669
1959	2,847	1969	6,968	6,967	1979	16,590	29,454

Year	Set apart in year	Total in Field	Year	Set apart in year	Total in Field
1980	16,600	29,953	1990	26,438	43,651
1981	17,800	29,702	1991	25,416	43,395
1982	18,260	26,606	1992	28,084	46,025
1983	19,450	26,850	1993	29,460	48,708
1984	19,720	27,392	1994	28,198	47,311
1985	19,890	29,265	1995	29,214	48,631
1986	20,798	31,803			
1987	21,001	34,750			
1988	22,619	36,123			
1989	25,609	39,739			

Total to date: 6,320,814

INDEX

Boston Massachusetts Region 508
Boston Massachusetts Temple 12,439,511
Botswana 291-92
Bountiful Utah Temple.........11,439-40,505
Bowen, Albert E. 53
Boy Scouts 519
Boynton, John F. 50
Bradford, William R. 23
Brady, Rodney H. 9
Brazil...292-97
Brazil Area 182
Brazil Belem Mission......................295,431
Brazil Belo Horizonte East Mission 296
Brazil Belo Horizonte Mission 295,427
Brazil Belo Horizonte South Mission 431
Brazil Brasilia Mission 296,426
Brazil Campinas Mission...............296,426
Brazil Curitiba Mission 296,425
Brazil Florianopolis Mission 296,430
Brazil Fortaleza Mission 296,427
Brazil Manaus Mission 296,428
Brazil Marilia Mission 296,431
Brazil Porto Alegre North Mission ..296,429
Brazil Porto Alegre South Mission..296,416
Brazil Recife Mission....................296,425
Brazil Recife South Mission 296,430
Brazil Ribeiro Preto Mission 296,430
Brazil Rio de Janeiro Mission 296,419
Brazil Rio de Janeiro North Mission296,430
Brazil Salvador Mission.................296,428
Brazil Salvador South Mission 296,431
Brazil Sao Paulo East Mission 296,429
Brazil Sao Paulo
Interlagos Mission 297,429
Brazil Sao Paulo North Mission 297,421
Brazil Sao Paulo South Mission 297,421
Brazilian Mission 414
Brewerton, Ted E........................68,8,511
Brigham Young University 75:F33,
.......................'76:G46, '77:294, '78:296
degrees offered: ....'79:294-98
enrollment, ...'75:F32, '76:G45, '77:293,
....'78:296
law library 509
library 12,519
president 12
science building...............................12
Brigham Young University-Hawaii Campus
athletics 9-10
enrollment and presidents ....'75:F34,
..........................'76:G47, '77:295, '78:298
president 505,516
British-born members, ...'74:255, '80:276,
....'81:256
British Columbia, Canada 300-301
British Mission 410
Brockbank, Bernard P. 66
Brooklyn (ship) 518
Brough, Monte J. 20
Brown, George Washington 125-26
Brown, Harold C. 9
Brown, Hugh B........................44-45
Brown, John 126
Brown, L. Edward......................33,8,515
Brown, Nathaniel T. 126
Brown, Victor L. 76,8,515
Buehner, Carl W. 78
Buenos Aires Argentina Temple............440
Bulgaria 297

Bulgaria Sofia Mission 297,429
Bullock, Thomas.............................126
Burke, Charles A.............................126
Burnham, Jacob D. 126-27
Burton, H. David.....................39,8,515
Burton, Robert T. 77
Burton, Theodore M. 65-66
Burundi 297-98
Busche, F. Enzio.............................23
Butterfield, Josiah 57

C

Caldwell, C. Max 33
Calendar, perpetual................ '82:298-99,
..................................'83:300-301
California....................................194-201
California Anaheim Mission 200,419
California Arcadia Mission 200,420
California Carlsbad Mission 200,430
California Fresno Mission 200,422
California Los Angeles Mission......201,410
California Oakland Mission 201,420
California Riverside Mission 201,429
California Roseville Mission 201,430
California Sacramento Mission 201,415
California San Bernardino Mission 201,425
California San Diego Mission 201,422
California San Fernando Mission ..201,431
California San Jose Mission 201,424
California Santa Rosa Mission 201,426
California Ventura Mission..............201,424
Call, Waldo P..69
Callis, Charles A. 53
Camargo, Helio R. 69
Cambodia...........................298,11,516
Cameroon...................................298-99
Canada 299-307
Canada Calgary Mission...............300,415
Canada Halifax Mission 303,421
Canada Montreal Mission 306,421
Canada Toronto East Mission 305,430
Canada Toronto West Mission.......305,413
Canada Vancouver Mission...........301,417
Canada Winnipeg Mission 302,423
Canadians, ...'79:255, '80:281, '81:255
Canary Islands 390
Cannon, Abraham H. 51-52
Cannon, Carol H. 10
Cannon, Elaine A. 93
Cannon, George I. 69
Cannon, George Q. 43
Cannon, John Q. 78
Cannon, Lucy Grant.........................92
Cannon, Sylvester Q. 53
Cape Verde, Republic of 307-8
Caracas Venezuela Temple 12,440,511
Carmack, John K. 24
Carrington, Albert 47,127
Carter, William 127
Case, James 127
Catholic Church 506,515
Catholic Community Services of Utah ..505
Cayman Islands 345
Celebrations, historical ....'80:316-20,
'81:298-302
Central Africa Republic 308
Central America Area........................180
Chamberlain, Solomon 127

Rodgers, Ralph G., Jr. 10
Rojas, Jorge A. 74,519
Rolfe, Benjamin W. 147
Romania..................................381
Romania Bucharest Mission 381,431
Romney, George W. 10
Romney, Marion G. 45
Rooker, Joseph 147
Rota (island)..............................369
Roundy, Shadrach 147-48
Rudd, Glen L. 70
Russell, Gardner H. 70
Russia 381-83,505
Russia Moscow Mission 383,429
Russia Novosibirsk Mission 383,431
Russia Rostov Mission 383,431
Russia St. Petersburg Mission 383,430
Russia Samara Mission 383,431
Russia Yekateringburg Mission 383,431

S

Sackley, Robert E. 70
Saipan (island)........................369
St. George Temple 458
St. George, Utah 513
St. Kitts (island) 383
St. Louis Missouri Region 508
St. Louis Missouri Temple 458-59
St. Maarten (island) 364
St. Vincent..............................383-84
Salt Lake City, historic photographs,
...................................'80:130-132
original ward boundaries map,
...................................'85:317
parks...........................511-12,518
Salt Lake Mormon Tabernacle Choir,
history, ...'76:F18
performances..................508-10,513,518
recordings 506-7
'77:298-99
Salt Lake Tabernacle organ, ...'87:327
Salt Lake Temple.....................459-60
Samoa Apia Mission 407,413
Samuelson, Cecil O., Jr. 31,504
San Diego, California 515
San Diego California Temple 460
Sandwich Islands Mission.............411,412
San Francisco, California 518
Santiago Chile Temple 460-61
Santo Domingo
  Dominican Republic Temple....11,461,519
Sao Paulo Temple 461
Saskatchewan, Canada 306-7
Sato, Tatsui 10-11
Scandinavian Mission 410
Scandinavians, ...79:256, '80:275,
...................................'81:255-56
Schaerrer, Neil D. 87
Schofield, Joseph S. 148
Scholes, George 148
Schools, Church......................'83:285-86
Schwendiman, Kay 9
Scotland 400-401
Scotland Edinburgh Mission 401,417
Scott, Jeanene W. 10
Scott, Richard G. 18,11,518-19
Seattle Temple.........................462
Second Quorum

of the Seventy......................33-38,72-75
Seminaries
  enrollment, ..'75:F36-37, '76:F49 '77:297-
...................................98, '78:300-301, '83:279-80
  statistics 6
Seoul Korea Temple 462-63
Serbia..................................384
Seventy, First Council of the 56-61
  First Quorum of the 22-32,65-72
  Presidency of the 63-65
  Presidency of the Quorums of the 20-21
  Second Quorum of the 33-38,72-75
Sherman, Lyman R. 57
Sherwood, Henry G. 148
Shimabukuro, Sam K. 74,519
Ships, Mormon emigrant.................159-67
Shumway, Andrew P. 148
Shumway, Carolyn M. 10
Shumway, Charles 149
Shumway, Eric B. 9,11,505
Shumway, Naomi M. 89
Siam Mission 412
Sierra Leone 384-85
Sill, Sterling W. 65
Silva, Ricardo Garcia 10
Simmons, Dennis E....................36,8,515
Simpson, Robert L. 66
Singapore..............................385
Singapore Mission 385,420,425
"60 Minutes" (TV program) 513
Slovakia 385-86
Slovenia 386
Smith, Barbara B.........................96
Smith, Bathsheba W. 96
Smith, David A. 77
Smith, Douglas H. 70
Smith, Eldred G. 56
Smith, Emma Hale 95
Smith, G. Carlos 86
Smith, George A. 43,149
Smith, George Albert 41
Smith, Hyrum 42-43
Smith, Hyrum G. 56
Smith, Hyrum Mack 52
Smith, John 48
Smith, John (patriarch)...................56
Smith, John Henry 46
Smith, Joseph 40
children, '83:283
Smith, Joseph, Sr. 48
Smith, Joseph F. 40-41
Smith, Joseph Fielding...................41
Smith, Joseph Fielding (patriarch) 56
Smith, Nicholas G. 62
Smith, Sylvester 57
Smith, William 49,56
Smoot, Reed 52
Smoot, William C. A. 149-50
Snow, Eliza R. 95
Snow, Erastus 50-51,150
Snow, Lorenzo 40
Society Islands Mission.................410,413
Somalia 387
Sonne, Alma 65
Sonnenberg, John 68-69
Sonntag, Philip T. 68
Sorensen, David E. 31,8,508
Sorensen, Lynn A. 70
South Africa 387-88,515